Encyclopedia of Jewish History and Culture
Volume 6
So–Z

Editor in Chief
Dan Diner

Advisory Board

Marion Aptroot (Düsseldorf)
Jacob Barnai (Haifa)
Israel Bartal (Jerusalem)
Omer Bartov (Providence, RI)
Esther Benbassa (Paris)
Dominique Bourel (Paris)
Michael Brenner (Munich)
Matti Bunzl (Urbana-Champaign)
Lois C. Dubin (Northampton, MA)
Todd M. Endelman (Ann Arbor, MI)
David Engel (New York)
Shmuel Feiner (Ramat Gan)
Norbert Frei (Jena)
Saul Friedländer (Los Angeles)
Sander L. Gilman (Atlanta)
Frank Golczewski (Hamburg)
Andreas Gotzmann (Erfurt)
Michael Graetz* (Heidelberg)
Raphael Gross (London/Frankfurt am Main)
Heiko Haumann (Basel)
Johannes Heil (Basel)
Susannah Heschel (Hanover, NH)
Yosef Kaplan (Jerusalem)
Cilly Kugelmann (Berlin)
Mark Levene (Southampton)
Leonid Luks (Eichstätt)
Ezra Mendelsohn* (Jerusalem)
Paul Mendes-Flohr (Chicago/Jerusalem)
Dan Miron (New York)
Gabriel Motzkin (Jerusalem)
David N. Myers (Los Angeles)
Jacques Picard (Basel)
Gertrud Pickhan (Berlin)
Anthony Polonsky (Waltham, MA)

Renée Poznanski (Beer Sheva)
Peter Pulzer* (Oxford)
Aron Rodrigue (Stanford)
Manfred Rudersdorf (Leipzig)
Rachel Salamander (Munich)
Winfried Schulze (Munich)
Marcos Silber (Haifa)
Gerald Stourzh (Vienna)
Stefan Troebst (Leipzig)
Feliks Tych* (Warsaw)
Yfaat Weiss (Jerusalem/Leipzig)
Christian Wiese (Frankfurt am Main)
Carsten L. Wilke (Budapest)
Susanne Zepp (Berlin/Leipzig)
Moshe Zimmermann (Jerusalem)
Steven J. Zipperstein (Stanford)

deceased

Encyclopedia of Jewish History and Culture

Volume 6
So–Z

Editor in Chief

Dan Diner

On behalf of the Saxonian Academy of
Sciences and Humanities in Leipzig

Editorial Staff of the German Edition

Markus Kirchhoff (Head)　　　　　　Daniel Ristau
Philipp Graf　　　　　　　　　　　Frauke von Rohden
Stefan Hofmann　　　　　　　　　Ulrich Schuster
Ulrike Kramme　　　　　　　　　Želmíra Urra Muena
Regina Randhofer　　　　　　　　Robert Zwarg

Lukas Böckmann, Marcel Müller, Momme Schwarz
(*Assistants*)

Consulting Editors of the English Edition

Francis G. Gentry
Jessica Kley
Patricia Casey Sutcliffe

Editorial Staff of the English Edition

Ralf Balke　　　　　　　　　　　Helena Schöb
Sara Bellomo　　　　　　　　　　Diana Steele
David Johst

BRILL

LEIDEN | BOSTON

Cover *illustrations*: The Jewish May, Lithograph by Ephraim Moses Lilien (1902). From: Lothar Brieger, E. M. Lilien. Eine künstlerische Entwicklung um die Jahrhundertwende. Mit 226 Abbildungen nach Radierungen und Zeichnungen des Künstlers, Berlin/Vienna: Verlag Benjamin Harz 1922, p. 129; The Orient report on the Damascus Affair, May 9, 1840. Georg Olms Verlag, Hildesheim; Newspaper boys waiting for the release of *Forverts* in front of the publishing building in New York at night (1913). Library of Congress (rightsholder unknown); Jewish Savanna, painting by Pierre Jacques Benoit (1830). Private property; Advertisement for the copper house in the Jüdische Rundschau, June 30, 1933 (Excerpt). Private property; Armillary sphere; Model of the celestial mechanics of the geocentric world view; image from Ma'aseh Toviyah (Jeßnitz 1721). Private property; Title page from Mortiz Lazarus's and Chajim Heyman Steinthal's Zeitschrift für Völkerpsychologie und Sprachwissenschaft (1860) Leipzig University Library; Protest in Wadi Salib, 1959. Photo by Oskar Tauber, Josef Tauber

Original German Language Edition: Enzyklopädie Jüdischer Geschichte und Kultur. Im Auftrag der Sächsischen Akademie der Wissenschaften zu Leipzig herausgegeben von Dan Diner. © J.B. Metzler, Stuttgart/Springer-Verlag GmbH Deutschland 2011–2017.

The translation of this work was funded by Geisteswissenschaften International – Translation Funding for Work in the Humanities and Social Sciences from Germany, a joint initiative of the Fritz Thyssen Foundation, the German Federal Foreign Office, the collecting society VG WORT and the Börsenverein des Deutschen Buchhandels (German Publishers & Booksellers Association).

Library of Congress Cataloging-in-Publication Data
LC record available at https://lccn.loc.gov/2017029003

Typeface for the Latin, Greek, and Cyrillic scripts: "Brill". See and download: brill.com/brill-typeface.

ISBN VOLUME 6: 978-90-04-30947-0 (hardback)
ISBN 978-90-04-30940-1 (Set)

Copyright 2023 by Koninklijke Brill NV, Leiden, The Netherlands.
Koninklijke Brill NV incorporates the imprints Brill, Brill Nijhoff, Brill Schöningh, Brill Fink, Brill mentis, Brill Wageningen Academic, Vandenhoeck & Ruprecht, Böhlau and V&R unipress.
All rights reserved. No part of this publication may be reproduced, translated, stored in a retrieval system, or transmitted in any form or by any means, electronic, mechanical, photocopying, recording or otherwise, without prior written permission from the publisher. Requests for re-use and/or translations must be addressed to Koninklijke Brill NV via brill.com or copyright.com.

This book is printed on acid-free paper and produced in a sustainable manner.

PRINTED BY DRUKKERIJ WILCO B.V. - AMERSFOORT, THE NETHERLANDS

Contents

Instructions on Use VII
Transcription and Spelling VIII
Citation Guide to Biblical and Rabbinical Literature XI
List of Articles XII
List of Authors XIV
List of Translators XVI
List of Images and Maps XVIII
Articles 1

Instructions on Use

The EJHC makes no claims to factual completeness. Its status as an encyclopedia inheres in the topographies of knowledge and remembrance that emerge through its lemmatization. The carefully balanced architecture of entries taken from various spheres of Jewish history and cultures is quite independent of hierarchical subdivision of the subject matter by topic area and, in many cases, the title is not the obvious choice for the subject matter of the article in question. This approach is justified in detail in the editor's introduction. The introduction also contains an overview of the areas of focus, the fields of knowledge, and the subject matter belonging to them, along with examples illustrating how the lemmata were named.

With the exception of the article *Alef Bet*, which opens the encyclopedia, the articles in the EJHC appear in alphabetical order. The alphabetical list of articles provides an overview. A detailed list in Volume 7 indexes the articles in their totality. This list is especially important for its listing of persons and places that have no dedicated article for conceptual reasons.

Article Structure

Each article begins with an exposition outlining the central aspects and orientation of the article. The body of the article follows, preceded in the case of longer articles by an overview of the subsections. A bibliography is included at the end; this generally begins with source literature (although this is not always explicitly marked), followed by secondary literature. All bibliographical entries are numbered consecutively.

Numbers in square brackets within the text refer to entries in the bibliography. These numbers can include page numbers or a volume number, e.g. [5. 140–162] or [5. vol. 1, 450].

Cross references are signaled with an arrow (→).

Identification of Authors

The name of the author appears at the end of the article and is collected in a list of authors. Translators are identified in a list of names along with the articles each translated.

Transcriptions

Transcribed words are italicized in the article text. See the notes and lists that follow on p. viii.

Place names

The use of place names generally follows the naming conventions for the place (or region) during the period under discussion. The conventional English spellings are used for places. In Volume 7, each place is referenced by all the name variants used within the encyclopedia.

Orthography and Spelling

The orthography generally follows the standard of *Merriam-Webster's Collegiate Dictionary, Eleventh Edition*. In a few cases, preference is given to a different spelling, for example with *antisemitism*.

Abbreviations

For the sake of readability, the EJHC uses a of minimum abbreviations, retaining only standard abbreviations in common use or in line with academic norms.

Figures

The EJHC contains figures and maps. Details on authorship and copyright are shown in the List of Images and Maps, p. xviii.

Transcription and Spelling

A. Transcription of Non-Latin Writing Systems

For Arabic and the Slavic languages that use the Cyrillic script, the transcription guidelines of the Library of Congress are used, which are currently the international standard in scholarly works and popular science works. The Library of Congress transcription style is based on English orthography. It has been slightly modified (simplified) in the case of the Cyrillic alphabet (see section D. below). Hebrew transcription follows the YIVO (Institute for Jewish Research, New York) transcription standard, which follows closely the Library of Congress transcription style with the following exceptions: Library of Congress, though in slightly simplified form (e.g., using *k* to represent both *kaf* and *kuf* [*qof*], *s* for both *sin* and *samekh*, and *t* for both *tet* and *tav*. Transcription of Yiddish follows the transcription guidelines of YIVO, which are widely recognized as the standard.

Transcribed words are italicized, except for personal names, article keywords, and bibliographical items.

B. Personal Names

The rendition of names presents a special problem. Many individuals spelled their named in multiple ways, especially in the context of polyglot regions like medieval Spain or Eastern Europe. Additionally, there are various transcription traditions in the different European languages.

For persons from the medieval and early modern periods, biblical first names are generally rendered in their English forms and according to English orthography, e.g. Solomon ben Isaac (Rashi), Israel ben Eliʿezer (Baʿal Shem Tov), but Arabic names are transcribed, e.g. ʿUmar ibn al-Khaṭṭāb, al-Samawʿal ibn ʿĀdiyāʾ. Jews in the Islamic world often had Arabic as well as Hebrew names, and so they may be referred to using both, e.g. Ismāʿīl ibn al-Naghrīlah or Samuel ha-Nagid. If there is an established spelling, that is what is used, e.g. Judah Halevi, Sabbatai Zevi, Faisal (the King of Iraq), Muhammad (the prophet).

Names of persons from modern times are not transcribed but rendered in the usual version (e.g. Yitzhak Rabin, Salima Murad). The names of modern authors are cited in the spelling most commonly used in their publications in the Latin alphabet, with preference for the spelling used in English publications, where available; thus the American-Yiddish spelling Sholem Yankev Abramovitsh or Mendele Moykher-Sforim, Sholem Aleichem, and Samir Naqqash.

C. Notes on Transcription and Pronunciation

1 *Hebrew*

The YIVO guidelines have been simplified in the following ways: A *Shwa* is only transcribed with an "e" when necessary for the pronunciation of a word (e.g. *kehillah*); otherwise, it is omitted (e.g. *b'rit; tshuvah*). The *Yud* in construct forms is only rendered by "e" (*baṯe̱; Nevukhe̱*). The *Alef* and the *Ayin* are transcribed when within a word (e.g. *baʿal*) but are omitted from both the beginning and ending of words. The spellings, for example, of *Bezalel, Hannukah, Hasidism*, and *Sepharad/Sepharadim* have been modified to the common spellings in English.

TRANSCRIPTION AND SPELLING

			Pronunciation
'		*bi'ur*	stop, as in uh'oh
ḥ and kh		*ḥakham*	like ch in loch
v		*avodah*	like v in vote
s		*musar*	like s in sidestep
sh		*shanah*	like sh in shape
ts		*tsedakah*	like ts in tsar
z		*zakhor*	like z in zest

2   Yiddish

		Pronunciation
ay	*haynt*	like ai in hide
ey	*keyt*	like ay in weight
kh	*tkhines*	like ch in loch
oy	*Toyre*	like oy in toy
s	*mayse*	like s in sidestep
sh	*shul*	like sh in shape
tsh	*mentsh*	like ch in bench
v	*levone*	like v in vote
z	*zikhroynes*	like z in zest
zh	*zhurnal*	like zh in pleasure

3   Arabic

		Pronunciation
'	*ra's, fuqarā'*	stop, as in uh'oh
ā, ī, ū	*zamān, dīn, rasūl*	long vowels
th	*thalāth*	like voiceless th in think
j	*jamal*	like j in James
ḥ	*ḥadīth*	voiceless, pressured h (no English equivalent)
kh	*kharf*	like ch in loch
dh	*dhimmah*	like voiced th in the
r	*rasūl*	rolled r

		Pronunciation
z	*zamān*	like z in zest
s	*rasūl*	like s in sidestep
sh	*shams*	like sh in shape
ṣ	*ṣabāḥ*	emphatic s (voiceless and dark; no English equivalent)
ḍ	*faḍl*	emphatic d (voiced and dark; no English equivalent)
ṭ	*waṭan*	emphatic t (dark; no English equivalent)
ẓ	*ẓalla*	emphatic dh (voiced, dark th; no English equivalent)
'	*ya'lamu*	guttural (no English equivalent)
gh	*mughlaq*	voiced velar r (no English equivalent)
q	*qamar*	velarized dark k (no English equivalent)
w	*waṭan*	like w in world
y	*yaktubu*	like y in yesterday
aw	*yawm*	diphthong like au in how
ay	*'ayn*	diphthong like ei in sign

4   Cyrillic

The following deviations from the Library of Congress guidelines were adopted for the Cyrillic letters: the Cyrillic "e" is rendered with "ye" at the beginnings of words, after Russian vowel letters, and after soft and hard signs; everywhere else, it is rendered with "e" (e.g. *yeyevrei*, but *entsiklopẹdiya*). The Cyrillic "ё" is rendered with "o" after ж, ч, ш, щ; everywhere else, it is rendered with "yo" (*yeshchọ*, but *vsyọyo*). й is rendered "j" (e.g. *yevrejskiy*). ц is transcribed as "ts" (*entṣiklopediya*).

		Pronunciation
zh	*zhurnal*	like zh in pleasure
z	*zavtra*	like z in zest
kh	a) *kharasho*	like ch in loch (before a, o, and u)
	b) *khimiya*	like ch in the German dichten (before e and i) (no English equivalent)
ch	*uchit'*	like ch in bench
sh	*shkola*	like sh in shape
shch	*Borshch*	as in the Russian borschtsch

Citation Guide to Biblical and Rabbinical Literature

Citations from the books of the Bible generally follow the Jewish Publication Society (1917). The names and abbreviations of the books of the Hebrew Bible are as follows:

1 Torah (Pentateuch)

Genesis (Gen), Exodus (Exod), Leviticus (Lev), Numbers (Num), Deuteronomy (Deut).

2 Prophets

Joshua (Josh), Judges (Judg), 1 Samuel (1 Sam), 2 Samuel (2 Sam), 1 Kings (1 Kgs), 2 Kings (2 Kgs), Isaiah (Isa), Jeremiah (Jer), Ezekiel (Ezek), Hosea (Hos), Joel (Joel), Amos (Amos), Obadiah (Obad), Jonah (Jonah), Micah (Mic), Nahum (Nah), Habakkuk, (Hab), Zephaniah (Zeph), Haggai (Hag), Zechariah (Zech), Malachi (Mal).

3 Writings

Psalms (Ps/Pss), Proverbs (Prov), Job (Job), Song of Songs (Song of Solomon) (Song) *or* Canticles (Cant), Ruth (Ruth), Lamentations (Lam), Ecclesiastes (Eccl) *or* Qohelet (Qoh), Esther (Esth), Daniel (Dan), Ezra (Ezra), Nehemia (Neh), 1 Chronicles (1 Chr), 2 Chronicles (2 Chr).

List of Articles (So–Z)

Cross-reference entries indicate the main entry with an arrow. Cross-reference entries are not included in the main text of the Encyclopedia.

Sobibór
Soccer
Social Democracy → Reichstag
Society for Jewish Folk Music
Sociology
Sociology of Knowledge
Solal
Sonnet
Spanish Civil War → Botwin Company
Spielmacher
Sport
St. Matthew Passion
Stalingrad
Star of David
[The] Star of Redemption
Statelessness → Citizenship;
   → Nansen Passport
Statistics
[The] Street of Crocodiles
Struma
Student Corporations
Students → Universities
Style of Thought
Sufis
Sukkot → Course of the Year
Sulamith
Sultan's Jews
Superman
Sweatshop → New York
Synagogue
Tafsīr
Talmud
Talmud Torah
Tanakh
Tancred
Tangier
Tarbut
Tavern
Technion
Tekhelet
Tel Aviv

Tell Halaf
Temple
Teshuvah
Tevye
Territorialists → Colonization
Textile Industry → Łódź
al-Thaqāfah
[The] Thaw
Theatre Criticism
Theory
Theory of Relativity
Theresienstadt
Thesaurus of Hebrew Oriental Melodies
Thessaloniki → Salonika
Tiberias
Tikkun olam
Time
Tin Pan Alley
Tish'ah be-Av
Tkhines
Tłomackie Synagogue
Todesfuge
Tohuwabohu
Toledo
Torah → Tanakh
Tractatus Theologico-Politicus
Transfer Agreement → Ha'avarah
   Agreement
Transit
Translation
Transportation
Treblinka
Trieste
[The] Truce
Tsaddik
Tsedakah
Tsene-rene
Tunis
Tur Malka
Turin Group
Twelve-Tone Music

LIST OF ARTICLES (SO–Z)

Type
Typography
Übervolk
Ultra-Orthodoxy
Undzere Kinder
Universities
University in Exile → New School for Social
    Research
Utopia
Vaudeville
Venice
Verein für Cultur und Wissenschaft
    der Juden
[Der] verwaltete Mensch
Vichy
Vienna
Vienna Circle
Vienna Werkbund Estate
Vilna
Vilna Troupe
Vitebsk
Völkerpsychologie
Voskhod
Wadi Salib
Warburg Library
Warsaw
Watchmaker
Weintraubs Syncopators
Weißensee
Weizmann Institute
Weltbühne
Weltende
Weltgeschichte
West Side Story
Westerbork

Westminster
White Christmas
Wiener Library
Wirklichkeit der Hebräer
Wissenschaft des Judentums
Wolkenbügel
Woman Rabbi
World Jewish Congress
World Union for Progressive Judaism
World's Fair
Worms
Yad Vashem
Yankele
Yekkes
Yentl
Yeshiva University
Yeshivah → Talmud Torah
Yevsektsiya → Birobidzhan
Yiddish
Yiddishland
Yishuv
YIVO
Yom Kippur → Course of the Year
Yung-yidish
Zakhor
Zeitschrift der Deutschen
    Morgenländischen Gesellschaft
Zelig
Zeno
Židovská Strana
Zikhron Ya'akov
Zikhroynes
Zion
Zionism → Basel; → Old New Land
Zohar → Mysticism
Żydokomuna

List of Authors

Abd El Gawad, Walid (Leipzig): Tafsīr

Ancselovits, Elisha (Jerusalem): Talmud Torah

Aptroot, Marion (Düsseldorf): Yiddish

Ariel, Yaakov (Chapel Hill, NC): Temple, Teshuvah, Ultra-Orthodoxy, Yeshiva University

Aust, Cornelia (Mainz): Transportation

Balke, Ralf (Berlin): Struma, Tekhelet, Tunis (with U. Schuster), Weizmann Institute

Barkow, Ben (London): Wiener Library

Bartal, Israel (Jerusalem): Zikhron Ya'akov

Battegay, Caspar (Basel): Superman

Beller, Steven (Washington D.C.): Vienna, West Side Story

Ben-Artzi, Yossi (Haifa): Technion

Ben-Naeh, Yaron (Jerusalem): Sultan's Jews, Tiberias

Berg, Nicolas (Leipzig): Style of Thought, Theory of Relativity, Völkerpsychologie

Bönnen, Gerold (Worms): Worms

Breysach, Barbara (Berlin): [The] Street of Crocodiles

Brook, Vincent (Los Angeles): Zelig

Bułat, Mirosława M. (Cracow): Vilna Troupe

Consonni, Manuela (Jerusalem): [The] Truce, Turin Group

Crhová, Marie (Olomouc): Židovská Strana

Dahm, Annkatrin (Cologne): St. Matthew Passion

Deonna, Emmanuel (Lausanne): World Jewish Congress

Deventer, Jörg (Leipzig): Venice

Diner, Dan (Jerusalem/Leipzig): Weltgeschichte

Dreyfus, Kay (Melbourne): Weintraubs Syncopators

Dubin, Lois C. (Northampton, MA): Trieste

Dunkhase, Jan Eike (Marbach am Neckar): Tractatus Theologico-Politicus

Dykman, Aminadav (Jerusalem): Translation

Dynner, Glenn (New York): Tavern, Tsaddik

Endelman, Todd M. (Ann Arbor): Westminster

Feinberg, Anat (Heidelberg): Spielmacher, Yekkes

Finder, Gabriel N. (Charlottesville): Undzere Kinder

Flavin, Michael (London): Tancred

Gallus, Alexander (Chemnitz): Weltbühne

Gilibert, Alessandra (Berlin): Tell Halaf

Goldberg, Chad Alan (Madison): Sociology (with M. Müller)

Goldberg, Sylvie Anne (Paris): Time, Tish'ah be-Av

Graf, Philipp (Leipzig): Transit

Gray, Alyssa M. (New York): Tsedakah

Griffioen, Pim (Amsterdam): Westerbork

Gur, Golan (Cambridge): Twelve-Tone Music

Hájková, Anna (Coventry): Theresienstadt

Hamberlin, Larry (Middlebury): White Christmas

Hart, Mitchell B. (Gainesville): Statistics

Hüttenmeister, Nathanja (Essen): Weißensee

Isenschmid, Andreas (Berlin): Solal

Kanarek, Jane L. (Brookline): Talmud

Kara, Cem (Munich): Sufis

Kassow, Samuel D. (Hartford): Warsaw, YIVO

Keßler, Katrin (Braunschweig): Synagogue (with U. Knufinke)

Kettler, David (Annandale-on-Hudson): Sociology of Knowledge (with V. Meja)

Klibansky, Ben-Tsiyon (Tel Aviv): Vilna

Knapp, Alexander (London): Tin Pan Alley (with R. Randhofer)

Knufinke, Ulrich (Braunschweig): Synagogue (with K. Keßler)

Koller, Sabine (Regensburg): Vitebsk

Kramer, Sven (Lüneburg): [Der] verwaltete Mensch

LIST OF AUTHORS

Krone, Kerstin von der (Berlin/Braunschweig): Verein für Cultur und Wissenschaft der Juden

Kühne, Jan (Jerusalem): Tohuwabohu

Kuzar, Ron (Haifa): Yishuv

Lavitt, Pamela Brown (Seattle): Vaudeville

Lisek, Joanna (Wrocław): Yung-Yidish

Liska, Vivian (Antwerpen): Weltende (with B. Witte)

Liss, Hanna (Heidelberg): Tanakh

Lohmann, Ingrid (Hamburg): Sulamith

Mahrer, Stefanie (Jerusalem): Watchmaker (with J. Picard)

Marx, Peter W. (Cologne): Theatre Criticism

Maurer, Trude (Regensburg/Göttingen): Universities

Meder, Iris (Vienna): Vienna Werkbund Estate

Meja, Volker (St. John's, Newfoundland): Sociology of Knowledge (with D. Kettler)

Mendes-Flohr, Paul (Chicago/Jerusalem): [The] Star of Redemption, Utopia

Michlic, Joanna B. (Bristol/Waltham, MA): Żydokomuna

Miron, Dan (New York): Tevye, Tur Malka

Morgan, Michael L. (Toronto/Bloomington): Tikkun Olam

Morris-Reich, Amos (Haifa): Type

Müller, Marcel (Leipzig): Sociology (with C. A. Goldberg)

Nadell, Pamela S. (Washington D.C.): Woman Rabbi

Nemtsov, Jascha (Potsdam): Society for Jewish Folk Music

Neuberg, Simon (Trier): Tkhines, Tsene-rene

Norich, Anita (Ann Arbor): Yentl

Norkina, Ekaterina (St. Petersburg): Voskhod

Oegema, Gerbern S. (Montreal): Star of David

Pareigis, Christina (Berlin): Yankele

Picard, Jacques (Basel): Watchmaker (with S. Mahrer)

Poznanski, Renée (Beer Sheva): Vichy

Randhofer, Regina (Leipzig): Thesaurus of Hebrew Oriental Melodies, Tin Pan Alley (with A. Knapp)

Rohden, Frauke von (Leipzig): Zakhor

Rürup, Miriam (Hamburg): Student Corporations

Schächter, Elizabeth (Canterbury): Zeno

Schick, David (Munich): [The] Thaw

Schmid, Ulrich M. (St. Gallen): Stalingrad

Schoell-Glass, Charlotte (Hamburg): Warburg Library

Schuster, Ulrich (Leipzig): Tunis (with R. Balke)

Ščrbačić, Maja (Leipzig/Jerusalem): al-Thaqāfah

Serels, M. Mitchell (Scarsdale): Tangier

Silber, Marcos (Haifa): Tarbut, Tłomackie Synagogue, Yiddishland

Silbergklang, David (Jerusalem): Sobibór

Soltes, Ori Z. (Washington D.C.): Wolkenbügel

Sonder, Ines (Potsdam): Tel Aviv

Sparr, Thomas (Berlin): Todesfuge

Stadler, Friedrich (Vienna): Vienna Circle

Stauber, Roni (Tel Aviv): Yad Vashem

Tamari, Ittai J. (Munich): Typography

Thulin, Mirjam (Mainz/Frankfurt am Main): Zeitschrift der Deutschen Morgenländischen Gesellschaft

Ticotsky, Giddon (Tel Aviv): Sonnet

Turniansky, Chava (Jerusalem): Zikhroynes

Umansky, Ellen M. (Fairfield): World Union for Progressive Judaism

Voigt, Sebastian (Munich/Leipzig): Treblinka

Voigts, Manfred (Potsdam): Wirklichkeit der Hebräer

Warneck, Dorothea (Halle, S.): World's Fair

Weiss, Yfaat (Jerusalem): Wadi Salib

Wiese, Christian (Frankfurt am Main): Wissenschaft des Judentums

Wilke, Carsten L. (Budapest): Toledo

Witte, Bernd (Düsseldorf): Weltende (with V. Liska)

Wussow, Philipp von (Frankfurt am Main): Theory, Übervolk

Zank, Michael (Boston): Zion

Zimmermann, Moshe (Jerusalem): Soccer, Sport

List of Translators

Tim Barnwell
  Student Corporations
Mike Chase
  Sobibór
  Stalingrad
  Sulamith
  Tarbut
  Tell Halaf
  Theatre Criticism
  Theresienstadt
  Tiberias
  Tikkun olam
  Tłomackie Synagogue
  Todesfuge
  Translation
  Universities
  Venice
  Vichy
  Völkerpsychologie
  Watchmaker
  Weltbühne
  West Side Story
Gwendolin Goldbloom
  Sociology
  Sociology of Knowledge
  Solal
  Spielmacher
  Sport
  St. Matthew Passion
  [The] Star of Redemption
  Statistics
  [The] Street of Crocodiles
  Struma
  Sufis
  Sultan's Jews
  Superman
  Tafsīr
  Talmud
  Talmud Torah
  Tanakh
  Tangier
  Technion

Tevye
al-Thaqāfah
[The] Thaw
Theory
Theory of Relativity
Thesaurus of Hebrew Oriental Melodies
Time
Tin Pan Alley
Tohuwabohu
Toledo
Tractatus Theologico-Politicus
Transit
Transportation
Treblinka
Trieste
Tsene-rene
Tunis
Tur Malka
Turin Group
Twelve-Tone Music
Type
Typography
Undzere Kinder
Utopia
Vaudeville
Verein für Cultur und Wissenschaft der Juden
[Der] verwaltete Mensch
Vienna
Vienna Circle
Vienna Werkbund Estate
Vilna
Vilna Troupe
Vitebsk
Voskhod
Wadi Salib
Warburg Library
Warsaw
Weintraubs Syncopators
Weißensee
Weizmann Institute
Weltende

LIST OF TRANSLATORS

Weltgeschichte
White Christmas
Wiener Library
Wirklichkeit der Hebräer
Wissenschaft des Judentums
Wolkenbügel
World Jewish Congress
World Union for Progressive Judaism
World's Fair
Worms
Yankele
Yekkes
Yentl
Yeshiva University
Yiddish
Yiddishland
YIVO
Yung-yidish
Zakhor
Zeno
Zikhron Ya'akov
Zikhroynes
Zion
Żydokomuna
Ela Harrison
   Star of David
   Style of Thought
   [The] Truce

Tina Jerke
   Soccer
   Society for Jewish Folk Music
   Sonnet
   Tekhelet
   Tish'ah be-Av
   Tkhines
   Tsaddik
   Tsedakah
   Übervolk
   Ultra-Orthodoxy
   Westerbork
   Westminster
   Yad Vashem
   Yishuv
   Zeitschrift der Deutschen
   Morgenländischen Gesellschaft
   Zelig
   Židovská Strana
Nik Myers
   Synagogue
   Tancred
   Tavern
   Tel Aviv
   Temple
   Teshuvah
Janina and Julia Peschke
   Woman Rabbi

List of Images and Maps

Images

Soccer (p. 9): Béla Guttmann (1899–1981). picture-alliance/dpa

Sociology (p. 20): Émile Durkheim (1858–1917). picture-alliance/Leemage

Sociology of Knowledge (p. 25): Karl Mannheim (1893–1947). Henk Woldring

Sonnet (p. 40): Lea Goldberg (1911–1970). Central Zionist Archives, Jerusalem

Spielmacher (p. 44): George Tabori (1914–2007). Bayerische Staatsbibliothek / Felicitas Timpe

Sport (p. 57): Spectators during a handball match between Makkabi Absalom from Petah Tikva (Palestine) and a selection team of Makkabi Berlin, June 24, 1937, photo by Herbert Sonnenfeld. Herbert Sonnenfeld, Jüdisches Museum Berlin

St. Matthew Passion (p. 65): Felix Mendelssohn Bartholdy (1809–1847). picture alliance / United Archives/DEA

Stalingrad (p. 71): Wassily Grossman (1905–1964). picture-alliance/dpa

Star of David (p. 77): The American heavyweight boxer Max Baer (l.) fighting Joe Louis (1935). Though not Jewish himself, Baer regularly fought wearing a Star of David – also in his knockout victory over Max Schmeling in June, 1933 (→ Boxing). picture-alliance/dpa

[The] Star of Redemption (p. 79): Franz Rosenzweig (1886–1929). Courtesy of the Leo Baeck Institute

[The] Street of Crocodiles (p. 94): *Józef by his sick father Jakub's bedside*, Drawing by Bruno Schulz (1926). Jewish Historical Institute Warsaw

Student Corporations (p. 102): Students of the Jewish association KC Ghibellinia in front of a picture of the Freiburg Minster (taken in 1912). Jüdisches Museum Berlin, Schenkung

Style of Thought (p. 108): Ludwik Fleck (1896–1961). Archiv für Zeitgeschichte, ETH Zürich, FD Thomas Schnelle / 8

Sulamith (p. 120): Title page of the first issue of the journal *Sulamith*, Leipzig 1806. Gidal-Bildarchiv im Steinheim-Institut

Synagogue (p. 139): View of the Oranienburger Straße and Neue Synagoge (New Synagogue) in the Mitte district of Berlin, taken 1934. bpk / Abraham Pisarek

Talmud Torah (p. 162): Students discussing the Chumash in ḥeder (Jewish elementary school), [Brod], ca. 1938. Photo by Roman Vishniac. © Mara Vishniac Kohn, courtesy of International Center of Photography

Tancred (p. 178): Benjamin Disraeli (1804–1881). bpk / W. D. Downey

Tel Aviv (p. 206): Allenby Square (today: *Kikar Magen David*) in Tel Aviv (picture from 1940). ullstein bild – Pachot

Tell Halaf (p. 211): Max von Oppenheim (1860–1946) beside a statue excavated at Tell Halaf (1930). ullstein bild – Martin Munkacsi

Tevye (p. 226): Sholem Aleichem (b. Shalom Rabinovitch, 1859–1916). www.sholom-aleichem.org, Robert Waife

[The] Thaw (p. 242): Ilya Ehrenburg (1891–1967). ullstein bild – RIA Novosti

Theory (p. 258): Title page of Georg Lukács's treatise *Die Theorie des Romans*, published in Stuttgart in 1916. Staatsbibliothek zu Berlin

Theory of Relativity (p. 263): Albert Einstein (1879–1955). The Granger Collection, NYC

Theresienstadt (p. 271): *Backdrops for the the International Commission (Theresienstadt)*, Sketch by Bedřich Fritta (1943/1944). Jüdisches Museum Berlin, Dauerleihgabe von Thomas Fritta-Haas

Thesaurus of Hebrew Oriental Melodies (p. 277): Abraham Zevi Idelsohn (1882–1938). From the Abraham Zwi Idelshon

LIST OF IMAGES AND MAPS

Archive, The National Library of Israel, Jerusalem

Tikkun olam (p. 290): Emil Fackenheim (1916–2003). Herlinde Koelbl

Tłomackie Synagogue (p. 315): View of the Tłomackie Synagogue in Warsaw (postcard, ca. 1936). Emanuel Ringelblum Jewish Historical Institute Collections

Todesfuge (p. 319): Paul Celan (orig. Paul Antschel, 1920–1970). ullstein bild / Imagno

Tohuwabohu (p. 326): Sammy Gronemann (1875–1952). bpk

Toledo (p. 334): The Alhambra Decree of 1492 featuring the signatures of King Ferdinand II of Aragón and Queen Isabella of Castile (excerpt). Archivo Municipal de Avila

Tractus Theologico Politicus (p. 340): *Spinoza*, Painting by Samuel Hirszenberg (1907). The Kursk Deineka Picture Gallery

Transit (p. 347): Anna Seghers (orig. Netty Radványi, née Reiling, 1900–1983). ullstein bild – ADN-Bildarchiv

Trieste (p. 369): Interior view of the Scuola Grande Synagogue in Trieste, built 1797. Riccardo Camerini/Archivio Alinari, Florence

[The] Truce (p. 373): Primo Levi (1919–1987). Marcello Mencarini

Tsedakah (p. 386): Donation box with the Hebrew inscription *Erets Yisra'el* (Land of Israel), Halberstadt Synagoge (17th century). Städtisches Museum Halberstadt

Tur Malka (p. 399): Uri Zvi Grinberg (1896–1981). National Photo Collection Israel

Turin Group (p. 411): Natalia Ginzburg (1916–1991). picture alliance/Gattoni/Leemage

Twelve-Tone Music (p. 415): Arnold Schönberg (1874–1951). ullstein bild

Type (p. 420): Georg Simmel (1858–1918). The Granger Collection, NYC

Undzere Kinder (p. 444): Shimen Dzigan (l., 1905–1980) and Yisroel Shumacher (1908–1961). Anat Zeltser

Utopia (p. 455): Ernst Bloch (1885–1977). ullstein bild – Würth GmbH/Swiridoff

[Der] verwaltete Mensch (p. 473): Mensch H. G. Adler (1910–1988). ullstein bild – dpa

Vienna (p. 491): Arthur Schnitzler (1862–1931). ullstein bild/Imagno/Archiv Setzer-Tschiedel

Vienna Werkbund Estate (p. 501): Advertisement poster for the Vienna Werkbund Estate (1932). University of Applied Arts Vienna, Collection and Archive

Vilna (p. 508): Elijah ben Solomon (1720–1797), the Vilna Gaon. Schwadron Portrait Collection. Courtesy of The National Library of Israel, Jerusalem

Vilna Troupe (p. 514): Members of the Vilna Troupe around 1919, among them David Hermann (standing, 1st left), Sonia Alomis (seated, 1st left), and Leib Kadison (seated, 1st right). YIVO Institute for Jewish Research, New York

Vitebsk (p. 518): Marc Chagall (1887–1985). ullstein bild – Photo12

Völkerpsychologie (p. 523): Titel page of the *Zeitschrift für Völkerpsychologie und Sprachwissenschaft* (1860), edited by Moritz Lazarus and Chajim Heymann Steinthal. Universitätsbibliothek Leipzig

Wadi Salib (p. 535): Protest in Wadi Salib, 1959. Photo by Oskar Tauber. © Josef Tauber

Warburg Library (p. 539): The Reading Room of the Kulturwissenschaftliche Bibliothek Warburg in Hamburg, photo of 1926. ullstein bild

Watchmaker (p. 550): Headquarters of the Swiss Watch Company Movado in La Chaux-de-Fonds (photo montage, 1948). Christian Pfeiffer-Belli

Weißensee (p. 558): Jewish cemetery Berlin-Weißensee, memorial to the wine merchant and restaurateur Berthold Kempinski (1843–1910). ullstein bild – Straub

Weltbühne (p. 570): Kurt Tucholsky (1890–1935). ullstein bild – Keystone

West Side Story (p. 586): Leonard Bernstein (1918–1990). ullstein bild – Gräwert

White Christmas (p. 602): Irving Berlin (1888–1989). picture alliance

Wiener Library (p. 606): Alfred Wiener in his London office (1952). Wiener Library, London

Wissenschaft des Judentums (p. 619): Leopold Zunz (1794–1886). bpk/Julius Löwensohn

Wolkenbügel (p. 626): *Der Wolkenbügel*, Sketch by El Lissitzky (1925). picture alliance/Heritage Images

World Jewish Congress (p. 641): Nahum Goldmann (1895–1982). Courtesy of Leo Baeck Institute, New York

World Union for Progressive Judaism (p. 649): Lily H. Montagu (1873–1963). Courtesy of Jewish Museum London

Yad Vashem (p. 663): Yad Vashem director Ben-Zion Dinur (third from left) presents Israeli President Yitzhak Ben-Zvi (second from right) with documents from the Oyneg Shabbes Collection (photo from 1956). Yad Vashem Photo Archives

Yankele (p. 669): Mordechai Gebirtig (1877–1942). public domain

Yekkes (p. 671): Café Mugrabi in Tel Aviv, 1935. Pia Gidal / Jüdisches Museum Berlin

YIVO (p. 700): Simon Dubnow (standing, center) at an international YIVO conference, Vilna, 1935. YIVO Institute for Jewish Research, New York

Zeno (p. 724): Italo Svevo (orig. Aron Hector Schmitz, 1861–1928). ullstein bild

Zikhroynes (p. 739): *Bertha Pappenheim dressed as Glikl*, Painting by Leopold Pilichowski (ca. 1925). Moshe and Alice Shalvi

Maps

Tangier (p. 186): The Jewish exodus from the Maghreb states after the Second World War

Zydokomuna (p. 748): Anti-Jewish violence at the time of the foundation of the Polish state 1918/1919

All maps were created by the Leibniz Institute for Regional Geography (IfL), Leipzig. The English version maps were created by Erik Goosmann.

S

Sobibór

Site of a National Socialist extermination camp in eastern Poland. From May 1942 to October 1943, between 150,000 and 250,000 persons were murdered in Sobibór. Like the other two large camps of the "Aktion Reinhard" (Operation Reinhard), Bełżec and Treblinka, which were built for killing the Jews of the General Government in Poland, Sobibór was initially intended for the extermination of Jews from the district of Lublin. In addition, several tens of thousands of Jews from Slovakia, the Czech Republic, Germany, Austria, the Netherlands, France, Lithuania, and Belarus were deported to the camp. Together with Auschwitz-Birkenau and Treblinka, Sobibór was, in the autumn of 1943, one of the death camps in which a revolt and mass escape by Jewish inmates took place.

1. Organization and personnel
2. Camp operation and day-to-day life of the prisoners
3. Rebellion and flight
4. Closing of the camp and documentation

1. Organization and personnel

During the Second World War, the small village of Sobibór near the river Bug, today situated in eastern Poland close to the border with Belarus and Ukraine, was part of the Lublin District within the General Government. National Socialist mass killings in the region began in December 1939, when at least 320 Polish-Jewish prisoners of war were deported in cattle cars from Lublin to Włodawa. More than half of them died during the transport, while most of the rest of them were shot in the forest by the SS and the Volksdeutscher Selbstschutz, an auxiliary force of the SS, made up of Polish so-called ethnic Germans. When a delegation from the → Judenrat of Włodawa went to the forest near Sobibór at the behest of the local SS members to receive a group of these prisoners of war, they found corpses in tattered uniforms at the site.

The extermination camp situated in the vicinity of the village of Sobibór was, along with Bełżec and → Treblinka, one of the killing facilities that were set up in the context of the operation, ordered by Himmler in October 1941, which aimed at the complete plundering and murder of all Jews in the General Government. The extermination program, called "Aktion Reinhard" beginning in the summer of 1942 – apparently named after Reinhard Heydrich, organizer of the "final solution of the Jewish Question," who had been assassinated in June 1942 – was under the command of Odilo Globocnik, head of the SS and the police of the Lublin District. By means of the systematic deportation and extermination set in motion here, the vast majority of Polish Jews were killed by the end of 1942. Within a very short time, the operation was also extended to the Jews of many other countries, who were ultimately deported from all of Europe to the three camps. In all, approximately two million Jews were murdered from March 1942 to November 1943 in the course of "Aktion Reinhard." Between

1.6 and 1.7 million of them died by gas in the extermination camps, and the rest by shooting and → forced labor, during deportation, or from the unbearable living conditions in the camps [1. 541–548].

Sobibór was chosen because the village met the essential requirements that were also crucial for the other extermination camps of "Aktion Reinhard": isolation and accessibility as a guarantee of efficient transportation routes with concurrent secrecy. All three camps were located in isolated areas that were linked by major railway lines: Sobibór was near the line from Lublin via Chełm to Brest-Litovsk.

SS Oberstumführer Richard Thomalla, who had already supervised the construction of the Bełżec camp from November 1941 to mid-February 1942, was also responsible for the construction of the Sobibór camp, which began in February or March 1942 and was completed by the end of April. Guarded by a small unit of some ten Ukrainians, about 80 Jews from the environs were forced to carry out the construction work. They were shot after its completion. The gas chambers were then tested on Jews from the nearby forced labor camp at Krychów. SS Hauptsturmführer Franz Stangl was named commander of the camp at the end of April; after his transfer to Treblinka in August, he was succeeded by SS Hauptsturmführer Franz Reichleitner (1906–1944).

Sobibór was considered an optimized variant of the Bełżec prototype. It was 600 × 400 meters in size, and was subdivided into three areas, separated from one another. Camp I included the barracks of the Jewish worker-prisoners and the workshops, in which the possessions of the Jews were sorted and various skilled handiworks were carried out for the Germans. Camp II and the front camp, situated between Camp I and Camp III, formed the largest area. The front camp included the railway ramps, the quarters of the SS and the Ukrainian guards, as well as storage rooms; Camp II, with shacks for

disrobing, storerooms for valuables, as well as a room in which womens' hair was shorn, served as an immediate preparation to the killing of the Jews who had been brought to it. Camp III was the extermination zone and consisted of gas chambers, mass graves, and the barracks of the Jews who worked there. There was no contact at all between the prisoners working in the various camps. A path, 255 meters long and five meters wide, which prisoners and guards called "Heaven Street" or "the hose," connected Camp II and III. It was along this path that the prisoners were driven into the gas chambers. As in the other camps of the "Aktion Reinhard," the gassing was carried out by carbon monoxide. The gas was produced by a 200 hp engine, and directed to the three chambers there. By an order from Himmler in 1943, the construction of a fourth camp area was planned, which was to serve for the treatment of Soviet ammunition.

Each camp had its own "Lagerältester" (Camp Elder) or "Oberkapo" (chief prisoner functionary), who sometimes behaved decently to the prisoners, other times with brutality and corruption. The personnel consisted of 20 to 30 German SS men and policemen, most of whom had previously taken part in the murder of disabled persons in the context of the "euthanasia program" known as "Operation T4." Added to these were 90 to 120 Ukrainians, most of whom had been members of the Red Army and had switched sides after being captured, along with other Ukrainians and ethnic Germans from the Soviet Union; they were all called "Ukranians" in the camp. The Ukrainians were trained in the SS training camp of Trawniki (west of Chełm), and were therefore also known as "Trawnikis" in the camp; they were employed as guards and work supervisors and were also used in gassings and shootings. The number of Jewish prisoners who performed forced labor in the camp was usually between 600 and 700 [1. 157–164].

2. Camp operation and day-to-day life of the prisoners

The first Jews from the Lublin District were deported to the extermination camp of Sobibór in May 1942. Within a few days, they were followed by transports from Germany, Slovakia, the Czech Republic, and Austria. Sometimes, Jews who did not come from the General Government were told after their arrival to inform their family members via postcard that they had reached their destination safely. They were to give "Włodawa Labor Camp" as the return address. Nearly all Jews were killed immediately after their arrival.

Prisoners helped new arrivals down from the train, after which they were usually divided by gender, with small children remaining with the women. They were given a speech by one of the SS men, who announced that healthy prisoners would be assigned work, while children and the elderly would be cared for. The vast majority of each transport were then driven into the disrobing rooms, with the women having their hair cut off as well. After that, they had to walk through the camouflaged "hose" to Camp III, where they were crammed into the gas chambers and killed.

Prisoners from Camps I and II sorted through their belongings, while prisoners in Camp III had to look after the corpses. Whoever was too old or fragile to make the journey to Camp III was taken in a horse-drawn cart to the "infirmary," which was really a place of execution, and was shot there. The entire process of murder, from arrival to extermination, lasted scarcely more than an hour.

The prisoners chosen for labor carried out various tasks. In Camp II, qualified workers were used in the workshops as so-called "Hofjuden" (court Jews), where they worked as cabinet makers, tailors, jewelers, and shoemakers, or had to perform services for the Germans, such as cleaning or cooking. Those who had to receive incoming transports at the platform, remove the corpses of those who had died along the way, or sort the clothes of the murdered were called "Platzjuden" (Square Jews); "Goldjuden" (gold Jews) had to search for gold and other valuables among the belongings of the newly arrived deportees; "barbers" had to cut off the women's hair. As "dentists," the inmates of Camp III were used to remove gold teeth from the corpses, to take them to mass graves, and to burn them. The life of the Jewish prisoners depended on a continuous influx of Jews to be murdered, as well as goods to be sorted and packaged, and was forfeit as soon as that influx came to an end.

Transports to Sobibór were interrupted in the summer of 1942. Since the Wehrmacht needed railway cars for the German summer offensive in the Soviet Union, deportations to Bełżec and Sobibór slowed down in June and July. Moreover, the killing capacity of the gas chambers of both camps had proved insufficient for the task assigned to them. In Sobibór, the capacities were exhausted by the arrival of 19,000 Jews from the Lublin District, as well as an additional 10,000 from throughout Europe in July 1942 alone. In addition, the tracks near Sobibór, which led through swampy land, had not withstood the large number of transports, and the camp was therefore closed temporarily. The available documents, such as deportation numbers for specific places, police records, and eyewitness testimonies, indicate that until June 20, 1942, at least 90,000 Jews had been murdered in Sobibór [8. 146–158].

The shortage of transports was used to build new gas chambers. By the time it reopened in October, the camp's killing capacity had more than doubled. Henceforth, the six chambers held over 1,200 people. Once the transports began again, more than 42,000, and perhaps even more than 60,000 Jews, who came from the Lublin District or had been deported there from Slovakia, were brought to Sobibór. The deportation of 2,000 Jews from France followed in March 1943. At the same time, the first of 19 trains carrying Dutch Jews reached the camp: by July 1943, a total of 34,000 Jews from the Netherlands arrived at Sobibór. From July to October 1943, several thousand Jews from Belarus and Lithuania (primarily from → Vilna) were carried off to the extermination camp in the wake of the liquidation of the ghetto there [9. 48–57, 197–226].

One of the cynical features of the prisoners' daily lives in the extermination camps of "Aktion Reinhard" was that Jewish forced laborers who had to work in the death zone were often allowed more food and, in general, better everyday conditions than Jews in many other places under German dominion. Their work day began early and ended late with a roll call; beatings and killings by the Germans were usual. However, if they "stole" any of the belongings of the murdered Jews, the Germans sometimes overlooked it. They could also consume food that they found in the baggage of arriving Jews and could also make music, dance, and, to a limited extent, lead a social life. Sometimes there were even musical performances also attended by camp personnel. Many women were among the working prisoners in Camps I and II. In these surreal surroundings, in which an already-pronounced death sentence hovered over the heads of all, friendships and even love affairs developed among the prisoners.

3. Rebellion and flight

Unlike in Sobibór, the extermination procedures in Bełżec had already been declared complete in December 1942, and the camp was closed early. It had fulfilled its task in the sense of the "final solution": almost 500,000 Jews from the districts of Cracow, Galicia, and parts of the Lublin District fell victim to genocide in Bełżec. The Jewish forced laborers who remained behind had to burn their corpses and dismantle the camp. Afterwards, the 300 men were brought to Sobibór and shot. When the prisoners there received, as ordered, the clothing of the murdered victims, they found a note in the pockets of one of the victims, which gave information on the identity of the group and warned the finders of what was in store for them. As a result, some tried to flee, while others planned a mass escape.

Since Himmler had ordered the establishment of Camp IV to recondition captured Soviet munitions, a "Waldkommando" (Forest Commando) was set up, which felled trees outside the camp for construction. This facilitated attempted escapes, which became more frequent in the summer of 1943. Alongside increasing partisan activity in the area, this once again caused the Germans to lay a cordon of landmines around the camp. Thus, Jews and Ukrainian guards, some of whom had deserted to the → partisans, were to be prevented from escaping, and the partisans kept far from the camp. Almost all the fugitive Jews, moreover, were caught, and drastic collective punishments were imposed: ten Jews were shot for every escapee.

In mid-July 1943, an underground group took shape among the prisoners in Camp I, led by Leon Feldhendler (1910–1945), former head of the → Judenrat in Żółkiewka. In view of the cordon of mines and the imminent punishment, they decided to organize a mass escape of all prisoners, so that no one should be punished for the escape of another. After many deliberations had been rejected, in August 1943 a former officer of the Dutch navy, Joseph Jacobs (1900–1943), began to organize a plan for a revolt and an escape, which also included arrangements with some Ukrainian guards, who intended to escape with the Jews and join the partisans. However, the plan was thwarted after details were passed on to the Germans by one of the Ukrainian guards, and Jacobs and an additional 72 Dutch Jews from the camp were executed.

In September 1943, the Oberkapo Moshe Sturm planned an escape together with five other Kapos; however, another Kapo informed the Germans of their plan, and all six were immediately killed. Other prisoners later took revenge on the Kapo who had betrayed the group by beating him up and poisoning him. The prisoners in Camp III planned a breakout by means of an escape tunnel, which, however, was discovered in mid-September, before it was completed. As a result, all the camp's prisoners were shot, and replaced by a new detachment.

In the wake of the liquidation of the ghettos in Belarus, the Germans deported thousands of more Jews to Sobibór. Among them was a group of Soviet-Jewish prisoners of war. The approximately 80 men under the command of Lieutenant Alexander (Sasha) Pechersky (1909–1990) arrived in late September 1943 with a transport of more than 2,000 Jews from Minsk. Their arrival proved to be the decisive factor for planning and carrying out a revolt and mass escape. At the end of September 1943, Pechersky and Feldhendler agreed to plan the escape of all 600 Jews in Camp I. The group around Feldhendler brought to the plan their precise knowledge of the camp, while the prisoners of war led by Pechersky brought with them military experience. They were not able to include the inmates of Camp III, since no contact could be established with them. This placed the group in an almost insoluble dilemma for it meant abandoning the inmates to certain death. In addition, they had to remain silent about the plan.

Because of negative experiences with Ukrainian guards, none of them was in on the plan. Nevertheless, the planning group included two Kapos, who enabled Pechersky to get a position in the carpenters' workshop in order better to coordinate the underground work. Two plans were developed in parallel. One envisaged a nighttime breakout through a tunnel, while the other involved killing most of the Germans and fleeing through the main gate. Meanwhile, heavy rain on the 8th and 9th of October impeded the tunnel, the construction of which had been begun a few days beforehand, leaving the group only with the second plan. October 13th was fixed as the date for the revolt and escape. Owing to the unexpected arrival of a group of German inspectors, the operation was postponed for one day.

The revolt was planned as a three-stage operation, and was to begin shortly before the end of the working day, and as close as possible to the beginning of dusk, so that the inmates could flee under cover of darkness. In a concerted operation between 15:30 and 16:45, SS men were to be lured into the workshops on the pretext of a fitting for shoes and clothes, and were to be killed there; next, telephone lines and electricity were to be cut, and ammunition, grenades, and weapons were to be seized from the quarters of the SS and the Ukrainian guards. Then (around 16:45), the two participating Kapos were to muster the inmates, along with the prisoners of war and those who were in on the plot forming the first rows. Finally, the inmates would be led to the main gate, whereupon the Ukrainian guards would come under fire. Meanwhile, the inmates were to flee to the safety of the nearby woods and try to join up with the partisans.

On the day of the uprising, work proceeded as usual. The rebels executed the first part of the plan without being noticed: eleven SS men were killed without a sound. The SS man Erich Bauer suddenly appeared in the workshop, realized what was going on, and opened fire at the same moment that the leader of the Ukrainian guards was killed on the parade ground. The guards noticed what was happening and began to shoot at the inmates. In return, the rebels mortally wounded four of them, while the prisoners were able to run toward the fence and escape. Some 300 inmates left the camp; at least half of them reached the woods, while all the others were shot by the guards or killed by mines. The remaining 300 inmates, who were sick and unable to escape, or who came from Central and Western Europe and therefore could neither understand the local language nor find their way in the environs, were killed, like the prisoners in Camp II, either on the same or the next day [1. 299–348].

On the morning after the revolt, a contingent of 400 men, made up of members of the Wehrmacht, the SS, and the police, as well as the Ukrainian guards, supported by two to three reconnaissance aircraft, began to hunt the escapees. The latter split up into small groups and searched for partisans to join. Pechersky and a few others were able to cross the Bug river and meet up with Soviet partisans; others joined the Communist People's Army (Armia Ludowa) or the Jewish partisan group led by Yehiel Grynszpan in the Parczew forest. Within a week, about 100 of the escapees had been recaptured and killed. The others had been helped initially by the protection of darkness and a mistake by the Germans: most inmates fled north to the Parczew forest, not eastwards to the Bug, where most of the German search troops were stationed. Nevertheless, most of the escapees were captured and killed, or otherwise fell in battle. The Germans received active assistance from the local population in their hunt, but there were also farmers who helped the fugitives.

Only about 50 escapees survived until the liberation of the area. Many of them fell victim to the antisemitic pogroms in Poland after the end of the war, as did Feldhendler, for instance, who was killed in Lublin in April 1945.

Most of the Jewish forced laborers who remained in the Lublin District were shot during the "Aktion Erntefest" (operation harvest festival) on November 3 and 4, 1943.

Research often interprets this operation as Himmler's reaction to the revolts in → Treblinka and Sobibór, as well as to the one in the → Warsaw ghetto in April and May, as well as in Białystok in August 1943 [1. 365f.]; [5. Introduction 13–18]; [3. 328f.]; [10. 404].

4. Closing of the camp and documentation

After the execution of all remaining inmates, the Germans razed the entire camp complex in Sobibór to the ground. All the barracks were removed, and the land was partially reforested in order to conceal all traces of mass murder.

Estimations of the number of Jews killed at Sobibór vary considerably. The most important preserved document on the industrial-scale killing in the camps of "Aktion Reinhard" is the Höfle telegram of January 11, 1943, deciphered by the British. In it SS Sturmbannführer Hermann Höfle, as deputy head of the operation, informed the Berlin headquarters of the Reichssicherheitshauptamt (Reich Main Security Office; RSHA) of the number of Jews murdered by the end of 1942: 713,555 in Treblinka, 434,508 in Bełżec, 101,370 in Sobibór, and 24,733 in Majdanek, for a total of 1,274,166 in 1942 [11]. It is not certain, however, that this information accurately conveys the number of the murdered [1. 381–382].

Even the number of Jews deported to Sobibór in 1942 seems to clearly exceed the information given by Höfle. One may assume tens of thousands of additional murder victims in the Sobibór camp for 1943. Owing to the destruction of the site and the systematic elimination of documentary material by the Germans, reconstruction of the events and the number of victims of the Sobibór extermination camp beyond the facts established by historical research and in court proceedings hardly seems possible now.

Bibliography

[1] Y. Arad, Belzec, Sobibor, Treblinka. The Operation Reinhard Death Camps, Bloomington 1987. [2] Y. Arad, Sobibór, in: Encyclopaedia of the Holocaust, ed. by I. Gutman et al., vol. 4, New York/London 1990, 1373–1378. [3] H. Grabitz/W. Scheffler (eds.), Letzte Spuren. Ghetto Warschau, SS-Arbeitslager Trawniki, Aktion Erntefest, Berlin 1988. [4] Y. Haimi/W. Mazurek, Uncovering the Remains of a Nazi Death Camp. Archaeological Research in Sobibór, in: Yad Vashem Studies 41 (2013) 2, 55–94. [5] W. Lenarczyk/D. Libionka (eds.), Erntefest 3–4 listopada 1943. Zapomniany epizod Zagłady ["Operation Erntefest" November 3–4, 1943. A Forgotten Chapter in the Murder of the Jews], Lublin 2009. [6] M. Novitch, Sobibor, Martyrdom and Revolt. Documents and Testimonies, New York 1980. [7] R. Rashke, Escape from Sobibor. Revised and Updated Edition, New York 2013. [8] A. Rückerl (ed.), Nationalsozialistische Vernichtungslager im Spiegel deutscher Strafprozesse. Belzec, Sobibor, Treblinka, Chelmno, Munich 1977. [9] J. Schelvis, Sobibor. A History of a Nazi Death Camp, New York 2007. [10] D. Silberklang, Gates of Tears. The Holocaust in the Lublin District, Jerusalem 2013. [11] P. Witte/S. Tyas, A New Document on the Deportation and Murder of Jews during "Einsatz Reinhardt" 1942, in: Holocaust and Genocide Studies 15 (2001) 3, 468–486.

DAVID SILBERGKLANG, JERUSALEM

Soccer

Jews have been involved in the game of soccer (or "football," in a European context) since the late 19th century. While they were not among the earliest pioneers of this massively popular → sport between 1863 and 1871, when soccer was given its body of rules and regulations in England, Jews have since the last decades of the 19th century contributed to its spread across Europe and America. After the turn of the century, soccer was also used to dispel the image of the sickly Jew of the Diaspora. With the Holocaust, however, the strong and vibrant Jewish soccer culture largely came to an end.

1. Beginnings
2. Professionalization and antisemitism
3. After 1933
4. In Israel

1. Beginnings

The history of soccer is closely associated with two modernizing developments that accompanied industrialization in the 19th century. For one, cities saw a rapid increase in their bourgeois and working class populations; another factor was the restructuring of work processes toward a highly mechanized, rigid schedule, which called for new types of leisure-time activities, and sport ranked prominently among these. By the end of the 19th century, soccer had become as much a symbol of modernization as of the cultural influence of England. Citizens of the United Kingdom, or persons who had grown up in the country, took the sport to the European mainland and to other continents; a number of Jews were at the forefront of this movement as players, managers, sponsors, and journalists. The London-born brothers Gus (1873–1953) and Fred Manning (1871–1960), as well as John Bloch from Birmingham, not only played the game, they were also among the founding fathers of the German Football Association (DFB, 1900). The trailblazers for soccer in Germany furthermore included Berlin-born Walther Bensemann (1873–1934), an admirer of English culture, who was involved in the founding of soccer clubs in Montreux (Switzerland), Munich, and Karlsruhe. Jews moreover had no small part in exporting the sport to America: in 1913 Gus Manning promoted the founding of the United States Soccer Association in New York; the English Jew Nathan Agar

(1887–1978) – player, referee, coach (manager), official, and club owner all rolled into one – in the 1920s held a key position with the American Soccer League.

The late-19th-century debate over the character of modern Judaism and the problems of an allegedly degenerate Jewish body, gave rise to the idea of the → muscular Jew. Proponents of the concept at first recommended gymnastics and athletics as a modern method to achieve physical fitness and social integration (→ Bar Kochba Berlin), but soccer was gaining in popularity across the board and quickly became an attractive sport for assimilated Jews as well. Even among those Zionists who were aiming to establish an autonomous Jewish identity and who were promoting the muscular Jew, soccer ranked as a useful tool. As early as 1902 in his futuristic novel *Altneuland* (→" Old New Land," 1941) Theodor Herzl describes how young Jews play soccer (and cricket) in Palestine – for him the sign of a new vital force and national regeneration.

Especially young Zionists or Jews with national Jewish inclinations, both in the Diaspora (primarily in Europe) and in Palestine, turned to soccer. The best-known and most successful team was → Hakoah Vienna, among whose supporters was none other than Franz Kafka (→ Prague). Founded in 1909, the club defined itself as *national-jüdisch* (i.e. in favor of Jewish nationhood) and became the 1924/1925 champions of the Austrian professional league. The 5–0 Hakoah victory over the English team of West Ham United in 1923 served "national" and assimilated Jews alike as a popular argument in combating prejudices about the alleged physical inferiority of Jews.

Soccer clubs modeled after Hakoah Vienna often formed where Jews decided to express their self-confidence as a people or as a national minority. Hakoah's 1923 victory over Hertha BSC led to a Hakoah club being established in Berlin. Other clubs followed in Germany and Austria, but none

of these were as successful as the Vienna original. Soccer saw an upswing in the → Yishuv after Hakoah Vienna traveled to Palestine. When Hakoah visited the United States in 1926, they were celebrated by a frenetic crowd of 46,000 at the New York Giants' stadium – illustrating the extent to which soccer helped shape the Jewish self-confidence in the New World. At the same time, paradoxically, the visit heralded the demise of Hakoah Vienna as the Jewish soccer club *par excellence* because some of its players received attractive offers and stayed on to play for American professional teams. Hakoah New York, later Hakoah All Stars, was founded as early as 1928, but never rose to prominence in sporting circles due to the relative insignificance of soccer in American sports. As it was never on a par with the "Big 4" major league team sports – American football, hockey, baseball, and basketball – its main task in the New World was to preserve the pre-emigration European tradition. It never became a vehicle for integration in the way → boxing or → baseball did; at any rate not among the first generation of Jews who had emigrated from Eastern Europe beginning in the 1880s.

In the interwar period, all-Jewish soccer teams also gained great popularity in Eastern Europe. Many belonged to the Maccabi organization and pursued social goals not unlike those promoted by Hakoah in Central Europe. Some even made it into the Premier League. Maccabi Czernowitz played in the Romanian league and won the regional championships in 1927, 1931, and 1932; Vívó Budapest played in the Hungarian and Maccabi Brno in the Czech league, ŻTS Jutrzenka Kraków at the top level in the regional league, and Hakoah Riga and Dijsk Dwinsk played in the Latvian league. Founded in 1908, the most popular Jewish soccer team in Poland was ŻKS Hasmonea Lwów, and even the small Polish town of Oświęcim (→ Auschwitz) had a Jewish soccer team: ŻKS Kadimah. A sizeable number of Jewish soccer players played for Jewish workers' sporting organizations, which were especially popular between the wars. The Gwiazda (Yidd. *Shtern*) clubs offered a Zionist-socialist alternative. *Morgnshtern* teams, supported by the socialist → *Bund*, played in various leagues; their declared enemy was the bourgeois Maccabi.

2. **Professionalization and antisemitism**

Professional soccer reached the European mainland between the wars. Players now received wages (instead of expenses), and transfer fees were paid when players changed clubs – these had both been common practices in England since the 1880s. Austria was the first country in continental Europe to create a professional league in 1924/1925; Hakoah Vienna won the first championship. The professional league that France established in 1931 owed its existence in large part to Jean Bernard-Lévy (1897–1940), the Jewish president of the soccer section within the Racing Club de France. In Germany, a professional league was about to be launched in 1932, but after the National Socialists' takeover, professionalism in sport was discouraged. The same policy would later be implemented in the areas annexed or controlled by the Third Reich. At the time, those debating the professionalization of soccer in Europe, especially in Central Europe, made frequent allusions to prejudices about the Jewish character of professional sport, and the alleged influence of Jewish greed on amateur soccer, which was considered morally superior.

Jewish soccer players played for both Jewish and non-Jewish clubs; some were also called up to play on national teams. Before the First World War two Jews played in the German selection: Gottfried Fuchs (1889–1972), who scored ten goals in a 1912 match against Russia, and Julius Hirsch (1892–1943). Gyula Bíró (1890–1961), Béla Guttmann (1899–1981), and Gyula Mándi (1899–1969) played for Hungary, and the Polish national team had three Jewish players as well: József Lustgarten (1889–1973), József Klotz (1900–1941), and Zygmunt Steuermann (1899–1941). While Fuchs, Hirsch, and Lustgarten played for non-Jewish German (Karlsruher FV) and Polish (Cracovia) clubs respectively, as did the three Hungarian players, Klotz and Steuermann played for the Jewish clubs Maccabi Warsaw and Hasmonea Lwów respectively. Hirsch, Klotz, and Steuermann were murdered by the Nazis. Fuchs emigrated to Switzerland in 1937, and from there to Canada; Lustgarten was deported to a Soviet gulag, which ultimately saved his life.

Jews were also among the best soccer coaches in Europe: Hugo Meisl (1881–1937), head coach of the Austrian "Wunderteam" in the 1930s, which placed fourth in the 1934 World Championship, was one of them. Gyula Bíró coached FC Nuremberg, Hasmonea Lwów, and FC Saarbrücken in the 1920s; Jenő Konrád (1894–1978) was in charge of FC Nuremberg until 1932. Béla Guttmann, a former player for Hakoah Vienna, coached Austrian, Hungarian, and Dutch teams before the war. After returning from his Swiss

Béla Guttmann (1899–1981)

exile he became one of the most successful coaches of the post-war years, first in Brazil, then for Benfica Lisbon in Portugal. With Benfica he won the European Cup in 1961 and 1962 [5]. During the same period, however, with few Jewish players left in Europe, the number of Jewish coaches declined as well.

The activities of Jewish soccer enthusiasts were not limited to those of players and coaches on the pitch. Walther Bensemann, dubbed "the man who brought soccer to Germany" [3], delivered his greatest contribution to German soccer in 1920 by establishing the magazine *Kicker*, which to this day remains the most popular and the most influential soccer publication in Germany. Another famous Jewish soccer journalist was the Austrian Willy Meisl (1895–1968), in the 1930s the "king of the sports journalists" in Berlin. In 1934 he emigrated to London, where he came to be known as "the world's No. 1 football critic" in the 1950s.

The conspicuous presence of Jews on the pitch, among officials and spectators prompted antisemites to brand certain teams with the stigma of being Jewish. As early as the 1920s, FK Austria Wien was labeled a *Judenklub* ("Jews' club"). Unlike the supporters of Hakoah Vienna who were predominantly of Eastern European origin and relatively poor, its numerous Jewish fans came from the better-off bourgeois families of Vienna. The *Judenklub* epithet was attached to a number of other clubs as well: in Germany to Eintracht Frankfurt, Tennis Borussia Berlin, and FC Bayern Munich, in Poland to Cracovia Kraków, and in England to Tottenham Hotspurs, whose supporters adopted the derogative antisemitic label as their own, and continued to call themselves "Yids" in a spirit of defiance. Even after the Holocaust, various clubs are still thought of as "Jewish." Some fans of teams playing against Ajax Amsterdam in the recent past used the rallying cry "Hamas, hamas, joden aan het gas!" ("Hamas, hamas, Jews into

the gas!"). Since 2003, Chelsea London has been described as "Jewish" because the club was bought by the Russian-Jewish oligarch Roman Abramovich. Jewish owners, particularly of soccer clubs, are relatively rare in Europe. This contrasts with the United States, where the fact that many teams in American football, baseball, and basketball are owned by Jews does not provoke antisemitic reactions, but rather belongs to normalcy.

3. After 1933

Jewish soccer players and coaches were among the first victims of the anti-Jewish policies of the Nazis. In March 1933, Kurt Landauer (1884–1961), President of FC Bayern Munich since 1919, and Richard Dombi Kohn (1888–1963), the coach from Austria who in the previous year had led the club to its first title, lost their posts [9]. Both Landauer and Kohn left Germany. Since Jews were expelled from German clubs, those who wished to keep on playing soccer had to join Jewish clubs, which for the most part belonged to either the Zionist Maccabi group or the assimilatory *Schild* association. In 1935, some 40,000 German Jews were officially members of Jewish sports clubs – a clear indication of the vital role sport played in the expression of Jewish self-confidence under the National Socialists. The Jewish press reported extensively about soccer. At the same time Jews still rooted for German clubs. For the historian Peter Gay (Peter Fröhlich) the matches of Eintracht Frankfurt and later those of Herta BSC Berlin made life bearable: "From 1933 on, the reason for my posture as a fan was that sports could serve as a screen blocking out the oppressive world of Nazi Germany" [9. 107].

The 1938 Anschluss (annexation) of Austria marked the end of Jewish participation in sporting activities. They were expelled from non-Jewish clubs; Jewish clubs were banned from the leagues; the stadium of

Hakoah Vienna was confiscated, and many players and officials were imprisoned or murdered. Among them was Max Scheuer, the captain of the legendary Hakoah Vienna team of 1925. Having fled from the Third Reich, the exiled Jewish soccer players founded new clubs or joined existing organizations such as Eintracht New York, which played in the German-American Soccer League alongside the Wiener Sports Club, among others, or the soccer section of the German-Jewish Club. Former members of Hakoah Vienna who had fled to Palestine founded Hakoah Tel Aviv in 1938. Other Hakoah players reached Australia, where new teams constituted themselves in → Melbourne and Sydney. Soccer even spread to China: many Jews found refuge from the National Socialists in the Jewish quarter of → Shanghai, and a regular soccer league was formed with eight Jewish teams.

After the → November pogrom of 1938, Jewish soccer clubs were banned in the Third Reich, along with other cultural and social activities. From that time on, playing soccer was only permissible in Jewish schools, which operated until the deportations began. In the territories occupied by Germany and the Soviet Union after 1939 all soccer activities ceased. Nazi cynicism, meanwhile, produced the extraordinary absurdity of a soccer league in the → Theresienstadt concentration camp, the so-called Liga Terezín. The composition of the teams was determined by the players' places of origin or their professions. One of their matches is documented in the 1944 propaganda film *Der Führer schenkt den Juden eine Stadt* (called "Theresienstadt. A Documentary Film" in English), which Kurt Gerron was forced to make.

In the aftermath of the war, the administrations of the → displaced persons camps (DPs; → Munich) offered organized sporting events, among them soccer, in addition to other cultural activities. Regional leagues were the result, with clubs such as Hapoel,

Maccabi, and Iḥud (unity), which at their height counted 169 teams. The matches were played while the camps remained in existence; they were dismantled step by step between 1948 and 1957. In Eastern Europe and in the Soviet Union Jewish soccer clubs became a rarity. Between 1945 and 1949 there were still a number of clubs in Poland; branches of the Gwiazda network of Jewish workers' clubs existed in twelve cities. However, the players left the country as soon as they could, and when Jewish organizations were successively prohibited, this era also came to an end.

In Western Europe it was primarily the international Zionist sporting organization Maccabi which was involved in establishing new Jewish sports and soccer clubs. But none of these clubs was able to recapture the great successes of the interbellum soccer teams. Participation in the Maccabiah Games, a quadrennial event held in Israel, was their only opportunity to compete with other, albeit Jewish, teams. Of those Jews who had been active before the war, few came back to Europe after 1945. One of them was the aforementioned Béla Guttmann. Having been invited by FC Bayern, Kurt Landauer resumed his Munich presidency; Dombi Kohn worked as coach for Feyenoord Rotterdam. Jewish players were a rarity in European soccer. Sándor Gellér (1925–1996), a Hungarian goalkeeper, was a member of the Hungarian national team which won the Olympic gold medal in Helsinki in 1952, and of the Hungarian team in the World Championship finals in 1954. George Cohen (b. 1939) won the World Championship with England in 1966.

4. In Israel

Soccer in Palestine during the 1920s developed under the influence of the British Mandate. As an indicator of the sport's popularity and of its significance as a national symbol, the 1930 cup final between

Maccabi Tel Aviv and a selection from the Northamptonshire Regiment of the British Army was attended by some 10,000 spectators – roughly one quarter of the city population of Tel Aviv: the Maccabi team won the cup. An amateur league was formed in 1932 with clubs from the British army and police, as well as Jewish teams such as Maccabi, Hapoel, and Beitar. Despite Palestine being a British mandate, the style of soccer played in the territory was heavily influenced by the Austrian short passing game. This style was introduced by Simon (Lumek) Rotner, a player from the early days of Hakoah Vienna; Egon Pollak (1898–1984), a famous personality from the Austrian National Championship of 1924/1925, came to coach Maccabi Tel Aviv and later the Israeli national team. The Hakoah Tel Aviv team was an exception among Israeli sports clubs as it did not belong to any centralized association like Maccabi, Hapoel, and Beitar, each of which represented a particular political persuasion. It was only when the traditional hegemony of the Israeli workers' parties came to an end in the 1970s that professional soccer found a home in Israel.

After the foundation of the State of Israel, Israeli teams, and especially the national squad, were regarded as symbols of the "new Jew." In the early years of the state's existence, they were sent abroad in order to establish contacts with the Jewish Diaspora. Significantly, the first away game of the Israeli national team in September of 1948 took place in New York, the city with the largest Jewish population outside of Israel: the opponent was an American team. During the Cold War, but also in view of the Middle East Conflict, soccer became a proxy for politics. In the qualifier matches for the Olympics that pitted Israel against the Soviet Union in 1955 (0–5 and 1–2), the Soviet team was perceived as an ally of the Arabs. In 1954 the Israel Football Association joined the Asian Football Confederation

(AFC), only to be boycotted by the Arab member states. Since the 1970s Arab soccer players also belong to the Israeli national team. Following expulsion from the AFC in 1974 and the rejection of Israel's application for membership of UEFA because of the no-votes of numerous Eastern Block states, Israel played against teams from the Oceania Football Confederation. In 1991 UEFA finally accepted the Israel Football Association as a member; full membership followed in 1994. Israeli soccer has since been working to reconnect with its European roots.

Bibliography

Sources
[1] J. Bunzl (ed.), Hoppauf Hakoah. Jüdischer Sport in Österreich, Vienna 1987. [2] P. Gay, My German Question. Growing up in Nazi Berlin, New Haven/London 1998.

Secondary literature
[3] B.-M. Beyer, Der Mann, der den Fußball nach Deutschland brachte. Das Leben des Walther Bensemann. Ein biografischer Roman, Göttingen 2003. [4] M. Brenner/G. Reuveni (eds.), Emancipation through Muscles. Jews and Sports in Europe, Lincoln 2006. [5] D. Claussen, Béla Guttmann. Weltgeschichte des Fußballs in einer Person, Berlin 2006. [6] H. Kaufman/H. Harif (eds.), Tarbut ha-guf veha-sport be-Yisra'el ba-me'ah ha-'esrim [Body Culture and Sport in Israel in the 20th Century], Jerusalem 2002. [7] T. Niewerth et al. (eds.), Jüdischer Sport und jüdische Gesellschaft = Jewish Sport and Jewish Community, Berlin 2010. [8] D. Schulze-Marmeling (ed.), Davidstern und Lederball. Die Geschichte der Juden im deutschen und internationalen Fußball, Göttingen 2003. [9] D. Schulze-Marmeling, Der FC Bayern und seine Juden. Aufstieg und Zerschlagung einer liberalen Fußballkultur, Göttingen 2011.

MOSHE ZIMMERMANN, JERUSALEM

Society for Jewish Folk Music

The Society for Jewish Folk Music (Russ. *Obshchestvo yevrejskoj narodnoj muzyki*; Yidd. *Gezelshaft far Yidisher Folks-Muzik*, 1908–1920) was founded in St. Petersburg under the influence of the Eastern European Haskalah. As the first secular Jewish musical institution in Russia, it promoted the emergence of a national Jewish style in Russian art music and enabled composers to organize themselves in the New Jewish School (*Novaya yevrejskaya shkola*). The Society became a model for other Jewish associations in Eastern and Central Europe, America, and Palestine that continued to develop the idea of a Jewish national music.

1. Beginnings in Saint Petersburg
2. Successor society in Moscow
3. The New Jewish School in the 1930s

1. Beginnings in Saint Petersburg

The founding of the Society for Jewish Folk Music was an expression of a growing national self-confidence by the Jews of Russia in the second half of the 19th century (→ Maskilim). Among musicians it nourished the idea of a national music combining traditional and modern elements. They took their cue from the national Russian composers of the "Mighty Handful": not only had Alexander Borodin (1833–1887), César Cui (1835–1918), Mily Balakirev (1837/1838–1920), Modest Mussorgsky (1839–1881), and Nikolai Rimsky-Korsakov (1844–1908) created a national style aligned with Russian culture and tradition, they had moreover discovered Russian folklore as a rich source for the renewal of music. Particularly Rimsky-Korsakov's composition class at the St. Petersburg Conservatory had many Jewish attendees.

A piano student at the Conservatory, Leonid Nisvitzky (later Arie Abilea, 1885–1984), eventually proposed the creation of a Society for Jewish Music. On March 4, 1908, he and two of his fellow students – the music composition student Solomon Rosowsky and the singer Iosif (Joseph) Tomars – applied for the registration of such a society. The composer Lazare Saminsky (1882–1959), also a member of the initiative group, remembered: "Three members of our group appeared before the St. Petersburg police board presided over by General Dratchevsky, the capital's governor, to register our new Society for Jewish Music. Dratchevsky pondered a moment and said: 'No, I cannot allow a Jewish music society. It's misleading. Jewish music does not exist, or at any rate, is debatable. But why not call your group, "Society for Jewish Folk Music?" Here you are on firm soil. [...] The idea was accepted'" [1. 12].

None of the participants had a clear idea at first of how to organize the Society's activity. Jewish → music included works by composers of Jewish descent such as Felix Mendelssohn (→ St. Matthew Passion), Fromental Halévy, or Giacomo Meyerbeer, which in the early documents of the society was described as "Jewish art music," as well as works by non-Jewish composers such as Mussorgsky, Rimsky-Korsakov, or Balakirev that were inspired by Jewish music, but also Yiddish operettas (→ Pomul Verde), countless types of folklore, or synagogal music (→ Organ).

The society's profile was developed over time. After the failure of early attempts to foster "Jewish art music," members focused instead on the systematic collection of folk songs and their adaptation for performance and publication. A decisive contribution in this regard came from Susman Kiselgof and Joel Engel. The folk song collector Susman Kiselgof (1884–1939) had in 1907 travelled to the center of Chabad → Hasidism in the village of Lubavitch, where he transcribed more than 100 folk melodies; he placed his collection at the disposal of the Society for Jewish Folk Music. The Muscovite music critic and composer Joel Engel (1868–1927) was invited to St. Petersburg in April 1909. He gave a lecture before members of the Society and presented his folk song adaptations in a subsequent performance. Engel demonstrated his methods for setting the songs to music: the folk melodies were furnished with basic chords or accompanying voices and were arranged in simple patterns for different scorings popular with amateur performers.

It did not take long for some of the Society's composers to express their dissatisfaction with such simple adaptations. Their annual concert on March 10, 1912 focused on new tendencies: before an audience of over 1,500 people, works by Moshe (Michail) Milner (1886–1953), Joseph Achron (1886–1943), and other musicians, which went well beyond the strict limitations of an adaptation, were presented. The compositions were either large and complex orchestral arrangements based on folk songs, or they were entirely composed in the Eastern European Jewish idiom.

Russian music publications spoke of an interesting new phenomenon in Russian musical life. The art historian and professor of aesthetics at the St. Petersburg Conservatory, Liveri Antonovich Sakketti (Liberio A. Sacchetti, 1852–1916), first used the term "New Jewish School" in a lecture to refer to the composers of the Society for Jewish Folk Music. The program notes for the concert of March 10, 1912, described for the first time the core idea of this school: "The Society for Jewish Folk Music seeks to uncover the treasures of the folk song and, whenever possible, to bring to it all the achievements of modern musical culture" (cited in [4. 55]).

Membership of the Society continually grew; between 1912 and 1913 alone, the number rose from 389 to 884. In the autumn of 1913, local chapters were opened in Moscow, Kiev, and Kharkiv. In 1914 the Society already had more than 1,000 members. Between 1914 and 1916, further members were added with the opening of chapters in Odessa, Rostov, Ekaterinoslav (today Dnipro), and Simferopol.

Ethnographic material was only gathered sporadically and on the initiative of individual members, who received financial support for their undertakings. In 1913 the Society cooperated with the ethnographic expedition of S. An-Ski (1863–1920; → Dybbuk; → Jewish Society for History and Ethnography), but it was very active staging concerts in Russia and throughout Europe. Between 1909 and 1913, beside the St. Petersburg concerts, there were 146 concerts in other cities, most of which were given by the Society's own established ensembles. In 1912, the company headed by the singer Jakov Medvedev was the first to tour abroad in Germany and Austria-Hungary; later it gave concerts in England, France, and the United States. The Society's publishing arm saw similarly intense activity; during the 12 years of its existence it issued more than 80 musical works.

The organization of the Society's concerts and the publication of the music were the domain of the Music Committee, which also played a vital role in the compositional work of the Society's members: its regular sessions provided a unique opportunity for the Society's young composers, all of whom also belonged to the committee, to play their new pieces before an audience of their peers, to discuss technical and stylistic problems, or to ask for advice from more experienced colleagues. The intensive exchange of opinions and the high artistic standards of the committee were essential for the rapid artistic development that many composers experienced within a very short time span.

Beginning in 1912 the Society's composers turned increasingly toward religious music. The reasons for the new direction were manifold: one was the fact that the expeditions of 1912 and 1913 yielded a body of new and diverse material for the composers who, up to that point, had largely worked with the Hasidic songs collected by Kiselgof. Not only did they now have a wider variety at their disposal, but for the first time they were able to compare the different genres, such as Yiddish songs, Hasidic *niggunim* (→ Niggun), cantillations, *mi-Sinai* chants, or *zemirot* (→ Piyyut) according to musical criteria, as well as their origin. Another factor was the increasingly target-oriented work of the composers. The initial enthusiasm for all things Jewish, and the efforts to popularize Jewish music, to make it accessible for a wider audience, over time gave way to a yearning for works to be created of superior artistic value. In their search for authentic material the composers eventually turned to religious music, which they believed had preserved older layers of the Jewish musical tradition (→ Thesaurus of Hebrew Oriental Melodies).

The outcome of the 1917 October Revolution also affected the work of the Society for Jewish Folk Music; all cultural institutions came under state control. The last major concert under the Society's auspices took place on March 28, 1919. Their activities are documented until 1920.

2. Successor society in Moscow

In 1922, former activists of the Moscow chapter of the Society for Jewish Folk Music took steps to establish a Moscow-based Society for Jewish Music. At the inaugural meeting on October 8, 1923, 39 of those present joined the new society. The pianist David Schor (1867–1942) was elected chairman. Schor's tenure ended with his emigration to Palestine in 1927.

Soon it became clear that the activities of the Society for Jewish Music would not be as extensive as those of its predecessor organization. The lack of funds meant that many projects were doomed to fail. The St. Petersburg Society had enjoyed the support of generous, culturally committed patrons such as the Gintsburg Family (→ Bankers). After the Revolution, the few wealthy Jews in the country either had their assets seized, or they fled abroad. The Moscow Society for Jewish Music thus depended on the contributions and small donations of its members.

The new Society almost completely dispensed with the costly ethnographic research in favor of a more narrow focus on concerts, which were a stimulus especially for young composers to dedicate themselves to Jewish music. Between 1924 and 1929 hundreds of new compositions were written, mostly in the field of chamber music. The programs were compiled by a Music Commission, whose members included the composers Michail Gnesin (1883–1957), Alexander and Grigori Krein (1883–1951 and 1879–1957), and Alexander Weprik (1899–1958). The artistic standards were exceptionally high. Not only Jewish musicians, but also top-ranking Russian artists such as the Moscow Beethoven Quartet or the pianist Maria Judina (1899–1970), maintained their association with the society throughout its existence.

Beginning in 1925, cultural officials began to criticize the repertoire of the Society for Jewish Music. Because its nationalities policy strove to assimilate the Jewish population, the Communist Party could not tolerate any measures intended to solidify a religious or national Jewish identity. Even the use of the Hebrew language was prohibited. Many musical pieces could no longer appear in the programs under their Hebrew titles and had to be renamed; thus Milner's *Agenda* became *Fairy Tale* and Weprik's *Kaddish* turned into *Sad Poem*.

Toward the end of 1927, membership peaked at 669, after which it saw a steady decline. By early 1928 the Society encountered serious financial problems. In February the board felt it had no option but to cooperate with other Jewish cultural institutions. These organizations were already under communist control, and their officials demanded full compliance from the Society and, in particular, a new repertoire to meet the needs of the Jewish workers.

The days of most Jewish cultural institutions were numbered – disbandment came in 1930/1931. The Society for Jewish Music hosted its final event at the Communist Club in Moscow on December 22, 1929.

3. The New Jewish School in the 1930s

The New Jewish School (*Novaya yevrejskaya shkola*) spread beyond Russia's borders. From 1932 to 1941 the American Palestine Music Association was active in New York. Also known under its Hebrew acronym, MAILAMM (*Makhon Erets Yisra'eli le-Mada'e ha-Muzikah*), it was the most important Jewish-American organization for the care and promotion of Jewish music. Its members were American Jews, emigrants from Russia and Eastern Europe and refugees from Nazi Germany, among them Joseph Achron and Lazare Saminksy, who were former members of the Society for Jewish Folk Music. The group organized concerts with the repertoire of the New Jewish School and collected funds for the development of Jewish Music in Palestine. The year 1939 saw the founding in New York of the Society for the Advancement of Jewish Musical Culture. Renamed the Jewish Liturgical Music Society of America in 1963, it became the American Society for Jewish Music in 1974 and to this day continues the work of the Russian musical societies.

In 1929 David Schor, together with a group of colleagues, established the Universal Society for the Promotion of Jewish Music (Hanigun) in Palestine, with the goal of transforming Palestine into a global center for Jewish music and musicologists. Schor's activities came to the attention of the → Hebrew University, and in the early

1930s he found employment with the university at their still-rudimentary Department of Music. During the 1930s, German immigrants in Jerusalem, on the initiative of the Frankfurt dentist and amateur musician Salli Levy, created the World Center for Jewish Music in Palestine (1936–1940). Its aim was to establish a new Jewish musical culture and be a contact point for Jewish musicians from around the world. Difficult economic and political conditions, however, left both institutions with only a modest range of projects to pursue.

As the creators of new Jewish music experienced increasing oppression in Russia, the German-speaking cultural area became their predominant sphere of activity. As early as 1922, a number of St. Petersburg protagonists came to Berlin and started two Jewish music publishers, Jibneh and Juwal. Both promoted young composers who were seeking a specific Jewish form of expression.

Vienna became the focal point for the New Jewish School in the 1930s after the foundation of the Verein zur Förderung jüdischer Musik in October 1928. Apart from the established repertoire of the Russian group, the numerous concerts of the society also showcased new works by Viennese composers such as Joachim Stutschewsky (1891–1982), Israel Brandmann (1901–1992), or Juliusz Wolfsohn (1880–1944). Whereas the earlier works of Jewish classical music had in the main referred to Yiddish folklore and synagogal music, composers now showed a growing interest in Hebrew folk songs from Palestine, which embodied a new free sense of life.

The program curation in Vienna was the same as in Russia. The concerts were a means to help audiences school their musical tastes while the performance of complex works were aimed towards broadening the appreciation of a new Jewish music. The dedication to the musical cause was by no means an end in itself, it was seen as a contribution to the creation of an autonomous Jewish national culture. In this respect, the Verein was able to form a close cooperation with the Zionist organizations of Vienna, without whose support the Verein's limited funds would have forced it to cease operations. This concerned above all the major, representative concerts, such as the orchestral concert of the youth organization "Erets Israel" in the Grosser Konzerthaussaal (February 1931), with the participation of the Vienna Symphony Orchestra, the Jewish Choral Society, and several prominent soloists.

The Vienna Verein and its protagonists organized and coordinated a network of Jewish musical talent that, in addition to Austria, encompassed countries such as Hungary, Poland, Romania, Czechoslovakia, the Netherlands, Yugoslavia, Latvia, Italy, and Switzerland. Within this network, concerts, presentations, and seminars were organized, while amateur orchestras and choral societies were supplied with sheet music and material for their programs. There was moreover a close cooperation with a range of other musical and cultural societies.

With the German "Anschluss" (annexation) of Austria on March 13, 1938, it became illegal for Jewish organizations to continue their operations. Persecutions during the period of National Socialism in Europe and Stalinism in the Soviet Union halted the development of the New Jewish School toward the end of the 1930s; later the School was largely forgotten. Not until the mid-1990s did the School see a systematic exploration and reintegration into musical life.

Bibliography

Sources

[1] Lazare Saminsky's Years in Russia and Palestine. Excerpts from an Unpublished Autobiography, ed. by A. Weisser, in: Musica Judaica 2 (1977/1978), 1–19.

Secondary literature

[2] P. Gradenwitz, The Music of Israel. From the Biblical Era to Modern Times, Portland 1996. [3] J. Loeffler, The Most Musical Nation. Jews and Culture in the Late Russian Empire, New Haven 2010. [4] J. Nemtsov, Die Neue Jüdische Schule in der Musik, Wiesbaden 2004. [4a] J. Nemtsov, From St. Petersburg to Vienna. The New Jewish School in Music (1908–1938) as Part of the Jewish Cultural Renaissance, Wiesbaden 2023. [5] J. Nemtsov (ed.), Jüdische Kunstmusik im 20. Jahrhundert. Quellenlage, Entstehungsgeschichte, Stilanalysen, Wiesbaden 2006. [6] J. Nemtsov, Enzyklopädisches Findbuch zum Archiv der Neuen Jüdischen Schule, Wiesbaden 2008. [7] J. Nemtsov/E. Kuhn (eds.), Jüdische Musik in Sowjetrussland. Die "Jüdische Nationale Schule" der zwanziger Jahre, Berlin 2002. [8] A. M. Rothmüller, The Music of the Jews. An Historical Appreciation, trans. by H. S. Stevens, Cranbury 1975. [9] L. Saminsky, The Music of the Ghetto and the Bible, New York 1934. [10] L. Sitsky, Music of the Repressed Russian Avant-Garde, 1900–1928, Westport 1994. [11] A. Weisser, The Modern Renaissance of Jewish Music, New York 1954.

JASCHA NEMTSOV, POTSDAM

Sociology

Institutionalized as a new discipline of cultural and social sciences at the end of the 19th century, sociology was not least a reaction to the upheaval within modern societies as a consequence of democratization, → nationalism, industrialization, urbanization, and modern science and scholarship. As the "science or study of society," it faced a triple task: analyzing social order as an internally linked whole that follows its own logic; understanding and explaining social life, frequently regarded as being in crisis; investigating the possibilities of reconstructing existing forms of coexistence under modern conditions or constructing new ones. Jews participated in establishing the subject, in particular Émile Durkheim (1858–1917) and Georg Simmel (1885–1918) in Europe and Louis Wirth (1897–1992) in the United States. The remit of the discipline provided the foundation of both the Jewish interest in sociology and the sociological interest in the modern experience of the Jews. While European sociology studied the Jews in connection with democratization and capitalism, American sociology addressed them in the context of migration, urbanization, and the emergence of the so-called "marginal man."

1. Establishment as a discipline and Jewish participation
2. Sociological perspectives concerning the Jews
3. The Jews in the modern world

1. Establishment as a discipline and Jewish participation

In 1838, the mathematician and philosopher Auguste Comte (1798–1857) coined the term sociology (derived from Lat. *socius*, companion) to refer to an academic discipline. His objective was to establish a field of study that followed the methods of natural science and would provide the means for a rational organization of society through the discovery of laws of development.

The institutionalization of sociology in France was essentially the work of Émile Durkheim. Born the son of a rabbi in Lorraine in 1858, he was destined to become a rabbi, too, and consequently studied → Hebrew and read the → Talmud. However, he enrolled as a student at the École Normale Supérieure. He would remain in intellectual opposition to his fellow-student Henri Bergson (1859–1941; → Lebensphilosophie) for his entire life. Following his studies he worked as a philosophy teacher at a secondary school. After returning from several months of research in Germany (1885/1886),

he held a professorship in pedagogy and sociology in Bordeaux from 1887 onward. In 1898, he founded the academic journal *L'Année sociologique*; in 1902 he was called to the Sorbonne in spite of antisemitic hostility. He endeavored to found a school here; his nephew Marcel Mauss and Maurice Halbwachs are regarded as its most important representatives.

According to Durkheim, society was a "synthesis *sui generis*" whose specific reality one could come to terms with only by means of investigating social facts (*fait social*). He defined these social facts – such as legal norms, moral rules, religious concepts – as specific "ways of acting, thinking and feeling which possess the remarkable property of existing outside the consciousness of the individual. Not only are these types of behaviour and thinking external to the individual, but they are endued with a compelling and coercive power by virtue of which, whether he wishes it or not, they impose themselves upon him." As they find expression in institutions, he regarded sociology as a "science of institutions, their genesis and their functioning" [1. 39, 51, 45].

In contrast with the positivist approach in France, an influential tradition of interpretive sociology dominated in Germany. Max Weber (1864–1920), who had studied political economy and law, sought to unite explanation and understanding "as belonging together." In his posthumously published study *Wirtschaft und Gesellschaft* (1921; "Economy and Society," 1968), he explained sociology as "a science concerning itself with the interpretative understanding of social action and thereby with a causal explanation of its course and consequences" [6. 4]. Similar to its French counterpart, German sociology, too, was a young academic discipline that had to hold its own beside neighboring fields such as political economy, historical science, philosophy, psychology, and → Völkerpsychologie. Together with Werner Sombart (1863–1941) and Edgar Jaffé (1866–1921), Weber edited the *Archiv für Sozialwissenschaft und Sozialpolitik* beginning in 1904. In 1909, he founded the Deutsche Gesellschaft für Soziologie (German Sociological Association) together with Georg Simmel (→ Type). Antisemitic discrimination contributed to Simmel becoming marginalized professionally; despite his achievements he remained a "Privatdozent" for 15 years.

In 1892, the first sociological faculty in the United States with the right to award doctorates, the Department of Sociology, was established at the University of Chicago, which also published the most important academic journal in the field, the *American Journal of Sociology*. The Chicago faculty also played a part in the foundation of the American Sociological Society. Contrary to the widespread misunderstanding that the so-called Chicago School focused on purely empirical and descriptive sociology, its representatives did in fact combine empirical research with theoretical reflection. Despite some influences from European sociology, the theoretical orientation was firmly rooted in the American tradition of pragmatism.

There were no Jews among the founders of sociology as an academic discipline in the United States; in fact, only very few were until the 1930s. This is due to the reluctance of the Anglo-Saxon establishment to entrust the study of American history, literature, or society to members of minorities [8. 731]. It was not until the second half of the 20th century that Jews were represented in American sociology in an appreciable number, although the focus of their research and publications was only rarely on Jewish life. One reason for this might be that American Jewish sociologists took care not to be identified with their Jewish background in their research [10].

During the second half of the 20th century, the Jewish presence in sociology shifted to Israel and, above all, the United States. Exceptions were, for instance, Raymond Aron in France or Norbert Elias (→ Civilizing Process) in Great Britain. Demographic changes in the wake of two world wars and the Holocaust as well as migration from Europe to Israel and the United States may be seen as the reasons for this shift. In the Soviet Union, sociology was regarded as a bourgeois discipline and consequently was not institutionalized until very late.

For a large number of Jewish sociologists, their origin in and emigration from Eastern Europe provided core experiences. Thus, for instance, the well-known Israeli sociologist Shmuel Eisenstadt as well as several chairpersons of the American Sociological Association, such as Erving Goffman, Seymour M. Lipset, and Frances Fox Piven, were the children or grandchildren of Jewish immigrants from Eastern Europe. German or Austrian origins also informed some Jewish sociologists in Israel and the United States, namely Arthur Ruppin (→ Palestine Office) and Martin Buber (→ Dialogue), who emigrated to Palestine in 1908 and 1938 respectively, as well as the heads of the American Sociological Association Louis Wirth, Paul Lazarsfeld, and Lewis A. Coser (born Ludwig Cohen, sometimes Cohn).

The remarkably strong Jewish presence in sociology fed the belief that Jews are particularly astute observers of society and that Jewish affiliation provides an important source of sociological insight. Whether expressing appreciation for or aiming to discredit the discipline, such claims are problematic in that they identify sociology as a kind of Jewish thinking or as the expression of an intrinsic Jewishness [11. 1–15]. Rather than searching their sociology for a hidden ethnic or religious core, we must locate the scholars and their work in the real Jewish world, that is in the particular societal and social context within which they developed their ideas.

Émile Durkheim (1858–1917)

2. Sociological perspectives concerning the Jews

Within the differing sociological traditions in France, Germany, and the United States, it is possible to identify particular topics in the context of the late 19th and early 20th centuries that were discussed specifically with reference to Jews to a significant extent. In France, the Jewish attitude to democracy was the subject of a sociological debate in the late 19th century; in Germany, sociologists devoted unprecedented attention to the relationship between Jews and capitalism in the two decades before the First World War; in the United States, well-known representatives of the Chicago School viewed Jews during the 1910s and the 1920s as the personification of the mixture of different peoples and cultures in modern cities.

In the Third French Republic, conservatives like Édouard Drumont (1844–1917) or Maurice Barrès (1862–1923), who rejected the legacy of the → French Revolution, attacked the Jews as its agents and beneficiaries. They employed religious terminology when pursuing the restoration of a hierarchical social order in the ecclesiastical mold or racial terms where they sought to revive the aristocratic principle of hereditary inequality in a new form. Left-wing antisemitic radicals, however – such as Albert Regnard (1836–1903) – viewed the Jews as posing a threat to the democratic principles of 1789. They accused them of pursuing a novel financial feudalism or religious obscurantism. Durkheim, who was a member of the → Alliance israélite universelle, challenged the contemporary antisemitic imputations by presenting counter-arguments about the Jews and indirectly by re-interpreting the French Revolution.

He inverted the image presented by the right that the Jews were the vanguard of a menacing modernism. Rather, he held, they were exemplary of a traditionalist, premodern type of solidarity, precisely the one to whose restoration the conservatives in France were aspiring. An adequate understanding of the French Revolution furthermore showed that it was not a source of social dissolution but of new religious ideals potentially serving to restore societal solidarity. Durkheim also challenged the scientific pretensions of racial antisemitism by proving that "race" was not an adequate explanation of fluctuations in the suicide rate (→ Race) [2. 82–103].

Durkheim differed firmly from the leftwing antisemitic radicals in the question of how the work of the French Revolution could be completed. While this left wing believed itself to be the most faithful heir to the Revolution, in Durkheim's view it was deeply reactionary. He regarded their understanding of solidarity as bigoted and based on the Jews being the scapegoat. His own understanding of socialism was more strongly universalist, affirming, and broadening the principles of 1789. Durkheim expected the new civil religion advocated by the Revolution to overcome the religious fault lines of the past and create a foundation for the integration of the Jews [9].

In the discussion on the Jews and modern capitalism conducted in German sociology before the First World War, Marx's changing views on the subject provided essential points of reference. As a young man, Marx had claimed in *Zur Judenfrage* (1843/1844; "On the Jewish Question," 1926) that the modern monetary economy universalized a "Jewish spirit" (→ Jewish Question). Later, too, Marx identified Jews with trade and usury, by then, however, not regarding these as the essential traits of but rather merely as historical preconditions for modern capitalism. According to this view, the Jews had encouraged the development of capitalism by contributing to the emergence and concentration of monetary capital and ultimately to sophisticated industrial production. Trade and usury, according to Marx, finally became subordinate to industrial production on an extended scale, to whose implementation they had originally contributed. These perspectives were now reformulated by Georg Simmel (→ Type), Werner Sombart, Ferdinand Tönnies (1855–1936), and Max Weber in different ways.

Simmel devoted himself to the subject in his *Philosophie des Geldes* (1900; "The Philosophy of Money," 1978). In his view, the monotheism of the Jews, their social deprivation under Christian rule in the Middle Ages, and their role as strangers in Christian communities encouraged an affinity with the modern monetary economy [4. 221–228, 252–255]. While this was more ambivalent in his opinion than in Marx's, he did agree with the latter's understanding that the Jewish interest in money became more generalized over time, as "the money form of transactions has now been taken up by the whole economic community" [4. 228]. Sombart in his turn claimed in *Die Juden und*

das Wirtschaftsleben (1911; "The Jews and Modern Capitalism," 2001) that the form as well as the spirit of modern capitalism were shaped by Jews. He traced this back to objective conditions that allowed the Jews to shape the capitalist system; further factors he mentioned were the Jewish religion as well as subjective forces, as he called Jewish characteristics. His analysis equated modern capitalism with the domination by a "Jewish spirit" internalized by non-Jews and objectivized in modern economic institutions. In *Individuum und Welt in der Neuzeit* (1913), Tönnies characterized the Jews as foreign to and alienated from Europe, as in opposition to medieval society and instead in league with modern capitalism and self-serving individualism. He avoided an essentialist explanation of these qualities, which according to him were at least in part a product of the Jews' position as strangers in society, but like Marx, Simmel, and Sombart diagnosed their becoming increasingly generalized in the modern world.

According to Max Weber, the Jews had contributed to the development of modern capitalism but were later ousted. He claimed that they had contributed to disenchanting the world and paving the way for a modern economic rationalism based on calculation. Some traits of Judaism, however, limited this rationalizing effect in Weber's view. In particular, it did not provide a spiritual basis for developing a rational organization of capital and labor, for which reason the Jews had become a → pariah people making gains from moneylending and favorable constellations of world events instead. The rational organization of capital and labor, in Weber's view the defining characteristic of modern capitalism *par excellence*, had its spiritual source in Protestant ethics according to him. Just as in Marx's later writings Jewish trade and usury was subordinate to modern industry, in Weber's representation puritanical-rational capitalism replaced Jewish pariah capitalism.

In the United States, William Thomas (1863–1947) and Robert Park (1864–1944) were the defining influences within the Chicago School of sociology. Neither Thomas nor Park were of Jewish origin but, like Park's pupil Louis Wirth, pursued a sociological interest in Jewish life in the United States. In *Human Migration and the Marginal Man* (1928), Park argued that the modern Jew was exemplary of a personality type he called the "marginal man." The product of cultural conflicts in the wake of conquest and migration, the marginal man had a part in the cultural life and the traditions of two peoples according to Park, as he neither could nor wished to break with his past and its traditions on the one hand but was not fully accepted by the new society in which he now sought a place on the other.

Moreover, Thomas, Park, and Wirth characterized the Jews as an urban people. It is true that European and American Jews were highly urbanized at the beginning of the 20th century, no city testifying to this more impressively than → New York, where 1.6 million Jewish inhabitants – predominantly immigrants and their children – constituted the largest urban community of Jews that had ever existed. In the Jews' own experience as the epitome of marginal men as well as in the reality of the cities described by Park and Wirth as a social and ethnic → melting pot, cultures interacted. With mass immigration and internal migration driving the growth of cities in the United States, American society in general could be grasped in similar terms. The Jewish marginal man, the city, and America all formed ciphers of cultural contact and collision in which Park recognized the sources of civilization and essential characteristics of the modern age.

The Chicago School regarded this cultural development as a cause of individual and societal dissolution but also as a potential impulse for creative reorganization. Thus, Wirth observed tendencies of deviant behavior in his research into Jewish immigrant families but added that "not every case of culture conflict inevitably leads to delinquency," as the person in question might also develop into a "prophet, a reformer or a political leader" [7. 491]. Similarly, Thomas declared that through new customs and institutions, immigrants were able to overcome disintegration. While in the Old World, Jews had had a dissolving influence due to migration and trade, in the New World they represented the potential of creative innovation. Thomas, Park, and Herbert Miller (1875–1951) pointed to the association of New York Jewish organizations known as "kehillah" as a promising indication of this development. This experiment during the years from 1908 to 1922 intended to provide the growing Jewish population of New York with a unified and democratic community structure [3. 236–238]. If the Jewish population of New York, deeply divided between wealthy, assimilated Jews of German origin in Uptown Manhattan and poor, → Yiddish-speaking Jews from Eastern Europe in the Lower East Side, the Bronx, and Brooklyn, was able to create an inclusive, democratic, and pluralist kind of community, the United States as a whole, they believed, could also hope to achieve this. In this concept, disintegration was a transitional phenomenon ultimately followed by – as long as the respective crisis could be overcome successfully – the re-integration of the individual into a new, more comprehensive societal order that would be "better adapted to the changed demands of the group," as William I. Thomas and Florian Znaniecki (1882–1958) put it [5. 4].

3. The Jews in the modern world

It was in keeping with their middle-class, Western European background that the founders of sociology such as Durkheim or Weber expected the Jews to assimilate (→ Assimilation) to modern societies.

Durkheim, rooted in French republicanism, continued to adhere to the objectives
of → emancipation and assimilation even
after the → Dreyfus affair. He welcomed the
→ February Revolution in Russia in 1917, as it
appeared to promise that these ideals would
now also come into their own in those
regions where most European Jews were
living. Durkheim's own biography suggests,
however, that he did not expect the characteristics of Jewish affiliation to vanish completely. He aspired to a more comprehensive
kind of solidarity that would transcend particular affiliations and ties without negating
them altogether.

Weber saw the Jews facing a more drastic alternative. He did not seem to be able
to imagine a future for them other than
either an obstinate insistence on an (admittedly mitigated) pariah status (→ Pariah
People) or complete absorption. He made
a distinction between Germany and the
Puritan countries: in his own country, Jews
would not become German but "remain –
even after long generations – 'assimilated
Jews'," while the "Puritan countries" (especially the United States) would absorb Jewish immigrants completely, as long as they
abandoned their → orthodoxy and thus the
religious basis of their self-imposed pariah
status [6. 623]. In Europe, the expectations of Jewish assimilation were of course
destroyed in the mid-20th century by the
Shoah, an event that was simply unimagina-
ble to Weber or Durkheim.

Where the future of the Jews was concerned, none of the early academic sociologists adopted the answer Marx had
suggested to the "Jewish question," namely
revolutionary socialism. Zionism (→ Basel)
was evaluated differently. Weber regarded
its prospects with skepticism. Ruppin,
however, was a confirmed believer in the
objectives of Zionism and collated dates
concerning the situation of the Jews in
Europe and America intended to document
that only in Palestine would the survival

and renaissance of the Jewish people be
probable (→ Statistics). In *Die Zukunft der
Juden* (1912), Sombart also supported Jewish
emigration to Palestine, but only for the so-
called → Ostjuden; he expected the German
Jews to stay in the country and accept their
social discrimination.

In spite of their attitude, which was
ultimately oriented towards the concept
of assimilation, the Chicago sociologists
Thomas, Park, and Miller regarded nationalist movements among immigrants – in
which definition they explicitly included
Zionism – as positive; they described them
as forms of expression capable of counter-
acting social disintegration and encouraging
respect as well as participation in American
life. Challenging Americanization in this
way was close to the type of cultural → pluralism championed by some intellectual dissidents such as John Dewey, Horace Kallen,
Randolph Bourne, and Alain Locke, but
did not entirely coincide with it. After the
Second World War, Jewish sociologists and
anthropologists continued to their investigation of assimilation.

The foundation of the State of Israel
and the new beginning of Jewish life revi-
talized the sociological interest in Zionism. In *La fin du people juif?* (1965; "The
End of the Jewish People?," 1967), Georges
Friedmann (1902–1977) pointed to the tension between Jewish affiliation and Israeli
national consciousness. Shmuel Eisenstadt
(1923–2010) returned to the topic of assimilation in *Israeli Society* (1967), researching
the absorption of immigrants into Israeli
society. Yonina Talmon (1923–1966) studied
kibbutsim in *Family and Community in the
Kibbutz* (1972). From new perspectives such
as Marxism, feminism, and post-Zionism,
Israeli sociologists have investigated and
discussed more recent changes and problems in their society. The constant reshaping of Jewish social life, in Israel as well as
in the Diaspora, remains an important topic
for the sociology of the Jews in the present.

Bibliography

Sources

[1] E. Durkheim, The Rules of Sociological Method, ed. by S. Lukes, trans. by W. D. Halls, New York 1982. [2] E. Durkheim, Suicide. A Study in Sociology, trans. by J. A. Spaulding/G. Simpson, New York 1966. [3] R. E. Park/H. A. Miller, Old World Traits Transplanted, New York 1921. [4] G. Simmel, The Philosophy of Money, trans. by D. Frisby/T. Bottomore, London 2004. [5] W. I. Thomas/F. Znaniecki, The Polish Peasant in Europe and America, New York 1958. [6] M. Weber, Economy and Society. An Outline of Interpretive Sociology, vol. 1, Berkeley 1978. [7] L. Wirth, Culture Conflict and Misconduct, in: Social Forces 9 (1931), 484–492.

Secondary literature

[8] W. J. Cahnman/H. Hartman, Sociology, in: Encyclopaedia Judaica, vol. 18, Detroit 2007, 728–737. [9] C. A. Goldberg, The Jews, the Revolution, and the Old Regime in French Anti-Semitism and Durkheim's Sociology, in: Sociological Theory 29 (2011), 248–271. [10] S. M. Lipset, Jewish Sociologists and the Sociology of the Jews, in: Jewish Social Studies 17 (1955), 177–178. [11] I. Strenski, Durkheim and the Jews of France, Chicago 1997.

CHAD ALAN GOLDBERG, MADISON
AND MARCEL MÜLLER, LEIPZIG

Sociology of Knowledge

The sociology of knowledge was developed in the 1920s and early 1930s as an independent theory within the field of → sociology, as a method with which to research the social genesis of ideas. The Hungarian-Jewish sociologist and philosopher Karl Mannheim (1893–1947) contributed significantly to its development and dissemination. His main work *Ideologie und Utopie* (1929; "Ideology and Utopia," 1960) triggered a debate in

which criticism of the sociology of knowledge was linked to the so-called Jewish question, among other things.

1. Origins
2. Karl Mannheim
3. The analysis of ideology
4. Politics as a science
5. Reception

1. Origins

Before the sociology of knowledge developed into a full subdiscipline of → sociology in German universities in the 1920s, it was merely the subject of debates among German humanities scholars. It became known to a broader public thanks to two opposing developments: the perception of a crisis in traditional humanist education, on the one hand, and the Marxist approach to explaining society by means of interest-driven ideologies that are based in materialism, on the other. As a consequence, the new discipline was polarized from the very beginning.

The first studies related to the sociology of knowledge were published in 1924 by the philosopher Max Scheler (→ Phenomenology) [6]. Together with the municipal researcher Hugo Lindemann and the sociologist Leopold von Wiese, he led the research institute for social sciences at the University of Cologne. Scheler studied the social conditions under which one of three forms of knowledge dominated: the practical knowledge of the positive sciences aimed at changing the world in practical terms, the educational knowledge of philosophy that could contribute to shaping personality, and the redemptive knowledge of religion that taught humans to participate with love in the process of being [7. 250].

In view of the perceived preponderance of positivist sciences in both academic and public life, which was seen as a crisis of culture and education, Scheler spoke of the powerlessness of the spirit [5. 37]. He began with a critique of Auguste Comte's law of three stages and his faith in progress; in his methodical recourse to contemporary ethnological literature on the genealogy of "primitive" or "religious" beliefs (→ Anthropology), Comte's cognitive interest overlapped with Max Weber's (→ Pariah People) and Alfred Weber's in Germany, Émile Durkheim's (→ Sociology) in France, and Leonard Hobhouse's in England. Scheler's sociology of knowledge, however, did not question the truth claims of the forms of knowledge whose social genesis he was striving to reveal.

Karl Mannheim was the first to place the concept of ideology at the core of the analysis of all types of knowledge. He published a series of academic articles as well as excerpts from his postdoctoral dissertation *Konservatismus. Ein Beitrag zur Soziologie des Wissens* ("Conservatism. A Contribution to the Sociology of Knowledge," 1986) in 1927. When he published the more provocative and political collection of essays *Ideologie und Utopie* in 1929, his sociology of knowledge became a cause célèbre [13].

2. Karl Mannheim

Karl (originally Károly) Mannheim was born to Jewish parents in Budapest in 1893. He began to study history, literature, and philosophy, and acquired his PhD in 1918 with a thesis on epistemology. In 1919 he moved to Germany and had already studied in Berlin for a year under Georg Simmel (→ Type), among others, before the First World War. In Hungary he feared being persecuted by the antisemitic and anti-communist Horthy regime (→ Numerus Clausus), not least because of his personal connection with Georg Lukács (1885–1971; → Class Consciousness). In the short-lived Hungarian Republic of Councils, Lukács had been the deputy minister of culture, and in the preceding

Karl Mannheim (1893–1947)

years, as a member of culturally dissident groups, he had been Mannheim's mentor. Mannheim himself never had communist leanings.

After a short stay in Berlin, Mannheim moved to Heidelberg in 1921, where he married the psychologist Juliska Láng. When he failed to persuade either of the prominent Heidelberg philosophers Karl Jaspers or Heinrich Rickert (→ Neo-Kantianism) to supervise his dissertation, he approached the sociologists and economists Alfred Weber and Emil Lederer (→ New School for Social Research) with more success. When, having finished his habilitation, Mannheim requested the title of Privatdozent in 1926, prominent members of the faculty opposed this with specious arguments. Furthermore, the department sought to have Mannheim's naturalization officially reviewed. While some aspects of these proceedings bear the mark of antisemitism, the outcome was in Mannheim's favor. He was granted the teaching license, but his naturalization procedure dragged on until 1929 [10. 17–19].

The Weimar Republic opened up opportunities for social advancement to Jews. When Mannheim applied for a professorship in Frankfurt at the end of the 1920s, his request was refused; however, several of his fellow applicants and the majority of the professors on the appointment committee were themselves Jews [9]. Even so, in 1930 Mannheim succeeded in becoming a professor of sociology at Frankfurt University as the successor of the political economist Franz Oppenheimer, moving into a floor in the building of the → Institute for Social Research. In the following years he became increasingly active in teaching as well as research, supported by his assistant Norbert Elias (→ Civilizing Process).

In 1933 he was dismissed as a result of the National Socialist "Gesetz zur Wiedrherstellung des Berufsbeamtentums" (Law for the Restoration of the Professional Civil Service). Together with his wife, he fled to England via the Netherlands. At first he became an extraordinary lecturer at the London School of Economics, which enabled him to continue his sociological research. He joined the Moot circle, a group of Christian intellectuals, and studied questions of the rational planning of social processes. In 1945 – two years before his death – he was finally granted an ordinary professorship for education science at the University of London.

3. The analysis of ideology

After the publication of *Ideologie und Utopie* in 1929, Mannheim's theories gave rise to a controversial discussion. A particular irritant was his belief that all thought relevant to human action had an underlying structure of political ideology, at least since the French Revolution. In his view, rival parties' inability to understand each other was not merely due to rhetorical distortion, strategic manipulation, or – as the Marxists would have it – an expression of class interests. Proletarian class consciousness did not provide a "scientific" alternative, nor did politicians' actions guided by the ethics of responsibility as envisioned by Max Weber. However, Mannheim also met conservative thinkers with skepticism. They longed for the political restitution of a cultivated elite and were outraged at their ideals being rejected and at the exaltation of the "pseudo-science" of sociology, which they regarded as sophistic – and Jewish [15]. These attitudes were also the motivation of some of the Heidelberg professors in their refusal to academically accept Mannheim [13. 90f.].

Initially, Mannheim classified the multitude of ideas in the modern world according to a structure with a small number of types of ideology. The most important ones were liberalism, conservatism, and socialism. He interpreted them as functions of a concrete way to exist in the social world that was determined in accordance with classes and generations as a position within the historically changeable patterns of stratification [4. 165–171]. Each of these ideologies, he held, found expression in a characteristic → style of thought that structured the perception of space, time, and reality, of human action, and of knowledge itself. According to Mannheim, styles of thought are best visible in the process of concept formation as well as in the logic with which concepts are linked with one another; consequently, styles of thought are closely connected to the situation of one of the historically existing social classes. Thus the task of the sociology of knowledge was to decipher the self-declarations that groups emphasized in their ideologies and utopias.

For example, the study of generations served to determine ideological phases to the extent that the existence of historical experiences that shaped the community could be proven with regard to groups [3]. Similarly, it was necessary to document the attribution of political demands to a concrete social group – proof of the dependence of knowledge on social existence – by means of historical data and concepts peculiar to the specific group. Mannheim, who was aware of the potentially circular nature of this process, denied that this might be detrimental to his project, not least because his aim was less to find causal explanations of convictions and more to elucidate social knowledge in the context of a comprehensive, or "total," view of society. The sociology of knowledge aimed to comprehend the ideological field as a whole in its historical changeability, placing it into a context with the historically changeable situation of classes and generations. Mannheim believed that this kind of unifying and integrating approach might succeed whereas an ideologically aligned approach would only be able to perceive segments [4. 52].

4. Politics as a science

Mannheim illustrated this approach in his essay *Ist Politik als Wissenschaft möglich?*, placing the opposing ideological concepts concerning the relation between theory and practice in their respective societal contexts. In this, the concept of situation became particularly relevant to the characterization of politics and political knowledge. Understanding a section of the historical world as a situation, Mannheim argued, meant observing it from the point of view of a prescient and far-seeing political actor. A situation consequently comprised a complex of meaningful factors and conditions: opportunities and prospects, dangers and promises [4. 97].

In order to illuminate situations, and in their search for intellectual means to achieve effective political actions, sociologists of knowledge as well as followers of

political ideologies seek valid knowledge. However, according to Mannheim, only the former possess the comprehensive and synoptic view that allows them to diagnose the time in which they live. To achieve this, it is not sufficient to be a mere observer; the precondition, in his opinion, had to be the will that gives direction to the sociological style of thought. In order to determine it, Mannheim employed the basic concepts of Marxist social theory. Elements originally of the proletarian-socialist ideology would change their character as soon as they became components of the sociology of knowledge as the latter did not, by any means, pursue the revolutionary objectives of the proletariat. Once the ideological vocabulary was no longer employed as a means to discredit and demoralize the opponent, this new understanding brought the cognitive achievements of ideologies to light.

The sociology of knowledge was motivated just as little by a Marxist way of thinking as by a universalist and rationalist one, which Mannheim attributed to the social position of the capitalist bourgeoisie and identified with the liberalist style of thought. The sociology of knowledge, he said, emphasized the historical character of societal knowledge as well as the element of will and choice. Mannheim thus identified the particularity of the main political styles and their social originators, convinced "that mutually opposing views and theories [... were] mutually complementary" and allowed "mutually complementary partial insights" into the political field. Only their integration into the sociology of knowledge made "politics as a science for the first time possible." He made it clear that this form of thinking was peculiar to the urban, educated, and relatively classless intellectuals – with recourse to a concept presented by Alfred Weber, he called it the "socially unattached intelligentsia" [4. 132, 137].

While Mannheim regarded the conflict of ideologies as based in the social situation of the times, he doubted that political competition alone would be able to provide all the knowledge required to overcome it. He was skeptical of positions such as that championed by Hans Kelsen (→ Pure Theory of Law) and Ernst Fraenkel, according to which politics corresponded to a liberal parliament as the forum of rational disputes in which knowledge was tested and affirmed. He considered this kind of view to be too "rationalist." He called upon Marxism to develop a concept of politics as a dialectic interplay of various factors that was more realistic than the competing opinions of liberal theory.

This corresponds to the political crisis of the Weimar Republic in which all the ideological parties presented their demands in absolute terms and employed the concept of ideology in a purely destructive manner, depriving one another of trusting their own view, instead treading a path toward senseless violence. According to Mannheim, none of the political forces was the bearer of comprehensive rationality and chosen by history to integrate the warring irrationalities into a higher, pacified order. Under such conditions it was impossible to realize true politics. The sociology of knowledge alone was capable of doing so by recognizing the diverse kinds of knowledge while restricting the application of every single one: "It accepts no theoretical contention as absolutely valid in itself, but reconstructs the original standpoints, viewed from which the whole world appeared thus and such, and tries to understand the whole of the views derived from the various perspectives through the whole of the process" [4. 152].

This concept of the sociology of knowledge as the organon of politics as a science, however, was difficult to verify and attracted a number of critics. Still, the sociology of knowledge came to be regarded as a subdiscipline of the social sciences whose applicability was subject to the standards of value-free science.

5. Reception

Mannheim's German contemporaries reacted mainly to his ambitious conception of the sociology of knowledge as the organon of politics, while later authors, especially from the English-speaking world, focused more on the concept of the sociology of knowledge as a positive discipline, a specialist subfield of academic sociology. For instance, Robert K. Merton (originally Meyer Robert Schkolnick) and Kurt H. Wolff both critiqued Mannheim's sociology of knowledge in different ways. Wolff had studied under Mannheim in Frankfurt before moving to Italy in 1933 and then emigrating to the United States six years later [14].

Mannheim's sociology of knowledge was a decisive attempt at forging a path through the crisis of liberal civilization beyond the relativizing insights of a fashionable cultural and political commentary. Mannheim's aim was to reveal the historical and social conditionality of all cultural products, including knowledge. Throughout, Mannheim emphasized the regulative idea of the philosophy of history, which was informed above all by a Hegelian interpretation of Marx and by Max Weber's realism. Weber's thought strategies benefited Mannheim's professionalism when his speculations led him into the vicinity of contemporary cultural essayists. Moreover, in all of the changing interpretations of the historical situation, his thinking was imbued with a strong sense of political responsibility.

The sociology of knowledge had its enthusiasts as well as its critics. Between 1925 and 1930, Weimar found itself in its most optimistic intellectual phase, and Mannheim was moved by it as well. Later his sociology of knowledge was interpreted as an idiosyncratic attempt at formulating a scientific cultural sociology that should more correctly be understood as the investigation of certain means by which convictions (rather than knowledge) were formed. Its cultural relevance was reduced to that of a further academic specialization and ceased to be controversial.

Reactions to Mannheim's sociology of knowledge always contained explicit and implicit accusations against Mannheim, imputing that he was indifferent to the truths of German culture as a foreigner and a Jew. Yet his personal background did not define his work in any way. The reception of his sociology of knowledge during the interwar years, in fact, is an instance of the complex and contradictory nature of the "Jewish question" in the intellectual life of the Weimar Republic, contradicting the simplifying theory of a steady antisemitic drumbeat that reached its climax in the National Socialist regime. Many of the numerous and influential critical reviews of *Ideologie und Utopie* were the work of Jewish authors who would find themselves in exile soon afterwards – including Helmuth Plessner, Günther Anders (originally Günther Siegmund Stern; → Hiroshima), Herbert Marcuse (→ Institute for Social Research), and Hannah Arendt (→ Judgement) [16].

Even so, the polemic linking of Mannheim's sociology to his Jewish background did take place. Among his antagonists in German academia was the renowned literary scholar Ernst Robert Curtius, who, though certainly not a staunch antisemite, explicitly criticized the openness to Jews that Mannheim's sociological project revealed [1]. A similar attitude is evident in a passage in an obituary by Leopold von Wiese, Mannheim's main rival in the Weimar years, whose arrangement with the National Socialist regime did not harm the reception of his formal sociology in the United States in any way. Writing in 1947, Wiese recalled a debate with the late Mannheim on the meaning of

liberty. He concluded that Mannheim's idea of liberty might lead to a "tyranny of the cunning" and had to remain strange to all those "whose ancestors did not come from a ghetto" [8. 99].

Bibliography

Sources

[1] E. R. Curtius, Sociology – and its Limits, in: V. Meja/N. Stehr (eds.), Knowledge and Politics. The Sociology of Knowledge Dispute, London/New York 2015, 113–120.   [2] K. Mannheim, Das konservative Denken. Soziologische Beiträge zum Werden des politisch-historischen Denkens in Deutschland, in: Archiv für Sozialwissenschaft 57 (1927) 1, 68–142, 470–495.   [3] K. Mannheim, The Problem of Generations, in: P. Kecskemeti (ed.), Karl Mannheim. Essays, London 1952, 276–322.   [4] K. Mannheim, Ideology and Utopia. An Introduction to the Sociology of Knowledge, trans. by L. Wirth and E. Shils, London 1960.   [5] M. Scheler, Problems of a Sociology of Knowledge, trans. by M. S. Frings, New York 2013.   [6] M. Scheler (ed.), Versuche zu einer Soziologie des Wissens, Munich/Leipzig 1924.   [7] M. Scheler, Cognition and Work. A Study Concerning the Value and Limits of the Pragmatic Motifs in the Cognition of the World, trans. by Z. Davis, Evanston 2021.   [8] L. v. Wiese, Karl Mannheim (1893–1947), in: Kölner Zeitschrift für Soziologie und Sozialpsychologie 1 (1948/49) 1, 98–100.

Secondary literature

[9] D. Kettler, Karl Mannheim in Frankfurt. A Political Education, in: M. Epple et al. (eds.), "Politisierung der Wissenschaft" – Jüdische Wissenschaftler und ihre Gegner an der Universität Frankfurt vor und nach 1933, Göttingen 2016.   [10] D. Kettler et al., Karl Mannheim and Conservatism. The Ancestry of Historical Thinking, in: American Sociological Review, vol. 49, no. 1, 1984, 71–85.   [11] D. Kettler et al., Karl Mannheim and the Legacy of Max Weber. Retrieving a Research Programme, Aldershot 2008.

[12] D. Kettler/V. Meja, Karl Mannheim's Jewish Question, in: Religions 3 (2012) 2, 228–250. [13] D. Kettler/V. Meja, Karl Mannheim and the Crisis of Liberalism. The Secret of These New Times, New Brunswick 1995. [14] D. Kettler/V. Meja, Karl Mannheim in America. The Loyalty of Kurt H. Wolff, in: G. Backhaus/G. Psathas (eds.), The Sociology of Radical Commitment. Kurt H. Wolff's Existential Turn, Lexington 2007, 93–113. [15] R. Laube, Platon und die Sophisten, in: H. Lehmann/O. G. Oexle (eds.), Nationalsozialismus in den Kulturwissenschaften, vol. 2, Göttingen 2004, 139–164. [16] V. Meja/N. Stehr (eds.), Knowledge and Politics. The Sociology of Knowledge Dispute, London/New York 2015.

DAVID KETTLER, ANNANDALE-ON-HUDSON
AND VOLKER MEJA, ST. JOHN'S,
NEWFOUNDLAND

Solal

Solal is the protagonist of a four-volume novel cycle written in French by Albert Cohen (1895–1981). When its most famous and successful part *La Belle du Seigneur* appeared in 1968, French criticism perceived Solal as a great tragic lover in the tradition of Tolstoy's *Anna Karenina*. It was not until the 1969 re-edition of the almost forgotten first two volumes of the tetralogy, *Solal* (1930; "Solal of the Solals," 1933) and *Mangeclous* (1938; "Nailcruncher," 1940) and the publication of the final volume *Les Valeureux* that the complete figure of Solal emerged. His biography is the exemplary representation of the fortunes of a Jew who is born in the Sephardic ghetto of a Greek island, rises to the highest ranks of French and international politics as an "Israelite," and finally takes his own life in despair at the Shoah and the inactivity of the political world. Solal's life reflects the period between the antisemitism of the French Dreyfus Affair and the National Socialist mass murder of Jews and is strongly influenced by Albert Cohen's own biography.

1. Albert Cohen
2. Writing and experience: the *Solal* tetralogy
2.1 France 1924: the cellar of St. Germain Castle
2.2 Germany 1935: Rachel Silberstein's cellar in Berlin

1. Albert Cohen

Albert Cohen was born in 1895 as the only child of Jewish parents whose ancestors had lived on the Greek island of Corfu for several generations. The family lived right next to the Jewish ghetto in a house belonging to the paternal grandfather Abraham Cohen, owner of a soap factory founded around 1840 and head of the Jewish community.

After the factory found itself in economic difficulties, and considering the precarious situation of the Jews in Corfu, the family emigrated to Marseille in 1900. The parents kept a small shop trading in eggs and oil. Cohen attended a Catholic primary school and from 1904 onward the Lycée Thiers, graduating with the baccalaureate in 1913. These years laid the foundations for Cohen's lifelong ambivalent relationship with France and the French language. Cohen, who spoke the Judeo-Venetian dialect of the Corfu Jews at home, discovered his love for the French language and literature during his school years; Marcel Pagnol (1895–1974), the future dramatist and script writer, was one of his closest school friends. However, a disturbing antisemitic incident on the day of his tenth birthday poisoned Cohen's relationship with all things French. A street peddler swore at him, calling him a "friend of Dreyfus," "parasite," and "traitor," reinforcing his sense of being excluded from French culture due to his origin.

In 1917, Cohen finished his three-year law course at the University of Geneva; in

1919 he became a Swiss citizen. During his years as a student, he became interested in Zionism, which significantly influenced his professional career. In 1917, he became friends with the Zionist poet André Spire (1868–1966); three year later, he met Chaim Weizmann (→ Balfour Declaration), who employed him to carry out smaller tasks in Geneva, before entrusting the *Revue juive*, co-financed by the World Zionist Organization, to him in 1924. Six editions were published under Cohen's editorship, featuring contributions by many famous scholars such as Martin Buber (→ Dialogue), Albert Einstein (→ Theory of Relativity), Gershom Scholem (→ Kabbalah), and Sigmund Freud (→ Psychoanalysis). In 1925/1926, Cohen acted as deputy for Victor Jacobson (1869–1935) who headed the Geneva office of the World Zionist Organization. In 1939/1940, he was active in a double role as general secretary for the → World Jewish Congress and, under Nahum Goldmann (1895–1982), for the Jewish Agency. At first, he tried to win the support of the French government for the "Légion juive," a project dear to his heart, which would provide 200,000 to 300,000 Jewish volunteer soldiers to the Allies (→ Military). When the project was rejected by the Daladier government on November 13, 1939, Cohen endeavored to establish a support committee named Pro Causa Judaica that was to consist of influential personalities with the aim of endorsing Jewish concerns in future peace negotiations. However, it was disempowered by the German invasion while constituting itself in the author Jules Romains's apartment on May 10, 1940. Cohen tried to find accommodation for the Paris Zionist organizations in the South of France before fleeing to London on June 20 of the same year. Here he continued to maintain contacts on their behalf, especially with the → Résistance organization La France Libre headed by Charles de Gaulle [11].

In addition to his engagement on behalf of the Zionist organizations, Cohen was repeatedly active as a political representative between 1926 and 1951: in Geneva with the Bureau international du travail and the Organisation internationale pour les réfugiés and in London with the Comité international pour les réfugiés. The fact that he was able to serve the London Committee as the author of the report on the basis of which, on October 15, 1946, an intergovernmental conference adopted the agreement on the issuance of a provisional travel document for stateless refugees, filled him with great satisfaction. It was adopted in substance into the → Geneva Convention of July 28, 1951, valid to this day. Cohen referred to the 32-page travel document projected by the report as his "most beautiful book" [5. XCVII]. Cohen returned to Geneva in 1947.

Until 1951, Cohen wrote his books during breaks from his political activities. After his two debut works, the collection of poems *Paroles juives* (1920) and the drama *Ézéchiel* (first version 1928), *Solal*, the first volume of the Solal saga, appeared in 1930 ("Solal," 1933). The subsequent volumes experienced a multifarious publishing history. In 1938, Cohen had written his first draft of the later volume *La Belle du Seigneur* (Engl. 1995) on 3,000 pages. At the request of the publisher Gallimard, he removed the section *Mangeclous* ("Nailcruncher," 1940) which leaves out Solal's love story, focusing instead on the adventures of the group of the "Valeureux," the "Gallants," who surround Solal in the story. A similar sequence of events occurred in 1967 with Gallimard initially rejecting a more substantial version of *La Belle du Seigneur*, only publishing it under this title in 1968 after the adventure and love stories had once again been separated. In the same year, the novel was awarded the Gran Prix du roman de l'Académie française. The story of the "Gallants" was moved into the eponymous final volume *Les valeureux*, published in 1969. At the end of 1951, Cohen concluded his political career, dedicating himself entirely to his literary activity in Geneva. In 1954, he published a volume of recollections *Le livre de ma mère* ("Book of My Mother," 1997); further recollections followed in 1972 with *Ô vous, frères humains* and 1979 with *Carnets 1978* ("Notebooks," 1978). Albert Cohen died in Geneva in 1981. His death marked the beginning of extensive, initially French, research into his much-read books, mostly, however, ignoring his early works.

2. Writing and experience: the *Solal* tetralogy

When Cohen published *Solal* in 1930, he was already planning a multi-volume work, which he sometimes referred to as "La geste des Juifs" (The heroic epic of the Jews) or "Saga des Solals." Over the course of four books, Cohen follows his successful protagonist Solal and his cousins who wander between the Jewish Orient of Cephalonia, based on Corfu, and the Occident, represented by Paris and Geneva during the Nazi era. *Solal* is the only one among the four novels in which Hitler plays no part. The plot takes place in the years between 1894 and 1925, most of it located in the historical milieu of France during the → Dreyfus affair. The second volume *Mangeclous*, originally published in August 1938, begins in April 1934. While Hitler is present as a threat to the Jews, Cohen still has the heroic group of the five "Gallants" make salacious jokes about him. The two subsequent novels, which appeared at the end of the 1960s, were composed in complete awareness of the Shoah. The approach to Judaism has changed entirely in its subject as well as its style. The last volume, *Les Valeureux*, takes place in 1935; the murder of Cohen's uncle and cousin in → Auschwitz as well as the death of Cohen's mother in German-occupied

Marseille on January 10, 1943, are the subject of author's comments which Cohen weaves into the plot of the novel [6. 93, 236].

Cohen's Solal saga is remarkable for great inventiveness of powerful images and a multitude of entirely unrealistic styles. All the same, large parts of this work are – in keeping with Cohen's writing strategy in general – highly autobiographically inspired. Especially the author's Jewish experiences were incorporated into the novels: the Sephardic influence from Corfu, the lebenswelten (worlds of lived experience) of the French Jews between → assimilation and the antisemitism of the time of the Dreyfus affair, Zionism, and the extermination of the Jews.

In *Ô vous, frères humains*, Cohen refers to the episode of his ten-year-old self being subjected to antisemitic invective by the street peddler in Marseille. His words – "You can clear out, we've seen you, this is not your home, this is not your country, you have no right to be here" – destroy the child's trust in the world, providing the seed for the topics and the attitude to life of his literary works. As a boy, Cohen already loved France and hated Germany. Every night he would kneel before the secret altar he had constructed in his room out of images of French classics, Napoleon, Pasteur, and little bags of French colonial soil. France was all the world to him; he was led by an "insane desire to belong" [4. 1063].

In his autobiographical text, Cohen describes the aimless wanderings of a child as a variation on the motif of the "eternally wandering" Jew (→ Ahasver), developing first into a daydreaming and then into a delirious examination of Judaism and nearly all the registers of its historical expression [4. 1098]. The boy shifts his focus from all things Jewish onto Israel and Masada, deliberating whether he should call himself an Israelite rather than a Jew. His lost wandering transforms into the regal strides of a proud Jew, blessing the evil fair-haired ones with the few words of → Hebrew with which he is familiar in the name of "Israel, who I had become" [4. 1102].

Cohen tied these experiences to two traumatic primal events in the history of the Jews: on the one hand to the Dreyfus affair, to which the street peddler referred and which he mentioned at the beginning of his autobiography *Ô vous, frères humains*; on the other hand to the Shoah, which the 77-year-old author correlates with his childhood memories in the final chapters of his book. The street peddler, he says, sent the small Cohen "into an invisible concentration camp for eternity, [...] a camp for his soul only" [4. 1064]. His hatred "announced" the gas chambers "where two relatives of mine, my uncle and his son" died [4. 1106].

All the elements of these childhood memories return – unfolded and transformed – in Solal's fictional life story. Cohen describes his experience as the archetype of the lifelong flight he devised for the hero of his novel and draws on the elements of his youthful desire to belong and his creative drive of the time in his depiction of the figures of the "Gallants," Solal's Quixotic cousins.

A further Jewish conditioning that left a deep impression on Cohen were the 15 days he spent on Corfu at the age of 13 with his parents on the occasion of his bar mitzvah. Cohen called these days "the most important of my life" [1. LXXVII]. Three impressions recur in his books: firstly the Corfu countryside with its orange and olive groves, the crystal-clear sea, the scents of jasmine and honeysuckle on the sea breeze. Cohen has three of the four Solal novels begin on Cephalonia, as he calls his poetic version of Corfu. The second deep impression of Cohen's journey also makes an appearance in these novels: in three of the four novels, there is a vividly drawn Jewish quarter, similar to that next to which the villa of Albert Cohen's grandfather stood. Solal is born in such a quarter, a hero who attempts

everything in order to escape this "oriental" origin and become French. The "Gallants," Solal's five cousins, come from the same background; they come back to haunt him regularly, reminding him of his Sephardic origins (→ Sephardim). Corfu's picturesque Jewish quarter provided Cohen with a counter-image to the assimilated lifestyle of the French Israelites. The greatest importance, however, was attached to the third defining experience of his visit, Albert Cohen's encounter with his grandfather Abraham Coen (it was not until later that Cohen added an h to his name). Cohen experienced him as a "patriarch," living with his family in "almost monasterial seclusion, with barely any contact with the Christian community, and in strict Orthodoxy" [3. 1177]. The grandfather introduced the young Cohen to Jewish tradition, its laws, and its holy scriptures.

His grandfather's instruction left visible traces in Cohen's literary work. He refers to it in his first publication, the collection of poems *Paroles juives*, which he wrote in order to explain the essence of Judaism to his Protestant wife Elisabeth Brocher. The beginning and the end of his Solal tetralogy, too, are informed by his encounters with tradition. In the first volume, Cohen revisits the circumstances of his journey to Corfu by having the story in Cephalonia begin on the eve of Solal's bar mitzvah; the law appears in the form of a satirically distorted bar mitzvah sermon. And Cohen even weaves the ancestral legacy of the one God and the motif of being rescued from captivity into the last sentence of *La Belle du Seigneur* in 1968.

Cohen had encountered a counter-image to Sephardic culture, the world of the assimilated "Israelites," in international organizations. This experience is reflected in particular in *La Belle du Seigneur* in Cohen's satirical description of the bureaucratic rituals among the functionaries of the League of Nations. The description of Solal's attempt at persuading the League of Nations to save the German Jews is informed by Cohen's experience in these organizations too. In this context it is significant that Cohen's political activity and his fiction were mutually influential. Long before his diplomatic deployment, Cohen had written literary pieces on the misery and the politically precarious status of refugees. The idea of a Jewish army is hinted at in the 1938 novel *Mangeclous*. And in a letter of April 5, 1939, Cohen asked Chaim Weizmann's forgiveness for the novel's protagonist who uses Weizmann's name in a fake telegram in order to be able to present a plea before the League of Nations for the borders of the future State of Israel to be expanded.

All the same, the novel cycle's main feature is the cesura marking the time as before and after the Shoah. Nowhere does the change in the writer's attitude become clearer than in the comparison of two underground scenes in *Solal* and *La Belle du Seigneur*, which may be regarded as the key scenes of the Solal saga. Nowhere else does Cohen discuss the issues of Jewish belonging in such a concentrated way. In both scenes the narrative changes to the first person in order to emphasize the identification with the Jewish people. And both scenes depict Jewish spaces that must be hidden from their hostile environment in the underground. When it comes to their interpretation and subject focus, however, the chapters are entirely different.

2.1 France 1924: the cellar of St. Germain Castle

In *Solal*, the eponymous protagonist, having risen to the position of minister in France, acquires the Chateau de St. Germain. In its upstairs apartments, he lives in an unhappy marriage with Aude de Maussanne, who comes from Protestant French nobility. In the sprawling cellars of the chateau, he shelters the "Gallants" together with half the ghetto of his Cephalonian home in complete secrecy. "A Biblical city swarms under

His Excellency's house. [...] In the night, I return to my country. And day and night, I am sad, so sad" [2. 242]. In this imaginary setting of an underground Israel in the heart of France, Cohen paints a multifaceted picture of the French Jews' assimilation dilemma. While the marriage and the relocation are expressions of the desire to belong to French society, this desire is thwarted by sadness and the simultaneous presence of Jewish tradition.

Once again topographically spacious and furnished with a great wealth of imagination, the cellar in which Rachel Silberstein found sanctuary from the Nazis in *La Belle du Seigneur* in 1935, and into which she has rescued Solal, is a powerful literary image as well; not, however, a freely invented one. It ties into the genuine mortal danger to which Berlin Jews were exposed during the years of National Socialism, which drove them into hiding.

The historical distance between the two underground scenes is further demonstrated in the different emphasis on the issue of Jewish self-understanding and in the difference between genre and style. In *Solal*, Cohen approaches these issues on the literary terrain of the grotesque, of carnivalesque exaggeration. The group of people embodying this stylistic level are the five "Gallants" with whom the colorful, effusive, "oriental" spirit of the Cephalonian ghetto invades the culture of France. They appear on the scene at the time when Solal has just become engaged to the Protestant Aude de Maussane, the daughter of a minister of state, and they compromise Solal to such an extent that he loses his fiancée and his position because of these "grotesques of the ghetto" [2. 183]. The passage culminates in a nighttime scene in which the "Gallants" "in-toned a synagogue psalm" [2. 183] by candlelight in the French Ministry of Foreign Affairs, with Solal joining in (like ten-year-old Cohen, according to his recollections). Finally Solal wins back his fiancée and when he, having risen again, becomes a government minister himself, the "Gallants" reappear, causing trouble at diplomatic receptions. "No ambiguity. French, only French, and all it implies," his father-in-law, by now Prime Minister, admonishes him. "Oh Sol! Come back to your self, to your holy nation," his uncle counters [2. 225, 228]. Outraged, Solal refuses to receive his father, to whom he only ever refers as the "Jewish rabbi." When the latter forces his way in, disrupting the reception, the son first considers hitting his father but then, "cast a venmous look [,] slowly crossed himself" and sends his father and uncle packing. However, as he sees "the two despairing old men" walk away, he experiences a change of heart: "Poor Solal, you have sold your soul" [2. 229, 230f., 233, 234].

Solal provides accommodation for the Cephalonian relatives in the cellar of his chateau and endeavors to "explain the beauty of Israel" to his wife. She converts with the words of Ruth: "'Thy people shall be my people, and thy God my God'" [2. 243]. However, she is unable to bear the whole 18-page walk through the never-ending cellars, staged by Cohen as a grotesque retelling of the entire Jewish cultural history. As Solal begins to sing the praises of his people and the narrator changes to the first-person perspective, she apostatizes: "'What have you in common with those people? You are [...] not like those worms. Beloved, send them away" [2. 259]. The tension between cultural affiliation and the demands of assimilation at the center of the novel as well as taking stock of the "mixed marriage" have reached their climax.

2.2 *Germany 1935: Rachel Silberstein's cellar in Berlin*

In the cellar scene in *La Belle du Seigneur*, the historical system of references has changed completely. Rather than in France in 1924, it is set in 1935 Germany. Dreyfus-related antisemitism is replaced with the Nazis'

murderous antisemitism. The point at issue is not assimilation and its boundaries but collective survival, saving the Jews of Germany. Consequently, this scene in *La Belle du Seigneur* is infinitely more complex than the scene in *Solal*. For reasons that remain unclear, Solal is wandering around 1935 Berlin dressed as an Orthodox Jew. "[B]lond beasts" attack him, gouging swastikas into his chest and beating him senseless [7. 484]. The family of the second-hand bookseller Silberstein from Łódź rescues him, hiding him in the sprawling cellar, where they hide together with innumerable works of art, two horses, and the carriage belonging to Rachel's grandfather, the "miraculous rabbi" [7. 493] of → Łódź.

Rachel, malformed as the result of a → pogrom during her mother's pregnancy, announces two insights to Solal that will change his destiny. She predicts that the National Socialists, who are currently satisfied with torture, in "one year, three years, and they'll be doing much worse [...] and will kill us all" [7. 484–488]. And she teaches him an understanding of Judaism that will define him for the rest of his life. Of the many interpretations circulating in the cellar at St. Germain, one now moves to the fore: the one focusing on Jewish law (→ Halakhah). This is a concept of the law that goes beyond the grandfather's lessons in Corfu. In *La Belle du Seigneur*, Cohen has imbued the concept of law with anti-National Socialist energy. It is now entirely focused on juxtaposing the Germans as "a people who live under the sway of nature" and Israel as "a people who live under the rule of anti-nature," as "people of the Holy Law"; Germans follow the law of nature of strength and killing, while ever since the Law was revealed to Moses, Israel has been symbolic of "the same end [...] which is the humanization of man" [7. 876–879].

The situation in the Berlin cellar is presented as a scene with multilayered narrative and styles, in which the sentences grow increasingly longer, finally flowing as a broad stream free from punctuation, the embodiment of seeking Jewish consciousness that draws everything along with it. Cohen transfers the cellar dialogue between Rachel and Solal into the phantasmagoria of a "special Purim festival" [9. 1184]. The two of them put on Purim masks, Rachel becomes Esther, Solal falls in love with her, she drapes the prayer shawl around his shoulders and "placed in his hands the sacred scrolls of the Commandments." [7. 496]. They sit in the carriage, the horses harnessed, for an ironical celebration of the Jews being saved, as the singing of "joy of the blood of Israel spurting beneath German knives" is heard in the street [7. 496]. In the neighboring cellar, Jews sing their songs of David and Solal stands by the window in his prayer shawl holding up "the Holy Law, [...] in gold and velvet crowned in silver" to "the young hopes of the German nation" [7. 496f.].

This scene is exactly in the middle of the book. Its central position is emphasized by the narrator's voice changing to the first person: it represents the decisive turning point in Solal's life. From the League of Nations' armchair strategist, he transforms himself into a warlike diplomat campaigning in the capital cities of the Western world for the League of Nations to take steps to save the German Jews. When he berates his colleagues for their hostile attitude, he is dismissed and, as the result of a masochistic self-denunciation, even loses his French citizenship. Now he retains his "country" [7. 823] only in the physically passionate love affair with Ariane, his employee Adrien's wife whom he seduced. However, this love, too, finds itself in crisis, on the one hand because the sexual attraction soon passes but on the other because Solal's longing is increasingly focused on Rachel Silberstein and her sister. He dreams of living with them in the underground community of their Berlin cellar, together with the Jews he failed to save. Here, the competition between two

types of love becomes a topic that is found throughout Cohen's entire work. Cohen juxtaposes the concept of occidental love in the sense of *Anna Karenina*, in which a connection grows out of passion and love, with his mother's "oriental" love: "She had not married for love. A husband had been found for her and she had meekly accepted. And biblical love had been born, so far removed from my Western passions" [7a. 15].

In the second half of *La Belle du Seigneur*, the decline of Solal's passion for Ariane and his return to his Jewish roots develop parallel to each other. The decline of the love affair is described with disillusioning psychological realism. The road to Judaism continues the phantasmagorical procession of the cellar scene. Having moved on to Paris, Solal dreams his hotel room into a ghetto in which he speaks Hebrew, wears his shawl and shivers in awe of the eternal, praying. In his mind he slips back into the cellar in Berlin, dons the Purim nose and crown and beholds: "Yes! Standing there in his mirror is Israel entire" [7. 842]. His imaginary identification with Jewishness grows steadily more comprehensive. He invents the, unfavorably drawn, Rosenfelds, a Jewish family of vulgar show-offs, only to include them, too, in his love for the Jewish people. Although himself Sephardic, he joins a group of Orthodox Eastern European Jews in the street – in the novel *Mangeclous*, the "Gallants" had still despised the so-called → Ostjuden – sings with them and "rocks his head and shoulders, rocks in time to the immemorial rhythm" [7. 847]. From the political present, he has stepped into a different time. Cohen ensures that everything that could shape and injure the fate of a European Jew in the 1930s flows into his narrative stream, alive with reality and truly universal. The narrative first flows to Masada, then Solal imagines a Résistance in National Socialist Berlin. Decked out in his Purim raiment, carrying the law scroll in his arm, he rolls out of the Silbersteins' cellar into the streets of Berlin, converts the bloodthirsty Germans to love the Jewish law, until the scene changes and he dies an imaginary death in the company of Rachel.

When, a hundred pages later, the novel ends with the actual suicide of Solal and Ariane, with his last breath the protagonist returns to this scene with Rachel in which he wept for the Jewish "children whom he had not saved" [7. 974] and speaks his last words: "Hear O Israel the Lord our God the Lord is One" (→ Shema) [7. 882]. Thus at the conclusion of Cohen's tetralogy, Solal has returned to the Jewish community he had intended to leave in favor of France at the beginning. He was a Frenchman, a Catholic, married to a Protestant woman, and is none of those things now. He is with Rachel Silberstein, who came for him when he was lying in the street in Berlin, bleeding, senseless, and in Orthodox attire.

Bibliography

Sources

[1] A. Cohen, Belle du seigneur, Paris 1968. See [7] and [7a] for English. [2] A. Cohen, Solal, trans. by W. Benson, New York 1933. [3] A. Cohen, Carnets 1978, in: A. Cohen, Oeuvres, ed. by C. Peyrefitte/B. Cohen, Paris 1993, 1111–1199. [4] A. Cohen, Ô vous, frères humains, in: A. Cohen, Oeuvres, ed. by C. Peyrefitte/B. Cohen, Paris 1993, 1039–1110. [5] A. Cohen, Oeuvres, ed. by C. Peyrefitte/B. Cohen, Paris 1993. [6] A. Cohen, Les valeureux, Paris 1969. [7] A. Cohen, Belle du Seigneur, trans. by D. Coward, London 1995. [7a] A. Cohen, Book of My Mother, trans. by B. Cohen, Brooklyn [2]2012.

Secondary literature

[8] J. I. Abecassis, Albert Cohen. Dissonant Voices, Baltimore 2004. [9] M. Joseph, Purim, in: Jüdisches Lexikon, vol. 4/2, Frankfurt am Main [2]1987, 1182–1186. [10] C. Nicault, Albert Cohen et le comité Pro causa judaïca. Nouveaux documents, in: Cahiers Albert Cohen 10 (2000), 9–49. [11] C. Nicault, Albert Cohen et les sion-

istes, in: A. Schaffner et al. (eds.), Albert Cohen dans son siècle. Actes du colloque international Cerisy-la-Salle, septembre 2003, Paris 2005, 99–118.

ANDREAS ISENSCHMID, BERLIN

Sonnet

The sonnet is the most frequently found poetic form in the Western world. Hebrew literature has a particular affinity for the sonnet, and from time to time the far from insubstantial contribution of Hebrew literature to the early development of the sonnet has been accorded to it. From Immanuel ha-Romi in the 13th century to present-day composers, many Hebrew poets have mastered the format – one that demands a high degree of poetic virtuosity – and often they have varied or challenged the strict formal framework. The relative foreignness of the sonnet to both historic and modern → Hebrew phonology, among other things, has meant that the Hebrew sonnet acquired a number of special characteristics. The most significant Jewish writers of Hebrew sonnets in the 20th century were Shaul Tchernichovsky, Jacob Steinberg, Lea Goldberg, and Yehuda Amichai.

1. Development
2. The sonnet in Hebrew literature
3. Tchernichovsky, Steinberg, Goldberg, and Amichai

1. Development

The sonnet is one of the oldest and most common forms of poetry; the earliest occurrence of the poetic shape we recognize today can be dated to the first half of the 13th century in the works of Giacomo da Lentini (ca. 1200–ca. 1260). Lentini was a member of the Sicilian School of Poetry at the court of the Holy Roman Emperor, Frederick

II – who according to Jacob Burckhardt was the "first ruler of the modern type who sat upon a throne" [5. 2]. Through their innovative use of the vernacular, instead of Latin, the poets of the Sicilian School heralded the beginning of modern Italian culture. A theory also reinforced by the name suggests that the format probably originated in the Provençal language (perhaps at an even earlier stage): *sonnet* denotes a "small poem" or "small song" and could be a diminutive of the Provençal *son*, which means "song," as well as a genre of poetry.

Dante Alighieri (1265–1321) interspersed his poetry with sonnets; in *La Vita Nuova* (1294; "The New Life," 1846) the format occurs more frequently than any other. His contemporary Immanuel ha-Romi (ca. 1265–1330), whose poetry drew on the Sephardic tradition (→ Sepharad), refined it. The 38 Hebrew sonnets preserved in *Maḥberot Immanu'el ha-Romi* ("The Cantos of Immanuel ha-Romi," 1957) are probably the oldest sonnets documented in a non-Italian language. Immanuel preceded Francesco Petrarca (1304–1374; known as Petrarch in English) by fifty years. Known not only as the father of Humanism but also as the father of the sonnet, Petrarch perfected its form in 317 poems and, in so doing, laid down its rules. The Petrarchan or Italian sonnet consists of 14 lines: one octave and one sestet with eight and six lines respectively. The octave is itself subdivided into two quartets, the sestet into two tercets. While the rhyme in the octave follows the bracketing ABBA pattern, it varies in the sestet (CDE). The differences between the two parts of the poem are also reflected in the content. The octave poses a question which is then answered in the sestet. Even though Petrarch never explicitly refers to Immanuel's poetry, which only had a very limited influence on the literature of the time, both men felt inspired by Dante in similar ways.

Petrarch's formative achievements made the sonnet famous and ensured its quick absorption into the national literatures of Europe. An important variation emerged in England at the beginning of the 17th century with the Shakespearean sonnet. In the 154 sonnets extant under his name, Shakespeare (1564–1616) preferred the model developed by Henry Howard, Earl of Surrey (ca. 1516–1547) to the Italian one and the popularity of the new format was such that it came to be named after him. The English, or Shakespearean, sonnet still has 14 lines, but they are subdivided into three quartets and culminate in a concluding, aphoristic couplet with the rhyme scheme ABAB, CDCD, EFEF, GG.

These two original forms of the sonnet, the Italian and the English, co-exist to this day; each generation of poets fills the traditional forms with new content, and often the poets are tempted to modify them, for example, by omitting a line or varying the rhyme scheme.

2. The sonnet in Hebrew literature

Since Immanuel ha-Romi no other secular literary form has had a presence in Hebrew → poetry as sustained as the sonnet. Immanuel gave the sonnet a finalized, pure form even before Petrarch established his, and he also brought to poetry mundane and previously untreated subjects of everyday life such as boasting and gluttony. Ha-Romi's powerful thematic innovations are also remarkable in the Jewish cultural context because his sonnets gave indirect expression to certain tendencies from the contemporary non-Jewish environment, for instance elements of the *dolce stil novo*, and because they were composed in a realistic style replete with eroticism, satire, and a defiant spirit. Ha-Romi's sonnets brought Hebrew poetry into close contact with Italian literature. It built a bridge between the two cultures, enabling new subjects, motifs, and ideas to reach Jewish writers and readers. While specific subjects were given new literary interpretations in his sonnets, they remained rooted in the Hebrew-Sephardic tradition of the → maqam (rhymed prose with origins in Arabic music).

After ha-Romi's time, the Hebrew sonnet lost some of its significance, probably as a result of the ban on *Maḥberot Immanu'el ha-Romi* pronounced by Joseph Caro (1488–1575) in his legal codex *Shulḥan Arukh* (Set Table). Caro cited their erotic content, but a more likely reason behind the ban may have been ha-Romi's use of Christian models for his love sonnets, which – inspired by the *dolce stil novo* – alluded to the Virgin Mary. The tension always associated with the form of the sonnet in non-Jewish literatures between the old and the new, between preservation of and break (or divergence) from the tradition, thus received an additional dimension in Hebrew culture: the tension between Hebrew and non-Hebrew form (→ Literature).

Around 1500 the Hebrew sonnet experienced a resurgence in popularity, especially outside of Italy, and often as commissioned poetry – for instance in the Jewish communities of the Netherlands (→ Esnoga), in → Salonika, and North Africa. The period up to the 19th century saw several dozen Hebrew poets emerge who composed sonnets, and even Ashkenazi Jews (→ Ashkenaz) appropriated the format. Poets of the Enlightenment appreciated its rationalistic aspects. Their general tendency to avoid the purely lyrical form of expression gave an often allegorical and – in Georg Lukács's (1885–1971; → Class Consciousness) terminology – "worldless" character to their compositions. However, in the poetry of the → Haskalah the sonnet never rose above the status of a minor offshoot.

3. Tchernichovsky, Steinberg, Goldberg, and Amichai

The most prominent composers of Hebrew sonnets in the 20th century were Saul Tchernichovsky (1875–1943), Jacob Steinberg (1887–1947), Lea Goldberg (1911–1970), and Jehuda Amichai (1924–2000).

Published in Berlin in 1922, Shaul Tchernichovsky's (→ Poetry) *Maḥberet ha-sonetot* (Book of Sonnets) comprised 46 poems. The earliest, *Ḥoravot* (Ruins), was a composition from 1895 by the then twenty-year old author. Moreover, Tchernichovsky published an essay on the history of the sonnet for the volume. The publication clearly pointed to the renewed theoretical and practical interest in the sonnet form, owing to the growing use of the tonal syllabic meter in Hebrew poetry as well. Because of the *Maḥberet*, Tchernichovsky was considered to be the "father of the sonnet" in modern Hebrew poetry. Some years later he added a monograph on the poetry of Immanuel ha-Romi, whose *Maḥberot* had inspired the title of his own book of sonnets.

What emerges in retrospect is Tchernichovsky's three-fold significance as a trailblazer for the sonnet in modern Hebrew poetry: he took the original form of the Petrarchan sonnet and preserved its clear separation between octave and sestet; he reintroduced serious, elevated subjects, in contrast to the Hebrew-Italian tradition which favored playful, lightweight themes; and he practiced the cyclical form, including the wreath of sonnets. The small, lyrical format of the individual sonnet thus took on additional perspectives and gained the character of a larger work.

Compared to Tchernichovsky, Jacob Steinberg was clearly less bound by formal criteria. He moreover used the sonnet format to create some of the most daring love poems of his time. Steinberg seems to have reinvigorated the Hebrew sonnet with a lyrical, almost confessional, power of expression whereas Tchernichovsky – in this regard inspired by Neoromanticism – had chosen a more descriptive and contemplative voice.

Steinberg rose to prominence as one of the outstanding poets of the generation after Tchernichovsky and Ḥayim Naḥman Bialik (1873–1934; → El ha-tsippor). Unchallenged by his contemporaries and clearly influenced by Charles Baudelaire (1821–1867), Steinberg was able to capture the modern city-dwelling experience mostly with an attitude of despair, bitter austerity, and decadence, and in this way became the urban poet *par excellence*. Often seen as confessional and pessimistic, Steinberg's poetry has also been noted for its "rhetoric of honesty" and celebration of life. He composed more than 20 sonnets in three cycles, of which the *Sonetot mi-bet ha-kafeh* (Coffee House Sonnets) he wrote while visiting Germany in 1922 would become his most popular. The eight sonnets together form a "poetic novella" depicting the coffee house as a microcosm of the entire universe. In the spirit of the interwar cultural climate and Oswald Spengler's simultaneous publication, *Der Untergang des Abendlandes* ("Decline of the West," 1928), Steinberg describes how the world vanishes in the night, and its fate seems as sealed as that of the cigarette; its smoke surrounds the sonnet and obscures the face of the narrator.

Steinberg had already moved to Palestine in 1914. Unlike other literary émigrés he declined to abandon the Ashkenazi pronunciation of Hebrew to embrace the Sephardic one, even though the latter, with its male and alternating rhymes, brought to the Hebrew sonnet some of the musicality of the original Italian. Steinberg's contemporary Jacob Fichman (1881–1958), by contrast, followed the prevailing tendency and changed his poetry, including his sonnets, by adapting the meter to the Sephardic pronunciation. Fichman also paved the way for the career of Lea Goldberg with a sympathetic review of her first book *Tab'ot Ashan* (1935; Smoke Rings).

Born in Königsberg (today Kaliningrad) in 1911, Lea Goldberg spent her early childhood years in Russia before moving to Kaunas (→ Kovno) in Lithuania, where she also

Lea Goldberg (1911–1970)

attended university. In 1930 Goldberg continued her studies in Bonn with a focus on Semitic languages, history, and pedagogy. Goldberg began to write poetry at a young age. Later her work comprised literary criticism, translations, children's books, stage plays, and prose for adult audiences. In Hebrew poetry she ranks as the mistress of the sonnet, being only the second female Jewish writer of sonnets after Trieste-born Rachel Morpurgo (née Luzzatto; 1790–1871; → Maskilah), who composed around 30 Hebrew sonnets. Goldberg wrote some 65 sonnets largely in the Italian-Petrarchan style, that is on the subject of love, and she arranged them in cycles. She also produced → Hebrew translations of 40 sonnets, particularly by Petrarch and Dante, and excerpts from the Italian works of Immanuel ha-Romi, of Baudelaire, and from English poets, in addition to a short monograph on the poetry of Petrarch.

In her first cycle of poems, *Mizmor la-or* (1927; Hymn to the Light), which she published at the age of 16, Goldberg claimed she could not write sonnets and stressed the disparity between the urge to express her emotions and the strict formal criteria of the sonnet. However, two years later she presented her first two sonnets under the title *Be-minzar Foz'iseli* (1929; In Pažaislis Monastery), marking the beginning of her literary career. The poems were inspired by her visit to one of the best-known Italian Baroque style buildings in her home country of Lithuania. The central theme highlights the conflict between the fascination for the aesthetics of the Christian rite and its prohibition by Jewish (religious and national) regulations. Their content therefore corresponds to the form: while it is considered to be aesthetically pleasing, the sonnet also constitutes an element that is essentially alien to Hebrew culture.

Following her emigration to Palestine in 1935, Goldberg joined the circle of modernist Hebrew poets around Avraham Shlonsky (1900–1973; → Poetry) but clearly distinguished her poetry from that of the other members of the group. Distancing herself from the idea of modernity, Goldberg deliberately chose to work with traditional forms of European poetry as a translator, scholar, and composer of sonnets. The choice of conventional aesthetic formats was for her the pursuit of an enduring and persistent practice – sophisticated and steeped in historical responsibility: "The artist accounting in the present for the development, the rise and fall of European culture, asks how to begin it all anew, and builds his new Europe, by living, primarily, with the memories of the past and by repeating it" [11. 270]. Goldberg composed and published the majority of her sonnets between 1942 and 1955, in the shadow of the Second World War, the → Holocaust, and the breakdown of Humanist culture in Europe – the very culture she was associated with and whose prominent "ambassador" people in Palestine believed her – and others alongside her – to be.

Contrary to her mostly conservative reputation, which also stemmed from her sonnets, Goldberg brought innovation and diversity to both form and content of the genre. This process was manifest in the appropriation, by a woman, of what was essentially considered to be a male form of expression. In this, she was preceded by a line of female pioneers of the European sonnet tradition: the Italian Gaspara Stampa (1523–1554), the French poetess Louise Labé (ca. 1520–1566), and Elizabeth Barrett Browning (1806–1861) in England. The innovative nature of the female-authored love sonnets emerges from the very fact that they followed the "male" tradition in every way – which in turn can be read as an act of subversion in and of itself. With a specific female voice they approached the hegemonic form of expression, and as a result their poems took on opposing or paradoxical layers of meaning.

Lea Goldberg mentored the next generation of Hebrew poets and advanced the careers of, among others, Tsherni Karmi, Dan Pagis, Dahlia Ravikovich, and Tuvya Rübner by publishing their first poems (→ Poetry).

In 1949, a 25-year old Yehuda Amichai wrote to Goldberg requesting her opinion on some of his earliest efforts, one of which was a sonnet. Much like Goldberg, the Würzburg-born Amichai was influenced by German sonnets, namely Rainer Maria Rilke's *Sonnette an Orpheus* (1922; "Sonnets to Orpheus," 1936). While Goldberg had also drawn on Russian poets, Amichai turned more often to their modernist English and American counterparts, especially W. H. Auden and T. S. Eliot. This created a new voice in Israeli poetry overall and for the Hebrew sonnet in particular – a more secular, colloquial voice that downplayed its poetic character and tended to cultivate a deliberate formal laxity. Amichai's poetry stands at the center of the transition in Hebrew literature away from a modern Russian dominance in favor of an Anglo-American (and to an extent even German) influence. In his first volume *Aḥshav uwa-yamim ha-aḥerim* (1955; Now and in Other Days), Amichai included 23 sonnets evidently inspired by the sonnet cycles of Auden, most notably *In Time of War* (later renamed *Sonnets from China*). Also in his second volume, *Be-merḥak shte tikvot* (1958; Two Hopes Away), the sonnet form occupies a similarly prominent position. The further development of Amichai's poetry saw an increasingly loose approach to the form of his sonnets, eventually prompting critics to remark that they no longer deserved to be described as such.

Amichai's affinity for the sonnet, especially at the outset of his career, does however stand in stark contrast to the almost complete avoidance of the form by his contemporary Nathan Zach (b. 1930). Modern Hebrew literature, therefore, is home to a succession of sonnet devotees – Judah Leib Gordon (→ Kotso shel Yud), Tchernichovsky, Steinberg, Yehuda Karni, Shin Shalom (Shalom Joseph Shapira), Fichman, Goldberg, and Amichai – mirrored by an equally distinguished group of poets adamantly, even vehemently, opposed to the format: Nathan Alterman (→ Silver Platter), David Avidan, Bialik, Uri Zvi Greenberg (→ Tur Malka), Shlonsky, and Zach.

After Amichai, the most important composer of – sometimes explicitly erotic – sonnets in Israeli poetry today is Aharon Shabtai (b. 1939). In the early 2000s, the *Ho!* literary circle led a revival of the regular rhythm in Hebrew poetry; members of the circle – primarily Dory Manor, Sivan Beskin, and Anna Herman – promoted the cause in the numerous sonnets they either composed or translated.

Bibliography

[1] D. Bregman, Le-parashat ha-hitkablut shel ha-sonet ha-ivri [On the Problem of the Acceptance of the Sonnet in Hebrew Literature], in: Tarbiz 56 (1987) 1, 109–124. [2] D. Bregman,

The Golden Way. The Hebrew Sonnet during the Renaissance and the Baroque, trans. by A. Brener, Tempe 2006. [3] D. Bregman, Sharsheret ha-zahav. Ha-sonet ha-ivri le-dorotav [The Golden Chain. The Hebrew Sonnet through the Ages], Tel Aviv 2000. [4] Y. Bronowski, Al tavuz la-sonet, ha-mevaker. Kitsur toldotav shel ha-sonet [Critic, do not Despise the Sonnet. A Short History of the Sonnet], in: Moznayim 74 (2000) 5, 34–37. [5] J. Burckhardt, The Civilization of the Renaissance in Italy (1860), trans. by S. C. G. Middlemore, London ¹1878. [6] L. Goldberg, Sfarim Aharonim [Recent Works], in: Itim 1 (March 26, 1948), 3. [7] A. Komem, Shalshelet shirah. Al shirah u-meshorerim [A Chain of Poetry. On Poetry and Poets], Be'er Sheva 2004. [8] D. Landau, Hitpatḥutah shel ha-sonetah ba-sifrut ha-ivrit [The Evolution of the Sonnet in Hebrew Literature], Ramat Gan 1970. [9] U. Shavit, Kavim la-prozodya shel shirat Amiḥai [Basic Outline of Prosody in the Poetry of Amichai], in: Z. Ben-Porat (ed.), Aderet le-Binyamin: sefer ha-yovel le-Binyamin Harshav [An Overcoat for Benjamin. Papers on Literature for Benjamin Harshav], vol. 2, Tel Aviv 2001, 36–49. [10] S. Tchernichovsky, Maḥberet ha-sonetot [Book of Sonnets], Jerusalem/Berlin 1922. [11] O. Yeglin, The Sonnets of Lea Goldberg, in: Hebrew Studies 50, 2009, 265–276.

GIDDON TICOTSKY, TEL AVIV

Spielmacher

The Hungarian Jewish director and dramatist George Tabori (1914–2007) regarded himself as a "Spielmacher" (lit. playmaker) who shaped performances in close cooperation with the actors. In plays that broke taboos and focused on National Socialism and the → Holocaust, he confronted the West German public with its past from the late 1960s onward, becoming one of the most important theatre artists of the Federal Republic. Deliberately challenging and disturbing, he opposed the dominant approach to National Socialist crimes, seeking to establish the stage as a live place of memory where wounds would be reopened and pain inflicted ancw.

1. "Don't play, act"
2. George Tabori
3. Theatre of embarrassment

1. "Don't play, act"

George Tabori's work as a director was characterized by close, egalitarian cooperation with the actors. He saw himself as a "Spielmacher," mediating between all those contributing to the dramatic process. Consequently, his advice to the actors was "Macht kein Theater" ("don't play, act"; cited in [8. 91]). As a playmaker or "animateur," he saw his task in creating a conducive working atmosphere, in which actors could transform the "energy of fear" into creative energy (cited in [7. 63]). He often held back during rehearsals in order to give the actors free rein in the interpretation. With his presence and reserved intervention, he was able to encourage the actors to use their own initiative to explore their possibilities and boundaries. To him the fusion of art and life, discipline and freedom, seriousness and fun, were indispensable preconditions for captivating theatre.

Tabori's understanding of stagecraft, as well as his practical work as a director, were influenced by the founders of avant-garde theatre, all of whom rejected the traditional mainstream of the established stage. He took his cue from Peter Brook's experimental theatre, putting himself in opposition to classic → Regietheater ("director's theatre"). In accordance with Grotowski's concept of "poor theatre," Tabori, furthermore, endeavored to reclaim all that he saw as the loss of sensuality, life, and magic in the theatre.

Especially with regard to the "pathological symptoms of the German stage" (cited in [7. 54]), he diagnosed two grave ones: the

excessive respect for authoritarian directors among German actors, and their desire, or even craving, for a powerful father figure who imposes his interpretation on them. Tabori rejected the all-powerful position for directors as he regarded the German word for theatre director, "Regisseur," as having connotations of regime and "Regierung" (government). He preferred to work with the ensemble as *primus inter pares*. The unchallenged center of his theatre was the actor as a creative *homo ludens*. In his eyes, the ideal performer – "the last messenger of humanism" – was duty bound to the existential imperative of being faithful to himself [3. 9f.].

While Konstantin Stanislavsky advocated that actors should feel their way into a part, Tabori encouraged them to discover it in their own selves as he assumed that all humans bore elements of this role in themselves. Accordingly, he preferred to use the English word "to act" over the German word "schauspielen," which he associated with dissimulation and dishonesty. The linking of being and acting, he held, would enable them to endeavor to "not reproduce art but rather produce life" [4. 85]. Hardly any other director in the German theatre landscape after 1945 had such a high degree of confidence in his actors or accorded them so much freedom, initiative, and responsibility. At the same time, his theatre practice was inseparably linked to political and other topics of his theatre activity, which, in turn, were determined by his biographical experience.

Tabori, who had lost the majority of his family in the Holocaust, unconventionally focused his stage plays on the mass murder of European Jews from the mid-1960s onward. His productions were disturbing as they frequently blurred the differences between victims and perpetrators in order to neither draw out pity as an emotion nor to assign guilt. He deliberately endeavored to break with taboos and mythicization and to immediately confront the audience with the crimes of National Socialism.

2. George Tabori

George Tabori was born in → Budapest in 1914. The second son of the Hungarian journalist and author Cornelius Tábori and his wife Elsa, who came from a Habsburg-Slovenian family, he grew up as György Tábori in an assimilated Jewish family of the educated middle class. Both he and his older brother Paul were brought up bilingually by their parents, speaking German and Hungarian. While their father was a cosmopolitan and agnostic, their mother professed Catholicism. Both children took part in Catholic religious education and regularly went to confession. The young Tabori never visited a synagogue, had no → bar mitzvah, and was indifferent to his Jewish origins. His Jewish affiliation was imposed on him from the outside: "One is reminded by others that one is Jewish," Tabori said in retrospect, explaining: "Fascism in Germany and Hungary brought to my notice that I am one. At some point I accepted that role. This was the most important experience of all" [1. 329].

As a schoolboy, Tabori was already full of enthusiasm for the theatre and films he attended with his brother. After graduating from secondary school, Tabori went to live in Berlin, where he worked in several grand hotels. In 1934 he returned to Budapest, but as antisemitism was rife, he followed his brother to London in 1936. During the war years, Tabori worked as a correspondent for several European newspapers in Sofia, Belgrade, and Istanbul. Beginning in 1942, he was simultaneously employed by the British secret service. Under the pseudonym Turner he worked in the BBC's Hungarian section in Jerusalem and Cairo, returning to London in 1943. Tabori, who lived in seventeen countries on three continents over the course of his life, rejected a geographical definition of home, stating instead: "The books are my home. The stage is my home. And my bed" [1. 333].

In London he turned to fiction, making a name for himself during the postwar years as the author of English novels (such as *Beneath the Stone the Scorpion*, 1945; *Original Sin*, 1947). Having been recruited by an American agency as a screenwriter, he moved to Los Angeles in 1947, working with leading directors such as Alfred Hitchcock and Joseph Losey in → Hollywood. During this time he gradually began to take a more active interest in the stage. In the circle of intellectuals and artists in exile in Santa Monica (→ Pacific Palisades), Tabori met Bertolt Brecht, among others, in 1947. The encounter with Brecht, some of whose plays he translated into English, as well as the experiences he gathered as an observer in Lee Strasberg's well-known Actors Studio in New York, encouraged him to direct plays himself. Between 1956 and 1969, Tabori

George Tabori (1914–2007)

became prominent as both a director and playwright. For instance, he directed the successful text-and-song collage *Brecht on Brecht: An Improvisation* (1961) and wrote the play *The Niggerlovers* (1967), "sort of mini-Brecht [...] on the opposition of white conservatives against the integration of Black people," as he wrote to Brecht's widow Helene Weigel (cited in [8. 72]). In addition, his production of *The Merchant of Venice as performed in Theresienstadt* (1966) was one of the first attempts ever at setting Shakespeare's play in the context of the Holocaust.

During the years immediately after the war, Tabori intended to make his family's fate and the murder of the European Jews the focus of his artistic creativity. However, his first attempt at a literary treatment of Jewish experiences in a concentration camp in a novel entitled *Pogrom* failed. He did not find a publisher, and he felt that his own experience as someone who escaped the Holocaust made an "authentic" approach problematic. For twenty years he concentrated on other subjects [15. 54]. Nonetheless, he did not find great success on the stages on or off → Broadway.

In 1968, Tabori returned to the story of his father, who had been murdered in → Auschwitz, writing *The Cannibals* his first stage play on the Holocaust. In 1969 he visited Germany on the occasion of the European premiere of this play in the Schillertheather in Berlin, and in 1971 he decided to make a fresh start in the Federal Republic. Among his most significant theatre projects in Germany and Austria were his "Theaterlabor" (theatre laboratory) in Bremen (1975–1978), where he was able to carry out numerous experiments broadening and sharpening his concept of theatre acting, the theatre *Der Kreis* that he founded in Vienna (1987–1989), the Vienna Akademietheater (1990–1999), and (from 2000 until his death in 2007) the Berliner Ensemble.

3. Theatre of embarrassment

Tabori's rise in German-speaking theatre was accompanied by scandal, outrage, and, frequently, harsh criticism. *The Cannibals* marked the prelude to his "theatre of embarrassment" (Jörg W. Gronius) – a theatre that deliberately intended to hurt and disturb. Tabori described the piece as "a black mass" dedicated to his father's memory [3. 37].

The story of twelve prisoners in Auschwitz is reproduced by the role-playing of their sons and two survivors – Hirschler and Heltai. At the center of the plot is a camp scene in which fellow inmate Puffi is killed in a brawl by the inmates because he had managed to obtain a piece of bread. While the body is cooking on the fire as a cannibalistic supper, the hungry prisoners tell stories of everyday life and relive their hopes, fears, and conflicts as self-staged episodes and moments of the past. They recall their deportation and the plan to kill the guard, which was foiled by an inmate named "Uncle." Accompanied by a kapo, a member of the SS with the telling name of Schrekinger enters as the "angel of death," looks into the cooking pot, and orders everyone to eat. Only Hirschler and Heltai obey – and survive. Schrekinger condemns those who refused to eat to be killed in the gas chambers.

The American reception of the premiere in 1968 was reserved. Maria Müller-Sommer (b. 1922), who would become Tabori's publisher and had supported and accompanied his career in German-speaking countries from the outset, acquired the manuscript but had doubts about it: "Is it permissible, advisable, necessary to put on this play in Germany?" [14. 49]. In her considerations, one can discern the public opinion that would dominate in the Federal Republic for years to come, characterized by shame and self-consciousness as well as suppression, when people were confronted with the Shoah. Sommer saw the limitations of presenting Auschwitz on stage, regarding them as a moral challenge, but ultimately championed the German premiere.

This was fundamentally different from previous approaches to the Holocaust in the German theatre, which were rare in any case. Until then, German stages had occasionally put on plays in which a Nazi recognizes his error, or even feels obliged to make amends in an act of delayed repentance, for instance, in Carl Zuckmayer's *Des Teufels General* (1946). Occasionally, melodramas on the fate of individual Jews were performed. The stage adaptation of *Das Tagebuch der Anne Frank* (1955/1956; "The Diary of a Young Girl," 1952; → Diary) was particularly successful, although it did not demand any personal conscience examination or a collective discussion of the Holocaust. Characteristically, Tabori had declined to adapt Anne Frank's diary for the stage in the past. During the 1960s, German stages also put on documentary plays on the subject of National Socialism; however, these presented the suffering of the Jews as incidental, as in Peter Weiss's *Die Ermittlung* (1965; "The Investigation," 1966).

In this context it becomes clear why Tabori felt that he had to force a public confrontation with the past with regard to his own family history: "There are taboos that must be broken if we are not to gag on them forever" [3. 37]. The reaction of audiences and critics to Tabori's drastic productions was often confusion. He was not concerned with guilt or accusation or with evoking pity in the audience. He neither glorified the murder victims nor cast them as martyrs. Indeed, with the deliberately chosen "we," by means of which he exhorted the public to engage with the past, and which would become the maxim of his work, he addressed – *horribile dictu* – Germans and Jews, perpetrators and victims, and not least their descendants together.

The Cannibals was Tabori's first attack on the convention of maudlin Holocaust sentimentality displayed unconvincingly, as well as on "good taste." The critic Friedrich Luft (1911–1990) wrote on December 14, 1969, in *Die Welt* that the play broke a taboo by presenting the celebration of a macabre cannibalistic ritual. He was convinced that this play may well have been the first to allow questioning, feeling empathy, and even laughing in the face of the worst. By contrast, Heinz Galinski (1912–1992), himself a Holocaust survivor and at the time the head of the Jewish community in Berlin, was incensed. He attempted to prevent the play from being produced. He found the play, with its flippant turns of phrase, disgusting, and he justified his harsh criticism with his own experience of Auschwitz. The two Jewish actors Michael Degen (b. 1932), who played the part of the uncle, and Herbert Grünbaum (1903–1981) as the survivor Heltai, were troubled and considered leaving the production more than once. Tabori had an unambiguous explanation for their unease: "The play was constantly destroying their mythology" [3. 23]; [7. 203–208]. He himself was astounded at the attention his production garnered.

His other plays provoked criticism and disturbed audiences as well. In 1978 he had thirteen Shylocks – men wearing caftans and black velvet hats, some of them sporting fake hook noses – appear in a Munich boiler room. He advised the actors to each find his inner Jew as well as his inner antisemite. In this project, entitled *Ich wollte meine Tochter läge tot zu meinen Füßen und hätte die Juwelen in den Ohren. Improvisationen über Shakespeares Shylock*, Tabori employed anti-Jewish prejudice and cliché with the aim of reflecting them back to the public.

In 1979 he returned to his personal story with his play *Mutters Courage* ("My Mother's Courage"), which also premiered in Munich. Without mystification or mythicization, the piece narrates the story of the miraculous escape of his mother Elsa Tábori. She was being deported from Budapest in the summer of 1944 together with 4,000 Jews and was able to save herself only by telling the SS officer in charge that she had a safe-conduct pass from the Red Cross but had unfortunately left it at home. With reference to Brecht's *Mutter Courage* and his epic theatre, Tabori presented seemingly a fairytale about concrete danger and awful terror, miraculous escape and a happy ending, fracturing the enchantment by means of ironic twists and turns. This play was simultaneously Tabori's response to the US television drama → Holocaust, which had sparked unprecedented interest in the history of the Shoah among the German public in 1979.

Another unconventional play was Tabori's memory play *Jubiläum* (1983). It was intended to recall the transfer of power to the Nazis in 1933 on the occasion of its 50th anniversary. The action is set in a cemetery by the Rhine where the dead, victims of National Socialism, cannot find rest. The play recounts antisemitic and violent episodes as evidence of continuing antisemitism as well as of hatred of strangers and outsiders after 1945. Over the course of the plot, the dead emerge from their graves. Characteristically, participants in Tabori's eerie danse macabre include not only Jews but also others persecuted by the National Socialists, among them homosexuals and a spastic woman. In *Jubiläum*, Tabori presented a production that once again undermined the expectations of the audience and the contemporary politico-cultural discourse. He did not present a ceremony of remembrance on stage, decisively rejecting the institutionalized forms of commemoration that were beginning to become established in the Federal Republic.

In his opinion these forms of staged collective commemoration, namely the ritualized and formalized remembrance events for the victims of National Socialism, resulted at best in a reflexive reaction, in

questionable dismay whose main symptoms were melancholy and reverence, rather than in a deeply and genuinely felt sadness. Consequently, Tabori later spoke out against the construction of the memorial for the murdered Jews in Berlin. He had experienced the Auschwitz concentration camp during a visit as a lifeless museum that kindled no emotions; this ran counter to his own strategy of commemoration. It is thus no coincidence that Tabori's memory play *Jubiläum* resembles Sigmund Freund's (→ Psychoanalysis) therapeutic approach of remembering, repeating, and working through. In this context, the theatre becomes a place of remembering, of memory, where wounds are reopened and pain reawakened: "It is impossible to come to terms with the past unless one has re-experienced it with one's skin, nose, tongue, backside, feet, and belly" [3. 202].

Tabori described his most successful stage play *Mein Kampf* (1987) as "a banal love story [...]. A Great Love Story – Hitler and his Jew. A horrifying case" [2. 24f.]. The farce noire was a further attempt at encircling Tabori's own dictum "the wound must understand the knife," that is to fathom the German–Jewish love-hate relationship [3. 30f.]. It tells the story of a men's shelter in the Blutgasse in Vienna, where Schlomo Herzl, a Jewish bookseller whose last name recalls the founder of political Zionism (→ Old New Land), meets the failing painter Adolf Hitler. With loving masochism, Herzl looks after the narcissistic malcontent, tries to teach the violent antisemite some manners, trims his mustache, giving him the typical Führer face – all to the amazement and chagrin of Lobkowitz, Herzl's roommate. When Hitler returns, frustrated, from the Academy of Arts, Herzl consoles him, advises him to go into politics, and prophesies: "you'll be a king walking on a carpet of bones" [5. 68].

The failed "love story" culminates in a nightmare of cruelty. On Yom Kippur, the highest of Jewish holidays, seven Tyrolean bumpkins as well as Hitler appear together with Herzl's childlike lover, whose name is Gretchen as an allusion to Goethe's *Faust* and who now wears the uniform of the Bund Deutscher Mädel. Hitler's henchman, named Himmlischst with a nod to Heinrich Himmler, master of a pseudo-religious sacrificial ceremony, plucks Herzl's beloved chicken Mizzi, carves it up, and drops it into a frying pan that is, significantly, placed on top of an oven. In this context, the Jewish *tarnegol kaparot* is no longer the traditional object of the transfer of a repentant believer's sins on the Day of Atonement but rather the signal for future disaster. "If you start burning birds, you'll end up burning people," Herzl says in a variation of Heinrich Heine's (→ Entreebillet) famous dictum [5. 81].

The play is characterized by the use of different genres and stylistic devices ranging from allegory and folk play to slapstick – a furious phantasmagoria in which Tabori juggles pettifogging jokes, shocking moments, and situation comedy. In *Mein Kampf* Tabori takes aim at affected reverence and maudlin piety, trying to free the audience – often by means of black humor – from conditioned partiality in order to put the banal evil as well as the true dimension of suffering into relief. The humoristic level was a constitutive element: The subject of a joke always represented a catastrophe, Tabori emphasized, adding that he regarded corny jokes in the face of horror as a "lifesaver" [15. 140–142].

Tabori's *Mein Kampf* firmly defied the ruling political correctness. As a consequence, there were voices among the public who criticized his tastelessness and reproached him for banalizing the Shoah in spite of the play's success. Other reactions, however, conceded him a special right, even a privilege, to cause political offense because of his Jewish origin. Jewish theatre artists like George Tabori and the director Peter Zadek (1926–2009) provided the impetus for a new cultural-political discourse in the Federal Republic, in which Jewish stage characters were no longer sacrosanct and untouchable and in which – twenty years before Dani

Levy's (b. 1957) film parody *Mein Führer* (2007) – even a farcical meeting between Hitler and a Jew was possible on stage.

Bibliography

Sources

[1] H. Koelbl, Georges [sic!] Tabori, in: Jüdische Portraits. Photographien und Interviews, ed. by H. Koelbl, Frankfurt am Main 1998, 328–334. [2] R. Palm/U. Voss, "Es ist das große Welttheater, jedes Leben." Gespräch mit George Tabori, in: Theater heute 7 (1987), 24–26. [3] G. Tabori, Unterammergau oder die guten Deutschen, Frankfurt am Main 1981. [4] G. Tabori, Betrachtungen über das Feigenblatt. Handbuch für Verliebte und Verrückte, Frankfurt am Main 1993. [5] G. Tabori, "Mein Kampf," in: Drama Contemporary. Germany, ed. by C. Weber, Baltimore 1996, 37–84.

Secondary literature

[6] H.-P. Bayerdörfer/J. Schönert (eds.), Theater gegen das Vergessen. Bühnenarbeit und Drama bei George Tabori, Tübingen 1997. [7] A. Feinberg, Embodied Memory. The Theater of George Tabori, Iowa City 1999. [8] A. Feinberg, George Tabori, Munich 2003. [9] J. W. Gronius/ W. Kässens, Tabori, Frankfurt am Main 1989. [10] C. Guerrero, George Tabori im Spiegel der deutschsprachigen Kritik, Cologne 1999. [11] B. Haas, Das Theater des George Tabori. Vom Verfremdungseffekt zur Postmoderne, Frankfurt am Main et al. 2000. [12] P. Höyng (ed.), Verkörperte Geschichtsentwürfe. George Taboris Theaterarbeit = Embodied Projections on History. George Tabori's Theater Work, Tübingen 1998. [13] A. Huth, "In meiner Geisterstunde." Intertextualität und Gedächtnis in Werken von George Tabori, Marburg 2008. [14] G. Ohngemach (ed.), George Tabori, Frankfurt am Main 1989. [15] J. Strümpel, Vorstellungen vom Holocaust. George Taboris Erinnerungsspiele, Göttingen 2000. [16] J. Strümpel (ed.), George Tabori, Munich 1997. [17] A. Welker (ed.), George Tabori. Dem Gedächtnis, der Trauer und dem Lachen gewidmet, Vienna et al. 1994.

ANAT FEINBERG, HEIDELBERG

Sport

An invention of the 19th century, sport became one of the characteristic recreational activities in modern industrial societies. To Jews, sport provided opportunities for societal inclusion and social advancement. However, anti-Jewish prejudice as well as growing antisemitism soon imposed limits, especially through denying Jews membership in sports clubs. As a result, Jewish sports clubs – mainly with a Jewish national ideology – were founded in Central and Eastern Europe. Independently of the respective organizational form, Jewish athletes countered the image of the unathletic, physically weak Jew. In Europe they achieved numerous sporting successes during the interwar years. After the Second World War, Jewish athletes were successful primarily in the United States, while sport in Israel was beset by numerous difficulties in the context of the Middle East conflict.

1.   19th and early 20th century
1.1   Contexts
1.2   Gymnastics
1.3   Muscles, spirit, and nerves
1.4   Competitive sport
1.5   England and the United States
2.   Europe during the interwar years
2.1   Jewish sports clubs
2.2   Achievements
3.   National Socialism and the Shoah
4.   After 1945
4.1   Europe
4.2   The United States
5.   Sport in the Yishuv and in Israel

1. 19th and early 20th century

1.1 *Contexts*
The terms "Jewish sport" or "Jews in sport" are fuzzy, as they generally refer to the ethnic origin or the affiliation with the Jewish religious community rather than to the individual athlete's self-understanding.

Different types of "Jewish sport" are conditioned by regionally specific peculiarities. Thus in England from the 1880s onward, the objective of Jewish workers' and youth clubs was to transform the Jewish immigrant into an English gentleman by means of sport. In a country of high assimilation such as Hungary, Jewish athletes were part of the first squad of many sports during the first decades of the 20th century, while in neighboring Romania, which had long refused to allow Jews to integrate, Jewish athletes were the exception during the same period. The function of Jewish sport in Europe with its long history of anti-Judaism differed from that in America, where the immigration society facilitated the integration and assimilation of Jews.

The part Jews played in sport in their respective countries depended not only on the comparative size of the respective Jewish communities and local traditions but also and essentially on their legal and societal status. Where individual Jews took part in general sporting activities, especially in clubs that accepted Jewish members, this was commonly a sign of → assimilation and integration. If they were forced to establish separate clubs and associations, this indicated limited inclusion during the period of the → emancipation.

1.2 *Gymnastics*
Jewish participation in gymnastics, which spread in Central Europe from the beginning of the 19th century onward, was determined by assimilation endeavors and the will to prove themselves. The German "Turnerbewegung" (gymnastics movement) had a nationalist ideology; its founder Friedrich Ludwig Jahn ("Turnvater Jahn"; "father of gymnastics") evolved the concept of physical exercise as a component of patriotic education in preparation for the wars of liberation against Napoleon. Gymnastics was to provide premilitary training and strengthen the German national consciousness. The idea of

national self-discovery according to Jahn's understanding, but also that of other early German nationalists such as Ernst Moritz Arndt or Johann Gottlieb Fichte, was based on a particular distinction as defined by their ideas of *völkisch* (ethnic-nationalistic) affiliation. One of the consequences of this idea of national affiliation in delimitation from the values of the → French Revolution was to deny the Jews equality as citizens (→ [Die] Germanomanie).

Even so, in the second half of the 19th century many Jews striving for assimilation joined German sports clubs. During a period of increasing bourgeoisification and legal equality, in doing so they expressed their sympathies with the German nation state (→ Middle Class). The majority of Jewish athletes were organized in German clubs during this time. Around the turn of the 20th century, the Verband der Deutschen Turnerschaft (DT), founded in Weimar in 1868 and which Austrian clubs could join as well, had an estimated 10,000 to 15,000 Jewish members [17. 143].

However, in Germany and even more vehemently in Austria, antisemitism emerged at this same time (→ Conspiracy). Just as in many student associations, singing clubs, reading circles, and the emerging youth movements, the concept of an exclusive, *völkisch* community became more influential in the context of gymnastics too. As early as 1887, the Erster Wiener Turnverein included an "Arierparagraph" ("Aryan clause") in its statutes. Of the 1,100 members, 480 Jews and 20 other "non-German persons" had to leave the club [7. 37]. During the Wiener Turntag of 1901, all Austrian clubs who made up the "Turnkreis 15" and were members of the DT decided to make membership in their clubs dependent on "Aryan" origins.

The first Jewish sports clubs were founded in this climate of rejection and exclusion. In a direct reaction to their exclusion, the Jews of the Erster Wiener Turnverein founded the Deutsch-Österreichischer Turnverein in 1887. In the German Empire, the foundation of the Jüdischer Turnverein → Bar Kochba Berlin (JTV) followed in 1898, with ten additional Jewish sports clubs being founded in, among other places, Cologne, Freiburg, Halberstadt, → Leipzig, and Posen (→ Poznań), by 1902. By 1914, Jewish clubs had also been founded in Budapest, Bucharest, Groningen, Constantinople, Łódź, Sofia, Salonika, Warsaw, Zagreb, and several other cities.

From 1900 onward, the *Jüdische Turnzeitung* was published. At first the organ of Bar Kochba Berlin, it soon developed into the mouthpiece of the entire national Jewish gymnastics movement beyond Germany and Austria-Hungary, explicitly stating the claim to self-assertion. Thus, the first edition proclaimed: "We want to restore the lost tone to the flaccid Jewish body, and make it fresh and powerful, agile and strong. We wish to do all this within a Jewish club, in which we can simultaneously strengthen our dwindling feeling of belonging and raise our declining self-confidence. [...] We want to face antisemitism [...] courageously and full of energy" [1. 1].

1.3 Muscles, spirit, and nerves

In the religious tradition of Judaism, the spiritual exercise of studying the sacred texts was considered more commendable than early forms of physical exercise. The Bible tells us: "Not by might, nor by power, but by My spirit—said the LORD of Hosts" (Zech 4:6). In the modern age, the idea of the physically feeble Jew was precisely based on these historical clichés of the Jews as "people of the book" and of the persecuted Jew unable to defend himself by physical force. When modern sport spread in industrial societies, Jews were disparagingly seen as stay-at-homes, coffee house visitors, or → Luftmenschen.

This was not exclusively an antisemitic cliché. The idea that emerged in the context of the Zionist movement, namely to regard sport as a means to improve the collective, even the national consciousness of the Jews, was based on the idea that Jews were physically weak. The physician and author Max Nordau (1849–1923), for instance, postulated during the Second Zionist Congress in → Basel 1898 that modern Judaism should evolve into "Muskeljudentum" (→ "muscular Judaism") [2. 24] in order to create the "new Jew." Nordau and other champions of muscular Judaism maintained that during their time in the Diaspora, the Jewish people had undergone a process of degeneration, which they could liberate themselves from through exercise and sport. The Eastern European Zionist and oculist Max Mandelstamm (1839–1912) thought along similar lines, concentrating his attention on the "ghetto Jews of the East" [3. 117] in Russia, Romania, and Galicia in particular (→ Ostjuden). The living conditions found there, he said, were detrimental to the health of the Jews. In Mandelstamm's view, introducing physical education lessons and founding sports clubs contributed to the socio-economic transformation of Jewish living conditions in Eastern Europe which should, however, also be accompanied by legal equality and economic support.

The model of the "muscular Jew" aspired to was not only the counter-image of the spiritual Jew but also of the "nervous Jew." Jews believed themselves to be particularly susceptible to neurasthenia (or enervation), which was considered a symptomatic affliction of the times from the late 19th to the early 20th century. The contemporary therapy recommended for this ailment was exercise. → Bar Kochba Berlin stated in the *Jüdische Turnzeitung* in 1900: "A healthy mind resides in a healthy body! [...] We are fighting the one-sided education of the mind which has caused our nervousness and mental fatigue!" [1. 1]. The claim that Jews in their "original state," namely before the time

of exile, had been physically healthy and strong, and that consequently their bodies could certainly be regenerated, clearly distinguished the Zionist champions of sport from the antisemites who regarded Jews as racially inferior.

1.4 *Competitive sport*

Besides gymnastics, competitive sport became increasingly popular in Central Europe around the turn of the 20th century. However, this originally English invention was initially regarded by protagonists of gymnastics as detrimental to health and an arrogant pastime of the "high society." From the point of view of "German" sport, the purely individual striving for one person's achievement did not appear compatible with encouraging national cohesion. Many gymnasts – including Jewish ones – considered sport around the turn of the century to be "un-German."

At the same time, sport offered the Jews a broader and initially less nationalistically defined area of cultural participation. This became particularly apparent as → soccer (called football in Europe) spread throughout Germany. While soccer was a team sport, the competition between teams was the dominant aspect, and its English origin was regarded as negative. At the end of the 19th century, Jewish soccer players, some of whom had their first experiences with soccer in other Western countries, played prominent roles as club founders and officials in soccer becoming established in Germany. Walther Bensemann (1873–1934) founded several soccer clubs in southern Germany and organized the first international matches between German, French, and English selection teams. Bensemann was among those who founded the Deutscher Fußball-Bund (DFB) in 1900. Gus Manning (1873–1953) played a similarly important part, contributing to the foundation of several clubs in Berlin and southern Germany as well as being present at the inaugural meeting of the DFB.

In the end, Jewish gymnasts overcame the traditional distance from sport sooner than the majority society. During the Olympic Games in Athens in 1896, the first Olympic medals won by Jews were awarded to two German Jewish gymnasts, for whom gymnastics was a competitive discipline – Alfred (1869–1942) and Gustav Flatow (1875–1945). In 1913, the *Jüdische Turnzeitung* was renamed the *Jüdische Monatshefte für Turnen und Sport*. In the same year, an article published in this periodical came to the conclusion that "Jewish gymnasts had acknowledged sport to be physical exercise of equal value." The "sense of order and discipline" that was part of gymnastics might be supplemented by developing "initiative in order to win in competitions" [5. 187]. Jewish gymnasts' acceptance of sport was based on the fact that like gymnastics it could be a form of self-assertion.

This aspect was also reflected in the names chosen for Jewish gymnastics and sports clubs which referred to biblical and post-biblical heroes. Clubs were called "Samson" (→ Samson), "Gideon," "Bar Kochba," "Hasmonean" or began with Hebrew words denoting strength and power, such as Hakoah ("The strength") or Gibor ("Hero"). The name Maccabi, which was selected with reference to the Jewish freedom fighter Judah Maccabee, was also common as a name for clubs even before the First World War. Recourse to historical figures of Antiquity served to legitimize sport in the Jewish community. Academic studies in which Antiquity was presented as the model for the modern Jewish enthusiasm for sport, such as by the expert on Maimonides Süssmann Munter (*Leibesübung bei den Juden von der ältesten Zeit bis zur Gegenwart*, 1926) or by Felix Pinczower (*Der jüdische Läufer*, 1937), were written in this context too.

1.5 England and the United States

Sport not only offered Jews a framework for social acculturation, integration, and collective self-assertion. Sporting excellence was accompanied, initially mainly in England, by individual recognition, and in the United States in particular, sport produced famous figures of identification who strengthened the immigrants' self-confidence and nourished their hope of social advancement.

This perception was particularly prevalent in → boxing. One of the first prominent English boxers at the end of the 18th century, Daniel Mendoza (1764–1836), was a Jew. He was joined by several more beginning in the 20th century: Ted "Kid" Lewis (Gershon Mendeloff, 1893–1970), born in London's East End, was the British featherweight champion in 1913 as well as the world welterweight champion in 1915 and the European champion nine years later.

Until the Second World War, two dozen US world boxing champions in the various weight categories were of Jewish origin. In the Jewish communities of American cities such as → New York and Chicago, they became celebrated stars. One of the first was the lightweight Benny Leonard (1896–1947), whose first boxing experiences were in a Jewish gang on New York's Lower East Side and who became a professional boxer at the age of 15 against the initial opposition of his Orthodox parents. The Polish Jewish wrestler and strongman Siegmund (Zishe) Breitbart (1883–1925; → Samson), who had attracted audiences numbering in the thousands to variety shows in Europe, also excited the audiences on → Broadway.

Besides boxing, team sports also offered similar opportunities for distinguishing oneself. Basketball, invented in America, was considered to be particularly suited to Jews in the early 20th century, as it was believed that intelligence was of higher importance in this sport than physique and muscular strength. This assumption appeared to be borne out by, for instance, the impressive career of Barney Sedran (Sedransky, 1891–1964), who was a mere 1.63 meters (5ft, 4in) tall and one of the best shooting guards in 1910s and 1920s basketball.

The surest path into American sporting culture, however, was by playing the national sport of → baseball. Second-generation Jewish immigrants in particular were enthusiastic about the game, expressing their willingness to integrate and their growing distance from their parents' Eastern European Jewish tradition, where education, religion, and family life were more valuable than enthusiasm for sport, let alone professional sporting careers.

2. Europe during the interwar years

2.1 *Jewish sports clubs*

After the First World War, sport became a forum of Jewish self-determination more than ever before, in particular in Central and Eastern Europe. Where Jews regarded themselves as a national minority (→ Minority Rights), but also in Western countries where rising antisemitism had to be fought, the numbers of Jewish sports clubs rose considerably, as did the number of members registered with them. Competitive sports were increasingly appreciated compared to traditional gymnastics. Clubs such as Bar Kochba established their own sections for athletics, soccer, handball, and hockey. Other clubs focused exclusively on sports, such as → Hakoah Vienna, founded in 1909, which became the Austrian soccer champion in 1925 and was also famous for international successes in the 1920s. Hakoah members were also very successful in the fields of swimming and fencing, which led to the foundation of more Hakoah clubs with a national Jewish ideology within Austria and beyond.

On the occasion of the 12th Zionist Congress in Carlsbad in 1921, the Maccabi World Union was founded as the umbrella organization of all Zionist gymnastics and sports clubs. Numerous Jewish clubs were furthermore founded independently of it. During the interwar years, new Jewish sports clubs were founded in Soviet Russia, Poland, the Baltic States, Romania, Czechoslovakia, France, England, and other European countries, with different political and ideological orientation.

Immediately after the Revolution, several Jewish sports clubs were founded in Russia, and Maccabi was even accepted as their umbrella organization. After 1923, however, the Soviet government increasingly limited the activities of Jewish sports clubs, forbidding them outright in 1926.

Since 1923, there had been clubs named Gwiazda (Star) in Poland, with a left-wing Zionist orientation. In 1926, the sports organization *Morgnshtern* (Morning star) was founded, supported by the Socialist → *Bund*. Both organizations were united in their rejection of the Maccabi and Bar Kochba clubs as "bourgeois." In addition, they championed the use of → Yiddish, especially as the language for commands and rules during sporting competitions; they regarded this as an expression of progressive popular affiliation, while → Hebrew to them was associated more with a backward-looking religious understanding of the community. Differences between the Socialist organizations were reflected in the value they attributed to different types of sport. *Morgnshtern* clubs preferred gymnastics, hiking, and cycling, as these – unlike competition and the cult of stars of "bourgeois" sports – encouraged class-linked collectivity. Because of this perspective, *Morgnshtern* was against boxing for many years, as it was seen to encourage brutality and egotism. Gwiazda did not share these assessments, approving of boxing as a contribution to shaping a militant class consciousness. The number of athletes organized in Jewish clubs in Poland (190 Maccabi clubs, 107 *Morgnshtern* clubs, and 44 Gwiazda clubs) increased from around 3,000 after the First World War to around 30,000 on the eve of the Second World War [9. 52].

In Germany, the number of active members of Jewish sports clubs amounted to around 11,000 before 1933 (nearly two percent of the Jewish population). Of these, around 8,000 were organized within Maccabi and around 3,000 in the Verband jüdisch-neutraler Turn- und Sportvereine (VINTUS; Association of Jewish Neutral Gymnastics and Sports Clubs) as well as in the Turn- and Sportbund Schild, the sporting association of the → Reichsbund jüdischer Frontsoldaten (Reich Federation of Jewish Front-Line Soldiers) [8. 38]. The two last-named organizations were openly Jewish while aspiring to full Jewish integration in German society.

2.2 *Achievements*

The heyday of the Jewish presence in sport in Europe was during the interwar years. This was reflected in a multitude of successes and record achievements. In team sports, Jews were particularly active in → soccer – especially in Germany, Austria, and Hungary – and in ice hockey and water polo. Jewish athletes won Olympic medals in a number of sports, from boxing and wrestling to horse riding and figure skating. Their presence in some sports, such as fencing and swimming, was noticeable, which led to these sports occasionally being regarded as typically "Jewish."

The remarkable presence of Jewish athletes in certain types of sport must also be regarded as a country-specific phenomenon. In Austria, swimming was a widely practiced sport. In Germany, where jujitsu was popular, sportsmen from the Schild achieved eleven German championship titles between 1926 and 1932. In Hungary, there were large numbers of Jews in fencing; Ilona Elek (1907–1988) was national foil champion, and Endre Kabos (1906–1944) was national sabre champion. Other successful Jewish athletes

in Hungary were Miklós Szabados (1912–1962) and Victor Barna (1911–1972), who won national championships in table tennis and were mixed doubles world champions, Ferenc Gerő (1900–1974), who won the Hungarian championships in the 100 meters, and Emília Rotter (1906–2003) and László Szollás (1907–1980), who were national figure skating champions. In Poland, Bronisław Czech (1908–1944) was skiing champion in several disciplines between 1927 and 1937; in Romania, Angelica Rozeanu (1921–2006) was the ladies' table tennis champion at the age of 15 and defended her title until 1957, with the exception of the war years.

The number of Jewish women among medalists and national champions is particularly noticeable. It indicates a connection between Jewish emancipation and women's emancipation. In the course of the bourgeoisification of European societies in the 19th century, numerous Jews had indeed become middle-class but quickly faced the limits of the realization of middle-class equality principles. Jewish women encountered not only anti-Jewish but also gender-specific discrimination (→ Jüdischer Frauenbund). Sport offered the opportunity of overcoming both of these social barriers. One exemplary sporting career is that of Lilli Henoch (1899–1942), who was called "the female Nurmi" with reference to the Finnish athlete Paavo Nurmi, winner of nine Olympic gold medals and world famous in his day. Henoch, a member of the Berliner SC, was German champion in shot-put, discus, and long jump. In 1926, she took part in the world record race of the 4×100 meter relay. In addition, she was a successful handball player. Martha Jacob (1911–1976) was German javelin champion in 1929. She had begun her career in the Jewish sports club Bar Kochba Berlin and continued in the Berliner SC and Sportclub Charlottenburg, where she was a member of the hockey and handball teams too. Ilse Friedleben (1893–1963) dominated German ladies' tennis in the early years of the Weimar Republic. Between 1920 and 1926, she was German champion six times, only losing in 1925 to Nelly Neppach (1898–1933), another tennis player of Jewish origin. Helene Mayer (1910–1953), daughter of a prominent Offenbach Jew and a non-Jewish mother, won six German foil fencing championships from 1925 to 1930, also winning medals in the European championships (1929, 1931), a world championship (1937), and an Olympic gold (1928) as well as a silver medal (1936). "Die Blonde He," who was considered a "Halbjüdin" ("half-Jew") under the Nuremberg Laws of 1935 but had no ties to Judaism and did not identify with Jewish sports associations, was exploited by the Nazis during the 1936 Olympic Games in Berlin. Mayer's nomination was intended to temporarily signal the regime's alleged tolerance towards Jews.

In America, Lilian Copeland (1904–1964) had a similar career to that of multi-talented Lilli Henoch in Germany. She was national javelin, discus, and shot-put champion in 1926 and Olympic discus champion in 1932. Other women played a major role in institutionally establishing sports considered to be the preserve of men in the United States. Senda Berenson (1868–1952) began in the late 19th century to establish women's basketball and worked as the editor of the *Basketball Guide for Women* until 1917. Charlotte Epstein (1884–1938) founded the Women's Swimming Association (WSA) in the United States in 1920, training its Olympic team in 1920, 1924, and 1928.

3. National Socialism and the Shoah

1933 was a turning point in the history of Jewish sport in Germany. While the National Socialist rulers feared a boycott of the Olympic Games in Berlin and did not at first issue any central orders concerning the participation of Jews in sports, sports associations and clubs began to exclude Jewish members in accordance with the predominant antisemitic discourse. The Deutsche Turnerschaft, then the largest individual association, compelled its member clubs as early as April 1933 to cancel the membership of Jewish members. The exclusion affected sports journalism too. Both Walter Bensemann (1873–1934), the founder and editor of the *Kicker*, and Willy Meisl (1895–1968), the well-known sports editor of the *Vossische Zeitung*, fled abroad in 1933. For some, being excluded from German sporting life was so unbearable that they committed suicide. Nelly Neppach took her life after being excluded from the Deutscher Tennis Bund. Fritz Rosenfelder (1901–1933), the press officer of the ski section in the TV Cannstatt, shot himself on April 6, 1933, as he could not bear to live knowing that the German gymnastics movement "regarded him as a traitor to the fatherland" [21. 242].

As a result of the new situation under National Socialist rule, many Jewish members of general clubs changed to Jewish clubs or joined them in reaction to the omnipresent persecution. For Jews in Germany, sport had become more than ever a means of self-assertion in German society. Between 1933 and 1938, Jewish clubs saw an enormous increase in membership. The German Maccabi federation grew to around 20,000 members in 1937, and the number of members in the Schild rose from 7,000 at the end of 1933 to 20,000 in 1936 [20. 47]. Both organizations also held regional and national championships attended by thousands of spectators. However, direct competition between Jewish and "Aryan" clubs was not permitted by the Nazis.

While the Austro-fascist regime governing Austria from 1933 onward did not enact any anti-Jewish laws, there were numerous instances of antisemitic discrimination in public life, including sport. On the occasion of the torch relay in anticipation of the 1936 Olympic Games, which passed through Vienna on its way from Athens to Berlin, a procession of Vienna sports clubs through the city center was arranged, during which the participating members of → Hakoah Vienna were forced to run past onlookers lining the streets who spat on and threatened them. Austrian Jews were excluded from sport after the "Anschluss" (annexation) of March 1938 more quickly than had happened in the "Altreich." Hakoah was dissolved, athletes and officials were removed from the "Aryan" clubs, and Jewish clubs were retrospectively deleted from championships lists.

On the part of Nazi politics, the 1936 Olympic Games in Berlin were to be exploited as a propagandistic *Gesamtkunstwerk* with the aim of influencing public opinion especially abroad. The German government responded to the international boycott movement by presenting itself as particularly tolerant. Thus, the Nazis were able to avert the threatened non-participation of the Olympic team of the United States, a team indispensable for sporting comparisons. Hitler and his sports officials agreed to "negroes" and foreign Jews taking part in the Olympic Games in Berlin as well as the Winter Games in Garmisch-Partenkirchen and accepted the ruling of the International Olympic Committee (IOC) that German Jews able to prove the relevant achievement were accorded the qualification for the national Olympic team. In the end, however, only two "Halbjuden" were part of the German Olympic team: Helene Mayer in foil fencing and Rudi Ball (1911–1975) on the ice hockey team; Meyer won silver. The high jumper Gretel Bergmann (1914–2017) – a "Volljüdin" ("full Jew") according to the Nazis and a member of Schild Stuttgart since being excluded from the Ulmer Fußball-Verein 1894 in April 1933 – achieved the German record of 1.60 meters during preparation for the Games. Although this made her the best female high jumper in Germany, her name was deleted from the list of the German team one day after the ship carrying the American Olympic team had set sail.

The fact that no nation followed the call to boycott the Games was also due to the flexible attitude of decision-making officials at the IOC. The reaction of Avery Brundage, at the time chairman of the American Olympic Committee (AOC), became particularly notorious. He travelled to Germany in July 1934 in order to investigate the conditions of Jewish sport there. In conversation with the deputy of the Reichssportführer (Reich sport leader) Arno Breitmeyer and representatives of Jewish sports clubs it was pointed out to him that Jews were prohibited from being members of German sports clubs, to which he replied: "Jews are also not allowed in my club in Chicago" [4. 141].

Of the Jewish athletes who were able to take part in the 1936 Olympic Games, 16 won medals. Nine of these were won by the Hungarian national team. Some Jewish athletes refused to take part in protest against the Nazis' politics. Among them were the three swimmers of Hakoah Wien Judith Deutsch (1918–2004), Lucie Goldner (1918–2000), and Ruth Langer (1921–1999), the Czech water polo player Franz Fischer (Hagibor Prag), and the American track-and-field athletes Herman Neugass (1915–1991) and Lillian Copeland (1904–1964).

On October 23, 1938, the celebration of the 40th anniversary of the foundation of Bar Kochba Berlin was staged in the Grunewald stadium. Three weeks later, after the → November pogrom, Jewish sports clubs in the German Reich were dissolved.

Jews who succeeded in emigrating or fleeing joined Jewish sport clubs in the countries of exile or founded new ones. After their escape, Jewish soccer players from Europe played for, among others, Eintracht New York or in other clubs of the German American Soccer League founded in 1923. In Shanghai, soccer enthusiasts in exile founded the Jewish League in 1940.

Some Jewish top athletes were able to continue their careers after emigrating or fleeing to America, Canada, Great Britain,

Spectators during a handball match between Makkabi Absalom from Petah Tikva (Palestine) and a selection team of Makkabi Berlin, June 24, 1937, photo by Herbert Sonnenfeld

or Palestine/Israel. Among them was Daniel Prenn (1904–1991), the German tennis champion of 1928, who was forbidden to represent Germany in the semi-finals of the February 1933 Davis Cup and emigrated to England. The German boxing middleweight and light-heavyweight champion Eric Seelig (1909–1984), who was not allowed to defend his title on March 31, 1933, emigrated to France and then, like the high jumper Gretel Bergmann, to the United States. Gottfried Fuchs (1889–1972), former member of the German national soccer team, emigrated via Switzerland to France in 1937, finally moving to Canada in 1940. The swimmer Judith Deutsch continued her swimming career in Palestine. Soccer player Emanuel Schaffer (1923–2012), who grew up in Germany, emigrated to Poland in 1933, and escaped the advancing German army to Kazakhstan in 1940, became the most successful coach of the Israeli national soccer team after the foundation of the State of Israel.

The period of successful Jewish sport in Europe came to an end with the expansion of Nazi rule in the Second World War. Jewish sports clubs were dissolved in the occupied regions in accordance with the immediately applied antisemitic measures. Many prominent Jewish athletes from all over Europe were among the victims of the Holocaust: Lilli Henoch and the national soccer player Julius Hirsch (1892–1943) were murdered in → Riga and → Auschwitz, respectively. The sabre fencer János Garay (1889–1944), who won medals for Hungary at the 1924 and 1928 Olympic games, was murdered in Mauthausen and his famous team mate Attila Petschauer (1904–1943) by Hungarian guards in a labor camp in Ukraine. The Hungarian national soccer player József Braun (1901–1943) died in a labor camp too. Three of the 1928 Dutch gymnastic gold medalists – Helena Nordheim (1903–1943), Anna Polak (1906–1943), and Estella Agsterribe (1909–1943) – were murdered in → Sobibór and → Auschwitz. The Dutch boxer and 1924 Olympic athlete Heinz Levy (1904–1944) and the gymnast and 1928 Olympic athlete Elias Melkman (1903–1942) were also killed in Auschwitz. Further victims of the Holocaust include the Polish Jewish soccer player Leon Sperling (1900–1941) and his team mate from the Polish international team Zygmunt Steuermann (1899–1941 or 1943), both of whom were probably shot in Lemberg. The Tunisian French Jewish flyweight boxer Victor "Young" Perez (1911–1945) survived Auschwitz but died during the → death march to Gliwice.

In Poland, Szapsel Rotholc (1912–1996), a member of Gwiazda Warsaw, had made a name for himself in the interwar years as the Polish flyweight champion of 1933. After 1933, Rotholc beat several German boxers and was consequently popular not just among Jewish audiences in Poland. After the establishment of the → Warsaw ghetto, he served in the Jewish police service; in November 1946 he was convicted of collaboration by a Polish Jewish court and condemned to two years' exclusion from the Jewish community and three years' loss of his civic rights. In June 1948 this verdict was annulled. Rotholc later emigrated to Canada.

Even in some of the ghettos and concentrations camps established by the Germans, Jewish sport continued. Photographs and memoirs from the ghettos in Warsaw, Łódź, and Vilna, or from the concentration camps → Westerbork and Auschwitz, document sport in the shadow of death. German Jews, deported to → Riga from October 1941 onward, were able to engage in sports in the ghetto before it was liquidated. The best-known instance of organized sport was in the → Theresienstadt concentration camp, which was also documented in the Nazi propaganda film *Theresienstadt. Ein Dokumentarfilm aus dem jüdischen Siedlungsgebiet* (1944; "Theresienstadt. A Dcoumentary Film"). The Nazis used the sporting activities in the camp, among them soccer and table tennis league matches, to show a pretense of normalcy and humanity; the prisoners were able to engage in sport to take their minds off camp life and received bigger food rations.

In his recollections of Auschwitz, the Polish writer Tadeusz Borowski remembered that soccer was played next to the ramp of Birkenau camp too. These players, however, were kapos and privileged detainees, among whom there were probably no Jews. The soccer games, did, however, succeed in deceiving the deported prisoners heading to their death regarding the true nature of the extermination camp. In addition, the "absolute perversion of the sporting idea" [11. 334] was found in the ghettos and concentration camps: exercises were euphemistically called "sport" by the SS, with the sole objective of tormenting and humiliating the Jews.

In Auschwitz, the SS recruited a boxing team in which the deported Greek Jewish boxing champion Salamo Arouch (1923–2009) had to train and take part in fights for the guards' entertainment. Arouch survived and emigrated to Palestine. His story was retold in films and books after 1945. Noah Klieger (1926–2018), a member of a Jewish underground organization during the German occupation of Belgium and a well-known Israeli sport journalist after the war, recalled the boxing team in Auschwitz after his liberation.

4. After 1945

4.1 *Europe*

After the Shoah, the Displaced Persons (DP) camps in the American and British occupied zones of Germany became centers of Jewish sporting activity in Europe (→ Munich). Jewish sports clubs and soccer, boxing, or track and field leagues were formed there. As early as October 1945, a friendly match between Ichud Landsberg and Maccabi Türkheim took place in front of over 2,000 spectators [12. 190]. DP sport reached its peak in

1947. Around one hundred clubs took part in twelve different sports. The matches of the soccer league were attended by hundreds, sometimes thousands of spectators. More than once there were violent incidents between the fans of different camp teams. Sport acted as an outlet for aggressions that must be understood in the context of the frustrating everyday life in the camps.

Above all, the inhabitants of the DP camps regarded sport as an opportunity for being active, which tied in with their longing for normalcy and a better life. These ideas went hand-in-hand with strict delimitation from their past tormentors. In DP camp sport, teams did not allow non-Jewish German members, and matches against German teams were prohibited and punishable.

Some Jewish athletes and officials were able to continue their activities in their countries of origin. Kurt Landauer (1884–1961), who had already been the long-standing president of FC Bayern Munich from 1919 to 1933, returned to his old club from exile and became its president once again from 1947 to 1951. Béla Guttmann (1899–1981), a former player with → Hakoah Vienna, survived the war, probably in Budapest, and started a successful international career as a soccer coach.

In Europe, a few Jewish competitive athletes returned to the top. Angelica Rozeanu, a table tennis player, succeeded in Romania. Ágnes Kelei (b. 1921), who had become Hungarian champion in gymnastics at the age of 16, was in hiding in 1944 avoiding the deportations and returned to sport, winning a total of ten medals for Hungary at the Olympic Games of 1948, 1952, and 1956. Róbert Antal (1921–1995) won a medal with the Hungarian national water polo team in 1952, while the swimmer Éva Székely (1927–2020) returned to the Hungarian Olympic team and won gold and silver medals in 1952 and 1956. The fencer Claude Netter (1924–2007) was a member of the French Olympic team

in 1948, 1952, 1956, and 1960 and won one gold and one silver medal with the team. There are only rare instances of renowned athletes who survived the Shoah as children. One of them was the canoeist Leon Rotman from Romania (b. 1934), who won two gold medals at the 1956 games and a bronze medal at the 1960 games in the Canoe Sprint Canadian Singles.

New generations of Jewish top athletes were able to come to the fore especially in those countries that had the largest percentage of Jewish inhabitants after the Second World War, above all in the United States but also in the Soviet Union. Among the Jewish athletes of the Soviet Union were the gymnast Vladimir Portnoy (1931–1984) and the discus thrower Faina Mel'nik (1945–2016). As the ethnic or national affiliation of athletes in the Soviet Union did not, according to the official doctrine, play a role, it was usually not mentioned in the case of Jewish athletes either. In Poland, Irena Szewińska (née Kirszenstein, 1946–2018), born in the Soviet Union, became a world class track-and-field athlete, who won numerous medals at European championships as well as the Olympic Games during the 1960s and 1970s in the 100, 200, and 400 meters and also in the long jump.

In countries not directly affected by the Holocaust such as England or Algeria, the fencer Allan Jay (b. 1931) and the boxer Alphonse Halimi (1932–2006) were among the few prominent and successful Jewish athletes.

4.2   *The United States*

The postwar world of Jewish sport was dominated by American athletes and team members. For some Jewish athletes, a door had opened to show business too. Thus, the boxer Max Rosenbloom ("Slapsie Maxie"; 1907–1976), the 1933 light heavyweight world champion, became a → Hollywood star, appearing in more than 100 films, among them works such as *To the Shores of Tripoli* (1942) or *Follow the Boys* (1944) produced to raise American morale during the Second World War.

As early as the 1930s, Hank Greenberg (1911–1986) from an Orthodox middle-class family in the Bronx had become the greatest Jewish → baseball star of his age. He was very popular among Jews, not only because of his sporting achievements and his forthright reactions to antisemitic comments. Due to his particularly long military service during the Second World War, which unlike many other league professionals he did not finish early, he earned the appreciation of many of his compatriots, becoming a national hero. Greenberg's legendary home run in the deciding game between the Detroit Tigers and the St. Louis Browns shortly after his discharge in 1945 illustrates the popularity of Jewish athletes in the United States; the baseball career of Sandy Koufax (b. 1935) in the 1950s was the crowning glory of this success story.

On the US Olympic teams, the absolute number of Jewish members did not increase significantly from 1948 onward compared to the prewar years. What did change were the disciplines in which Jews competed. There were no Jewish boxers on the American Olympic team from 1948 onward. The number of fencers, on the other hand, rose to 61 by 2004, amounting to around a third of all Jewish US Olympic team members. 37 of a total of 85 Olympic medals won by Jews for the United States between 1948 and 2004 were won by swimmers. The third place of the Jewish American medal table was occupied by equestrianism [15. 133f.].

In the course of the successful integration and social advancement of the Jews in the United States from the 1950s onward, individual sports such as tennis or swimming grew more popular among them. Like their social environment in the American middle class, Jews now regarded sports more as a leisure activity and less as a means to integration and equality. A further result of social advancement was the more noticeable presence of Jewish coaches, club officials, and team owners. The careers of William "Red" Holzman (1920–1998), who coached the New York Knicks from 1967 to 1982, of David Stern (1942 –2020), who was Commissioner of the National Basketball Association from 1984 to 2014, of the former owner of the New York Yankees George Steinbrenner (1930–2010), of Jeffrey Lurie (b. 1951), the owner of the Philadelphia Eagles, or Steve Tisch (b. 1949), whose family are co-owners of the New York Giants, to name but a few, are exemplary of this development.

5. Sport in the Yishuv and in Israel

After Max Nordau had called upon the Zionist organization to nurture "muscular Judaism," the Maccabi Association active within this remit became the central Jewish sports organization globally. On the eve of the Second World War, it had around 200,000 members in 38 countries.

In the → Yishuv in Ottoman Palestine, the first Jewish sports club was founded in 1906. By 1914, ten clubs with around 500 members had been founded, organized within the Maccabi umbrella organization from 1912 onward. After 1918, sport in Palestine was influenced on the one hand by the Zionist sporting tradition of Central European immigrants and on the other hand by the idea of sport as embraced by the British mandatory government. Immigrants from Germany, who had come in contact with the tradition of Jahn's ideal of physical exercise as contributing to the national defensive force as members of Jewish sports clubs or Jewish student associations, influenced the understanding of sport in the Yishuv and later in Israel in positions as sports teachers, club founders, and educators. Foremost among them was Arthur Biram (1878–1967) who moved from Germany to Palestine in 1913. Biram, who came from Bischofswerda in Saxony, had a PhD in Islamic Studies, and was a former rabbi in Potsdam, became head of the Realgymnasium in Haifa. He implemented an educational concept that informed the education debates in Erets Israel, with sport being regarded in the context of promoting health, individual self-discipline, paramilitary defensive capabilities, and national cohesion. In view of incidents of anti-Jewish violence in the British mandate, especially during the Arab uprising of 1936–1939, Biram's educational concept gained acceptance among the Jews in the mandatory region and the Yishuv.

Sport in Palestine and later in Israel was informed by a strong tie to political parties. Besides the Maccabi organization, which over time developed into an association in the middle-class camp, the youth and sports organizations of the Revisionist Betar movement (1923; → Altalena), the sport organization of the workers' parties Hapoel (1926), which split from the Maccabi Association, and the organization of the national-religious wing Elitzur, were also founded.

Meanwhile soccer, originating in England and imported into the mandatory area by British soldiers and immigrants, grew increasingly popular among the Jewish as well as the Arab population. When the famous team of → Hakoah Vienna came to Tel Aviv in 1925 and beat a Maccabi selection team 11:2, 10,000 spectators watched the match. In 1928, Jewish and Arab representatives founded the Palestine Football Association, which was accepted by FIFA as a regular member a year later. This was accompanied by the establishment of regular league activities in which Jewish, Arab, and British teams took part.

Spurred by the achievements of top Jewish athletes from Europe, the idea of forming an Olympic team for Palestine emerged in the early 1920s. Initiated by the Maccabi official Yosef Yekutieli (1897–1982) and under the patronage of the British High Commissioner Herbert Samuel, competitions took place in mandatory Palestine in 1923 in which Jewish, Arab, and British athletes participated. Yekutieli also inspired the organization of world Jewish sports championships, which took place for the first time in 1932 under the name Maccabiad (later Maccabiah) in → Tel Aviv. Yekutieli's engagement aimed at presenting Palestine as the center of Jewish national sport, buttressing his intention of having a national Jewish Olympic team. After a decade of preparations, the National Olympic Committee in Palestine was founded in 1933 and recognized by the IOC a year later.

There were even winter sports Maccabiahs in the 1930s, but only two, and outside of Palestine, which was not suited for winter sports. They took place in 1933 in Zakopane (Poland) and in 1936 in Banská-Bystrica (Czechoslovakia).

At the second Maccabiah of 1935, once again in Tel Aviv, 1,350 athletes from 28 countries competed, and up to 50,000 spectators watched the competitions. The great popularity was seen as the Jewish response to events in Germany. Both Maccabiahs were also used as a gateway for Jewish immigration into Palestine above the numbers permitted by the British government.

It was only possible to hold the third Maccabiah after the foundation of the State of Israel. From 1953 onward, Maccabiahs were held every four years in Israel. Outstanding sporting achievements, however, were rare. During the fourth Maccabiah in 1957, Isaac Berger (b. 1936), who had emigrated to America from Palestine, set a weightlifting (featherweight) world record, and the swimmer Mark Spitz demonstrated his outstanding abilities at the eighth Maccabiah in 1969 – three years before the Olympic Games in Munich.

Overall, however, the achievements of Israeli athletes remained rather modest compared to those of Jewish athletes in the Diaspora. For decades after the foundation of the State of Israel, Israeli athletes failed to win any Olympic medals. The first time it happened was in 1992, indicating a lower degree of importance attributed to competitive sport in Israel. One reason may be found in the influence exerted by Zionist sporting traditions under the conditions during the emergence of the State of Israel and the subsequent endeavors to consolidate the State. The Zionist message of "muscular Judaism" had already emphasized self-defense more than sport. In view of the conflicts in British Mandatory Palestine and the Arab–Israeli wars following the foundation of the State of Israel, the purpose of physical education was paramilitary or military rather than encouraging sporting activity in general.

The attempts at isolating Israel further internationally influenced the opportunities Israeli athletes had to compete in international events. After the Suez Crisis, for instance, Turkey, Indonesia, and Sudan refused to play against the Israeli team in the qualification round for the 1958 soccer world championship. In subsequent qualification rounds for soccer world championships, Israel was assigned to a number of different continental groups, namely the European group (1962, 1966, 1982), Oceania (1970, 1990), the Asian group (1974, 1978, 1986), and only since 1994 permanently to the Union of European Football Associations (UEFA). Until 1968, Israel took part in the Asian championships in soccer, where it was boycotted by the Arab countries. In 1974, Israel was excluded from the Asian Games Federation.

A particularly dramatic expression of the political implication of the Middle East conflict for Israeli sport occurred during the 1972 Olympic Games in Munich. Palestinian terrorists from the Black September organization attacked the Israeli team, taking several team members hostage. In the course of the hostage crisis and during the failed liberation attempt by the German police, eleven athletes of the Israeli Olympic team lost their lives.

Bibliography

Sources

[1] Was wir wollen!, in: Bar Kochba (ed.), Jüdische Turnzeitung 1 (1900), 1–5. [2] Stenographisches Protokoll der Verhandlungen des II. Zionisten-Kongresses gehalten zu Basel, Vienna 1898. [3] Stenographisches Protokoll der Verhandlungen des IV. Zionisten-Kongresses in London, Vienna 1900. [4] R. Atlasz (ed.), Bar Kochba. Makkabi – Deutschland 1898–1938, Tel Aviv 1977. [5] S. Hirsch, Die jüdische Turnbewegung in Deutschland, in: Jüdische Monatshefte für Turnen und Sport. Organ der jüdischnationalen Bewegung 6 (1913), 186–188.

Secondary literature

[6] J. Aviram, Entsiklopedya li-sport ule-tarbut ha-guf [Encyclopedia of Sport and Body Culture], vol. 2, Tel Aviv 1966. [7] H. Becker, Antisemitismus in der Deutschen Turnerschaft, Sankt Augustin 1980. [8] H. Bernett, Der jüdische Sport im nationalsozialistischen Deutschland 1933–1938, Schorndorf 1978. [9] D. Blecking, Marxism versus Muscular Judaism. Jewish Sports in Poland, in: G. Eisen et al. (eds.), Sport and Physical Education in Jewish History. Selected Papers from an International Seminar Held on the Occasion of the 16th Maccabiah, Jerusalem 2003, 48–55. [10] A. Bodner, When Boxing Was a Jewish Sport, Westport 1997. [11] G. Eisen, Changing Meanings – Changing Context. Play & Sport in the Mirror of the Holocaust, in: T. Niewerth etal. (eds.), Jüdischer Sport und jüdische Gesellschaft/Jewish sport and Jewish community, Berlin 2012, 319–337. [12] P. Grammes, Sports in the DP Camps, 1945–1948, in: M. Brenner/G. Reuveni (eds.), Emancipation Through Muscles. Jews and Sports in Europe, Lincoln 2006. [13] H. Kaufman/H. Harif (eds.), Tarbut ha-guf veha-sport be-Yisra'el ba-me'ah ha-esrim [Body Culture and Sport in Israel in the 20th Century], Jerusalem 2002. [14] P. Levine, Ellis Island to Ebbets Field. Sport and the American Jewish Experience, New York 1992. [15] P.Y. Mayer, Jews and the Olympic

Games. Sport: A Springboard for Minorities, London 2004. [16] T. Niewerth et al. (eds.), Jüdischer Sport und jüdische Gesellschaft/ Jewish Sport and Jewish Community, Berlin 2010. [17] L. Peiffer/H. Wahlig, Ein Treffpunkt der Gemeinde. Sport im deutsch-jüdischen Sozialleben vor und nach 1933, in: D. Diner et al. (eds.), Deutsche Zeiten. Geschichte und Lebenswelt, Göttingen 2012, 141–159. [18] J. Siegman, Jewish Sports Legends. The International Jewish Sports Hall of Fame, Washington 1997. [19] P. Taylor, Jews and the Olympic Games. The Clash between Sport and Politics – with a Complete Review of Jewish Olympic Medallists, Brighton 2004. [20] H. J. Teichler, Jüdische Sportler in der Weimarer Republik, in: B. Bahro et al. (eds.), Vergessene Rekorde. Jüdische Leichtathletinnen vor und nach 1933, Berlin 2009, 44–53. [21] H. Wahlig, Selbsttötung jüdischer Sportler im Nationalsozialismus. Die Beispiele Fritz Rosenfelder und Nelly Neppach, in: D. Blecking/L. Peiffer (eds.), Sportler im "Jahrhundert der Lager." Profiteure, Widerständler und Opfer, Göttingen 2012, 241–247. [22] D. Wildmann, Der Körper im Körper. Jüdische Turner und jüdische Turnvereine im Deutschen Kaiserreich 1898–1914, in: P. Haber et al. (eds.), Jüdische Identität und Nation. Fallbeispiele aus Mitteleuropa, Cologne 2006, 50–86.

MOSHE ZIMMERMANN, JERUSALEM

St. Matthew Passion

The St. Matthew Passion by Johann Sebastian Bach, one of the greatest masterpieces of Protestant sacred music, marks a central moment in the career of its "re-discoverer" Felix Mendelssohn Bartholdy (1809–1847). The grandson of the great Jewish Enlightenment thinker Moses Mendelssohn, Felix Mendelssohn was baptized a Protestant, his biography combining Judaism and Christianity, as well as German middle-class and English culture. At the same time, his pluralistic self-image, positioned between Jewish

affiliation and the anticipation of becoming integrated into the Protestant majority culture, indicates tensions specific to assimilated Jews in the first half of the 19th century. This aspect is also reflected in the varied reception history of Mendelssohn and his works.

1. The new performance of 1829
2. Felix Mendelssohn Bartholdy
3. Perception of self – perception by others

1. The new performance of 1829

The *Passio secundum Matthaeum*, composed by Johann Sebastian Bach in the late 1720s, is considered a central work of Protestant sacred music. After its creator's death in 1750, it stopped being played in public and only came to public notice again nearly eighty years later. The point of departure of the phenomenon called "the 19th-century Bach renaissance" was marked by three memorable performances by the Berliner Singakademie in the spring of 1829. Audience members at these performances included notable figures such as King Friedrich Wilhelm III of Prussia, Friedrich Schleiermacher, Friedrich Hegel, Heinrich Heine (→ Entreebillet), Rahel Varnhagen (→ Salon), Johann Gustav Droysen, and Gasparo Spontini. Twenty-year-old Felix Mendelssohn conducted the two performances on March 11 and March 21 while the director of the Singakademie Carl Friedrich Zelter, who was also Mendelssohn's composition teacher, conducted the third one on April 17 because Mendelssohn had set off on his first journey to England by that time.

In the context of the public perception of Bach and the development of a new focus in performance practice, the Berlin performances of the St. Matthew Passion are regarded as a turning point in music history that continues to be closely linked to Mendelssohn. The question of "Who has reawakened J. S. Bach's St. Matthew Passion?," asked by the musicologists Georg Schünemann and Friedrich Smend in the late 1920s, informed the search for traces within a complex history, the search itself having been in part ideologically charged. Mendelssohn's own remark, quoted by his friend Eduard Devrient, that "a Jew" brought back "to the people the greatest of Christian works" [2. 57] led not only to controversial discussions on the achievements of the people involved but also to the mythification of the "re-discovery" of Bach at the hands of Mendelssohn. In addition, the anecdote claiming that Devrient and Mendelssohn had to push their teacher Zelter into agreeing to the performance against his will, while not detracting from Mendelssohn's initiative and great achievements concerning the organization and work on the score, suggests mythification. The new performance in 1829 was the result of numerous factors.

The basic requirement was that various manuscripts of the St. Matthew Passion had survived. Zelter, who possessed a manuscript copy of the early version, began to rehearse parts of the St. Matthew Passion from June 1815 until 1820 and even later with the Berliner Singakademie. Zelter was probably considering a performance; however, he also saw fundamental problems, such as providing a double orchestra and double choir as indicated in the score, issues with the instrumentation due to the absence of an organ, as well as the necessity of abridging the work in places. In October 1820, Felix and his sister Fanny Mendelssohn joined the academy, where they first learned about the Passion. In 1823/1824, at the age of 14, Felix was given a manuscript copy by his grandmother Bella Bartholdy (actually Salomon, née Itzig). He then studied it intensively, hoping that the work would find broad public appreciation.

The performance can be positioned within multiple contexts, without which its success would hardly have been possible. Among them were the institutional circumstances and the premises of the Berliner Singakademie, the cultivation of Bach in bourgeois circles (→ Middle Class) during the first third of the 19th century, the growing lay music movement, which resulted in mixed-gender choirs rehearsing a repertoire of sacred music, and the growing importance of the Protestant music press in northern Germany. The press campaign in Berlin's *Allgemeine Musikalische Zeitung* both before and during the period of the performances, contributed significantly to the revival of the St. Matthew Passion and the public's new perception of Bach. It had been initiated by the paper's editor Adolf Bernhard Marx (1795–1866), a friend of Mendelssohn's who had converted from Judaism to Protestantism in 1819 and enthusiastically exalted Bach's St. Matthew Passion as a national return to home-grown musical traditions. Marx prompted the development of an edition of a complete piano score with the Berlin publishing house Schlesinger (1830). Additional (new) editions as well as complete collections of Bach's works followed. This raising of Bach to the status of a national figurehead accompanied the secularization of his works beyond denominational boundaries and their integration into the canon of bourgeois concert culture.

2. Felix Mendelssohn Bartholdy

Felix Mendelssohn was born in Hamburg in 1809. He was the grandson of the Jewish philosopher and Lumière Moses Mendelssohn (→ Bi'ur); his father Abraham Mendelssohn was a partner in the bank Mendelssohn & Co., and his mother Lea was a granddaughter of the Prussian → court Jew Daniel Itzig (→ Bankers). In 1811 the upper middle-class family fled from the Hanseatic city (then under French occupation) to Berlin. In the context of the *Edikt, betreffend die bürgerlichen Verhältnisse der Juden in dem Preußischen Staate* (→ Prussian Emancipation Edict of 1812), Abraham Mendelssohn had

Felix Mendelssohn Bartholdy (1809–1847)

his four children Fanny, Felix, Rebecka, and Paul baptized as Protestants. In keeping with his own desire, as well as following external pressures urging → assimilation, the father made use of the option to modify the family name by adding Bartholdy on the occasion of his own conversion in 1822.

Abraham and Lea Mendelssohn brought up their children in accordance with the idea of a comprehensive middle-class education (→ Bildung). All four children had music lessons, especially Fanny and Felix, both of whom displayed a talent for composition early on. The private teacher for harmony and composition engaged by Abraham was his friend Carl Friedrich Zelter, to whom he had donated numerous Bach autographs for the Singakademie in 1811. Zelter's intensive dedication to Bach determined Felix Mendelssohn's musical education and complemented the focus on Bach that Lea Mendelssohn encouraged in family music.

In October 1821 Zelter wrote Goethe to introduce the twelve-year-old Felix Mendelssohn to him. In his letter, he used the phrase "Admittedly, he is the son of a Jew, but no Jew himself" (October 21, 1821; cited in [3. 288]). After 1832, the Mendelssohn family found out about this from the posthumously published correspondence between Goethe and Zelter; they were deeply hurt. Mendelssohn's friendship with Goethe, whom he visited three times in Weimar, was characterized by mutual esteem. In addition to the poet, the guiding lights Handel, Beethoven, Mozart and especially Bach influenced Mendelsohn's career and work.

After gaining his first public recognition as the conductor of the St. Matthew Passion, Mendelssohn went on several educational journeys to England, Scotland, Italy, and France between 1829 and 1832. His travel impressions inspired many of his compositions. In addition, he took an active part in the musical life of the great European cultural centers he visited on his journeys. In London, in particular, Mendelssohn celebrated great successes as a composer, conductor, pianist, and organist. He was popular with the Philharmonic Society of London, and a cult of Mendelssohn emerged in Victorian England over the subsequent years; these factors contributed to his finding a second home in England, which he visited no fewer than ten times.

After his return to Germany, Mendelssohn held various positions. Between 1833 and 1835, he served as the head of the Niederrheinische Musikfeste (Lower Rhenish Music Festivals) and municipal director of music in Düsseldorf, where he placed particular emphasis on sacred music. Thanks to his endeavors to revive Handel's oratorios, the city became known for promoting and performing Handel's music. Düsseldorf was also where Mendelssohn composed the first of his own oratorios, *Paulus* (premiered in 1836).

From August 1835 to March 1847, Mendelssohn was the musical director of the Leipzig Gewandhaus. In addition to performances of works by contemporary composers such as Schumann and Schubert, he focused on works by Bach, Beethoven, Mozart, Handel, and Gluck in the "Historische Konzerte." His interest in music history derived from his progressive understanding of the connection between past and present. Other instances of the progressive nature of Mendelssohn's work are his transformation of the Gewandhaus orchestra into a modern symphony orchestra and his founding of the Leipzig Conservatorium in 1843, which he then developed into one of the most famous music schools of his time.

In 1837 Mendelssohn married Cécile Charlotte Sophie Jeanrenaud, the daughter of a French pastor of the Reformed Church. The couple had five children. During the last years of his life, he worked in Berlin, Frankfurt, and Leipzig. In addition he went on four concert tours to England (1842, 1844, 1846, and 1847) and directed music festivals in Düsseldorf (1842), Zweibrücken (1844), and Aachen (1846). Six months after the death of his sister Fanny Hensel, Felix Mendelssohn died unexpectedly in Leipzig on November 4, 1847, at only 38 years of age. His death led to great public expressions of sympathy. In the opinion of his contemporaries, he stood alongside Beethoven as one of the most important composers of the 19th century. The breadth of his compositions, which included vocal, orchestral, and chamber music, as well as symphonic, sacred, and theatre works, and his activity as a pianist, organist, and as a director and patron of music brought him recognition from the British, Prussian, and Saxon royal houses.

3. Perception of self – perception by others

In all probability, Mendelssohn's reception was more changeable than that of most composers. Revered all over Europe during his lifetime, he suffered posthumous devaluation in which aesthetic judgment and antisemitic invective were combined. Richard Wagner's article *Das Judenthum in der Musik* ("Judaism in Music," 1907; → Music), published first in 1850 and in an extended version in 1869, catalyzed and popularized this attitude. To Wagner, Mendelssohn was an instance of the snappy formula of the Jewish will to be creative combined with a lack of ability. He imputed to him a lack of "depth" and "originality," suggesting that Mendelssohn's focus on Bach and on sacred music appeared as a form of superficial imitation and meaningless mastery of form and technique. By bringing together the virulent stereotyped of Jewish incompetence in all things creative, Wagner subsumed composers as unlike as Giacomo Meyerbeer and Felix Mendelssohn Bartholdy under the label of "Jews in music."

In the debate that followed, critics of an antisemitic bent perceived "smoothness," "shallowness," "softness," and "sentimentality" in Mendelssohn's compositions, dismissing him as an ambitious and hardworking talent ranking with second-rate lesser masters. Critics documented this using various facets of his life and work. Among the evidence adduced to prove the imputation of "smoothness" and "shallowness" were Mendelssohn's precociousness as a musical prodigy, his seemingly unproblematic conversion, and the apparent ease with which he had an extremely productive professional career as an artist. The alleged musical equivalent of these indicators were works such as *Lieder ohne Worte* (Songs without Words) and the music for *A Midsummer Night's Dream*. Contradicting the then-current ideas of the nature of genius was also the cliché circulating about Mendelssohn's "softness," which was based on the numerous images of Mendelssohn in his youth, as well as on the personally and artistically significant close relationship between him and his sister Fanny. Attacks went so far as to accuse Mendelssohn of deliberately deceiving his non-Jewish surroundings – in antisemitic terms, this was referred to as "Jewish mimicry."

Despite efforts to have Mendelssohn reassessed as a composer, such derogatory judgments persisted until the end of the 20th century. The view of his compositional work was narrowed so that the compositions by Mendelssohn that were performed in concerts were limited to his 3rd and 4th symphonies ("Scottish" and "Italian"), the music for *A Midsummer Night's Dream*, the overtures, and the violin concerto in E minor. This, likewise, contributed to the persistence of negative views, such that even the well-known musicologist Carl Dahlhaus spoke of a "Mendelssohn problem" (1974). This unfortunate phrase evokes the unpleasant connotations of a "Jewish problem."

Other creative musicians of the time, such as Julius Stern, Joseph Joachim, and Louis Lewandowski (→ Organ), however, saw Mendelssohn – together with his sister Fanny – as emblematic of successful assimilation in the sense of embodying a Jewish-Christian synthesis. This raises the question of Mendelssohn's own self-image, positioned between Jewish tradition, Christian conversion, and Protestant sacred music. There can be no doubt that Mendelssohn lived in an intercultural environment, within which his search for self-understanding and belonging on the spiritual, social, political, and aesthetic levels determined his life [12. XXVIII]. Even so, it is difficult to determine verifiable parameters of his culturally pluralistic self-image between Christianity and Judaism, past and present, as well as German bourgeois and English culture.

As a Protestant, Mendelssohn found his spiritual home in sacred music. Beginning with the new performance of the St. Matthew Passion in 1829, his numerous works of sacred music such as choral cantatas, psalms set to music, and the two complete oratorios *Paulus* and *Elias* (1846; a third one, *Christus*, remained a fragment), mark

his compositional profession of his Protestantism. Within the family, J. S. Bach was a guiding star, as Abraham Mendelssohn pointedly expressed in a letter to his son: "I first became aware of the fact that Bach was the musical representative of Protestantism when listening to the Passion, and it becomes evident to me anew with every new piece of his that I hear" (March 3, 1835; cited in [1. vol. 4, 560]). In addition, Mendelssohn also regarded himself as part of a humanist tradition that saw music as a means to education, inspiration, and edification. In this context, he oriented his activity towards linking historical and contemporary, temporal and sacred, as well as national and European culture. In musical matters, in particular, he achieved the high standards of his own integrity: "I take music very seriously and consider it forbidden to compose something I do not truly feel throughout my entire being. It is as though I were telling a lie," he wrote to his Viennese relative Henriette von Pereira-Arnstein (July 3 and 4, 1831; cited in [1. vol. 2, 303]). He had this same sincere attitude concerning family matters and was especially proud of his grandfather's achievements. He felt that Moses Mendelssohn embodied the unity of traditional Judaism, Enlightenment ideals, and Humanist tolerance and saw this as an essential legacy. This explains his refusal to follow his father's wish that he use Bartholdy as his only family name.

Many composers and musicians born shortly after 1800 who decided in favor of → assimilation had ambivalent self-images, as well [6. 15]. However, there is hardly any evidence of this in Mendelssohn's case in his own testimony and other surviving materials. Nor is there anything to suggest that he struggled to deal with Jewish religion and culture or with anti-Jewish resentment, to which he was no doubt exposed. The absence of such testimony – whether due to them being taboo or to self-censorship – may indicate that he had hidden ambivalences like other artists who endeavored to assimilate during this period. Even so, the question of Mendelssohn's potentially ambivalent self-images has repeatedly prompted problematic assessments. On the one hand, for example, his explicit emphasis on his Protestant faith and his national integrity and integration is dubiously ascribed to the pursuit of a targeted assimilatory strategy that ultimately led to his hyper-assimilation. On the other hand, Mendelssohn is sometimes co-opted by Jews seeking specific cultural or religious characteristics in his biography and work, but such an assessment misses the point as the emphasis on his origin leads to a split that fails to do justice to his place within the context of music history. Above all, Mendelssohn was able, through his musical creativity, to unify opposite moments of his life and work. In this respect, many of his contemporaries between 1815 and 1845 saw him as embodying the ambiguity and complexity of Jewish self-images, of different kinds of belonging, and of culturally variable orientations in the modern era.

Bibliography

Sources

[1] F. Mendelssohn Bartholdy, Sämtliche Briefe in 12 Bänden auf Basis der von Rudolf Elvers angelegten Sammlung, H. Loos/W. Seidel (eds.), vols. 1–6, Kassel 2008–2012. [2] E. Devrient, My Recollections of Felix Mendelssohn-Bartholdy, and His Letters to Me, trans. by N. Macfarren, Cambridge 1869. [3] L. B. Bodley. Goethe and Zelter. Musical Dialogues, Farnham 2017.

Secondary literature

[4] C. Ahrens, Bearbeitung oder Einrichtung? Felix Mendelssohn Bartholdys Fassung der Bachschen Matthäus-Passion und deren Aufführung in Berlin 1829, in: Bach-Jahrbuch 87 (2001), 71–97. [5] C. Applegate, Bach in Berlin. Nation and Culture in Mendelssohn's Revival of the St. Matthew Passion, Ithaca/London 2005. [6] B. Borchard/H. Zimmermann (eds.), Musikwelten – Lebenswelten. Jüdische Identitätssuche in der deutschen Musikkultur, Cologne 2009. [7] C. Dahlhaus (ed.), Das Problem Mendelssohn, Regensburg 1974. [8] M. Geck, Die Wiederentdeckung der Matthäuspassion im 19. Jahrhundert. Die zeitgenössischen Dokumente und ihre ideengeschichtliche Deutung, Regensburg 1967. [9] A. Glöckner, Zelter und Mendelssohn. Zur "Wiederentdeckung" der Matthäus-Passion im Jahre 1829, in: Bach-Jahrbuch 90 (2004), 133–155. [10] J. H. Schoeps, Christliches Bekenntnis oder modernes Marranentum? Der Übergang vom Judentum zum Christentum: Das Beispiel Abraham und Felix Mendelssohn-Bartholdy, in: J. H. Schoeps, Die missglückte Emanzipation. Wege und Irrwege deutsch-jüdischer Geschichte, Berlin et al. 2002, 169–182. [11] M. P. Steinberg, Mendelssohn and Judaism, in: P. Mercer-Taylor (ed.), Cambridge Companion to Mendelssohn, Cambridge 2004, 26–41. [12] R. L. Todd, Mendelssohn. A Life in Music, Oxford 2003.

ANNKATRIN DAHM, COLOGNE

Stalingrad

A city on the Volga, founded as Tsaritsyn, was renamed Stalingrad in 1925 and in 1961 to Volgograd. From September 1942 to February 1943, it was the scene of the battle between German and Soviet units that led to the encirclement of the German 6th Army and ended in its crushing defeat. The Battle of Stalingrad became the central war experience of the author Vassili Grossman (1905–1964). In his epic *Zhizn' i sud'ba* (1960; "Life and Fate," 2011), he gave literary form to the Second World War, the → Holocaust, and the Stalinist crimes, on the basis of the battles that occurred there. As a war reporter, Grossman reached the concentration camps of Majdanek and Treblinka with the → Red Army, and he was one of the first authors to introduce the subject of the murder of European Jews by Nazi Germany into Soviet literature.

1. Vasily Grossman
2. *Life and Fate*
3. Publication history
4. Influence

1. Vasily Grossman

Iosif Solomonovich Grossman was born in 1905 in the East Galician → shtetl of Berdychiv. His mother called him Vasily, and he later adopted this name, in order to reinforce his Russian self-image. From 1910 to 1912, he lived with his mother in Switzerland, probably in Geneva. After his schooldays in Kiev (Kyiv), he studied chemistry at Moscow University from 1923 to 1929. He subsequently took up a position as an engineer in the heavy industry of the Donbas but returned to Moscow in 1932 after falling ill with tuberculosis.

Until the German attack on the Soviet Union in the summer of 1941, Grossman had scarcely concerned himself with his Jewish origins: on the contrary, he was convinced that such questions of affiliation were transcended in socialism. Thus, in 1937, he published the short story *Vesna* (Spring), in which a Jewish Bolshevik is taken prisoner by Ukrainian nationalists during the Russian Civil War (1917–1920). During his interrogation, he refuses to answer a question about his Jewish origins. His last thought before his execution reflects the Soviet policy on nationalities in the 1920s: "'questions like that will be irrelevant in the future'" (cited in [9. 67]). Grossman himself was firmly convinced that he was living in such a future.

He had made his debut in 1934 with the short novel *Glyukauf* (Good luck!), in which a communist mine captain urges his miners and himself to work at maximum capacity and finally dies of consumption. Maxim Gorky gave the work a lukewarm review: Grossman had indeed confronted an important subject, but his tale was "poorly 'presented'," and did not exhibit a correct ideological perspective (cited in [9. 106]). Socialist Realism, which had been declared a obligatory stylistic trend in literature at the first Congress of Soviet Writers, required "to depict reality in its revolutionary development" (cited in [2a. 21]). Abuses could therefore be described, but at the same time a solution corresponding to the system must be offered. There is no such happy ending in Grossman's novel, which could therefore be categorized as potentially defeatist naturalism.

The publication of two volumes of stories in 1935 and 1936 fulfilled the requirements for Grossman's acceptance into the Writers' Union in 1937. Professionalized writing led him to the style of great prose. The Bildungsroman *Stepan Kol'chugin* (four volumes, 1937–1940 and 1947; "Kol'chugin's Youth," 1946), written in the style of Socialist Realism, assumed semi-epic proportions. In it, Grossman traces the tortuous biography of the protagonist, shortly before the October Revolution. The novel, which appeared during the culmination of the Great Terror, received generally positive reviews. Nevertheless, Stalin personally crossed Grossman's name off the list of nominations for the Stalin Prize on the grounds that the novel was "Menshevist" [3. 180].

The German attack on the Soviet Union marked a turning point in Grossman's creative work. From August 1941, he worked as a war reporter for the military newspaper *Krasnaya zvezda* (Red Star). During his deployment, Grossman carefully kept a diary, noting individual episodes that were appropriate for reporting. At first, Jewish questions played a subordinate role in these notes. Grossman's criticism of the incompetence of military leaders grew. He soon progressed to gathering his sketches together into a novel, which he entitled *Narod bessmerten* (1943; "The People Immortal," 2022).

Individual chapters appeared in the *Krasnaya zvezda* in July and August 1942, while an edition in book form followed in 1943.

Grossman took part in the Battle of Stalingrad as a military reporter. Shaken by the ferocity of the battles, in 1943 he began to work up his collected experiences in the form of a novel. During the war, he published individual chapters under the title *Stalingrad* (1943; "For a Just Cause," 1952).

After the Red Army's victory over the German 6th Army, Grossman returned to the West with the Soviet troops. He thus reached the sites of the Nazi murder of the Jews, including Berdychiv, where his mother had fallen victim to a massacre by the SS. In this period, the Holocaust came to occupy center stage in Grossman's writing. In 1943, he wrote two essays on the murder of the Ukrainian Jews: *Ukraina bez yevreev* (Ukraine without Jews) and *Staryj uchitel'* (The Old Teacher).

Grossman's literary preoccupation with this theme, however, was delicate in general. The official party line did not tolerate any particularism among victims nor could the Ukrainian collaboration be mentioned. *Ukraina bez yevreev* could therefore not appear in → Russian and was published in the Soviet Union only in a Yiddish translation in the newspaper *Eynikayt* (Unity) of the → Jewish Anti-Fascist Committee (*Yevrejskij antifashistskij komitet*; JAC). The American Zionist newspaper *Jewish Frontier* published an English translation.

In August 1944, Grossman reported as an eyewitness on the Red Army's arrival at the site of the → Treblinka concentration camp, already dismantled by the SS. His disturbing text *Treblinskyj ad* (The Hell of Treblinka) was able to be published in 1944 in the literary journal *Znamya* (The Banner), which was affiliated with the → military. A Russian book edition appeared in 1945, and only one year later, the *Izdatelstvo inostrannoy literatury* (Foreign Languages Publishing House) even produced a German translation. This text was the first eyewitness report on a German extermination camp and was used as evidence in the → Nuremberg trials. However, publication was not possible in the Soviet Union until immediately after the war. Representations of the Nazi mass murders committed against European Jews were increasingly suppressed in official Soviet culture or even prohibited. Not until after Stalin's death could the text be included once again in a volume of stories, which appeared in the Moscow Military Press in 1958.

Grossman had already taken part in the liberation of the Majdanek concentration camp in July 1944. Nevertheless, it was the military writer Konstantin Simonov (1915–1979), who towed the party line, who was commissioned to write a report on Majdanek for the journal *Krasnaya zvezda*. Simonov followed the official phraseology. To be sure, he described the Nazis' cruelty in the most somber tones, but he suppressed the Jewish affiliation of most of the victims. After the war, Grossman challenged Simonov, in vain, to write a text on the murder of the Jews in Majdanek. For his part, as chief editor of the journal *Novyj mir* (New World), in 1948 Simonov made ideological corrections to Grossman's book *Stalingrad*, corresponding to the schematic worldview of the party leadership. Thus, Grossman had to distinguish between the American people and the US government; Hitler was not to be compared with Napoleon, and no reports should be made on corruption in the kolkhozes [9. 221].

Together with Ilya Ehrenburg (→ [The] Thaw), Grossman began work on the *Chornaya Kníga* ("The Complete Black Book of Russian Jewry," 2003) which was to document the murder of Jews in the territory of the Soviet Union. The sponsoring institution behind this book project was the JAC. When the printing plates were ready in 1947, publication was forbidden at the last moment, in the wake of Stalin's antisemitic campaign against → Cosmopolitans. The complete version did not appear until 1980 in Jerusalem. Grossman wrote many contributions to the *Chornaya Kníga*, and contributed a chapter on the murder of the Jews of Berdychiv.

In the latter half of the 1950s, Grossman worked on his magnum opus *Zhizn' i sud'ba* (1959; "Life and Fate," 2011), which can be read as a continuation of his first Stalingrad novel. In this period, he lived together with the wife of the poet Nikolaj Zabolotsky; however, both returned to their respective families in 1958. Grossman incorporated his private life into the plot of *Zhizn' i sud'ba* (hereafter we use the English title, *Life and Fate*).

In his last novel *Vsyo techyot...* (1970; "Forever Flowing," 1972), which he had begun in 1955, Grossman criticizes the Soviet system, as he had already done in *Life and Fate*, and describes Lenin as the originator of the Communist terror. He thereby contravened the official version under Khrushchev, which had criticized Stalinism merely as a cult of personality and a deviation from the principles of Leninism. He also took up another taboo subject by describing the famine in the Ukraine and Southern Russia in 1931/1932, which had claimed millions of victims, and was later referred to as *Holodomor*.

In 1961, Grossman took a trip to Armenia, and wrote a report *Dobro vam* (1967; All the Best). Grossman was inspired by an Armenian greeting formula for his title. In the essay, he makes a connection between the genocide carried out against the Armenians and the Holocaust. The text was first published posthumously in 1965, in a censured version, in the journal *Literaturnaya Armeniya* (Literary Armenia).

2. *Life and Fate*

The book *Life and Fate* depicts, with epic scope, events during the Second World War. The focus is on the Battle of Stalingrad, but subplots lead the reader to German concentration and extermination camps, to the Gulag, and the Soviet hinterland, among other locations. In addition to the Second World War, the central themes include the Holocaust, as well as Stalinist persecutions and their effects on daily life in the Soviet Union. The main characters of the storyline are the members of the Schaposchnikov family.

In *Life and Fate*, the Battle of Stalingrad is not depicted as an isolated event. Instead, Grossman interprets the war of destruction in the city on the Volga as a consequence of complete moral collapse, manifested equally in the Stalinist terror and in the Holocaust. For Grossman, Stalinism and Nazism are related phenomena. Nevertheless, in *Life and Fate* he is careful not to attest the proximity of the two systems as a narrator, but puts this thought in the mouth of an SS officer. For Grossman, Stalingrad, lying in ruins, becomes a metaphor for a destroyed spiritual landscape. He thereby turns away from the thematic orientation of his war

Wassily Grossman (1905–1964)

reporting of 1941 and 1942, which was still oriented toward the opposition between the progressive Soviet state and barbaric Nazi Germany, and was underlaid with heroic pathos.

However, he remained faithful to the realistic style of the great novelists of the 19th century. *Life and Fate* also shows clearly autobiographical features. Since Grossman's second wife Olga Guber was not willing to receive another person in their confined common Moscow apartment, he hesitated to fetch his mother from Berdychiv to the relatively safe capital, thereby sealing her fate. The anniversary of her death in an SS massacre was an important date for Grossman, on which he engaged in an intense conversation with his mother. In 1950 and 1961, he wrote long letters to the murdered woman on the anniversary of her death: "Your awful fate is the fate of humankind in an inhuman age. All my life, I have maintained the belief that all that is good, honorable, and generous in me – as well as my love – comes from you" (cited in [3. 615f.]). In *Life and Fate*, there is a long letter from a Jewish mother, crammed into a ghetto by the Germans, to her son, who is safe.

Grossman intentionally fashioned his novel after the model of Tolstoy's *Vojna i mir* (1868/1869; "War and Peace," 1886), the only novel he was able to read during the street battles in Stalingrad, as he wrote in a letter to his daughter. As in Tolstoy, the individual biographies in *Life and Fate* are inseparably tied to the circumstances of the time. World history and life destiny are entangled within the individual episodes, leaving little room for individual actions. The war appears as a vast chaos of isolated acts of war. The tragic, in the ancient sense of the term, was of central importance for the creation of both authors.

In Grossman, the tragic manifests itself especially in his depiction of the Holocaust. In *Life and Fate*, the gas chambers of the extermination camps are described from an internal perspective. A female childless doctor takes a small boy by the hand in the gas chamber and and accompanies him into death. Her last thought is: "I've become a mother" [1. xxxiv]. Moreover, in the face of the Holocaust, the doctor finds her way to a Jewish self-understanding: previously, she had defined herself solely by means of a professional self-image.

A locus of the resistance in the Battle of Stalingrad is depicted in a similarly tragic way. House no. 6/1, situated close to the Soviet front lines, is given high symbolic value in the novel's plot. The Red Army soldiers who have entrenched themselves in the house, which is in a tactically important location, realize that their death is certain. Grossman depicts the commander in House no. 6/1 as a charismatic figure. Hierarchy matters little to him. His soldiers are on an equal level with him; they all eat and sleep in the same space and renounce military ritual. When their superiors hear of this, they send a political commissar to the house, in order to restore military discipline. The heroic occupants of House no. 6/1 are killed on precisely the same day when the commissar sends off his denunciatory report on the ringleader. Grossman leaves the reader with no doubt that true communism already exists in House no. 6/1, while others are only concerned about their privileges and ensuring their careers. Thus, the soldiers die in anticipation of the communist ideal. However, the commissar is also caught up in the machinery that he himself drives forward with his indictments: he is captured and tortured. The circuit of slander is completed, and all the characters in the plot suffer a tragic fate, conditioned by delusion and heroism.

Grossman describes war as a situation in which social contradictions come to the fore with particular clarity. Like Tolstoy, he depicts individual persons from an alienated perspective. Each character represents a specific idea, the validity of which is measured against the demands of reality. Like Tolstoy, Grossman reveals his political beliefs in programmatic digressions. With a narrator's authority, he lays claims to a truth that is above all ideologies. In *Life and Fate*, this is the belief in kindness and friendship.

3. Publication history

In 1950, Alexander Tvardovski (1910–1971) was named editor-in-chief of *Novyj mir*, the most important literary journal of the Soviet Union. Grossman sent him his Stalingrad manuscript, which he had previously published only in extracts; he thus hoped to have the best chances for publication. Tvardovski was impressed by the work's literary quality but harbored doubts about the ideological orientation. He saw three problems: the reality of war was described too darkly; Stalin was not mentioned often enough, and the protagonist should not be a Jew. For the book's publication, Tvardovski sought to win the support of Mikhail Sholokhov, who, as the highly decorated author of the revolutionary epic *Tikhij Don* (1928–1932 and 1937–1940; "And Quiet Flows the Don," 1934), had considerable influence on the cultural scene. Yet Sholokhov spoke out unconditionally against leaving a subject so important for official Soviet patriotism to a Jewish author. Tvardovski finally succeeded in publishing the novel; yet Grossman had to make some changes. The Jewish protagonist faded into the background, the role of the positive hero was taken over by a Russian, and a special chapter was devoted to Stalin. Borrowing from a famous quotation from Molotov, the novel was given the innocuous title *Za pravoe delo* (For a Just Cause) and appeared in 1952 in four editions of *Novyj mir* [10. 30].

When Grossman had completed *Life and Fate* in 1960, he offered the manuscript to the journal *Znamya*, which followed the orthodox party line more strictly than *Novyj mir*, but in 1954 had published Ilja Ehrenburg's novel *The Thaw*, whose title became symbol of de-Stalinization under Khrushchev. The chief editor Vadim Kozhevnikov, himself a war author who followed the party line, passed the manuscript on directly to the Literary Committee of the Central Committee of the Communist Party. There, it was soon realized that *Life and Fate* had to be considered much more dubious than, for instance, Boris Pasternak's novel *Doktor Zhivago* (1957; "Doctor Zhivago," 1958), which had triggered a vehement debate only two years previously: after Pasternak won the Nobel Prize for Literature, the Soviet authorities unleashed a smear campaign that finally forced the poet to renounce the distinction. The regime had indeed prevailed in its demands, but the prestige of the Soviet Union had suffered, on both the domestic and the international level as a result of the campaign against the famous author. A repetition of such a fiasco could not be risked. The Soviet secret police, or KGB, therefore decided to take the unprecedented step of seizing Grossman's work on February 14, 1961. With Grossmann present, three KGB agents searched his apartment and confiscated a copy of the novel. Three other copies were found among relatives and acquaintances. Two official reports were later presented on the novel's ideological harmfulness.

Grossman reacted to this in 1962 with a strongly-phrased letter to Nikita Khrushchev, in which he designated his novel as a contribution to de-Stalinzation: "Why was my book, which answers the urgent questions of the Soviet people, and contains no lie nor slander, but only truth, pain, and love for mankind, forbidden?" (cited in [3. 602]). A few months later, Grossman received a phone call from the Kremlin: he was to discuss the matter with Mikhail Suslov, chief ideologue of the Communist Party. The conversation was fruitless. Suslov admonished Grossman to return to his politically reliable early work and not to turn away from

Soviet society. The novel *Life and Fate* could be published "in two or three hundred years" [11. 68].

Grossman had hidden two other copies of *Life and Fate* with distant acquaintances. In the 1970s, the atomic physicist Andrei Sakharov helped to produce a microfilm of the manuscript, which was smuggled out of the Soviet Union. *Life and Fate* appeared in Russian in 1980 in a publishing house for exiles in Lausanne, and was quickly translated into the most important European languages. Not until 1988, during Perestroika, could Grossman's novel be published in the Soviet Union.

4. Influence

Grossman's themes were taken up by other Soviet artists. Thus, in 1967 the director Aleksandr Askol'dov shot a film entitled *Kommissar'* (The Commissar), based on motifs from Grossman's story *V gorode Berdicheve* (1934; In the Town of Berdichev). The film describes how a very pregnant female commissar finds shelter with a poor Jewish family during the Russian Civil War. After the child's birth, the family retreats with the commissar into the cellar during an attack by the Whites. The father conceals the family's fear with a common dance, which, however, transforms into a prophetic vision of horror, when the commissar sees the Jewish family march into a concentration camp with the → Star of David. Promptly branded as "anti-Soviet" and prohibited, the film could not be shown in the Soviet Union until 1988.

The prohibition was symptomatic of the tabooization of the Nazi murder of the Jews in the Brezhnev period. In the official discourse, only Soviet citizens could be named categorically as victims. A specifically Jewish culture of remembrance with regard to the Holocaust was excluded. This was manifested, above all, in the difficulties that confronted various artists in the 1960s who concerned themselves with this topic.

Thus, Yevgeny Yevtuschenko was criticized because of his poem → *Babi Yar*, as was Dmitri Shostakovich, who set this poem to music in his 13th symphony. The film director Mikhail Romm was also not able to film any explicit sequences on the Holocaust in his documentary film *Obyknovennyj fashizm* (1965, The Usual Fascism).

In the West, because of his narrative depiction of the Holocaust and the Stalinist terror, Grossman attracted attention from those historians who studied the similarities between Nazism and Stalinism. The French historian François Furet (1927–1997), for instance, attributed great importance to Grossman in the depiction of Soviet communism's potential for violence [8. 469–472]. Grossman was a welcome witness for Furet, since, with his thesis of the kinship of communism and fascism, he corroborated the theory of totalitarianism of Carl Joachim Friedrich and Zbigniew Brzeziński in the 1950s. The historian Henry Rousso (b. 1954) also refers to Grossman; Timothy Snyder (b. 1969) draws upon Grossman in his book *Bloodlands* (2010).

Grossman had significant influence on the philosopher Emmanuel Lévinas (→ Alterity). Like Grossman, Lévinas was also marked by the catastrophes of the war. Nevertheless, both authors believed in the possibility of morality after → Auschwitz. Grossman formulated this post-traumatic *credo quia absurdum* in various passages of *Life and Fate*. Lévinas read the novel in the early 1980s. The Jewish philosopher adopted the nucleus of Grossman's narrative interpretation of history, which also has an ethical point: there is neither God nor the Good, but only kindness. Thus, a character in the novel *Life and Fate* declares: "I saw the sufferings of the peasantry with my own eyes – and yet collectivization was carried out in the name of Good. I don't believe in your 'Good'. I believe in human kindness" [1. 13].

In addition to the treatise on kindness, Lévinas singles out a scene at the end of the novel, which takes place after the victory of the Soviet troops at Stalingrad. Here, German prisoners of war are forced to clean out a cellar and recover the corpses rotting in it. While an officer suffers noticeably in this situation, a woman who particularly detests the Germans, initially takes delight in his suffering. Finally, however, she hands him her last remaining piece of bread. Lévinas is struck by this unusual act, since it shows that even in hatred, there is a mercy that is stronger than hatred. There are acts of foolish, senseless kindness [14. 89].

Bibliography

Sources

[1] V. Grossman, Life and Fate, trans. by R. Chandler, London 2011. [2] H.-J. Schmitt/G. Schramm (eds.), Sozialistische Realismuskonzeptionen. Dokumente zum 1. Allunionskongress der Sowjetschriftsteller, Frankfurt am Main 1974. [2a] Soviet Writers' Congress 1934. The Debate on Socialist Realism and Modernism in the Soviet Union, H. G. Scott (ed.), London 1977.

Secondary literature

[3] M. Anissimov, Vassili Grossman. Un écrivain de combat, Paris 2012. [4] A. Beevor, A Writer at War. Vasily Grossman with the Red Army 1941–1945, London, 2005. [5] K. Clark, Ehrenburg and Grossman. Two Cosmopolitan Jewish Writers Reflect on Nazi Germany at War, in: Kritika 10 (2009), 607–628. [6] F. Ellis, Vasiliy Grossman. The Genesis and Evolution of a Russian Heretic, Oxford/Providence 1994. [7] S. Fitzpatrick/M. Geyer (eds.), Beyond Totalitarianism. Stalinism and Nazism Compared, Cambridge (MA) 2009. [8] F. Furet, The Passing of an Illusion. The Idea of Communism in the Twentieth Century, trans. by D. Furet, Chicago 1999. [9] C. Garrard/J. Garrard, The Life and Fate of Vasily Grossman, Barnsley 2012. [10] S. Lipkin, Stalingrad Vasiliya Grossmana [Vassili Grossman's Stalingrad], Ann Arbor 1986. [11] S. Lipkin/A. Berzer, "Zhizn' i sud'ba" Vasilya Grossmana [Vassili Grossman's "Life and Fate"], Mos-

cow 1990. [12] S. Markish, Le cas Grossman, Paris 1983. [13] A. S. Nakhimovsky, Russian-Jewish Literature and Identity. Jabotinsky, Babel, Grossman, Galich, Roziner, Markish, Baltimore 1992. [14] J. Robbins (ed.), Is It Righteous to Be? Interviews with Emmanuel Levinas, Stanford 2001. [15] K. Sherman, Wassili Grossman's Treblinka, in: Brick 82 (2009), 138–146. [16] J. Zarusky, Wassili Grossmans "Leben und Schicksal." Zur Entstehung und historischen Konzeption eines Jahrhundertromans, in: F. Anton/L. Luks (eds.), Deutschland, Russland und das Baltikum. Beiträge zu einer Geschichte wechselvoller Beziehungen. Cologne et al. 2005, 245–276.

ULRICH M. SCHMID, ST. GALLEN

Star of David

Symbol comprising a six-pointed star, in widespread use in various cultures since Antiquity, which became a Jewish emblem (Hebr. *magen David*) in the Late Middle Ages. During the 19th and 20th centuries, the Star of David gradually developed into a symbol of affiliation to the Jewish people; it became the national symbol when the State of Israel was founded in 1948.

The six-pointed star (hexagram) is known in many cultures as a decorative, magic, or symbolic element, along with the five-pointed star. It is attested within Jewish cultures beginning in the first millennium BCE but did not yet have any specifically Jewish significance then. The numerous theories on the ancient history of a "Jewish" Star of David, like the attempts to link it with personages like King David or Bar Kokhba, or to explain it as a symbol composed of two Greek deltas, mostly originate from the early 20th century and cannot be proven.

Beginning in the Late Middle Ages, the six-pointed star was increasingly perceived as a Jewish symbol and referred to as the *magen David* (shield of David). From the

13th century onward, Jews often consciously used it as an emblem, although not yet as an exclusive Jewish symbol. It was used to decorate seals, cards, and flags, as well as Bible manuscripts and magical texts. Beginning in the 15th century, it became increasingly significant as a magical symbol of protection; around this time it began to replace the → menorah as an emblem of Jewish affiliation. In the early modern era, the Star of David was also used as the symbol of goldsmiths, in Kabbalistic and theosophical interpretations, as a printer's sign, and as a symbol in sacred art.

The appearance of the six-pointed star in sacred art accelerated its development into a Jewish symbol. From the end of the 18th century, the increasing use of the Star of David in → synagogue architecture, on Jewish huppah stones and cult objects like seder cups, havdalah cups, Torah covers and pointers, Hannukah menorahs, and bookstands ran parallel to Jewish → emancipation. In this period of increasing secularization, the Star of David became a visible distinguishing mark of Judaism, analogous to the cross for the Christians as a symbol of religious affiliation, without partaking in the religious content represented by the cross.

The evolution of the Star of David on huppah stones (→ Marriage) reflects the close interconnection between religious, social, and cultural aspects, which were being recalibrated in the course of secularization. The huppah stones or wedding stones in widespread use among Ashkenazi Jews were usually located inside synagogues or on the outer walls of synagogues; the young couple would break a wineglass or other fragile object on it during the marriage ceremony. The broken glass was supposed to bring them luck; hence, the words *mazal tov* (lit. "good star") was often engraved on the huppah stone. Similar to other customs, the Star of David had an ambivalent significance on the huppah stones. Alongside its increasing perception as a sign of Jewish affiliation,

it was also considered to have magical properties. Thus, it became subject to criticism as one of the superstitious aspects of Judaism, both in the context of longstanding anti-Judaism and from proponents of the → Haskalah (→ Emden-Eybeschütz-Controversy). Enlightened Jewish religious reformers saw to it that from 1836 onward, huppah stones were no longer placed in synagogue walls.

With the emergence of the Zionist movement at the end of the 19th century, the *magen David* increasingly became a political and nationalist emblem. Its dissemination as a Jewish, albeit not clearly religious symbol allowed it to be charged with a Zionist meaning expressing the hope for the establishment of a Jewish state. The Star of David has been used in various artistic manifestations for Zionist purposes since 1881. The Zionist weekly paper *Die Welt* (1897–1914), published by Theodor Herzl, had it on the masthead from its first issue of June 4, 1897. A few weeks later, the Star of David was used as the official symbol of Zionism at the First Zionist Congress in → Basel.

In the period of National Socialism, the Star of David became an antisemitic symbol, in subversion of its Jewish significance, under which Jews were excluded, expelled, and murdered. It was printed on anti-Jewish texts, pamphlets, and placards and smeared across the facades and windows of Jewish establishments and businesses. Its use as the "Judenstern" which went back to the "yellow patch" with which the Jews were distinguished in the Middle Ages (→ Dress Regulations), served the purpose of stigmatization. The two were now combined into a single symbol; Jews were forced to attach it to their clothing.

With the foundation of the State of Israel in 1948, the Star of David was finally incorporated as the national Jewish symbol. On a white background, bordered by two blue stripes (→ Tekhelet), associated with the blue tassels of the *tallit* (prayer shawl), it

The American heavyweight boxer Max Baer (l.) fighting Joe Louis (1935). Though not Jewish himself, Baer regularly fought wearing a Star of David – also in his knockout victory over Max Schmeling in June, 1933 (→ Boxing)

is at the center of the Israeli flag. An early design was the banner of the First Zionist Congress in Basel in 1897, initially without the star, but on the resolution of the 1933 Zionist World Congress, with the star. This version was finally introduced as the flag of the State of Israel.

Bibliography

[1] G. S. Oegema, Zur Erforschung der Geschichte des Davidschildes. Eine kritische Betrachtung, in: Frankfurter Judaistische Beiträge 20 (1993), 175–209. [2] G. S. Oegema, The History of the Shield of David. The Birth of a Symbol, Frankfurt am Main et al. 1996. [3] W. G. Plaut, The Magen David. How the Six-Pointed Star Became an Emblem for the Jewish People, Washington D.C. 1991. [4] G. Scholem, Das Davidschild. Geschichte eines Symbols, Frankfurt am Main ²2010.

GERBERN S. OEGEMA, MONTREAL

[The] Star of Redemption

Der Stern der Erlösung (1921; "The Star of Redemption," 1971) is the magnum opus of the German Jewish philosopher Franz Rosenzweig (1886–1929). The title alludes to the Star of David, not however as a symbol of the Jewish people but in the sense of the ontological truth of biblical faith. Rosenzweig ascribed different but complementary roles to Judaism and Christianity in the anticipatory realization of the last truth of human existence, which he identified with the term *Erlösung* (redemption). The re-adoption of traditional religious practice and faith by Rosenzweig, who had grown up in an assimilated family, became emblematic of religious renewal within German Jewish life in the years preceding the Holocaust.

1. Introduction
2. Franz Rosenzweig
3. *Der Stern der Erlösung*

1. Introduction

Der Stern der Erlösung is a systematic work through and through. Rosenzweig reconceptualizes the titular symbolism of the Star of David as a layered triadic structure. The structure of the text, accordingly, is arranged in three steps: "Die Elemente" ("The elements"), "Die Bahn" ("The course"), and "Die Gestalt" ("The configuration"). To each of these is assigned a historic-philosophical situation, "Die immerwährende Vorwelt" ("The ever-enduring proto-cosmos"), "Die Allzeiterneuernde Welt" ("The always-renewed cosmos"), and "Die Ewige Überwelt" ("The eternal hyper-cosmos"). Each part is in turn divided into three "books." The telos of *Stern der Erlösung* is a specific intellectual attitude shared by a liturgical community – the church and the synagogue – and expressed in the biblical categories of creation, revelation, and redemption. Revelation, the central concept of Rosenzweig's system, takes place within time and is thus not accessible to reason, which recognizes timeless essences only. All the same, this conception is not directed against reason but merely limits its applicability. In Rosenzweig's eyes, philosophical reason and faith are, when understood correctly, complementary. As a philosophical project, *Der Stern der Erlösung*'s most important objective was to develop a new relationship between theology and → philosophy in which both retain their integrity while recognizing their mutual dependence.

By placing the revelation at the center of his work, Rosenzweig recognized in transmitted religion a theocentric faith of enduring existential significance. While assimilated Jews of his generation had overall abandoned this kind of idea, Rosenzweig understood the Jews – whom he remarkably referred to as "the synagogue" – as a meta-historical community. Their spiritual and intellectual life unfolded within liturgical time, leading it to redemption – beyond the struggles and delusions of history. The synagogue, blissfully situated in the lap of eternity, formed a "star of redemption" that exhorted the church not to forget that the divine task was to lead history beyond itself and to the eschaton, the redemption. In Rosenzweig's eyes, the Christian church had grown out of a covenant that was just as valid as the covenant God entered into with the Israelites. Both are mutually dependent in that they, each in its own way, implement God's plan for salvation: unfolding redemption within human history. In light of his meta-historic view of Israel's spiritual destiny, it is not surprising that Rosenzweig remained reserved when it came to Zionism and its aim of the Jews' secular return into history.

2. Franz Rosenzweig

Franz Rosenzweig, born in Kassel in 1886, came from a prominent, assimilated German-Jewish family. His maternal grandfather, Samuel Meyer Ehrenberg (1773–1853), teacher and headmaster of the Samson-Schule in Wolfenbüttel, was a respected figure in the Jewish educational landscape of the first half of the 19th century and supported the values of the Enlightenment as well as integration into German culture. Rosenzweig's father was a successful businessman and also active in city life in Kassel.

Franz Rosenzweig began studying medicine in 1905 but from 1907 onward dedicated himself entirely to philosophy in Freiburg and Berlin. One of his teachers was his older cousin Hans Ehrenberg (1883–1958), also of Jewish origin and co-founder of the Bekennende Kirche. Through Rudolf Ehrenberg (1884–1969), another cousin, Rosenzweig made the acquaintance of Eugen Rosenstock-Huessy (1888–1973), who became a very close friend. Like Rosenzweig, Rosenstock was the son of assimilated Jewish parents but had converted to Christianity early in life.

As a historian of philosophy, Rosenzweig was at first attracted by the Neo-Hegelianism of the 1900s. He wrote his dissertation under Friedrich Meinecke in 1912, on the subject of Hegel's philosophy of the state. Soon, however, Rosenzweig came to believe that Hegel's understanding of history could not overcome the emerging philosophical relativism, instead strengthening

Franz Rosenzweig (1886–1929)

it. Encouraged by his friends Ehrenberg and Rosenstock, he turned increasingly to "Offenbarungsglaube," faith based on revelation, which believed in revelation as a historical fact, understood as the experience of divine discourse that offered a continuous existential option.

In 1913, Rosenzweig moved to Leipzig, not least in order to hear Rosenstock's lectures. The philosophical-theological discussions between Rosenzweig and Rosenstock culminated in the "Leipziger Nachtgespräch," conducted in private in the company of Rudolf Ehrenberg. The confrontation of philosophical relativism and Rosenstock's belief in the revelation plunged Rosenzweig into a deep crisis. He would later write to his teacher Friedrich Meinecke: "In 1913 something happened to me for which the only fitting name, if I ever were to speak of it, is collapse. I suddenly found myself on an expanse of rubble" [3. vol. 2, 679]. Subsequently Rosenzweig considered, as he himself recalls, to have himself baptized. However, in the autumn of 1913 he attended an Orthodox Yom Kippur service in Berlin, probably his first encounter with traditional Jewish religious practice. After the service he wrote to Rudolf Ehrenberg on October 31, 1913, that he did not consider baptism necessary any more: "I shall remain a Jew" [3. vol. 1, 133]. In research, it is disputed whether Rosenzweig's affirmation of Judaism actually goes back to a religious experience. In any case, he did not refer to it as the basis of his religious philosophy.

In the winter semester of 1913/1914, Rosenzweig began his studies in Berlin in order to gain comprehensive understanding of Judaism, with among others Hermann Cohen (→ Concept of God), who was teaching at the → Hochschule für die Wissenschaft des Judentums after his retirement. Rosenzweig's first essay on religious topics, "Atheistische Theologie" (written in 1914, published posthumously), already contained the argument that theology, and consequently religious faith, had to start with divine revelation, with the fact that a transcendent God communicated with humans [4. 697].

Because of the First World War, Rosenzweig interrupted his studies. He served in Belgium at first and from 1916 onward on the Macedonian front. During this time, he maintained a detailed correspondence with Rosenstock, who encouraged him to clarify the theological premises for his profession of Judaism. On postcards from the front, which he sent to his mother for safekeeping, Rosenzweig finally wrote down the manuscript of *Stern der Erlösung*, which clearly shows Rosenstock's influence in places. After finishing the book, Rosenzweig gradually endeavored to incorporate more extra-liturgical aspects of Judaism into his life and thought, from observing → Shabbat through keeping a kosher kitchen (→ Kashrut) to studying the Torah. His relationship with the → mitsvot, on the other hand, was idiosyncratic. Unlike Orthodox Jews, he did not accept the mitsvot based on rabbinical authority. His approach to the "law" was, as he explained in an open letter of 1923 to Martin Buber (→ Dialogue), to encourage every Jew to explore individually the sacramental and existential options of the mitsvot in order to determine which of these rules he personally was willing to observe. In this letter, which he called *Die Bauleute*, he developed his position with reference to a rabbinical commentary on Isaiah: "'And all your children shall be disciples of the LORD; And great shall be the happiness of your children' (Isa 54:13) – do not read banayikh: your children, but bonayikh: your builders" [4. 699]. Each generation, Rosenzweig held, had the option, indeed the task, to create the law anew for itself. Rosenzweig discovered a similar approach to the → Talmud and the Torah. It was not necessary to profess the faith beforehand in order to study the classical Jewish sources; all that was needed was an open, dialogic mindset. This idea found philosophical expression in the 1925 essay "Das neue Denken" ("The New Thinking," 1999) [4. 139–161]. It discusses the act of speech as the fundamental organon of truth. While Western philosophy had been guided by reason as the most important key of time-less and universal truth from the pre-Socratics until the present, new thinking believed truth – be it divine or human – to have been revealed in an intersubjective dialogue that takes place in a concrete space-time constellation of specific individuals each with their own respective biography.

From 1920 onward, Rosenzweig developed this dialogic conception of Jewish study in the program of Jewish adult education in Frankfurt am Main that he called the → Freies Jüdisches Lehrhaus. Attending this "Lehrhaus" – a translation of the Hebrew *bet ha-midrash* (→ Talmud Torah) alluding to the fact that the synagogue was also a place in which to study sacred texts – was "free" but not free of charge; on the contrary, Rosenzweig insisted on a comparatively high enrollment fee to ensure that the students took their studies seriously. It was free in the sense that all questions were permitted. Lectures were given by, among others, the Frankfurt rabbi Nehemias Anton Nobel and Martin Buber. Among the younger teachers were Siegfried Kracauer (→ Film), Ernst Simon, Nahum N. Glatzer, and Erich Fromm. Rosenzweig perceived contemporary Jews as being more or less alienated from the conceptual and rhetorical world of classical Judaism and consequently considered all questions that might be brought to the study of the sources to be legitimate. Only the willingness to listen to the answers emanating from these sources was necessary. In 1923, Rosenzweig was awarded the status of rabbi by Leo Baeck (1873 –1956; → Leo Baeck Institute), together with the title *morenu* (our teacher).

In order to open up this dialogue with the Hebrew Bible (→ Tanakh) as the founding source of Judaism, Rosenzweig together with Martin Buber embarked on a new translation of the Bible into German (→ Bible Translation). The guiding principle of their translation was that the Bible should be "heard" and not merely read. The auditive quality of → Hebrew with all its tonal inflections, its cadence, and its semantic force was to be expressed in German. To this end, Rosenzweig and Buber felt compelled to change individual German expressions, and even to reinvent them to a certain degree, in order to give a new voice to the spoken word of the Hebrew Bible. They also created, by reflecting their understanding of the texts through classical Jewish → commentary, not only a unique but also decidedly *Jewish* translation. Even on his deathbed in 1929, Rosenzweig read the galley proofs of his translation of the book of Isaiah; afterwards Buber continued to work on the translation on his own, completing it only a few years before his own death in 1965.

Rosenzweig applied similar principles to his translation of the Hebrew poetry of the Spanish-Jewish philosopher Judah ha-Levi (→ Kuzari), with whom he felt a deep spiritual affinity. In his afterword to the *Sechzig Hymnen und Gedichte des Jehuda Halevi* (1924; an extended version was published in 1927 under the title *Zweiundneunzig Hymnen und Gedichte des Jehuda Halevi*) he discussed not only the theological commentary on the poems but also the challenge presented by translating the Bible and sacred texts. The translator's task, he explained, was not to present the text in a form that would be easily understood by the reader but rather to change the target language in such a way that it would absorb the specific qualities of the source language. Consequently, he tried to transfer the phonology, the "units of breath" of ha-Levi's Hebrew into German in a similar way to that which he practiced in his Bible translation regarding the "Geprochenheit" (spokenness) of Biblical Hebrew. The ultimate aim of the translation, he held, was the redeeming harmonization of all languages.

3. *Der Stern der Erlösung*

The epistemological starting point of the philosophical system Rosenzweig formulates in *Der Stern der Erlösung* is the assumption that reason and existence are not identical. In contrast to the tradition stretching from the pre-Socratics to Hegel, he argues that reality does not correspond to the rules of reason but that existence precedes reason and remains independent of the latter. A "new theological rationalism" was to be established in the cooperation between the previously antagonistic disciplines of theology and philosophy [2. 102]. Rosenzweig recognizes that there was occasionally a kind of truce "between the two hostile powers" [2. 6]. In the modern era, it was above all Hegel's attempt at establishing an inner connection between philosophy and theology that failed, insofar as reason ultimately subsumed the revealed doctrines of religious faith. In agreement with Kierkegaard, Rosenzweig insists that true religious faith is characterized by the individual's existential longing for redemption and divine love. Thus, faith cannot accept the Hegelian view that philosophy "involuntarily confirms the truth of what revelation has declared" [2. 7]. Rosenzweig elucidates the Danish philosopher's protest by inverting Hegel's theory and states that divine revelation fulfils the promise of philosophy. Philosophy, Rosenzweig says enigmatically, is transformed into "in a manner of speaking the 'Old Testament' of theology" [2. 108].

The development of philosophy and theology as understood by Rosenzweig led both to a dead end from which they can escape only through mutual assistance. After the end of Hegelian philosophy, philosophy would be forced to find an Archimedean point outside of the "cognitive world" [2. 9], a world that does not know contingent, autonomous facts. After the internalization of faith in the 19th century, theology, in turn, was lacking an objectively binding link to the truth. Theology needed philosophy for the sake of preserving its founding experience – that is the revelation. Philosophy is thus given the task by Rosenzweig of restoring the *auctoritas* of religious faith. "What was for philosophy a demand in the interests of objectivity, will turn out to be a demand in the interests of subjectivity for theology" [2. 106]. The challenge for both is to remain simultaneously connected to subjectivity while reaching objectivity.

In the case of philosophy, the "bridge" between subjectivity and objectivity is built by the theological concept of revelation. In Rosenzweig's eyes it was a misunderstanding to comprehend revelation as a purely subjective, internal experience. Understood correctly, it is anchored within the concept of creation, in the world in its entirety in which the presence of God manifests itself. "Thus creation has once more to be placed next to the experience of revelation in the full gravity of its substantiality" [2. 103]. By bearing witness to God's active connection with the facts of existence, creation is the *archē* – the first principle – towards which the philosophers should orient their research. "And precisely creation is now the gate through which philosophy enters into the house of theology" [2. 103].

The concept of creation had, however, been almost expunged from modern theology. By reinstating the concept of creation, philosophy restored theology's epistemological inheritance as well as its authority. Once, religious faith had been guaranteed by tradition, the vessel of the very doctrine and knowledge that bore witness to the fundamental "miracles" of the faith. Just like the kindred concept of creation, the concept of miracles went against modern sensibility and was consequently studiously ignored by the theologians of the time. Rosenzweig quotes Goethe's (→ Elective Affinities) maxim that "the authentic miracle [is] belief's dearest child" [2. 108], asking

ironically which true faith could exist without reference to the concept of the miracle.

Philosophy as Rosenzweig understands it reveals the wondrous dimension of existence as creation; meaning that it recognizes "signs" within the existence which point to God's providential relation with the independent "factualities" of being. God, world, and human, the three central "factualities," are not entirely accessible to the conceptual approach of reason. In order to reformulate the relationship between thought and being, Rosenzweig adopted one of Hermann Cohen's (→ Concept of God; → Neo-Kantianism) core ideas. According to this, thinking per se is not *the* origin or *the* principle establishing the existence complete with uniformity and inner coherence; rather, thought achieves unity *with* existence by means of the "correlation" (Cohen). Rosenzweig regarded this insight as a radical break with idealism. "For here for the first time a philosopher who himself still considered himself an 'Idealist' [...] recognized and acknowledged that what confronted reasoning when it set out in order 'purely to create' was not Being but–Nought" [2. 21]. Rosenzweig marks this "Nought," situated beyond the spiritual web of reason, with the prefix "meta-" and consequently uses the terms metalogical, metaethical, and metaphysical. In Rosenzweig's eyes, Cohen's theory of the origin also revealed the dynamics of the encounter between the "Nought" and the elements. As opposed to the "static" logic of the "old thinking" that had dominated philosophy until then, the "new thinking" initiated by Cohen is dynamic. It moves from Nought to Aught and back, establishing a continuous motion between negation and affirmation, proximity and distance, concealment and revelation (in the sense of revealing). The central paradox guiding Rosenzweig's philosophical mediations consists in the "concealed" reality of the elements not being accessible to reason but to experience and to "common sense." Rosenzweig interprets this relationship in the sense that thinking anticipates experience. Unlike Kant, Rosenzweig did not see experience as being limited to the world of phenomena. The "anticipated" experience of a relationship between the elementary factualities of existence – God, world, and human – becomes manifest in the life of faith. In the vocabulary of faith, the triadic interrelations are known as creation (namely, the relation between God and the world), revelation (the relation between God and human), and redemption (the relation, initiated by the revelation, between human and world). The elements thus emerge from their "nothingness" in order to reveal themselves and establish a mutual relationship.

Referred back to the concept of philosophy Rosenzweig extrapolates in the first part of *Stern*, philosophy anticipates the "theological contents" or, more precisely, acts as "a foundation, to demonstrate the precondition on which it rests" [2. 108]. Rosenzweig further elucidates this "Grundlegung" (foundation) by ascribing a primary word to each of the vectors of the dynamism demonstrated by Cohen's theory of the origin: "yes," "no," and "and." The latter here denotes the relation between the thinking spirit and the unknowable differentness of the elements of reality. These primary words, Rosenzweig held, establish the quiet, inaudible structure of language. As mute words they are the language of logic, the foundation and precondition of real language: they constitute the "soundless realm of the Faustian Mothers" and establish "the ideational possibilities of arriving at an understanding" [2. 109]. In the relation between the mute "logic of language and its grammar," that is its audible expression as real language, Rosenzweig recognizes the connection between creation and revelation by means of an analogy [2. 110].

Rosenzweig calls the world as revealed by philosophy the "protocosmos" [2. 110], being the world before its complete illumination by the experience of faith. This protocosmos, he suggests, may be understood as the world of the creation – the world within which the relation between it and God remained mute because it had not yet been touched by the divine revelation to humans that would transform the relation into an apparent and living one.

Insofar as philosophy illuminates the miracle of creation, it restores the *auctoritas* of the experience of faith of the revelation. The miracle once again becomes "belief's dearest child" [2. 108]. Only experience, however, provides the necessary affirmation and proof of the philosophical "prediction." This seemingly circular argument is absolved from the accusation of arbitrariness by the primacy of existence over reason. In order to fulfil what Rosenzweig sketched in the first part, the new thinking is necessary. The second part of *Der Stern der Erlösung* is dedicated to extrapolating this. Epistemologically the new thinking is based within the existential logic of speech: in the common language of true conversation which – in "ecstatic" amazement (Schelling) – absorbs the unfolding facts of reality. In fact, Rosenzweig regards speech as the "organon of revelation" [2. 110]; in the wider sense it becomes the comprehensive fact of experience through which divine revelation becomes believable. To this end, however, a religious community must exist who experience God's revelatory love in anticipation in their liturgical life. The experience of the revelation, Rosenzweig argues in the third part of *Stern*, is not a preferential grace granted to only a limited number of the blessed but a universal promise to be realized at the end of time – or, more precisely, beyond time at the moment of ultimate redemption. This promise draws its force of being through a concrete ontological possibility from the praying community, especially the synagogue and the church. These spiritual forms, which Rosenzweig evaluated as objective sociological essences, generated a "supra-world" that anticipated the kingdom of God in which all of humanity would experience the presence of God.

We could thus refer to Rosenzweig's system as a system of revelation. He projects his vision of a new covenant between theology and philosophy onto the framework of this system. The philosophical cogency of this covenant ultimately rests in the testimony of the praying community and its anticipatory experience of the eschaton in which the universal reality of God's revealing love manifests itself and revelation becomes truth. Rosenzweig noticed, of course, that this kind of affirmation is not genuinely philosophical. In fact, his system rests on a dialogic concept of truth: it must always be truth for someone and is thus of necessity imagined as plural. "Truth ceases to be that which 'is' true and becomes that which wants to be verified as true. The concept of the probation of truth becomes the basic concept of this new epistemology" [4. 158f.]. Maybe Rosenzweig was thinking of this "messianic epistemology" [4. 159] when he wrote that *Der Stern der Erlösung* was not a philosophy of religion or philosophy of Judaism but a Jewish book all the same. It is Jewish in its method, namely its linguistic way of thinking and its recourse to quotations and commentaries, but not in its contents.

Bibliography

Sources

[1] F. Rosenzweig, Der Mensch und sein Werk. Gesammelte Schriften, Vol. 4: Sprachdenken im Übersetzen, Part 1: Jehuda Halevi. Fünfundneunzig Hymnen und Gedichte, ed. by R. N. Rosenzweig, Den Haag 1983; Part 2: Arbeitspapiere zur Verdeutschung der Schrift, ed. by R. Bat Adam, Dordrecht et al. 1984. [2] F. Rosenzweig, The Star of Redemption, trans. by W. W. Hallo, New York et al. 1971. [3] F. Rosenzweig, Der Mensch und sein Werk. Gesammelte

Schriften, Vol. 1: Briefe und Tagebücher, ed. by R. Rosenzweig/E. Rosenzweig-Scheinmann, The Hague 1979. [4] F. Rosenzweig, Der Mensch und sein Werk. Gesammelte Schriften, Vol. 3: Zweistromland. Kleinere Schriften zu Glauben und Denken, ed. by R. and A. Mayer, Dordrecht et al. 1984.

Secondary literature

[5] U. Bieberich, Wenn die Geschichte göttlich wäre. Rosenzweigs Auseinandersetzung mit Hegel, St. Ottilien 1990. [6] M. Bienenstock, Cohen face à Rosenzweig. Débat sur la pensée allemande, Paris 2009. [7] M. Brasser (ed.), Rosenzweig als Leser. Kontexuelle Kommentare zum "Stern der Erlösung," Tübingen 2004. [8] B. Casper, Das dialogische Denken. Eine Untersuchung der religionsphilosophischen Bedeutung Franz Rosenzweigs, Ferdinand Ebners und Martin Bubers, Freiburg im Breisgau et al. 1967. [9] B. Casper, Religion der Erfahrung. Einführung in das Denken Franz Rosenzweigs, Paderborn et al. 2004. [10] H.-J. Görtz, Tod und Erfahrung. Rosenzweigs "erfahrende Philosophie" und Hegels "Wissenschaft der Erfahrung des Bewußtseins," Düsseldorf 1984. [11] P. Mendes-Flohr (ed.), The Philosophy of Franz Rosenzweig, Hanover 1988. [12] S. Mosès, System and Revelation. The Philosophy of Franz Rosenzweig, trans. by C. Tihanyi, Detroit 1992. [13] W. Schmied-Kowarzik (ed.), Franz Rosenzweigs "neues Denken." Internationaler Kongress Kassel 2004, 2 vols., Munich/Freiburg im Breisgau 2006. [14] W. Schmied-Kowarzik, Rosenzweig im Gespräch mit Ehrenberg, Cohen und Buber, Freiburg im Breisgau/Munich 2006.

PAUL MENDES-FLOHR,
CHICAGO/JERUSALEM

Statistics

Over the course of the 19th century, statistical investigations and analyses acquired increasing importance for Jews in Europe and North America. Within the Jewish discourse, they served to register and interpret phenomena of the modern era. In Germany, institutionalized Jewish statistics became established around 1900. These expressed the relevance accorded to statistical findings in the perception of the Jews by that time – whether in the general public, antisemitic agitation, Jewish defense against antisemitism, or among followers of the various Jewish trends, in particular, the Zionist movement.

1. General statistics and Jewish statistics
2. Statistical discourse
3. The Jewish statistics movement
4. Controversies

1. General statistics and Jewish statistics

Ever since the end of the early modern age, data regarding the observation of nature and social life have been collected increasingly systematically. Early statistical surveys covered subjects such as the climate, geography and agriculture, demography, poverty, and crime.

The first official instance of the gathering and use of statistics is regarded as those gathered by the French economist Jean-Baptiste Colbert, who surveyed data of France's commercial activities and compiled them in 1665. In 1683 Elector Friedrich Wilhelm of Brandenburg in Prussia commissioned the first population statistics; in 1719 housing stock and communal finances were statistically surveyed, and in 1778 the price of grain, the flax and tobacco harvests, factories, and shipping as well as trade were all surveyed statistically. These early statistics were usually treated as official secrets and were concealed from the public as much as possible. It was not until the 19th century that statistical data were used as material by the humanities, as well as the social and natural sciences. Statistics were seen as particularly suited to recording the complexity of frequently occurring phenomena and to

discovering patterns in them – modern society was permeated by statistics [15. 1].

The first significant mention of statistics by Jewish scholars occurred in the context of the developing → Wissenschaft des Judentums. In 1823 Leopold Zunz (1794–1886) was still using the term in the sense of the prevailing understanding in the 18th century, wherein statistics were a means of understanding historical processes: "Accordingly, statistics are available only for the duration of infinitely small moments of time (differentials of history), and, conversely, history is the result of an infinite series of statistics" [13. 523]. In this context, Zunz formulated the tasks of the Wissenschaft des Judentums as being the study of the entire people or the sum of its constituting individuals, integrating all aspects of Jewish life. His understanding of statistics was related to the field of historiography that would later be interpreted as social history.

From the second half of the 19th century onward, various Jewish associations and institutions published statistical information concerning their activities. In its bulletin, the → Alliance israélite universelle, founded in 1860, published data on the Jewish education structure and on the schools it maintained in various countries. The → Deutsch-Israelitischer Gemeindebund, established in 1869 as an umbrella organization of the Jewish communities in Germany, published its *Statistisches Jahrbuch* beginning in 1885; it contained extensive data on individual communities, their members, and their budgets. The Jewish → Colonization Association, which existed from 1891 to 1978, published detailed statistics on the colonization projects it sponsored.

Institutionalized "Jewish statistics," however, only emerged towards the end of the 19th century. The field drew on Zunz's approach as well as the further development of the general statistical discourse. Joseph Jacobs (1854–1916) and Alfred Nossig (1864–1943) provided essential initial influences.

Born in Sydney, Jacobs studied in Cambridge (England) and Berlin, made a name for himself as a literary scholar and anthropologist, and moved to New York in 1900, where he worked as one of the editors of the *Jewish Encyclopedia* (→ Encyclopedias) between 1901 and 1906. In the 1880s Jacobs published statistical articles in the → *Jewish Chronicle* and the *Journal of the Anthropological Institute of Great Britain and Ireland*; his *Studies in Jewish Statistics: Social, Vital and Anthropometric* appeared in 1891. Nossig was born in → Lemberg (today Lviv) and, before becoming a staunch Zionist, had been a confirmed champion of Jewish acculturation to Polishness. He developed an interest in the colonization of Palestine years before the First Zionist Congress (→ Basel), publishing his first Zionist text in → Polish in 1887. In the same year he also published *Materialien zur Statistik des jüdischen Stammes*, a collection of population statistics according to country; in 1902 he was the (co-)founder of the Verein für Statistik der Juden (Association for Statistics of the Jews) in Berlin.

Specifically Jewish statistics of Eastern Europe became an established field somewhat later. The sociologist, economist, and statistician Jakob Lestschinksy (1876–1966), above all, focused on this subject. Having grown up near Kyiv, he studied in Switzerland and, after his return to Russia, became interested in Labor Zionism, among other things. After the First World War, he emigrated to Berlin, where he worked as the editor of the *Bleter far yidisher demografye, statistik un ekonomik* (Journal of Jewish demographics, statistics, and economics) from 1923 to 1925. He was also among the initiators of the → YIVO in Vilnius, founding and heading its Economic-Statistical Section in 1926.

2. Statistical discourse

Jewish statisticians usually incorporated superordinate scientific questions from the fields of anthropology, → demography, biology, → medicine, or political economics, or focused primarily on these. In parallel with the scientific and societal debates of the late 19th century, their objective was to describe and evaluate the dramatic shifts in Jewish life in Europe. In view of the demographic, social, and economic developments or upheavals, Jewish statistics centered on migration movements and settlement patterns, professional structures, as well as specific features, whether real or assumed, of the health of Jews.

However, the antisemitic discourse in Germany, which peaked for the first time in the late 1870s, was also dedicated to these topics. In order to provide evidence of their alleged objectivity and scientific approach, antisemites specifically adduced statistical data that appeared to attest to the "abnormal" and "pathological" behavior of the Jewish population. This was intended to explain the failure of → emancipation and → assimilation, which they preemptively insinuated would be impossible to realize.

The censuses carried out in Prussia between 1843 and 1861 already contained tendentious anti-Jewish professional and social statistics entitled "Juden-Tabellen" (Tables of Jews) [14. 87]. In the → Berlin debate on antisemitism during the years from 1879 to 1881, protagonists quoted statistics in order to show the presumed disproportionate influence of Judaism, or to warn against the dangers of Jewish immigrants pouring in from Eastern Europe. Two of the four main demands of the antisemitic petition submitted to Reich Chancellor Otto von Bismarck urged him to reinstate the official statistics on the Jewish population and to prohibit further Jewish immigration. Jews, in turn, used statistics to refute these claims. One instance of this is *Die Fabel von der jüdischen Masseneinwanderung*, a paper published in 1880 by the physician, statistician, and Berlin city councilor Salomon Neumann (1819–1908), a close confidant of

Zunz and founder of the Zunz Foundation, who had already made a significant contribution to the methodological improvement of the previous census of 1861.

In spite of their opposing objectives, Jews and antisemites appear to have agreed that statistical data made significant conclusions concerning modern mass society possible. In perceiving and interpreting the modern age on the basis of statistics, both sides focused less on the individual and more on the collective. Arthur Ruppin (1876–1943), who became known as a political economist, sociologist, and demographer before joining the Zionist Organization in 1905 and assuming the leadership of the → Palestine Office a few years later, was greatly in favor of this means of gathering insights. In his paper *Die Juden der Gegenwart*, published in 1904, he stated: "It is improbable that one will be able to say anything for certain from individual observation. Only mass observation provides the opportunity of arriving at an objective conclusion" [10. 195]. Yet this practice also shifted the standards of causal explanation. For instance, interpretations based on statistical arguments marginalized the factors influenced by an individual's morality while they elevated social factors, as well as anatomy and even racial-biological criteria, to dominating research characteristics.

Followers of the Zionist movement, as well as its Jewish opponents who wished to assimilate, ascribed great significance to statistics. Around the turn of the 20th century, both camps began to focus on the theory of degeneracy and adduced all manner of data: on birth and death rates, professional patterns among Jews, the distribution of certain diseases, and the number of suicides. In June 1902, *Die Welt*, the main publication of the Zionist movement, featured the headline: "Ist das jüdische Volk degeneriert?" (Are the Jewish People Degenerate?). The article opened with the statement: "That Jewry is degenerating is not only adduced by assimilationists to buttress their point of view, but, strangely, it is also believed by many Zionists." The author, however, vehemently rejected the presumed susceptibility of Jews to certain illnesses, such as neurasthenia or diabetes mellitus: "In order for such a conclusion to be permissible, one would have to, at the very least, provide proof that the spread of these ailments increases among us from one generation to the next, and that the increase represents a greater percentage among us than among non-Jews." There was, he added, not a single convincing statistic to back this up. He altogether rejected as unscientific the thesis that Jews were inclined to degeneracy because such a degenerative process would have had to have started 18 centuries previously [6]. Those contributing to the discussion, in any case, believed they could answer the question exclusively by means of statistics.

3. The Jewish statistics movement

The Verein für Statistik der Juden was founded in Berlin in 1902 at the initiative of Alfred Nossig. The initiators of the association were members of the democratic faction, founded the previous year, of the Zionist movement, which was particularly oriented towards → Cultural Zionism and its program of comprehensive renewal. Alongside Nossig, the members of the association board were the Orientalist Moritz Sobernheim (1872–1933), the lawyer Bruno Blau (1880–1954), who had published *Die Kriminalität der deutschen Juden* in 1906, and the political economist Hans Gideon Heumann (1882–1918).

Under Nossig's leadership, *Jüdische Statistik* was the association's first publication in 1903. The 111-page systematic bibliography included in the volume documents the quantity of data available on Jewish life that had been collected and published throughout the 19th century by official authorities, institutions, and scholars, the majority from non-Jewish sources. In addition, the volume provides an overview of the statistical work done by Jewish organizations and contributions to the statistics on Jews in individual countries as well as on overall statistics of Jews. Thus, the publication was intended, above all, to be the basis of further statistical research.

In the foreword of *Jüdische Statistik*, the board wrote that "the reawakening of Jewish national consciousness [has] strongly contributed to giving substance to the idea of Jewish statistics." The protagonists of the Jewish statistics movement were interested in gaining the approval of non-Zionists for their concerns as well. According to Nossig, Jewish statistics was born "from the needs of Judaism as a whole, and no less of the non-Jewish general public, thus, from the spirit of the age." Furthermore, the association professed to be committed to "the most stringent objectivity" [7.1, 2]. The movement frequently reiterated that the project of Jewish statistics did not adhere to a particular political or ideological trend; this attests to the association's intention of getting other Jewish groups to involve themselves with statistics.

The association set itself the task of systematically viewing and scientifically evaluating the data concerning Jews kept in state and community archives that had not yet been included in their project. To this end, working groups were formed, which led to statistics offices being established in Munich, Hamburg, Vienna, Warsaw, and other European cities. Similar institutions were founded in New York and London independently of the Verein für jüdische Statistik. In 1904 a central office was established in Berlin; Arthur Ruppin and his assistant Jakob Thon (1880–1950) were persuaded to join the staff. From 1905 onward, the Berlin Bureau für Statistik der Juden published the *Zeitschrift für Demographie und Statistik der Juden*, initially edited by Ruppin himself. It included original essays, summaries

of academic and popular articles on Jewish topics, as well as official statistics. Only occasionally did it undertake its own data collection – the authors and researchers of Verein für jüdische Statistik contributed little to statistical methodology. Their work focused on the professionalization of discourses on the population and social structure of the Jews. Arthur Cohen, a professor of economics in Munich and one of the association's initiators, praised its method in 1914: "Thanks to statistics, rhythm, measure, and order are introduced into the confusing multitude of social phenomena: they arrange themselves neatly and become a mere number within the social group to which they belong" [3. 149].

4. Controversies

Among the German Jewish statisticians who became leading figures in this field after 1900, the predominant view was that → assimilation was the greatest danger to the existence of the Jews as a community. In the eyes of Ruppin and his fellow campaigners, the objective as well as the merit of statistics was that it rendered certain consequences of → assimilation comprehensible. These included, among others, falling birth rates, increasing numbers of "mixed marriages" and → conversions to Christianity, increasing alcoholism, a rise in crime and suicides, as well as a growing number of persons with physical and mental disabilities. Listing dangers presumed to be caused by assimilation was the central topic of the numerous essays and books Ruppin wrote between 1902 and 1940. His 1904 work *Die Juden der Gegenwart* (amended new edition 1930/1931 entitled *Soziologie der Juden*) remains the best-known. Ruppin's hypotheses were amplified by the Munich physician and demographer Felix Theilhaber (1884–1956). In his 1911 book *Der Untergang der deutschen Juden*, he went so far as to prophesize the complete disappearance of Jews. Theilhaber and Ruppin both championed strengthening Jewish national consciousness as a possible way to reverse this trend. To them and other authors committed to the Zionist idea, statistical data seemed suited to affirming the belief in the unity of the Jewish nation. They occasionally used the term "race," rejecting, however, the biologistic determinism antisemites associated with this term; rather, they tended to explain evolutionary processes in accordance with Lamarck's theory of evolution as the heredity of socially acquired changes. They regarded statistical findings as powerful arguments when courting the liberal German Jewish majority with its commitment to emancipation and acculturation. As the Zionist *Die Welt* put it in 1902, the "optimism of the assimilationists" could be countered only by means of "plain numbers" [1. 6].

This provoked disagreement. Jacob Segall (1883–1959), also a physician and statistician, roundly rejected Theilhaber's book with reference to its method as well as its conclusions, giving rise to a years-long and at times relentless debate. Segall's review appeared in 1911 in the journal *Im deutschen Reich*, published by the → Central-Verein deutscher Staatsbürger jüdischen Glaubens (Central Association of German Citizens of Jewish Faith), a liberal and anti-Zionist organization. Segall wrote that although Theilhaber utilized "the heavy artillery of statistics," he was "not meticulous" about the figures and also possessed insufficient knowledge of modern scientific methodology. Segall's own interpretation was that the decline of the Jewish section of the total population of Germany from 1.3% to 1% resulted from the continuing emigration of German Jews [11]. In Theilhaber's opinion, however, this hypothesis was "scientific nonsense" [12. 94].

Like Segall, other Jewish social scientists and statisticians committed to social integration, such as Heinrich Silbergleit (1858–1939), the director of the statistical bureau in Berlin from 1906 to 1923, relied on the sort of data that they believed proved that assimilation did not pose the dangers invoked by Zionist authors. They did, however, maintain that Jewish nationalism was a threat to the Jews' welfare. The Russian-born American anthropologist and medical scientist Maurice Fishberg (1872–1934) was the most prominent champion of this trend. His 1911 magnum opus *The Jews. A Study of Race and Environment* was the most comprehensive statistical compilation of modern Jewish life of its day. Fishberg explicitly criticized the deeply pessimistic Zionist attitude towards the contemporary living conditions of the Jews. Similarly, Arthur Cohen of the Central-Verein rejected the Zionist approach to statistical interpretation, stating in 1914 that "the Jewish question" was "not a purely Jewish question but a cultural question" [3. 148]. A decade later, the mathematician, political economist, and statistician Julius Rotholz (1864–1939) pointed to the doubling of the membership of the Central-Verein from 35,248 in 1913 to 70,104 in 1924, and, consequently, to the "victoriousness of the C. V.-organization" [9. 39, 40].

During the first decades of the 20th century, attitudes based on statistical observation shaped the debates on the circumstances of modern Jewish life; these attitudes were reflected in scholarly monographs as well as → encyclopedias and almanacs, publications by Jewish communities, as well as popular journals and magazines.

German antisemites made use of the findings provided by Jewish statistics. The same logic was applied in the decree on the "Nachweisung der beim Heere befindlichen wehrpflichtigen Juden" (Evidence of the participation of conscript Jews in the army) published by the Prussian war ministry on October 11, 1916, the so-called → Judenzählung (census of Jews). It was undoubtedly a reaction to the claim made in antisemitic circles that Jews did not take part in the war in numbers commensurate with their percentage in the population as a whole. The justification given by the war ministry that its objective was merely to refute this claim did not convince anyone, and the fact that the results of the census – which the responsible offices failed to carry out completely – were never published potentially exacerbated this. For the German Jews, the entire process was devastating. The Central-Verein, the Deutsch-Israelitische Gemeindebund, the Zionistische Vereinigung für Deutschland, and other Jewish associations had presciently appointed a committee for war statistics. In 1921 Segall published the collected data in the study *Die deutschen Juden als Soldaten im Kriege*, refuting the theory that Jews had been underrepresented on the frontlines. The well-known Frankfurt political economist, sociologist, and Zionist Franz Oppenheimer (1864–1943) also documented the war ministry's methodological errors in his 1922 study *Die Judenstatistik des Preußischen Kriegsministeriums* and found that the percentage of Jews among soldiers, the wounded, and the fallen corresponded with the Jewish portion of the population. He countered the rampant racial polemic by pointing out: "If one also includes, as one must if the basis for the argument is the 'race community,' the thousands of baptized and dissident Jews as well as the innumerable half-Jews from mixed marriages, it would seem that the Jewish race community contributed more than its fair share to the horrendous blood sacrifice" [8. 42]. Oppenheimer knew full well that the findings of the Jewish associations would not impress the antisemites in Weimar: "The swastika gentlemen will never be convinced that this is more than merely a Jewish falsification" [8. 12f.].

Bibliography

Sources

[1] Die sozialen Verhältnisse der deutschen Juden, in: Die Welt 31, August 1, 1902, 6–7.   [2] Bureau für Statistik der Juden (ed.), Statistik der Juden.

Eine Sammelschrift, Berlin 1917.   [3] A. Cohen, Judenfrage und Statistik, in: Zeitschrift für Demographie und Statistik 11–12 (1914), 146–151.   [4] M. Fishberg, The Jews. A Study in Race and Environment, New York 1911.   [5] J. Jacobs, Studies in Jewish Statistics. Social, Vital and Anthropometric, London 1891.   [6] M. Jungmann, Ist das jüdische Volk degeneriert?, in: Die Welt 24, June 13, 1902, 3–4.   [7] A. Nossig (ed.), Jüdische Statistik, Berlin 1903.   [8] F. Oppenheimer, Die Judenstatistik des preußischen Kriegsministeriums, Munich 1922.   [9] J. Rothholz, Die deutschen Juden in Zahl und Bild, Berlin 1925.   [10] A. Ruppin, Die Juden der Gegenwart. Eine sozialwissenschaftliche Studie, Berlin 1904.   [11] J. Segall, Der Untergang der deutschen Juden, in: Im deutschen Reich 9 (1911), 485–499.   [12] F. Theilhaber, Der Untergang der deutschen Juden, Berlin ²1921.   [13] L. Zunz, Grundlinien zu einer künftigen Statistik der Juden, in: Verein für Kultur und Wissenschaft der Juden (ed.), Zeitschrift für die Wissenschaft des Judenthums, Berlin 1823, 523–532.

Secondary literature

[14] A. Barkai, Jüdische Minderheit und Industrialisierung, Demographie, Berufe und Einkommen der Juden in Westdeutschland 1850–1914, Tübingen 1988.   [15] I. Hacking, The Taming of Chance, Cambridge 1990.   [16] M. Hart, Social Science and the Politics of Modern Jewish Identity, Stanford 2000.   [17] T. Porter, The Rise of Statistical Thinking, 1820–1900, Princeton 1986.

MITCHELL B. HART, GAINESVILLE

[The] Street of Crocodiles

Title of a prose volume by Bruno Schulz (1892–1942) about the living environment of the Galician Jews published in 1933 by the prestigious Warsaw publishing house Rój (dated 1934). The fifteen prose texts in *Sklepy cynamonowe* ("The Street of Crocodiles," 1934/1963; lit. "Cinnamon Shops") owe their artistic imprint to the language rich in images in which childhood myths, the Galician province, and Jewish family topoi are fused together to form an artificial reality. The texts are characterized by binary subject fields such as province and metropolis, sacredness and profaneness, the masculine and the feminine, son and father, writing and image, perversion and norm, imagination and Jewish tradition, as well as torment and lust. In his work, Schulz provided important stimuli for the Polish-Jewish avant-garde.

1. Bruno Schulz
2. Liberating the imagination
3. Schulz as a visual artist
4. Readings and legacy

1. Bruno Schulz

Bruno Schulz was born in 1892 as the youngest child of a Polish-Jewish family in the Galician town of Drohobych, situated in a region that was part of Austrian Galicia from 1772 to 1918. As Drohobycz it was part of Poland from 1918 onward and is today in Ukraine. Other artists born in Drohobych were the painter Maurycy Gottlieb (1856–1879; → History; → Art) and the painter and book artist Ephraim Moses Lilien (1874–1925; → Art Nouveau). Together with the spa town of Truskawiec and Borysław, a city grown wealthy thanks to the oil industry, Drohobych formed a triangle of modern productivity in the Galician province in the immediate vicinity of the centers of Hasidic (→ Hasidism) spirituality.

Bruno's father Jakub Schulz owned a textiles shop; his mother Henriette (Hendel, née Kuhmerker) came from a family of small industrialists and wood merchants. Bruno Schulz, a pupil showing talent for language as well as drawing, attended a → Polish-language secondary school. In view of the family's precarious situation, rather than pursuing his passion for painting, he studied → architecture at the Technical University of Lemberg, also undertaking several study trips to → Vienna. His delicate health, his father's early death in the summer of 1915, and continuing financial difficulties made it impossible for him to live as an independent artist. As a consequence, Schulz worked as a teacher of drawing and handicraft in his home town from 1924 onward.

Beginning in the 1920s, Schulz contributed to exhibitions in the cities of → Lemberg, → Cracow, Warsaw, and → Vilna, as well as in Drohobych and Truskawiec. *Sklepy cynamonowe* was the visual artist's literary debut in 1933. He found recognition in the Galician and the Warsaw artistic communities, established a network of contacts, and had a prominent sponsor in the Polish writer Zofia Nałkowska. Men of letters such as Antoni Słonimski and Julian Tuwim (→ Shmontses; → Skamander) recommended *Sklepy cynamonowe* for the literature prize of the prestigious journal *Wiadomości Literackie* (Literary News). Henceforward Schulz led a double life between artistic Bohemianism and small-town norms. Intending to marry, he left the Jewish community in July 1936. However, his wedding to the Pole Józefina Szelińska, who had translated Kafka's novel *Der Prozeß* ("The Trial," 1937; → Prague) into Polish with Schulz's assistance, never took place.

Schulz's second prose volume, *Sanatorium pod Klepsydrą* ("Sanatorium under the Sign of the Hourglass," 1997), dedicated to Szelińska, appeared in 1937. A last journey, undertaken in the hope of finding sanctuary abroad, took Schulz to Paris in the summer of 1938. Besides visits to galleries and exhibitions and encounters with the artists Ludwik Lille and Naum Aronson, the visit to France did not bring success. In addition, Schulz's request to be transferred to Warsaw was rejected; he was also depressed by the "Anschluss" (annexation) of Austria and the Sudeten crisis. With his lost → German novella *Die Heimkehr*, he tried to establish contact with Thomas Mann, then living in exile in Switzerland, whom he admired just as much as Rainer Maria Rilke.

When Drohobych was occupied by the → Red Army in September 1939 and by the Wehrmacht in June 1941, Schulz was already in a physically and mentally weakened condition. The immediate consequences of the German occupation were → pogroms, mass executions in the nearby Bronica forest, and deportations to the Bełzec extermination camp (→ Buchach; → Holocaust). A ghetto was established in Drohobych in October 1942, into which Schulz was forced to move. Until then he had been protected by the Viennese Gestapo officer Felix Landau, for whose children he had to paint murals with motifs from fairy tales.

In November 1942, while Schulz was preparing to flee from the ghetto with fake documents, he was shot in the street, apparently by a rival of Landau's. Evidence that Schulz's body was buried in the Jewish cemetery has not been confirmed; the location of his grave is unknown. Shortly after his murals were rediscovered in the house formerly inhabited by the Gestapo officer, they were transferred to Israel in a spectacular secret mission in the summer of 2001. They are now exhibited in → Yad Vashem, the World Holocaust Remembrance Center as part of the "Holocaust Art" collection.

2. Liberating the imagination

The topics of the short stories in *Sklepy cynamonowe* focus on the narrow world of a small-town family and the mental and physical decline of the father Jakub; his decaying dignity and increasing degeneration into illness and embarrassment are described with brutal honesty: "I have never seen an Old Testament prophet, but at the sight of this man stricken by God's fire, sitting clumsily on an enormous china chamberpot [...] I understood the divine anger of saintly men" [2. 40]. In the attic of the family home Jakub develops his obsessive ornithological

passion, but "Father's bird kingdom" [2. 50] is destroyed by the powerful housemaid Adela, who later moves into the space that previously was the father's exclusive realm, desecrating it.

The family's Jewish living environment provides the narrative subtext. Their mealtime rituals (→ Kashrut) indicate Ashkenazi cooking (→ Ashkenaz); their decay is the expression of centuries of Jewish-East Polish isolation (→ Shtetl), and the father's humiliation reflects the specific criticism Kafka's and Schulz's generation felt for the alienation from Jewish tradition. At the surface of the texts, the birth of the artist-narrator takes its course. He visits the art school during a nighttime stroll, surrenders to the imaginary goings-on in the darkness of the town's parks and luxurious interiors, and goes on a carriage ride guided not by the coachman (→ Balegule) but rather by the horse to whom the first-person narrator is devoted in loving tenderness. He enters into the imaginary world of his childhood, while simultaneously being exposed to a clearly sexualized present. In the text, these nighttime fantasies become tangible along with the contemporary drawings in the image of the "ownerless horse-drawn cabs" and the omnipresence of shameless prostitutes: "Showily dressed in long lace-trimmed gowns, prostitutes have begun to circulate. They might even be the wives of hairdressers or restaurant bandleaders. They advance with a brisk rapacious step, each with some small flaw in her evil corrupted face; their eyes have a black, crooked squint, or they have harelips, or the tips of their noses are missing" [2. 108].

The next step in the process is the father's decline, his metamorphosis to becoming a cockroach, and the family's denying him. In his last appearance in the short story *Noc wielkiego sezonu* ("The Night of the Great Season"), Jakub has to justify himself on Yom Kippur. In accordance with Schulz's aesthetics of degradation and loss of control, a small-town mob surges forth, looting the father's shop, creating a pogrom mood. The spiritual authorities, however, do not intervene: "Meanwhile, the fathers of the city, members of the Great Synhedrion, walked up and down in dignified and serious groups, and led earnest discussion in undertones" [2. 135]. The libidinousness of the female physicality is contrasted with the powerlessness of patriarchal intellectualism. The massacre that takes place in the final scene, however, is directed against the stuffed birds of the father's collection which, in a process of estrangement, have become works of art. It shows the author as the master of provocative irony, linking the motifs of the pogrom, the father's degenerate passions, and the liberty of art as it reveals itself.

Schulz's own comment on *Sklepy cynamonowe* in 1937 was: "This book represents an attempt to recreate the history of a certain family, a certain home in the provinces, not from their actual elements [...] but by seeking their mythic content, the primal meaning of that history. [...] The ultimate given data of human life, he submits, lie in a spiritual dimension, not in the category of facts" [1. 153].

In another place, he defined the principle of *Sklepy cynamonowe* as that of a "universal disillusioning reality"; art "operates at a premoral depth, at a point where value is still in *statu nascendi*" [1. 113]. The language of images was based on a "Pan-maskerade": "Reality takes on certain shapes merely for the sake of appearance, as a joke or form of play. One person is a human, another is a cockroach, but shape does not penetrate essence, is only a role adopted for the moment, an outer skin soon to be shed" [1. 113]. Schulz's texts reveal the irony of human existence as well as the "clown's stuck-out tongue" of art: "I think of it [*Cinnamon Shops*] as an autobiographical narrative," as "a genealogy *par excellence* in that it follows the spiritual family tree down to those depths where it merges into

mythology, to be lost in the mutterings of mythological delirium" [1. 114]. In the same text, Schulz refers to Thomas Mann and his *Die Geschichten Jaakobs* (1933) as the models of his own mythical genealogy.

At the same time, Schulz's technique relies on putting a distance between himself and written Jewish tradition, which he then re-appropriates freely and without commitment in an artistic act. The art fantasies interspersed with traces of tradition form a kind of neo-mythology. The figure of the father as "a broken man," as "an exiled king who had lost his throne and his kingdom" [2. 50], is the leitmotif interpretation of the existence in exile, in which tradition, dream, and imagination appear to be equal quantities. The father's disappearance and the family's subsequent denial of him go hand in hand with the enthronement of the literary imagination.

3. Schulz as a visual artist

In Schulz's works of visual art, which include painting, drawings, etchings, book illustrations, and other styles, the power of the imagination is indissolubly tied to the artist's phantasm in that the barely concealed → self-portrait is a constant element in the creation of visual art. Especially when depicting male persons, Schulz repeatedly resorts to the principle of the more or less hidden self-portrait. The small, slight man with the large head, his devout desire for seemingly superior women as well as his helplessness in the face of emasculated father figures point to the man Bruno Schulz (see image).

To the eye of the visual artist Bruno Schulz, every figure and every thing in the restricted provincial world is an object of amazement and transformation. The shoes and hats of the alluring women become objects of the artist's reverence, while the heads of passersby or the unremarkable presence of a group of Hasidim in the townscape seem

Józef by his sick father Jakub's bedside, Drawing by Bruno Schulz (1926)

like questions emerging from deep perplexity, transformed into images. Every last profane human gathering has the potential to become a procession, while animals represent aspects of human character so perfectly that Józef becomes immersed in conversation with a mythical dog-man and horses push the coachman out of the picture but still strut like the "wingless Pegasus" (Jerzy Ficowski) of art. In the graphic works of the 1930s, dogs with human faces appear as allegories of the chained human instead.

Around 1920, when the book of prints *Xięga Bałwochwalcza* (The book of idolatry) appeared, in which Schulz employed the *cliché verre* technique, the omnipotence of sensual desires was already present in his visual language, earning him the reputation of an expert in female sadism and male masochism. Both the visual and the literary work distance themselves from female creativity and productivity, which are frequently – for instance in the case of female family members – devalued as a purely physical obsession: "It was an almost self-propagating fertility, a femininity without rein, morbidly expansive" [2. 32]. Schulz's friendship with the author Zofia Nałkowska, for instance, or the artist Debora Vogel contradict this misogynistic trait, which may thus be interpreted as the reflection of a cultural fault.

4. Readings and legacy

The tension between form and freedom are the characteristic and the subtext of Schulz's prose. The plots of all his short stories conclude within the cycle of a year (→ Course of the Year), structured by the holidays and with recourse to religious topics. In the prose volume *Sanatorium pod Klepsydrą*, Jewish topoi return as the objects of breathless desire, without, however, becoming meaningful and ordering symbols. This becomes clear, for instance, in the version of the topos of the desecrated original. Józef is outraged at his father, accusing Jakub of betraying the holy book: "I raised my reproachful eyes to Father. 'You must know, Father,' I cried, 'you must. Don't pretend, don't quibble! This book has given you away. Why do you give me that fake copy, that reproduction, a clumsy falsification? What have you done with The Book?'" [3. 3].

Walter Benjamin's (→ Angelus Novus) theorem of the technical reproducibility of a work of art is radicalized here with reference to the medialization of the Book of Revelation. The accusation of profaning the unmistakable, original book corresponds to the longing for a return to the symbiosis between father and son; it, rather than maternal love, becomes the relationship and world model, while the female maternal element finds itself under the constant suspicion of corruptibility at the hands of the modern temptations of consumption. This is also tangible in Schulz's graphic output, in which sophisticated, sometimes provocative or nude women appear as the seductresses of powerless men. Józef, the author's alter ego, is called Jakub in accordance with the biblical tradition, and obsessively seeks the "original" that his father is unable to hand down, while the women – like the housemaid Adele in *Sklepy cynamonowe* – engage in the shameless desecration of the fragments of the original.

Realities such as the city of Warsaw, Emperor Franz Joseph II, or allusions to the actress Asta Nielsen seemingly refer to concrete historical time in the later prose texts. However, Schulz's motivation as an artist who leaves the structure of space and time behind, formulated programmatically in "The Republic of Dreams," is valid in these cases too:

I have seen this person, I have spoken with him. His eyes were an improbably vivid sky-blue, not made for looking outward but for steeping themselves in the cerulean essence of dreams. [...] He heard a summons, an inner voice, like Noah did when he received his orders and instructions. He was visited by the spirit of this design, which wandered at large in the atmosphere. He proclaimed a Republic of Dreams, a sovereign realm of poetry. [...] That man who drags himself to the gates of this fortress, wolves or brigands hot on his trail, is saved. [1. 221f.]

Schulz's literary writing followed the principle of elevating the imagination to a public interest and to the touchstone of eternal truths, even making it the sanctuary of life under threat.

Bruno Schulz was among the early admirers of the works of Franz Kafka (→ Prague), recognizing in the latter's style a new primal force, the creator of "a species of parallel reality [...] a *Doppelgänger* or substitute reality." "He is a bard and worshipper of the divine order; a bard of a strange stripe, to be sure. [...] The sublime nature of the divine order, according to Kafka, can be rendered only by the power of human negation" [1. 88, 86]. In his eyes, Kafka was the mediator of human and absolute, of freedom and law. In Schulz's own work, human strength and imagination appear to have undergone a process of estrangement until they become disfigured, as well as realized through the inversions of worldly and divine authority. Compared to Kafka's at times sober prose, Schulz's search for law and tradition is inscribed with the sexualization and polarization of gender norms. Unlike Kafka, Schulz's autobiographical remarks and → essays contain few explicit comments on Judaism or on the circumstances of Jewish art in the interwar years. The entire sphere of Jewish life is elevated to the level of artificial fact. Renouncing the self-identification as a Jewish artist made Schulz a (Jewish) postmodern artist *avant la lettre*, characterized by playful, quoting recourse.

Posthumously, the works of the artist and writer Schulz developed a great fascination even beyond Europe. Traces and reflections of his artistic signature are found in the works of, among others, Primo Levi (→ [The] Truce) and Cynthia Ozick as well as John Updike and Philip Roth (→ Schlemiel), J. M. Coetzee, David Grossmann (→ Samson), Tadeusz Kantor, and most recently in Maxim Biller's prose *Im Kopf von Bruno Schulz* (2013; "Inside the Head of Bruno Schulz," 2015). Schulz's world of images inspired the theatre artist Tadeusz Kantor (1915–1990), born in Galicia as the son of a Jewish father and a Catholic mother, who staged the magic and materiality of soulless dolls and mannequins as the glittering alternative world to the uninspired adaptation to the reality principle.

Bruno Schulz's œuvre is a highpoint of Polish-Jewish artistic interaction during the interwar years and shows the force with which the Central European province was pushing into the cities, challenging the supremacy of the centers. In view of the partial survival of the work – the novel *Mesjasz* (The Messiah), the short story *Die Heimkehr* and the majority of the paintings are lost – any appreciation must include reservation. Still, a school of "Schulzology" has emerged, which includes a "Schulz dictionary" (*Słownik schulzowski*, 2006) in which the author's artistic coordinates are sketched and the numerous points linking him to the European avant-garde and modernism are made clear. The dictionary represents the reception that emphasizes the connection with Polish avant-gardists such as Witold Gombrowicz or Witkacy (born Stanisław Ignacy Witkiewicz) but also exponents of Polish postwar painting like Jan Lebenstein. A new edition of Schulz's *Sanatorium pod Klepsydrą* was published in 1957 against the socialist realism of the late 1950s, becoming the sensational, almost surrealist return of the previously ousted Polish-Jewish avant-garde of the interwar years.

Bibliography

Sources
[1] B. Schulz, Letters and Drawings of Bruno Schulz with Selected Prose, ed. by J. Ficowski, trans. by W. Arndt, New York, 1988. [2] B. Schulz, The Street of Crocodiles, trans. by C. Wieniewska, New York 1963. [3] B. Schulz, Sanatorium Under the Sign of the Hourglass, trans. by C. Wieniewska, Boston, 1997.

Secondary literature
[4] W. Bolecki (ed.), Słownik schulzowski [Schulz-Dictionary], Danzig 2006. [5] B. Breysach, Das Buch als Metapher und Materie. Bruno Schulz' Ästhetik der Grenzüberschreitung, in: S. Jaworski/V. Liska (eds.), Am Rand. Grenzen und Peripherien in der europäisch-jüdischen Literatur, Munich 2012, 134–150. [6] R. Lachmann, Der Demiurg und seine Phantasmen. Schöpfungsmythische Spekulationen im Werk von Bruno Schulz, in: P. Kosta et al. (eds.), Juden und Judentum in Literatur und Film des slawischen Sprachraums. Die geniale Epoche, Wiesbaden 1999, 131–154. [7] M. P. Markowski, Polska literatura nowoczesna. Leśmian, Schulz, Witkacy [Modern Polish Literature. Leśmian, Schulz, Witkacy], Cracow 2007. [8] J. Schulte, Eine Poetik der Offenbarung. Isaak Babel, Bruno Schulz, Danilo Kiš, Wiesbaden 2004.

BARBARA BREYSACH, BERLIN

Struma

At the beginning of 1942, Jewish refugees, mainly from Bessarabia and Bukovina, tried to reach Palestine from the Romanian Black Sea coast on the ship registered under the name Struma. After weeks of enforced stay in Istanbul, the ship was sunk after sailing by a Soviet submarine in the entrance to the

Bosporus on February 24, 1942. Of the almost 800 passengers, only one survived. The sinking of the Struma highlights the desperate attempts by Jews during the Second World War to reach Palestine, which was closed to them.

1. The sinking of the Struma
2. Background
3. Illegal immigration into Palestine
4. Consequences

1. The sinking of the Struma

The Struma, launched in Great Britain as a yacht in 1867, changed name and owner several times. Before her last journey as a refugee ship, she served as a livestock transporter on the Danube. The *Mosad le-Aliyah Bet* (Institution for the Second Aliyah), active on behalf of the Jewish Agency to enable illegal immigration into Palestine, had originally intended to send the Struma on her way by being towed by the steamer Darien sailing from Constanţa but abandoned this plan when the concomitant delays threatened to endanger the escape project. The Darien left the Romanian port on February 17, 1941, carrying several hundred Jews. After taking more refugees on board in Varna and Istanbul, it arrived in Haifa on March 19, 1941, carrying 789 passengers.

Subsequently, the Struma's Greek owner looked for a new contract for his ship and contacted representatives of the Revisionist Zionists (→ Altalena), who immediately expressed an interest. Internal disputes with their youth movement, Betar, on who could and could not board, delayed the endeavor. In September 1941, the Jewish owners of a travel agency placed advertisements in the Romanian press, promising passage on a technically restored and fully functional ship including full board. The cost given was 200,000 lei (1,000 US dollars) per person. All the greater was the horror of the 769 Jewish passengers when they first set eyes on the Struma in Constanţa on December 7, 1941. The ship was in a miserable state and suitable for carrying a hundred passengers at most. Their dismay was increased by the hostile treatment they suffered at the hands of the Romanian authorities who confiscated all valuables as well as the majority of the passengers' provisions [6. 39, 149, 150].

The Struma set sail on December 12, 1941, but made slow progress due to engine trouble, only reaching the Bosporus after four days. A Turkish tugboat towed the by then disabled ship into Istanbul harbor. The Turkish authorities instantly put the ship in quarantine. While they would have preferred to have immediately sent the Struma back to Romania, they were wary of an accident in Turkish waters and the attendant duty of rescuing the passengers and giving them sanctuary in Turkey. As a result, the Struma's engines were just barely repaired at the expense of the Jewish community in Istanbul. Even so, the overburdened ship was not seaworthy, as the Struma's concerned Bulgarian captain pointed out to the harbor authorities. Meanwhile the Jewish Agency sought to persuade the British Mandate authorities to allow the Struma's passengers to enter Palestine. On the ship itself the food situation, hygiene conditions, and health of the passengers continually deteriorated. After ten days, a representative of the → Joint Distribution Committee was allowed on board. An onboard committee organizing the care of passengers had already been formed; in negotiations with Turkish authorities, they tried to have the quarantine relaxed.

When after two months of negotiations between the Jewish Agency and the British for the passengers of the Struma no solution had been found, the Turkish authorities had the ship towed out to sea on February 23, 1942. The following day the Soviet submarine Shch-213 torpedoed the Struma, believing it to be an enemy transport. With the exception of then 19-year old David Stoliar

(1922–2014), all passengers perished. The cause of the catastrophe has only been known since 1964; previously it had been assumed that the ship was sunk by the attack of a German U-boat or had hit a mine [7. 96].

2. Background

On June 28, 1940, Soviet troops marched into Bessarabia and northern Bukovina. Two days later, in the Second Vienna Award, Germany and Italy induced Romania to cede Northern Transylvania to Hungary and southern Dobruja to Bulgaria. Within a few months, Romania lost a third of its territory.

In view of the resulting protests, King Carol II of Romania appointed General Ion Antonescu prime minister on September 4, 1940, granting him full dictatorial powers. Under his leadership, Romania moved closer to Germany, joining the Tripartite Pact on November 23, 1940. On their retreat from Bessarabia and Bukovina, Romanian soldiers murdered numerous Jews who were rumored to harbor sympathies for the Soviet Union. In addition, the government led by Antonescu passed special anti-Jewish laws, while their allies, the Iron Guards, carried out violence against Jews. The antisemitic measures and persecutions culminated in the pogrom of → Iaşi immediately before the German and Romanian attack on the Soviet Union. During the recapture of northern Bukovina and Bessarabia, German and Romanian *Einsatzkommandos* began mass executions of the Jews living there. From August onward, the remaining Jews were taken to temporary camps and ghettos and, if they survived the inhumane living conditions and the massacres carried out by the Romanian army, were deported to Romanian-occupied Transnistria beginning in September 1941. Of the over 150,000 Jews forced to walk from Bessarabia and Bukovina to Transnistria, around two thirds died from hunger, deficiency diseases, or were murdered [1. 30].

Romanian Jews seeking to escape persecution increasingly found their paths blocked. During the Balkan offensive, Yugoslavia and Greece came under German occupation in April 1941, closing the overland route to the Mediterranean for Jews hoping to reach Palestine. The only remaining option was to flee across the Black Sea, which became a theatre of war with the German attack on the Soviet Union on July 22, 1941. The 30th German submarine flotilla was stationed in Constanţa with the objective of preventing shipments reaching the Soviet Union; the Soviet navy, in turn, operated on the Black Sea.

3. Illegal immigration into Palestine

As a result of the → Balfour Declaration, Jewish immigration to Palestine increased considerably after the end of the First World War. The Arab population resorted to protests and violence directed against this development. In order to counteract this, the British authorities made Jewish immigration more difficult beginning in the 1930s. From 1934 onward, Zionist organizations like *He-Ḥaluts* (The Pioneers) or the Revisionists and their youth organization Betar responded by organizing illegal immigration. The Jewish Agency, as the official representative of Jewish interests in Palestine and the contact of the British mandatory authorities, at first was reserved concerning this practice.

In view of the antisemitic violence attendant on the "Anschluss" (annexation) of Austria, the failed → Evian conference on refugees, and the → November pogrom, endeavors to emigrate increased considerably among German Jews in 1938. This led to a shift in opinion on the part of the Jewish Agency. In April 1939, specifically for illegal immigration, it founded the *Mosad le-Aliyah Bet*, a subdivision of the *Haganah* (Defense) led by Shaul Avigur (1899–1978), with the task of preparing clandestine operations parallel with the legal *Aliyah Alef* (lit. Immigration A; → Aliyah).

Between September 1939 and May 1945, around 50,000 Jews reached Palestine via a variety of routes; 16,500 of these came illegally by sea. Almost 1,200 Jewish refugees perished in the war years during attempts to reach Palestine by ship [6. 167, 318, 327].

With the White Paper published by the British government in May 1939, which limited immigration to Palestine for the subsequent five years to 10,000 Jews annually and 25,000 additional refugees, and in addition made all future immigration subject to the consent of the Arab population, conditions for immigration deteriorated further. The more restrictive British approach in response to the Arab revolt (1936–1939) was aimed at placating the Arabs in Palestine out of imperialistic considerations. The British efforts to prevent illegal Jewish immigration were quite successful. In January 1940 the British navy captured the Hilda; all 707 Jewish refugees were interned in Atlit. In February it followed the same procedure with the Sakarya and her 2,228 passengers.

When Italy joined the war on June 10, 1940, the Mediterranean became a war zone. Refugee ships were in danger of being attacked as a presumed supplies transport for the combatants or of blundering into one of the numerous mine fields. Soon afterward an Italian submarine torpedoed a tanker off Haifa. Like many refugee transport ships, it had sailed under the Panama flag. In early September 1940 thousands of Jews from Germany and Poland, among them released inmates from the Dachau concentration camp, set off from Vienna on Danube steamers. They were headed for Romanian Black Sea ports where they intended to board the oceangoing ships Milos, Pacific, and Atlantic in order to travel to Palestine. Over the course of a few days in November, the Royal Navy captured these

three ships carrying 3,551 Jewish refugees off Haifa [6. 325f.]. Influenced by these events, the British high commissioner for Palestine, Sir Harold MacMichael, ordered illegally immigrated Jews to be deported to Mauritius. The steamer Patria was made available for this journey. Over 1,800 refugees were on board in the morning of November 25, 1940, when an explosive device attached to the ship detonated. It had been placed there by *Haganah* with the intention that the explosion should prevent the ship leaving the port of Haifa. As the amounts of explosives had been incorrectly calculated, the Patria sank, and 267 persons perished [2. 61].

As for the Struma waiting in the port of Istanbul, the British allowed humanitarian considerations to prevail. Thus the British ambassador in Ankara, Sir Hughe Knatchbull-Hugessen, declared that while the ship's passengers were not permitted to continue their journey to Palestine, he was reluctant to send it back into the Black Sea. It was to set course for the Dardanelles and thus enter the Mediterranean. Colonial Secretary Lord Walter Moyne, however, feared that this might be viewed as a signal by Jews in the Balkans. He ordered Knatchbull-Hugessen to inform the Turkish government that the Struma's passengers would not be permitted to enter Palestine but not to give any further advice. On February 12, 1942, the British government revised its attitude, granting permission first for children between 11 and 16 and, a few days later, for all 70 children on board to immigrate into Palestine. Turkey, however, refused to let them travel overland. As no British ship was available as transport, the children remained on board the Struma.

4. Consequences

Two days after the sinking of the Struma, the Jewish public in Palestine was informed of the event. While the BBC had reported it immediately, British censors had prohibited the news being carried by the Hebrew press, which instead published black-edged biblical quotations on disasters at sea. When the news became official on February 26, 1942, the → Yishuv went on a general strike for twelve hours. Pamphlets bearing the photo of the high commissioner and the words "Wanted for murder" were distributed. The Yishuv held Great Britain responsible for the death of the refugees. Over two years later, the militant underground organization Lehi justified its murder of the former colonial secretary Lord Moyne on November 6, 1944, in Cairo with reference to his involvement in this disaster.

After the Struma catastrophe became known, criticism of London's refugee policy grew among the British and American public, which promptly led to the revision of its restrictive approach. High Commissioner MacMichael was ordered to continue to prevent illegal immigration in the future but to avoid particularly dramatic incidents. Lord Moyne's successor in office Lord Robert Cranborne also favored greater flexibility when dealing with Jewish refugees. From that point on, whoever succeeded in reaching Istanbul was granted an entry permit for Palestine.

The Struma catastrophe did not stop Jews from Romania or Bulgaria from continuing to try and reach Palestine by sea from the Black Sea coast. In the months from March to August 1942 alone, seven further boats arrived carrying over 200 refugees from Romania [6. 167]. They came on their own initiative without help from the Jewish Agency. Under pressure from Germany, Romania prohibited escape via the Black Sea. Even so, individual ships continued to put out to sea. One of these was the Mefkure, which was also torpedoed by a Soviet submarine in August 1944 with a loss of 379 lives.

When after the end of the war, the *brihah* (Hebr.; escape) – the second phase of illegal immigration bringing primarily → Holocaust survivors to Palestine – began, the British Mandatory authorities once again attempted to limit Jewish immigration. The most prominent instance is the fate of the → Exodus.

Bibliography

[1] W. Benz, Rumänien und der Holocaust, in: W. Benz/B. Mihok (eds.), Holocaust an der Peripherie. Judenpolitik und Judenmord in Rumänien und Transnistrien 1940–1944, Berlin 2009, 11–30. [2] M. Chazan, The Patria Affair. Moderates vs. Activists in the Mapai in the 1940s, in: The Journal of Israeli History 22 (2003), 61–95. [3] C. Collins/D. Frantz, Death on the Black Sea. The Untold Story of the Struma and World War II's Holocaust at Sea, New York 2003. [4] T. Friling, Between Friendly and Hostile Neutrality. Turkey and the Jews During World War II, in: M. Rozen (ed.), The Last Ottoman Century and Beyond. The Jews in Turkey and the Balkans 1808–1945, Tel Aviv 2002, 309–423. [5] M. Greenfield, The Jews' Secret Fleet. The Untold Story of North American Volunteers Who Smashed the British Blockade of Palestine, Jerusalem/New York 2010. [6] D. Ofer, Escaping the Holocaust. The Illegal Emigration to the Land of Israel, 1939–1944, Oxford/New York 1991. [7] J. Rohwer, Die Versenkung der jüdischen Flüchtlingstransporter Struma und Mefkure im Schwarzen Meer (February 1942, August 1944), Frankfurt am Main 1965. [8] J. Rohwer, Jüdische Flüchtlingsschiffe im Schwarzen Meer (1934–1944), in: U. Büttner (ed.), Das Unrechtsregime. Internationale Forschung über den Nationalsozialismus, Vol. 2: Verfolgung, Exil, Belasteter Neubeginn, Hamburg 1986, 197–248.

RALF BALKE, BERLIN

Student Corporations

Since the end of the 19th century, Jewish student corporations emerged in Germany as a response to increasing antisemitism at → universities. The majority of these associations were arrayed in German-patriotic or national Jewish umbrella organizations. Beyond programmatic differences, members of the Jewish corporations internalized ritualized forms of behavior. Moreover, they developed a sense of belonging and self-consciousness in these male societies, which, under the conditions of exclusion and pressures to conform, proved to be a strategy of self-assertion.

1. Background
2. Organizations and objectives
3. Significance

1. Background

With the foundation of the German Reich in 1871, Jews gained legal equality in the Empire (→ Emancipation). Since Jews adapted rapidly to the → middle class (Bürgertum) and strove for social advancement, they were disproportionately represented among the students at → German universities (→ Bildung). Thus in 1886/1887, 1,344 Jews from the territory of the Reich studied at Prussian universities. This corresponded to a 9% share of students and thus seven times their share of the population [3. 359].

At the end of the 19th century, universities became places of everyday antisemitism. Thus, on the occasion of the → Berlin debate on antisemitism in 1881, the first Vereine Deutscher Studenten (VDSt; Associations of German Students) were established, which soon had a broad resonance. They came out of the committee for the dissemination of the so-called "Antisemitenpetition" (antisemite's petition; → Ostjuden). Among other things, the petition called for the removal of Jews from key positions in society, such as the civil service and education. In fact, this aimed at the abolition of constitutionally guaranteed rights for German Jews. In November 1880, Berlin and Leipzig students had sent the petition to all German universities with an accompanying letter. Nationwide, only about 0.6% of the population signed the petition, but 19% of the students were in favor. In Berlin alone, 41% of all students there signed the petition [6. 57]. In April 1881, it was handed over to Chancellor Otto von Bismarck with about 265,000 signatures.

While Jews could still become members of German student corporations relatively unproblematically until the 1880s, antisemitism increasingly took hold in them as a social practice in the 1890s. Within the universities, various forms of corporations were competing for influence and prestige among the students, such as *Landsmannschaften* (territorial cooperations), *Corps*, confessional corporations, and *Burschenschaften* (student brotherhoods) which originated during the time of the anti-Napoleonic wars of liberation. Jewish members were now regarded as a status-reducing blemish. Already in the 1880s, the aristocratic *Corps* began to introduce "Aryan paragraphs." The *Burschenschaften* occasionally followed suit beginning in 1896 with the Waidhofen Principle adopted in Austria, according to which Jews were regarded as fundamentally dishonorable; however, it was only after the First World War that the majority of the student corporations adopted regulations for the exclusion of Jews in their statutes.

In Imperial Germany as well as in the Weimar Republic, corporations had a significant influence on academic life. They formed an indispensable part of student sociability. Membership in a corporation was linked to an elevated social status at the university, as well as better opportunities for career advancement. In the 1880s, the labor market situation for academics in Germany worsened, so the protection afforded by the "old boys networks" became all the more valuable for young professionals. Jews at universities were increasingly viewed as illegitimate contenders in the competition for social advancement. The aspiration of many Jews for education was not acknowledged as a basic willingness to undergo → assimilation, but disparaged as an attempt to gain further advantages by a group overrepresented in the academic professions. Before the First World War, only about a third of all Jewish students joined corporations, while in the case of non-Jews this was almost 80% [6. 84].

2. Organizations and objectives

The first Jewish corporation was founded in autumn 1886 under the name Viadrina by twelve medical students in Breslau. One aim of the association was to actively fight against antisemitism and strengthen Jewish self-confidence. Thus their motto went: "Nemo me impune lacessit" (No one provokes me with impunity). The members of Viadrina shared a German patriotic self-understanding. This was emphasized by their colors of black, red, and gold, with which they adopted a positive reference to the *Urburschenschaft* (original student brotherhood) from the time of the anti-Napoleonic wars of liberation. The coat of arms of the Viadrina showed, on the one hand, the national-romantic symbol of Germania and three crossed swords. On the other hand, three interlinked rings were located on the coat of arms in an allusion to Lessing's ring parable [6. 87–88] – the students of Viadrina combined their national allegiance with the call for religious tolerance.

Further Jewish corporations were established following the model of the Viadrina. In 1890, seven students, among them the later founder of the Institut für Sexualwissenschaft (→ Sexology) Magnus Hirschfeld, founded the Badenia corporation in Heidelberg. The Sprevia was founded in Berlin in 1894, and the Licaria in Munich in 1895. In August 1896, these corporations joined together in the umbrella organization the Kartell-Convent der Verbindungen Deutscher Studenten jüdischen Glaubens (Cartel Convent of Associations of German

Students of the Jewish association KC Ghibellinia in front of a picture of the Freiburg Minster (taken in 1912)

Students of the Jewish Faith; KC). The KC strove for recognition of its members as Germans and Jews. With a self-assured demeanor, physical training, and the willingness to react to antisemitic insults with challenges for duels, they hoped to push through their acceptance in the student milieu.

With the program geared towards defending against antisemitism and the aspiration of national integration, the KC was close to the Central Association of German Citizens of Jewish Faith (→ Central-Verein), the largest and most important Jewish organization in Imperial Germany and the Weimar Republic. Part of the student members of the KC later took over leading positions in the Central-Verein. New corporations joined the umbrella organization in the following years. In 1896, the Friburgia was admitted, of which Ludwig Haas was a cofounder. Haas later served as the interior minister of Baden and as a representative in the German Parliament (→ Reichstag) for the Deutsche Demokratische Partei (German Democratic Party). The Saxo-Bavaria was founded in → Leipzig in 1912; its members included the law student Franz Neumann (→ Institute for Social Research). Other corporations which joined the KC were founded at the universities of Bonn, Cologne, Karlsruhe, Frankfurt, Hamburg, Göttingen, Marburg, and some others. By 1924, 21 fraternities with some 2,000 members, including around 1,200 "old boys," were organized in the KC [6. 93].

Parallel to the German-patriotic student corporations, national Jewish and Zionist ones were also established. Thus already in 1882, law student Nathan Birnbaum (→ Czernowitz Conference) and the medical student Moritz Schnirer founded the Kadimah corporation in → Vienna. Among its honorary members were the writers Leo Pinsker (→ Auto-Emancipation) and Peretz Smolenskin (→ Maskilim) as well as the founder of → psychoanalysis Sigmund Freud. Kadimah also saw it as its task to strengthen Jewish self-confidence; its motto read "Mit Wort und Wehr für Juda's Ehr!" ("By word and weapon for Judah's honor") (cited in [6. 100]). Besides opposing antisemitism, Kadimah also championed national Jewish aspirations and supported Jewish settlements in Palestine (→ Aliyah; → Palestine Office). When Theodor Herzl's (→ Old New Land) programmatic work *Der Judenstaat* ("A Jewish State," 1896) appeared in 1896, the corporation invited the author to an official event and was one of the first Jewish organizations to give the project their approval.

In Germany, the first national-Jewish student corporation was founded in 1895 with the Berlin Vereinigung jüdischer Studierender (Association of Jewish Students; VJSt). The corporation distanced itself from non-sectarian student fraternities, that is to say, those which were equally open to Jews and non-Jews, as well as from assimilatory tendencies. Its endeavors included

the "development of a living Jewry" and the "physical regeneration of the Jewish people" (cited in [6. 103]). Growing Jewish self-confidence was accompanied by a rejection of the → Diaspora that had allegedly softened the Jewish body and was why the promotion of physical exercise was regarded as necessary for the national future (→ Muscular Judaism). Students in the VJSt practiced fencing and furthermore devoted themselves to gymnastics and other disciplines of → sport.

Some renowned representatives of Zionism emerged from the members of the Berlin VJSt. These include the later head of the political department of the Jewish Agency Chaim Arlosoroff (→ Basel; → Ha'avarah Agreement) and the philosopher of religion Martin Buber (→ Dialogue). Buber himself moved to Leipzig in 1898 to establish a branch of the VJSt. Besides an additional VJSt corporation at the Technical Academy of Berlin, fraternities of the same name arose in Breslau, Freiburg im Breisgau, Munich, Frankfurt am Main, Königsberg, Marburg, Bonn, Straßburg, and Heidelberg. Together these formed the Bund jüdischer Corporationen (Federation of Jewish Corporations; BJC) in 1901. By 1910, the organization had about 600 members, half of them "old boys" [6. 108].

The influence of the corporations organized in the BJC can also be gauged by the fact that seven of the eight presidents of the Zionistische Vereinigung für Deutschland (Zionist Federation for Germany; ZVfD) were previously active in their individual corporations [6. 104]. Among them was the young Nahum Goldmann (→ Claims Conference; → Luxembourg Agreement), who led the ZVD from 1926 to 1933 and later served as chairman of the → World Jewish Congress. During his studies in Heidelberg in 1912–1914, Goldmann was a member of the local VJSt Ivria. Among his fraternity brothers was the historian of Antiquity Eugen Täubler (→ Akademie für die Wissenschaft des Judentums).

Besides the BJC, further corporations emerged at the beginning of the 20th century whose political self-understanding was directly aligned with the → Basel program of the Zionist Organization. For example, in 1902 the Freie Verbindung Hasmonaea (Hasmonaea Free Corporation) was established in Berlin and the Jordania in Munich in 1905, which joined together in the Kartell Zionistischer Verbindungen (Cartel of Zionist Corporations; KZV) in the following year. Up to the First World War, corporations from Freiburg im Breisgau and Breslau were added. The Viennese Kadimah also became part of the KZV. Even before the beginning of the war, the two national Jewish umbrella organizations were united into the Kartell Jüdischer Verbindungen (Cartel of Jewish Corporations; KJV). After the war, new corporations emerged in many cities, including Rostock, Göttingen, Gießen, Hamburg, Hanover, and Frankfurt am Main, which joined the KJV. In 1932, the KJV numbered around 2,000 members, of whom 1,440 were "old boys" and the rest students. The majority studied medicine and law [6. 113f.]. Hence only around a tenth of all Jewish students joined Zionist corporations. Compared to the rather weak dissemination of Zionism among German Jews as a whole, however, this was a relatively high proportion.

Besides the German-patriotic and national Jewish corporations, in 1906 a religious umbrella organization was founded with the Bund Jüdischer Akademiker (Federation of Jewish Academics; BJA). It was created as a merger of the Vereinigungen Jüdischer Akademiker (Associations of Jewish Academics; VJA), founded in 1903. Only devout Jews could become members. The BJA rejected the student traditions of the other Jewish umbrella organizations, and behaved neutrally toward political questions. Its goal was rather to combine secular scholarship (→ Science) with religious education

(→ Talmud Torah). In 1913, the BJA was represented at seven universities, in Berlin, Heidelberg, Marburg, Munich, Straßburg, Würzburg, and Breslau, and had about 700 members; unlike the patriotic and national Jewish corporations, this included women.

Finally, Jewish students were able to join nonsectarian corporations such as the Freie Wissenschaftliche Vereinigung (Free Scholarly Association), which united Jewish and Christian students under liberal auspices. Within a very short time, Jews were *de facto* the predominant, if not the exclusive, members of these corporations. Nevertheless, they rejected any specific Jewish aspects in their program.

Active Jewish student corporations in Germany existed until 1933. The "old boys" networks" were able to continue their meetings and the publication of their organizational magazines until 1937. The regional corporation of the Zionist KJV in Palestine, that had already been founded in 1924, partially took over the work of the former headquarters in Berlin in 1933, holding regular meetings until the 1970s and producing a magazine.

3. Significance

The Jewish corporations chose to be represented by flags, coats of arms, uniforms (regalia), and ribbons in a symbolic choice of color, which corresponded to their self-understandings. The colors most commonly used as distinctive marks in all Jewish corporations were yellow and blue. Blue was considered the color of Israel (→ Tekhelet), which is why it was often utilized by national Jewish and Zionist corporations. Yellow referred to the medieval "Jewish patch" (→ Dress Regulations) and experienced a positive reinterpretation as the color of many Jewish fraternities corporations. For instance, the Berlin VJSt stated in a

1895 proclamation that they wished "to wear the color yellow, that was stitched onto our fathers' garments as a disgrace, as a badge of honor" (cited in [6. 251]).

The corporations' educational programs also contributed to the Jewish self-perception among their members. In the Zionist student corporations that learnt → Hebrew and undertook exploratory trips to Palestine. Conversely, within the KC, lectures and seminars on various topics of Jewish history were offered, which mainly focused on the modern history of the Jews in Germany and Europe emphasizing the fundamentally successful nature of → emancipation.

Like the other fraternities, the Jewish corporations were also characterized by regimentation and rituals. Academic fencing (mensur), drinking sessions, and commercia occupied a large part of the student corporations' daily routine. The drinking sessions were recurring, strictly standardized rituals, in which the excessive consumption of alcohol (according to a set of rules) and the accompanying singing were intended to educate, the participants in disciplined cohesion and masculinity. Mensur, a fencing bout between students of different corporations, also served this goal. On so-called mensur-days, the entire corporation competed against other groups in order to demonstrate community, strength, and self-confidence to the outside world. Defending honor with the bare weapon came to be of central importance in the internal education of the dueling corporations.

For Jewish fraternity members, this understanding of honor had a particular significance, since antisemitic attacks targeted their background and were associated with the experience of rejection and exclusion. In 1911, for example, the Zionist students in the corporation magazine of the BJC called for a militant defense of Jewish honor: "And with this, the answer as to how we should approach the question of satisfaction is given: fight back! Fight back so manfully and so forcibly that not only is every attack effectively repulsed, but that folks lose their traditional desire to make us the objects of their loutishness!" [1. 153]. At both the KC and the KJV, mensur was abolished after the First World War, but the principle of obligatory satisfaction remained unchanged in the KC. For this purpose, martial arts groups were formed in the corporations after 1918, which trained in → boxing and Jiu-Jitsu for defense against antisemitic attacks.

However, the defense of Jewish honor was not only associated with the direct encounter with attacks. The positive assumption of qualities with masculine connotations such as strength, courage, and defensive readiness also matched the dominant stereotypical roles in broader society. Fencing exercises and mensur sought to outwardly achieve recognition from non-Jewish students, and inwardly they shaped the habitus of the proud man. The goal was to educate a young fraternity student – according to a member of a Zionist corporation – "to the vigorous personality, manliness, and a ready-for-action attitude for the honor of the Jewish nation" (cited in [6. 306]).

The student corporations proved to be a place for national and masculine becoming, especially for the marginal group of Jewish students – both the Zionists and non-Zionists. Conversely, the rituals practiced, through their ideological overload, which were often charged with "Jewishness," led in turn to a "re-Judaization" of the fraternity students as they learned more about their Judaism in the corporation than ever before.

Bibliography

Sources

[1] W. Stein, Zur Satisfaktionsfrage, in: Der Jüdische Student 5/6 (1911), 151–157.

Secondary literature

[2] N. Hammerstein, Antisemitismus und deutsche Universitäten 1871–1933, Frankfurt am Main 1995. [3] N. Kampe, Jews and Antisemites at Universities in Imperial Germany (I). Jewish Students. Social History and Social Conflict, in: Leo Baeck Institute Year Book 30 (1985), 357–394. [4] N. Kampe, Jews and Antisemites at Universities in Imperial Germany (II). The Friedrich-Wilhelms-Universität of Berlin. A Case Study on the Students' "Jewish Question," in: Leo Baeck Institute Year Book 32 (1987), 43–101. [5] N. Kampe, Studenten und "Judenfrage" im Deutschen Kaiserreich. Die Entstehung einer akademischen Trägerschicht des Antisemitismus, Göttingen 1988. [6] M. Rürup, Ehrensache. Jüdische Studentenverbindungen an deutschen Universitäten 1886–1937, Göttingen 2008. [7] T. Schindler, Studentischer Antisemitismus und jüdische Studentenverbindungen 1880–1933, Erlangen 1988. [8] L. F. Zwicker, Dueling Students. Conflict, Masculinity, and Politics in German Universities, 1890–1914, Ann Arbor (MI) 2011.

MIRIAM RÜRUP, HAMBURG

Style of Thought

The term Denkstil (style of thought) came into widespread use in philosophy at the end of the 19th century. Its broad semantic content is connected with various philosophical and socio-psychological concepts based on the history of ideas; the term received a specific theoretical denotation in the sociology of the 1920s and early 1930s. In this context, it is especially associated with the name of the long-forgotten Polish-Jewish doctor, microbiologist, and epistemologist Ludwik Fleck (1896–1961). He used the term in his work *Entstehung und Entwicklung einer wissenschaftlichen Tatsache* (1935) for the relationship between the collective and the individual in the establishment and dissemination of knowledge and scientific ideas.

1. Introduction
2. Ludwik Fleck
3. "Wandering knowledge" and cognition
4. Jewish and antisemitic versions
5. Experience and method

1. Introduction

The concept of "Denkstil" was first articulated by Ludwik Fleck in his work *O niektórych swoistych cechach myślenia lekarskiego* (1927; "Some Specific Features of the Medical Way of Thinking," 1986), published in German as *Über einige spezifische Merkmale des ärztlichen Denkens*. He discusses the thesis that the doctor's profession leads to "a specific way of treating medical phenomena" and, thus, to a "specific style in the grasping of its problems" [8a. 39]. What he here calls "style of thinking," "type of thinking," or "way of thinking" [8a. 41, 39, 40] and exemplifies through the professional activity of the doctor was a conglomeration of intuition, prior knowledge, professional education, and abstraction, from which, he claims, the fundamental terms of all knowledge was assembled. Herewith, Fleck devotes himself less to explanations themselves (of whichever kind of phenomena) and more to the question of which fundamental processes and mechanisms lead to the canonization of knowledge or, vice versa, how positive knowledge can be "refuted" and hence removed from the canon again: "Medical observation is not a point but a small circle. It is placed not in the system of coordinate straight lines inclined to one another at a constant angle, but in a system of optional, mutually intersecting, curves which we do not know closely" [8a. 45].

His book *Entstehung und Entwicklung einer wissenschaftlichen Tatsache* ("Genesis and Development of a Scientific Fact," 1981), which appeared eight years later in German in Switzerland, was inspired by this basic idea. Fleck remained true to his interest in the "social factor in the genesis of cognition"

[8a. 49]. Some of the work's important ideas can already be seen in the essays *Zur Krise der Wirklichkeit* (1929) and *Über die wissenschaftliche Beobachtung und die Wahrnehmung im Allgemeinen* (1935). Fleck later published the central axioms of his œuvre (partly in the context of the scholarly controversies of his day) several times in a summarized form, especially in the essays *Das Problem einer Theorie des Erkennens* (1936), *Schauen, Sehen, Wissen* (1947), and, finally, in *Krise der Wissenschaft* (1960).

While Fleck emphasized in *Entstehung und Entwicklung einer wissenschaftlichen Tatsache* that "scientific work" was "collective effort" [7. 41], so that the culture of understanding between scholars should be researched with respect to relationships between group coherence and the progress of knowledge, he stressed the plurality of realities and the significance of overcoming boundaries of language, tradition, and textbooks. The rather unsystematic, essayistic text, clearly written in haste, was in reality a patchwork of essays (see [8. 31]). It represents a byproduct of his studies in the history of medicine and in bacteriology that dealt with the origins of the concept of syphilis and with the Wassermann reaction. Fleck's position in his own field was based primarily on an experimental procedure with which the so-called leucergia (clumping of white blood cells) could be proved. Today, he is scarcely known for his medical work; instead, he is far better known for his general theoretical work that transcended the bounds of medicine – his thesis that "cognition" was "the most socially-conditioned activity of man" [7. 42] is exemplified in his life's work itself.

Fleck's work was not particularly successful in the period when he first published it; it was first rediscovered by Thomas S. Kuhn. In the introduction to Kuhn's book *The Structure of Scientific Revolutions* (1962), which examines changes in scientific "paradigms" and the significance of the "scientific

community" in terms of communications theory for the production of knowledge, he emphasizes that Fleck had anticipated many of his own thoughts ([12. 10] see [25]). After that, the term Denkstil proliferated in the theory of knowledge several times. Kuhn compared the paradigm of Denkstil, still somewhat statically, with "chess problems" and with "geographical maps"([12. 38]; see [20. 243]). More recent uses can be found in the context of historical epistemology, which researches knowledge and the milieu of characteristics that lead to the development of knowledge, like curiosity, competition, disorders, chance, translations, and intersections between fields of knowledge, along with their chosen forms of self-justification.

2. Ludwik Fleck

Ludwik Fleck was born in 1896 to Jewish parents in Lvóv (Galicia), where, after attending a Polish secondary school, he studied medicine, soon specializing in microbiology. At the same time, he read books on philosophy and the history of science on the side. In the 1930s, his scientific interests turned to serological questions, on which he published in Polish, German, and English professional journals. In 1939, when Lvóv was occupied by the Soviets, Fleck held an important position in the university's Department of Medicine and was director of the city's sanitary biological laboratory. He was deported to Auschwitz at the beginning of February 1943, and then to the Buchenwald concentration camp in January 1944. There, he was put to work as a prisoner functionary where the typhus vaccine was being developed.

After the Holocaust, Fleck went to Lublin and later to Breslau where, in 1946, he qualified as a professor with Ludwik Hirszfeld and was named an extraordinary professor shortly thereafter. In 1948, he was present at the IG-Farben trial in Nuremberg as a medical expert on the criminal research conducted by the SS in the German

Ludwik Fleck (1896–1961)

concentration camps. From 1952 onward, he researched and taught in Warsaw, now also on the subjects of diphtheria and leucocytosis. In 1957, Fleck resettled in Israel, where he continued his work at a research institute for biology in Nes Ziona; from 1959 onward he was also a visiting professor in microbiology at the → Hebrew University of Jerusalem at the same time.

3. "Wandering knowledge" and cognition

The place of origin of Fleck's theory of knowledge – like that of the sociology of knowledge in general – was the multilingual, multinational empire of the late Habsburg monarchy. Around 1900, forms of social differentiation typical of modernization became much more important in this Central European region on account of cultural, ethnic, and national differences. In this situation, multiple affiliations were not unusual; in fact, they were the rule [23. 351f.]. For Fleck and many other Jewish intellectuals, Judaism was documented, not through closeness to the religion nor through positive personal assertions of Jewish affiliation, but through the experience typical for the time of multilingualism, success in education, and mobility, as well as the experience of the "elemental force" of communities, as Fleck put it [8a. 156].

These experiences influenced Fleck's conception of the sociology of knowledge and the theory of science. Increasingly, he emphasized the epistemological significance of phenomena of movement and translation not only in the dissemination of knowledge but in its generation. The expression of the "socio-cognitive migration of fragments of personal knowledge" constituted a mobile, dynamic metaphor whose imagery is closely connected with Fleck's doctrine of Denkstil and Denkkollektiv (thought collective) [7. 118]. For him, communication was not only the (more or less formalized) exchange of fixed knowledge but the locus in which knowledge first came into existence: the "intra-communal exchange," Fleck stated, strengthened the available knowledge; the "inter-communal exchange," by contrast, altered "the sense of notions, gives them a [...] new meaning, and can thus be a source of new ideas" [8a. 156]. Before the publication of his book, he stressed in a letter to Moritz Schlick, the Viennese champion of logical empiricism, "the transmission of [the] knowledge," or, as he wrote, "its migration from man to man" and from "a scientific journal to a textbook," still received too little attention in scholarship [8a. 79].

In order to recognize a fact, according to Fleck in 1935, one must first be prepared in one's Denkkollektiv: a fact does not exist independently of the thinker, but the latter must first learn to see and interrogate it in order to get to know it as such [7. 84]. Language for Fleck was not a means of communication but this specific "something" that one struggles with before knowledge arrives. It appears in his works as an independent and lively third actor in between researcher and subject in the production of knowledge: it is necessary, and it presents itself or fails to appear. Knowledge for Fleck is not a "discovery" but a creative "touch," a regular "modelling" and a "reshaping and being reshaped" [8a. 48ff.]:

> The first, chaotically styled observation resembles a chaos of feeling: amazement, a searching for similarities, trial by experiment, retraction as well as hope and disappointment. Feeling, will, and intellect all function together as an indivisible unit. The research worker gropes but everything recedes, and nowhere is there a firm support. Everything seems to be an artificial effect inspired by his own personal will. Every formulation melts away at the next test. He looks for that resistance and thought constraint in the face of which he could feel passive. Aids appear in the form of memory and education. At the moment of scientific genesis, the research worker personifies the totality of his physical and intellectual ancestors and of all his friends and enemies. They both promote and inhibit his search. The work of the research scientist means that in the complex confusion and chaos which he faces, he must distinguish that which obeys his will from that which arises spontaneously and opposes it. This is the firm ground that he, as representative of the thought collective, continuously seeks. These are the passive connections [...]. The general aim of intellectual work is therefore maximum thought constraint with minimum thought caprice. [7. 94–95]

In this context, "thought constraint" does not mean the renunciation of freedom; it refers to the direction in which as individuals we "look," but in so doing always "see with the eyes of a collective body" [8a. 134]. Fleck's arguments are neither determinist nor relativist but context dependent and relational. For him, the theory of knowledge was an artifact of culture; its "direct perception of form" was unrelated to objective physical elements, being based instead on "cultural-historical context" [8a. 243, 48]. With Fleck's strong emphasis on social-scientific factors, the "thinking individual" appears primarily as a member of a social community and has "his own reality"; indeed, "even many, sometimes contradictory, realities" [8a. 49]. Thus, the process of science occurs to a significant degree unconsciously, according to Fleck, but this does not mean it lacks direction:

> However, the research worker has no consciousness of choice; on the contrary, the choice is imposed on him directly and in a binding manner, following from his mood of thought, from the set of its mental readiness, from his mental thinking practices – in short from what we call the *thought-style* (*Denktstil*). The *thought-style* thus understood is the result of the theoretical and practical education of the given individual; in passing from teacher to pupil, it is a certain traditional value which is subjected to a specific historical development and specific sociological laws. [8a. 66]

According to Fleck, knowledge is a productive capacity, "an act of creation" [8a. 49], and, especially, not a positive property with validity for all time.

At the same time, Fleck relativized static perspectives of truth and error, right and wrong, both of which, in consequence of his cultural-theoretical turn, could be a construct and artifact of a negotiation process that could always begin anew: "Whether an individual construes it as truth or error, understands it correctly or not, a set of findings meanders throughout the community, becoming polished, transformed, reinforced, or attenuated, while influencing other findings, concept formation, opinions, and habits of thought" [7. 42]. Thus, the system of knowledge creates "constructions"; not the kind that follow willful and arbitrary periods but those that depend on long traditions of "seeing forms" and "communal styles of thinking" and, hence, are also always dependent on the experiences of the individuals involved. Fleck was convinced that scientific truth could only reasonably be conceived of if it was converted "from something stiff and stationary into dynamic, developing, creative human truth" [8a. 131, 157].

4. Jewish and antisemitic versions

Fleck's book was a reaction and response to a tendency toward lack of clarity in epistemology that was becoming increasingly problematic. The term Denkstil had been in use in a growing philosophical and sociological literature from the 1870s onward to differentiate specific intellectual attitudes and ways of thinking and to categorize the supposedly identified differences typologically – often as diametric opposites. In the early texts of French social psychology, like Gabriel Tarde's Les lois de l'imitation (1890), the few original intellectual states and the regular intellectual iterations and imitations were differentiated. For Tarde, imitation was not purely negatively valued since it brought with it a group style and thus also made comparison possible. Georg Simmel, an early positive recipient of Tarde's theory, even saw in the principle a "socializing force" since imitation passes "through the whole group" and results in a "uniform way of living together" [17. 411].

In the German-language context, Simmel's interest in the French sociology of forms and style constituted an exception. In this context, the goal of completely dissolving the individual into the collective dominated. The constitutional lawyer and sociologist Ludwig Gumplowicz, who taught in Graz and wrote in a polemically extreme form, became well-known (which Fleck later took up on several occasions): "it

is not man himself who thinks but his social community; the source of his thoughts is in the social medium" [9. 148]. In particular, a younger generation of Jewish intellectuals who had grown skeptical of assimilation, among them Hans Kohn (→ Nationalism), committed themselves in their early writings to the fundamental conviction that it befitted the times to "adjust one's self to supra-individual interconnexions" and "to go beyond the individual." The crisis in spiritual life, as Kohn wrote when he was still a young student in Prague, revealed "the supra-individual of all culture, all life, of the spirit" so that one learned – "outside of and still inside our deepest and very own self" – to get a firm footing in collectives and to perceive oneself as part of a "higher supra-individual course of events" [11. VI]. In the early 20th century, a time when nationalism and collectivism were becoming ever more essentialist, such positions quickly intensified. It is even generally stated in Grundzüge der Soziologie (1930) by the Jena constitutional and legal theorist Franz W. Jerusalem, who joined the NSDAP in 1937, that the "most important peculiarity of the human mind" was not at all its individuality but "its collective character": "All mind is [...] collective mind" [10. 34].

Furthermore, the suggestion of dividing thoughts into formal types was often equated with the intention of capturing the conceptually developed types in reality, that is, in specific social groups, nations, or religions. For example, in Die Juden und das Wirtschaftsleben (1911), Werner Sombart related his hypostatized "capitalist mind" to the Jews causally and genealogically since, in his view, Jews had not only historically disseminated the principle of the modern economy but also embodied it as a group in their psychology. Such collective constructions were not only in Sombart's case provided with clearly articulated ideological valuations. The philosopher Rudolf Eucken, a representative of a metaphysically elevated Germanness, was convinced that the multiplicity of opinions of his day could be derived from a handful of thought forms. In *Die Einheit des Geisteslebens* (1888), Eucken distinguished "naturalism" and "intellectualism" as the two most powerful fundamental attitudes among people shaping their ideals, their political convictions, and their guiding principles in their surrounding world. He devoted himself in his works to the advantages and disadvantages of such "types of thinking" [5. 120]. In contrast to Eucken, the philosopher Hans Leisegang sought out not universal laws of thought but "worldview images" in his "Phänomenologie des Denkens" (1928). Leisegang favored a typological method "that from the outset does not assume a straight line or a dialectical movement of the one world reason but recognizes different forms of thought side by side and tries to do justice to each" [13. 8, 457].

Both Eucken and Leisegang took positions on the concept and content of supposedly Jewish thought, albeit in rather different ways. Whereas Leisegang distanced himself from a "physiologial conditionality" of typical thought forms and strictly rejected the idea of fixed styles of thinking for a people or race, Eucken's typologization of thought was accompanied by antisemitic sentiments: "creative" or "inventive" thought and the specification of "German style" thought were contrasted via folk psychology and determinism with the pejoratively depicted "isolated intellect" whose "free-floating cognitive work," according to Eucken, was "hopeless" [4. 299]. Leisegang also connected the traditional distinction "between oriental and Occidental thinking," according to which the oriental was deep, mystical, and naturally predisposed toward the metaphysical, whereas the Occidental was distinctly rationalist and empirical [13. 452]. However, Leisegang held that this opposition did not account for the Jews;

although they had an oriental history, they had a rational religion devoid of mysticism. Thus, Spinoza, the only Jewish philosopher of the modern era, had worked through mystical thought motifs but he had not argued against science and mathematics; rather, he had joined the two together. Here, Leisegang attempted to connect the history of Jewish thought with the universal model of reason, which is why he emphasized the leading role of Jewish scholars and intellectuals in the "formation of traits considered typical of western cultures." In his view, the democratic forms of government and modern economic life could not be contrasted to a construct of the "Jewish oriental mind" but rather were generated "in the sense and with the help" of this mind [13. 453].

The term Denkstil appeared in Jewish publications of the day, such as in S. M. Melamed's *Psychologie des jüdischen Geistes* (1913). It was used in this context not so much to refer to a determination of the individual through his origins but rather to the individual contribution of the "fate-forging personality" to the collective [14. VII]. Diesendruck, in his essay *Vom Denkstil Achad-Haams* (1916), distinguished between a "thinker of Judaism" and a "Jewish thinker." Only the latter attended "to the method," and it was only in this context that a "primacy of mind, rooted in prophesy" was to be found. Here, the term Denkstil becomes a paraphrase for "world perception" and "worldview" and a cipher for the "awakening of a genuine national feeling, the spiritual in the Jew." Diesendruck describes a "Jewish style of thought" as a double, a "bioptic" thinking that contains thoughts, themes, and designs; the "interlaced nature of journalism and philosophy" that emerges from this, he claimed, was "characteristic of Jewishness." Denkstil appears here as an "inner constitution" that cannot be learned [3. 272].

Martin Buber (→ Dialogue) also criticized "the application of the method of the natural sciences [...] to psychology" in his treatise *Der Geist des Orients und das Judentum* (1916), starting likewise from the juxtaposition of an "Occidental" and an "Oriental type of human being." "He found his distinction between "motor or sensory types" in the antinomy between "Occident" and "Orient"; he concretized the differentiation between "Germans" and "Jews" with reference to two collectives of peoples. Following the idealist tradition of German classicism, wherein the multiplicity of peoples were acknowledged in their historical and literary traditions, as in the universalist → Völkerpsychologie of the 18th century, Buber held that one should always look "through the shell of diversity [into] its unified spiritual core" [1. 56–57].

Tracking the secret of a "unifying" form of thinking also led to some universalist theses after 1900. However, the antisemitism of these years, with its special interest in determining a collective unity of thought, emphasized the exact opposite. In their books *Rasse und Stil* and *Rasse und Seele*, both of which appeared in 1926, Hans Günther and Ferdinand Clauss distinguished a "Nordic" style from all other, inferior styles. They both defined "style" as a distinguishing feature of "the soul's unique manner of perceiving" that was allegedly different and considered "formative activity" as the "unity of style" [2a. 65–66]; [2b. 63]. In the early 1940s, the Berlin philosopher August Faust described a specifically German style of philosophy with an accompanying worldview and categorically separated these from "Jewish thinking." Max Mikorey's presentation "Das Judentum in der Kriminalpsychologie," which he gave in October 1936 at the conference titled *Das Judentum in der Rechtswissenschaft* and organized by Carl Schmitt, exemplifies the antisemitic appropriation of the sociology of knowledge and of the concept of Denkstil. Mikorey introduced his presentation with a warning and a confession. The warning declared the necessity of preventing

unsuspecting students from getting lost and losing their way "in the labyrinths of Jewish techniques of thought." Here, the author used the term Denkstil, or "style of thought," in a decidedly antisemitic spirit when he claimed he was exposing "the multiplicity of criminal psychological faces of Judaism" resulting from their "homelessness" and a "dialectics uprooted from the Labyrinth" – to him, this was precisely the "common denominator of a racially conditioned style of thought conditioned in criminal psychology" [15. 62].

Against this background, it is no surprise that when Ludwik Fleck's work *Entstehung und Entwicklung einer wissenschaftlichen Tatsache* appeared in German in 1935, reviews from within the field of National Socialist medicine, which had become very nationalist, explicitly agreed with its theses. For example, in the *Klinischen Wochenschrift*, it was explicitly stated that Fleck had, in "a peculiar and from this side a little unexpected way," adapted to "our new German style of thought, which rejects any unconditional, absolute science" [16]. However, Fleck represented the exact opposite of such a "German style of thought" and always defended the axiom that only theory and theoretical concepts that opened up "new fields of research, new mental possibilities" should be recognized as valuable; not those "that close the path to future research" [8a. 63].

5. Experience and method

From a present-day perspective, Ludwik Fleck's text is an especially apt example of its own theoretical formation because it took up available, "migrating" knowledge and simultaneously held onto it, "learned to see" with it, and developed something new from it. In the context of the sociology of knowledge, Fleck thus followed the thinking of Karl Mannheim (→ Sociology

STYLE OF THOUGHT

of Knowledge), who used the term Denk-stil primarily with reference to the relation-ship between collectivity and individuality in thought. Yet Fleck did so in order to go beyond Mannheim's typology to arrive at a generalizability of knowledge that would extend beyond linguistic, communication, and generational communities. Epistemo-logically speaking, the book was significant in terms of a theory of science not least because of how Fleck interwove natural science and epistemology, applying social metaphors from his own personal experi-ences as a model of transmission. Thus, the concept of Denkstil is itself the result of a specific Denkstil. As such, it reflects a "soft," immaterial definition of modern collectiv-ity that contains a historical experience of community and belonging beyond nation, religion, denomination, and ethnicity. The shaping of social science concepts by a whole series of Jewish scholars is, thus, in no way disproved by the antisemitism that appropriated serious reflections on thought collectives and styles of thought and used them as confirmation for their own view of a supposedly absolute, insurmountable difference between Jewish and non-Jewish thought.

Bibliography

Sources

[1] M. Buber, On Judaism. An Introduction to the Essence of Judaism by One of the Most Impor-tant Religious Thinkers of the Twentieth Cen-tury, ed. by N. N. Glatzer, New York 1996. [2] F. Clauß, Rasse und Seele. Eine Einführung in die Gegenwart, Munich 1926. [2a] L. F. Clauss, Racial Soul, Landscape, and World Domination, in: G. Lachmann Mosse (ed.), Nazi Culture. Intel-lectural, Cultural and Social Life in the Third Reich, Madison 2003, 65–78. [2b] R. Bernas-coni, Ludwig Ferdinand Clauss and Racializa-tion, in: L. Embree/T. Nenon (eds.), Husserl's Ideen, Dordrecht 2013, 55–70. [3] W. Diesen-druck, Vom Denkstil Achad-Haams, in: Der

Jude 4 (1916), 271–274. [4] R. Eucken, Die Ein-heit des Geisteslebens in Bewusstsein und That der Menschheit, Leipzig 1888. [5] R. Eucken, Gesammelte Aufsätze zur Philosophie und Leb-ensanschauung, Leipzig ²1913. [6] A. Faust, Wesenszüge deutscher Weltanschauung und Philosophie, in: Zeitschrift für deutsche Kultur-philosophie 8 (1941/1942), 81–168. [7] L. Fleck, Genesis and Development of a Scientific Fact, ed. by T. J. Trenn and R. K. Merton, trans. by F. Bradley/T. J. Trenn, Chicago 1981. [8] L. Fleck, Denkstile und Tatsachen. Gesammelte Schrif-ten und Zeugnisse, ed. by S. Werner/C. Zittel, Frankfurt am Main 2011. [8a] R. S. Cohen/T. Schnelle, Cognition and Fact. Materials on Lud-wik Fleck, Dordrecht 1986. [9] L. Gumplowicz, The Outlines of Sociology, trans. by F. W. Moore, Kitchener, Canada 1999. [10] F. W. Jerusalem, Grundzüge der Soziologie, Jena 1930. [11] H. Kohn, Geleitwort, in: Vom Judentum. Ein Sam-melbuch, ed. by Verein jüdischer Hochschüler Bar Kochba, Leipzig 1913. [12] T. S. Kuhn, The Structure of Scientific Revolutions, vol. II, no. 2, Chicago 1970. [13] H. Leisegang, Denkfor-men, Berlin/Leipzig 1928. [14] S. M. Melamed, The Psychology of the Jewish Mind, in: Jew-ish Chronicle, 26 May 1911, 26. [15] M. Miko-rey, Das Judentum in der Kriminalpsychologie, in: Das Judentum in der Rechtswissenschaft. Ansprachen, Vorträge und Ergebnisse der Tagung der Reichsgruppe Hochschullehrer des NSRB am 3. und 4. Oktober 1936, Berlin o.J., 61–82. [16] H. Petersen, Ludwig Flecks Lehre vom Denkstil und dem Denkkollektiv, in: Kli-nische Wochenschrift 15 (1936) 7, 239. [17] G. Simmel, Rez. G. Tarde, Les lois de l'imitation, in: G. Simmel, Gesamtausgabe, ed. O. Rammstedt, vol. 1, Frankfurt am Main 2000, 411f.

Secondary literature

[18] I. Hacking, Styles of Scientific Thinking or Reasoning. A New Analytical Tool for Histo-rians and Philosophers of the Sciences, in: K. Gavroglu et.al. (eds.), Trends in the Historiog-raphy of Science, Dordrecht et al. 1994, 31–48. [19] W. Höppner, "Rasse ist Stil." Anmerkungen zum Wissenschaftsstil in der germanistischen

Literaturwissenschaft des "Dritten Reiches," in: F.-M. Kirsch/B. Almgren (eds.), Sprache und Politik im skandinavischen und deutschen Kontext 1933–1945, Aalborg 2003, 73–88. [20] H. Knoblauch, Wissenssoziologie, Konstanz ²2010. [21] T. Schnelle, Ludwik Fleck. Leben und Denken. Zur Entstehung und Entwicklung des soziologischen Denkstils in der Wissenschaftsphilosophie, Freiburg im Breisgau 1982. [22] H. Schüling, Denkstil. Beschreibung und Deutung der Denkformen, Gießen 1964. [23] P. Stachel, "Was ist eine Tatsache?" Ludwik Flecks Beitrag zur Wissenssoziologie und Erkenntnistheorie, in: Jahrbuch des Simon-Dubnow-Instituts 4 (2005), 351–382. [24] G.-R. Wegmarshaus, Vom Denkstil zum Paradigma. Zum Schicksal einer unzeitgemäßen Einsicht, in: B. Choluj/J. C. Joerden (eds.), Von der wissenschaftlichen Tatsache zur Wissensproduktion. Ludwik Fleck und seine Bedeutung für die Wissenschaft und Praxis, Frankfurt am Main et al. 2007, 49–63. [25] D. Wittich, Das Verhältnis von Wissenschaft und Kultur in der Wissenschaftstheorie von Ludwik Fleck, in: Zeitschrift für Deutsche Philosophie 31 (1983), 852–855.

NICOLAS BERG, LEIPZIG

Sufis

Members of an Islamic-mystic movement the origins of which date back to the early Islamic period and which became more differentiated thanks to contacts with non-Muslim faith communities. From the very first, a close connection developed between Sufis and Jews with an interest in → mysticism. Notwithstanding occasional conflicts, the religious views of both groups were easily translatable, ensuring lively spiritual exchange, especially in Muslim centers with numerous Jewish population such as → Baghdad, al-Andalus (→ Sepharad), → Damascus, → Salonika, and → Mashhad.

1. History of Sufism
2. Exchanging religious ideas and practices
3. Sufi mysticism and Jewish literature
4. Contacts, interrelations, and conversions
5. Delimitations and conflicts

1. History of Sufism

Sufism (Arab. *taṣawwuf*) is the collective term for a variety of mystic trends within Islam. As opposed to Islamic orthodoxy, these emphasize the spiritual dimension of Islam and seek to achieve an experience of the divine using different teachings and practices depending on the different interpretations. The term "Sufi" is derived from the Arabic *ṣūf*, the name for the woolen garments of the first Sufis.

Sufi groups are found in nearly all regions of the world influenced by Islam. They display considerable differences in their cultural characteristics, their approach to faith, and their ritual practices. In some cases, these can be traced back to contacts with non-Muslim faith communities, varying depending on the place and the time. The element common to all the various Sufi trends is the hope of achieving a connection with God in this world and experiencing the unity of God. The path (Arab. *ṭarīq*) receives impulses from divine love (Arab. *'ishq, maḥabbah*), includes certain rites such as the commemoration of God (Arab. *dhikr*) or religious dance (Arab. *samā'*); the Sufi progresses along it under instruction from a master (Arab. *murshid, shaykh*). After a long process of gradual human perfection (Arab. *al-insān al-kāmil*) it leads to the complete absorption into God (Arab. *fanā' fī Allāh*).

In the self-understanding of many Sufis, the origins of the movement go back to the Quran, read applying special and often allegorical hermeneutics, and to the Prophet Muhammad, who is particularly revered in Sufism. The oldest surviving historical sources point to the early 8th century.

They record above all the ascetic piety of the Sufis in Basra and → Baghdad, who were presumably influenced by the early Christian concepts of asceticism and hermit life that had developed within the Eastern Church. Junayd al-Baghdādī (ca. 830–910) and his pupil Manṣūr al-Ḥallāj (857–922) achieved enduring importance for the further development of Sufism. Although they were close, they represented opposing views: while Junayd devised a sober type of Sufism mostly in accordance with the Sharia, sources describe his pupil al-Ḥallāj as an ecstatic and enraptured God-loving man. Al-Ḥallāj's polarizing mysticism contributed to many theologians and law scholars rejecting Sufism.

Abū Ḥāmid al-Ghazālī (1058–1111; → Falsafah), whose works are among the most important of Islamic intellectual history, sought the harmonization of orthodox theology (Arab. → *kalām*) and Sufism. Two further Islamic mystics whose influence throughout history was similarly significant were Muḥyī al-Dīn ibn al-ʿArabī (1165–1240) and Mawlānā Jalāl al-Dīn Rūmī (1207–1273). Born in Spain, Ibn al-ʿArabī is regarded as the great systematist among the Sufi scholars whose ontology, anthropology, and epistemology were significantly influenced by Neo-Platonism. His principle of the "unity of being" (Arab. *waḥdat al-wujūd*), according to which all creation manifests the divine and consequently had a part in it, has often been assumed to be the foundation for the universal tolerance exhibited by many Sufis. Similar maxims are also found, besides spirited verses rich in metaphors about the love of God, in the poetry of the Persian mystic Rūmī. His ideas provide the foundation for the Mevlevi order, who were politically as well as culturally influential in the Ottoman Empire – those Sufis who became famous in Europe by the 19th century as "whirling dervishes" because of their spinning dances.

In the 12th century, the Sufi movement acquired institutional form with fixed organizational structures in the shape of religious orders (Arab. *ṭarīqah*). Further orders were founded during the 13th century, soon encompassing all regions influenced by Islam. The orientation of the communities differed considerably: while the Qadiri and Naqshbandi, influential in wide regions of the Islamic world, embraced moderate views and practices and continued to follow the rules of orthodox Islam on the whole, other orders emerged who inclined to antinomianism, such as the Bektashi, who were influential in Anatolia and southeastern Europe and were influenced by Twelver Shiʿism (→ Dönmeh). Many of these communities did not live secluded from the world but contributed to the cultural life of the region with music, art, and literature (→ Maqam). Some, like the Mevlevi and the Bektashi, and the Naqshbandi from the 18th century onward, exerted great influence on society and politics in the Ottoman Empire. The Persian Safavid Empire (1501–1722) even originated in a Sufi community, the Safavi order.

Even in the modern era, the Sufis did not completely lose their influence. The orders reacted differently to the challenges of modern times. In some countries they were officially forbidden in the course of secular or fundamentalist endeavors, such as in Turkey under Atatürk and in Wahhabi Saudi Arabia. Even so they retained their social position. Beginning in the early 20th century, several orders expanded their networks into Western Europe and North America, such as for instance the Sufi Order International, founded by the Indian Sufi master Hazrat Inayat Khan (1882–1927) in London in 1917.

2. Exchanging religious ideas and practices

Cultural and spiritual exchanges between Sufis and non-Muslim groups took place over centuries, for instance in the region of India and Pakistan (Hindus and Sikhs), in southeastern Europe (Greek Orthodox and Armenian Christians), or in Egypt (Copts). There were interrelations between Sufis and Jewish mystics as well, leading to a blending of religious ideas. As early as the 8th and 9th centuries, some Jews joined the first Sufis in → Baghdad and converted to Islam (→ Conversion). In this way, ideas embraced by Jewish *merkavah* → mysticism, which goes back to the biblical vision of the throne-chariot (Hebr. *merkavah*) seen by Ezekiel, probably made their way into early Sufism. In particular the Sufi view of Muhammad's journey to heaven (Arab. *miʿrāj*), which is regarded as the central instance and model of being close to God, appears to have been influenced in this way. A number of Sufi narratives on the subject of ascensions to heaven, for instance by Bāyazīd al-Bisṭāmī (803–874 or 877/878) display remarkable parallels with *merkavah* mysticism [8. 148–153]. However, it is not always possible to clearly distinguish between the concrete transfer of religious ideas and the legacy of a shared history of ideas.

Just to what degree Islamic mysticism influenced Jewish mysticism is a matter of dispute; doctrines range from constructs of dependence to total negation. Without doubt elements of Islamic mysticism made their way into the teachings of Abraham ben Moses ben Maimon (1186–1237), the only son of Maimonides (→ Guide for the Perplexed) and his successor as the *Nagid* (religious leader) of the Jews in Egypt. In his magnum opus *Kifāyat al-ʿābidīn* (Arab.; Guide for the servants of God), he referred explicitly to Sufi religious beliefs and ritual practices. He traced many of their rites back to traditions of biblical prophets: while these survived among the Sufis, they had been forgotten among the Jews living in the → Diaspora. Abraham even institutionalized some customs in the course of his reforms of the Jewish rite, among them the Sufi

practice of the so-called *khalvah*, in which believers retired to a hermitage for forty days in order to devote themselves to contemplation of God in seclusion. Abraham's son Obadiah (1228–1265) continued this tradition, as we know from his only surviving work *Maqālat al-ḥawḍīyah* (Arab.; Treatise on the cistern), a guideline for the spiritual path [6]. As the presumably last descendant of the Maimonides dynasty to hold the position of *Nagid*, David ben Joshuah (1st half of the 14th cent. – 1414) practiced the *khalvah*, it is safe to assume that this Jewish-Sufi form of piety was alive for nearly 200 years.

Some Jewish ritual practices of the early prophetic-Kabbalistic movement (beginning in the 13th century) were also probably modeled on Sufi customs: the descriptions concerning the contemplation of God, for instance, as provided by Abraham Abulafia (1240–1291/1292) and his followers, especially Nathan ben Saʿadyah and Isaac ben Samuel of Acre (both 13th/14th cents.), recall the Sufi spiritual exercise of *dhikr* – the genuine Sufi practice during which the various names of God are repeated in a sometimes ecstatic manner.

3. Sufi mysticism and Jewish literature

Sufis and Jews encountered one another in the medium of written texts as well. The Jews in Damascus, for example, are said to have studied Maimonides's philosophical magnum opus *Dalālat al-ḥāʾirīn* (Arab.; Hebr. *Moreh Nevukhim*; → Guide for the Perplexed) under the guidance of the Sufi al-Ḥasan ibn Hūd (13th cent.), reinterpreting it in the Sufi spirit. Sufi influence also extended to written texts themselves. In the field of Judeo-Arabic literature (→ Arabic), the mysticism of the Sufis informed works written in al-Andalus (→ Sepharad), for instance by Solomon ibn Gabirol (1021–1058), Yehudah ha-Levi (ca. 1075–1141), and Bahyah ibn

Pakudah (11th cent.). Ibn Pakudah's main work *Kitāb al-hidāyah ilā al-farā'iḍ al-qulūb* (Arab.; Book on the guidelines for the duties of the heart, 1080) was a religious guidebook in ten chapters, each of which presents one of the duties of the heart, with the entire book demonstrating the individual spiritual path to God. In it, he combined elements of the rationalistic-Islamic theology embraced by the *mu'tazilah* (→ Kalām), of Jewish rabbinic theology (→ Talmud), and of Sufism in a unique manner [9]. Numerous further Jewish works with references to Sufism were preserved in the Cairo → Genizah, among them the treatises on Sufi-Jewish piety by the Maimonides family. Besides these, we find writings of Rabbanite as well as → Karaite Jews, who wrote about the lives and works of well-known Sufis such as Junayd al-Baghdādī and Manṣūr al-Ḥallāj or translated their works into → Hebrew and Judeo-Arabic.

Judeo-Persian literature, too, includes works informed by Sufism. Particularly worth noting among these is the *Ganj-nāma* (Pers.; Book of the treasure) by the poet 'Imrānī (1454 – after 1536) from Isfahan, whose entire literary creation followed the tradition of classical Persian and mystic poetry by Sa'dī (ca. 1210–1292) and Ḥāfiẓ (ca. 1320–1389). The *Ganj-nāma* is 'Imrānī's verse commentary on the Mishnah treatise *Pirke Avot* (Hebr.; Sayings of the fathers; → Talmud), employing explicitly Islamic-mystic concepts and doctrines. A comparable work from the late 18th century is the *Ḥayāt al-rūḥ* (Arab.; The life of the soul) by the poet and scholar Siman Tov Melammed (d. 1800, 1823, or 1828) from → Mashhad, which may be regarded as an amalgam of Jewish and Islamic mysticism and philosophy (→ Falsafah) [2]. In a poem from the *Ḥayāt al-rūḥ*, Melammed lists the virtues of the Sufis, calling them "Godly and radiant like roses" (cited in [2. 260–265]) in the chorus; in classical Persian Sufism, the rose is the most widely-used metaphor for divine beauty.

4. Contacts, interrelations, and conversions

Contacts between Sufis and Jews were particularly visible on the field of music. In the 16th century, the paraliturgical Sephardic hymns (→ Piyyut) found themselves influenced by the Ottoman Turkish → maqam, which would over time encompass the entire Sephardic Jewish → liturgy. The contact was due to, among other things, Sufi orders in the Ottoman Empire, mainly the Mevlevis, who contributed significantly to the development of Ottoman art music. From the 16th century onward, continual exchanges between Mevlevi dervishes and Jewish musicians are documented in → Smyrna, → Salonika, and Edirne. Autobiographical accounts, such as by the Jewish composer Behor Menahem (1908–2003) from Edirne, document that Jewish musicians visited Sufi convents and attended the musical rites of the Mevlevis, among them the dervishes' ritual spinning dance. The Mevlevis, in turn, visited the synagogue in order to listen to the → cantor (Hebr. *ḥazan*). The remarkable connection between the two groups was demonstrated when Atatürk declared all Sufi orders illegal in Turkey in 1925; after the Mevlevi convents had been closed, the Jews in Edirne let the dervishes use the premises of the Great Synagogue (El Kahal Grande) for their ceremonies.

The missionary Joseph Wolff (1795/1796–1862), whose activities led him to Persia in the 1830s, confirmed the close contacts between Sufis and Jews in → Mashhad that are indicated by works such as Melammed's *Ḥayāt al-rūḥ*. Wolff, who had converted from Judaism to Christianity and sought to convert Jews, Muslims, and members of other religious communities on his numerous journeys in the → Orient, reported Persian works inspired by Sufism in the possession of the Jews of Mashhad. These were written in the Judeo-Persian variant of the → Hebrew script. A group of Mashhad Jews, he said, even studied with a Sufi master named Muḥammad ʿAlī. Wolff described these "Jewish Sooffees" as Sufis and Jews at the same time: while they had not converted to Islamic Sufism, they studied Sufi doctrines and practices without abandoning their original faith. According to their own testimony, they had two different religions: Judaism as the "exterior" faith in their dealings with society and Sufism as an "interior" faith practiced in the Sufi convents [3. 93–127]. It is probable that the dichotomy of an external, manifest (*ẓāhir*) and an inner, spiritual (*bāṭin*) dimension of the faith, found especially in Shiʿite and Sufi hermeneutics, built a bridge between Sufis and Jews, as Jewish philosophers also referred to it, for instance Saʿadyah Gaʾon (→ Kalām) and Maimonides. Similar Sufi-Jewish interrelations were also found in other cities of present-day Iran, such as Hamadan at the end of the 19th and Tehran at the beginning of the 20th century. While the sources rarely name a concrete order, the Sufi groups in question probably belonged to the influential Shiʿite Nimatullahi order.

There were individual cases of Jews converting to Islam as well as Sufism. The poet Muḥammad Saʿīd Sarmad (d. 1659) was born in Kashan in the province of Isfahan. He was from a Jewish family, converted to Islam, and followed Sufi mysticism. In 1632 he moved to the Mughal Empire in India where he translated parts of the Torah (→ Tanakh) into Persian and composed verses about the love of God. His unorthodox lifestyle – he often appeared without clothes and embraced free-thinking ideas – led to the Mughal Emperor Aurangzeb (1618–1707) having him executed. The best-known → conversions of Jews to Islam are without a doubt those of the pseudo-Messiah Sabbatai Zevi (1626–1676; → Smyrna) and his followers, the → Dönmeh. This (originally involuntary) conversion was also linked to a Sufi impulse. Sabbatai Zevi probably visited the Bektashi convent Hızırlık in Edirne, adopting its rites; he also appears to have been in direct contact with the famous Sufi Niyāzī-i Mıṣrī (1617/1618–1694). After Sabbatai Zevi's death, his followers became divided into three main groups which joined different Islamic trends: while the Yakubiler were close to orthodox Sunni Islam, the Kapancılar were influenced by the Mevlevis and the Karakaşlar by the Bektashis. Kapancılar and Karakaşlar were distinct groups who wove Jewish mystical and Islamic mystical religiousness into their own doctrines in an eclectic fashion [5. 33f., 55–60].

5. Delimitations and conflicts

In the regions where the Jewish and Muslim faiths had close contacts, dedication to Sufi mysticism also met with criticism among the Jews. Abraham ben Moses ben Maimon's openness to Sufi rites had already aroused suspicion and resistance among some Egyptian Jews. A poem written in Judeo-Persian by a poet named Jacob also testifies to rejection, painting a polemic picture of the initiation into a Sufi order and emphasizing in contrast the poet's own deep connection with the Mosaic faith.

In Sufi circles, however, there was criticism of the universal interpretation of religion that often was the basis of the encounters and exchanges between Sufis and Jews. Individual Sufi trends claimed the authority of interpretation concerning the "correct" faith, excluding other religious communities. Thus some subgroups of the Naqshbandi order rejected non-Muslim faith communities as well as Muslim ones that diverged from orthodox Sunni Islam.

The coexistence of Sufis and Jews was not always harmonious either. In some cases, open conflict broke out, for instance in 17th-century Morocco: when the Nasiri order gained influence in the Zagora region and established its center in Tamgrut, it brought about the emigration of the local Jewish community first through economic policy and later by means of repressive measures.

Notwithstanding individual difficulties, the encounters between Jews and Sufis documented in a variety of places at different times are testament to a fundamental shared understanding of religion that either permitted religious ambivalence or relativized differences.

Bibliography

Sources

[1] 'Obadyah Maimonides, The Treatise of the Pool, trans. by P. Fenton, London 1995. [2] V. B. Moreen, In Queen Esther's Garden. An Anthology of Judeo-Persian Literature, New Haven 2000. [3] J. Wolff, Researches and Missionary Labours among Jews, Mohammedans, and Other Sects, London 1835.

Secondary literature

[4] M. Amanat, Jewish Identities in Iran. Resistance and Conversion to Islam and the Bahā'ī Faith, London 2011. [5] M. D. Baer, The Dönme. Jewish Converts, Muslim Revolutionaries, and Secular Turks, Stanford 2010. [6] P. B. Fenton, Judaism and Sufism, in: S. H. Nasr/O. Leaman (eds.), History of Islamic Philosophy, vol. 1, London/New York 1996, 755–768. [7] M. B. Jackson, Mixing Music. Turkish Jewry and the Urban Landscape of a Sacred Song, Stanford 2013. [8] R. C. Kiener, Jewish Mysticism in the Lands of the Ishmaelites. A Re-Orientation, in: M. M. Laskier (ed.), The Convergence of Judaism and Islam. Religious, Scientific, and Cultural Dimensions, Gainesville et al. 2011, 147–167. [9] D. Lobel, A Sufi-Jewish Dialogue. Philosophy and Mysticism in Baḥya Ibn Paqūda's Duties of the Heart, Philadelphia 2007. [10] A. Schimmel, Mystical Dimensions of Islam, Chapel Hill (NC) 2011.

CEM KARA, MUNICH

Sulamith

The first Jewish periodical in the German language and the Latin alphabet, which was published in Dessau in nine volumes between 1806 and 1848. Indebted to the Jewish Enlightenment in its self-understanding, its declared goal was to advance → Bildung and assimilation into the → middle class, as well as equal rights for Jews in the German territories. Following upon the early → Haskalah, *Sulamith* devoted itself to the reform of Jewish worship and schools, the traditional forms of which their authors considered to be the main obstacle to → Emancipation. The journal, addressed both to a Jewish public and to the surrounding society as well, made a key contribution to the creation of a public for Jewish questions and the modernization of Jewish life in Germany.

Around 1800, the efforts of Jewish proponents of the Enlightenment, as well as debates about emancipation and acculturation brought about far-reaching changes in the communicative structures of Jewry in the German territories. In the wake of the Haskalah, a new intellectual elite made its appearance, which promoted the formation of a public for Jewish topics through their publications. By the end of the 18th century, however, their leading figures and pioneers had died, for instance Moses Mendelssohn (Bi'ur) in 1786 and Isaak Euchel (→ Reb Henokh) in 1804. In addition, the first modern Hebrew journal, *Ha-Me'assef* (The Collector), edited by Euchel, had ceased publication in 1797.

In 1806, *Sulamith* was founded as a successor publication to *Ha-Me'assef*. The Dessau pedagogues David Fränkel (1779–1865) and Joseph Wolf (1762–1826) acted as editors of the first issues. In 1802, Fränkel had taken over the presidency of the Jewish Haupt- und Freischule in Dessau, which he had co-founded, and in 1806 had inaugurated the Israelite Töchterschule (girl's school); later, he took over the direction of the Jewish schools of Dessau. Wolf had taken up a position as teacher of German at the Dessau Freischule in 1797, and had, moreover, come to the fore as a preacher in the Jewish community, where he introduced worship in German in 1805 (→ Sermon) [10. 108f., 119f.]. From 1808 onward, Fränkel was solely responsible for the journal.

Unlike its Hebrew predecessors, or the *Jüdisch-deutsche Monatsschrift*, typeset in German and Hebrew script, which had appeared in Prague in 1802, *Sulamith* used German in Latin script. By means of this programmatic decision, the editors united, on the one hand, the hope of accelerating the cultural modernization of the Jews; on the other, they expected, from a stronger orientation to the general public, a positive echo for Jewish themes and acceptance from the surrounding society [6. 15]; [7. 446]. In addition, they concluded from the cessation of *Ha-Me'assef* that the disappearance of the Hebrew-speaking readership would give expression to a changing need for reading and communication, which would be met by the new journal. In addition, the decision in favor of German in *Sulamith* abolished the separation, which had previously reigned, between internal literature in Jewish languages and apologetic literature, which was directed especially to Christian readers in their respective vernaculars [9. 82].

Many of the journal's authors were, like Fränkel and Wolf, also pedagogues, writers, and proponents of the Haskalah as well, for instance, Aaron Halle-Wolfssohn (1754/1756–1835) or David Caro (ca. 1782–1839), and had already published previously in *Ha-Me'assef*. The authors also included David Friedländer (1750–1834) the main representative of the Berlin Haskalah, the teacher, translator, and publisher Moses Philippson (1755–1814), and Ludwig Philippson (1811–1889), the later founder of the *Allgemeine Zeitung des Judentums*. The editors also persuaded individual Christian scholars to contribute to the journal.

Whereas the publication of the first year's issues took place in Leipzig, *Sulamith* was moved to Dessau beginning in 1807. Here, the journal's publication was favored by the relatively tolerant policies, sustained by the ideas of the Enlightenment, of Duke Leopold III Friedrich Franz von Anhalt-Dessau. In 1810, Fränkel temporarily moved the journal's place of publication to Kassel, where he was active as a member of the Westphalian Consistory of Israelites. In addition to sales by subscription, the issues were also available in select bookstores, for example in Leipzig and Vienna. After only half a year, the editors found themselves forced to switch from their planned monthly rate of publication to an irregular rhythm. The number of subscribers remained manageable overall;

Title page of the first issue of the journal Sulamith, *Leipzig 1806*

thus, in 1834/1835, exactly 214 persons committed themselves in advance to purchasing the journal. It may be assumed, however, that individual issues came into the hands of several readers and thus reached wider circles of readers [7. 487f.].

Sulamith was addressed primarily to an educated public, which represented the middle-class attitude to life of a liberally oriented Jewry and combined professional success with a citizen's loyalty to the state [7. 450]. It was aimed at Jewish readers of various milieus, from schoolteachers to bankers. *Sulamith* also reached influential personages from politics, science, and trade. As early as the first issue, Fränkel could allude to the fact that he had won over the prince of Anhalt-Dessau as a subscriber [2. 36]; he was later joined by the kings of Württemberg, the Netherlands, and Belgium. Moreover, several Christian scholars were among its readers and disseminators [5. 161].

Against the background of the legal equality achieved by Jews in the wake of the → French Revolution, from the dissemination of which in the German territories and from the establishment of the Kingdom of Westphalia, where Fränkel worked in the Consistory of Israelites, the editors of *Sulamith* also hoped for the implementation of complete emancipation. They therefore gave a favorable report of the Grand → Sanhédrin, which Napoleon convoked in 1807. They adopted the idea that only an alignment of the Jews with the middle class, as had already been demanded by Christian proponents of the Enlightenment in debates over the → improvement of the Jews, would create the preconditions for it. A political demand thus became a question of pedagogy [9. 86]. In the same vein, Joseph Wolf named as its "sole purpose" the "development of the powerful educational ability of the Jews" in the foreword to the first issue of the journal [3. 11]. This program, the claim to affiliation with the surrounding society, and

the current status of these questions were also expressed by the changing subtitles: *Eine Zeitschrift zur Beförderung der Kultur und Humanität unter der jüdischen Nation* (A Journal for the Promotion of Culture and Humanity among the Jewish Nation, 1806–1809); *Eine Zeitschrift zur Beförderung der Kultur und Humanität unter den Israeliten* (A Journal for the Promotion of Culture and Humanity among the Israelites, 1810–1834); *Eine Zeitschrift* (A Journal, 1834–1848).

Like its predecessor *Ha-Me'assef*, *Sulamith* followed the model of the Enlightenment periodicals in choice of subjects and in format. It addressed moral and religious questions, printed → Bible translations and traditional literature, and reported on the lifestyles of other peoples as well as of other Jewries, but also dealt with technical and economic topics [9. 82]. Contributions on education, culture, and pedagogical reform occupied a central position. In addition, the journal rendered outstanding services in popularizing the philosophy of the Enlightenment and German literature. Individual contributions to the journal were united by their focus on the religious and cultural renewal of individuals and society.

Here, the turn toward German and culture was conceived as a key presupposition for the rise to the middle class. Although dissenting opinions also came to the fore, which demanded acceptance of the plurality of Judaism, the efforts of *Sulamith* were oriented primarily toward the reform of traditional customs and cult, as well as the occupational structure (→ Professions). It supported the tendency toward confessionalization and reform of worship after the model of Protestantism, for instance by its advocacy of sermons in German. It consistently pled for loyalty to the State and conformity to secular laws. Here, the efforts at reform of Jewish ways of life popularized in the journal were addressed, on the one hand, to Jewish readers; on the other, the contributions were to make the Jews' readiness for acculturation obvious to Christian readers. In this context, Christian scholars who appeared as authors of the journal were presented as authorities on culture and education. In their contributions, moreover, they sometimes expressed a certain degree of criticism of state policies concerning the Jews, which seldom happened with Jewish authors [8. 4].

Sulamith was also deliberately directed to a female readership. Thus, in the first edition, Fränkel recommended the journal particularly to the "mothers and daughters in Israel" as "loyal friend and advisor" [2. 38]. In view of the crisis of → marriage and family, which manifested itself especially in urban centers between 1770 and 1830 in the growing number of conversions, divorces, and out-of-wedlock → births, *Sulamith* fashioned a new image of Jewish women. It advocated their withdrawal into domestic life; it was here alone that feminine morality was to have its effects. The normative conception of women as protectresses of religiousness as lived in private was to mitigate the sociocultural assimilation to the surrounding society that was demanded of Jewish men in public and in working life.

Fränkel ceased publication of *Sulamith* in 1848. Against the background of the March Revolution, he now considered the journal obsolete since emancipation seemed to be immediately imminent. Thus, the citizens of Dessau called for the equal rights for the Jews, which was granted in an edict by Leopold IV Friedrich, Duke of Anhalt-Dessau. In addition, in a decree from April 1848 on some principles of the future Prussian constitution, the Prussian king Friedrich Wilhelm IV had declared, among other provisions, that the exercise of citizens' rights was independent of creed. Fränkel hoped from these developments that "the situation of most German Jews" would now enter into a "new, beautiful era," if "unconditional emancipation" were now realized [1]. At the same time, however, the now seventy-year-old Fränkel

could no longer keep up with the discussions that resulted from this development: the long interval between the publications of the last volumes may be considered an indication of this. The younger generation, in particular, demanded more appropriate and more political journalistic formats, to which the moral air of *Sulamith* no longer corresponded. By the mid-19th century, periodicals such as Gabriel Riesser's *Der Jude* (1832–1835), the → *Allgemeine Zeitung des Judentums* (1837–1922), and → *Der Orient* (1840–1851) appeared, which, for their part, reflected and carried on the modernization of Judaism that was originally promoted by *Sulamith*.

Bibliography

Sources

[1] D. Fränkel, Schlußbemerkungen. Ein Wort zu seiner Zeit, in: Sulamith. Neue Folge 1 (1847/1848) 3, 272. [2] D. Fränkel, Vorläufige Bemerkungen über die zweckmäßigsten Mittel zur Beförderung der Kultur und Humanität unter der jüdischen Nation, in: Sulamith 1 (1806) 1, 12–40. [3] J. Wolf, Inhalt, Zweck und Titel dieser Zeitschrift, in: Sulamith 1 (1806) 1, 1–11.

Secondary literature

[4] M. Eliav, Jewish Education in Germany in the Period of Enlightenment and Emancipation, Jerusalem 1960. [5] W. Grossert, Sulamith (1806–1848), die erste jüdische Zeitschrift in deutscher Sprache und in deutscher Schrift, in: E. J. Engel/B. G. Ulbrich (eds.), Judentum. Wege zur geistigen Befreiung, Dessau 2002, 158–169. [6] K. von der Krone, Wissenschaft in Öffentlichkeit. Die Wissenschaft des Judentums und ihre Zeitschriften, Berlin 2012. [7] S. Lässig, Jüdische Wege ins Bürgertum. Kulturelles Kapital und sozialer Aufstieg, Göttingen 2004. [8] K. Oppermann, "... ich ersuche ihn herzlich, uns recht oft mit seinen vortrefflichen Aufsätzen zu erfreuen." Christliche Autoren in der Zeitschrift Sulamith, in: Medaon. Magazin für jüdisches Leben in Forschung und Bildung 5 (2011) 8,

1–7. [9] D. Sorkin, The Transformation of German Jewry 1780–1840, New York 1987. [10] D. Sorkin, Preacher, Teacher, Publicist. Joseph Wolf and the Ideology of Emancipation, in: F. Malino/D. Sorkin (eds.), From East and West. Jews in a Changing Europe 1750–1870, Oxford/Cambridge 1991, 107–125. [11] M. Will, "Die Philosophie im Weiberrocke wird kein Vernünftiger achten ...." Zur Ambivalenz in den Mädchenbildungskonzepten der Zeitschrift Sulamith (1806–1848), in: B. L. Behm et al. (ed.), Jüdische Erziehung und aufklärerische Schulreform, Münster 2002, 369–391.

INGRID LOHMANN, HAMBURG

Sultan's Jews

Due to their business acumen and wide-ranging connections, individual Jews were able to rise to high positions and offices in the Ottoman sultans' courts of the early modern age. As Sultan's Jews they could exercise influence on domestic as well as foreign policy in the Ottoman Empire, acting in addition as mediators, intercessors, and supporters of the Jewish community. Among their most prominent representatives were members of the Sephardi Nasi family who, after settling in Constantinople, acquired the reputation of being political actors, → patrons of the arts, and advocates of Jewish concerns.

1. Jews at the Sultan's court
2. Significance
3. The Nasi family
4. Decline

1. Jews at the Sultan's court

From the 15th century until the Tanzimat reforms in the 19th century, Jews lived at the sultans' courts and acted as high- and low-ranking public servants. The first ones were Jews from Central Europe (→ Ashkenaz), who arrived in waves in the Ottoman Empire from the 14th century onward as they hoped for better living conditions under Muslim rule than in Christian Europe. Sephardic Jews found a home among the Ottomans in large numbers after the expulsions from Spain in 1492 and Portugal in 1497 (→ Sepharad). Sultan Bayezid II (r. 1481–1512) invited them explicitly to settle in his realm, guaranteeing freedom of religion and → autonomy. Numerically as well as culturally, they soon surpassed the Ashkenazi Jews, → Karaites, and Byzantine Romaniotes. In the 16th century, especially after the 1506 massacre in Lisbon and the initiation of the Portuguese Inquisition 1536 (→ Toledo), a growing number of → Conversos immigrated wishing to practice Judaism openly once more. The fact that the frequently wealthy Jewish new arrivals were not only familiar with the political and economic circumstances in Europe but often also had valuable business contacts and other connections with the ruling houses there, positively predestined them for the role as diplomats and advisers to the sultans.

Many of the Sultan's Jews were physicians at the court. Depending on their rank, their activities ranged from the medical care of the palace inhabitants – most of whom were slaves – to treating the ruling family or the sultan himself. Jewish merchants supplied the court with wine, spices, jewelry, and other goods. They frequently unlocked additional lucrative sources of income by leasing the collection of taxes and customs duties (→ Leaseholding). In addition, a number of Jewish musicians worked at court, teaching instruments or playing in ensembles for the entertainment of the courtiers. Some of them rose to become the sultan's personal music teachers. Jewish women, too, acquired influence at court. As intermediaries between the world beyond the court and the ladies of the harem, they provided the latter – who were forbidden to leave the palace – with medical services, cosmetics, and valuables.

Their activities at court brought the Sultan's Jews wealth and influence. Born in Portugal, the Converso Solomon Abenaes (1520–1603), for example, lived in several European capitals during his flight from the Inquisition and established valuable connections with the respective rulers. Visiting the Ottoman Empire on a diplomatic mission in 1585, he decided to settle there and re-convert to Judaism. He established close connections with Sultan Murad III (1546–1595), who would soon entrust him with the position of governor of the Greek port of Mytilene; in 1579 he assumed the lordship of → Tiberias. Furthermore he worked on establishing an alliance between England and the Ottoman Empire that would be directed against Catholic Spain.

Some of the sultans' Jewish physicians also served as diplomats. Born in northern Italy, Solomon Nathan Ashkenazi was a merchant as well as the Venetian *bailo*'s (ambassador) physician before becoming the medical attendant to all Venetians in Constantinople. Eventually the grand vizier Sokollu Mehmed Pasha appointed him his personal physician. Esteemed by Sokollu for his diplomatic skill, Ashkenazi succeeded in negotiating the peace agreement between the Ottomans and Venice in 1573 on behalf of the grand vizier. He also played a significant part in the election of Henry of Valois, the Ottomans' preferred candidate, to become king of the Polish–Lithuanian Commonwealth in the same year.

Besides access to the Sublime Porte, the Sultan's Jews also cultivated connections with courtiers and high-ranking officials. Among these were the Agha of the Janissaries, the chief eunuch, the grand vizier, the sultan's mother, and members of the Islamic clergy (*'ulemā'*).

2. Significance

Materially as well as culturally, the life of the Sultan's Jews differed fundamentally from that of the majority of their fellow believers in the Ottoman Empire. As early as the mid-16th century, the scholar Moses ben Baruch Almosnino listed them besides the working population and the elected community leaders as a third prominent group within the Jewish community [6. 43f.]. In view of their position as mediators with the non-Jewish population, they could claim various privileges – such as maintaining private synagogues and exemption from community taxes. In addition, they lived in magnificent buildings and looked to the culture of the Ottoman elite. As a consequence, their lifestyle was not always in accordance with the requirements of the → Halakhah as embraced by religious Jewish authorities.

Many Sultan's Jews supported the poor in the Jewish communities (→ Tsedakah). As → patrons, they also sponsored book → printing, art, and scholarship. Solomon Abenaes, for instance, promoted the dissemination of an edition of the → Talmud produced by the printers *Yabets* in Constantinople [17. 134–137]. Families such as Nasi, Abenaes, or Elnekave were also prominent as the founders of important yeshivot (→ Talmud Torah) in the capital, and they employed renowned Jewish scholars to lead them. Their charity meant that, as members of a religion based on divine revelation (→ Ahl al-kitāb) with protected status (→ Dhimmah) in the Ottoman Empire, they also observed the commandment of leading a modest life.

Sultan's Jews also used their connections to the ruling dynasty in their function as intercessors (→ Shtadlanut) for the Jewish community. Tobias Hakohen (1652–1729; → Ma'aseh Toviyah) for instance, who was born in → Metz and later became court physician to the sultan's courts in Adrianople and Constantinople, boasted of having achieved "splendid things" on behalf of his Jewish co-religionists in the service of the grand vizier Rami Mehmet Pasha [2. Fol. 84a]. Sources even report that in 1579 Solomon Nathan Ashkenazi was able to persuade Sultan Murad III to commute an edict preparing the prosecution of Jews in the Ottoman Empire into a regulation to limit luxury among Jews and Christians (→ Dress Regulations) [14. 10f., 347f.]. Moses Hamon (ca. 1490–ca. 1554) from Granada and physician to Selim I and Süleyman I, in his turn succeeded in persuading the latter to issue a *firman* to protect the Jews from the accusation of ritual murder (→ Blood Libel); under this decree, plaintiffs were not permitted to bring the accusation before a common judge but had to present their suit directly to the Sublime Porte. The Sultan's Jews demonstrated their influence when, at the request of the Jewish authorities, they obtained the expulsion of the charismatic Kabbalist and self-styled messiah Sabbatai Zevi (→ Smyrna) from the city in 1666 and his ensuing exile to Albania [3. 2]; [15. 747f., 752].

Many Jewish dignitaries in the Ottoman capital were also active on behalf of the concerns of the Jews in Erets Israel. Thus, in the 17th century, we find numerous petitions from the Jerusalem community addressed to influential Sultan's Jews in Constantinople. In the 18th century, the physician of the grand vizier and subsequent Sultan Ahmed III, Joseph Ashkenazi, acted as the mediator in negotiations concerning the debts incurred by the Jerusalem community [11. 309–317]. Individuals also requested support for their concerns from the Jewish elite at court. Joseph Mataron in → Safed approached the Sultan's Jew Aharon Garsi in Constantinople requesting him to obtain a decree from the Sultan that would exempt him and his family from the Ottoman *sürgün* policy of forced resettlement; according to a *sürgün* edict, around two thirds of the Jewish community of Safed were to be resettled

on Cyprus which had recently (1571) been conquered by Selim II [8. 23].

In view of the extent of their power, Sultan's Jews usually did not consider themselves to be bound by all the regulations of Jewish community life. Some even distanced themselves from the Jewish community or decided to convert to Islam. The Jews working at the Sultan's court were linked among themselves by a close network of kinship and interest-based connections that was repeatedly shaken by bitter rivalries.

Not infrequently members of the Jewish elite would demand remuneration for their activities as intermediaries, a common practice in the Ottoman Empire. Another compensation for their services was in the form of professions of gratitude and honor from the Jewish community, bestowing on them a reputation as pious and self-sacrificing community members. Rabbis composed inscriptions for houses and synagogues belonging to the Sultan's Jews, while gravestones praised their work as well as their significance in the network of connections between the economic and the rabbinical elites [4].

By acting on behalf of the Jewish community, they acquired the status of authorities, which in turn increased their prestige among the Ottoman elite. This is reflected in the honorific "Supreme Leader of the Jewish Nation" bestowed retrospectively on Jews such as the businessman Abraham de Castro (16th cent.), who was in charge of the mint in Egypt, or Joseph Nasi, even though they had not held any official position in a community [1].

3. The Nasi family

The members of the Nasi family are among the most famous Sultan's Jews, foremost of all Doña Gracia Nasi (1510–1569), born Beatriz de Luna into a wealthy Lisbon family of Conversos. In 1528, she married into the Mendes family whose members served as merchants and → bankers at several European royal courts. After the death of her husband Francesco Mendes, she fled from the Inquisition (→ Toledo) to → Antwerp with her family. She contributed to managing the bank founded by her brother-in-law Diego Mendes, carrying out transactions all over Europe. After Diego's death in 1543, she continued the business with support from her nephew João Miguez Nasi (ca. 1520–1579).

In order to circumvent Emperor Charles V's and his sister Mary of Hungary's ploy to lay their hands on the family fortune by marrying Beatriz Mendes's daughter Reyna to a nobleman, Beatriz and her family first fled to → Venice in 1544, and – after a brief incarceration as the result of being denounced as a crypto-Jew by her sister Brianda Mendes – finally in 1550 to Ferrara in northern Italy, where numerous Sephardic Jews were living. Here, Beatriz Mendes openly re-converted to Judaism, adopting the Hebrew name Gracia (Hannah, Hebr. *Ḥanah*) Nasi. She supported the Jewish community and helped Jews leave the Iberian Peninsula after forced conversions and settle in Italy or the Ottoman Empire. By funding a Jewish Castilian → Bible translation, she intended to facilitate the Marranos' re-conversion to Judaism who were unfamiliar with → Hebrew.

Fearing the Inquisition, Doña Gracia finally settled in Constantinople in 1553. João Miguez followed her a year later, converting to Judaism as well and calling himself Joseph Nasi from then on. Marriage with his cousin Reyna strengthened the familial ties of the family, who soon made their way into the economic elite of the Ottoman Empire thanks to their business activities.

Gracia Nasi was able to draw on a network of trade agents, particularly in the maritime trade with Italian cities. Joseph Nasi established connections with the court of Sultan Süleyman I, allowing him to provide the sultan with detailed information regarding the political situation in Europe

within a short time. He also gained the trust of Süleyman's son. When the latter became Sultan Selim II (1524–1574) in 1556, Nasi rose to becoming a favorite courtier and close adviser in foreign matters. As a sign of his favor, Selim II appointed him Duke of Naxos and the Cyclades in 1566. Joseph's great wealth also enabled him to lease (→ Leaseholding) some of the most lucrative sources of income, among them the tax on imported wine. In a bitter competition with his rival Sokullu Mehmed Pasha, a convert from Serbian Orthodox Christianity to Islam who was appointed grand vizier of the Ottoman Empire in 1565, Nasi endeavored to bring Ottoman diplomacy in line with his own projects. Selim II's death, however, shook his position as a Sultan's Jew with lasting effect, as the new sultan Murad III initially favored Sokullu Mehmed Pasha above all other advisers.

The Nasi family's palace in the Ortaköy district on the Bosporus became a center of → philanthropy, of Torah studies, and of universal scholarship. Gracia Nasi founded a yeshivah (→ Talmud Torah) and appointed as its head the famous rabbi Joseph Ben Lev (1502–1588) from → Salonika. In Salonika, she supported the institution of a new → kahal that was named after her – *Kahal Kadosh Livyat Ḥen* (a play on her Hebrew name *Ḥanah*) – and intended primarily for the Conversos who had reconverted to Judaism. The establishment of a yeshivah led by the Talmud scholar Samuel de Medina (1505–1589) is attributed to her as well. Moreover the family sponsored the copying of manuscripts and book → printing; in the 1590s Reyna Nasi, by then a widow, ran her own printing press in Constantinople [17. 32].

Politically, too, the family members stood up for other Jews and Marranos. When Pope Paul IV had a group of Conversos burnt at the stake in Ancona in 1556 because of a suspicion that they secretly practiced Judaism,

Gracia Nasi endeavored to organize an international trade boycott against the city, which was part of the Papal States, in which she was supported by Jewish merchants and religious authorities in the Ottoman Empire. One of her economic initiatives was to strengthen Pesaro, establishing it as the new maritime base for trade between Italy and the Levant, but this was never realized. Another project embraced by the Nasi was the development of → Tiberias and the surrounding area. In 1560, Gracia Nasi obtained the concession for Tiberias and the surrounding villages, which had been conquered by the Ottomans a few years earlier, from Süleyman I in return for an annual payment of a thousand gold coins. Her intention was to transform the region, which had been stagnating since the 13th century, into a center of Jewish scholarship and economic activity. In the mid-1560s Joseph Nasi completed the construction of the city walls, the majority of residential dwellings, and a synagogue. For the projected silk production, the Nasi had mulberry trees planted for the silk worms. It is possible that they even imported merino sheep prized for their wool from Spain and planted palms and citrus trees in the region around Tiberias. However, in spite of all these endeavors, they were not successful in their plan of a long-term settlement of Jews in the region.

4. Decline

Conflicts and crises weakened the Ottoman Empire from the 17th century onward. Jews continued to play an important part at court. Even at the end of the 18th century there were instances of them acting as mediators between the Ottoman Empire and European powers. However, they gradually lost their leading position as financiers and diplomats to members of the competing Greek and Armenian minorities or to Muslim elites. When the Janissaries were abolished in 1826, the Jews finally lost their

economic connections with these military units as well.

During the 19th century, the Jews in the Ottoman Empire experienced profound changes as the → millet system and the position of → Ḥakham Bashi were introduced, and Western practices of modernization spread more widely. They also found themselves facing anti-Jewish hostility (→ Blood Libel). Now their advocates in these cases were no longer Sultan's Jews but representatives of Western European Jewish communities (→ Damascus; → Alliance israélite universelle).

Bibliography

Sources

[1] H. Gerber, Mismakh turki al Avraham de Castro. Manhig yehude Miẓrayim ba-me'ah ha-16 [A Turkish Document Concerning Avraham de Castro. Leader of the Jews in Egypt during the 16th century], in: Tsiyon 45 (1980), 158–163.   [2] T. Hakohen, Ma'aseh Toviyah [Work of Tobias], Venice 1707.   [3] Y. Tishbi (ed.), Sefer Tsitsat Novel Tsvi le-rabbi Ya'akov Sasportas [The Book of the Withering Flower of Zvi, by Jakob Sasportas], Jerusalem 1954.

Secondary literature

[4] Y. Ben-Naeh, Ḥibbat Tsiyon al gdot ha-Bosporus [Love of Zion on the Banks of the Bosphorus], in: Et-mol 29 (2004) 6, 28–29.   [5] Y. Ben-Naeh, Jews in the Realm of the Sultans. Ottoman Jewish Society in the Seventeenth Century, Tübingen 2008.   [6] M. Z. Bnaya, Mosheh Almosnino, ish Saloniki. Po'olo u-yetsirato [Mosheh Almosnino of Salonika. His Life and Work], Tel Aviv 1996.   [7] L. Bornstein-Makovetsky, Yehudim portugezim be-ḥatser ha-malkhut ha-otomanit ba-me'ah ha-16. Don Yosef Nasi [Portuguese Jews at the Ottoman Sultan's court in the 16th century. Don Yosef Nasi], in: Z. Ankori (ed.), Mi-Lisbon le-Saloniki ve-Kusta [From Lisbon to Salonica and Constantinople], Annual Conference on the Jews of Greece (1986), Tel Aviv 1988, 69–94.   [8] J. R. Hacker, The Sürgün System and Jewish Society

in the Ottoman Empire during the Fifteenth and Seventeenth Centuries, in: A. Rodrigue (ed.), Ottoman and Turkish Jewry. Community and Leadership, Bloomington 1992, 1–66. [9] U. Heyd, Te'udot turkiyot al binyanah shel Teveryah ba-me'ah ha-16 [Turkish Documents on the Construction of Tiberias in the 16th Century], in: Sefunot 10 (1966), 175–210. [10] M. Orfali, Dona Gracia Mendes and the Ragusan Republic. The Successful Use of Economic Institutions in 16th Century, in: E. Horowitz/M. Orfali (eds.), The Mediterranean and the Jews. Society, Culture and Economy in Early Modern Times, Ramat Gan 2002, 175–202. [11] I. Rivkind, Tsror ktavim le-korot ha-yehudim be-erets Yisra'el [Collected Writings on the History of the Jews in Palestine], in: Reshumot 4 (1926), 301–324. [12] C. Roth, The House of Nasi. Doña Gracia, Philadelphia 1948. [13] C. Roth, The House of Nasi. The Duke of Naxos, Philadelphia 1948. [14] S. A. Rozanes, Divre yeme Yisra'el be-Togarmah [History of the Jews in Turkey], vol. 3, Husiatyn et al. 1913. [15] G. Scholem, Sabbatai Ṣevi. The Mystical Messiah, 1626–1676, Princeton 1973. [16] Y. Tsur, On the Importance of Unseen Institutions. The Jewish Notables of Istanbul and the Intisab [Hebr.], in: M. Winter/M. Shefer (eds.), Turkiyah: he-avar ha-Ot'mani veha-hoveh ha-republikani [Turkey. The Ottoman Past and the Republican Present], Tel Aviv 2007, 121–138. [17] A. Yaari, Ha-defus ha-ivri be-Kushta [Hebrew Printing in Constantinople], Jerusalem 1967.

YARON BEN-NAEH, JERUSALEM

Superman

Endowed with supernatural powers, so-called superpowers, Superman, appearing as the journalist Clark Kent in everyday life, is the protagonist of several US comic book, television, and film series. Through its wide reception the character was merged into a wide-ranging superhero mythology, developing into an icon of popular culture.

Created by the descendants of Jewish immigrants from Eastern Europe, Superman is the counter-image of the stereotyped feeble Jew, symbolizing the strength of those originally powerless. Consequently, the character of the comic book hero born as Kal-El on the distant planet Krypton can also be read in the context of the integration of Jewish immigrants into American society.

1. Introduction
2. Development of the character
3. Material from Jewish tradition
4. The discourse of popular culture

1. Introduction

Joseph "Joe" Shuster (1914–1992), the artist of the first Superman comic strip, and Jerome "Jerry" Siegel (1914–1996), the inventor of the character Superman, were of Jewish origin, as indeed were many others involved in the production of the first Superman comic strips. Shuster and Siegel came from Eastern European Jewish immigrant families and grew up in a traditional, Yiddish-speaking environment in Cleveland (Ohio). Siegel recalled having created the character in 1933 as a result of his experiences of anti-semitic hostility and based on the biblical character of → Samson in the hope that the powerless and defamed would one day find justice. The comic-book character Superman himself recalls Samson's destruction of the temple of the Philistines in an episode from 1939, when he shakes the pillars of the negotiation room to urge the hostile parties in a civil war to find a solution to their conflict, shouting: "A guy named Samson once had this idea!" [14. 28]. While Samson lost his invincibility with the loss of his hair, Superman's powers wane when he comes in contact with kryptonite, the element of his home planet. This addresses the dilemma of → assimilation. Every reference to one's own origin could complicate the acculturation aspired to, might be interpreted as suspicious by one's environment, and even provoke antisemitic slander [1. 60].

With his origin on the lost planet Krypton and the various guises in which he appears, Superman recalls the challenged self-understanding of American Jews in the 1930s and 1940s (→ America) [12]. The plots of the comics furthermore allude repeatedly to the American Jewish experience. In addition, various archetypical images used in the Superman stories symbolize elements of Jewish tradition. Thus, the story of the extraterrestrial baby in a space capsule being raised by a terrestrial couple may be read as a variation on the biblical Moses narrative. Since the 1990s, these scenes have been adopted into popular culture, where they have been repeated and varied, contributing to Superman becoming a figure of identification in the eyes of American Jews. Jerry Seinfeld (→ Humor), for instance, called Superman his Jewish brother-in-arms [13. 67]. The appropriation of the figure bears witness to the transformation of American Jews into a self-confident and successful population group.

2. Development of the character

Ever since his inception in the 1930s, the character of Superman – whose name has also been linked to Nietzsche's "Übermensch" (Superman) – has undergone several transformations. His first appearance was in 1933 in "The Reign of the Super-Man," a short story written by Jerry Siegel and illustrated by Joe Shuster published in their fanzine *Science Fiction: The Advance Guard of Future Civilization*. In this instance, Superman is a villain endowed with supernatural intellectual abilities by a mad scientist, who then plots world domination. In the end, however, he loses his extraordinary powers. The first comic strip that showed Superman wearing the insignia valid to this day: the

blue suit, red "S" on a yellow background on his chest, and the red cape, appeared in 1938.

At first, the Superman stories were part of the *Action Comics* series published by DC, which became one of the largest comic publishers in the US, thanks not least to the success of this character; since 1969 it has been a subsidiary of Warner Bros. (→ Hollywood). Besides other comic-strip heroes developed in the 1930s, such as Dick Tracy or Flash Gordon, the character of Superman was influenced by contemporary cinema. Thus, the main scene of the character's activities, → Metropolis, a reflection of New York, owes its name to Fritz Lang's film of 1927. Shuster's and Siegel's experiences during the Great Depression (1929–1941) and their support for the → New Deal made their way into the stories too. We see the hero fighting corrupt politicians as well as a mine owner who refuses to provide labor protection for his workers. While Superman appeared as an aggressive, violent, and simple fighter at first, from the 1940s onward he increasingly acted as the idealistic representative of an altruistic-humanist ethics. It is less his physical superiority than his moral attitude that make him an idealized figure.

Even before the United States entered into the Second World War, Superman fought against the Axis powers as well as against communism. Here, too, he shows himself to be a faithful follower of Franklin D. Roosevelt. In 1940, Shuster and Siegel published a comic strip in which Superman captured Hitler and Stalin. Grabbing the intimidated Hitler by the collar, he expresses the wish to land a "strictly non-Aryan sock on [his] jaw" – giving expression to a desire felt by many Jews [6]. However, Superman does not use violence, instead delivering both dictators – in keeping with his lofty moral code – to the League of Nations (→ Geneva). Typically, he lets even his archenemies live, for instance the supervillain Lex Luthor. The SS reacted to the comic strip in their weekly paper *Das Schwarze Korps*, highlighting the Jewish origin of Superman's creators and accusing the character of morally corrupting young Americans [12].

During the war, Superman was an icon of American propaganda. The War Department organized for Superman comics to be distributed among the troops overseas. Publication figures increased threefold between 1940 and 1945, every fourth book making its way into the hands of a soldier. Military censorship did, however, stop the publication of three episodes whose plots contained references to nuclear weapons, fearing, presumably, that they might give the Nazis a hint to the development of the nuclear bomb (→ Manhattan Project). They were published only after the end of the war.

The incarnation of good, Superman supported the American troops against their Japanese and German foes. Considering his "superpowers," it would have been easy for the "Man of Steel" to intervene decisively in the war. The author and artist avoided this utopian storyline by simply declaring Clark Kent unfit for service after he failed an eye test. From then on, Superman helped on the home front, training soldiers (whom he subsequently addressed as "super soldiers") or advertising war bonds. He also fought American followers of Hitler – before the United States even intervened in the Second World War – resulting in Joe Shuster receiving threatening letters from members of the German American Bund, who sympathized with the Nazis. The superheroes of the second great American comic book publisher Timely Production, founded in 1939 by Moses Goodman and renamed Marvel Comics in 1961, engaged much more aggressively in the Second World War. For Captain America (created by Jack Kirby and Joe Simon), the fight against the Nazis was at the core of innumerable stories. This is a reflection of the different attitudes of American Jews towards the United States entering the Second World War [3. 66–69].

In the 1940s the "Man of Steel" appeared not only in comic strips but also in the cinema and on the radio; in 1966 an entire → Broadway musical was dedicated to the character. Significant stages in the development of Superman were the 17 ten-minute animations (Paramount Pictures) of the years 1941–1943 as well as the radio series *The Adventures of Superman* broadcast from 1940 to 1951, which is the source of the famous lines "Up in the Sky, look! It's a bird! It's a plane! It's Superman!" From 1946 onward, the producers of the radio series endeavored to impart values such as tolerance and fair play to their young audience, cooperating with education experts to this end. In a 16-part feature, Superman faces the "Guardians of America," a shady association with the aim of sowing hatred between the different population groups of the United States. In the end, Superman is able to unmask the leader of the group as a former Nazi agent. The plot drew on the experiences of the journalist Stetson Kennedy who worked for the Anti-Defamation League (→ B'nai B'rith) and had infiltrated the Ku Klux Klan after the Second World War [2].

Superman's childhood and adolescence are presented as unremarkable. He grows up in rural Kansas as an average American boy with the farmers Jonathan and Martha Kent, who bring up the foundling. The film *Man of Steel* (2013) also takes up this narrative, at the same time adding an ironic facet when Superman asks at the end, what could be more American than being from Kansas. The town Smallville – at the opposite end of the scale from urban Metropolis – also allows the neutral background description of an average town in which the American mainstream audiences could discover their own experience.

Superman's alter ego is a classic nebbish. The journalist Clark Kent is a shy, socially awkward, bespectacled, quasi-intellectual corresponding to the "feeble Jew" type [3. 7].

In the four great cinema productions filmed between 1978 and 1987 starring Christopher Reeve, the character finally grew in complexity. Clark Kent underwent a re-adjustment, imbuing the films with an ironic aspect. Especially his relationship with the journalist Lois Lane, one of the few people who are aware of his true self and who, being an emancipated woman, indicates Superman's modern nature, breaks the figure's pathos. The TV series *Lois & Clark. The New Adventures of Superman* (1993–1997), for instance, highlights the relationship between the two journalists more than the muscular superhero.

The dilemma of the dual identity has been a core topic of the stories at least since the revision of Superman's universe at the hands of DC Comics in the mid-1980s. A key publication documenting this transformation is the comic *Whatever Happened to the Man of Tomorrow?* (1986) by Alan Moore. Devised as an alternative history or meta-fiction outside of Superman's regular universe, it shows a world in which Superman has retired. The plot is determined by Superman having to give up his invulnerability and physical strength in order to be able to marry Lois. An even more faceted image of the character is presented in the various series collected under the title *The Death and Return of Superman* (1992–1993), which reflect his role as a superhuman-human hero. As Clark Kent, Superman is wholly human, just as Kal-El is Kryptonian. This ambivalence is symbolically manifested in the relationships with his two fathers too; the true (super-)father Jor-El and Jonathan Kent, to whose upbringing Superman owed his indelible human moral code.

3. Material from Jewish tradition

While there is no obligation to discover a specifically religious interpretation in the films and comic-strip narratives, Superman's Kryptonian name Kal-El evokes → Hebrew and the Bible with its theophorous part "El" (God). In addition, the narration of the story of his home planet – its origin, the prophecy of its fall and destruction – uses the language of Genesis. Superman's flight from Krypton resembles an Exodus [13. 66]. From the point of view of the Kabbalah (→ Mysticism), the destruction of Krypton can be interpreted as the "shattering of the vessels," while Superman's endeavors on behalf of good may be read as an attempt at restoring the damaged world (→ Tikkun olam). He is also the survivor of a catastrophe. His ambivalent attitude towards this legacy appears as the feeling of guilt experienced by those who got away, analogous to a similar phenomenon in survivors of the → Shoah. In a 1962 episode (One Minute of Doom), Superman encounters other Kryptonians who escaped the destruction of the planet, celebrating a "Krypton Memorial Day" – similar to the Holocaust Memorial Day *Yom ha-Shoah veha-Gevurah* [5. 14].

Superman's actions are guided by the rule of charity (→ Tsedakah) – he helps the weak, the oppressed, and the destitute. Thanks to his moral code he may well be called a → tsaddik, albeit an altogether worldly one. In the radio series of the 1940s in particular, Superman is presented as a figure fighting for truth, justice, and the American way of life that combines these virtues within itself.

Besides the creators of Superman, the artists of many other famous comic characters were of Jewish origin too. Superheroes such as The Spirit (Will Eisner), Green Lantern (Milton "Bill" Finger), Spider-Man (Stanley Martin Lieber, known as Stan Lee), or the X-Men, which feature openly Jewish connotations in places (Jacob Kurtzberg alias Jack Kirby), developed out of a specific socio-historical milieu. Because of antisemitic hostility, their creators were often unable to find employment in advertising agencies. As a result, during the so-called Golden Age of Comics, the sons of Eastern European immigrants turned to this art form, which was generally despised as trash, established it, and, as a consequence, asserted its social acceptance. The depiction of the characters might suggest influences of Yiddish popular culture or kinship with the saviors and heroes of Jewish tradition such as the → golem. However, the objective of the artists and authors was to fit into American society by way of their acceptance within popular culture while ensuring to keep the cultural and religious markers of their origin under cover. Superman, with his superhuman but always failing attempts to assimilate, in the guise of Clark Kent, seamlessly into American society, has become a reflection of these difficulties encountered in Jewish acculturation. Being vulnerable only to the material kryptonite that made up his home planet Krypton, he is identified unmistakably as a Kryptonian – or, indeed, a crypto-Jew.

4. The discourse of popular culture

The invention of comic-strip superheroes by American-Jewish artists has been repeatedly linked to events in National Socialist Germany and the Shoah. Since the 2000s, this dimension has been the subject of detailed reflections in popular culture. In his play *The History of Invulnerability* (2010) about the life of Jerry Siegel, for instance, David Bar Katz emphasizes that awareness of the Jewish experience and the → Holocaust was a determining factor in the development of Superman. This connection was highlighted in several episodes of the comic strip itself in 1998, on the occasion of the 60th anniversary of the character's first appearance: Clark Kent visits, among other places, a → shtetl in German-occupied Poland, where he meets two boys, Moishe and Baruch, who are clearly recognizable as Joe Shuster and Jerry Siegel, Superman's "inventors." Clark, however, does not reveal his true self for fear of only making things worse. In another story, Superman, after liberating Lois Lane from a transport headed

for → Treblinka, finally takes part in the Jewish uprising in the → Warsaw ghetto, fighting side by side with, among others, Mordechai Anielewicz [14. 32f.]. The link between the comic strips creators and historical events becomes clearest in Michael Chabon's novel *The Amazing Adventures of Kavalier & Clay* (2000). The Pulitzer-Prize-winning novel describes the lives of two Jewish immigrants integrating into American society during the 1930s and inventing a comic-strip hero with the telling name "The Escapist."

Various adaptations, some of them parodistic, of the figures also document the search for a secular American-Jewish self-understanding especially in the media of popular culture. One of them is Shaloman (from 1985 onward), a Jewish superhero defending Israel. Identifying Jewish references as such in the discourse of popular culture is not infrequently emblematic of the new self-confidence of a previously marginalized immigrant population. The poster boy of this social transformation of American Jewry is Woody Allen (→ Zelig). Although heroic, muscular Superman is his direct opposite, as a character he is also devised in such a way that he swings back and forth between the mainstream and the margins of society. This ambivalence is precisely what makes Superman a paradigmatic Jewish figure of popular culture.

Bibliography

[1] T. Andrae, Funnyman, Jewish Masculinity, and the Decline of the Superhero, in: T. Andrae/M. Gordon (eds.), Siegel and Shuster's Funnyman. The First Jewish Superhero. From the Creators of Superman, Port Townsend 2010, 49–83. [2] R. Bowers, Superman versus the Ku Klux Klan. The True Story of How the Iconic Superhero Battled the Men of Hate, Washington 2012. [3] H. Brod, Superman Is Jewish? How Comic Book Superheroes Came to Serve Truth, Justice and the Jewish-American Way, New York et al. 2012. [4] D. Fingeroth, Disguised as Clark

Kent. Jews, Comics, and the Creation of the Superhero, New York/London 2007. [5] A. Kaplan, From Krakow to Krypton. Jews and Comic Books, Philadelphia 2008. [6] J. Mcinrenken, Eine jüdische Geschichte der Superhelden-Comics, in: M. Kampmeyer-Käding/C. Kugelmann (eds.), Helden, Freaks und Superrabbis. Die jüdische Farbe des Comics, Berlin 2010, 24–41. [7] F. Musall, Star(s) of Redemption. The Maginei David of Kitty Pryde and Benjamin Grimm, in: Transversal 10 (2009) 1, 63–78. [8] J. Neuman, The Religion of Jewish Popular Culture, in: Jüdisches Museum Berlin Journal 4 (2011), 60f. [9] R. Palandt, Jüdische Identitäten von SuperheldInnen in Comics, in: K. Hödl (ed.), Nicht nur Bildung, nicht nur Bürger. Juden in der Populärkultur, Innsbruck 2013, 131–158. [10] E. Portnoy/P. Buhle, Comic Strips/Comic Books, in: P. Buhle (ed.), Jews and American Popular Culture, vol. 2, Westport 2007, 313–341. [11] R. Reynolds, Super Heroes. A Modern Mythology, London 1992. [12] L. Tye, 10 Reasons Superman Is Really Jewish. Sort of Semitic Superhero Celebrates 75th Birthday, in: The Jewish Daily Forward, June 21, 2013. [13] L. Tye, Superman. The High-Flying History of America's Most Enduring Hero, New York 2012. [14] S. Weinstein, Up, up, and oy vey! How Jewish History, Culture, and Values Shaped the Comic Book Superhero, Baltimore 2006.

CASPAR BATTEGAY, BASEL

Synagogue

The institution of the synagogue (Gr. *synagogé*, assembly) as a place where the Jewish community assembles probably originated in the Babylonian exile (6th cent. BCE). Over time, the synagogue took on a defined form as an architectural facility with numerous functions of both a sacred and secular nature. After the destruction of the → Temple (70 CE), its primary function became the implementation of a non-sacrificial religious service (→ Liturgy), defined by prayer and the reading of the Torah. Although its role as the social and religious center of the Jewish community remained unchanged, architecture and interior furnishings were transformed. The synagogue buildings constructed in Western and Eastern Europe over the course of the centuries reflect the relationships between the Jewish communities and their surrounding cultures, in a spectrum ranging from stylistic conformation to self-representation. The synagogues constructed in Germany after 1945, which filled the void left by the → November pogrom, tie in with the ancient purpose of the synagogue as an establishment with a range of functions, and at the same time serve as a visible sign of Jewish life which was being newly established.

1. Introduction
2. Biblical and rabbinical eras
3. Sepharad and Ashkenaz
4. The modern era
5. Worship service reform
6. Jewish citizenship
7. National Socialism
8. After 1945

1. Introduction

After the → Temple in Jerusalem, the synagogue is Judaism's most important structural institution. It distinguishes itself from the Temple through the daily prayer that is celebrated there in lieu of the sacrifice reserved for the inner sanctum of the Temple, and has found a continuation in the practices of communal prayer in Christianity and Islam. The synagogue did not at first represent a substitute for the Temple and its rituals, but instead enabled the community to assemble locally, and as a result contributed to the strengthening of those communities that were situated a great distance from Jerusalem and only undertook the onerous journey to the Temple during the pilgrimage festivals of Pesaḥ, Shavuʿot, and

Sukkot (→ Course of the Year). The significance of the synagogue increased after the destruction of the Temple in 70 CE.

Jewish religious law (→ Halakhah) defines a synagogue as a room in which, in contrast to a private prayer room, a public religious service is regularly held. After the destruction of the Temple it was self-evident in Erets Israel that any place with *minyan* (the number of religious adherents required by tradition to hold a public religious service) should have access to a synagogue, failing which the inhabitants of a locality could be forced to contribute at least a portion of the funds toward the construction of a synagogue. It is the presence of a Torah scroll and the community assembled there for prayer (→ Liturgy) that imbues the room with its sanctity. It is not subject to any architectural specifications; usually, the room contains the Torah shrine with the Torah scrolls and the bimah – the pulpit from which the Torah is read (→ Art) – as well as seating.

2. Biblical and rabbinical eras

The synagogue probably dates from the Babylonian exile (597–538 BCE); ritual assemblies would have served the purpose of filling the void created by the loss of the Temple as a religious center. It is also conceivable that the synagogue developed after the return of the exiles to the land of Israel in the context of the religious reforms of Ezra and Nehemiah: Jewish tradition often sees the prototype for the synagogue as a public religious institution in the public reading of the Torah in front of the city gates of Jerusalem on Tishri 1, 444 BCE by the scribe Ezra (Neh 8:1–8) [13. 23].

The first archaeological evidence in the form of dedication inscriptions dates from the 3rd century BCE (for example in Leontopolis, Egypt), but it is only in the 1st century CE that descriptions of synagogues in Palestine and the → Diaspora increasingly appear. There is a great accumulation of archaeological finds from the period after the destruction of the Temple. There were synagogues in many places in the Roman Empire, such as Rome, Sardis, and Ostia. Philo of → Alexandria states that there were several synagogues for different nationalities in his home city. Reports of synagogues in Palestine come from Josephus Flavius (Tiberias, Dor, Caesarea), the New Testament (Nazareth, Capernaum, Jerusalem), and also rabbinic literature. They describe synagogues as centers for the community, where court proceedings (→ Bet din), political or social assemblies, and communal meals took place alongside prayer and religious services. One could study there (→ Talmud Torah), store the charity box safely (→ Tsedakah), and travelers could spend the night.

It is conceivable however that the synagogue developed out of the public place in or close to the city gate which had been used in earlier centuries for public and religious gatherings. The discovery of stone benches in the gate chambers and cult objects around the gates of Meggido, Beersheba, and Tel Dan dating from the Solomonic era (10th cent. BCE) suggests that these gathering places had a religious purpose [13. 27]. It was probably during the Hellenistic period that a shift toward the allocation of a building for functions which were important for communal life took place. The *agora*, the gathering place of Greek Antiquity, underwent a corresponding development. The organization of ancient synagogues, with banked steps for seating and pillars, is reminiscent of the Hellenistic assembly room of the town councils (*bouleutérion*).

The synagogue building was the Jewish community's largest monumental structure and usually also its only public building. It constituted the secular and religious focal point for Jews in Palestine as well as for the Jewish communities scattered throughout the → Diaspora, for whom it represented an even more significant reference point for community life [13. 119]. While Israelite synagogues were usually also in the locality's geographical center, synagogues in the Diaspora could be situated alongside non-Jewish structures. According to a series of reports, non-Jews also visited synagogues. According to Josephus Flavius, it was normal for synagogues to be constructed close to the sea, and Paul's statements in the New Testament also suggest that positioning them on river banks was not unusual; it is possible that this proximity to water was connected to cleanliness rituals (→ Mikveh).

In the Greek-speaking Diaspora, the term used for "synagogue" fluctuated according to setting between *synagogé*, *proseuché* (prayer), and *hierós tópos* (holy place). The external appearance of the structures varied, as each was adapted to the architecture of its respective environment. Synagogues in the Diaspora (for example in Alexandria, according to Philo) were decorated in part with inscriptions, golden crowns, steles, or statues, while archaeological finds in modern-day Israel show simple plastered walls. The first archaeological evidence for designated places of honor was found in the synagogues of the Talmudic era (Korazim, 5th cent.; Horvat Kur, 6th cent.), although they probably already existed at the time of the Temple. These suggest particular offices in the synagogue or the community, as referenced in the Theodotos inscription (1st cent.) discovered in 1913, the earliest archaeological evidence of a synagogue in Jerusalem. The *archisynagogós* mentioned there was the head of the synagogue and probably also of the community. As the title was later applied to women and children, it could also have been an honorary title.

After the destruction of the Temple, communal prayer in the synagogue, which had developed into an established institution, replaced the sacrifice in the Temple, and the ritual of daily assembly maintained the memory of the loss of the sanctuary. The perception of the synagogue in its role as the house of God, and its designation as holy (→ *kadosh*), were correspondingly strengthened. During the Talmudic era, it retained its designation as a house of assembly and a center for the community in which secular announcements were made and probably also served as a hostel. This double usage, as a building for both sacred and secular assemblies, is made clear in the Hebrew terms for synagogue: *bet knesset* (house of assembly), *bet tefillah* (house of prayer), or *bet am* (house of the people).

Reminders of the Temple are to be found in the → liturgy as well as in the furnishings of the synagogue building, for example in the depiction of ritual objects from the Temple on mosaic floors in Dura-Europos (2nd–3rd cents.), Hammat Tiberias (4th cent.), Beth Alpha (6th cent.), or Beit She'an (6th/7th cent.). At the same time, edifices or objects modeled on the Temple were strictly avoided in order to emphasize the uniqueness of the destroyed sanctuary. There is also evidence of Hellenistic influences, such as the 12-part zodiac as a floor mosaic in Beth Alpha, Ein Gedi, Susya, or Tiberias. According to the Jerusalem → Talmud, walls began to be decorated with paintings in the 3rd century, and floors were furnished with mosaics from the 4th century onward (Avodah Zarah 3:3). Inscriptions dedicated to the memory of individual members of the community mark the synagogue as a place of collective commemoration. There are no references to regular separation of the sexes in the synagogue (→ *meḥitsah*) in Talmudic texts; women were permitted to read the Torah until the 1st/2nd century CE.

3. Sepharad and Ashkenaz

In Spanish → Sepharad, synagogues were built not only by the flourishing communities, but often also by influential donors, who not infrequently held diplomatic or other government offices. The community synagogues comprised the social and religious center of the Jewish residential quarter, known as the *juderías* and not strictly separated from non-Jewish residential areas. The architecture and features of these synagogues were oriented toward Islamic architecture, mosques in particular. Separation of the sexes seems to have been less strict in comparison to → Ashkenaz; Maimonides (1135–1204; → Guide for the Perplexed) does not mention it, and women are depicted in a room of a synagogue in the illuminations of a Spanish haggadah from around 1350. Galleries or annexes suggest a separation of the sexes, which could perhaps have been suspended on festival days such as Pesaḥ (→ Course of the Year). In many respects, Sephardic synagogues served as places of remembrance where one could commemorate significant members of the community as well as the Temple in Jerusalem. The Hebrew donor inscription of a synagogue in → Córdoba designates the building, built in 1315, as *mikdash me'at* (small sanctuary) in reference to the Temple, while another inscription designates the bimah – called the *teva* in a Sephardi context, and usually clearly elevated – in front of a niche in the western wall as the *migdal David* (tower of David).

After the expulsion of Jews from Spain in 1492, numerous synagogues were transformed into churches. The religious services of those Jews threatened with forced baptism (→ Conversos) were carried out in the utmost secrecy in private rooms. Although the public ritual and with it all of the synagogue's functions came to a standstill in Sepharad in the 16th century, refugees exported their synagogal traditions to the countries in which they took refuge around the Mediterranean, in the Ottoman Empire, in the Balkans and the Middle East, Northern Europe, India, and America. Sephardi synagogues exhibit clear similarities to one another, above all in their interior arrangement, although their external form and decoration are oriented towards their respective surroundings.

In → Ashkenaz, the region in Western Europe where Jews settled during the Middle Ages, the term *schola iudaeorum* (Jewish school) indicates that here, too, the synagogue was not reserved exclusively for the purpose of religious services, although it was not used as diversely as had been the case in Antiquity. It continued to constitute the religious and social center of the community, was laid out with the Torah shrine oriented toward the East (→ Orient), and were, in most cases, located in a central place in the Jewish quarter, a part of the city which was initially an open part of the city but which, as Jews became increasingly isolated, was closed off, often with gates. This isolation was not motivated exclusively by anti-Jewish sentiment, but could sometimes have been desired by the Jewish communities as it made the creation of a Shabbat boundary (*eruv*), within which one is permitted to carry items during → Shabbat, easier.

The synagogue courtyard was of particular significance for community life. It was bordered, especially in larger communities, by other Jewish public buildings, the purposes of which as dance hall, Jewish hostel, study center (*batei midrash* or yeshivot), → *mikvot* (ritual baths), or bakehouse had, to some extent, been fulfilled by the synagogue in Antiquity. Most of the ceremonies which took place in both the courtyard and the synagogue were those in which the community participated, such as customs connected to the cycle of life like → circumcision, weddings and divorces (→ Marriage), or the ritual of *ḥalitsah* (release from the obligation of levirate marriage). Furthermore, the rabbinical court (→ *bet din*) met in the synagogue. The authorities also used it as a place for the administration of justice or for the swearing of the Jewish oath (→ Oath More Judaico).

Synagogue buildings were often constructed on urban or sovereign land. Jewish communities were not always able to take ownership of the buildings. The construction of new synagogues, which had to be

SYNAGOGUE

authorized by the authorities, was often subject to restrictions or even entirely prohibited by church rulings, such as those of the Council of Oxford (1222) or the Synod of Prague (1349), although in practice these bans were frequently disregarded. The construction of synagogues close to churches was not permitted, and in height and appearance they were to be as inconspicuous as possible [14. 42]. The enforced modesty of the external architecture stood in contrast to the interiors, which often featured magnificent structures for the Torah ark and bimah designed by the Jewish community according to their vision, and often at great financial expense. Both archaeological finds and contemporary accounts attest to the exquisite furnishings, custom-built by Christian craftspeople. The bimah in the synagogue in Cologne (ca. 1267), for example, was furnished with a structure featuring a slender arcade decorated with foliage, grapes, dogs, an ape, and birds. The religious-legal (→ Halakhah) permissibility of representational depictions and other design characteristics (→ Aniconism), also a cause for discussion in Christianity and Islam, was the subject of numerous rabbinical responses (→ Responsa). Consistent rules on the matter were however only set up to a point.

The orthodoxy of the Middle Ages also held true for the Jewish living environment and led to increasing separation of the sexes in the synagogues (→ Meḥitsah). In smaller buildings this was probably achieved by means of simple partitions, as can be seen in historical representations. In the large communities along the Rhine (→ Ashkenaz), annexes for women were added to existing synagogues in the 13th century. The earliest example of this is the women's synagogue in Worms, which was constructed in 1212/1213; the small openings in the wall connecting it to the main room only allowed the women seated at the front to follow the service. Often, the prayers of the women were led

by their own female prayer leader (Yidd. *firzogerin*), but the reading of the Torah only took place in the men's room. The furnishings were limited to seating. Corresponding annexes can be found later in Speyer, Nuremberg, Mainz, Würzburg, and Trier, among other places.

As in Antiquity and in the Sephardic world, here too the synagogue served as a place of remembrance. Donor inscriptions on religious objects and memorial candles placed in front of the ark served as collective commemorations of the dead (→ Kaddish; → Death). At the same time, the synagogue also reflected the social structure within the community. Seats close to the ark on the eastern wall were awarded to those members who enjoyed the greatest recognition.

4. The modern era

In Eastern Europe, medieval building traditions continued into the early modern era, but were now influenced by the ideas of the Renaissance via Italian architects. This led to the development of the "fortress synagogue" construction model, which was typical for Eastern European synagogues, and was externally reminiscent of military fortifications due to its crenellations, highly-placed windows, and closed facades (Old Synagogue in Cracow, rebuilt 1570; Great Synagogue in Zhovkva/Żółkiew, today Ukraine, late 17th cent.; the synagogue in Lutsk, today Ukraine, 1629). Some of these synagogues were in fact intended to be used defensively if the city were under threat, thereby going beyond their sacred function and also serving the non-Jewish population. The interiors of these structures could be subdivided into nine bays by four massive pillars, with these supports surrounding the free-standing bimah in the center of the space. This style further developed into the bimah-support, a pillar and canopy construction in which the bimah was embedded, thereby inseparably combining it with the synagogue's overall architecture [12]. In the 17th century the "wooden synagogue" form developed out of traditional craftsmanship in Eastern Europe (Poland, Lithuania, Belarus, Ukraine) parallel to church construction. The interior of such synagogues was occasionally grandly painted by Jewish artists [15].

In addition to the large structures, rooms were needed in which to hold the less well-attended services during the week, and which could be heated during colder times of the year. This commonly called "winter synagogue" or "warm school" (Yidd. *shul*) was usually integrated into the building (the "cold school") as a vestibule. From the 17th century onward, individual vestibules were added to synagogue buildings, which not only served as porches but also fulfilled other social roles. The donation box (→ *tsedakah*), washing facilities, and often a room for community meetings or even the "warm school" itself could be located here, for example [7. 237f.].

The synagogue also continued to be the religious and social center of the Jewish residential quarter during the modern era. In larger towns and → shtetls there were often multiple synagogues and numerous prayer rooms, which were visited by representatives of different professions (artisans, merchants, scholars) and of various Hasidic groups (→ Hasidism). Small prayer houses or prayer rooms known as *shtibl* (small room) or *kloyz* (cell) were widespread among Hasidic Jews, who used them for prayer, teaching, and eating meals. The flow of migrants which began in the late 19th century took the Eastern European synagogue tradition to the United States, Western Europe, and Palestine.

After the → pogroms and expulsions of the Middle Ages, the remaining Jews in Western Europe were only guaranteed continuity of settlement in a few places, resulting in widespread interruption to the tradition of synagogues there. Jewish communities, which were in most cases small

in number, held services in private rooms, which were often rented due to the restrictions surrounding land acquisition. These prayer rooms were usually situated in the houses of wealthy members of the community, who also contributed significantly to their upkeep. The rooms were equipped for services with the necessary furnishings (ark, bimah, kneelers), the design of which was oriented toward the corresponding medieval objects but which were fashioned in the respective style of the time. The synagogue rooms retained their role as places where the authorities made announcements to the entire Jewish community. Important celebrations such as weddings (→ Marriage) or → circumcisions continued to take place in the synagogue or in an adjoining courtyard. In addition to the synagogue, larger communities constructed a *bet midrash* as a place of teaching and learning; this could also be called a "klaus" (as in Halberstadt, for example) in reference to the Hasidim of Eastern Europe.

In the German-speaking world, the construction of new synagogues only recommenced in the late 17th century, primarily in southern Germany (Fürth, Frankfurt am Main) at first. These large constructions were frequently supported or financed by influential → court Jews, such as in Halberstadt (Gemeindesynagoge, 1712) or Berlin (Old Synagogue, completed 1714). Since Jews had been denied entry to guilds since the High Middle Ages, the buildings were mostly constructed by Christian craftspeople and were architecturally oriented toward Protestant church construction. Such buildings in fact remained a largely invisible part of the cityscape but constituted important landmarks in their immediate vicinity. The interior furnishings were influenced by contact with Eastern European Jewish communities. The magnificent wall paintings of various southern German synagogues for example were by Elieser Sussmann (18th cent.), an itinerant synagogue painter from → Brody.

Also arks decorated with woodcarvings refer to models in the wooden synagogues of Eastern Europe, although they also demonstrate a close affinity with Baroque church decoration. The areas for men and women were increasingly brought together into one space, although women were restricted to latticed galleries with separate entrances [17]; [13]; [7].

Sephardi communities in Western Europe and America, which had close contact with the community in Amsterdam, took the → Esnoga (1675) as the model for their places of worship in Hamburg, London, and New York. The room layout of this synagogue can be observed in medieval Spain, and was retained by the entire Sephardic Diaspora: the pulpit for reading the Torah was located against the wall opposite the ark, with the two forming a longitudinal axis toward which the seating was oriented.

View of the Oranienburger Straße and Neue Synagoge (New Synagogue) in the Mitte district of Berlin, taken 1934

5. Worship service reform

The significance of the synagogue as a social and religious institution was initially changed little by the Enlightenment and early → Haskalah. The establishment of schools with programs shaped by the Enlightenment, such as the → Freischulen or the → Philanthropin in Frankfurt am Main, can however be understood as a sign of the gradual separation of the secular and religious lebenswelten (worlds of lived experiences). In the German-speaking world, the synagogue was increasingly understood as the "house of God" in the same way as the Christian church. The interest of the authorities in sacred buildings that were visible parts of the cityscape or landscape grew correspondingly. As a result, territorial lords exerted influence over the external appearance of synagogues and community buildings as representative structures of their own residences (such as the synagogue in Kassel, an unrealized project of 1781), or even commissioned them themselves (Wörlitz, 1789–1790).

In addition to spatial-functional changes, the → reform in the early 19th century also entailed a change in the significance of synagogues to Jewish communal life. Many elements of the new worship service, as introduced in 1810 by Israel Jacobson in the → temple of the Freischule he had founded in Seesen (→ Hamburg Temple Dispute), can be understood in terms of a stricter arrangement: the chronological flow of the ritual was regulated by a musically durchkompaniert liturgy, accompanied by → organ and choral singing, together with a → sermon routinely carried out in the national language. A new arrangement of the most significant furnishings prompted a greater spatial restructuring: the increased significance of the sermon caused the pulpit, only recently introduced into the synagogue, to adopt the form of a chancel (used in churches), which was placed in front of or to the side of the Torah shrine; the bimah moved eastward from the center of the space to a position in front of the Torah shrine, which together with the bimah and the pulpit now comprised a single focal point rather than the traditional arrangement of two spatially separated centers. Over the course of the 19th century, the trend toward the aggregation of the liturgically important places on the eastern side of the synagogue led to a further innovation: a separate area emerged for the platform carrying the Torah shrine, pulpit, and bimah, which occupied the space opposite the congregation and was often furnished with seating for the community council (→ Kahal). This area tended to be consistent with the separation of the congregation into the laity on one side and the participants (prayer leaders, cantors, preachers) as well as the community council on the other. In place of the individual movable prayer stools which had previously been standard, fixed pews were introduced positioned one behind the other. The organ and choir were positioned on the gallery, which no longer only served as the area for women. Furthermore, the lattices and curtains which had restricted the visual connection between the men's and women's areas were removed. The stricter temporal and spatial ordering of the synagogue service was clearly oriented toward the ritual of churches, in particular the Protestant church, especially since the Reform movement began in the Protestant regions of Germany [2].

In order to implement the new arrangements that reform-oriented forces were seeking in the synagogues, synagogue ordinances were issued from the early 19th century onward. These ordinances, written in the national language and often printed, regulated the service structure and made offenses subject to intracommunity punishments. One can assume that old customs in traditional synagogues – such as walking around, loud prayer, speaking with others, or arbitrarily leaving – continued, since it

was necessary to use such measures to take action against them. The emergence of the synagogue ordinances coincided with the issuing of community statutes (→ Pinkasim), which were also written in the national language and had to be approved by the authorities. Here too, stricter organization and a certain level of state oversight of the Jewish community's self-administration (→ Autonomy) was enforced, which was intended to lead to the development of the communities as legal bodies.

The envisaged formal organization of the religious service was accompanied by a professionalization of important synagogal offices. In accordance with the requirements of the → liturgy, which was set to music in the style of Western art music, the office of the prayer leader or → cantor changed from being an honorary post to a career requiring academic learning. While prior to the reforms the rabbi had hardly played a role in the religious service, now as a preacher he was afforded a central significance (→ Rabbinate; → Sermon). As a result, the synagogue became a place of moral-theological, and ultimately civic education (→ Bildung) for the whole community, imparted by a professional theologian. The cultural significance of this change was demonstrated by the accentuation of the pulpit. In reform-oriented communities, the synagogue lost its earlier function as a space for individual religious study in the sense of the *shul*.

Synagogues did however continue to be educational institutions, albeit there was a spatial division between the school and the synagogue as the location of the religious service. Frequently, school rooms for religious education were established in the buildings attached to the synagogue, for example in the houses on the front. Jewish schools with their own buildings were usually located close to the synagogue or were planned together with them as a structural unit. The proximity of the (religious) school and synagogue accommodated the professionally trained staff known as *Kultusbeamte* (cultural officers), who combined multiple offices (teacher, cantor, and others) in one individual, especially in smaller communities. Their apartments were often located in the synagogue complex. The → mikveh, another religious institution, could also be found in the synagogue buildings. Some reform-oriented communities, however, rejected the construction and maintenance of ritual baths, the usage of which generally declined over the course of the 19th century.

6. Jewish citizenship

While synagogues in Germany and Western Europe were mostly concealed behind houses built onto the front, and were therefore not visible elements of the cityscape during the early modern era, over the course of the 19th century Jewish communities openly strove to construct buildings on public streets, including even in public squares, in order to make their claim to participation in civil society known. The question of appearance and construction style became increasingly relevant, especially as the architectural-theoretical basis of stylistic pluralism, which followed on from the architectural historicism of the mid-19th century, sought to establish the identification of the construction project, builder, and construction style. The responses found for synagogues ranged from solutions which were similar to churches and knowingly drew upon regional tradition, such as the neo-Romanesque buildings in Hannover (New Synagogue, 1870) or Munich (Main Synagogue, 1887), to those which made use of an architectural language that was explicitly different from the local one, such as the Moorish-style synagogues in → Leipzig (Community Synagogue, 1855), → Budapest (Great Synagogue, 1859), or St. Petersburg (Grand Choral Synagogue, 1893). By means of their size and stylistic design, together the

historicist synagogues advanced the "sacralization" of construction, which, so to speak, "confessionalized" Jewish prayer houses as they took their place alongside Christian houses of God.

The antisemitism of the late 19th century incorporated synagogues into its (visual) propaganda strategy as symbols of Jewish culture, for example by depicting them in caricature as "alien" buildings. Jewish communities, especially in Germany, responded by emphasizing the "down to earth" nature of the architectural language chosen for their synagogues. Even though the sacred character of the synagogues was increasingly architecturally accentuated and became appreciably more visually prominent in the cityscape over the course of the 19th century, the buildings remained multifunctional complexes, housing assembly rooms, community administrations, schools, and social amenities. As a result, they were centers not only in the more narrow sense of religious life, but also of the cultural and social community.

The fact that large Jewish schools and homes, as well as hospitals and other social amenities, contained their own prayer rooms, and that synagogue rooms were even established in prisons, can be viewed as evidence of the differentiation of the institutionalized Jewish social welfare system over the course of the 19th and early 20th centuries. These "Anstaltsbetstuben" (institutional prayer rooms) also continued the early modern tradition of religious services in poorhouses and hospices.

By the late 19th century, the → reform of the ritual had established itself in Germany, at least in urban communities, in a more or less distinctive form. There were also many communities in neighboring regions of Europe and in North America which configured their services and synagogues accordingly; this is evidenced by different designations such as "choral synagogue" (Vilna, St. Peterburg) or → "Temple"

(Seesen, Hamburg, Vienna, Paris). Platforms with the Torah shrine, bimah, and preaching pulpit, as well as organ and choir galleries, were standard in the now numerous new buildings, and existing synagogues were remodeled accordingly [3]. A further spatial expansion began, so that from the 1860s onward synagogues in the large cities of Europe and North America such as Berlin (New Synagogue, begun 1859), Budapest (Great Synagogue), or New York (Temple Emanu-El, 1868) could contain over a thousand seats. In doing so they came close to, or even surpassed, the municipal church buildings of the time. The frequency of synagogue attendance however noticeably declined among many members of the community. By contrast, services on high feast days were often so crowded that some communities in large cities hired public halls and used them as festival synagogues from the late 19th century onward (for example in Berlin, where this was increasingly the case from around 1880).

The process of reforming the religious service in the synagogue lasted for many decades and yielded differing results. Numerous pamphlets show evidence of the fact that it was accompanied in many places by disputes within communities. These could lead to the temporary or even permanent secession of individual groups, which either promoted an even more dramatic reconfiguration than the majority ("Reform congregations") or opposed the liturgical changes ("Austrittsgemeinden," secession communities; → Neo-Orthodoxy).

Similar phenomena of a process of diversification, with different preconditions and characteristics, can be observed not only in Germany but throughout Europe and in other non-European countries: where multiple synagogues existed in one city during the modern era, they were first and foremost differentiated by national identity according to the place of origin of the community members. After the start of the reform process, this was augmented by the degree of implementation of service reform, such that in large cities the most markedly different synagogues could be located next to one another. The migrations of the 19th and early 20th centuries, in particular emigration in response to → pogroms in Czarist Russia, considerably contributed to further differentiation in Western Europe and in those non-European countries which were destinations for the migrants.

7. National Socialism

Due to the increasing level of persecution during the early years of National Socialist rule in the German Reich, synagogues and Jewish community houses became important havens for those sections of the population whom racial ideology identified and stigmatized as Jewish. Synagogues became centers of Jewish life by virtue not only of religious services and theological lectures and courses, but also of non-religious cultural events such as educational and training opportunities, concerts, or theatre evenings (→ Kulturbund), particularly as Jews were forbidden from attending other venues. Schooling was occasionally provided in the community rooms, but also where assistance for the persecuted and impoverished was organized and support offered for efforts to leave Germany.

This phase ended with the Kristallnacht on November 9, 1938 (→ November Pogrom). The systematic destruction of the synagogues as visible signs of the Jewish religion and culture was an initial step on the path toward the extermination of Jews in Germany and later in Europe. Almost all of the synagogues in the German Reich were affected by the November pogrom. Not all of the buildings were torn down; the ownership of those religious buildings that avoided destruction was transferred to non-Jews, who reconfigured them for different purposes. Only a few of the ruined prayer

SYNAGOGUE

rooms could be restored by the Jewish community and used for religious services (Hannover, Old Synagogue), so relief synagogues had to be established in other community institutions (Halberstadt, Jewish retirement home). In the last phase prior to deportation, the law concerning "Mietverhältnisse mit Juden" (Jewish tenancy) of April 30, 1939, which abolished tenant protections and free choice of housing for Jews, created the preconditions for the concentration of the Jewish population in certain parts of the city; community structures and also synagogues together with their adjoining buildings were declared Jewish housing into which Jews were forced to move (such as in the Levetzowstraße Synagogue in Berlin). Transportation to the labor and extermination camps was carried out from here.

8. After 1945

Countless synagogues across the whole of Europe fell victim to the devastation and destruction initiated by the National Socialists. After the → Holocaust, the surviving buildings could only in a few cases be used by the newly founded Jewish communities for their original function. Most were given new purposes and to this end were rebuilt in a more or less disfiguring manner, or even demolished. With few exceptions, interest in preserving the remaining former synagogues in Germany as memorials to Jewish culture was not aroused until the 1980s. They were restored and made publicly accessible as places of remembrance and commemoration of the victims of the Holocaust. In other European countries, this process of museumization often began even later (→ Museums).

After 1945, modern rebuilt synagogues continued the development toward multifunctional centers for the community that had been introduced in the early 20th century by liberal communities in particular (Hamburg, Temple, 1931; Zurich, Projekt

für ein liberales Gemeindezentrum, 1929). The concept of the community center, with facilities for religious, cultural, and social activities, had been established since 1945, especially in the United States. The modern community center is a hub for a wide range of different activities, among which the holding of religious services continues to be afforded great significance. This is reflected in the fact that the synagogue component of the building is usually accentuated by its design, and is often made recognizably "sacred" from the outside, although it by no means necessarily constitutes the largest share of the construction volume. Community centers have emerged and continue to do so in numerous countries around the world. In Israel, corresponding facilities are located next to those that perpetuate the framework of the more complex prayer and teaching houses of the Eastern European tradition. With their synagogues sometimes containing hundreds of seats and multiple rooms for prayer and teaching, these can also be understood as community centers (for example the Belzer Hasidim synagogue complex in Jerusalem, 2000).

Since the 1950s, the community center's equivalent *Gemeindezentrum* has also been the most frequently realized concept of Jewish community facilities in the Federal Republic of Germany. As well as the practical aspect of spatial consolidation, the concentration of all functions under one roof also performed the role of giving survivors and their families quasi self-contained protective and identity spaces within the majority society. The wave of newly constructed synagogues and community centers in Germany, which can be observed since 1990, is a response to immigration from the states of the former Soviet Union. The enormous growth of Jewish communities has been accompanied by an increased religious-cultural differentiation, provided for by the establishment of Orthodox, liberal, or conservative Ashkenazi and Sephardi synagogues. High public interest, both politically and among the population in general, demonstrates the great significance of Jewish facilities in the contemporary discourse of culture of memory, in which synagogues are still architecturally symbolic of Jewish and non-Jewish communal life.

Bibliography

[1] S. Coenen Snyder, Building a Public Judaism. Synagogues and Jewish Identity in 19th-century Europe, Cambridge (MA) 2013. [2] A. Cohen-Mushlin/H. H. Thies (eds.), Synagogue and Temple. 200 Years of Jewish Reform Movement and Its Architecture, Petersberg 2012. [3] T. Frühauf, The Organ and Its Music in German-Jewish Culture, Oxford 2009. [4] S. Gruber, American Synagogues. A Century of Architecture and Jewish Community, New York 2003. [5] H. Hammer-Schenk, Synagogen in Deutschland. Geschichte einer Baugattung im 19. und 20. Jahrhundert (1780–1933), Hamburg 1981. [6] R. Jütte/A. P. Kustermann (eds.), Jüdische Gemeinden und Organisationsformen von der Antike bis zur Gegenwart, Wiesbaden 1998. [7] K. Keßler, Ritus und Raum der Synagoge. Liturgische und religionsgesetzliche Voraussetzungen für den Synagogenbau in Mitteleuropa, Petersberg 2007. [8] S. Korn, Synagogenarchitektur in Deutschland nach 1945, in: H.-P. Schwarz (ed.), Die Architektur der Synagoge, Frankfurt am Main 1988, 287–343. [9] S. Korn, Synago-genarchitektur in Frankfurt am Main, in: K. E. Grözinger (ed.), Jüdische Kultur in Frankfurt am Main von den Anfängen bis zur Gegenwart, Wiesbaden 1997, 287–320. [10] R. Krautheimer, Mittelalterliche Synagogen, Berlin 1927. [11] C. H. Krinsky, Synagogues of Europe. Architecture, History, Meaning, New York 1985. [12] T. Lamey, Bimot in Polish Stone Synagogues until 1650. Forms, Function, and Religious Aspects, in: A. Cohen-Mushlin/H. H. Thies (eds.), Jewish Architecture in Europe, Petersberg 2010, 109–116. [13] L. I. Levine, The Ancient Synagogue. The First Thousand Years, New Haven/London 2000. [14] S. Paulus, Die Architektur der Synagoge im Mittelalter. Überlieferung und Bestand, Petersberg 2007. [15] M. Piechotka/K. Piechotka, Heaven's Gates. Wooden Synagogues in the Territories of the Former Polish–Lithuanian Commonwealth, trans. by K. Cieszkowski, Warsaw 2015. [16] M. Piechotka/K. Piechotka, Heaven's Gates. Masonry Synagogues in the Territories of the Former Polish–Lithuanian Commonwealth. trans. by K. Cieszkowski, Warsaw 2017. [17] R. Wischnitzer, The Architecture of the European Synagogue, Philadelphia 1964. [18] W. S. Zink, Synagogenordnungen in Hessen 1815–1848. Formen, Probleme und Ergebnisse des Wandels synagogaler Gottesdienstgestaltung und ihrer Institutionen im frühen 19. Jahrhundert, Aachen 1998.

ULRICH KNUFINKE, BRAUNSCHWEIG
AND KATRIN KEßLER, BRAUNSCHWEIG

T

Tafsīr

Arabic technical term for the exegesis of the Quran. Due to the proximity between the older Jewish and the still young Islamic textual culture in linguistic as well as lebenswelt terms, Jews were regarded as models and authorities on the field of Quranic exegesis even during the Prophet Muhammad's lifetime. The influence of Jewish scholarship on the interpretation of Islamic sacred texts extended through the various types of medieval Quranic exegesis into the modern age. Following the example of the → Wissenschaft des Judentums, Jewish and Muslim scholars of the 19th and 20th centuries placed the → Quran and its exegesis on the basis of enlightened scholarship.

1. Etymology
2. Qirā'āt and wujūh
3. First authorities
4. *Isra'īlīyāt*
5. The Middle Ages
6. The modern era

1. Etymology

Muslim sources disagree on the origin of *tafsīr* meaning "exegesis." They frequently trace *tafsīr* to the roots *f–s–r*, *s–f–r*, and *f–r–s*, which are regarded as metatheses. In → Arabic, these three roots originally denoted practical matters from the everyday life of the Arabs and had no connection with exegesis scholarship. However, as the older → Hebrew and → Aramaic equivalents of these roots bear the meaning of scholarship, scripture, and exegesis, it should be assumed that they were adopted from Jewish scholarly culture to the designation for Quranic exegesis.

In Arabic, the root *f–s–r* has the meaning "to uncover," "to reveal." The verb *fasara* derived from it originally denoted the examination of urine in order to diagnose illnesses; in the Quran the noun *tafsīr* refers to the "interpretation" of questions with which the heathen Meccans intended to challenge the Prophet's credibility (Surah 25:33). The corresponding Aramaic and Hebrew root *p–sh–r* with the meaning of "to convey," "to explain," "to interpret," and "to comment" is more strongly scripture-related. In the Aramaic-Hebrew Book of Daniel, for instance, the verb form derived from this root is used to refer to the explanation for the writing that appeared to King Belshazzar in his dream (Dan 5:7). In the Qumran texts and in the → Midrash, the Hebrew verbal noun *pesher* denotes the continuous → commentary of a book of the Bible (such as *pesher habbakuk*) as well as the exegeses of specific passages.

In Arabic, form 1 of the root *s–f–r* bears not only the meaning of "to illuminate," "to uncover," "to unveil" but also "to travel." In Hebrew, however, the root *s–f–r* refers to the semantic field of "book," "written text," "message," and "writer, scribe." The Hebrew derivatives *sefer* (book) and *sofer* (writer, scribe, conveyor [of information]) occur in their Arabized forms *sifr* and *sāfir* or *safīr* in the Quran and its exegesis in unmistakably Jewish contexts. The definitive Arabic dictionary *Lisān al-ʿarab* (completed by Ibn

Manzūr in 1290), too, explains the word *sifr* as a "great book or part of the Torah."

Form 1 of *f–r–s* originally implies content relating to horses in Arabic. The noun *faras* means "horse" and the verb *farusa* "to understand horses and their characteristics." *Lisān al-'arab* lists the noun *farsan* unexpectedly as a synonym of *tafsīr* in the sense of "exegesis and precise explanation of scripture." The corresponding Hebrew root *p–r–sh* may be adduced in explanation once again: in the Hif'il verb stem, it refers to the cloven hooves of animals, while the Pu'al derivative *meforash* means "to distinguish precisely between individual words" and to read, translate, or interpret a text (Neh 8:8; Ezra 4:18). The corresponding Pi'el verb *peresh* is consequently used to mean "to interpret." The connection between *tafsīr* in Arabic and *p–r–sh* in Hebrew can probably be traced back to the exemplary role of the *perushim* (exclusive, separated scribes; Pharisees). In analogy, early authorities of Quranic exegesis were honored with the scholarly titles of the Pharisees.

2. Qirā'āt and wujūh

The first step to Quranic exegesis is to choose a particular reading (Arab. *qirā'ah*), which may be variable due to the Arabic consonant script and the lack of diacritical marks in the original text. Besides language competence and mastery of the art of reciting the Quran, knowledge of the contents of the text is indispensable. Many of these originate in Jewish sources. In the story of Moses and the Israelites, for instance (Surah 2:54), it is not clear what precisely the punishment of the Jews was for venerating the golden calf: the phrase *fa-qtulū anfusakum* may be interpreted as "kill yourselves," "kill your souls," or "kill one another" in the sense of "kill the guilty among you." The last of these corresponds to the recognized reading as well as the majority opinion of the exegetes and also agrees with the Jewish origin of the Quranic text (Exod 32:27). For the interpretation of this verse, Muslim commentators had to rely on Jewish sources and did indeed refer to them.

The defective Arabic script and the Jewish origin of many Quranic passages also explains in part why Muhammad and his companions preferred the Quranic recitation by Jewish scholars. Muhammad appointed his close confidant, the Yemeni Jewish convert Abū Mūsā al-Ash'arī (ca. 614–662) as the head of the Quran reciters, for he "[had been] given one of the *mazamir* (sweet melodious voices) of the family of David" [12. book 66, Hadith 72/vol. 6, book 61, Hadith 568]. One of the three authorized codices for reading the Quran is also attributed to Abū Mūsā. In addition, Jewish scholars had the advantage over their Muslim colleagues as a result of the textual kinship between the Quran and the Torah (→ Tanakh). This manifests itself in particular in a phenomenon called *wujūh al-Qur'ān* (Arab.; faces of the Quran) by Muslim scholars and *panim la-torah* (Hebr.; faces of the Torah) by Jewish exegetes: in both texts the same wording allows numerous, in some cases differing, ways of interpretation. Jewish as well as Muslim scholars do not regard the manifold interpretability of their scriptures as unclear or contradictory but rather as a sign of the wealth of ideas that characterizes their sacred texts.

3. First authorities

The first Muslim exegetes of the Quran studied under Jewish authorities. Muhammad's cousin 'Abdallāh ibn 'Abbās (619–687) founded one of the first schools of Quranic exegesis, influential to this day. Thanks to his outstanding scholarship, he was awarded the Arabic, originally Jewish, honorific titles *Rabbānī* and *ḥabr al-ummah* (master and scribe of the community). The word *ḥabr* and its plural *aḥbār* are used in the Quran exclusively to denote Jewish scribes

(Surah 5:44 and 63; Surah 9:31 and 34). This usage may be derived from the Hebrew equivalent *ḥaver* (pl. *ḥaverim*; companions) used by the Pharisees as designation for the members of their scholarly circles. In later times, the term was transferred to other Jewish scholars, and later still onto Christian and Muslim ones as well.

The Jewish background of Ibn ʿAbbās's school found its expression in the titles of its founding father as well as his lively exchanges with Jewish scholars. Thus, Ibn ʿAbbās primarily drew on the knowledge of Kaʿb al-Aḥbār (d. between 652 and 655), a Jewish convert from Yemen who had distinguished himself through scholarship even before his conversion to Islam. Abū al-Jald Jaylan ibn Farwah (7th cent. CE), a Jewish authority on the Torah as well as the Quran, taught Ibn ʿAbbās the meaning of the words in the Quran. The Jewish convert ʿAbdallāh ibn Salām (d. 663) from Medina, one of Muhammad's confidants, was another of his teachers. Ibn ʿAbbās, in turn, had Jewish pupils such as Muḥammad ibn Kaʿb al-Qurazī (664–726), who was regarded as one of the most reliable transmitters and most learned Quranic exegetes of his time.

The influence of Jewish scholarship and tradition extended onto the later canonic works of Islamic tradition. Recognized authorities such as Ibn Jarīr al-Ṭabarī (839–923) in his Quranic commentary and Muḥammad ibn Ismāʿīl al-Bukhārī in his canonic hadith collection (compilation of traditions about the Prophet Muhammad) included numerous exegetical traditions from Ibn ʿAbbās and his pupils that originated in Jewish sources.

4. *Isrāʾīlīyāt*

As a result of the exchanges between Muslim authorities and Jewish scholars, but also through Jewish tales being adopted into Arab oral popular literature, numerous traditions from Judaism made their way into Muslim written texts. These so-called *isrāʾīlīyāt* (Israelite traditions; → Ahl al-kitāb), which in some cases also included Christian stories, provide important links between Jewish and Muslim textual tradition in the contexts of Quranic exegesis, hadith, and the *qiṣaṣ al-anbiyāʾ* (legends of the prophets).

Jewish scholars were involved in Quranic exegesis from the very beginning. The medieval historian Ibn Khaldūn (1332–1406) believed the reason for this to be that the first recipients of the Quran were uneducated Bedouins, who might have been interested in its stories but were unable to comprehend all the background knowledge implied in the text. Jews, in contrast, came from centers of scholarship, had enjoyed a wealthy written culture for centuries, and were consequently seen as authorities, also for the elucidation of the Quran. The Muslim chronicler Muḥammad ibn ʿUmar al-Wāqidī (747–823) reported of the Jews in Medina that they taught Arabs and Muslims reading and writing in the early Islamic period.

Jewish converts were among the main sources of *isrāʾīlīyāt*. ʿAbdallāh ibn Salām, for instance, had been among the leading Jewish scholars of Medina before his conversion, and Muhammad himself called him a "dweller in Paradise," "scribe," and "witness of the sons of Israel" in whose honor God had even sent down Quranic verses [16. 7f.]. As an expert in the Torah and the Quran, in Jewish as well as Muslim traditions, he enjoyed great respect. A great number of his traditions were included in Muslim canonic texts. Aḥmad ibn ʿAbdallāh ibn Salām (d. 836) further transmitted this knowledge and translated, among other works, the Torah (→ Tanakh) and the Prophetic Books from → Hebrew as well as the Gospel from Greek into → Arabic.

One of the most important transmitters of the *isrāʾīlīyāt* was Kaʿb al-Aḥbār, whose traditions testify to his in-depth knowledge of Jewish scripture. Even after his conversion, he continued to feel connected to Judaism;

he recited the Torah in the mosque, and was not afraid to praise Jerusalem (→ Zion) in front of Muhammad's companions. Ka'b's traditions and their later emendations, undertaken by the Umayyads for political purposes, played a significant part in Jerusalem becoming established as a sacred place in Muslim memory.

It is known that Abū Hurayrah (602–679), Muhammad's most famous companion, turned to Ibn Salām and Ka'b al-Aḥbār in matters of exegesis. He asked them, for instance, which hour the Prophet had referred to precisely when he promised that God would hear a Muslim's prayer "at that hour." Abū Hurayrah asked Ka'b al-Aḥbār to search for an answer to this question in the Torah, and he requested Ibn Salām "not to keep his knowledge to himself and to find an answer to this question" [2. vol. 2, 190]. There can be no doubt that the scriptures of the Jews were regarded as a source of knowledge concerning questions from the still young Islamic faith.

However, depraved elements also crept into the *isra'īlīyāt*. Firstly, not only learned but also uneducated Jews spread stories, which the simple Bedouin were not able to distinguish from those transmitted by Jewish authorities. Secondly, the listeners were captivated by the *isra'īlīyāt* with their tales of the beginning of creation, their eschatological ideas, accounts of events, peoples, and prophets of times past, and their fantastical descriptions of the otherworld. They passed them on, changing them in the process. New *isra'īlīyāt* were added too. The *quṣṣāṣ* (storytellers) found a wealth of exciting material in these fables, which they wove into their own tales and stories. As this placed them in competition with the scholars, the intellectual elite and the rulers attacked them vociferously.

The prestige enjoyed by Jewish scholars and exegetes also led to numerous Muslim scholars endeavoring to rely on the authority of Jewish traditions. If there were no suitable ones, they were simply invented, composed in the style of the respective scholar, and attributed to him. The conflations and falsifications that occurred in the course of the history of the *isra'īlīyāt* for cultural, theological, or political reasons, cast an unfavorable light on Jewish scholars in later times. Muslim scholars doubted their credibility, imputing clandestine intentions to them. The high point of anti-Jewish polemic on the part of Islamic Orthodoxy was reached with the conservative scholar Ibn Taymīyah (1263–1328), who played a significant part in the term *isra'īlīyāt* becoming established as the name for the genre.

5. The Middle Ages

Rationalistic Quranic exegesis, too, was subject to Jewish influence. One of the most important representatives and founders of this trend was Abū 'Ubaydah Ma'mar ibn al Muthannā (728–824), who was of Jewish origin. He regarded the philological, literary, cultural-historical, and historical approach as the primary key to Quranic exegesis, referring to explanatory traditions only if the text could not be understood otherwise. Similar to Ibn 'Abbās, he adduced numerous instances of pre-Islamic poetry in his Quranic exegesis. Because of his revolutionary methods based on reason and language, he attracted the hostility of the greatest scholars of his time, among them the poet and philologist 'Abd al-Malik ibn Qurayb al-Aṣma'ī (740–831) and the grammarian Abū Zakarīyah Yaḥyā ibn Ziyād al-Farrā' (761–822).

During the High and Late Middle Ages, the convergences between Jewish and Muslim exegesis continued. The overlap between Jewish and Mu'tazilite Islamic hermeneutics is exemplary of these. The rationalist school of the *mu'tazilah* (→ Kalām) founded in the 8th century, whose exegetic methods rested primarily on philology and Greek philosophy (→ Falsafah), entered into a lively exchange with the rationalist scholars of rabbinic as well as → Karaite

Judaism from the 9th century onward. One prominent example of this cultural contact was Saʿadyah Gaʾon (882–942; → Prophecy), whose theological and exegetic work has fundamental parallels with Muʿtazilite paradigms. Similar to the Muʿtazilite exegesis of the Quran, Saʿadyah in his Bible exegesis applied sophisticated philological methods to reinterpret terms that appeared to contradict God's dignity. The Karaite Yūsuf al-Baṣīr (d. 1040) studied the teachings of the reformed branch of the *muʿtazilah* and subsequently, like many other Karaite and rabbinic authorities of his time, decided to follow the arguments of the original *muʿtazilah* concerning the existence, essence, qualities, and deeds of God. This explains why there were Muʿtazilite texts preserved in the Cairo → Genizah – thanks to their authoritative character they were translated and copied by Jews in the Middle Ages. In *Dalālat al-ḥāʾirīn* (Hebr. *Moreh Nevukhim*; → Guide for the Perplexed) Maimonides (1138–1204) finally reinterpreted the anthropomorphistic phrases used in the Torah, such as for instance "the face of God" (Hebr. *pne Adonai*) homonymically in analogy with Muʿtazilite theological teaching and exegesis [11. 222]. In addition, he sought to integrate principles of Aristotelian moral philosophy into biblical and rabbinic statements using hermeneutical methods similar to those of the *muʿtazilah*.

6. The modern era

In the 19th and 20th centuries, Quranic exegesis received strong impulses from the → Wissenschaft des Judentums under whose influence Christian Hebraists lost their theologically inspired prerogative of the interpretation of Jewish and Islamic texts to modern, scientific research (→ Semitic Studies). Its representatives in the 19th and 20th centuries were predominantly Jewish scholars who had received a traditional education and discovered the philological and historical-critical method of → biblical

criticism as a way of accessing the Jewish as well as the Islamic textual corpus suitable to the modern era.

In his groundbreaking study *Was hat Mohammed aus dem Judenthume aufgenommen?* (1833; "Judaism and Islam," 1896), Abraham Geiger (1810–1874) subjected the → Quran to a historical-critical investigation, reconstructing its links with the Hebrew Bible and the rabbinic texts. Geiger was the first to indicate the adoption of central Hebrew terms with religious connotation such as *sefer* or *ḥaver* into the Quran.

Gustav Weil (1808–1889) deserves the credit of having been the first to research the Prophet's biography from a historical-critical perspective in *Mohammed der Prophet, sein Leben und seine Lehre* (1843), highlighting its connections with Jewish and Christian tradition. In his study *Historisch-kritische Einleitung in den Koran* (1844, revised in 1878), he drew on the Prophet's biography in order to work out a new sequence of the chapters and verses of the Quranic text in accordance with historical-critical, philological, and literary criteria, which the profound expert in classical Arabic literature Theodor Nöldeke (1836–1930) took as the basis for his *Geschichte des Qorans* (1860; "The History of the Qurʾān," 2013). In *Biblische Legenden der Muselmänner* (1845; "The Bible, the Koran and the Talmud," 1846), a contribution to the study of the *israʾīlīyāt* (→ Ahl al-kitāb), Weil collected narratives from the earlier prophetic legends mentioned in Islamic literature, searched for their Jewish origins in the → Talmud and the Midrash, and analyzed the modifications they had undergone in Muslim texts, which he explained with the specific style of the → Arabic language.

This European Jewish Orientalist tradition reached its zenith in the founder of modern Islamic Studies Ignaz Goldziher (1850–1921), whose two-volume *Muhammedanische Studien* (1888/1890; → "Muslim Studies," 1967/1971) represent a turning point in the historical-critical investigation of the canon of Muslim traditions that had previously been regarded as sacred texts. He introduced the term *isra'īlīyāt* into Western scholarship and defined it in terms of cultural history. In his 1920 study *Die Richtungen der islamischen Koranauslegung*, Goldziher pursued the political and theological influences on Islamic Quranic exegesis, uncovering the links between Jewish and Islamic exegetic traditions. He adduced a great number of previously neglected classical and medieval Muslim as well as Jewish sources for his analysis, as well as appreciating the achievements of contemporary Muslim scholars. Thus, he devoted the main part of the book's last chapter "Der islamische Modernismus und seine Koranauslegung" to the Quranic commentary *al-Manār* (The lighthouse; 1906–1927) written by the Egyptian reformer and Quranic exegete Muhammad Abduh (1849–1905), a text informed by the ideas of the Enlightenment.

Israel Wolfensohn (1899–1980) was the first to make the philological and historical-critical methods of European and, above all, German Orientalists of the 19th and 20th centuries accessible in Arabic and consequently to the Islamic world. In 1922, Jerusalem-born Wolfensohn was the first Jewish student at the philosophical faculty of the Egyptian University in Cairo (today Cairo University in Gizeh), writing his PhD thesis *Tārīkh al-Yahūd fī bilād al-ʿArab fī al-jāhilīyah wa-ṣadr al-Islām* (The history of the Jews in the Arabian lands in the pre- and early Islamic period) in Arabic in 1927 under the Egyptian intellectual Taha Hussein (1889–1973; → al-Thaqāfah). He highlighted numerous connections between Judaism and Islam, the kinship between the two cultures being his primary theory. Wolfensohn's second dissertation *Kaʿb al-Aḥbār und seine Stellung im Ḥadīth und in der islamischen Legendenliteratur* was written in Frankfurt under the supervision of the Jewish Orientalist Gotthold Weil (1882–1960) and completed in 1933. This study in the tradition of Geiger, Gustav Weil, and Goldziher may

be regarded as the first detailed historical-critical monograph on a traditionist in Western research; based on the influence Kaʿb al-Aḥbār's *isra'īlīyāt* exerted on the Islamic canon of hadith and Quranic exegesis, it documented "Quranic ideas with regard to their dependence on Jewish thought" [16. 52]. In his Arabic work *Mūsā ibn Maymūn* (Moses ben Maimon; 1936), Wolfensohn made Maimonides's writings accessible to Arab readers, providing further clarification of the links between Jewish and Islamic philosophy and exegesis in the Middle Ages.

The research initiated by Jewish scholars fell on fertile soil among Arab Islamic and Quranic scholars of the 20th century. The Egyptian reformer Amin al-Khuli (1895–1966) stood in the tradition of Muhammad Abduh's modernist Quranic exegesis as well as of the Wissenschaft des Judentums. There are unmistakable parallels between his view of the Quran as a literary work of art to be investigated in the style of Protestant → biblical criticism using literary-critical, historical-critical, and philological methods and Weil and Geiger; al-Khuli himself referred mainly to Nöldeke and Goldziher. He also recognized the Enlightenment potential of Muʿtazilite exegesis and endeavored to integrate its texts into the canon of Sunni Quranic exegesis. With reference to Israel Wolfensohn, he regarded the *isra'īlīyāt* as a symbol of the mutual influence of Judaism and Islam that contributed to shaping the consciousness of every Muslim exegete and whose study without prejudice was the duty of comparative religious studies.

After 1945, the contributions of Jewish scholars to Islamic Studies received barely any attention in the Islamic world. Remarkably, the name al-Khuli was not mentioned in the entry *Tafsīr* in the second edition of the *Encyclopaedia of Islam* (1960–2004), although he had contributed to the translation into Arabic of parts of the first edition (1913–1938) as well as annotating and editing them.

Bibliography

Sources

[1] Ibn Khaldūn, The Muqaddimah. An Introduction to History, trans. and intro. by F. Rosenthal, abr. and ed. by N. J. Dawood, Princeton 1967. [2] Aḥmad ibn Muḥammad al-Qasṭalānī, Min irshād al-sārī fī sharḥ ṣaḥīḥ al-Bukhārī [A Guide to the Interpretation of the Sahih of al-Bukhārī], 10 vols., Cairo 1889. [3] Abū ʿUbaydah Maʿmar ibn al-Muthannā, Majāz al-Qurʾān [Figures of Speech in the Quran], Cairo 1955. [4] A. al-Khuli, Tafsīr, in: Dirāsāt Islāmīyah [Islamic Studies], Cairo 1996, 17–46. [5] E. Ben-Yehuda, Thesaurus totius hebraitatis et veteris et recentioris, 16 vols., Jerusalem 1980. [6] A. Geiger, Judaism and Islam. A Prize Essay, trans. by F. M. Young, Charleston 2010. [7] I. Goldziher, Schools of Koranic Commentators, trans. by W. H. Behn, Leipzig 2006. [8] I. Goldziher, Muslim Studies, 2 vols., ed. and trans. by S. M. Stern and C. R. Barber, London 1968. [9] Ibn Jarīr al-Ṭabarī, The Commentary on the Qurʾān, ed. by W. Madelung, trans. by J. Cooper, W. Madelung, A. Jones, Oxford 1987. [10] Jamāl al-Dīn ibn Manẓūr, Lisān al-ʿArab [The Arab Language], 6 vols., Cairo n.d. [11] M. Maimonides, The Guide for the Perplexed, trans. by M. Friedlander, New York 2000. [12] Muḥammad ibn Ismāʿīl al-Bukhārī, Ṣaḥīḥ. Being Traditions of the Sayings and Doings of the Prophet Muḥammad, trans. by M. Asad (L. Weiss), Lahore 1938. [13] G. Weil, Mohammed der Prophet, sein Leben und sein Werk, Stuttgart 1843. [14] G. Weil, The Bible, The Koran, and The Talmud. Biblical Legends of the Mussulmans, New York 1855. [15] I. Wolfensohn, Tārīkh al-Yahūd fī bilād al-ʿArab fī al-jāhilīyah wa-ṣadr al-Islām [The History of the Jews in the Arabian Lands in the Pre- and Early Islamic Period], Cairo 1927. [16] I. Wolfensohn, Kaʿb al-Aḥbār und seine Stellung im Ḥadīth und in der islamischen Legendenliteratur, Gelnhausen 1933.

Secondary literature

[17] C. Adang et al. (eds.), A Common Rationality. Muʿtazilism in Islam und Judaism, Würzburg 2007. [18] A. Neuwirth, The Qurʾan and Late Antiquity. A Shared Heritage, trans. by S. Wilder, Oxford 2019.

WALID ABD EL GAWAD, LEIPZIG

Talmud

The Talmud – transmitted in two separate works as a Palestinian and a Babylonian Talmud – is the literary founding document of post-biblical Judaism and rabbinic traditional literature. The extensive work, which was composed over several centuries during Antiquity, combines Jewish law (→ Halakhah) as well as multi-layered narrative traditions (Haggadah), intertwined in a complex fashion. It reflects not only the self-understanding and worldview of the class of rabbinic scholars who contributed to its compilation but also offers insights into Jewish society as a whole during Antiquity and its multifarious connections with the non-Jewish culture surrounding it. To this day, the Babylonian Talmud constitutes the most important textual foundation of Jewish religious practice.

1.   Historical background
2.   The Mishnah
3.   Two Talmuds
3.1 Shared characteristics
3.2 Yerushalmi
3.3 Bavli
4.   Relevance in the present

1. Historical background

The Talmud (Hebr.; lit. "study," "teaching," "instruction") is the most eminent literary product of the "rabbinic era." This term usually denotes the Jewish living environment between 70 CE, the year of the destruction of the Second Temple, and the middle of the 7th century. The word "rabbinic" is derived from "Rabbis" (Hebr. *rabbanim*, "masters," "teachers"; → Rabbinate), the learned members of a distinct group within the Jewish community who claimed the authority over Jewish life and knowledge. While the term "rabbinic era" implies, certainly incorrectly, that the majority of the Jews of Antiquity were members of the rabbinic scholar class – in fact, we must presume the existence of a majority of varied non-rabbinic Jewish communities (→ Diaspora) – it is correct in terms of their influence on later eras of Jewish history. While there are many individual studies concerning this historical period, the image of the Jewish community during Antiquity is still very incomplete. One reason for this is the small number of written documents by non-rabbinic Jews during this time. It is also due to the rather small degree of interest devoted to the study of rabbinic culture in Sasanian Persia compared to Roman Palestine.

In the works of rabbinic literature, however, the members of this group ascribe to themselves a central role in the re-establishment of Jewish life in Palestine after the destruction of the Temple and the loss of independent statehood, above all, in the transformation from Temple-centric to Torah-centric Judaism. Rabbinic scholars' rise to becoming the social, regulatory elite took several centuries; they probably developed their full societal domination no earlier than the 7th century. Essentially, the rabbinic Jews were not only a minority within the Jewish community, but they also lived in two separate majority communities – one in Roman Palestine, and one in Sasanian Persia. Both Talmuds reflect the respective interactions between rabbinic and Roman-Hellenic or New Persian-Sasanian culture and society. Intensive contacts between the different cultures are documented not only by the numerous Greek, Latin, and Persian loanwords in both versions of the Talmud; narrative passages also point out that the rabbis were familiar with, for instance, non-Jewish belief systems,

such as the Zoroastrian religion (e.g. Bavli, Sanhedrin 39a).

The main feature of the essentially male rabbinic living environment was the study of the Holy Scriptures and their exegesis – women were exempt from this duty. Lessons were held in the form of gatherings of a "master" (Hebr. *rav* or *rabbi*) and his students, usually in the master's house, but also in public places or in the *bet midrash* (house of exegesis). The early scholars, mainly based in Palestine (70 to ca. 220 CE), were called "repeaters [of the rabbinic teachings]" (Aram. *tanna'im*; Eng. usually in the form "Tannaim"). They were succeeded by the *amora'im* ("speakers"; Amoraim) who "spoke" about and added to the teachings of their predecessors from about 220 to 500 CE. The rabbinic scholars were well aware of the significance of their community and their activity; as early as the early Middle Ages, their post-Talmudic successors composed texts about the history of rabbis. From the 12th century onward, the Tannaitic period was divided into five generations of scholars (according to more recent research into four or six), and the Amoraic period into seven (nowadays, eight). Smaller study groups or Talmud academies (Hebr. *yeshivah*; Aram. *metivta*; → Talmud Torah) led by important Tannaitic scholars were located in Yabneh, Usha, Beit She'arim, and Sepphoris in Palestine. During the Amoraic period, Tiberias and Caesarea were Palestinian centers of scholarship, while the "Babylonian" academies of the Neo-Persian Sasanian Empire were situated along the Euphrates in Nehardea, Sura, Pumbedita, Maḥoza and Mata Meḥasva.

2. The Mishnah

The Hebrew Mishnah is the first comprehensive post-biblical collection of laws and forms an integral literary part of the Talmud, whose formal structure corresponds to that of the Mishnah. The word *Mishnah* (Hebr.;

lit. "repetition [of the teachings of the Bible]") was at first used to denote a variety of early rabbinic teachings, some in written form and some long transmitted only orally. In the end, the version that, according to tradition, Judah ha-Nasi (Yehudah the patriarch) or his school had edited conclusively after the middle of the 3rd century was given preference. It became known as "our Mishnah," or simply, "the Mishnah" [7. 299]. Of this version, too, different types of text are extant, of Palestinian as well as Babylonian origin, respectively. Many rabbinic rulings that were not included in the Mishnah would later be known as *Baraita* (Aram.; approx. "extra-canonical doctrine"); many of them were included in the Talmud. The Tosefta (Aram.; "addition," "continuation"), which was collated around the same time as the Mishnah with the same formal structure but on a rather more extensive scale, did not, on the whole, become included in the Talmud.

From the 3rd century onward at the latest, rabbis regarded the Mishnah – calling it as well as the Talmud "oral Torah" (Hebr. *torah shebe-al peh*) – as complementary to the "written Torah" (*torah shebi-ktav*), the Holy Scriptures. Unlike the latter, however, the oral Torah was understood as a growing corpus to which new teachings could be added. Their transmission from master to students is an essential feature of the oral law.

While much time passed between the destruction of the Temple and the Mishnah acquiring its fixed written form, a significant section of the text is devoted to Temple laws. Besides these there are a large number of additional religious ritual laws, as well as those applying to a variety of aspects of everyday life. This mixture made the Mishnah the normative foundation for the transformation from a more or less Temple-centric past to a rabbinic future.

Unlike the → Midrashim composed at the same time, which usually follow the structure of the book of the Bible they interpret, the Mishnah overall presents its discussions of religious law independently of the structure of the Hebrew Bible (→ Tanakh). All the discussions are arranged according to their subject matter in a total of 63 "tractates" (Hebr. *masekhtot*, sing. *masekhet*), which are structured into six "orders" (Hebr. *shishah sedarim*): *Zera'im* ("seeds": blessings and agricultural laws), *Mo'ed* ("festival": → Shabbat and religious festivals; → Course of the Year); *Nashim* ("women": → marriage, divorce, and oaths), *Nezikin* ("damages": civil and criminal law), *Kodashin* ("holy things": sacrifice and Temple laws), and *Toharot* ("purities": purity and impurity laws; → Kashrut). The six orders are the defining feature of rabbinic-Halakhic literature; besides the Mishnah, this structure is observed in the Tosefta, the Talmud, and the medieval Ashkenazi *Tosafot* (supplementary Talmud commentary). The latter (Sanhedrin 24) uses the Hebrew acronym *Shas* as the abbreviation for the "six orders." In order to avoid the word "Talmud," to which Christian censorship objected, the acronym was used for the first time as a synonym for Talmud in the Talmud of 1578 to 1581 printed in Basel; it has been used this way ever since.

3. Two Talmuds

3.1 *Shared characteristics*

The Hebrew word *talmud* originally referred to the Bible and its teachings, among other things. Thus, the phrase *talmud lomar* frequently documented in rabbinic discussion means "the Bible teaches," and *yesh talmud* means "there is a biblical instance." *Talmud Yerushalmi* (also abbreviated as *Yerushalmi*; Jerusalem Talmud) and *Talmud Bavli* (or *Bavli* for short; Babylonian Talmud) appear, above all, as commentaries on the Mishnah. A short Mishnah passage (quoted in *Bavli* only) is followed by an extensive disquisition in Hebrew and Aramaic, the Gemarah (Aram.; "completion," "conclusion," "learning"); a uniquely Talmudic component, this term has frequently been used since the early Middle Ages as a synonym for Talmud. However, in spite of their sometimes detailed legal (Halakhic) discussions of the Mishnah teachings, these disquisitions are much more than legal commentaries. They contain reflections – often digressing considerably from the Mishnah passage – on God and biblical exegesis, the revelation and man, a wealth of narrative material containing folk tales and proverbs, as well as comprehensive discussions of subjects from the fields of → medicine, magic, the interpretation of dreams, astronomy, geography, and → history. The two Talmuds may safely be regarded as → encyclopedias of the rabbinic wisdom of Antiquity and as condensations of their view of the world. That they are by no means mere law codices is confirmed by the fact that they frequently do not offer a conclusive decision in cases of conflicting rabbinical opinions.

For historical as well as demographic reasons, the more extensive *Bavli*, edited in the 6th or probably even the 7th century CE, was regarded as the more important Talmud during the early Middle Ages. The *Yerushalmi*, edited in the early 5th century in Galilee and Tiberias, has since then not been studied as an independent Halakhic work – except in Palestine – and was also copied much less frequently, but it was never forgotten all the same. While at first glance both versions of the Talmud give the impression of repeating learned discussions from the Talmud academies, the texts are in fact more or less extensively edited, Tannaitic and Amoraic doctrines and anonymous statements interwoven into literary units (*sugyah*, pl. *sugyot*; approx. "course of the argumentation") with a complex structure of argument. The comparatively brief Tannaitic and early Amoraic dicta are frequently in → Hebrew. Detailed and complex manners of argumentation presumably by post-Tannaitic and post-Amoraic scholars (Hebr. *stamma'im*) in → Aramaic imbue the *Bavli*, in particular,

with its characteristic dialectic style. One *sugyah* (Bavli, Pesaḥim 4a) is exemplary of this dialectic; its basis is the biblical prohibition of consuming fermented foods during Pesaḥ (→ Course of the Year). The rabbinic law rules that on the eve of Pesaḥ, the 14th of Nisan, every house must be searched for remnants of fermented foods. The *sugyah* is concerned with the question of whether the tenant or the landlord of a dwelling rented on this day is responsible for searching the house for fermented foods:

They raised a dilemma before Rav Naḥman bar Yitzḥak: [With regard to] one who lets a house to another on the fourteenth [of Nisan], upon whom [is it incumbent] to search [for leaven]? [Is it incumbent] upon the lessor to search [for leaven], as the leavened bread is his; or perhaps [incumbent] upon the lessee to search, as the [source of the] prohibition is in his domain [since he will be living in the house during Passover? He answered:] Come [and] hear [an answer from a *baraita*: With regard to] one who lets a house to another, [the obligation is] upon the lessee to affix a *mezuza* for it. [Apparently, the person renting the house is obligated to perform the mitzvot connected to the house. The Gemara rejects this proof:] There, [in the case of *mezuza*,] didn't Rav Mesharshiya say: [Affixing] a *mezuza* is the obligation of the resident? [The fact is that the owner of an uninhabited house is not obligated to affix a *mezuza* to its doors. If so, the question remains,] what is [the *halakha*] here? Rav Naḥman bar Yitzḥak said to them [that] we [already] learned [the resolution to this dilemma in a *baraita*]: One who rents a house to another, if before he delivered the keys to [the renter] the fourteenth [of Nisan] began, [the obligation] is upon the lessor to search [for leaven]. And if [it was] after he delivered the keys to him [that] the fourteenth began, [the obligation is] upon the lessee to search [for leaven]. [1. 320]; [1a]

This brief *sugyah* combines a few typical characteristics of Talmudic discourse: an Amoraic scholar is asked a Halakhic question; an anonymous scholar interjects, pointing out an underlying legal implication and proposing a possible answer based on a comparable Halakhic decision; the suggested solution is rejected because of the differences between the Halakhic problem under discussion and the older decision; the Halakhic decision is applied to the present case; finally, the scholar who was asked in the first place answers with reference to an older tradition. Like most *sugyot*, this one, too, presumes knowledge of rabbinic categories and practices as well as the reader's or listener's ability to deduce a greater Halakhic context based on abridged statements. Here, as in numerous other instances, the answer does not follow the Halakhic query immediately but is based on a similar train of argument that, in turn, is based on older authoritative texts. In addition, the *sugyah* opens up a path to ambiguity in its phrasing: Why, for instance, does it suggest that a mezuzah and Pesaḥ are parallel cases? For what reasons is the analogy rejected? These and other questions are asked and answered by later commentators. Thus, the *sugyah* is not only evidence of rabbinic thought but also the starting point for continued Halakhic as well as non-Halakhic discourse.

The literary material of the Talmuds is usually classified according to whether it is part of the Jewish law (→ Halakhah) or of the narrative, non-legislative Haggadah (Hebr.-Aram. *aggadah*; "sayings"). This terminological division conceals just how closely interwoven the two genres are. Occasionally, the Halakhah is described as elite discourse in the Talmuds (Bavli, Sotah 40a; Bavli, Ta'anit 7a), but the interrelations between Halakhah and Haggadah are emphasized at the same time: Bible stories are presented as the sources of rabbinic laws, normative practices are elucidated in narratives (Hebr. *ma'asim*, sing. *ma'aseh*) about the actions of

rabbis, and court cases are reported in narrative form. While rabbinic scholars since the Geonic era (2nd half of the 6th cent. to 11th cent.) have regarded Halakhah and Haggadah as two entirely separate discourses, ascribing to the Haggadah an inferior, non-authoritative role, this interpretation cannot be inferred from the Talmuds by any means.

3.2 *Yerushalmi*

The compilation of the *Yerushalmi* in Galilee can be dated to around 400 CE; it is consequently the older of the two Talmuds. While it was known as *Talmud di-Vne Ma'arava* (Talmud of the inhabitants of the West) or *Talmud de-Erets Yisra'el* (Talmud of the land of Israel) in the Babylonian Diaspora, it was called simply "the Talmud" in the land of Israel itself. Nowadays, the title *Talmud Yerushalmi*, in use since the early Middle Ages, has become established, although the term "Palestinian Talmud" used in scholarly texts is more correct considering its geographical place of origin.

The *Yerushalmi* is written in a mixture of → Hebrew and West → Aramaic, commenting 39 (of 63) Mishnah tractates from the orders *Zera'im*, *Mo'ed*, *Nashim*, *Nezikin*, and a few chapters from the tractate *Niddah* (order *Toharot*). Its *sugyot* are overall briefer and more concrete than those of the *Bavli*, as unlike the latter they contain only few anonymous discussions. The comparison between the layers of Tannaitic and Amoraic contribution in the *Yerushalmi* and the *Bavli* shows a shared literary origin, with the *Bavli* additionally containing later Amoraic traditions as well as detailed anonymous commentaries. Consequently, stylistic differences between the two Talmuds should not be explained primarily as due to cultural or historical factors, but rather to the *Yerushalmi* being compiled at an earlier point in time. While around a third of the material in the *Bavli* may be classified as Haggadic (narrative), only a sixth of the *Yerushalmi* is Haggadic. This difference may be due to the circumstance that the great → Midrash collections containing extensive narrative material originate in Palestine, while these traditions were incorporated into the *Bavli* in Babylonia and did not circulate as independent tradition [9. 484]. Unlike the *Bavli* with its encyclopedic layout and tendency to abstract concepts and legal principles, the *Yerushalmi* was primarily the place for Halakhic Mishnah commentary [6. 841f.].

The *Yerushalmi* was studied and appreciated in the schools of North African commentators such as Chanan'el ben Chishi'el (990–1053) and Isaac Alfasi (1013–1103) – this is affirmed by medieval *Yerushalmi* fragments found in the → genizah. That its importance was secondary all the same may be deduced from Alfasi's remark, which states that the legal ruling of the *Bavli* was to be given precedence in cases where it disagreed with a ruling of the *Yerushalmi* (Alfasi on Bavli Eruvin 104b). In the immediate post-Talmudic era, the *Yerushalmi* as well as the *Bavli* probably commanded comparable authority among the Jewish scholars in Erets Israel and Babylonia, respectively. With the establishment of the caliphate in → Baghdad in the 8th century, the Babylonian *ge'onim* (sing. *ga'on*; heads of the Talmudic academies) consolidated their authority over the Jewish → Diaspora in that region, endeavoring to assert the *Bavli* as superior to the *Yerushalmi* for good. Overall, only very few *Yerushalmi* texts have been transmitted from the period up to the 10th century, but it appears that from the 12th century onward, *Yerushalmi* study increased among the northern French and Rhenish Talmud scholars in → Ashkenaz. The oldest and only complete manuscript (Leiden Or. 4720) dates from 1289; based on this text, the printer Daniel Bomberg (→ Printing) produced the first printed version in Venice in 1523. He decided to print the medieval commentary beneath the Gemara – a layout design that would be retained in later editions too.

3.3 *Bavli*

The prominent position of the *Bavli* in Jewish scholarly culture is the result of the Babylonian *ge'onim*'s religious-political authority and the concomitant continuity of studying (→ Talmud Torah), transmitting, and commenting on the *Bavli*. In accordance with its geographic origin, it was composed in → Hebrew and – predominantly – East → Aramaic. It contains the Halakhic discussions as well as Haggadic traditions of rabbis living in Sasanian Persia between the 3rd and 6th or early 7th centuries CE; the text reached its present final form at the end of this era. It was long assumed that the compilation was concluded in the 5th century, but new research (David Halivni, Shamma Friedman) date the final edition to the 6th and 7th, possibly even the early 8th century. This later date is based on the assumption that anonymous post-Amoraic scholars (*stamma'im*) might have made interpolations in older Halakhic and Haggadic sections and occasionally changed their meaning. The *Bavli* consists of three textual layers: the Tannaitic, the Amoraic, and the anonymous; the last is the most extensive. While there is no consensus, most scholars regard the anonymous commentary as the most recent layer in the *Bavli*.

The *Bavli* contains a total of 37 tractates of the orders *Mo'ed*, *Nashim*, *Nezikin*, and *Kodashim*; only one tractate (*Niddah* and *Berakhot*) of the orders *Toharot* and *Zera'im* is included. It thus comprises even fewer tractates commenting on the Mishnah than the *Yerushalmi*. One reason for the *Bavli*'s being incomplete may be that it only included laws that were relevant to the Babylonian post-Temple → Diaspora community. Missing tractates are those from the order *Zera'im*, which contains the commentary on the agricultural laws for the land of Israel, as well as those from the order *Toharot*, in which matters of the purity of the Temple are discussed, among other things. It is not clear why the sacrificial laws *Kodashim* were included. One possible reason may be found in the rabbinic claim to priestly authority and authority over the Temple ritual.

Despite the smaller number of tractates, the *Bavli* is significantly more substantial than the *Yerushalmi*, which is predominantly due to the larger volume of the anonymously transmitted material. The Palestinian Haggadic tradition is much shorter in comparison. Another literary characteristic concerns the historicity of the traditions included in it. Some scholars assume that the anonymous final editors reworked the older material so thoroughly that it now contains only information about the time of the latest additions but not on the older Tannaitic and Amoraic sources. However, other Talmudic experts regard the *Bavli* as a multi-layered testimony of the time and circumstances preceding the final compilation. Consequently, the historical reliability of the sources should be neither accepted *a priori* and uncritically nor rejected outright. By means of a variety of analytic-hermeneutic and comparative-investigative methods, it may indeed be possible to gain new insights into rabbinic culture and its times.

Many medieval fragments of the *Bavli*, unlike the *Yerushalmi*, have survived – but only one complete manuscript (Munich Cod. Hebr. 95 [1342]). The printer Daniel Bomberg (ca. 1475–1549) from → Antwerp, being a Christian, was permitted to run a printing shop in Venice. He employed a number of learned Jews and published the first complete printed version of the *Bavli* between 1519/1520 and 1523 (→ Printing). The layout of the pages would become the foundation for all subsequent printed editions of the Talmud. The Mishnah text was placed in the middle of the page, followed by the Gemara, although the medieval manuscript had already used this clear separation of Mishnah and Gemara. The space to the sides and sometimes underneath the main text was reserved for various columns of commentary: The commentary by Rashi (→ Worms) as well as additional notes were printed on the inside margin, whereas the commentaries by the Tosafists (medieval Ashkenazi Talmudic commentators) appeared on the outside and bottom margins. This design, which comprised more than 10,000 pages in the first impression, became the template for all subsequent editions. In order to create an improved version of the *Bavli*, the edition published by Witwe und Brüder Romm in Vilna (today Vilnius) between 1880 and 1886 was the first to include further manuscripts and commentaries that had not been taken into account for the Bomberg edition. This publication, known as *Vilna Shas*, became the standard for all subsequent printed editions of the Talmud. Its folio pagination is the standard for quoting the *Bavli*.

4. Relevance in the present

The Talmud *Bavli*'s prominent significance is also reflected in the large number of commentaries produced since the Middle Ages, although many of the several dozen commentaries focus on only a selection of Talmud tractates. The number of commentaries on the *Yerushalmi* is comparatively small, and it was not until the 18th century that works were composed that became standard commentaries.

Until the early modern age, Talmud commentators referred directly to the Talmud; since then, they have mainly composed supra-commentaries on older Talmud commentaries, especially Rashi (→ Worms) and the Tosafists [12. 479–481]. However, all Halakhic writings, be they medieval codices or modern-age → responsa, are based on a specific reading of the Talmud. Although it was never the only text of the rabbinical curriculum, and the study of the Bible and works of Jewish ethics and other religious subject areas increased in importance after the emergence of the Jewish → Reform movement and Conservative Judaism (→ Breslau), the study of the Talmud and its exegesis enjoyed the highest esteem until well into the 20th century. The awareness that many rituals, such as the lighting of the Hannukah candles, are based on Talmudic laws (Bavli Shabbat 21a–21b; → Course of the Year) exists to this day, even among followers of liberal denominations that do not observe the Orthodox Halakhah.

Currently, Talmud studies are experiencing a renaissance insofar as they are conducted in many → synagogue communities and at public universities, as well as by independent study groups. They regard the Talmud not only as a religious text but also as a historical document. In addition, an increasing number of women now dedicate themselves to Talmud studies, which were long denied them under the traditional Halakhah (→ Talmud Torah; → Meḥitsah). The growing interest in the Talmud is due not least to the new translations of the *Bavli* into → Hebrew and → English, namely, by Adin Steinsaltz (Hebrew until 2010; English 1989–2000) and by Schottenstein/ArtScroll (English 1990–2005); ArtScroll also published a Hebrew–English edition of the *Yerushalmi*. The founder of the Ḥakhme-Lublin yeshivah Me'ir Shapiro proposed the idea of the *daf yomi* ("the daily page") in 1923, envisaging the study of the entire *Bavli* in a cycle of seven and a half years. This idea, too, has gained great popularity far beyond his following among ultra-Orthodox Jews.

Bibliography

Sources

[1] L. Goldschmidt, Der Babylonische Talmud, vol. 2, Berlin 1930. [1a] A. E.-I. Steinsaltz, Koren Talmud Bavli, Noé Edition, in: The William Davidson Talmud, digital edition, https://www.sefaria.org/Pesachim.4a.

Secondary literature

[2] E. S. Alexander, The Orality of Rabbinic Writing, in: C. E. Fonrobert/M. S. Jaffee (eds.), The Cambridge Companion to the Talmud and Rabbinic Literature, New York 2007, 38–57. [3] R. Brody, The Geonim of Babylonia and the Shaping of Medieval Jewish Culture, New Haven/London 1998. [4] D. W. Halivni/J. L. Rubenstein, The Formation of the Babylonian Talmud, New York 2013. [5] C. E. Hayes, Between the Babylonian and the Palestinian Talmuds, New York/Oxford 1997. [6] R. Kalmin, The Formation and Character of the Babylonian Talmud, in: S. Katz (ed.), The Cambridge History of Judaism, Vol. 4: The Late Roman-Rabbinic Period, Cambridge 2006, 840–876. [7] D. Kraemer, The Mishnah, in: S. Katz (ed.), The Cambridge History of Judaism, Vol. 4: The Late Roman-Rabbinic Period, Cambridge 2006, 299–315. [8] S. Lieberman, The Publication of the Mishnah, in: S. Lieberman, Hellenism in Jewish Palestine, New York 1994, 83–99. [9] L. I. Rabinowitz/S. G. Wald, Art. "Talmud, Jerusalem," in: Encyclopaedia Judaica, vol. 19, Detroit 2007, 483–487. [10] G. Stemberger, Introduction to the Talmud and Midrash, trans. by M. Bockmuehl, Edinburgh 1996. [11] Y. Sussman, "Torah shebe-al peh." Peshutah ke-mashma'a [The Oral Tora. Its Literal Meaning], in: Y. Sussman/D. Rosenthal (eds.), Meḥkere Talmud. Talmudic Studies Dedicated to the Memory of Professor Ephraim E. Urbach, vol. 1, Jerusalem 2005, 209–384. [12] S. G. Wald, Art. "Talmud, Babylonian," in: Encyclopaedia Judaica, vol. 19, Detroit 2007, 470–481.

JANE L. KANAREK, BROOKLINE

Talmud Torah

Since Antiquity, the study (Hebr. *talmud*) of the Holy Scriptures, the "teachings" (Hebr. *torah*), has been considered a religious duty of Jewish men. It ultimately came to include studying the ancient and early medieval rabbinic texts in which biblical commandments were discussed and expanded. As a consequence, *talmud torah* developed increasingly into the study of Jewish traditional literature. In view of the social changes of the early modern age, medieval study traditions changed, too, with the ideal of lifelong study becoming an increasingly practical option. Interest in the Jewish Enlightenment and secularization tendencies led Orthodox and ultra-Orthodox Jewish communities to engage in new forms and subjects of study to this day. The "study of the teachings" continues to be one of the fundamental ideals of Judaism.

1. Biblical and rabbinic foundations
2. *Pilpul*
3. *Talmud torah* and the Jewish Enlightenment
4. *Lomdus*
5. More recent developments

1. Biblical and rabbinic foundations

The central importance that studying the Holy Scriptures holds in Judaism may be traced back to passages in the Hebrew Bible (→ Tanakh). The instruction recorded there – to transmit the divine commandments to every following generation (Deut 11:19) – was included in one of the most important Jewish prayers (→ Shema). In fact, the legal codices collected in the Torah (Hebr. "teachings"), which – with the exception of provisions concerning impurity and sacrifices – consist of a few succinctly expressed laws, required interpretation from an early stage. The Book of Ezra, composed during the age of the Second Temple around 400 BCE, informs us that the priest and scribe Ezra "had dedicated himself to study the Teaching of the LORD so as to observe it, and to teach laws and rules to Israel" (Ezra 7:10). The "law of the Lord," the Torah, was not only the authoritative legal foundations for priests and scholars of the law but also served as a source of moral reflection and wisdom (Ps 19:8).

Precise oral and written reiteration of Torah passages was closely linked to the idea of a binding holy (→ *kadosh*) text, as was their exegesis with relevance to their practical application. Prophets, priests, and scribes – frequently one and the same person – were responsible for the application of the Torah, its transmission, and for instructing the people (Ezra 22:26). This practice is similar to that of the ancient Oriental non-Jewish scribe schools, where mytho-historical narratives, laws, and books of wisdom were transmitted.

The forced Hellenization under Seleucid rule (2nd cent. BCE) and the simultaneous decline in the importance of Temple service led to a flourishing of Torah studies in the 1st century BCE. It manifested itself in two sectarian movements engaged in ideological conflict. The priestly-aristocratic Sadducees recognized only the Torah as divine law, accepting at best a new written compilation of biblical laws together with succinct explanations. The Pharisees, on the other hand, who were scribes and scholars, insisted on the necessity of reflecting on biblical laws and applying them to further areas of life. In spite of all these differences, the representatives of both groups regarded the daily study of the Torah as a religious duty (→ Mitzvah). The phrase *bet ha-torah* (house of teaching; CD 20,8–14), which was found in a Qumran text, as well as the term *bet midrash* (house of interpretation/explanation; Sir 51:23), which was transmitted from the apocryphal Ben Sira (early 2nd cent. BCE), support the assumption that Torah studies were institutionalized early on. One scroll (4Q Instructions) found among the Qumran texts, for instance, was composed specifically for instructing the poor. There are also references to Torah instruction by Pharisaic scribes (Matt 23:2f.).

After the destruction of the Temple in 70 CE, the scribes endeavored to preserve the knowledge and understanding of all commandments regarding cultic matters as well as those concerning everyday practice, even without a Temple and an independent state. The discussion of biblical laws and traditional doctrines by the Tannaim (from Aram. *tanna'im*; repeaters [of the teachings]), the successors of the Pharisaic scribes, were written down in the *Mishnah* (repetition [of the teachings]). The → Midrash works, in turn, reflect the ancient studies concerned, above all, with the exegesis of the biblical text itself. The scholars were always also teachers, called *rav* and *rabbi* (master; my master), or under Aramaic influence, *rabban* (→ Rabbinate). The Tannaim coined the Hebrew phrase *talmud torah* (lit. study of the teachings) to refer to the study of the Torah and the discursive exegetic practice. They regarded it as one of the most deserving activities of a Jewish man (Mishnah, Pe'ah 1:1), one that he ought to pursue every day (Mishnah, Avot 1:5); accordingly, an equivalent or even higher religious merit was ascribed to teaching.

While rabbinic doctrine did not prohibit girls and women from studying in theory, they were considered to be "exempt" (→ Mehitsah) from the duty of studying because of their domestic tasks. The moral verdict according to which girls studying the religious laws was an "impropriety" and "nonsense" (Mishnah, Sotah 3:4) led to girls being almost always excluded from the institutions of *talmud torah*, but it did not prohibit them from reading the Bible or receiving appropriate instruction. Learned women who dedicated themselves to *talmud torah* via the informal route – usually supported by their fathers – remained an exception.

In order to abide by the biblical command to study, and to prepare *talmud torah*, elementary schools were established simultaneously in Palestine and in Babylonia (*bate sefer*; houses of the book), in which boys from around five to fifteen years of age learned the Bible, the Targum (→ Bible Translation), and the Mishnah more or less thoroughly by means of reading aloud. Gifted boys subsequently studied Jewish religious law (→ Halakhah) in the *bet midrash* or *bet talmud* (house of study). The gatherings of teachers and pupils, as well as the subject matter itself, were called *yeshivah* (Hebr., pl. *yeshivot*; session); the term was used for the institutions of higher rabbinic education (academies) emerging in Palestine and Babylonia (where they were called Aram. *metivta*) from the 3rd century onward. The "wise men" (Hebr. *ḥakhamim*) who taught there and their pupils (*talmide ḥakhamim*) repeated, commented on, and added to the discussions of the Tannaim. Because of this, they were called Amoraim (from Aram. *amora'im*; repeaters, commentators). Together with the Mishnah, their debates conducted in → Aramaic constitute the Talmud. The scholars accorded the same merit to studying the Talmud as to studying the Torah itself. They regarded the Holy Scriptures as the "written" and the Talmud as the "oral" Torah, and, in their view, knowledge of the oral Torah was virtually a precondition for understanding the written Torah (Bavli, Shabbat 31a).

Besides encouraging observance, the value of *talmud torah* was that it led a man to wisdom. The study was to be undertaken for its own sake or for the glory of God but not to raise one's social status. The image conveyed in ancient rabbinic texts of a Judaism in which all men – with the exception of a few *ame ha-arez* (untaught ones) – were fluent in biblical-Mishnaic → Hebrew and Talmudic → Aramaic and devoted many hours of every day to studying the scriptures is hardly realistic. Rather, it corresponds to the rabbinic scholars' ideal and claim to religious-normative leadership; however, they always remained in the minority.

2. *Pilpul*

Talmud torah was also firmly established in the urban Jewish culture of the European Middle Ages (→ Ashkenaz). Boys and sometimes also girls had private or elementary school lessons with a *melammed* (teacher [for children]). Male adolescents studied in a *bet midrash* run privately by a scholar. In order to pursue higher education, young men (*baḥurim*) moved to locations where the Jewish community maintained a yeshivah headed by a respected scholar. Some students left the yeshivah after a few years as *ḥaver* (members) in order to teach in a smaller community. Others, if they were financially secure thanks to a wealthy family, continued their studies for years or decades until they achieved the status of being a *talmid ḥakham* or *ḥakham*. As the leader of a yeshivah, the latter bore the title of *morenu* (our teacher/instructor).

Medieval Ashkenazi scholars studied the Talmud, composing commentaries and legal additions (Hebr. *tosafot*). The Tosafists endeavored to make their Halakhic rulings (→ Halakhah) compatible with Talmudic teachings. Their systematic application of hermeneutic rules could often lead to rather theoretical discussions instead of orthopraxic exegesis. This led to the *pilpul* (approx.: keen penetration; pointed argument) method in the Late Middle Ages with the objective of finding innovative explanations for any Talmudic passage. Every detail of the content as well as the wording would be interpreted, even seemingly minor ones, and even their absence. The scholars pursued the question of why a Talmudic passage adduced a *specific* question or reasoning if a *different* one entailed the same Halakhic conclusion. The frequently very

subtle interpretations were the result of discussions between two or more scholars. These small groups (*ḥavurah*) soon became the normative *talmud torah* practice. *Pilpul* itself was seen not only as a hermeneutic method but also as a form of instruction. The oldest instances of the application of this method are the *Tosafot Gornish* (additions by Gornish) from the 14th century.

Scholars in medieval → Sepharad neither applied *pilpul* nor were they fixated on Talmud studies or the Halakhah. Rather, they attached great importance to → ethics and religious-philosophical questions. Maimonides (→ Guide for the Perplexed) was of the opinion that *talmud torah* should consist of a third each of Torah, Talmud, and methodological reflection (Hilkhot Talmud Torah, 1:11). In fact, linguistic and systematic-methodical discussions were an important part of Sephardic Talmud studies; the work *Darkhe ha-Talmud* (Paths of the Talmud) by Isaac ben Jacob Canpanton (1360–1463), the head of the Talmud academy in Zamora in Castile, Spain, is exemplary of this.

The spread of the plague and the accusation that the Jews had "poisoned the wells" and were thus responsible for the outbreak led to the expulsion of many Jewish communities from → Ashkenaz to Central Eastern Europe. Economic → privileges and legal → autonomy further encouraged migration, resulting in prosperous communities whose members possessed sufficient income to allow an increasing number of men to pursue *talmud torah* as a long-term or even exclusive occupation. With the increasing numbers of students, demand rose for professional teachers. Unlike community rabbis in the *bet midrash*, such teachers did not necessarily have to concern themselves with rulings on the practical side of religious law but could devote themselves exclusively to the theoretical and intellectual investigation of the Talmud.

In the yeshivot of Eastern Europe, *pilpul* was further perfected; its heyday was during

Pupils in a Jewish elementary school (ḥeder) in Brod (Czechoslovakia); photo by Roman Vishniac (ca. 1938)

the 17th and 18th centuries, when it was the definitive method of *talmud torah*. While most communities had neither a yeshivah nor a well-known scholar, they at least had a *bet midrash* in which *pilpul* could be studied. Great Talmud academies (yeshivot) were established in some communities, where leading scholars would harmonize contradicting *pilpulim* using older commentaries and a new exegetic ruling (*ḥilluk*, lit. distinction). Along with *pilpul*, the *ḥilluk* that complemented it became the most important hermeneutic method of *talmud torah*.

Some other famous scholars, such as Jehuda Löw ben Bezalel (1512/1525–1609) and Isaiah Horovitz (1565–1630) from Prague, were opposed to *pilpul*; instead, they called for the study of the entire biblical and rabbinic literature. Champions of *pilpul* argued against their critics that in view of the increasing availability of printed Halakhic codices (→ Printing) and the expanding scope of the rabbinate as the Halakhic authority, proficiency in *pilpul* was more important than comprehensive knowledge of Jewish traditional literature.

3. *Talmud torah* and the Jewish Enlightenment

The followers of the Jewish Enlightenment movement (→ Haskalah) that emerged in the mid-18th century turned against the rabbis' claim to authority and their demand that Talmudic "ceremonial law" enjoy absolute applicability, branding this stance "rabbinism." Haskalah followers considered *talmud torah* to be outdated, and from the 1740s onward called for secular, general education. They sought not only a → reform of the Jewish education system but also the end of rabbis' authority of interpretation over the genuine "sensible" Judaism *per se*. They criticized traditional teachers for children (*melammdim*) and especially the poorly educated itinerant Talmud teachers in Poland, who only taught recitation of the Bible and Talmudic laws without ensuring pupils' understanding thereof.

Indeed, many of the teachers from Eastern Europe had themselves only received the traditional elementary education. Their search for a source of income took them to Berlin and other parts of Prussia, where, in the opinion of the followers of the Jewish Enlightenment, they engaged in "subtle casuistry" to justify "unreasonable" Talmudic customs. Enlightenment criticism of traditional *talmud torah* became increasingly severe by the early 19th century. While allegorical Bible interpretation and the "hairsplitting" of *pilpul* had at first been regarded as insufficient religious knowledge, they would later be seen as the cause of continuing "ignorance" and "folly."

Alongside the first champions of the Haskalah, wealthy middle-class merchants, → court Jews, and → bankers advocated a reformed system of general education. They supported the foundation of private schools where mathematics, German, and bookkeeping were taught in addition to the Talmud and religious studies – such as the Ephraim'sche Lehranstalt, endowed in 1775 by the Berlin mint master and court banker Veitel Heine Ephraim (1703–1775). The Berlin → Freischule founded in 1778 proved more successful, reducing the share of religious education even further. It became the model for many other Jewish Reform schools.

When compulsory education was introduced in Prussia in 1794, the maskilim were required to formulate their ideas of religious education – this became even more urgent in 1824, when the Prussian circular decree prohibited all private schools and introduced public super-denominational community schools (Christian and Jewish schools were counted among these). The maskilim's aim was not to abolish but to reform the traditional style of education; some favored the Bible and the Mishnah as the focus of modern religious education, while others emphasized more in-depth understanding of the Talmud. They were all in agreement, however, that younger pupils should initially be instructed in the Bible exegesis in accordance to the "simple meaning of the words" (*pshat*). Complex mystical and allegorical interpretations were to be reserved for advanced pupils. This program was implemented in the curricula of the modern community schools from the early 19th century onward (→ Bildung). Particular emphasis was to be placed on the Torah in religious studies as a matter of principle, as during a time of political and social upheaval it would be able to provide moral orientation. Besides biblical → Hebrew, Jewish community schools were to teach a wide range of secular subjects with → German as the language of instruction.

While only few Jews still advocated *talmud torah* as the sole ideal of education in enlightened Western Europe at the beginning of the 19th century, and the schools of the Jewish → Reform movement, of modern → Orthodoxy, and of the conservative middle ground (→ Breslau) offered a sufficient range of alternatives, the shift away from traditional *talmud torah* began noticeably later in Eastern Europe. It was not until the middle of the 19th century that Russian Lumières (→ Maskilim; → Maskilah) began to found Jewish reform schools. The Russian authorities, in turn, tried to find ways to place the "backward" traditional schools and the training of rabbis under state control. They convened a commission in St. Petersburg in 1843, whose Jewish members included Hasidic and Orthodox rabbis as well as one representative of the maskilim. In the following year, a law was passed providing for the introduction of state-run elementary and secondary schools as well as state supervision of traditional religious educational institutions. However, this law had little effect as hardly any Jewish children attended state schools, and the supervision of Talmud Torah schools as well the yeshivot failed in practice.

4. *Lomdus*

In pre-Enlightenment Eastern Europe, elementary education for Jewish boys did not differ much from medieval practice, with the exception that increasing numbers of girls took part in lessons from the late 18th century onward. As the lessons were privately organized and often took place in the teacher's house, the traditional elementary school was called *ḥeder* (Hebr.; chamber). After two to five years of elementary instruction, during which knowledge of the Bible and the basics of Hebrew as well as the Mishnah were taught, many boys went on to receive instruction in the Talmud in one of the community schools until the age of 14. From the 16th century onward at the latest, these were called Talmud Torah, each teaching their own curriculum with a variety of subject teachers and fixed budgeting. Some were housed in the local → synagogues, which were also occasionally called Talmud Torah for this reason. The *bet midrash* for Talmud studies, whose head was often the leader of the local religious court (→ *bet din*), was often also within the synagogue building; because of this, it was called the *kloyz* (cell, cubicle) in vernacular Yiddish. Here as well as in the yeshivah, adolescents and adults studied together.

Even within strict Orthodox Judaism, the practice of *talmud torah* underwent some changes from the 19th century onward. Many scholars preferred teaching in their own yeshivot rather than being teachers in a community yeshivah and dependent on the financial support of the local Jewish community only. Ḥayyim ben Isaac (1749–1821) founded a *yeshivah gedolah* (Talmud academy; lit. great yeshivah) in Volozhin, Lithuania (today Valozhyn, Belarus) in 1803.

It became the model for many other Lithuanian yeshivot thanks to its intercommunal character as well as the matter-of-fact, text-focused method of study associated with the specifically "Litvak" scholarship (Yidd.; Lithuanian; → Litvaks) – *pilpul* was rejected in favor of straightforward textual understanding (*peshat*). As a pupil of Elijah ben Solomon (the Gaon of → Vilna; 1720–1797), Ḥayyim ben Isaac was a staunch opponent (*mitnagged*) of → Hasidism and its practice of mystical-popular piousness; like his teacher, he supported traditional Talmud studies based on in-depth knowledge of the biblical and Mishnaic sources, as well as of thorough mastery of both Hebrew and Aramaic. Yeshivot such as this trained Talmud students to become rabbis as well as Halakhic scholars. Jewish communities recognized the value of such "elite schools" that were famous beyond their own region and supported suitable students financially. In rare cases, even individual married Jews – it was the custom for men to leave the institutionalized *talmud torah* after marriage – joined a group (Hebr. *kollel*; this was also the name of yeshivot for married men), in which they would complete three to five years of intensive studies that even carried a small financial remuneration.

In the 1840s, the → *musar* movement emerged among the followers of Litvak scholarship. Studies focused on the Halakhah were complemented by studies of works of moral philosophy, ethics (Hebr. *musar*), and kabbalah (→ Mysticism), as well as some exercises of practical piety; some of these *musar* practices were later adopted into classic Litvak scholarship.

A decisive innovation occurred in Litvak *talmud torah* only with the introduction of a new, analytical-conceptual method of study. In their yeshivah in Brisk in Lithuania (the Yiddish name for Brest, in present-day Belarus), Ḥayim Soloveitchik (Reb Chaim Brisker, 1853–1918) and his son Isaac Ze'ev

Soloveitchik (the rabbi of Brisk, 1886–1959) developed the so-called Brisk *lomdus* (Hebr.-Yidd.; scholarship). Like other advocates of the Litvak method, they dispensed with studying the Talmud using classic *pilpul* or *ḥilluk*, preferring instead the analysis of individual *halakhot* (religious laws) with regard to the laws on which they were based (*dinim*).

While the first generation of the leading exponents of *lomdus* still appreciated the comprehensive knowledge of classical rabbinic literature as the counterweight to abstract-logical derivations, later followers championed a theoretical *lomdus* with no ties to the practical → Halakhah; as a consequence, most of them refused to assume a position as practicing rabbi (→ Rabbinate). This truly academic direction of the Lithuanian yeshivot gave rise to a class of scholars who contributed significantly to the development of the religious science of Talmudic law. While non-*pilpul* scholars criticized this method for transforming *talmud torah* into a kind of "chemistry," it did in fact set new standards of Talmud scholarship and was still supported in a new interpretation by the Orthodox US-American rabbi and philosopher Joseph Dov (also Joseph B.) Soloveitchik (1903–1993; → Halakhic Man), Ḥayim Soloveitchik's grandson.

All the same, the influence of the Brisk *lomdus* remained limited to the *kloyzn* and Talmud academies in Lithuania. The traditional form of Litvak *talmud torah* continued to be practiced in Galicia, while Hungarian yeshivot were hardly influenced by this at all, as they followed the traditional Orthodox Halakhic tradition of studying established by Moses Sofer (1762–1839; → Orthodoxy). Separate forms of Talmud studies had evolved within Hasidism from the late 1880s onward, and Hasidic scholars continued to employ their own hermeneutic instruments. In Germany, traditional *talmud torah* was practiced only in Esriel Hildesheimer's (1820–1899) Orthodox → rabbinical seminary, where the emphasis was on thorough, well-grounded knowledge of rabbinic literature and the process of Halakhic rulings.

5. More recent developments

After the → Holocaust, all Jewish communities were located in predominantly secular societies. As a result, familiarity with the traditional Orthodox way of life and its reflections in rabbinic literature declined, with dramatic effects on Jewish education and its institutions. *Talmud torah* was not the means of perpetuating rabbinical Orthodox Judaism anymore, but the starting point for a neo-traditional one. This development was accompanied by two significant changes in the Orthodox education system:

First, the education in Talmud Torah schools was organized from the elementary to the secondary level. Even ultra-Orthodox circles that had previously rejected the Orthodox → Bais Ya'akov girls' schools now accepted girls being admitted to suitable schools (→ Ultra-Orthodoxy). The *talmud torah* in a *yeshivah gevohah* (high yeshivah), which followed secondary school, became the norm for ultra-Orthodox men; women studied in separate colleges. An increasing number of married men devoted themselves to full-time *talmud torah* in the *Kollel* without aspiring to a position as rabbi or as judge in a religious court (→ *bet din*). In the last quarter of the 20th century – after decades of Talmud studies for girls, academic Talmud classes for men and women within the conservative movement (→ Conservative Judaism), as well as targeted *talmud torah* courses for adult Orthodox women – Jewish women in Israel (*Midreshet En ha-Netsiv*) and in the United States (Stern College) could finally complete the entire traditional Orthodox Talmud education.

Second, a new, factual analysis of Talmudic terms and concepts was sought. While the majority of neo-traditional Orthodox Jews avoided the Judaic Studies of American universities and *Maḥshevet Yisra'el* (Jewish thought) and *Limmude Talmud* (Talmud studies) at Israeli academic establishments, nearly all yeshivot and *kollelim* of the Litvak tradition as well as modern Orthodox institutions adopted *lamdanut* (scholarship) as their predominant method of *talmud torah*. This was the concrete analysis of Talmudic terms and concepts with a focus on philology that also became the basis of Halakhic rulings (*pesak*). A smaller, modernist sub-group adopted certain elements of academic study into the *talmud torah* curriculum of their yeshivot, replacing, however, the historical-philological method that appeared alien to them with Orthodox study of history (→ Zikhron Ya'akov) and archeological insights. Among the champions of this form of study are Adin Steinsaltz (1937–2020), who produced a popular, modern-Orthodox translation of the Talmud in modern Hebrew, and Ze'ev Safrai (b. 1948), who is working on a socio-historical commentary on the Mishnah.

Several representatives of Orthodox Judaism also pursued the popularization of *talmud torah*. The Hasidic Rabbi Me'ir Shapira (1887–1933) invented the *daf yomi* – "daily (Talmud) folio" – in 1923, and it proved to be the most influential method. It is laid out in such a way that the entire Babylonian Talmud can be read in a cycle of seven and a half years; it is now available in digital form complete with an English translation.

New developments in traditional *talmud torah* at the beginning of the 21st century include the increasing contribution of women, inter-denominational yeshivah studies as practiced in the United States (National Center for Jewish Learning and Leadership) and Israel (Pardes Institute of Jewish Studies), as well as the integration of socio-historical academic methods of research (neo-*lamdanut*) at individual Orthodox yeshivot.

Bibliography

[1] I. Aron/M. Zeldin, Contemporary Jewish Education, in: D. E. Kaplan (ed.), The Cambridge Companion to American Judaism, Cambridge 2005, 145–168. [2] J. M. Baumgarten, Common Legal Exegesis in the Scrolls and Tannaitic Sources [Hebr.], in: M. Kister (ed.), The Qumran Scrolls and Their World, Jerusalem 2009, 649–665. [3] I. Etkes (ed.), Yeshivot u-vate midrasot [Yeshivot and Bate Midrash], Jerusalem 2006. [4] I. Lohmann, Tora und Vernunft. Erneuerung der Religion als Medium der Verbürgerlichung in der jüdischen Aufklärung, in: Zeitschrift für Erziehungswissenschaft 9 (2006) 2, 203–218. [5] L. Moscovitz, Talmudic Reasoning. From Casuistics to Conceptualization, Tübingen 2002. [6] D. Rappel, ha-Vikuaḥ al ha-pilpul [The Debate over Argumentation], Jerusalem 1979. [7] J. L. Rubenstein, The Culture of the Babylonian Talmud, Baltimore 2003. [8] C. Saiman, Talmud Study, Ethics and Social Policy. A Case Study in the Laws of Wage-Payment as an Argument for Neo-Lamdanut, in: Jewish Law Association Studies 25 (2014), 225–261. [9] N. Solomon, The Analytic Movement. Hayyim Soloveitchik and His Circle, Atlanta 1993. [10] G. Stemberger, Introduction to the Talmud and Midrash, trans. by M. Bockmuehl, Edinburgh 1996 [11] I. M. Ta-Shma, Ha-sifrut ha-parshanit le-Talmud be-Eropa uve-tsfon Afrika [Talmudic Commentary in Europe and North Africa], 2 vols., Jerusalem 1999/2000.

ELISHA ANCSELOVITS, JERUSALEM

Tanakh

The Hebrew Bible (Hebr. *Tanakh*) containing the creation myth about the origins of the world and the account of the history of the Jews from the beginning to the Babylonian exile is an important testimony of ancient Oriental narration as well as religious and historical experiences. Insofar as the Tanakh reports on the special and indissoluble covenant between God and the people of Israel, it is the religious and historical foundation of Judaism. Since the emergence of Christianity and Islam, the text has not been received and interpreted exclusively within Judaism, a fact that has influenced Jewish understanding of the Bible ever since. As a leading thinker of the Enlightenment, Moses Mendelssohn endeavored to harmonize the rabbinic and medieval understanding of the Bible with modern linguistic and philological insights. In the 19th century, scholars of the Wissenschaft des Judentums found themselves at the center of tensions between the fruitful investigation of the historiographical and philological methods of modern Bible criticism while simultaneously dissociating themselves from its propositions.

1. Origins
2. Use in synagogues
3. Rabbinic understanding of scripture
4. The Middle Ages and the early modern period
5. Modern Era
6. Tanakh and modern biblical studies

1. Origins

In Hebrew, the Jewish Bible is most commonly referred to by the acronym TaNaKh, consisting of the initial consonants of its three sections *Torah* (Pentateuch), *Nevi'im* (Prophets), and *Ketuvim* (Writings). Other Hebrew names for the Bible are *Ha-Mikrah* (lit. "that which must be read") and *Ha-Katuv* (lit. "that which is written" or *Kitve ha-Kodesh* ("holy writings"). In the post-Talmudic era, the Torah (lit. "instruction," "teachings") was also called *Ḥamishah Ḥumshe Torah* after the books included in it ("five fifths of the teachings"; Pentateuch or *Ḥumash*).

According to Jewish understanding, the Tanakh is a text revealed by God and thus is Holy Scripture. Besides a universal creation myth, it contains the account of the choosing of the people of Israel sealed by a covenant between God and the Israelites. This covenant was based on a mutual obligation, namely, God's unlimited protection of the people and the Israelites' concomitant observance of all the commandments set down in the Torah. In addition, the Tanakh contains ancient historiography and provides insights into the mythological, religious, political, and anthropological ideas of the ancient Near East.

The biblical texts were composed in the Babylonian, Persian, Palestinian cultural area between the end of the 7th and the 3rd century BCE and were originally transmitted unpunctuated (without vowel signs) as purely consonantal texts. They are written in → Hebrew; only a few sections of the books of Daniel and Ezra, as well as individual glosses, were written in → Aramaic. Due to characteristics of form and content, individual psalms (Hebr. *tehillim*) can be attributed to cultic usage during the period of the First → Temple (8th century BCE), while some prophetic dicta had circulated among certain groups since the fall of the Northern Kingdom (late 8th cent. BCE) and were gradually compiled into larger collections, which were reworked repeatedly well into the 3rd century. The collation of the parts of the Torah took place only during the postexilic period, between 450 and 400 BCE. The clearly discernible breaks and contradictions, above all, in the extensive legal compendia in Leviticus and Deuteronomy, indicate that different Jewish groups and religious trends in Babylonia and Erets Israel contributed to its development.

The first collection of religious law, the Mishnah (→ Talmud), was compiled around the year 300 CE. At that time, no biblical canon, that is, a fixed number of books with clearly defined textual inventory, existed as yet. It was only in the Babylonian Talmud, whose final version was edited around the mid-6th century CE, that 24 books (the basis for the later name of the Bible *Esrim ve-Arba'ah*, lit. "twenty-four"), their sequence, and their authors were named (Bava Batra 14b–15a). The Torah was postulated as a normative document as early as Ezra/Nehemiah (4th cent. BCE; these were originally a single book); its validity is affirmed by the translation into Greek in the 3rd century BCE. This → translation of the Bible, known under the title Septuagint, differed from the canon of the Hebrew Bible in the chronological sequence of the books, as well as the stronger emphasis on the tradition of wisdom. The present-day canon, that is the number and sequence of the texts as well as their consonantal inventory, are documented only from the 3rd/4th century CE, a time when Jewish scribes (rabbis; → Rabbinate) joined together in a movement and their formative impulses entering into their first phase of stabilization. The final compilation of the canon presumably took place in the 4th century CE.

In the 1st century CE, the individual Hebrew books gradually began to be standardized. Accordingly, the biblical texts found in Qumran (4th cent. BCE – 1st cent. CE; → Archaeology), the oldest extant manuscripts of all, were still unpunctuated, and the orthography of words was not standardized. In addition, the markers identifying sections surviving in the Qumran scrolls only corresponded to the present-day division into weekly segments (Hebr. *parashiyot*) in some cases. The system of vocalization and cantillation, the *masorah* (lit. "tradition") that unifies the Hebrew text, was developed by textual scholars from the 5th century CE.

These so-called Masoretes noted deviations in the ways the texts were read or written, as well as the frequency of certain words, their pronunciation in each case, and grammatical deviations and corrupt text passages. Their work allowed the textual inventory to become fixed. The earliest documented versions of Masoretic Bibles are the Codex Cairensis (896), the Codex Aleppo (925), as well as the oldest complete Bible manuscript, the Codex Petropolitanus/Leningradensis (1008).

2. Use in synagogues

In the post-exilic book of Nehemiah (chap. 8) there is already an account of the solemn reading of the book containing the teaching of Moses on the first day of the seventh month. Apparently, the text was read aloud in sections and subsequently elucidated. When Neo-Assyrian Imperial Aramaic superseded Hebrew as the vernacular, a translation of the biblical text became necessary; there were numerous Aramaic → Bible translations among the Qumran texts dating from the 3rd century BCE.

Since the classical rabbinic era (2nd – 6th cent. CE), reading from the Torah and a selection from the Prophets and Writings has been obligatory in synagogue worship services. This was the reason for the term *mikrah* becoming established to denote the Tanakh. Reading successive sections of the Torah on → Shabbat became a central component of the → liturgy (Mishnah, Megillah 4.1f.). The scroll for this reading must be of leather inscribed with ink (*sefer torah*; Talmud Yerushalmi, Megillah 1.9). The cycle begins in the autumn with *Simḥat Torah* (Festival of Rejoicing of the Torah; → Course of the Year). Specific passages are read not only on Shabbat but also on feast days, on days of the new moon, on Mondays, Thursdays, and during the days of fasting. Since the 4th/5th century CE, the Torah has been divided into different reading portions. With the Palestinian division into 452 portions (*sedarim*), typically used in Erets Israel, a cycle probably took three years. The Babylonian division into 53 weekly sections (54 for leap years; → Calendar), which is employed to this day, allows a reading cycle of one year. In certain years, it is possible to combine some weekly sections in double readings; for instance, *Be-Har* (Lev 21:1–26:2) and *Be-Ḥukotai* can be combined to ensure that the section *Va-Ethanan* (Deut 3:23–7:11) can always be read on the Shabbat following the 9th of Av (→ Tish'ah be-Av), with the cycle concluding on *Simḥat Torah*.

The Torah reading on Shabbat concludes with the reading from the Prophets (*haftarah*, pl. *haftarot*), consisting of a text selected from either the so-called Former Prophets (Joshua to 2 Kings) or Latter Prophets (Isaiah to Malachi). The Writings occupy a considerably less important position than the Torah and the Prophets. There are, however, certain festivals during which the five scrolls (*megillot*) that constitute them are read in their entirety: Kohelet during Sukkot, Esther during Purim, The Song of Songs during Pesaḥ, Ruth during Shavuot, and the Lamentations on the 9th of Av (→ Course of the Year). In addition, some of the songs and prayers in the psalms are a fixed part of the liturgy.

The public Torah reading during the worship service reiterates and presents the revelation of God's word on Mount Sinai in a ritualized fashion. Only unadorned Torah scrolls without vowels, accents, or chrysography may be used, as the text is not intended to be seen but exclusively to be recited – according to the different → Ashkenazi or → Sephardi tradition. Once the prescribed quorum (Hebr. *minyan*) of ten persons has been gathered – according to the Orthodox rite, only men count – the weekly section must be read out loud in the prescribed style of recitation. These ritual instructions tie the liturgical performance closely to the Torah scroll to this day, while it is permitted to use a printed book for the exegesis of the biblical text, its intellectual acquisition (grammar, lexicography), and for practicing the recitation.

3. Rabbinic understanding of scripture

The rabbinic textual scholars approached the Holy Scriptures in a special way from the beginning by regarding the "written teachings" (*torah shebi-khtav*) as equivalent to the rabbinic "oral teachings" (*torah shebe-al peh*). Rabbis were less concerned with developing a sacred text, or its correct exegesis, and more with their own specific understanding of the scripture that could not be inferred from the Tanakh itself – an understanding that they wished to establish in spite of the biblical text. It rested on two premises: for one, the assumption that in and by means of the text, God was sharing his revelation with the people of Israel, and, for another, the understanding that Israel would adopt this revelation and accept it as valid at all times. The context of the Holy Scriptures is thus always the exegete's context. According to rabbinic understanding, Israel encounters God in the text and does not encounter God in → history but rather in spite of history – that is, by carrying out the exegesis (→ Commentary). In consequence, Israel always also encounters itself. The exegesis and the renewed sanctification (→ Kadosh) of the text resulting from it constitute the Jewish community.

This understanding of scripture was simultaneously the cause and the consequence of rabbinic self-understanding. The scholars never regarded biblical events and actors as independent of the biblical people of Israel but measured them according to their own standards. Accordingly, they criticized the priest Pinchas for murdering an idolatrous priest and his Midianite woman (Num 25:7f.) – although God had been appeased by Pinchas's deed and subsequently entered into a covenant of eternal priesthood with him and his descendants – with the words: "Pinchas did not act 'with the agreement of the Sages'" (Talmud Yerushalmi, Sanhedrin 9,7). The rabbinic scholars' view of the Tanakh reflects their religious and social endeavor, after the loss of independent political statehood and the Temple as their cultic center, to place the Jewish people on the new foundation of the Torah, led not by kings, priests, or prophets, but instead by the scholars themselves.

As the Torah was regarded as God's only revelation, it was necessary for scholars to interpret God's word in relation to their respective present. Consequently, rabbinic exegesis began immediately at the place where the written revelation had been received: "And all the people see the voices (Exod 20:18) [...], for when they were all standing before Mount Sinai in order to receive the Torah, they heard God's word and interpreted it" (Mekhilta de-Rabbi Yishma'el, *Ba-Ḥodesh* 9 [Horovitz-Rabin], 235). The dominant endeavor was to erect a critical counterweight next to the synagogical reception with its firm adherence to textual form and performance. The main hermeneutic precondition was that every exegesis had to be inherent in the Scripture. This entailed not only the concept that the Scripture as such fundamentally contained multiple meanings but, above all, that there was an infinite multitude of exegetic possibilities.

The texts of religious law of rabbinic Judaism go even further in their independence from the Tanakh than the exegetic commentaries. Accordingly, the earliest collection of biblical laws, the Mishnah, says that exegesis on the subjects of "Shabbat, Festival peace-offerings, and misuse of consecrated property are like mountains suspended by a hair, as they have little written about them in the Torah, and yet the details of their halakhot are numerous" (Mishnah, Ḥagigah 1,8). Many rules of religious law thus hang on the proverbial string of rabbinic interpretation, rather than being derived from a biblical passage. It is true that the 517 chapters of the Mishnah contain only 265 Bible quotations. In an exceedingly self-confident way, rabbis appear to have had the religious laws fixed

long before they began to engage in exegesis. In the early period, they even called a law that could not be inferred from the Torah a *halakhah le-Mosheh mi-Sinai* (Halakhah [given] to Moses on Sinai). The development of a hermeneutic principle that continued to tie rulings of religious law to the Bible text thus aimed to uphold the absolute authority of the written Torah, as well as to provide scope for allowing the → Halakhah to be adapted to changed circumstances if needed. Ultimately, the scholars sought not so much to establish a "people of the book" but rather a "people of the exegesis of the book."

The close connection between the text and its exegesis tied the Tanakh and the post-biblical Jewish community together just as much as it separated them. After losing statehood and the Temple cult, rabbis emphasized the discontinuity of the national history of the Jews (→ Diaspora), while pointing out the continuity of God's choosing of Israel. Rabbinic Judaism consequently drew its strength from the reception of the Hebrew Bible while simultaneously emancipating itself from it. This allowed for the successful ideological reinvention of the national community as a community of → exile.

4. The Middle Ages and the early modern period

The medieval understanding of scripture evolved in two geographical areas and cultural contexts that only slowly began to grow together in the middle of the 11th century: in Muslim North Africa and Spain (→ Sepharad) and in Christian West and Central Europe (*Tsarfat* and → Ashkenaz). Under the influence of Arab Islamic culture and scholarly tradition – and always in contrast to the Quran and its exegesis (→ *tafsīr*) – Jewish scholars in medieval Spain and North Africa approached the Bible through lexicographical and grammatical research.

In 10th-century Spain, in particular, scholarship and politics became closely intertwined. The Umayyad caliph of Córdoba, ʿAbd al-Raḥmān III (891–961), an art and architecture enthusiast, granted minorities religious freedom and gathered intellectuals of all faiths around himself. His court physician Ḥasdai ibn Shaprut (ca. 915 – ca. 975), a Jewish scholar whom the caliph also entrusted with diplomatic missions, instructed the grammarian Menahem ben Saruq (910–970), whom his father had sponsored before him, to compile an comprehensive dictionary of biblical → Hebrew. The result, *Maḥberet Menaḥem* (Menachem's booklet) was used not only in Spain but long remained the most important source for Tanakh scholars working in the field of lexicography in medieval northern France.

The focus of Spanish Jewish scholarship lay increasingly on the translation of linguistic and philosophical works from → Arabic to Hebrew, with many Arabic terms being adopted or adapted. The Jewish scholars' mastery of Arabic, another Semitic language, alongside → Aramaic, allowed them to compare difficult or unique Hebrew words (hapax legomena) with Arabic lexical meanings in their lexicographical studies of the Holy Scriptures. The linguists Yehudah Ḥayyūj (Abū Zakariyyā Yaḥyā ben David al-Fāsī Ḥayyūj) and Yona ibn Janāḥ (Abū al-Walīd Marwān ibn Janāḥ), both of whom worked in Spain in the 10th and 11th centuries, wrote their works in Arabic. Various biblical exegetes frequently quoted Yona, most prominent among them Abraham ibn Ezra (ca. 1092 – ca. 1167). They above all etymologically and morphologically investigated the Hebrew language as used in the Tanakh, prioritizing secular, linguistically oriented questions over the study of biblical narratives and religious laws.

The Spanish commentators of the 11th and 12th centuries, notably Ibn Ezra and members of the learned Kimchi family, studied the Bible with an understanding of Islamic universal scholarship. Instead of following the four traditional rabbinical methods of biblical exegesis, Ibn Ezra combined universal scholarship (linguistics, → philosophy, astronomy, → mathematics, and → medicine) with Tanakh → commentary. Thus, he opened up an entirely new approach to the Holy Scriptures, paving the way for an exegesis that could be measured against reason and ranked among the general canon of science. Even more explicitly than earlier biblical exegetes from northern France and the Rhineland, this universal scholarship approach implied a deliberate examination of and clear demarcation from earlier forms of biblical exegesis that had been oriented primarily towards religious or pedagogic objectives. For this reason, Abraham Ibn Ezra and David Kimchi prefaced their commentary with a detailed introduction that clearly distinguished it from the earlier understanding of the scriptures.

By contrast, Jewish biblical exegesis in Western Europe in the 11th and 12th centuries featured an intensive interest in the transformation within the Christian scholarly culture in the region. A number of cathedral (Paris, Chartres, Reims) and monastery (Fleury, Laon) schools were founded in northern France in the 10th and 11th centuries or reached their heyday during this period. They promoted the development of new intellectual and spiritual trends that, thanks to the porous borders, spread comparatively freely into the Rhineland to the east. Consequently, a renewal movement gained ground; its followers pursued a more rational approach to religious matters.

In this flourishing intellectual climate, a Jewish school of exegesis emerged in northern France that informed the understanding of scripture like no other. To this day, it is counted among the most important of all schools. Its most famous exponent was Solomon ben Isaac, called Rashi (1040–1105; → Worms). He composed his commentary in Troyes after 1070 and was the first commentator in the northern France-Rhineland region to base his exegesis on the linguistic-semantic and contextual analysis of the Hebrew Bible text despite taking the traditional → Midrash literature into account. Moreover, the lists of synonyms and Old French glossaries compiled by the northern French exegetes testify to their intensive study of Old French – the language the Jews of northern France spoke among themselves and which they used to explain difficult words of the biblical text. It is possible that the Jewish scripture experts' lexicographical works were composed in the context of inquiries originating from their Christian environment concerning the vernacular version of the Bible.

In France and Germany, the → Talmud had long become the standard work of rabbinical scholarship and religious practice. This allowed a freer approach to the Bible, which occasionally and very tentatively revealed a more secular understanding of scripture that diverged from the most common method of exegesis based on the immediate lexical meaning (Hebr. *pshat*). Glossing the Tanakh had revealed the literary nature of its texts. For instance, Rashi's grandson Samuel ben Me'ir (Rashbam, ca. 1085 – ca. 1158) – also a famous Bible commentator – presented the Song of Songs as a Hebrew counterpart to the *chansons de femme*; in his Torah commentary, he referred to the literary structures of Old French romances (*aventure*). These comparisons suggest that the readership was comprehensively educated and probably included women, and that there was widespread acceptance of the new understanding of the Bible with its more literary focus. This development was probably influenced by the changes in literature in the Christian culture of the time, which divided into Christian-Latin (spiritual) and Anglo-Norman and Old French (worldly) branches. Marie de Champagne (1145–1198) was the financial sponsor of the first Old French Bible → translation; this

suggests that at least part of Christian society perceived the Holy Scriptures as a text related to secular literature.

In the 13th century, however, the Jewish understanding of scripture again became more religiously oriented; reasons for this were internal Jewish debates, as well as the confrontation with Christian exegesis and dogmatic-theological questions pushed on Jewish scholars by Christian theologians. The Torah commentary by Nachmanides (Moses ben Nachman, Ramban, 1194–1270) displays clear influences of philosophical exegesis, especially the Maimonidean controversy on the question of the createdness or eternal duration of the world (→ Guide for the Perplexed). His commentaries contain many theological deliberations, among them polemics against Christianity and its increasingly missionary intentions. Nachmanides is usually regarded as the first Jewish theologian because he was the first person in Jewish exegetical history to systematically investigate subjects that had previously been reserved for philosophers on the basis of the biblical text and its exegesis.

During the Renaissance and the early modern period, a new Jewish understanding of the Bible developed, especially in Italy. Christian humanism, with its enthusiasm for *hebraica veritas*, exerted a great influence on this, along with book → printing. In 1455, Gutenberg printed the first Latin Bible in Mainz; printed versions of the Hebrew text of individual books of the Bible, such as the Psalms, soon followed (Bologna, 1477). As a consequence of this development, the Tanakh once again moved into the center of Jewish interest. With Christian society in Italy becoming more tolerant towards the Jews, the latter were able to pursue the study of sciences, technology, medicine, and art to a previously unknown extent and to take up the same professions as Christians. The increasing intermingling of Jewish and Christian lebenswelten also found expression in Jewish commentators' understanding of scripture and choice of subjects. They discovered that the Bible contained texts applicable to nearly all areas of (men's) public life, such as politics, kingship, the art of war, and poetry. Judah Abravanel (Leone Ebreo, ca. 1460 – ca. 1523) felt this applied especially to politics and society. In their Bible commentaries, various exegetes focused on different aspects: Profiat Duran (ca. 1340 – ca. 1415) on specific aspects of biblical Hebrew, Judah Messer Leon (1420–1498) on rhetoric, Azariah de' Rossi (ca. 1511–1578) on biblical archeology, and Abraham Portaleone (1542–1612) on the reconstruction – including the musicological aspects – of sacrifice and divine service. The intellectual confrontation with Italian Renaissance culture provided the standard for their study of the Holy Scriptures.

5. Modern Era

Until the late 18th century, Jewish scholars studied the (Babylonian) Talmud almost exclusively, along with rabbinic literature and Kabbalah (→ Mysticism). In the case of members of the old → Orthodoxy, this self-restriction continued even to the beginning of the 20th century. Only with the emergence of the Jewish Enlightenment (→ Haskalah) did the Tanakh move into the focus of Jewish interest once again. Enlightened scholars attempted to base their work on the foundations of philological biblical studies established at universities (→ Classical Studies). While the majority of traditional Talmud scholars rejected modern academic research on the subject of the Bible altogether, open-minded Jewish intellectuals did not yet find any non-theological courses on the Bible and the Talmud at → universities. In 1848 Leopold Zunz (1794–1886; → Verein für Cultur und Wissenschaft der Juden; → Wissenschaft des Judentums) applied to have a chair for Jewish history and literature established at the University of Berlin. The philosophical faculty of Berlin rejected his application on the grounds that such a subject was ultimately "Jewish theology" and served to train rabbis – a service the faculty felt should be performed exclusively by seminaries rather than universities. However, Zunz was interested in the academic investigation of his own tradition with the aim of strengthening the core of the Jewish faith on the basis of non-Jewish scholarly insights.

Nevertheless, among the Jews, a denominationally influenced, pedagogical reading of the Tanakh was preserved. From Moses Mendelssohn's (1729–1786; → Bi'ur) enlightened works of → philosophy of religion to the Halakhic writings of the neo-Orthodox scholar David Zvi Hoffmann (1843–1921), the relationship between the written and the oral Torah, especially the weighting of the Masoretic text, on the one hand, and the relevance of the religious law, on the other, was the starting point for their approach to modern scholarship. The idea that the text of the Hebrew Bible had been deliberately or accidentally changed and, thus, falsified over the course of history was entirely unacceptable to the representatives of → Orthodoxy. The Protestant theologian Johann Gottfried Eichhorn (1752–1827) claimed that the biblical text as transmitted by humans contained many corrupt words and passages; these required elucidation and correction by means of philological criticism. Mendelssohn, however, in his introduction *Or la-Netivah* (Light for the Path) to the annotated translation of the Pentateuch *Netivot ha-Shalom* (Berlin 1780–1783; → Bi'ur), declared the oral tradition of the biblical text to be the guarantor of its purity and unfalsified transmission. Mendelssohn regarded the Torah as *the* medium of divine revelation. As it contained truths of reason, it contained not only written but also oral teachings, without which the written form would have gradually become unintelligible. Eichhorn's attitude, he thought, undermined the authority of the oral Torah, which was able to derive a Halakhah or narrative exegesis from any biblical phrase.

Still, Mendelssohn and his fellow campaigners did not simply insist on the unconditional authority of the oral Torah. Rather, they sought to integrate rabbinic writings and commentary literature into the Jewish understanding of the Bible in a way that was comprehensible to Christian theologians as well. For instance, they emphasized the philological quality of the exegetic texts. Naphtali Herz Wessely (1725–1805; → Divre Shalom ve-Emet) exemplified this in the preface to his Leviticus commentary, a part of Mendelssohn's *Netivot ha-Shalom*: "There is hope only when God shows me the grace to thoroughly grasp the meaning of the [lexicographical] roots. For, when we understand them, we realize that the words of the Midrash are nothing less than the depth of the literal meaning of scripture. And those who are far from each other will grow close to each other" [2. 309f.]. Wessely was referring here to the exegetical method based on the plain lexical meaning of the word (*pshat*); medieval commentators had already based their study of Hebrew grammar, as well as of the Masoretic text with its readings and cantillations, on this method. In competition with Christian exegesis, Wessely also advocated scholarly philological commentary. Mendelssohn's *Bi'ur* (commentary, exegesis) represents the endeavor to provide modern linguistic and philological insights as evidence for the harmony between the rabbinic and the medieval understanding of the Bible.

By focusing on → Hebrew and its grammar and poetics, Jewish biblical exegesis at first avoided the historical paradigm. This changed during the 19th century, when Protestants increasingly tied the concept of truth to issues of literary history. This is most clearly observable in the works of David Zvi Hoffmann, who studied the influential "higher criticism" of the Bible, championed most prominently by his contemporary Julius Wellhausen (1844–1918). Hoffmann, a member of the "law-abiding" → neo-Orthodoxy, was searching to make his traditional education compatible with his academic work. Between 1873 and his death in 1921, he taught the Talmud and Codex literature, as well as the Pentateuch, at the Orthodox → rabbinical seminary in Berlin, which his teacher Esriel Hildesheimer (1820–1899) had founded. Hoffmann's work focused on the Halakhic sections (→ Halakhah) of Jewish traditional literature, as well as on the Torah. Like the representatives of the → Wissenschaft des Judentums, he sought to find common ground with academic research, engaging in intensive study of the form as well as the content of the historiographic and philological methods. In his commentaries on Leviticus and Deuteronomy, the books of religious law, for instance, he attempted to refute the four-source hypothesis of the composition of the Pentateuch introduced by Karl Heinrich Graf (1815–1869) and Wellhausen (→ Biblical Criticism). In addition, concerning the age of the so-called priestly codex (P), he endeavored to prove that it was chronologically earlier and older than the other source texts, especially the book of Deuteronomy (D). This literary historical claim, which Yehezkel Kaufmann (1889–1963), in particular, took up, was later continued by Orthodox Bible scholars such as Menahem Haran (1924–2015), Israel Knohl (b. 1952), and even Moshe Greenberg (1928–2010) and Jacob Milgrom (1923–2010), each of whom put his own exegetic spin on it. The weakness of Hoffmann's exegetic approach was that it intended to provide historical verification of a quasi-dogmatic statement – the biblical text as God's revealed teaching – and historical proof of Moses being the guarantor of the divine nature of the scripture. Nor was it possible to historically verify the literary-historical reconstructions of the biblical text. This remains true today as well.

The Reform-oriented scholar Abraham Geiger (1810–1874; → Quran) took a different route. He too pursued literary-historical research but dispensed with denominational readings. His magnum opus of Bible criticism, *Urschrift und Übersetzungen der Bibel*, appeared in 1857. In it, he endeavored to prove that the evolution of the biblical text was influenced by the conflicts between different Jewish sects, especially the Pharisees and Sadducees, during the period of the Second → Temple. However, Geiger ignored the later reception history of the Tanakh from the rabbinic period onward and advocated that the Hebrew Bible be treated as an inter-religious research matter.

Both Geiger's and Hoffmann's understanding of the Bible proved to be barely compatible with the way denominations interpreted it. Geiger turned the Bible into a object of study exclusively from Antiquity, without integrating the later exegetic literature meaningfully; Hoffmann's approach failed, in effect, because he refused to abandon Jewish reception history, although he sought to use this history to help answer historical and literary-historical questions. Thus, neither the representatives of the → Reform nor of neo-Orthodoxy succeeded in developing a coherent hermeneutics, equal to Protestant biblical studies, that might have contributed to bridging the chasm between the two trends.

6. Tanakh and modern biblical studies

Biblical studies became established as a university subject in Germany and other European countries, as well as in the United States and Canada. Establishing biblical studies in the → Yishuv in Palestine proved to be extremely difficult due to the question of whether "higher criticism" could be permitted to form part of the curriculum. The treatment of the subject there was influenced by the newly awakened Jewish national consciousness. In 1925, biblical studies first began to be taught in the Faculty of Humanities of the → Hebrew University in Jerusalem as part of Palestine studies, with a focus on historical geography. Soon afterwards, it came to be taught there in the context of biblical → archaeology as championed by Samuel Klein (1886–1940), a graduate of the Orthodox → rabbinical seminary in Berlin. In 1926/1927, the rabbi and linguist Moshe Zvi Segal (1876–1968) accepted a teaching position on Jewish Bible commentators. From 1931/1932 onward, the field of biblical studies had a curriculum of its own and could be studied at least as a minor. In 1939, Umberto Cassuto (1883–1951) became the first appointed professor for biblical studies.

Nowadays, the content and methodological orientation of Israeli biblical studies presents a disparate picture; this is because the various academic institutions have different academic emphases, and the individual scholars each have their own religious orientation. Some focus on archeological research on ancient Israel and its neighboring societies; others focus on textual and manuscript studies concerning the biblical tradition or on the texts of biblical exegesis. Research focusing on the literary history of the Pentateuch, as Hoffmann advocated in the early 20th century, does not exist to this day.

In Israel, the Tanakh occupies an important place outside of the scholarly community – as well as outside the religious sphere – for two reasons. For one, many Israelis claim to be the descendants of the biblical Israelites and increasingly turn to the Holy Scriptures and biblical history. For another, writers and poets, influenced by topics and usage of the Tanakh, reinterpret these to a greater or lesser extent in their modern Hebrew works (→ Literature; → Poetry). They are inspired by the wish to liberate Jewish secular history from biblical and rabbinic stereotypes and elevate the Tanakh to the status of being Israel's – partially secularized – national epic.

In the United States, the exegetic parameters of both modern Christian and Jewish biblical studies shifted earlier than in Germany. Synchronic textual analysis is no longer required to prove the historical unity of the text. A more comprehensive concept of scholarship has led to *close reading* and exegesis as *reader response criticism* – adopting a reader-oriented hermeneutics as formulated by, for instance, Umberto Eco (1932–2016) and Wolfgang Iser (1926–2007); this hermeneutics is almost equal to "classical" biblical studies focused on literary history or historical realities. The multitude of receptions and interpretations of the Tanakh, thus, also allows for Jewish-denominational biblical exegesis to be regarded as scholarly. Methodologically, this means turning away from historism and reverting to interpreting the literary level of the text, including the multi-layered culture of its reception, to arrive at one meaning among the infinitely many possible meanings.

Bibliography

Sources

[1] M. Cohen (ed.), Mikra'ot Gedolot "Haketer." A Revised and Augmented Scientific Edition of "Mikra'ot Gedolot." Based on the Aleppo Codex and Early Medieval Mss, 28 vols., Ramat Gan 1992–2012. [2] M. Mendelssohn, Gesammelte Schriften. Jubiläumsausgabe, begun by I. Elbogen, J. Guttmann, E. Mittwoch. Continued by A. Altmann, E. J. Engel, M. Brocke, D. Krochmalnik, Vol. 9.3: Schriften zum Judentum III, Stuttgart-Bad Cannstatt 2009.

Secondary literature

[3] M. Z. Brettler et al. (eds.), The Bible and the Believer. How to Read the Bible Critically and Religiously, Oxford 2012. [4] S. Carmy (ed.), Modern Scholarship in the Study of the Torah. Contributions and Limitations, Northvale/London 1996. [5] J. C. Gertz, T&T Clark Handbook of the Old Testament. An Introduction to the Literature, Religion and History of the Old Testament, London/New York 2012. [6] H. Liss, Creating Fictional Worlds. Peshat Exegesis and Narrativity in Rashbam's Commentary on the Torah, Leiden/Boston 2011. [7] H. Liss, Tanach. Lehrbuch der jüdischen Bibel, Heidelberg ³2011. [8] M. Sæbø (ed.), Hebrew Bible/Old Testament. The History of Its Interpretation, 3 vols., Göttingen 1996–2013.

HANNA LISS, HEIDELBERG

Tancred

Tancred, or, The New Crusade was the title of a novel by Benjamin Disraeli (1804–1881), who as a leading member of parliament for the Conservative party and two-time prime minister (1868, 1874–1880) had a significant impact on the politics of Great Britain during the Victorian era. As well as facilitating his ambitious social life, his successful literary career served as a means for Disraeli, who was from a Jewish family and was baptized at the age of 12, to formulate political visions. In *Tancred*, Disraeli addresses his understanding of Judaism, of Christianity as the consummation of the Jewish religion, and also of "race" as one of the driving forces of history. The world of ideas outlined therein continued to have an effect on his domestic and foreign policies as prime minister.

1. The Middle East as projection
2. Benjamin Disraeli
3. Judaism and "race"
4. Domestic and foreign policy

1. The Middle East as projection

Tancred is the protagonist of the novel of the same name published in 1847. As an aristocrat who has just come of age, he rejects the seat reserved for him in the British parliament and refuses to pursue the career path which has been predetermined for him. Tancred also avoids marriage to a bride whom his mother has chosen, arguing that he first wishes to seek answers to the central questions of life: "What is duty, and what is faith? – What ought I to do, and what ought I to believe?" [2. vol. 1, 37]. Instead, Tancred decides to undertake a pilgrimage to the Middle East.

Tancred's repudiation of both a typical career and the amenities of high society pick up on a central theme of the Young England movement of the 1840s, that of noble altruism. The literary character Tancred's actions have connections with his own family history; as evoked by his name, one of his own ancestors had taken part in the Third Crusade (1189–1192) and had visited the same region. His intentions are met by his parents with divided opinions. To his father, it seems that the planned trip to Jerusalem "[is] at least better than going to the Jews" in order to finance an extravagant lifestyle by incurring debt like many of his contemporaries. By contrast, his mother declares "I would rather that he should be ruined than die" [2. vol. 1, 53].

Having arrived in Palestine, Tancred makes the acquaintance of the Emir Fakredeen, who is portrayed as both charismatic and manipulative, and his attractive foster-sister Eva Besso, the daughter of a Jewish banker from Jerusalem, "who embodies the spirit of Judaism" [4. 208]. The protagonist falls victim to an abduction initiated by Fakredeen, regains his freedom, and returns to Jerusalem, where he meets Eva again and professes his love for her. At first she refuses him, but as the pair physically approach one another, Tancred's parents unexpectedly make an appearance. At that point, the novel abruptly ends. Whether Eva and Tancred are reconciled, and what his family would think of this norm-defying union between an English noble and a Syrian Jew, remains unanswered.

In *Tancred*, Disraeli portrays the Middle East as a place full of exoticism and spirituality. The extremely lyrical descriptions of Jerusalem and Palestine were particularly positively received by his English readers. Although the setting is repeatedly identified as Syria, it was intended to be Palestine, which was in Syrian territory; Disraeli widely used Syrian as a synonym for → Hebrew [15. 231].

During an attack of encephalitis on Mount Sinai, Tancred has a vision. The "angel of Arabia" had appeared to him, and spoke:

> power is [...] ideas, which are divine. [...] but the intellect of Arabia comes from the Most High. Therefore it is that from this spot issue the principles which regulate the human destiny. [...] a Galilean Arab advanced and traced on the front of the rude conquerors of the Caesars the subduing symbol of the last development of Arabian principles. Yet again - and Europe is in the throes of a great birth. The multitudes again are brooding [...]. [2. vol. 2, 15f.]

The message of the angel can be understood as a spiritually expressed variant of Disraeli's own political convictions: industrialization had shredded the social fabric of England, and visionary leadership was required to restore the symbiotic relationship between the different classes.

Furthermore, the novel's character Fakredeen makes the suggestion that the British monarchy be relocated abroad and designate Delhi as the seat of government instead of London. He would have the Ottoman Empire split between it and the Egyptian viceroy Mehmet Ali (Muhammad Ali Pasha; → Board of Deputies; → Damascus), and subsequently both would acknowledge the British monarch as overlord. With the emir's words, *Tancred* anticipates the coronation of Queen Victoria as Empress of India, which she would fulfill – on the advice of Disraeli during his second term as British prime minister (1874–1880) – three decades later in 1877.

The more intensively Tancred engages himself in the Middle East, the more strongly Judaism becomes a theme. Thus Tancred declares: "Christianity is Judaism for the multitude, but still it is Judaism [...]." He himself "sprung from a horde of Baltic pirates" who were heathens [2. vol. 2, 205]. However, the novel also integrates the classical civilization of Greece into its portrayal of the Middle East. Tancred meets the young queen Astarte, in whose dominion the ancient deities are still worshipped. The spiritual convictions expressed in *Tancred* represent not least Disraeli's intention to reveal a core of pure truth in a present experienced as chaos by using a return to original, thoroughly oppositional formations of Antiquity [7. 133].

2. Benjamin Disraeli

When *Tancred* was published in 1847, Disraeli had already been a representative for the Conservative party in the lower house (House of Commons) of the British parliament for a decade. Born in → London in 1804, he grew up in a family home whose surname D'Israeli indicated their Sephardic origin. The family had initially settled in → Venice in the 16th century, moving to England around the mid-18th century. Benjamin's father, the literary historian and biographer Isaac D'Israeli, saw himself as being committed to the ideas of the → Enlightenment, in particular those of Voltaire. He was little interested in religion, but cherished his Jewish origin; he advised his son to learn → Hebrew. In 1817, he had his children baptized as Anglicans.

In keeping with his societal ambitions, Benjamin Disraeli – like the hero of his novel, Tancred – showed an early inclination toward an extravagant lifestyle. Growing up in the age of the stock exchange, with London its emergent center, he invested in stocks as early as the 1820s, but lost his fortune and fell heavily into debt. In 1826/1827,

Benjamin Disraeli (1804–1881)

still only in his early 20s, he published his debut novel *Vivian Grey*, composed in his idiosyncratic and polished style. The novel was a portrait of high society and was immediately a great success. Published anonymously at first, the work was intended to suggest that the author (unlike Disraeli) was himself a member of the upper class. The revelation of the true author caused a mild scandal. As a result, Disraeli embarked upon a grand tour lasting three years, which took him as far as the Levant. The often overwhelming impressions that the → Orient made on him were later inserted into *Tancred*.

Disraeli subsequently attempted to make his mark as a politician for the Tories, later the Conservative party. After two unsuccessful candidacies in 1832 and 1835, he won his first seat in the House of Commons in 1837 thanks to the financial support of a fellow party member. His entry into parliament was possible due to his conversion to the Anglican state church; by contrast,

Jews were initially barred from sitting in the House of Commons as they could not swear an oath to the Church of England (→ Westminster). As a member of parliament, in 1837 Disraeli voted against exempting Quakers, members of the free churches, and Jews from the requirement to take an oath. After his friend Lionel → Rothschild became the first Jewish candidate to gain a mandate in a parliamentary election (for the City of London) ten years later, Disraeli now demanded that he should take the designated parliamentary seat. He repeated his conception of Christianity as the consummation of the Jewish religion, as formulated in *Tancred*, in the House of Commons in 1847: "Where is your Christianity if you do not believe in their Judaism?" (cited in [7. 125]). In 1858 the upper house finally granted each chamber autonomy in their handling of the oath formulation.

Meanwhile, Disraeli conceived of literature as a testing ground for his personal image, and as a means of formulating political ideas which were integrated into his actions as a politician. In 1834 he presented his interpretation of a conservatism in *The Revolutionary Epick*, which he intended to dedicate to the Duke of Wellington, who however rejected this offer. After the Conservatives' victory in the election in 1841, he perceived it as a bitter affront that Prime Minister Peel did not include him in the government. In 1844 he joined with the aristocracy in opposition to Peel's free trade policies. During this time, the Young England trilogy of *Coningsby or The New Generation* (1844), *Sybil or The Two Nations* (1845), and *Tancred* served Disraeli in the formulation of his political position.

Disraeli had already developed conceptions of a benign aristocracy in *Vivian Grey*, and in doing so had anticipated a central idea of the Young England movement of the early 1840s. Under this designation a group of young parliamentarians from aristocratic backgrounds gathered together. In the face of the social upheaval resulting from the Industrial Revolution, they reproached the clergy and aristocracy for not having discharged their moral obligations to the lower classes. Closely aligned politically with the Tories, the group promoted a strongly idealized form of feudalism. Disraeli was their only representative who neither had an aristocratic background nor had studied at Eton or Cambridge and, moreover, was from a Jewish family. The Young England novels invariably expressed his political belief in a benign and responsible aristocracy. Only they could alleviate the social tensions generated by the industrial revolution. Even the hero Tancred is the "grandson of a mere country gentleman" [2. vol.1, 10].

Disraeli's broad literary œuvre, which encompassed novels, satires, and other writings, furthered his reputation and contributed to safeguarding his financial existence. For a long time he remained deeply in debt as a result of bad speculations in South American mining stocks, his extravagant lifestyle, as well as the expenses of his election campaigns [11. 314].

After his rift with Peel, Disraeli sought to improve his position within the Conservative party. This goal was aided by his biography of his friend Lord George Cavendish-Bentinck, a prominent advocate of the emancipation of Catholics and Jews, which was published in 1852. Here Disraeli drew a most positive and sympathetic portrait of his long-term rival Peel, who had died two years previously. He served in the governments of Lord Derby three times as Chancellor of the Exchequer (1852, 1858–1859, 1866–1868), until taking over the office of prime minister from him in 1868. While this first term of office only lasted a few months as the result of lost elections, Disraeli served as British prime minister for over six years beginning in 1874.

3. Judaism and "race"

Judaism and → race are two topics which repeatedly reappear in Disraeli's literary output. In the works of his Young England trilogy, he is particularly able to deal with Judaism as the origin of the Christian religion in *Tancred*, by moving the setting from Great Britain to the Middle East and Palestine, which was perceived as the Holy Land.

In *Tancred*, Disraeli highlights the historical significance and merits of the Jewish people. Moreover, he expresses the conviction that "race" is one of the driving forces of history, and that it plays a significant role in the development of human character. The Sephardi banker Sidonia, a character who had been introduced in *Coningsby*, makes an appearance for this purpose. In *Tancred*, Sidonia declares: "All is race; there is no other truth" [2. vol. 1, 169]. Sidonia is well-to-do and influential, but as a Jew he is barred from holding any political office. Because of his wealth Sidonia is similar, at first glance, to the → Rothschilds; in the novel he serves primarily to articulate Disraeli's own political views. By showing that the Jew Sidonia is both "of pure race" and in some regards superior to his aristocratic counterpart, Disraeli confronts his own adversaries who attempted to impede his steady political ascent with antisemitic attacks [11. 218].

An antithesis to everything bad and corrupt in *Tancred* is provided by the Jewess Eva, whose moral superiority is highlighted in particular by her passionate defense of Judaism in comparison with Christianity: "We have saved the human race, and you persecute us – for doing it" [2. vol. 1, 223]. Disraeli's opinions on the supposed purity of the Jews as a race is also communicated through her: "The Hebrews have never blended with their conquerors" [2. vol. 1, 219]. The characters of Eva and Fakredeen, who are not biological siblings but who grew up together as brother and sister, allows the author to present members of two peoples side by side. In doing so, Disraeli accentuates rather the commonalities between Jews and Arabs than the differences: "The Arabs are only Jews upon horseback" [2. vol. 1, 286].

Disraeli had previously dealt literarily with Judaism in his 1833 novel *Alroy*. In the novel, Disraeli retells the story of the 12th century Jewish scholar and pseudo-Messiah David Alroy, who initiated an uprising against the Seljuq dynasty because they oppressed the Jews in their empire. Disraeli's depiction of a messianic warrior is obviously intended to make reference to the strength and superiority of Jews in earlier times, as a result of which they could feasibly be affiliated with the heroes of English history. In his biography *Lord George Bentinck*, he dedicated an entire chapter to the Jews without once mentioning the person who is supposedly the subject of the book. "We hesitate not to say that there is no race at this present [...] that so much delights, and fascinates, and elevates, and ennobles Europe, as the Jewish" [1. 491f.].

In his books, Disraeli positions himself as an advocate for the full acceptance of Jews by the British elite. He took up the discourse about "race" in terms of its meaning at the time, in that the term referred to a common origin and not a biological classification [15. 216].

The millenarian idea of a restoration of Zion, which was present in British Christian circles at the time, is also a recurring motif in Disraeli's work. *Alroy* was the expression of an "ultimate heroic fantasy" in which the Jewish people returned to Zion [8. 44]. In *Tancred*, Eva explains: "The vineyards of Israel have ceased to exist, but the eternal law enjoins the children of Israel still to celebrate the vintage. A race that persist in celebrating their vintage, although they have no fruits to gather, will regain their vineyards" [2. vol. 2, 152].

Similar proto-Zionist allusions were not a feature of Disraeli's activities as a politician. The memoirs of Prime Minister Lord Derby describe a conversation, not reported anywhere else, between the two politicians in

January 1852, in which Disraeli is reported to have spoken about the purchase of land for Jews in Palestine, a purchase which he said could have been made financially possible by the Rothschilds [8. 45]. "Tancred" was also the alias which Theodor Herzl (→ Old New Land) used as a member of the student association Albia; it cannot be demonstrated that reading Disraeli's book was the impetus for this.

4. Domestic and foreign policy

Disraeli, especially during his second term as prime minister, initiated the passage of a series of new laws that contributed to the improvement of the living conditions of large sections of the population and mitigated the social conflicts which he had already addressed in the Young England trilogy of the 1840s. These laws were also a manifestation of the concept of a provident aristocracy that he had repeatedly sketched in his novels; his legislative initiatives thus also served to safeguard a paternalistically structured society in the long term. The social legislation adopted in 1875 include the Employers and Workmen Act, which granted employers and employees equality under civil law; the Conspiracy and Protection for Property Act, which legalized trade union activity; the Artisans' and Labourers' Dwelling Improvement Act to eliminate the slums in large cities, as well as the Agricultural Holdings Act to provide coverage for tenant farmers.

As both an author and a politician, Disraeli was convinced that the global British Empire had a particular mission. He had a close relationship with Queen Victoria, who recommended his appointment as prime minister, allowed herself to be crowned Empress of India on his recommendation in 1876, and thanked him by elevating him to the aristocracy as the Earl of Beaconsfield.

At the heart of his foreign policy as prime minister was a region, related to the Eastern Question, which he had once visited, and

where *Tancred* also takes place. In 1875 he secured England's domination over the Suez canal, an extremely important connection to India, by means of the acquisition of shares in its operating company that had been owned by Khedive Isma'il Pasha, who had fallen into financial hardship; this coup was made possible for the British government by credits from the English Rothschilds.

The resolutions of the 1878 → Congress of Berlin, through which the great powers ended the preceding Balkan and Oriental crises and established a new peace framework for southeastern Europe, were among his greatest foreign policy triumphs. These enabled Disraeli to prevent the increase of Russian power in the eastern Mediterranean, and also to secure British control over Cyprus.

Tancred is not Disraeli's most significant literary work, an accolade normally reserved for *Sybil*. He nonetheless repeatedly explained that it was his favorite work from among all his books; as a result, *Tancred* is also key to understanding his personality. By referring in his writing to the merits and cultural heritage of the Jews, Disraeli gained recognition and respect as an aspiring and ambitious actor on the political stage of 19th century England.

Bibliography

Sources

[1] B. Disraeli, Lord George Bentinck. A Political Biography, London 1905.   [2] B. Disraeli, Tancred, or the New Crusade, 2 vols., Paris 1847.   [3] B. Disraeli, Vivian Grey, London 1833.

Secondary literature

[4] R. Blake, Disraeli, New York 1967.   [5] T. Endelman, The Emergence of Disraeli's Jewishness, in: T. Endelman (ed.), Broadening Jewish History. Towards a Social History of Ordinary Jews, Oxford 2011, 201–224.   [6] E. J. Feuchtwanger, Disraeli, London 2000.   [7] M. Flavin, Benjamin Disraeli. The Novel as Political Discourse, Brighton 2005.   [8] B. Glassmann,

Benjamin Disraeli. The Fabricated Jew in Myth and Memory, Lanham 2002. [9] C. Hibbert, Disraeli. A Personal History, London 2004. [10] N. Miller, Nachwort, in: B. Disraeli, Tancred oder Der neue Kreuzzug, Zurich 2004, 877–899. [11] R. O'Kell, Disraeli. The Romance of Politics, Toronto 2013. [12] M. Ragussis, Figures of Conversion. "The Jewish Question" and English National Identity, Durham (NC) 1995. [13] J. Ridley, The Young Disraeli, London 1985. [14] P. Smith, Disraeli. A Brief Life, Cambridge 1996. [15] S. Weintraub, Disraeli, London 1993.

MICHAEL FLAVIN, LONDON

Tangier

City in the far north of Morocco, home to a significant Jewish community for many centuries. Tangier's status as a center of European diplomacy in Morocco from the late 18th century onward along with the International Zone established here between 1923 and 1956 meant that the history and social structure of the Jewish community of the city differed considerably from those of other communities in the Maghreb. Looking to Western languages and European education, Tangier's Jews became pioneers of the modern age in Morocco. After Moroccan sovereignty over the city was re-established in 1956, nearly all its Jews emigrated.

1. Origins
2. Between Europe and North Africa
3. Social and economic structures
4. The International Zone

1. Origins

Tangier was founded in the 5th century BCE as a Carthaginian colony named Tingis in the territory of a village previously inhabited by Berbers. Thanks to archeological excavations, numerous Jewish artefacts from the Carthaginian period are documented. In the 5th and 6th centuries CE, Jews sought sanctuary from persecutions in the Visigoth Empire in Tangier, which became part of the Byzantine Empire in 533 and fell under Arab rule in the early 8th century. As the chronicler Abraham ibn Da'ud (→ Falsafah) reports in his 1160/1162 Sefer ha-Kabbalah (Hebr.; Book of tradition), the Almohad dynasty (1147–1269) put a violent end to all Jewish life in the city in 1148. After the expulsion of the Jews from Spain in 1492, Jews settled anew in Tangier, which was now under Portuguese rule. From 1538 onward, a Jewish community existed in the city once more. When Spain took control of the city and the laws of the Inquisition (→ Toledo) were introduced, the Jews were once again forced to leave Tangier.

When England assumed control of Tangier in 1662, there were a mere 51 Jews living there, most of them from nearby Tétouan [2. 54]. Many of them were employed by the English, for instance the merchant Salomon Pariente, who was a translator and adviser to four governors. The influx of Jewish merchants from the Netherlands during English rule led to tensions between Moroccan and European Jews; the rabbis of Tétouan to whom Tangier was formally subject as a community, imposed a → ban against the immigrants in 1675 because they were said to have drunk unkosher wine and traded in pork (→ Kashrut).

As a result of being accused of spying for the sultan, all Jews were expelled from the city in 1677. While they were permitted to return to Tangier in 1680, they had to stay outside the city walls overnight. At the end of English rule in 1684, most Jewish merchants left the city, which would henceforth be governed by the Alawites, leaving only a few craftsmen behind.

In 1725, Abraham Benamor was the only Jewish merchant residing in Tangier. He came originally from Meknes, from where more Jews would move to Tangier. By the middle of the 18th century, around 150 Jews were living in the city once more [1. 305]. By 1744 they had their own *dayan* (Hebr.; judge), the rabbi Judah Hadida, and were organizationally subject to the community in Tétouan. It was only towards the end of the 18th century that the approximately 200 Jewish families in Tangier adopted an *askama*, the traditional Sephardic set of regulations (→ Sephardim) for the administration of internal matters; this meant that they were a small independent Jewish community from that point forward [14. 486].

2. Between Europe and North Africa

In 1772, Sultan Muḥammad III tried to limit European influence by prohibiting Christians from settling in Morocco, the only exception being Tangier where the European powers and the United States subsequently established their consulates. Many of the city's Jews entered into employment with these diplomatic missions; not infrequently a Jew would hold the position of consul of a European power. The Jews of Tangier were predestined for the role as professional mediators as they were familiar with the European Christian culture as well with that of North African Muslims and furthermore possessed good contacts with the Moroccan hinterland that was regarded as dangerous by Europeans. The extensive knowledge of languages Jewish merchants and their families had acquired was a further point in their favor. Besides Essaouira, Tangier was the only Moroccan port that reported significant trade with Europe in the second half of the 18th century [9. 46]. A particularly close economic relationship linked Tangier to British Gibraltar, which it supplied with food and everyday commodities.

In many cases, the Jews working in the consulates were granted → citizenship of the countries they represented or were declared their protégés; concomitantly, they adopted a Western style of dress. Sultan ʿAbd

al-Raḥmān regarded this as an infringement of the traditional ethnic-religious boundaries (→ Dress Regulations) and reacted with restrictions; faced with British pressure, however, in 1831 he allowed Jews from Gibraltar who often came to Tangier to wear European clothing for the period of up to a month. He unsuccessfully attempted to have Jews from Algeria who settled in Tangier classed as foreign nationals; according to his understanding of the law, they were persons subject to the protection of → *dhimmah* and consequently to his authority only.

European citizenship meant those Jews were exempt from traditional everyday rules, such as the prohibition of riding a horse; the same applied to the local jurisdiction which favored Muslims. This contributed to a perception of the Jews of Tangier as representatives of European interests and values. In 1846, Sultan ʿAbd al-Raḥmān banned the Jews of Tangier from leaving the city, giving as justification that in this way they evaded the poll tax (Arab. *jizyah*) and would plot against him once outside Morocco; however, due to economic reasons he did not implement the ban. Jewish traders, being non-Muslims, allowed the sultan to profit from trade with the Europeans without exposing himself to the influence of "infidels," which was presumed to be harmful.

Over the course of the 19th century, tensions between the European powers and Morocco increased. The sultanate was among the so-called Barbaresque states of North Africa which profited from capturing merchantmen, ransom and protection money, kidnapping, and the → slave trade (→ Pirates). When Morocco conducted negotiations with Great Britain, Sardinia, Naples, and Austria on safe trade in the Mediterranean in the 1820s and 1830s, the merchant Judah Benoliel from Tangier served as Sultan ʿAbd al-Raḥmān's diplomat.

Piracy, which was virulent along the North African coast, repeatedly led to military punitive expeditions by European naval powers also affecting Tangier. In 1844 the French navy shelled the city. As no Jews were hurt during the attacks, which took place during Purim (→ Course of the Year), the Jewish community subsequently celebrated the event as *Purim de las bombas*. By signing the British-Moroccan trade agreement (1856) and treaties with Spain (1861) and France (1863), Europeans were ensured free access to the Moroccan market as well as customs and tax privileges, even establishing their own jurisdiction. Morocco's defeat in the Spanish–Moroccan War (1859/1860) contributed to the sultan's gradual loss of sovereignty.

From 1805 onward, diplomatic missions of European states in Tangier were granted the right to monitor the port for the medical protection of their citizens, including the introduction of quarantine measures. For many Muslim pilgrims from West Africa, the city was a stopover point on the way to and from → Mecca and was repeatedly beset by pestilence. The authority vested in the Conseil Sanitaire de Tanger was confirmed by Sultan 'Abd al-Raḥmān in 1840. In 1892, Sultan Hassan I granted the sanitary council the additional right of constructing streets and ensuring they were kept clean. The council transferred the right onto the hygiene commission founded on the initiative of the inhabitants of the city in 1870, who could raise taxes to this end. The hygiene commission was a board of 26 representatives appointed by the European consulates, the sultan, the chief rabbi of Tangier, and by a group of wealthy and mainly foreign inhabitants of the city. Under the aegis of the French and Spanish consuls, it gradually acquired the authority of Tangier's true city council.

3. Social and economic structures

Between 1844 and 1904, the population of Tangier quadrupled to 40,000. The Jewish community increased from 2,000 persons in 1830 to over 8,000 in the late 19th century

[11. 11]; [8. 24]. In 1864, a community council, the junta, was established, whose members were exclusively drawn from the wealthiest families. In contacts with the outside world, this committee represented the concerns of the Jews with the Moroccan authorities, collected the poll tax, oversaw social issues, and punished the non-observance of religious commandments (→ Mitsvot) [8. 24]. As a result of their mercantile activities, close relations existed between members of the junta and the French Consistoire central israélite (→ Israelite Central Consistory) and the British → Board of Deputies.

The vernacular used by the Jews in Tangier was *ḥaketía*, the Judeo-Spanish dialect (→ Ladino) of northern Morocco. In 1864, the → Alliance israélite universelle opened its second education institution in Morocco in Tangier. Lessons were held in French with Spanish, → English and, from the 1920s onward, → Hebrew taught as additional subjects. → Arabic was not part of the curriculum. Education in French corresponded to the degree of acculturation among the higher and middle classes, but also met the needs of the majority of poorer Jews, many of whom were craftsmen or small traders hoping that an education in the European style (→ Bildung) would better their children's chances of social advancement. With the newspapers *Al-Moghreb al-Aksa* in English, *El Eco Mauritano* in Spanish, and *Le Réveil du Maroc* in French published in Tangier, the city became the center of the non-Arabic press in Morocco.

A further special feature was the unique freedom of movement and settlement enjoyed by the Jewish population of Tangier. Unlike other communities in the sultanate, they never had to live in a → mellah, the walled district exclusively inhabited by Jews. Even Beni Ider, a district considered to be a Jewish quarter, was home to numerous Muslims and Christians as well. The living situation of the Jews of Tangier was similar to those living in the port cities → Alexandria or → Salonika. Their exceptional status within Morocco also found expression in their attitude to the Jews of Fes or → Marrakesh who spoke Arabic or Tamazight, the Berber language, whom they called *foresteros* (Judeo-Span.; foreigners). The Jews of Tangier regarded themselves as *rumi* (from Arab. *rūm*, Byzantines), in Morocco a synonym for Europeans or Christians.

From the late 18th century onward, larger groups of Jews from the city had lived as merchants in Gibraltar, Oran, Cairo, → London, or Manchester. Their cultural and linguistic ties to the Iberian Peninsula led some of them to Latin America in the 19th century. The majority returned to Tangier as wealthy men, where they frequently challenged the old-established system represented by the junta and the rabbinate [6. 200]. Small groups also settled in Portuguese Cape Verde, Angola, and Mozambique [12. 100].

At the beginning of the 20th century, the two Jewish bankers Isaac Abensur and Salvador Hassan founded a real estate company together with the German financier Max Haessner and the British journalist Walter Burton Harris and began to construct buildings outside the city walls. Their syndicate was exemplary of the international orientation of the leading Jewish families in Tangier: Isaac Abensur was a British subject and Knight of the French Legion of Honor; Salvador Hassan was vice-consul of Spain as well as Italy. Jewish investors like David Benelbas and the brothers José and Mimouni (Mimón) Bendahan, who had acquired their fortunes in Latin America, constructed Morocco's first street in the European style in 1905, marking the transition from the traditional medina to a modern residential area.

4. The International Zone

As a consequence of the so-called Moroccan crises of 1904–1906 and 1911, which were an expression of the growing rivalry between the great powers, decisions concerning Tangier were made as well. The special status of Tangier, governed primarily by foreign diplomats, was confirmed by the European signatory powers and the United States during the 1906 Algeciras Conference. In 1912, France asserted its protectorate of Morocco, conceding to Spain a zone of influence in the north of the country. Tangier and its surrounding region were officially declared an International Zone.

In 1923, this status was confirmed by a number of other states. Formally, the Sultan of Morocco continued to exercise sovereignty over Tangier, represented, however, by a *mandūb* (Arab.; authorized representative), whose appointment had to be confirmed by France and who was assisted by a French adviser. The legislative assembly established in 1923 corresponded to a large degree to the earlier hygiene commission. The sultan's subjects were granted nine seats, six of which were reserved for Muslims and three for Jews. In addition, the members of the committee included four Spaniards, four Frenchmen, and three Britons as well as representatives of the other contracting states – who were not infrequently Jews as well.

Politically, the Jews of Tangier possessed a degree of autonomy unique in Morocco. The Moroccan authorities and the Legislative Assembly of Tangier guaranteed their rights. Usually the *mandūb* accepted all the candidates the Jewish community suggested for the junta, even if it consisted of foreigners. Thus, in 1950/1951 there were only seven Moroccan nationals among the 16 community councilors, but five former consulate protégés as well as four Jews who held European → citizenship [4. 176]. In addition, the community had its own rabbinate court (→ *bet din*). After the First World War the court, like the *mandūb*'s residence, was housed in the building of the former German consulate, the size of which reflected the ambitions of the Wilhelmine German Empire in Morocco.

Towards the end of the 1930s, the International Zone, for which there were no immigration restrictions, developed into a contact point for Jewish refugees. Until 1939, approximately 1,500 Jews had found sanctuary in the city, around half of them → Ashkenazim from Hungary and Poland and the other half → Sephardim from the Dodecanese Islands, where the Italian race laws had been introduced in 1938 [4. 178]. The French defeat in 1940 marked a turning point for the refugees as well as for the old-established Jews. Under the pretense of protecting the neutrality of the International Zone, Spain occupied Tangier, placing the city under its protectorate administration in Tétouan. For the Jews of Tangier, the Spanish occupation entailed above all a higher tax burden as well as discrimination in administrative issues, for instance the awarding of business licenses. The rabbinate court had to vacate its premises to make room for the reopened German consulate; the *mandūb* was dismissed, and Spain from then on determined the representatives from the Jewish community. The administration's financial support for the community was abolished too. In addition, the Spanish authorities revoked work permits for Jewish refugees, with the result that the → World Jewish Congress, the → Joint Distribution Committee, and the → Alliance israélite universelle were obliged to ensure they were supplied with the essentials.

Compared to the antisemitic measures passed in the French protectorate Morocco (→ Marrakesh) under the influence of the → Vichy Regime, living conditions for Jews in Tangier under Spanish occupation were much better. The antisemitic propaganda of German agents on the ground showed little effect. Over the course of the Second World War, Tangier received a further 3,000 Jewish refugees. Among them were the married couple Renée and Samuel Reichmann, who became known in Europe for their commitment to persecuted Jews. The Reichmanns had fled from → Vienna via → London to Paris, from where they had reached Tangier at the end of 1940 using a safe-conduct document from the chief rabbi of Spanish Morocco. Renée Reichmann founded the Tangier Committee for Aid to Refugees,

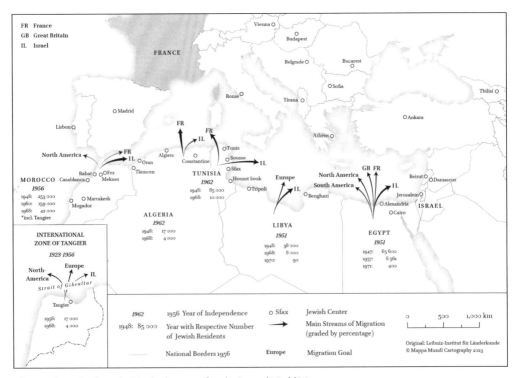

The Jewish exodus from the Maghreb states after the Second World War

which sent care packages to Jews in German-occupied Europe with the aid of the Spanish Red Cross from 1942 onward. Together with *Va'ad Hatsalah* (Hebr.; rescue committee), she obtained 500 visas for Jewish children in Hungary in the summer of 1944, saving them from deportation in → Budapest [11. 155].

After the withdrawal of the Spanish forces in October 1945, Tangier's status as an International Zone was restored. Until the beginning of the 1950s, the population grew to 172,300 of whom 15,000 were Jews [13. 185]. The rich families of the junta, such as the British Abensurs, the Portuguese Hassans, the Spanish Laders, and the Dutch Bendelacs, once again assumed their former positions. The foundation of the State of Israel in 1948 did not entail many changes at first. While a Zionist committee had existed since 1919, it mainly devoted itself to philanthropy. The readiness for → *aliyah* (lit. ascent) to Israel remained low at first, as most of the Jews felt secure in the International Zone in spite of the Moroccan nationalism emerging under Sultan Muhammad V. The special position was also beneficial to the emigration organization *Kadimah* (Hebr.; ahead), which worked for the Jewish Agency in Morocco from 1949 onward, using Tangier as a transit port for Jews wishing to emigrate to Israel.

The situation was different in the Spanish and French protectorates, where the emigration of the Jewish population began at the end of the 1940s. Of the approximately 250,000 Jews living there in 1948, over 100,000 left their homes before the independence of Morocco in 1956, most of them moving to Israel (→ Mizrahim). In October 1956, Moroccan sovereignty was established in Tangier too. Once the international status had been abolished, Tangier was not a free port any more, and all goods became liable to customs duty. The subsequent economic decline compelled the Jews as well as most of the Europeans of the city to leave. In 1968, around 4,000 Jews were still living in Tangier; by 1970 their number had fallen to 250.

While approximately 230,000 Moroccan Jews emigrated to Israel by 1970, the majority of the Jewish inhabitants of Tangier moved to Europe and America [5. 502]. The fact that Jews of the middle and upper classes frequently held European citizenship made it easier for them to start a new life especially in France, Spain, or England. Banks owned by Jews (→ Bankers) were dissolved or transferred to other countries, such as the Banque Pariente to Switzerland and the Banque Nahon to Spain. After the June War of 1967, hostility against the Jews who had remained in Morocco – including a knife attack on the chief rabbi of Tangier – boosted emigration. By the end of 1967, only 40,000 Jews were living in Morocco, and by 2000, their number had fallen to 6,000 [3. 321]; [5. 503]. The Jewish community in Tangier numbered around 200 members at the turn of the century; the Benchimol Hospital, Morocco's oldest Jewish hospital, was torn down in 2010, and of once over a dozen places of worship, only the Chaar Rafael Synagogue is still in use.

Bibliography

Sources

[1] I. Laredo, Memorias de un viejo tangerino. Leyendas y resúmenes históricos de Tánger, desde los tiempos más remotos hasta hoy, Madrid 1935. [2] E. Routh, Tangier. England's Lost Atlantic Outpost, 1661–1684, London 1912.

Secondary literature

[3] J. Baïda, The Emigration of Moroccan Jews, 1948–1956, in: E. Gottreich/D. J. Schroeter (eds.), Jewish Culture and Society in North Africa, Bloomington 2011, 321–333. [4] M. M. Laskier, The Alliance Israélite Universelle and the Jewish Communities of Morocco 1862–1962, Albany 1983. [5] M. M. Laskier/E. Bashan, Morocco, in: R. S. Simon et al. (eds.), The Jews of the Middle East and North Africa in Modern Times, New

York 2003, 471–504. [6] S. G. Miller, Kippur on the Amazon. Jewish Emigration from Northern Morocco in the Late Nineteenth Century, in: H. E. Goldberg (ed.), Sephardi and Middle Eastern Jewries. History and Culture in the Modern Era, Bloomington 1996, 190–209. [7] S. G. Miller, Making Tangier Modern. Ethnicity and Urban Development, 1880–1930, in: E. Gottreich/D. J. Schroeter (eds.), Jewish Culture and Society in North Africa, Bloomington 2011, 128–149. [8] S. G. Miller, The Mellah without Walls. Jewish Space in a Moroccan City, Tangier 1860–1912, in: D. Maghraoui (ed.), Revisiting the Colonial Past in Morocco, London 2013. [9] D. J. Schroeter, The Sultan's Jew. Morocco and the Sephardi World, Stanford 2002. [10] D. J. Schroeter, From Dhimmis to Colonized Subjects. Moroccan Jews and the Sharifian and French Colonial State, in: E. Mendelsohn (ed.), Jews and the State. Dangerous Alliances and the Perils of Privilege, New York 2003, 104–123. [11] M. M. Serels, A History of the Jews of Tangier in the Nineteenth and Twentieth Centuries, New York 1991. [12] M. M. Serels, Jews of Cape Verde. A Brief History, New York 1997. [13] G. H. Stuart, The International City of Tangier, Stanford 1955. [14] J. Tolédano, La saga des familles. Les Juifs du Maroc et leurs noms, Tel Aviv 1983.

M. MITCHELL SERELS, SCARSDALE

Tarbut

In the interwar years, *Tarbut* (Hebr.; culture) was the most important network of Jewish-secular education in Eastern Europe. Especially in Poland, the association maintained a widely-ramified system of educational institutions for children and adults. It had its international legal basis in the educational autonomy for minorities, codified in the Paris Peace Treaties. The network was run by Zionist parties of the center as well as the moderate left to guarantee Hebrew-language training in keeping with the times.

Tarbut had a lasting influence on the cultural self-understanding of an entire generation; many graduates later settled in Palestine and helped to shape the State of Israel.

1. Russia and Poland
2. The Baltic states and Romania
3. Graduates in Palestine/Israel

1. Russia and Poland

The first efforts to establish secular Jewish educational institutions in Eastern Europe date back to the end of the 19th century. This was the time at which members of → *Hoveve Tsyion* in Russia founded reformed schools (*ḥadarim metukanim*), in which, to be sure, traditional educational principles (→ Talmud Torah) were provided, but the pedagogy and curriculum were modernized in the spirit of European educational reforms. After the → February Revolution, the association previously called *Hoveve Sefat Ever* (Friends of the Hebrew Language) changed its name to *Tarbut* (Culture) and worked for the foundation of Hebrew schools. The victory of the Bolsheviks soon made this commitment impossible .

In the territory of Poland, the organization of modern Hebrew (as well as Yiddish) schools began after the occupation of Western areas of Russia by German and Austrian troops in the First World War. Thus, for instance, a Hebrew elementary school was founded in Goniądz near Białystok in 1915. The efforts received a decisive boost beginning in February 1919, when the Polish Republic introduced compulsory schooling, which had not existed in the previously Russian areas. In June of the same year, Poland explicitly acknowledged the Jews' right to set up an independent educational system in Article 10 of the Minorities Treaty (→ Minority Rights) that it signed with the Principal Allied and Associated Powers. The most important political and religious movements among Polish Jews – the *Bund*, the Zionists, *Agudat Yisra'el* (→ Bais Ya'akov), and the *Mizraḥi* – immediately founded their own educational networks.

The newly founded schools of the Zionist camp were united into a confederation at a conference in Warsaw in 1921, at which 178 delegates from Hebrew-language schools took part. Initially subordinate to the Zionist Education Department (Kuratorium oświatowe), it was continued, after the latter's dissolution in 1922, as a *Tarbut* school network, whose co-founder and most prominent leader was Ozjasz Thon, the Zionist Cracow rabbi and member of the → Sejm. The Central Committee in Warsaw coordinated the numerous regional committees. Like the other networks, *Tarbut* initially received funds from the → Joint Distribution Committee. When payments were halted in 1929, financing was based on tuition and occasional contributions from Jewish organizations but only rarely from public resources.

In Poland, *Tarbut* schools were run especially in the eastern regions that had previously belonged to Russia, and, as far as education was concerned, presented a less advanced stage of development than the rest of the country. In 1924, eight of the nine Hebrew secondary schools were in the East. Later, *Tarbut* operated 31 elementary schools, two secondary schools, three kindergartens, 16 night schools, and one teachers' college in the Voivodeship of Vilna alone [4. 53f.]. Although as many as 75% of Jewish children studied at state schools in Poland, *Tarbut* nevertheless continuously grew, especially in elementary school education. The number of students rose from 16,625 in the school year 1925/1926 to over 27,000 in 1937/1938. In Poland in the mid-1930s, approximately 9% of the 500,000 Jewish schoolchildren and about one quarter of the 180,000 students at educational facilities attended institutions belonging to *Tarbut* [5. 36].

Because of their relatively high fees, the secondary schools and teacher colleges, pedagogical classes, and especially the kindergartens were utilized mainly by more affluent families sympathetic to Zionism. In Białystok, for instance, 60% of these parents were merchants or shopkeepers, 10% representatives of liberal professions, and only 9% craftmen [7. 441f.]. More young men than women received instruction at the secondary schools and higher classes of Polish (as well as Baltic) *Tarbut* schools. Most of the teachers were also male, and only in kindergartens and lower grades did women predominate.

The curriculum prescribed by the Ministry of Religious Affairs and Public Education for elementary schools stipulated the subjects of Polish, geography, history, and contemporary regional studies as compulsory, all of which were to be taught in → Polish. *Tarbut* thereby promoted Polish patriotism but at the same time distinguished it from mere assimilation. The curriculum was shaped primarily by Hebrew, which the Zionist teachers considered as fundamental for the formation of a new Jewish nation, as well as of the establishment of a Jewish homeland in Palestine. Language instruction followed the "natural method" of *Ivrit be-Ivrit* ("Hebrew in Hebrew," that is, without translation), with the Sephardic pronunciation being preferred. Jewish and general subjects were taught in → Hebrew. The students became acquainted with the most important Jewish works, including the → Talmud, of rabbinical and modern literature, as well as prayers and religious usages.

The contents were determined not so much by tradition or religion as by nationalist Jewish motives. The → Tanakh was handled with great respect but was considered first and foremost as a work of national culture and evidence of an ongoing connection to the Land of Israel. Zionism was at the center of the educational program, which included Jewish → history, contemporary subjects, Zionist anniversaries such as the death of Theodor Herzl or the signing of the → Balfour Declaration, but also traditional holidays. *Tarbut* schools constantly tried out new educational models, for instance emphasizing child developmental stages and enlivening face-to-face teaching with experimental learning in workshops and laboratories, by physical activity and excursions. The more apparent the discrepancy became between Jewish cultural autonomy and the progressive Polonization of youth from about 1925 onward, the more intensely *Tarbut* concentrated on issues concerning emigration to Palestine, for instance the acquisition of agricultural knowledge and physical fitness.

Economic and sociocultural changes within Jewish communities led to a slow diminution in the number of students, as well as in the number of Hebrew-speaking secondary schools. Nevertheless, *Tarbut* maintained bilingual (Utraquist) schools, which emphasized the need for life "in two cultures," and, until 1937/1938, developed into the largest group among Jewish secondary schools. Some of them received state recognition, which granted their graduates the right to study at Polish universities.

2. The Baltic states and Romania

In addition to Poland, centers of the *Tarbut* network existed in the Baltic states and in Romania.

The three Baltic states were accepted into the League of Nations (→ Geneva) in 1921, on the condition that, on the model of Poland, they would sign declarations on protection of the rights of minorities. Especially in Lithuania, additional factors favored the development of Jewish schools, such as the frequent changes in official language between 1914 and 1919 and the limited extent of acculturation of Lithuanian Jewry, but above all the basic stance of the State, which

was initially oriented toward the integration of its many national minorities.

The Lithuanian Law on Elementary Education ascribed responsibility for the basic schooling of minorities to the Ministry of Education; its (partial) financing was tied to a minimum number of students. Teachers were officially appointed, and the curriculum and school organization had to meet State regulations. In the 1920s, State and communal contributions made up 40% of the annual budget of the Jewish elementary schools, while tuition accounted for an additional 30%. *Tarbut* and local Jewish communities made up the difference, which resulted in a chronic deficit. Nevertheless, the network prospered until 1924. The number of students first began to decline with the reduction of State contributions, beginning in 1925. The practice of subventions was basically maintained, however, even under the authoritarian governments of the second half of the 1920s, and until the incorporation of the Republic of Lithuania into the Soviet Union in 1940. In 1928, 75% of Jewish children were taught in the 81 recognized and publicly supported schools of the Lithuanian *Tarbut* system (including associated schools) [6. 137–146].

All private secondary schools and gymnasia required recognition by the Lithuanian Ministry of Education, which also partially specified the curricula. Nevertheless, such establishments had relatively broad freedoms as compared to the state schools. Since State and communal contributions were granted only to a limited degree, they were largely dependent on tuition fees and hence on the financial possibilities of the parents. The preschool sector as well, which never received public grants and was entirely financed by contributions from parents and support by the Jewish communities, developed continuously from the opening of the first Lithuanian *Tarbut* kindergarten in 1922 until the school year 1927/1928, with as many as 760 children accommodated in 26 institutions. However, these figures diminished in the 1930s [9. 143f.]. In Lithuania as well, the most important goal of the *Tarbut* was humanistic education, with general course content combined with Jewish materials, and an emphasis on Jewish culture and Zionist thought.

In Latvia and Estonia, essential contributions to the development of Hebrew- and Yiddish-language schools, which were to some extent financially supported by the State and the communes, were made by an initially largely tolerant policy toward minorities, as well as the low level of acculturation of the local Jewries. In Latvia, Jewish schools were organized by a committee appointed by the Ministry of Education, which represented supporters of Yiddish as well as the Orthodox and Hebraists. The Hebrew-language schools were associated with *Tarbut* and with *Tushiyah* (a network of the *Mizraḥi*); one third of the Jewish children in Latvia attended the *Tarbut* schools [1. 16–22]. In Riga, there was a Jewish kindergarten teachers college for all three Baltic states. The Estonian community, which counted fewer than 4,500 Jews, maintained schools with instruction in Yiddish and Hebrew in Tallinn and Tartu, with *Tarbut* running a kindergarten in each city [8. 305f.].

Romania had signed an agreement on the protection of minorities in December 1919, half a year after Poland. However, *Tarbut* remained a marginal phenomenon in the Romanian Old Kingdom. Only in Bucharest was a Jewish school successfully founded; Hebrew courses for adults and teachers were also offered [3. 232–239]. In Romania, secularly-oriented *Tarbut* schools were especially popular in the eastern parts of the country, except for the traditionally-inclined educational landscape in Bukovina. In Bessarabia, *Tarbut* had been founded under Bolshevik rule in 1918; since the union with Romania in the autumn of the same year,

the network quickly expanded, in view of the underdeveloped educational system of both the Romanian state and the Yiddish-speaking community. In 1937, it maintained 14 kindergartens, 35 elementary schools, and ten secondary schools, and half of the Jewish children of Bessarabia attended *Tarbut* schools [2. 258–266].

Conditions in Transylvania were also favorable for the *Tarbut* network of schools. The Jews there were largely Magyarized, but the Romanian government made it difficult for them to be accepted in Hungarian schools, with the quality of Romanian schools being considered poor. Beginning in November 1920, *Tarbut* founded two elementary schools in Transylvania, as well as a secondary school, and maintained as many as 17 kindergartens. Hebraism, which was elsewhere important, found no resonance here, especially since, on the one hand, most of the children came from Orthodox, → Hungarian-speaking families, while on the other, knowledge of → Hebrew among the teachers there was limited [10. 361–377].

3. Graduates in Palestine/Israel

Many graduates of educational institutions directed by *Tarbut* who immigrated to Palestine or Israel, especially women, took up positions in the educational system there; higher positions were more likely held by men. Shmuel Rosenheck, Chairman of the Faculty of Education of the University of Haifa, and his colleague in Tel Aviv, Eliyahu Rosenboim, one of the founding fathers of the university, had previously worked as prominent functionaries of the network. The Israeli historians Chaim Wirszubski (in → Vilna until 1934) and Menahem Stern (in Białystok until 1938), the poets Lea Goldberg (→ Sonnet) and Abba Kovner (→ Partisans), and the painter and photographer Moshe Vorobeichic (→ Photography) had also attended *Tarbut* schools.

Bibliography

[1] N. Bistritski, Ha-ḥinukh ha-ivri ba-golah [Jewish Education in the Diaspora], Jerusalem 1933. [2] M. Brayer, Ha-ḥinukh ha-ivri be-Bukowinah, be-Besarabyah uve-Transilvanyah [Jewish Education in Bukovina, Bessarabia and Transylvania], in: Z. Scharfstein (ed.), Ha-ḥinukh veha-tarbut ha-ivrit be-Eropa ben shte milḥamot ha-olam [Hebrew Education and Culture in Europe between the Two World Wars], New York 1957, 248–272. [3] M. Brayer, Toldot ha-ḥinukh ha-ivri be-Romanyah [History of Jewish Education in Romania], in: Z. Scharfstein (ed.), Ha-ḥinukh veha-tarbut ha-ivrit be-Eropa ben shte milḥamot ha-olam [Hebrew Education and Culture in Europe between the Two World Wars], New York 1957, 201–247. [4] M. Eisenstein, Jewish Schools in Poland. Their Philosophy and Development, 1919–1939, New York 1950. [5] S. Frost, Schooling as a Socio-Political Experience. Jewish Education in Interwar Poland, Jerusalem 1998. [6] B. Kahn, Ha-ḥinukh ha-ivri be-Lita ha-atsma'it [Hebrew Education in Independent Lithuania], in: Z. Scharfstein (ed.), Ha-ḥinukh veha-tarbut ha-ivrit be-Eropa ben shte milḥamot ha-olam [Hebrew Education and Culture in Europe between the Two World Wars], New York 1957, 135–170. [7] K. S. Każdan, Di geshikhte fun yidishn shulvezn in umophengikn Poyln [The History of the Jewish School System in Independent Poland], Mexico City 1947. [8] D. Levin, Toldot yehude Estonyah [History of the Jews of Estonia], in: Pinkas ha-kehillot. Encyclopaedia of Jewish Communities from Their Foundation till after the Holocaust. Latvia and Estonia, Jerusalem 1988, 299–318. [9] Š. Liekis, "A State within a State?" Jewish Autonomy in Lithuania 1918–1925, Vilnius 2003. [10] I. Peri [Friedman], Toldot ha-Yehudim be-Transilvanyah ba-me'ah ha-esrim [History of the Jews in Transylvania in the 20th century], Tel Aviv 1995.

MARCOS SILBER, HAIFA

Tavern

In the small towns and villages of premodern Eastern Europe, taverns provided not only places of hospitality, but were also popular meeting places for the discussion of commercial and public affairs, as well as for religious celebrations. They were predominantly operated by Jews who had leased the premises and alcohol licenses from Polish landowners. Both social reformers and government officials blamed Jewish innkeepers for the epidemic of drunkenness among the rural population, despite the role assigned to them in local economic and social life. Attempts to hinder Jews from selling alcohol by means of draconian fees, restrictions, bans, and evictions grew from the 19th century onward.

1. Jewish innkeepers in the Polish–Lithuanian Commonwealth
2. In the Partitions of Poland
3. Decline

1. Jewish innkeepers in the Polish–Lithuanian Commonwealth

Jewish taverns emerged in the 16th century as part of a non-agrarian leasing system (*arenda*; → Leaseholding). In addition to monopoly rights on collecting taxes, as well as tolls on both goods and roads, Polish landowners also leased their mills and inns to Jews, thereby securing a lucrative source of income for themselves. This model was so successful that by the mid-18th century, 40% of the Jewish population were employed in the tavern industry; this represented approximately 85% of all innkeepers in the Polish-Lithuanian Commonwealth. Furthermore, in the 18th century the export of grains declined, while the price of spirits rose proportionally. As a result, landowners decided to convert an increasing amount of their grains into spirits. In doing so, they also further enhanced the value of tavern leases, which was of great significance to a rural economy based on land ownership.

Landowners did not consider either farmers or members of the lower gentry to be suitable innkeepers, as they could not offer any knowledge of bookkeeping and financial investment. The lower gentry were also thought of as quarrelsome and politically ambitious. Jews, however, who were considered to be hardworking and prudent, appeared to possess the skills necessary to work as innkeepers. Furthermore, they were better able to understand the needs of the numerous traveling Jewish merchants (→ Peddlers) who frequently carried out their business in taverns. In the autobiography of the philosopher and writer Salomon Maimon (→ Lebensgeschichte), the sight of the Jewish merchant and innkeeper appears to be almost paradigmatic of the everyday rural constellation of the 18th century: "The Jews in this neighbourhood are continually moving about from place to place; and as there was a great traffic at our village, they were frequently passing through it, and of course they had always to stop at my grandfather's inn" [2. 10f.].

The business of the Jewish innkeeper extended far beyond the sale of spirits. They acted as brokers for credit (→ Money Lending), goods, and remedies, and also gave advice and mediated conflicts. Christians living in the area gained access to local markets through Jewish innkeepers. They also customarily organized their religious festivals, weddings, and family celebrations in the taverns.

Jewish prominence in the tavern industry however increased hostility between Christians and Jews. Many Polish Christians were deeply suspicious of Jewish innkeepers. It was insinuated that they only remained sober in order to get their guests drunk, ultimately intending to swindle them and inflate their drinking debts. Jews in turn

fostered their own cultural stereotypes of the *goy* (non-Jew) constantly getting themselves drunk. Ḥayim Naḥman Bialik (→ El ha-tsippor), himself the son of an innkeeper, described what effect the sight of incessantly intoxicated members of the majority society had on the perception of cultural superiority that the Jews of the region had in his Hebrew poem *Avi* (1933; "My Father," 2000): he contrasted the yelling and vomit pouring out of the "tongues of filth" of the "drunks" with the words of the Torah coming out of his father's mouth [1. 20].

Rabbinic authorities were conflicted about the Jewish tavern industry. Some feared that the depraved surroundings could taint the leasers. Even more problematic for them were the consequences of this profession on religious practice, as Jewish innkeepers opened their inns on → Shabbat and on holidays for the sake of profitability. While some rabbis wanted to issue strict edicts (*takkanot*) banning this practice, most of them reluctantly drafted agreements enabling the innkeepers to enter into hypothetical partnerships with non-Jews which enabled them to relinquish the taverns temporarily on holidays.

The writings of Polish social reformers were a far greater threat to the existence of Jewish innkeepers. From the mid-18th century onward, they blamed innkeepers for widespread drunkenness and the ruin of the farmers. In his work *O przyczynach szkodliwości Żydów* (On the reasons of Jewish noxiousness), published in 1816, the journalist and politician Stanisław Staszic (1755–1826) warned: "Allowing the Jews to distribute alcohol with its terrible consequences means entrusting the property of our peasants to non-believers who are hostile to Christians. They are given a weapon to deal with the peasant's property as they please, without punishment" [4. 300]. Journalists repeatedly demanded the expulsion of Jews from rural taverns in order to protect farmers, both during the final attempts at reform during the Four-Year Sejm (→ Sejm) in the Polish-Lithuanian Commonwealth (1788–1792) and later in Congress Poland, which was established in 1815 and ruled by Russia. Most landowners however retained the right to appoint innkeepers themselves; most of the recommended proscriptions were invalid as a result.

2. In the Partitions of Poland

After the partitioning of Poland (1772, 1792, and 1795), legislation on spirits was handled in different ways in the respective areas. What the policies of the partitioning powers had in common was that they directed the cameralistic order toward maximizing state revenues: ethnically dominated economic niches were to be dissolved and the population as a whole was to be economically "productivized." For Jews, this meant a trend toward the cancellation of lease contracts, the gagging of small businesses, and transferal to supposedly "useful" work in agriculture or → crafts. These specifications did in fact correspond with the demands of Polish social reformers, but the edicts and bans created unrest in the population. Not infrequently, state officials found themselves forced to reverse their restrictions during periods of increased political instability.

The first attempt to ban Jewish inns by law in partitioned Poland was undertaken in Galicia in 1784 as part of the reforms of Joseph II (→ Edicts of Toleration). Initially, a ban on the leasing of tavern rights to Jews was enacted; leasing to Jews in general was abolished in the following year. Both measures resulted in the exodus of roughly 15,000 Jewish families. In 1790, the new ruler Leopold II reacted to the protests of Polish landowners by almost completely abandoning implementation of the edicts. The politics of toleration that was predominant during the 19th century resulted in Jewish involvement in the selling of spirits flourishing again. This was fully utilized for propaganda

purposes by the proponents of a new political antisemitism, who made the liquidation of taverns operated by Jews a principal demand of their program.

The sale of spirits by Jews in rural areas was also officially banned in the parts of Poland taken over by Prussia. Here too, however, the edict of 1793 was only partially implemented by Prussian officials, who feared a rural exodus of Jewish innkeepers robbed of their livelihoods.

The most significant measures were enacted in those Polish regions which were incorporated into the Russian Empire, and which formed most of the so-called → Pale of Settlement. At first, Governor General Pyotr Bogdanovich Passek withdrew the right to distill alcohol from Jews in 1783, although in response Polish landowners forced the senate to reinstate it two years later. The situation of Jewish innkeepers was most significantly exacerbated as a result of the statutes issued by Czar Alexander I in 1804. Article 34 of these statutes stated that "No Jew (...) in any village or in the countryside, is allowed to hold a lease on a tavern, drinking house, or inn, either in his own name or in another's, nor to sell liquor, nor even to live where this is done, except when passing through" (cited in [11. 141]). The eviction of 60,000 Jewish families was planned in 1808, but this was only hesitantly implemented. Concerned that these measures would jeopardize Jewish loyalty in the face of a looming military conflict with Napoleon, the Czar suspended the evictions by decree. Subsequently, no fewer than 20,000 Jews were chased out of the provinces of Chernigov and Poltava in 1821, officially in order to protect the peasant population. There was also a campaign against the Sabbateans (→ Dönmeh), who were active as missionaries in both provinces; it is possible that the intention was to keep the region free from Jewish settlement. The evictions were stopped in 1835. In order to be able to administrate and regulate the activities of the increasingly numerous Jewish innkeepers in the provincial capital of Kam'yanets-Podilskyy, Czar Nicholas I decided to lease the levying of alcohol taxes to Jews.

In the Duchy of Warsaw, which was under Napoleonic rule between 1807 and 1814, an edict of 1812 which remained in effect until July 1814 prohibited Jews from selling alcohol. During this period, Jewish innkeepers had to acquire alcohol licenses. After the defeat of Napoleon and the establishment of the Kingdom of Poland ruled by the Russian Czar (Congress Poland, 1815), Polish journalists demanded the complete exclusion of Jews from the alcohol business. In fact, alcohol licenses proved to be extremely lucrative for the state, and Jewish advocacy proved effective. As a result, the legitimacy of the Napoleonic era edict was repeatedly deferred, while the price of alcohol licenses was gradually driven up. In this way, Jews were forced out of the spirits trade, although not without first providing the state with a respectable profit.

Rhetoric and national policy were primarily targeted toward the restriction of Jewish taverns located on remote country roads and villages. It was argued that people living in cities were less easy for Jewish innkeepers to manipulate than the rural population. City dwellers were assumed to have the education and business acumen to operate taverns themselves, thereby opposing the Jewish taverns with "ethical" alternatives. Jewish innkeepers in urban environments were indeed confronted with obstacles. Alcohol licenses were more expensive in cities than in the country, surveillance by the police was stricter, and the competition from other taverns was tougher. The biggest problem, however, was the tightening of establishment restrictions which was intended to eliminate Jewish innkeepers. This resulted in expulsions in over 50 cities, including Warsaw. Nevertheless, throughout the 19th century the legality of Jewish

taverns in urban areas was never fundamentally abolished.

As a result of their visibility in public life and controversial status, a typified form of the Jewish innkeeper found its way into 19th century Romantic Polish literature. Probably the best-known example is the character of Jankiel in Adam Mickiewicz's epic poem → *Pan Tadeusz* (1834). For Mickiewicz, the Jew and his inn are simultaneously a natural part of the landscape and a unifying force in the joyless daily life of partitioned Poland. The Jewish innkeeper and his daughter perform a similar function in Stanisław Wyspiański's drama *Wesele* (1901; The Wedding). In many works however, the Jewish innkeeper appears as a source of deep discomfort, portrayed as having a less quaint effect on their peasant customers and noble landowners.

3. Decline

A ban on the sale of spirits by Jews in rural areas was issued in 1844 in the regions of Poland under Russian rule in the course of a general campaign against drunkenness. The only consequence of this edict was an increase in Jewish black market activity involving alcohol. With the approval and support of local landowners who disapproved of state interference in their local economies, rural Jews gave their taverns a Christian look while continuing to provide the inns with alcohol, oversee its sale, and pursue other activities traditionally incumbent upon an innkeeper. In the cities, Jewish innkeepers could continue to operate their inns publicly provided they acquired the necessary licenses, which were later also required of Christian innkeepers.

In the late 19th century, Jewish innkeepers gained new competition as the result of an increasingly emancipated peasantry. Prior to the turn of the century, the authorities in the partitioned territories had abolished the traditional monopoly on alcohol that the Polish nobles had held, thereby destroying the traditional economic symbiosis between nobles and Jews. One consequence of this was the diversification of Jewish trade; this was promoted by developments such as urbanization, industrialization, and the opening up of branches of the economy and education to which access had previously been restricted. Many Jews, nevertheless, persisted in the production and sale of alcohol or the levying of alcohol taxes, thereby provoking the displeasure of the Christian population. "Sober Jews won a decisive victory over us intemperate people in a peaceful economic struggle," complained one Catholic priest on the eve of the First World War (cited in [5. 229f.]).

Jews initially continued to work in the spirits trade in Poland after the country was restored following the end of the First World War. When the Polish government nationalized the production and distribution of alcohol in the early 1920s, Jews were able to acquire a majority of the necessary licenses. In doing so they incurred the wrath of right-leaning Polish nationalists. The Narodowa Demokracja (National Democracy Party) in particular agitated against any Jewish involvement in the alcohol industry. In February 1939, the → Sejm's budget committee passed a resolution limiting the issuing of alcohol licenses to non-Jews. Jews who were operating under such licenses at the time were required to liquidate their taverns and alcohol stores within a year.

Bibliography

Sources

[1] H. N. Bialik, Songs from Bialik. Selected Poems of Hayim Nahman Bialik, ed. and trans. by A. Hadari, Syracuse 2000.   [2] S. Maimon, An Autobiography, trans. by J. C. Murray, ed. by A. Gardner, London et al. 1888.   [3] S. Staszic, O przyczynach szkodliwości Żydów i środkach usposobienia ich, aby się społeczeństwu użytecznymi stali [On the Reasons of Jewish Noxiousness and the Measures to Make Them Useful for Society], in: Pamiętnik Warszawski 4 (1816), 390–429.   [4] S. Staszic, Żydzi. Przestrogi dla Polski [Jews. A Warning for Poland], in: Pisma filozoficzne i społeczne [Philosophical and Social Writings], ed. by Bogdan Suchodolski, Warsaw 1954.

Secondary literature

[5] J. Burszta, Społeczeństwo i karczma. Propinacja karczma i sprawa alkoholizmu w społeczeństwie polskim XIX wieku [Society and Inn. Taverns and Alcoholism in Polish Society during the 19th Century], Warsaw 1951.   [6] G. Dynner, "A Jewish Drunk Is Hard to Find." Jewish Drinking Practices and the Sobriety Stereotype in Eastern Europe, in: Jewish Quarterly Review 104 (2014) 1, 9–23.   [7] G. Dynner, Yankel's Tavern. Jews, Liquor and Life in the Kingdom of Poland, New York 2013.   [8] D. Fajnhauz, Dwór i karczma żydowska na Litwie w połowie XIX w. [Jewish Mansions and Inns in Lithuania around the Mid-Nineteenth Century], in: S. Yeivin (ed.), Studies in Jewish History, Tel Aviv 1974, 62–76.   [9] J. Goldberg, Tavernkeeping, in: G. Hundert (ed.), The YIVO Encyclopedia of Jews in Eastern Europe, New Haven/London 2008, 1849–1852.   [10] G. Hundert, Jews in Poland-Lithuania in the Eighteenth Century. A Genealogy of Modernity, Berkeley/Los Angeles 2008.   [11] J. D. Klier, Russia Gathers Her Jews. The Origins of the "Jewish Question" in Russia, 1772–1825, DeKalb 1986.   [12] R. Mahler, Hasidism and the Jewish Enlightenment. Their Confrontation in Galicia and Poland in the First Half of the Nineteenth Century, Philadelphia et al. 1985.   [13] M. Opalski, The Jewish Tavern-Keeper and His Tavern in Nineteenth-Century Polish Literature, Jerusalem 1986.   [14] H. Rożenowa, Produkcja wódki i sprawa pijaństwa w Królestwie Polskim, 1815–1863 [Vodka Production and Intoxication in the Kingdom of Poland, 1815–186], Warsaw 1961.

GLENN DYNNER, NEW YORK

Technion

Technical educational institution founded in Haifa at the beginning of the 20th century on the initiative of the → Hilfsverein der deutschen Juden (Aid Association of German Jews). After conflicts regarding the status of → Hebrew as the language of instruction, courses began to be taught at the Technion in 1924. During the first decades of its existence, it was characterized by German teaching and research methods and by the German education system in general. By 1950 it had grown into a renowned technical university that, in accordance with its founding idea, contributed to the development of technology and infrastructure in the → Yishuv through scientific research and the training of engineers and architects.

1. Foundation
2. Technical college and Realschule (1907–1914)
3. The early years (1914–1930)
4. Establishment as a technical university (1931–1950)

1. Foundation

In 1902 Martin Buber (→ Dialogue), Berthold Feiwel (→ Jüdischer Verlag), and Chaim Weizmann (→ Chemistry; → Balfour Declaration) submitted a plan to the World Zionist Organization (→ Basel) to establish a Jewish university in Palestine. Their proposal included a technical department for the local training of engineers, teachers for various technical disciplines, as well as "expertly educated practitioners" and the pursuit of "the technological development of the country" [1. 17, 21]. They also planned to develop a "preparatory technical college" for future students that would train technicians, craftsmen, and agricultural, as well as industrial professionals [1. 21].

The training was subdivided into an academic and a vocational department and was based on the hierarchically structured professional training that had been widespread at technical schools and universities in Germany and other Central European countries since the 19th century. The professional and pedagogical approach of, above all, the Königliche Technische Hochschule Berlin-Charlottenburg (Royal Technical Academy of Berlin-Charlottenburg; TH), where Weizmann himself had studied, informed the concept of the institution, which was initially called the Technikum. Two professors of the TH, Georg Schlesinger and Wilhelm Franz, headed the scientific and technical advisory board, which first convened in 1909. They developed recommendations for the course offerings in view of what would be needed in Palestine [9. 128–130].

The → Hilfsverein der deutschen Juden assumed management of implementing the plans, with goal of providing material support to the Jews of Eastern Europe and the Middle East and to financially promote their emigration overseas (→ Bremerhaven). It also campaigned for the establishment of schools and vocational training institutions in order to enable impoverished Jews in the Balkans and in the Middle East to make a living via independent work. This was linked to the aim of spreading German culture and education (→ Bildung). The activities of Jewish organizations, such as the → Alliance israélite universelle and the Hilfsverein, were decidedly in line with the foreign policy aims of the European powers in which they were located to exert greater influence in the Ottoman Empire. Thus, the Hilfsverein's educational and philanthropic projects were linked to a political objective, especially with regard to German-French competition, namely the support of the endeavors to expand German influence in the Ottoman Empire, which had been intensified under the rule of Emperor Wilhelm II.

2. Technical college and Realschule (1907–1914)

After a journey through Palestine in 1907, Paul Nathan, the chairman of the Hilfsverein, suggested Haifa as the location for the planned technical college and the preparatory Realschule. Besides Jerusalem, Jaffa, with its satellite town of → Tel Aviv, and Haifa had become the most important places of Jewish immigration around 1900, growing into economic centers of the new Yishuv. The small coastal town of Haifa was considered a future center for the industrial and technological development of the country. Thanks to its sheltered bay, Haifa had grown in importance as an anchorage for ships of greater draft since the opening of the Suez Canal in 1869. When a branch line of the Hejaz Railway connecting Darʿā, a city between Damascus and Amman, with Haifa began service in 1905, the coastal town's development further accelerated. Long-term planned projects included a connection with the Baghdad railway via Aleppo as well as the construction of a deep-water harbor. Arthur Ruppin (→ Brit Shalom), who was overseeing the establishment of representation of the Zionist Organization in Palestine (→ Palestine Office), and Ahad Ha-Am (→ Encyclopedias; → Cultural Zionism), a representative of Zionist organizations for the founding of the Technikum, likewise approved of the selection of Haifa as the location for the new institution.

During his visit, Nathan found that there were already institutions of higher education for the arts, law, and the economic sciences in Istanbul and Beirut. Acquiring academic technical knowledge, however, was possible only outside the Ottoman Empire at that time. Based on his travel observations, Nathan drafted a detailed curriculum for the planned institution. Initially it included three to four years of technical training. Beginning with the first year of study, the students were to benefit from guided work in the laboratory, in workshops, and in the university's own garden. Suitable graduates could subsequently train to become engineers, while all other students would leave the institutions as qualified craftsmen or technicians. Nathan envisaged the language of instruction as Hebrew; new students were required to learn → German and → Arabic as well: German would enable them to keep abreast of the latest technological developments, while Arabic would ensure integration into their everyday environment.

Nathan estimated the cost of implementing the project, including the purchase of a plot in Haifa and constructing the buildings, at around half a million Reichsmarks. Ahad Ha-Am and the journalist Shmaryahu Levin supported the campaign for procuring funds. Thanks to their mediation, David Wissotzky, the son of the late tea entrepreneur Kalonymus Ze'ev Wissotzky, provided 100,000 rubles for the purchase of a suitable plot. Jakob H. Schiff (→ Railway), one of the most renowned Jewish → bankers in → New York, donated 100,000 US dollars for the project. Simultaneously, the society Jüdisches Institut für technische Erziehung in Palästina (Jewish Institute for Technical Education in Palestine) was constituted in Berlin, which would be responsible for further decisions regarding the development of the planned institution. Schiff appointed eight members of the board of trustees and Wissotzky five, among them Ahad Ha-Am, who was employed by the tea company. The Hilfsverein appointed five members, including Paul Nathan and James Simon (→ Patrons). Simon contributed 100,000 Reichsmarks to the project.

In 1908 the association acquired a plot of land for the Technikum and the affiliated Realschule on Mount Carmel [9. 79–93]. The board of trustees appointed the German-Jewish architect Alexander Baerwald – also a graduate of the Berlin TH – to plan the construction project. From 1909 onward, Baerwald familiarized himself with particulars of the site, as well as the local → architecture in Haifa [3]. In his draft design for the Technikum and the Realschule, he combined elements of Central European and Palestinian-Arab architecture. The result was an eclectic, so-called Zionist Erets-Israeli style that became the inspiration for many new buildings in Jewish settlements. The foundation stone was laid in 1912; the frames of the main building, the workshops, and the Realschule were completed the following year. In 1913 the complex of the Technikum was ready for use.

In the same year, the first curriculum was agreed upon, and it was based on that of the Berlin TH. The board of trustees initially agreed not to set an official language of instruction. Nevertheless, since Hebrew lacked terminology in engineering and natural sciences, it was determined that courses in these fields should be taught exclusively in German. This decision caused the so-called → language conflict. A compromise was arrived at in 1914, providing that mathematics and physics should be taught in → Hebrew from the start. The outbreak of the First World War, however, prevented its implementation [9. 200].

3. The early years (1914–1930)

As a consequence of the war, at the end of 1914 the association that sponsored the Technikum became insolvent. In the following year, the Hilfsverein purchased the property, selling it to the World Zionist Organization in 1920 [9. 211–226]. During the war years, the building complex was commandeered for military purposes.

After the end of the war, the World Zionist Organization focused on the inauguration of the → Hebrew University in Jerusalem and did not take any steps to develop the Technikum. It was not until 1921 that the Hebrew Realschule, a combination of Realschule and Gymnasium, founded during the languages conflict, moved into one of the buildings. Headed by Arthur Biram, it soon became one of the leading education institutions, opening branches in the Merkaz HaCarmel and Aḥuzat Shmu'el districts of the city. After the British army returned the main building in the same year, the engineer Max Hecker – who had been on the intended staff list of the Technikum since 1913 – was commissioned to complete the construction that was still required. Hecker also worked towards redefining the training objectives of the Technikum, favoring a purely technical university without the inclusion of a training college for technicians and skilled workers. Weizmann and the World Zionist Organization, however, supported a practical-technical training institution in accordance with the requirements of the Yishuv. Although Albert Einstein (→ Theory of Relativity) also championed the establishment of a technical college after a visit in 1923, the precise status of the Technikum remained undetermined for nearly a decade [4. 337–344].

Courses began at the institute in late 1924 under the leadership of the English board member Arthur Belock, initially as evening classes for workers and craftsmen teaching the subjects electrical engineering, metal engineering, postal systems, and telegraphy. In early 1925, lessons began in the department of structural engineering and road construction. At the official opening in the same year, the institute was given the name *Tekhniyon*, derived from the biblical Hebrew lexical root *tav–khaf–nun* ("to measure, calculate"), the sound of which resembled the Hebrew adjective *tekhni* ("technical," from Greek, and spelled with *tet* instead of *tav*). In 1945, the spelling of *Tekhniyon* with *tet* as the first letter was introduced; this has been the official name of the institution since that time.

As a consequence of budget cuts and the fact that the management of the institute changed every two years, the Technion was initially a vocational college for training technicians. Although it was able to recruit renowned teaching staff – in addition to Hecker and Baerwald, for instance, it also hired the physicist Aharon Tchernavsky – it faced closure in the summer of 1930 [7. 27–29]. Regular teaching and studying activities became established only when Biram took over the management of the Realschule as well as the Technion temporarily in 1931. During the 17th Zionist Congress, which took place in the same year in → Basel, those who sought to see the Technion upgraded to a university finally prevailed.

4. Establishment as a technical university (1931–1950)

At the end of 1931, Shlomo Kaplansky – a member of *Po'ale Tsiyon* of Austria, graduate of Vienna's Polytechnikum, and head of the settlement department of the World Zionist Organization from 1927 to 1929 – became head of the Technion. Under his leadership it developed into an institution of university-level teaching and research, playing a central part in the construction of infrastructure, especially (road) construction, industry, electrical engineering, chemistry, and physics in the → Yishuv. In addition to engineering courses, the Technion offered training and further education opportunities for technicians and technical assistants. It benefited from the increasing number of European Jews arriving in Palestine in the course of the Fifth → Aliyah between 1932 and 1939. The BASMAT (*Bet Sefer Miktso'i Tikhoni le-Handasa'im ve-Tekhna'im Musmakhim*) vocational college for engineers and technicians founded in 1933, as well as the nautical college *Bet ha-Sefer ha-Yami* (later the Naval Officers School of Acre), established in 1938, complemented the Technion. The Faculty of Technology was established in 1936. By 1947, 14 additional research and study laboratories were added, which were used for teaching and basic research, as well as serving the Yishuv economy.

On the eve of the foundation of the State of Israel, the Technion had a staff of 55 academic employees in the Institute for Engineering with its four departments – civil engineering, architecture, technology, and chemistry – the vocational college BASMAT, as well as the nautical college. In 1946, the first expansion of the Technion was planned, including the introduction of transportation and aeronautics as well as shipbuilding in new educational structures. By 1947, a total of 762 graduates, including thirty women, had completed courses at the Technion. Approximately 600 students enrolled that same year.

During the Arab-Israeli war from 1947 to 1949, the Technion was used as an arms cache; some employees produced ammunition, explosives, and weapons. At this time, the Technion already covered almost all technical requirements of the Yishuv in the fields of construction and industry. It established itself as an international research institute and renowned technical university, whose significance in Israel soon equaled that of the → Hebrew University and the → Weizmann Institute of Science.

Bibliography

Sources

[1] M. Buber et al., Eine jüdische Hochschule, Berlin ²1902.

Secondary literature

[2] C. Alpert, Technion. The Story of Israel's Institute of Technology, New York/Haifa 1982. [3] Y. Ben-Artzi, "Massa ha-limud" shel Aleksander Berwald [Alexander Baerwald's "Study Trip"], in: Zemanim. Riv'on le-historyah 96 (2006), 14–21. [4] Y. Dror, Reshit ha-Tekhniyon ha-ivri be-Ḥeifa 1902–1950. Meha-tokhnit le-vet sefer gavohah yehudi ve-ad tom tekufat nihulo shel Shlomoh Kaplanski [The

Beginnings of the Hebrew Technion in Haifa 1902–1950. From the Planning of the Jewish University until the End of Shlomo Kaplansky's Presidency], in: Iyunim bi-tkumat Yisra'el 6 (1996), 330–357. [5] Ha-maḥlakah le-kishre tsibbur shel ha-Tekhniyon [The Department of Public Relations of the Technion] (ed.), Toldot ha-Tekhniyon be-reshito 1908–1925 [History of the Technion's Formation 1908–1925], Haifa 1953. [6] Ha-Tekhniyon (ed.), Ha-Tekhniyon ha-ivri be-Ḥeifa bi-shnot tartsat ad tashaz (October 1939 – October 1946). Din ve-ḥeshbon la-kongres ha-Tsiyoni ha-esrim u-shnayim be-Bazel [The Hebrew Technion in Haifa from 1939 to 1946. A Report for the 22nd Zionist Congress in Basel], Haifa 1946. [7] U. Kirsh, Hebetim yihudiyim be-hitpathut ha-Tekhniyon. Met-suyanut akademit, trumah le'umit we-tarbut nihulit [Special Aspects of the Development of the Technion. Academic Excellence, National Contributions and Management Culture], Haifa 2013. [8] R. Lavi, Technology and Nation, Haifa 1999. [9] Z. W. Sadmon, Die Gründung des Technions in Haifa im Lichte deutscher Politik 1907–1920, Munich 1994.

YOSSI BEN-ARTZI, HAIFA

Tekhelet

Hebrew name for a blue color and a dye that was applied in the production of textiles for ritual use during the Temple period. Beyond the original significance of the color as a magical shield against evil, *tekhelet* symbolizes the connection of Jews with Erets Israel, as well as their religious autonomy. The Zionist movement (→ Basel), in its endeavor to create national symbols such as the flag for the State of Israel, separated the color from its sacred, magical context and charged it with secular meaning.

In the → Temple period, the textile fittings of the Tabernacle (*mishkan*) and the fabrics used for the garments of the High Priest were dyed in the blue *tekhelet* color. Today, as in Talmudic times and earlier, one or more cords in the tassels (*tsitsit*) of the prayer shawl (*tallit*) are once again dyed in this color. While the term occurs numerous times in the → Tanakh and in rabbinic sources, there are no equivalents in either Latin or Greek.

Production of the dye ceased in Late Antiquity. Its exact identification has remained controversial until relatively recently. Proceeding from the crustacean *ḥilazon* (lit. snail), which is mentioned in the Talmud, albeit without further specification, the Hasidic rabbi Gershon Chanoch Leiner located the source of the dye in the common cuttlefish (*sepia officinalis*) and in the 1880s began to dye his *tsitsit* with it. The practice was widely emulated. However, in his 1913 dissertation Isaak Herzog (Yitzhak Halevi Herzog), the first Chief Rabbi of Ireland and first Ashkenazi Chief Rabbi of Israel, concluded that *tekhelet* had to be a substance harvested from a particular species of sea snail (*Murex trunculus*, now *Hexaplex trunculus*). This theory was corroborated in the early 1980s due to research conducted by the chemist Otto Elsner at the Shenkar College in Ramat Gan and the marine biologist Ehud Spanier (b. 1945) at the University of Haifa.

Since ancient times, the color blue has held positive connotations throughout the Near Eastern and Middle Eastern regions. It is thought to be an auspicious color and to have apotropaic qualities. For this reason door or window frames are often painted in blue, and children wear blue fabric ribbons and amulets to protect against the evil eye (Hebr. *ayin ha-ra*). This popular belief in the magical efficacy of the color blue is reflected in the 13th century *Sefer ha-Zohar* (Book of Splendor), the central work of Jewish → mysticism. Its authors ascribe the *tekhelet*-dyed *tzitzit* with the power to ward off evil and to protect Torah-abiding Jews.

In addition to its wider magical applications, *tekhelet* has sacred semantic value in Judaism. The Bible frequently mentions *tekhelet* and *argaman* (purple) in the same context, but the two colors are used differently; while *argaman* refers to the aristocratic status of its wearers, *tekhelet* has a specific Jewish and religious connotation. In the Book of Numbers, God commands the Israelites through Moses to affix tassels with blue cords on the corners of their garments (Num 15:38); the blue cords are to remind the wearer of God's commandments. The sanctity of the color *tekhelet* was thus established, but when the knowledge about its production and exact ingredients were lost, the commandment itself was no longer viable.

Depending on the interpretation, *tekhelet* either symbolizes the color of the sea or the sky. This has frequently caused the term to be translated as "azure." It was thought that to behold the color was equal to beholding either God himself, or his heavenly throne [3. 198f.]. Furthermore, *tekhelet* is etymologically related to *takhlit*, which means "goal" or "purpose." The Hasidic rabbi Nachman of Breslov correlated the two concepts and explicitly linked the color and its spiritual dimension to the Jewish goal of a return to Jerusalem (→ Aliyah). *Tekhelet* was also exclusively associated with Erets Israel, enabling the → Karaite scholar Yefet ben Eli ha-Levi to declare in his *Sefer ha-Mitsvot* (Book of Commandments; 10th cent.) that the color was "unknown in the → Exile" [1. 68].

In the history of the Jewish people, wearing the blue cords on the *tallit* symbolizes the religious autonomy of Jews in Erets Israel. After the knowledge about the origin and exact shade of *tekhelet* was lost, only white cords continued to be worn up until the present day. Since this loss was accompanied by the dispersal of the Jews (→ Diaspora), the color white was increasingly associated with the condition of exile. In the 19th century, Orthodox authorities engaged in debates about *tekhelet*, its origins and its meanings, which then found their way into the Zionist

imagination. One of the first to describe white and blue as the colors of the Jewish people and the "precious land" [2. 127f.] was Ludwig August Ritter von Frankl-Hochwart (elevated to the nobility in 1876), a Jewish physician and writer from → Vienna, in his poem "Judas Farben" (1864).

The blue and white colors as an expression of the Jewish existence in a secular context are first attested for Palestine, where in 1885 the settlers raised a blue-and-white flag to commemorate the third anniversary of the foundation of Rishon Le-Zion (→ Ha-Tikvah). In 1891 the founders of Nahalat Reuven followed this example; their blue-and-white flag bore the inscription *nes Tsiyonah* (Sign of Zion), the later name of the settlement. The founding father of political Zionism, Theodor Herzl (→ Old New Land) in his Zionist manifesto *Der Judenstaat* (1896; "A Jewish State," 1904) envisioned a white banner with seven → Stars of David denoting "the seven golden hours of our working-day" [4. 39].

Herzl's concept of the seven stars met with no success. Finding favor instead was the flag originally developed by David Wolffsohn, one of the early Zionist activists, intended as a festive decoration for the First Zionist Congress in → Basel (1897). He then realized: "We have a flag: its colors are blue and white. The *tallis* we use to wrap around us during prayer is the Jewish symbol. This is the flag [...] we need to rediscover. It will be the standard of our pride in the face of all Israel and all nations" (cited in [5. 112]). The flag proposed by Wolffsohn closely predicted elements that were later adopted for the national flag of Israel after the independent state came into being (1948); its two blue stripes on the borders recall the *tsitsit* dyed with *tekhelet*.

The term *tekhelet* came to feature in the names of Zionist organizations and societies. Thus, for instance, a German-Czech youth group founded after the First World War called itself *Tekhelet-Lavan* (*tekhelet*-white).

In contrast to many other groups that used the name *Kaḥol-Lavan* (blue-white), it referred to the spiritual significance of the color from ancient Israel, despite its secular orientation.

With the Star of David now blue as well and placed in the middle of the flag, the transformation of yet another protective symbol into a secular national emblem was complete. Because the star had rarely held a religious connotation in ancient times it could, according to Gershom Scholem (→ Kabbalah), be filled more easily with symbolic content: "But it seems that the hexagram as a sign charged with magic exercised a greater attraction on the Shield of David until it finally defeated the Menorah on the battlefield of modern Jewish symbolism" [7. 270]. The → menorah also took on meaning as a national symbol; since 1948 it has been the official coat of arms of the State of Israel.

In the same way that the end of the Jewish presence in Palestine had coincided with the loss of knowledge about the production of the dye and the origin of its ingredients, the reintroduction of the dye corresponds to the return to Erets Israel. Today the shade of blue evokes associations with popular beliefs as well as religious Jewish traditions while simultaneously representing the sovereign statehood of modern Israel.

Bibliography

[1] D. Frank, Search Scripture Well. Karaite Exegetes and the Origins of the Jewish Bible Commentary in the Islamic East, Leiden et al. 2004. [2] A. Frankl, Ahnenbilder, Leipzig 1864. [3] K.-E. Grözinger, Ich bin der Herr, dein Gott! Eine rabbinische Homilie zum Ersten Gebot (PesR 20), Bern/Frankfurt am Main 1976. [4] T. Herzl, A Jewish State. An Attempt at a Modern Solution of the Jewish Question, trans. by S. D'Avigdor and J. De Haas, New York ³1917. [5] I. Meybohm, David Wolffsohn. Aufsteiger, Grenzgänger, Mediator. Eine biographische Annäherung an die Geschichte der frühen Zionistischen Organisation (1897–1914), Göttingen/Bristol (CT) 2013. [6] Z. Ruder, The National Colors of the People of Israel. Tradition, Religion, Philosophy, and Politics Intertwined, Jerusalem 1999. [7] G. Scholem, The Star of David. History of a Symbol, trans. by M. A. Meyer, in: The Messianic Idea in Judaism and Other Essays on Jewish Spirituality, New York 1971, 257–281. [8] B. Sterman/J. Taubes Sterman, The Rarest Blue. The Remarkable Story of an Ancient Color Lost to History and Rediscovered, Guilford 2012. [9] J. Trachtenberg, Jewish Magic and Superstition. A Study in Folk Religion, New York 1939.

RALF BALKE, BERLIN

Tel Aviv

Tel Aviv is considered to be the first Jewish city of the present era. Founded as a Jewish garden suburb of Jaffa in 1909 and named the following year after the Hebrew title of Theodor Herzl's utopian novel *Altneuland* ("Old New Land," 1941), the location soon developed into the urban center of the new Yishuv, and the secular antipode to the religiously-molded Jerusalem. In the 1930s, Jewish architects, who came to Palestine from Central Europe with the Fifth Aliyah, transformed the city into a laboratory of modernism: the so-called White City, a unique architectural ensemble of the international style and Bauhaus, emerged on a plot of land along the coast.

1. Founding history
2. The 1920s
3. The "White City" – international style and Bauhaus
4. "The Big Orange" – Israel's cultural metropolis

1. Founding history

In the second half of the 19th century, Christian, Muslim, and Jewish suburban settlements were founded outside the old city of Jerusalem and other cities in Palestine. During these decades, the old harbor and mercantile city of Jaffa, which had served as a point of arrival and transit for pilgrims to the Holy Land for centuries, and from the 1880s onward increasingly for Jewish immigrants as well, experienced a rapid demographic boom. Fewer than 3,000 people lived in the largely Muslim old city at the beginning of the 19th century; their number rose to roughly 10,000 at the start of the Zionist immigration. At the time of the founding of the settlement from which Tel Aviv would soon after emerge, Jaffa had some 47,000 inhabitants [3. 146–152].

Following an 1867 Ottoman edict permitting foreigners to purchase land, and especially from the 1870s when the demolition of the fortifications began, twenty suburban settlements – eleven of them Jewish – emerged outside Jaffa until after the turn of the century. The first Jewish residential settlement was Neve Zedek, northeast of the old city, founded in 1887 by immigrants of the First → Aliyah (1882–1903). This was followed by Neve Shalom (1890) and Mahane Yehuda (1896), as well as adjoining living complexes. Unlike the settlements of the Württemberg Templers, such as the German colonies in Haifa (1869), Sarona (1871), and Wilhelma (1902), with their wide streets and cultivated gardens at every house, it was scarcely possible to distinguish most of the Jewish residential districts externally from the densely populated city. The settlements were characterized by narrow alleys, enclosed courtyards bounded by high walls, and wretched sanitary conditions resulting from a lack of sewer systems and ventilation.

In the summer of 1906, Jewish immigrants to Jaffa founded the home building society *Ahuzat Bayit* (homestead) with the goal of constructing a modern residential district based on a European model. Among the initial 66 members, the majority of whom had come to Palestine from the Russian

Empire in the Second Aliyah (1904–1914), were wealthy business people, academics, and teachers. Under the leadership of Akiva Arie Weiss, members included the Hebrew writer Simhah Alter Gutmann, Me'ir Dizengoff, who would later become the first mayor of Tel Aviv, and the Zionist official Menahem Sheinkin. It was Sheinkin who recommended naming the settlement after the Hebrew title of Theodor Herzl's novel *Altneuland* (1902; → Old New Land) in honor of the author; the novel appeared in Hebrew translation under the title *Tel Aviv* (hill of spring) the year of its first publication.

As part of their project to construct a modern residential district at both a physical and cultural distance from the Arabian Jaffa, the members of *Ahuzat Bayit* also intended to create a Hebrew urban center that distinguished itself from the religiously-influenced Jewish settlements in Palestine. These considerations were drawn from the ideas of → cultural Zionism, which expounded a cultural renewal through the revival of the → Hebrew language, → literature, and culture, which would also include the creation of an intellectual center for a new Jewish society in Palestine. The most important project was the reconstruction of the Hebrew academic secondary school Herzliya, which had been founded in Jaffa in 1905. By contrast, the construction of a synagogue, which had been customary in previous Jewish residential districts in Palestine, was not planned. This decision underscored the secular character of this foundation.

The plot of land acquired by *Ahuzat Bayit*, which had been called Karm al-Jabali (vineyard of the al-Jabali family) by the previous owners, was to the northwest of Jaffa. To the south it bordered the railway track between Jaffa and Jerusalem, which had been opened in 1892. It was separated from the Mediterranean to the west by a sand dune strip roughly a kilometer wide which was under Arab ownership. Initially a purely residential district, without commercial amenities, was envisaged. The intention was to construct broad, paved streets planted with trees and illuminated by street lighting, detached houses with gardens, a public park, an educational institute, and modern plumbing and sewer systems. The model for the planning of the suburb was Ebenezer Howard's garden city concept [8. 114–126].

One of the most important personalities during the planning phase, and the man who made the founding of Tel Aviv possible, was Arthur Ruppin, the leader of the → Palestine Office founded in 1908. As a result of his influence, *Aḥuzat Bayit* was the first city construction project in Palestine supported by credit from the Jewish National Fund; its ground plan was authorized by a set of building regulations. The guidelines established in these regulations constitute the first building legislation following a European model in the new → Yishuv.

As the first modern Jewish city, Tel Aviv was afforded enormous significance upon its emergence. The act of foundation was the allocation of the first 66 parcels of land by lottery on April 11, 1909; it was recorded photographically by Avraham Soskin. The image, "The housing plot lottery in the sand dunes in front of Jaffa, 1909," established Tel Aviv's urban iconography. It significantly contributed to the myth of the "city built out of the sand," and the narrative of a creation *ex nihilo*; a group of people in the middle of the sand dunes, with neither the sea nor Jaffa, from where the founders came and which is distantly visible on a hill, appearing in the photograph. The first Hebrew city was from then on imagined as a *tabula rasa*, where Zionist ideology and ahistorical modernity united in a metaphor for the new beginning in the land of Israel. Artists such as Reuven Rubin and Naḥum Gutman promoted this perception with their depictions of small houses scattered in the sand [1. 33–123].

The development of the residential district did not follow a uniform construction plan, as was characteristic for European garden cities. The first houses reflected the individual preferences and resources of their residents, with, in some cases, clear reference to their countries of origin, which, for the most part, were in Eastern Europe. An eclecticism of traditional European architectural styles and Middle Eastern form elements predominated. Tiled gable and tented roofs competed with accessible flat roofs inspired by local examples. The first public green space in a Jewish residential area in Palestine developed in the middle of Rothschild Boulevard. The new building for the Hebrew secondary school Herzliya was constructed in an exposed location at the upper end of Herzl Street. Built between 1909 and 1911 according to plans by the architect Joseph Barsky, it was part of the search for a new Hebrew national style of → architecture.

As an urban manifestation of practical Zionism and a secular alternative to the religiously-influenced Jewish residential districts of the old Yishuv, Tel Aviv exerted a significant appeal on both new immigrants and long-established residents after it was founded. In the following years, newly established building societies such as *Naḥalat Binyamin* (Binyamin's Property, 1910) and *Ḥevrah Ḥadashah* (New Society, 1911–1914) acquired neighboring land and divided it into plots taking the existing street network and building regulations into consideration. On the eve of the First World War, a chaotic structure comprising 139 houses, in which 1,419 people lived, developed out of the small garden suburb.

2. The 1920s

After the end of the First World War, a modern civil administration was introduced in Palestine under the British mandate, which also led to far-reaching innovations in urban planning. Among the first measures taken by the mandate authorities was the publication in 1921 of the "Palestine Town Planning Ordinance," the country's first urban development ordinance in which general regulations for cities' structural development were codified. Since then, the issue and approval of land development plans for new phases of construction in Tel Aviv and their authorization by the British Town Planning Commission was obligatory.

In 1921, Tel Aviv was declared an autonomous urban community following anti-Jewish riots in Jaffa. As a result of this administrative detachment from the Arabian core city, the first independent Jewish city was born. Jewish economic and trading activity increasingly relocated to Tel Aviv. Jews who left Jaffa as a result of anti-Jewish attacks, as well as the new, urban-inclined immigrants of the Third Aliyah (1919–1923), who did not want to join the cooperative communities of the kibbutzim and moshavim without any agricultural training, were accommodated, at first, in temporary barracks and tents due to a lack of housing space.

Tel Aviv's development into a coastal city was made possible by the acquisition of oceanfront building land. In 1921, the newly founded Tel Aviv city administration commissioned the German-born architect and city planner Richard Kauffmann to plan a district in the northern, coastal expansion area. His design envisaged a broad seafront promenade which expanded into the dunes to create a large recreational space. Duplexes with gardens, as well as squares, markets, and cultural centers, would be built along an orthogonal street network. However, as a result of rapid demographic development, the greatest possible exploitation of the construction space was given priority over considerations of urban planning, which prevented a systematic layout of the beach district. The dunes were transferred to private ownership and became a lucrative object of speculation; the land envisaged

Allenby Square (today: Kikar Magen David) in Tel Aviv (picture from 1940)

as parkland was built on and only a narrow beach survived.

As a result of unification with neighboring Jewish city districts in 1922, and the flow of immigrants during the Fourth Aliyah (1924–1931), by 1925 the population of Tel Aviv had grown to roughly 34,200 people living in some 2,600 houses as well as 1,500 temporary barracks and tents. Unlike earlier groups of immigrants, most of whom had Socialist-Zionist inclinations, this so-called middle class aliyah brought business people and small traders in particular, predominantly from Poland, to Tel Aviv, where they discovered promising opportunities for economic activity in the growing urban infrastructure.

In view of the previously chaotic growth of the young city, in 1925 the Scottish sociologist and town planner Patrick Geddes was commissioned to draft an urban development plan by the Tel Aviv city administration. This encompassed an area reaching to the river *al-Auja* (known today as the Yarkon) to the north and to the road linking Jaffa with the Arabian town Salama (today called Ibn Gabirol Street) to the east. Geddes had previously worked as an advisor on other urban development projects for the Zionist executive. His "Town-Planning Report – Jaffa and Tel Aviv," submitted at the end of 1925, envisaged the development of Tel Aviv into a port city with 100,000 inhabitants [9].

Like Kauffmann, Geddes was guided by the garden city concept. He envisioned a hierarchical street system for Tel Aviv's area of expansion, with main streets running from north to south and residential streets running from west to east. The blocks that emerged from this grid system would include smaller housing units and semipublic amenities, including kindergartens and laundries, as well as fields and gardens for communal use which were accessible via short inner streets closed to traffic. Duplexes with at most two levels were planned, which

were to have small windows and accessible flat roofs in keeping with regional models. There were to be parks, green spaces, and playgrounds throughout the whole city district. Cultural centers and educational institutions were envisaged at topographically prominent locations. A yacht and commercial port was planned in the north of the city.

The Geddes plan was adopted by the Tel Aviv city administration in 1926, and certified by the city planning commission after several modifications. It formed the foundation of the later development of the city. In particular the spreading of the city along the coast to the north, the hierarchical street grid, and the position of the most important public spaces all remain references to this first development plan to this day. A development along garden city lines, as proposed by both Kauffmann and Geddes, was however not realized when faced with the political and cultural upheavals of the 1930s.

3. The "White City" – international style and Bauhaus

During the Fifth Aliyah (1932–1938/1939) some 250,000 Jews from Central Europe, of whom roughly a quarter were from Germany, reached Palestine. During this time, the population of Tel Aviv quadrupled, and the city experienced a previously unknown construction boom. As a result of the influx of capital, new construction projects were realized which corresponded to the visions of the immigrants, who predominantly came from a metropolitan middle-class milieu.

Among the emigrants were numerous architects who had completed their training at German and international schools of art and architecture such as the Bauhaus, and who counted famous avant-garde architects such as Le Corbusier, Walter Gropius, Ludwig Mies van der Rohe, or Erich Mendelsohn (→ Einstein Tower) among their teachers. They adapted the formal vocabulary of architectural modernity to suit the climatic conditions of Palestine. At the pinnacle of this development was an association of architects called *Ḥug* (ring), founded in 1934, among the initiators of which was the Bauhaus graduate Arieh Sharon. Their official organ was *Ha-binyan be-mizraḥ ha-karov* (Construction in the Middle East, 1934–1938), the first Hebrew-language architectural periodical in Palestine. In the 1930s, these architects created a globally unique architectural ensemble of the international style and Bauhaus on the plot of land covered by the Geddes plan. These white plastered cube structures shaped the image of Tel Aviv as the "White City."

The unexpectedly large population growth required modifying the housing construction envisaged in the Geddes plan. Instead of two-story duplexes, four-story housing blocks modeled on Viennese residential complexes developed with internal garden courtyards. In these cooperative apartment blocks for workers (*me'onot ovdim*), the first of which was constructed in 1935 according to plans by Arieh Sharon, leftist Zionist ideas of collective living were combined with avant-gardist architectural concepts in order to solve the housing shortage.

Geddes had envisaged a plaza, planned as a hexagon with uniform peripheral structures, as the centerpiece of the new city. In 1934, the architect Genia Averbouch won the competition to develop Zina Dizengoff Square, named after the wife of the first mayor of Tel Aviv. The cultural center which Geddes had recommended was realized through the construction of the → Habima Theatre (1935) according to designs by Oskar Kaufmann. When Jaffa's harbor was strikebound in the course of the Arab revolt between 1936 and 1939, the harbor of Tel Aviv emerged at the mouth of the Yarkon alongside the grounds of the Levant Fair. Opened in 1938, it developed into a symbol of the independence of the new Yishuv and turned Tel Aviv into a harbor city.

Tel Aviv is frequently referred to as a "Bauhaus city," even though its architectural appearance was shaped in the years before the Second World War by a range of modernist currents summarized by the general term "international style." Typical characteristics of the international style as it is expressed in Tel Aviv, which can be traced back, for example, to Le Corbusier's "five points of a new architecture," include accessible flat roofs and the mounting of the main structure on pilotis (supporting pillars), which create shade, ventilation, and green areas within the courtyards underneath the building. The first building on pilotis was the Engel House on Rothschild Boulevard, built in 1934 according to plans by Zeev Rechter. Ribbon windows, which are typified by large glazed openings in European modernism, find their equivalent in Tel Aviv by means of horizontally accentuated balconies, which are sometimes rounded and lead around corners. As a result of the intensive sunlight, windows are usually scaled down and furnished with projecting sunshades. Alongside the cuboid character of the buildings, there are numerous elements of maritime architecture. Circular oriels, accentuated stairwells, and dynamic corner solutions evoke Erich Mendelssohn's European structures [6].

In the decades after the founding of the state, the modernism of Tel Aviv's architecture was forgotten and the city's historical buildings were falling into disrepair. A return to this architectural heritage only began in the 1980s. Since then, building historians and architects have made efforts to renovate this globally unique ensemble. In 2003, the "White City" with its roughly four thousand structures in the international style was declared a UNESCO World Heritage Site.

4. "The Big Orange" – Israel's cultural metropolis

The significance of Tel Aviv as a laboratory of national independence reached its climax with the proclamation of the State of Israel in 1948 in the historical house of Me'ir Dizengoff on Rothschild Boulevard (today known as "Independence Hall"). Tel Aviv initially functioned as the seat of government until Jerusalem was declared the capital of Israel in 1950. In the same year, Tel Aviv and Jaffa were combined into a single municipal entity. Since then the city bears the name Tel Aviv-Yafo. Jaffa, which with 4,000 years of history is one of the oldest cities in the world, became a historical annex to the first Jewish city, the symbol of Zionist modernity. The flight and expulsion of Jaffa's Arab population during the Palestine war from 1947 to 1949 and its later revitalization continue to play a central role in debates about the self-perception of the Jewish-Arabian double city and its architecture today [4].

The growing commercialization and Americanization of Israeli culture and society since the 1960s, which is architecturally reflected in Tel Aviv, for example, by the construction of numerous hotels along the coast as well as skyscrapers and shopping malls based on the American model, and also by the demolition of historical structures such as the Hebrew secondary school Herzliya in the course of urban renewal, promoted a new self-image for Tel Aviv as a Western metropolis. In the late 1980s, following New York's nickname "The Big Apple," the designation "The Big Orange" – also an allusion to the leading regional export, the Jaffa orange – gained currency for Tel Aviv. The urban culture of Tel Aviv during the early 21st century, its so-called Tel Avivness, is a synonym for a hedonistic style of life with a European-Mediterranean-Oriental atmosphere, with cafes, lascivious beach culture, and nightlife, summarized in the *bon mot*: "Jerusalem prays, Tel Aviv plays, and Haifa works."

Today with 405,000 inhabitants the cultural metropolis of Tel Aviv-Yafo is Israel's second largest city, which since its inclusion on the list of World Heritage Sites presents itself as the "White City" of modernity on the Mediterranean coast, irrespective of its heterogeneous urban fabric and multiform architectural heritage.

Bibliography

[1] M. Azaryahu, Tel Aviv. Mythography of a City, Syracuse 2007. [2] M. Azaryahu/S. I. Troen (eds.), Tel-Aviv. The First Century. Visions, Designs, Actualities, Bloomington 2012. [3] R. Kark, Jaffa. A City in Evolution, 1799–1917, Jerusalem 1990. [4] M. LeVine, Overthrowing Geography. Jaffa, Tel Aviv, and the Struggle for Palestine, 1880–1948, Berkeley/Los Angeles 2005. [5] B. E. Mann, A Place in History. Modernism, Tel Aviv, and the Creation of Jewish Urban Space, Stanford 2006. [6] N. Metzger-Szmuk, Des maisons sur le sable. Tel-Aviv, mouvement moderne et esprit Bauhaus/Dwelling on the Dunes. Tel Aviv, Modern Movement and Bauhaus Ideals, Tel Aviv 2004. [7] J. Schlör, Tel Aviv. From Dream to City, trans. by H. Atkins, London, 1999. [8] I. Sonder, Gartenstädte für Erez Israel. Zionistische Stadtplanungsvisionen von Theodor Herzl bis Richard Kauffmann, Hildesheim et al. 2005. [9] V. Welter, The 1925 Master Plan for Tel-Aviv by Patrick Geddes, in: Israel Studies 14 (2009) 3, 94–119.

INES SONDER, POTSDAM

Tell Halaf

An ancient settlement hill near the northern Syrian town of Ras al-Ayn, discovered in 1899 by Max Freiherr von Oppenheim (1860–1946). His privately-financed excavations at Tell Halaf are among the highlights of German Near Eastern → archaeology. Oppenheim, who came from a converted Jewish banking family (→ Bankers), repeatedly tried to act in the interests of Germany, including through plans for inciting Muslims against the enemies of the German Reich in the First as well as in the Second World War. In Oppenheim's biography, resentments against Jewish members of high finance overlapped with an almost unbridled striving for assimilation, unconditional devotion to a conservative worldview, and a thirst for adventure.

1. Tell Halaf
2. Oppenheim as an orientalist, diplomat and patron
3. The Jihadization of Islam
4. From the First to the Second World War

1. Tell Halaf

In 1899, Max von Oppenheim undertook a seven-month long reconnaissance expedition through northern Syria and Upper Mesopotamia. On commission from Deutsche Bank, he was to ascertain the most appropriate route for the planned Baghdad railway. The project was to contribute to the economic development and political consolidation of the Ottoman Empire. Through the construction of the line, finally (from 1903) financed by an international banking consortium and carried out under the direction of German companies, German foreign policy hoped to increase Germany's influence in the region. In the course of the expedition, Oppenheim discovered the settlement mound of Tell Halaf. Within three days, he began, with the help of natives, to dig exploratory trenches, by means of which he came across the entrance hall to a palace complex. The excavation of several monumental basalt sculptures convinced him that he had made an extraordinary find, although he could not initially attribute it to any culture. At first, Oppenheim devoted

only a brief mention of his discovery in his report of the expedition.

Since the mid-19th century the ancient Orient awakened the interest of → archaeology, and powers like England, France, and Germany strove to outdo one another in the discovery of ancient Near Eastern monuments and the acquisition of finds from excavations. German archaeologists were among the pioneers of the excavations in Babylon (from 1899) and Assur (from 1903). Not until a few years later did Oppenheim return to Tell Halaf, and in 1908 he published a brief monographic essay on his find, which did not go unnoticed in professional circles. In the following year, he applied for an excavation license for the settlement hill. With the help of a scientific report by twenty prominent orientalists, he persuaded his father, the Cologne → banker Albert von Oppenheim (1834–1912), to financially support the undertaking.

The excavations at Tell Halaf from 1911 to 1913 and from 1927 and 1929 led to the uncovering of ancient Guzāna (also Gozan/Gosan), capital of the Aramaic princedom Bit Bahiani from the early 1st millennium BCE. This was a sensational find, especially because material remains of the Arameans, as opposed to their language and script (→ Aramaic), were scarcely known before then. Oppenheim earmarked most of the finds for exhibition in the halls of the Königliche Museen zu Berlin. The overall costs for the first excavation alone amounted to 750,000 Reichsmarks, two thirds of which was provided by Oppenheim's father, and one third by Oppenheim himself [10. 65]. The excavation was thus the most expensive private archaeological undertaking to ever take place in the Near East.

2. Oppenheim as an orientalist, diplomat and patron

Max von Oppenheim was born in Cologne in 1860 as a scion of the Oppenheim banking

Max von Oppenheim (1860–1946) beside a statue excavated at Tell Halaf (1930)

family (→ Bankers). Since Salomon Oppenheim (1772–1828) moved the bank he had founded, Bankhaus Sal. Oppenheim Jr. & Cie., from Bonn to Cologne in 1798, and was the first Jew named to the Chamber of Commerce of Cologne, the family, one of the most affluent in the German states, found itself obliged to acculturate to the elite of Cologne. Contributions to this goal included their involvement in general → philanthropy, their emergence as → patrons, and a pragmatic policy of → marriage. Max's grandfather Simon (1803–1880) raised his children for a life in a majority Christian society; his father had himself baptized into the Catholic faith (→ Conversion) shortly before his marriage to Paula Engels (1837–1919), a merchant's daughter from the upper classes of Cologne. In 1867, Simon Oppenheim was elevated to the Austrian rank of baron (confirmed by Prussia in the following year).

Max Oppenheim opposed his father's wishes that he become involved in the family banking business. As a compromise, he began studying law at Strasbourg in 1879, graduating with a doctorate in Göttingen in 1883. During his legal clerkship in the winter of 1883/1884, he accompanied his uncle Eduard von Oppenheim (1831–1909) to Constantinople by way of Athens and Smyrna. This first trip to the East was followed by many other trips through North Africa and the Near East, including a large-scale expedition from the Mediterranean to the Persian Gulf, and thence to German East Africa; Oppenheim's two-volume report *Vom Mittelmeer zum Persischen Golf durch den Hauran, die syrische Wüste und Mesopotamien* (1899/1900) is now considered one of the classics of Oriental travelogues.

Oppenheim's ambition was a diplomatic career, and he repeatedly applied to the Foreign Ministry, but was rejected because of his Jewish origin. Upon his first application in 1887, Herbert von Bismarck, son of the Reichskanzler and State Secretary for Foreign Affairs, called him a "Jewboy" in a private letter. Against admitting him to the diplomatic service, he remarked that "Jews, even if they have talent, always become tactless and pushy as soon as they reach a privileged position" (cited in [7. 111]). Oppenheim's second application, submitted in 1891, was rejected by the diplomat Friedrich August von Holstein, on the grounds that his qualities as a "a full-blooded Semite [...] and member of a family of bankers" disqualified him from the diplomatic service (cited in [7. 112]).

Oppenheim finally obtained the status of a member of the Foreign Service, but not that of a career diplomat: in 1896, he was provisionally assigned as an attaché to the German Consulate General in Cairo. In Cairo, Oppenheim learned fluent → Arabic, and developed a deep knowledge of the Orient. He saw himself as connected to the intellectual world and lebenswelt (world of lived experience) of the people of the Orient, maintained contacts with Sufi brotherhoods (→ Sufis), and attended Muslim prayer and discussion events. He was particularly interested in the Bedouins, whose notions of values, property, and law appeared to him as an alternative to Western modernity. At the same time, he remained linked to the European world, and especially to the German Empire. He provided the Foreign Ministry with reports on political developments in Egypt, which had been under British rule since 1882, and supported the project, led by German interests, of the Baghdad railway, which led him to Tell Halaf in 1899. The discovery of the Aramaic buildings and images lent him the aura of an important amateur archaeologist.

In the British and French diplomatic milieus of Cairo, Oppenheim's unclarified official position at the German Consulate General and his opulent lifestyle gave rise to rumors that he was a German secret agent. In German diplomatic circles, he was considered a servile busybody possibly working for foreign powers. In 1909, these speculations led to Oppenheim's leave of absence and in November 1910 to his ultimate discharge from the diplomatic service.

With the excavation at Tell Halaf, which began the following year, Oppenheim hoped to achieve wide recognition, especially since he acted as a benefactor. With his decision to leave the sculptures brought to light at Tell Halaf to the Königliche Museen zu Berlin, he, like James Simon (→ Kaiserjuden; → Patrons), supported the prestige-oriented museum policies of Wilhem II. During the excavation campaigns of 1911–1913, Oppenheim continued to carry out negotiations with the Sublime Porte over the transfer of important finds to Germany. In this process, the fact that his excavation was not official, but had been carried out on private initiative and at his own expense, turned out to be an obstacle. In exchange for financial compensation, he was finally granted permission to export 43 crates of clay tablets, minor finds, and smaller sculptures; another 31 crates of finds, which Oppenheim had declared as household goods, was seized on the high seas by a British warship in 1914, and later given to the British Museum in London.

Whereas Oppenheim had held out the prospect of donating the finds to the Berlin museums, the high excavation costs forced him to charge a fee; but the museums announced they would not be able to pay it. At the same time, he tried to convince Wilhelm von Bode, General Director of the Königliche Museen zu Berlin, to officially take over the excavations. According to the stipulations of a German-Ottoman agreement, this would have meant a division of all finds made under the direction of the Königliche Museum between both contracting parties. The First World War prevented this plan.

3. The Jihadization of Islam

During his time in Cairo, Oppenheim had already become interested in the pan-Islamic movement, which aimed at the preservation of the Ottoman Empire. He presented his reflections on a jihad of Muslims, which was to be ignited for the benefit of both the German and the Ottoman Empires against the powers of the Entente, in a memorandum to the Kaiser in 1898, and in another memorandum to Reichskanzler Bernhard von Bülow in 1908. At the end of October 1914, just before the definitive entry of the Ottoman Empire into the First World War on the side of the Central Powers, Oppenheim presented his memorandum *Die Revolutionierung der islamischen Gebiete unserer Feinde* to the Foreign Ministry. The essential consideration of this and of the earlier memoranda was the intention of inciting Muslims from Morocco to India to fight against England, France, and Russia. The highest Islamic authority of the Ottoman Empire was to call for a "Holy War" of the Muslims, and the requisite propaganda was to be organized by German experts and supported by German financial means.

Oppenheim's plans met with the approval of the Foreign Ministry and of Emperor Wilhelm II. In fact, the hoped-for jihad fatwa was issued in November 1914 by order of the Ottoman Sultan-Caliph in Constantinople. At the same time, the Nachrichtenstelle für den Orient (Intelligence Bureau for the East; NfO) was established under Oppenheim's supervision. Its many collaborators, both German and from the Orient, in loose association with the Foreign Ministry, worked together with the foreign missions of the Empire and German military offices, among other agencies. Oppenheim himself contributed private funds by the millions. Arabic and Turkish native speakers, as well as German orientalists and translators, diplomats, and publicists with knowledge of the relevant languages produced, in twenty languages, leaflets and brochures, journals and newspapers, books, or films. The addressees were the Muslim population under colonial rule and Muslim prisoners of war from the armies of the Entente. Oppenheim was sent to Constantinople in 1915, where he was to coordinate propaganda: among other activities, he set up information halls in the Ottoman Empire in which propaganda was posted in words and, with a view to those who were illiterate in the respective languages, in images.

Despite huge expenses on the German side, uprisings against the Entente in Muslim lands failed to materialize. In contrast, the British, with Thomas E. Lawrence (Lawrence of Arabia), were able to induce Arabs to rise up against Ottoman rule. Oppenheim's direction of jihad propaganda in the World War strengthened British policies in their view that the Turkish government was controlled by a secret group of Jews friendly to Germany.

4. From the First to the Second World War

After the First World War, Oppenheim devoted himself once again to Tell Halaf and the management of the excavation finds. In 1922 he established a privately financed Orient-Forschungsinstitut (Oriental Research Institute) in Berlin, with a large specialized library. However, the hyperinflation of 1923 created substantial financial problems for the adminstration of his archaeological collection, and he lost the bulk of his wealth. Negotiations with the Berlin museums were also unsuccessful. In 1929, he set up a foundation to ensure his legacy, and, with the help of private loans, had a factory building in Berlin-Charlottenburg converted into a museum, in which he exhibited his finds. To be sure, the opening in July 1930 attracted a great deal of attention among both public and press, yet the underlying financial problems remained, and several ancient sculptures had to be pawned.

Even in National Socialist Germany, Oppenheim remained true to his unconditionally patriotic and politically compliant views. It remains an open question whether this was his conviction or due to constant pressure to adapt. Although the Nazis classified him as a "half-Jew," he largely continued to be spared harassment. In 1933, Hitler's Vizekanzler Franz von Papen granted him a monthly stipend to conclude publication of the excavation report of his Tell Halaf project, which was initially suspended after the enactment of the Nürnberger Rassegesetze (Nuremberg Laws) of 1935, but was paid out again in 1941. In May 1935, Eduard von der Heydt, a staunch Nazi and owner of Bankhaus von der Heydt, tried to take advantage of the situation and, as one of the many creditors, laid claim for himself to Oppenheim's share of the Tell Halaf collection, yet he failed in his attempt.

During the Second World War, Oppenheim, now in his eighties, once again sought contact with the Foreign Ministry. After the surrender of France in 1940 and the installation of the → Vichy regime, which also administered Syria and seemed to offer new perspectives for German interest in the Orient, he wrote letters of recommendation to Syrian dignitaries for Werner Otto von Hentig, head of the Orientreferat (Orient section). He sent Theodor Habicht, the Nazi official and Head of the Information, Press, and Radio Section of the Foreign Ministry, a brief memorandum on uprisings taking place especially in Arabia. With reference to the memorandum of 1914, it also contained operational suggestions for putting an end to British rule in the Near East [8. 55], including the assassination of the pro-British Iraqi Prime Minister Nuri al-Said and the expulsion from Palestine of the Jews who had emigrated there after the First World War.

The Tell-Halaf-Museum in Charlottenburg was largely destroyed in November 1943 in an Allied bomb attack. The remnants of those Aramaic statues that could be saved were able to be reconstructed from 2001 to 2010 in one of the most expensive restoration projects of the Staatliche Museen zu Berlin. As Oppenheim had originally planned, they found their permanent home in the Pergamon Museum on the Museum Island Berlin. Oppenheim spent the last year of his life with relatives in Landshut, where he died in 1946.

Bibliography

[1] N. Cholidis/L. Martin (eds.), Tell Halaf. Im Krieg zerstörte Denkmäler und ihre Restaurierung, Berlin 2010. [2] N. Crüsemann, Max von Oppenheim und die Berliner Museen. Ein schwieriges Verhältnis, in: N. Cholidis/L. Martin (eds.), Die geretteten Götter aus dem Palast vom Tell Halaf. Regensburg/Berlin 2011, 231–236 [exhibition catalogue]. [3] T. Epkenhams, "Geld darf keine Rolle spielen," Part 1, in: Archi-vum Ottomanicum 18 (2000), 247–250. [4] T. Epkenhams, "Geld darf keine Rolle spielen," Part 2, Max Freiherr von Oppenheim's Memorandum "Die Revolutionierung der islamischen Gebiete unserer Feinde" (October 1914) from the Politics Archive of the Foreign Ministry in Bonn, in: Archivum Ottomanicum 19 (2001), 120–163. [5] L. Gossman, The Passion of Max von Oppenheim. Archaeology and Intrigue in the Middle East from Wilhelm II to Hitler, Cambridge 2013. [6] S. M. Kreutzer, Dschihad für den deutschen Kaiser. Max von Oppenheim und die Neuordnung des Orients (1914–1918), Graz 2012. [7] M. Kröger, Mit Eifer ein Fremder. Im Auswärtigen Dienst, in: G. Teichmann/G. Völger (eds.), Faszination Orient. Max von Oppenheim. Forscher – Sammler – Diplomat, Cologne 2001, 106–139. [8] W. G. Schwanitz, Max von Oppenheim und der Heilige Krieg. Zwei Denkschriften zur Revolutionierung islamischer Gebiete 1914 und 1940, in: Sozialgeschichte 19 (2004), 28–59. [9] W. G. Schwanitz, The Bellicose Birth of Euro-Islam in Berlin, in: A. Al-Hamarneh/ J. Thielmann (eds.), Islam and Muslims in Germany, Leiden et al. 2008, 183–212. [10] G. Teichmann, Grenzgänger zwischen Orient und Okzident. Max von Oppenheim 1860–1946, in: G. Teichmann/G. Völger (eds.), Faszination Orient. Max von Oppenheim. Forscher – Sammler – Diplomat, Cologne 2001, 10–105.

ALESSANDRA GILIBERT, BERLIN

Temple

As Judaism's central holy site, the Temple in Jerusalem was an intrinsic element of the political and religious life of the ancient Israelites. After the destruction of the Second Temple in 70 CE, Jews expressed their hopes of its reconstruction during the promised messianic era in their writings and → liturgies. In Europe and the United States, the term "temple" developed into a cipher used by proponents of → reform from the 19th century onward. The "temple" of more liberal communities constituted a modern alternative to the traditional → synagogue. This, combined with a turning away from the messianic concept of a return to → Zion, entailed the reinterpretation both of Jewish traditions as well as of the relationship with non-Jewish society.

1.   Antiquity
2.   Reform temples in Germany
2.1 Seesen and Berlin
2.2 Hamburg and Vienna
3.   Europe and the United States
4.   Messianic aspirations

1. Antiquity

Use of the term "Temple" for the central holy site in Jerusalem can be traced back to the Vulgate (4th cent. CE), where the Latin *templum* (beam, board, also extended to mean a finished house) is used to translate the Hebrew word *hekhal* (palace, temple), itself borrowed from Akkadian. Initially, *hekhal* was the name of the local holy site in Shiloh (1 Sam 1:9; 3:3). The term was only rarely used for the First Temple in Jerusalem (→ Zion), which according to tradition was built around 960 BCE under King Solomon, instead denoting the Temple's sanctuary (main interior space), which was separated from the Holy of Holies and the porch. After the destruction of this Temple in 586 BCE (→ Tish'ah be-Av) and the Babylonian → exile, *hekhal* prevailed as the standard term for the new Temple building constructed in the 6th century BCE. The designations *bayit* (house), *bet YHWH* [*Adonai*] (house of Yahweh) or *bet elohim* (house of God) were also common, although these were used for other sacred buildings as well and not just the holy site in Jerusalem. The → synagogue (Gr. *synagogé*; assembly) as a place where Jews gathered or prayed together probably emerged during this time. To differentiate it from the Temple, this was designated as *bet knesset* (house of assembly), *bet tefillah* (house of prayer), or *bet am* (house of the people).

Also recorded in the Bible is the Hebrew term *mikdash* (sanctuary; → Kadosh) for a sacred place (e.g. Exod 15:17; 25:8), emphasizing that the holiness of a place resulted from its identification as God's place of residence. The recurrent designation of the Second Temple in Jerusalem as a *mikdash* emphasizes its significance. The phrase *bet ha-mikdash* (house of the sanctuary) only predominated in post-Biblical times [4. 47f.]. At the time, the central sanctuary was considered the place of entcounter between man and God; it was also the place where priests, by means of sacrificial rites, sought atonement for the whole of Israel. Even during the time of the First Temple, the priesthood in Jerusalem attempted to establish it as the only legitimate center for the worship of God. Pilgrimages (→ Aliyah) to the Temple were considered a duty (→ *mitsvot*), the observance of which expressed → piety and loyalty to the one God.

As a result of its symbolic importance, the Second Temple achieved a significant position in the religious conception of the Jewish communities in Palestine, the Near East, and the Mediterranean. Rival institutions also existed, such as the Samaritan Temple on Mount Gerizim from the 4th century until 129 BCE and the ritual building constructed in Egyptian Leontopolis by Onias IV in 164 BCE, which was modeled on the Temple in Jerusalem. With the destruction of the Temple in 70 CE after it had been considerably expanded under Herod the Great, ancient Judaism lost its religious and communal center.

The temple ritual, which was tied to a specific place, was replaced by the divine → liturgy, which could be performed anywhere. The → Shabbat rituals, from the purification of the body with special prayers and food to the lighting of the candles, maintained the distinction between the sacred and the profane; for Jews in the → Diaspora, Shabbat served as "a temple in time" (A.J. Heschel). The right to bless bread and wine, which had been reserved for priests in the Temple, was henceforth the prerogative of every male adult Jew. Synagogues and rooms where the holy texts were studied were designated as *mikdash me'at*: the little temple.

After the destruction of the temple, messianic ideas (→ Messianism) were associated with its reconstruction. As well as liturgically, these ideas were expressed through sacred art, for example through the use of images of the Temple candelabra (→ Menorah) in synagogues, on grave stones, and in book decorations. In the early modern era, the Temple became a subject of scientific interest and the focus of attempts at archaeological reconstruction among Christian scholars; models of the Temple became display objects in the art collections of European ruling families. The Jews involved in this debate were almost exclusively Italian and Sephardi writers, such as Solomon Ibn Verga (d. ca. 1530) who described the Temple in detail in *Shevet Yehudah* (1554, Scepter of Judah).

2. Reform temples in Germany

The foreign designation "temple" for → synagogues – which was also used in Catholic regions to describe Protestant churches – was common in Europe as early as the early modern period [8. 42]. Similar usage of the term by Jews is first recorded in 1802, when members of the → Breslau "Gesellschaft der Brüder," a healthcare association founded in 1780 whose members were committed to the ideas of the → Haskalah and to modern → Bildung (education), called their new prayer room "Tempel." The term developed among proponents of Jewish → reform into a cipher for the modernization of the Jewish religious service; it was associated, for example, with the abolition of inherited liturgical traditions, striving for more significant aestheticization, the introduction of German → sermons, choral singing, and → organ, and also the removal of the wall separating the spaces for men and women (→ *mehitsah*).

In their use of the term "temple," Lumières turned away from traditional messianic concepts of the reconstruction of Jerusalem and a return to → Zion. They explicitly acknowledged life in the → Diaspora, while also invoking the historic Jewish heritage associated with the term with similar self-confidence. This was accompanied by the definitive rejection of sacrificial rituals and priesthood, that is with tasks previously reserved for priests increasingly performed not only by members of the → rabbinate but also by lay people; this rejection shaped the early phase of the temple movement. Rabbis and preachers with university educations increasingly became more significant, a fact which was publicly manifested at → rabbinical conferences and synods (→ Deutsch-Israelitischer Gemeindebund) from the 1840s onward. From that point forward, use of the term "temple" indicated a position taken by liberals who wanted to distance themselves from conservative and orthodox advocates of tradition. Heinrich Heine (→ Entreebillet) derisively picked up on this internal Jewish disagreement in his poem *Deutschland, ein Wintermärchen* (1844, "Germany: A Winter's Tale," 2007): "The Jews are however divided again / Into two very different parties / the old one goes to the synagogue, / In the temple the new one's heart is" [2. 91].

In fact, use of the term "temple" harbored further potential for conflict. While some advocates of reform appropriated it even then for substantive delimitation if their places of worship operated officially as synagogues, most majority liberal communities avoided it so as not to cause internal community dissent or disputes that might become externally evident. In general, they retained instead the traditional designation of synagogue.

2.1 Seesen and Berlin

The first temple with a decidedly reformist agenda was established in the small city of Seesen by Israel Jacobson (1768–1828; Hamburg Temple Dispute; → Reform), who was active in the Napoleonic Kingdom of Westphalia as a court financier, consistorial president, and philanthropist. The temple, located in the grounds of the → Freischule which had been founded in 1801, was dedicated in 1810. The authorities in Brunswick in fact refused permission for an ambitious building with a cupola as well as a tall clock and bell tower. The completed building, with its simply curved roof and small tower, did however stake a claim to being a smaller copy of the Temple in Jerusalem, as Jacobson stressed in his opening speech. In addition to moving the *almemor* (lectern) from its traditional place in the center of the room to the Torah shrine, where a pulpit had been added for the sermon, an organ was constructed in a Jewish place of worship for the first time [8. 42–46]. Together with the newly introduced weekly sermons in → German, the singing of a male choir, and contemporary musical compositions, the temple aimed for a modernized, esthetically impressive divine service, and in doing so was oriented toward Protestant ideals (→ Protestantization).

After the breakup of the Kingdom of Westphalia, Jacobson took up residence in Berlin. There, initially in his private home, he led services with German sermons and organ and choir accompaniment until this was banned by the government at the end of 1815. While the community synagogue was being repaired, from 1817 onward there was a temple with reformed rite in the house of the sugar manufacturer Jacob Herz Beer, which primarily attracted young, acculturated Jews. Prayers that were considered to be no longer contemporary or esthetically appealing such as the → *Kol Nidre*, as well as those with messianic overtones, were omitted. The number of – halakhically

motivated – innovations were, however, kept within narrow limits; many traditional elements were retained. Following disagreements between advocates of tradition and modernization, and also as a result of the attitude of the King of Prussia Friedrich Wilhelm III, according to whom reforms in Judaism weakened Christianity and undermined proselytization of Jews, the government closed Beer's temple in September 1823.

It was the Jüdische Reformgenossenschaft, founded in Berlin in 1845 and shaped in particular by Samuel Holdheim (1806–1860), that founded a new temple, the imposing new building of which was dedicated in 1854. The most striking innovation, which was unique in Europe, was the offering of an additional → Shabbat service on Sundays; this was discontinued after a few years due to a lack of popularity. It nonetheless spawned imitators in the United States, where for some decades a Sunday service was held in a few American Reform congregations, such as Temple Sinai in Chicago [3. 79–100].

2.2 Hamburg and Vienna

In → Hamburg, reform-oriented members of the Neuer Israelitischer Tempelverein opened their own place of worship in 1818. Although they continued to belong to the Jewish community, members expressly set themselves apart from the synagogue, which was no longer considered to be in keeping with the times, through both their designation of the building as a temple and the name of their society. They wanted an "ordered" and "worthy" service with preaching, songs, choral singing in the German language, and organ accompaniment, which led to conflict with the traditional community leadership. The catalyst for the so-called → Hamburg temple dispute was the publication in 1819 of the Tempelverein's prayer book, the first comprehensive Reform liturgy to appear in print. As a result of the temple in Hamburg, and the services held during the trade fair in

→ Leipzig which used it as a template, the "temple" achieved notoriety across Europe and was the model for numerous similar Jewish reform projects.

During the first half of the 19th century, synagogues that operated under the designation "temple" were also established in → Vienna; in the Stadttempel, which was dedicated in 1826 and constructed in Empire style with a rotunda and cupola, Rabbi Isaak Noah Mannheimer (1793–1865; → Sermon) and the → cantor Salomon Sulzer (1804–1890; → Organ) successfully combined traditional liturgy with modern preaching and aesthetics. The Jewish Viennese art historian Max Eisler however retrospectively criticized the building for appearing "from the outside – since the Jews were not permitted to make their places of worship recognizable – like an apartment building, and from the inside like a theatre," and for being, if only in its architectural design, not a temple [1. 157].

Between 1854 and 1858 another temple emerged in the form of the Israelitische Bethaus in the Viennese suburb of Leopoldstadt, the "moorish" style of which referenced the golden age of medieval Jewish life in al-Andalus (→ Sepharad) and North Africa – also in order to distinguish the building from church architecture. During the 1860s, the Temple Synagogue in → Cracow, the Templul Coral in Bucharest, the synagogue in Zagreb, and the Spanish Synagogue in → Prague were also constructed based on this model.

3. Europe and the United States

Temples and synagogues aligned with the reform program were also established in other Jewish communities in Europe, often inspired by German temple structures. Choral synagogues, including the Great Synagogue in Pest, were constructed in Hungary from the 1820s onward by representatives of the moderate reform-focused Neology (→ Neolog). These were not always explicitly

named "temples." As a result of their pro-reform orientation, they primarily attracted members of the acculturated middle class. Traditional elements, such as the wall separating the areas for men and women, were however retained.

In Eastern Europe, where Jews were largely or even predominantly adherents of → Orthodoxy and → ultra-Orthodoxy, most remained with traditional synagogues. In Great Britain, where most prominent Jews were affiliated with traditional synagogue congregations, reformers refrained from referring to their prayer houses as temples.

In the United States, larger reform projects began in Jewish communities as a result of the wave of immigration from German speaking countries from the end of the 1840s onward. With the support of their congregations here, too, leading minds of reform turned away from the messianic hope of the reconstruction of Jerusalem, and from then on regarded their synagogues as "little temples." The Sephardi Beth Elohim congregation in Charleston (South Carolina) was the first to establish a synagogue which was referred to as a temple. In his speech on the occasion of the dedication of the new place of worship (which was furnished with an organ) in 1841, the religious head of the community, Gustavus Poznanski (1804–1879) from Poland, emphasized: "This synagogue is our temple, this city our Jerusalem, this happy land our Palestine" (cited in [8. 234]).

Jews in the United States usually attached less significance to the different designations given to their places of worship than Jews in Europe. The former group used the word "synagogue" even for those places of worship of Reform congregations which had the word "temple" in their official name, such as the Temple Shalom in Dallas and the Temple Sholom in Chicago. The traditional Yiddish name *shul* was often used by modern Orthodox Jews to refer to their synagogues and those of the Conservative movement, but not to Reform synagogues or temples. Members of Conservative congregations (→ Conservative Judaism) were aware of the origins of the term "temple" and mostly refrained from using it, even though members of other religions used the term to describe Conservative synagogues.

4. Messianic aspirations

Many American temple congregations founded offshoots in Israel. There they remained more strictly loyal to the traditional liturgy and continually renegotiated the relationship between reform and tradition. Reform congregations in Israel entirely refrained from using the term "temple" for their synagogues; they expressly distanced themselves from the idea of a re-establishment of the Temple.

In contrast to the Reform movement, several groups associated with → ultra-Orthodoxy have pursued plans, especially since the 1970s, for the construction of a new Temple, faithfully reproduced after the ancient model, with priests and sacrificial rituals as a symbol of both a reanimated Jewish religion and of the Jewish State. This aspiration was strengthened by the reconquest of the historical Old City of Jerusalem in the Six-Day War in 1967. Organizations such as *Ateret Cohanim* (Crown of the priests) train priests for future service in the Temple. The "Temple Mount and Land of Israel Faithful" movement concentrates on prayer and possesses a corner stone, showcased in a way designed to attract media attention, for the new construction to be built on the Temple Mount. The groups most closely affiliated with Jewish settlers in the West Bank, which combine religious-messianic piety and nationalistic-expansionist ideas, receive additional financial and spiritual support from evangelical Christian groups who see in the reconstruction of the Temple the transition to the return of Jesus to earth. Thus, Jewish interpretations of the Temple in the postmodern era span a spectrum from historical localization to a future project with unvaryingly strong symbolic power.

Bibliography

Sources
[1] M. Eisler, Der Seitenstetten Tempel, in: Menorah 4 (1926) 149–157. [2] H. Heine, Germany. A Winter Tale, ed. by A. Moore, trans. by E. A. Browning, New York 2007.

Secondary literature
[3] T. Brinkmann, Sundays at Sinai. A Jewish Congregation in Chicago, Chicago 2012. [4] V. Fritz, Tempel. Alter Orient und Altes Testament, in: Theologische Realenzyklopädie, ed. by G. Müller, vol. 33, Berlin/New York 2002, 46–54. [5] M. Inbari, Jewish Fundamentalism and the Temple Mount. Who Will Build the Third Temple?, Albany 2009. [6] L. A. Jick, The Americanization of the Synagogue, 1820–1870, Hanover 1976. [7] J. Katz, A House Divided. Orthodoxy and Schism in Nineteenth-Century Central European Jewry, Hanover 1998. [8] M. A. Meyer, Response to Modernity: A History of the Reform Movement in Judaism, Detroit 1995.

YAAKOV ARIEL, CHAPEL HILL, NC

Teshuvah

Since Antiquity, the Hebrew term *teshuvah* (lit. reversal; return) has designated the confession and repentance of sins in order to achieve forgiveness and reconciliation with God. Teshuvah is a central component of the Jewish faith. From the Middle Ages onward it was sometimes also linked with ascetic ideas. Movements of cultural-religious returning to tradition developed during the modern era, initially among secular, religiously liberal Jews in Germany and Italy, among other places. After the Second World War, the Hasidic teshuvah movement made overtures toward hippie culture in the United States; a significant teshuvah movement has developed in Israel since the 1980s.

1. Literary and liturgical foundations
2. Modern *teshuvah* movements
3. After the Second World War

1. Literary and liturgical foundations

The term *teshuvah* is derived from the Hebrew root *shin-vav-vet* (in *Pa'al* "to turn [away]"; "to return"). The metaphorical meaning "to return to God" is biblical, first recorded in Deuteronomy: "when you are in distress because all these things have befallen you and, in the end, return [*ve-shavtah*] to and obey your God" (Deut 4:30). In later biblical writings (→ Tanakh), especially in the prophets, this meaning is more specifically defined: man should turn from his "wicked ways" – especially the honoring of other gods – and improve his behavior (Jer 18:11; 2 Kgs 17:13); his loyalty should exclusively be to YHWH and his commandments. The commandment for repentance can apply collectively to the whole people, for example when they are defeated by an enemy as a result of their sins against God; provided Israel responds with repentance and praising God, it can hope for forgiveness (2 Chr 6:24f).

Derived from the biblical verb, the noun *teshuvah* – translated under Christian theological influence as "repentance" – is first used in the Damascus Document (2nd cent. BCE) found in Qumran (19. 16ff.). Rabbinic scribes also engaged intensively with *teshuvah* as a response to sins which had been committed. In the Mishnah (→ Talmud), the first major legal compendium, it is written: "A sin-offering [...] and a definite guilt-offering [for sins which have unquestionably been committed ...] atone for those sins. Death and Yom Kippur atone for sins when accompanied by repentance. Repentance itself atones for minor transgressions,

for both positive mitzvot and negative mitzvot." (Yoma 8:8). In the Mishnah, the word is also used for the first time – albeit only once – for an actively engaged subject, one who is returning (Heb. *ba'al teshuvah*): "Just as there is a prohibition against exploitation [*ona'a*] in buying and selling, so is there *ona'a* in statements [...]. If one is a penitent [*ba'al teshuvah*], another may not say to him: Remember your earlier deeds" (Bava Metziah 4:10).

In the Talmud – as in → midrash – more attention is given to the idea of the penitent and repentance is considered the highest form of ethical righteousness: "As Rabbi Abbahu said: In the place where penitents [*ba'ale teshuvah*] stand, even the full-fledged righteous [*Tsaddikim*] do not stand, [...] who was distant from an act of transgression from the outset, [... and] the penitent who was close to an act of transgression but has now distanced himself from it" (Talmud Bavli Berakhot 34b).

Particular times in the liturgical → calendar are dedicated to *teshuvah* as the confessing of and repenting for sins. The monthly day of the new moon (*Rosh Ḥodesh*) has a somewhat ancillary – albeit originally liturgically evident – significance as a day of remorse. More importantly, particular *seliḥot* (penitential prayers) are recited in the morning religious service during Elul, the last month of the year. Liturgical remorse and prayer for the forgiveness of sins culminate in the annual ten "Days of Awe" (*Yamin Nora'im*) between Rosh ha-Shanah (new year) and Yom Kippur (the day of atonement; → Course of the Year). These are also called the "ten days of repentance" (*aseret yeme teshuvah*). According to Jewish tradition (Talmud Bavli Rosh Hashanah 16b), during these days the book of life and the book of death are opened, in which good and evil people respectively are recorded. Provided someone repents of their sins during these days and asks for forgiveness, it is bestowed upon them that they are recorded in the book of life. Fasting on the day after new year (Tzom Gedaliah) is also conducive to remorse. The prayer *Avinu malkenu* ("Our father is our king"), which has its origins in the Talmudic era and which is recited in morning and afternoon services (→ Liturgy) on weekdays during the high festivals, as well as on Rosh ha-Shanah and Yom Kippur, also contains an acknowledgement of sins and a request to be inscribed in the book of life. The climax of the days of repentance is Yom Kippur (→ Course of the Year), which is celebrated with fasting as an expression of remorse and a service with prayers for forgiveness.

While the rabbinic discussion of *teshuvah* was less systematic – the term *kapara* ("atonement") was used more often for the phenomenon – the question of the correct form of practical repentance received new momentum during the Middle Ages. In his *Hilkhot Teshuvah* (remorse laws), Maimonides (1135/1138–1204; → Guide for the Perplexed) systematized the requirements concerning this matter. He stated that there were six different steps to the process of complete repentance: casting off sins, removing them from your thoughts, the determination to do so, regret for sins committed, the expression of truthfulness toward God, and the oral acknowledgement of sins committed.

In → Ashkenaz the paradigm of bodily mortification, especially by means of fasting, also contributed to the discussion. The significance ascribed to personal as well as collective fasting for the purpose of repentance during the High and Late Middle Ages is documented in the four forms of penitence in *Sefer ha-Rokeah* (ch. *hilkhot teshuvah*) by Eleazar of Worms (ca. 1176–1238) or the *Sefer ha-mitzvot ha-Katan* (small book of commandments; 1277; → Mitsvot) by Isaac ben Joseph of Corbeil, as well as by a multitude of → responsa [2. 77f.].

2. Modern *teshuvah* movements

Traditional notions of *teshuvah* remained fundamentally unchanged until the era of the → Enlightenment (→ Haskalah) and → secularization, even though some practices such as collective fasting became less important. In the modern era, the call to repentance was applied to individuals, although more rarely was it also applied to entire communities. Thus the Moroccan rabbi Joseph Maimon (Maman Maghrabi, 1741–1822), who moved from → Safed to Bukhara in 1793 as an official emmisary (*shaliah*), decided that the Jewish community there required a religious revival in order to strengthen their → piety and their knowledge of the traditional literature; this development was understood as *teshuvah*.

A fundamentally new meaning of *teshuvah* arose in the 19th century. Against the backdrop of European nationalism, the Sephardic rabbi (→ Sephardim) Yehudah Alkala'i (1798–1878), who was born in Sarajevo and grew up in Jerusalem, interpreted the traditional concept of a return to religious righteousness as a return to the Land of Israel. Traditionally this manner of return was reserved for the messianic era, but Alkala'i reformulated it as a precondition for the arrival of the Messiah (→ Messianism) [4. 221]. He expounded upon this completely original idea in works such as *Minhat Yehudah* (The offering of Judah, 1843) and *Goral le-Adonai* (A lot for the Lord, 1857), in which he also discussed better living conditions for Jews in Palestine. To this end, he called for the purchase of land from the Ottomans, the development of agriculture, and the introduction of → Hebrew as a generally spoken language. Alkala'i developed his ideas after meeting Yehudah Bibas (1780–1852), who was from Gibraltar and was working in Corfu as a rabbi. Bibas had studied in → Livorno and had already promoted the link between *teshuvah* and returning to the Holy Land during his travels to various European countries.

Another *teshuvah* movement, which essentially promoted a cultural → renaissance, manifested itself in Germany during the early 20th century, with its zenith occurring during the interwar years. Advocates of this movement held the view that their Judaism was weak or diluted, and that the price which they had paid for integration into German society – specifically the loss of Jewish knowledge and customs (→ Minhag) – was too high. They portrayed Eastern → Europe as the refuge of an authentic Judaism and were fascinated by its customs, which were considered exotic (→ Ostjuden). As a result, *Erzählungen der Chassidim* (1949), published by the philosopher of religion Martin Buber (→ Dialogue), was just as popular as German translations of the Hebrew novels and short stories of Shmuel Yosef Agnon (→ Shira; → Anthology), which were full of rich allusions to Jewish tradition.

After the First World War, the philosopher Franz Rosenzweig (→ [The] Star of Redemption) emerged as a leading proponent of a religious return to tradition that was rooted in philosophy. His personal commitment as a *ba'al teshuvah* to Jewish culture followed a period of fascination with Christianity and was made as an alternative to → conversion: repentance offered a spiritual reorientation that was bold enough to integrate secular values into a religious worldview [7. 787]. Rosenzweig and other representatives of the cultural *teshuvah* movement considered education (→ Bildung) and not proselytism to be the driving force behind an awakening interest in Judaism. The → Freies Jüdisches Lehrhaus in Frankfurt attracted acculturated Jews who combined their interest in Jewish thought and their moderate form of observance with a sustained participation in German culture. Many of them valued the writings of Martin Buber very highly; these writings would also become popular a generation later among members of the American return movements. Some of Rosenzweig's supporters, such as the journalist and author Bertha Badt-Strauss (1885–1970), sent their children to Orthodox Jewish schools.

Although the circle around Rosenzweig was not focused on Zionism, during the Weimar period a series of *ba'ale teshuvah* nonetheless combined their new interest in Jewish tradition with liberal-national ideas and emigrated to Palestine. Among them was Ernst Simon (1899–1988), founder of the Department of Educational Science at the → Hebrew University in Jerusalem and cofounder of → Brit Shalom, an academic-political association founded in 1925 which advocated for Jewish-Arab coexistence.

A comparable *teshuvah* movement also emerged during this period in Italy. Under the influence of Enlightenment and emancipatory ideas, as well as the → *risorgimento*, most Italian Jews were to a great extent socially acculturated. Around the start of the 20th century they lived a secular life, for which piety or traditional scholarship (→ Talmud Torah) had no appreciable significance. → (Neo-)Orthodoxy and conservative Judaism (→ Breslau), which were followed by roughly 20% of German Jews, had almost no adherents in Italy. In the early 20th century, a broad Jewish revival movement emerged there under the leadership of acculturated intellectuals such as the rabbi and journalist Dante Lattes and the lawyer Alfonso Pacifici. The followers of this movement also supported the idea that the survival of Judaism depended to a great extent on knowledge and observance. Many of them joined the Zionist movement (→ Basel) and emigrated to Palestine. Some, including the pacifist and journalist Enzo Sereni as well as the engineer Giacomo Hirsch, who was involved in agricultural training (*hakhsharah*), returned to secular life and affiliated themselves with the kibbutz and workers movement. Others meanwhile, such as the musicologist Leo

Levi, the historian Joseph Baruch Sermon-eta, and the diplomat and author Vittorio Dan Segre, remained observant and were engaged in political and cultural life in Israel.

The *ba'ale teshuvah* of this generation had hardly any interest in → ultra-Orthodoxy. The Dutch-Jewish lawyer, politician, and poet Jacob Israël de Haan (1881–1924) was an exception. He initially aligned himself with Zionist → neo-Orthodoxy, but after his immigration to Palestine in 1920 he advocated an ultra-Orthodox way of life and became a spokesperson for the non-Zionist Orthodox group *Agudat Yisra'el* (abbr. *Agudah*; → Bais Ya'akov). As a result of his activities in opposition to the founding of a Jewish national community in Palestine, the *Haganah* (Defense; → Military) had him assassinated in 1924. This act is today considered the first political murder in the Yishuv. To his ultra-Orthodox companions, he became "martyr (*ha-kodesh*) de Haan."

3. After the Second World War

The first notable *teshuvah* movement in the United States emerged in the 1950s and 1960s and comprised a fundamentally new form and practice of repentance. In 1949 Yosef Yitshak Schneersohn (→ Hasidism), the messianically influenced leader of the Lubavitch Hasidim (Chabad), sent his emissaries (Hebr. *shluhim*) to American colleges and universities in order to generate interest in Hasidic-Jewish customs (→ Minhag) and ways of life among secular, non-observant Jews. The first two emissaries were Zalman Schachter, born in Polish Żółkiew (today Zhovkva, Ukraine), and Shlomo Carlebach, who had grown up in Berlin; their efforts shaped the later Hasidic *teshuvah* movement. Both were influenced by the American beat culture of the 1950s and 1960s, as well as by their interest in other religious movements.

They believed that negative experiences and events, in particular those of the → Holocaust, gave young Jews the impression that Judaism could offer neither joy nor consolation, and therefore considered it their mission to refute this impression. They gradually moved away from Chabad and developed ideas that were more strongly egalitarian and liberal. Carlebach accompanied his events with music in order to make Hasidism and its folklore more accessible to his audience. Together with Schachter, he created a genre of neo-Hasidic stories, in which Hasidic culture was portrayed from a beatnik or hippie perspective, for example in Schachter's *Wrapped in the Holy Flame* (2003) or in Carlebach's *The Holy Beggars' Gazette* (1972–1979) or *Shlomo's Stories* (1994). The rise of this counterculture in the late 1960s and early 1970s was the basis for manifold expressions of the *teshuvah* movement.

Although ultra-Orthodox Hasidism and hippy counterculture appeared to be irreconcilable, and were initially considered to be so, they nonetheless shared some viewpoints and values. Both rejected the basic premise of a rational, skeptical → Enlightenment and were open to mystical concepts. Furthermore, neither of them trusted modern commercial enterprises to manage people's wellbeing in a responsible manner. For Hasidic Jews this was evidenced by the Holocaust, while hippies found proof of this in the Vietnam War. While moderate, normative forms of Christianity and Judaism both gained ground after the Second World War, from the late 1960s onward, religious movements that promised a novel spirituality while simultaneously offering clear guiding principles were more successful.

The "House of Love and Prayer," a significant *teshuvah* center inspired by Carlebach and Schachter which operated in San Francisco between 1968 and 1975, followed a program that blended neo-Hasidic elements with contemporary hippie culture. It was based on the model of the outreach centers introduced by Chabad which appeared in their hundreds throughout the world from the 1970s onward, where nonobservant Jews were instructed in Jewish-Hasidic teachings. Under the leadership of the seventh Lubavitcher *rebbe* Menaḥem Mendel Schneerson, Chabad transformed from an ultra-Orthodox Hasidic group into an order of (male) emissaries.

Although the contemporary American *teshuvah* movement is usually associated with → ultra-Orthodoxy, liberal forms also developed at first. Schachter turned away from Chabad, and from the 1970s onward promoted a progressive trend within which, for example, elements of Sufiism (→ Sufis) were adopted. As a founder of the religious left-liberal Jewish Renewal movement, in 1962 he constructed the center B'nai Or ("sons of the light"), later renamed P'nai Or ("faces of the light") for reasons of inclusivity.

In the late 1960s the *teshuvah* movement spread from the United States to Israel, where it initially received little support. Israeli society emerged from the Six Day War (1967) with a reinforced confidence in itself; the preeminence of secular Zionism (→ Basel) was as yet unchallenged, and modern → Orthodoxy functioned at best as a junior political partner. Some Israelis, such as the rabbis Adin Steinsaltz and Dov Bigon, were nonetheless starting to move away from secular, socialist ideas and turn toward Orthodoxy. At that time the Diaspora Yeshivah (*Yeshivat ha-Tefuẓot*) was founded on Mount Zion in Jerusalem by Mordechai Goldstein, who was influenced by Carlebach. This first outreach yeshivah, which based itself on American models, primarily offered study courses on Jewish traditional literature for beginners and advanced learners.

The American rabbis Nota Schiller and Noah Weinberg expanded the model established by Carlebach and Schachter, founding the outreach yeshivah *Ohr Somayach* in Jerusalem in 1970. The designation of outreach centers as yeshivot (→ Talmud Torah) became an established practice, and lent the *teshuvah* movement a greater legitimacy among Orthodox Jews. In 1974 Weinberg founded the organization *Aish HaTorah* ("fire of the Torah") in Jerusalem. Both establishments transformed into significantly more conservative educational networks, which offered seminars for men and women (in separate centers) in various countries. They increasingly rejected their neo-Hasidic origins and shifted more closely toward Orthodoxy. Just as the Chabad emissaries had previously wanted to offer alternatives to non-Jewish spiritual groups, so too the *teshuvah* movement now saw itself as being in competition with Orthodoxy.

Following the Yom Kippur War of 1973, and especially the Lebanon War in 1982, public support for secular Zionism waned. Many Israelis, including artists, soldiers, kibbutzniks, and children of the political and administrative elite, turned toward new or traditional religious groups, as a result of which the *teshuvah* movement increasingly began to align itself with ultra-Orthodoxy. In the 1980s and 1990s a significant *teshuvah* movement emerged among → Mizraḥim. Prior to this, Jews from countries in the Middle East and northern Africa had mostly been only moderately religious. The new *teshuvah* movement promoted a non-Ashkenazi Orthodox way of living, which combined the preservation of Mizraḥi and Sephardic culture (→ Sephardim) with pride in one's own ethnic affiliation. The *teshuvah* movement arose in the same time period during which the women's movement was advancing. From the 1980s onward a series of yeshivot and outreach centers for women were founded. Most of the women returning to Judaism chose this route fully aware of the religious or social alternatives; they made their decision based on a preference for strictly regulated, family-oriented community life [9. 120f.].

Bibliography

[1] Y. Ariel, From Neo-Hasidism to Outreach Yeshivot. The Origins of the Movements of Renewal and Return to Tradition, in: B. Huss (ed.), Kabbalah and Contemporary Spiritual Revival, Beer Sheva 2011, 17–37. [2] E. Baumgarten, Practicing Piety in Medieval Ashkenaz. Men, Women, and Everyday Religious Observance, Philadelphia 2014. [3] B. Beit-Hallahmi, Despair and Deliverance. Private Salvation in Contemporary Israel, Albany 1992. [4] A. Ben-Ur (ed.), A Ladino Legacy. The Judeo-Spanish Collection of Louis N. Levy, New York 2001. [5] S. B. Benor, Becoming Frum. How Newcomers Learn the Language and Culture of Orthodox Judaism, New Brunswick 2012. [6] M. Brenner, The Renaissance of Jewish Culture in Weimar Germany, Princeton 2013. [7] A. A. Cohen/P. Mendes-Flohr (eds.), 20th Century Jewish Religious Thought. Original Essays on Critical Concepts, Movements, and Beliefs, Philadelphia 2009. [8] M. H. Danzger, Returning to Tradition. The Contemporary Revival of Orthodox Judaism, New Haven 1989. [9] L. Davidman, Tradition in a Rootless World. Women Turn to Orthodox Judaism, Berkeley 1991.

YAAKOV ARIEL, CHAPEL HILL, NC

Tevye

Tevye, the Yiddish form of the Hebrew-Biblical Tovyah (Tobias), is the most nuanced and three-dimensional literary figure in the works of Shalom Rabinovitch (1859–1916), published under the pen name of Sholem Aleichem. The writer, whose popular-humoristic texts (→ Humor) played a significant part in the evolution of modern literary → Yiddish, described the confrontation between the traditional → shtetl and the European modern age in tragicomical monologue form in a series of nine short stories published between 1895 and 1914 under the title of *Tevye der milkhiker* ("Tevye the Dairyman," 1994). The stories are regarded as the highpoint of his literary work and influenced entire generations of readers and critics in Europe and North America. The idealization of the character of Tevye, adapted by theatre, musical, and film, and of the shtetl in Sholem Aleichem's exaggerated depiction influence the idea of Jewish life in its supposedly original guise in Eastern Europe to this day.

1.	Shalom Rabinovitch
2.	Literary works
2.1	Early texts (1883–1889)
2.2	Artistic self-discovery (1892–1899)
2.3	Greatest creative period (1899–1905)
2.4	Late work (1906–1916)
3.	*Tevye der milkhiker* (1895–1914)
4.	Autobiographical legacy
5.	Reception

1. Shalom Rabinovitch

As well as Sholem Y. Abramovitsh (Mendele Moykher-Sforim, 1836–1917; → Fishke) and Isaac Leib Peretz (1852–1915; → Bontshe), Shalom Rabinovitch is regarded as one of the founding fathers of modern Yiddish → literature. His literary œuvre, translated again and again as well as adapted for stage and screen, comprises literary newspaper and journal articles, stories, → novels, plays, and silent film scripts that found a wide audience throughout Europe and North America. With their tragicomical figures, they especially depict the confrontation between traditional Jewish life in the Eastern European → shtetl and the challenges and upheaval of the modern era.

Rabinovitch was born in 1859 in the Ukrainian provincial town of Pereyaslav. His parents earned their living in the timber trade and timber rafting (→ Transportation). He spent his childhood and early adolescence in the small shtetl Voronkov in Poltava province, the mainly Jewish inhabitants of which made a living selling consumer goods such as clothes, shoes, and agricultural equipment to the non-Jewish farmers of the region. He would later mythologize the Jewish living environment in the imaginary shtetl Kasrilevke, a place exalted by many of his readers and theatre audiences – and not least emigrated Jews – as the epitome of the old homeland and Jewish community life in Eastern Europe (→ Yiddishland).

The correspondence between the fiction and historical reality was, of course, at best meager; the writer's greatness was not measured against the standard of a faithful chronicler but rather the inspired creator of myths. Rabinovitch received a traditional ḥeder education (→ Talmud Torah) in Voronkov and also benefited from his father Nahum Rabinovitch's interest in → Hebrew and the educational objectives of the → Haskalah. A moderate Maskil (→ Maskilim), he not only read the Hebrew weekly papers *Ha-Melits* (The Advocate) and *Ha-Tsefirah* (The Advent) but also admired the romantic biblical novels by Abraham Mapus (1808–1867; → Ahavat Tsiyon) written in stylized Hebrew. Shalom Rabinovitch had Hebrew lessons and learned almost the entire Bible by heart at an early age. Because of economic difficulties, the family returned to Pereyaslav in poverty. His father now worked as an innkeeper (→ Tavern); his mother died in a cholera epidemic. From then on, a stepmother looked after him and his siblings. These distressing experiences drove him into daydreams and phantasies that later found their way into his stories and dramas in humorous form.

Between 1873 and 1876, Rabinovitch attended a Russian secondary school where he improved his knowledge of → Russian and learned to appreciate Russian literature, above all Gogol and Turgenev. After graduating with honors, in 1877 he found employment with the wealthy landowner Elimelekh Loyev as his sons' tutor for three years. When he was dismissed because of having started a love affair with Loyev's eldest daughter

Sholem Aleichem (b. Shalom Rabinovitch, 1859–1916)

Olga, he successfully ran for the position of government rabbi in the city of Lubny, keeping the position from 1880 to 1883. While he had previously written some articles for *Ha-Melits* and *Ha-Tsefirah*, the separation from Olga Loyev and the intricacies of small-town life gave the real impulse for his literary career. He used the experience of his affair in his first tragic-melodramatic love story for the young Yiddish weekly paper *Dos yidishe folksblat* (The Jewish People's Newspaper) published in St. Petersburg. For the paper, he also wrote witty → feuilletons, in which he often used the form of correspondence to unmask the untruths and dirty secrets of the rich inhabitants of Lubny. His decision to write in → Yiddish rather than in Russian, as he had originally planned, proved to be fateful. Before long, he found his head spinning with *meshuges*, as he called it, the craziness, carnivalesque vitality and elan of the language [15. 78]. Now a confirmed Yiddish writer – his few texts in Hebrew and Russian met with little resonance – he would feel close to his not very educated but constantly growing Yiddish readership for all his life.

In order to keep his identity a secret in view of his revelations about the Lubny upper class, Rabinovitch chose the pseudonym "Sholem Aleichem": originally a Hebrew welcome (*shalom alekhem*; peace be with you), the phrase picked up on the author's given name, immediately turning it into a joke with its own dynamism. To begin with, the author created the storyteller "Sholem Aleichem," who suddenly appeared on railway stations or came flying in with balloons, as a literary figure coming home as a welcome guest from far away to be with his faithful readers at home once more. The figure captured the spirit of the 1880s, which brought great upheaval for the Jews of Eastern Europe due to the → pogroms and the restrictive → May Laws after the murder of Czar Alexander II in 1881 as well as the beginning of mass emigration (→ Bremerhaven). The figure of Sholem Aleichem embodies the unrest, the speed, the garrulousness, and the unconventionality of these years, ultimately becoming a *leyts*, as it were, which in Yiddish means a mocking rascal as well as an evil spirit (→ Badkhn). Finally, Rabinovitch adopted the name of his colorful → folklore figure, the diabolical trickster greatly adored by the readers, as his pseudonym. Under the name of Sholem Aleichem he became the most popular writer of the entire Yiddish-speaking world on both sides of the Atlantic.

2. Literary works

2.1 *Early texts (1883–1889)*
The year 1883 marked the beginning of a hectic six-year period of creativity for Sholem Aleichem. The fact that he was able to marry Olga Loyev after all in 1883 and managed the family's wealth after his father-in-law's death in 1885 gave him financial independence. He moved to Kyiv, where he dedicated himself to stock market transactions, but above all writing. He continued tirelessly to compose

humorous satirical dialogues for the mass of readers with little education, in which the figure of Sholem Aleichem held the post of impetuous conferencier. In the texts, he invented a whole army of minor characters who attacked Sholem Aleichem, his writings, and his misdemeanors in fictitious polemic, bringing him more public attention. One of these minor characters, the newly married Menakhem-Mendl, used his time of living at the expense of his in-laws – most → marriage contracts of the time did indeed provide for this – in order to try his hand at writing. In lengthy novels he satirized the personality of the cantankerous mother-in-law.

The main part of Sholem Aleichem's literary ambition was directed at composing short → novels with serious plots, six of which appeared by 1889. In these stories, he combined the light romantic love stories favored and bought by Yiddish readers with a more sophisticated realistic novel in the style of modern French and Russian authors. Within his concept of the "Jewish novel," the limits of reality such as traditional Jewish morals and customs were not transgressed in spite of the central love story [21. 12]. His best-known "Jewish novel" is *Stempenyu. A yidisher roman* (1888; "Stempenyu. A Jewish Romance," 1913), which describes the failed love affair between the → klezmer musician Stempenyu and a prudish, married, lower-middle-class woman. The sparse love story is covered up by the colorful descriptions of Jewish community life in the Ukrainian province accompanied by the usual "Sholem Aleichem" chattiness. Sholem Aleichem regarded this and the following novel *Yosele solovey* (1889; "The Nightengale," 1985), the story of a young → cantor, as *Künstlerroman*, a sub-genre that was intended to slowly widen the horizon of his readership and gradually lead them towards the modern era. In fact, they reveal his own bourgeois admiration for the ideal of the "Jewish woman," who was able due to her particular pudicity and morality to hold her erotic desires in check. This reverence was balanced by the romantic glorification of → music as the greatest of all arts, which was able to exert great emotional power but could at the same time be seductive, destructive, and cause social instability.

Finally, as a literary critic and publisher Sholem Aleichem endeavored to make Jewish → literature socially acceptable. In many articles he attacked the Yiddish → publishing sector and its preference for unrealistic trashy and kitsch novellas. The high point was his 1888 pamphlet *Shomers mishpet* (Shomer's trial), in which he described an imaginary trial in which the popular Yiddish writer Nokhem-Meyer Shaykevitch (1849–1905) had to defend the wordy and overblown penny novels he produced by the dozen and was then condemned and pilloried. Sholem Aleichem himself was working to establish a Yiddish "tradition" of realistic literature, which for him meant the satirical → Yiddish literature, the foundation of which had been laid since the 1860s mainly by Sholem Y. Abramovitsh to whom he dedicated *Stempenyu*. In the Dedication, he called him "dear grandfather," presenting himself has his "devoted grandchild" and rightful heir [7. 1, 8].

In addition, he published two volumes of a Yiddish almanac in the style of Russian literary journals in 1888/1889, entitled *Di yidishe folks-bibliyotek* (The Yiddish people's almanac). Besides a few forgotten Yiddish texts of the early → Haskalah, he included instalments of new works by prominent Yiddish authors such as Abramovitsh and Isaac Joel Linetzky (1835–1915) but also works by talented newly discovered writers such as Isaac Leib Peretz (→ Bontshe). He published his two *Künstlerromane*, *Stempenyu* and *Yosele solovey*, as substantial supplements to the almanac.

His writing and publishing activities came to an end when his family's fortune was lost in speculative stock market transactions in 1889/1890. Confronted with complete poverty and the loss of his social status for the second time in his life, he first moved with his family to → Odessa, later fleeing the country for several months to be safe from his creditors. Once his bankruptcy had been formalized, he returned to Kyiv penniless, scraping a living as a stockbroker and trying at the same time to revive his writing career.

2.2 *Artistic self-discovery (1892–1899)*

Besides Sholem Aleichem's financial difficulties, the ever more severe state → censorship made publishing in → Yiddish more difficult in the 1890s. The Yiddish journals that had flourished in the 1880s were suppressed altogether. In addition, Sholem Aleichem, who had political ties to Zionism (→ Basel), struggled to overcome his image as backward and traditionalist due to his connections with the Jewish petty bourgeoisie, unlike Peretz who oriented himself towards the increasingly relevant Jewish proletariat.

Despite all the tribulations, Sholem Aleichem's work gained depth during this time in particular. Having abandoned his ambitions to write the great Jewish romance novel or the great Jewish family saga, and after a few shorter, less ambitious texts, in the 1890s his creative genius emerged in *Menakhem-Mendl* and *Tevye der milkhiker*, two series of interdependent short stories. In different and seemingly contradictory ways, they reflected his own way of life as well as the social, economic, and cultural processes in the lives of Jews in Eastern Europe.

Menakhem-Mendl, the first series of short stories, begun in 1892 and continued until 1913, returned to the comic character with whom his readers were already familiar. Parodying his own Jewish romantic novels, Sholem Aleichem depicted him, a → Luftmensch and → schlemiel, and his small-town wife Sheyne-Shendl as eternally estranged but at the same time entirely dependent on each other. The couple do not live together, as rather than using the dowry to establish a little business in the → shtetl, the enthusiastic young husband is seduced by the promises of stock market speculations in Odessa and Kyiv and loses all his money in the process. Interspersed with periods of despondency, he rushes headlong into further speculation whenever money is sent to him; his family does not see him again. As his wife is the only person who listens attentively to him, he describes his exciting transactions in regular letters to her. She, in turn, expresses her anguish and vexation at being an abandoned wife, revealing among other things the skepticism, crude realism, and deep-seated conservatism of the pre-modern shtetl. Even so, the two do not understand each other; Menakhem-Mendl ignores his wife's worries entirely. This comical, dysfunctional correspondence was the subject matter of Sholem Aleichem's epistolary novels. Menakhem-Mendl presents himself quite innocently, without having the slightest idea of even the rudiments of the functioning of the capitalist economy, as a successful *homo oeconomicus* sacrificing his basic human needs to his hope for imminent wealth. His wife does not understand this and in turn bestows sexual innuendos on her formerly passionate husband. With their parodistic style, Sholem Aleichem's subtle → novels on the one hand focused on the confrontation between shtetl Jews and the urbanization process but highlighted the modern Jewish battle of the sexes on the other. By virtue of their circular and repetitive nature, the stylistic and formal components employed, such as the flowery phrases of traditional Jewish correspondence, show up the aspirations of the supposedly modern Jews. In leaving the shtetl, they frequently imagined to have left their traditional origins behind them, believing they have become successful in the urban capitalist society. In fact, however, they usually found themselves transported into a socio-economic vacuum or a proletarian environment without the shtetl mentality having been challenged at all.

The epistolary stories around Menakhem-Mendl, which Sholem Aleichem continued until 1913, are regarded as among the author's best, if not the best, works. As to their artistic merit, however, they rank behind his second serialized novel about the dairyman Tevye.

2.3 *Greatest creative period (1899–1905)*

A slight loosening of Czarist censorship policy fundamentally changed the Yiddish literary landscape around 1900. Yiddish periodicals, among them the groundbreaking fortnightly Zionist journal *Der yud* (1899–1902; The Jew), multiplied rapidly, competing for the ever-growing readership. In the literary environment of the Yiddish press, Sholem Aleichem soon became the most popular author, receiving the highest pay of all Yiddish writers in return for producing weekly instalments of short stories, → feuilletons, humorous stories, and other short texts. From then on, he made writing his main occupation, producing hundreds of comparatively short, and not infrequently mediocre, texts over the next six years. Despite his tremendous popularity, Sholem Aleichem was constantly in economic difficulties. He was naïve in negotiations with his publishers, with the result that in times of financial crisis they pressured him to sign contracts so disadvantageous that only a minimal portion of the income from his book sales reverted to him. His main income was popular readings of his works for which he travelled the entire Eastern European → Pale of Settlement. The permanent travel required not only drained his strength but also undermined his health in the long term.

Prominent among the texts of this creative period were a series of short stories, written between 1901 and 1905, in the monologue form with which Sholem Aleichem had already experimented in his earlier Tevye stories. He not only convincingly reproduced the diction and tone of numerous fictional characters, mainly simple, worldly, common Jews of Eastern Europe with all their financial, social, and family problems, but also imbued them with a bubbling, occasionally even vulgar, garrulousness that revealed the tragic depth of the superficially amusing stories. In *Dos tepl* (1901; The little pot), for instance, the young widow Yente, a poultry seller in the market, consults the rabbi of her town concerning her only ceramic pot that she uses to prepare chicken broth and which may have become unkosher (→ Kashrut) from a few drops of milk. This is the background of her monologue, a long meandering story telling us about her life, commenting on her neighbors, nagging, and gossiping. Besides the seemingly Halakhic reason behind the untidy, witty, and chatty narrative, the story is really about Yente's other "single remaining pot": her son, who suffers from tuberculosis and who she fears may die young like his father, leaving her alone in the world. Behind this tragedy is a seething, almost unconscious fury at all those by whom Yente feels oppressed: at men who despite their weakness and unreliability dominate women in the structures of a patriarchal society, at physicians (→ Medicine) who cannot heal, at the rabbi as the representative of the repressive → Halakhah, and thus implicitly at God. In nearly all of Sholem Aleichem's monologues, several layers are superimposed on each other: comedy edges on top of tragedy, and both are permeated by a deeper and almost imperceptible anarchism. Seemingly irrelevant asides, Freudian slips, and unexplained changes of pitch allow the reader to uncover hidden truths and deeply-rooted resentment. These monologues are undoubtedly among Sholem Aleichem's greatest achievements as an artist as well as a chronicler of contemporary Jewish life on the realistic-mimetic level and beyond.

During the first years of the 20th century, he composed innumerable short stories. He was considered a master of the festival story that appeared on the occasion of the feast days in the Jewish → course of the year in the supplements of Jewish newspapers, dealing with historical topics, the Jewish family, and social life. While he followed the basic rules of the genre and showed some aspects in a positive light, at the same time he undermined them subtly by means of dark undertones emphasizing fears, suffering, poverty, and the marginalized position of the Jewish inhabitants of the → shtetl. He frequently developed the festival atmosphere from the point of view of the weak and oppressed. Consequently, the protagonists of his stories, some of which are characterized by guilt and fear, are frequently poor children growing up in social insignificance and with family pressures, who perceive the ceremonies with some distance. Thus in the story *Der esreg* (1902; The etrog), a boy feels the irresistible urge to put the stem of the fruit (etrog) used for blessings during Sukkot into his mouth, although the fruit must be entirely unblemished for its ritual role. Despite several admonishments, the stem breaks off by accident and tastes bitter and repulsive in the child's mouth. His emotions of guilt, fear, and anger reveal several surprising psychological insights. For stories like these, Sholem Aleichem developed a special hybrid-monologue narrative style that interweaves the child's innocent narrative with the illuminating comments of the adult he would one day become.

In texts with an omniscient narrator, Sholem Aleichem also employed tradiional, pseudo-folkloristic techniques such as the ones used in the Yiddish *mayse bikhl* (little books of stories). Texts of this genre consisted of brief chapters each of which was introduced by ceremonial → Hebrew and then continue in an idiomatic everyday slang, for instance the short story *A mayse on an ek* (A story without an end), better known under the title *Der farkishefter shnayder* (1900; The bewitched tailor). It is based on a well-known story about Chełm: a naïve teacher from Chełm, the proverbial Jewish town of fools, buys a nanny goat in a nearby town. On his way home, it is secretly exchanged for a billy goat, and the angry melammed returns to the previous owner as he believes he has been cheated. However, the billy goat is exchanged for the nanny goat again on the way. This game continues until the teacher has a mental breakdown and the foolish rabbi of Chełm explains the sex change with a devilish trick. With recourse to the *mayse bikhl* structure, Sholem Aleichem shines a light on the growing discrepancy between the original trick and the mental breakdown of the protagonist, who gradually loses his masculinity in the process. The motif of the gender metamorphosis provides the background for a deep and subtle disquisition on the subject of gender and gender roles in traditional Jewish life.

2.4 *Late work (1906–1916)*

In 1905, Sholem Aleichem and his family at first experienced the hope and excitement gripping the entire Czarist Empire. After the failed revolution, they found themselves once again confronted with the horrors of escalating → pogroms. Via Galicia, Germany, and England, the family emigrated to → New York. Sholem Aleichem had toyed with this idea for some time, but it took the anti-Jewish attacks to remove his last doubts. He had reached the conclusion that he could not continue to produce short stories and → feuilletons at the same high speed and that the → shtetl motifs he used would soon be exhausted; as a consequence he would require new sources of income. The success of his drama *Tsezeyt un tseshpreyt* (1903; Scattered and dispersed), performed in → Polish in Warsaw in 1905, gave him the idea of trying his luck at the theatre. New York was the best port of call as it was the only one at the time that boasted a commercially successful theatre landscape (→ Broadway; → Second Avenue), and Sholem Aleichem believed he was the man to raise its supposedly low cultural level. He spent most of 1906 in New York, at first welcomed enthusiastically by the American and Yiddish local press as the "Jewish Mark Twain" [12. 185]. His plays, however, failed, as he had barely any skills in dramatic presentation and ignored the taste of the Jewish audiences in the city almost with arrogance.

Discouraged, Sholem Aleichem and his family returned to Europe. With no fixed abode, decreasing financial resources, and failing health, all that was left to him was to tour the provincial towns of the → Pale of Settlement by train as a travelling artist. He read, mainly in improvised lecture rooms, excerpts from his œuvre to Yiddish-speaking audiences. While his return to the Ukrainian and Belarussian provinces was a triumph, he suffered a life-threatening breakdown in the summer of 1908 when he developed open tuberculosis. From then on, he was forced to spend the winters in the Mediterranean and the summers mainly in Swiss or Bavarian health spas. With the exception of a few months in 1908, he was unable to leave his bed again. However, he tirelessly continued to write new texts, which appeared in the Yiddish daily papers of Warsaw and New York. From 1909 onward, the publishing rights to his collected works at least guaranteed him a regular income.

Sholem Aleichem returned to writing novels on an epic scale, the genre he had favored in his early work. Until his death, he composed five more → novels two of which remained unfinished. Now his shtetl-born protagonists were transplanted from their original provincial home to new surroundings such as the urban centers of Eastern Europe or the great cities of North America, which took into account the contemporary perspectives of Eastern European Jews. Literary requirements demanded the large-scale epic form with an omniscient narrator rather than the short story reflecting the limited intellectual world of the backward protagonists of his monologues.

In addition, Sholem Aleichem was influenced by the new Russian literature of the "Silver Age" and intended to openly discuss subjects and issues that he had only indirectly alluded to in his earlier works, such as women's struggle for autonomy. In his first new novel *Der mabl* (1907; The flood), he depicted the developments within the Jewish cultural landscape and society from 1905 onward, describing the lot of raped Jewish women who had become pregnant as a consequence at the center of the plot. In *Der blutiker shpas* (The bloody hoax), which he composed in 1912 under the influence of the trial of Mendel Beilis for → blood libel, he investigated the possibility or impossibility of romantic attachments between Jews and non-Jews, who cannot exchange roles, in the context of official antisemitism. In the longest novel of this creative period, *Blondzhende shtern* (1909–1911; Wandering stars), finally, he portrayed the life and the art of Jewish actors in Eastern Europe, Vienna, → London, and New York, including the anarchical elements of the alternative lifestyle prevailing in the Yiddish theatre milieu.

In his novels, Sholem Aleichem also considered the changes in the increasingly sensation-seeking Yiddish newspaper business (→ Press) and its serialized publications, positioning himself on the fine line between serious art and entertainment. In spite of cleverly laid out plots and character sketches, the novels of that period in particular lack depth and the tragicomical impact the Tevye stories, for instance, conveyed. In view of the modern psychological novels by young Yiddish writers such as David Bergelson (1884–1952; → GosET; → Khurbn), Sholem Asch (1880–1957; → Motke), and Joseph Opatoshu (1886–1954; → Di Yunge), his narrative style could only appear antiquated and superficial. His great successes during this creative period rested on the genres he had perfected between 1900 and 1905, which he now adapted in such a way that they could convey new and more complex information. The monologizing narrator of the short story *Dray almones* (1907; Three widows), a city-dweller attracted by the modern era is drawn much more consciously and subtly than the protagonists of the earlier popular monologue stories. Furthermore, his secret does not concern socioeconomic difficulties but rather his latent homosexuality, because of which he decides against marrying one of the three widows, indeed seeing himself as the fourth widow. The childlike-adult hybrid narrator was used successfully in the unfinished masterpiece *Motl Peyse dem khazns* (1907/1908; "Motl the Cantor's Son," 2009). In interlinking stories, a child, the half-orphan Motl, narrates the story of the decline of a middle-class family respected in the shtetl as if it were a wonderful adventure. At first, the family, hopelessly impoverished after the early death of the father, who served as the community cantor, wanders all over Western Europe, finally emigrating to → America where proletarianization and exploitation await them. Motl regards the concomitant anarchism as a liberating and serene force. He celebrates the decline of shtetl society and its traditional, repressively regulated culture without regrets, enjoying every minute of his newly-won freedom. He understands the metamorphosis as the rebirth of a people whose former lifestyle is doomed. In this way, the character transports Sholem Aleichem's revolutionary interpretation of the decline of shtetl culture that is replaced by a coarse and vulgar immigrant society.

Because of his deteriorating health, after 1908 Sholem Aleichem initially focused on a new series of monologues. The *Ayznbangeshikhtes* (Railway stories) a commercial traveler claims to have overheard or been told by Jewish passengers in the slow trains of the Pale of Settlement were shorter, more simply structured, more direct as to their narrative style, and less reliant on uncontrollable garrulousness to move them forward. They portrayed Jews outside of their habitual living environment in ambiguous interactions with a foreign world they barely knew and completely misunderstood. This informed the comedic as well as the tragic mood of the stories, nearly all of which build on incorrectly decoded signs. Thus, the naïve commercial traveler does not understand that his companion, a Jew from → Buenos Aires allegedly on a pilgrimage to his impoverished home in Courland in order to pray at his parents' grave and find a wife, is in fact a trafficker who supplies poor Jewish and non-Jewish girls from Europe to American brothels (→ Jüdischer Frauenbund). While some misunderstandings end surprisingly positively, most lead to difficulties for which the monologizing protagonists are no match. All the same, despite all the turmoil the stories radiate an almost uncanny calm.

Nearly all Sholem Aleichem's important new works looked at people who had been removed from their ancestral place or their customary roles. Even Tevye abandons his work as a dairyman in the last stories, sells his cows and farm, is evicted from his native village, and is forced to become an itinerant without a destination (→ Ahasver); the cantor's son Motl suffers a similar fate. In the unfinished novel *Der misteyk* (The mistake) begun 1915, a Jewish girl arriving in America misses the relatives who were coming to meet her and wanders through the new country on her own. In the short epistolary novel *Marienbad* (1911), however, the comedy of intrigue and puzzlement is based on the protagonists leaving their home in Warsaw in order to enjoy the comforts of the famous spa of → Marienbad.

3. *Tevye der milkhiker* (1895–1914)

At the beginning of the 1890s, Sholem Aleichem began working on his brilliantly conceived second series of novels *Tevye der milkhiker* with the first story appearing in 1895; until 1914, eight more followed in irregular intervals. It is regarded as the highpoint of his creative work and of modern Jewish → literature in general. Unlike the obvious parallels discernible between his life and the failed character Menakhem-Mendl, his connection with Tevye, an equally impoverished paterfamilias, is not easy to recognize. The figure of the narrator, too, in whom facets of Sholem Aleichem himself may be found, has lived through the deceptive seduction of making a quick fortune and lost all his savings.

Tevye is commonly seen as a fictional representative of the deeply religious traditional Jewish society of Eastern Europe, a hard-working, loving father of a family and charitable member of the traditional → shtetl community, who weathers the devastating effects of the modern age and the deteriorating living conditions for Jews in the Czarist Empire thanks to his trust in God. As he retains his dignity, sense of → humor, and innate optimism in spite of everything, he appears to embody everything that is positive and relevant in traditional Jewish civilization. The actual character created by Sholem Aleichem, however, diverges considerably from this idealized and simplified image, being much darker, more complex, and more nuanced. Instead of a typical traditional Jew, Tevye is in fact a character in transition, in whose life the old norms are not only subject to constant compromise forced by poverty and drudgery but also to elements of the humanist modern age imparted to him by his → assimilated daughters whose Jewish education he has woefully neglected. Moreover, Tevye is not a typical shtetl Jew, although he frequently wishes he were. He lives on a farm not far from a Ukrainian village among non-Jews with whom he has developed a comparatively neighborly relationship, and he earns his living with the agricultural activity of milk production. He conducts a constant and lively dialogue with the Jewish God, which is frequently filled with deep irony expressing the pent-up bitterness caused by his poverty. Even the education (→ Bildung) and scholarship he displays, and shares most obtrusively and tiresomely with uneducated women in particular, is based on a fraud: his knowledge comes from merely a few basic texts of the canon (→ Tanakh). Everything else consists of made-up quotations from other texts. Tevye thus possesses all the usual flaws of a society in which actions belie the ostensible spirituality; he loves money, but is incapable of managing it wisely and dreams of acquiring wealth by finding rich husbands for his daughters; he despises women and craves recognition.

He is a master only when it comes to telling chatty, very lively and witty anecdotes. This saves him from an aesthetic point of view and wins him the readers' favor, while those having to live with him – such as his wife Golda – grow increasingly and terribly impatient with him. His stories, meandering between half-truths and self-deception, are his protection from the horrors of his everyday life. By splitting hairs and presenting pseudo-Talmudic arguments, he is even able to soften the blows of fate when one of his daughters, whom he had hoped to marry to a millionaire, commits suicide and when his wife dies miserably. Tevye does thus not represent any Jewish values but the eloquence and vulnerability of art in general and narrative art in particular. In the figure of Sholem Aleichem – the writer himself – Tevye sees not only the audience of his confession of seemingly innocent, accidental mistakes but also the artist who appreciates his delightful stories, even identifies with them and as a consequence might grant him a kind of aesthetic absolution.

The Tevye stories enjoyed great popularity with the Yiddish readership and were translated into innumerable languages. Stage adaptations were performed at, among others, the Warsaw Yiddish Art Theatre (*Varshever Yidisher Kunst-Teater, VYKT*; → Kaminski Theatre). Directed by Maurice Schwartz (→ Second Avenue), who also played the main character, the story made it to the screen in 1939 as *Tevya*, becoming a classic of American Yiddish film. On → Broadway, the character Tevye premiered in the musical *Fiddler on the Roof* – the title of a painting by Marc Chagall (→ Vitebsk) – in 1964. The piece became a global success and was performed in the Federal Republic of Germany from 1968 onward under the title *Anatevka* – the name of Tevye's shtetl in the musical. The 1971 → Hollywood film adaptation of the same title won three Academy Awards, among others.

4. Autobiographical legacy

In the last years of his life, Sholem Aleichem worked on an extensive autobiographical novel but finished only two of the planned eight chapters. *Funem yarid* ("From the Fair," 1986) follows the writer's artistic journey through the vanity "fair" that is the world of Yiddish literature. The → novel also represents the entire course of his life, beginning with the journey "to the fair" and continuing all the way to old age, infirmity, and death. It charts the rise of the successful author as well as that of Yiddish → literature and the Jewish people in general. The novel does not, however, achieve the standard of his earlier works, as the text lacks the self-analysis and self-revelation the contemporary readership expected in an autobiographical confession. Instead, *Funem yarid* presents a very selective view of the author's childhood and adolescence that informed his understanding of art as the union of fancy and caricature, free imagination, and mimetic truthfulness, but limited it at the same time. However, the volume is hardly able to explain the complex personality of Sholem Aleichem or his understanding of art.

Funem yarid was composed mainly in → New York in 1915. Despite the deep dislike for the country he felt after his failed stay in 1906, the outbreak of the First World War forced Sholem Aleichem to return to the United States. Cut off from their main sources of income, the newspapers and publishing houses of Warsaw, as citizens of an enemy state living in Berlin, the family succeeded in crossing the Atlantic from neutral Denmark. The son Micha Rabinovitch, who was suffering from tuberculosis, stayed behind in a Swiss sanatorium, where he died in 1915. Sholem Aleichem used the escape to America, without a clear prospect of a new home and new sources of income, as the background for a series of monologues published in the same year. Entitled *Mayses fun toyzent eyn nakht* (Stories from the thousand and one nights), their protagonist is a lonely and destitute Polish Jew narrating the story of the destruction of his community and the decimation of his family in the first months of the war. As a consequence of his → shtetl being occupied by German troops and then reconquered by the Russians, the Jews become the victims of the graphically described brutality of both sides. While the series is in some ways a forerunner of later → Holocaust literature (→ Khurbn), it also reflects Sholem Aleichem's old-fashioned style: the insurmountable chasm between the events described, such as the narrator's hopeless situation in the present, and his immutable habitual self-importance, pompousness, and the arrogance of a smug community leader, provide the basis for the tragicomical story. The stylistic device, used by Sholem Aleichem in his Tevye stories above all, acquired an unexpected breadth and menace in this his last work. Sholem Aleichem died in May 1916 in New York from kidney failure and aggravated heart trouble.

5. Reception

Sholem Aleichem stands for many things: a Jewish comic genius, the chronicler of the shtetl civilization in the last phases of disintegration, the successful dramatist who merged comedy and melodrama into a formula for a long and fruitful life on stage, finally the writer who more than any other made use of the rhythmical resources of the language and, after Mikhah Yosef Berdyczewski (1865–1921), achieved for → Yiddish what Rashi (→ Worms) had achieved for → Hebrew. His Yiddish readership regarded Sholem Aleichem above all as a national provider of consolation who created a sensation of familiarity and comfort in his cheery, often serene stories, while the readers themselves faced the challenges and difficulties of dealing with everyday life in the modern age.

Yiddish-speaking intellectuals of his time, who were aspiring to modernize and Europeanize Yiddish culture, criticized him good-humoredly as a backward popular entertainer who was unable to cut the cord tying him to the → shtetl. After a → Russian edition of selected works by Sholem Aleichem appeared in 1911, Russian writers and critics rejected this accusation, attesting his work an unexpected forcefulness. Franz Kafka (→ Prague), who regarded all modern Yiddish works as the continuation of naïve popular literature, changed his view after reading a → German translation of some of Sholem Aleichem's stories. Having first trusted Max Brod's verdict and recommended them as children's books, he now recognized the incredible complexity of the subject matter [10. 711].

Sholem Aleichem's growing to be one of the greatest modern Yiddish writers was mainly due to his ability to subtly translate the innermost human emotions and fears into words while retaining the multilayered structure of intentions, uncontrollable and often unconscious afflictions, dissimulations, and truths concealed by them. The speech form was the only resource, the only weapon of the weak in danger of being swallowed by the maelstrom of life and clinging to every straw. It was precisely the literary form of the monologizing protagonist, not that of the epic omniscient and allegedly objective narrator, that became the *conditio sine qua non* of Jewish → literature in the 20th century. In addition, the discourse written down by Sholem Aleichem assumed the special function of employing literature to convey the message of the often defenseless and persecuted Jews. The reason why Sholem Aleichem can be regarded as a great writer of the 20th century is because he succeeded, particularly in his stories about Menakhem-Mendl and Tevye, in finding the raw nerve that conveyed authentic emotions.

Bibliography

Sources

[1] Sholem Aleichem, From the Fair. The Autobiography of Sholom Aleichem, Harmondsworth 1986. [2] Sholom Aleichem, Marienbad, trans. by Aliza Shevrin, New York, 1984. [3] Sholem Aleykhem, Nineteen to the Dozen. Monologues and Bits and Bobs of Other Things, trans. by T. Gorelick, Syracuse 1998. [4] Sholem Aleykhem, Favorite Tales of Sholom Aleichem, trans. by J. and F. Butwin, New York 1983. [5] Scholem Aleichem, Tevye the Dairyman. And Motl the Cantor's Son, trans. by A. Shevrin, New York 2009. [6] Scholem Alejchem, The Letters of Menakhem-Mendl and Sheyne-Sheyndl; and, Motl, the Cantor's Son, trans. by H. Halkin, New Haven 2002. [7] Scholem Aleichem, Stempenyu. A Jewish Romance, London 1913. [8] Scholem Alejchem, Tevye the Dairyman and the Railroad Stories, trans. by H. Halkin, New York 1987. [9] S. Aleykhem, Tevye the Dairyman, trans. by J. Simon, Malibu 1994. [10] F. Kafka, Letters to Felice, ed. by E. Heller/J. Born, trans. by J. Stern/E. Duckworth, New York, 1973.

Secondary literature

[11] Y. K. Brenner, On Sholem Aleykhem, in: Prooftexts 1 (1986) 6, 17–22. [12] J. Dauber, The Worlds of Sholem Aleichem. The Remarkable Life and Afterlife of the Man Who Created Tevye, New York 2013. [13] M. Erik, Menakhem Mendl, in: Prooftexts 1 (1986) 6, 23–40. [14] D. Miron, The Image of the Shtetl and Other Studies of Modern Jewish Literary Imagination, Syracuse 2000. [15] D. Miron, From Continuity to Contiguity. Toward a New Jewish Literary Thinking, Stanford 2010. [16] D. Miron, Mi-peh la-ozen: sihot u-mahashavot al omanut ha-monolog shel Shalom Alekhem [Verbatim. Sholem Aleichem's Art of the Monologue], Tel Aviv 2012. [17] S. Niger, Sholem Aleykhem. Zayne vikhtikste verk, zayn humor un zayn ort in der yidisher literatur [Scholem Alejchem. His Most Important Works, His Humor and His Position in Yiddish Literature], New York 1928. [18] D. Roskies, A Bridge of Longing. The Lost Art of Yiddish Storytelling, Cambridge (MA)/London 1995. [19] D. Sadan, Three Foundations, in: Prooftexts 1 (1986) 6, 55–63. [20] E. Spivak, Sholem Aleykhems shprakh un stil [Sholem Aleichem's Language and Style], Kiev 1940. [21] J. Weitzner, Sholem Aleichem in the Theatre, Northwood 1994. [22] M. Wiener, Tsu der geshikhte fun der yidisher literatur in 19tn yorhundert [On the History of Yiddish Literature in the 19th Century], 2 vols., New York 1946. [23] R. R. Wisse, Sholem Aleichem and the Art of Communication, Syracuse 1980.

DAN MIRON, NEW YORK

al-Thaqāfah

Title of an Egyptian cultural journal published between 1939 and 1953 that was of central significance for the literary life of Egypt. It served as the mouthpiece of liberal intellectuals interested in modern knowledge and education and moreover occupied a position open to the emigration of Jewish academics. In the early 1940s, the exiled

Semitic and Islamic scholar Paul Kraus (1904–1944) used *al-Thaqāfah* as a forum to present his research and findings to the interested Arabic-speaking public.

1. *al-Thaqāfah* and the liberal tradition
2. Paul Kraus

1. *al-Thaqāfah* and the liberal tradition

Al-Thaqāfah (The Culture) appeared in Cairo from 1939 to 1953 and was one of the most influential Egyptian cultural journals of the first half of the 20th century, together with *al-Hilāl* (The Crescent, 1892–1930), *al-Muqtaṭaf* (The Digest, 1876–1952), and *al-Risālah* (The Message, 1933–1953). Published weekly with an estimated circulation of 20,000 copies, it reached a broad readership among officials and the educated urban middle class [3. 187]. As the organ of the influential *Lajnah al-ta'līf wa-al-tarjamah wa-al-nashr* (Committee for Composition, Translation and Dissemination of Books) it was edited by the committee's chairman Ahmad Amin (1886–1954) and was associated with the tradition of some reform-oriented and liberal-minded Egyptian intellectuals around Amin and his writer colleague Taha Hussein (1889–1973).

Like many of their liberal contemporaries, Amin as well as Hussein had grown up in a traditional Cairo environment informed by religion before an impulse of modernization emerged in Egyptian society at the beginning of the 20th century. The resultant establishment of educational institutions in the European mold brought them into contact with Western, secular educational curricula as well as the ideas of the Islamic reform movement inspired by the Egyptian grand mufti Muhammad Abduh (1849–1905). In the early years, they both attended courses at the Egyptian University in Cairo, newly founded in 1908. With its orientation towards the French and British university tradition, it provided an alternative to the religious Islamic Al-Azhar University. In the absence of qualified Egyptians, the teaching staff in the first decades consisted mainly of European academics, above all Oriental scholars fluent in → Arabic such as Carlo Nallino, Ignazio Guidi, Louis Massignon, and Enno Littmann, who influenced the two young students greatly. Alumni of the Egyptian University like Amin and Hussein were part of a generation of intellectuals who represented the historical-critical method of modern Oriental studies (→ Orient; → Semitic Studies) in their country. Amin's three-part cultural history of early Islam – *Fajr al-Islām* (Dawn of Islam, 1928), *Ḍuḥā al-Islām* (Morning of Islam, 1933–1936), and *Ẓuhr al-Islām* (Noon of Islam, 1945–1955) – published in Cairo is an explicit example of the influence of the European academic tradition and also the first attempt by an Arabic-speaking Muslim to pursue Islamic historiography on a modern scholarly basis.

Committed to critical, modern scholarly writing, *al-Thaqāfah* occupied a progressive-liberal position, contributing significantly to the cultural production in Egypt during the war years in particular. At the same time, it remained aloof from the nationalist narrative that had been growing stronger since the 1930s, seeking to homogenize Egyptian society and attempting to exclude ethnic and religious minorities such as Jews, Armenians, and Greeks from participating in the societal discourse [4. 174–195]. Instead, the periodical provided a forum where Egyptians of all and any ethnic and religious background as well as exiled European scholars could publish their academic, literary, and journalistic works. It also published 15 journal articles by the Jewish Semitic and Islamic scholar Paul Kraus.

2. Paul Kraus

Paul Kraus was born in → Prague in 1904. He studied Oriental languages in his home city and moved to Palestine in 1925 as a member of the Zionist (→ Basel) youth movement *Tekhelet-Lavan* (Blue-White). Disillusioned with life in a kibbutz, he began studying biblical studies (→ Biblical criticism), → Semitic studies, and → archaeology at the recently founded → Hebrew University in Jerusalem as well as studying at the American School of Oriental Research, the École archéologique française in Jerusalem, and later at the École française orientale in Damascus. In 1927, he enrolled at Friedrich-Wilhelms-Universität in Berlin.

Kraus went to Berlin because of his interest in ancient Oriental studies. Joining the Berlin Institut für Semitistik und Islamkunde introduced him to the still-young discipline of Islamic studies (→ Muslim Studies), represented at the Institute above all by the Oriental scholars Carl Heinrich Becker (1876–1933) and Hans Heinrich Schaeder (1896–1957). Soon after his arrival in Berlin, Kraus began to focus on Arabic studies as well as researching the cultural and religious history of the Islamic world.

During his years of study in Prague and Berlin, Kraus acquired profound philological competence in a number of Near Eastern languages from cuneiform idioms of the ancient Near East such as Akkadian through → Aramaic to languages still spoken in the present like → Arabic, → Hebrew, Turkish, and Persian. The intellectual environment at the Berlin Institute honed his insight into matters of cultural history. At the same time, his academic self-understanding was formed by the philological tradition of German Oriental studies of the 19th century, which had received significant impulses from the → Wissenschaft des Judentums. While his dissertation was devoted to a topic of ancient Oriental studies, his postdoctoral thesis on the alchemist Jābir ibn Ḥayyān, with which he qualified as a professor in both Semitic and Islamic studies, shows his growing interest in Islamic civilization. Thanks to his research activities at the Berlin Institut für Geschichte der Naturwissenschaften, founded in 1927, he became one of the most prominent scholars on the field of medieval Islamic intellectual history. His studies on the history of Arabic alchemy focused on one of the central questions of research into the history of alchemy at the time, furnishing an important contribution to the more precise dating of the reception of Greek knowledge from Late Antiquity through the Islamic world.

After the first Jewish academics were removed from their positions at university of Berlin as a consequence of the Gesetz zur Wiederherstellung des Berufsbeamtentums (Law for the Restoration of the Professional Civil Service) in 1933, Kraus was obliged to abandon his academic career in Berlin. His mentor Becker advised him to emigrate to France, recommending him to the French Oriental scholar Louis Massignon (1883–1962); Kraus's increasing interest in mystical and heterodox trends within Islam during this time is due to the influence of Massignon who was fascinated by mysticism.

Besides working as a lecturer at the Institut d'histoire et de philosophie des sciences et des techniques of the Sorbonne founded in 1932 and headed by the French philosopher and historian of science Abel Rey (1873–1940), Kraus was mainly active at the École pratique des hautes études, which had become a first port of call for many Russian and German émigrés, many of them of Jewish origin, in the 1920s and 1930s. Like Kraus they frequently came from the educated middle class of Eastern or East Central Europe and had arrived in Paris after the transfer of power to Hitler, having previously studied at German → universities. Here, Kraus found a fertile academic environment among international émigrés, allowing him to communicate with prominent European scholars. Since their shared Paris exile, he and Leo Strauss (1899–1973; → Law), his future brother-in-law, for instance, had found a common interest in the writings of Arab philosophers of the Middle Ages

(→ Falsafah) such as al-Fārābī and Maimonides (→ Guide for the Perplexed); Kraus was able to help Strauss translate them. His lectures in Paris dealt with topics of Islamic studies and with the reception of ancient Hellenistic philosophers in the Arabic language-area, continuing his research in the Islamic and cultural history of the Near East. However, despite support from leading French Orientalist scholars, Kraus did not succeed in establishing himself as an academic in France; because of his Czechoslovak nationality he was never granted a university position.

Consequently Massignon, who had been a guest professor at the Egyptian University in 1912 and 1913, referred him to his former student Taha Hussein in Cairo. From 1936 onward, Kraus was able to teach Semitic philology, textual criticism, and editorial techniques at the Egyptian University, and from 1942 onward at the newly founded Farouk I University in Alexandria. In Egypt, Kraus was able to acquire considerable standing, especially among the local academic community. In 1942, he was unanimously voted into the prestigious Institut d'Égypte. It was also in Cairo that Kraus published his two-volume magnum opus *Jābir ibn Ḥayyān. Contribution à l'histoire des idées scientifiques dans l'Islam* in 1942–1943.

At the time when Kraus moved his exile to Cairo, Hussein was a full professor of Arabic literature and had just been appointed dean of the Faculty of Philosophy at the Egyptian University. One of his first official acts was to appoint Kraus a lecturer in the philological department of his faculty. However, with his liberal attitude, his critical publications, and his connection with the ruling *Wafd* party, Hussein had also made powerful enemies. His emphasis on European scholarly traditions in particular met with determined opposition. Many conservative contemporaries protested vehemently against the use of the methods of modern Orientalist scholarship. His study *Fī al-shiʿr al-jāhilī* (On

pre-Islamic poetry), in which he challenged the authenticity of pre-Islamic poetry, had given rise to a wide-ranging scholarly controversy in 1926, especially among the religious circles of the Islamic Al-Azhar University, triggered by the question of whether the methods of critical research should be applied to the study of sacred subject matter. In 1932 this resulted in his temporary suspension from university service and subsequently led to Hussein's academic position remaining uncertain and dependent on favorable political constellations.

In the 1930s, the political situation in Egypt was overall unstable. The Egyptian University became the main scene of political conflicts, accompanied by large-scale student protests. Those involved were in part drawn from fascist groups like *Miṣr al-Fatāh* (Young Egypt Party) and its paramilitary wing, the so-called Green Shirts. These nationalist movements were not only directed against the political leaders in the country but increasingly displayed signs of being influenced by European nationalism as well. Antisemitic and xenophobic attitudes were directed noticeably against the foreign scholars at the Egyptian University of whom Kraus was one.

With the beginning of the Second World War and military combat operations in North Africa, the political situation in Egypt deteriorated. While fascist Italy had been engaged in military action against the British in North Africa since September 1940 and been joined by German troops from March 1941 onward, the threat posed by Rommel's Afrikakorps became more acute in June 1942 (→ El-Alamein). Constant air raids on Alexandria by the Axis powers unsettled the local population. The climax of hostilities in North Africa, for the time being, came at the end of June 1942, when the Egyptian civilian population as well as the British military prepared for the invasion of Alexandria by the Axis powers. It was not until November that the 8th British Army, under its commander General Montgomery, was able to defeat the German and Italian armed forces at the gates of Egypt for good.

Despite the defeat of the Axis powers in North Africa, Kraus's position in his Egyptian exile became increasingly precarious. At the same time, he endeavored tirelessly to present the results of his research to an Arab expert audience. His contributions to *al-Thaqāfah*, which appeared between February 1943 and June 1944 in the category *Min minbar al-sharq* (From the pulpit of the East), discussed Greek-Arab subjects as well as his new theory on the metrics of Arabic poetry, which he expanded into a metrics of Semitic languages by applying it to kindred languages like Assyrian and → Hebrew. A lecture on the subject he presented at the → Hebrew University in Jerusalem in 1943 met with skepticism among the audience; the historian of religion Gershom Scholem (1897–1982; → Kabbalah) in particular rejected Kraus's assumptions. As the latter was considering emigrating to Palestine at this time, Scholem's rejection had far-reaching consequences.

In Cairo, Kraus continued to be dependent on Taha Hussein's protection. As a result of political change in October 1944, Hussein had to resign his post as the dean of the Faculty of Philosophy once again and informed his protégé Kraus of the latter's dismissal. A few short hours later, Kraus took his own life in his apartment in the Zamalek quarter of Cairo. In the presence of a small community of mourners, he was buried in the local Jewish cemetery. Besides the Arabist, diplomat, and future Israeli foreign minister Abba Eban, those present included the scholar Albert Hourani and his brother, the politician Cecile Hourani [6. 181]. Even after his death, Paul Kraus enjoyed a great reputation in Cairo for his comprehensive scholarship, his publications of eminent works of Oriental studies and his comprehensive knowledge of medieval Arabic [2. 38].

Bibliography

[1] R. Brague, Paul Kraus. Person und Werk (1904–1944), in: P. Kraus, Alchemie, Ketzerei, Apokryphen im frühen Islam. Gesammelte Aufsätze, ed. by R. Brague, Hildesheim/Zurich/New York 1994, vii–xiii. [2] R. Burger (ed.), Encounters and Reflections. Conversations with Seth Bernadete, Chicago/London 2002. [3] I. Gershoni, Reconstructing Tradition. Islam, Modernity, and National Identity in Egyptian Intellectual Discourse, 1930–1952, in: Tel Aviver Jahrbuch für deutsche Geschichte 30 (2002), 155–211. [4] A. Gorman, Historians, State and Politics in Twentieth Century Egypt. Contesting the Nation, London/New York 2003. [5] L. Hanisch, Die Nachfolger der Exegeten. Deutschsprachige Erforschung des Vorderen Orients in der ersten Hälfte des 20. Jahrhunderts, Wiesbaden 2003. [6] J. L. Kraemer, The Death of an Orientalist. Paul Kraus from Prague to Cairo, in: M. S. Kramer (ed.), The Jewish Discovery of Islam. Studies in Honor of Bernard Lewis, Tel Aviv 1999, 181–223. [7] A. M. H. Mazyad, Aḥmad Amīn (Cairo 1886–1954). Advocate of Social and Literary Reform in Egypt, Leiden 1963. [8] D. M. Reid, Cairo University and the Orientalists, in: International Journal of Middle East Studies 19 (1987), 51–75. [9] M. Ščrbačić, Von der Semitistik zur Islamwissenschaft und zurück. Paul Kraus (1904–1944), in: Jahrbuch des Simon-Dubnow-Instituts 12 (2013), 389–416.

MAJA ŠČRBAČIĆ, LEIPZIG/JERUSALEM

[The] Thaw

Title of the 1954 novel by the Soviet-Jewish author and journalist Ilya Ehrenburg (1891–1967). Published one year after Stalin's death, *Ottepel'* ("The Thaw," 1955) marked the start of extensive discussions on socialist realism, but also on the political conditions during and after Stalin's rule; the novel's title became synonymous with the beginning, short though it was, of Soviet reform. Characterized by ambivalences and abrupt breaks, Ehrenburg's work referred to the specific experiences of Jewish communists in the Soviet Union. The highpoint of Ehrenberg's fame was during the Second World War, when he distinguished himself with journalistic and propagandistic texts.

1. A code for a new time
2. Ilya Ehrenburg
3. Belonging, adaptation, dissidence

1. A code for a new time

In September 1954, Ilya Ehrenburg published his last novel *Ottepel'* ("The Thaw," 1955) after its first part had been published in April in the literary journal *Znamya*. Despite its limited literary quality, the book caused a sensation in the Soviet Union, as it showed one of the best-known Soviet writers breaking with the formal and aesthetic rules of socialist realism along with its subject matter. Ehrenburg included topics in the plot of the novel that had been taboo for the Soviet public, such as the Stalinist purges of the 1930s and the antisemitic campaign after the end of the Second World War (→ Cosmopolitans).

In the → novel, Ehrenburg gave literary expression to the criticism of socialist realism he had already expressed in October 1953 in his essay "O rabote pisatelya" (On the work of the writer). He had demanded the protagonists' inner life to be more clearly shown instead of describing, as was often the case in Soviet novels, the material contexts and manufacturing processes around them [4].

Two characters, Dmitri Koroteev and Lena Zhuravlyova, are at the center of the plot, which is set in the winter of 1953/1954 in a small town on the Volga and described by an auctorial narrator. A love affair burgeons between Koroteev, an engineer in the local machine factory, and Lena, a teacher married to the factory director. At first, they do not acknowledge their feelings, hanging on to their existing relationships. They justify the impossibility of change with moral concepts based on the Soviet ideal in which individual endeavors take second place to the expectations of the collective. Over the course of the novel, these concepts are weakened and ultimately overcome.

In the novel, Ehrenburg tried to contrast complex figures with inner struggles with each other and used this as the starting point for a discussion of the relationship between the private and working lives in the Soviet Union and of the function of art. Not only in the title but throughout the text, weather phenomena are used as metaphors of social and interpersonal relationships. At the end of the plot, the beginning thaw heralds the optimism of the coming spring which will bring the solution of many of the conflicts described in the book.

The image of the dawning of a new age as the novel's leitmotif could be seen as the author distancing himself from Stalin's rule without directly naming the latter. The title became the signum of the times after Stalin's death, times characterized by the end of political terror and the trend to opening up. In the Russian Empire of the 19th century, the term *ottepel'* ("thaw") had already denoted the period of political reforms after the death of Czar Nicholas I (→ Cantonists) [18]. The metaphor that provides the novel's title also expresses the political uncertainty of the time: the thaw is the first sign of spring, but it may still be followed by frost. While a certain degree of criticism of the Stalinist system became possible after Khrushchev's secret speech about Stalin's crimes on the occasion of the 20th Party Congress in 1956, regime critics and dissenters continued to be persecuted.

Beyond its political significance, the book also exerted considerable influence on the development of Soviet literature. Following the Second Congress of Soviet Writers in 1954, which Ehrenburg attended and during which he defended his writing strategy, a liberal and a conservative faction emerged among the writers, who would remain irreconcilably opposed until the fall of the Soviet Union in 1990/1991. The Soviet leadership made it known that while the party would not relinquish its claim to controlling literature, there would be an end to systematic arrests. As a consequence, numerous Soviet authors abandoned the previously prevailing schematic style of socialist realism; the dogma, however, was officially retained. With censorship being relaxed, novels such as Vladimir Dudintsev's *Ne khlebom yedinym* (1957; "Not by Bread Alone," 1957) could be published, which pointed to the ills in Soviet society and discussed subjects still considered sensitive.

2. Ilya Ehrenburg

Ilya Ehrenburg was born in Kiev (today Kyiv) in 1891 and grew up in a middle-class family in which Jewish religion and tradition had barely any significance. In his autobiography, he recollected having grown up among Russian children and only understanding → Russian [3. 12, 19–20]. Still, he emphasized that he was always aware of his Jewish origin and had never been ashamed of it. In 1895, the family was permitted to move to Moscow, where his father had a position as the director of a brewery. At his secondary school, Ehrenburg came across communist ideas early on and met Nikolai Bukharin (1888–1938), who was two years his senior. Electrified by the Russian Revolution of 1905, he began to be active in Bolshevik circles. In 1908 he was arrested by the Czarist secret police and imprisoned for five months. Afterwards, his father succeeded in obtaining a permit for him to leave the country.

Paris became Ehrenburg's new home, where he began to write. He was familiar with the circles of artists and bohemians who met in the cafés Closerie des Lilas and the Rotonde (→ École de Paris). He became friendly with Amedeo Modigliani, Pablo Picasso, Max Jacob, Fernand Léger, and Diego Rivera. His relationship with the revolutionary movement in Russia remained ambivalent. After a period in which he identified with the objectives of the Bolsheviks, Ehrenburg distanced himself from the revolutionaries after a meeting with Trotzky (→ Non-Jewish Jew; → Red Army) in 1909 and also resigned from the Russian Social Democratic Labor Party (RSDLP; *Rossijskaya sotsial-demokraticheskaya rabochaya partiya*, RSDRP).

During the First World War, Ehrenburg worked as a war correspondent for two Russian newspapers, writing reports of trench warfare on the Western Front at close range. After the → February Revolution, he returned to Russia in the summer of 1917. However, he found the civil war, the violence on both sides, and the anti-Jewish

Ilya Ehrenburg (1891–1967)

→ pogroms perturbing and deeply unsettling and decided in 1921 to return to Paris. Before he left, he applied for a Soviet passport. In Paris, he was expelled as an undesirable foreigner and settled in Berlin for two years, keeping company with Russian émigré circles. He also stayed in touch with representatives of the Soviet Union, meeting, among others, Vladimir Mayakovsky, Nikolai Bukharin, El Lissitzky (→ Wolkenbügel), and Isaac Babel (→ Red Cavalry). He helped other Soviet writers to be published in Western Europe.

In 1924, Ehrenburg was able to settle in Paris once more. He continued his activities as a mediator between Soviet and Western European art and literature. Towards the end of the 1920s, his views grew gradually closer to the official Soviet policy line – at a time when Stalin had already consolidated his leadership and enforced stricter regulations not least in cultural politics. Ehrenburg justified himself in his memoirs by saying that he realized during this time that there was no middle course in Europe between fascism and communism and that, consequently, he had to adopt a clear position.

From 1932 onward he became the France correspondent of the official government newspaper *Izvestiya*, placing himself at the service of Soviet propaganda. He used his contacts with French intellectuals, emerging as one of the organizers of the authors' conferences for the defense of culture in 1935 and 1937. He wrote articles on the Spanish Civil War (→ Botwin Company) in which reportage mixed with propaganda. Beginning in April 1939, in the run-up to the political change of course that led to the Molotov–Ribbentrop Pact, his articles were no longer printed. This situation changed only after the German invasion of the Soviet Union in June 1941, as a result of which Ehrenburg was appointed correspondent for the organ of the → Red Army *Krasnaya zvezda* (Red Star) [13. 203]. Until 1940, Ehrenburg had stayed in Paris, leaving for the Soviet Union only after the German army entered the city [13. 196].

During the Second World War, Ehrenburg developed extensive journalistic activity, publishing more than 1,500 articles many of which also appeared in the Western press, making him the most influential Soviet propagandist. He mainly aimed at mobilizing the Soviet population, highlighting a downright Manichaean contrast between fascism and anti-fascism and deliberately fanning hatred of the enemy. This culminated in the phrase "The Germans are not human beings" and in the order "Kill the Germans!" [6]. Ehrenburg was aware of the significance of his images, writing in 1942: "Hatred was not easy for us. [...] But now we understood that there was no place on earth for the fascists and us at the same time" (cited in [10. 300]).

Because of his importance for Soviet mobilization during the war, Ehrenburg became a figure of hate for National Socialist propaganda. He represented the Nazis' absolute enemy image, being a Jew, Russian, and a Bolshevik all in one person. This even persisted in the Federal Republic of Germany: after the publication of his memoirs was announced by Kindler Verlag in 1960, there were protests referring to his allegedly calling for the rape of German women in 1944; there was not, however, any evidence of this [10. 300].

The part played by Ehrenburg during the Stalinist terror before and after the Second World War, too, was a constant topic of Western and later post-Soviet discussion. While his attitude during the Great Terror of 1937 was criticized merely with regard to a degree of demonstrative indifference, serious accusations were levelled in the context of the antisemitic campaign of the postwar years (→ Cosmopolitans). Any active involvement on Ehrenburg's part has been refuted, but his responses to the Western media were often evasive or incorrect regarding the fates of individual Jewish writers and artists in the Soviet Union. Even so, his own life was in great danger during the antisemitic persecution. At the beginning of 1949, his name appeared on a list of members of the → Jewish Anti-Fascist Committee (*Yevrejskij antifashistskij komitet*) who were to be arrested. Stalin initialed the list in person but jotted a question mark next to Ehrenburg's name, thus saving him from arrest [1. 468]. Stalin was probably worried that Ehrenburg's disappearance might cause a stir, making it more difficult to conceal the antisemitic cleansings [7. 472].

At the time, Ehrenburg continued to comment publicly on Jewish issues. Thus, on the occasion of the foundation of Israel he wrote an article for *Pravda* in September 1948 discussing the relationship of Soviet Jews with the Jewish state. He pointed out that the Soviet Union was the first state to recognize Israel and that he welcomed its existence; at the same time he maintained that only the victory of socialism over capitalism could provide the "solution of the 'Jewish question,'" namely its societal abolition. He rejected Zionism as well as emigration to Israel [5].

Ehrenburg was able to observe the trial of the former members of the Jewish Anti-Fascist Committee in the summer of 1952 and the pogrom-like mood in January 1953 in the wake of the so-called Doctors' Plot at close range.

3. Belonging, adaptation, dissidence

Towards the end of his life, Ehrenburg repeatedly emphasized that his experiences made their way into his novels "as material for various inventions" [3. 10]. His literary work reflects the changeable and contradictory phases of his life in a multitude of text forms.

The beginning of his literary career went hand in hand with his disillusionment with the Bolsheviks in 1909, which plunged him into a deep existential crisis. For a time, he flirted with converting to Catholicism

(→ Conversion), dedicating his first volume of poetry, self-published in 1910, to Pope Innocent VI. His works of the time are characterized by Catholic mysticism [17. 182]. He distanced himself from his Jewish background, writing, for instance, in 1912: "I cannot live with you, Jews / You are strangers to me, I hate you" (cited in [8. 16]). Ehrenburg's poetic reaction to the October Revolution was also informed by mysticism and religiosity, now of the Russian Orthodox kind. In the poem *Molitva o Rossii* (1918; Prayer for Russia) we read: "Russia, that has lost its way on its hidden path / Forgive, Lord! / Rise, golden sun, / Churches white, domes sky-blue, / You, pious Rus!" (cited in [8. 17]).

The experiences of the First World War and during the Russian Civil War honed Ehrenburg's awareness of the upheavals of the modern age. In 1922, he wrote his first novel *Neobychajnye pokhozhdeniya Khulio Khurenito i yego uchenikov* (1930; "The Extraordinary Adventures of Julio Jurenito and his Disciples," 1930), which made him not only famous overnight but also the most-read author in the Soviet Union. This satirical text mocks the culture of Western Europe as well as the young, revolutionary movement in the Soviet Union, leaving the reader without hope. The main character Julio Jurenito explains that humanity is accustomed to cure its illnesses by shedding Jewish blood. The anti-Jewish violence of the Russian civil war appears as the symbol of the loss of all moral categories.

Between 1922 and 1931, Ehrenburg composed no fewer than 19 novels without, however, achieving the incisiveness, poignancy, and independence of his debut novel *Khulio Khurenito*. The plots of his subsequent books focused on love. Furthermore, his literary activity during the 1920s was characterized by distance to the emerging Soviet society. His short stories and novels were severely criticized in the Soviet Union but were still published – albeit in censored versions. His picaresque novel *Burnaya zhizn'*

Lazika Rojtshvanetsa (1960; "The Stormy life of Lasik Roitschwantz," 1960) was the only one prohibited in the Soviet Union until 1989. Ehrenburg drew on the motif of the wandering Jew (→ Ahasver), sketching a Jewish figure whose wanderings through many lands, searching for a place where he belonged, seems similar to the situation of the Soviet writer in exile and his existence between the worlds.

The beginning implementation of the first five-year plan and the start of collectivization in 1928 were the first incisive changes in the Soviet Union, which were reflected in Ehrenburg's literary activity. Jewish topics and characters, and in fact experimental characters altogether, vanished from his work. He dedicated himself to the principle of socialist realism, producing literature in accordance with the Soviet party line. His novel *Den' vtoroj* (1933; The second day), for example, focused on the implementation of the first five-year plan. At the center of the story is the inner conflict experienced by an intellectual desperately trying to commit entirely to the party, but whose conscience rebels against this submission; in the end, he commits suicide.

As a political writer, Ehrenburg unreservedly championed the regime in the 1930s but did not join in the hate campaigns initiated by the party that took place at the time of the first wave of terror. Subsequently, he published his world war epics *Padenie Parizha* (1942; "The Fall of Paris," 1943), *Burya* (1948; "The Storm," 1949), and *Devyatyj val* (1953; "The Ninth Wave," 1955), all of them appearing in large print runs and translated into a number of languages.

In *Burya*, Ehrenburg explicitly mentioned the → Holocaust. At the center of the plot are the two Jewish brothers Leo and Osip. One grows up in France, the other one in the Soviet Union. Ehrenburg emphasizes the differences between the two protagonists, which become particularly significant during the Second World War. While Osip fights in the ranks of the → Red Army, becomes a hero, and rises to the position of leading Soviet official, Leo dies in a gas chamber. In this clearly ideologically motivated juxtaposition of hero and victim, Ehrenburg also draws attention to the National Socialists' mass murder of Jews on Soviet territory and, unlike Soviet propaganda, reveals the Jewish victims among the Soviet population. In other texts as well Ehrenburg discussed the mass murder of the European Jews. In 1945, he had published the poem → *Babi Yar* about the mass shooting of Jews at the hands of German task forces in the ravine of that name near Kiev.

In addition to his literary activity, Ehrenburg also was active as a founding member of the → Jewish Anti-Fascist Committee. Together with Vasily Grossman (→ Stalingrad), he edited the *Chernaya kniga* ("The Black Book of Soviet Jewry," 1981) on the extermination of the Soviet Jews, the publication of which was prohibited by the Soviet authorities. Ehrenburg's ties to his Jewish background were strengthened by the Holocaust. In a radio interview in 1961, he declared that he would insist on being a Jew for as long as there were antisemites [17. 175].

Ehrenburg's last transformation occurred after Stalin's death: from a political writer he evolved into a prophetic one, trying to find his role as an artist anew and perceiving it in rather more visionary depictions of the future. To the surprise of many contemporaries, he transformed from an intellectual whose loyalty lay with Stalin to the spokesman of a group of writers demanding an end to the cult of personality and desiring to overcome the constricting rules of socialist realism. As a result, Ehrenburg was fiercely criticized by literary critics as well as the political leadership. In communist circles in the West his critical remarks also met with rejection.

His last great project was his six-volume memoir *Lyudi, gody, zhizn* ("People and

Life," 1961–1966). Ehrenburg died in 1967. The public was to be excluded from his burial, but a large crowd gathered at the gates of Novodevichy cemetery in Moscow. Security forces prevented them from joining the ceremony. At the end of his changeable life, Ehrenburg had finally become a symbolic figure for Soviet dissidents.

Bibliography

Sources

[1] K. Clark et al., Soviet Culture and Power. A History in Documents, 1917–1953. New Haven, 2007. [2] I. Ehrenburg, The Thaw, trans. by M. Harari, Chicago/London, 1955 [3] I. Ehrenburg, People and Life, Vol. 1: Memoirs of 1891–1917, trans. by A. Bostock/Y. Kapp, London, 1961. [4] I. Erenburg, O rabote pisatelya [On the Work of the Writer], in: Znamya 23 (1953) 10, 160–184. [5] I. Erenburg, Concerning a Certain Letter, in: Documents on Israeli-Soviet Relations 1941–1953, part 1, 1941–May 1949, London 2000, 352–360. [6] I. Ehrenburg, Ubej! [Kill!], in: Krasnaya zvezda [Red Star], July 24, 1942, 4.

Secondary literature

[7] K. Clark/E. Dobrenko, Soviet Culture and Power. A History in Documents, 1917–1953, New Haven 2007. [8] V. Dohrn, Il'ja Erenburg. Ein sowjetischer Schriftsteller jüdischer Herkunft, Bremen 1992. [9] B. Ya. Frezinskij, Ob Il'e Erenburge. Knigi. Lyudi. Strany [On Ilja Ehrenburg. Books. People. Countries], Moscow 2013. [10] K. Grüner, Ilja Ehrenburg in und über seine Zeit, in: Osteuropa 5 (1963), 294–306. [11] R.-R. Hammermann, Chassidisches Gedankengut in Ehrenburgs "Lazik Rojtsvanec," in: Wiener Slavistisches Jahrbuch 20 (1974), 37–52. [12] R. Lauer, Il'ja Ėrenburg und die russische Tauwetter-Literatur, Göttingen 1975. [13] L. Marcou, Ilya Ehrenbourg, un homme dans son siècle, Paris 1992. [14] B. M. Paramonov, Portret yevreya. Erenburg [Portrait of a Jew. Ehrenburg], in: Zvezda 1 (1991), 132–150. [15] J. Rubenstein, Tangled Loyalties. The Life and Times of Ilya Ehrenburg, New York 1996. [16] D. Rytman, Russian-Jewish Literature as a Mirror of the Fate of Russian Jewry. The Special Case of Ilya Ehrenburg, Ann Arbor 1994. [17] E. Sicher, Jews in Russian Literature after the October Revolution. Writers and Artists between Hope and Apostasy, Cambridge 1995. [18] P. Thiergen, "Tauwetter." Zur politisch-literarischen Sprache Rußlands, in: Zeitschrift für Slavische Philologie 40 (1978), 129–133. [19] A. Tippner, Bewegung und Benennung. Jüdische Identität bei Il'ja Ėrenburg, in: Osteuropa 58 (2008) 8–10, 331–340.

DAVID SCHICK, MUNICH

Theatre Criticism

Theatre criticism developed into an independent branch of journalism in 19th century Germany. In the Empire and Weimar Republic, it was especially Jewish authors who left their mark on the genre. Like journalism in general, theatre criticism opened up a field of activity for the academically trained, regardless of their origins, and, moreover, enabled participation in key cultural and social debates. In parallel, an antisemitic stereotype of "Jewish theatre criticism" developed.

1. Introduction
2. Symbolic participation
3. Anti-Jewish polemics

1. Introduction

The first reviews of dramas had already been appearing in early modern journals since 1688. Theatre criticism, which judged both text and staging in their artistic components, first developed as an independent genre in German-speaking lands in the 18th century as a part of the formation of a journalistic public sphere. As early as the late 18th century, two central moments in middle-class self-conception were combined in theatre criticism: on the one hand, the

THEATRE CRITICISM

theatre was perceived, in Schiller's sense, as a "moral institution"; on the other, criticism was assigned the role of public debate [15. 86]. In their combination, both point to the prominent role of theatre criticism in public debates, in which art was still understood, precisely in the 18th century, as separate from the political and economic sphere.

The first theatre critic is considered to have been Gotthold Ephraim Lessing, who, as a dramaturg at the Nationaltheatre at Hamburg, also acted as a critic. In his *Hamburgische Dramaturgie*, which appeared twice weekly between 1767 and 1769, he laid the central foundations for the emergence of theatre criticism and its criteria through his critiques, in which he discussed plays and their performances. According to Lessing, the critic monitors the work in the theatre and explains to his readers the literary repertoire, as well as the achievements of actors and poets [9. 16f.].

With the establishment of fixed state theatre houses, the number of publications on the theatre also grew from the second third of the 18th century. Thus, in 1802, the *Spenersche Zeitung*, which appeared in Berlin, introduced a continuing segment on the theatre in the → feuilleton. In the first half of the 19th century, theatre criticism was often written by authors, among whom were many Jewish writers. Whereas Ludwig Börnes's (1786–1837) critiques concerned the political and social role of the theatre, Moritz Gottlieb Saphir (1795–1858) excelled in polemical texts, which sometimes contained pungent ridicule and gossip. From 1827 onward, Saphir published, in the form of the *Berliner Courier*, a morning paper devoted to theatre, fashion, and urban life. He also established so-called night criticism, in which he discussed the respective staging on the very morning after the premiere, thus getting the jump on the competition and avoiding pre-censorship.

In the last third of the 19th century, theatre criticism developed, especially in Berlin, into a central component of the emerging mass press. The introduction of freedom of trade in Prussia and the North German Confederation in 1869 simplified the opening of theatres, which led to many new foundations and the diversification of the theatre landscape. Theatre and press contributed to the formation of an urban attitude toward life and created a modern public sphere [12]. The journalistic practice of theatre criticism deeply influenced Jewish authors. For them, the journalistic form of presentation, which had very high social importance, appeared as a possibility of symbolic participation in social life.

2. Symbolic participation

Toward the end of the 19th century, the field of theatre criticism was still relatively manageable. Moreover, many critics also worked in other areas, especially as writers, directors, playwrights, or theatre managers. In addition to Theodor Fontane (1819–1898), who worked as a theatre critic at the *Vossische Zeitung* beginning in 1870, and Paul Schlenther (1854–1916), who, from 1886, worked as Fontane's colleague, and later as his successor, taking over as head of the Vienna Burgtheatre in 1898, it was especially Oscar Blumenthal (1852–1927) and Otto Brahm (1856–1912; → Piscator Stage; → Regietheatre) who left their mark on Berlin theatre criticism in the late 19th century German Empire. Like most Jewish theatre critics, Blumenthal and Brahm had received doctorates in German studies and philology, but, because of the their Jewish origins, could hardly hope for a university career or a position in the civil service.

Oscar Blumenthal came from a family of Jewish merchants, and studied philology in Berlin and Leipzig from 1869. After receiving his doctorate in 1875, he worked until 1887 as critic and editor at the *Berliner Tageblatt*, where the ironic/sarcastic tone of his critiques earned him the nickname "bloody Oscar." Blumenthal cultivated the subjective quality of his contributions, which came to be the key component of the literary construction of his critiques. Thus, in a short piece from 1885, he fought against the demand for State control of the aesthetic and moral standards of the theatre, which was to take place as soon as a license was granted. As he phrased it with high irony, instead of paternalism from State authorities, one should "simply leave the surveillance of taste to the aesthetic security service of critique" [2. 351]. In 1888, he opened the newly constructed Lessingtheatre as its director, with the programmatic intention of dedicating it to contemporary drama [21]. Nevertheless, his first production was Lessing's play *Nathan der Weise* ("Nathan The Wise"). Both his own hit plays, such as the comedy *Im weißen Rößl* (1897; "The White Horse Inn," 1935), and the dramas of Hermann Sudermann, which were popular at the time, could be seen in his private, profit-oriented "Theatre der Lebenden" (Theatre of the Living). Blumenthal was among the most often-performed stage authors in the 1890s, and advocated a variety of forms and genres of the theatre, both as a critic and as a theatre director.

In contrast, Otto Brahm promoted naturalism in the theatre, and imposed it on Berlin stages. Brahm, the son of a Jewish merchant, studied German language and literature at Berlin, and received his doctorate in Jena in 1897. He was first employed, together with Fontane and Schlenther, as a theatre critic at the *Vossische Zeitung*, before founding, together with other personalities of literary and cultural life, the *Freie Bühne* association after the French model in 1889. On the one hand, it championed the staging of naturalistic dramas and organized their performance as private events in order to circumvent censorship laws. On the other hand, beginning in 1890, it published the eponymous journal, which reported on cultural and intellectual life . In 1894, Brahm

took over the direction of the Deutsches Theater, and correspondingly reduced his activity as a critic [19]. Unlike Blumenthal, whose opinions and personal taste formed the nucleus of his critiques, Brahm understood theatre criticism as part of social criticism and a project of political reform, which he articulated by his advocacy of naturalism.

Around 1900, theatre criticism became considerably professionalized. Critics such as Alfred Kerr (1867–1948) and Siegfried Jacobsohn (1881–1926; → Weltbühne) now devoted themselves exclusively to their profession and achieved the status of widely-respected voices of the journalistic public sphere. Against the background of the large number of competing newspapers and journals, critics often courted readers with particularly sharp phrasing, which artists often lamented. Thus, in 1902, the dramatist Hermann Sudermann wrote a polemic pamphlet with the accusatory title *Verrohung in der Theatrekritik*, in which he lamented the commercialization and sheer joy in destruction. He was answered by one of the highest-profile contemporary theatre critics, Alfred Kerr, who declared criticism itself to be a form of art *sui generis* and the critic a poet.

Kerr studied German language in Breslau and Berlin, completing his doctorate in 1894 at the University of Halle. He had written theatre criticism for various newspapers and journals since his student days. In 1909, he wrote as theatre critic for the Berlin newspaper *Der Tag*, and in 1912 edited the weekly *Pan*. Kerr brought the subjectivity of his critiques to a zenith, which also found formal expression: even externally, his reviews were easily recognizable by their division into subsections marked off by Roman numerals. Kerr advocated naturalism, but polemicized against Max Reinhardt (→ [The] Great World Theatre).

Besides Herbert Ihering (1888–1977), Kerr was the most respected theatre critic in the Weimar Republic. His move to the *Berliner Tageblatt* in 1919 was considered a public political event. The fact that such incidents were widely debated corresponds to the increased importance of the theatre and theatre criticism in the Weimar period. In retrospect, the author, philosopher, and theatre critic Ludwig Marcuse (1894–1971; → Alexanderplatz) spoke about it in these terms: "In social gatherings, the talk was not about the Treaty of Versailles, nor even about a theatre performance, but about the theatre politics of theatre criticism. The theatre was the church of the time, and the theatre critic was its militant theologian" [4. 68].

In this context, a series of Jewish critics now appeared not only as authors but also published their own journals. Prototypical for this development was Maximilian Harden (1861–1927). This merchant's son first underwent training as an actor, converted to Protestantism in 1878 (Conversion), and, from 1884 onward, worked as a theatre critic for various periodicals. In 1892, he founded his own journal, entitled *Die Zukunft*. Harden vehemently advocated a liberal theatre landscape, independent of State structures. His pamphlet *Berlin als Theatrehauptstadt*, published in 1888, consequently focused primarily on private theatres, whereas for the court theatre he attested "the artistic bankruptcy, the complete renunciation of any leading position in the life of German theatre" [3. 153]. Less dogmatic than Brahm in his aesthetic judgments, Harden deliberately opposed the imperial court and used his journal as a forum for this purpose. This conflict culminated between 1907 and 1909 in the so-called Harden-Eulenburg Affair, in which Harden combined criticism of the policies of the imperial house with allusions to the homosexuality of close advisors to Kaiser Wilhelm II.

Other Jewish journalists took Harden, *qua* independent author and publisher, as their role model. In Vienna in 1899, Karl Kraus founded → *Die Fackel*, for which he acted not only as publisher, but also, from

1912, as the sole author. In the process, he extended the field of his criticism from artistic production to politics and society. Siegfried Jacobsohn followed in 1905 with *Die Schaubühne*, which, once renamed in 1918 as the *Weltbühne*, bore its extension to political criticism in its very name. With this politicization, theatre criticism achieved the status of a journalistic genre of its own. At first, its authors considered it as a substitute for political expression and broadened it accordingly. As the embodiment of an artistic form that was public because it was collectively absorbed, the theatre provided an important forum for dealing with social questions. It was precisely Jewish intellectuals who took part in discussions of → art in the context of a society in which an equal role in politics, administration, and scholarship often remained forbidden to them.

In the 1920s, journalistic theatre and cultural criticism developed into a discourse on the social conditions and the symptomatic significance of art and culture. Thus, for instance, the theatre critic, writer, and playwright Julius Bab (1880–1955) defined artistic experience as a social event as well: "In fact, an experience that is so thoroughly social must be supported by the society, also economically, if it is not to be damaged" [1. 160]. In the works of authors such as Walter Benjamin (→ Angelus Novus) or Siegfried Kracauer (→ Film) art criticism ultimately became a social philosophy and was opened up to academic writing.

3. Anti-Jewish polemics

Professionalized theatre criticism, which increased with the expansion of the newspaper business (→ Press), sometimes filled contemporaries with deep unease and became the object of antisemitic resentment (→ Conspiracy). Here, Jewish critics and journalists became the embodiment of a supposed cultural decline. Thus, in his 1852 comedy *Die Journalisten* ("The Journalists,"

1899), Gustav Freytag (1816–1895) depicted the Jewish editor Blumenthal and his author Schmock – the term, taken from the → Yiddish, soon became a suggestive synonym for a self-righteous, pushy journalist – as negative figures. Both embodied a fashion-oriented, superficial journalism that made public discourse degenerate into a business. In *Das Judenthum in der Musik* (1850; "Judaism in Music," 1910) Richard Wagner pointedly denied Jews any ability for art and for a "life replete with art-possibilities" [7. 25] (→ Music). In Wagner, the confrontation between the visionary artist, on the one hand, and the nit-picking, brooding Jew on the other, formed the nucleus of art criticism by Jews, whom he reproached with backwardness and otherness [7. 19f.]. He articulated that association of anti-modern fear of loss and antisemitic resentment that was typical of antisemitism in the Empire. In *Die fröhliche Wissenschaft* (1882; "The Joyful Wisdom," 1910, retranslated as "The Gay Science," 2006) Friedrich Nietzsche also attested that the Jews had a specific talent for criticism, which he traced back to their claim to be a chosen people, "because they are the moral genius among the nations (because they had a more profound contempt for the human being in themselves than any other people)" [6. 188]. It was from their Jewish → self-hatred that their inclination to acting and criticism emerged. As the alleged controllers of the European press and as born literati, Jews exerted public influence primarily on the basis of their acting abilities: that is, they played "the 'expert,' 'the specialist'" [6. 317]. To the activity of the critic, which he considered as corrosive and destructive, Nietzsche diametrically opposed a genuine, creative art.

The negative figure of the Jewish critic was also taken up by Jewish intellectuals. Thus, in 1888, the journalist and theatre critic Fritz Mauthner (→ Critique of Language) born in Bohemia in 1849, published a sharp polemic

against contemporary journalism in his satire *Schmock oder Die literarische Karriere der Gegenwart*. The work, which gives otherwise failed existences fictional and satirical advice for a successful career as a critic, plays with antisemitic elements in several passages. Among other things, Mauthner suggests changing Jewish-sounding names (→ Naming) and the → conversion of Jews, if they wanted to prove themselves as critics. Here, his contemptuous image of journalism and of criticism probably reflected his own ambivalent relation to his Jewish origins – Mauthner left Judaism in 1891, but never converted – and those attacks with which he found himself repeatedly confronted. He also opposed the "decay" of the German language, as well as the immigration of Jews from Eastern Europe (→ Scheunenviertel; → Ostjuden), which, in his view, exacerbated antisemitism and demanded a resolute → assimilation.

In general, the theatre criticism written by Jewish authors equally reflected the possibility of participating in society, which had been opened up to Jews since the late 19th century, but also their exclusion. The transfer of power to Hitler spelled the end of forthright criticisms and commentaries on social and theatrical life. From now on, the previous reviews by individual journalists were replaced by a national "art appreciation" that refrained from any individual evaluation and feigned objectivity. This was directed in particular against Jewish critics, who were reproached with wanting to put on airs in public with their subjective opinions. In May 1936, Joseph Goebbels, Reichsminister for Public Enlightenment and Propaganda, began by prohibiting opening night reviews; in November of the same year he forbade art criticism of any kind. In the following years, most of the Jewish theatre critics of the Weimar period emigrated, including Alfred Kerr.

Bibliography

Sources

[1] J. Bab, Das Theatre im Lichte der Soziologie, Leipzig 1931. [2] O. Blumenthal, Theatralische Eindrücke, Berlin 1885. [3] M. Harden, Berlin als Theatrehauptstadt, in: P. W. Marx/S. Watzka (eds.), Berlin auf dem Weg zur Theatrehauptstadt. Theatrestreitschriften zwischen 1869 und 1914, Tübingen 2009, 147–169. [4] L. Marcuse, Mein zwanzigstes Jahrhundert. Auf dem Weg zu einer Autobiographie, Zurich 1975. [5] F. Mauthner, Schmock oder Die literarische Karriere der Gegenwart, Berlin 1888. [6] F. Nietzsche, The Gay Science. With a Prelude in Rhymesand an Appendix of Songs, trans. by W. Kaufmann, New York 1974. [7] R. Wagner, Judaism in Music, trans. by E. Evans, London 1910.

Secondary literature

[8] H. Adamski, Diener, Schulmeister und Visionäre. Studien zur Berliner Theatrekritik der Weimarer Republik, Frankfurt am Main et al. 2004. [9] V. Boenisch, Krise der Kritik? Was Theatrekritiker denken – und ihre Leser erwarten, Berlin 2008. [10] G. Erken/T. Koebner, Gattungstheoretische Überlegungen zur Theatrekritik, in: Jahrbuch für Internationale Germanistik 3 (1971) 1, 96–105. [11] M. Fontius, Art. "Kritisch/Kritik," in: Ästhetische Grundbegriffe. Historisches Wörterbuch in sieben Bänden, ed. by K. Barck et al., vol. 3, Stuttgart/Weimar 2005, 450–489. [12] P. Fritzsche, Reading Berlin 1900, Cambridge (MA) 1996 [13] P. Gay, Weimar Culture. The Outsider as Insider, New York 2001. [14] J. Habermas, The Structural Transformation of the Public Sphere. An Inquiry into a Category of Bourgeois Society, Cambridge (MA) 1989. [15] P. W. Marx, Theatrekritik – ein Diskurs zwischen Theatrewissenschaft und Theatrepraxis?, in: H. Kurzenberger/A. Matzke (eds.), TheorieTheatrePraxis, Berlin 2004, 147–156. [16] P. W. Marx, Gab es eine "jüdische Theatrekritik"? Anmerkungen zur Situation und Bedeutung der Theatrekritik in Deutschland, 1870–1933, in: G. Nickel (ed.), Beiträge zur Geschichte der Theatrekritik, Tübingen 2007, 239–258. [17] D. Schaaf, Der Theatrekritiker Arthur Eloesser, Berlin 1962. [18] H. Schneider, Alfred Kerr als Theatrekritiker. Untersuchung zum Wertsystem des Kritikers, 2 vols., Rheinfelden 1984. [19] O. Seidlin, Der Theatrekritiker Otto Brahm, Bonn 1978. [20] S. Volkov, Antisemitismus als kultureller Code. Zehn Essays, Munich 2000. [21] J. Wilcke, Das Lessingtheatre in Berlin unter Oscar Blumenthal (1888–1898). Eine Untersuchung mit besonderer Berücksichtigung der zeitgenössischen Theatrekritik, Berlin 1958.

PETER W. MARX, COLOGNE

Theory

In modernity, the concept of theory (Gr. *theoría*) comprises both the explanatory modes of the sciences and the grand future concepts and theory movements that have spread virulently since the mid-19th century. In the second of these denotations, in particular, the concept of theory was tied to Judaism in manifold and often problematic ways in the imagination of the 20th century. After the expulsion from Europe and the reshaping of their work in exile, many Jewish thinkers transformed the concept of theory, with ramifications that lasted long into the postwar years.

1. Introduction
2. Marx, Nietzsche, Freud
3. A new Jewish self-understanding
4. Expulsion and exile
5. The logic of science
6. From Lukács to Adorno
7. After 1945

1. Introduction

In modern Jewish thought, theory is an umbrella term that brings various *topoi* of the Jewish history of knowledge, of ideas, and of politics into a comprehensive and unified perspective. It denotes the so-called contributions of the Jews to European sciences as well as their considerable share in revolutionary theory trends. These facts might alternatively be traced back to a complex interplay of social exclusion and inclusion, to the secularized legacy of traditional Jewish textual scholarship, to the compensation of metaphysical homelessness, or to a specifically Jewish → self-hatred – but all these *topoi* remain incomplete as long as they fail to address the common *problem* of theory in modern Jewish thought. In the Jewish history of theory, in fact, the paradoxes and blurrings of the general concept of theory are intensified. Modern Jewish thought was informed by the opposition of theory and practice, but also of theory and life, as expressed in Goethe's much-quoted lines: "My worthy friend, gray are all theories, / And green alone Life's golden tree" ("Faust," 1871; → Elective Affinities). Theory always claimed to be able to explain the world as it is, but it has always been suspected of growing increasingly removed from reality. Jews were considered to be the originators of the most important grand theories of the modern age; at the same time, they noted the problematic character of theory with particular keenness.

In the conceptual history of theory since Greek Antiquity, the theoretician was originally someone who observed the stars. Aesop's fable of the unnamed astronomer who, gazing up at the sky, trips over an obstacle on the ground, falls into a well, and is mocked by a handmaid, is an early instance. Plato changed the story in characteristic fashion in *Theaetetus*, transferring it from the unnamed astronomer onto Thales, the founder of → philosophy [7]. In this primal scene of theory, theoretical life is contrasted with reality, a contrast that was buried for a long time by the modern opposition between theory and practice. Around 1900, it also received a characteristic Jewish attribution tied in with the metaphor of the

→ Luftmenschen and the rootless Jewish intellectuals (→ Sociology of Knowledge).

Aristotle separated theoretical life from political-practical life (*bios politikos*, Lat. *vita activa*), as well as from the life of pleasure or appetite (*bios apolaustikos*; Lat. *vita voluptuosa*). Theoretical life is the only one not pursued for personal advantage, so it constitutes the highest form of human praxis. The Aristotelian concept of theory was subject to many changes during Antiquity and the Middle Ages but underwent its decisive transformation in modern philosophy. To begin with, theory was devalued in relation to praxis. Soon the term theory was used to refer to hypotheses that had to prove their validity by means of their agreement with phenomena. With the pluralization of the concept of theory from 1750 onward, the term could be used to denote partial conjectures (theories of this and that), whereas theory had previously always been *the* theory of the whole. Ultimately, theory was defined by its contrast with the abundance of life, as codified in Goethe's powerful verse. German idealism, above all, as represented by Hegel, expanded the concept of theory to comprise all thought and describe the gradual process of the mind becoming aware of itself [21]. The concept of theory characteristic of the history of Jewish thought between 1843 and 1941 denotes the post-Hegelian materialistic understanding of this specific growing self-awareness, an understanding that fed the universalist "grand narratives" (Jean-François Lyotard) of the modern age. This applies above all to Marxism (→ Class Consciousness), → psychoanalysis, and to a certain extent to Nietzsche's philosophy (→ Übervolk) as well.

2. Marx, Nietzsche, Freud

Between 1843 and 1941, the "grand narratives" of the modern age took shape, while the concept of science and scholarship on which they were based had not yet crumbled. History and the present were radically aligned towards the horizon of an open future. The grand theories of modernity were thus always directed at the ultimate sublation of theory within transformed societal praxis. This was nowhere expressed more clearly than in the words of Edmund Husserl (→ Phenomenology), one of the most vigorous proponents of the theory paradigm, who declared in 1920: "All theory is as nothing to me, unless it be for a new world" [13. 16].

Pathos formulas of this kind reached beyond all differences of political opinions and were not reserved for Marxist thinkers alone. Moreover, to Karl Marx the relationship between theory and practice was considerably more complex than the famous *Thesen über Feuerbach* (1845; "Theses on Feuerbach," 2010) would suggest. The eighth thesis states: "All mysteries which lead theory to mysticism find their rational solution in human practice and in the comprehension of this practice" [15. vol. 5, 5]. This concept of theory is closely linked with the opposition between mere interpretation of the world and changing it as conceived in the eleventh thesis: "The philosophers have only interpreted the world, in various ways; the point is to change it" [15. vol. 1, XIV]. However, the narrative of communist society was also a "theory," whose practical objective, as phrased in the *Communist Manifesto*, "may be summed up in the single sentence: Abolition of private property" [15. vol. 6, 498]. At the same time, Marx regarded the "contempt for theory [...] as an end in itself" as a prominent feature of Jewish religion [15. vol. 3, 172].

Despite converting to Protestantism (→ Conversion), Marx always remained recognizable as a Jew. To him, this recognizability of Jewishness was a problem that could be solved by means of theory. If we follow the genesis of Marxism out of the aporia

of his early text *Zur Judenfrage* (1843/1844; "On the Jewish Question," 1926; → Jewish Question), the metaphors (about which a controversial debate continues to this day) of Jewish participation in → money lending, with their antisemitic connotation, appear to have a compensatory function within the subsequently canonized theory of society. They become accessible in the context of Marx's attempt to solve the Jewish question through the "organisation of civil society" [15. vol. 3, 77]. This kind of organization, the context suggests, would abolish the preconditions for Jewish differentness in the non-Jewish majority society. Communist society was precisely designed in such a way to render the characteristics of Jewishness invisible.

The way Jewish thinkers interpreted Friedrich Nietzsche in the early 20th century led to his precarious incorporation into the Jewish theory canon (→ Übervolk). Jewish thinkers from Martin Buber (→ Dialogue) to Leo Strauss (→ Law) understood *Zarathustra* as a new Bible (or parody of the Bible) – as a comprehensive new explanation of the world that would replace the Jewish-Christian explanation of the world. Its central figure, the "Superman" (Übermensch), was supposed to establish new value concepts after the death of God.

In Sigmund Freud's writings, the concept of theory occurs primarily in the denotation of developing a scientific hypothesis, but → psychoanalysis as such is a grand narrative sort of theory that was supposed to supersede the Jewish faith. Freud may be seen as the prototype of the "psychological Jew" (Philip Rieff) – that is, one who adheres to a diffuse sense of Jewishness without being able to imbue it with any substance. In his few personal remarks on the subject, Freud explained that "dark emotional powers" he could not put into words bound him to Judaism [10. 368]. In his theoretical writings, however, he declared religion – and, with increasing explicitness, Judaism – to be a neurosis. His late work *Der Mann Moses und die monotheistische Religion* (1939, "Moses and Monotheism," 1939) was devised to contain the narrative of Judaism with the help of psychoanalytic theory and thus surpass its comprehensive explanatory claim. For Freud, theory promised a sense of belonging within which the characteristics of Jewish differentness would no longer be visible, guaranteed by Jews' ability to participate in the academic culture without being discriminated against – unlike Freud's experience (→ Numerus Clausus).

Marx, Nietzsche, and Freud are the originators of the modern concept of theory, understood as a comprehensive explanation of the world radically directed at a future horizon. All three of them aimed to produce a theory that would supersede the religious interpretation. Marx, Nietzsche, and Freud constitute the climax of the modern critique of religion. All three not only compared religion to drugs that kept the masses in a state of immaturity but also devised a grand theory to fill the vacancy left by the declining religious explanation of the world. They explained the origin of religion as class struggle, the will to power, or collective immaturity and posited a new objective for humanity to replace religion: the classless society, the Superman, or humanity as seen by a science free of prejudice. It was this concept of theory that found itself in a deep crisis in the late 1930s, when a profound change of the temporal horizon of theory emerged due to the rise of National Socialism and the expulsion of Jewish scholars and scientists. In retrospect, this change appeared to have been foreshadowed in the history of Jewish → emancipation, in which the aims of theory were closely associated with the hopes and failure of Jews being accepted into European academia.

3. A new Jewish self-understanding

When the universities opened to Jewish students and scholars in the 19th century, the project of theory presented a welcome alternative to Jews who no longer felt connected to Jewish tradition and who strove for → assimilation. In 1904 the philosopher Hermann Cohen (→ Concept of God), the first German Jew to be appointed to a professorship in 1876, expressed the hope that comprehensive systematic and historical studies on Jewish thought would "compel respect" and that tolerance would be "a consequence of theoretical culture" [8. 124]. This expectation was not fulfilled, because theory contributed little to the invalidation of antisemitic prejudice and the acceptance of Judaism. On the contrary, the model of the Jewish "contribution" to German culture that Cohen implied was increasingly regarded as part of the problem. Thus, Leo Löwenthal (→ Institute for Social Research), in his early series of articles *Judentum und deutscher Geist* (1926–1932), sought to dispel the "suspicion" that the objective was "to validate apologetically the Jews' having-been-present-as-well" [14. 9]. German Jews' aspiration to be recognized as Germans on the basis of their intellectual achievements found its ultimate expression in the entry "Philosophie, Juden in der" in the *Jüdisches Lexikon* (1930; → Encyclopedias), which was able to handle the plurality of Jewish thought from the mid-19th century onward only by providing a purely additive list of names.

Theory was all the more effective at articulating a new Jewish self-understanding that delimited itself equally from tradition and Jewish nationalism, appealing instead to the universalist elements of Judaism. This self-understanding was largely articulated on the fringes of Western European thought, and only in rare instances did it include a positive connection to Judaism. Rather theory, conceived as a universal metalanguage, was the paradigmatic medium for dissolving Jewishness into the general. The elementary process was to transfer religious concepts, or concepts with even the slightest religious connotation, into a social semantics that would erase all traces of origin and tradition or absorb them into a universal project. This concept of theory entered into a severe crisis from the late 1930s onwards, and most deeply in 1940/1941. The universalist program was limited in that external characteristics of Jewishness had never ceased to be visible to the non-Jewish surrounding culture. As early as 1937, the lawyer and author Franz Rudolf Bienenfeld wrote about the "type of non-religious Jew who relinquished Jewish customs, assumed those of his environment, and who yet in most cases could be distinctly recognised as a Jew" that emerged in the middle of the 18th century [6. 6].

This type was canonized in the figure of the → non-Jewish Jew, who stands "within a Jewish tradition" according to its originator Isaac Deutscher [9. 26]. Other relevant points of reference are Hannah Arendt's construct of a "hidden" Jewish tradition that takes as its basis the "conscious" position of the Western European Jews as society's outsiders [4. 99–101], and George Steiner's "Meta-Rabbis," who are primarily recognizable as the secularized heirs of the ancient rabbinical art of interpretation [17].

4. Expulsion and exile

From 1933 onward, approximately 2,000 academics and scientists were expelled from Germany, most of whom were Jews or socialists (or both) [22]. The places of exile were many, but from the point of view of the history of theory, transit locations such as Paris and → New York were particularly significant. Moreover, they were hubs

where German-Jewish scholarly traditions of theory encountered the traditions of the respective host countries, resulting in multifarious tensions but also in unexpected new perspectives. In the 1930s, Paris was a sanctuary for intellectuals such as Walter Benjamin (→ Angelus Novus) and Hannah Arendt (→ Judgement), who survived there in difficult material circumstances and with barely any opportunities to publish. A variety of scholarly circles and traditions came together in Alexandre Kojève's (→ Recognition) Hegel lecture in Paris beginning in 1933, in which Hegel's grand theory was ironically revived and, by projecting the end of history in which philosophy and theory would end as well, disbanded at the same time. Walter Benjamin, meanwhile, was experimenting with the possibility of construction and assembly superseding theory altogether. However, his numerous drafts of *Passagen-Werk* do not provide a conclusive result.

As a transit location, Paris was also a place of anticipated departures from Europe. New York was frequently the first port of call for academics who – facing increasingly severe immigration conditions – were able to emigrate to the United States. Siegfried Kracauer (→ Film), who reached New York on one of the last ships from → Lisbon, wrote to Max Horkheimer (→ Dialectic of Enlightenment): "It was the darkest time in eight dark years. Once I am even halfway to feeling calm again, I shall note down our experiences over the last two years under the title *Journey to America*. Either I shall succeed in putting Kafka in the shade, or I shall not have been capable of describing the events properly" [3. 428]. The primary host institutions that provided the exiled academics at least temporary employment included the → New School for Social Research, Columbia University – home to, among other things, the exiled → Institute for Social Research – as well as a number of non-university institutions. From these, most of them moved on to universities where they finally established their iconic status as representatives of a lost tradition.

Clear indications of their later fame were already present early in their extraordinary ability as seismographs of the transformations that theory had undergone in the meantime. As early as 1936, Husserl (→ Phenomenology) had written that "the dream [of pure philosophy as a strict science] is over" [11. xxxi]. However, he, too, stuck to theoretical work; when he discovered the "life-world" in his later works [11. xi], he arrived at a theoretical innovation that would only be honored many years later during a phase of normalization in the history of theory.

In exile, the problematic aspects of the German tradition of theory moved front and center. The change to another language of academic discourse, in itself, often brought changes in the concept of theory. At the same time, political developments prompted new questions that older theories did not seem to adequately answer. For example, Hannah Arendt presented contemporary human rights issues as a problem for which the German philosophical tradition did not have a language [5. 113f.]. Lastly, the readjustment of theoretical categories was also due to the foci set by the institutions where the exiled academics found employment.

At the New School for Social Research, research at the interface of economic theory and social politics was replaced, at least temporarily, with studies that sought to locate the origins of National Socialism in German → philosophy. In the frequently heated debates of 1940/1941, which shifted the boundaries of the discussions around 1915 only slightly, many German-Jewish exiles learned to reassess the essentially metapolitical German theoretical tradition that had been their own background in light of the political events. Franz Neumann and Herbert Marcuse had similar experiences when they placed their profound knowledge

of German politics and culture at the service of enemy intelligence with the Office of Strategic Services from 1942 onward. The crisis of exile forced even the radical theory program of the → Vienna Circle to restructure its conception of the theory of science and of politics.

5. The logic of science

Modern theory always served simultaneously a descriptive and a prognostic purpose; it added a progressive temporal horizon to the comprehensive analysis of reality, frequently inferring statements on the future course of events from its findings. This also applied to the teachings of the logic of science (also known as Logical Empiricism or Logical Positivism), which were frequently suspected of serving only the status quo. The project of the logic of science is primarily associated with the → Vienna Circle (Moritz Schlick, Otto Neurath, Herbert Feigl, Victor Kraft, Hans Hahn), but it had proponents in Berlin (Hans Reichenbach) and Prague (Rudolf Carnap) as well.

Furthermore, across all internal differences within the schools, the logic of science may be understood as the strongest variant of the ideal theory of science Husserl once described as "the self-contained system of propositions" [12. 101]. As the manifesto *Wissenschaftliche Weltauffassung* (1929) stated, the project of the Vienna Circle was characterized by "the search for a neutral system of formulae, for a symbolism freed from the dross of historical languages; [...] the search for a total system of concepts. Neatness and clarity are striven for, and dark distances and unfathomable depths rejected. There are no 'depths' in science; surface is everywhere: everything experienced forms a complex, not always discernible web that can often be grasped through its details only" [18. 11f.].

This program was vehemently directed against all religion and metaphysics, especially in the case of Rudolph Carnap.

Statements on God or the soul were, according to Carnap, simply meaningless sentences (*Scheinprobleme in der Philosophie*, 1928). This radical scientism was predominantly linked to a socialist ideology. While political views were programmatically intended to be strictly separate from theoretical work (*Theoretische Fragen und praktische Entscheidungen*, 1934), scientific doctrine was often directly linked to political programs, for instance, on the democratization of knowledge. A paradigmatic instance of this is Otto Neurath's invention of the statistical visual language Isotype, in which certain statistical ratios of populations were no longer represented by diagrams but by a corresponding number of human figures with the aim of making them vivid and comprehensible to a greater number of people.

It was not only through the connection with political practice but also within the scientific context itself that the logic of science occupied a paradoxical position in relation to theory. Ludwig Wittgenstein (→ Critique of Language), who had ties to the Vienna Circle for a time, formulated the empiricist position as follows: "[And] we may not advance any kind of theory. There must not be anything hypothetical in our considerations. We must do away with all *explanation*, and description alone must take its place" [19. 47e]. It was via this anti-theoretical tenet, whose coherence was controversial from the point of view of philosophy – after all, even the rejection of theory was obviously guided by a theory – that the logic of science was closely linked to the idea of Jewish "positivism" in the antisemitic imagination. The Vienna Circle, especially, was regarded as "Jewish."

Thus, the logic of science was a "theory" primarily in the sense of the hypotheses on which it based its articulation of the "scientific worldview" ("wissenschaftliche Weltauffassung"); however, on the basis of these hypotheses it simultaneously developed a grand theory intended to permeate all aspects of social life. The manifesto *Wissenschaftliche Weltauffassung* already displayed clear signs of a self-understanding according to which the new unified science was meant to prepare the progressive rebuilding of society along rational-logical criteria. At no point were there significant signs of Jewish self-understanding or reflections on a Jewish question of any kind. Otto Neurath's early study on Jewish colonization in Palestine was written from a purely professional perspective. The antisemitic perception of the Vienna Circle as Jewish did not refer to the background of individual members but rather to the "method," the school itself. Accordingly, after the philosopher Moritz Schlick was murdered in Vienna in 1936 by his former student Hans Nelböck, the theoretical method was explicitly associated with Jewish characteristics [23. 246].

The point at which the epistemological teachings of the Vienna Circle coincides with the Jewish question it had omitted, as well as with the political history of the 20th century, is in its conception of a rational society, cleansed of all contradictions. This society was not to be guided by premises of thought conditioned by tradition and origin. Scientific reason and unified language usage were to prepare a rational global society where all characteristics of differentness would be invisible. However, the concept of reason remained too narrow to bear the societal-political claims based on it. Consequently, this sociopolitical theory was never able to become widely influential.

With the majority of its proponents having emigrated to the United States, the logic of science soon lost its utopian-political dimension and limited itself to "technical" problems in the self-justification of the sciences. It survived the end of theory by reshaping itself from a grand future narrative – as still expressed in the title of Otto Neurath's last great work *Modern Man in the Making* (1939) – back into a normal science. In the United States, philosophers of science could also become visible as Jews but nearly all of them strictly separated their theoretical work from their religious faith. Hilary Putnam, one of the most eminent representatives of American philosophy of science and a student of Hans Reichenbach, sought to balance the tension between philosophy and religion late in his life by focusing on the Jewish philosophy of Franz Rosenzweig (→ [The] Star of Redemption), Martin Buber (→ Dialogue), and Emmanuel Levinas (→ Alterity) [16].

6. From Lukács to Adorno

Theory was not a primarily Jewish discourse but one in which Jews *also* had a share and which, for a time, appeared to offer them extraordinary opportunities, promising them a place that would deliver them from their "transcendental homelessness" (Georg Lukács). Such messianic transformations become visible at significant junctures in the respective œuvre, where the Jewish question left out of the theory becomes visible in the very moment of its disappearance. In the works of Georg Lukács (→ Class Consciousness), this moment may be found in his conversion from esthetic → messianism – fueled in part by Jewish sources – to communism. The fragmented world devoid of meaning, which would – according to his original conception – reconstitute itself in an act of metaphysical reawakening (*Theorie des Romans*, 1916), would henceforth become a whole in "orthodox Marxism" (*Geschichte und Klassenbewusstsein*, 1923). The career of Siegfried Kracauer (→ Film) displays a similar watershed moment inspired by Lukács. During the early 1920s, Kracauer had had close ties to the → Freies Jüdisches Lehrhaus before radically turning his back on Franz Rosenzweig and Martin Buber (*Die Bibel auf Deutsch*, 1925) and embracing "society" to search for traces of transcendent meaning in the abysses of the secular world.

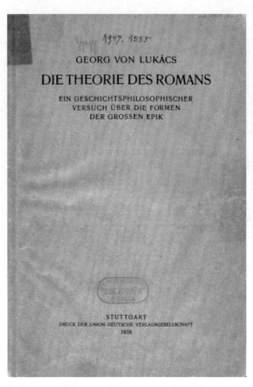

Title page of Georg Lukács's treatise Die Theorie des Romans, *published in Stuttgart in 1916*

Leo Löwenthal, who, like Kracauer, was influenced by Lukács, also sought salvation in converting to theory. In Löwenthal's works, the transition occurs in his series of articles *Judentum und deutscher Geist* (1926–1932), in which he endeavored to translate German-Jewish intellectual history into materialist categories. He wrote programmatically that the lives of leading Jews reflected the history of the rising bourgeois society and its contradictions. For example, he says about Moses Mendelssohn (→ Bi'ur) that he was "a reflex of the lack of independence of his social stratum, – but he also represents its progressive tendencies" [14. 14]. Löwenthal was applying a theory that, in its consistent distinction between "progress" and "reaction," always focused on the sublation of theory into societal practice. At the latest with Lukács's *Die Zerstörung der Vernunft* (1954), this distinction arrived at a dead end since it could be used to disqualify all positions that were not "orthodox Marxist" as bourgeois and reactionary.

The so-called Critical Theory, named after Max Horkheimer's essay *Traditionelle und kritische Theorie* (1937; "Traditional and Critical Theory," 1937), largely operated with reference to a similarly progressive concept of theory intended to be distinguished from the static Cartesian understanding of philosophy (→ Institute for Social Research). But despite some narrowing into possible societal progress, Critical Theory retained the flexibility of its categories. As a result, the seismic shifts in the concept of theory around 1940/1941 were noted most keenly by members of the exiled Institute for Social Research. "We are now left with our theory as the disgraced Hebrews" [1. 16], Adorno wrote on September 8, 1939, to his parents on the outbreak of the Second World War, after the official theory of the institute, according to which there was not going to be a war, had been proven wrong. As if in a last reflex, the Hegelian-Marxist explanation of the world was ironically shifted into the grandest possible perspectives once more at the very moment of its demise: "If it really is true, then the world spirit has had an occupational accident, and the world of appearances has gained control over the intrinsic order – or rather disorder – of the present historical phase in a truly demonic fashion" [1. 17].

This type of grand explanation would soon yield to an entirely different understanding of theory, intended to bring the gestural function of theory to bear. In August 1940 Adorno wrote to Horkheimer regarding the latter's essay *Art and Mass Culture*: "It really is the starting point of an experience – one might almost say that the essay represents a gesture even more than an idea. Rather as if, left behind on an island, one were to desperately wave a shawl to capture the attention of a ship sailing away once it is too far away to call. Our pieces will increasingly have to become such gestures from concepts, and less and less theories in the traditional sense. Only, of course, this requires the full exertion of the concept" [2. 200]. This conception of theories as "gestures from concepts" was diametrically opposed to the understanding of theory as a self-contained system of propositions. Gestural thought also had the function of referring once more to the perishing content of the European tradition of theory at the moment of its disappearance.

However, this conception was not able to resolve the fundamental problem of theory in view of the political events of the 20th century. Adorno noted: "That the force of facts has become so horrifying that all theory, even the true one, appears to be mocking it – this has been branded onto the very organ of theory, onto language itself. Praxis that disempowers theory comes to light as an element of destruction within theory, without a view to possible praxis. In effect, one cannot say anything more" [2. 224]. The surprising insight resulting from this destruction of theory consisted in the fact that theory was now more necessary than ever. In November 1941 Horkheimer wrote to Löwenthal: "Our task in life is theoretical work. [...] From the results the meaning of our earlier work – indeed, of our existence – will become clear. In view of the horror that prevails outside and gathers inside, and in view of the fact that we see no-one around us anywhere, the responsibility is immeasurably great" [14. 233]. The envisaged theory of the present age was supposed to show how the Enlightenment project of using theory to establish a rational society, liberated from all particular characteristics of origin and tradition, had been turned on its head. The *Dialektik der Aufklärung* (1944/1947; → "Dialectic of Enlightenment," 2002) is an early example of the paradox of a comprehensive, grand theory that outlived the end of theory.

7. After 1945

Horkheimer and Adorno were not the only ones to react to the new situation of theory in light of political events; nor was the caesura within theory ever implemented unambiguously. Until the late 1960s, Critical Theory continued to fluctuate between a new conception of theoretical work and a self-understanding according to which the end of theory would have to be overtaken by a grand Freudian-Marxist theory. Overall, changes in the concept of theory were frequently announced before older, long-established forms of theoretical work reasserted themselves. The → New School for Social Research reverted to grand conceptions of planned economy as early as 1942/1943 when the German defeat could be foreseen. These were composed with a view to re-educating the Nazified German masses and the aim of not surrendering Europe to blind market forces alone. The members of the New School were less influential in the re-education than, for instance, Franz Neumann, Ernst Fraenkel, and Franz Borkenau (→ Congress for Cultural Freedom), all of whom played an important role in the development of political science in Germany as well.

The orientation towards politics led to profound changes in theory, inasmuch as the political sector, with its conceptual pairs of asymmetrical oppositions, had always undermined every self-contained system of concepts. Hannah Arendt dissolved the concept of philosophy tied to the Aristotelian *bios theoretikos* in favor of "political theory," emphasizing thinking and judging in contrast to the traditional concept of theory (→ Judgement). Both thinking and judging no longer took place within a reasoned theoretical context; rather, they could only be comprehended on the basis of the thinker's individual experiences and ways of reacting. Among Jewish intellectuals, in particular, these redirections of the concept of theory were due not least to reflections on the latency of the → Holocaust within theory.

The frequently unfathomable reflections on latency *in* theory, however, were hardly noticed anymore by the 1960s at the latest, when the desire for societal change in praxis significantly changed the meaning of theory. Theory as pursued in academic reading groups and in alternative political discourse had now, paradoxically, been elevated to the rank of a societal praxis whose objective was to prepare a radical transformation of politics and society [20]. This model retained much of its suggestive force until 1989. The age of theory came to an end only with the end of the "grand narratives." Since then, normative grand theories of society have increasingly been suspected of being anachronistic, as have grand explanatory models based on the theory of science. This also applies to theories that promise to resolve the Jewish question in a universal, rational global society. Nevertheless, theory, in a new guise, is always required wherever observed reality must be described and its mere being must to some degree be transcended. Jewish intellectuals were groundbreaking when it came to transforming grand theories into small, minimal theoretical formations primarily directed against hegemonic discourses.

Bibliography

Sources

[1] T. W. Adorno, Letters to His Parents: 1939–1951, Cambridge 2006. [2] T. W. Adorno/M. Horkheimer, Briefwechsel, Vol. 2: 1938–1944, C. Gödde/H. Lonitz (eds.), Frankfurt am Main 2004. [3] T. W. Adorno/W. Kracauer, Correspondence 1923–1966, trans. by S. Reynolds/M. Winkler, Cambridge 2020. [4] H. Arendt, The Jew as Pariah. A Hidden Tradition, in: Jewish Social Studies 6 (1944), 99–122. [5] H. Arendt, Antisemitism. Part One of the Origins of Totalitarianism, New York/London, 2012. [6] F. R. Bienenfeld, The Religion of the Non-religious

Jews. A Lecture Delivered to the Sociological Society of Vienna on November 10th 1937, London 1944. [7] H. Blumenberg, The Laughter of the Thracian Woman. A Protohistory of Theory, trans. by S. Hawkins, New York/London 2015. [8] H. Cohen, Jüdische Schriften, vol. 2, Berlin 1924. [9] I. Deutscher, The Non-Jewish Jew, in: I. Deutscher and T. Deutscher, The Non-Jewish Jew and Other Essays, London 1968, 25–42. [10] E. Freud (ed.), Letters of Sigmund Freud 1873–1939, London 1961. [11] E. Husserl, The Crisis of European Sciences and Transcendental Phenomenology. An Introduction to Phenomenological Philosophy, Evanston 1970. [12] E. Husserl, Formal and Transcendental Logic, trans. by D. Cairns, The Hague 1969. [13] E. Husserl, Briefwechsel, vol. 3, ed. K. Schuhmann, Dordrecht 1994. [14] L. Löwenthal, Schriften, vol. 4, ed. H. Dubiel, Frankfurt am Main 1990. [15] K. Marx/F. Engels, Collected Works, vols. 1–6, 2010. [16] H. Putnam, Jewish Philosophy as a Guide to Life. Rosenzweig, Buber, Levinas, Wittgenstein, Bloomington/Indianapolis 2008. [17] G. Steiner, Some "Meta-Rabbis," in: D. Villiers (ed.), Next Year in Jerusalem, London 1976, 64–76. [18] M. Stöltzner/T. Uebel (ed.), Wiener Kreis. Texte zur wissenschaftlichen Weltauffassung, Hamburg 2006. [19] L. Wittgenstein, Philosophical Investigations, trans. by G. E. M. Ascombe, Oxford 1967.

Secondary literature

[20] P. Felsch, Der lange Sommer der Theorie. Geschichte einer Revolte 1960–1990, Munich 2015. [21] G. König, Theorie, I., in: Historisches Wörterbuch der Philosophie, J. Ritter/K. Gründer (eds.), vol. 10, Basel 1998, 1128–1146. [22] C.-D. Krohn (ed.), Handbuch der deutschsprachigen Emigration, Darmstadt ²1998. [23] F. Stadler, The Vienna Circle: Studies in the Origins, Development, and Influence of Logical Empiricism, vol. 4, Vienna/New York 2015. [24] P. v. Wussow, Jüdische Theoriegeschichte (1843–1941).

Ein methodologischer Vorschlag, in: Transversal. Zeitschrift für Jüdische Studien 14 (2013), 61–94.

PHILIPP VON WUSSOW,
FRANKFURT AM MAIN

Theory of Relativity

Albert Einstein's (1879–1955) theory of relativity revolutionized the understanding of the laws of nature that had been established since Kepler and Newton and provided the basis for modern physics. Its influence was felt beyond the boundaries of the sciences in philosophy, epistemology, literature, and art (→ Einstein Tower); it has grown to become the synonym for modern knowledge in general. Einstein composed its seminal texts in 1905, an exceedingly productive year for him, in Bern. Among "völkisch" (ethnic) nationalists, the theory of relativity became the target of antisemitic resentment; National Socialist authors construed an antagonism between "German" and "Jewish" physics. Throughout his life Einstein, known for his cosmopolitism and pacifism, lived entirely in the universalism of science.

1. Albert Einstein – a life in science
2. On the sociology of knowledge of the "annus mirabilis" in Bern
3. Physics in the age of ideology
4. Cosmopolitanism and pacifism

1. Albert Einstein – a life in science

His main achievement, Einstein once said about himself, was to remain "independent of the customs, opinions, and prejudices of others" [13. 50]. It is true that he belonged less to a country, state, or religion than to a profession; the former might change, and he remained true only to the latter. Insistence on collective community remained alien to him throughout his life. "The state to which I belong as a citizen does not play any role in my feelings [*Gemütsleben*], because I see it more like a matter of business, such as the relations with a life insurance company" [5. 97]. He frequently characterized his faith as "cosmic," his political beliefs as cosmopolitan or international (cited in [18. 284, 355]). In his public correspondence with Sigmund Freud (→ Psychoanalysis), Einstein described himself "as one immune to nationalist bias" [6. 188]. He regarded neither the place of his birth nor his respective places of residence as his home. Marriage, family, and friendships were not life-defining ideals to him either. The state, human communities, and his place of work all failed to provide a feeling of home for Einstein; only natural science and its timeless questions and ideas could do that.

Einstein was born in 1879 in Ulm into a family that leaned toward religious → reform. His father Hermann Einstein worked in the electrical industry, one of the most innovative and expansive sectors of the time. Einstein displayed an interest in → mathematics and geometry early on. As an adolescent he read classics of the history of science as well as philosophical books, many of them suggested by Max Talmud (1869–1941), a Polish Jewish medical student for whom the Jewish community had arranged free meals with the Einstein family [18. 50]. Due to frequently moving from one place of residence to another, Einstein attended the Catholic primary school and the Luitpold Gymnasium in Munich as well as a Gymnasium in Pavia in Lombardy before completing the Matura (school exit exam) in the canton school in Aarau in Switzerland in 1897. He began studying in Zurich in the same year.

He had already relinquished German → citizenship a year earlier. After his graduation as a teacher for mathematics and physics from the Eidgenössisches Polytechnikum, he repeatedly applied for assistant posts at Leipzig University but was rejected. After some months as a private tutor in Schaffhausen, he started in a position with the patent office in Bern in the spring of 1902.

Einstein's scientific breakthrough came in 1905. In that year, alongside his doctoral thesis, he composed further sensational papers, such as the essay "Zur Elektrodynamik bewegter Körper" ("On the Electrodynamics of Moving Bodies," 1920), which contains the ideas of the theory of relativity. His application for Swiss citizenship was granted in the same year; he simultaneously relinquished his formal religious affiliation, writing "dissident" on the relevant documents from then on. However, Einstein did not adopt a purely positivist worldview; on the contrary, the most incomprehensible thing about the universe to him was that it was comprehensible. He firmly rejected "professional atheists" who were proud of having "removed Gods and miracles" from the world. He referred to himself as a "believing physicist" (cited in [18. 357]); his creed praised Spinoza's (→ Tractatus Theologico-Politicus) God "who reveals himself in the orderly harmony of what exists" (cited in 18. 324]), and with it pantheism and Goethe's Spinozism (→ Elective Affinities). In a letter looking back over his life, Einstein wrote: "I have found no better expression than 'religious' for confidence in the rational nature of reality insofar as it is accessible to human reason. Wherever this feeling is absent, science degenerates into uninspired empiricism" [9. 105].

In 1909 Einstein was offered an associate professorship in theoretical physics at the University of Zurich. In 1911 he was appointed to the German university in → Prague as a full professor. Only one year later he returned to Zurich, where he became a professor for theoretical physics at the Eidgenössische Technische Hochschule. Shortly before the First World War, the physicist – whose name was by now well-known in professional circles – received a call to the Königlich-Preußische Akademie der Wissenschaften (Prussian Academy of Sciences) in Berlin. Exempt from teaching duties, he found the conditions for research in Berlin ideal. It was there that he succeeded in harmonizing Newton's theory of gravitation with his own theory of motion, arriving at the theory of general relativity. In Berlin Einstein also began to develop a deeper interest in Jewish matters. He became a prominent voice of the German Zionists, championed Jewish settlement in Palestine (→ Yishuv), and later actively supported the establishment of the → Hebrew University in Jerusalem.

Once power had been transferred to the National Socialists, Einstein was excluded from the Akademie der Wissenschaften. He chose the United States as his place of sanctuary, where he was able to pursue his own research interests at the recently founded Institute for Advanced Study in Princeton, exempt from all teaching and organizational duties. Einstein died in 1955 when events and conferences to celebrate the fiftieth anniversary of the theory of relativity were being prepared in several places.

Einstein's convictions and principles often differed from the majority opinion of his time, such as his speaking out against the First World War or against the veneration of the "shrine of patriotism" practiced by most of his contemporaries. In return, his every step was closely watched by the authorities with unconcealed suspicion [14. 13–23]. Like a cursed independent of any place or time, this official suspicion pervaded Einstein's life as a public person, from being spied on by the military and police authorities of the German Empire during the First World War to the years of surveillance by the FBI under John Edgar Hoover in the United States during the McCarthy era (→ Rosenberg Trial). Political reservations about the Jewish scholar, which officials of the administration had absorbed, manifested themselves obviously in a heightened wariness toward him.

When it became known in 1921 that Einstein was to be awarded the Nobel Prize for physics, diplomatic skirmishes broke out behind the scenes on the question of which state would send an emissary to the award ceremony, Germany or Switzerland, as the laureate himself was in Japan at the time and unable to attend. In the end, the German ambassador in Stockholm, Rudolf Nadolny, expressed thanks in Einstein's absence, resulting in a paradoxical situation; the German ministry for foreign affairs, in particular, regarded the invitations for Einstein to visit foreign countries as positive diplomatic missions and a way of representing the voice of Germany abroad. The Akademie der Wissenschaften, however, expressed criticism of, among other things, the fact that Einstein had visited Palestine on the way home from Japan; the travels of its member could thus not be regarded as expressing the institution's own views, as they were carried out "in the service of Zionist propaganda" [14. 19].

Einstein's fame and his appropriation by an enthusiastic public that made him a star grew in proportion to the question of whom

Albert Einstein (1879–1955)

he represented. In whose name did he speak on the international stage? He remained suspicious of this popularity, seeking always to keep his distance from it.

This was apparent in 1922, for instance, when Einstein became a member of the International Commission for Intellectual Cooperation of the League of Nations. He resigned his post some months later, after the murder of Walther Rathenau (→ Kaiserjuden), having noticed that, as he wrote to Marie Curie, "very strong antisemitism is prevalent in the class which I am supposed to represent, as it were; and that I am not suited to be a representative or mediating person" (cited in [14. 20, n. 39]). Einstein's time with the Institute for Advanced Study in Princeton, as well as his support of Zionist ideals and his championing matters of cultural and educational politics in the young State of Israel, were among the most significant constants in his life.

Again and again Einstein ironized the scurrilous appropriation of his person and his work, which turned him into a hero or a traitor, depending on the position of the wheel of politics. In a speech given in Paris in 1921, the year he was awarded the Nobel Prize, he said: "If I am proved right in my theory of relativity, the Germans will say that I am a German and the French will say that I am a citizen of the whole world. Should my theory be proved wrong, the French will say that I am a German, and the Germans that I am a Jew" (cited in [17. 7]). This criticism of the reflexes of the time to regard knowledge as a national achievement reveals a fundamental issue of the paradoxical Jewish modern age: Whereas it was theoretically possible to lead a universalistic life in science during the age of nationalism and essentialism, traditional models of perception and conventional justifications of collective affiliation always called one back to the reality of the time.

2. On the sociology of knowledge of the "annus mirabilis" in Bern

As a young man in his mid-twenties and without ties to any university, Einstein had published over twenty scientific papers over the course of just one year in 1905, among them four remarkable discoveries. With his special theory of relativity, he submitted a new interpretation of the physical relation between mass, motion, and energy. At the same time, he wrote a study of the connection between energy and mass that would later lead to the famous formula: Energy equals mass times the speed of light squared ($E = mc^2$) [20. 93]. Biographers and historians of science use the phrase "annus mirabilis"; it has been said that the achievement of this one year would have been enough for an entire life [18. 325].

The perception of Einstein as a singular scientific genius has its own history. Without intending to qualify his achievement, an approach based on the perspective of the → sociology of knowledge directs our eyes towards the young scholar's formative years in Zurich and Bern, as well as the social backgrounds of the theory of relativity [11]. Especially in retrospect, Einstein himself took such a perspective, which included the social aspect and looked beyond his specific, individual talent at the wider European Jewish experience, regarding his Swiss time in general and "those happy years in Bern" in particular [2. 148]; [22].

Switzerland occupied a special position in Europe in 1900 [21]. After the federal constitutional reform of 1866, which liberalized citizenship law, Swiss → universities had become a promising sanctuary for emigrants from Eastern Europe who were denied the opportunity to study in their home countries or who had fled for political reasons. These young, politically active intellectuals were mostly destitute but idealistic and ambitious. Among them in the 1890s were the student Rosa Luxemburg (1871–1919) from Zamość, as well as the siblings Maria, Samuel, and Chaim Weizmann (1874–1952; → Balfour Declaration), who were born near Pinsk. Luxemburg was enrolled in Zurich in the law and philosophy departments and would later become one of the most important theoreticians of the workers' movement. Chaim Weizmann, the future first president of the State of Israel, was an unknown → chemistry Ph.D. student in Fribourg, but even in those days his debate with Georgi Plekhanov, the leader of Russian social democracy, which had its headquarters in Geneva at the time, had a signaling effect in the context of Jewish matters. To Plekhanov's amazement, students from Bern led by Weizmann formed the first Zionist section in Switzerland. The fact that the first three Zionist congresses in 1897, 1898, and 1899 took place in → Basel is part of this development. In retrospect, Weizmann said that the Swiss university cities of Zurich, Bern, Basel, and Geneva were special in that the revolutionary forces of all of Europe met in them [11. 279].

While Einstein was anything but a political revolutionary, he did have friends in this intellectual environment. His Swiss years offered not only cosmopolitan flair but also protection and security. One did not need to come from places of unrest or from Eastern Europe in order to appreciate this spirit. This was precisely the case with Einstein. He arrived in Zurich in 1897, moved to Bern in 1902 as a 23-year-old tutor and "temporary resident not of any canton," sharing in the security of middle-class society as well as in the stimulating milieu of the universal search for new knowledge [12. 11]. Furthermore, in 1903, he joined the Naturforschende Gesellschaft Bern (Society of Natural Sciences Bern), an association of experts and non-experts before whom Einstein gave his first lecture on "Die Theorie der elektromagnetischen Wellen" ("The

Theory of Electromagnetic Waves") [20. 89]. Still without an academic position and without a secure income, he was uninhibited enough to offer the first papers he had written himself to the *Annalen der Physik* edited by Max Planck (1858–1947).

The international character of the intellectual environment of his Swiss years was among the most influential factors in his scientific biography. The intellectual exchange with his Italian Jewish friend, the future engineer Michele Besso (1873–1955), whom he had met as a student in Zurich, continued throughout their lives. They worked together in what Einstein called the "secular monastery" of the patent office, and it was Besso who first drew Einstein's attention to, among other things, the writings of the theoretician of science Ernst Mach. In his essay on relativity, Einstein mentioned Besso with gratitude. The mathematician Marcel Grossmann (1878–1936), an old school and university friend whose father had arranged for Einstein's father to be given the position in Bern, came from Budapest; Einstein would later stress his profound gratitude to him [2. 152]. The young philosopher and mathematician Maurice Solovine (1875–1958), Einstein's best friend during these years, came from Romania; they had met as the result of a newspaper advertisement looking for a private tutor. He later translated Einstein's works into French. Einstein's connection with Friedrich Adler (1879–1960) from Vienna, with whom he studied in Zurich and who later published scientific essays on Einstein's kinematics, was one of friendship as well as competition. In retrospect, when commenting on their time together, Adler maintained that "our development was fairly parallel" [11. 282]. Mileva Marić (1875–1948) from the Austro-Hungarian Vojvodina region was particularly close to Einstein's ideas and subjects. In 1900 they formed a veritable intellectual partnership for physics, married in 1903, and had three children (1902, 1904, and 1910).

Einstein regularly met the Habicht brothers, Paul (1884–1948) and Conrad Habicht (1876–1958), in private or in a restaurant to read and converse. They shared his love for mathematics, music, and physics as well as for inventions and epistemology; they jokingly called their meetings "the Olympia Academy." They discussed and played music, spoke about newly published scientific writings, and read classic texts on natural philosophy and epistemology. Their reading list included Plato's *Dialogues*, Ernst Mach's *Mechanik* ("The Science of Mechanics," 1960) and *Analyse der Empfindungen* ("The Analysis of Sensations," 1890), John Stuart Mill's *Logic*, works by David Hume and Hermann von Helmholtz, as well as recent books by the French mathematician Henri Poincaré. In a circle of immigrants of similar age who shared scientific interests and whose exchanges were characterized by liberty and mutual respect, there was a consolidation of ideas, questions, and hypotheses that fostered Einstein's formulation of the theory of relativity. It was during this time that Einstein began a specialist scholarly correspondence with the epistemologist Moritz Schlick (1882–1936; → Vienna Circle) and also corresponded with Max Planck, one of the most famous physicists of the time. Indeed, it was Planck who recognized and appreciated the significance of Einstein's ideas and consequently became the young scholar's most important sponsor.

3. Physics in the age of ideology

The reception of the theory of relativity has been characterized by waves of enthusiastic agreement and harsh rejection, and it has given rise to an entire branch of literature popularizing it. In Germany alone, nearly 1,500 publications by more than 350 authors either defending or criticizing Einstein had appeared by 1924; there were more than 1,000 publications on the subject in England, as well as another 1,000 in France, Italy, the Netherlands, and Russia combined [16. 67].

In the country of Einstein's birth and in Switzerland, expatiating on the substance, meaning, and position of the theory of relativity had its own tinge. There was resistance against the theoretical dissolution of solid matter into invisible rays and currents; in Germany this was called "zersetzend" (dissolving, disintegrating) with particular frequency [10]; [19]. The attacks against the theory of relativity often derived from the resentments of self-styled scholars who perceived the subject as an opportunity to articulate their criticism against the modern age in anti-Jewish slogans. Some examples of such scholars include Johann Heinrich Ziegler (1857–1936), a Swiss industrialist who championed his own theory of primordial light who accused Einstein of plagiarism and published over twenty texts against his theory, and the infamous antisemitic agitator Theodor Fritsch (1852–1933) from Leipzig who held forth on *Einstein's Truglehre* in 1921. These scholars, too, could refer to internationally respected scientific experts in their works because criticism of Einstein in the 1920s comprised, alongside eccentric naturalists and self-styled "solvers of the mystery of the universe," private persons, lecturers, and engineers who sought to outdo one another in refutations of Einstein's theory, as well as the "völkisch" scientists of academic renown who even founded an academy of Einstein opponents in the United States in 1921 [23].

Within the scientific network aligned against Einstein, the Berlin physicists Ernst Gehrcke (1878–1960) and the physics Nobel laureate of 1915 Philipp Lenard (1862–1947) stood out. Lenard had made a name for himself with research on the theory of rays and had at first – including in direct exchanges with Einstein – adhered to the academic rules of debate culture. Later, when Lenard occupied leading positions in scientific organizations, he abandoned this consensus,

THEORY OF RELATIVITY

and, in keeping with the spirit of the times that had elevated him, he published his *Deutsche Physik* (1936), which promised to overcome all "Jewish relativism."

The antagonism between "German" and "Jewish" physics constructed an antinomy between "sensory-demonstrable" and "abstract." Other Jewish scientists besides Einstein also found themselves in the crossfire of criticism, for instance, Hermann Minkowski (1864–1909) from Kaunus, Einstein's teacher in Zurich. The young physicist and astronomer Bruno Thüring (1905–1989), a rising man in the "Third Reich" who joined the NSDAP early on and enhanced Lenard's criticism of Einstein, attempted to demonstrate the presumed formal similarity between the → Talmud and the works he attacked. Paul Weyland (1888–1972), who was described in contemporary Jewish journalism as the "stage director of the persecution of Einstein," agitated against the "abstract spirit" of modern physics as well. He was a political organizer rather than a physicist, founding the Arbeitsgemeinschaft deutscher Naturforscher zur Erhaltung reiner Wissenschaft (Working Association of German Natural Scientists for the Preservation of Pure Science) and, above all, making a lot of noise.

The collection *Hundert Autoren gegen Einstein* ("A Hundred Authors against Einstein"), containing excerpts of previously published texts, a few original contributions, as well as a list of signatures against Einstein, appeared in 1931. It was typical of the criticism of those years in that only one physicist and hardly any mathematicians were among the contributors to the compilation [15]. Besides Lenard and Gehrcke, the professor of physics from Aachen Wilhelm Müller (1880–1968) also belonged to the established anti-Einstein front at German universities. In his 1936 pamphlet *Judentum und Wissenschaft*, he denounced the theory of relativity as a symbol of the "malign spirit of international cultural Judaism," regarding it as merely "desk-based research removed from reality." In addition, Müller agitated against all "speculative science," against "mathematicala formalism," and against "theoretical confusion of concepts," evoking the dangers of a "dead physics of mechanical 'relativity'." Overall the wrath of this exorcism was aimed at determining a presumed categorical, absolute difference between German and Jewish science (→ Style of Thought); consequently, he intended for his writings to contribute to "drawing boundaries between types" and "identifying contrasts" that had been rendered invisible by "the fog of liberalist-abstract leveling" [8. 5, 47f., 50].

4. Cosmopolitanism and pacifism

Calls for international understanding and peace signed by Einstein had established his reputation as a pacifist during the Weimar era. However, in view of the political developments in National Socialist Germany, especially after the discovery of nuclear fission in Berlin at the end of 1938, the reports of the → November pogroms, and the German attack on Poland, he retracted his position. At the beginning of August 1939, Einstein wrote to the president of the United States Franklin D. Roosevelt (→ New Deal), urging him to preempt the threat of a German nuclear bomb through intensive American research in the field of nuclear physics (→ Manhattan Project).

Later, Einstein reverted to the role of the globally respected Nobel laureate who argued equally and without partisanship against nationalism, militarism, and war. In the end, he became a figurehead of reason and without a doubt one of the most famous contemporaries to be so viewed. His "already mythical authority" for having "rescued the honor of humanity" (Thomas Mann) was less the result of his public activism; it was his status as a scientist that lent his words authority. As a global admonisher during the Cold War, he was respected on both sides of the Iron Curtain; the Soviet Union and the GDR, too, regarded him as a model for the "global community of all peace-building forces" [1. 6]. Finally, he was even compared to figures such as Mahatma Gandhi. Shortly before his death, he spoke out against the development of the hydrogen bomb together with the philosopher Bertrand Russell and other Nobel laureates in the Russell–Einstein Manifesto, which made headlines.

Nevertheless, Einstein did not begin to perceive himself as a political thinker only in the 1930s; rather, he had done so all his life. In 1914 he was already convinced that the educated class in all of Europe had "sinned when they neglected to care for general political questions"; in the future, only supra-national organizations would be able to prevent violent conflict [5. 97]. Einstein also first spoke out in the context of collective Jewish concerns during the First World War. He chose to speak in public both in particular emergencies as well as in favor of general legal equality. He advocated for help for Jewish immigrants from Eastern Europe (→ Ostjuden; → Scheunenviertel), supported the establishment of → Brandeis University, and championed the establishment of the State of Israel.

Einstein's writings, above all, the theory of relativity, were translated into → Hebrew by the mathematician Jacob Greenberg for the Dvir publishing house as early as the 1920s. On the occasion of the foundation of the → Hebrew University of Jerusalem, Einstein went on a lecture tour of America together with its future president Judah L. Magnes (1877–1948) and Chaim Weizmann, canvassing for public support and donations for this institution. During his life, Einstein donated the manuscript of his essay on the theory of relativity of 1905 to the university, which regards him as its intellectual founder. Today it holds his complete estate. His lecture on the occasion of the opening of the university in 1925 illustrates just how much he held the intellectuals and universities in Europe responsible for the political failure of the entire era. When Israel offered him the highest political position of president of the state in 1953, however, he declined. His personal ideal of life was neither politics nor representation, and he preferred to remain connected with the scientific cosmos of his institute at Princeton.

Einstein did not stop at traditional boundaries between the sciences and the humanities. He did not regard textbook science as an authority, committing instead to experiments, the discoverer's intuition, and to close communication within the field as well as beyond it. Unbiased openness and anticipation were the values he prized most highly, whereas routine and submission to authority were the dangers he avoided most. He spoke of "the greatest wonderment" and loathed drill, snobbery, and obedience, which to him were antithetical to all science and scholarship. He valued nothing greater than personal liberty, loved nothing more than the harmonic clarity of pure mathematical axioms symbolizing reason. In a contemporary portrait of the scientist on the basis of conversations with him and in which Einstein himself had editorial input, he was introduced with logical consistency as a "discoverer" and "inventor" rather than as an intellectual [7. 79, 100, 221]. His contemporary colleague Ernest Rutherford did not misrepresent Einstein's self-perception either when he called the theory of relativity a "great work of art" [20. 212]. When Einstein wrote in an obituary of his great mentor Ernst Mach that "the direct joy of seeing and understanding – Spinoza's *amor dei intellectualis* – was so prevalent that he could look into the world with the curious eyes of a child, even in his old age, and thus be perfectly happy to enjoy himself by understanding interwoven connections" [3. 141], he was also painting a picture of himself.

Bibliography

Sources

[1] M. Born/L. Infeld, Erinnerungen an Einstein, Berlin 1967. [2] A. Einstein, Erinnerungen – Souvenirs, in: Schweizerische Hochschulzeitung (Sonderheft "100 Jahre ETH") 28 (1955), 145–153. [3] A. Einstein, Ernst Mach, in: A. Kox et al., The Collected Papers of Albert Einstein, Vol. 6, The Berlin Years: Writings 1914–1917 (English translation supplement), trans. by A. Engel, Princeton 1997, 141–145. [4] A. Einstein, The World As I See It, trans. by A. Harris, New York 1949. [5] A. Einstein, My Opinion on the War, in: A. Kox et al., The Collected Papers of Albert Einstein, Vol. 6, The Berlin Years: Writings 1914–1917 (English translation supplement), trans. by A. Engel, Princeton 1997, 96–97. [6] A. Einstein, Einstein on Peace, ed. by O. Nathan and H. Norden, New York 1960. [7] A. Moszkowski, Einstein, the Searcher. His Work Explained from Dialogues with Einstein, trans. by H. L. Brose, New York 2014. [8] W. Müller, Judentum und Wissenschaft, Leipzig 1936. [9] A. Einstein/M. Solovine (ed.), Letters to Solovine. 1906–1955, New York 2011.

Secondary literature

[10] C. Asendorf, Ströme und Strahlen. Das langsame Verschwinden der Materie um 1900, Gießen 1989. [11] L. Feuer, The Social Roots of Einstein's Theory of Relativity, in: Annals of Science 27 (1971), 277–298; 313–344. [12] M. Flückiger, Albert Einstein in Bern. Das Ringen um ein neues Weltbild. Eine dokumentarische Darstellung über den Aufstieg eines Genies, Bern 1974. [13] P. Frank, Albert Einstein. His Life and Times, trans. by G. Rosen, Cambridge, MA 2002. [14] F. Gilbert, Einstein's Europe, in: H. Woolf et al., Some Strangeness in the Proportion. A Centennial Symposium to Celebrate the Achievements of Albert Einstein, Reading, MA 1980. [15] H. Goenner, The Reaction to Relativity Theory in Germany, III. "A Hundred Authors against Einstein," in: J. Earman et al. (eds.), The Attraction of Gravitation. New Studies in the History of General Relativity, Boston et al. 1993,

248–273. [16] K. Hentschel, Interpretationen und Fehlinterpretationen der speziellen und der allgemeinen Relativitätstheorie durch Zeitgenossen Albert Einsteins, Basel et al. 1990. [17] R. Jessen/J. Vogel, Die Naturwissenschaft und die Nation. Perspektiven einer Wechselbeziehung in der europäischen Geschichte, in: R. Jessen/J. Vogel (eds.), Wissenschaft und Nation in der europäischen Geschichte, Frankfurt am Main 2002, 7–37. [18] J. Neffe, Einstein. A Biography, trans. by S. Frisch, New York 2007. [19] R. Panek, The Invisible Century. Einstein, Freud and the Search for the Hidden Universes, London 2005. [20] J. Renn (ed.), Albert Einstein. Chief Engineer of the the Universe: Einstein's Life and Work in Context, Berlin 2005. [21] A. Schwarzenbach, Das verschmähte Genie. Albert Einstein und die Schweiz, Munich 2012. [22] J. Stachel, Einstein's Jewish Identity, in: J. Stachel (ed.), Einstein from "B" to "Z," Boston et al. 2002, 57–84. [23] M. Wazeck, Einstein's Opponents. The Public Controversy about the Theory of Relativity in the 1920s, trans. by G. S. Koby, Cambridge 2013.

Nicolas Berg, Leipzig

Theresienstadt

Fortress town in northern Bohemia and during the Second World War a transit camp, to which over 143,000 Jews were deported. From here, over 60,000 Czech, more than 16,000 German, and 7,500 Austrian, as well as over 3,000 Dutch Jews were deported to the ghettoes and extermination camps of the East; about 34,000 died in the camp itself. The SS also used Theresienstadt as a "Vorzugslager" (privileged camp) for elderly or prominent Jews from Germany and the Netherlands, as well as for propaganda purposes, with a view to which they granted access to the International Red Cross and had a film made. However, the use of prisoners for propaganda purposes had little effect on their life in Theresienstadt, where the decisive factor was constant fear of deportation.

1. Construction
2. Everyday Life
3. Self-governance
4. Liberation

1. Construction

Theresienstadt (Czech, Terezín), named after Empress Maria Theresia, is a fortress town constructed between 1780 and 1790 by order of Emperor Joseph II, and situated approximately 60 kilometers northwest of Prague on the river Ohře, a few kilometers from where it flows into the Elbe. The town, built in the classical style and aligned in strict symmetry, where civilians also lived, is divided into the garrison town and the small fortress, located on the other side of the Ohře. Both complexes are surrounded by an extensive rampart, which made it easy to seal the place off. Originally built for defense against a possible attack by Prussia, Theresienstadt was used as a garrison, first by the Imperial and Royal Army, and then, after 1918, by the Czechoslovakian military. As a result of the German annexation of the "rump of Czechoslovakia" in March 1939, the town was included in the so-called Reichsprotektorat Böhmen und Mähren (Reich Protectorate of Bohemia and Moravia).

A Gestapo prison existed in the Lesser Fortress beginning in June 1940, in which, until the end of the war, a total of 32,000 political prisoners were detained, primarily from Bohemia and Moravia. The decision to intern large numbers of Jews in Theresienstadt dates from October 10, 1941, when Adolf Eichmann initially planned the construction of a transit camp for Bohemian and Moravian Jews, from which they, too, were to be deported "to the East." The "Theresienstadt ghetto," as it was officially called until the summer of 1943, was under the authority of the Zentralstelle für jüdische Auswanderung in Prag (Central Office for Jewish Emigration in Prague; from August 1942: Zentralamt für die Regelung der Judenfrage in Böhmen und Mähren [Central Office for the Resolution of the Jewish Question in Bohemia and Moravia]); however, influence was also exerted by the commanding officer of the Sicherheitspolizei (security police) and of the SD (security service) in Prague, and Department IV B4 of the Reichssicherheitshauptamt (Reich Main Security Office) (Adolf Eichmann's so-called "Judenreferat") in Berlin.

In November 1941, the Jewish community of Prague was ordered to send a group of men, the so-called first Aufbaukommando (construction commando), of 342 persons to Theresienstadt, which was to prepare the site to receive thousands of people. While in the first eight months part of the town was initially destined for the internment of Jews, the entire locality was declared a "ghetto" on July 1, 1942, by a decree that ordered the local population to evacuate. To accelerate the transports and conceal them still further from the public, the town was connected by a stretch of track built by prisoners to the Prague-Dresden railway line; until its activation in June 1943, the prisoners had to travel either on foot or by truck to the next station Bauschowitz (Bohušovice), 2.5 kilometers away.

From the outset, Theresienstadt served as a transit camp. Until the summer of 1942, thousands of Czech Jews were removed from the Protectorate to Theresienstadt, from where they were deported to the East. The first transport took place on January 9, 1942 to Riga. From the perspective of the plans of Eichmann's office IV B4, Theresienstadt initially functioned here within the context of the German Reich: that is, early transports from Theresienstadt had the same destinations as deportations from Berlin, Frankfurt am Main, or Vienna, namely the ghettos in Riga, Minsk, or Piaski. From October 1942, the extermination camp of

Auschwitz was the sole destination of transports from Theresienstadt. Until the end of the Second World War, the number of Czech Jews taken to Theresienstadt totaled 73,608; 60,382 of them were deported to the "East," and approximately 4,000 survived [12. 158]; [3. 87, n. 36].

In addition to its function as a transit camp for Czech Jews, beginning in June 1942 Theresienstadt also assumed the significance of a "Vorzugslager" (privileged camp) for specific groups of German and Austrian Jews. These included Jews older than 65, partners from terminated mixed marriages, "Geltungsjuden" (counted as Jews), decorated war veterans, and collaborators in the Reichsvertretung der deutschen Juden (Reich Representation of German Jews) or other Jewish institutions, including the long-time leader of the Reichsvertretung and rabbi Leo Baeck (1873–1956; Leo Baeck Institute), but also the first ordained → woman rabbi Regina Jonas (1902–1944) or the composer of the *Sportspalastwalzer* (Sports Palace Waltz), Siegfried Translateur (1875–1944). Until the end of the war, 42,956 Jews from the "Altreich" (Old Reich), as well as from the Sudetenland, Danzig, and Luxembourg were deported to Theresienstadt; another 15,324 came from Austria. 16,098 and 7,572 of them respectively were taken to the extermination camps [1. 31–60].

In all, over 143,000 Jews were deported to Theresienstadt. In addition to the Jews from the Protectorate and the Reich, these included 1,447 Slovakian, 4,897 Dutch, 466 Danish, and 1,074 Hungarian Jews. Nearly 34,000 Jews died in the "ghetto" [1. 38, 33–34].

2. Everyday Life

With the transportation of mainly older German and Austrian Jews beginning in the summer of 1942, the occupancy of Theresienstadt increased sharply: by mid-September 1942, the number of inmates reached its highest point at 58,491 prisoners [1. 451]. Living conditions deteriorated correspondingly. The Gestapo had touted

Backdrops for the the International Commission (Theresienstadt), *Sketch by Bedřich Fritta* (1943/1944)

Theresienstadt to the elderly Jews from the "Altreich" as a health resort, and had made them pay for accommodation expenses in the form of so-called "Heimeinkaufsverträge" (home purchase agreements). The overwhelmed self-government authorities, however, found themselves obliged to house most of the newcomers in the remaining houses and in the attics of the barracks. The situation in the attics was particularly degrading, since residents had no access to furniture, light, windows, running water, or toilets, and people, often over 80 years old, were forced to lie down on the bare floor. Because of the overcrowding and the resulting catastrophic hygienic conditions, the mortality rate in early autumn 1942 rose to 156 persons per day. The SS solved the crisis in its typical way: in September and October 1942 alone, they sent 19 shipments, mainly of elderly people, to the extermination site at Maly Trostinez and the extermination camp at → Treblinka.

From November 1942 onward, the situation in Theresienstadt improved somewhat. Separated by gender, rooms or halls were occupied by 8 to 200 persons. Adolescents up to 18 years could be lodged in youth centers, and most parents took advantage of this, since there was a general requirement to work, and conditions in the homes were better. Medical care also improved, since the SS feared epidemics. The older occupants were at greatest risk. Detainees over 60 (women) and 65 (men) respectively usually no longer had to work, were often much too weak to do so, and received by far the most meager rations of food. This was reflected in mortality. 84% of those over 65 died in Theresienstadt, most of them from illnesses caused by malnutrition; 92% of those who died in Theresienstadt were over 60 years old; in contrast, 2.7% were under 45 years old [5. 173f.]. Younger detainees often suffered from hunger, but as long as they were able to stay in Theresienstadt, were not immediately at risk of dying. Given the SS fear of epidemics, Theresienstadt had adequate medical care available by 1944 at the latest.

As the first to arrive, the young Czechs assumed the status of a social elite and could often work in better positions as cooks, bakers, or technicians. They had access to food, often had their own accommodations, and were often protected from transport. Throughout their detention, the Czechs remained the dominant group in the "ghetto," not only because they were the largest group, and this was reflected in the use of Czech in life at the camp. The privileged position of many young Czechs was often echoed in romantic and sexual relations. Thus, many women offered sex in exchange for food, an act that was not unusual at the time, but which was repressed or depicted in a moralizing light in later testimonies [1. 243, 316]. Meanwhile, the German and Austrian Jews who arrived later found themselves subject to a great deal of anti-German resentment. In addition, the camp society tended to reject elderly people, and the overwhelming majority of German and Austrian Jews were seniors.

Transports from the Netherlands were different. Two thirds of them were German and Austrian emigrants, who were better able to cope. One-third were native-born Netherlanders, who were rather disoriented, and adopted a primarily passive attitude. The small group of Danish Jews consisted in members of old Danish families, Russian refugees from the pogroms of 1905, as well as members of the youth aliyah from Germany in 1938–1939. Beginning in March 1944, they received food packages from the Danish government, which made them seem privileged in the eyes of the detainee population. For the Slovakian and Hungarian Jew, as well as the Jewish partners in mixed marriages, who arrived during the last four months, Theresienstadt was merely one more stopping point on their long odyssey of deportation.

No common Jewish self-understanding developed in the "ghetto." The Theresienstadt of privileged young cooks was different from that of a poor, elderly, Viennese Jew. In addition, many prisoners saw their identification as Jews as imposed upon them externally. Not a few inmates were atheists or Christian believers; Theresienstadt had an active Catholic and Protestant community. Nevertheless, the Theresienstadt community developed a master narrative that understood the camp as a place in which the inhabitants worked hard, contributed to the community's well-being, accomplished outstanding cultural achievements, and thus confirmed their affiliation to Central European culture.

Among the inmates were many artists and intellectuals, some of them prominent, such as the Romanian composer Rafael Schächter (1905–1944/1945), the German philosopher and psychologist Emil Utitz (1883–1956), or the Czech pianist Alice Herz-Sommer (1903–2014); but laypersons also made cultural contributions. Music (S'brent), particularly vocal music, which was easier to present, was performed and heard, although its origins were various. While German Jews enthusiastically attended staged readings of *Faust* by Philipp Manes (1875–1944), Czech Jews went to Rafael Schächter's staging of the *Verkaufte Braut* (The Bartered Bride) or Vlasta Schönová's (Nava Shan, 1919–2001) adaption of František Langer's (1888–1965) comedy *Velbloud uchem jehly* (Camel Through the Eye of the Needle). Many events were apparently of outstanding quality, and certain opera stagings or Verdi's *Messa da Requiem* were so popular that onlyinfluential or affluent prisoners were able to attend them. Sometimes women, who worked in one of the agricultural sections, obtained tickets in exchange for highly-prized smuggled pickles and attended a performance of Mozart. Soccer, which was a part of the recreational activities, also played an important role, giving rise to a kind of league in which teams organized according to work assignments played against one another.

The rich cultural life in the camp was convenient for Nazi propaganda. Eichmann's office, which changed its name in July 1943 to the "Jüdisches Siedlungsgebiet" (Jewish settlement area), tried to project a false image of humane treatment of Jews in German concentration camps to the outside world. Visits by representatives of the International Red Cross and of the Danish government in June 1944 and March 1945, which had been preceded by extensive renovations and beautification work in Theresienstadt – such as the planting of flowerbeds – were aimed at this goal, to such an extent that the delegations did indeed get the impression that the inmates' situation was satisfactory. It was concealed from them that in order to reduce the occupancy of the camp, more than 17,500 mostly Czech Jews had been deported to Auschwitz between September 1943 and May 1944. There they were initially interned in the so-called Familienlager Theresienstadt (Theresienstadt family camp), but most were murdered in March and July 1944.

The best-known example of propaganda is the film shot in the course of 1944 on the initiative of Hans Günther, head of the Prague Zentralamt, *Theresienstadt. Ein Dokumentarfilm aus dem jüdischen Siedlungsgebiet* ("Theresienstadt. A Documentary Film"). It was directed by two non-Jews from the Prague film company Aktualita, together with the Jewish prisoner Kurt Gerron (1897–1944), who was a well-known actor, singer, and director. Through its depiction of a schematized daily routine, the film presents the seemingly idyllic life of the inhabitants of Theresienstadt. When it was projected in Theresienstadt in the spring of 1945, in a showing reserved for the representatives of foreign organizations, most of the protagonists were no longer alive. After shooting was concluded in September 1944, transports to Auschwitz were resumed. Gerron, who had believed he could save his own life and that of many of his fellow-prisoners by means of the film, was also deported to Auschwitz.

3. Self-governance

In Theresienstadt, it was part of the Nazis' practice to assign the immediate regulation of the daily realities of life in the "ghetto" to a Jewish self-governing body (Judenrat). Nevertheless, the bureaucratic apparatus here was presumably more extensive than in other camps. In Theresienstadt, it consisted in a threefold system of management: the Judenältesten (Jewish Elder) with their staff, the Ältestenrat (Council of Elders), which was subordinate to them, and the "Abteilungen" (sections), which were called the departments of management, central labor exchange, internal administration, economy, technical division, finance, health and welfare, child care, and leisure activities. The Abteilungen were further divided into areas of responsibility, which were themselves subdivided, so that self-government ultimately encompassed several hundred units (schema from September 1944 in [1. 182–204]). For Jewish functionaries, bureaucracy became a means by which they believed they could cope with the squalor and anguish around them, and, to a certain extent, actually did manage to keep them under control.

The first leadership consisted in Czech Zionists in the circle of the first Judenältester Jakob Edelstein (1903–1944) and his deputy, the architect Otto Zucker (1892–1944). In January 1943, Edelstein was replaced by the President of the Reichsvereinigung, the German Jew Paul Eppstein (1902–1944; Reichsvertretung der deutschen Juden); Edelstein now became his deputy, together with the Viennese Rabbi Benjamin Murmelstein (1905–1989). Once again, Murmelstein was named Judenältester in late September 1944; he was the only one to survive. Edelstein was deported to Auschwitz in December 1943,

where he was shot to death six months later; Eppstein was murdered in the same way in the Lesser Fortress, shortly before the great transports in September 1944.

Eppstein used his position to bring collaborators of the Reichsvereinigung into office, and ordered (perhaps at the command of the SS) that every Abteilung must have a German or an Austrian Jew in a management position. However, the extant leadership was not disbanded, so that the number of officials grew, especially because the Directors better: directors were accompanied by deputies and department heads. Self-administration continued to increase, when in the summer of 1943 the last members of the Jewish communities in the Reich and the Protectorate, whose work had obviously been so important that they had been initially spared, were deported to Theresienstadt. In the camp, an effort was now made to find positions for them, in order to make them exempt from transports. Where this was successful, these functionaries usually took positions that were clearly lower than before. At the same time, this makes it evident that the administration of Theresienstadt was essentially a male-dominated world of primarily younger, Czech, often Zionist-oriented men. Thus, colleagues who had previously been equally valued, such as Martha Mosse (1884–1977) from Berlin or Hannah Steiner (1894–1944) from Prague, where they each held high-ranking positions in the community administration, were now given subordinate, advisory positions at best.

Ultimately, the management was to guarantee that deportations proceeded smoothly. This implied making selections, for which the self-administration was responsible until October 1944. The command gave the order that a transport had to be dispatched. At this point, the self-administration convened the Transport Commission, which called the roll of all prisoners who qualified for the transport. The members of the commission now had the opportunity to speak out in favor of their collaborators. In addition, each Abteilungsleiter (head of section) and each representative of the Ältestenrat had the right to a personal protection list of up to 60 persons [1. 236–245]. This procedure, which, according to the information given by the former prisoner and chronicler of Theresienstadt H. G. Adler (1910–1988; → [Der] verwaltete Mensch) could take days, ended with the autumn wave of transports in September and October 1944, by means of which two thirds of the remaining inmates were transported to Auschwitz. Beginning on October 6, 1944, the SS arranged the transports under its direct control. In the last two October transports, the command also deported almost all functionaries together with their families, and persons named on the protection lists, many of whom were shot to death as soon as they arrived.

4. Liberation

When they liberated the site on May 9, 1945, the Red Army still found more than 17,500 long-interned inmates in Theresienstadt; another 15,000 prisoners, among them many non-Jews, had arrived since the end of April on so-called → "death marches." After the liberation, it took until the end of August before all the inmates, many of whom were ill or elderly, could be released. Many of the German Jews, often those whose homes in the formerly German areas were now located in Polish territory, could not or did not wish to return to their home towns, so that they gathered in the Displaced Persons camp at Deggendorf (Munich).

Theresienstadt itself was once again used by Czechoslovakian (Czech after 1993) troops as a garrison, and civilians also resettled in the garrison town. In 1945 the National Cemetery, dedicated to all the victims of the camp, was dedicated in front of the Lesser Fortress, while a permanent exhibition opened in the Lesser Fortress in 1949. In the course of the 1960s, the history of the "Theresienstadt ghetto" was integrated into the exhibition of the Theresienstadt Memorial (*Památník Terezín*), as it has been known since 1965.

Bibliography

[1] H. G. Adler, Theresienstadt 1941–1945. The Face of a Coerced Community, trans. by B. Cooper, Cambridge 2017. [2] R. Bondy, "Elder of the Jews." Jakob Edelstein of Theresienstadt, New York 1989. [3] A. Hájková, "Poor Devils" of the Camps. Dutch Jews in the Terezín Ghetto, 1943–1945, in: Yad Vashem Studies 43 (2015) 1, 77–111. [4] A. Hájková, Sexual Barter in Times of Genocide. Negotiating the Sexual Economy of the Theresienstadt Ghetto, in: Signs. Journal of Women in Culture and Society 38 (2013) 3, 503–533. [5] A. Hájková, The Prisoner Society in Terezín Ghetto, 1941–1945, unpublished dissertation, University of Toronto 2013. [6] A. Hájková, Der Judenälteste und seine SS-Männer. Benjamin Murmelstein und seine Beziehung zu Adolf Eichmann und Karl Rahm, in: R. Loewy/K. Rauschenberger (ed.), "Der Letzte der Ungerechten." Der Judenälteste Benjamin Murmelstein in Filmen 1942–1975, Frankfurt am Main 2011, 75–100. [7] P. Hallama, Nationale Helden und jüdische Opfer. Tschechische Repräsentationen des Holocaust, Göttingen/Bristol (CT) 2015. [8] K. Lagus/J. Polák, Město za mřížemi [City behind Bars], Prague 1964. [9] Z. Lederer, Ghetto Theresienstadt, London 1953. [10] K. Margry, Der Nazi-Film über Theresienstadt, in: M. Kárný et al. (eds.), Theresienstadt in der "Endlösung der Judenfrage," Prague 1992, 285–306. [11] B. Meyer, "Altersghetto," "Vorzugslager" und Tätigkeitsfeld. Die Repräsentanten der Reichsvereinigung der Juden in Deutschland und Theresienstadt, in: Theresienstädter Studien und Dokumente 12 (2005), 124–149. [12] P. Škorpil, Jüdische Opfer Nazi-Deutschlands aus den Böhmischen

Ländern 1938–1945. Versuch einer Bilanz, in: Theresienstädter Studien und Dokumente 1 (1994), 152–165.

ANNA HÁJKOVÁ, COVENTRY

Thesaurus of Hebrew Oriental Melodies

This is the title of a ten-volume collection of traditional Jewish chants from the Orient, as well as from Western and Eastern Europe, which was compiled by the Latvian cantor and music researcher Abraham Zevi Idelsohn (1882–1938). The *Thesaurus* is regarded as the founding document of modern Jewish musicology. The impetus for the work came from the Zionist call to build a new Jewish culture in Palestine. Idelsohn endeavored to document the existence of a genuinely Jewish → music on the basis of traditional melodies from East and West and place it on a par with Western music. The collection shows that both Zionist ideas and European tradition informed his work.

1. Introduction
2. Abraham Zevi Idelsohn
3. *Kibbuts galuyot*
4. East and West

1. Introduction

Between 1907 and 1921 Idelsohn, using a phonograph, collected around 4,000 orally transmitted chants and pronunciation samples in Palestine from the Oriental Jews from Yemen, Iraq, Syria, Persia, Morocco, the Caucasus, Central Asia, and Ethiopia, as well as from Sephardic Jews. He also added some instances of Christian chants and Arabian vocal and instrumental music to the collection. He was supported in this monumental undertaking by the phonogram archives in Vienna and Berlin (→ Comparative Musicology), which sent recording equipment, sound storage media, and sound meters to him in Palestine. The project was largely funded by the Kaiserliche Akademie der Wissenschaften (Imperial Academy of Sciences) in Vienna, with which the phonogram archive was affiliated.

The core work in which Idelsohn documented his material was the ten-volume *Thesaurus of Hebrew Oriental Melodies*, published between 1914 and 1932. The first five volumes appeared in three editions in German, English, and Hebrew; they comprise the melodies from Oriental and Sephardic traditions collected in Palestine. Idelsohn wrote the remaining five volumes after moving his home and creative base to the United States in 1922. They appeared in a German and an English edition, supplementing the phonographed examples from oral traditions with melodies from written sources representing the traditional music of Ashkenazi Jews in Germany and Eastern Europe and including Hasidic chants. The melodies cover a variety of functions, ranging from liturgy – the cantillation of the Torah, above all – to paraliturgical and folk songs. Each volume contains an introduction focusing on the historical background, customs, peculiarities of pronunciation, and the musical idiosyncrasies of the respective tradition. The *Thesaurus* was accompanied by numerous additional publications that commented on and evaluated the collection.

When comparing the melodies, Idelsohn found that the divergent musical idioms that had developed in the → Diaspora over centuries possessed a shared musical essence. This essence, which he deemed constant over time and across space, seemed to him to be the genuine and authentic Jewishness that linked all the traditions and indicated a common legacy. By uncovering this presumed constancy of transmission, Idelsohn believed he had provided empirical proof of an original Jewish music whose origins had to be found in the East.

2. Abraham Zevi Idelsohn

Abraham Zevi Idelsohn was born in 1882 in Filzberg, a fishing village near Libau (today Liepāja) in Latvia. As his father was a *shoḥet* (Hebr.; ritual slaughterer) and *ba'al tefillah* (Hebr.; "master of prayer," honorary prayer leader), he had an Orthodox upbringing from the first, to which he felt indebted all his life. His father and the Libau cantor Abraham Mordechai Rabinowitz introduced the synagogal chants and Jewish folk songs to him at an early age. The synagogue would determine Idelsohn's professional career. Having first attended the yeshivah after graduating from the Gymnasium (secondary school), he decided to become a cantor after a short period of deliberation. He began his training with Rabinowitz in Libau and then moved on to Eduard Birnbaum in Königsberg (today Kaliningrad), a man of profound expertise in synagogal music and a collector of manuscripts of Jewish liturgical music from Central Europe. Rabinowitz not only taught him the traditional art of the cantor but also introduced him to the works of reform composers like Hirsch Weintraub, Salomon Sulzer, and Louis Lewandowski (→ Organ; → Cantor), as well as to Western music theory and harmonics and, not least, to Western classical music composers including Bach, Handel, Haydn, Mozart, and Schubert.

From 1901 to 1903, Idelsohn deepened his knowledge of Western music, completing a degree in classical music at the Stern'sches Konservatorium in Berlin and at the Konservatorium in Leipzig. This provided him with the intellectual foundations he needed for his project of studying traditional Jewish music, which led him to Palestine after four years of employment as a cantor in Leipzig, Regensburg, and Johannesburg.

In 1907 Idelsohn came to Jerusalem in the course of the Second → Aliyah, working as a teacher at one of the schools run by the → Hilfsverein der Deutschen Juden (Relief Organization of German Jews). This was where he wrote his numerous studies on Jewish liturgy and music that made him famous as the "father of Jewish musicology." Collecting and studying the traditional vocal music of the Jews living in the region was at the center of all his work. Alongside his academic activities, he also supported the establishment of musical life in the Yishuv, developing plans for an institute of Jewish music, founding choirs, teaching cantors and music teachers, and working as a composer. Among the songs he set to music, *Havah Nagilah* is now one of the best-known popular songs in Israel. In 1912 he compiled the *Sefer ha-shirim* (Song book) published by the Hilfsverein, the first more extensive collection of songs in Hebrew for nursery, primary, and secondary schools; in addition to the *Thesaurus*, it is among the most important works dating from Idelsohn's time in Palestine. In between his years in the Yishuv, Idelsohn went on a longer sojourn to Europe in 1913/1914, at the center of which was the presentation of his research to the Wiener Akademie der Wissenschaften.

Abraham Zevi Idelsohn (1882–1938)

After returning to Jerusalem, Idelsohn changed sides in the controversy between the Hebraists and the liberal aid agency, joining the Hebraists – probably influenced in part by his friend and mentor Eli'ezer Ben-Yehudah (→ Hebrew) – and began to work at Hebrew schools. When the First World War started in 1914 – the year in which the first volume of the *Thesaurus of Hebrew Oriental Melodies* appeared – his research activity came to an almost complete halt. During the war, he served in the Ottoman army, and it was not until 1919 that he was able to resume his work as a teacher and researcher.

In 1921 Idelsohn first returned to Europe in order to publicize his research in further lecture tours and to promote the publication of his work. In 1922 he settled in America, taking up a position at the Hebrew Union College in Cincinnati, which established a chair of Hebrew, Liturgy, and Jewish Music for him in 1924. There he had access to and catalogued Eduard Birnbaum's extensive collection of written sources of Central European synagogal music of the 19th century, which the college had acquired in 1918. Using material from the Birnbaum Collection, Idelsohn was able to expand the *Thesaurus* from five to ten volumes.

Volumes 6–10 of the *Thesaurus* were published in 1932. By this time Idelsohn had abandoned his professional career due to a serious illness. In 1937 he once again moved with his family to Johannesburg, where died in 1938.

3. *Kibbuts galuyot*

Idelsohn's work in Palestine was informed throughout by his desire to create a national style of Hebrew music. A vocal opponent of assimilated life, which he had primarily encountered during his years as a student in Germany, he felt a profound unease concerning the modernization of Jewish traditions that had begun in Central Europe. Above all, he rejected the "Germanized"

singing in German synagogues, which was in line with the musical aesthetics of the surrounding culture [6. 20]. From then on, the search for the "Jewish sound" became the mainspring of his life and work. In Germany, Idelsohn first became interested in Zionist ideas. The works of Aḥad Ha-Am (→ Cultural Zionism), in particular, gave him guidance. In 1901 he first thought of going to Palestine as a farmer. When the president of the Zionist Organization (→ Basel) David Wolffsohn invited him to Palestine during a visit to South Africa in 1906, suggesting that he should undertake the leading role in a renewal of music there, Idelsohn accepted, moving to Jerusalem at the end of 1906.

The more than 300 synagogues he found in the Yishuv represented the traditions of various countries of origin (→ Liturgy). Idelsohn, who until then had known only the European *ḥazzanut* (→ Cantor), the works of Reform composers, and Western classical music, discovered that the melodies of the various → *minhagim* (among them the chants of the Oriental Jews, which were unknown in Europe up until then) differed greatly from one another. The traditions gathered in the Yishuv provided the concrete framework for his project of the cultural renewal of Jewish music in accordance with the Zionist *kinnus* (→ Anthology), the creation of a new national culture on the basis of select fragments of Jewish → folklore.

When Idelsohn began his research in Palestine, scholarly interest in Jewish music had not come very far. To be sure, the → Society for Jewish Folk Music (Russ. *Obshchestvo yevrejskoj narodnoj muzyki*; Yidd. *Gezelshaft far Yidisher Folks-Muzik*), which was dedicated to collecting traditional Jewish music, had been founded in St. Petersburg in 1908 on the initiative of some Jewish musicians. However, it was not guided by Zionist ideas and was less interested in researching the sources of music than in creating a Jewish national style within the framework of Russian classical music. In Central Europe, too, cantors had collected and published the music of European synagogues since the mid-19th century. Nevertheless, these aligned with the liberal course set by the → Wissenschaft des Judentums. Idelsohn had no links to either of these two trends but determined from the very first to present his research in the Zionist press of Europe and Palestine [14. 392].

When Idelsohn began to collect the music of Diaspora traditions, his project accorded entirely with the concept of *kibbuts galuyot*, the "gathering of the dispersed" that had been promised to the people of Israel ever since the days of Babylonian exile and realized as a Zionist ideal through the → Aliyah. He began to publish his work in the same year, developing a Zionist music theory that he explored in various publications [14. 392–407].

A fundamental assumption Idelsohn had was that the significant differences between the transmitted melodies must have come about due to the traditions in the Diaspora absorbing foreign elements under the influence of the surrounding culture, and that these elements were now superimposed on the core like an external shell. Furthermore, Idelsohn criticized Jewish musicians who had assimilated to European musical aesthetics. He joined in the heated debate triggered by Richard Wagner's antisemitic 1850 pamphlet *Das Judenthum in der Musik* ("Judaism in Music," 1907) that had attacked Jewish composers (→ Music). He turned Wagner's accusation of the "Judaization of modern art" on its head, arguing that the problem was not, in fact, that Jews were reshaping European music but, conversely, that Jewish music was becoming Europeanized; salvation for Jews, however, could not be achieved through assimilation as it was impossible for them to escape their Jewish soul but by returning to Zion, where a national rebirth could take place and artistic creativity could connect to the time before the exile. Another essential building block

of his theory was the assumption that the Oriental Jewish communities, having never had contact with Europe, had transmitted the purest and oldest strands of Jewish music. Unlike the European traditions, their music, he held, had not been contaminated by foreign elements because the Jews, a Semitic tribe, had not had any contacts in the Orient beyond the surrounding Semitic tribes. Idelsohn came back to the idea of a music shared by all Semites in his 1920 article *Neginah shemit* ("Semitic-Oriental Song," 1992) [5]. In this article, he expanded his Zionist theory into a music theory of the Semitic race, whose three branches – Arabian, Hebrew-Jewish, and Aramean – demonstrated shared characteristics in their music. For him, this indicated an underlying common Semitic prototype. He declared Jewish music to be a part of Semitic music, irrespective of later reshaping resulting from exile.

With the first five volumes of his *Thesaurus*, Idelsohn joined a radical form of the Zionist *shlilat ha-golah* (rejection of the Diaspora) as represented by the writers Micha Joseph Berdyczewski (Bin Gorion; → Anthology) and Joseph Chaim Brenner. In this line of thought, experience of the Diaspora is rejected in favor of an essentialist nationalism along biblical lines, which regards all things European as contamination and wishes only to return to an ancient Hebrew purity [14. 396]. The title – *Thesaurus of Hebrew Oriental Melodies* – was already programmatic. The highest ranking is reserved for the inquiries into the origin, authenticity, and the most ancient strata of tradition, answers to which Idelsohn discovered in the traditions of the East. He believed that the traditions of the Yemenite Jews were especially old. Due to his assumption that they had been isolated and not exposed to the influences of either European or Arabian-Persian classical music for many centuries, he saw them as preserving a tradition dating back to biblical times.

By linking older traditions to Oriental origin, Idelsohn conveyed several messages. First, he established for music what Jewish folklore studies, unlike their European counterpart, had not been able to achieve: a connection between the forms of the present and those of the past. Consequently, an abridged version of his study of the Yemenite Jews became the opening text in 1918 of the first issue of the *Reshumot* (Records) series, a publication of Zionist folklore scholars with the objective of creating folklore for a new Hebrew nation [13. 265–266]. Second, by discovering an ancient "genuinely Jewish music," he introduced a counterargument into the contemporary discourse that was founded on antisemitic resentment and regarded the Jews as an un-creative race (→ Music). In so doing, he turned against assimilated Jews in Europe, accusing them of justifying their abandonment of Judaism with the argument that there was no original specifically Jewish characteristic. Another – and not the least important – objective that Idelsohn's empirical proof of an original, pure Jewish tradition had was to support his plans for the foundation of a music institute that would put *kibbuts galuyot* into practice, purifying the transmitted melodies from all over the world of foreign elements. However, the institute never came into being as the Zionists did not support the project and the Orthodox Ashkenazi rabbis fought it. In the end, it failed due to the lack of funding.

While the second part of Idelsohn's *Thesaurus*, dedicated to Western and Eastern European traditions and compiled during his creative years in America, was no longer guided by Zionist ideas – he wrote it in the context of liberal Reform Judaism [10] – it does complement the first part, forming an organized whole in the sense of constructing a unity of Jewish music whose origin and *telos* are located in the East [8. 29]. The starting point in volumes 1 and 2 is provided by the presumably oldest and most authentic traditions of the Jews of Yemen and Iraq

(Babylonia). These are followed by volumes 3–5 containing the other traditions of the Mediterranean and the Orient. In the next two volumes, Idelsohn moves from the Orient to Europe and into the center of modernity, Germany (volumes 6 and 7). Volumes 8–10 conclude the collection with the chants and melodies of Eastern Europe, his own home. Through this deliberately chosen spatial arrangement, in which the modern style represented by the West is positioned within the enclosure of an East that is doubly traditional, Idelsohn not only anchors Jewish music in the Orient but also abolishes the traditional demarcations between Eastern and Western European Judaism, Europe and the Orient, traditional and modern styles – entirely in accordance with the Zionist idea of *kinnus* [8. 29].

4. East and West

At first glance the *Thesaurus*, at least as far as the section compiled in Palestine is concerned, appears to be informed wholly by the concept of *shlilat ha-golah*. However, Idelsohn was simultaneously part of a network of Western scholarly traditions, technologies, and discourses, without which the realization of the project would not have been possible and which, paradoxically, ensured that the *Thesaurus* was a profoundly European work.

Idelsohn's combination of biblical Hebraism and an ostensible Oriental-Semitic purity is part of European Orientalism, a complex conglomerate of Western ideas and projections regarding the East that many Jewish intellectuals adopted, too. The idea of the Orient as a spiritual constant had been alive in the → Diaspora ever since the destruction of the ancient nation and the dispersal of the people, and it had found manifold expression in rites of prayer and divine service. In the 19th century, the orientation towards the East and, consequently, the common Islamic-Jewish legacy assumed more concrete forms: Synagogues in the Moorish style evoked a romanticized version of the golden age of al-Andalus, Zionists like Aḥad Ha-Am (→ Cultural Zionism) and the painter Ephraim Moses Lilien (→ Art Nouveau) saw the return of the Jews to Palestine also as a return to their spiritual center, comprising the past as well as the future. Jewish Oriental scholars like Ignaz Goldziher (→ Muslim Studies) sought historical connections between Judaism and Islam, and Jewish enthusiasts of all things Oriental, such as Benjamin Disraeli (→ Tancred) and Ármin Vámbéry, recalled the roots of Judaism in Asia. Idelsohn's endeavors to imbue Jewish music with a new center of gravity by proving its Oriental-Semitic descent fit seamlessly into this framework.

Idelsohn's ideas owed their authority, above all, to the scholarly field of → comparative musicology, which had developed in the early 20th century in the German language area. It was a corollary of progress in the field of audio media: The invention of the phonograph by Thomas Edison (1877) and the → gramophone by Emil Berliner (1887), as well as Alexander Ellis's introduction of the cent system (1885) to determine precise pitch, allowed sounds to be preserved, reproduced, and descriptively copied for the first time. They could also be broken down into primary parameters and measured, so that scholars could examine oral traditions in depth. Subsequently, the first sound archives were founded in Vienna (1899) and Berlin (1901); these archives used phonographs to collect the languages and music of foreign peoples; they also provided Idelsohn with equipment. According to Erich Moritz von Hornbostel, the founding father of comparative musicology in Berlin and Idelsohn's adviser, the aim of the field was "the introduction of a certain way of looking at things" that allowed for "the analysis and precise description of isolated phenomena" by "contrasting these with other phenomena and emphasizing their distinguishing peculiarities," as well as "recording similarities and formulating them as 'laws'" [3. 40]. The new discipline relied heavily on linguistic research, which its practitioners had conceived as comparative-historical from the early 19th century. Musicologists adopted the search for universal patterns and cultural contexts, as well as the investigation of origins (in this case, of music) and efforts to reconstruct proto-forms from such linguistic research.

Comparative musicology aligned with Idelsohn's inclinations in two ways. Its research interest in languages and music as oral phenomena coincided with Idelsohn's primary interest, as an Orthodox cantor, in the "oral Torah": the biblical text, its pronunciation, and its cantillation. It also contributed the modern scientific methods that enabled him to develop his own field of research in a way that would be useful for addressing contemporary concerns. Intending to (re-)construct authentic Jewish music, Idelsohn used the phonograph to record the "oral Torah" of various living traditions. He then utilized a sound meter to dissect these recordings into physically measurable units and classified them according to similarities and divergences, uncovered chronological and spatial layers within the tradition, and endeavored to explain these. Just how much this approach shook the foundations of handed-down religious ideas is evident from the reaction of the Orthodox camp, which accused him, among other things, of carrying out "vivisection" [15. 57].

Idelsohn's striving for recognition in academic circles probably played a part that should not be underestimated in his linking of his *Thesaurus* to European scholarly tradition. Indeed, it may be the reason he sought to make the results of his studies fruitful for general musicology as well. The latter had long either ignored the existence of living Jewish music or devalued it as being mere imitation of the respective surrounding cultures, devoid of its own history. While experts on the whole agreed that there had been Hebrew music in the biblical past, they did not see any link to the songs of the present day – if, indeed, the music of the Bible was not regarded as belonging to a distant "primitive" past. August Wilhelm Ambros, whose three-volume *Geschichte der Musik* (1862–1868) may be considered the first scholarly study of the subject, was emblematic of this attitude. While the first volume *Die Musik des griechischen Altertums und des Orients* devotes more than 330 pages to the music of the Greeks, barely 200 are concerned with the peoples of the ancient Orient, and only 20 of these pages deal with the Hebrews. Ambros does concede that they had original music, but he draws the following conclusion regarding contemporary traditions: "The melodies along the lines of which the Jews sing their psalms nowadays do not provide any indication [of their origin] as the German, Italian, Spanish, etc. Jews sing the same psalm to melodies that are completely different from one another. The Jews, however firmly they have always adhered to the essence of their nationality and their faith, adapt with a wondrous elasticity to the peoples among whom they have lived since their dispersal" [1. vol. 1, 414]. In the second volume, Ambros goes one step further: "In fact, it seems as though the Jews never possessed their own national or religious music" [1. vol. 2, 9, n. 1].

Around the turn of the 20th century, musicology increasingly turned to researching the musical past of Europe, especially Gregorian chant, which was seen as the link between Antiquity and Western music history. Researchers inquiring into the earlier history of the forms and genres of the chants, which are found in written form dating from the 10th century, limited themselves to the sources from the Latin-speaking region, although many suggested that they consider the music of the Middle East and the synagogue as well. The newly awakened interest in Gregorian chant and the music of Antiquity played into Idelsohn's hands. When he met Guido Adler, professor of musicology in Vienna, during his visit to that city in 1913/1914, he announced that he hoped his *Thesaurus* had provided material for research into ancient and ecclesiastical music. During his stay in Vienna, he maintained regular contact with Adler, who had acquired an influential position in the musical life of the city as well as the university, despite his Jewish heritage. Adler, the founder of the Vienna Musikhistorisches Institut and one of the founding fathers of modern musicology, also provided a decisive impetus for the study of Gregorian chant. At his invitation, Idelsohn attended Adler's lectures on Gregorian chant and gave some lectures at the university. It was probably during their exchanges that the concept Idelsohn placed at the beginning of the first volume of the *Thesaurus of Hebrew Oriental Melodies* almost like a motto first emerged (Adler would later raise it to the status of dogma in his *Handbuch der Musikgeschichte* [1922]): "A systematic collection of the traditional melodies of the Oriental Jews is of paramount importance to the elucidation of synagogal chant in general and not less so to the investigation of the origin of Roman ecclesiastical chant; for both have their root in the sacred chant of the Oriental Jews" [4. vol. 1, XI]. Idelsohn's theory, which he set forth in a series of further publications, met with international appreciation, quickly becoming the *opinio communis*. That he was concerned not exclusively with the subject matter but also with achieving recognition within the scholarly community is reflected not least in his later dogged negotiations with Adler over being awarded the title of Ph.D. "in absentia." He believed he was entitled to this on account of his research.

With its fusion of Orientalist, Zionist, and European ideas, the *Thesaurus of Hebrew Oriental Melodies* appears to be an expression of a search for direction that Idelsohn himself ascribed to the "perplexity of a modern

Jew" in his autobiography [6.19]. In the later reception of this work, this tension – born of the debate about Europe and its Jewish questions – proved to be extremely fruitful. By asserting his sources as the progenitors of Christian liturgical music and thus placing Western music on the foundation of Hebrew music, Idelsohn introduced a change in perspective. He raised the status of Jewish music from "primitive" to "ancient and authentic" and located it within Western music history, thereby succeeding – in spite of general anti-semitic tendencies – in gaining recognition for Jewish music and justifying its inclusion in the canon of musicology. With his collection of Oriental melodies, he contributed to the shaping of Israeli music culture in Palestine. There, the melodies from the first five volumes were adopted, above all, during the nation's phase of consolidation and made their way into popular music as early as the 1920s and 1930s. When composers who had immigrated from Europe turned away from the Western legacy in their efforts to develop a new national style of classical music, they sought new models in the music of the Eastern Mediterranean and the Orient (→ Mediterranean Style). In doing so, they frequently borrowed specific melodies from the *Thesaurus*. Finally, the combination of Zionist ideas with the European scholarly tradition led to the emergence of a new discipline, Jewish musicology, which has long since freed itself from the ideological constraints of its beginnings.

Bibliography

Sources

[1] A. W. Ambros, Geschichte der Musik, 5 vols., Hildesheim 1968 [Reprint of Breslau/Leipzig 1887–1911]. [2] M. Brod, Zum Problem der "jüdischen Musik," in: M. Brod/F. Weltsch, Zionismus als Weltanschauung, Mährisch-Ostrau 1925, 96–107. [3] E. M. v. Hornbostel, The Problems of Comparative Musicology, in: E. M. v. Hornbostel/K. Wachsmann et al., Hornbos-

tel Opera Omnia, vol. I, section 12, The Hague 1975. [4] A. Z. Idelsohn, Thesaurus of Oriental Hebrew Melodies, 10 vols., Berlin/Jerusalem/Vienna 1923–1933. [5] A. Z. Idelsohn, Semitic-Oriental Song, in: A. Z. Idelsohn, Jewish Music. Its Historical Development, New York 1992, 24–34. [6] A. Z. Idelsohn, My Life. A Sketch, in: I. Adler et al. (eds.), The Abraham Zvi Idelsohn Memorial Volume, Jerusalem 1986, 18–23.

Secondary literature

[7] I. Adler et al. (eds.), The Abraham Zvi Idelsohn Memorial Volume, Jerusalem 1986. [8] P. V. Bohlman, Abraham Zvi Idelsohn and the Reorientation of Jewish Music History, in: The Collection of Abraham Zvi Idelsohn (1911–1913), ed. by D. Schüller, Vienna 2006 [3 CDs, 1 CD-ROM, booklet]. [9] P. V. Bohlman/R. F. Davis, Mizrakh. Jewish Music and the Journey to the East, in: M. Clayton/B. Zon (eds.), Music and Orientalism in the British Empire, 1780s – 1940s. Portrayal of the East, Aldershot 2007, 95–128. [10] J. M. Cohen, Rewriting the Grand Narrative of Jewish Music. Abraham Z. Idelsohn in the United States, in: Jewish Quarterly Review 100 (2010) 3, 417–453. [11] I. Heskes, Passport to Jewish Music. Its History, Traditions, and Culture, Westport 1994. [12] J. Hirshberg, Music in the Jewish Community of Palestine, Oxford 1995. [13] M. W. Kiel, Ideologies of Jewish Folklore. Reshumot – The Russian Years, in: E. Lederhendler/J. Wertheimer (eds.), Text and Context. Essays in Modern Jewish History and Historiography in Honor of Ismar Schorsch, New York 2005, 256–282. [14] J. Loeffler, Do Zionists Read Music from Right to Left? Abraham Tsvi Idelsohn and the Invention of Israeli Music, in: Jewish Quarterly Review 100 (2010) 3, 385–416. [15] E. Schleifer, Idelsohn's Scholarly and Literary Publications. An Annotated Bibliography, in: I. Adler et al. (eds.), The Abraham Zvi Idelsohn Memorial Volume, Jerusalem 1986, 53–180. [16] E. Seroussi, Music. The "Jew" of Jewish Studies, in: Jewish Studies 46 (2009), 3–84.

REGINA RANDHOFER, LEIPZIG

Tiberias

Tiberias, situated on the West Bank of the Sea of Galilee, is, along with Jerusalem, Safed, and Hebron, one of the four holy cities of Judaism. After an initial blossoming period in Late Antiquity and the early Middle Ages, the city only again regained importance near the end of the 16th century. Even before the beginning of the Zionist-motivated immigration from Eastern Europe in the late 19th century, Tiberias had become one of the most important Jewish centers in northern Palestine (Galilea; → Yishuv) and was characterized by close relations to the Diaspora in the Ottoman Empire.

1. Establishment and early history
2. The Northern Yishuv
3. Relations to the Ottoman Diaspora
4. After 1881

1. Establishment and early history

Tiberias (Hebr. Tverya; Arab. Ṭabarīyah) was founded around 18 CE by Herod Antipas, a son of King Herod I, presumably on the ruins of the biblical settlement of Rakkath; the city received its name from the Roman emperor Tiberias, who was reigning at the time. The town, situated approximately 210 meters below sea level, was known for its hot springs and therefore destined to be a spa. At the same time, the settlement was named capital of the short-lived Roman province of Galilea. The population at this time consisted primarily of Jews, who, because of the scarcity of arable land, primarily engaged in fishing. → Crafts such as pottery, (wool-) weaving, woodwork, and fish-farming were widespread.

In Late Antiquity, Tiberias achieved the status of the most important Jewish town of Palestine, even before Jerusalem. Its importance was based mainly on the fact that Tiberias was chosen as the official residence of the Jewish patriarch (→ Nasi). Added to this was the fact that the Jewish inhabitants of Jerusalem had been expelled from the city as a result of the unsuccessful Bar Kokhba revolt and settled here. In the 3rd century, the Sanhedrin, the highest Jewish court in Jerusalem until 70 CE and which now assumed the function of an academy as the "House of Great Counsel," was transferred to Tiberias. Such important learned authorities as Rabbi Jochanan ben Sakkai (ca. 180–279?) or Shim'on ben Lakisch (200–275) belonged to this influential rabbinic academy.

The Mishnah (edited around 300; → Talmud), and certainly large parts of the Palestinian Talmud (edited in the early 5th century) were presumably compiled in Tiberias. Between the 8th and the 10th centuries, Tiberias was the place of activity of the Massoretes (From the Hebr. *masorah*, tradition) around the Ben Asher and Ben Naphtali families, who worked on their text-critical → commentaries on the Bible there.

The city's influence began to fade when, as a result of the Arabic conquest of Palestine in the 7th century, the religious authorities returned to Jerusalem. However, as late as the 12th century, Maimonides (1135–1204; → Guide for the Perplexed) considered Tiberias so important that he directed his remains to be buried there.

The importance of Tiberias was rather minor even after the Ottoman conquest in 1516–1517: at the most, one can speak of a living community over a period of barely one hundred years, while its golden age lasted only about fifty years (ca. 1525–1575; → Sultan's Jews). Thus, at the beginning of the 17th century, the Jewish inhabitants of → Safed still made up about half the Yishuv, that is the Jewish population living in Palestine.

2. The Northern Yishuv

In all, the Galilean → Yishuv was rather limited in numbers in the 17th century, especially after the economic and demographic decline of Safed. The number of

Jews oscillated between a few hundred and 2,000 to 2,500 around the mid-18th century [12. 202–206]. Jews lived in several Galilean villages with populations of mixed religions, such as in Ein al-Zeitun, Shfar'am, Kfar Hananya, Kfar Kana (probably the largest rural Jewish community of the time), Kfar Yasif (which still had a Jewish community in the 18th century and where the Jews from Acre were buried) as well as in Peki'in, which featured a Jewish community without interruption down to the 20th century. According to Ottoman folk tales from the 17th century, each village with a Jewish population comprised between ten and fifteen Jewish families, most of whom belonged to the autochthonous Must'arabim [12. 202]. At the time, Tiberias was a place of little importance for Jews; by the end of the 17th century, the settlement had no Jewish inhabitants.

The economic power of the Jews in Galilea was variously strong, among other things as a result of their respective origins. Thus, the → Arabic-speaking autochthonous Jews, Jews from North Africa (Maghrebim), and, albeit to a lesser extent, also immigrants from other parts of the Ottoman Empire, such as Turkey or the Balkans, were able to integrate into the local market more easily than the Jews who came from → Ashkenaz. For the latter, their lack of knowledge of the language and greater cultural differences made it much more difficult to adapt. In the rural communities of Galilea, Jewish men worked primarily in agriculture, where vegetables, grains, legumes, and cotton were grown, and honey and dairy products were produced, but also in → crafts and as suppliers of agrarian and artisanal products. In contrast, significantly more Jewish traders, merchants, translators, and commercial agents, but also more craftsmen had settled in the towns, especially the larger ones on the coast. Here, Jews were also represented in the fishing and navigation sectors. Little is known about the economic activity of Jewish women. Many were probably employed in their husbands' crafts and some in wool processing (spinning and weaving). Older widows and Talmud students traditionally did not take part in local economic life but had to rely on donations (→ Tsedakah).

The increase in the Jewish population in the 18th century was essentially based on immigration from other countries. In contrast, the natural growth rate was low, owing to the high average age of the immigrants – particularly the many widows among them – as well as the high infant mortality rates. At this time, Jews immigrated to Erets Israel primarily for religious reasons: they wanted to study, pray, and be buried in the Holy Land.

Ashkenazi immigrants to Erets Israel settled increasingly more often in Galilea, since in the early 18th century the infrastructure of the Ashkenazi community of Jerusalem had broken down due to excessive debt, impoverishment, and immiseration. Particularly important in this process was the year 1740, when the Bedouin Arab sheikh Dhaher al-Omar (ca. 1690–1775) had the Galilean towns of Tiberias, Haifa, and his governmental seat Acre secured with fortifications. Previously, Dhaher had consolidated his power over the northern regions of Palestine by means of skillful policies that integrated the ethnic and religious groups, and after the central Ottoman power had made unsuccessful attempts to subjugate him, it had finally acknowledged him. In the following years, Acre rose to become the de facto capital of the province. At the same time, Dhaher promoted the settlement of European merchants who were interested in cotton and other products of the region.

For the further development of Tiberias, Dhaher had recourse to settling Jews, who remunerated his pledge of protection by paying taxes. It was on these conditions that the scholar Chaim Abulafia (1660–1744), who came from → Smyrna, arrived in Tiberias in 1740 with a group of his students and their families. In the course of the century, they were joined by *maghrebim* as well as by Ashkenazi Jews, especially Hasidim from Eastern Europe, who arrived in Palestine beginning in the 1760s. For instance, in 1764/1765, there was a group among them under the leadership of Nachman of Horodenka and Menachem Mendel of Przemyśl. Above all, after the immigration of the Hasidic Rebbe Menachem Mendel of → Vitebsk, Abraham of Kalisk, and Israel of Polotsk in 1777, increasing numbers of East European followers of → Hasidism settled in Galilea. They preferred Tiberias over → Safed, where, after the 1808 immigration of a group of students of the anti-Hasidic Elia ben Salomo, the Gaon of → Vilna, a hostile attitude was apparently adopted toward them. In 1798/1799, the famous Rabbi Nachman of Breslov (1772–1810) stayed in Galilea and his brief presence steadily attracted more Hasidim.

Settlement by well-known non-Hasidic personalities also led to increased immigration in the 18th century. Among them was the Torah commentator and Kabbalist Chaim ibn Attar (1696–1743), who came from Morocco – and had resided since 1739, with interruptions, in → Livorno and other Italian communities – in order to collect funds for the foundation of a Jewish community in Palestine. For Ibn Attar, the settlement of Chaim Abulafia in Tiberias was also the reason for him to set out for the Holy Land. In 1741, he reached Acre, along with his followers, where, two years later, the Italian Kabbalist scholar Moses Chaim Luzzatto (1707–1746; → Mysticism), who had lived for a few years in Amsterdam (→ Esnoga) after accusations of Sabbatianism, settled.

In the first half of the 18th century, there was a fundamental change in the composition of the immigrants according to their country of origin. Since then, most Jewish immigrant no longer came from the Ottoman Empire in the strict sense (although most Jerusalem Jews came from there), but from North Africa (especially from Morocco and Algeria), Eastern Europe, and from what

is now Iran. Thus, in 1839 approximately 150 Jews lived in Haifa; many of them were *maghrebim*. By this time, the port of Acre had long replaced Jaffa as the most important gateway to the nation, although the spatial proximity to Jerusalem, now as before, was an advantage for Jaffa's Jewish community. Similarly, the significance of Acre strengthened the Jewish community of Tiberias, as it did for the Galilean Yishuv as a whole, along with Caesarea and the smaller settlements in the Jezreel Valley in the interior. In this period, the number of immigrant Jews with letters patent of protection from Europe increased steadily: Jews worked increasingly more often in the coastal cities of the state as consuls for England, Austria, and other countries.

In the meantime, domestic migration to Galilea was added to the immigration from overseas. The reasons for this included the earthquakes of 1822 and especially 1837, recurrent epidemics, and the problematic security situation. As late as the first half of the 19th century, European travellers constantly reported on poverty among the Beduins and city-dwellers and the omnipresent dangers, including frequent cases of robbery and murder [3]. The legal status of Jews as protected (*dhimmī*; → Dhimmah) had little value.

3. Relations to the Ottoman Diaspora

Northern Palestine, which was under Ottoman rule, belonged to the provinces (Vilāyets) of Damascus and Sidon (later Acre). Whereas the Jewish communities in the area south of the Jerusalem-Jaffa line maintained only loose connections to those of the Khedivate of Egypt and its capital Cairo, the Jewish communities in Galilea were closely connected to the other Jewish communities of the Vilāyêt. The multiple contacts with Syria, and especially with the Jewish community of Damascus, which, for its part, maintained close connections with the community of Istanbul, made a substantial contribution to saving the Jews from Tiberias when it was besieged by Ottoman troops in 1742. Jacob ben Chaim Berab (Beirav) described these events in detail in his *Zimrat ha-Arets* (Song of the Land, Mantua 1745), but also described the emergence of the Jewish community shortly before the siege and emphatically spoke out in favor of its reconstruction.

The relations between the Jewish communities of Galilea and those of the Ottoman Diaspora were primarily financial in nature. In addition to the funds which official envoys (Hebr. *shadarim*) of the Jewish communities of Palestine collected in Europe (→ Ḥalukkah), benevolent organizations or individuals, primarily from Turkey and the Balkans, supported needy communities in northern Palestine by donations, foundations, or gifts (→ Tsedakah). The Jews of Istanbul also appeared as their spokespersons (→ Shtadlanut) at the sultan's court, usually to obtain assistance against persecution or relief from excessive tax burdens. Letters to the Jewish community of Istanbul document the requests of Galilean Jews for assistance for those in need or, faced by imminent desecration of tombs and destruction of synagogues, expressed their concern for the continued survival of their community [11. 113].

In fact, the Jewish communities in Galilea were permanently dependent on the Committee of Defenders of Erets Israel in Istanbul (*Va'ad Pekide Erets Yisra'el be-Kushtah*), which had been founded in 1726 for the support of the Jews of Jerusalem and was the model for the subcommittees in → Safed (before 1742) and Tiberias (1740). The committee members issued letters of recommendation for their envoys who collected funds, examined the account books of the Palestinian communities, and, with the help of local representatives, supervised the expenditures and utilization funds on site, as well as the overall administration of the communities. Finally, they even regulated the distribution of immigrants among the communities. This strongly centralized apparatus managed the affairs of the Yishuv and its communities for about fifty years until its influence waned. It was replaced in the early 19th century by the organization *Pekidim ve-Amarkalim* (Representatives and Adminstrators), which had its seat in Amsterdam.

Another example of the close connection between the Galilaean Yishuv and the Jewish community of → Damascus is the work of the well-to-do Farḥi family of → bankers and goldsmiths from Damascus. Until the interim Egyptian conquest and administration of Syria (1831–1840), they sent financial and practical support to the Jews of Galilea, specifically by the promotion of mutual trade, the exchange of emissaries and scholars, as well as grants for pilgrims and couples wishing to marry. Galilaean Jews also repeatedly fled to Damascus on the occasion of epidemics or other crises.

Jewish pilgrims also arrived in Galilea from the northern vilayêts, especially for the pilgrimage festivals Pesaḥ and Shavu'ot (→ Course of the Year). Since the Mamluk period (1291–1516), Upper and Lower Galilea assumed particular importance for pilgrimages, while Jerusalem and its environs, as well as the Cave of Machpelah in the Hebron, were only marginally significant for pilgrims. This phenomenon was reinforced by the strong presence of Kabbalists in Safed. Thus, Isaac Luria (→ Mysticism) believed he had discovered the tombs of famous Tannaim and Amoraeans (→ Talmud) in Galilea and suggested they be considered places of individual retreat and prayer. They located the cave and the tomb of Shim'on bar Jochai (→ Safed), the purported author of the *Zohar* (→ Mysticism) on Mount Meron, where ceremonies are held to this day at the Lag BaOmer festival (→ Course of the Year).

There were also ritual sites used in common by different religious communities, such as the Cave of Elijah on Mt. Carmel. The increasing number of pilgrimages and their institutionalization were accompanied by newly-built walking paths, the introduction of prayers with reference to places in the Holy Land, and visual representations in the form of hagiographical maps. Thus, the Land of Israel now appeared as a collection of holy places with Galilea as its center.

4. After 1881

The Zionist settlement of Galilea proceeded sluggishly, with the exception of the Jezreel Valley on the southern border, and was selective. Nevertheless, beginning in the early 20th century, Tiberias attracted a comparatively large number of Jewish immigrants. In 1922, more than 4,000 Jews lived in the town and thus represented the majority of the population. Around the same time, the construction of new residential quarters began outside the town walls (Shekhunat Aḥva, 1912; Kiryat Shemu'el, 1922). The transition to Jewish ownership of the mineral springs in 1922 marked the beginning of the development of Tiberias into a modern resort.

After the town fell to Israeli forces in 1948, and the Arab population was forced to abandon it, the number of Jewish inhabitants consistently grew through new immigrants from the Maghreb (→ Tangier). Today, tourism is the town's major source of revenue; the tombs of the rabbinic scholars Jochanan ben Sakkai and Rabbi Akiva, as well as of Maimonides, have great appeal.

Bibliography

Sources

[1] M. Benayahu, Zimrat ha-arets le-Ya'akov Beirav [The Song of the Land by Jacob Berab], Jerusalem 1946. [2] U. Heyd, Ottoman Documents on Palestine, 1552–1615. A Study of the Firman According to the Mühimme Defteri, Oxford 1960. [3] M. Ish-Shalom, Masa'e notsrim le-erets Yisra'el. Reshumot ve-eduyot le-toldot ha-yishuv ha-yehudi [Christian Travels in the Holy Land. Documents and Testimonies on the History of Jewish settlements], Tel Aviv 1965. [4] Y. M. Toledano (ed.), Otsar Genazim: osef igrot le-toldot Erets-Yisra'el mi-tokh kitve-yad 'atikim [Archival Treasure. Collection of Letters on the History of Erets Yisrael from Ancient MSS], Jerusalem 1960.

Secondary literature

[5] Y. Ben-Zwi, Erets Yisra'el ve-yishuvah be-shilton ha-otmanit [The Land of Israel and its Jewish Settlements under Ottoman Rule], Jerusalem ³1976. [6] A. Cohen, Palestine in the 18th Century. Patterns of Government and Administration, Jerusalem 1973. [7] A. Cohen (ed.), Historyah shel Erets-Yisra'el 7: Shilton ha-Mamlukim veha-Ot'omanim (1260–1804) [The History of Erets Yisrael, Vol. 7: Under Mamluk and Ottoman Rule (1260–1804)], Jerusalem 1981. [8] A. Cohen/B. Lewis, Population and Revenue in the Towns of Palestine in the 16th Century, Princeton 1978. [9] B. Lewis, On History. Collected Studies, ed. by R. Simon, Jerusalem 1988 [Hebr.]. [10] M. Ma'oz (ed.), Studies on Palestine during the Ottoman Period, Jerusalem 1975. [11] M. Pachter, Mitsfunot Tsefat: meḥkarim u-mekorot le-toledot Tsefat ve-ḥakhameha be-me'ah ha-16 [From Safed's Hidden Treasures. Studies and Sources on the History of Safed and its Sages in the 16th Century], Jerusalem 1994. [12] M. Rozen, The Jewish Settlement in Erets-Yisrael on the Eve of Modern Times (1516–1804) [Hebr.], in: A. Cohen (ed.), Historyah shel Erets-Yisra'el 7: Shilton ha-Mamlukim veha-Ot'omanim (1260–1804) [The History of Erets Yisrael, Vol. 7: Under Mamluk and Ottoman Rule (1260–1804)], Jerusalem 1981, 199–274.

YARON BEN-NAEH, JERUSALEM

Tikkun olam

The expression *tikkun olam*, which goes back to the early period of Rabbinic Judaism, designates the restoration of the (damaged) world. Especially after it was developed in Lurianic Kabbalah (→ Mysticism; → Safed), this notion was widespread. The rabbi and philosopher Emil Fackenheim (1916–2003; → Philosophy) discussed the concept in a central part of his main work *To Mend the World. Foundations of Future Jewish Thought* (1982), in which he understands the → Holocaust as a radical break in history. The question of how resistance in the face of extermination was necessary and possible demanded the Jewish concept of *tikkun olam*. It contributes to reflection on the Holocaust, a moment which philosophy urgently needs in view of the extermination of European Jewry.

1. History of the term
2. Fackenheim's life and work
3. *Tikkun olam* in *To Mend the World*

1. History of the term

The Hebrew Bible (→ Tanakh) uses the root *t–k–n* in the sense of "to smooth out" or "to repair" (for instance, Eccl 1:15). The noun derived from it, as a part of the expression *tikkun ha-olam* (healing or restoration of the world), however, is rarely found in the Jewish → liturgy and in the → Talmud, and only in quite specific contexts. Thus, for instance, adaptations of rabbinic legal norms, considered as necessary, were justified by reference to the "improvement of the world" (e.g. Talmud Bavli, Gittin 45a, 47a). In addition, the expression was used in the *Aleinu* prayer, which arose in the 3rd century CE and is based on motifs from *Merkavah* mysticism but did not enter into daily prayers until after 1300. Here, in any case, the attainment of salvation was still left up to the action of God alone.

After the term had been used since at least the second half of the 13th century in the *Sefer ha-Zohar* (Book of Splendor), it was the subject of increased attention from the 16th century onward in Lurianic Kabbalah (→ Mysticism). Since then, it was used most often without the definite article, as *tikkun olam*. In the Kabbalistic notion of the breaking of the vessels and the distribution of the divine sparks throughout the world, human action now achieved greater significance. It was incumbent upon the Jews of the → Diaspora to contribute to the healing of the world and the cosmos through regular prayer, keeping of the → mitsvot, study of the Torah (→ *talmud torah*), and good deeds by means of the healing of the soul. Transmitted through further elaborations, for instance by Ḥayyim ben Joseph Vital, Sabbatai Zevi (→ Smyrna), Jehuda Löw ben Bezalel, and in → Hasidism, *tikkun olam* finally entered the thought of the 20th century.

Since the 1970s, the expression has been increasingly used for political engagement, especially in the United States, by followers of → Conservative Judaism, prominent among whom was Rabbi Abraham Joshua Heschel (→ Civil Rights Movement), as well as in Reform Judaism, for instance Arnold Jacob Wolf. In particular, *tikkun olam* now designated efforts aiming at social justice. Soon, the expression was so widespread for designating efforts to heal, repair, and improve the world in general that in 1986 a newly-founded journal for Jewish renewal chose the title *Tikkun. To Heal, Repair, and Transform the World*. Unlike these quite universal uses in a sociopolitical context, Fackenheim related the term to a specific historical situation in his work.

2. Fackenheim's life and work

Emil Ludwig Fackenheim was born in Halle in 1916. At the gymnasium, he devoted himself primarily to ancient languages, but after graduation he did not follow the advice of his teacher, Adolf Lörcher, to study classical philology. Instead, in 1935 he began rabbinic studies in Berlin at the → Hochschule für die Wissenschaft des Judentums, under such teachers as Leo Baeck (→ Leo Baeck Institute), Ismar Elbogen (→ Historiography), and Max Wiener (→ Secularization); he also attended courses at the University of Halle in preparation for a philosophical dissertation.

Fackenheim's father Julius was a well-known lawyer with offices in Berlin and Halle; for a while, he held the presidency of the local lodge of the → B'nai-B'rith, founded a Jewish sports club, and became involved in the → Reichsbund jüdischer Frontsoldaten. The parents of Fackenheim's mother ran a warehouse (→ Department Stores) in Halle. The family celebrated the Jewish holidays together with his grandparents (→ Course of the Year), as Fackenheim reports in his memoirs [4. 17].

After the transfer of power to Hitler, Emil's father could no longer practice his profession as a result of the Gesetz über die Zulassung zur Rechtsanwaltschaft (Law on Admission to the Bar) of April 1933. In Berlin, he henceforth advocated extrajudicially for Jewish entrepreneurs who were threatened by expropriation, for which he was arrested in 1935 and incarcerated for six weeks. After the → November Pogrom of 1938, the Nazis took Emil Fackenheim temporarily to the concentration camp of Sachsenhausen. Following his release in 1939, and after successfully passing his rabbinical examination, he fled to Aberdeen in Scotland, where he continued his philosophical studies at the university there. In 1940, together with other Germans who had fled to the British Isles, he was detained as an enemy alien in various camps on the Isle of Man. In the following year, hewas again freed, and reached Canada, where he was once again taken into custody, this time in a transit camp in Sherbrooke, Quebec. He was released after several months.

Emil Fackenheim (1916–2003)

Fackenheim went to Toronto, where he was accepted into the doctoral program in the Department of Philosophy at the university. He earned his doctorate in 1945 with a dissertation on medieval Arabic and Jewish philosophy (→ Falsafah), which contained introductory chapters on Aristotle and Neoplatonism. From 1943 to 1948, Fackenheim held the → rabbinate of the Reform community, founded in the 1850s in Hamilton (Ontario). In 1948, he obtained a position in the Department of Philosophy of the University of Toronto, where he taught, later as full professor, until he moved with his family to Jerusalem in 1983 and taught at the → Hebrew University.

In the postwar period, Fackenheim published primarily on questions of Jewish theology and → philosophy. His subjects extended from medieval philosophy through defenses of the revelation, to a modern concept of faith inspired by the Existentialist thought of Sören Kierkegaard (→ Alterity), Martin Buber (→ Dialogue), and

Franz Rosenzweig (→ [The] Star of Redemption). In 1956/1957, Fackenheim received a Guggenheim Fellowship for a study of reason and revelation from Kant (→ Concept of God; → Lebensgeschichte) to Kierkegaard. However, he set this project aside to concentrate instead on the philosophy of Hegel (→ Recognition). The result was the 1967 book entitled *The Religious Dimension in Hegel's Thought*, in which he criticized Hegel's system since it did not attribute an appropriate place to revelation.

In the two decades following the Second World War, theology in North America hardly dealt with the catastrophe that was only later called the → Holocaust and for which the Yiddish word → *khurbn* (destruction, annihilation) was customary. This changed in the mid-1960s with the appearance of Richard Rubenstein's works (for instance, *After Auschwitz. History, Theology and Contemporary Judaism*, 1966), but above all after the → Eichmann trial. Hannah Arendt's (→ Judgement) work *The Origins of Totalitarianism*, which appeared in 1951, was widely diffused, but was nevertheless understood in the first instance as a historical and theoretical study of Western culture. In the early 1960s, the works of Raul Hilberg (→ Judenrat), George L. Mosse, Primo Levi (→ [The] Truce), and Elie Wiesel, which dealt with the Holocaust, were indeed available in → English, but were little known.

Fackenheim's own work from the late 1940s to 1965 scarcely mentions National Socialism and avoids an explicit consideration of the theological or philosophical questions that arose in view of the extermination camps and the Holocaust. Not until 1965/1966 did he take up the theme of the Nazi atrocities and their effects on Judaism and on Western culture. His book entitled *God's Presence in History* (1970) emerged from his reflections on the implications of → Auschwitz for history and the philosophy of religion. In the mid-1970s, Fackenheim began a large-scale project on the meaning of these questions for the future of both Jews and non-Jews: the result was his magnum opus, *To Mend the World* (1982). The subjects it dealt with occupied him for the rest of his life. Among other themes, his discussed the special role of the State of Israel for Judaism after the Holocaust. Fackenheim died in Jerusalem in September 2003.

3. *Tikkun olam* in *To Mend the World*

In 1975, Fackenheim undertook a study of Jewish thought and Jewish → philosophy, at the center of which was to be the thesis that Auschwitz marked a historical break and should therefore be characterized as an "epoch-making event" [3.15]. By this formulation, which went back to Hegel, Fackenheim described extraordinary historical phenomena that entailed a completely changed way of understanding history, and therefore posed entirely new intellectual and moral demands for mankind in general, as well as for Judaism. As examples, he adduced the destruction of the → Temple, → emancipation, as well as the founding of the State of Israel. In 1982 the only completed part of the study, originally planned to be much more extensive, appeared under the title *To Mend the World*. In this book, Fackenheim brings about a meeting between Spinoza (→ Tractatus Theologico-Politicus) and Franz Rosenzweig (→ [The] Star of Redemption), in order to determine the desiderata of a genuinely Jewish thought. It must be based on relation between the divine and the human, which is essentially indebted to → history, and must therefore take a position with regard to its traumas and horrors.

To meet these requirements, Fackenheim, going back to Hegel and the Hegelian tradition in philosophy, sketched a specifically Jewish conception of revelation. All future Jewish thought must face up to the possibility of a historical break, which was documented in Auschwitz in the attempt to completely annihilate Judaism. In order to show how Judaism can and must continue to exist in the face of such events, Fackenheim developed the category of unconditional resistance against horror. In so doing, he had recourse to the ideas of *tikkun olam* and → *teshuvah* (repentance) and discussed which meaning they assumed for Judaism, Christianity, and philosophy after the → Holocaust.

Fackenheim tries to show how the Holocaust is to be understood as an epoch-making event, the monstrosity and evil of which demands a response that simultaneously enables acts of rebellion and of resistance. In a powerful phenomenological and dialectical argumentation, it is explained how, in many victims, the Nazis' atrocities and the horror of the extermination camps entailed a behavior that was "at once a *surprised acceptance* and a *horrified resistance*," all in one. "[S]ince the thought that is *in* this surprise is forced to accept what is yet in all eternity unacceptable, *thought is required to become 'ecstatic,' such as to point beyond resistance within its own native sphere, to a resistance that is beyond the sphere of thought altogether, and in the sphere of life*" [3. 247].

Fackenheim draws two conclusions from this: the first is that the evil of the world of the Holocaust today "*is philosophically intelligible after Auschwitz only in the exact sense in which it is already understood in Auschwitz* [...] *by the resisting victims themselves* [...]. This *grasp—theirs no less than ours—is epistemologically ultimate.*" The second conclusion is that rebellion against the Holocaust was a proper "*way of being. For our thought now*" – insofar as it is in opposition to the goals of the Nazis – this resistance therefore constitutes an "*ontological category*" [3. 248].

By this argument, Fackhenheim points out that revolt against National Socialism and its goals is also necessary today, and even obligatory, precisely because it was possible then. However, if this is so, Fackenheim asks: "*Butcan this imperative be obeyed?*" [3. 249]. The Holocaust marks a radical break. If we

can continue with our lives, this continuity is not possible by the use of old-fashioned categories or modes of thought but must be based on a new concept: according to Fackenheim, the idea of *tikkun olam*.

Philosophy needs this idea. Judaism has it at hand, and it is be found in the Kabbalah (→ Mysticism). It connects the acknowledgement of a complete break – a fracturing of cosmic as well as historical events – to a "healing" that is at the same time divine and human and yet always remains incomplete. Fackenheim points out explicitly that his concise presentation of Kabbalistic imagery and symbolism goes back to Gershom Scholem's (→ Kabbalah) *Die jüdische Mystik in ihren Hauptströmungen* (1957; "Major Trends in Jewish Mysticism," 1961) and admits that his own engagement with Kabbalistic terms first began in *To Mend the World*. Whereas in the past, Kabbalists pursued a *tikkun* from below – by means of "Torah, prayer and '*mitzvot*'" –, in order to elicit a divine response, complete *tikkun* had become impossible both during and after the Holocaust. The rupture still existed. At the same time, however, according to Fackenheim, "the impossible *Tikkun* is also necessary." Resistance during the Holocaust can therefore be considered as *tikkun*, even if it seemed impossible at the time. As a result, it is established that *tikkun* is necessary today and correspondingly possible, even if it should occur in a fragmented, incomplete way. "Hence in our search for a post-Holocaust *Tikkun* we must accept from the start that at most only a fragmentary *Tikkun* is possible. This is because we are *situated in* a post-Holocaust world. We must accept our situatedness. We must live with it." [3. 254, 256]. Fackenheim thereby suggests that Judaism has an intellectual figure at hand that is lacking in traditional Western philosophy.

To Mend the World attracted broad attention in contemporary Jewish thought and may be considered Fackenheim's most important and lasting contribution to 20th century Jewish philosophy. Nevertheless, it does not easily fit within established categories and traditions. Fackenheim's mode of thought and argumentation form a particular synthesis, which is indebted to his reading of Kierkegaard and Hegel, Buber and Rosenzweig, and could be designated as "dialectical existentialism." The book also contains Fackenheim's most developed confrontation with Heidegger (→ Davos Disputation) without, however, taking part in the discussions of the philosophical implications of Heidegger's proximity to National Socialism. Despite its richness and originality, *To Mend the World* was only occasionally the subject of further study. Thus, for instance, Emmanuel Levinas referred to Fackenheim, although his philosophy of → alterity with regard to Western rationalism was based on a primacy of ethics, whereas Fackenheim gave preference to the "*sphere of life*" [3. 247].

Bibliography

Sources

[1] E. L. Fackenheim, God's Presence in History, New York 1970.   [2] E. L. Fackenheim, Encounters between Judaism and Modern Philosophy, New York 1975.   [3] E. L. Fackenheim, To Mend the World. Foundations of Future Jewish Thought, New York 1982.   [4] E. L. Fackenheim, An Epitaph for German Judaism. From Halle to Jerusalem, Madison 2007.

Secondary literature

[5] L. Cooper, The Assimilation of Tikkun Olam, in: Jewish Political Studies Review 25 (2013) 3/4, 10–42.   [6] L. Fine, Tikkun. A Lurianic Motif in Contemporary Jewish Thought, in: J. Neusner et al. (eds.), From Ancient Israel to Modern Judaism. Intellect in Quest of Understanding. Essays in Honor of Marvin Fox, vol. 4, Atlanta 1989, 35–53.   [7] L. Greenspan/G. Nicholson, Fackenheim. German Philosophy and Jewish Thought,

Toronto 1992.   [8] M. L. Morgan, The Central Problem of Emil Fackenheim's "To Mend the World," in: Journal of Jewish Thought and Philosophy 5 (1996) 2, 297–312.   [9] M. L. Morgan, Fackenheim's Jewish Philosophy. An Introduction, Toronto 2013.   [10] M. L. Morgan/B. Pollock (eds.), The Philosopher as Witness, Albany 2008.   [11] B. Pollock, Thought Going to School with Life? Fackenheim's Last Philosophical Testament, in: S. Portnoff et al. (eds.), Emil L. Fackenheim. Philosopher, Theologian, Jew, Leiden 2008, 55–87.   [12] G. S. Rosenthal, "Tikkun ha-Olam." The Metamorphosis of a Concept, in: Journal of Religion 85 (2005) 2, 214–240. [13] D. Shatz et al. (eds.), Tikkun Olam. Social Responsibility in Jewish Thought and Law, Northvale 1998.

MICHAEL L. MORGAN,
TORONTO/BLOOMINGTON

Time

The Jewish understanding of time rests on biblical foundations and was shaped by ancient rabbinic scholars as well as medieval thinkers and mystics. After the destruction of the Second → Temple (70 CE), and, above all, after the final compilation of the Babylonian → Talmud (6th or 7th cent. CE), the terminology and the concepts associated with time were standardized and unified. By means of legal and exegetic interpretation of the contradictions found in the Bible, the rabbis, who claimed the authority over the normative understanding of scripture, conferred a specific character onto various aspects of time. This ultimately led to the development of the principle of twofold temporality oscillating between universal time and Jewish time. This principle is based on the perpetual interplay among different registers of time, namely, cyclical, linear, historical, eschatological, and philosophical time.

1. Ancient concepts
1.1 Structures of time in the Bible and the Talmud
1.2 Cyclical time and linear time
1.3 Historical time
1.4 The determination of time
1.5 Eschatological time
2. Imagined time
2.1 Philosophers and mystics
2.2 Recourse to tradition
2.3 Dual temporality

1. Ancient concepts

1.1 *Structures of time in the Bible and the Talmud*

The concept of "time" can be understood as a complex whole consisting of the way in which it is experienced (duration, points in time, → calendar, time of day, rhythm), as well as the way in which it is approached intellectually (in astronomy, → mathematics, → philosophy, → phenomenology, psychology, theology, history, → sociology). The abstract concept, in fact, reflects a more comprehensive understanding of time that includes the world and the cosmos.

The Jewish perception of time is based on the interpretation of the biblical story of creation. The first division of time is undertaken in Genesis 1:5: "God called the light Day and called the darkness Night. And there was evening and there was morning, a first day." The chronological pattern applied here is a sequential one: day and night follow one another in a regular, eternally recurring sequence. On the fourth day, the divine word creates time: "Let there be lights in the expanse of the sky to separate day from night; they shall serve as signs for the set times-the days and the years" (Gen 1:14). In this Bible verse, Jewish tradition recognizes the anchoring of Jewish temporality within universal time. The heavenly bodies that provide the light of the first day of creation allow humans to distinguish between nocturnal darkness and daylight and thus recognize a chronological sequence of days and nights. Sun and moon would later serve to show the Jews the respective points in time of their feast days.

The word most frequently used to denote time in the Hebrew Bible is *olam* (eternity, world). This term may be used to refer to all the facets inherent in time: God's eternal existence as mentioned in Genesis 21:33 (*el olam*), and time past in Deuteronomy 32:7 (*yemot olam*; "days of old"). Rabbinic literature derived from this *olam ha-ba* (Mishnah Peah 1:1), time to come, but also the full duration of human life and ultimately the world in its entirety. In the → Talmud, the word indicates the categories of nature, existence, lifetime, and eternity. The term thus comprises the entirety of the possibilities inherent in time: eternity as well as the duration of time defined by a human life, the terrestrial world as well as the world to come, limited as well as unlimited time, measure and immeasurability, and what is concealed or unknown.

Historical time, in contrast, is referred to in the Bible as "days" (*yamim*; pl. of *yom*); the phrase *divre yamim* (lit. matters of the days) describes the narration of the "days of the world" (*yemot olam*) and its denotation, including history in general: "Remember the days of old, Consider the years of ages past" (Deut 32:7). In this sense, *olam* also includes *zeman* (time), a word not yet used in the Pentateuch, in that it passes, is calculated, and runs out, marking an indefinite point in time in the process (e.g. Eccl 3:1f.). In the sense of the time available, the word takes the – Aramaic – plural *zemanin* (e.g. Dan 6:11: "three times"). The adjective *zemani* is first used in → Bible translations into → Aramaic, denoting the passing or transitoriness of time. This is a time that eludes the idea of eternity and marks a passing and a movement. However, the word can also mean "allocated" time. It is used this way in Esther

(9:27, 31), Nehemiah (2:6), and Daniel (2:16; 3:7f.) when the history of Israel and other peoples coincide.

The term *mo'ed* (point in time) denotes a moment, an encounter or a meeting (e.g. Exod 9:5). In the context of the "tent of meeting" (*ohel mo'ed*) as the place of encountering the divine (e.g. Exod 27:21), it also refers to something enduring, a structured and meaningfully defined time, and as such to liturgical time. The plural *mo'adim* denotes the Jewish festivals (Lev 23:44; → Course of the Year), imagined as an extension of cosmic time (Gen 1:14). Even so, *mo'ed* also comprises the factor of change (Deut 7:25) or indeed reversal (Isa 1:13); used in this way, it describes the time of a past era or of an era on the brink of passing.

The most subtle of the biblical terms denoting time is the word *et*, used, for instance, in the phrase *ba-et ha-hi* ("at that time"; Gen 21:22), or in the proverbial *et* in Ecclesiastes 3:1f. "A season is set for everything, a time for every experience under heaven: A time for being born and a time for dying." This is the fleeting time of the moment often characterized by the absence of something: "The time has not yet come for rebuilding the House of GOD" (Hag 1:2). *Et* also describes the time that eludes human decision or human will as it follows the hour willed by God. *Be-et razon* ("at a favorable moment"; Ps 69:14) thus refers to a time beyond all chronology and can be understood only through a prophetic reading of time.

1.2 Cyclical time and linear time

Jewish temporality is arranged around the rhythm provided by the creation of the world in seven days, the last of these being of particular importance because "God finished the work that had been undertaken: [God] ceased on the seventh day from doing any of the work" (Gen 2:2; → Shabbat). The rhythm governed by the number seven determines the week as well as the cycles of the "weeks of the year." The fallow periods prescribed by the Bible as well as the jubilees align themselves in accordance with these. One day each week, the Shabbat, is withdrawn from time, as it were, and dedicated to the divine, leading to a division between profane and holy time, between existence on earth (time present) and the other world (time future). The Jewish week is referred to as *shavuah* (lit. sevenfold), corresponding to its cycle; its days are named by simply enumerating them: The sixth day ends with *erev shabbat*, the "eve of Shabbat." While the Shabbat week must be observed everywhere in the → Diaspora, the significance of the "weeks of the year," which determine the fallow periods and the concomitant social and agricultural regulations, is tied to Erets Israel.

Shabbat, being linked to the idea of rest and freedom, had led to the concept of the sabbath year and of the jubilee coinciding with every seventh sabbath year even in biblical times (Lev 25:6 and passim). This rhythm provides the basis for a cyclical → calendar that enables a link between everyday life and religious life, as well as between the time on earth and the time of the other world. In the Diaspora, where the direct connection between the rhythm of the seasons in Erets Israel and the time lived by the Jews was interrupted, the significance of Jewish temporality increased further.

Jewish chronology begins with the biblical narrative of the origin of the world, which also marks the beginning of the → history of → Israel. By preserving the recollection of the origin of monotheism, the narrative continues the history of humanity as the story of Jewish history. The editors of the biblical canon understood human temporality as being oriented towards the future; historical events are recorded on a "Jewish" timeline bearing various chronological markers, thus forming a historical, mathematical, and eschatological chain. Because the Bible itself is divided into *parashiyot* (weekly sections), the sequence of biblical readings on Shabbat and the holidays observes a tempo that harmonizes with their exegesis. From this perspective, the Torah symbolizes the passing of time. For one, its reading arranges religious duties in the way prescribed by the cyclical → course of the year; for another, the Torah, by starting with the creation of time and the world, may serve simultaneously as both a universal and Jewish chronology. Thus, the Torah makes it possible to locate the present in the past or, indeed, to revive the latter within lived time.

Accordingly, the biblical narrative endeavors to write the Hebrews into a specific history, albeit without concretely determining the time of the events described. This time, whether left vague or linked to certain rulers, retains the character of narrated time throughout, events and people following one another as the result of specific narrative topics: "He led Israel for twenty-three years; then he died and was buried at Shamir. After him arose Jair the Gileadite, and he led Israel for twenty-two years" (Judg 10:2f.). While Ezekiel's prophecy may be rather more eloquent, his date "[i]n the thirtieth year, on the fifth day of the fourth month" (Ezek 1:1) does not specify whether the year mentioned was calculated based on a Babylonian rulership or on King Jehoiachin's exile. The late books Daniel, Ezra, and Nehemiah, however, name the exact year of the respective rulership (e.g. Dan 9:1; Ezra 6:3).

As Jewish concepts of time from Antiquity onward included cyclical elements originating in a cosmic order, as well as linear elements from the history of humankind, these are also found in the Jewish calendar. Calendar and chronology allow the individual to find his way in cyclical as well as passing time. The calendar comprises different registers: time is ordered by religious, eschatological, seasonal, historical, and ethnical elements. In its essence, however, the calendar is cyclical; it determines the term

of a life following the rhythm of recurring events such as the seasons and the festivals.

Yet, the measure for past time, which already contains the computation of eras that would be used later, is organized by the biblical Israelite chronology. This is detached from the course of nature, adopting a linear character instead. It rests on the sequencing of time segments defined by the beginning and end of ruling periods during which the respective realm undergoes change in the wake of the passage of time. Time segments may also be delimited by an unexpected event that imparts meaning to the way history evolves.

1.3 Historical time

A postbiblical text from the Tannaitic (→ Talmud) and Pharisaic tradition adds a further dimension to the Jewish understanding of time. *Megillat Ta'anit* (Scroll of Fasting) contains a list of 35 days of the year on which mourning and fasting are prohibited. The holidays mentioned are linked to events such as military victories during the Hasmonean period or the Pharisees prevailing over the Sadducees in the question of legislation. These events are not referred to on other occasions and, if it is indeed possible to date them, would have happened before 66/67 CE. The sequence of holidays, beginning with the month of Nisan in the spring, corresponds to the observation of the Jewish historian Josephus (The Antiquities of the Jews, 169). In his view, Nisan began the rhythm of the liturgical cycle since Moses, even though this contradicts the Mishnah collection of laws (Rosh ha-Shanah 1:1). According to the latter, Nisan represented merely the "date that the years of a king's rule are counted [...] and] the order of the Festivals." It seems that until the destruction of the Second → Temple, the year began *de facto* in spring; since then, Rosh ha-Shanah, the beginning of the year, has been celebrated in the autumn. Consequently, the memorial celebrations mentioned in the Scroll of Fasting, which were abandoned with the exception of the historical feast days Purim and Hanukkah (→ Course of the Year) after the destruction of the Second Temple, confirm the existence of a national → calendar, even if it was recognized only by some Jewish groups and abandoned after the destruction of Jerusalem and the Temple. The rabbinic rejection of such a calendar of feast days based on the commemoration (→ Zakhor) of concrete historical events, which, thus, implied the register of historical time, manifested the sudden change in the Jewish relationship to politics. Furthermore, it testifies even more to Jews' relationship to time, now giving preference to diversity over irreversibility.

During the time that the law books, the Mishnah (1st–3rd cents. CE) and the Talmud (3rd–late 6th cents.), were compiled, the tendency emerged in rabbinic thought to insert the history of humanity into Jewish chronology. This may be inferred from the introduction of a universal dating system that takes the Jewish idea of the creation of the world as its reference point.

While the counting of years beginning with a presumed date of the creation of the world has its roots in Antiquity, it was applied only sporadically and not systematically in the Talmud and only later became institutionalized. The most ancient chronographies – in particular, the annals mentioned in the biblical Books of Kings – have not survived the centuries. However, fragments survive of the Patristic works – transmitted by Clement of Alexandria (2nd–3rd cents.) and Eusebius of Caesarea (3rd–4th cents.) – which document the lively chronographical activity of the last three or four centuries before the beginning of the Christian era and its adoption by rabbinic Judaism. Thus, the Hebrew work *Seder Olam* (Order of the world; probably 1st cent. CE) introduces an exegetic chronology leading from the Bible to Alexander the Great to the Bar Kokhba rebellion (132–135 CE). Overall,

the commonality of the texts of this period, written in Greek (→ Alexandria), → Hebrew, or → Aramaic, and among which Josephus's *Antiquitates Judaicae* ("The Antiquities of the Jews," 2006) may also be counted, is that they present the episodes reported in the Bible from the creation of the world to the destruction of the Temple in the form of a coherent historical narrative. Based on the numerical information found in the Greek Septuagint (→ Bible Translation) or the Masoretic Bible text (→ Tanakh), all these chronographies start with the creation of the world. However, the chronographies mentioned do not employ a system that aligns with eras. The "present moment" is defined by a movable temporality that corresponds to the reign of the respective rulers. A Jewish era thus finds itself in a state existing merely according to the principle. One → Midrash mentions an era from the exodus to the construction of the Temple: "Once the Temple was built, they began to count from (the time of) its building [...] If they did not merit numbering from its building they numbered from its destruction" (Mekhilta de-Rabbi Yishma'el, Yitro, *Ba-ḥodesh*, 1).

According to the rabbinic view, the counting of years advances on each Rosh ha-Shanah (Talmud Bavli, Rosh ha-Shana 2b). In addition, it should be universally valid and, at the same time, demonstrate specifically Jewish implications. The editor of the Midrash compilation *Pesikta de-Rav Kahana* (after 250 CE) embraced this view, affirming the idea that God gave the Torah to the Jews for them to make time their own and control it. He also shows that managing time was a prerogative monopolized by the rabbinic scholars in which not even divine providence could intervene: "All the ministering angels assemble with the Holy One, blessed be He, saying to him, 'Lord of the ages, when will it be the New Year?' And he says to them, 'Me do you ask? You and I should ask the court below.'" (Pesiqta 5:13). The Midrash refers to the solemn proclamation of the new counting of the year that had previously been the prerogative of the tribunal, the Sanhedrin. Furthermore, the rabbinic authority implied that time did not exist in and of itself but was determined by humans. Consequently, time was more of a convention in the eyes of the Talmudic rabbis.

1.4 *The determination of time*

The process leading to fixing the creation of the world in time and introducing it as the beginning of the dating system was by no means straightforward. The Books of the Bible Haggai, Daniel, Zechariah, Ezra, Nahum, and Esther date events in accordance with the Persian dynasties or the Arsacids; the Mishnah (→ Talmud) names the Median and Greek kingdoms (Gittin 88:45), the Talmud the Seleucid era (Bavli, Avoda Zara 9a). The oldest archaeological sources document jubilee cycles of 49 or 50 years, as well as the era of the destruction of the → Temple, and briefly also the era of *ge'ulat Yisra'el* (redemption of Israel) during the Bar Kokhba rebellion with its messianic connotation.

The dating system that follows the era of the creation of the world was used with increasing frequency from the 4th and 5th centuries onward and was regarded as established throughout the Jewish world around the 11th and 12th centuries. Epigraphy has left behind snapshots of the dating practices. In addition to individual catacombs and gravesites, cemeteries also testify to the introduction of the global era. Some of the grave inscriptions in Brindisi, Venouse, and Lavelle still refer to the era of the destruction of the Temple (there are dates featuring the years 730 to 770), while others refer to the creation of the world (in this context, we find dates from 4579 to 4599).

Even so, during the High Middle Ages, dating followed a variety of chronologies; among these were not only the creation of the world but also Seleucid rule, the construction and destruction of the Temple, and the Exodus from Egypt. The system that began with the creation of the world appears to have been established in the 15th century, as Jacob ben Asher reported in his Halakhic compendium *Arba'ah Turim* (1475; → Halakhah).

The Hijra and the birth of the savior sealed the break of Islam and Christianity with the timekeeping system of the Hebrew Bible. The institutionalization of the Jewish era of the creation was accompanied by the transcendence of Jewish temporality. While the points of reference linked to historical events lost some of their importance, by no means did they become invalid; to this day they permeate another register of temporality – that is, the religious one.

From the autumn celebrations marking the beginning of the year through the exodus from Egypt to the giving of the Torah, biblical history permeates Jewish ritual, embedding it in the eternal recurrence of sacral temporality. Rather than fitting everything into one single frame, the ritualized transitions between profane time and sacral time (→ Kadosh) ensure the parallel existence of several temporalities. The historical events and references to heroic or charismatic figures, who are limited to the transitory register, allow Judaism to persist beyond time as it must inscribe itself into all times. In this sense, the Jewish → calendar harmonizes human life, the rhythm of nature, and divine time. The era and the calendar are linked to the same event, namely, the creation of the world. They anticipate the same expectation: the universal redemption that will complete the course of the historical and exclusively human time and unite it with the order of divine time.

1.5 *Eschatological time*

The registers of time have a dual purpose. On the one hand, they are based in lived time and, as such, form the core of Jewish life. The handing down of the tradition and the societal organization of time, thus, has decisive significance in Judaism. On the other hand, time *per se* is understood as an eschatological framework. As long as the concept of time is not precisely defined, there is no requirement to lock the arrow of time into place. As soon as time is understood as leading from an origin to a conclusion, its linearity demands that the creation situated at the beginning of time should inescapably move towards its completion: towards the end of its development and the arrival of the messiah (→ Messianism).

The eschatological register of time emerges in the postbiblical texts. Those that do contain indications concerning a calendar and/or astronomy bear witness to the existence of a solar calendar, such as the Book of Jubilees, the First Book of Enoch, and some of the fragments found in Qumran. Beyond the calendars, some of these texts also contain biblical chronologies characterized by an eschatological perspective. Their temporality is completely absorbed into the expectation of redemption and is entirely removed from societal as well as historical time. However, as formulated in a prayer (*Adon Olam*) of the daily → liturgy, God is the one "who was, who is, who shall be": God is thought as existing before the creation of the world, he has existed ever since, and he will exist in the world to come. God is thus transferred into a something beyond the temporal that is eternal, unmoved, and unchanging. Moving and irreversible, time is the authentic space, as it were, in which all being moves. The reflections of medieval philosophers and kabbalists (→ Mysticism) repeatedly endeavored to penetrate this aporia.

2. Imagined time

2.1 *Philosophers and mystics*
The → Midrash literature and the Aggadic parts of both → Talmuds document that the learned rabbis were by no means unfamiliar

with metaphysical problems. The ancient philosophers' topics, such as the one discussed by Plato in *Timaeus*, whether the world was created out of nothing or out of some pre-existing eternal matter, occupy considerable space in the deliberations of medieval Jewish scholars, usually in literary-allegorical form. The question of whether the world was created within a temporal continuum or whether, conversely, time was a product of creation was bound up in the question of the origin of the world and the divine itself. Thus, it is written in the Midrash *Genesis Rabbah* (1:4): "In the beginning, God created. Six things preceded the creation of the world; some of them were actually created, while the creation of the others was already contemplated. The Torah and the Throne of Glory were created. [...] The creation of the Patriarchs [...] Israel [...] the Temple [...] the name of Messiah was contemplated" [1a. 6]. The Midrash *Pirke de-Rabbi Eli'ezer* (ch. 3; also in the Talmud Bavli, e.g. Pesaḥim 54a) has a similar phrase: "Before the world was created, the Holy One, blessed be He, with His Name alone existed, and the thought arose in Him to create the world. [...] Seven things were created before the world was created. They are: The Torah, Gehinnom, the Garden of Eden, the Throne of Glory, the Temple, Repentance, and the Name of the Messiah."

The corpus of rabbinic literature is based on three great cosmological traditions, all of which originated during the Hellenistic period. They refer to the account of the creation according to Genesis and reflect the multitude of Hellenistic interpretations. The first one, embraced by the apocryphal book Wisdom of Solomon (11:18), develops the idea of a creation on the basis of pre-existing, eternal matter. The second one inclines to a creation out of nothing (*creatio ex nihilo*) and is found in the Second Book of Maccabees (7:28) and a few epigraphical texts such as the Slavonic Enoch and the Fourth Book of Ezra. The noticeably more speculative third tradition, a theory of emanation referring to the "garment of light" mentioned in Psalm 104:2, employs the concept of *logos* developed by Philo (→ Alexandria). It is found in the Book of Jubilees, in the Midrash literature, and in the early mystic *Sefer Yetsirah* (Book of Formation; 2nd–6th cents.), before re-emerging explicitly in mystical texts like the *Sefer ha-Bahir* (Book of Brightness; 12th cent.) and the *Sefer ha-Zohar* (Book of Splendor; 13th cent.).

In contact with Muslim culture, and especially with → *kalām* (Arab.; "divine word"; "theological debate"), various speculative and theological approaches to addressing problems were developed. Their formulations overcame the ancient, allegorical investigation of the question and illustrate how the Jewish scholars contributed to the theological and philosophical debates of their contemporaries. They conceived of time along the lines of Aristotelian, neo-Aristotelian, and neo-Platonic trends, which interpreted time as movement. God is removed from human time and is likewise outside of the process of creation: God the unmoved mover creates but is not created; he is located in unchanging time and embodies eternity. In their endeavors to reconcile the Jewish doctrine of creation and the doctrine of the finiteness of time with these philosophical trends, medieval philosophers like Sa'adyah Ga'on (882–942), Ḥasdai Crescas, Maimonides (→ Guide for the Perplexed), Levi ben Gerson (Gersonides; → Prophecy), and Joseph Albo developed different understandings of the creation out of nothing (*yesh me-ayin*), the cause of the world, the miracles, and the revelation. Others like Abraham bar Hiyya (1065–1136) and Abraham ibn Ezra conceived of time in millennial cycles in a universal space, not restricting their cosmic idea to the concepts relevant to Jews.

The blurring of the boundary between the earthly world and heavenly worlds, and the crossing of this boundary as projected in texts of Jewish → mysticism from the Middle Ages onward, shifted the concept of time that had positioned God outside of human space and time in order to transcend it and to penetrate the ultimate meaning of existence and the world. This developed into ideas and representations of God, → history, and time, with time occasionally being regarded merely as one of the divine attributes. From the *sifrut ha-hekhalot* (Literature of the heavenly palaces; 2nd–5th cents.) to Polish → Hasidism (which emerged in the late 18th cent.), a massive messianic project can be discerned that intended to observe all commandments (→ Mitsvot) through the prism of a vision, wherein time was understood as an experience tied to actions. The idea that it is possible to influence the source of time and history by means of theurgically affecting the *sefirot* (divine hypostases) was expressed, for instance, by the kabbalist Moses Cordovero (1522–1570; → Safed): "[As] we are the people of God, all our actions and the progression of time are precisely calculated in accordance with the *sefirot* [...], and He has ordered the moments of the year and the movement of the heavenly bodies in such a way that, thanks to their signs, we are able to understand the heavenly instructions" [3. 190a]. From the perspective of mysticism, the observance of the commandments is an active contribution to divine action. A kabbalist is able to transform every moment into sacred time by carrying out specific rituals. Frequently, the most common actions suffice to transcend history and reinterpret the understanding of time – an idea also elaborated in Polish Hasidism.

2.2 Recourse to tradition

The rhythm of the → calendar organizes the everyday life of Jews, strengthening their collective sense of belonging. This rhythm is, furthermore, one of the indicators of the multitude of temporal registers they have at their disposal. Even during Antiquity, the calendar was the object of fierce conflicts.

In the Middle Ages, the debate flared anew as a result of the → Karaites' dissidence. The Karaites primarily attacked the traditional calendar, and in its defense, a new genre of religious literature emerged that linked scientific and religious arguments (→ Science). Jewish scholars of the Middle Ages investigated calendar issues, among them Sa'adyah Ga'on in his Arabic *Kitāb al-'ibbūr* (Book of the calendar; first half 10th cent.), Abraham bar Hiyya in *Sefer ha-Ibbur* (Book of the calendar; 1122/1123), and Abraham ibn Ezra in his work of the same title (composed ca. 1147 in Verona). While the rules for calculating the calendar in the Jewish world had been fixed, they did introduce some innovations, such as scientific → Hebrew terminology and an exact mathematical concept (→ Number). In addition, they referred to insights from Greek-Arab astronomy in order to explain the rules of the Jewish calendar, transforming it from a divine secret to a system resting on rational foundations. They insisted that the calculation then in force was based on the rabbis, yet they simultaneously adopted non-Jewish insights into the tradition by linking exegetic interpretations with scientific explanations, as Abraham bar Hiyya had done. After Maimonides's *Ḥibbur be-Ḥokhmat ha-Ibbur* (Essay on calendar science) appeared, these works took on great pedagogical significance.

Ashkenazi literature on the calendar calculation is neither speculative nor theological but of a practical orientation because of its connection to the Bible and prayer books. With the rise of book → printing, *sifre evronot* (Books of intercalations) circulated increasingly beginning in the 15th century. These works were intended as a kind of instruction manual for time and followed the example of Christian almanacs. In the early modern era, Jewish calendars transformed into small illustrated compendia of Jewish life. Alongside the usual contents, such as times for prayer, they contained information on the kosher preparation of meat (→ Kashrut),

medical advice (→ Medicine), such as the correct time for bloodletting, as well as the times of sunrise and sunset and community duties.

Moreover, calendars offered an overview of Jewish and Christian holidays. Many contained a complete Christian calendar including saints' days and, depending on the region, the dates of significant trade fairs. Characteristic of this new genre, the introduction to one such calendar of 1577 makes the following remark: "Until now I have written for you ... how to calculate the molad ... and to weigh (check) your calculations on 'scales of justice'. And now I shall also write for you how to know the Christian calendar, and to know how to fix the date of the birth of Jesus, which is their New Year, called in their language *Jahrestag*, as well as the holidays of the saints that occur every year, according to the months of our year" [9. 123].

Paradoxically, it was early modern science that made it possible to fully fathom the symbolic value inherent in the observance of the traditional calendar. The astronomical achievements of bar Hiyya, Ibn Ezra, Isaac ben Solomon Israeli (840/850–ca. 932), and even by the commentator and mathematician Levi ben Gerson (→ Mathematics) in the Middle Ages, however, had no influence on the perception or calculation of the calendar – on the contrary, this knowledge was utilized to buttress the validity of the traditional calendar. Only the debate emerging in the 16th century, which took early modern scientific methods into account, succeeded in proving that the Jewish calendar was not founded on scientific exactitude but only on the authority of tradition [11].

For example, Azariah dei Rossi (ca. 1511–1578) showed in his three-volume work *Me'or Enayim* (Light of the eyes, 1573–1575) that the era of creation had only been introduced into Jewish practice during Shrira Gaon's time (906–1006). He also adduced numerous sources to document contradictions and gaps in the temporal calculations of the *Seder Olam*, ultimately refuting the correctness of Jewish chronology as well as that of the Jewish calendar as a whole. In addition, he demonstrated that barely any details were known about the process of introducing mathematical calendar calculations in spite of a tradition transmitted by Maimonides (*Kiddush ha-Ḥodesh*, 5,3). He likewise showed that the belief that the patriarch Hillel bar Judah (330–365) introduced the calendar could merely be traced back to a → responsum by Hai Gaon (939–1039). After Jehuda Löw ben Bezalel of Prague (→ Golem) sharply criticized him and Joseph Caro threatened to → ban his work (→ Halakhah; → Minhag), dei Rossi felt compelled to retract his statements. His followers included the mathematician and astronomer David Gans (1541–1613; → History), a pupil and assistant of Tycho Brahe and Johannes Kepler. In his chronicle *Zemah David* (Offspring of David; 1592), which had one part dedicated to Jewish history from the beginnings and a second part to universal history, he emphasized: "There is no mistake in our customary calculation of the creation that would contradict a law or a commandment. Even where the calculation of the first new moon after creation (counted from the second day of creation) is concerned, it will not be possible to add or detract a whit from the sublimity of its fixed date, nor indeed move it for as long as the world shall exist [6. §448, 24].

The question of continuing the tradition arose anew in the 19th century. The introduction of historical-critical methods of research in all disciplines revolutionized the view of religion as well. The philosopher Nachman Krochmal (1785–1840) began the investigation of the historicity of Judaism. In his *Moreh Nevukhe ha-Zeman* (→ Guide for the Perplexed of Our Time), he tried to show that Aristotelianism was finished and the time had come to secure Jewish tradition by means of a modern orientation. Krochmal endeavored to respond to the challenges facing Judaism from atheism, deism, Protestant theology, and even more from scholarly approaches such as → biblical criticism and the → philosophy of religion. In Krochmal's assessment, Jewish tradition required regeneration to prevent its being hollowed out on two fronts: by Pietist fanaticism and by scholarly criticism. From his perspective, the existence of Jews was a challenge to history in that their notion of time eluded the frame of metaphysics established by medieval tradition. According to Krochmal, → prophecy and miracles had been replaced by rabbinic scholarship (→ Talmud Torah) that had left a lasting mark on the strictly monotheistic expression of the faith. Krochmal believed this to be a dead end, and in order to find a way out he devised a theory of the history of Judaism as being torn between two extremes: the search for the spiritual absolute and total immersion in the historical process. In this theory, time is not made material or embodied in ritual or in → history – it exists in and of itself and must be thought of as such. Following the example of medieval philosophers, Krochmal developed the idea of a time whose nature was purely metaphysical. Aware of the immeasurable chasm separating humans from the search for the absolute or from God in time, he transferred the proof onto history by postulating time to be its engine.

2.3 Dual temporality

The exegesis (→ Commentary) of the Hebrew Bible (→ Tanakh) introduced the concept of a universal time in which Jewish temporality unfurls. In their Bible chronologies, Jewish authors of Late Antiquity added the belief that the succession of centuries follows a directional movement. Past time was calculated by linking universal history and Jewish history. As these chronologies were in part directed at establishing parallels between episodes of Jewish history and rulers whose existence is affirmed by historical sources, and in part at locating the narrative entirely within the temporality of their surroundings, as Josephus did in his writings, they developed a Jewish history that evolved within the dual temporality of historical time. *Seder Olam*, in contrast, ignores any form of reconstruction that diverges from the biblical narrative. Its subsequent adoption into the rabbinic corpus proves the contemporaneity of a dual development that reached its end over the course of the 2nd century CE. One of them was aimed at inscribing Jewish chronology into the chronology of nations, while the other ignored this idea. Insofar as the chronologies based on the Septuagint make allegorical use of the Bible with a universalistic orientation, they simultaneously document the existence of exegetic historical activity that gained entry into tradition only in the strictest version of literal Bible interpretation. The emergence of rabbinic Judaism thus led to the abandonment of traditions that had sought to integrate Jews into history in multiple ways in favor of one single biblical narrative. Ever since, a time scale has been at the core of Jewish history. Even so, the dual time register inherent in Israel's diasporic situation (→ Diaspora) continues beyond the biblical narrative, enabling the Jews to adhere simultaneously to both a Jewish temporality and a different one. Furthermore, these chronographies of Late Antiquity attest that the global era, although mostly unknown at the time, was already used by chronographers.

Tradition had shown that time could be experienced through ritualization and the peculiar relationship with God, namely, through → Shabbat. The delicate dosage of profane and sacred time allowed Jewish temporality to transcend the idea of the "transient" as opposed to "spiritual," as developed by Augustine in the context of Christianity. As → philosophy and the ideas of the → Enlightenment seeped in, they made the aporia inherent in this concept of the link between Jewish history and the time of immanence apparent. Abandoning the ritualization of time, modern thinkers such as Heinrich Graetz (→ Historiography), Franz Rosenzweig (→ [The] Star of Redemption), and Walter Benjamin (→ Angelus Novus) reified mystical thought by dissolving the connection between Judaism and time, placing the former into a kind of supertemporality. Conversely, Samson Raphael Hirsch (→ Neo-Orthodoxy) and Abraham Joshua Heschel (→ Civil Rights Movement), who were more strongly rooted in tradition, insisted that the order and the rhythm of the Jewish calendar had to be regarded as the fundamental bearers of time and of Jewish temporality.

Bibliography

Sources
[1] Megillat Ta'anit: ha-nusakhim, pishram ve-toldotehem [Megillat Ta'anit. The Versions, Their Interpretation and History], ed. by V. Noam, Jerusalem 2003. [1a.] Midrash Rabbah, trans. by H. Freedman and M. Simon, London 1939/1961. [2] Seder Olam: mahadurah mada'it, perush u-mavo [Seder Olam. Critical Edition, Commentary and Introduction], ed. by C. Milikowsky, 2 vols., Jerusalem 2013. [3] M. Cordovero, Sefer Tefillah le-Mosheh [Book of the Prayer of Moses], Premislany 1892. [4] Flavius Josephus, The Antiquities of the Jews, in: The Works of Josephus. Complete and Unabridged, trans. by W. Whiston, Peabody 2006. [5] S. Gandz (ed.), The Code of Maimonides. Book III, Treatise 8: Sanctification of the New Moon, New Haven 1956. [6] D. Gans, Tsemah David [Offspring of David], ed. by M. Breuer, Jerusalem 1983. [7] N. Krochmal, Moreh Nevukhe ha-Zeman: sefer moreh emunah tserufah u-melamed hokhmat Yisra'el [Guide for the Perplexed of our Time. Guide to Pure Faith and Instruction of the Wisdom of Israel], ed. by L. Zunz, Lviv 1851.

Secondary literature
[8] A. I. Baumgarten, The Flourishing of Jewish Sects in the Maccabean Era. An Interpretation,

Leiden 1997. [9] E. Carlebach, Palaces of Time. Jewish Calendar and Culture in Early Modern Europe, Cambridge/London 2011. [10] E. Frank, Talmudic and Rabbinical Chronology. The System of Counting Years in Jewish Literature, New York 1956. [11] S. A Goldberg, Clepsydra. Essay on the Plurality of Time in Judaism, trans. by B. Ivry, Stanford 2016. [12] J. M. Harris, Nachman Krochmal. Guiding the Perplexed of the Modern Age, New York/London 1991. [13] W. Z. Harvey, Physics and Metaphysics in Hasdai Crescas, Amsterdam 1998. [14] C. R. Holladay, Fragments from Hellenistic Jewish Authors, Vol. 1: Historians, Society of Biblical Literature, Texts and Translations, Chico 1983. [15] M. Idel, Some Concepts of Time and History in Kabbalah, in: E. Carlebach et al. (eds.), Jewish History and Jewish Memory. Essays in Honor of Yosef Hayim Yerushalmi, Hanover/London 1998, 153–188. [16] M. Idel, "Higher than Time." Observations on Some Concepts of Time in Kabbalah and Hasidism, in: B. Ogren (ed.), Time and Eternity in Jewish Mysticism, Leiden/Boston 2015, 179–211. [17] T. Rudavsky, Time Matters. Time, Creation, and Cosmology in Medieval Jewish Philosophy, New York 2000. [18] S. Saulnier, Calendrical Variations in Second Temple Judaism. New Perspectives on the "Date of the Last Supper" Debate, Leiden 2012. [19] J. Strugnell, The Angelic Liturgy at Qumran. 4Q Serek Širot "Olat Haššabat," in: Vetus Testamentum Supplement 7 (1960) 3, 318–345. [20] J. C. VanderKam, Calendars in the Dead Sea Scrolls. Measuring Time, London/New York 1998.

SYLVIE ANNE GOLDBERG, PARIS

Tin Pan Alley

This name was given to Twenty-Eighth Street between Fifth and Sixth Avenues in the New York borough of Manhattan, where the majority of American music publishing houses settled towards the end of the 19th century. The works these houses distributed laid the foundation for a closely interconnected music industry. The Tin Pan Alley genre of songs, created by Jewish songwriters on commission from these publishers, amalgamated various styles imported into America and defined American musical tastes until the mid-1950s.

From around 1885 onward, when the American music industry began to be concentrated more and more in New York, the first publishing houses specializing in popular music were established there. In order to satisfy the increasing demand of a public enthusiastic about music, they were constantly on the lookout for pieces that promised to be commercial successes. Unlike in Europe, which had a naturally evolved middle-class music culture and corresponding traditions, the system of music production and dissemination that developed in the United States was oriented more strongly towards the business practices of the free market economy.

Towards the end of the 19th century, many New York publishing houses moved to Twenty-Eighth Street between Fifth and Sixth Avenues, on both sides of the intersection with → Broadway. The street was soon given the nickname "Tin Pan Alley," probably with reference to the cacophony of cheap pianos with their thin, tinny sound that could be heard emerging from the publishers' offices all day long [1. 2].

There was a high degree of Jewish participation in the Tin Pan Alley music industry from the very beginning. By 1900, around half a million Jewish refugees from Eastern Europe had crossed the Atlantic to America; a further million and a half followed by 1924, most of whom settled in → New York, their place of arrival (→ Ellis Island; → Demography). Between 1890 and 1920, over 70% of the renowned publishing houses were owned by first or second generation Jewish immigrants, among them M. Witmark & Sons, T. B. Harms & Co., Howley, Haviland & Co., Joseph W. Stern & Co., Feist & Frankenthaler, and F. A. Mills. The centuries during which the choice of professions for Jews had been limited to trade (→ Professions) had endowed them with mercantile skills that now benefited them in the music business [5. 59]. Leo Feist (1869–1930), for instance, the sales manager of a corset firm and a music lover, first tried his luck as a songwriter but without success. He abandoned composition but not the music business, having recognized its potential. He teamed up with Joe (Joseph) Frankenthaler, and together they founded a music publishing house that successfully published songs written by songwriters, not least hits such as *Peg O' My Heart* (1913), which was set to music by Fred Fisher, and *My Blue Heaven* (1927), which was performed by Gene Austin [4. 133f.]; [2. 32].

Enterprising publishers continued to rationalize music production, adapting it to the industry processes. While at first the composers approached the publishing houses and offered their songs, they were soon signed by the publishers to compose on demand. In order to further increase the number of new creations, the composers were required only to provide musical ideas that arrangers would then work into songs. In the 1920s, further specialization led to the emergence of lyricists who added lyrics to newly composed songs.

Afterwards, contracted song pluggers had to play the songs to performers and expert listeners; if the songs passed this test, they were printed. As soon as they were printed, they had to be turned to account. The task of the song pluggers was to perform the songs to Broadway producers and → vaudeville stars with the aim of having them add the songs to their stage repertoire, arousing potential buyers' interest in the sheet music. In turn, publishers would pick up popular songs from Broadway or vaudeville shows, printing and advertising them.

In 1909 the United States introduced copyright law for printed music, which protected not only the rights of the composer but also the publishers' property rights to the music. In 1914 prominent representatives of Tin Pan Alley founded the performing rights' organization ASCAP (American Society of Composers, Authors and Publishers), which concluded a contract with broadcasting stations guaranteeing that its products would be exclusively transmitted.

Until 1910, Tin Pan Alley songs were more famous than the names of their creators. On the road to integration into American society, Jewish musicians soon discovered Tin Pan Alley as a commercial milieu open to cultural and musical syncretisms. Some of them were influenced by musical traditions that were also reflected in → klezmer or in the golden age of cantorial music (→ Cantor). They sought to preserve the accent, intonation, and → humor of → Yiddish, emphasizing sentimentality and nostalgia, in songs such as *My Yiddishe Momme* (1925) by Jack Yellen and Lew Pollack and *Bei Mir Bistu Sheyn* (1933) by Sholom Secunda. These songs had long-term influence on the musical tastes of the wider American population.

The majority of Jewish song writers soon fell in line with the American ethos. In their songs aimed at the mainstream of white urban society, they created an image of America with sentimentality, romantic love, peace, and prosperity at its heart. Among the composers of this style were Ira (→ Broadway) and George Gershwin (→ Rhapsody in Blue) – George Gershwin had started his career as a song plugger at the age of 15 – as well as Irving Berlin (→ White Christmas), who represented the Tin Pan Alley style like no other in the first half of the 20th century, Harold Arlen, Fanny Brice, Sammy Cahn, Eddie Cantor, George M. Cohan, Benny Goodman (→ Jazz), and Jerome Kern.

The songwriters found inspiration in a rich repertoire fed by the musical traditions of the early English settlers, the subsequent immigrants like the Irish, Italians, Germans, and Scandinavians, as well as the African Americans brought to the country as slaves.

They owed many ideas to the "father of American music," songwriter Stephen Foster (1826–1864): He composed around 200 sentimental songs in the style of minstrel pieces (→ Blackface), in which he drew on the different styles of the American musical landscape, and in whose texts he evoked moods of nostalgia and pathos, of longing for home and family.

Tin Pan Alley songs were subject to strong standardization, including simple diatonic melodies, major and minor keys, straightforward harmonic cadence, and symmetrical phrase lengths of 16 or 32 bars in verses and choruses. In addition to the use of sequences, an increasingly pronounced sense of intensification ensured memorable melodies. Furthermore, musicians like George Gershwin, Jerome Kern, and Cole Porter included stylistic influences from Romantic and Impressionist composers, such as Claude Debussy (→ Polytonality), Edvard Grieg, Giacomo Puccini, and Sergey Rachmaninoff, but also from blues and → jazz. Employing sevenths and ninths, added seconds and sixths, augmented and diminished chords, as well as modulations to ever more distant keys, added more complexity to their harmonies.

However, Tin Pan Alley songs owed their very special tension to the characteristics shared by traditional Jewish music and African-American jazz. For example, both Eastern Ashkenazic (→ Ashkenaz) cantorial chants and jazz are unwritten, ex tempore music. The blue notes typical of jazz – especially the bending of the third and seventh degree of the scale – also have parallels in the double subdominant, the third, seventh, and tenth degrees of the Eastern Ashkenazic *Adonoi Molokh* style. Finally, the syncopation typical of African-American music is also common in klezmer and in Hasidic dance (→ Hasidism; → Niggun).

The multifarious relationships that emerged among published sheet music,

piano, pianola, jukebox, gramophone, record, radio, television, and film (→ Cinema) resulted in Tin Pan Alley music being disseminated in numerous, frequently competing forms. While a total of several million music scores had been sold by 1900, by 1910 there were 100 songs that had each reached a circulation of more than a million printed copies. Around the turn of the century, new songs were mainly performed in the context of stage productions, such as → vaudeville, revue theatre, and musical comedy, and the music industry profited primarily from selling sheet music. There were more than a hundred piano manufacturers in America; families with an interest in education owned a piano, and popular songs and piano pieces were played in the home. Soon the production of sheet music declined in favor of music recordings. As early as the 1890s, jukeboxes could be found in many public places, and in the early 1900s, firms experimented with cylinders and records (→ Gramophone). By 1920 there were almost 200 record companies in the United States, and the sales figures for the recorded version of a song soon exceeded those of the sheet music.

By 1930 around 600 commercial → radio stations broadcasting popular music had been founded in the country. Meanwhile in 1927 the first feature-length talking film *The Jazz Singer* (→ Blackface) was produced starring Al Jolson. In the 1930s, → Hollywood films became the most important entertainment medium in the United States. In many cases the films were accompanied by songs, and film studios employed hundreds of musicians they often contracted away from → Broadway or Tin Pan Alley.

Neither the Great Depression of 1929 nor the rise of fascism in Europe and the Second World War were able to change the style of Tin Pan Alley songs that had developed in the 1890s. Ultimately, however, the increasing control record labels, radio stations, and television networks had over the American music market broke the dominant position of Tin Pan Alley. When ASCAP tried to negotiate a new contract with American radio networks in 1940, negotiations failed due to the sum it had demanded. Instead, broadcasters turned to the products of BMI (Broadcast Music, Inc.), which had been founded the previous year. The new union of songwriters, lyricists, publishers, and radio stations removed ASCAP from its monopoly position and ensured that the *lingua franca* of Tin Pan Alley gave way to a greater variety of popular styles, such as country, African-American genres like → jazz and rhythm 'n' blues, Latin-American music, and, finally, → rock 'n' roll. The early 1950s marked the end of an era of American song culture in which Jews had significantly shaped American mainstream music for half a century.

Bibliography

[1] K. Charlton, Rock Music Styles. A History, New York 2011. [2] J. Gottlieb, Funny, It Doesn't Sound Jewish. How Yiddish Songs and Synagogue Melodies Influenced Tin Pan Alley, Broadway, and Hollywood, Albany 2004. [3] C. K. Harris, How to Write a Popular Song, Chicago 1906. [4] D. A. Jasen, Tin Pan Alley. The Composers, the Songs, the Performers and Their Times. The Golden Age of American Popular Music from 1886 to 1956, New York 2003. [5] J. Karp, Of Maestros and Minstrels. American Jewish Composers between Black Vernacular and European Art Music, in: B. Kirshenblatt-Gimblett/J. Karp (eds.), The Art of Being Jewish in Modern Times, Philadelphia 2008, 57–77. [6] D. Lyman, Great Jews in Music, Middle Village (NY) 1986. [7] J. Shepherd, Tin Pan Alley, London et al. 1982. [8] N. E. Tawa, The Way to Tin Pan Alley. American Popular Song, 1866–1910, New York 1990.

ALEXANDER KNAPP, LONDON
AND REGINA RANDHOFER, LEIPZIG

Tish'ah be-Av

Since Antiquity, the Ninth of Av (Hebr. *tish'ah be-Av*) has been one of the most important Jewish days of mourning, lament, and fasting. Tradition holds that the greatest catastrophes and calamities in Jewish history occurred on this day, and many historical events have for this reason been retroactively assigned the same date. The liturgical customs associated with Tish'ah be-Av also award special significance to this day in the Jewish calendar.

Tish'ah be-Av is the ninth day of the fifth month in the Jewish religious calendar and the eleventh month in the civil → calendar (July/August in the Gregorian calendar). According to Jewish tradition (Talmud Bavli, Ta'anit 29a), the "original catastrophe" that occurred on Tish'ah be-Av and came to define the day was the 586 BCE destruction of the → Temple in Jerusalem. The same Talmudic source also associates the destruction of the Second Temple in 70 CE with this day. Moreover, in the Jewish calendar it marks the last day and, thus, the culmination of the three-week period of mourning which begins on the Seventeenth of Tammuz – the day that saw the city wall of Jerusalem razed in 70 BCE – and commemorates the end of Jewish statehood (→ Midrash Eichah Rabbati 1:29).

The Ninth of Av thus serves as a day of collective remembrance (→ Zakhor) to mark the greatest Jewish catastrophes and tragedies of Biblical and ancient → history. Many subsequent catastrophic events have in the Jewish tradition been assigned this date; examples include the fall of the Betar Fortress in 132 CE, the 1095 call by Pope Urban II for the First Crusade, which led to the massacres of 1096, the expulsion of Jews from England in 1290, and the expulsion of Jews from Spain in 1492. The practice of symbolic calendrical allocation continued into the

20th century and was for instance applied to the declaration of war by the Central Powers in 1914, the mass deportations of Jews from Warsaw in 1942, and the 1994 attack against the Asociación Mutual Israelita Argentina (AMIA) in → Buenos Aires.

The calendrical and also liturgical identification of historical events with direct or long-term negative consequences for Jews has its origin in the Jewish notion that the Jewish calendar contains theological "lessons." Fast days, for instance, are generally seen as expressions of punishment but at the same time they signal repentance (→ *teshuvah*) and hope. Thus in Jeremiah 36:9, a fast day is described where the predictions of the prophet are read out in public to encourage repentance. The ancient scholars of Talmudic literature defined the fatefulness of the day from the very beginning: when the scouts sent out by Moses returned with false reports about the Promised Land, the people complained, revolted, and declared their intention to return to Egypt (Num 14:1–4). Rabbinic authorities claim this episode occurred on the eve of the Ninth of Av, which prompted God to give the needlessly complaining Israelites of every generation a valid reason and a particular day to → lament (Talmud Bavli, Ta'anit 29a). Another rabbinic tradition (Talmud Bavli, Gittin 55a–b) holds that the Second Temple was destroyed for a different reason, "baseless hatred" (*sin'at ḥinnam*) among the Jews, but still on the Ninth of Av.

Recalling both historically distant and more recent events on the same date conveyed a message: since the ominous prophecies of Jeremiah and Ezekiel had been fulfilled, those of Zechariah (8:19) would be equally correct, and days of mourning would in the future become days of joy. This idea is reflected in the name used for the month since Antiquity: *menaḥem* (*Av*) – Comforting (Av).

The end of the Babylonian → exile and the rebuilding of the Temple around 518 BCE probably meant that Tish'ah be-Av was no longer considered a day of mourning (Talmud Bavli, Rosh ha-Shanah 18b). However, after the destruction of the Second Temple it was once again claimed as such; reaffirmed by the historical events that followed the destruction (Tosafot Rosh ha-Shanah 18b), the modalities for this day were confirmed:

> Five calamitous matters occurred to our forefathers on the seventeenth of Tammuz, and five other disasters happened on the Ninth of Av. On the seventeenth of Tammuz the tablets were broken [...]; the daily offering was nullified [...]; the city walls of Jerusalem were breached; the general Apostemos publicly burned a Torah scroll; and Manasseh placed an idol in the Sanctuary. On the Ninth of Av it was decreed upon our ancestors that they would [...] not enter Eretz Yisrael; and the Temple was destroyed the first time [...] and the second time [...]; and Beitar was captured; and the city of Jerusalem was plowed [...]. [F]rom when the month of Av begins, one decreases acts of rejoicing. (Mishnah, Ta'anit 4:6f.)

Contemporary historian Josephus (37–100 CE) had already stressed the significance of the Ninth of Av as the day that brought the destruction of the First and the Second Temples: "it was fate that decreed it so to be [...] For the same month and day were now observed, as I said before, wherein the holy house was burnt formerly by the Babylonians" [2. book 6, chapter 4]. The commemoration of multiple catastrophic events on a single day seems to have emerged as a result of the Talmudic rabbis' decision to re-dedicate the day of mourning for the destroyed temples into a day that commemorates the oppression and exile of the Jewish people (Talmud Bavli, Ta'anit 29a).

The most important stipulation associated with the day of commemoration is the 25-hour fast, during which no food or drink may be consumed. Shaving is forbidden, as is washing oneself and festive clothing – the usual prohibitions for periods of mourning (→ Death). If Tish'ah be-Av falls on a → Shabbat, the prohibitions go into effect the following day; this corresponds to the practice by which all mourning rituals are suspended throughout the Shabbat because of its joyful character.

While many ancient customs for the Ninth of Av have seen changes over the centuries, others have remained untouched. Among the latter are the prohibition on wearing leather, and in particular leather shoes – a material that was costly and therefore associated with opulence and festivity –, bodily hygiene, marital intercourse, or Torah study (→ Talmud Torah), all of which were considered sources of pleasure and well-being. Obligations include sitting on the floor or on a low bench, reading of the biblical lamentations (*Eichah*), the Book of Job, the curses in Leviticus, the dark chapters of Jeremiah, the Talmudic descriptions of the destruction of Jerusalem (e.g. Bavli, Gittin 55b–58a), and the Talmudic laws of mourning. The non-canonical Talmudic tractate Soferim, probably composed in 7th-century Palestine, contains one of the oldest descriptions of the Tish'ah be-Av → liturgy: "Some congregations read the Book of Lamentations in the evening while others postpone it to the [following] morning after the reading of the Torah, when the reader stands up, his head covered with ashes, his clothes torn, and reads it with weeping and lamentation" (Soferim 42b).

Under the influence of local practices around Tish'ah be-Av, the element of mourning gained in intensity during the medieval period. The 11th century Talmud commentator Rashi (Shlomo Yitzchaki, 1040–1105; → Worms) records a custom that involved visiting the graves of the deceased to request their intercession and to remember the destruction of the Temple (Rashi on Bavli, Ta'anit 16a). In the immediate aftermath

of the Crusades, a number of innovations found their way into the synagogue service of → Ashkenazi communities: on Tish'ah be-Av it became customary to read *kinot* (laments) that demand vengeance for those who have been slain and others containing passages from the Hebrew chronicles of the Crusades. The elegy *Sha'ali Serufah ba-Esh* (Ask, you who were burnt in the fire), composed by Me'ir ben Baruch of Rothenburg (ca. 1215–1293) after the 1242 burning of the Talmud in Paris, also came to be incorporated into the liturgy for the Ninth of Av.

Other traditions marked the proximity of ritual commemoration and the private mourning for a loved one (Talmud Bavli, Ta'anit 30a). Moses of Coucy described in the 13th century how on the Ninth of Av men wore neither prayer shawl (*tallit*) nor phylacteries (*tefillin*) in the → synagogue [3. Hilkhot Tish'ah be-Av, 249b]. Likewise the meal preceding the fast of the Ninth of Av (*seudah hamafseket*), like the one of mourners, should consist of lentils and hard-boiled eggs. Earlier, in the 12th century, Maimonides (→ Guide for the Perplexed) had prescribed as appropriate attire a dark cloak and bare feet (Mishneh Torah, Hilkhot Ta'anit 5:8). Other widespread customs included sprinkling ash on one's head covering, placing a stone under one's pillow as a symbolic gravestone, or sleeping on the ground. There was also the practice of covering a window arch in the synagogue with a black cloth to darken the interior. Adults sometimes did not consume meat or alcohol until the afternoon of the following day because a traditional account of the event held that the Temple had remained ablaze for the same length of time. This bundle of customs contributed to the Ninth of Av gaining the character of a day of mourning. As on Yom Kippur (→ Course of the Year), work is prohibited on the ominous Ninth of Av. Some communities, especially those following the Yemeni and Sephardic rites (→ Minhag), continue the practice of reciting the years that have passed since the destruction of the Temple.

Nevertheless, Tish'ah be-Av is also a source of solace: according to the Talmudic tradition the Messiah will be born on the Ninth of Av. This and the fact that it is followed by the *Shabbat Naḥamu* ("Sabbath of Consolation"; after Isaiah 40:1: "Comfort, oh comfort My people") enhance the element of hope and joy (Talmud Yerushalmi, Berakhot 2:4). A → midrash confirms this messianic component and lends weight to the notion that the Messiah was conceived on the day the Temple fell, and he was waiting for a generation worthy of his arrival (Eichah Rabbati 1:15).

The notorious "pseudo messiah" Sabbatai Zevi (1626–1676; → Smyrna) seized on this tradition and let it be known that he was born on the Ninth of Av. Zevi abolished the fast and re-defined the day as a day of joy. This practice was widely adopted in the 17th century among his Orthodox followers.

In the 19th century it was the leaders of the Jewish → Reform movement who decided to dispense with the fast. This rule is today binding for many liberal and conservative currents, and only observant circles uphold the fast. Nonetheless, in Israel bars, restaurants, → cinemas, and similar venues are closed on the Ninth of Av, and many religious Jews travel to the Western Wall in Jerusalem for services with a specially modified liturgy.

Bibliography

Sources

[1] Y. Culi/Y. Bakhor Agruiti, The Story of Tisha B'Av. The Torah Anthology Me'Am Lo'ez, trans. by A. Kaplan, New York/Jerusalem 1981. [2] Flavius Josephus, The Jewish War, trans. by W. Whiston, London 1737. [3] Moses of Coucy, Sefer Mitsvot ha-Gadol [The Great Book of Commandments], Venice 1522.

Secondary literature

[4] A. P. Bloch, The Biblical and Historical Background of Jewish Customs and Ceremonies, New York 1980. [5] C. M. M. Brady, The Rabbinic Targum of Lamentations. Vindicating God, Leiden 2003. [6] I. Elbogen, Jewish Liturgy. A Comprehensive History, ed. by J. Heinemann et al., Philadelphia 1993. [7] D. Goldschmidt, Seder ha-kinot le-Tish'a be-Av ke-minhag Polin u-kehillot ashkenazim be-erets Yisra'el [Order of Lamentations for the Ninth of Av in the Polish and Ashkenazi Rites], Jerusalem 1968. [8] D. Sperber, Minhage Yisra'el. Mekorot ve-toldot [Customs of Israel. Sources and History], 8 vols., Jerusalem 1998–2007. [9] D. Sperber, Why Jews Do What They Do? The History of Jewish Customs throughout the Cycle of the Jewish Year, trans. byY. Elman, Hoboken 1999.

SYLVIE ANNE GOLDBERG, PARIS

Tkhines

Tkhines (Yidd.; Hebr. *teḥinnot*) are supplications, or petitions, mostly in Yiddish, to be recited in situations where the fixed Hebrew → liturgy provides no standard texts. They are aimed primarily at women and deal with all aspects of daily life but in particular with personal and private requests, such as an easy delivery, healthy children, a safe income, or protection against "evil thoughts." Originating in the early modern period, the genre has remained extraordinarily popular to this day.

1. Emergence and early history
2. Linguistic style
3. Uses

1. Emergence and early history

Tkhines texts appear to have been spread since the end of the 16th century in manuscripts and prints. Initially they took the form of small octavo fascicles; some were added as fillers at the end of other Yiddish books, for instance in *Maese bess-Dovid bime Pras* (Story of the House of David in Persian Times; Basel 1599). Anonymous transmission is typical for these texts, and the early manuscripts carry no explicit location or date. Where a name is given in the print editions, it is more likely referring to collecting activities rather than to authorship.

From the beginning, the *tkhines* genre was fully developed in terms of style and structure [8. 258], which suggests a wide dissemination at the time and a prehistory. Larger *tkhines* collections are first documented for the middle of the 17th century; the very first, with 37 texts, was published in Amsterdam in 1648. It continued to be reprinted there, but also at various German locations and in Prague, while its contents grew over time to eventually include some 120 petitions. By the end of the 18th century, the number of print editions was already incalculable; to this day their bibliographical documentation remains unsatisfactory. Since it is a matter of "functional literature," as indicated, for example, by the numerous fragments of used copies that have come to light in the → *genizot* of rural synagogues in southern Germany, the rate of loss was substantial and the incentive to attempt a systematic collection all the lower.

An explanation for the need to provide women with prayers in → Yiddish is offered by the editor of the Amsterdam collection who, in his preface, makes an explicit reference to the *Sefer Hasidim* (Book of the Pious; 12th/13th century): if women, who do not speak the holy language (→ Hebrew), desire to understand the prayers "one is obligated to teach her so that she understands well. For prayer comes from the heart, and when the heart does not know what the mouth speaks, the prayer helps but little" (cited in [9. 18]). Similar views were still expressed by

editors in the 18th century. Their reasoning may indeed be seen as the impetus for the emergence of the *tkhines* genre.

2. Linguistic style

Tkhines are composed in an emotional language but also inspired either directly or indirectly by Hebrew prayer texts. This gave them a peculiar, archaic-sounding style even in the early stages that came to be known as *loshn-tkhine* or *tkhine-loshn* (*tkhine* language). Thus, in the period shortly before 1700, the tragic events during an outbreak of the plague in Prague are reported *be-loshin-tkhine* (in the style of a *tkhine*) in Yiddish songs of mourning, namely those of the Prague poet Taube bat Loeb Pisker. The term is still current even in the artistic prose composed during the classic age of Eastern European Yiddish. For instance, Mendele Moykher-Sforim's (born Sholem Yankev Abramovitsh; → Fishke) novel, *Dos vintsh-fingerl* (1865; author's own Hebrew trans. 1880; "The Wishing Ring," 2003), book five, chapter five, his character "Hudl" speaks "in a tone of prayerful supplication" [3. 178], which the original Yiddish text compares to the language of the *tkhines*.

The particular style of the *tkhines* is characterized, among other things, by the speaker addressing God directly, the use of paratactic sentences, which often begin with *un'* ("and"), emphatic periphrastic verbal constructions with *tun* (+ infinitive), and other syntactic peculiarities, as well as the presence of lexical elements otherwise associated with Yiddish → Bible translations. To this must be added the specific intonation, or singsong, of the *tkhines*, which is often referenced in modern Yiddish → literature. For instance in Sholem Aleichem's (→ Tevye) story for Jewish children, *Bashefenish* (1903; "Creature," 1996): "Tsugegangen tsu der tir, derher ikh a modne geveyn mit a shreklekh yomern, mit a meshune-vildn nign fun vaybershe tkhines: – Vey iz mir, vind iz mir, tsu vos hob ikh dikh badarft geboyrn, a make iz mir a groy-se?" [5. 183]. – "And I went into the rebbe's room [...] and heard a strange crying and heart-rending keening like the drawn-out wailing accompanying women's prayers: 'Woe is me, alas, why did I give birth to you, may I be cursed?'" [4. 190]. The subsequently repeated separation of the last syllable at the end of the sentence has a decelerating effect and creates a strong emphasis at the end of the syntactic unit.

3. Uses

The *tkhines* texts draw on the linguistic tension between natural expression, aided by the use of the vernacular and their focus on concrete private situations, and the artificiality of a pre-formulated, stereotypical hand-out, where the textual and linguistic elements are informed by supra-individual considerations. In concrete personal situations, however, it is precisely this feature which can have a calming effect where those praying would otherwise be struggling to find the appropriate expressions.

The burgeoning of Yiddish book → printing also gave rise to a rapid increase in the availability of printed *tkhines*. They became an integral component of nearly every → Ashkenazi book collection; some were bound up with the standard prayer book (→ Siddur) and pre-designed for this purpose at the print shop. Presumably the growing number of printed editions from around the middle of the 17th century was accompanied by an increasingly individualized prayer practice. Private prayer now replaced the earlier communal experience where a *firzogerin* (precentress) would lead other women in prayer reciting suitable texts. It is likely, although not proven, that the earliest *tkhines* manuscripts evolved from the practice of such female "specialists."

The path of specific *tkhines* up to their inclusion in standard collections is tangled and largely uncharted; a *tkhine* from the Yiddish Bible → commentary → *Tsene-rene* (ca. 1600) resurfaces nearly verbatim in the major compilation *Seder Tkhines u-Vakoshes* (Order of Supplications and Petitions; Sulzbach 1798). The latter volume and other collections still dominate the present-day *thkines* market. Among these collections, *Seder Tkhines* (Order of Supplications) contains both daily prayers and texts for foreseeable personal situations and constitutes a second prayer book alongside the siddur, plus the *Ma'ane Lashon* (Book of Supplications; Frankfurt am Main 1723/1724) offers the requisite prayers for visiting the cemetery.

The collections of the 18th century also incorporate *tkhines* based on Hebrew prayers with a Kabbalistic background (→ Mysticism). First attested in 1662 and 1717 respectively, the Hebrew prayers were by all appearances adapted for use as *tkhines* soon after publication. This, however, does not imply that *tkhines* convey complex Kabbalistic themes; rather, it is an expression of the need for a complementary set of personal prayer texts that were better suited to specific situations and gave comfort to the supplicant.

A remarkable facet of the great collections, beyond the variety of the women-specific subjects they cover, is the frequent invocation of female figures from the Bible. As well as the matriarchs Sarah, Rebecca, Rachel, and Leah, the worshippers also sought help from Hannah and Esther (→ Edom; → Purim-sphil) whose prayers, according to the Biblical tradition, were answered by God.

Each *tkhine* has its theme explained in the heading, for ease of access when looking for a specific prayer to match a specific purpose (healthy children, safe travels for the husband, etc.). Often included are directions on how to speak the prayer, for example "tearfully," "with humility," "not too quickly," or "with reverence."

The prayers dealing with special requests are joined by others dedicated to the traditional commandments assigned to women (→ Mitsvot), such as the lighting of the → Shabbat candles and the preparation of the Shabbat breads. Only a small number of *tkhines* are composed especially for men. Some that do not deal with women-specific issues can also be used by men, but purely female prayers are in the majority by far.

Tkhines belong to the works of old Yiddish literature that – apparently because of their religious, edifying nature – have in the past enjoyed great popularity at least in Orthodox circles, and continue to do so. They live on in reprints and are to some extent included in modern editions such as *Tkhine Sore Rokhl* (Brooklyn 1994). Like → *Tsene-Rene* or the Yiddish morality tractates *Simhat ha-Nefesh* (Song of the Soul; by Elhanan Hendel ben Benjamin Wolf Kirchhan, Frankfurt am Main 1707) and *Lev Tov* (Good Heart; by Yitshak ben Elyakim of Poznań, 1626, 1709), *tkhines* can be appreciated by new audiences after only minimal linguistic revision. Due in part to their relatively young age, even in their modernized form they remain immediately recognizable when compared to earlier versions. Significantly older Yiddish works, if they survive at all, only do so in a completely new guise (→ Bobe-Mayse). Attempts to make *tkhines* more accessible to a wider group of interested women within → Orthodox Judaism through English translations, for example with *The Merit of Our Mothers* (1992), have not yet seen a response to match the success of the original texts.

Bibliography

Sources

[1] Seder Tkhines u-Vakoshes [Order of Suplications and Petitions], Sulzbach 1798.   [2] Sefer Tkhine Sore Rokhel, Brooklyn 1994.   [3] Mendele Moykher Sforim, The Wishing-Ring. A Novel, trans. by M. Wex, Syracuse 2003.   [4] Sholom Aleichem, Creature, in: A Treasury of Sholom Aleichem Children's Stories, trans. by A. Shevrin, Northvale, NJ/London 1996, 181–196.   [5] Sholem Aleykhem, Bashefenish [Creature], in: Ale verk fun Sholem Aleykhem [Collected Works of Sholem Aleykhem], vol. 8, Vilnius 1925, 173–189.

Secondary literature

[6] S. B. Freehof, Devotional Literature in the Vernacular, in: Yearbook of the Central Conference of American Rabbis 33 (1923), 375–424.   [7] T. G. Kliers (ed.), The Merit of Our Mothers. A Bilingual Anthology of Jewish Women's Prayers, Cincinnati 1992.   [8] M. Weinreich, History of the Yiddish Language, New Haven 2008.   [9] C. Weissler, Voices of the Matriarchs. Listening to the Prayers of Early Modern Jewish Women, Boston 1998.

SIMON NEUBERG, TRIER

Tłomackie Synagogue

The Great Synagogue in Tłomackie Street, built in the last quarter of the 19th century, was the representative center of the Warsaw's → Reform-oriented Jewish community. Corresponding to its progressive orientation toward the Polish → middle class, sermons were held in → Polish, and national Polish festivals were celebrated. In addition, the Tłomackie Synagogue was known for its important liturgical music performed by the best → cantors of the time. In the interwar years, the complex of buildings housed the Main Judaic Library and the Institute of Judaic Studies, which were considered centers of Jewish learning far beyond the boundaries of Warsaw and of Poland.

1. Origins
2. The Great Synagogue
3. Socio-religious characteristics
4. In the public sphere
5. Destruction

1. Origins

The Great Synagogue in Tłomackie Street, consecrated in 1878, originated from a prayer room which the affluent Jew Isaac Flatau, who had moved there from Prussia, had built in his house for private purposes in 1802. After his death in 1806, the → Synagogue developed into the place of worship of the German Jews of Warsaw, for whom → sermons in German and other typical features of → Reform were important. In the first decades of the 19th century, they were joined by progressive Warsaw Jews who admired enlightened German Jewry (→ Haskalah), and strove to emulate it. As its members copied German fashion in clothing, no longer wore beards, and spoke → German, the Synagogue in Daniłowiczowska Street was called *Di Daytshe Shul* (the German Synagogue), and its members were known as *daytshe*. A new building was erected for the growing community in an adjacent area in 1843.

The innovations in the → liturgy which their Rabbi Abraham Meyer Goldschmidt (1812–1889), in particular, took over from the German-speaking world, did not infringe upon the Jewish religious law (→ Halakhah), but did sharply contrast with the predominantly Orthodox or Hasidic-leaning rituals of Polish Jewry (→ Orthodoxy; → Hasidism). Goldschmidt, who came from the province of → Poznań and presided over the community from 1840 to 1858, gave a more strict form to the divine service: he forbade loud talking, walking around, and bringing children younger than five, and he established a → cantor and a choir. The other communities of Warsaw and their religious authorities interpreted the Western habits cultivated in this synagogue as a dangerous departure from tradition and a step in the direction of apostasy. Nevertheless, matters never went so far as a schism between the two camps, probably because of the important social influence of the well-to-do "German" community.

Throughout their existence, important rabbis and preachers had led the synagogues of the progressive Warsaw community. Goldschmidt, who took up a position in Leipzig in 1858, was followed by Markus Jastrow (1829–1903), who was deeply beloved in Warsaw circles, and whose pro-Polish attitude in the context of the January Uprising is prominently expressed in the painting *The Funeral of the Five Fallen in 1861* (see figure, vol. 3, 437). Identification with Poland and with the → Polish language increasingly prevailed in the community. At the latest when Jastrow took office in 1858, sermons in German were given up in favor of Polish, under the influence of the growing Polish nationalist movement. After the suppression of the January Uprising, however, sermons in Polish were initially forbidden by Russian authorities.

2. The Great Synagogue

Wealthy members of the community usually exercised a right to a permanent seat in the → synagogue, which obviously embodied a certain social prestige [6. 196]. As the number of members grew, so did the demand for a new, larger house of worship in the style of the great synagogues of Central and Western Europe, which, moreover, should occupy a prominent location inside the city. 1872 saw the purchase of the site on Tłomackie Street, a main thoroughfare between the Jewish Quarter (→ Nalewki Street) and the adjacent city center. Warsaw's most renowned architect of the time, Leandro Jan Marconi, was charged with the planning and construction of the edifice. Participants in the dedication ceremony in 1878, on the Jewish New Year

View of the Tłomackie Synagogue in Warsaw (postcard, ca. 1936)

5639, included the Russian governor Paul von Kotzebue, who had the honor of opening the Synagogue, high-ranking Polish and Russian authorities, the mayor, and the rector of the university, as well as representatives of social associations and the press.

The Synagogue was built in the neoclassical style. The men's area on the main floor accommodated up to 1,142 worshippers, while the two galleries, reserved for women, offered 1,050 places. The interior was decorated with precious materials and equipped with such modern technology as heating and gas lighting. A frieze in the choir apse cited the → *shema* prayer; the fact that the name of God was written out in it represented a monstrous breach of taboo for most Warsaw Jews.

Owing to its exposed location, architecture, and size, the Great Synagogue came to be a symbol of Jewish Warsaw. Even Jews who rejected → reform felt a certain pride at the sight of the imposing edifice. The frieze, displayed at an impressive height and surrounding the portico, with the Hebrew inscription "May the One, who has provided this house with His Name, bring love and brotherhood, peace and friendship among you," and the *magen David* (→ Star of David), enthroned on the gilded copper dome and visible from afar, symbolized the community's self-awareness. A square installed directly in front of the Synagogue around the turn of the century made it appear even more magnificent.

3. Socio-religious characteristics

The construction of the Great Synagogue occurred in the term of office of Rabbi Izaak Cylkow (1841–1908), who led the community from 1864 to 1908, and distinguished himself as a translator of the Bible into → Polish. He was followed by the Arabist and student of Moritz Steinschneider (→ Bibliography) Samuel Abraham Poznański (1864–1921). The last officially appointed preacher at the Great Synagogue before its destruction was the great historian of the Polish Jews Moses (Mojżesz) Schorr (1874–1941).

Aesthetics and questions of representation were always of considerable importance in the rituals of the Synagogue. The clothing and hats of the women, the top hats of the men, as well as the sober character of the service were expressions of a middle-class morality that was to earn respect for Judaism among the Christian population. In his opening address of 1878, Rabbi Cylkow returned to Polish as the language of the → sermon, without being contradicted by the Governor, who was present. The Tłomackie community distinguished itself by this affinity to Polish from the other modern synagogues of Warsaw, such as Sinai, Nożyk, or Moriah. These also stood apart from the hundreds of very simple Jewish houses of worship by imposing buildings, elaborate → liturgy, the use of → cantors and choirs, as well as Yiddish sermons (primarily Zionist-oriented). Its mainly petit bourgeois members maintained a recognizably Jewish habitus and → Yiddish as their vernacular, without yielding to Orthodox (→ Orthodoxy) or Hasidic fervor (→ Hasidism). The Tłomackie Synagogue stood out from all these by the very fact that its members generally belonged to the upper middle class, which was assimilated to Polish culture. The practice of religion was correspondingly associated with the Polish national consciousness as well; thus, for instance, after Poland regained its statehood in 1918, prayers were held on Independence Day.

An important legacy of Rabbi Samuel Abraham Poznański was the construction of the Main Judaic Library (Główna Biblioteka Judaistyczna), founded in 1879 – Poland's first public Jewish library. In 1936, it was accommodated, together with the Institute of Judaic Studies (Instytut Nauk Judaistycznych), founded in 1928 by Majer Bałaban, Moses Schorr, and Markus Braude, which housed one of Europe's most important Judaica collections in an extension on the northeast side of the square in front of the Tłomackie Synagogue. In addition to the founders, luminaries of Warsaw's Judaic studies also belonged to the Institute's teaching staff, including Ignacy Schiper, Abraham Weiss, Arieh Tartakower, and Edmund Stein. As Poland's only Jewish university-level academic institution, the Institute required its students be enrolled in the University of Warsaw, in addition to solid religious and secular knowledge.

4. In the public sphere

Warsaw's broader Jewish public viewed the Tłomackie Synagogue with a combination of rejection and interest. To be sure, it still seemed unheard-of that, as a journalist emphasized pointedly, "a shaven rabbi dared to call upon the Lord in Polish" [1. 9], but the experience of the splendor and magnificence of the services also appealed to many. Cantoral and liturgical music were very popular among Warsaw Jews, and the offerings in the Great Synagogue, in which the cantors and preachers, accompanied by an → organ and a choir, "appeared in costumes like opera singers," attracted them as a "well-staged show" [2. 327].

The first → cantor was the tenor Simon Grützhändler (1842–1920). In 1908, Gershon Sirota (1874–1943), the "king of the cantors" and the "Jewish Caruso," was appointed principal cantor. Sirota often travelled to → New York for High Holidays, since his salary there was much higher than in Warsaw; from 1927 onward, he devoted himself exclusively to his concert career. The cantor was accompanied by a choir, led by important musicians, which also found itself called upon to perform at the highest level. Guests streamed into the → Synagogue *en masse*, especially to services on the → Shabbat, at which Sirota, his successor Moshe Koussevitzky (1899–1966), or famous guest cantors were to be heard. As a rule, the Synagogue announced in the press who would be the cantor on the following Shabbat and which quota of tickets would be available. This procedure, and more generally the closeness of spectacles in the Great Synagogue to forms of modern entertainment, were vehemently criticized in the Jewish press. Because of the large crowds, masses of people often gathered in front of the Synagogue as well, in order to listen to the cantor and the choir; sometimes, the faithful also tried to obtain entry without a ticket to take part in the prayers. Occasionally, the leadership of the Synagogue asked the authorities to send two mounted policemen, who, much to the consternation of most Warsaw Jews, were posted in front of the portico to prevent the crowd from penetrating into the Synagogue.

On High Holidays, especially Rosh ha-Shanah, but always on Yom Kippur (→ Course of the Year), non-Jewish representatives of the government and city authorities attended the services; special seats for official visitors were reserved for them. Local opera singers, such as the Polish star tenor Jan Kiepura, also came to hear the cantor and the choir. The concerts that took place with liturgical music at Hanukkah came to be a fixed component of Warsaw's musical calendar. During the reading of the Megillah at the Purim festival and at Simchat Torah, the Synagogue opened its doors, so that those who were interested could glimpse how the *daytshn* celebrated these festivals. Weddings of the upper class, which took place during the week with considerable pomp, were a popular spectacle among the public.

5. Destruction

After the German attack on Poland, Moses Schorr fled to the Ukrainian city ofOstroh in Soviet territory. There, he was arrested in late October 1939 by the NKVD as a representative of the Polish bourgeois elite, and sentenced to five years imprisonment in an Uzbek labor camp, where he died in July 1941. In his stead, Majer (Meir) Tauber (1880–1942), previously rector of the seminary and Director of the Institute of Judaic Studies, took over Schorr's position as preacher.

During the German occupation, the Great Synagogue was part of the ghetto known as the "Jewish Residential District" (→ Warsaw). The holdings of the Library, which had become extremely important, and of the Institute of Judaic Studies were plundered by the Germans in order to supply Nazi → Judenforschung. The Synagogue buildings and forecourt were then used as a storage place for furniture that had been carried off during the plundering of the ghetto in 1940. On May 16, 1943, one day after the quashing of the ghetto uprising, the SS commander Jürgen Stroop had the Synagogue blown up, as a symbol of the completion of his mission to obliterate all Jewish presence from Warsaw.

The outbuilding in which the Institute of Judaic Studies was formally housed survived the war. From 1947 onward, it accommodated the newly founded Żydowski Instytut Historyczny (→ Jewish Historical Institute). After the war, many anticipated that the Synagogue would be rebuilt. In the 1950s, however, the neighboring financial district was redesigned, and a modern highrise (Błękitny Wieżowiec) was erected on the old site of the Synagogue. After technical problems that lasted decades, the building was finally authorized for use in 1993. A modern legend ascribed this delay to a "rabbinic excommunication" (*klątwa rabina*), according to which the Great Synagogue henceforth haunted the site as a sort of spirit.

Bibliography

Sources
[1] B. Singer, Moje Nalewki [My Nalewki Street], Warsaw 1993. [2] Z. Turkow, Di daytshe shul [The German Synagogue], in: M. Ravitsch (ed.), Dos amolike yidishe Varshe. Biz der shvel fun dritn khurbn [The Former Jewish Warsaw. Until the Beginning of the Third Destruction], Montreal 1966, 323–329.

Secondary literature

[3] M. Beizer/I. Bartal, The Case of Moses Schorr. Rabbi, Scholar and Social Activist, in: Polin. Studies in Polish Jewry 21 (2009), 426–459. [4] M. Dold, "A Matter of National and Civic Honour." Majer Bałaban and the Institute of Jewish Studies in Warsaw, in: East European Jewish Affairs 34 (2004) 2, 55–72. [5] A. Guterman, The Congregation of the Great Synagogue in Warsaw. Its Changing Social Composition and Ideological Affiliations, in: Polin. Studies in Polish Jewry 11 (1989), 112–126. [6] A. Guterman, The Origins of the Great Synagogue in Warsaw on Tłomackie Street, in: W. T. Bartoszewski/A. Polonsky (eds.), The Jews in Warsaw. A History, Oxford 1991, 181–211. [7] R. Zebrowski, Geneza biblioteki wielkiej synagogi na Tłomackiem [Genesis of the Library of the Great Synagogue in Tłomackie Street], in: Biuletyn Żydowskiego Instytutu Historycznego 189 (1999), 14–33. [8] A. Zimmermann, Ha-ḥazanim be-bet ha-kneset bi-reḥov Tlomatski be-Varsha [The Cantors of the Synagogue in Warsaw's Tłomackie Street], in: Areshet 6 (1987), 74–80.

MARCOS SILBER, HAIFA

Todesfuge

The title of a poem, published in 1947, by the Bukovina-born German-language poet Paul Celan (1920–1970). Although the work initially met with a mixed reception in Germany, Celan later publicly turned away from the poem and no longer allowed it to be printed; today it is one of most famous poetic works that recall the → Shoah. Like no other work or art, Celan's *Todesfuge* embodies the genre of poetry after Auschwitz, in form and content, as a text and in its influence.

1. Life and work
2. Poetological aspects
3. Significance and influence

1. Life and work

Paul Celan (→ Europe; → Gruppe 47) was born Paul Antschel in Czernowitz in 1920. The capital of Bukovina, which he described as an area "in which books and people lived" [2. 395], was an ethnically and linguistically multifaceted place at the time. His mother Friederike came from the neighboring Hasidic center of Sadagora, while his father Leo was a staunch Zionist. The family belonged to the middle class. Whereas his mother felt closely bound to German language and culture, his father set great store by his son's Jewish education. In Czernowitz, German was the language of everyday life, of education (→ Bildung), and of social advancement, while English and French were also widespread. The young Celan was influenced by Rilke, the French Symbolists, and Shakespeare (→ Shylock). Romanian was the national language; Russian the one learned later, and Yiddish was the language present in the day-to-day life of the city. Celan attended four schools before graduating: first the German elementary school, then the Hebrew Ssafa-Ivrija elementary school, where he was instructed in the study of the → Tanakh, then the Romanian school, followed by the Ukrainian state secondary school, where Celan completed his schooling in 1938. He wrote his first poems at the age of 15 or 16. He formed the name under which he was to become famous as an anagram of the Romanianized "Ancel."

In 1938, Celan began studies of medicine in Tours, which, however, he did not complete. On the way to France, he travelled through Germany, with a stop in Berlin on the morning after the → November Pogrom.

In the 1963 cycle *Die Niemandsrose* ("No One's Rose," 2021), one reads: "Via Krakow / You came, at the Anhalter / Bahnhof / a smoke floated toward your gaze, / it was already of tomorrow" [3d. 348] in which this stay is recalled. Celan could no longer return to France after the summer holidays of 1939 due to the outbreak of the Second World War and began to study Romance languages in Czernowitz, since Jews were forbidden to enroll in medical studies.

In 1940, Soviet troops occupied the area. After Romania's participation in the German attack on the Soviet Union in 1941, the city belonged to Romania again until 1944. In August 1941, general Ion Antonescu ordered the construction of a ghetto in Czernowitz, in which Celan's parents were also interned; their son avoided arrest only by chance. At the dissolution of the ghetto in June 1942, his parents were deported to the Michailovka camp (in the Ukranian Rajon of Kelmenzi in the Tschernowitz Oblast, established in 1940), and were presumably murdered there in the same year. Celan lived through the war years in Romania; he was temporarily interned in various labor camps (→ Forced Labor), and finally reached the Romanian capital.

Celan left Bucharest in 1947, and emigrated to → Vienna. It was in the local journal *Plan* that the first selection of his poems appeared in 1948; they were essentially perceived as surrealist avant-garde. Still in the same year, Celan came to Paris, where he met, and later married, the artist Gisèle Lestrange (1927–1991). He became a lecturer at the École normale supérieure in 1959.

He translated many works by European poets, and became one of the most renowned German lyric poets of the postwar period, if not of the 20th century. In Vienna, Celan met Ingeborg Bachmann, Milo Dor, and Reinhard Federmann, who had a key influence on his reception in Germany. In 1952, he contributed to the autumn session of the → Gruppe 47; in the same year

Paul Celan (orig. Paul Antschel, 1920–1970)

the volume *Mohn und Gedächtnis* ("Poppy and Memory," 2001) appeared, which made him known to a broader public. In 1969, he travelled for the first and only time to Jerusalem, where he met with Gershom Scholem (→ Kabbalah), among others. Celan died in unexplained circumstances in 1970, although it was assumed to be suicide.

Celan's work can be divided into three phases: the early poems, influenced by Symbolism, until the volume *Sprachgitter* (1959; "Language Mesh," 1988), was followed by the second phase, characterized by a radicalizing linguistic skepticism (→ Critique of Language), from *Die Niemandsrose* (1963) to *Atemwende* (1967; "Breathturn," 1995). The last period of his creative work is distinguished by an even greater destruction of units of meaning. It includes the poetry cycles *Fadensonnen* (1968; "Threadsuns," 2000), *Lichtzwang* (1970; "Lightduress," 2005), and the volume *Schneepart* ("Snowpart," 2007), published from his posthumous works in 1971. From an early stage, motifs became established that frequently emerge in later poems as well: the experience of the loss of language and home, the exile in Paris, and the memory of the murdered, especially his mother who was killed.

2. Poetological aspects

By his own account, Paul Celan wrote *Todesfuge* ("Deathfugue," 2001) in Bucharest in May 1945, after reading reports on the Lwów ghetto. In all probability, this was an article from the Soviet newspaper *Izvestiya* (News), entitled "On the Crimes of the Germans in the area of the Lemberg District" [13. 441f.]. The poem first appeared in Romanian in a translation by Celan's friend Petre Solomon that appeared in 1947 in the newspaper *Contemporanul*, under the title *Tangoul morţii* (Death Tango); it was Celan's very first publication. The first printing was followed by the explanation: "The poem whose translation we are publishing is built upon the evocation of a real fact. In Lublin, as in many 'Nazi death camps,' one group of the condemned were forced to sing nostalgic songs while others dug graves" (cited in [8. 28]). *Todesfuge* first appeared in German in 1948, in the thin volume of poetry *Der Sand aus den Urnen* ("The Sand from the Urns"); however, Celan had the book withdrawn soon after its publication, because oftypographical errors which distorted the meaning. The poem then appeared in 1952, both in the *Neue literarische Welt* and in the volume *Mohn und Gedächtnis*.

Todesfuge, structured in 36 verses and six stanzas, begins with the words "Black milk of daybreak we drink it at evening / we drink it at midday and morning we drink it at night / we drink and we drink / we shovel a grave in the air there you won't lie too cramped" [8. 31]. The lyric We is inserted without punctuation into the flow of an event, and contrasted with a lyric He: "A man lives in the house he plays with his vipers he writes / he writes when it grows dark to Deutschland your golden hair Margareta / he writes it and steps out of doors

and the stars are all sparkling he whistles his hounds to come close / he whistles his Jews into rows has them shovel a grave in the ground / he commands us to play up for the dance." [8. 31]. The principle of counterpoint is borrowed from the musical fugue, as are the two voices. The incomplete nature of the present determines the poem, which deals with the presence of a traumatic past experience of time. *Todesfuge* is structured by oppositions: of "we" to "him," of heaven and earth ("a grave in the air"), of light to dark, of indoors to outdoors.

Shortly after, allusions occur in the fifth stanza to Johann Wolfgang von Goethe's (→ Elective Affinities) Gretchen ("your golden hair Margareta") and the virgin Sulamith from the Song of Songs ("Your ashen hair Shulamith") – a pair of opposites with which the poem comes to a prominent end. There is also what is perhaps the best known formulation of *Todesfuge*, often re-used against the author's intentions: "this Death is a master from Deutschland" [8. 31]. *Todesfuge* is one of the first poems that takes up the Shoah – before the term became customary (→ Holocaust) – from the first line to the last, yet does not make it an explicit theme. The distance necessary for this was not granted to Celan, with millionfold murder in his memory. However unique *Todesfuge* may be in its effects and its value, its origin took up influences from others: the image of "black milk" presumably goes back to the poet Rose Ausländer (1901–1988) of → Czernowitz, Celan's older contemporary; the poem *Er* by Celan's childhood friend Immanuel Weissglas (1920–1979), which was not published until 1970 and had originated before Celan's, shows certain parallels in its motifs to *Todesfuge*. Years after writing it, Celan gave an account in his notes of the form and content of what was, as he emphasized, an "independent poem": "the meaning of what occurs fills them both {Marg/Sul} | braids = snakes | the poem becomes ever more lethal (more concise) | A poem with death and 'to death' | milk of dawn – the nurturing | of the other | it is the dying who speak" (cited in [3. 607]).

Todesfuge opens a broad resonance chamber, which has not ceased to occupy interpreters, and which extends from the Song of Songs to the Dance of the Dead and the musical lament for the dead (→ Lamentation). Celan himself seems to have understood the poem as a burial in and through the text. Thus, as he wrote in 1959 to Ingeborg Bachmann, to whom he was both bound and separated from the late 1940s to the early 1950s, by a multi-year amorous relationship: "You know – no, you knew – and now I must remind you of it, that the Deathfugue also has this meaning for me: that of an epitaph and a tomb. [...] My mother, too, has only this as a grave" (cited in [3. 608]). In this sense, Celan conceived his work as the burial of a burnt offering, and as a monument to the dead [12].

Despite many changes in his work, *Todesfuge* is nevertheless paradigmatic for Celan's poetry. *Engführung* ("Stretto") is the title of a poem from the volume *Sprachgitter* (1959), also composed after the model of a fugue, and which for that reason takes up *Todesfuge* once again, but gives it a decisively new turn. The poem, which no longer describes something to the readers but leads them into the terrain, begins: "Driven into the / terrain / with the infallible trace" [3a. 231]; they are "driven" "déportés," as it reads in the French version. "Grass, written asunder. The stones, white, / with the shadows of grassblades: / [...] Read no more – look! / Look no more - go!" [3a. 232–233]. The literary scholar Peter Szondi (1929–1971), born in → Budapest of Hungarian-Jewish origins, who had escaped deportation to Auschwitz with the Kasztner transport (→ Kasztner Affair) and was a friend of Paul Celan, has shown in his last essay *Lecture de Strette*, originally written in French, how the *Engführung* follows the path through the extermination camp. However, this was no depiction of the terrible

place, but a textual path; it was not about representation, but about the realization of the past, which assumes the form of the present in this poem as well: "The text itself is refusing to serve reality, to go on playing the role that has been assigned to it since Aristotle. Poetry is ceasing to be mimesis, representation; it is becoming reality" [6. 31]. The poem emerged in the mid-1950s, when Celan was creating the German version for the film *Nuit et brouillard* ("Night and Fog") by Alain Resnais (1922–2014). There are many correspondences between the image sequences, the commentary on *Nuit et brouillard*, and Celan's poem *Engführung*, which can be understood as a drastically modified poetic conception of *Todesfuge*.

3. Significance and influence

The reaction to Celan's works, which became known to a broader public with *Mohn und Gedächtnis* at the latest, oscillated between rejection and acceptance in Germany. As early as 1952, he read *Todesfuge* in Niendorf on the Baltic, at a session of the → Gruppe 47 that later became famous: "a flop," as Walter Jens later reported (cited in [7. 92]). Hans Werner Richter, who led the session, was said to have compared Celan's presentation to Goebbel's manner of speaking [7. 92]. Nevertheless, Celan received the Bremer literary prize in 1958, and two years later the Büchner prize, the nation's highest literary distinction, which was awarded for the first time to an author of Jewish descent. In the 1950s and 1960s, the reception of *Todesfuge* was marked by either complete disregard or a by an exaggeration of its historical content.

These experiences from the postwar period left a deep influence on Celan. In his posthumously published poem *Wolfsbohne* ("Wolf's-bean," 2002), he writes: "(Far away, in Mikhailovka, in / the Ukraine, where / they murdered my father and mother: what / flowered there, what / flowers there? What / flower, Mother, / hurt you there / with its name? // You, Mother, / who said *wolf's-bean*, not: / lupin. // Yesterday / one of them came and / killed you / once more in / my poem. // Mother. / Mother, whose / hand did I clasp / when with your / words I went to / Germany?" [3b. 341, 343]. The occasion for this poem was a critique by Günter Blöcker, written in the autumn of 1959. According to the journalist, Celan's lyric verse was detached from reality. *Todesfuge* and *Engführung* were "contrapuntal exercises on notepaper or mute keys – eye-music, optical scores." In an ambiguous formulation, moreover, Blöcker spoke of how Celan's origins permitted him "greater freedom" in his dealings with the German language (*Der Tagesspiegel*, October 11, 1959).

In the same year as Celan received the Büchner prize, he also received public accusations from Claire Goll, that he had plagiarized the poems of her late husband Yvan Goll (1891–1950). Celan had met this Jewish poet, who wrote in German, in Paris in 1949, and had translated his poems. Despite protests and defense by renowned advocates such as Walter Jens or Peter Szondi, Celan never got over this accusation, despite all his recognition.

Nevertheless, the more time elapsed from the origin of the poem, the more its historical contents came to light. Over the decades, *Todesfuge* became a symbol of the literary depiction of the Shoah. It had found in the poem a literary expression which, to be sure, the author himself submitted to revision in *Engführung*, but which nevertheless also underwent criticism. Thus, Reinhard Baumgart wrote in 1965: "Celan's *Todesfuge* [...] and its motifs, the 'black milk of the morning', death with a violin, 'a master from Deutschland', all that thoroughly composed in a refined score – didn't this show too much enjoyment in art, in the despair that, by its means, has become 'beautiful' again" (cited in [10. 274]).

Celan's poem was thus situated within the forcefield of a problematization which

Theodor W. Adorno (→ Dialectic of Enlightenment) had emphasized in 1951, through the affirmation that to write a poem after → Auschwitz was barbaric [1a. 34]. Celan later noted: "No poem after Auschwitz (Adorno): what kind of concept of 'poem' is being assumed here? The arrogance of the person who has the audacity to consider Auschwitz, in a hypothetical/speculative way, from the perspective of a nightingale or a song thrush" (cited in [7. 131]). In fact, Adorno later retracted his verdict: "Perennial suffering has as much right to expression as a tortured man has to scream; hence it may have been wrong to say that after Auschwitz you could no longer write poems" as one reads in *Negative Dialektik* (1967; "Negative Dialectics," 2005) [1b. 362]. The poet and the philosopher knew one another. In his posthumously-published *Ästhetischen Theorie* ("Aesthetic Theory," 1997), Adorno engaged intensively with Celan's poetry; again, Celan wrote his own prose text, *Gespräch im Gebirg* ("Conversation in the Mountains," 2003) about a failed meeting with Adorno in the Engadine in the summer of 1959.

Translated into many languages, *Todesfuge* became a part of world literature: the poem was considered almost as standard against which to measure all works that dealt with the extermination of European Jews. Among the many poets who referred, directly or indirectly, to Celan and his poetry, Nelly Sachs (1891–1970) was particularly associated with him. After growing up in an assimilated Jewish family of the Berlin middle classes, she began to write in her early years, and published her first collection in 1921, with the help of Stefan Zweig (→ [The] Royal Game). She also regularly wrote for various Berlin newspapers. A later recipient of the Nobel Prize (she received the distinction in 1966, together with Samuel Joseph Agnon; → Shira), she shared with Celan, in addition to the influence of Jewish → mysticism on her work, primarily the experience of exile. It was persecution by the Nazis that first led Sachs to make her Jewish origins as her subject. In 1940, she was able to flee to Sweden under difficult circumstances. Her 1947 volume *In den Wohnungen des Todes* comes closest to *Todesfuge* in both date and content. Thus, it includes the poem *O die Schornsteine* ("O the Chimneys," 1969), which, like Celan, makes use of the image of rising smoke: "On the ingeniously devised habitations of death / When Israel's body drifted as smoke / Through the air" [5. 3]. In 1949 the poem → *Hiob* appeared in the volume of verse entitled *Sternverdunklung*, in which she dealt with the failure of speech when faced with the Shoah.

In 1953, Sachs came into contact with Celan, and a deep friendship developed between them. Celan dedicated many texts to Sachs, and the connection between the two of them is impressively attested in their correspondence. Even more strongly than in Celan, there are, however, religious references in Sachs's work that Celan did not share [8. 239–240]. In 1960, on the day of an unsettling meeting with Martin Buber (→ Dialogue), Celan wrote the poem *Die Schleuse* ("The Sluice," 2001), addressed to himself and to his "sister" Nelly Sachs: "Over all this / Grief of yours: no / second heaven. / .... / To a mouth / for which it was a thousandword, / lost — / I lost a word / that was left to me: / Sister" [3c. 151]. At that time, Nelly Sachs was suffering increasingly from a mental illness, which forced her to spend several years in a Stockholm mental hospital. In 1970, on the day of Paul Celan's burial, Sachs succumbed to cancer.

The influence of *Todesfuge*, as a closed literary cosmos of the Shoah, is discernible in many other works as well. References to Paul Celan's verse is found in poets as diverse as Peter Weiss, Hilde Domin, Michael Hamburger, Erich Fried, Dan Pagis (→ Poetry), or Tuvia Rübner. At first it was primarily Jewish authors for whom the experience recorded in Celan's poem was unavoidable, and who

approached it in a variety of ways. Only later were non-Jewish authors such as Peter Rühmkorf or Richard Exner added to the list.

In the 1980s, moreover, the poem seemed to develop an influence on the politics of remembrance. On November, 10 1988, Ida Ehre (1900–1989), an actress persecuted as a Jew and, after 1945, Director of the Hamburg Chamber Theatre, recited Celan's *Todesfuge* in the German Bundestag. Two days later, Philipp Jenninger, President of the Bundestag, resigned from his position, since he had given a speech in commemoration of the 1938 *Pogromnacht* in a way that was – rhetorically albeit not on the level of content – ambiguous. It seems that two cultures of remembrance – the recitation of a poem from 1945 and the political discourse of remembering – had clashed. Finally, *Todesfuge* was prominently evoked at the beginning of the novel *Kaddis a meg nem született gyermekért* (1990; "Kaddish for an Unborn Child," 2004) by the Nobel Prize winner Imre Kertész: "more darkly now stroke your strings then as smoke / you will rise into air / then a grave you will have in the clouds / there one lie unconfined" [4. Epigraph]. The Hungarian Nobel Prize winner writes: "the book, which contains the endless names of the dead and of those who were never born," in the clouds: "Because this too is just a hoe's scratch towards the trench, the burial pit that I am digging in the air (because there I shall be able to lie down in comfort)" [4a. 357–358]; [4. 9]. "[T]hey have whistled out the signal," writes Kertész "to dig a grave for myself, and at present, even though so much time had already passed – God help us! – I am still just at the digging stage." [4. 25].

The reception of *Todesfuge* also left traces outside of literature. There were numerous musical adaptations of the poem in East as well as in West Germany. A particularly impressive artistic treatment the poem comes from the poet and sculptor Anselm Kiefer. In the early 1980s, Kiefer took up the last two verses: "your golden hair Margareta / your ashen hair Shulamith" in a series of (double) portraits, which show allegorical female figures in the midst of devastated, burned fields with yellow straw or black symbols stuck to them, mixed with particles of ash. Significantly, these works arose as part of the artist's confrontation with "myths of German history." They show what Celan's poem has become in the decades since its origin: a part of this history, more influential than anywhere else.

Bibliography

Sources

[1] T. W. Adorno, Gesammelte Schriften, ed. by R. Tiedemann, 20 vols., Frankfurt am Main 1997. [1a] T. W. Adorno, Prisms, trans. by S. and S. Webel, Cambridge, Massachusetts 1981. [1b] T. W. Adorno, Negative Dialectics, London/New York 2005. [2] P. Celan, Speech on the Occasion of Receiving the Literature Prize of the Free Hanseatic City of Bremen, in: Selected Poems and Prose of Paul Celan, trans. by J. Felsiner, New York 2001, 395–396. [3] P. Celan, Die Gedichte. Kommentierte Gesamtausgabe, ed. by B. Wiedemann, Frankfurt am Main 2003. [3a] P. Szondi, D. Caldwell, S. Esh, 'Reading "Engführung." An Essay on the Poetry of Paul Celan', in: Boundary 2, vol. 11, no. 3, 1983, pp. 231–264. [3b] P. Celan, Wolf's-bean, in: Poems of Paul Celan, trans. by M. Hamburger, New York 2002. [3c] P. Celan, Selected Poems and Prose by Paul Celan, trans. by J. Felstiner, New York 2001. [3d] K. Leeder, M. Pajević, M. Eskin, Paul Celan Today. A Companion, Berlin/Boston 2021, 348. [4] I. Kertész, Kaddish for an Unborn Child, trans. by T. Wilkinson, New York 2004. [4a] L. F. Földényi: Schicksallosigkeit. Ein Imre-Kertész-Wörterbuch, Reinbek bei Hamburg 2009, 357–358. [5] N. Sachs, 'O the Chimneys'. Selected Poems, Including the Verse Play 'Eli', trans. by M. Roloff, New York 1967. [6] P. Szondi, Celan Studies, Stanford 2003.

Secondary literature

[7] W. Emmerich, Paul Celan, Reinbek 1999. [8] J. Felstiner, Paul Celan: Poet, Survivor, Jew, New Haven 1995. [9] H. Kiesel/V. Stepp, Paul Celans Schreckensmusik, in: U. Bermbach/H. R. Vaget (eds.), Getauft auf Musik. Festschrift für D. Borchmeyer, Würzburg 2006, 115–131. [10] D. Lamping, Dein aschenes Haar Sulamith. Dichtung über den Holocaust, Munich 1992. [11] T. Sparr, Zeit der Todesfuge. Rezeption der Lyrik von Nelly Sachs und Paul Celan, in: S. Braese et al. (eds.), Deutsche Nachkriegsliteratur und der Holocaust, Frankfurt am Main/New York 1998, 43–52. [12] U. Werner, Textgräber. Paul Celans geologische Lyrik, Munich 1998. [13] B. Wiedemann, Welcher Daten eingedenk? Celans "Todesfuge" und der "Izvestija"-Bericht über das Lemberger Ghetto, in: Wirkendes Wort 3 (2011), 437–452.

Thomas Sparr, Berlin

Tohuwabohu

In the Hebrew Bible (→ Tanakh), the words *tohu va-vohu* (unformed and void; Gen 1:2; Jer 4:23) describe the mythical, incomplete original state of the earth at the beginning of the creation story. The German-Jewish lawyer and writer Sammy Gronemann (1875–1952) used the words as the title of his satirical social novel *Tohuwabohu*, published in Berlin in 1920, a critical insight into the relationship between German Jews and Jews from Eastern Europe. In his literary works, which are permeated by juristic and religious motifs and characterized by witty and conciliatory humor, Gronemann devoted himself to questions of assimilation and the foundation of a new Jewish self-confidence. After his move to Palestine in 1936, his comedies, written in German, contributed significantly to the development of Hebrew theatre.

1. A new creative stage
2. Sammy Gronemann
3. Zionist comedy
4. Theatre in Israel

1. A new creative stage

In his → novel *Tohuwabohu* ("Utter Chaos," 2016), written between 1916 and 1920, Gronemann used the relationship between German Jews and Jews from Eastern Europe to describe the state of Jewish tradition in the modern era, issues of → assimilation, and also the effects of antisemitism (→ Conspiracy). He contrasts the imponderabilia of Jewish existence in East and West with the evolution of a new creative stage. This would be the foundation for a new Jewish consciousness by means of which internal Jewish schisms would be overcome and the future of the Jewish people secured in a home in Palestine.

The storyline of the satirical novel begins in the spring of 1903 in the imaginary town of Borytshev near Vilna, where law-abiding Yossel Schlenker and sharp-witted Chana Weinstein debate on the religious rules for → Shabbat. Yossel's arguments, based on the Halakhah, are defeated by Chana's wit and irony. Subsequently, Yossel and Chana fall in love, marry, and move to Berlin in order to pursue their desire for freedom and knowledge as university students, and flee the constricting existence of Eastern Europe without leaving Jewish tradition behind [15. 358f.]. Gronemann uses Yossel's and Chana's experiences to draw a scintillating as well as humorous portrait of Jewish life in Berlin, a kaleidoscope of Jewish traditions grotesquely distorted as a consequence of → emancipation – a strict observance of rigid religious rules (→ Halakhah) on the one hand and assimilation and → conversion to Christianity leading to apostasy from Judaism on the other. Jewish life in Eastern Europe as embodied by Yossel is presented as a natural harmony against which the ways of life of German Jews are contrasted satirically.

In Berlin, Yossel meets his second cousin Heinz Lehnsen, representative of the second generation of converts in the family. He invites Heinz to Borytshev, where he experiences Pesaḥ (→ Course of the Year) for the first time. When during the ritual seder the door is symbolically opened for the prophet Elijah, the noise of a → pogrom approaching can be heard. Heinz understands that self-defense and political action are necessary; his understanding of himself and of the world are profoundly shaken.

After returning to Germany, he represses this experience, believing himself to be safe. He travels to Baden-Baden to distract himself. Yossel and Chana are travelling on the same train, but Heinz avoids them. Heinz is on the way to the races and concerned with the question of whether "Ice Wind or Faust will reach the finish line as victors" [4. 255]. This is contrasted with Yossel's awareness of tradition and his experience of the existential threats in Eastern Europe which lead him to Zionist activism. While Heinz's behavior appears to lead him astray, Yossel and Chana are travelling to the sixth Zionist Congress in → Basel.

In his other anecdotic books, Gronemann also distances himself from the assimilation of German Jews, contrasting them with a positive image of the → Ostjuden. He repeatedly relys on the word "Tohuwabohu," referring to his diagnosis of the time. Thus, in his 1927 book *Schalet. Beiträge zur Philosophie des "Wenn Schon,"* he wrote: "The creation phase of Tohuwabohu in which we find ourselves will one day be overcome, there will be light, and perhaps we are perceptibly approaching the age of revelation" [1. 56].

2. Sammy Gronemann

Sammy Gronemann was born in 1875 in Strasburg in West Prussia, the son of Rabbi Selig Gronemann. His father was

→ neo-Orthodox and had studied at the rabbinical seminary in → Breslau under Zacharias Frankel and Heinrich Graetz (→ Historiography). In 1897, he distanced himself from the protest of German rabbis against the first Zionist Congress (→ Basel).

Gronemann spent the greater part of his childhood and school years in Hannover. After his Abitur, he spent one year at the Klaus Synagogue in Halberstadt, a center of neo-Orthodoxy. In the following year, he continued his studies at Esriel Hildesheimer's → rabbinical seminary in Berlin but soon abandoned them, switching to jurisprudence and graduating in 1898. After judicial service training at the local court of Nienburg, he was transferred as prosecutor to Hannover in 1900.

Here, Gronemann attended a Zionist conference for the first time and founded the Hannover Zionist local branch, representing it as a delegate at the fifth Zionist Congress. From then on, he attended all Zionist Congresses as a delegate, from 1911 to 1933 as the head of the Zionist court of honor founded by him, and between 1921 and 1947 as the chief justice of the Congress Court. As a lawyer, he had represented, among others, Theodor Herzl (→ Old New Land), Aḥad Ha-Am (→ Cultural Zionism), Arthur Schnitzler, and Richard Beer-Hofmann from 1904 onward. He moved to Berlin in 1906, where he specialized in family law, international law, and copyright law. In 1910 he was one of the founders and, until 1933, company lawyer of the Schutzverband deutscher Schriftsteller (Association for the Protection of German Authors).

Gronemann had first begun to write at the age of only 14, later continuing alongside his studies and work. He composed short plays, newspaper articles, and short stories, in which he focused on Jewish self-perception with a Zionist tendency. His characteristic → humor already appeared in these early works, which remained free from the pathos

Sammy Gronemann (1875–1952)

of the Zionist movement, for instance *Ein Mordskerl* (1904).

In the First World War, Gronemann served in the press office in Ober Ost near Kovno and → Vilna after being wounded. Here, he came in contact with the Jewish population, became acquainted with the → Vilna Troupe, and together with German Jewish intellectuals such as Arnold Zweig (→ Hiob; → Lied der Partei) and Hermann Struck developed a positive image of the so-called → Ostjuden. Gronemann was familiar with the living conditions of the Jewish population – his parents and his wife came from Eastern Europe. In *Hawdoloh und Zapfenstreich – Erinnerungen an die ostjüdische Etappe 1916–1918* (1924) he drew on his experiences in the region, contrasting the life and religious practice of the Jews in Eastern Europe with that of the German Jews. He supported the Vilna Troupe and → Habima, founding the Jüdischer Theatreverein Berlin in 1921, which he led until it was disbanded. He was active in the German-Jewish committee for the East and supported Jewish refugees from Eastern Europe in arbitration courts.

When the Great Depression began to have an adverse effect on his work as a lawyer from 1929 onward, Gronemann hoped to be able to begin a new career as a freelance writer following the success of *Tohuwabohu*, which had gone through 18 editions by 1930. The career change was doomed to failure with the transfer of power to Hitler. In 1933, Gronemann fled to Paris where he dedicated himself to refugee aid and to establishing Zionist associations.

In 1936, Gronemann emigrated to Palestine. He was not able to pursue his calling as a lawyer here, instead becoming a justice of the peace. After his wife Sonja (née Gottesmann; 1877–1936) died in an accident, he lived with his sister Elfriede's (m. Bergel-Gronemann; 1883–1958) family, composed his *Erinnerungen*, wrote six stage plays, ten one-act plays, numerous cabaret songs, poems, and newspaper articles, in which he depicted the society and culture of the new → Yishuv in a humorous as well as critical fashion. While Gronemann's Hebrew was excellent, he continued to write in → German. To him, the German language was his spiritual home and a Jewish cultural language that should not take second place to the demand for → Hebrew to be the sole official language. All the same, his plays were performed in Hebrew translation on the stages of the Yishuv. Gronemann appeared as the conferencier in → cabaret and gave lectures on Jewish traditions of humor and theatre, becoming a dominant figure in the cultural milieu of German Jews (→ Yekkes).

3. Zionist comedy

While still in Germany, Gronemann had established the genre of the Zionist comedy with his theatre plays, characterized by satirical criticism of → assimilation and parodistic references to texts of the Jewish and humanist educational tradition. It links two motifs from the Jewish festival calendar (→ Course of the Year): the Purim motif of the inversion of hierarchical structures during carnival in the → Diaspora and the Pesaḥ motif of the Exodus from Egypt and the return to the Land of Israel.

Thus, his 1926 → Purim-shpil *Hamans Flucht* narrates the dream of an assimilated boy named Heinz who spends a night in a → library in order to improve his knowledge of Jewish history. There, he dreams the story of Esther, but with Haman evading his execution on the gallows. Utilizing the mythological bearer of the world, Atlas, Heinz follows him through different epochs of the history of the Jews, with Haman concealing himself in anti-Jewish key figures from Vespasian to Hitler. In the end, Heinz understands that the only answer to the persecution of the Jews is to establish a Jewish state. The final scene of the dream shows Jewish farm workers in Palestine while Haman hangs himself in the background. In this prospect, Gronemann links the diasporic tradition of the Purim play to the Pesaḥ motif of the return to the Land of Israel.

In his internationally successful play *Jakob und Christian*, completed in Palestine in 1937, Gronemann once again built on the topic of contrasting German Jews and Jews from Eastern Europe. The comedy concerned two infants switched at birth one of whom grows up to become an Orthodox Jew (→ Orthodoxy), the other a National Socialist. Thirty years after their birth they – Jakob and Christian – face each other and discover the switch that took place when they were infants. Further role changes ensue, adapting the Rabbinic dictum *ad de-lo-yada* (lit. "until no-one knows any more"; Talmud Bavli, Megillah 7b), with the conclusion that during Purim one should aspire to a state of consciousness in which it is impossible to distinguish between "cursed is Haman" and "blessed is Mordechai" any more – the protagonist and the antagonist are inverted, Jakob and Christian are each exposed to the opportunity of being the other. In the end it is left open which of the two is a Jew or a non-Jew. In this satirical inversion, Gronemann leads the National Socialist race ideology *ad absurdum*. In this way the play is doubly encoded: Christian, the Nazi, also represents the assimilated German Jew who becomes reconciled with his counter-myth, the stereotypical → "Ostjude."

4. Theatre in Israel

Gronemann employed a theatrical metaphor in his ironic take on his own move and Jewish immigration into Palestine in 1936: "The Jewish people are returning from their world tour. They played major and minor parts in all theatres, and now they are returning in order to play in their own theatre. This is where the comedy ends and the drama begins" (cited in [8. 153]). "Comedy" to Gronemann meant Jewish → assimilation and denial of their identity (→ Self-hatred); conflicts between Israeli reality and the diasporic past (→ Diaspora) appeared to be the drama. He diagnosed that his contemporaries possessed a diasporic mentality. By means of his comedies, he endeavored to bring to life the seemingly paradoxical Jewish tradition in the land of the Jews.

In his comedies, Gronemann spoke out against the melancholy pathos of early Zionism. Thus, the Talmudic suspension of biblical capital punishment became a *leitmotif* of his plays – and at a time when the heroes of early Israeli drama tragically sacrificed themselves for the community and the heroic → martyr was a figure of identification. Gronemann avoided the motif of → death in order to be able to continue to employ the genre of comedy [9].

In his *Was hat ein Goij mit Chasanut am Hut?* (1938), an Orthodox community in Tel Aviv sues its German-Jewish → cantor who accompanied the Yom Kippur (→ Course of the Year) prayers with an intonation of Wagner arias (→ Music; → Polytonality). During the trial the British, non-Jewish judge calls on the parties not to make their disagreements

public and to liberate themselves from their diasporic faith in the authorities.

Gronemann's greatest success that endures to this day was the 1942 comedy *Der Weise und der Narr* ("The King and the Cobbler," 1952), which became a classic of Israeli theatre in Nathan Alterman's (→ Poetry; → [The] Silver Platter) translation entitled *Shlomo ha-melekh ve-Shalmai ha-sandlar* (King Solomon and Shalmai the cobbler). Shalmai, a reincarnation of → Schlemiel, changes places with King Solomon. While the former succeeds in changing the affairs of state for the better, Solomon's melancholic wisdom reaches its limitations beyond the confines of his palace. Enriched by each other's point of view, both of them gratefully return to their original lives and more experienced in the end. Set to music by Sasha Argov and with songs by Alterman added, Gronemann's comedy became Israel's first successful musical in the 1960s.

The success of Gronemann's plays in the → Yishuv was due to the quality of the translations. His other comedies, however, enjoyed only small success. In *Der Prozess um des Esels Schatten* (1945), he adapted C. M. Wieland's metaphor of the trial of the donkey's shadow from *Die Abderiten*, using it to illustrate the party disputes within the Zionist movement as well as the demands that → Hebrew should be the only language used in the Yishuv. In his last comedy, *Die Königin von Saba* (1951), he dramatized the mythical encounter between King Solomon and the Queen of Sheba. In this sequel to *Der Weise und der Narr*, Gronemann also reflected the tensions between European and Oriental Jews (→ Mizraḥim; → Wadi Salib).

Towards the end of his life, Gronemann became disillusioned with the political conditions in the State of Israel. In a text published posthumously in 1953, he criticized the repressive language policy that affected above all → German- and → Yiddish-speaking Israelis. He also noted that although he was "a long-standing champion of the national Zionist idea" in view of the mentality prevalent in Israel even he found it difficult "not to despair." All the same, he remained optimistic: "If freedom of thought and speech, liberality in every sense, can be realized anywhere in the world, it will be in Israel; if not in this generation, then in a future one that will have freed itself from the ballast of Exile" [2]. His plays rehearse this very liberation from Exile.

Bibliography

Sources

[1] S. Gronemann, Schalet. Beiträge zur Philosophie des "Wenn Schon," Leipzig 1998. [2] S. Gronemann, Zu meiner Entlastung, in: Yediot Ḥadashot, March 30, 1953, 13. [3] S. Gronemann, Havdoloh und Zapfenstreich. Erinnerungen an die ostjüdische Etappe 1916–1918, Königstein 1984. [4] S. Gronemann, Utter Chaos, trans. by P. Milbouer, Bloomington 2016. [5] S. Gronemann, Erinnerungen, ed. by J. Schlör, Berlin 2002. [6] S. Gronemann, Erinnerungen an meine Jahre in Berlin, ed. by J. Schlör, Berlin 2004.

Secondary literature

[7] S. E. Aschheim, Brothers and Strangers. The East European Jew in German Jewish Consciousness, 1800–1923, Madison 1982. [8] J. Kühne, Das Ende einer jüdischen Welttournee. Sammy Gronemann und die zionistische Rückkehr in die Geschichte, in: Tel Aviver Jahrbuch für deutsche Geschichte 41 (2013), 143–160. [9] J. Kühne, "Das schönste Theatre bleibt doch das Gericht." Todesstrafe und Talion im Drama Sammy Gronemanns, in: Aschkenas 24 (2014) 2, 305–323. [10] J. Kühne, "Wer ist Wer?" Sammy Gronemanns Jakob und Christian, in: Pardes 19 (2013), 191–206. [11] H. Mittelmann, Das Problem der deutsch-jüdischen "Symbiose" im zionistischen Roman, in: S. Moses/A. Schöne (eds.), Juden in der deutschen Literatur. Ein deutsch-israelisches Symposon, Frankfurt am Main 1986, 226–236. [12] H. Mittelmann, Sammy Gronemann (1875–1952). Zionist, Schriftsteller und Satiriker in Deutschland und Palästina, Frankfurt am Main 2004. [13] H. Mittelmann, Das Theatre von Sammy Gronemann. Vermittlung zwischen Alt und Neu, in: M. Zimmermann/Y. Hotam (eds.), Zweimal Heimat. Die Jeckes zwischen Mitteleuropa und Nahost, Frankfurt am Main 2005, 172–181. [14] H. Mittelmann, Sammy Gronemann. Ein Leben im Dienste des Zionismus, Berlin 2012. [15] J. Schlör, Tohuwabohu. Einige Klärungen und viel mehr Fragen, in: S. Gronemann, Tohuwabohu, ed. by J. Schlör, Leipzig 2000, 357–376.

JAN KÜHNE, JERUSALEM

Toledo

After the Christian conquest in 1085, Toledo was the residence where the Castilian court stayed most frequently in the Middle Ages and was the ecclesiastical primatial seat of Spain. The capital of New Castile was also home to the largest Jewish community existing on the Iberian Peninsula (→ Sepharad) before the expulsion of 1492. Collective conversions to Christianity, in part by means of forced baptism during the pogroms of 1391, in part due to social pressure in the subsequent period, led to an elite of → Conversos rising into leading municipal and ecclesiastical positions. Crushing this influence was the original function of the Inquisition, who accused the converts of secretly practicing Judaism. For a time, the Inquisition tribunal active in Toledo beginning in 1485 was the most powerful one in Spain; besides Old Christians, it persecuted thousands of Conversos as late as the 18th century. Because of its former importance and thanks to the two surviving medieval → synagogues, Toledo holds a place in Jewish remembrance culture and in Spanish cultural politics since the second half of the 20th century as a central memorial location of Sephardic Judaism (→ Sephardim).

1. Origin legends and the medieval community
2. Topography and culture
3. The Conversos and the Inquisition tribunal
4. Toledo as a place of remembrance
5. Cultural legacy

1. Origin legends and the medieval community

Medieval tradition tends to present Toledo as the oldest Jewish settlement on the Iberian Peninsula (→ Sepharad). A legend narrated by the archbishop Rodrigo Jiménez de Rada around 1243 and repeated by the Jewish Bible commentator Isaac Abravanel (→ Jewish National and University Library) in 1483 has the legendary Iberian king Pyrrhus as an ally of Nebuchadnezzar's. After the Babylonian conquest of Jerusalem in 587 BCE, he deported Jewish nobles, among them descendants of the Davidian royal dynasty, to Toletum/Toledo as prisoners. The prisoners named the city after the Hebrew word *tiltul* (migration, wandering) or *toledot* (line of succession). By means of this foundation legend, the Jews of Toledo affirmed their claim of being the aristocracy among the European Diaspora. In encounters with Christians, they adduced this legend as evidence that their ancestors had immigrated before the Roman era and had consequently no part in the death of Jesus. In the Middle Ages even a correspondence was faked, indicating that the Jews of Toledo had interceded with the Jerusalem Synhedrion on behalf of the accused Jesus [5. 321–323].

Historical evidence of Jewish settlement in Spain from the Mediterranean coast into the Castilian heartlands first appears in the 6th century during the Visigothic era. According to Ibn 'Idhārī, the Muslim conquerors were met by only "a handful of Jews" in the depopulated city of Toledo in 715 [8. 14]. After their number remained insignificant under Moorish rule, from the Christian conquest of 1085 onward, and

because of the religious persecutions under the Almohads, Toledo became a sanctuary for Jews from the Islamic south after 1140. In 1300, the community was estimated to number slightly over 350 families, making it the presumably largest in Europe [6. vol. 1, 190, 196]. The second Castilian community, the one in Burgos, was less than half the size; only in the Kingdom of Aragón did half a dozen urban communities number 200 to 250 families. Toledo was the richest community of Castile as well. While it was home to around a tenth of the Jews of the kingdom, it paid 40% of their total tax. The majority of the Toledan Jews were craftspeople working in the manufacture and processing of wool, silk, leather, and precious metals.

The presence of the Jews in the city was never unchallenged. Local urban groups or knights passing through on their way to fight the Moors committed several massacres (1090, 1108, 1212). The community owed its most important protection to the presence of the court and especially the services provided to the royal house by Jewish chamberlains and tax collectors. In the early 12th century, the Andalusian physician and minister Joseph ibn Ferruziel, called Cidellus (d. ca. 1145) was the first of these to be documented. He bore the title of → *Nasi* (Hebr.; head, leader) of all Castilian–Leonese Jews. After him, members of the aristocratic Jewish families Ibn Ezra and Ibn Shoshan, whose history goes back to Moorish Toledo, occupied the positions of Castilian finance minister (Span. *almoxarife*). Community elders (Hebr. *mukdamim*; Span. *adelantados*) also came from this oligarchy, whose members were permitted to bear the noble title "Don."

During the reign of King Alfonso X the Wise from 1252 to 1284, the wealth as well as the rivalry of the powerful families grew. Meir ibn Shoshan and Isaac ibn Sadok competed for the profits from the extensive conquests in southern Spain, but both were embroiled in Prince Sancho's court intrigues and fell from grace in 1279. Even after the end of the Reconquista in Castile, the Castilian-Jewish financial elite retained its ruling position, unlike in neighboring Aragón, but found itself under pressure from several directions. While their tax burden grew, the church as well as the estates demanded drastic economic restrictions from 1273 onward, going beyond even the discriminatory provisions the Castilian law book *Fuero real* (1265) had adopted from the decrees of the Lateran councils. In addition, there was growing displeasure among the majority of Jewish craftsmen and small traders regarding the privileges and the lifestyle enjoyed by the crown agents. The position of court rabbi (Span. *rab de la corte*) instituted by Alfonso X became an increasingly important arbitration authority.

During the 14th century, Toledan Jewish finance ministers from the Ibn Wakar, Abulafia, and Abravanel families continued to carry out their risky activities. However, even royal protection proved to be insufficient against social violence in times of crisis. In the civil war against Peter the Cruel, the followers of his rebellious brother Henry of Trastámara invaded the Jewish quarters, committing arson and massacres. During the pogrom wave that started in Seville in 1391, a mob incited by clerics fell on the Jews of Toledo. The majority of the latter were murdered or baptized by force. In July 1411, the Dominican preacher Vincent Ferrer was active in the city, had several synagogues re-consecrated as churches, and forced hundreds more Jews to be baptized. The reorganization of the Castilian Jews undertaken in the decrees of Valladolid of 1432 was arranged above all by the Toledan Don Abraham Benveniste of Soria, who was court rabbi as well as a financial agent of the realm.

Contemporary sources give the high but not entirely improbable figure of 200,000 persons for the Jewish population expelled from the two kingdoms of Castile and Aragón as a result of the Edict of Expulsion. In Toledo, 48 Jewish families left real estate behind [7. 289f.]. The majority of those expelled first crossed the border into Portugal, while other groups boarded ships on the Mediterranean. As they had witnessed the Inquisition's persecution of the Conversos, only a few Spanish Jews sought refuge in conversion to Christianity.

2. Topography and culture

Toledo is a natural fortress situated on a granite promontory bounded to the south by the river Tagus. Under Moorish rule, the Jewish city (Arab. *madīnat al-Yahūd*) occupied the extreme northwestern corner of the old city center between the Jewish Gate (today Puerta del Cambrón) and the San Martín bridge. After the Christianization of the city, a commercial street led from this bridge to the northeastern city gate, the Puerta de Bisagra. Several quarters mainly inhabited by Jews grew up along this street, as the separation of residential districts was implemented only in 1412. According to the reconstruction undertaken by Jean Passini, these quarters occupied nearly a fourth of the area inside the city walls.

The older quarter, Alcaná, was a market district north of the cathedral. The Great Jewish Quarter (Span. *Judería Mayor*) was a sprawling web of alleyways in the parish of Santo Tomé in the west of the city. Below the commercial street that bisected it was the Arriaza quarter with the old synagogue, the hospital, the slaughterhouse, and a bastion. The area above the commercial street was dominated by the five-nave → synagogue believed to be the most magnificent in Spain during the Middle Ages. Converted into the church Santa María la Blanca (La Blanca) in the 15th century, it survives as a museum today. Its foundation is attributed to the financier Joseph ibn Shushan. The *Judería Mayor* was surrounded by smaller Jewish quarters, among them Hamanzeit with its bathhouse to the south, where the royal chamberlain Samuel ha-Levi Abulafia had a magnificent private synagogue built in 1357 that would later be consecrated as the church of Nuestra Señora del Tránsito (El Tránsito). Both synagogues display characteristics of the Mudéjar style employed by Muslim master builders under Christian rule. The community cemetery was to the north of the city on the Cerro de la Horca.

Literary greats like Abraham ibn Ezra (→ Hebrew; → Commentary) and Judah ha-Levi (→ Kuzari), both of whom were born in Tudela in the Navarre region, were probably linked incorrectly to Toledo by tradition. Prominent among the scholars immigrated from Andalusia in the 12th century is Abraham ibn Da'ud (ca. 1110–1180), who wrote the historical chronicle *Sefer ha-Kabbalah* (1161) and is regarded as the first Jewish Aristotelian due to his philosophical work *al-ʿaqīdah al-rafīʿah* (The sublime faith, 1168). A lively controversy surrounds the question of whether ibn Da'ud was identical with the (converted?) Jew Johannes Hispalensis who worked with Dominicus Gundisalvi on the → Arabic-Latin scientific → translations initiated by Archbischop Raymond de Sauvetat in the years between 1126 and 1151. The Toledo school of translators included numerous further Jewish scholars, especially once interest turned to the exact → sciences, the Bible, and some esoteric fields during the reign of Alfonso X. Don Isaac ibn Said, the editor of the astronomical tables of dates *Tabulae Alfonsinae* (1272), exerted the most enduring influence of all these translators.

The founder of rabbinical literature in Christian Spain was the Toledan Halakhist Me'ir ben Todros Abulafia (1170–1244). In the Maimonides controversy (→ Guide for the Perplexed), the traditionalist trend he represented fought successfully against the increasingly worldly spirit of the age articulated most expressively in the sensual and even erotic early work by the Hebrew poet Todros ben Judah Abulafia (1247–1306). While the poet vowed to mend his ways after his sponsor Isaac ibn Sadok's execution, the court rabbi Todros ben Joseph Abulafia (1220–1298) used the catastrophe as an opportunity to proclaim a thorough moral reform in 1281. A mystic of rigid faith, he criticized the Jewish upper class's display of splendor, their oligarchic demeanor, the charging of interest among Jews, their non-Jewish concubines, and their study of Maimonidean rationalism.

The return to traditionalist values was sealed in 1304 with the appointment of an Ashkenazi rabbi (→ Ashkenazim) from Cologne, Asher ben Jehiel called "Rosh" (ca. 1250–1327), the author of a compendium of Talmudic glosses much studied to this day. He founded a dynasty of scholars, his son Jacob ben Asher (1269–ca. 1343) composing *Arba'a Turim* (Four pillars), the most important Jewish legal codex of the Middle Ages. There was still a renowned Talmud academy in Toledo at the time of the expulsion. Its tradition influenced Joseph Caro (1488–1575), a born Toledan, who codified Jewish law for the modern era in his *Shulḥan Arukh* (Set Table; first printed 1565; → Halakhah).

3. The Conversos and the Inquisition tribunal

Under the name → Conversos, the Jews who had been baptized by force in Toledo in 1391 and 1411 and their descendants constituted a separate group – and were perceived as such – among the Christian inhabitants of the city. In the majority, they continued to be craftspeople like their ancestors. An elite among the converts, however, established an influential patriciate in the central quarter

La Magdalena. Unlike the unbaptized Jews with whom they cooperated, they were able to hold royal, municipal, and ecclesiastical positions of power.

Segregating this rising population was one of the main concerns of the Toledan majority population over the subsequent centuries. When the unpopular minister Álvaro de Luna was supported by them in his taxation policy, the cathedral canons incited a → pogrom in 1449. The rebels, led by the mayor Pero Sarmiento, murdered the state chamberlain Álvaro de Cota, breached the Conversos' armed defense, looted their possessions, and declared them incompetent to occupy any municipal or ecclesiastical positions henceforth. This unprecedented act gave rise to a theological and legal controversy on the admissibility of discriminating against neophytes in Christianity that anticipates some of the traits of racial discrimination [6. vol. 2, 279–282].

After Prince Henry had crushed the revolt, Pope Nicholas V condemned Sarmiento's legislation in the bull *Humani generis inimicus* (1449) and declared it null and void as well as un-Christian. During the dispute over the throne between King Henry IV and his brother Alfonso, the violence between the two parties in the city erupted once more. Royalist, well-armed, and allied with members of the nobility, the Conversos were defeated after only days of fighting. Their district went up in flames; their leaders Fernando and Alonso de la Torre were hanged, and many of the survivors expelled from the city.

Towards the end of the 15th century, these Conversos found themselves under increasing pressure throughout the country. In 1478, the Dominicans in Seville attempted to limit their influence by means of an Inquisition into genuine or presumed heresies. Unlike its medieval predecessors, the Holy Office of the Inquisition, which was active in Spain until 1820, was subject only nominally to the pope, while its administration was part of the royal government. In the end, the Grand Inquisitor and his high council (*Suprema*) headed 20 regional tribunals – 15 in the motherland, three in Spanish America, and two in Italy. The trials took place in secret, with the exception of the proclamation of the verdict in public *autos-da-fé*. The most common punishment for those who had confessed was confiscation of property and loss of honor, while those who were found guilty or relapsed would be burned at the stake after being executed by means of a garotte.

During its first three decades, the Spanish Inquisition was concerned nearly exclusively with Conversos accused of not having completely abandoned Judaism. When the short-lived regional tribunal of Ciudad Real was moved to Toledo in June 1485, the work of the Inquisition began here too. In early 1486, hundreds of semi-naked men and women were driven through the city in humiliating penitential processions. In summary trials, the tribunal imposed penance on 5,221 persons, conducting regular trials against 1,290 others; the victims of the 250 death sentences even included high-ranking officials and clerics. Some Conversos were safe at court, among them political-historical authors of Jewish extraction like Mosén Diego de Calera (1412–1488) and Hernán Pérez del Pulgar (1451–1531), according to whose estimates the Spanish Inquisition tribunals condemned 2,000 persons to death in the 1480s and sentenced 15,000 more to other punishments [2. vol. 1, 168f.]; [6. vol. 2, 343]; [10. 145, 149].

After 1495, the Inquisition commuted the loss of honor imposed on the Conversos remaining in Toledo and their descendants into fines. As a result, 2,180 families from the jurisdiction of Toledo, around a quarter of them from the city itself, tried to regain their place in society [9]. Commercial gains were employed to purchase municipal positions,

The Alhambra Decree of 1492 featuring the signatures of King Ferdinand II of Aragón and Queen Isabella of Castile (excerpt)

once again provoking embittered resistance on the part of Old Christian antagonists. With reference to Pero Sarmiento's older decrees, Archbishop Juan Martínez Silíceo issued the first statute on the purity of the blood, which required that all those in positions dependent on the cathedral chapter had to prove they were free from Jewish or Moorish ancestors. The Toledan statute on race was affirmed by Emperor Charles V and received the blessing of the Church at the hands of Pope Paul IV in 1555. Even so, many Converso families were able by means of clever power and marriage strategies to establish durable networks that included the municipal, noble, and ecclesiastical elites. The foundation of the Carmelite monastery of San José in 1572, for instance, was in part due to a legacy from the wealthy Toledan merchant Martín Ramírez and the initiative of St. Teresa of Ávila, both of whom were from Converso families.

With its political influence and numerous employees, the Inquisition found new groups of victims to ensure its continued existence even after most crypto-Jewish communities had been dissolved. It discovered a new sphere of activity in disciplining the Catholic community in accordance with the Council of Trento. In the 16th century, the tribunal of Toledo alone conducted 7,862 trials, the majority of which targeted Old Christians on charges of blasphemy, superstition, homosexual acts, or having criticized the Church. Others were directed against Protestants and moriscos; only 506 trials involved accusations of Judaism [10. 145, 148]. Among these, the severity of the proceedings, the near-universal use of torture, and the comparatively high percentage of women (39%) are, however, remarkable. Some Conversos found refuge in the villages of military orders, until the Inquisition and its web of informers (Span. *visitadores*) sought them out there too.

After the counter-reformatory social discipline subsided, the Spanish Inquisition turned its attention to the Jews with renewed intensity from the 1590s onward. It now persecuted immigrant Portuguese traders of Jewish descent, many of whom had come to the neighboring country fleeing the Inquisition at home, which had been established in 1536. At the time, the tribunal in Toledo was the most powerful one in Spain, as it was also responsible for monitoring the capital Madrid where the court tribunal (*despacho de corte*) achieved independence only gradually. During the 17th century, 926 persons were incarcerated in Toledo because of crypto-Judaism; most of them Portuguese living in Madrid, who had maintained contacts with the Diaspora in France (→ Bordeaux), Italy (→ Livorno), and the Netherlands (→ Esnoga). These trials took a comparatively long time in Toledo, two years on average. With an eye to self-promotion, the Inquisition of Toledo used the central square in Madrid for its elaborate *autos-da-fé* in 1632 and 1680. The repression of the Conversos with Jewish roots reached its historical climax around 1654, continuing until a last wave of persecutions in the years from 1721 to 1723. The Inquisition tribunal in Toledo, which even in the 18th century brought charges of Judaism against 129 persons, carried out the last death penalty in 1738 and the last torture and confiscation of property of a man accused of Judaism in 1756 [4]. When it was dissolved in 1820, it was the only tribunal on the Spanish mainland besides Cuenca whose archives survived.

4. Toledo as a place of remembrance

A book of examples of 1292 is the first to tell the story of a Toledan Jewish woman of whom King Alfonso VIII had been so enamored a century previously that his realm was in danger of becoming ruler- and defenseless, until the Castilian grandees finally killed the mistress. This most famous female Jewish character of Spanish literature was given the name of Fermosa in Florián de Ocampo's *Crónica General* (1541) and Raquel in Luis de Ulloa's *La Raquel* (1650). The most popular version of the tragic legend was penned by Lope de Vega in his drama, printed in 1617, *Las paces de los reyes y judía de Toledo*.

In the 15th and 16th centuries, the Jews of Toledo were the subject of many myths about → conspiracies. Thus, they were accused of having taken the opportunity of surrendering the city to the Muslims during a Christian pilgrimage to the chapel of St. Leocadia in 715. An accusation of ritual murder (→ Blood Libel), as a result of which the Inquisition of Ávila sentenced and burned three → Conversos and two Jews in 1491, was also linked to Toledo in retrospect. According to this version, the five had plotted after an *auto-da-fé* in that city that they would bewitch the Inquisition by means of a stolen host and the heart of a Christian child. This legend, too, was put on the stage in an impressive version by Lope de Vega in his play *El niño inocente de La Guardia* (1617; "The Innocent Child," 2001). A further instance of similar conspiracy fantasies is a letter falsified by Archbishop Silíceo in the mid-16th century to support his incitement against the Conversos. The rabbis of Constantinople, it claimed, had ordered the Jews of Saragossa during the expulsion of 1492 to let themselves be baptized in order to then become lawyers, physicians, and clerics who would rob the detested Christians of their money, lives, and souls [5. 323–325].

Local traditions from Toledo are documented among the → Sephardim in North Africa (Fez) as well as in the Ottoman Empire (→ Salonika) and in Israel (→ Safed). The city is present in the frequent family name "Toledano," the "Toledo" synagogue community in Istanbul, and in family recollections according to which the key to the living quarters in Toledo were passed on

from generation to generation in Salonika until the → Holocaust. Toledo also appears as the location of the → Ladino romances sung following medieval models, for instance the → romancero ballad *Diego León*, whose eponymous hero proves himself worthy of the love of a girl from a good family by his perseverance. However, in the Sephardi versions of the ballad of the ride of Peranzules, a Toledan hero in the fight against the Moors, the connection to the location has been lost.

The revaluation of the city in Jewish memory began with the romantic view of Spain in the 19th century. It also refers to the → Haskalah topos of the urbane Sephardic philosopher. In the novella *Der Rabbi von Bacherach* (ca. 1825; "The Rabbi of Bacherach," 1891/2005), Heinrich Heine (→ Entreebillet) has his Ashkenazi hero study the Talmud in Toledo, adopting "freygeistige Denkungsart" ("habits of free thinking") while there. For his *Romanzero* (1850), he invented a religious dispute at the court of Peter the Cruel in Toledo. The literary subject matter of the "Jewess of Toledo" was made popular by Franz Grillparzer (1855) and Lion Feuchtwanger (1955). The so-called Moorish style employed in → synagogues built in the 19th century referred not least to the synagogues of Toledo.

In Moritz Steinschneider's Jewish literary history (1850; → Bibliography), the Toledo school of translators symbolizes a place of communication and translation between the religions; indeed, a non-violent counterculture to the Crusades: "Toledo had become the Jerusalem where the fighters with pens went" (cited in [17. 182]). A polemic stereotype still found in the *Jüdisches Lexikon* in the 1930s, which contrasted Christian intolerance with Muslim tolerance, recognized the achievements of the Jews in Christian Toledo as, at best, "a brilliant after bloom of Jewish-Arab culture" [1. 531]. Since then, Yitzhak Baer's work *A History of the Jews in Christian Spain* (1961/1966) has laid the foundations for a more differentiated view.

5. Cultural legacy

After the court moved away from Toledo in 1561, the city was mainly an archbishopric and seat of the Inquisition, becoming the symbol of a unified Catholic Spain. After the expulsion, the Jewish quarter was divided into new lots, with the intention of removing all traces of the previous inhabitants. Noble families and religious orders built new residences here. As a result of impoverishment in the 18th century, the buildings degenerated into barracks and shelters for the homeless. An epigraphic study (F. Pérez Bayer, *De Toletano Hebraeorum templo* 1752) and a collection of plates (*España artística y monumental*, 1842) were early references to the historical significance of the → synagogues. This encouraged official institutions to restore La Blanca in 1856 and El Tránsito in 1888 as memorials; the historizing restoration practices destroyed much of the medieval substance. It would be some time, however, before the buildings became → museums – as in → Córdoba – in the course of a cultural policy implemented during the later years of Franco's dictatorship in order to gain international recognition.

The first Jewish museum of Spain, the *Museo Sefardí* opened in El Tránsito in 1964; on the occasion of the inauguration, a public Jewish service was permitted for the first time in modern Spain. Together with the entire city center, the two synagogues became UNESCO World Heritage Sites in 1986. Since then, the association *Caminos de Sefarad / Red de juderías de España* (Routes of Sepharad / Network of Jewish Quarters in Spain) has worked successfully to attract part of the flood of tourists, with several hundred thousand visitors coming to Toledo and the *Museo Sefardí* each year these days.

Bibliography

Sources

[1] F. Baer, Art. "Spanien," in: Jüdisches Lexikon, vol. 4, Berlin 1930, 523–538.   [2] C. H. Lea, A History of the Inquisition of Spain, 4 vols., London 1906–1907.   [3] J. Sierra, Procesos en la Inquisición de Toledo (1575–1610). Manuscrito de Halle, Madrid 2005.

Secondary literature

[4] M. Alpert, Crypto-Judaism and the Spanish Inquisition, New York 2001.   [5] R. Amram, Calumnias y falsificación histórica. Dos casos de correspondencia apócrifa relacionadas con judíos hispanos durante el medioevo, in: Cahiers de linguistique hispanique médiévale 29 (2006), 317–326.   [6] Y. Baer, A History of the Jews in Christian Spain, 2 vols., Philadelphia 1978.   [7] H. Beinart, The Expulsion of the Jews from Spain, Oxford 2002.   [8] H. Beinart, The Jews in Castile, in: H. Beinart (ed.), Moreshet Sepharad. The Sephardi Legacy, Jerusalem 1992, 11–43.   [9] F. Cantera Burgos/P. León Tello, Judaizantes del Arzobispado de Toledo habilitados por la Inquisición en 1495 y 1497, Madrid ²2009.   [10] J.-P. Dedieu, Les causes de foi de l'Inquisition de Tolède (1483–1820), essai statistique, in: Mélanges de la Casa de Velázquez 14 (1978), 143–171.   [11] A. Fidora, Abraham Ibn Daud und Dominicus Gundissalinus. Philosophie und religiöse Toleranz im Toledo des 12. Jahrhunderts, in: M. Lutz-Bachmann/A. Fidora (eds.), Juden, Christen und Muslime. Religionsdialoge im Mittelalter, Darmstadt 2004, 10–26.   [12] P. León Tello, Judíos de Toledo, 2 vols., Madrid 1979.   [13] L. Martz, A Network of Converso Families in Early Modern Toledo. Assimilating a Minority, Ann Arbor 2003.   [14] D. Nirenberg, Deviant Politics and Jewish Love. Alfonso VIII and the Jewess of Toledo, in: Jewish History 21 (2007) 1, 15–41.   [15] J. Passini, Reconstitution de la 'judería' de Tolède, in: P. Salmona/L. Sigal (eds.), L'archéologie du judaïsme en France et en Europe, Paris 2011, 103–114.   [16] M. Saperstein,

The Preaching of Repentance and the Reforms in Toledo of 1281, in: B. M. Kienzle (ed.), Models of Holiness in Medieval Sermons. Proceedings of the International Symposium (Kalamazoo, 4–7 May 1995), Louvain-la-Neuve 1996, 155–172. [17] C. Schapkow, Vorbild und Gegenbild. Das iberische Judentum in der deutsch-jüdischen Erinnerungskultur 1779–1939, Cologne et al. 2011. [17a] C. Schapkow, Role Model and Countermodel. The Golden Age of Iberian Jewry and German Jewish Culture during the Era of Emancipation, trans. by C. Twitchell, London 2016. [18] L. Suárez Fernández, Judíos españoles en la edad media, Madrid 1980.

CARSTEN L. WILKE, BUDAPEST

Tractatus Theologico-Politicus

In his *Tractatus Theologico-Politicus* (Eng. "Theological-Political Treatise") published anonymously in 1670, Baruch de Spinoza adopted a position in the power struggle in the Dutch Republic at the time. The Dutch philosopher of Sephardic origin set down his reasons for the necessity of freedom of opinion, of the separation of philosophy and theology, and of religious authorities being subordinate to secular ones. The basis of his argument was biblical criticism unprecedented in its radicality. Spinoza systematically adhered to the identification of God with nature in his posthumously published magnum opus, *Ethica, ordine geometrico demonstrata* ("Ethics, Demonstrated in Geometrical Order," 1883); in this political polemic, he already hinted at this as well. It was widely condemned as being blasphemous and would soon be banned. Spinoza's reception among Jews was hindered from the first by the ban, which excommunicated him from the Jewish community in Amsterdam as early as 1656. During the German

Spinoza renaissance in the time of Goethe, however, the heretical early exponent of the Enlightenment evolved into a figure of identification for secular Jewish intellectuals, ultimately reaching his national apotheosis in Zionism.

1. Spinoza
2. Biblical criticism and politics
3. God or nature
4. Jewish reception

1. Spinoza

Baruch (Port.: Bento; Lat.: Benedictus) de Spinoza was born in Amsterdam in 1632 and died in The Hague in 1677. His parents, being → Conversos, had fled from the Inquisition in Portugal to the Netherlands, where they openly returned to Judaism. His father Michael de Spinoza (also: d'Espinosa) ran a merchant business in Amsterdam and for a time was a member of the board of the Portuguese Jewish community (→ Esnoga), which had been founded at the beginning of the 17th century and was soon flourishing. As a consequence of this family background, Spinoza grew up not only among heterogeneous cultural influences but also with several languages: Portuguese as his mother tongue, Spanish as the secular academic language of the Iberian Jews, Dutch to communicate with the urban environment, which was not isolated by ghettoization, and not least → Hebrew as the liturgical language, which he learned in the community school, clearly to a high level, as a boy. Religious education focused primarily on the study of the Hebrew Bible. After only five years, the gifted pupil had to leave school in order to work in his father's business. Even so, the intellectual life of the community undoubtedly continued to influence him afterwards as well. The community counted famous rabbis such as Isaac Aboab da Fonseca, Menasseh ben Israel, and Saul Levi Mortera among its members, but it also had to face the challenge posed by heretics like Uriel da Costa and later Juan de Prado.

The young Spinoza soon felt drawn more to the direction of these heretics, discovering an interest in more education than the Jewish community could satisfy. He began to study Latin, choosing as his teacher Franciscus van den Enden, a former Jesuit regarded as a heretic and atheist. In his Amsterdam house, Spinoza was introduced not only to the authors from Antiquity but also to modern philosophers, such as Machiavelli, Hobbes, and above all Descartes, and made friends with young Protestant freethinkers. Openness towards the liberal and even heterodox intellectual climate of his hometown was encouraged by the merchant's trade. When his father died, Spinoza and his brother – who emigrated to the Caribbean soon afterwards – inherited the family business, which was heavily in debt as a consequence of the First Anglo-Dutch War.

Freethinking trends coinciding with financial ruin provided the background for Spinoza's falling out with the Jewish community. In accordance with Dutch law but in breach of Jewish law, he took on a non-Jewish custodian in order to free himself from the debt burden of his father's business without losing the inheritance of his mother, who had died earlier. The community responsible for the Portuguese Jews could tolerate this even less than his simultaneous and increasingly clear rejection of the Jewish faith and social norms. After the community leaders had tried in vain to mediate, he was put under a → ban in July 1656, which expelled him from the Jewish community with reference to "the horrible heresies which he practiced and taught" and "the monstrous actions which he performed" (cited in [5. 145]) – henceforth, no one was permitted to maintain contact with him or read anything he had written. Clearly, he had deliberately provoked this verdict; he is traditionally believed to have stated that he had not been forced to do anything

he would not have done of his own accord [5. 51]. Consequently, throughout his life Spinoza never endeavored to have the ban overturned, although this might well have been possible. He did not convert to Christianity either and remained without religious affiliation.

In 1660, Spinoza settled in a small house in the village of Rijnsburg not far from the university city of Leiden, moving to the even more southerly Voorburg three years later; in 1669 he finally settled in The Hague. Until his death, he lived a very modest solitary life focused on contemplation, although he did not lack scholarly or social interaction. His friends and sponsors included members of the Dutch ruling class, and his correspondence went beyond the Netherlands to the European Republic of Letters.

After he left Amsterdam, Spinoza's philosophical work began to take shape. The only text published under his name during his lifetime, *Renati Descartes principia philosophiae, more geometrico demonstrata* ("The Principles of Descartes' Philosophy," 1905), appeared in 1663 and was composed in Latin, as was his entire œuvre. Even more than this small epistemological critique, his two early works composed in the preceding three years, *Korte Verhandeling van God, de mensch en deszelvs welstand* ("A Short Treatise on God, Man, and His Well-Being," 1909) and Tractatus de Intellectus Emendatione ("On the Improvement of the Understanding," 1901), may be seen as preliminary studies for his magnum opus *Ethica, ordine geometrico demonstrata* on which he began to work during that time. In 1665, however, political developments in his country compelled Spinoza to put the great synthesis of his ideas on hold in order to write a text of an entirely different kind.

2. Biblical criticism and politics

After the ban, Spinoza was able to live free of harassment as a philosopher with no religious affiliation. That he could do so was due not least to the political status quo in the Dutch Republic, which was characterized by tolerance. However, in the mid-1660s, this began to falter. Johan de Witt, who as Grand Pensionary of the province of Holland had led the government of the entire republic – now weakened by a new war with England – during the period from 1652 onward when there were no governors and a protector of the interests of the liberal republican citizens and merchants, saw himself and his politics threatened by the supporters of the Orange and Calvinist Orthodoxy. Simultaneously, the influence of Protestant fundamentalism grew, which derived its political principles, in accordance with the motto *sola scriptura* (by means of Scripture only), from the Hebrew Bible. Theology and politics could thus not be separated. As a consequence, Spinoza composed his intervention on behalf of de Witt's republicanism as *Tractatus Theologico-Politicus*.

The preface of the work begins with a brief elucidation of superstition resulting from the affect of fear. In this, Spinoza refers to the fact that "we have the rare good fortune to live in a commonwealth where freedom of judgment is fully granted to the individual citizen and he may worship God as he pleases, and where another is esteemed dearer and more precious than freedom" [7. 3]. He claimed that his intention was to show "that not only can this freedom be granted without endangering piety and the peace of the commonwealth, but also the peace of the commonwealth and piety depend on this freedom" [7. 3].

Ultimately, however, the treatise went far beyond merely defending freedom of thought and opinion; its objective, stated explicitly in the last chapter, was to fundamentally justify a state whose "ultimate purpose is [...] in reality, freedom" [7. 232] – a secularly-constituted "democratic state" that

Spinoza, *Painting by Samuel Hirszenberg* (1907)

was above theological claims of interpretation. To do so, Spinoza once again referred to the example of Holland and Amsterdam, idealizing this example all the more as he saw the status quo achieved under de Witt as endangered: "In this flourishing state, a city of the highest renown, men of every race and sect live in complete harmony; [...] religion or sect, that is of no account, because such considerations are regarded as irrelevant in a court of law" [7. 236].

According to Spinoza, this condition, which he invoked at the end of the treatise, was the opposite of the theocratic model. He provided the fate of the biblical state of the Hebrews – which followers of Calvinist Orthodoxy had, in turn, taken as their model – as an example of the failure of the theocratic model. In order to be able to deconstruct their political theology, the philosopher employed the sort of → biblical criticism that pervades the entire theological part of the work. This part, with fifteen chapters, is much more voluminous than the following political part, with five chapters.

In the context of the history of ideas, Spinoza's criticism of the belief in the Bible as revealed religion has probably remained the core legacy of the polemical text. It is also the basis of the widespread misunderstanding that the treatise was Spinoza's reaction to being banned from the Portuguese Jewish community, "to settle accounts with the Jewish people and their traditions," as it were, as one standard work on Jewish history put it [9. 720]. Certainly, the text contains much that must have run contrary to traditional Jewish self-understanding; above all, the core of Spinoza's biblical criticism, which held that the Holy Scripture had to be seen as a literary work composed by human hands rather than being the word of God, contradicted a fundamental consensus of Judaism. No earlier exegetes, such as Maimonides (→ Guide for the Perplexed) or Abraham ibn Ezra, had ever made such a denouncement. Even so, Spinoza aimed

his criticism at Protestant Christianity rather than at his former fellow believers. Christianity, after all, was ultimately much more strongly affected by his deconstruction of the principle of Scripture than Judaism with its more openly interpretable tradition of oral teachings alongside written doctrine.

As the early reaction of contemporary philosophers – above all, the young Gottfried Wilhelm Leibniz – shows, the impact of Spinoza's biblical criticism was due precisely to the Hebraist expertise its author had at his disposal thanks to his Jewish origin and education. Although he wrote in Latin, this expertise distinguished him within the intellectual mixture of political philosophy and Christian Hebrew studies of the time. In this context, the seventh chapter of the treatise, "On the interpretation of Scripture" [7. 88], is of central importance. In it, Spinoza explains his new philological approach, wherein the Holy Scripture is placed entirely within the confines of human history. He introduces the argument by saying that "the method of interpreting Scripture is no different from the method of interpreting Nature, and is in fact in complete accord with it"; therefore "interpretation of Scripture and study of its contents [...] can be gathered only from Scripture itself" [7. 89]. For historical reasons, though, the necessary prerequisite – "a thorough knowledge of the Hebrew language" – was no longer a given [7. 96]. He also pointed out that, because of the ambiguities characteristic of → Hebrew due to its linguistic peculiarities – which Spinoza described with insight and a wealth of examples – it was impossible to clarify the meaning of all biblical passages, let alone of acquiring the requisite "history of all the Biblical books" [7. 99]. Spinoza expressed an important corollary of this philological secularization of Hebrew in the twelfth chapter on "The reason why Scripture is called holy and the Word of God":

Words acquire a fixed meaning solely from their use; if in accordance with this usage they are so arranged that readers are moved to devotion, then these words will be sacred, and likewise the book containing this arrangement of words. But if these words at a later time fall into disuse so as to become meaningless, or if the book falls into utter neglect, whether from malice or because men no longer feel the need of it, then both words and book will be without value and without sanctity. [7. 151]

By explicitly referring to the motto *sola scriptura* repeatedly throughout his argument, Spinoza prepared to conquer Calvinist dogmatism with its own weapons.

This did not escape the notice of the authorities of ecclesiastical Orthodoxy at whom the criticism was directed, and they condemned the treatise as blasphemous soon after its publication in 1670. As Spinoza's Amsterdam publisher and friend Jan Rieuwertsz had published the work without giving the author's name, having also stated Hamburg as the fictitious place of printing, it was safe from being prohibited for the time being. A ban was further delayed because the censorship process was complicated by the federal structures in Holland; Johan de Witt may also personally have undermined efforts to ban it. After de Witt was hanged by an angry mob in the course of the political upheaval in the country in 1672, Spinoza's adversaries intensified their activities – since by then he was generally identified as the author. In July 1674, the *Tractatus Theologico-Politicus* was finally officially banned by the Dutch authorities, together with other texts such as Thomas Hobbes's *Leviathan*. However, by this time the text had traveled beyond the Dutch borders to early Enlightenment circles, who disseminated it in all of Europe. Just how far the influence of the treatise spread into the Western world may be inferred from the fact that Thomas Paine, for instance, quoted it in his work of biblical criticism *Age of Reason* (1794) from a French edition, and one of the founding fathers of the United States, Benjamin Franklin, possessed an English translation.

3. God or nature

The banning of the treatise and the political developments that led to it convinced Spinoza not to publish the *Ethica*, which he had completed in 1675, during his lifetime. His main work consequently appeared some months after his death – like the *Tractatus politicus* that he subsequently began but left unfinished, in which he modified his political theory with reference to the guiding principle of humans being bound by affect. In the context of the history of philosophy, the *Ethica* was of greater significance than his political polemical text of 1670. His novel understanding of God and His relationship with humans and the world, based on the idea of an all-embracing substance, expressed in the formula "deus sive natura" (God, or nature), proved to have a particularly strong impact.

Spinoza had already hinted at this idea, though he did not fully explicate it, in his *Tractatus Theologico-Politicus*; this contributed to the universal condemnation of the work. Examples of such hints include Spinoza's statement that it amounts to one and the same thing: "the universal laws of Nature according to which all things happen and are determined are nothing but God's eternal decrees." "Again, since the power of Nature in its entirety is nothing other than the power of God through which alone all things happen and are determined," he continued, "it follows that whatever man—who is also a part of Nature—acquires for himself to help to preserve his own being, or whatever Nature provides for him without any effort on his part, all this is provided for him solely by the divine power, acting either through human nature or eternally to human nature" [7. 37]. In correspondence with Heinrich Oldenburg, who after reading the book had expressed criticism of "the passages that seem to speak ambiguously about God and Nature," Spinoza admitted in 1675 that "I favor an opinion concerning God and Nature that is far different from the one Modern Christians usually defend": "For I maintain that God is, as they say, the immanent, but not the transitive, cause of all things" [4. 464, 467].

In the *Ethica*, Spinoza defined God initially as an "absolutely infinite being, i.e. substance consisting of infinite attributes, each one of which expresses eternal and infinite essence" [6. 3]. In this way he positioned himself outside the major trends of Judaism and Christianity; after all, this God-substance was not, as those of theist views held, a transcendent being possessing intelligence and will with whom humans are in some kind of partnership. However, Spinoza did not – as the secularizing message of the *Tractatus Theologico-Politicus* might have suggested – renounce the positive concept of God altogether. That this is by no means a kind of merely religious atavism is affirmed not least by the principle of the (intellectual) love of God (*amor dei*), which Spinoza embraced as an ideal of life in the *Ethica*, whereby his *deus sive natura* retains religious substance as a love motif.

While the dilemmas resulting from this continue to occupy philosophers to this day, it was for this very reason that Spinoza's metaphysics, from the 18th century onward, grew increasingly attractive as the point of reference for an alternative, secular type of religiosity, especially in the German language area. The term "pantheism" came to denote this phenomenon, although conservative forces in politics and church alike battled against it as being atheistic. The pantheism, or Spinozism controversy, which began in 1785, brought Spinoza into the focus of Germany's debate on religious philosophy. Hardly any of the well-known poets and intellectuals between the "Sturm und Drang" and Romantic periods, or Late Enlightenment, Idealism, and Natural Philosophy, remained unaffected by it – least of all Goethe, who professed a lifelong → "elective affinity" with Spinoza [2. 26]. In 1835 Heinrich Heine (Entreebillet) called pantheism "the clandestine religion of Germany" and Spinoza the one thinker "who in our present day has achieved a unique spiritual authority" [3. 59, 50].

4. Jewish reception

In the German Spinoza renaissance, Spinoza's work truly began to have an impact in Jewish circles. While Orthodox Judaism has maintained a strict rejection of Spinoza's work to this day, Moses Mendelssohn (→ Bi'ur) displayed a clear softening of this stance in his *Philosophische Gespräche* (1755). All the same, in his defense of the late Lessing, the father of the → Haskalah took a clear position against the Jewish heretic. From the early 19th century onward, the increasingly secular climate of German Jewish thought, however, meant that reservations gradually waned. Spinoza became an intellectual model who appeared to guarantee the compatibility of Jewish and German ideals of education (→ Bildung) in the modern world. One can observe this view not only in Heine but also in the co-founder of the → Wissenschaft des Judentums Immanuel Wolf and in the writer Berthold Auerbach. After the German Jews, those in Eastern Europe also began to discover Spinoza for themselves over the course of the 19th century.

The direction Moses Hess (→ Geldwesen) took, in turn, seems visionary in retrospect. The German-Jewish early socialist attributed a major role to Spinoza in his historico-philosophical doctrine of salvation *Die heilige Geschichte der Menschheit. Von einem Jünger Spinozas* (1837; "The Holy History of Mankind. By a Young Disciple of Spinoza," 2004). In his proto-Zionist work *Rom und*

Jerusalem (1861; "Rome and Jerusalem," 1918), Hess exalted Spinoza as a precursor of the idea of the Jewish nation-state. He referred to a passage in the *Tractatus Theologico-Politicus* in which Spinoza declared in passing: "Indeed, were it not that the fundamental principles of their religion discourage manliness, I would not hesitate to believe that they will one day, given the opportunity—such is the mutability of human affairs—establish once more their independent state, and that God will again choose them" [7. 47]. While this remark should be interpreted neither as a prophesy nor as wishful thinking, it took on greater significance in the chapter "Of the vocation of the Hebrews" in that the author undertook a consistent secularization of Jewish history; in the context of this history, even the discourse about Jews being God's chosen people had to be understood as only metaphorical. Consequently, Zionist intellectuals invoked this passage until well into the 20th century to recognize in Spinoza one of their own. A significant station in this process of appropriation – criticized by philosophers such as Leo Strauss (→ Law), Emmanuel Levinas (→ Alterity), and Karl Jaspers – was the unauthorized symbolic annulment of the ban by the historian and literary scholar Joseph Klausner in a lecture given at the → Hebrew University in Jerusalem in 1927. And a quarter of a century later, the founder of the State of Israel David Ben-Gurion (→ Raison d'état) was still championing Spinoza as "the most original and profound philosopher the Hebrew people have produced in the past two thousand years" [1]. Ever since then, the author of the *Tractatus Theologico-Politicus* has been accorded attention in the Israeli context whenever the relationship between religion and the state is discussed anew.

And even in other contexts that have no connection with Zionist or Israeli issues, Spinoza has represented a means of secular Jewish self-understanding – be it as the "first secular Jew" or, in the tradition of the → Epikoros, as the epitome of the → "non-Jewish Jew." It is obvious that this does not exhaust his philosophical legacy. However, neither Spinoza's work nor his influence can be grasped fully unless their Jewish aspects are taken into consideration. In addition, any discussion of Spinoza possesses a seismographic function for the understanding of the variety of Jewish encounters with the modern age, of which he was undoubtedly a precursor.

Bibliography

Sources

[1] D. Ben-Gurion, Netaken ha-me'uvat [Let us straighten out the crooked], in: Davar, 25. December 1953. [2] J. W. v. Goethe, The Auto-Biography of Goethe. Truth and Poetry. From my Own Life, vol. 2, trans. by J. Oxenford, Cambridge 2013. [3] H. Heine, Heine. On the History of Religion and Philosophy in Germany, ed. by T. Pinkard, trans. by H. Pollack-Milgate, Cambridge 2007. [4] B. de Spinoza, The Collected Works of Spinoza, vol. II, trans. by E. Curley, Princeton 2016. [5] J. M. Lucas/A. Wolf, The Oldest Biography of Spinoza, London 1927. [6] B. de Spinoza, Ethics. Proved in Geometrical Order, ed. by M. J. Kisner, trans. by M. Silverthorne, Cambridge 2018. [7] B. de Spinoza, Theological-Political Treatise (Gebhardt Edition, 1925), trans. by S. Shirley, Indianapolis/Cambridge 1998.

Secondary literature

[8] W. Bartuschat, Baruch de Spinoza, Munich 2006. [9] H. H. Ben-Sasson, The Social Ideals of Jewry at the End of the Middle Ages, in: H. H. Ben-Sasson (ed.), A History of the Jewish People, Cambridge, Massachusetts 1976, 691–726. [10] J. E. Dunkhase, Lingua, non Scriptura. Spinozas hebräische Säkularisierung, in: Jahrbuch des Simon-Dubnow-Instituts 12 (2013), 319–335. [11] J. E. Dunkhase, Spinoza der Hebräer. Zu einer israelischen Erinnerungsfigur, Göttingen/Bristol (CT) 2013. [12] S. James, Spinoza on Philosophy, Religion, and Politics. The Theologico-Political Treatise, Oxford

2012. [13] S. M. Nadler, Spinoza. A Biography, Cambridge/New York 1999. [14] S. M. Nadler, A Book Forged in Hell. Spinoza's Scandalous Treatise and the Birth of the Secular Age, Princeton/Oxford 2011. [15] R. H. Popkin, Spinoza, Oxford 2004. [16] W. Schröder, Deus sive natura. Über Spinozas so genannten Pantheismus, in: Deutsche Zeitschrift für Philosophie 57 (2009), 471–480. [17] D. B. Schwartz, The First Modern Jew. Spinoza and the History of an Image, Princeton/Oxford 2012. [18] S. B. Smith, Spinoza, Liberalism, and the Question of Jewish Identity, New Haven/London 1997. [19] O. Vlessing, The Excommunication of Baruch Spinoza. The Birth of a Philosopher, in: J. Israel/R. Salverda (eds.), Dutch Jewry. Its History and Secular Culture (1500–2000), Leiden et al. 2002, 141–172. [20] J.-H. Wulf, Spinoza in der jüdischen Aufklärung. Baruch Spinoza als diskursive Grenzfigur des Jüdischen und Nichtjüdischen in den Texten der Haskala von Moses Mendelssohn bis Salomon Rubin und in frühen zionistischen Zeugnissen, Berlin 2012. [21] Y. Yovel, Spinoza and Other Heretics: The Adventures of Immanence, Princeton 1992.

Jan Eike Dunkhase, Marbach am Neckar

Transit

Transit is the title of the German-Jewish author Anna Seghers's (1900–1983) autobiographical novel, first published in 1944 in English. It describes the situation of refugees from the German-occupied area in Marseilles at the beginning of the Second World War, and the existential distress attendant on obtaining visas, transit permits, and ship passages. Being a communist author, Seghers was essentially committed to Socialist Realism in her narrative work; after years of fleeing from National Socialism and of exile in Mexico, she assumed the chairmanship of the Schriftstellerverband (Writers' Association) of the GDR (German Democratic Republic). *Transit* stands out among her

work as the least ideological novel, as if the state of being powerless and at the mercy of circumstances had momentarily suspended her usually forward-looking optimistic writing style.

1. The novel as an exception
2. Anna Seghers as "the chronicler of the German unemployed"
3. *Transit* as experience
4. Failed return to Germany

1. The novel as an exception

The novel is mainly set in the southern French port city of Marseilles some months after the capitulation of France in the summer of 1940. The plot begins with the first-person narrator inviting a listener (who remains silent throughout) to keep the narrator company at dinner in a pizzeria overlooking the old harbor, with the aim of "[telling] the whole story, just for once, from the beginning" [5. 5]. This is followed by the detailed description of the narrator's adventurous life since escaping from a German concentration camp in 1937, being interned as an "enemy alien" in a French camp, and fleeing to the south of unoccupied France after the Wehrmacht attacked.

The narrator himself does not at first have the intention of leaving the country via Marseilles. Centered around his efforts to secure his residence in the city, the novel unfolds a panorama of the desperate endeavors of innumerable refugees wishing to leave the European continent to escape from the Nazis. In their desire to depart from Marseilles, the refugees are met with an almost Kafkaesque concatenation of, at times, seemingly insurmountable bureaucratic obstacles. For example, an elderly bandmaster from Prague saw his Venezuelan visa expire when it took too long for his exit permit, the so-called *visa de sortie*, to be issued. Now, with the exit visa finally issued, he is awaiting the renewal of his employment contract in Caracas, but this contract is only valid if his visa is renewed. Another man who has collected all the necessary documents failed to receive the final stamp from the harbor authorities because he escaped from a French internment camp and, consequently, cannot produce a certificate of release. These administrative odysseys culminate in the so-called transit: the permit required in order to travel through a third country on the way to one's destination.

Introduced to this world, the narrator reacts with unbounded astonishment: "'What purpose is there in holding on to people who want nothing more than to leave a country where they would be imprisoned if they stayed?' [...] 'Why aren't people allowed to travel through countries on their way to their new homes in other countries?'" [...] "'My son, it's all because each country is afraid that instead of just traveling through, we'll want to stay'" [5. 39f.]. In addition, there was the threat of being picked up by French officials (→ Vichy) and interned or, worse, handed over to the Germans.

The novel *Transit*, which appeared in English in 1944 and was published in German in Konstanz in 1948, allows for many readings. Seghers drew on her own experiences while a "transitaire" in Marseilles. Having come from Paris, she stayed in the city with her children from December 1940 onward, while her husband was interned in the transit camp Les Milles. Furnished with Mexican visas, the family finally succeeded in continuing to the United States in March 1941, and on to → Mexico City from there. Their departure benefited from favorable circumstances as Seghers was traveling under her civilian name Netty Radványi. This enabled her to slip through the net of the German authorities, who had applied for her to be extradited.

In addition to being the literary description of her escape from Paris, *Transit* is an account of the fate of an entire milieu surging into exile once again after the beginning

of the so-called Battle of France: among them, some of Seghers's close friends, comrades, and companions in mortal danger, like Egon Erwin Kisch (→ Reportage), Lion Feuchtwanger (→ Pacific Palisades), Heinrich Mann, and Franz Werfel (→ Musa Dagh). For them, as well as for thousands of not only German-speaking anti-fascists and former volunteers of the Spanish Civil War, Marseilles became the hub between Europe and America (→ Lisbon).

Moreover, *Transit* documents its author's temporary ideological uncertainty. In this sense, one can interpret the narrator's wish to "tell the whole story, just for once, from the beginning," in light of being in a state in which everything was "temporary" and no-one knew whether it would "last till tomorrow, another couple of weeks, years, or our entire lives" [5. 5, 32]. The narrator expresses the hope of establishing a degree of certainty concerning his own life in times of perpetual rumors and deep insecurity. In this hope, Seghers displayed an uncommon openness that has little in common with the heroism of her anti-fascist global success *Das Siebte Kreuz* (1942; "The Seventh Cross," 2018) or with the rigorism of her socialist novels *Die Entscheidung* (1959) and *Das Vertrauen* (1968).

2. Anna Seghers as "the chronicler of the German unemployed"

Anna Seghers was born Netty Reiling in 1900 in Mainz. Her father Isidor Lutz Reiling (1867–1940) ran a flourishing art and antiques business and was a member of the → neo-Orthodox community in Mainz; in accordance with the image of women of her class, her mother Hedwig (née Fuld; 1880–1942) did not have a profession but was a founding and board member of the → Jüdischer Frauenbund. Seghers attended a private school and the secondary school for girls, graduating in 1920 with the Abitur, qualifying her for university admission. Her parents brought her up in accordance with the commandments of Jewish tradition; → philanthropy and social commitment were a matter of course, as was the presence of art. Together with the experience of the First World War, when Seghers and her fellow pupils were drafted to carry out auxiliary service, this upbringing conditioned her from an early age to take the side of the weak and oppressed.

After finishing school, Seghers studied history, art, and Sinology at the universities of Cologne and Heidelberg, gaining her Ph.D. in 1924 with the art history thesis *Jude und Judentum im Werk Rembrandts*. Inspired by the lively intellectual climate at the University of Heidelberg, and influenced by her fellow student and future husband László Radványi (Johann Lorenz Schmidt; 1900–1978), who had fled from → Budapest in 1919, Seghers embarked upon her transformation into a communist during her study years. She transferred her previous desire to "alleviate" social ills by means of philanthropy into her concept for overcoming these ills through the socialist revolution. Towards the end of her studies, she decided to become a writer rather than, as her parents had hoped, taking over her father's business.

After marriage and their move to Berlin, where her husband was first an employee and later the head of the Marxistische Arbeiterschule (MASCH; Marxist Workers' School), Seghers made a name for herself as a writer. She became known to the wider public in 1928 when she was awarded the Heinrich Kleist Prize for her novellas *Grubetsch* (1927) and *Aufstand der Fischer von St. Barbara* (1928; "Revolt of the Fishermen of Santa Barbara," 1960). Since 1924 she had used the pseudonym Anna Seghers, borrowed from the Dutch painter and Rembrandt contemporary Hercules Seghers. In 1928 she became a member of the KPD (Communist Party of Germany) as well as the Bund Proletarisch-Revolutionärer Schriftsteller (Association of Proletarian-Revolutionary Authors). After joining the Communist Party, interpreted as a meaningful turning point in her life [11. vol. 1, 221f.], Seghers increasingly turned to concerns of the present in her narrative work. In quick succession, she wrote the novels *Die Gefährten* (1932), *Der Kopflohn. Roman aus einem deutschen Dorf im Spätsommer 1932* (1933; "A Price on His Head," 1962); in exile in Paris, she also wrote *Der Weg durch den Februar* (1935) and *Die Rettung* (1937), as well as her global success *Das Siebte Kreuz* (written 1938/1939, published 1942). *Das Siebte Kreuz* is about the escape of seven German prisoners from the fictitious German concentration camp Westhofen, only one of whom survives – the one who can rely on the solidarity of the Communist Party.

In these early stories and novels, Seghers always focuses on the world of laborers, whereby the changeability of humans and their circumstances emerges as a recurrent topic – as if humans, given information about their situation within the contradictions of society, would become class conscious and,

Anna Seghers (orig. Netty Radványi, née Reiling, 1900–1983)

consequently, change their existence. Seghers would later characterize this trait of her writing as follows: "If you write, you have to write in such a way that one can feel opportunity beyond despair, and a way out beyond doom" (cited in [11. vol. 1, 241]). The pedagogical impetus she based this on aligned with the educational idea of her parental home as well as with her materialist worldview; in both, individuals are regarded as products of their environment and, thus, as theoretically capable of change.

In terms of literary theory, Seghers adhered to Socialist Realism, which Stalin had declared mandatory in 1934, elevating the "truthful historical representation of reality in its revolutionary development" accompanied by "ideological reshaping and education" to the universally normative art form of Soviet literature and literary criticism (quoted in [4. 168f.]). While Seghers expressed mild criticism of these guidelines in the context of the so-called Expressionism debate in 1937/1938 in a series of letters to Georg Lukács (→ Essay; → Class Consciousness), insisting on her individual creative scope as an author [2], she nevertheless took on the task of writing in this style out of the deepest conviction. On the occasion of the publication of her novel *Die Rettung* in 1937, Walter Benjamin (→ Angelus Novus), with whom she was in touch during her years of exile in Paris, described her admiringly as "the chronicler of the German unemployed" [1. 129].

3. *Transit* as experience

Little of Seghers's confidence that all challenges could be met with solidarity and the right frame of mind remains in *Transit*. Rather, the novel, a book of flight and not of resistance, eludes the principles of Socialist Realism. The narrator characterizes himself as "a somewhat courageous, somewhat weak, somewhat unreliable fellow, who might with a lot of effort become more courageous, less weak, and a little bit more reliable without others even noticing" [5. 237]. Consequently, his suitability as a positive identification figure is limited. Instead, he appears to be an egoistic and dispassionate person who is helpless and at the mercy of the tide of events. Whereas Seghers usually placed the working class at the center of her writing, it is no longer the subject of the story in *Transit* but only a timeless backdrop and part of the port city: "The newspaper boys, the fishermen's wives on the Belsunce, the shopkeepers opening their stores, the workers going to work the early shift – they were all part of the masses who would never leave no matter what happened. [...] Wars, conflagrations, and the fury of the powerful has passed over them" [5. 242]. Only the wounded veteran of the Spanish Civil War, the communist Heinz, whom the narrator helps to escape, symbolizes something like Seghers's certainty from the old days in the description of him as having something steadfast about him "that will never be broken" [5. 132].

From September to December 1940, Seghers and her two children, aged twelve and fourteen, were in the French town of Pamiers at the foot of the Pyrenees in order to be near her husband who, like hundreds of other "enemy aliens," was interned in the nearby camp Le Vernet. Alone with her children, without luggage, without friends, and without sufficient means, Seghers made every effort necessary in order to leave Europe, finding herself confronting precisely the adversities she would condense into literature in *Transit* shortly afterwards. She wrote to friends in the United States, above all, F. C. Weiskopf in New York, imploring them to expedite the granting of visas for her family; she begged international aid organizations for money, only to be rejected with reference to her political stance; she tried to obtain a visa confirmation for her husband, without which he would not be able to leave the camp; and she traveled several times – without the children – to Marseilles several hundred kilometers away. Moreover, she knew of the vicissitudes of applying for papers, of which "one has always just expired when the other arrives"; and she worried about her own residence permit. She was also concerned about whether her literary works, such as the manuscript of *Das Siebte Kreuz*, a copy of which she had entrusted to friends for safekeeping, would survive. In addition to everything else, she constantly feared that all her efforts might have been in vain [7. 76–104]. In November 1940, her despair reached its peak: "I cannot describe to you how we live," she wrote to Weiskopf, "Dante, Dostoevsky, Kafka – oh! those were mere trifles. Small discomforts that passed. This here – this is serious" [7. 459]. Even if Seghers was presumably unlikely to choose suicide at a moment of such deep hopelessness due to concern about her children, some news, such as that of Walter Benjamin's (→ Angelus Novus) death in 1940, may well have led her to consider at least that they might not succeed in escaping the Nazis.

In early December 1940, Seghers's situation began to ease slightly as she now had a guarantee of passage and was permitted to stay in Marseilles in order to arrange the modalities of leaving the country. Even so, the uncertainty and restlessness reflected in *Transit* remained ever present: "I have [...] never written anything so immediately located in experience," Seghers remarked. Continuing, she claimed that she wrote most of the manuscript in Marseilles "in the mentioned cafés, probably even when I had to wait for too long in the waiting rooms of consulates, then onboard ship [...], and the ending in Mexico" [6. 43f.]. These circumstances etched themselves so deeply into the novel as though the author had been tasked with being their chronicler. Thus, her account became a document of the insight that the experience she had lived through in Paris, Pamiers, and Marseilles, this "waiting

for nothing" [5. 186], could not be apprehended with the traditional political categories of Marxist understanding.

In retrospect, the vividness and quality of *Transit* benefited from the disintegration of a positive anticipation of the future. Reality prevailed over distorting ideological filters. In a certain sense, Seghers was illustrating by means of factual dramatic literary description the experience that Hannah Arendt was beginning to reflect on politically and theoretically at the same time. Arendt (→ Judgement) shared Seghers's fate as a refugee in France (moreover, she had been stateless since 1937) before she managed to travel to New York from → Lisbon in the spring of 1941. She would later base her magnum opus *The Origins of Totalitarianism* (1951) on the dramatic refugee crisis in France and on the concomitant phenomenon of expiring → citizenship. Seghers worked the loss of rights considered to be inalienable into the atmosphere of the entire novel, and she did so explicitly, for instance, in having her narrator observe two sleeping tramps, remarking that "[t]hey were unaffected by what was happening" and sleeping "in their country" [5. 74f.]. With hindsight, the narrative expression with which the communist Seghers imbued this life reduced to bare existence during the liminal period of transit reads like an illustration of Arendt's "Aporias of Human Rights."

4. Failed return to Germany

The state of transition in which Seghers found herself after her escape from Paris continued for years, and grew more extreme. Until 1946 she lived in → Mexico City, where she was part of the group of exiles around Paul Merker, a high-ranking functionary in the Communist Party of Germany. In June 1943, she suffered multiple serious injuries in a traffic accident, recovering only slowly and with difficulty after a lengthy hospital stay. In the autumn of the same year, she received the news that her mother had been deported to Piaski near Lublin; this affected her all the more because she had endeavored to the very last to enable her to leave Germany. Her father had died in the spring of 1940, only a few days after the complete "Aryanization" of his property. Seghers drew on both of these events for what is probably her most famous novella, *Der Ausflug der toten Mädchen* (written 1944, published 1946; "The Excursion of the Dead Young Girls," 1995), which is about a dream on several time levels that flow into one another. The dream follows the life stories of girls who were classmates in a school in Mainz. Like *Transit*, this disturbing story, too, is entirely free of heroism. It ends in one girl's failed attempt to re-establish contact with her mother one last time, her image fading like a gradual loss of consciousness; only the vow to witness this as well as the girls' fates may be seen as a bridge to the future.

Her return to Germany in April 1947 marked the end of Seghers's exile; however, it had left lasting traces. Seghers dedicated herself, outwardly at least, to the development of the GDR. In 1952 she assumed the chairmanship of the Deutscher Schriftstellerverband. She became a role model for an entire generation of primarily younger authors. The subject of transformation remained the central motif of her literary work, for instance, in the novella *Der Mann und sein Name* (1950/1952) and in the large-scale industrial novel *Die Entscheidung* (1959). Even so, Seghers was unable to return to the incisiveness and vividness that had characterized her writing before the war.

Seghers's existential experiences during the war years and the mentality of the Germans could only rarely be reconciled with expectations of socialism. While she escaped the party cleansings of the early 1950s, she could not help but notice that all "Mexicans" were under suspicion, so that she was threatened as well. Her loss of confidence in

the future, which first became apparent in *Transit* and had increased with her experience of the → Holocaust, continued as the Stalinist crimes came to light from 1956 onward. However, she did not dare write openly about these issues, or about whether the GDR fulfilled her socialist vision, but did so only in coded terms. To the outside world she presented herself as true to the party line, but the damage to her anticipations for the future in the light of the devastations she found, as well as the loss of family members and close friends, is reflected in her early letters after her return. She felt out of place and unable to find much in common with the Germans, who struck her as "strangely undiscriminating and deformed" [7. 219]. In her later literary work, Seghers increasingly employed smaller formats in which she made contemporary observations using historical subjects in distant settings. Examples of this in a Caribbean setting are the novellas *Die Hochzeit von Haiti* (1949) and *Das Licht auf dem Galgen* (1961).

Ultimately, seeing no alternative to the GDR, Seghers refrained from publicly criticizing the party. Manès Sperber (→ Renegades) had already remarked on Seghers's attitude during her French exile that all "mocking remarks, all critical allusions she made in personal conversation quite unreservedly and even with visible enjoyment, were forgotten as soon as things got serious, namely, when she wrote or appeared in public" (cited in [11. vol. 1, 303]). During the Cold War, her manner of reacting in line with partisanship hardened when it came to protecting the utopian GDR state. In this way, she protected herself from regarding her return to Germany and, indeed, her biography as failures. Thus, she revealed herself as belonging to an entire generation of Jewish communists who, in spite of all doubts concerning their conversion from Judaism to the communist utopia of equality, adhered unconditionally to communism in the end.

Bibliography

Sources

[1] W. Benjamin, A Chronicle of Germany's Unemployed. Anna Seghers' novel 'Die Rettung,' in: Walter Benjamin. Selected Writings. Volume 4, 1938–1940, trans. by E. Jephcott and others, ed. by H. Eiland and M. W. Jennings, Cambridge and London 2003, 126–134. [2] G. Lukács/A. Seghers, Ein Briefwechsel zwischen Anna Seghers und Georg Lukács, in: H.-J. Schmitt (ed.), Die Expressionismusdebatte. Materialien zu einer marxistischen Realismuskonzeption, Frankfurt am Main 1973, 264–301. [3] M. Reich-Ranicki, Bankrott einer Erzählerin, in: Die Zeit, 11. March 1969, 28. [4] H.-J. Schmitt/G. Schramm (eds.), Sozialistische Realismuskonzeptionen. Dokumente zum 1. Allunionskongreß, Frankfurt am Main 1974. [5] A. Seghers, Transit, trans. by M. B. Dembo, New York 2013. [6] A. Seghers, Briefe an Leser, Berlin/Weimar 1970. [7] A. Seghers, Ich erwarte Eure Briefe wie den Besuch der besten Freunde. Briefe 1924–1952, ed. by C. Zehl Romero/A. Giesecke, Berlin 2008.

Secondary literature

[8] H. Arendt, The Origins of Totalitarianism, New York 1973. [9] M. Melchert, Heimkehr in ein kaltes Land. Anna Seghers in Berlin 1947 bis 1952, Berlin 2011. [10] L. Winckler, Eine Chronik des Exils. Erinnerungsarbeit in Anna Seghers "Transit," in: Exilforschung 28 (2010), 194–210. [11] C. Zehl Romero, Anna Seghers. Eine Biographie 1900–1983, 2 vols., Berlin 2000/03.

PHILIPP GRAF, LEIPZIG

Translation

Because of the diasporic multilingualism of the Jews, translation is crucially important in both religious and secular contexts. The transition to new speech areas entailed the need both to integrate influences from the surrounding cultures into Hebrew and to open up to the respective local languages. Here, the traditions of Jewish translations are characterized by a lack of continuity for there is a continuing tension between striving for and rejecting translations, as well as adapting linguistic elements from other cultures.

1. Introduction
2. The Middle Ages
3. Haskalah
4. Reawakening

1. Introduction

The Hebrew Bible (→ Tanakh) contains direct references to translation activities. In the story of Joseph and his brothers, we read "They did not know that Joseph understood, for there was an interpreter between him and them." (Hebr. *melits*; Gen 42:23). The explanation by the medieval commentator Rashi (→ Worms) of the passage runs: "For whenever they spoke with him, the interpreter, who knew both Hebrew and Egyptian, was between them, and he would translate (*hayah melits*) their words for Joseph and Joseph's words for them." Already in Biblical medieval Hebrew, the word, a substantivized present participle in *hif'il* of the Hebrew root *lamed – yud – tsadi*, can be understood in the sense of "interpreter" as well in that of "translator." The term *melits* is rendered in the Vulgate by *interpres*, which means both "exegete" and "expositor" or "interpreter." In Rabbinic literature, the corresponding verb had assumed the meaning of "to explain," or (in a poetic or homiletic sense) "to expound," while *metargem* was customarily used for the participle and substantive of "to translate." A word from the same root is used once in the Bible for translating from Hebrew to Aramaic (Ezra 4:7).

It is undisputed in scholarship that many passages in the Hebrew Bible exhibit connections with texts of Near Eastern origin. Thus, there are striking parallels between the Flood in Genesis and in the Gilgamesh Epic, and well as of several sections in the Books of Psalms and various hymns from Canaanite Ugarit. The paths of transmission cannot, however, be followed, since no information of any kind has been transmitted that provides information on the precise source of texts, translators, or translation techniques.

The subsequent history of translation in Jewish culture is closely bound to the → Diaspora and to the fate of → Hebrew. While it increasingly tended to lose importance as a spoken language – a process that was presumably completed by the time of the collection of oral traditions in the Mishnah (→ Talmud) around 300 CE –, translation activity did not cease to increase. The oldest attestation to this comes once again from the Bible itself. The Book of Nehemiah contains a description of a Torah reading in Hebrew, followed by a translation for the → Aramaic-speaking community, who no longer understood the original text (Neh 8:8).

In the period of the Second Temple, a number of individual books of the Bible were rendered into Aramaic (presumably beginning with the Book of Job [Hiob]), which were collectively called *targumim* (Aram.; translation, interpretation; sing. *targum*). There are also various references to translation practices and the importance of translations in Talmudic literature as well. Thus, a saying attribute to Rabbi Yehuda bar Ilai ran as follows: "One who translates [*metargem*] a verse literally is a liar, since he distorts the meaning of the text, and conversely, one who adds his own translation is tantamount to one who curses and blasphemes God" (Bavli, Kiddushin 49a). The remark is presumably connected to the dissatisfaction with the large number of paraphrases in the contemporary Aramaic → Bible translations. Renderings of the Torah into other languages were also considered clearly inferior to the Hebrew Bible: translated books of the Bible "does not defile

the hands" (Mishnah, Yadayim 4,5), this is, they are not holy (→ *kadosh*).

Translations were nevertheless indispensable for orientation to the Holy Scripture, as is also shown by the Septuagint, prepared in Hellenistic Egypt in the 3rd century BCE. Like the Jewish inhabitants of pre-exilic Palestine, the Greek-speaking Jews could no longer speak Hebrew. The common denominator of all translations, however different they might be, consisted in the fact that they originated in an intracultural act of translation, as opposed to a transcultural one. In the large corpus of Talmudic literature, there is never even a single line translated from any tradition stemming from those cultures with which the Jews were in direct contact. Presumably, the clash with the Greek and Roman lifeworlds at the time of the Second Temple promoted the unfavorable attitude which the Rabbinic authorities displayed to all non-Jewish sources for centuries.

2. The Middle Ages

Insofar as translation can be understood as a process of the transfer of sacred and profane texts from one culture to another, the true history of translation into → Hebrew begins in the Middle Ages. In the 10th century, the commentator and grammarian Dunasch ben Labrat (920–990) introduced – not without resistance – the prosody of Arabic poetry into Hebrew, thereby laying the foundation for the most important innovation in the system of Hebrew literature: secular poetry.

With the expansion of Arabic culture, the Jews in → Sepharad increasingly wrote their works in → Arabic. As long as their readers knew this language, translations into Hebrew were not necessary. However, beginning in the 12th century, large Jewish communities arose in areas where no Arabic was spoken, especially in northern Italy and southern France. The elites of these communities were anxious to familiarize themselves with writings on the religious law and with → ethics, which they knew only by rumor. Hebrew therefore acquired once again the function of a *lingua franca*, and united Jews from different linguistic areas, who otherwise had no possibilities of communicating with one another.

The important intracultural translations of Baḥya ibn Pakuda's *Kitāb al-hidāyah ilā al-farā'iḍ al-qulūb* (Book on the Guidelines for the Duties of the Heart; Hebr. *Sefer Ḥovot ha-Levavot*; 1080), Maimonides's *Dalālāh al-ḥā'irīn* (Hebr. *Moreh Nevukhim*, ca. 1190; Guide for the Perplexed) and Judah Halevi's *Kitāb al-Khazarī* (Hebr. *Sefer ha-Kuzari*; Book of the Khazars, ca. 1140; Kuzari) were soon followed by a broad wave of transcultural translations, which covered every area of human knowledge. Moritz Steinschneider's monumental → bibliography *Die hebräischen Übersetzungen des Mittelalters und die Juden als Dolmetscher* (1893) cites hundreds of Hebrew translations of → philosophy, → medicine, → mathematics, and astronomy, as well as religious works and other books and essays. Through the Arabic translations, many Greek and Latin words also found their way into Hebrew. The outstanding example is provided by some terms from the works of Aristotle (Falsafah). Compared to the large number of works from the fields of → science and general knowledge, the corpus of translated literary works is strikingly small, with a half dozen books.

Beginning with the 12th century, two diametrically opposed conceptions of translation emerged. On one side were the Tibbonids, an exceptionally productive Jewish family of translators who lived in southern France, who translated scientific texts into Hebrew for generations. Orders were usually placed by communities or Jewish patrons. Following the head of the family Judah ibn Tibbon (1120–1190), who came from Granada, → Arabic was considered a highly developed language, which was in many respects superior to Hebrew, a frozen

language that had not further developed for centuries. As a result, the translations of the Tibbonids remained very close to the Arabic original. Judah ibn Tibbon translated Judah Halevi's *Kuzari* into Hebrew, while his son Samuel did the same for Maimonides's *Moreh Nevukhim*. At the same time, the Tibbonids' translations made a large contribution to the development of the Hebrew language itself, since they brought with them changes in the meaning of current Hebrew words, new loanwords from Arabic, and some important morphological innovations. On the other side, the Spanish poet and translator Yehudah Al-Ḥarizi (1165–1225) – who also prepared a translation of Maimonides's *Moreh Nevukhim* – advocated the view that Hebrew is superior to all other languages with regard to its sacredness and originality: hence, every translation automatically increased the value of a work. The Tibbonid approach was primarily applied to non-fictional texts, while Al-Ḥarizi's view strongly influenced the later approach to the translation of literary texts.

3. Haskalah

From the second half of the 18th century, translations played a key role in the → Haskalah's project of modernizing Jewish life. Because of religious restrictions, the introduction of non-Jewish works in theHebrew sphere was a difficult task at first. The work of the first modern translators from Hebrew was, moreover, made more difficult by the attitude that only classical, Biblical Hebrew was an appropriate means of expression for literary production. Jewish proponents of the Enlightenment sought first and foremost to fill the large gap between Central and Western European culture and the Jewish world. Therefore, scientific works, oriented toward general education (→ Bildung), or fictional texts were considered for translation, especially when they were considered morally or intellectually useful.

Despite the pathbreaking, polemical character that many translations from this period possess, central taboos were maintained: texts that contained heathen or Christian elements remained untranslated or were carefully purged. Friedrich Schiller represents a typical example; although he was the favorite poet of many 19th century Enlightenment translators, and many of his works were translated repeatedly, none of his poems on classical themes, except for *Der Ring des Polykrates* ("The Ring of Polycrates," 1879), found its way into → Hebrew. Texts with Biblical themes, in contrast, had a good chance of being translated. Biblical dramas by Racine, Klopstock, and Metastasio were translated early on. Texts in → German long constituted the main source for translations for the Haskalah, even in cases in which it served as an intermediary language (for → English or French). Jewish proponents of the Enlightenment also took journalistic models from German culture, which they imitated, such as the edition of periodicals (→ Ha-Me'assef). An entire series of ideas and literary genres (e.g. dialogues of the dead, odes, or ballads) can be traced back to German literature, whence they were adapted through imitation or direct translation.

The lack of developed institutional structures, such as publishing houses (→ Publishing), ensured that translation activity remained largely sporadic and incomplete. Literary works were seldom translated completely, and translations of fragments and excerpts were much more frequent. There was an additional problem in the field of → poetry, which impeded an easy influx of foreign language texts into Hebrew: the incompatibility of metrical systems. Most European poetry used syllabotonic (syllable-counting) meters, while Hebrew poetry, in contrast, used quantitative meters. Another reason for the nearly complete disregard for the autonomy of translated texts resided in the fact that translators felt bound first and foremost to Jewish culture and the Hebrew language and only secondarily to the adapted text. Thus, many translations acquired new proportions: omissions and additions were not considered translational violations, as long as they served the end product. The text of the first Hebrew translation of Goethe's *Hermann und Dorothea – Neve ha-Tsedek* (1857; lit. Treasury of Justice; → Elective Affinities), for instance, is one third longer than the original. There was also a series of strategies for making texts acceptable to the reader. Thus, the names of characters were often Hebraized: *Ram ve-Ya'el* instead of *Romeo and Juliet* is a well-known example of the quest for phonetic correspondence. Textual passages extolling the author were also inserted.

Among the leading translators of the Haskalah were, for instance, Meir Letteris (ca. 1800–1871), who translated Racine's two Biblical dramas *Athalie – Geza Yishai* (1835; The Stock of Jesse) and *Esther – Shlom Ester* (1843; The Peace of Esther), as well as the first part of Goethe's *Faust – Ben Abuyah* (1865). Isaac Edward Salkinson (1820–1883) saw to the translations of the first two plays by Shakespeare (→ Shylock): *Othello – Ithi'el ha-Kushi* (1874; Iti'el the Kushite) and *Romeo and Juliet – Ram ve-Ya'el* (1878), as well as Milton's *Paradise Lost – Va-Yegaresh et ha-Adam* (1871; And He Drove Out Adam). In all, the translations of that period resemble an accumulation of arbitrarily chosen works of the Central European canon, which are loosely connected by general features of Hebrew style and by similarities in translation techniques. No single work and no significant author was appropriately represented by the translations. Nevertheless, the Haskalah did produce a few lasting masterpieces, introduced new stylistic tools into Hebrew prose and poetry, inspired the emergence of Hebrew-language children's literature, and made a large contribution to the secularization of the whole of Hebrew → literature.

4. Reawakening

Translations (especially literary) into Hebrew underwent one final important revaluation during the Jewish → renaissance, from the last quarter of the 19th century to the 1910s, as well as in the immediately following period of Hebrew modernism between the 1910s and the late 1940s. This period is characterized by several parallel processes. On the one hand, translation activity shifted to the East: the center of Hebrew literature migrated from Germany to the Slavic regions, and thus Russian culture became the model to be emulated. On the other, Hebrew experienced a continuing revival, not least through the influence of Zionism (→ Basel) and the incipient Jewish emigration to Palestine (→ Aliyah), as the spoken language of the → Yishuv.

The strict, puristic style of the first generation of Lumières was replaced by a more flexible, inclusive kind of modern Hebrew. From the second half of the 19th century, an increasing number of reference works (→ Encyclopedias) appeared for all areas of knowledge, many of which were translated or adapted from → German and → Russian. The translators' efforts to find suitable parallels for various terminologies and nomenclatures supported this process of revival. In the field of poetry, the adaptation of syllabotonic verse structure, which had begun around 1880 under the influence of Russian models, eliminated one of the last major obstacles that had impeded the translation of European poetry into Hebrew.

The end of the 19th century, which brought with it the stabilization of secular Hebrew → printing, saw the beginning of collective efforts to make the works of world literature accessible to Jewish culture. Translated works made up an important part of the production of nearly all publishing houses. Most active in this regard were the publishers Stybel, founded in Warsaw in 1918 with the specific purpose of translating classical literature into Hebrew, and Dvir, established in → Odessa in 1919, but based in Tel Aviv since 1924. Many contemporary Jewish intellectuals, especially Hebrew poets, willingly undertook translations, the supply of which more than doubled in a relatively short time. The range of source languages was broadened, and modern translation standards made their appearance. Partial translations of originals and censored or highly manipulated editions were no longer acceptable to readers, and even the use of secondary translations as sources continued to wane. David Frishman (1859–1922), who, among other works, translated Nietzsche's *Also sprach Zarathustra* ("Thus Spoke Zarathustra," 1909–1911; → Übervolk) into Hebrew, was probably one of the last important translators to use the old techniques for making texts accessible to Jewish readers. The best example is a version, published in 1895, of Andersen's Christmas story *Den Lille Pige med Svovlstikkerne* ("The Little Match Girl," 1846), which Frishman transformed into a Hanukkah fable.

The prominent status of Hebrew in Zionist culture also contributed to creating a more or less homogeneous style for both poetry and prose. In the 1920s, → poetry was largely determined by the norms of Russian translations, which demanded a formal, metrically precise rendering. The nucleus of the canon of literary translations into modern Hebrew dates from this period. Thus, for instance, Saul Tchernichovsky (1875–1943) translated works by Homer, Sophocles, Shakespeare, and Moliere. Avraham Shlonsky (1900–1973) produced a highly-praised translation of Pushkin's verse epic *Eugene Onegin*, but also translated other authors, primarily Russian, such as Gogol, Chekhov, or Isaac Babel (→ Red Cavalry).

Translation activity was given another boost with the formation, consolidation, and rapid diffusion of Hebrew publishing in Palestine. Since 1942, a prestigious prize, named after Saul Tchernichovsky, has been given for outstanding translations. Although many gifted translators were murdered in the → Shoah, and many important translation projects remained unfinished, Palestine developed into the undisputed center of literary efforts in Hebrew.

After the founding of the State of Israel, a radical change in Hebrew literature took place, beginning in the mid-1950s. Its ties to the Russian language were replaced by an Anglo-American orientation, and an extreme change in linguistic sensitivity took place. The grandiloquent cadences of Hebrew that were hegemonic at the time were replaced by a new style that strove to cover the middle and lower registers of Hebrew as well. Both translators and readers clearly realized that many translations were outdated. This gave rise to a veritable flood of works that had already been translated.

Bibliography

[1] D. Almagor, Shakespeare in Hebrew Literature of the Enlightenment and Revival Periods. A Bibliographical Survey and a Bibliography [Hebr.], in: B. Shakhevitch/M. Peri (eds.), Sefer ha-yovel le-Shim'on Halkin. [Simon Halkin Jubilee Volume], Jerusalem 1975, 721–784. [2] A. Dykman, Tchernichowsky's Homer, in: B. Arpaly/Zivah Golan (eds.), Sha'ul Tshernihovski: mehkarim u-te'udot [Saul Tchernichovsky. Studies and Documents], Jerusalem 1994, 421–473. [3] A. Dykman, The Secret of a Kiss, Be It through a Veil [Hebr.], in: A. Reich (ed.), Ha-neshikah mi-ba'ad la-mitpahat: mivhar hashva'ot targume shirah [A Kiss through a Veil. Hebrew Verse Translations by Many Hands Compared], Tel Aviv 2001, 9–22. [4] I. Even-Zohar, Polysystem Studies, in: Poetics Today 11 (1990) 1 [Special issue]. [5] I. Even-Zohar, Papers in Historical Poetics, Tel Aviv 1978. [6] S. Feiner, The Jewish Enlightenment, Philadelphia 2004. [7] M. Pelli, Haskalah and Beyond. The Reception of the Hebrew Enlightenment and the Emergence of Haskalah Judaism, Lanham 2010. [8] R. Singerman, Jewish Translation History. A Bibliography of Bibliographies and Studies, Amsterdam/ Philadelphia 2002. [9] G. Toury, Descriptive Translation Studies and Beyond, Amsterdam/ Philadelphia 2002. [10] I. Zinberg, A History of Jewish Literature, 12 vols., New York 1972–1978.

AMINADAV DYKMAN, JERUSALEM

Transportation

During the early modern and modern periods, Jews in Europe were involved in various ways in the transport of goods and passengers, in hauling and shipping, and later on the → railways and in motorized long-distance passenger transport. They occupied a leading position in transportation especially in the Polish–Lithuanian Commonwealth of the early modern period as well as the Russian Empire of the 19th and 20th centuries.

1. Traditional sectors
2. Eastern Europe in the modern era

1. Traditional sectors

Jews were active in the maritime trade as early as the Middle Ages. They were mainly merchants, agents, or insurers active predominantly in the Mediterranean. These, as well as related activities, continued in the early modern period; many Portuguese Jews, for instance, were involved in shipbuilding [4. 186f.]. Shipping itself, however, remained mostly closed to them as specific privileges such as anchoring rights, tax benefits, and other measures facilitating trade were limited to Christians or Muslims.

Jewish shipowners are documented since the second half of the 16th century; the first mention of a Jewish ship proprietor is probably Christopher Marlowe's *The Jew of Malta* (1592; → Shylock). Jewish shipowners relied on official protection of their ships; at first they were limited to the Ottoman Empire and → Livorno but were later also found among Portuguese Jews (→ Sephardim) in Hamburg, Amsterdam (→ Esnoga), and other cities of Western Europe. In the 17th and 18th centuries, too, the owners and merchants traveling in Europe and the New World were mainly Portuguese Jews (→ Slave Trade). In the mid-17th century, the Netherlands granted Jews the right to own ships and to sail under the Dutch flag. In the New World, ship names such as *Königin Esther*, *Pinhas*, *Mazal Tov* (Good luck), *Ha-Melekh David* (King David), or *Shmuel ha-Katan* (Little Samuel) in Curaçao point to Jewish shipowners [1. 56f., 61–66].

Jews were barely represented in continental transportation in Western and Central Europe during the early modern period, but the situation was different in Eastern Europe. In the Polish–Lithuanian Commonwealth, many worked as wagoners (Yidd. → *balegules*), and less frequently we find porters, rafters, ferrymen, and lockkeepers. According to a census of 1764, two to three percent of the Jewish population of Polish towns and shtetlach (→ Shtetl) made a living in this sector [6. 144].

Jews were active above all as merchants in river transport in Eastern Europe in the 18th century. This is demonstrated, for instance, by shipping traffic on the Vistula from southeast Poland to Gdansk and on the Neman River from Lithuania to Königsberg. On these and other rivers in Poland–Lithuania, trade was predominantly in the hands of wealthy Polish noblemen (magnates). On the Vistula they mainly transported grain and forest products to Gdansk, acquiring Western and colonial goods as well as clothing. In order to make these transports profitable, they offered merchants who did not own their own ships space as well as protection during the journey. This opportunity was taken mainly by Jewish merchants who sold produce such as linen, hemp, wax, and animal skins in Gdansk, and bought sugar, spices, household and metal goods, as well as clothes, among other things.

Compared to non-Jewish merchants, Jewish traders were more likely to seize the opportunity to transport goods on the Vistula and usually also carried goods of higher quality. Some of the bills of lading were written in Yiddish [9]. From the 1720s onward, river trade on the Neman River intensified. Here, too, merchants from cities and towns along the river who transported their wares on boats were influential for the efficiency of this transport route. Just under half of these merchants were Jews [11. 172–177].

The presence of Jews in the hauling and transportation sector and their involvement in inland shipping in the 18th century were closely linked to the most important economic activities of the Jewish population in the countryside, as well as with trade, → leases, and innkeeping (→ Tavern). Trade demanded in-depth knowledge of transport routes and required transporting goods over short and long distances; army suppliers also needed these skills. The prevalent practice of Jews leasing and administering the country estates of the nobility also required a high degree of mobility. Taverns run by Jews holding the "propinacja," the privilege of distilling and serving alcohol, were usually situated on important trade routes, offering travelers food and accommodation at affordable prices.

In the 19th century, Jews in Eastern Europe continued to play an active part mainly in the traditional sectors of hauling and transportation. In some areas, their percentage rapidly increased as urbanization caused the profession of wagoner to grow in importance, offering employment to untrained persons, in particular. In the → Pale of Settlement and in Congress Poland, Jews managed a large number of post offices and, in this capacity, were exempt from some of the anti-Jewish regulations. After the introduction of the railways, the horse and cart remained an important means of transport; as late as 1897, there were more than 25,000 Jewish wagoners in the Pale of Settlement, amounting to 21% of all independent wagoners. Overall around 4% of the Jewish population earned a living via activities in the transport sector. In Galicia, just under 18% of all those employed in this sector were Jews [6. 144f.].

2. Eastern Europe in the modern era

In the second half of the 19th century, transportation in Eastern Europe underwent a fundamental transformation as the result of industrialization and urbanization. The percentage of Jewish employees and workers in the new sectors remained small.

For instance, they were hardly able to establish themselves as employees of urban passenger transport (streetcars and buses). In → Łódź this career was entirely forbidden to them. In 1897 four prominent Jewish entrepreneurs withdrew from a syndicate for streetcar network construction established two years previously as it had been decided that only Christians were to be employed in the streetcar sector [5. 21]. In all of Russia, as well as in Poland and Galicia, the number of Jewish employees in the postal, telegraph, and telephone sectors remained small.

During the interwar years, this number shrank even further in Poland and Galicia, with Jews increasingly pushed out of the civil service [6. 145–148]. The only exception was long-distance overland transport, where the percentage of Jews among the workforce was high. Jewish motor bus proprietors appear to have been inclined to prefer Jews when recruiting employees. The number of Jewish owners of motor buses was considerable; in the Białystok voivodeship, 47 of 66 motor buses belonged to Jews in 1933 (71%). That same year, over 90% of the conductors on long-distance buses and around 20% of the drivers in Poland as a whole were Jews [6. 145–149].

During the first decades of the 19th century, Jewish merchants and entrepreneurs in Congress Poland and Russia had begun to

become involved in the banking sector. Over the course of the century, Jewish → bankers there as elsewhere in Europe became more active in establishing and expanding the → railways. Jewish financiers in Eastern Europe thus played an important role in this between the 1830s and the early 20th century because they were willing to bear the risk of these investments more frequently than others.

After the Russians were defeated in the Crimean War in 1856 – an outcome caused not least by the technical and structural backwardness of the country – the Russian government recognized the importance of the railways and the Grande Société des Chemins de fer Russes was founded in 1857. Among its founders were the Jewish bankers Émile and Isaac Péreire, as well as the latter's son Eugène; others were Alexander von Stieglitz (St. Petersburg), the bank S. A. Fraenkel (Warsaw, represented by Fraenkel's son Antoni Edward F.), and the Mendelssohn bank (Berlin). The Poliakov brothers Lazar, Samuel, and Yakov invested, above all, in domestic Russian lines, for instance, between Kharkov and Taganrog. In 1857 a private company headed by Herman Epstein and later the convert Leopold Stanisław Kronenberg took over the management of the line between Warsaw and Vienna. Kronenberg had also completed the line between Warsaw and Brest-Litovsk and managed stock corporations for the expansion of the railway network between Poland, Ukraine, and South Russia together with Jan Gotlib Bloch and other Jewish entrepreneurs between 1862 and 1902.

Jewish businessmen also occupied technical and administrative positions in the railway sector, such as Henryk Toeplitz as the managing director of the Russian Southwest Railways in the second half of the 19th century. Among railway workers, however, there were hardly any Jews; in the → Pale of Settlement and Poland they accounted for two percent of the workforce, and in Poland

TRANSPORTATION

between the wars less than one percent [6. 145–148]. Towards the end of the 19th century, mistrust of private investors, the trend towards state control, and, to some degree, an interest in income from lucrative lines led to the increasing nationalization of railway networks all over Europe. In Russia the state took over the management of all railway lines in 1912.

The expansion of modern transportation and, above all, the construction of the railways in Russia had far-reaching consequences for the Jewish populations in the regions concerned. In the Russian Empire, the expansion of the railway network increased the mobility of the population in general. It also led to the grain trade shifting eastward from the traditional transportation hub in → Odessa to ports further east on the Black Sea. At the same time, customs policy encouraged grain export via the Baltic ports, prompting heavy losses for the Jewish merchants and agents dependent on the grain trade in Odessa. The decline of the Odessa grain trade, in turn, incited anti-Jewish resentment especially among non-Jewish merchants, triggering the first anti-Jewish riots in Odessa in 1871 [10. 128–131]. During the wave of anti-Jewish → pogroms in Russia ten years later, a number of attacks spread from larger cities into the areas surrounding the railway lines. Railway workers, the itinerant unemployed, as well as workmen and farmers who often traveled in groups by train, contributed to the spread of the pogroms [2. 47, 49].

Jewish businessmen in 19th-century Russia not only had a share in railway construction but also in the development and expansion of motorized domestic shipping. In 1876 Evzel Gintsburg (Joseph Günzburg) and his son Goratsi (Horace Günzburg; → Bankers; → Philanthropy), both of whom were already involved in the development of the railway industry, took over the management of shipping on the Volga. The businessman David Margolin founded a shipping

line on the Dnieper River in 1883 that grew into a fleet of 62 steam ships by 1911 [4. 188]. Subsequently, Grigori Abramovich Poliakov expanded transportation on the Volga and the Caspian Sea. Water freight increasingly gained importance for the transport of crude oil and other oil products.

With Eastern European Jews emigrating in ever larger numbers to → America, Jewish businessmen found that transporting their fellow-countrymen could produce additional income. From the late 1860s onward, Jewish entrepreneurs founded offices in Hamburg, Rotterdam, and London, buying tickets for the crossing to America in bulk, often during the winter months, in order to resell them at a profit in the summer (→ Bremerhaven). The Russian Jewish émigré Sender Jarmulowsky, who settled in Hamburg in 1868, was one of these entrepreneurs. Five years later, he relocated to → New York, where he founded the Jarmulowsky Bank, which sold tickets on an installment plan, enabling Jews who had already immigrated to have their families join them. Such ticket reselling practices, however, were short-lived because the shipping companies soon enacted stricter rules.

Once official restrictions had been abolished in the wake of the → February Revolution, the number of Jewish workers in the transport and communications sector increased in post-revolutionary Russia. The number of Jewish railway workers and employees in Belarus rose from 29 to 82% from 1926 to 1928. At the same time, the number of Jewish employees in the postal and telegraph sectors doubled [3. 214]. Overall, however, their number remained small in these professions; in the Ukrainian Soviet Republic, only 1.1% of railway workers were Jews in 1929 [7. 157].

Bibliography

[1] B. Arbel, Shipping and Toleration. The Emergence of Jewish Ship-Owners in the Early Modern

Period, in: Mediterranean Historical Review 15 (2000) 1, 56–71. [2] I. M. Aronson, The Anti-Jewish Pogroms in Russia in 1881, in: J. D. Klier/S. Lambroza (eds.), Pogroms. Anti-Jewish Violence in Modern Russian History, Cambridge 1992, 44–61. [3] S. W. Baron, The Russian Jew under Tsars and Soviets, New York 1976. [4] S. W. Baron/A. Kahan, Economic History of the Jews, ed. by N. Gross, New York 1976. [5] F. Guesnet, Lodzer Juden im 19. Jahrhundert. Ihr Ort in einer multikulturellen Stadtgesellschaft, Leipzig 1997. [6] R. Mahler, Yehude Polin ben shte milḥamot olam. Historyah kalkalit-sotsiyalit le-or statistikah [Polish Jews during the Interbellum. Socio-economic History in the Light of Statistics], Tel Aviv 1968. [7] A. Nove/J. A. Newth, The Jewish Population. Demographic Trends and Occupational Patterns, in: L. Kochan (ed.), The Jews in Soviet Russia since 1917, Oxford 1972, 125–158. [8] T. Presner, Mobile Modernity. Germans, Jews, Trains, New York 2007. [9] M. Rosman, Polish Jews in the Gdansk Trade in the Late Seventeenth and Early Eighteenth Centuries, in: I. Twersky (ed.), Danzig between East and West. Aspects of Modern Jewish History, Cambridge 1985, 111–120. [10] L. Siegelbaum, The Odessa Grain Trade. A Case Study in Urban Growth and Development in Tsarist Russia, in: The Journal of European Economic History 9 (1980) 1, 113–151. [11] A. Teller, Money, Power, and Influence in Eighteenth-century Lithuania. The Jews on the Radziwill Estates, Stanford 2017.

CORNELIA AUST, MAINZ

Treblinka

Extermination camp northeast of Warsaw, where around a million Jews were systematically murdered between July 1942 and August 1943. On August 2, 1943, prisoners staged an armed revolt which enabled around 200 detainees to escape. This event was the basis for Jean-François Steiner's novel *Treblinka: la révolte d'un camp d'extermination* ("Treblinka," 1967) published

in France in 1966. With its depiction of the → Holocaust, the novel rocked the French postwar narrative of a population united in the myth of the → Résistance, leading to an interest in the widespread collaboration in France (→ Vichy). Simultaneously, the question of the possibilities of armed resistance discussed in the novel informed Jewish self-understanding in postwar France.

1. Treblinka extermination camp
2. Jean-François Steiner
3. Steiner's novel
4. The Treblinka affair
5. Resonance

1. Treblinka extermination camp

The construction of the Treblinka camp in May 1942 marked the beginning of the implementation of "Aktion Reinhard," the plan for the systematic murder of all Jews in the General Governorate. It was the third camp besides Bełżec and → Sobibór that was entirely dedicated to the project of extermination. Treblinka was the name of a small village northeast of Warsaw halfway to Białystok. Four kilometers from the railway station, the extermination complex was constructed in a densely wooded area. During only 13 months, around a million Jews and several thousand Roma were gassed there [7. 468]. The majority of the victims came from the → Warsaw ghetto and the Radom District. Later, Treblinka would also be the final destination of transports from the German Reich, the Protectorate of Bohemia and Moravia (→ Theresienstadt), Slovakia, Greece (→ Salonika), and Bulgaria (→ Peshev Protest).

The first three gas chambers were constructed by specialists from the National Socialists' euthanasia program ("Aktion T4"), which was discontinued in 1941. In order to expand the extermination capacity, a building containing ten further gas chambers was built from August to October 1942. The camp grounds measured 400 by 600 meters and consisted of three zones – a residential complex for the guard teams and prisoners' barracks, the reception camp, and the death camp. The staff comprised no more than 20 to 30 SS men and around one hundred Ukrainian volunteers, so-called "Trawnikis" or "Trawniki men" [3. 15]; [8. vol 3., 898].

The first transport with Jews from the Warsaw ghetto arrived on July 23, 1942, in Treblinka. Arriving trains with around 40 to 50 wagons and up to 7,000 detainees first stopped at the railway station in Treblinka village where a smaller number of wagons were uncoupled and gradually brought into the camp. In order to prevent panic and guarantee a smooth process, a train station furnished with a clock, a ticket office, time-tables, and a sign bearing the fictitious name "Obermajdan" gave the impression that this was merely a stopover. SS men forced the Jews out of the wagons and a commander explained that they had reached a transit camp; before they could be sent on to labor camps, they would have to disinfect their clothes, temporarily hand over their valuables, and shower. Women and children were separated from the men; both groups had to strip naked. Women and children were pushed through a long, narrow corridor called "the hosepipe" into the gas chambers into which carbon monoxide was introduced, suffocating them within thirty minutes. During this time, the men had to wait at the "transfer yard" before they, too, were taken to the gas chambers, once the bodies had been removed, and gassed.

From autumn 1942 onward, it was possible to murder 12,000 persons in Treblinka every day. Jewish Sonderkommandos (special units) were deployed to remove the bodies, which were initially thrown into mass graves, to remove gold teeth, to search bodily orifices for hidden valuables, and to collect valuables and send them to the Reich. Their members were usually murdered after a short time and replaced with newly arrived deported prisoners. When it became clear that it was more efficient not to replace the "Arbeitsjuden" ("Jewish workers") constantly, their respite was extended. In Treblinka, between 500 and 1,000 inmates had to work in the Sonderkommandos.

First endeavors to conceal the traces of mass murder began in the spring of 1942. This project, called "Aktion 1005," was of great urgency in view of the military successes of the Allies, especially after the battle of → Stalingrad. From the end of February 1943, bodies were burned immediately in Treblinka. Tens of thousands of corpses buried in mass graves had to be exhumed and cremated by the inmates. Once separated from bone residue, the ashes were mixed with sand and rubbish and then buried once more. In spring 1943, the elimination of traces was personally inspected by Himmler.

The Nazis' project to eliminate all traces of the mass murder made it clear to the prisoners in the Sonderkommandos that the camp would be completely liquidated and all witnesses eliminated in the near future. A small group of no more than five prisoners at its core began to plan an uprising in the spring of 1943. Among this committee were Julian (Ilya) Chorążycki, a physician and captain in the → Polish Home Army (Armia Krajowa), Marceli (Alfred) Galewski, an engineer from → Łódź, as well as Rudolf Masárek and Želo Bloch, both officers from the Czechoslovak army. As members of the work detail, they had the opportunity to obtain the valuables and money of the murdered Jews with which they intended to bribe the Ukrainian guards. The Trawniki, who were known to be bribable, took the money but did not provide weapons. When the SS found a considerable sum of money with Chorążycki, he took poison to escape certain torture and execution. When numerous prisoners fell ill during an epidemic of yellow fever in the camp, plans for an uprising came to a temporary halt.

In July 1943, the exhumation and cremation of the bodies neared their end; fewer transports arrived in Treblinka. In addition, news of the landing of Allied troops in Italy and of the German Wehrmacht suffering defeats on the eastern front spread among the inmates. The members of the Sonderkommandos concluded that their murder was imminent and that an uprising had to take place immediately. They succeeded in copying a key for the weapons store and taking possession of several dozen grenades. They also had a few pistols, guns, and petrol bombs. The uprising broke out on August 2, 1943, with several hundred prisoners taking part. The insurgents opened fire on the SS and the Trawniki and set fire to several buildings and the petrol tank. In the initial chaos they were able to get hold of more weapons and storm the fence of the camp. However, the Ukrainian Trawniki and the SS quickly rallied and shot several hundreds of insurgents. Around 200 prisoners succeeded in escaping, but most of them were soon hunted down by the SS. Others were handed in by peasants or murdered by → partisans. Only around 60 of those escaped lived to see the end of the war.

The gas chambers remained functional despite the uprising. Even so, the revolt accelerated the liquidation of the camp. On August 21, 1943, the last prisoners of Treblinka were gassed. Afterwards the camp was razed to the ground by the Germans and covered up by a farm built on the site.

2. Jean-François Steiner

When the novel *Treblinka: la révolte d'un camp d'extermination* ("Treblinka," 1967) was published by Fayard publishers in Paris in 1966, its author Jean-François Steiner was unknown. He was born in 1938, the son of Isaac Kadmi Cohen, a Jew originally from Poland, and a French Catholic woman who had converted to Judaism. His father was a lawyer and well known in France as a follower of Revisionist Zionism (→ Altalena) founded by Vladimir Ze'ev Jabotinsky, who had come to public notice because of his articles in the journal *Mercure de France*, among others. Later, Isaac Kadmi Cohen developed his own ideas of a Jewish state in the Middle East and beginning in 1942 even attempted to come to an agreement with the → Vichy regime, intending to facilitate the emigration of Jews from France. In the spring of 1944, he was deported via → Drancy to Gleiwitz, a subcamp of → Auschwitz, and murdered there.

After the liberation of France, Jean-François's mother married the Jewish physician Ozias Steiner, who adopted her son in 1952. The stepfather imparted knowledge of Jewish history and religion to Jean-François as well as the left-leaning politics which he, a former communist who had fought in the international brigades in the Spanish Civil War (→ Botwin Company), still embraced. Steiner dedicated the novel to his two fathers.

As an adolescent, Steiner spent two years in Israel but did not regard himself as a follower of Zionism. Back in France, he spent his military service with an airborne unit deployed in the war with Algeria. His first article in *Les Temps modernes* dealt with this experience. From this time onward, Steiner kept in touch with the editing team of the journal, especially with Simone de Beauvoir who supported him. For a time, Steiner worked in Paris as a journalist, writing for *L'Express*, *Réalités*, and *Le Nouveau Candide*.

Steiner's interest in Treblinka was influenced by the works of the former partisan commander Abba Kovner from Vilna (→ Partisans). In 1964, Steiner read the French translation of a lecture Kovner had given in → Hebrew before the foundation of the State of Israel to a unit of the Palmach (→ El-Alamein; → Raison d'état) in a French journal. Kovner's lecture focused on the issue of Jewish passivity during the Second World War. As one of the leaders of the armed resistance in the Vilna ghetto, Kovner had exhorted its Jewish inhabitants not to let themselves be led like lambs to the slaughter. Steiner decided to write a novel on the subject of the history of Jewish resistance. He spent several months in the Centre de documentation juive contemporaine (→ Center of Contemporary Jewish Documentation) in Paris, but it was only during another visit to Israel that he discovered the real history of the Treblinka uprising. Steiner then studied the records of the second Treblinka trial held at the Landgericht Düsseldorf in 1964/1965 and interviewed survivors in Israel. This research became the basis for his novel.

3. Steiner's novel

The first sentence of the novel states from the point of view of the auctorial narrator that the Nazis' extermination program is the background of the plot. "Since they had not succeeded in deporting all the Jews of whom they had wanted to rid their empire, the builders of the Thousand Year Reich decided to exterminate them" [5. 15].

The narrator's eye then turns to → Vilna in Lithuania (today Vilnius). For the Jews living there, he describes, the antisemitic → pogroms committed by Poles and Lithuanians were part of their existential experience. The project of planned extermination, which was adopted upon the arrival of the "Technicians of the Final Solution" in the course of the German invasion, however, went beyond their powers of imagination, as it combined the previously known irrational zeal of the antisemites with the technical rationality of the Nazis [5. 16]. Over the course of the story, the author repeatedly emphasizes the specific peculiarity of the → Holocaust, which should never be regarded as merely a part of Nazi crimes in general. In the person of the novel's narrator, he states: "When people talk about the war of 1939–1945, they confuse two wars that have absolutely nothing in common: a world war, the war Germany made on the world, and a universal war, the war of the Nazis against the Jews, the war of the principle of death against the principle of life. In their war the Jews were alone, but it could not be otherwise" [5. 216].

The peculiarity of the crime is thus the starting point from where Steiner follows Jewish behavior. From the construction of the camp through the extermination of human beings to the uprising and escape of the prisoners, the narrator describes his protagonists' thoughts and emotions, reveals the mechanisms of entanglement, and delivers moral judgments. This approach is visible for instance in the depiction of the real person of Jacob Gens, the head of the → Judenrat and police chief of the Vilna ghetto, whose authority was used by the Nazis to ensure the smooth exploitation and deportation of the ghetto inhabitants. To this end, Gens was encouraged to retain the illusion that by means of higher productivity and unconditional obedience the Jews would be able to avoid deportation. In the novel, Steiner describes the fact that Gens fell for this illusion as partially due to his self-congratulatory and authoritarian character who enjoyed being granted privileges and power.

The subject of Jewish entanglement is also discussed where Steiner describes the Treblinka camp as an incomprehensible hell, in which the German "Technicians" succeeded in turning the Jews in the Sonderkommandos into "accomplices of their own executioners" [5. 71]. Simultaneously, Steiner unfolds a panorama of human behaviors – the will to survive, resignation, hopelessness, deadening, suicide – with which members of the Sonderkommandos reacted to their monstrous position. About one of the members, Meir Berliner, who finds himself unable to act against the orders of the SS guards and give water to the thirsty and doomed prisoners on a newly arrived transport, he says:

"On that day he ceased to be a man. There was no room for men in Treblinka, either on one side or on the other. Then he learned to hide his face, not to see the blows coming, to run like a blind man, to work like a robot. His world contracted" [5. 78].

Against this tendency of dehumanization, however, the will to rise up grows in Steiner's protagonists. The author characterizes the uprising as the prisoners' attempt to recover their humanity by once more becoming agents able to decide their own fate – even if that means only the moment of their death. They are also inspired by the desire to → bear witness. Humanity must be shown that the Jews were not only resigned to their fate but that they also fought back. Steiner has one of the leaders of the uprising, Ze'ev Kurland, put this into words: "We must show the world that even in the bottom of hell man does not abdicate. We must tell of our martyrdom. Therefore it is essential that the revolt take place, that it succeed, and that there remain at least one witness to relate both the martyrdom and the supreme revolt" [5. 226].

The description of the planning and execution of the uprising conveys the message that even in the extreme conditions of an extermination camp, there were possible courses of action that might serve as examples for posterity. Here, Steiner's novel links to the controversies that had accompanied attempts at comprehending the dimension of the Holocaust, above all in Israel. In the first years after the foundation of the state, there was a distinction between honorable armed resistance on the one hand and complicity through passivity and collaboration on the other (→ Kasztner Affair; → Yad Vashem). The recollection of resistance was linked to the self-understanding of militant Zionism, while the presumed complicity was regarded as the negative consequence of the kind of Diaspora Judaism that had become accustomed to conformity and submissiveness. Steiner, too, intended to

commemorate the armed uprising with his novel. Simultaneously, his description of the dilemmas of Judenräte, ghetto police, and overseers, however, focused on the borderline situations that arose in the conditions of the extermination program systematically executed by the Nazis.

4. The Treblinka affair

Steiner's book quickly became a bestseller in France; more than 100,000 copies were sold in the first year of publication alone [12. 1]. The wide reception of the book was probably significantly promoted by the preface written by Simone de Beauvoir. First reviews, such as by Edmond Michelet and Pierre Vidal-Naquet in *Le Monde*, Pierre Daix in *Les Lettres françaises*, and François Mauriac in *Le Figaro littéraire* were extremely positive. Some reviewers had been → Résistance fighters and interned in concentration camps. In the year of publication, Steiner was awarded the prestigious *Prix littéraire de la Résistance*.

However, Steiner's fundamental theory regarding the peculiarity of the murder of the Jews had been overlooked, even in the preface in which de Beauvoir presented the difficulties of developing a stance of resistance against the Nazis as a universal challenge faced by "all peoples" in "the world of concentration camps" [2. 7]. Only a heroic attitude could have awakened the spirit of resistance against the social technology of the SS, the objective of which was segregation and dehumanization. This kind of reception could indeed be integrated with the dominating image of the Nazi era in postwar France, where until the end of the 1960s all relevant political camps were joined together under the narrative of a French nation united in its resistance against the German occupation. The → Vichy regime's collaboration with Nazi Germany and the cooperation of French police in the deportation of Jews (→ Drancy) had no place in this narrative, and neither did the Molotov–Ribbentrop Pact and the initially cooperative stance of the Communist Party. It was not the Nazi extermination camps that were seen as the symbol of the cruelty of National Socialism, but rather the → Buchenwald concentration camp, in which the inmates were nearly exclusively political prisoners, among them numerous Résistance fighters and communist anti-fascists.

The actual starting point of the Steiner affair that would exercise the public was an interview with Steiner in *Le Nouveau Candide* shortly after the publication of his novel in March 1966. The title page of the Gaullist journal provocatively featured a swastika and the headline "Les juifs: Ce qu'on n'a jamais osé dire" in large letters. In answer to the question why he wrote a further book about the death camps, Steiner said that although books about the "camp universe" had been written, hardly any had focused on extermination camps, with the result that the victims' involvement in their own extermination had not become apparent. Steiner also confessed the shame that filled him as a Jew looking at the implementation of the → Holocaust. By telling the story of Treblinka as a heroic uprising, however, he was able to overcome this sensation [12. 4–6].

By concentrating on the Jewish resistance that in his view formed in the face of the extermination program, the young author broke new ground in the French postwar debate and in some cases encountering vehement opposition. Thus, the journalist and author David Rousset, who as a former concentration camp prisoner himself had informed the perception of National Socialist camps decisively with his books *L'univers concentrationnaire* (1946; "A World Apart," 1951) and *Les jours de notre mort* (1947), criticized Steiner's emphasis on Jewish particularity in a detailed review in *Le Nouveau Candide*. To distinguish between Jewish victims and political deported, namely between extermination and concentration camp, Rousset

maintained, shook the foundations of his universalist conviction [12. 58–63]. Steiner's book was also met with protest from Jewish survivors, above all those with whom he had spoken during his research. Rachel Auerbach, an archivist with → Yad Vashem, even took legal action against the author, endeavoring to have corrections made in the novel and prevent its translation. She especially criticized that Steiner explicitly mentioned her in his afterword, giving the impression that she supported the publication. The Holocaust historian Léon Poliakov (→ Center of Contemporary Jewish Documentation) also accused the author of factual errors and flawed scholarship. In addition, Poliakov perceived an essentialist argument in the emphasis on Jewish specificity that he believed demonstrated the characteristics of mystical nationalism and bore racist connotations [4].

Having read the novel in French in 1968, the Czech Treblinka survivor Richard Glazar addressed an open letter to Steiner sent, however, to Yad Vashem. Glazar had written an account of his experiences shortly after the war (which was only published in 1992) and had been called as a witness in the second Treblinka trial. Reading the novel was a shock for him, Glazar wrote, as it stylized events in a way that did not correspond to the realities of Treblinka. Categories such as courage, shame, and cowardice, for instance, had had an entirely different meaning for the prisoners, who were closer to death than to life, than for people outside the camp [12. 137–140].

In the Federal Republic of Germany, the publication of *Treblinka*, even in 1966, did not lead to public debates. In view of the specific situation in the country of the perpetrators (→ Frankfurt Auschwitz Trial; → [The] Deputy), it was primarily Jewish survivors who commented on the topics of the French debate. Thus, the former inmate of Auschwitz Jean Améry (→ Breendonk) described Steiner's novel, independently of its factual accuracy, as a legitimate literary approach to Treblinka. The decisive factor was that the author described the "aloneness of the Jews in this war, their absolute loneliness" more clearly than anyone before him [1. 174].

The historian and Auschwitz survivor Joseph Wulf assessed the novel critically in a review for the Südwestfunk broadcasting company. While he agreed that it was a unique description presented with literary force, in his view Steiner suggested erroneously that the uprising in Treblinka was proof that resistance was possible under all circumstances. This, he argued, made the behavior of those who did not revolt seem all the more reprehensible [10. 332f.]. In 1973, taking the 30th anniversary of the uprising in Treblinka as his cue, Wulf commented on the book once more in a radio broadcast. Reinforcing his earlier deliberations, he argued that not only should an armed uprising be considered to have been resistance, but that the concept would have to be expanded to include the conditions of the ghetto as well as the concentration and extermination camps [6. 8].

5. Resonance

The actual Steiner affair in France lasted only a few months; the topics debated – the understanding of the → Holocaust within the context of the Nazi crimes and the question of the appropriateness of the way in which the Jews acted – however, had a long-term influence on the French view of history. For the first time since the liberation, the murder of the European Jews moved into the consciousness of a broader French public. Since then, the symbol of the Holocaust in France has been Treblinka and not primarily → Auschwitz.

Consequently, the Steiner affair was also the beginning of throwing light upon the French postwar myth of a nation united

in its resistance against the Nazis. Interest in the → Vichy regime and the deportation of French Jews (→ Drancy) received new impulses in May 1968 in Paris, eventually culminating in the 1969 documentary film *Le chagrin et la pitié. Chronique d'une ville française sous l'occupation* ("The Sorrow and the Pity") by Marcel Ophüls which focuses on the Vichy regime's collaboration with the German occupiers. For the first time, it was documented through numerous interviews that a considerable part of the French population not only did not take part in the resistance, as had been insinuated for decades by the Résistance myth, but had in fact been in sympathy with the Vichy regime. This introduced the period of the "miroir brisé" ("broken mirror"; Henry Rousso) in the French postwar era, that is, of the critical approach to French collaboration and the revocation of previous concepts of history.

After the debate surrounding his novel, Jean-François Steiner did not appear publicly in the French media for some time. When he made the news again in the 1990s with the problematic defense of the Vichy official Maurice Papon, he was widely criticized in view of the changed landscape of memory that had emerged not least as a result of the publication of his novel.

Bibliography

Sources

[1] J. Améry, Erlösung in der Revolte, in: Der Spiegel, November 7, 1966, 173–175. [2] S. de Beauvoir, Preface, in: J.-F. Steiner, Treblinka, trans. by H. Weaver, New York 1967, xix-xxiv. [3] R. Glazar, Trap with a Green Fence, Survival in Treblinka, trans. by R. Theobald, Evanston 1995. [4] L. Poliakov, Tréblinka. Vérité et roman, in: Preuves 183 (May 1966), 72–76. [5] J.-F. Steiner, Treblinka, trans. by H. Weaver, New York 1967. [6] J. Wulf, Vor 30 Jahren: 2. August 1943. Revolte im Konzentrationslager Treblinka, Radiobeitrag für Deutsche Welle (July 1973), Nachlass

Joseph Wulf, B 2–1, series b, nr. 954, p. 1–8, Zentralarchiv zur Erforschung der Geschichte der Juden in Deutschland, Heidelberg.

Secondary literature
[7] F. Golczewski, Polen, in: W. Benz (ed.), Dimension des Völkermords. Die Zahl der jüdischen Opfer des Nationalsozialismus, Munich 1996, 411–497. [8] R. Hilberg, The Destruction of the European Jews, 3 vols., New York 1985. [9] J. Hoffmann, "Das kann man nicht erzählen." "AKTION 1005" – Wie die Nazis die Spuren ihrer Massenmorde in Osteuropa beseitigten, Hamburg 2008. [10] K. Kempter, Joseph Wulf. Ein Historikerschicksal in Deutschland, Göttingen/Bristol (CT) 2014. [11] S. Klarsfeld, Memorial to the Jews Deported from France, 1942–1944. Documentation of the Deportation of the Victims of the Final Solution in France, New York 1993. [12] S. Moyn, A Holocaust Controversy. The Treblinka Affair in Postwar France, Waltham 2005. [13] H. Rousso, The Vichy Syndrome. History and Memory in France since 1944, trans. by A. Goldhammer, Cambridge 1991.

SEBASTIAN VOIGT, MUNICH/LEIPZIG

Trieste

From the late 18th century until the First World War, Trieste served as the most important sea access point for the Habsburg Monarchy. Due to its free port, the city developed into one of the leading trade and business centers of Europe with connections to East Asia as well as North and South America. The history of the Jews of Trieste is paradigmatic of the specific position of Port Jews, who were granted comprehensive rights in the early modern period and who were integrated into urban society to a considerable degree. With the endeavors to establish an Italian national state, nationalist tensions in Trieste increased from the second half of the 19th century onward, similar to other cosmopolitan port cities in the multinational empires (→ Salonika).

1. Free port
2. The Jewish community
3. Port Jews
4. From cosmopolitism to nationalism

1. Free port

Trieste was part of the Habsburg Empire from the late 14th century onward, providing it with access to the Mediterranean. Due to its geographical position, the city's importance for the Habsburg endeavors to expand their sphere of influence increased in the 18th century. After the military successes in the Ottoman–Venetian War (1714–1718), Charles VI (1685–1740) sought to restructure the Habsburg monarchy as a unified economic area in the course of his mercantilist politics, establishing new trade ties with the Ottoman Empire and exerting pressure on Venice which was in decline. In 1717, he declared the freedom of navigation in the Adriatic in contravention to the preceding Venetian control of shipping; vessels calling at Habsburgs ports were guaranteed the protection of the imperial navy. In 1719, he granted the status of free port to the Adriatic ports Trieste and Fiume, which exempted these cities from the usual customs duties on naval trade.

Charles VI and his successor Maria Theresa (1717–1780) remodeled the free port of Trieste into an independent economic and political unit. They had new port facilities as well as districts and streets constructed, enacted specific decrees regarding trade, and restructured the administration. The free port patents invited people "of any nation, condition, and religion" [5. 11] to settle in Trieste and engage in trade, at the same time offering protection as well as immunity regarding unlawful acts committed elsewhere. After losing Silesia to Prussia in the

War of the Austrian Succession (1740–1748), Maria Theresa increased trade on the Adriatic. In spite of her overall hostile attitude to non-Catholics, she explicitly permitted Trieste to implement a policy of tolerating non-Catholic groups of the population. The attendant status of corporations provided the legal and social framework for the settlements of Jews, Greeks, Serbian-Orthodox Christians, Protestants, and Armenians. Being "nazioni" they were granted considerable autonomy in the organization of their religious and educational institutions; their members enjoyed many of the civil and economic liberties to which Catholic merchants were entitled as well.

As a result, the small Adriatic town, which had only between 3,000 and 5,000 inhabitants around 1700, rapidly grew into a busy port city; by 1800 the population had grown to approximately 20,000 to 24,000, with a further 5,000 people having settled in the immediate outskirts. The volume of the goods handled grew considerably too, and by the mid-1780s a third of the exports from the Habsburg Empire passed through the free port. International trade and the concomitant agency, financial, and insurance businesses were the main economic sectors; on a smaller scale, manufacturing industries were also present. Magnificent new residential and office buildings, the neo-classical commodity exchange ("Borsa"), and the theatre as well as sumptuous places of worship represented the wealth of the prosperous port city. As Trieste was organized by the Habsburg authorities in cooperation with the multiethnic, multireligious, and multilingual merchant elite, there were neither guilds nor landowners nor powerful nobles who restricted the new political and economic forces.

2. The Jewish community

Jews had settled in Trieste as early as the Middle Ages. From the 13th century onward,

Jewish moneylenders (→ Money Lending) from → Ashkenaz are documented in the town. In the 16th and 17th centuries, extensive imperial → privileges were awarded to individual Jews, granting them – similar to → Court Jews – the right of settlement, protection, and unrestricted economic activity. At the beginning of the 18th century, around ten to twelve Jewish families numbering sixty to eighty people in total lived in the ghetto which had been established in 1697 but was not kept rigidly separate (→ Venice).

Free port politics brought about rapid growth of the Jewish community of Trieste in the 18th century. Most immigrants came from the dominions of Venice and → Mantua; they were joined by Ashkenazi Jews from the Habsburg Empire as well as Sephardim (→ Sepharad). In 1746, a Jewish community was officially founded, which was responsible for regulating internal Jewish concerns (→ Autonomy) and representing Jewish interests with the authorities (→ Shtadlanut). The community built a → synagogue and appointed a rabbi. By 1800, there were already four synagogues, two of which followed the → Ashkenazi and two the → Sephardic rite. In addition, religious and charitable societies had emerged. Italian was the dominant language in everyday life, in trade, and for community activities. In 1802, there were approximately 1,250 Jews living in 220 households. After their proportion of the total population had grown from approximately three percent in 1735 to five to seven percent between 1802 and 1818, Jews constituted around half of the non-Catholic population of Trieste.

The legal status of the Jews of Trieste had been decreed by Maria Theresa in a statute and a privilege in 1771, inviting Jews because of their mercantile abilities and business acumen to settle in the city. In addition, she guaranteed them unusually far-reaching economic, religious, and legal liberties. Jews, like the other inhabitants of the city, were not only permitted to engage in trade, pursue → crafts, and manage factories, but also to acquire land. Unlike most Jews in the Habsburg Empire, they were exempt from toleration tax, protection money, and humiliating identifying markers (→ Dress Regulations). Their number was not subject to restrictions, but the community was advised to keep destitute Jews out. Particularly wealthy Jews were permitted to settle outside the ghetto boundaries. Ever since the foundation of the Borsa in 1755, which also functioned as a chamber of commerce, they had held a seat and a voice there too. Out of consideration for Jewish agents, its meetings were moved from Saturday to weekdays; in the early 1780s, 14% of the members of the exchange were Jews [5. 33]. Local officials as well as the Jews of Trieste were well aware that the Jewish inhabitants of the city – as a community and as individuals – enjoyed a much more privileged status than most of their fellow believers in the Habsburg Empire or in Italy. In fact, before the 1781 → Edicts of Toleration they were almost equal to other non-Catholic merchants.

The Josephine decrees were accompanied by a new public discourse on the Jews, who were now regarded as useful and valuable subjects. The Jews of Trieste endeavored on the one hand to retain their existing privileges insofar as these went further than the policies of the Patent of Toleration. On the other hand, the positive transformation in the political climate entailed noticeable changes for them too. The ghetto was abolished in 1785. Jewish members could be elected to the board of directors of the Borsa. Jews were admitted to public schools, and the existing Jewish school became a standard school – the "Scuola Pia Normale sive Talmud Torà" – in which the state curriculum was taught in addition to Jewish religious education. Due to its modernized education system and its overall support for the Josephine legislation, the Jewish community of Trieste was considered exemplary by the followers of the → Haskalah, not least because it also supported Naphtali Herz Wessely who was under pressure for publishing the enlightened treatise → *Divre Shalom ve-Emet* (Words of Peace and Truth). In their cultural and political attitudes, the Jews of Trieste related to the comparatively liberal Italian tradition and to their role as social actors in the dynamic and cosmopolitan port city.

3. Port Jews

For the Habsburg authorities, the Tuscan free port → Livorno served as a model. In order to facilitate international trade, merchants of different origins were encouraged to settle in the city with promises of tolerance and openness. The authorities expected them to generate shared norms of behavior and a civic morality. In this way, trade and culture would be fused into a kind of secular virtue. In the 1780s, the Trieste authorities

Interior view of the Scuola Grande Synagogue in Trieste, built 1797

published an almanac containing "useful and pleasing notices for Roman Catholics, Lutherans, Calvinists, non-Uniate Greeks, Jews, Turks" living in their city, which they described as "not only tolerant, but also friendly" [5. 201]. Trieste thus embodied the reformatory potential of an absolutistic state while still acting within the framework of an estates-based corporative order.

The historiography of the late 20th century considered the history of Jewish merchants in Trieste under the topos of "Port Jews." This term was applied to Sephardic and Italian Jewish merchants who lived in dynamic early modern port cities on the Mediterranean, the Atlantic Ocean, and in the New World – Livorno, → Bordeaux, Amsterdam (→ Esnoga), → London, or → Recife. With their engagement in international maritime trade, they contributed to European expansion into overseas territories. In the mercantile milieu, Port Jews often evolved gradual, non-ideologically-charged modes of adapting to the surrounding society, benefiting from their privileged position. They thus found their own distinctive way toward acculturation and integration, which differed from that of the → court Jews or the followers of the Jewish enlightenment (→ Haskalah; → Maskilim). The connection between trade, culture, and politics in the communities and networks of the Port Jews provided them with their own road into the modern age. As Salo W. Baron (→ Jewish Social Studies) has emphasized, the lebenswelt of the Port Jews provides a concrete example for the significance of a gradual path generated by socio-economic circumstances that led from the Old Regime order of privileges to civil inclusion and, ultimately, to legal equality in modern states.

4. From cosmopolitism to nationalism

During the 19th century, Trieste developed into one of Europe's trade hubs. Jews were active as merchants, → bankers, landowners, and industrialists; they worked in the free → professions and as craftsmen (→ Crafts). The majority belonged to the bourgeoisie (→ Middle Class) and gained access to the multiethnic economic, financial, and social elite of the city. In businesses and corporations, Jews worked together with members of other population groups, especially Greeks, for instance in the large insurance companies Riunione Adriatica di Sicurità and Assicurazioni Generali founded in the early 19th century, and cultivated extensive kinship as well as business networks in Italy and the Habsburg Empire.

The Jews of Trieste received legal equality for the first time, and only temporarily, under French occupation between 1809 and 1813 and finally as a result of the Constitutional Law (→ Austrian Imperial Council) enacted after the → Austro-Hungarian Compromise of 1867. In the newly founded Italian national state (→ Risorgimento), whose development the Jews of Trieste followed closely, the emancipation of Jews had already been confirmed seven years earlier. Societal integration of the Jews of Trieste had, however, preceded their legal equality. During the last third of the 19th century, their integration displayed increasingly assimilatory characteristics (→ Assimilation). They married non-Jews (→ Marriage), turned their backs on religion, or decided to convert (→ Conversion) in greater numbers than elsewhere. Even so, the approximately 5,000 Jews were the largest non-Catholic population in the city. Full of self-confidence, the community celebrated the dedication of an impressive new → synagogue in 1912.

When Jews from Central and Eastern Europe, Hungary, the Balkans, and especially the island of Corfu immigrated, the Jewish community became increasingly diverse. Many Jews in Trieste spoke Italian and → German. Both languages were used for trade, and German was required for official administrative concerns as well. Traditionally, the Jews of Trieste were cultural intermediaries between Central Europe and Italy, between Ashkenazi, Italian, and Sephardi Jews. In 1869, the physician and writer Saul Formiggini (1807–1873) from Trieste published the first translation of Dante's *Divine Comedy* into → Hebrew (*Sefer Mar'ot Elohim*).

Cultural and national diversity contributed to the open intellectual climate of Trieste. In the early 20th century Italo Svevo (1861–1928; → Zeno) and Edoardo Weiss (1889–1970) played a significant part as intermediaries of modernist literature and → psychoanalysis from Central Europe to Italy. Essential characteristics of Jewish as well as non-Jewish Trieste of this era are portrayed in Italo Svevo's novels *Una vita* (1892; "A Life," 1963), *Senilità* (1898; "As a Man Grows Older," 1932; "Emilio's Carnival," 2001), and *La coscienza di Zeno* (1923; "Confessions of Zeno," 1930; "Zeno's Conscience," 2003).

In the late 19th century, the social and political fabric of the cosmopolitan port city gradually dissolved. At a time of industrialization and mass politics, social divisions and nationalist endeavors grew stronger. The abolition of the free port and rescission of the customs exemption in 1891 were a cesura in the economic history of Trieste. Trade and financial services in the city fell behind the transport economy and industry. Slovenes from the hinterland provided a pool of industrial workers, contributing significantly to population growth in the city. While the inhabitants had numbered 70,000 in 1869, their number had grown to 230,000 by 1910; the proportion of Jews sank to 3.2% over this period.

For primarily economic reasons, a large part of the Trieste elite were loyal to the Habsburg monarchy, while the middle class increasingly identified with Italian culture and the new Italian state. Irredentist hopes for Trieste becoming united with Italy increased negative attitudes toward Slavs generally, and against Slovenes and Croats particularly. Of the many Jews who shared these outlooks, several were prominent in local politics. From the late 19th century onward, nationalist tensions grew above all between Italians and Slovenes; anti-Slavic as well as antisemitic sentiments became important political factors.

During the First World War, nationalist tensions in Trieste increased further. After the disintegration of the Austro-Hungarian Empire, the city fell to Italy and lost its previous importance. Economic decline and its position on the border contributed to the growth of nationalist tendencies. Racist trends increased parallel to the rise of Italian Fascism and German National Socialism.

The fascist regime in Italy was supported by the majority of the middle class as well as most of the Jews in Trieste, until the race laws of 1938 essentially excluded the latter from urban life. At the time, approximately 5,400 Jews were living in the city, of whom around half subsequently emigrated. Until the capitulation of Italy, the port of Trieste was of some importance as a hub of the escape routes of persecuted Jews. After the German occupation of Northern Italy, the Operationszone Adriatisches Küstenland (Operational Zone of the Adriatic Littoral) was established in September 1943, which entailed the systematic persecution and murder of the approximately 2,300 to 2,500 Jews still remaining in Trieste. Antonio Santin, bishop of Trieste and Capodistria, protested in vain to church dignitaries and the German authorities against the anti-Jewish measures. In a suburb of Trieste, the Germans erected the Italian concentration camp and crematorium Risiera di San Sabba for the internment of political prisoners and partisans. But it also served as a holding camp for Jews. Most of the 1,200 Jews interned here were deported to extermination camps, primarily → Auschwitz. At the end of the war in May 1945, around

400 to 500 Jews remained in Trieste; by July 1945 the Jewish community had grown to approximately 900 members thanks to the return of survivors and emigrants.

Bibliography

[1] A. Ara/C. Magris, Trieste: un'identità di frontiera, Turin 1983.　[2] S. Bon, Gli ebrei a Trieste 1930–1945. Identità, persecuzione, risposte, Gorizia 2000.　[3] T. Catalan, The Ambivalence of a Port-City. The Jews of Trieste from the 19th to the 20th Century, in: Quest. Issues in Contemporary Jewish History 2 (2011), 69–98.　[4] T. Catalan, La comunità ebraica di Trieste (1781–1914). Politica, società e cultura, Trieste 2000.　[5] L. C. Dubin, The Port Jews of Habsburg Trieste. Absolutist Politics and Enlightenment Culture, Stanford 1999.　[6] L. C. Dubin, Researching Port Jews and Port Jewries. Trieste and Beyond, in: D. Cesarani (ed.), Port Jews. Jewish Communities in Cosmopolitan Maritime Trading Centres, 1550–1950, London/Portland 2002, 47–58.　[7] L. C. Dubin, "Wings on Their Feet ... and Wings on Their Head." Reflections on the Study of Port Jews, in: D. Cesarani/G. Romain (eds.), Jews and Port Cities 1590–1990. Commerce, Community and Cosmopolitanism, London 2006, 14–30.　[8] A. Dugulin (ed.), Shalom Trieste. Gli itinerari dell'ebraismo, Trieste 1998.　[9] R. Finzi et al., Storia economica e sociale di Trieste, 2 vols., Trieste 2001/03.　[10] D. Sorkin, The Port Jew. Notes Toward a Social Type, in: Journal of Jewish Studies 50 (1999) 1, 87–97.

LOIS C. DUBIN, NORTHAMPTON, MA

[The] Truce

Title of the second book by the Italian author and chemist Primo Levi (1919–1987), which describes the Odyssey-like return to Italy by the Auschwitz survivor and his slow return to a life free from hunger and fear. Metaphorically, the "truce" can be seen as a moment of relaxation, a respite from the

horrors of the concentration camp and the moral tension that brand Levi's life and writings. The word takes on its precise meaning in the context of the question dealt with in the novel: whether the Holocaust was a historical anomaly or a continuation of normal human behavior.

1. Primo Levi's journey from Auschwitz to Turin
2. Chemistry and literature
3. Resistance, deportation, concentration camp
4. Poetological Aspects
5. In the Gray Area

1. Primo Levi's journey from Auschwitz to Turin

Levi's autobiographical novel *La Tregua* ("The Truce," 2015), written in 1961/1962 and published in 1963, has always been overshadowed by his earlier novel *Se questo è un uomo* (1947; "If This is a Man," 2015), which describes his year in the Buna-Monowitz camp factually and yet humanely and is considered a masterpiece of Holocaust literature. *The Truce* deals with the period between the last "dawn command" in → Auschwitz – "*Wstawać*," Eng. "get up" – and his return to Italy, where the command recurred over and over in a "dream within another dream" [9. 397f.].

In the opening chapter of *The Truce*, Levi reminisces about the first Russian patrol that came in sight of the Auschwitz-Monowitz camp on January 27, 1945:

Four young soldiers on horseback, machine guns under their arms, proceeded warily along the road that followed the perimeter of the camp. [...] They seemed to us miraculously physical and real [...]. They didn't greet us, they didn't smile; they appeared oppressed, not only by pity but by a confused restraint, which sealed their mouths, and riveted their eyes to the mournful scene. It was a shame well-known to us, the

Primo Levi (1919–1987)

shame that inundated us after the selections and every time we had to witness or submit to an outrage: the shame that the Germans didn't know, and which the just man feels before a sin committed by another. It troubles him that it exists, that it had been irrevocably introduced into the world of things that exists, and that his goodwill availed nothing, or little, and was powerless to defend against it. [9. 216]

The arrival of the Russian soldiers and the return of this sense of shame initiates the process through which Levi becomes "human" again, although the memory of the horrors of the camp seems to preclude a return to normality.

At the end of February 1945, after a month in the new "Infectious Diseases Ward" [9. 224] in the main Auschwitz camp, Levi leaves the camp and finds himself on a transport to a Soviet transit camp in Katowice. During this transport, he meets Mordo Nahum, a Jew from Salonika, and they engage in an unequal, controversial discussion on the nature of war. In Katowice, Levi works as a nurse and writes his report, commissioned by the Red Army, on the hygienic conditions in Auschwitz together with Leonardo Debenedetti, another Italian-Jewish former camp inmate [10. 19–44]. Mid-July 1945 he sets out for Odessa with 800 Italian former prisoners (mostly prisoners of war and slave laborers) without Russian escort or sufficient supplies. The train journey across a devastated Europe, which lasted until October 19, 1945, follows a grotesque route. Initially, they travel eastward to Zhmerynka, a railroad hub in central Ukraine. Instead of heading for Odessa, the train then goes farther north, initially to Slutsk, sixty miles south of Minsk, and then to the small town of Staryya Darohi, where Levi and 1,400 Italians are housed in a huge building on the edge of a forest (the "Red House" [9. 333]). A long portion of *The Truce* deals with life in this place, the farthest from Levi's homeland of all stations of the journey. After a long trip southward to eastern Romania, the train reaches the border with Hungary on September 26. Here, Levi believes himself in Europe again, "under the wing of a civilization" for the first time [9. 388]. Passing through Budapest and Szób, on October 7 the train reaches Bratislava in Slovakia, "in view of the Beskids, the very mountains that obstructed the grim horizon of Auschwitz" [9. 390]. Now Katowice is only 200 kilometers away, and Levi recalls his apprehension that they would have to make the exhausting journey around Europe all over again. Then, the train reaches Austrian territory, where he feels as if he is "almost home" [9. 390]. But the devastation in Vienna provokes feelings of sorrow and fear, the dread of an "irreparable und ultimate evil, present everywhere, hidden like a cancer in the bowels of Europe and the world, the seed of future harm" [9. 392]. In St. Valentin, a few miles from Linz, the group leaves the train and is handed over to the Americans.

Levi's next stop after that was Munich. The feeling of having his feet on German soil for the first time – "an edge of Germany – not of Upper Silesia or Austria but of Germany itself" [9. 394]– overlaid his exhaustion with a complex state of mind, a mix of sensitivity, frustration, and tension. "It seemed to me that each one should interrogate us, read in our faces who we were, and listen humbly to our tale. But no one looked us in the eye, no one accepted the challenges; they were deaf, blind, and mute, locked in their ruins as in a fortress of deliberate ignorance" [9. 395]. After the stop in Munich, the train had 61 carriages where before it had had only 60; the new carriage was full of young Zionists from all over Eastern Europe who hoped to get to Palestine – a key event that was significant for the later novel *Se non ora quando?* (1982; "If Not Now, When?" 2015). Finally, Levi – who wanted to survive to tell the tale – arrived in Turin, his birthplace.

2. Chemistry and literature

Born on July 13, 1919, in Turin, Primo Levi's ancestors were Spanish Jews who had come to Piedmont through Provence. In 1934, he began studying at the Ginnasio-Liceo Massimo D'Azeglio, a center of Italian anti-Fascism and especially of the Italian-Jewish anti-Fascist intelligentsia, united in the → Turin Group. In his years at the D'Azeglio secondary school, Levi discovered a love for the mountains and his dual vocations of chemistry and literature. The two were connected for him in that the periodic table of chemical elements reflected his appreciation of order – an order that translates into the natural discursive form of words. He regarded chemistry as a form of linguistic communication. Levi recalled, "I was substantially a romantic, and also in chemistry it was the romantic aspect that interested me. I hope to go very far, to the point of possessing the universe, to understanding the why of things. Now I know it doesn't

exist, the why of things, at least that's what I believe" [11. 13]. This connection between his early experience and later knowledge becomes apparent in the chapter titled "On the bottom" [4. 18]in *If This is a Man*, where Levi, desperately thirsty, snaps an icicle off the window of his barracks, which is immediately snatched away from him by a bigger, stronger man. In his poor German, Levi asks "*Warum*?" The brutal response: "'*Hier ist kein warum*' (there is no why here)" [4. 25].

At the end of 1937, Levi enrolled in chemistry at the University of Turin. Here, his linguistic experience begins to take shape. In his view, chemistry was expressed in a linguistic style that he liked very much – "without useless words [...] also from a literary point of view: a definite language" [11. 19]. At the same time, Levi saw chemistry as an alchemy of language, in that the combination of heteronomous elements creates a composition that is ordered by language. Hence, the concept of a harmonious language conflicted with one of Levi's basic principles: the necessity of imperfection. Similarly, his attitude to literary language oscillated between obsessive adherence to high Italian and recognition of the presence of dialects in the spoken language. In this context, too, chemistry is crucial. Following its model, he created a linguistic palette unusual for the Italian prose of his period: every word has its place in an invisible order, creating a tension between the imperfection of spoken Italian and the perfection of the written word. Thus, writing becomes an autonomous and at the same time dedicated action that requires courage and decisiveness – a liberating experience against the background of Fascism and at the same time a lesson in patience and objectivity. Levi saw chemistry as representing the most natural opposition to the regime. He wrote in *Il sistema periodico* (1975; "The Periodic Table," 2015), "that the chemistry and physics on which we nourished ourselves were, apart from vital nourishment themselves, the antidote to fascism [...] because they were clear and distinct, at every step verifiable" [2. 787]. The importance of linguistic rigor that emanated from chemistry and his love for the subject led him to include his old textbook of practical and organic chemistry from his university days, Ludwig Gatterman's *Die Praxis des organischen Chemikers* ("Laboratory Methods of Organic Chemistry," 1934) in his personal anthology *La ricerca delle radici* (1981; "The Search for Roots," 2002). This book was also presented to him for the "chemistry examination" in Auschwitz – a grotesque entrance exam that enabled him to do laboratory work while at Buna [4. 96].

3. Resistance, deportation, concentration camp

In a manuscript added to the → Yad Vashem archive in 1960 (probably in connection with the collection of witness accounts for the upcoming → Eichmann trial) and discovered there in 2007, Levi recorded the earliest stages of his odyssey that ended with his return to Turin in October 1945:

> On 9 September 1943, along with some friends, I took refuge in the Val d'Aosta: to be specific, at BRUSSON, above St Vincent, 54 km from the regional capital. We had formed a partisan band which included a number of Jews [...] We were joined by an individual who went by the name of MEOLI and who, since he was a spy, lost no time in informing on us. With the exception of CESARE VITA, who managed to escape, we were all arrested on 13 September 1943" [1. 83f.]. In the interrogation that followed, Levi declared he was an "Italian citizen of Jewish race. [4. 10]

The fact that he emphasized his Jewish origins and not his political allegiance was undoubtedly due to fear for his life (he believed that he would be tortured and killed

as a partisan), but it also expresses the issues of self-understanding shared by many Jews who were interned and deported during the Repubblica Sociale Italiana (Fascist state in Northern Italy between September 1943 and April 1945) and the Nazi occupation.

Levi was initially taken to a camp run by the Fascist militia; in January 1944 he arrived at Fossoli di Carpi, the transit camp near Modena especially for Jews that was under the command of Italians and Germans. In February, he was deported to Auschwitz along with 650 Italian Jews, of whom only 96 men and 29 women reached the Buna-Monowitz camp and Birkenau. Compared to most of the prisoners there, the Italian Jews in → Auschwitz were unaware and helpless, "all lawyers, all university graduates, [...] who don't know how to work, and let their bread be stolen, and are hit from morning to night. The Germans call them *zwei linke Hände* (two left hands), and even the Polish Jews despise them, because they don't speak Yiddish" [4. 46]. They comprised a separate class and were thus exposed and unprotected. They also lacked the ability of, for example, the Greek Jews of dealing with discrimination and "of knowing how to get by in all circumstances" [9. 240]. The Italian Jews were utterly predestined to become "Muselmänner," downtrodden prisoners whose will to live had become enfeebled and whose selection was immediately impending. Levi later called these the true witnesses in whose name he, the survivor, told the story. His description of the *Muselmänner* is legendary:

> The easiest thing is to succumb: one has only to carry out all the orders one receives, eat only the ration, stick to the discipline of the work and the camp. Experience proved that very rarely could one survive more than three months in this way. All the Muselmänner who go to the gas chambers have the same story, or, more exactly, have no story. [...] Once they entered the camp,

they were overwhelmed either through basic incapacity, or through misfortune, or through some banal incident, before they could adapt; they are beaten by time, they do not begin to learn German and to untangle the fiendish knot of laws and prohibitions until their body is already breaking down, and nothing can save them from selection or from death by exhaustion. Their life is short, but their number is endless; they, the Muselmänner, the drowned, form the backbone of the camp, an anonymous mass, continually renewed and always the same, of non-men who march and labor in silence, the divine spark dead within them, already too empty to truly suffer. One hesitates to call them living; one hesitates to call their death death – in the face of it they have no fear, because they are too tired to understand. [4. 85]

Levi survived the camp due to a fortunate series of events: first and foremost, as a chemist he could work in the Buna laboratories instead of being set to labor outside in the much harsher conditions. He was sick with scarlet fever in the infirmary in January 1945 and so avoided the death marches. But it was not only through the working conditions that chemistry saved Levi from death. He saw his education in literature and chemistry as crucial to his survival, as it enabled him to view the camp as "a gigantic biological and social experiment" [4. 82]. In conversation with Philip Roth, Levi recalled: "I remember having lived my Auschwitz year in a condition of exceptional spiritedness," brought on by what some later commentators considered cynical "curiosity of the naturalist who finds himself transplanted into an environment that is monstrous, but new, monstrously new" [7. 17]. In the camp, the function of education and knowledge changed: they acquired the character of sublimation, of being saved from the horror through recognition of human suffering. As

late as 1986, he recollected that his education "saved" him in Auschwitz [3. 1512].

4. Poetological Aspects

In Levi's first book, *Se questo è un uomo*, the adverb "quivi" (there, then) appears several times – an allusion to Dante's Inferno. Placing Dante in Auschwitz represents an attempt on the part of the author to impose order on the chaos and nothingness of the camp through language. Dante is explicitly mentioned once, in the chapter titled "The canto of Ulysses" [4. 106]. Levi tries to explain a verse from Dante's *Divine Comedy* to his fellow inmate Jean, understanding the words themselves in their full meaning for the first time: "Consider well the seed that gave you birth: / you were not made to live your lives as brutes, / but to be followers of worth and knowledge" [4. 108]. In the midst of the horrors of Auschwitz, the lines seem to him "like the voice of God. For a moment I forget who I am and where I am" [4. 108]. This "quivi" registers that in the "perpetual Babel" of Auschwitz, "in which everyone shouts orders and threats in languages never heard before" [4. 34]; the word is not dead. Levi devotes himself to writing not only to narrate but also to restore communication, as if to prove that unclear writing is by no means a faithful expression of a constitutive ambiguity in human consciousness to which we are "condemned" [8. 2062]. In his article "On Obscure Writing" [8. 29–36], one of the most important documents of his poetology, he rejects the "obscure" language of the heart not because of a particular aesthetic but based on the idea that each individual has his own language of the heart, which, however, is "not a language at all," but "at most we can call it a vernacular, an argot, if not an individual invention"; hence, whoever writes in that language of the heart risks to be "understood by no one." Writing, according to Levi, serves to communicate and transmit information and sensations and includes the task of getting one's ideas across to the reader. Any writing that is incomprehensible "transmits nothing, is only a voice crying in the wilderness" [8. 2062–2063].

This affirmation of clarity is extremely important for understanding Levi's poetics. He wants to tell the story and at the same time experiences the fear of telling it, a fear that was already present in the camp. This is connected with the difficulty for survivors to believe that what happened in the camps really happened, which extends to a fear of returning to the civilized world, telling the story, and not being believed. Levi begins to write in order to shed light on an experience both for himself and for others, and he undertook the project with the conviction of a scientist exploring the possibilities of literary writing. The same poetological conception is true of Levi's poetry, which is published in *Ad ora incerta* ("Collected Poems," 1984). In an interview with Giulio Nascimbeni, recalling Adorno's dictum that it was impossible to compose poetry after Auschwitz, he asserts that his own experience – especially in 1945/1946, when he wrote his first works – was different: "[I]t seemed to me that poetry was more suitable than prose to express what weighed inside me. [...] In those years, if anything, I would have reformulated Adorno's words: after Auschwitz there can be poetry only about Auschwitz" ([6. 136f.]; cited in [6a. liii]).

The short stories, 20 of which Levi initially published under the pseudonym Damiano Malabaila as *Storie naturali* (1966; "The Sixth Day and Other Tales," 1990), express the tension between self-understanding as an author and the antiliterary attitude of a witness and scientist. By means of a change in genre, they pull the author away from a topic too close to his memories and emotions, for him to eventually be able to write about it again. The urge to explore his own literary potential ultimately led him to write his novel *Se non ora, quando?*, in which for the first time he turns to a decidedly Jewish subject matter. "I had made a sort of bet with myself," he explained in 1986 in conversation with Philip Roth: "after so much plain or disguised autobiography, are you, or are you not, a fully-fledged writer, capable of constructing a novel, shaping characters, describing landscapes you have never seen? Try it!"(cited in [12. 337]). Thematically, the book is based on the history of Jewish partisans in Belarus and the history of young Zionists on their way to Palestine like the ones he encountered on the train to Italy in 1945. To better understand the world of the Jews of Eastern Europe, which he found fascinating, Levi learned Yiddish and read accounts of the Jewish partisans in the original. The novel is also permeated with quotations from the foundational texts of Judaism, so that it can indeed be described as Levi's "Returning to Jewish Roots" [12. 337–355]. Israel, the partisans' destination, remains an idealized land – a land, as Levi explains, that does not exist in reality. His attitude toward the real Jewish state remained ambivalent.

5. In the Gray Area

In 1986, *I sommersi e i salvati* ("The Drowned and the Saved," 2015) appeared, the last book published during Levi's lifetime. It is an ethical reflection on human nature in view of his experience in the camp – a quiet and defiant dialogue with the condemned and an open and relentless one with the saved. There is a terrible, pervasive doubt due to the unclear line that Levi crossed as a victim and a survivor. The knowledge of this crossing is connected with shame, a complicity with the perpetrators for having become a witness to an unprecedented act of violence; he felt as though he was contaminated, which causes the ethical demarcation line between perpetrators and victims to disappear.

This reflective approach leads him to devote an entire chapter of the book to the "grey area" of collaboration between perpetrators and victims, of which the "Judenältester" ("Jewish Elder") in the ghetto of → Łódź, Chaim Rumkowski, was the most striking example (→ Judenrat). Levi writes: "Like Rumkowski, we, too, are so blinded by power and prestige that we forget our basic fragility. We make our deals with power, willingly or not, forgetting that we are all in the ghetto, that the ghetto is walled in, that outside the wall are the lords of death, and that not far away a train is waiting" [3. 2456]. The recapitulation that unfolds in the book, sustained by the hope of a real and lasting truce and with the awareness of a perpetually continuing war, in many ways builds on the encounter with the fierce Mordo Nahum, the strong and wild Greek, one of the central characters in *The Truce*. It is Mordo Nahum who wins the struggle. With merciless realism, he reminds Levi that actually there is no truce, but, to the contrary, "there is always war" [9. 251]. "'But the war is over', I objected; and I thought it was over, like many in those months of truce, in a more universal sense than one dares to think today. 'There is always war', Mordo Nahum answered, memorably" [9. 250]. Both of them were in the concentration camp, but whereas Levi initially "perceived it as a monstrous distortion, an ugly anomaly of my history and the history of the world" for the Greek, it was "a sad confirmation of well-known things" [9. 251]. The two positions recur regularly in Primo Levi's works, with great importance given to the voice of Mordo Nahum. Shortly after completing *The Truce*, Levi initially contemplated concluding the subject of Auschwitz; he believed that he had said everything there was to say about it. But the persistence of the memories made him reconsider Mordo's words after he had obviously tried to forget their meaning. In his poem "Partisans" (1981), Levi returns yet again to this subject as he calls resistance fighters to partake in new struggles: "Rise and stand, old men, your own worst enemies: / Our war is never over." [5. 1942].

The persistence of this subject in Levi's writings sheds light on the ending of *The Truce*. When he arrives home from his odyssey through Europe, he finds his family and friends, "the warmth of secure meals, the concreteness of daily work, the liberating joy of recounting" and a clean bed [9. 397]. In the months that follow, he slowly loses the habit of keeping his eyes on the ground when he walks and of looking out for food to hide or trade. Only a dream within a dream does not stop haunting him:

> I am at the table with my family, or friends, or at work, or in a verdant countryside – in a serene, relaxed setting, in other words, apparently without tension and pain – and yet I feel a subtle, profound anguish; the definite sensation of a looming threat. [...] Everything has now turned into chaos; I am alone at the center of a gray and murky void, and, yes, I *know* what this means, and I also know that I have always known it. I am again in the Lager, and nothing outside the Lager was true. The rest was a brief holiday, or a trick of the senses, a dream: the family, nature in flower, the house. Now this internal dream, the dream of peace, is over, and in the external dream, which continues coldly, I hear the sound of a well-known voice: a single word, not imperious, but brief and subdued. It is the dawn command of Auschwitz, a foreign word, feared and expected: get up, "*Wstawać.*" [9. 397–398]

Levi died on April 11, 1987. His unexplained fall from the third floor of his house was probably suicide. It appears that for Levi, too, despite all his literary efforts, the war never came to an end.

Bibliography

Sources

[1] P. Levi, Deposition for the Eichman Trial 1960, in: P.Levi/L. De Benedetti, Auschwitz Testimonies. 1945–1986, trans. by J. Woolf, Cambridge, UK/Medford, MA 2018, 83–86. [2] P. Levi, The Periodic Table, trans. by A. Goldstein, in: The Complete Works of Primo Levi, vol. II, New York/London 2015, 749–946. [3] P. Levi, The Drowned and the Saved, trans. by M. F. Moore, in: The Complete Works of Primo Levi, vol. III, New York/London 2015, 2405–2574. [4] P. Levi, If This Is a Man, trans. by S. Woolf, in: The Complete Works of Primo Levi, vol. I, New York/London 2015, 1–166. [5] P. Levi, Collected Poems, trans. by J. Galassi, in: The Complete Works of Primo Levi, vol. III, New York/ London 2015, 1865–2007. [6] P. Levi, Conversazioni e interviste 1963–1987, ed. by M. Belpoliti, Turin 1997. [6a] E. Ferrero, Chronology in: P. Levi, The Complete Works of Primo Levi, vol. I, New York/London 2015, xxv–lviii. [7] P. Levi, The Voice of Memory, trans. by M. Belpoliti/R. Gordon, Cambridge 2001. [8] P. Levi, Other People's Trades, trans. by A. Shugaar, in: The Complete Works of Primo Levi, vol. III, New York/London 2015, 2009–2255. [9] P. Levi, The Truce, trans. by A. Goldstein, in: The Complete Works of Primo Levi, vol. I, New York/London 2015, 207–398. [10] P. Levi/L. De Benedetti, Auschwitz Testimonies: 1945–1986, trans. by J. Woolf, Cambridge 2017. [11] P. Levi/T. Regge, Dialogo, trans. by R. Rosenthal, Princeton 1989.

Secondary literature

[12] M. Anissimov, Primo Levi. Tragedy of an Optimist, trans. by S. Cox, London 1998. [13] C. Cases, L'ordine delle cose e l'ordine delle parole, in: P. Levi, Opere, vol. 1, ed. by C. Cases/E. Ferrero, Turin 1993, IX–XXXI. [14] M. Consonni, Primo Levi, Robert Antelme, and the Body of the Muselmann, in: Partial Answers. Journal of Literature and the History of Ideas 2 (2009) 7, 243–259. [15] J. Farrell (ed.), Primo Levi. The Austere Humanist, Frankfurt am Main 2004.

MANUELA CONSONNI, JERUSALEM

Tsaddik

Since the late 18th century, it has become customary to refer to a charismatic Hasidic personality as *tsaddik* (lit. "righteous one"). According to the beliefs of the founder of → Hasidism, Israel ben Eliezer, the Ba'al Shem Tov (ca. 1700–1760), a tsaddik possessed special magical and spiritual powers which benefited his respective followers. Indeed the figure of the tsaddik gradually took on responsibilities and abilities ascribed to very diverse Jewish religious authorities in Eastern Europe.

1. Purpose
2. The court of the tsaddik

1. Purpose

The Hebrew word *tsaddik* (derived from *tsedek*, righteousness) originally referred to a person who is "righteous" in the sense of "pious." Such righteous personalities already appeared in rabbinic literature; one tradition (Talmud Bavli, Sanhedrin 97b) holds that every generation comprises 36 "hidden tsaddikim" (*tsaddikim nistarim*), whose efforts support the world and hasten redemption. According to the classic Kabbalistic interpretation of the world (Zohar I, 148b; → Mysticism), the tsaddik is a metaphor for *Yesod* (foundation), one of the ten divine emanations (*sefirot*). His task is to draw the flow of divine blessing down to earth. The followers of → Hasidism, the popular religious and mystical movement emerging in 18th-century Eastern Europe, agreed with this interpretation to a large extent.

In contrast to traditional rabbinic literature, the Hasidim (lit. "the pious") did not consider the tsaddik's obscurity a mark of his true power but the revelation of his work. Not only was he able to draw the flow of divine blessing down to earth but also to "penetrate" and reshape the material world that surrounds him. To the Hasidic tsaddik as a real, living person they accorded the spiritual rank of an ancient Biblical priest, king, prophet, or philosopher. Consequently, the tsaddikim assumed a regal demeanor, claimed prophetic status, and declared themselves the sole infallible interpreters of the Holy Scriptures (→ Tanakh). In Hasidic beliefs, these individuals were endowed with magical powers, among which were those of the cleansing of souls and the healing of the sick. In principle any person, male or female, regardless of their sinfulness or their social status, could attain superior spiritual skills, provided they joined such a tsaddik - who would be addressed by his followers as *rebbe* (Yidd.; master, teacher).

The movement founded by Israel ben Eliʿezer Baʿal Shem Tov (ca. 1700–1760; also known by the acronym of his name, "Besht") was indeed attractive to large numbers of uneducated Jews. He and his disciples adopted many ideas of the elitist Kabbalah (→ Mysticism) but not without radically simplifying them. They also discarded the Kabbalistic obligation to adopt an ascetic lifestyle. The Hasidic rebbe was not a traditional rabbi but an entirely new type of religious leader. Because of the magical powers ascribed to him he was most directly reminiscent of the miracle worker Baʿal Shem (Hebr. for "He who knows the [divine] name"; → Baʿal Shem); at the same time he also functioned as preacher (*maggid*; → Sermon), judge (*dayan*; → Bet din), and scholarly exegete (*rav/rabbi*; → Rabbinate) for his followers. His particular gift was the ability to enter into a close rapport (*devekut*; lit. "to attach"; derived from this "devotion")

with God by means of religious rituals but also through seemingly secular activities.

Besht's successor was his foremost disciple, Dov Ber (ca. 1704–1772) of Mezeritch (Międzyrzecz, today in Ukraine), also called "the Great Maggid." Dov Ber occasionally used the term *tsaddik* to distinguish Hasidic personalities from medieval mystics who had conducted their studies and their teaching in private or exclusively among their small circle of disciples. In his interpretation of Psalm 92:13 ("The righteous [*tsaddikim*] bloom like a date-palm; they thrive like a cedar in Lebanon"), he compared the cedar to the *tsaddik* of past generations, whose "justice [had] no influence on others" and who therefore would "not bear fruit," while the new Hasidic tsaddik "flourished like a palm tree," because he led sinners to repentance (→ Teshuvah) and thus enabled "the good to flourish and to spread in the world [...] and his reward will be immeasurably greater than that of the aforementioned *tsaddik* of earlier times" (Or Torah, 87; cf. Zohar, I:82a).

Another disciple, the Kabbalist Jacob Joseph (1710–1784) of Polonoye (today Polonne, Ukraine), wrote the first ever Hasidic book, *Toldot Yaʾakov Yosef* (1780; Story of Jacob Joseph), in which he used the term *tsaddik* to refer to a "true" spiritual leader whose sympathies lay with the uneducated Jews. Joseph distinguished the Hasidic tsaddik from the leading rabbinic voices, studious but arrogant, whom he described as "Jewish demons" and who, in his opinion, were ignoring the needs of the common people. Jacob Joseph sometimes likened members of Besht's inner circle to biblical heroes. For Hasidic Jews to follow a tsaddik unconditionally was of the greatest importance, as exemplified in the "devotion" shown by the Israelites toward Moses.

Elimelech (1717–1786) of Lizhensk (today Leżajsk, Poland), another Besht disciple, was the first Hasidic thinker to develop a tsaddik doctrine in his principal work *No'am Elimelekh* (The Grace of Elimelech, 1788): despite being mortal, the state of *devekut* meant that the tsaddik was at one with the divine to such an extent that he attained magical powers. With these powers he was able to heal the sick and even bring the dead back to life. Elimelech also referenced Lurianic Kabbalah (16th century), and in particular its concept of divine sparks which permeate the material world. He explained that the tsaddik had to release or redeem the fallen holy sparks – paradoxically – by pursuing earthly affairs. Recalling the ideas of Sabbatianism (→ Smyrna), Elimelech taught that the tsaddik had to "descend" in order to "join and become one with the common people before leading the way for them, ultimately, to the holiness above" (*No'am Elimelekh*, Balak). Notwithstanding his doctrine that a tsaddik must sin occasionally in order to redeem ordinary people, Elimelech and other tsaddikim affirmed the validity of the religious law (→ Halakhah). Even though Elimelech bestowed on his tsaddik a royal-messianic component, neither he nor his successors developed him into a fully formed Messiah (→ Messianism).

The first Hasidic rebbe to be pronounced tsaddik after his death was probably the Besht disciple Yechiel Michel (ca. 1731–1786) of Zlotshov (Yidd. for Złoczów; today Zolochiv, Ukraine). Subsequently the title was conferred on every Hasid who gained a following. Contrasting with the declared sympathy for the uneducated and the common people, most tsaddikim did have a traditional education (→ Talmud Torah), wealth, and a prestigious rabbinic ancestry (*yiḥus*). In homiletic → sermons, which they gave during the gathering known as the "Third Meal" (*se'udah shlishit*) on the → Shabbat and which the pupils would often write down from memory later that same night, the tsaddikim discussed their own ideas about the tsaddik. They paid particular attention to the "worship through corporeality" (*avodah be-gashmiyut*): according to the latter, the tsaddik could draw holiness from profane, albeit theoretically permissible actions such as eating, consuming alcohol, telling stories, singing folk songs, or dancing. Only in the 19th century did Hasidic tsaddikim begin to warn against the "worship through physical engagement" on account of its antinomic aspects.

A great-grandson of the Besht, Naḥman of Bratslav (Breslov; 1772–1810), developed a radical tsaddik ideology which allowed for only one true and quasi-messianic tsaddik. Rabbi Naḥman claimed this title for himself, so that after his death the Hasidim of Bratslav never conferred it to any of his successors. Today his tomb in Uman (today Ukraine; → Hasidism) draws thousands of pilgrims every year at Rosh ha-Shanah (→ Course of the Year).

2. The court of the tsaddik

In keeping with the later Hasidic concept of the tsaddik as the incarnation of a Biblical king, the tsaddikim made an effort to cultivate an aristocratic demeanor; however in the Polish regions, to begin with, the constitution was opposed to an absolutist model of domination. Dynastic succession – where a son or a favorite disciple inherited the title – could not take root among Polish Hasidim until the latter half of the 19th century when the Kingdom of Poland had effectively been absorbed into the empires of Russia or Austria. Here, the tsaddikim defended the founding and maintenance of their prayer houses and courts by citing the prescription of toleration guaranteed in the Polish constitution. The comparatively advanced pace of urbanization and industrialization in the the Kingdom of Poland moreover enabled the emergence of a Jewish mercantile elite, some of whom also lent their financial support to the tsaddikim. Several prominent Polish tsaddikim, such as Simḥah Bunem of Pshiskhe (Przysucha; 1765–1827), his disciple

Menachem Mendel (1787–1859) of Kotzk (today Kock, Poland), Isaac (Yitzchak) Me'ir Alter (ca. 1789–1866) of Ger (today Góra Kalwaria, Poland), and Israel (Yitzchok) Kalish (1779–1848) of Warka (Yidd.; Vurke, Poland) had themselves been merchants, the latter having also served as advocate for his community (→ Shtadtlanut). Their worldliness and intimate contacts with different social circles produced a more urbane, more cosmopolitan, and politically versatile → Hasidism [12. iii].

In Ukraine, Belarus, and Galicia the tsaddikim, in their large, ostentatious houses, imitated the courtly life of the monarchs. Israel Friedman (1796–1850) of Rushin (today Ruzhyn, Ukraine) surpassed all tsaddikim with his grandiose royalism. Friedman prided himself on his descent from the Maggid of Mezeritch but had very little education otherwise and may have been semiliterate at best. Friedman resided in palatial buildings and, among other things, maintained a klezmer band to accompany his magnificent processions.

The courts attracted a great number of pilgrims who sought the help of the tsaddik with petitionary letters (Yidd. *kvitlekh*), whom they rewarded with a "ransom payment" (Hebr. *pidyon*). Indeed, for many Hasidim the courts of the tsaddikim offered completely new experiences: those who had struggled to connect with the unapproachable Talmud authorities found a new spiritual directness at the court of the tsaddik. Women unable to conceive, young people suffering from depression, tradesmen seeking business advice as well as the poor always found a willing listener in the tsaddik. Attending to the mundane needs of their followers, however, meant that the tsaddikim had to, at the same time, descend from the elevated state of *devekut*; apparently they accomplished this reversion in the spirit of sacrifice and generosity. With their magical or theurgic rituals they knew how to support the pilgrims in achieving their desired outcomes.

Not only was the tsaddik an expert in the transcendental, but as a teacher, healer, miracle worker, moral authority, and personal counsel he also embodied a thoroughly secular authority. In regions where the tsaddikim were able to win a large following, the tsaddik also appointed important local officials such as the judge (→ Bet din), the kosher butcher (→ Sheḥitah), the → cantor, and the ḥeder teacher (→ Talmud Torah), as well as attendants of the synagogue and even the bathing house (→ Mikveh). Vagrant religious officials such as the → Ba'al Shem or the preacher (*maggid*), whose services were in part paid for by the Jewish communities themselves (→ Kahal), could be dismissed by the tsaddikim. The function of the traditional rabbi in such communities was largely limited to rulings on halakhic regulations (→ Halakhah). Apart from theological objections, it was this fusion and subversion of traditional offices, in particular, which drew the sharp criticism of the non-Hasidic authorities.

The challenge posed by → secularization prompted a quietistic, apolitical response from most tsaddikim. Exceptions were two tsaddikim who pursued a populist political agenda: Yehoshua Rokeach (1825–1894), youngest son and successor of the Belz Rebbe Sholom Rokeach (ca. 1780–1855), who in 1879 – together with others – founded the *Mahzike ha-Dat* (Supporters of the Faith) organization, which took up the defense of → ultra-Orthodox interests in Galicia. The Ger tsaddik Avraham Mordechai Alter (1866–1948) very successfully backed the Polish branch, established in 1916, of the ultra-Orthodox political party *Agudat Yisra'el* (Union of Israel, abbrev. *Agudah*; → Bais Ya'akov). The party was able to send delegates to the → Sejm and the Senate and had members in Polish municipal councils as well as in Jewish communities. In 1919 two of the eleven elected Jewish deputies in the Sejm were members of *Agudah*; in 1922 *Agudah* held six of 35 seats.

Although the tsaddikim endeavored to accommodate the needs of the Jewish population and sought to establish a broad Hasidic movement, they were in no way democratically minded. Nor did they set their followers on a path to a level of education corresponding to their own, for example through years of in-depth studies, let alone ensure a comparable social status by promoting the economic activities of their followers. Their populism nevertheless posed a direct challenge to the exclusivity so blatantly cultivated by the traditional authorities. The Orthodox opposition against the tsaddikim arose in three waves. As the most distinguished voice of the *mitnaggdim* (Hebr.; "opponents"), the eminent scholar Elijah ben Solomon (1720–1797), also known as the → Vilna Gaon, reacted to the first Hasidic *minyan* in Vilnius by issuing a → ban in 1772 against the Hasidim. The second wave arose in 1781 after the publication of *Toldot Ya'akov Yosef*. The third was ignited by Shneur Zalman of Liady (1745–1812/1813). His *Sefer ha-Tanya* (Book of Learning, 1796) became the key document of Chabad Hasidism, and the debate over the book lasted well into the 19th century (→ Megalle Temirin). Numerous bans and epistles accompanied the waves of opposition and expressed the non-Hasidic Orthodox objections against Hasidic concepts and practices such as kosher butchering with specially sharpened knives. Many accusations were also leveled directly against the tsaddikim, in particular their alleged avarice, their excesses, alcohol abuse, and exploitation of gullible women. Because many of their opponents had previously been driven from office by a tsaddik, these accusations had more to do with the accuser's loss of power, influence, and status than any basis in factual reality.

Bibliography

Sources

[1] Dov Ber of Mezhirech, Sefer Or Torah, Korets 1804. [2] Nachman of Bratslav, Rabbi Nachman's Stories, trans. by A. Kaplan, Jerusalem 1983. [3] Nachman of Bratslav, Likutei Moharan, New York 1957. [3b] Y. S. Klein, Sunlight of Redemption. An Illuminated Path Toward Inner Freedom - Rebbe Nachman Of Breslov's Likutei Moharan: Lesson One, Nanuet 2019. [3c] Integral online translation: https://www.sefaria.org/Likutei_Moharan

Secondary literature

[4] D. Assaf, The Regal Way. The Life and Times of Rabbi Israel of Ruzhin, Stanford 2002. [5] S. Brody, "Open to Me the Gates of Righteousness." The Pursuit of Holiness and Non-Duality in Early Hasidic Teaching, in: Jewish Quarterly Review 89 (1998) 1/2, 3–44. [6] G. Dynner, Men of Silk. The Hasidic Conquest of Polish Jewish Society, New York 2006. [7] S. Galley, Der Gerechte ist das Fundament der Welt. Jüdische Heiligenlegenden aus dem Umfeld des Chassidismus, Wiesbaden 2003. [8] A. Green, Tormented Master. A Life of Rabbi Nahman of Bratslav, Tuscaloosa 1979 ([2]1992). [9] A. Green, Typologies of Leadership and the Hasidic Zaddiq, in: A. Green (ed.), Jewish Spirituality II, New York 1987, 127–156. [10] G. Hundert (ed.), Essential Papers on Hasidism, New York 1991. [11] N. Lamm, The Religious Thought of Hasidism. Text and Commentary, New York 1999. [12] M. Unger, A Fire Burns in Kotsk. A Tale of Hasidism in the Kingdom of Poland, Detroit 2015. [13] E. Wolfson, Open Secret. Postmessianic Messianism and the Mystical Revision of Menahem Mendel Schneerson, New York 2009.

GLENN DYNNER, NEW YORK

Tsedakah

From the earliest stages in the development of rabbinic Judaism down to the present day, *tsedakah* has stood for Jewish poor relief and charity. If the word itself originally meant "justice," "merit," or "charity" in the Hebrew Bible, in the 2nd century BCE the focus began to shift heavily toward almsgiving. While charity has always been a religious commandment, its practices have been subject to continual change. The modern era has seen a widening of the concept, and *tsedakah* now embraces the imperative to promote universal social justice.

1. Bible
2. Charity in rabbinic Judaism
3. Middle Ages and early modern period
4. Modern period

1. Bible

In the Hebrew Bible (→ Tanakh), the noun *tsedakah* occurs 86 times; it signifies a religious merit earned for pleasing God. Thus in Genesis 15:6 we read: "And he put his trust in יהוה [Jehovah], who reckoned it to his merit." Frequently (23 times) *tsedakah* is paired with *mishpat* (law) for exemplary behavior, as in Genesis 18:19: "doing what is just and right."

The meaning of *tsedakah* as "almsgiving" has a more recent origin and is derived from the related Aramaic word *tsidka* ("righteous deed"; "charity") in the context of showing mercy to the poor (Dan 4:24). The Pentateuch still treats the subject of poor relief without using the term *tsedakah* by naming specific practices: the Covenant Code (Exod 21–23) prohibits the ill-treatment of strangers, widows, or orphans, and warns lenders not to exact usurious interest from the poor. One of the commandments of the Deuteronomic Code obligates Jews to donate the tithe (Hebr. *ma'aser*) of every third year for Levites, strangers, orphans, and widows (Deut 14:27–29; 26:12–15). In the Proverbs of Solomon, the admonition to be generous to the poor often comes with an appeal to be compassionate and merciful; he who shows compassion to the poor makes a "loan" to God (Prov 19:17) that God will repay.

The exact point in time at which *tsedakah* took on the meaning of giving alms is impossible to determine, but the evidence in Daniel, Sirach, and Tobit suggests that the shift occurred around the 2nd century BCE.

2. Charity in rabbinic Judaism

In rabbinic Judaism the concept of *tsedakah* as almsgiving was already fully formed, even though the term itself was initially scarcely used. The Tannaitic rabbis who were active in Palestine during the 2nd century (*tanna'im*: repeaters of the [Biblical] teachings) thus largely avoided mentioning *tsedakah* with that connotation in their halakhic writings. The Mishnah (→ Talmud) contains only two occurrences as *gabbai tsedakah* (*tsedakah* collector; Demai 3:1; Kiddushin 4:5). In the tractate *Pe'ah* on the laws concerning gifts to the poor, the phrase *matnot aniyim* (gifts to the poor) is used in place of *tsedakah*, paralleling *matnot kehunah* (priestly gifts), which is itself a reference to the usage in Leviticus and Deuteronomy. This semantic pattern emphasizes the parity of God's care for priests and the poor, neither of whom owned land from which they could have benefitted.

Beyond the contribution of the agricultural harvest, the Tannaitic rabbis provided new ways of caring for the poor. Thus an itinerant needy person, who arrives at a Jewish settlement, is to receive a loaf of bread worth one *dupondium* (Roman coin). If a poor person spends the night, the community is obliged to give him shelter; if he stays over → Shabbat, he is entitled to three meals (Mishnah Pe'ah 8:7). Clearly such acts of charity were to be provided by the community, which would explain the rule that a beggar going from door to door shall not receive any (additional) gifts (Tosefta Pe'ah 4:8). Mishnah and Tosefta distinguish two forms of community support, named after the vessels for the donations: *kuppah* (lit. "basket") described the money for the poor collected from community members every Friday, but the daily food donations for the needy were called *tamḥui* (lit. "bowl"). Depending on the degree of distress, the person in need was to receive both *kuppah* and *tamḥui*, but also produce or clothes (Mishnah Pe'ah 8:7, 8:8f.). The texts moreover specified which items of value among his possessions, if possessions there were, a poor person had to dispose of before he became eligible to receive help (Mishnah Pe'ah 8:8; Tosefta Pe'ah 4:11).

Alms were collected by community officers, *gabbai tsedakah*. The Mishnah does not state that only rabbis may hold the office, or that the *gabbai* alone can collect and distribute *kuppah* and *tamḥui*. While he probably did perform these duties himself at times, he had the *parnas* (provider, administrator) to assist him as the official in charge of poor relief. Like the *gabbai*, the *parnas* was not required to represent the halakhic authority of a rabbi; rather, he sometimes administered private properties or looked after economic interests involving more than one community [7. 564–569]. In towns with Jewish and non-Jewish inhabitants, *parnasim* were to collect contributions for the poor from both populations to support those in need and to "keep the peace" (Tosefta Gittin 3:13).

The Tannaim were succeeded by the Amoraim ("speakers," or commentators, of the Tannaim), whose key works included the Babylonian (*Bavli*) and the Palestinian (*Yerushalmi*) → Talmud. The Amoraim adopted and expanded the Tannaitic guidelines. Their halakhic literature (→ Halakhah)

discusses *tsedakah* and *mitsvah* ("duty"; → Mitsvot), along with other good deeds, under the heading of *zekhe imi* ("gain merit through me," or "give me alms"), and usually they are considered a form of "charity." For the authors of the *Yerushalmi* the *mitsvah* is more often associated with money for charitable causes, while *tsedakah* in particular evokes the concept of charity.

Unlike the Tannaim, the Palestinian Amoraim seem to have been actively involved in the collection and distribution of alms. They also seldom mentioned the *gabbai tsedakah* but invoked all the more frequently the *parnas* and his social functions (Yerushalmi, Pe'ah 8:7, 8:9). By so doing, the office of the *gabbai* clearly lost esteem: while the Mishnah conveys a positive image, the Palestinian Amoraic literature preserves critical depictions, possibly because of rivalries with the non-rabbinic form of poor relief. The → midrash *Leviticus Rabbah* 30:1 likens the *gabbai* to an "oppressor."

The Babylonian Talmud, however, favors the word *tsedakah* for poor relief over *mitsvah* or *zekhe imi*. Babylonian-Amoraim collectors and distributors of alms differed from the Palestinian *gabba'im* in that they alone held the office and, as a result, also controlled it. Giving alms was no longer viewed as a voluntary act; it could be "enforced" (Bava Batra 8b) or "imposed" (Megillah 27a–b). While the Palestinian Amoraim approved of direct poor relief, the Babylonian Amoraic rabbis preferred the anonymous giving already mentioned in the Mishnah (Ketubbot 67b; Bava Batra 10a–b).

Rabbinic literature also set the type and amount of alms to be given. In the *Bavli* (Ketubbot 50a) one finds the annual maximum of charitable donations set at 20% of one's yearly income, as previously mentioned in the *Yerushalmi*. Women without any income of their own, or very little, are mainly noted as food donors (Ketubbot 67b). Collectors of donations were therefore reminded not to ask women for money and, at most, only to accept a "small" offering (Bava Kamma 119a).

3. Middle Ages and early modern period

Under the heads of the Babylonian Talmud academies from the late 6th to the 11th century, the *ge'onim* (sing. *ga'on*), the *Bavli* gradually attained its central significance. Charitable practices in medieval Jewish communities, however, did not strictly abide by the Talmudic commandments but were first and foremost based on local community structures and local needs, which shaped the organization of poor relief.

In Cairo (Fustat) during the "classical" → genizah period from ca. 970 to ca. 1250, private charity was practiced alongside public measures [5. 6]. The Talmudic concepts of *kuppah* and *tamḥui* do not occur in the documents from Fustat; instead *mezonot* (food, provisions) was the term for the weekly food distribution in the community. It also undertook the provision of those in need with clothes, housing, and medical care. Another means of support granted to the poor were subsidies for the poll tax (Arab. *jizyah*), since in the case of failure to pay they would have been arrested by the authorities. In the event of that happening, the community made every effort to redeem them.

The *parnas*, as the collector of communal donations, was an established institution in the Jewish community of Cairo; even more colleagues joined than the two or three individuals prescribed in the Talmud. Additional public charity in Fustat was provided through the *hekdesh* (lit. "consecrated property"). Classical rabbinic literature used the term to denote gifts for the → Temple and the priesthood in Jerusalem. In medieval Egypt, by contrast, the *hekdesh* served as a pious foundation whose income supported communal welfare operations. In Fustat several foundations were known by the term "for the poor." While they did not, as a rule, distribute alms directly to the needy, they appear to have funded services for impoverished travelers and subsidized poll tax payments.

Donation box with the Hebrew inscription Erets Yisra'el (Land of Israel), Halberstadt Synagoge (17th century)

In the northern, Christian part of Spain, the institution of the *hekdesh* spread in the second half of the 13th century [8]. Here most of the donors designated that their *hekdesh* gifts go directly to the poor. Presumably this was motivated by the popular belief in the efficacy of conduct pleasing to God as a way to escape the threatening torments of hell. Both Jewish and Christian wills from late medieval Christian Spain express the hope that the souls of the deceased might benefit from their charitable bequests. This practice was a continuation of the theology of charitable giving already found in late ancient sources from both communities [10].

Regulated public poor relief developed in the Jewish communities of 14th-century Spain (→ Sepharad) [2. 318–323]. The deteriorating economic situation also fueled the need for other benevolent undertakings in the shape of "sacred societies" (→ *hevrah kaddisha*). Their spread points to the shortcomings of a system of welfare that depended entirely on the goodwill of wealthy members of the community and to the unease of the poor in light of the oligarchical management structures of the Spanish-Jewish communities. In many cases the sacred societies engaging in charitable work were established against the wishes of the community leaders.

After the expulsion of the Jews from the Iberian Peninsula in 1492/1497, sacred societies spread to Italy and the Ottoman Empire (→ Sephardim) in the 16th century. Here, too, the oligarchical character of the Jewish communities (*kehillot*) remained intact (→ Kahal); the leadership was drawn from the most affluent community members, whose concern for the needs of the poor was limited. In Italy, the creation of ghettos (→ Venice) was also conducive to the expansion of the *hevrot kaddisha*.

The Jewish communities of the 12th and 13th centuries who lived north of the Alps (→ Ashkenaz) practiced charity both through private donations – as a fulfillment of a religious duty (→ Mitsvot) – and as a communal responsibility. Some Ashkenazi communities, Frankfurt being one example, still existed in the 12th century without any kind of communal welfare; *gabba'im* nevertheless collected and distributed donations from members of the community [9]. According to Eliezer ben Nathan of Mainz (1090–1170), his city had a *kablah* (communal fund) and an alms collector. As a halakhic authority and reformer of poor relief, he went against the Talmudic decision and pronounced that communal alms collectors could also accept "large" sums from married women. Subsequent Ashkenazi scholars were however reluctant to follow this ruling [10]. Reports of his grandson Eliezer ben Yoel HaLevi of Bonn (1140–1225) indicate that in the Rhineland communal funds still existed in the 13th century. Explicit reference is made to an institution of the *kis shel kahal* (comunity pocket) already mentioned in the *Bavli* (Bava Batra 8b), which was apparently a fund from donations from the community. [9. 83f.].

In the late 13th century the general tendency throughout the Ashkenazi regions was one of increasing community participation in the practice of *tsedakah*. While prior to the early 13th century it had still been the custom to collect voluntary charitable donations, the second half of the century marked the transition to a compulsory system of taxation for the purpose of welfare. At the same time, the monetary tithe (*ma'aser*) already mentioned in the → Talmud ceased to be an individual religious duty and became a communal obligation [9. 91, n. 19]. The influential halakhic scholar Isaac ben Moses of Vienna (1180–1250; → Halakhah) stipulated that in an emergency charitable donations could also be used for other needs of the community. In addition to the reorganization of alms collection and communal poor relief practices, in the High Middle Ages the eligibility criteria for receiving communal poor relief were specified according to religious law. The scholar and halakhist Eliezer ben Samuel of Metz (ca. 1115–1198), who had been appointed alms collector in Mainz, ruled that a person found to be knowingly violating the halakhah (*avaryanim be-mezid*) be automatically disqualified from receiving *tsedakah*.

As the center of Ashkenazi Judaism gravitated into Eastern Europe, and in particular to Poland–Lithuania (→ Autonomy; → Demography), at the onset of the early modern period it was accompanied by what appeared to be mounting communal conflicts over *tsedakah*. In the middle of the 17th century Nathan Neta Hanover (ca. 1610–1683; → History; → Cossack Persecutions) praised the charity of the Polish Jews, their hospitality toward strangers and travelling scholars, and the care and attention given by "righteous women" to unmarried orphan girls [12. 146f.] A considerably less rosy picture was painted slightly earlier by Shlomo Ephraim Luntschitz (1550–1619), who lived in Poland and later in Prague. He reported serious tensions between rich and poor and community leaders favoring the rich. The scholar Yom-Tov Lipman Heller (1579–1654) also criticized the behavior of wealthy Jews and their claims to lead the communities. Already in the 16th century *Ḥevrot kaddisha* had been founded in Ashkenaz; their influence increased over the course of the 17th century in response to intra-communal tensions between wealthy and poor Jews, general economic crises, and the changing social conditions during the Counter-Reformation [3].

4. Modern period

From the 18th century onward, the institutions of the *hekdesh* charity and the → *ḥevrah kaddisha* gradually dissolved. In their place, Jewish communities increasingly began to found charitable establishments such as hospitals and orphanages. In the 19th century, Jewish welfare organizations were also combined under the umbrella of larger multi-communal structures; one example for this development is the founding of the Federation of Jewish Charities of Boston (1895). There were moreover Jewish welfare initiatives operating on the national and international level, such as the American aid organizations Jewish → Joint Distribution Committee and → Hadassah. Jewish organizations joined them in more recent times providing assistance to people regardless of their religious, ethnic, or national affiliation. Among these, the American Jewish World Service (AJWS) has since its foundation in 1985 epitomized the rise of "social justice" as a guiding principle of the 20th century.

Charitable practices transformed in this way were able to spread because religious motives gave way to secular philanthropic concepts (→ Philanthropy). The emergence of both → reform-oriented and conservative (→ Conservative Judaism) religious movements was another contributing factor.

A more recent reconfiguration of the traditional Jewish cultural value of *tsedakah* is the imperative to create "social justice." It was adopted as a Jewish-religious commandment especially – albeit not exclusively – by non-Orthodox religious movements. Like the more philanthropically-oriented organizations, they also sought to frame their work for social justice in universal terms and not as directed exclusively at Jews. To this end the Talmudic concept of → *tikkun olam* was appropriated; the original idea, which described a "well-ordered community," expanded into an ambitious agenda with the aim of "restoring" or "repairing the world." The modern reinterpretation of *tikkun ha-olam* as a Jewish religious obligation to heal a broken world is seen by critics as an unwarranted break with tradition or as a mere slogan. In any event it illustrates the capacity for change in the perception of *tsedakah* against the backdrop of a growing global awareness of oppression, poverty, and injustice.

Bibliography

[1] G. A. Anderson, Charity. The Place of the Poor in the Biblical Tradition, New Haven 2013. [2] Y. T. Assis, Welfare and Mutual Aid in the Spanish Jewish Communities, in: H. Beinart (ed.), Moreshet Sepharad. The Sephardi Legacy, vol. 1, Jerusalem 1992, 318–345. [3] Y. Ben-Naeh, Ben gildah le-kahal. Ha-ḥevrot ha-yehudiyot ba-imperiyah ha-otomanit ba-me'ot ha-17–18 [Between Guild and Community Council. Jewish Confraternities in the Ottoman Empire in the 17th and 18th Centuries], in: Ẓiyon 63 (1998), 277–318. [4] R. Brooks, Support for the Poor in the Mishnaic Law of Agriculture. Tractate Peah, Chico 1983. [5] M. R. Cohen, Poverty and Charity in the Jewish Community of Medieval Egypt, Princeton 2005. [6] L. Finkelstein, Jewish Self-Government in the Middle Ages, New York 1972. [7] S. D. Fraade, Local Jewish Leadership in Roman Palestine. The Case of the Parnas in Early Rabbinic Sources in Light of Extra-Rabbinic Evidence, in: S. D. Fraade, Legal Fictions. Studies of Law and Narrative in the Discursive Worlds of Ancient Jewish Sectarians and Sages, Leiden 2011, 555–576. [8] J. D. Galinsky, Jewish Charitable Bequests and the Hekdesh Trust in Thirteenth-Century Spain, in: Journal of Interdisciplinary History 35 (2005) 3, 423–440. [9] J. D. Galinsky, Public Charity in Medieval Germany. A Preliminary Investigation, in: Y. Prager (ed.), Toward a Renewed Ethic of Jewish Philanthropy, New York 2010, 79–92. [10] A. M. Gray, Married Women and Tsedaqah in Medieval Jewish Law. Gender and the Discourse of Legal Obligation, in: A. Gray/B. Jackson (eds.), Jewish Law Association Studies XVII. Studies in Mediaeval Halakhah in Honor of Stephen M. Passamaneck, Eastbourne 2007, 168–212. [11] A. M. Gray, Redemptive Almsgiving and the Rabbis of Late Antiquity, in: Jewish Studies Quarterly 18 (2011) 2, 144–184. [12] A. Grossman/M. Ben-Sasson, Ha-kehilla ha-yehudit bi-yeme ha-benayim [The Jewish Community of the Middle Ages], Jerusalem 1987. [13] Y. Wilfand, Poverty, Charity and the Image of the Poor in Rabbinic Texts from the Land of Israel, Sheffield 2014.

ALYSSA M. GRAY, NEW YORK

Tsene-rene

Ever since its first printing in the early 17th century, the voluminous Yiddish work entitled *Tse'enah u-Re'enah* (*Tsene-rene*; Go forth and see [O ye daughters of Zion]) has been the most frequently published, widely read, and probably the most influential Yiddish book ever. The work includes an exegetic rendition of the Pentateuch, the Megillot, and the Haftarot – those parts of the Bible which make up the obligatory readings over the course of the year – together with commentaries of a variety of authorities as well as Midrashic elements and stories. Its dissemination and reception can shed a light on numerous facets of the history of books and language but also of mentality and Jewish history in general.

1. Author, work, and title
2. Printing history and success
3. Content and form

1. Author, work, and title

Not much is known about the author of *Tsene-rene*. He calls himself Jacob ben Isaac Ashkenazi (1550–1623) of Janów. It is not clear which of the Polish towns of this name is meant. The kind of work he wrote gave him barely any opportunity for autobiographical information, and although the popularity of *Tsene-rene* had already become apparent during his lifetime, no information about him has been transmitted. Only the year of his death, 1623, has been established thanks to research by Moritz Steinschneider (→ Bibliography) and after him Haim Liberman.

The book was probably composed towards the end of the 16th century, but it cannot have been printed before the early 17th century, as the most recent work quoted, *Kli Yakar* by Shlomo Ephraim ben Aaron Luntschitz (1550–1619) was printed in Lublin in 1602. According to a note on the title page of the oldest surviving edition, Basel (in fact Hanau) 1622, *Tsene-rene* had already been printed three previous times in Cracow and Lublin. These early Polish editions have not survived, nor are any eyewitness descriptions known. It is certain that the work was printed four times over two decades during the author's lifetime, and that consequently its great success manifested itself very quickly. The author was not successful, however, in his attempt at publishing a supplement to *Tsene-rene* entitled *Melits Yosher* (Advocate). Besides the lost first edition printed in Lublin in 1622, only the Amsterdam reprint of 1687/1688 is known. Another unfinished work, *Sefer ha-Maggid* (Book of the preacher), for which the author had already collected rabbis' recommendations, was replaced with the text of an anonymous writer in the end and printed using the same title and the same recommendations between 1623 and 1627 in Lublin.

Steinschneider was of the opinion that the title of the book was in fact *Ḥamishah Ḥumshe Torah* (The five books of the Torah) and not the biblical quotation *Tse'enah u-Re'enah* (Song of Songs 3:11), pronounced "Tsene-rene" in Yiddish, that followed it on the title pages. In any case, *Tsene-rene* became the established title early on. In fact, in *Melits Yosher* the author himself referred to his book as *Tsene-rene*. And of course the title *Tsene-rene* also has a symbolic facet in that it is unequivocally in the feminine (imperative) form and thus explicitly addresses women. The male education ideal (→ Talmud Torah), in contrast, focused on the study of texts in the holy language → Hebrew. While less educated men were certainly also readers of this work as well as older → Yiddish literature in general, the image of the pious older woman reading *Tsene-rene* became established, primarily in the 19th century in classical Yiddish literature.

2. Printing history and success

After the initial phase during the 2nd half of the 17th century, over the course of the 18th century, *Tsene-rene* became a bestseller for several printing houses of southwestern and southern Germany thanks to the continually expanding Jewish → printing business. There can be no doubt that the success was due above all to the original combination of content and form, but another contributing factor was certainly that many printed versions (the first one being Sulzbach 1692) illustrated the text with, in some cases, rather attractive woodcuts. More than once, the models for these were unmistakably Christian Bible illustrations [7]; [10]. In total, hundreds of editions have been documented [5]; [6].

The fact that *Tsene-rene* was read continuously in the West, too, rather than just standing on the shelves of private libraries, is documented by the well-worn copies recovered in recent decades in the genizot of small country synagogues in southern Germany (→ Genizah); in Veitshöchheim alone, fragments of at least twelve different editions of *Tsene-rene*, mainly from the 18th century, were discovered [8]. Among the (ultra-)Orthodox, who have continued to use → Yiddish as their lingua franca, *Tsene-rene* continues to enjoy uninterrupted popularity, so much so that Brooklyn publishers took the risk of typesetting completely new editions, in addition to the photomechanical reprints of earlier editions. Thus *Tsene-rene* is one of the (mainly edifying) works of older Yiddish literature that lives on.

As the printing history documents, *Tsene-rene* served without competition as the family resource for imparting knowledge of the Bible at the time of the emerging → Haskalah. In the wake of the endeavors of Moses Mendelssohn (→ Bi'ur) and his fellow activists to achieve linguistic integration for German Jews, German printing houses gradually stopped printing Yiddish books nearly everywhere shortly after 1800. What the Lumières thought of *Tsene-rene* may be inferred from the "Vorerinnerung" (introduction) with which a printer from Sulzbach prefaced his edition of Mendelssohn's → Bible translation entitled *Ets Ḥayim* (Tree of Life) in 1810 – in High → German in Hebrew characters – which tells us that: "One may well object that we have a *Tsenerene*, which is true indeed, and this book is also useful in certain cases (for elderly women, for example), but on the whole it is not at all suitable, particularly not for half-grown girls: the language is too corrupt, the presentation intertwined with too many astute discussions and many sections too harsh for the delicate demands of decency" [8. 34]. The words of the editor from comparatively conservative Sulzbach sound ambivalent but on the whole follow the main trend of the Haskalah. Until 1799, he himself had printed *Tsene-rene* a number of times, and after his death his sons published one or two more, among them the presumably last one in Central and Western Europe in 1836.

In Eastern Europe, however, *Tsene-rene* – and indeed the Eastern Yiddish language in general – could not be ousted by the Lumières. From the end of the 18th century onward, *Tsene-rene* was printed here too (first surviving edition Lemberg 1786); its language remaining largely unchanged. In fact, the language was understood by everyone through the centuries. While some editors gently modernized the spelling, vocabulary, and word order, attempts at transforming the text comprehensively in the direction of New High German or at publishing straightforward Bible translations under the promising title *Tsene-rene* were not successful [5]. While those who thought along modern, enlightened, assimilatory lines considered *Tsene-rene* the epitome of an attachment to tradition that should be discarded, it remained – supported by the approval of rabbinical authorities (→ Censorship) – the most popular Yiddish book in Eastern Europe.

3. Content and form

Tsene-rene presents a vernacular paraphrase of the narrative parts of the Torah (→ Tanakh), structured in accordance with the weekly readings, followed by a second part comprising the five *megillot* (the scrolls of the Song of Songs, Book of Ruth, Lamentations including a section "Destruction of the Temple" primarily drawn from the → Talmud tractate Gittin, as well as Kohelet [Ecclesiastes] and Esther), traditionally read on the occasion of the five festivals of Pesaḥ, Shavu'ot, → Tish'ah be-Av, Sukkot, and Purim (→ Course of the Year), and the *haftarot*, the prophetic readings linked to the individual sections of the Torah. Some passages, especially of the second volume, may have been circulating even before the publication of *Tsene-rene* (in print only "The destruction of the Temple," Cracow 1595); because of linguistic peculiarities it is assumed that they were not composed by Jacob ben Isaac Ashkenazi. Beginning with the 1711 Amsterdam edition, the *haftarot* were usually inserted after the relevant weekly sections interrupting the sequence of the biblical narrative and consequently emphasizing the work's para-liturgical function more explicitly. Later editors occasionally attempted to embellish the text of *Tsene-rene* by inserting additional commentaries; these were not integrated into the main text but placed below the respective text on the lower half of the page, further increasing the similarity with the Hebrew Bible editions where commentaries are printed parallel with the text.

The crucial factor for the book's great impact, however, was probably the didactic principle following educational structures, which allowed the author to link the literal interpretation of selected verses or sections of the Bible with commentaries of several authorities such as Rashi (→ Worms), Nachmanides (→ Commentary; → Guide for the Perplexed of Our Time), and Bahya ben Asher. The main source appears to have been Bahya's very voluminous Hebrew Torah commentary, which was also based on compilation and was the model for the overall construction of the work. The interspersed stories and legends from the Talmud, the → Midrash, and other sources are particularly effective, being introduced with stylistic elements used in educational works. The author asks, for instance, "Why?" and then answers the question himself. At the very beginning, the question "Why does the Torah begin with the letter Bet and not with Aleph?" is thus answered with two interesting Midrashim. By means of the approximately 700 instances in *Tsene-rene*, it is easy to reconstruct how the interrogative "why" developed through syntactic reinterpretation to gradually come to mean "for, because" in the New Yiddish form *worem/worn* [9].

An almost direct impression of the style of presentation is conveyed by the peculiar translation of the section Genesis, carried out by Bertha Pappenheim (→ Jüdischer Frauenbund) and published in Frankfurt am Main in 1930. However, there is no German edition of the book's complete text; the German version printed in Hebrew characters a number of times in Paks (Hungary) at the end of the 19th and beginning of the 20th century has been adapted not only linguistically but also with regard to content in accordance with enlightened ideas.

One example of the way in which a self-contained story was integrated is the widely known legend of Elijah, which is most famous in the classic retelling by Isaak Leib Peretz (→ Bontshe) entitled *Zibn gute yor* (Seven good years). In the second volume of *Tsene-rene* it is embedded without a source reference in the Megillah Ruth (regarding 4:11) linked by means of a Psalms verse (98:3) as praise for a prudent housewife, while another version of the story appears simultaneously in the *Mayse-Bukh* (Basel 1602, no. 148) as an independent tale, in this instance with the correct reference to the Hebrew source ("Sefer Yalkut in the Section Ruth").

Thanks to the skillful selection from the commentaries, the sermon-like structure, and the style influenced by oral study, the book has great entertainment value for the whole family. The wealth of material and the intensive study of constantly recurring subject matter make *Tsene-rene* a source of biblical knowledge that should not be underestimated. This might be imparted directly or by retelling it to small children, including sons and grandsons who did not receive the traditional Ashkenazi ḥeder education (→ Talmud Torah) in the wake of the Haskalah.

Bibliography

Sources

[1] B. Pappenheim, Zeenah u-Reenah, Frauenbibel. Translation and Interpretation of the Pentateuch by Jacob ben Isaac Ashkenazi of Janow, ed. by B. Pappenheim, Frankfurt am Main 1930. [2] M. Steinschneider, Catalogus Librorum Hebraeorum in Bibliotheca Bodleiana, Hildesheim 1964 [Reprint of the Berlin 1852–60 edition]. [3] H. Libermann, Vegn dem "Seyfer ha-Magid" un zayn mekhaber [On Sefer ha-Maggid and its Author], in: Ohel Rahel, Part 2, New York 1980, 231–247 [Hebr. and Yidd.]. [4] S. Neuberg, Pragmatische Aspekte der jiddischen Sprachgeschichte am Beispiel der "Zenerene," Hamburg 1999. [5] C. Shmeruk, Di mizrekh-eyropeishe nuskhoes fun der "Tsenerene" [The Eastern European Versions of the "Tsenerene"],

in: L. S. Davidowicz (ed.), For Max Weinreich on his Seventieth Birthday, The Hague 1964, 195–211. [6] C. Shmeruk, Sifrut Yidish be-Polin: meḥkarim ve-iyunim historiyim [Yiddish Literature in Poland. Historical Studies and Perspectives], Jerusalem 1981. [7] C. Shmeruk, ha-Iyurim le-sifre Yidish ba-me'ot ha-16–17: ha-tekstim, ha-temunot ve-nim'anehem [The Illustrations in Yiddish Books of the Sixteenth and Seventeenth Centuries. The Texts, the Pictures and their Audience], Jerusalem 1986. [8] E. Timm/H. Süss, Yiddish Literature in a Franconian Genizah. A Contribution to the Printing and Social History of the Seventeenth and Eighteenth Century, Jerusalem 1988. [9] E. Timm (co-edited by G. A. Beckmann), Historische jiddische Semantik. Die Bibelübersetzungssprache als Faktor der Auseinanderentwicklung des jiddischen und des deutschen Wortschatzes, Tübingen 2005. [10] F. Wiesemann, "Kommt heraus und schaut." Jüdische und christliche Illustrationen zur Bibel in alter Zeit, Essen 2002.

SIMON NEUBERG, TRIER

Tunis

Capital of the French protectorate of Tunisia established in 1881 and home to a large Jewish community whose members included distinct groups of different regional origin and linguistic-cultural lifestyle. As a result of the six months of German-Italian occupation starting in November 1942, it was the only Jewish community in North Africa directly threatened by the National Socialist extermination project. German intentions were hampered by the moderating influence of the French protectorate administration and the objections of the Italians; ultimately the lives of the majority of the Jewish population were saved by the advance of British and American troops in May 1943. After Tunisia gained its independence in 1956, most of the Jews left the country.

1. Origins and protectorate era
2. Under German occupation
3. After independence

1. Origins and protectorate era

With the Arab conquest of the territory of modern Tunisia at the end of the 7th century, Tunis began its rise to supra-regional importance as a trading port and capital of the province of Ifrīqiyā. Between 1534 and the establishment of the French protectorate in 1881, the territory was part of the Ottoman Empire, with the beys of the ruling Ḥusaynid dynasty (1705–1957) being granted a considerable degree of autonomy.

Jewish communities already existed in the region during the era of the Roman Empire; for a long time, their centers were the city of Kairouan and the island of Djerba. In Tunis itself, from the 13th century onward Jews lived in the *ḥārah al-yahūd*, a district exclusively reserved for Jews similar to the → mellah in other North African cities. After 1492, these autochthonous inhabitants, who called themselves *touansa*, were joined by Jewish immigrants from the Iberian Peninsula and from the end of the 16th century onward also by Jewish merchants from → Livorno (Judaeo-Arab. *Gorna*), who called themselves *gornim* or *grana* after that city and were also of Sephardic origin (→ Sepharad).

At the beginning of the 18th century, relations between the Jewish population groups deteriorated. The *touansa* rejected the *grana's* lifestyle as "Christian," while the latter considered the longer-established group as backward. In 1710, a separate community structure was developed by the *grana*, which included their own → synagogues, slaughterhouses (→ Sheḥitah), a cemetery, and a → rabbinate. Moreover, they no longer lived in the *ḥārah al-yahūd* but in the city quarters preferred by Europeans. After 1881, they called themselves "La Communauté israélite portugaise de Tunis."

Being members of a monotheistic minority, all Jews were subject to the Muslim authorities (→ Dhimmah). They were able to organize their community affairs in comparative autonomy; they were headed by a representative (Arab. *qā'id*) appointed by the bey who was responsible for collecting taxes. All the same, they were subject to a series of restrictions. For instance, they were forbidden to wear the regional style of red fez or to own property in cities and villages.

As a result of the Tanzimat reforms (1839–1876), the legal position of the Jews in Tunis began to improve; however, only the *Pacte fondamental* (1857) guaranteed their equal treatment and abolished the ancient restrictions. The first Tunisian constitution was accompanied by a tax increase for all subjects of the bey, as he was heavily in debt to the European powers, with the result that riots broke out in 1864. In 1869, national bankruptcy was declared, and the country was placed under French–British–Italian financial control.

In 1878, the first school of the → Alliance israélite universelle (AIU) began to teach in Tunis – against the bey's opposition. School education not only permitted social and economic advancement but also persuaded many Jews of the attractiveness of the French language and culture. This, in combination with the secular tendency of the curricula, was a particular challenge for the *touansa*, and their community representatives insisted on a contract assuring them that sufficient time would be devoted to teaching religious matters too [11. 446].

The *grana* also resisted the Alliance's schooling project. At first, they welcomed the concept of a modern Jewish education institution in accordance with European standards; however, the dominance of French provoked rejection among those who preferred teaching to be oriented towards Italy. Thus, the physician Giacomo di Castelnuovo (1819–1886), born in Livorno and himself one of the school's founders, ended

his involvement in 1881 after the Treaty of Bardo asserted the right of France to establish the protectorate, rather than Italy which had also aspired to regional hegemony. As a result, Italophile grana no longer acted along religious but national commonalities, joining Christian Italians – by far the largest European population in Tunisia, numbering around 100,000 persons – in matters of education [12. 196f.]; [2. 313].

With the beginning of the French protectorate, the life of Jews in Tunis profoundly changed. The French colonial authorities abolished the status of *dhimmī* and brought the Jews economic and social freedom of movement. Previously, the majority of them had made a living as craftsmen in small towns and villages or had been dependent on support from the community. Now an increasing number of Jews moved into the capital, which offered a multitude of income opportunities thanks to the modernization initiated by France. More and more Jews worked in the liberal professions as lawyers or physicians, found employment with the French authorities, or were part of the growing labor force. The improved living conditions were also reflected in the growth of the Jewish population. At the establishment of the protectorate, 25,000 Jews lived in Tunisia; their number rose to 105,000 by the beginning of the 1950s [11. 447].

In 1899, France abolished the position of *qā'id* and prescribed a unified administration to both Jewish communities. The Conseil de la communauté israélite was founded in response to a French initiative in 1921. From then onward, this community council was elected every four years by taxpaying members. Assimilation-oriented Jews struggled for control of the council with representatives of the Fédération sioniste de Tunisie, which had been founded in 1920 and numbered around 3,000 members [11. 449].

French rule in Tunisia also led to the question of → citizenship becoming extremely topical. The Francophile Jewish population demanded the implementation of the → Crémieux Decree in force in Algeria to be extended to Tunisia too [3. 134]. In order to add authority to their request, the founder of the journal *La justice* Mardochée Smadja (1864–1923) organized a demonstration in Tunis in 1910. Due to its pro-French stance, it was viewed very critically by the Muslims, who protested in turn against Smadja and his followers. With the Morinaud Law of 1923, the naturalization process gradually became easier; by 1950, 7,311 Jews had been granted French citizenship and, as a result of extending citizenship to family members and descendants, 35,000 Tunisian Jews were French in 1956 [3. 134]. In particular, Jews oriented towards assimilation and living in Tunis obtained French citizenship. The more traditionally-minded Jews, such as those on the island of Djerba, kept their distance from France.

Orientation towards France also affected the relationship with Muslims; only a few hundred of whom received French citizenship during the protectorate. The desire for social integration and advancement alienated the majority of Jews looking towards Europe from the emerging Tunisian independence movement and its Destour (from Arab. *dustūr*, constitution) Party founded in 1920.

2. Under German occupation

The defeat of France in June 1940 and the establishment of the → Vichy regime did not remain without consequences for the Jews of Tunisia. Beginning on November 30, 1940, a slightly altered version of the *Statut des juifs* passed by Vichy barely two months earlier went into effect in Tunisia. It restricted the practice of liberal and medical professions and excluded Jews from public service, the law society, and → universities. The anti-Jewish legislation was passed as a decree in the name of Bey Ahmad II and signed by the

French resident-general in Tunisia, Admiral Jean-Pierre Esteva. Thanks to the benevolent attitude of Bey Ahmad II and his successor Muhammad VII al-Munsif as well as Esteva himself, most regulations remained theory or were applied rather negligently. The resident-general even went so far as to confer with the Jewish community of Tunis on how best to react to them [10. 206].

In addition, Italy, going against its own anti-Jewish legislation, acted against the application of the *Statut* to the around 5,000 Jews with Italian citizenship and against all attempts on the part of Vichy to take over Jewish possessions in the course of the planned "Aryanization." One of Italy's military aims had been to gain control over Tunisia, but by agreeing to an armistice with France, Germany had blocked access, considerably damaging relations between the two Axis powers. In this situation, Italy regarded the existence of the *grana* as a means of exerting influence, although many of them had distanced themselves from fascist Italy and applied for French → citizenship [4. 252].

While the Jews of Tunisia continued to feel relatively safe in spite of two → pogroms carried out by Muslims in Gafsa and Gabès, their situation suddenly changed with "Operation Torch," the landing of British and American forces in Morocco and Algeria on November 8, 1942 (→ Algiers). Now German and Italian units were deployed to Tunisia. Soon afterwards, the agent of the German Foreign Office with the Afrika Korps Rudolf Rahn declared to the French resident-general that from now on Germany would determine the guidelines of policies regarding the Jews. The first measures in November 1942 were to arrest the head of the community council Moïse Borgel as well as other dignitaries. After an intervention from the bey and Esteva, most of them were released again after a few days.

The occupiers, however, began to establish parallel structures. They installed commissions which included Italians as well as pro-German Vichy French and Tunisians who addressed administrative matters. On the one hand this implied the erosion of Resident-General Esteva's authority; on the other it could be read as a signal to the Tunisian national movement whose sympathies the Germans were trying to secure. In November 1942, for instance, they arranged for Habib Bourguiba to be released from a French prison. Bourguiba had led the modernist-secular Neo-Destour Party since 1934 and worked towards Tunisian independence more radically than the more religiously-oriented mother party. The future first president of Tunisia, however, eluded being co-opted, while the majority of the Neo-Destour Party were in favor of cooperating with the Germans.

On November 24, 1942, the SS Einsatzkommando headed by SS Obersturmbannführer Walther Rauff, whose original plan had been to annihilate the Yishuv in Palestine, was moved from Athens to Tunis. On December 6, 1942, the leadership of the Wehrmacht, the SS, and the German Foreign Office decreed that Jewish forced laborers would be detailed to erect the fortifications demanded by the Wehrmacht. On the same day, Rauff declared the Jewish community council to have been abolished and ordered a nine-person committee led by Haïm Bellaïche, the chief rabbi of Tunis, to be convened. In this, the SS followed the model applied in Europe by establishing a mandatory board comparable to the → "Judenräte" whose main purpose was to receive and implement orders from the Germans.

Two days later, Rauff ordered Bellaïche and Borgel to make 3,000 Jewish men available for this purpose within 24 hours; otherwise the Germans would begin to execute hostages. As a result, the community founded a dedicated Comité de recrutement de la main d'œuvre led by the lawyer Paul Ghez. As only 120 persons responded to the call on December 9, 1942, Rauff ordered

a raid during the course of which more than 1,500 Jews, many of whom had sought sanctuary in the Great → Synagogue of Tunis or in the AIU building, were arrested, with the younger ones among them being immediately deported to one of the around 40 labor camps. Forced recruitment was repeated over the following weeks, and soon 5,000 inadequately provisioned Jews had to erect fortifications or construct other military facilities. Furthermore, they were exposed to the combat operations going on around them. The majority of the 2,500 Tunisian Jews who died during → forced labor were the victims of Allied bombings; more than twenty Jews were accused of political activities and transferred to Europe where they were murdered in concentration camps [8. 390f.]; [6. 73f.].

In addition, heavy fines were imposed on the Jewish communities. In antisemitic propaganda directed primarily at the Muslim population, the Germans denounced the Jews as being responsible for the Allied air raids on Tunis, because of which the community should pay the city 20 million francs within 24 hours. Officially, the money benefited a committee compensating non-Jewish victims of bombings. In this way, Rauff initiated the theft of Jewish property, hoping at the same time to mobilize Muslim sympathies in favor of Germany. The communities at Sousse, Sfax, and Gabès were also forced to pay similar sums; the Jews of Djerba had to hand over several kilograms of gold. There were also uncontrolled lootings and confiscation of vehicles and companies owned by Jews.

The rapid advance of the Allies and the low manpower of the SS Einsatzkommando of no more than 100 people prevented the implementation of considerably more radical measures, such as the ghettoization of the Jews. The Germans also had to consider their ally Italy, which rejected the introduction of the *Judenstern* for its citizens and intervened repeatedly when Italian Jews were subjected to forced recruitment. The bey also refused to issue such measures in his name; instead, Muhammad VII al-Munsif declared: "The Jews, like the Muslims, are my children" (cited in [10. 207]). In view of France's weakness, he simultaneously presented himself as a Tunisian nationalist, seeking rapprochement with the Neo-Destour party. At the beginning of May 1943, the German and Italian units in Tunisia capitulated; Rauff and his colleagues were flown to Italy just before. Muhammad VII al-Munsif was deposed as he was accused of collaborating with Germany and Vichy.

3. After independence

The fact that France was unable to protect its citizens during the German occupation together with the discriminations imposed by Vichy and the increasing momentum of the Tunisian national movement had led to deep insecurity among the Jews of Tunisia (→ [The] Pillar of Salt). Thus, the establishment of the State of Israel sparked a first emigration wave; by 1952, 6,500 Jews had moved there. In view of the growing anti-colonial endeavors, France gradually granted its protectorate an increasing degree of autonomy, releasing Bourguiba from prison in 1955 and Tunisia into independence in 1956. In the same year, a further 6,500 Jews emigrated to Israel [11. 455].

The majority of the representatives of the Jews who remained in Tunisia preserved neutrality towards the independence movement. In 1952, the community leader in Tunis Charles Haddad reported to a conference held by the → World Jewish Congress in → Algiers that France and the Tunisian nationalists endeavored to secure their support in equal measure; consequently, he recommended a mediator's role be taken in this process [6. 262]. However, there were also attacks by Muslim adolescents on the *ḥārah al-yahūd* in the same year, during which one Jew was killed; several such attacks occurred despite the community repeatedly requesting increased police protection. Even so, the Jews of Tunisia supported Prime Minister Mendès-France's declaration of autonomy on July 31, 1954, which led to the formation of a first Tunisian government a year later that also included one Jew, Albert Bessis. Bourguiba, who followed Tahar Ben Ammar as prime minister after independence on March 20, 1956, abolished the monarchy in 1957, and held the position of president of the Republic of Tunisia from July 25, 1957, maintained good relations with the Jews of the country. In his first cabinet, the Jewish businessman André Barouch, who had supported the national movement and had been imprisoned by the French as a consequence, was a minister until 1957. The number of emigrants subsequently dropped. As a result of the difficult economic situation of many → mizraḥim and the discrimination they suffered in Israel (→ Wadi Salib), several hundred Jews even returned to Tunisia.

Events such as the brief armed conflict between France and Tunisia over the naval base in Bizerte which the French continued to use (1961) as well as the Six-Day War (1967), in the wake of which there were extensive anti-Jewish attacks in Tunis, led to more Jews leaving Tunisia. While there were only around 25,000 Jews living in all of Tunisia in 1966, their number shrank to a few hundred in the city of Tunis and around 1,000 on Djerba [3. 145]; [6. 306].

Bibliography

[1] M. Abitbol, The Jews of North Africa during the Second World War, trans. by C. Tihanyi Zentelis, Detroit 1989. [2] F. Cherif, Jewish-Muslim Relations in Tunisia During World War II. Propaganda, Stereotypes and Attitudes, 1939–1943, in: E. Gottreich/D. Schroeter (eds.), Jewish Culture and Society in North Africa, Bloomington 2011, 305–320. [3] A. Hirschberg, A History of the Jews in North Africa, vol. 2, Leiden 1981. [4] B. Hunger, Wer sind wir? Gruppeni-

dentitäten und nationale Einheit im kolonialen und postkolonialen Tunesien, Bern 2005. [5] S. La Barbera, Les Français de Tunisie (1930–1950), Paris 2006. [6] M. Laskier, North African Jewry in the Twentieth Century. The Jews of Morocco, Tunisia and Algeria, New York 1994. [7] L. Lévy, La nation juive portugaise. Livourne, Amsterdam, Tunis, 1591–1951, Paris 1999. [8] P. Longerich, Holocaust. The Nazi Persecution and Murder of the Jews, trans. by S. Whiteside, Oxford 2012. [9] K. M. Mallmann/M. Cüppers, Nazi Palestine. The Plans for the Extermination of the Jews in Palestine, New York 2010. [10] C. Nataf, Les Juifs de Tunisie face à Vichy et aux persécutions allemandes, in: La Revue Pardès 16 (1992), 203–231. [11] H. Saadoun, Tunisia, in: R. Spector et al. (eds.), The Jews of the Middle East in Modern Times, New York 2002, 444–457. [12] Y. Tsur, Religious Internationalism in the Jewish Diaspora, in: A. Green/V. Viaene (eds.), Religious Internationals in the Modern World. Globalization and Faith Communities since 1750, New York 2012, 186–205.

RALF BALKE, BERLIN
AND ULRICH SCHUSTER, LEIPZIG

Tur Malka

Literally "the king's mountain"; originally the → Aramaic name of a hill southeast of Jerusalem. It is also the pseudonym of the Hebrew-Yiddish poet Uri Zvi Grinberg (1896–1981; → Poetry), which he adopted during his → Aliyah in December 1923 and later also bore in civilian life together with his wife, the poet Aliza Gurevitch (b. 1926). While his early poems, influenced by Expressionism and Modernism, were published in → Hebrew and also in → Yiddish, after turning to Zionism, he dedicated himself exclusively to Hebrew. Impressed at first by Labor Zionism and the kibbutsim movement, he became radicalized in the wake of the 1929 Hebron massacre. Grinberg was politically active as a follower and spokesman for the Revisionists around Vladimir Ze'ev Jabotinsky and later stood for the Knesset for the Herut party, becoming a parliamentarian for a short time. His poetry reflects the tense and fraught development of the Zionist project in Palestine.

1. Uri Zvi Grinberg
2. Existentialist nihilism
3. Zionist Expressionism
4. Crisis and prophetism
5. Second career

1. Uri Zvi Grinberg

Uri Zvi Grinberg (also spelled Greenberg) was born on September 22, 1896, in the East Galician village of Bialikamin (today Bilyi Kamin) near the eastern border of Austria-Hungary. His family were part of a long-established Hasidic tradition. From an early age, Grinberg identified with Rebbe Uri of Strelisk (1757–1826), also known as "the Seraph"; an influential representative of → Hasidism in Galicia, the charismatic and ecstatic mystic had fought against the opponents of his faith in the early decades of the 19th century. His namesake Uri Zvi Grinberg, too, later embodied some of his characteristics: a very lively personality, religiousness, ecstasy, charisma, and the inner inclination to rush headlong into ideological and political battles.

He shared this temperament with his mother Bat-Sheva, who lavished possessive mother's love on her firstborn and only male offspring. Under her influence, he developed his self-image as a chosen one. His father Ḥayim, an introverted scholar, devoted himself to studying the sacred texts (→ Talmud Torah) and a life in religious seclusion. When the family moved from Bialikamin to → Lemberg (today Lviv), a much bigger city, the father earned a meager living as a semi-rabbinical local authority. The family lived on the brink of poverty. Uri passed through the conventional Jewish ḥeder education of the time, but he also immersed himself in the Hasidic atmosphere of his parents' house and its Kabbalistic traditions of → mysticism and legends. He began to compose his own poems from a young age. He was also permitted to learn → German and read books of his own choosing, including modern secular Hebrew and Yiddish → literature. He regularly met with a group of young Yiddish poets from Lemberg who had gathered towards the end of the first decade of the 20th century under the guidance of the Romantic poet and translator of Heinrich Heine's (→ Entreebillet) works Shmaryahu Imber, the father of the writer Shmuel Yankev Imber and brother of Naphtali Imber, the author of → *Ha-Tikvah* (Hope). At the age of 16, Grinberg celebrated his debut as a Yiddish and Hebrew poet, gaining a degree of recognition in the years before the First World War as the author of a series of brief, unpretentious, rhyming poems with loose scansion which expressed a youthful sadness and loneliness in an airy, sometimes gracefully musical fashion. He cannot be seen as an innovator during this phase; in their brevity, their dark tonality, and formal simplicity, his poems were typical of the Hebrew as well as Yiddish → poetry of these years, which may be called the "post-Renaissance" in modern Jewish culture, or the post-Bialik and post-Peretz era in modern Jewish poetry.

When the First World War broke out, the young poet was still living with his parents. As he had not yet reached the age at which men were drafted into the Austro-Hungarian army, he was able to concentrate on writing and publishing poems. After East Galicia was reconquered by the Austrians in June 1915, he was immediately drafted (→ Military) together with thousands of adolescents (many of them Jews). During his deployment to the Serbian front, the commander brought him the first volume of his poems *Ergets oyf felder* (1915; Somewhere in the fields), published in Lemberg in his

Uri Zvi Grinberg (1896–1981)

absence. The volume contains two cycles of short poems, the first one composed during the first months of the war at home, the second one sent home from the front. The form, style, and tonality of the book made it a direct continuation of his pre-war poetry. The poems, while pervaded by the doom and gloom of war, expressed a gentle, passive, elegiac mood entirely without true spiritual shock.

The Austrian offensive began soon afterwards. Under heavy bombardment from the Serbian positions, Grinberg crossed the Sava with his unit. While it was a military "success," the operation led to bloodshed on both sides that remained engraved on the young poet's mind. However, the creative consequences of this birth into 20th-century reality only gradually emerged. Stationed in occupied Serbia, Grinberg continued to write elegiac poetry for the time being. Only the prose of his diary-style narrative displayed a new note. It was published soon after the war under the title *In tsaytns roysh* (1919; In the turmoil of the times. The better-known title *Krieg oyf der erd* [War on earth], was that of the second, expanded edition of 1922). The narrative documents a state of mental fragmentation and loss of orientation which gradually slips into a calmer mood. The latter made it possible to step back from the overwhelmed self and empathically observe the ordinary Serbian people in their dogged struggle against the occupiers. Even so, *In tsaytns roysh* shows barely any sign of the new, revolutionary note that would characterize Grinberg's Yiddish poetry after the war and came into its own in the masterly long poem *Mefisto* (Mephistopheles), the poet's best work in Yiddish.

2. Existentialist nihilism

When the Austro-Hungarian army was disbanded in 1918, Grinberg fled to his home town, hiding in his parents' house. As a result of the disintegration of the Dual Monarchy, the entire Jewish community of East Galicia found itself in a dangerous position of neutrality between Ukrainian and Polish militias. When the provincial capital → Lemberg was conquered by the Poles in November 1918, the victors took revenge on the Jewish "traitors" (→ Żydokomuna) in a pogrom that lasted three days from November 22 to 24 and, according to cautious estimates, cost 74 lives. During the night, the entire Grinberg family including the poet were already lined up against the floodlit back wall of the city's cathedral awaiting their execution, when the shootings were halted due to an emergency. The experience of having narrowly escaped was no less influential for Grinberg than surviving the Sava crossing. In his recollection, both events merged into one insight that would never leave him: as soon as the thin veneer of liberalism and humanism had been peeled off the European people after the "death of God" (Nietzsche; → Übervolk) by nihilism and been burnt to ashes in

the horrors of the "Great War," the extermination of the European Jews would become inevitable due to the incurable → anti-Judaism inherent in Christianity. Grinberg foresaw the approaching catastrophe, including the gassing of Jews, with astonishing clarity as early as 1923, when he composed *In malkhes fun tseylem* (In the realm of the cross). His last Yiddish poem became a prophetic vision of extraordinary power born out of a unique combination of pathos, lyrical expression of profound despair, and surgical precision in the description of imminent horror. The poem is one of the most significant predecessors of the so-called → Holocaust literature (→ Khurbn).

Grinberg owed his ability to process his own experiences mentally and overcome the late-Romantic narcissism of his poetry not least to the influence of artistic and poetic Modernism which informed → Yiddish as well as → Hebrew secular culture and → literature after the war. Coming from the nascent Soviet Union, Futurism was influential through Yiddish poets like Moyshe Broderzon (1890–1956; → Łódź; → Yung-yidish) and Peretz Markish (1895–1952; → Shtetl); in addition, there was the "dawn of humanity" mood of Austrian and German Expressionism and the effect of Modernism on Polish literature; finally, the → Skamander circle of poets around Julian Tuwim (1894–1953) transformed contemporary Jewish literary culture. The great Romanticism built by Ḥayim Naḥman Bialik (1873–1934; → El hatsippor) and Isaak Leib Peretz (1852–1915; → Bontshe) on the idea of a national "renaissance" was pushed off its pedestal. The objectives of poetic Modernism resonated with the young writers formulating a new worldview founded on the assumption that present and future reality were irrevocably cut off from the middle-class era of the 19th century. History did not unfold in an "evolutionary" way or in the form of "progress," being instead barbaric and revolutionary and offering only two possible paths of development battling for supremacy: universal devastation and revolutionary Utopianism. Art and music had to steer a radically different course. They had to jettison not only the Romanticism and mimetic realism of the 19th century but also colorful Impressionism and the atmospheric, hyperaesthetic Symbolism that had taken their place. To overcome the aesthetic ideals and norms of the past, they had to tear down the boundaries between → art and inner reality in order to gain a foothold in this psychological as well as social reality. This was to be done in close contact with the "primary processes" in the Freudian sense (→ Psychoanalysis) and, consequently, in a "primitive" manner. Some variants of Modernism also encouraged direct involvement in the social and political struggles of the time. For most Jewish poets in Europe, this meant professing literary Expressionism (→ Weltende), whose general starting point was the rejection of Realism and Impressionism, both of which shared the "mimetic" approach to the object (→ Mimesis). It further implied strengthening subjectivism by means of replacing the descriptive style with direct and "coarse" expression of moods and emotions; also the creation of loud, hard, skeletal, and non-artistic means of expression, above all the search for immediate, unadulterated verbal expression of the self's inner life. Grinberg became a major representative of this trend in Yiddish as well as Hebrew literature. In Hebrew literature, he was regarded for decades as the essential Expressionist poet and most important polemicist, who campaigned against Hebrew Romanticism and mimetic realism with great energy on the theoretical level too.

The transformation was visible in part in the substantial volume of poetry *Farnakhtengold* (1921; Evening gold), but it only really came into its own in *Mefisto*. In this work he linked Nietzsche's dictum of the death of God and the resultant age of nihilism with a surprisingly varied version of the legend of Faust and Mephistopheles. As God is either dead or (as hinted at in some passages of the poem) incarcerated in a remote citadel, Mephisto rules the world. And as he is in the advantageous position of not having to steal the human soul from a kindly creator any more, he deceives humans twofold, taking from them sexual lust and everything else they valued and desired. He thus robs their existence of the last *raison d'être*, leaving them vegetating in pain, (psychological and political) chaos, and self-destruction. The "Faustian" human, speaking voice of the poem shares the sufferings of his fellow human beings but is distinguished from them by his greater intellectual ability. In his proverbial striving for truth and understanding, he now wants to "know" his master Mephisto. The insight to which he aspires is similar in principle to that of the mystic (→ Mysticism), who desires to "know" God. The speaking voice even conceives the idea of becoming Mephisto's "poet," of giving expression to his satanic being. Mephisto, however, avoids his endeavors to find closeness and intimacy. The whole poem is constructed around this vain endeavor: rather than Mephisto pursuing Faust in order to "serve" him, Faust tags along behind Satan in the hope of gaining his favor, while Mephisto refuses to reveal himself. It is not until the last section of the poem that the speaking voice begins to suspect the truth in an hour of deep reflection: Mephisto is a part of him and not an independent metaphysical entity [2. vol. 2, 377–378].

The long poem is structured as a sequence of variations on painful emotions, melancholy, and tracing a disappointing quest. Gradually, the extraordinary dynamism of the first sections fades, as though the speaking voice's "Faustian" energies are exhausted. The unordered subject matter, the harsh rhythms, the "raw," deliberately anti-harmonic tonality, the systematic avoidance of any traditional poetic from, and above all the obsessively repeated emotional navel-gazing imbued Grinberg's work with the status of being the representative and iconic Expressionist poem in Yiddish. What the poet explored was the universal constitution of the modern age and its metaphysical conditions; what he practiced was the poetic language by means of which this constitution could be grasped and expressed.

3. Zionist Expressionism

The success of *Mefisto* (a second, slightly improved edition soon followed the first one) made its author a prominent figure in Jewish literature. Grinberg was soon known as one of the preeminent young Yiddish poets. In 1923, he began to edit the literary journal *Albatros* first in Warsaw and later in Berlin, writing nearly all contributions himself [5. 130]. The substantial poems – written in ever longer verses in order to rule out any possibility of a traditional metrical reading – were accompanied by poetic manifestoes, political essays, and modernist graphics. Politically, Grinberg was demonstrating a kind of despairing anarchism nourished by a sense that neither socialism nor Zionism (→ Basel) were able to save the Jewish people from barbarism. When the League of Nations confirmed the British Mandate for Palestine in 1922 on the condition that the promise of the → Balfour Declaration would be honored and subsequently a considerable number of Eastern European Jews emigrated to Palestine, the poet's attitude changed overnight. In July 1923, while he was in Berlin in order to evade the strictures of Polish censorship, which criticized the blasphemous language used in *Albatros*, he professed himself a radical Zionist. As soon as he joined the Zionist Organization, he immediately set his sights on its leadership around Chaim Weizmann (1874–1952; → Chemistry), as it accepted the conditions set by the Balfour Declaration, the vague concept of a "national home." What was needed, rather, was a true Jewish state, which could be achieved quickly

through a "Hebrew revolution" [1. vol. 15, 22–26]. Grinberg, whose literary production in → Hebrew had been vanishingly small compared to his output in → Yiddish, now oriented his own literary activity entirely towards Hebrew, while at the same time preparing his → Aliyah. When he reached Jaffa in 1923, he immediately declared that he was turning his back on the "West," redefining himself through the real contact between his feet and "the earth here – not in Europe" [1. vol. 15, 29–30]. At that time, he began to publish poems under the pseudonym "Tur Malka," the name of a mountain southeast of Jerusalem known for its fertile soil and its olive trees whose oil had been used to anoint kings.

Now Grinberg's most hectic and fruitful creative period began. The voluminous and consistently original poems he published (beginning during his last months in Berlin) revolutionized Hebrew poetry and caused a great stir when they appeared in 1925 in his first volume of Hebrew poetry *Emah gedolah ve-yareaḥ* (Great fear and moon). Grinberg developed a form of Zionist Expressionism which not only did not retract the existentialist nihilism of *Mefisto* and the poet's other Expressionist Yiddish poems but rather heightened its expression to an unprecedented and almost unbearable pitch. In quick succession, he created giant formless poems, their topics out of center and their verses of prosaic length and substance, which required a printing format similar to that of a broadsheet. In this process, he deconstructed every stylistic and formal poetic norm to which modern Hebrew → poetry had adhered so far. *Emah gedolah ve-yareaḥ* began with a series of poems which systematically explored the various dimensions of the new age: social chaos, the terrors of the modern metropolis, spiritual nihilism, unlimited yet meaningless sexuality for fear of a meaningless death, the absolute sensation of consisting merely of flesh and blood that will ultimately decay, and so forth. On the basis of Jewish messianic traditions (→ Messianism), which interpreted the present time as the chaotic-apocalyptic era preceding the end of times and the beginning of the "Sabbatical" (→ Shabbat) beyond time, Grinberg's descriptions of the "sixth millennium" followed a downward spiral into hell or the dark night of the soul.

Emigration to Palestine did not end this downward trend entirely. The fragmented, repetitive, and in many places entirely annulled narrative strand of the poem that gave the volume its title unfolds before the backdrop of a Palestinian desert landscape and an ominous Jerusalem (→ Zion) torn between religions. A literary *tour de force* characterized by the automatized writing of crude and unsublimated raw sensations, the poem indicated that Palestine as such could be interpreted as a grotesque version of the universal collapse of civilization in a godless era. Only the present day of the Zionist pioneers struggling in the heart of the wastelands under impossible conditions allowed a positive view of reality. By interpreting their work as a form of divine service and their settlements as the temple of a revived "earthly Jerusalem," the poet was able in a renewed dialogue with God to preserve the latter from meaninglessness and himself from suicide.

Grinberg styled himself as the bard of the pioneers of the Jezreel Valley and was accepted as such by the majority among them. As he moved from one small settler community to the next and was invited by the members of these select communities living a very simple life, he recited poems such as *Ha-gavrut ha-olah* (Masculinity rising) or *Tur Malka* (both 1926) which, following the structure of descent and resurrection on a smaller scale, were more formally structured and noticeably less "wild" than earlier poems. Grinberg simultaneously engaged in frenetic journalistic activity, writing dozens of articles – for → *Davar* among others – in which poetic manifestos stood next to criticism of the day-to-day running of the Zionist project in Palestine. Once again, he founded a "private" newspaper, entitled *Sadan* (Anvil), which he, in the style of Karl Kraus's → *Die Fackel*, not only edited but also wrote himself using several pseudonyms.

4. Crisis and prophetism

All these activities came to a temporary standstill when the Zionist project found itself in a financial crisis in 1926/1927, during which the poet identified entirely with the despair of the unemployed and hungry town-dwellers and the suffering in the agricultural settlements. In Grinberg's eyes, however, the crisis was above all an ideological and political one. The unimaginative implementation of the Zionist plan, which could be traced back to it abandoning its revolutionary dynamism, gradually diminished the loyalty and financial support of the Jewish masses of Europe for Zionism, he held. Just as the political will to continue to support the project was dwindling among the British colonial administration, the emerging Palestinian nationalist movement felt encouraged to attack the still small and feeble Jewish community with the aim of "nipping it in the bud" either with the silent approval or the beneficial indifference of the Mandate administration, as the latter was forced to court the Arabs [1. vol. 2, 88]. Soon, Grinberg prophesied in 1928, there would be an Arab attack on the → Yishuv. This prediction came true in the spring and summer of 1929, when hostilities erupted around the Temple Mount, culminating in a bloody massacre of Jews in Hebron in August. Subsequently, Grinberg called on the political leaders he trusted – Berl Katznelson (1887–1944) and David Ben-Gurion (1886–1973; → Raison d'État) – to assume the leadership of the Zionist Organization (→ Basel) by non-democratic means if needed. When these leaders ignored his exhortation, he lost faith in them and increasingly turned to the main rival of Labor Zionism, the "Zionist Revisionists." In 1930, he joined Vladimir Ze'ev Jabotinsky's Revisionist movement (→ Altalena), rapidly rising to become one of their renowned leaders, spokespeople, and mentors.

Grinberg emerged from the crises of the late 1920s a different poet. In his series of poems *Anakre'on al kotev ha-itsavon* (Anacreon at the pole of melancholy), regarded as his best and "purest" work by the critics, he succeeded in creating a literary image of his predominant mood of passive despair during the years 1926/1927. His overall orientation, however, shifted from lyrical to prophetic-political texts, as witnessed in three publications of the following years: *Ḥazon eḥad ha-legyonot* (1928; Vision of one of the legionaries), *Kelev bayit* (1929; A house dog) and *Ezor magen u-ne'um ben ha-dam* (1930; Defensive shield and the word of the son of blood). *Anakre'on* sparked universal applause, yet it was misunderstood to some degree by his many admirers. With its central topic of fear of death and despair as the root causes of modern humans' unease and restlessness, the poem confronted its readers with a terrifying dialectical *salto mortale*. It began with a series of formally perfect short poems guiding the reader into a mood of resignation, acceptance of the unavoidable, and the bitter consolation of passivity that those who have failed are left with. The literary affirmation of this mood required Grinberg to jettison almost all of the fundamental traits of his Expressionist poetics. These new elegiac poems were short, focused on one topic, severely structured, and written in brief, rhyming and, in the main, scanning verses, which developed a warbling musicality in places – to wit, everything the poet had declared poetically insufficient and had overcome. Suddenly, however, the speaker openly rejects the silence of this gathering of failures who had settled passively and almost comfortably at the "pole of melancholy," declaring

his rejection of the finality of death and of his recognition of it in a return to the earlier Expressionist style. Instead, he unfolds a dialogue with "God the smith" in the context of metaphysical rebellion, promising a religious reversion to God in the name of modern man who is distant from religion – on the messianic condition that God must abolish death. The metaphysical rebellion and the firmly negotiated new covenant with God give rise to new vitality and creativity; the rebellion and the subsequent new testament can, however, only be realized with the sharp and heavy tools of Modernism. If God is a smith, man must adopt the toughness of durable metal or even counter the strikes of God's giant hammer by striking with his own tools. The topic of the poem which – at a superficial glance – was individual in its tone, simultaneously carried within it a collective political undercurrent: the correct political option was that embraced by the rebel and revolutionary, not the defeatist.

That this was part of the poet's message could be seen in the texts composed and published at the same time as *Anakre'on*, all of which featured political topics, rhetoric, and messages. By the time Grinberg produced the indisputably most important volume of political poetry in Hebrew, *Sefer ha-kitrug veha-emunah* (The book of accusation and faith), in 1937, he had already become a prominent public figure. In the poetry of those years, he attacked political opponents, the official Zionist establishment, and the representatives of Labor Zionism as well as the Arabs and the British, speaking in the name of a truth of almost divine authority. In order to endow himself with the necessary authority, a speaking voice with the qualities of a biblical prophet was required, a man chosen by God to be a messenger, chastiser, and harbinger of the redemption to come. The prophetization of Grinberg's speaking voice occurred gradually and not without inner conflicts.

At the outset, the speaker, although already a "seer," introduces himself simply as "one of the legionaries" (i.e. one of the betrayed pioneers whose crossing to Palestine is compared to that of the Roman legions who destroyed Jerusalem in the 1st century CE); he is only distinguished from his despondent comrades because he has been "cursed with the gift of incisive expression by the God of the Hebrew revolution" [1. vol. 2, 18]. Then the speaking voice assumes the form of a "prophetic dog," a lowly creature which is nevertheless able to sense danger before everyone else. The confirmation of his 1929 forecast enabled Grinberg to re-evaluate the character in his poems of the 1930s, presenting him as an experienced prophet. He even described himself as living "in fear of prophecy" [1. vol. 3, 34–35], as his predictions in which he saw the coming catastrophe came true against his will. In this as well as other aspects, Grinberg's political prophecy differed from that of his great predecessor Bialik (→ El ha-tsippor). Unlike Bialik's prophetic figure, Grinberg's was doubly tested: firstly, by having in fact predicted the future and, secondly, because his prophecy was located outside general beliefs and consequently led to rejection, vilification, and demonization of the prophet. While Bialik's figure enjoyed the august position of the "guardian over the house of Israel," Grinberg's prophet was reduced to being a wailing dog, barking fearfully into the darkness – a darkness only he could see at that time.

This in turn led to the development of a new poetics of prophecy. While Grinberg occasionally made use of the sublime voice of Bialik's pseudo-biblical prophecy, he was able – and very successfully – to employ "humble" forms of verse too: those used in ballads, primitive doggerel, scandalizing ad-hominem slander, and other types of popular comedy and scatological satire. This offered reading pleasure in a genre whose august and dark tones frequently evoked boredom. In fact, many of the poems replaced the overblown tragic style with one that might be described as wild abandon. Grinberg's collections of political poems appeared in succession like the chapters of a tragic picaresque novel narrating the life story of the true prophet as the story of a loathed and despised individual fouling his own nest, by mingling the sublime with the common, pathos with bathos, profound sadness with a sardonic cackle.

Grinberg's political voice was loud and effective, so much so that Labor Zionism regarded him as their most significant opponent after Jabotinsky. After the murder of the leading Labor Zionist Chaim Arlosoroff in 1933 (→ Ha'avarah Agreement), which was interpreted as a political murder encouraged by the Revisionist side, attacks against Grinberg increased to personal persecution, with the result that he had to leave Palestine. He spent most of the 1930s living in → Warsaw, editing a Revisionist Yiddish weekly journal and composing numerous political articles, mainly in → Yiddish. The publication of his *Sefer ha-ḳitrug veha-emunah* in Palestine caused an uproar that led to a kind of excommunication – his book vanished completely off the shelves of the bookshops – and paralyzed the poet's creativity for some years. The demonization of Jabotinsky and Grinberg was part of a successful campaign of Labor Zionism aiming to marginalize the Revisionist movement in Palestine. For years to come, Grinberg would be read only by members of the Revisionist youth movement Beitar and the anti-British underground militias Irgun and Leḥi ("Stern Gang"; → Exodus).

5. Second career

In September 1939, when the German army advanced with great speed in western Poland, Grinberg left Warsaw, which was subjected to daily air raids, and travelled to Palestine via the Romanian port of Galați, reaching his destination within a few weeks.

He could not even bid farewell to his parents, his sisters, and their families, as under the Ribbentrop–Molotov Pact, → Lemberg became part of Soviet Ukraine, where the agents of the NKVD would have arrested the well-known Hebrew "reactionary" and "fascist" poet. Indeed, rumors about his arrest and execution were rife. In Palestine, he hid in the house of friends for several years. Everything he now wrote, he kept to himself, giving the outward impression that his career as a poet had come to an end. However, his second career, in many ways as public and successful as the first one, began in July 1945, parallel to the defeat of National Socialist Germany. Aware since 1942 of all the dimensions of extermination, which he refused to call the → Holocaust because of that term's association with a "natural" and inevitable catastrophe, a great flood of emotions and insights, metaphysical as well as political, was churning inside him, erupting in a torrent of extraordinary, semi-liturgical dirges and → lamentations. Until 1948, Grinberg published unusual poems in the daily press in almost weekly succession – ballads, poems with historical and religious trains of thought, lyrical lists, horrendous visions of existing under water or in the sky among decaying corpses, all combined with profound Zionist soul-searching and self-incrimination. When the poet was the first to succeed to articulate in his works a collective narrative for the still overwhelmed and downright stunned people, he rose almost overnight to being a voice of the nation. All attempts by old enemies from the Left and a few ambivalent allies from the Right to put an end to his renewed greatness were washed away by a tidal wave of emotional empathy and applause from the critics.

Grinberg's Holocaust poetry, collected in 1951 in a weighty tome entitle *Reḥovot ha-nahar* (The streets of the river), is to this day the most comprehensive, coherent, and at the same time shocking work of Jewish poetry dealing with the historic catastrophe

(→ Khurbn). Unlike the works of those immediately faced with the horror, this collection grew out of the mind and intellect of a helpless and profoundly as well as personally affected observer. While this position to a certain extent diminished the immediacy characteristic of the best works of some other poets, it allowed a depth of emotion, intellectual clarity, and vehemence of the imagination that cannot be achieved in the state of numbness often induced by direct confrontation with the unthinkable. Grinberg explored the Holocaust and its after-effects on at least four levels, all of which he regarded as having been irretrievably damaged by the events. The first and most emotional level was personal mourning. The poet continually met members of his perished family in a variety of imagined encounters, all of which were informed to a degree by the awareness of their sheer non-existence. On a second, theological level, the poet followed the dead on their path to Heaven where they looked in vain for an avenging God who would answer for the injustice suffered and alleviate their suffering (→ Tikkun olam). The Holocaust created a theological vacuum or shunted God into the position of protector of murderers. On a third level of language and poetry, Grinberg explored the metaphors usually employed to describe the Jewish experience of abuse, torture, and extermination, only to find in the end that none of the metaphors was really linked to the experience. Thus, the poet reached the conclusion that language, robbed of the validity of its metaphors, had been demoted by the catastrophe to lead an existence "as a mere shadow" [1. vol. 6, 37–38] (→ Bearing Witness), and that, if this applied to language in general, the fate of poetry was much worse, as the latter was only possible where language achieved its highest semantic intensity. Grinberg had to admit that the expressive point of language had been broken forever. If poetry was to be possible in future, it would have to recur to the ancient, primitive, collectivistic, and formulaic conventions of → liturgy (which was attempted in many of the poems). The fourth level was historical and political. Here, the visions of the establishment of a great Jewish empire stretching from the Euphrates to the Nile were presented as the only possible "response" to the annihilation, which might reverse the process of decomposition started by the Holocaust. While these visions were not convincing intellectually and politically and led to disquieting displays of military might, at the same time they were relatable as compensatory phantasies.

The foundation of the State of Israel in 1948, celebrated by Grinberg as the realization of his prophecies, made him delve into party politics for a short while once more: he became a member for Menaḥem Begin's (1913–1992) Herut party in the first elected Knesset. Soon, however, parliamentary politics became unbearable to him. At the age of 52, he married the young poet Aliza Gurevitch with whom he had five children over the next decade, naming them after his murdered relatives. Together with Gurevitch, he adopted "Tur Malka" as his civilian name. Marriage and family, however, did not fit in with his habits of a reclusive and egocentric poet. Over the remaining two decades of his literary activity, he created works of a quality equal to those of his earlier days. He wrote innumerable political poems affirming his well-known ideas and attitudes and expressing his bitter disappointment in the politics embraced by Ben-Gurion, as the latter tacitly accepted the partition of Palestine and restrained the new Jewish army which could have "liberated" the entire area of the biblical homeland during the Arab-Israeli wars. He was particularly incensed by the division of Jerusalem between Israel and Jordan, which meant that the holy places and above all the Temple Mount remained in Jordanian hands. However, his new political poetry did not reach the intensity and

the sardonic humor of the early political poetry from the 1930s.

Grinberg's greatest achievement after *Rehovot Ha-Nahar* (Streets of the river; the last volume of poetry published during his lifetime; he refused to have his collected works published) was a series of around a dozen poetical "treatises." The series opened in 1950 with the publication of the grandiose *Min ha-ḥakhlil u-min ha-kaḥol* (Of the red and the blue) and then developed through the addition every few years of great parts under a variety of titles. In fact, the poet was now writing a titanic open poem, a formal conclusion of which was never envisaged. Following Whitman's model (→ Skamander), which he had always admired, Grinberg wrote his "Cantos" as a comprehensive philosophical monumental poem in which the entirety of his life experience was investigated in a multitude of forms and keys and then re-evaluated.

The poem, progressing in a zigzag line, highlighted the inner dialectic of Grinberg's work and personality. On the one hand, it penetrated deeper than ever before into the previously suppressed romantic stratum: the innocence and confidence under the wings of caring parents in an idealized Jewish Slavonian homeland; suffering and serenity of early love and the subsequent tragedy of losing the beloved; the excitement of the young man discovering poetry as an outlet for overwhelming emotions, and the deep longing of the aged poet for his first poem, however weak and childish it may have been; the temptations and joys of youthful sexuality, and so forth. On the other hand, Grinberg identified with the "mission" that tore him away from these charms, shaping him into a man "who eats fire, drinks fire, and is consumed by fire" [1. vol. 9, 216]. If he could have lived his life a second time, Grinberg said, he would not have stepped off the fateful path that guided him from the paradise of childhood into the hell of his mission. Above the dichotomy of the red (the mission, the "fiery" present) and the blue of the distant landscapes of a dreamlike childhood, a greater, metaphysical dichotomy appeared: on the one hand the relentless search for a new dialogue with the Jewish God whose presence was so difficult to discern in the age of → Auschwitz, on the other, the devouring reality of death and the ever deeper deliberations on the meaning of the finiteness of human existence. As the monumental poem grew, the conflict of the sexual and emotional vitality of adult masculinity was joined by the numbness and bleakness of old age.

The conflict was interpreted in three directions at least: personal experience; the heavy load of the national project the poet was shouldering; poetry and poetic achievement, which he explored by means of rereading the old poems from his earlier works in a parodistic, sometimes downright mocking, fashion. The landscapes before which these dramas of self-deconstruction unfolded were far distant from those of the Ukrainian village of his childhood. Rather, they show images of storm-tossed seas or dark, bare, and perilous mountains. The language the poet now employed was interspersed with → Midrash and Kabbalistic-Zoharistic (→ Mysticism) terminology. In many respects, Grinberg reached the peak of his lyric-metaphysical poetry in this late work. At the same time, the monumental poem, or at least parts of it, were perceived as distanced and solipsistic, its topics and style disconnected not only from the Israeli poetry of the time (the 1950s and 1960s) but also, despite obvious continuity in the subject matter as well as the style, from his own extraordinarily vivid poetry of the 1920s and 1930s. It is a rarely read, impenetrable corpus written in an Aramaizing idiom rather alien from spoken → Hebrew, with which Grinberg had successfully enriched the poetical vocabulary of his poems written in the 1920s and 1930s.

Around 1975, at the age of 79, Grinberg stopped writing. The last six years of his life he spent shut away and finally suffering dementia. The ordered publication of his enormous œuvre began in 1991, a decade after his death. A total of 21 volumes have been published as of 2023, and it will not be complete for some time.

Bibliography

Sources
[1] U. Z. Grinberg, Kol ketavav [Collected Works], ed. by D. Miron, 19 vols., Jerusalem 1990–2015.   [2] U. Z. Grinberg, Gezamelte verk, ed. by K. Schmeruk, 2 vols., Jerusalem 1979.   [3] U. Z. Grinberg, Ba-'avi ha-shir: mivḥar shirim [At the Hub. Selections from his Poetry], ed. by D. Miron, Jerusalem 2007.   [4] U. Z. Grinberg, Mephisto, Munich 2007.

Secondary literature
[5] S. M. Finnis/H. Valencia, Sprachinseln. Jiddische Publizistik in London, Vilna und Berlin 1880–1930, Cologne 1999.   [6] D. Miron, Akdamut le-ATsaG [Prolegomena to Uri Zvi Grinberg], Jerusalem 2002.   [7] D. Miron, Introduction to the Poetry of U. Z. Greenberg, in: D. Miron, The Prophetic Mode in Modern Hebrew Poetry, New Milford 2010, 191–307.

DAN MIRON, NEW YORK

Turin Group

Anti-fascist resistance group in Italy founded in the late 1920s by the Giustizia e Libertà (Justice and Freedom) movement in Turin, primarily supported by Jewish intellectuals. They were part of a tradition of outstanding political commitment among Piedmontese Jews during the → Risorgimento and the socialist movement, based on the close connection between Jewish self-understanding and belonging to the Italian nation. Even after the arrest or emigration of leading members of the group in 1934/1935 and the introduction of race laws in Italy in 1938, young Jews in Turin continued their resistance, with their Jewish ancestry gradually increasing in importance. From 1943 onward, they took an active part in the armed conflict, and many of them made an appearance on the political stage after the Second World War.

1. Jews in Piedmont
2. Turin as the center of the socialist movement
3. Jewish anti-fascism
4. Persecution, exile, and resistance

1. Jews in Piedmont

Jews have been documented in Piedmont since the Middle Ages. From the early modern era on, they lived in segregated quarters, ghettos (→ Venice) in the cities and were subject to numerous restrictions obliging them to attach special markers to their clothing (→ Dress Regulations). In 1761 around 4,200 Jews lived in Piedmont in 20 locations, around 1,300 of them in Turin. As a result of the first, short-lived French occupation and the proclamation of the Piedmontese Republic, they obtained legal equality in December 1798 and January 1799 (→ French Revolution). With Bonaparte's victory at Marengo in 1800 and the French annexation of the Subalpine Republic, close ties developed between the Piedmontese Jews and French culture and politics that continued beyond the end of French rule. Thus around half the representatives from the Italian regions taking part in the Grand → Sanhédrin in Paris in 1806 came from Piedmont.

The end of Napoleonic rule resulted in the restitution of the Kingdom of Piedmont–Sardinia under Victor Emmanuel I. The so-called Royal Patents (*Regie Patenti*) issued on March 1, 1816, restored the pre-1798 legal and social position of the Jews. The obligation to display discriminatory marks, however, was not reinstated, and the importance of the Jews for the Piedmontese economy was recognized. Around the same time, occasional anti-Jewish pamphlets (→ Anti-Judaism), some of which were widely disseminated, campaigned against the → emancipation of the Jews in Piedmont. Some of them emigrated to the Habsburg Kingdom of Lombardy-Venetia, where a patent of toleration guaranteed the Jews a large degree of equality, or to Ticino in Switzerland (→ Helvetic).

However, anti-Jewish attitudes were also one of the motives for the Jews of the region to take part in uprisings and the → Risorgimento, endeavoring to achieve emancipation as Italians [6. 80]. The Collegio Foa founded in Vercelli in 1829, the second most important training institution for rabbis and Jewish teachers in the Italian states after the → Collegio Rabbinico in Padua, served as a secret meeting place for the followers of Giuseppe Mazzini. Students at the college were involved in the Risorgimento, among them Isaac Artom, the secretary of Camillo Benso, count of Cavour, David Levi from Chieri, later rabbi of Asti, Marco Tedeschi, and Salvatore De Benedetti from Novara, who would become Italy's first Jewish professor when he was appointed to the chair for → Hebrew language and literature at the University of Pisa in 1862.

In 1848 King Charles Albert granted the Piedmontese Jews full emancipation [1], serving as a model for other regions of the Italian peninsula. Modernizing endeavors in the Piedmont Jewish communities found expression in *L'Educatore Israelita*, the first significant Italian-Jewish journal published by the rabbis Giuseppe Levi and Esdra Pontremoli from 1853 onward [8]. Their Judaism gradually became limited to the observance of important feasts and holidays (→ Course of the Year) as well as a kind of Jewish → piety that did not necessarily presume individual faith but was an expression of family unity [2. 5].

Emancipation strengthened the Piedmontese Jews' identification with the Italian nation and the Risorgimento. The Zionist movement (→ Basel) found little interest among them. The most visible expression of their loyalty to the Italian nation was the Mole Antonelliana in Turin. Originally conceived as a → synagogue and completed in 1889, the Jewish community sold it to the city council in 1878, and it became the landmark of the city.

2. Turin as the center of the socialist movement

Since the end of the 19th century, Piedmont had developed into a center of socialist and revolutionary movements in Italy. Jews were active in the workers' movement, founding socialist journals and associations, above all the Partito Socialista Italiano (PSI) founded in 1892 by Filippo Turati and his companion, the Russian-Jewish anarchist Anna Kulisci-off (born Anna Moisejevna Rosenstein). The future manufacturer of typewriters Camillo Olivetti, a graduate of Turin Polytechnic, took part in workers' protests in Milan in 1894/1895. Authors writing for socialist organs in Piedmont included the cousins Riccardo, Felice, and Adolfo Momigliano as well as Emilio De Benedetti, Donato Bachi, and Benedetto Morpurgo.

Coming from a wealthy assimilated Jewish family in Turin, Claudio Treves was one of the most prominent socialist politicians and journalists until he fled into exile in 1926. In Paris he led the semi-monthly *Rinascita Socialista* (publ. 1928–1930), the organ of the Partito Socialista dei Lavoratori Italiani, and beginning in May 1927 the weekly *La Libertà* of the opposition coalition Concentrazione Antifascista Italiana (CAI; 1927–1934). His supporter, Gustavo Sacerdote, had worked in Berlin as the correspondent of the socialist party organ *Avanti!* since the late 19th

century. Sacerdote also contributed to the socialist journal *Critica Sociale* in which, strengthened by the victory of the Bolsheviks in Russia in 1917, revolutionary and reformist positions confronted one another.

In 1921 the PSI split into the revolutionary Partito Comunista Italiano (PCI) and the reformist Partito Socialista Unitario (PSU) under the leadership of Turati and Giacomo Matteotti. The majority of the Jewish socialists from Piedmont joined the so-called "pessimistic socialism" of the PSU, among them well-known personalities such as the Turin economist Riccardo Bachi.

3. Jewish anti-fascism

After the First World War, the fascist movement, which transformed into the Partito Nazionale Fascista (PNF) in 1921, quickly gained momentum. Benito Mussolini, appointed prime minister of a coalition government in 1922, exploited his position to establish a fascist dictatorship in the following years.

The fascist movement also found followers among Turin Jews, including the banker Ettore Ovazza, a key figure of the Jewish community of Turin who had already been involved in the March on Rome in 1922. In 1934 he founded the journal *La Nostra Bandiera* which was first published weekly and then bi-weekly until 1938. The pro-assimilation and anti-Zionist publication intended to counteract any doubt of the patriotism and "Italian character" of the Jews as well as the antisemitic and pro-German tendencies within the fascist movement. However, the journal was powerless against the regime's growing antisemitism; Ovazza and his family were murdered by the SS in autumn 1943.

Numerous young Piedmontese Jews joined the anti-fascist resistance, the impact of which grew in Turin throughout the 1920s. After the assassination of Matteotti, many socialists decided to emigrate, among

Natalia Ginzburg (1916–1991)

Levi, Cesare Pavese, Massimo Mila, Luigi Salvatorelli, and Norberto Bobbio, who were also members of the Turin Group, as well as Elio Vittorini, he founded the Turin publishing house Einaudi in 1933. In 1938, Ginzburg married Natalia Levi from Palermo, who had published her first short story *I bambini* in the journal *Solaria* in 1933. Her works, including the 1963 autobiographical work *Lessico famigliare* ("Family Sayings," 1967), document the activities of the Turin Group.

The streets of Turin were where the group held conspiratorial exchanges. Other members included Natalia Ginzburg's brother Alberto Levi and his friend Vittorio Foa. Foa, later one of the leading men of the Resistenza, wrote that to him Turin, "with its style and its unwritten laws" was the hub: "Politics, even high politics, as a projection of everyday life; and beyond that, too, possibly with a slight moral emphasis, the imperative: work for Italy" [2. 58]. Since in his view fascism contradicted life, his opposition to it was unconditional. In 1933 Leone Ginzburg persuaded him to become involved in the Turin Group, for which he also worked as a journalist [7. 168].

While the members of the Turin Group did not consider themselves as belonging to the Jewish community, their Jewish origins united them in their fight against fascism and for Italy. The importance of this link grew during the years of persecution and the Second World War. Natalia Ginzburg, who had grown up in a secular family, even used the phrase "silent complicity" which united her with other Jews [11. 144–151].

them Turati who fled to Corsica and then to Paris in 1926 thanks to the help of members of Natalia Ginzburg's family, Ferruccio Parri and Sandro Pertini, both leading figures in the Comitato di Liberazione Nazionale Alta Italia (Committee of National Liberation for Northern Italy), and Carlo Rosselli, the son of a Jewish family from Florence.

The Turin Group of the liberal socialist movement Giustizia e Libertà (GL) founded in 1929 in Paris exile by Rosselli, Emilio Lussu, and Alberto Tarchiani acquired particular importance among the anti-fascist organizations. It was led by the writer Leone Ginzburg, who had moved to Italy from → Odessa with his family when he was a child and attended secondary school in Turin. With a grant he traveled to Paris in 1932, and established connections there with the GL leadership. Subsequently he taught Slavic studies at the University of Turin until 1934 when his license to teach was revoked for refusing to swear the oath of allegiance to the fascist regime. Ginzburg rooted his anti-fascism in his commitment to Italy and its history, which he regarded as being destroyed by the fascist movement. Together with Carlo

4. Persecution, exile, and resistance

Together with Sion Segre, Carlo Levi, and others including Natalia Levi's father Giuseppe and her brother Gino, Ginzburg was arrested in 1934 for anti-fascist activities. The press regarded those arrested, nearly all of whom were of Jewish origin, as a "Jewish → conspiracy." While Ginzburg was released,

Carlo Levi was exiled to the southern Italian region of Lucania (today Basilicata), an experience detailed in his best-known book *Cristo si è fermato a Eboli* (1945; "Christ Stopped at Eboli," 1947). In 1939 he escaped to France, returning to Italy only in 1942 to join the Resistenza.

Having been denounced to the Organizzazione di Vigilanza e Repressione dell'Antifascismo (OVRA) by the popular author Dino Segre (pseud. Pitigrilli), the brother of Sion Segre, Vittorio Foa, his father Ernesto Ettore and brother Beppe (Giuseppe), and Alberto Levi were arrested together with 40 others in 1935; this isolated the families from their environment, including the Jewish one. Vittorio Foa's sister Anna Foa noted: "Nobody came to visit anymore, and nobody called" [3. 178f.]. Numerous Jewish members of the Turin Group and Jews suspected of being members went into exile. The musicologist Leo Levi emigrated to Palestine in 1936; Beppe and Anna Foa settled in the United States two years after the fascist race laws had been passed in 1940. Vittorio Foa was sentenced to 15 years in prison for his anti-fascist activities but was released in 1943 and joined the resistance. Leone Ginzburg was exiled in 1940; Natalia Ginzburg followed her husband to Pizzoli in the Abruzzi mountains. After the fall of Mussolini, the couple lived in Rome from 1943, where Ginzburg became one of the masterminds of the Resistenza. Arrested in an underground printing shop by the Gestapo, he died in 1944 as a result of torture in the Regina Coeli prison.

The emigrated and arrested members of the Turin Group were succeeded by a younger generation of Jewish anti-fascists. They met at various places in Turin, such as the Liceo Classico Massimo d'Azeglio, which was a school of the educated middle class [14. 232]. The race laws passed in 1938 severely restricted the activities of Jewish intellectuals and excluded Jewish pupils, students, teachers, and lecturers from public schools and → universities. One intellectual affected was the historian of classical Antiquity Arnaldo Momigliano, who came from an → orthodox family and emigrated to England; another was the literary critic and Sigmund Freud scholar (→ Psychoanalysis) Giacomo Debenedetti, who published his writings under a pseudonym after 1938 and drew on his experiences in the ghetto of Rome in 1944 in the novellas *16 ottobre 1943* (1959; "October 16, 1943," 2001) and *Otto ebrei* (1961; "Eight Jews," 2001).

As a consequence, Jewish communities founded their own educational institutions. In Turin, where a Jewish kindergarten and a Jewish primary school had existed since the mid-19th century, a middle school, a humanistic secondary school, and a vocational school were founded within two months. Among the teachers was Emanuele Artom, who together with his brother Ennio Artom organized a group of young Jews who met in the school library of the Jewish community. Members of this group also included Franco Momigliano, Vanda Maestro, Silvio Ortona, Ada Della Torre, Giorgio Diena, Alberto Salmoni, Eugenio Gentili Tedeschi, Giorgio Segre, Bianca Guidetti Serra, the siblings Anna Maria, and Primo Levi (→ [T]he Truce), as well as Lino Jona. They directed their rediscovered humanistic and cosmopolitan Judaism against the fascist regime. Luciana Nissim, another member of this group, recalled the growing connection between the members [5. 77]. In his autobiographical novel *Il sistema periodico* (1975; "The Periodic Table," 1984), Primo Levi described their situation: "We had to start again from nothing, 'invent' our own anti-fascism, create it from the seed, the roots, our roots. We looked around us and took paths that didn't lead far. The Bible, Croce, geometry, physics seemed to us sources of certainty [...] the sky above us was silent and empty. He had let the Polish ghettos be wiped out, and slowly, chaotically, the idea dawned in us that we were alone, that […] we would have to find in ourselves the power to resist" [4. 795].

After Italy's armistice with the Allies and the German occupation, many members of the group joined the active anti-fascist resistance beginning in September 1943, for instance as part of the Partito d'Azione (Action Party) founded in 1942, with some such as Ortona, Momigliano, and Guidetti Serra occupying leading positions. Emanuele Artom, a member of the Turin group of partisans Monte Bracco, was captured and tortured to death in 1944. Others like Primo Levi and Luciana Nissim were not well prepared when they joined the Resistenza; they were soon arrested and deported to → Auschwitz [11. 152–160].

The surviving members of the Turin Group as well as the Jewish Resistenza fighters enriched Italian culture after 1945 not only with numerous literary and autobiographical works, but, in many cases, continued their commitment to politics – primarily for left-leaning parties and organizations – such as Vittorio Foa, who was a member of the Constituent Assembly. After the right-wing terrorist bombing of Milan's Piazza Fontana in 1969, Natalia Ginzburg became increasingly active in politics and was elected to parliament in 1983 for the list of the Partito Comunista Italiano.

Bibliography

Sources

[1] A. Foa, La Torino della giovinezza, centro di formazione culturale e sociale, in: A. Chiappano/A. Ferruta (eds.), Luciana Nissim Momigliano. Una vita per la psicoanalisi. Il paziente miglior collega, Rome 2012, 18–23. [2] V. Foa, Il cavallo e la torre. Riflessioni su una vita, Turin 1991. [3] D. Jona/A. Foa, Noi due, Bologna 1997. [4] P. Levi, The Periodic Table, trans. by A. Goldstein, in: The Complete Works of Primo Levi, vol. II, New York/London 2015, 749–946. [5] L. Nissim Momigliano, Ricordi della casa dei morti e altri scritti, Florence 2008.

Secondary literature

[6] A. Cavaglion, Notizie su Argon. Gli antenati di Primo Levi da Francesco Petrarca a Cesare Lombroso, Turin 2006. [7] M. Consonni, Fra Antifascismo ed Ebraismo. Intervista con Vittorio Foa, in: Italia-Israele. Gli ultimi centocinquanta anni. Atti della conferenza, Gerusalemme 16–17 May 2011, Milan 2012, 167–181. [8] B. Di Porto, Il giornalismo ebraico in Italia. "L'Educatore Israelita" (1853–1874), in: Materia Giudaica 6 (2000), 60–90. [9] A. D'Orsi, La cultura a Torino tra le due guerre, Turin 2000. [10] C. Ferrara degli Uberti, Making Italian Jews. Family, Gender, Religion and the Nation, 1861–1918, London 2017. [11] A. Lang, Resistance and Italian Jews in Wartime Italy, in: P. Henry (ed.), Jewish Resistance against the Nazis, Washington D.C. 2014, 138–160. [12] A. Lunel, Juifs du Languedoc, de la Provence, et des états français du pape, Paris 1975. [13] A. Milano, Storia degli ebrei in Italia, Turin 1963. [14] A. Monti, I miei conti con la scuola. Cronaca scolastica italiana del secolo XX, Turin 1965. [15] M. Sarfatti, The Jews in Mussolini's Italy. From Equality to Persecution, trans. by J. and A. C. Tedeschi, Madison 2007.

MANUELA CONSONNI, JERUSALEM

Twelve-Tone Music

Twelve-tone music, or dodecaphony, is primarily linked with the name of the Austrian composer Arnold Schönberg (1874–1951). Developed at the beginning of the 1920s, it marks the end point of Schönberg's endeavor to renew Occidental music out of its own tradition. The twelve-tone works he composed after 1933 in his American exile accompany his gradual abandonment of the idea of → assimilation as he increasingly committed himself to and eventually professed Judaism.

1. Origins
2. Arnold Schönberg
3. From "German music" to the "music of humanity"
4. The journey to professing Judaism
5. Reception

1. Origins

Similar to atonal music, Arnold Schönberg's twelve-tone technique represents an attempt to replace the traditional tonality of the music of the Christian Occident, which was based on cadence harmony, with a novel formal principle, the "Method of Composing with Twelve Tones Which are Related Only with One Another" [3. 218]. Schönberg elucidated the rules of twelve-tone technique as well as the motives that had inspired him to create the new method in several essays; the most detailed is the famous *Komposition mit zwölf Tönen* (probably written in 1934; "Composition with Twelve Tones," 1984). According to this, every dodecaphonic work is based on a tone row consisting of the twelve tones of the chromatic scale, which is reinvented for each new composition, as well as on the permutations of the tone row: retrograde, inversion, and retrograde inversion. All four transformations of the row may be transposed freely. The tone row may be used as the basis of one movement as well as a composition consisting of several movements. This construction process allows the composer, unlike in the case of tonal and atonal music, to determine the melodic and chordal "vocabulary" of a work in advance; this gives the composer control of the musical material even before the process of composition begins.

Schönberg spent twelve years working out this new method of composition. He finally created his first works using the twelve-tone technique in the early 1920s. Prior to this, an event had shaken his self-understanding as an assimilated member of German-Austrian culture to the core. Schönberg planned to spend the summer of 1921 in the Mattsee summer resort in the Austrian state of Salzburg. He arrived in the town with his family in early June; other Jews also visited this town in the summer. Shortly afterwards the local community council unanimously passed a resolution "to send a call to the landlords of summer apartments containing the request to keep the town of Mattsee 'free of Jews' this summer as it had been the previous year" (cited in [14. 24]). Schönberg was asked to prove that he was not of Jewish faith. While he, being a convert, could have provided the documentation, he decided to leave the town and spend the remainder of his summer break in Traunkirchen in Upper Austria. The "Mattsee Incident" gave Schönberg fundamental pause for thought, which found expression in a change of his attitude to twelve-tone technique and ultimately led to him professing Judaism.

2. Arnold Schönberg

Schönberg was born in Vienna in 1874 in a lower middle-class Jewish family. His father Samuel, a shoemaker, came from Pressburg (today Bratislava), and his mother Pauline (née Nachod) came from → Prague. He first had violin lessons at the age of eight and began to compose music shortly afterwards. After completing the Oberrealschule (secondary school), Schönberg began a bank apprenticeship in the private bank of Werner & Co. but did not abandon composition. In 1894 he met the composer Alexander Zemlinsky who supported him in his artistic endeavors. Schönberg took a few lessons in counterpoint with Zemlinsky, but otherwise he taught himself compositional skills.

In 1895 Schönberg resigned his position with Werner & Co., dedicating himself in the following years to composing and leading various choral societies; he conducted three workers' choirs, showing a sympathy for

Arnold Schönberg (1874–1951)

socialism he would, however, later abandon. In 1898 he left the Jewish religious community in Vienna and converted to Christianity (→ Conversion). A year later he achieved his artistic breakthrough with the string sextet *Verklärte Nacht*, Op. 4 (1899). Early compositions like *Verklärte Nacht* and the *Kammersymphonie Nr. 1* ("Chamber Symphony No. 1"), Op. 9 (1906), still recall the postromantic style of Richard Strauss with clear influences of Richard Wagner (→ Music) and Johannes Brahms, but they transcend the boundaries of traditional tonality in their use of unconventional chords and unresolved dissonances.

With the *Streichquartett Nr. 2* ("String Quartet No. 2"), Op. 10 (1907/1908), Schönberg not only broke through the framework of major-minor tonality but also deconstructed the conventional form by inserting two poems by Stefan George (→ George Circle) set for soprano voice in the last two movements. Moreover, his atonal period, which began with the *Streichquartett*, was informed by Schönberg's interest in Expressionist and Symbolist poetry as well as an aesthetic point of view emphasizing the subjective character of the artistic œuvre. His best-known work of this period is the melodrama *Pierrot Lunaire*, Op. 21 (1912), which combines three times seven poems by Albert Giraud into a song cycle; in the foreword Schönberg instructs the singer not to sing the melody suggested by the notes but rather to transform it into a "speech melody." The subjects as well as the musical form of these works express Schönberg's endeavor to break established artistic boundaries.

In the wake of the Mattsee Incident, Schönberg's first twelve-tone compositions marked the start of another creative period in the 1920s. At the same time he began to develop an interest in his Jewish origin, to which he had previously been indifferent. In 1925 he was appointed Ferruccio Busoni's successor as head of the composition masterclass at the Preußische Akademie der Künste in Berlin. In addition to his work at the academy, the years leading up to 1933 were filled with his composing numerous new works, conducting performances, and giving concert tours. After power had been transferred to Hitler, Schönberg was excluded from the academy.

Schönberg left Berlin and traveled first to Paris, where he rejoined the Jewish community; his reconversion took place in the Union libérale israélite in the presence of Marc Chagall (→ Vitebsk). From France, he emigrated to the United States, settling in Los Angeles in 1934 (→ Pacific Palisades). His life and work in America were characterized by a strong interest in Jewish concerns, among them Zionism (→ Basel). In some of his final works, such as → *Kol Nidre* ("All Vows"), Op. 39, for speaking voice, mixed-voice choir, and orchestra (1938), he returned to a tonal musical language. Schönberg died in Los Angeles in 1951.

3. From "German music" to the "music of humanity"

At first glance, the development of the twelve-tone technique was merely the solution to a technical composition problem. Numerous music theoreticians associated with Schönberg were also convinced that the traditional tonal system had exhausted its potential as an art form and effective artistic medium of expression, prompting the need for new musical forms. Schönberg's motives for creating twelve-tone music, however, had their roots in a specific view of music history that was closely linked to his Jewish background.

Like other Jews in the late 19th and early 20th centuries, Schönberg sought to liberate himself from the marginal status of Judaism through → assimilation. His → conversion provides the clearest indication of this, although it also reveals his ambivalence. While he, like Gustav Mahler (→ Resurrection), may have been encouraged to seek baptism in anticipation of professional success, he did not join the conformist Catholic majority in the Habsburg Empire but rather the Protestant minority [14. 120f.].

The aspiration to achieve great things, or, as Schönberg put it, the "faith in protection by achievement" (cited in [14. 122]) may be seen as another assimilation phenomenon. Educated Jews in particular (→ Bildung) found themselves compelled to prove that they qualified as worthy citizens and as part of the surrounding Christian culture through intellectual and artistic achievements within the tradition of the Western cultural canon. Schönberg regarded it as a duty to join the ranks of composers from Bach and Beethoven to Wagner, Brahms, Strauss, and Mahler, and to champion German-Austrian music. Consequently, the idea that the anticipated transformation of music had to come from "outside" was alien

to him. Unlike composers such as Claude Debussy or Darius Milhaud (→ Polytonality), Schönberg had no interest in non-European music cultures, and he did not consider the invention of new musical instruments as suggested by, for instance, the Futurists, a sensible undertaking either. He had no intention of abolishing the musical past but instead regarded himself as anchored in the German music tradition with its characteristics and formal principles.

However, his endeavors to continue along the path of tradition and to revive it in a novel and modern form prompted dislike of his work from two opposite directions. Conservative critics categorically rejected his theories of new methods of composition, and the avant-garde composers of the younger generation such as John Cage and Pierre Boulez had reservations concerning the perceived conservative dimension of Schönberg's œuvre, which remained faithful to the formal conventions of classical music.

Schönberg's experience of antisemitism initially increased his efforts at assimilation. He felt compelled to present his first twelve-tone compositions, which he created shortly after the Mattsee Incident, as a product of the German music tradition. Schönberg's pupil Josef Rufer quoted him as having said shortly after leaving Mattsee, "I have made a discovery which will ensure the supremacy of German music for the next hundred years" [6. 48]; [6a. 277]. And even at the end of 1921, he remained faithful to his idea of assimilation, completing his setting of *Es ist ein Ros entsprungen* intended for the Christian celebration of Christmas [14. 137].

Schönberg's dissimilation began in 1923, triggered by antisemitic remarks his long-term friend Wassily Kandinsky had made, which Alma Mahler-Gropius then told him. The widow of Gustav Mahler (→ Resurrection) and lover of Franz Werfel (→ Musa Dagh), Mahler-Gropius had endured harsh criticism from Kandinsky because of her relationships with Jewish men. Sensitized by his experience in Mattsee, Schönberg reacted by writing a letter vehemently attacking his friend's antisemitic accusations; this was the first time he took a stand against antisemitism in writing. While Schönberg and Kandinsky managed to avert a rift, Schönberg's dissimilation and his intensive study of religious and political Jewish subjects, as well as his inquiry into his own Jewish belonging, increased, as evident in the documentation [14. 137–140].

This was accompanied by Schönberg's re-evaluation of the twelve-tone technique: he now no longer justified it by referring to its music-historical or subject-immanent logic but positioned it instead in a new frame of reference outside of music [14. 141]. A letter written in 1930 clearly shows that in view of the increasing threat of the National Socialists, Schönberg no longer intended to secure the "dominance of German music" but rather hoped "to have shown humanity the paths of musical creativity for at least a hundred years to come" (cited in [14. 141]).

4. The journey to professing Judaism

With his forced emigration to America, Schönberg fully embarked on his journey to return to Judaism. He became a fervent advocate of Zionism (→ Basel) and came to public notice by giving lectures as well as publishing on Jewish political topics. In a lecture given in Los Angeles in 1935, he first admitted in public the distressing effect that Wagner's open antisemitism (→ Music) and the new racial theories had had on the young Jewish artists and intellectuals in *fin de siècle* Vienna: "And now here is the point where you can recognize the terrible influence of racial theories – not on Aryans, but on Jews. The latter, deprived of their racial self-confidence, doubted a Jew's creative capacity more than the Aryans did" [3. 504].

In the draft of an essay entitled *A Four-Point Program for Jewry* (1938), he declared that the struggle against antisemitism had proved to be futile and that the Jews now had to work towards solving the problem by creating an independent Jewish state.

Schönberg's return to Judaism was accompanied by a series of compositions that reveal a new approach to musical composition emphasizing the social content and social function of music, although he did not abandon his earlier aesthetic convictions. As early as 1925, the second of the *Vier Chorstücke*, Op. 27 ("Four Pieces"), which concerns Jewish → aniconism, announced the transformation. During this time Schönberg also worked on the drama *Der biblische Weg* (1926/1927, "The Biblical Way"), which he had begun to draft in 1922/1923; the work, whose plot was not set in biblical times, may be seen as Schönberg's first creative engagement with Jewish politics, the Jewish faith, and the way in which the Jews became a people. Similar to the drama, the opera *Moses und Aron* ("Moses and Aaron"), of whose projected three acts Schönberg completed only two between 1928 and 1937, used biblical history to celebrate God's covenant with the Jews. The 1938 work → *Kol Nidre* documents Schönberg's increasing closeness to the Jewish faith, which culminated in his las work *Moderne Psalmen* (1950/1951, "Modern Psalms"), which remained in draft form. *Kol Nidre* occupies a special position in Schönberg's creative œuvre as it was originally intended to be sung in the → synagogue but was only ever performed in a concert hall. The composition was commissioned by Jacob (Jakob) Sonderling, a German rabbi who had emigrated to America and founded the → Reform Fairfax Temple in Los Angeles, and who commissioned musical works from other composers in exile in the United States as well.

Schönberg composed the short oratorio *A Survivor from Warsaw*, Op. 46, in 1947. It is characterized by its complex symbolism pervading all layers of the composition. The vocal piece in twelve-tone technique is dedicated to the victims of the Holocaust, whose experience is presented by a male narrator. The initial sentence may be seen as Schönberg's personal creed: "I remember the grandiose moment when they all started to sing, as if prearranged, the old prayer they had neglected for so many years – the forgotten creed! But I have no recollection how I got underground to live in the sewers of Warsaw for so long a time" [14. 147]. In the prayer *Shema Yisra'el, Adonai elohenu, Adonai eḥad* ("Hear, O Israel! The LORD is our God, the LORD alone"; → Shema) sung by the choir, the piece recalls the binding force of the Jewish faith.

5. Reception

The Second World War and the → Holocaust led to a renewed interest in Schönberg's work and defined its reception. In retrospect it seems that the development that led to the rupture of civilization found concealed expression in Schönberg's uncompromising music. As early as 1934 Theodor W. Adorno (→ Dialectic of Enlightenment) stated in his Schönberg interpretation *Der dialektische Komponist* ("The Dialectical Composer," 2002): "Not the unaccustomed sounds, no, it is the rhythm of the extremes, the air of catastrophe that has inspired the fear of Schoenberg. This rhythm does not merely dominate the history of Schoenberg's œuvre in the abstract. It inhabits almost every one of his pieces, down to the most hidden compositional cells" [1. 204]. The fact that Nazis as well as the communists fought Schönberg's music exalted it to a symbol of the resistance and protest of a young Western European generation of composers.

Some of the most influential composers and musicians of the 20th century were among Schönberg's pupils, such as Anton Webern, Alban Berg, Hanns Eisler (→ Misuk), and Egon Wellesz. Some of his Viennese and Berlin pupils were of Jewish origin and had to leave their homes after 1933, building a new existence in the musical teaching institutions of their host countries.

Contrary to the original expectation of Schönberg and several of his followers, twelve-tone music did not establish itself as the universally recognized language of music. However, his ideas on musical parameters and musical organizing principles based on mathematical logic have accompanied numerous composers since the 1950s. At the same time, Schönberg's political and "Jewish" works are undergoing re-evaluation in the context of the growing interest in music as an expression of cultural affiliation.

Bibliography

Sources
[1] T. W. Adorno, Essays on Music, ed. by R. Leppert, trans. by S. H. Gillespie, Berkeley 2002. [2] J. Auner (ed.), Schoenberg Reader. Documents of a Life, New Haven/New York 2003. [3] A. Schönberg, Style and Idea. Selected Writings of Arnold Schoenberg, ed. by L. Stein, trans. by L. Black, Berkeley 1984. [4] A. Schönberg, Composition with Twelve Tones (1) (1941), in: Style and Idea. Selected Writings of Arnold Schoenberg, ed. by L. Stein, trans. by L. Black, Berkeley 1984, 214–244. [5] A. Schönberg, "Stile herrschen, Gedanken siegen." Ausgewählte Schriften, ed. by A. M. Morazzoni, Mainz 2007. [6] A. Schönberg/J. Rufer, Berliner Tagebuch, Frankfurt am Main 1974. [6a] H. H. Stuckenschmidt, Schoenberg. His Life, World and Work, trans. by H. Searle, New York 1977.

Secondary literature
[7] L. Botstein, Judentum und Modernität. Essays zur Rolle der Juden in der deutschen und

österreichischen Kultur 1848 bis 1938, Vienna et al. 1991. [8] J. Brown, Schoenberg and Redemption, Cambridge 2014. [9] C. M. Cross/R. A. Berman, Political and Religious Ideas in the Works of Arnold Schoenberg, New York 2000. [10] S. Feisst, Schoenberg's New World. The American Years, Oxford 2011. [11] P. Gradenwitz, Arnold Schönberg und seine Meisterschüler. Berlin 1925–1933, Vienna 1998. [12] G. Gur, Orakelnde Musik. Schönberg, der Fortschritt und die Avantgarde, Kassel et al. 2013. [13] E. Haimo, Schoenberg's Serial Odyssey. The Evolution of his Twelve-Tone Method, 1914–1928, Oxford 1990. [14] M. Henke, Schönberg, Mattsee und "A Survivor from Warsaw," in: E. John/H. Zimmermann (eds.), Jüdische Musik? Fremdbilder – Eigenbilder, Cologne et al. 2004, 119–148. [15] M. Mäckelmann, Arnold Schönberg und das Judentum. Der Komponist und sein religiöses, nationales und politisches Selbstverständnis nach 1921, Hamburg 1984. [16] A. L. Ringer, Arnold Schoenberg. The Composer as Jew, Oxford 1993.

GOLAN GUR, CAMBRIDGE

Type

Type and typology are basic terms widely used in the humanities and social sciences of the 19th and 20th centuries. The German-Jewish philosopher and sociologist Georg Simmel (1858–1918) used the term *type* in the context of his deliberations on the fundamental epistemological preconditions for the study of society. In his *Philosophie des Geldes* (1900/1907; "The Philosophy of Money," 1978) as well as in the *Exkurs über den Fremden* (1908; "The Stranger," 1971), he studied questions of belonging, discrimination, and integration in modern society, specifically on the basis of the economic and social position of Jews in their surrounding society.

1. The concept
2. Georg Simmel
3. Type as a sociological principle
4. From type to stereotype

1. The concept

The concept of type refers to the common characteristics of a number of individuals in order to distinguish between them according to kinds, classes, or groups. Typologies were developed with specific problems and goals in a variety of fields of knowledge, such as morphological biology, → anthropology, economic sciences, art history, → statistics, and → sociology. The concepts of Max Weber (1864–1920; → Pariah People) and Georg Simmel met with broad attention here.

Weber developed a concept of the ideal type to be applied in the social sciences. Ideal types (or pure types) are constructs derived from the characteristics and elements of empirical phenomena. To Weber they were valuable means of insight to unlock concrete cultural phenomena in their interconnections, causes, and comprehensive meanings; furthermore, they were the basis of causal explanations [14. 110–121]. The ideal type was deliberately conceived to allow the interpretation of the hypothetical course of an action in such a way as if it could be entirely explained by the underlying comprehensible motives and convictions. Weber's term served as a methodological as well as heuristic tool for entire generations of scholars of religious studies as well as comparative social research.

Weber adopted the concept of the ideal type from the constitutional lawyer Georg Jellinek, who used it in a legal context. Objectively, he was guided by the considerations of the economist Carl Menger, who developed "strict" or "exact" types to examine social regularities [14. 16f.], but also by Simmel's writings. In the book *Probleme der*

Geschichtsphilosophie (1892; "The Problems of the Philosophy of History," 1977), Simmel had already demanded that the concepts necessary for the investigation of historical events should be developed in an abstraction process ignoring mere side effects and coincidences [8. 122]. In his material studies, Simmel employed the concept of type in a more playful, associative way [7. 387–389]. At the same time, the concept to him was not only a methodological tool but, in the form of the social type, also a fundamental principle of social interactions.

In his research into great thinkers such as Johann Wolfgang von Goethe (→ Elective Affinities) or Friedrich Nietzsche (→ Übervolk), Simmel correlated type and individuality in such a way that on the whole the most individual overlaps with the typical. Goethe, for instance, as the "genius type," on the one hand appeared as an absolutely autonomous person, but on the other as a "vessel of objective necessity" [4. 2]. Simmel's → essays and treatises using the concept of type present a dense network of conceptual and rhetorical connections. Still, the implications of the deliberations on the concept of type are closely interwoven with his own background and biography.

2. Georg Simmel

Simmel was born in 1858 as the seventh child of a middle-class family in Berlin. Both parents were of Jewish origin but had, independently of each other, converted before his birth to Catholicism or Protestantism (→ Conversion). Born a Christian, Simmel passed through the general education system, sharing the beliefs and values of his generation. Even so, for his entire life he was aware of his Jewish background and the fact that he was identified as a Jew, although he had hardly any stake in the Jewish religion and tradition and was not brought up to regard himself as Jewish in any way.

Georg Simmel (1858–1918)

In 1876 Simmel began to study history and philosophy, with art history and Italian as minor fields, at the Friedrich-Wilhelms-Universität in Berlin, attending lectures by, among others, the philosopher Wilhelm Dilthey, the psychologist Moritz Lazarus (→ Völkerpsychologie), and the historians Theodor Mommsen and Gustav Droysen. His further academic career proved to be difficult. His dissertation on the origins of music was rejected in 1881, and the doctorate was eventually awarded on the basis of an earlier prize essay. He finished his habilitation thesis just two years later, but was not granted the *venia legendi* until 1885, after a second trial lecture had become necessary.

During the following decades, Simmel taught as an unpaid "ewige Privatdozent" (eternal lecturer) in Berlin. In 1889 an inheritance made him financially independent; he would not have been able to live on his income from lecture fees and publication royalties alone. He had already found international recognition in the 1890s. He was featured in the first issue of the journal *L'Année sociologique* founded by Émile Durkheim (→ Sociology) in 1896, and nine of his articles were published in the *American Journal of Sociology* between 1896 and 1910. The programmatic essay "Das Problem der Soziologie" (1894; "The Problem of Sociology," 1895) was translated into English, French, Italian, and Russian by 1900. Several books reached multiple editions, such as *Philosophie des Geldes, Kant und Goethe, Zur Geschichte der modernen Weltanschauung* (1906/1916), or *Die Religion* (1906/1912).

Despite everything, he was denied a full professorship for a long time. While Max Weber – with whom Simmel had been involved in the foundation of the Deutsche Gesellschaft für Soziologie – had sponsored him when a chair in philosophy opened at Heidelberg University in 1908, an antisemitic appraisal destroyed his candidature [10. 141f.]. It was not until 1914, nearly three decades after his habilitation, that he was offered a position at the University of Strasbourg, where he taught until his death in 1918. Among his students were Ernst Cassirer (→ Philosophy of Culture), Ernst Bloch (→ Utopia), Martin Buber (→ Dialogue), Georg Lukács (→ Class Consciousness), and Siegfried Kracauer (→ Film).

Simmel's Jewish origin had always been perceived by those around him, as documented in accounts by people close to him which were published many years after his death in a *Buch des Dankes* (1958). These impressions are pervaded by allusions to Simmel's alleged Jewish appearance, voice, or gestures, probably not even meant in a derogatory way. Thus for instance Max Weber's wife Marianne – both had often been guests in the house of Gertrud (née Kinel) and Georg Simmel – wrote: "He was barely of middle height, shorter than she, typically Jewish, unattractive; but then what does the appearance matter in the case of such a witty person!" (cited in [10. 132]).

From a modern perspective, the deep ambivalence and tensions in Simmel's deliberations on type cannot be detached from this background. They are an expression of experiences which enabled Simmel to understand seemingly self-evident aspects of culture and society from the very same distance from which members of the majority society regarded those who were "strangers" in their eyes [10. 149].

3. Type as a sociological principle

Simmel's œuvre exhibits a range of topics extending from formal sociology through philosophy of art and economics to the philosophy of life (→ Lebensphilosophie). The concept of type pervades many of his writings. While he sometimes argues by means of suggestive allusions, he does not neglect the conflicting aspects often concomitant with the processual formation of self-images in the context of social interactions; for these he uses the term "Wechselwirkung" ("reciprocal interaction"). His epistemology points out the close relationship between typing and stereotyping – in the case of the social actors as well as the social scientists studying their actions.

Simmel approaches two problems with the concept of social type. On the one hand he sought to reconcile Moritz Lazarus's → Völkerpsychologie with the philosophy of → Neo-Kantianism. This was particularly concerned with the objections Dilthey had expressed against Lazarus's supra-individual categories (for instance: "Volksgeist" [national spirit], "Volksseele" [national soul], nation) and which culminated in the rejection of the concept of society and sociology as a science [10. 380–397]; [9]. In the fundamental question "How Is Society Possible?" Simmel rendered Kant's epistemological inquiry regarding nature into one regarding society [3b. 372]. How can society, understood as a supra-individual subject, represent a delimited object of research while supra-individual authorities are denied? How is a theory of society possible without merging into individual psychology? Simmel's answer was that society is a legitimate object of research in that the reciprocal interactions between individuals "persist as forms, even though individual members withdraw and new ones join" [1. 16]. The concept of type mediates between individual phenomena and their supra-individual perception. A type is the form in which we recognize a certain constellation of individual interactions.

On the other hand, the concept of type aimed at clarifying the connection between human individuality and cognitive ability. Simmel maintained – like the founder of → Gestalt psychology Max Wertheimer – that only "totalities" could ultimately be comprehended. The fragmentary perception of individuals in social interaction would thus require a complement in the form of the subsumption under types: "In order to know a man, we see him not in terms of his pure individuality, but carried, lifted up or lowered, by the general type under which we classify him." Simmel defined this process of assessing individuals using the measure of a type as an *a priori* condition of sociation [3a. 10].

The theory of type was applied to social as well as political concerns, including Jewish ones. The brief *Exkurs über den Fremden* ("The Stranger," 1971) was particularly influential. Its subject matter was adopted and further developed by the sociologist Robert Michels in his *Materialien zu einer Soziologie des Fremden* (1924), by the founder of phenomenological sociology Alfred Schütz in *The Stranger. An Essay in Social Psychology* (1944), and included in the migration research of the Chicago School around Robert Ezra Park (→ Sociology).

Simmel's references to the social position of the Jews exemplified more general and universal insights into the constitution of modern societies. Thus in the history of economics, "the stranger everywhere appears as a trader, or the trader as a stranger." As someone who – in contrast to the understanding of common sense – "comes today, and stays tomorrow," the stranger could not find a "chance to make a living" except for trade within a self-contained economic area, in which functional positions such as in agriculture and crafts were already taken. "[T]he classical example is the history of European Jews" [3a. 402f.]. Simmel's stranger is not, in fact, restricted to a mere example, but represents a type characterized by specific and recurring forms of relationships within socially differentiated societies [13. 274–277]. In this respect, the self-understanding of the Jews results from the experience that they live in communities among non-Jews with whom they interact in certain ways.

By discussing Jews in the context of the type of the stranger, Simmel did not intend to catalogue the social types of German society in the way that August Sander's social-documentary photography did at the time. Rather, in Simmel's problematization, the analysis complied with the dynamics of processes of self-understanding (Selbstverständigung). He regarded the latter as deeply disharmonic processes, as they occurred at the interface of self-perception and external perception and were founded on intrinsic ideas of individuality as well as the projections of the social environment.

Wherever Simmel resorts to the Jewish example in illustration of his ideas on modern society, he is most interesting and challenging in his references to those Jews who did not see themselves as strangers in their society and not as defined primarily by their Judaism or their Jewish background. → Assimilation produces citizens who were, paradoxically, simultaneously close to and distant from the surrounding society. "The unity of nearness and remoteness involved in every human relation is organized, in the phenomenon of the stranger, in a way which may be most briefly formulated by saying that in the relationship to him, distance means that he, who is close by, is far, and strangeness means that he, who also is far, is actually near." The stranger was an integral part of the group without being recognized as an organically integral part. "The stranger [...] is an element of the group itself. His position as a full-fledged member involves both being outside it and confronting it" [3a. 402f.]. Here, Simmel transforms the significance of a person who is a stranger in a place into a type denoting a variant of social exclusion. He is formalizing a concrete historical moment that would be incomprehensible but for specific assumptions concerning the Jews and their surrounding society. However, one must also consider not only the type of the stranger but also the different forms of being a stranger. Simmel's belief that the Jews were strangers and thus practically excluded from extensive participation in society was linked to a specific conception of society that has by now lost its historical validity [11].

Simmel's theoretical framework of the social type and its application, the linking of Jews to the stranger type, are among the most ambivalent socio-philosophical reflections developed before the → Holocaust. This applies to the evaluation of the historical situation at the time as well as the anticipated future development of the self-understanding of Judaism, whose path to full integration or assimilation into European societies appeared blocked.

4. From type to stereotype

Simmel's concept of type clearly converges with the socio-scientific concept of the stereotype. The journalist and political commentator Walter Lippmann (1889–1974), for instance, described the stereotype as a prefabricated, standardized impression of a person or situation in his 1922 study *Public Opinion*.

Simmel himself observed that on the occasion of the first impression that the Ego forms of the Other, its perception is more strongly informed by stereotypes than by the processes he had described in his earlier, formal conception of the formation of social types. At a first encounter, he pointed out, one does not know "particular facts" about the other, but one does know "a tremendous amount: the person, and that which is unmistakable about the person." This first impression "merely deepens and increases" later [5. 66]. Furthermore, Simmel gradually arrived at the opinion that the subsumption of an individual under a type did not take place, as originally assumed, reciprocally, but was considerably more one-sided, at least in practice. This was similar to the way in which Jews were perceived through preconceived stereotypes by the majority society. Simmel's epistemology thus recognized the deep ambivalence of social attributions embedded in the knowledge of the social actors.

The possibly most pointed version of Simmel's reflections on modern Jewish self-understanding is derived from a further deliberation on the concept of type. In general terms, Simmel expresses the idea that the degree of correspondence between an individual and the type ascribed to him or her can also be judged aesthetically [2. 90–100]. The more type and individual correspond, the greater the beauty. Simmel did not mean beauty in the traditional sense, but rather authenticity. Transferred to Jews, this would mean that they appeared authentic, or beautiful, if they resembled their stereotype, but non-authentic or ugly, if they deviated from it. Everyone is free to endeavor to liberate him- or herself from the type others ascribe to them – but not without paying a price [12].

Bibliography

Sources

[1] G. Simmel, Über sociale Differenzierung. Sociologische und psychologische Untersuchungen, Leipzig 1890. [2] G. Simmel, Einleitung in die Moralwissenschaft. Eine Kritik der ethischen Grundbegriffe, vol. 2, Berlin 1893. [3] G. Simmel, Soziologie. Untersuchungen über die Formen der Vergesellschaftung, Leipzig 1908. [3a] G. Simmel, The Sociology of Georg Simmel, ed. and trans. by K. H. Wolff, New York 1964. [3b] G. Simmel, How Is Society Possible?, in: Georg Simmel, 1858–1918. A Collection of Essays, with Translations and a Bibliography, ed. by K. H. Wolff, Columbus 1959, 337–356. [4] G. Simmel, Goethe, Leipzig 1913. [5] G. Simmel, Rembrandt. An Essay in the Philosophy of Art, ed. and trans. by A. Scott/H. Staubmann, New York 2005.

Secondary literature

[6] L. Coser (ed.), Georg Simmel, Englewood Cliffs 1965. [7] H.-J. Dahme, Soziologie als exakte Wissenschaft. Georg Simmels Ansatz und seine Bedeutung in der gegenwärtigen Soziologie, Stuttgart 1981. [8] U. Gerhardt, Idealtypus. Zur methodologischen Begründung der modernen Soziologie, Frankfurt am Main 2001. [9] K. C. Köhnke, Four Concepts of Social Science at Berlin University, in: M. Kaern et al. (eds.), Georg Simmel and Contemporary Sociology, Dordrecht 1990, 99–107. [10] K. C. Köhnke, Der junge Simmel in Theoriebeziehungen und sozialen Bewegungen, Frankfurt am Main 1996. [11] K. C. Köhnke, Der Fremde als Typus und als historische Kategorie. Zu einem soziologischen Grundbegriff bei Georg Simmel, Alfred Schütz und Robert Michels, in: N. Berg (ed.), Kapitalismusdebatten um 1900. Über antisemitisierende Semantiken des Jüdischen, Leipzig 2011, 219–238. [12] A. Morris-Reich, The Beautiful Jew Is a Moneylender. Money and Individuality in Simmel's Rehabilitation of the 'Jew', in: Theory, Culture & Society 20 (2003) 4, 127–142. [13] O. Rammstedt, Georg Simmels "Frem-

der," in: W. R. Dombrowsky/U. Pasero (eds.), Wissenschaft, Literatur, Katastrophe. Festschrift zum sechzigsten Geburtstag von Lars Clausen, Opladen 1995, 268–284. [14] F. Ringer, Max Weber's Methodology. The Unification of the Cultural and the Social Sciences, Cambridge (MA) 1997.

AMOS MORRIS-REICH, HAIFA

Typography

Hebrew typography is closely connected to Hebrew book → printing. To begin with, it developed primarily on the basis of the tradition of religious texts, linking different typefaces with specific text groups. The dynasties of printers who emerged over time each cultivated their own particular typographical styles that spread throughout vast regions following the geographical dispersion of families. In the 19th and 20th centuries, the need for a precise modern typography that would foster a sense of belonging arose in the context of the revival of → Hebrew and its new encoding by Zionism (→ Basel).

1. Origins of Hebrew typography
2. Spread in Europe
3. Zionism, tradition, and modern style

1. Origins of Hebrew typography

The term typography is based on the Greek words *typos* (form) and *graphein* (to write). Distinct from handwriting or chirography (Gr. *cheiros*, hand), it refers to the production and arrangement of texts by means of movable types. Individual forms of writing are replaced with a superordinate system of standardized types. In addition, movable types allow larger and more uniform print runs of works, whose reach and radius of integration are greatly increased compared

TYPOGRAPHY

to manuscript culture. Characteristics of → Hebrew typography are, on the one hand, the emergence of particular styles of lettering for specific text groups, and, on the other, the comparative freedom granted the printers by the religious authorities, with the result that the production of books was not based exclusively on the → Halakhah but also on economical or aesthetic criteria.

Hebrew book → printing began approximately twenty years after Johannes Gutenberg's first prints appeared around 1450. Subsequently, Hebrew typography developed five fundamental typefaces on the basis of the square script for sacred texts, the semi-cursive used for Rabbinic texts, and the cursive script for everyday use. In printed books, two square types, one in Ashkenazi (→ Ashkenaz) and one in Sephardi (→ Sepharad) style, were predominantly reserved for sacred texts. To these were added two semi-cursive types – these, too, in Ashkenazi as well as Sephardi styles. The Ashkenazi variant, used exclusively for → Yiddish texts, is called *Vaybertaytsh* (Yidd.; women's Yiddish) or *mashket* or *masha'it*. The Rashi type, which is used to this day for Bible and Talmud → commentaries, was developed on the basis of the Sephardi variant. Finally, in Amsterdam (→ Esnoga), an independent interpretation of a cursive type in the Ashkenazi style was developed.

Ashkenazi square type was used in numerous stylistic variations. In Central and Eastern Europe, typography was often based on local manuscripts, occasionally adopting elements of the increasingly dominant Sephardi square script, too. In German-speaking regions, references to Gothic type can be detected [8. 23]. Rashi type, occasionally also termed Rabbinic type, dates back to the first dated Hebrew print, the scholar Rashi's (Solomon ben Isaac, 1040–1150; → Worms) commentary on the Pentateuch (→ Tanakh) printed in the southern Italian city of Reggio di Calabria in 1475. The printer

Abraham ben Garton, a Jew who had immigrated to Calabria from Spain, employed a semi-cursive Sephardi type, which was subsequently named after the medieval exegete.

In the 15th century, the three brothers Obadiah, Manasseh, and Benjamin of Rome are said to have printed the first incunabula in Hebrew type in the printing shop belonging to the printers Konrad Sweynheym and Arnold Pannartz, who had immigrated from Mainz and were active in Subiaco and Rome. The brothers employed an Ashkenazi Italian square script based on the manuscript traditions of the printers from Germany [8. 18]. From the early 16th century onward, Christian printers, too, employed Hebrew characters in the production of textbooks and grammar books for Hebrew and → Aramaic. They primarily employed Ashkenazi square types while Jewish printers producing Hebrew works increasingly moved on to using Sephardi square types almost exclusively [8. 20].

Over time, a variety of different type styles were used side by side in one and the same publication, especially in the editions of the Mishnah, the → Talmud, or the *Shulḥan Arukh* (Set Table; → Halakhah), which included numerous commentaries. Technical complications in the production of the letter types frequently led to differences between letters of the same type, with the result that readers could find it difficult to distinguish between graphically similar letters in a printed text [7. 3]. A further problem for printers arose from the vocalization and cantillation marks above and below the letters in biblical texts (→ Tanakh). In the early years of printing, these were often subsequently added by hand. Another challenge was the reproduction of the numerous special forms of Hebrew letters found in Bible manuscripts [9. 40].

While words were not allowed to break off at the end of a line in square script and empty spaces were not desirable either, *litterae dilatabiles* – letters stretched sideways – were developed to fill the space. Pagination was usually marked using Hebrew letters, in rare cases also using Arabic numbers. Title pages were unknown in early printed books [7. 4f.].

2. Spread in Europe

The first printing dynasties emerged in the wake of the invention of book printing and the development of a genuinely Hebrew typography at the end of the 15th century. Jewish and non-Jewish punchcutters, type founders, and typesetters developed their own styles and formats of letters; these may be regarded as the identifying features of the respective families, who were frequently widely dispersed and active at numerous locations.

A Jewish family originally from Speyer and Fürth achieved great prominence in Soncino near Milan. Gershom Soncino (ca. 1460–1533), above all, acquired great renown thanks to his prayer books, Bibles, and Talmud tractates that were particularly elaborate in their typography. In cooperation with the dyer Abraham ben Chaim, one of the most renowned typographers of his time, he published the first complete Bible in → Hebrew in 1488. This was followed four years later (1492) by the first complete edition of the Mishnah. In 1505 he published the first Hebrew book that included a title page, the *Sefer ha-Rokeah*, a book of advice by Eleazar ben Yehudah of Worms, to accompany the → Halakhah [2. 5]. Through five generations, the Soncino dynasty produced books on three continents. The printing formats employed, as well as their typography, were long regarded as being of such high quality that any alteration would have been a sacrilege [3. 24]. The Soncinos were also the first who based their style on the Sephardi square type in the hope of attracting the Jews expelled from the Iberian Peninsula after 1492 (→ Sephardim) as their customers; subsequently, Sephardi letters became the standard type for many printers.

Non-Jewish printers, too, set new standards in Hebrew typography, such as Daniel Bomberg (ca. 1475–1549) from Flanders. He settled in → Venice, where he acquired the privilege of being permitted to print Hebrew books in 1516 – the same year in which the Jews of the city had to move into the ghetto. With the first complete edition of the → Talmud (1520–1523), Bomberg made a decisive contribution to the city's becoming a center of Hebrew book printing. Bomberg, who possessed some knowledge of Hebrew, derived the system of pagination and folio numbering in the Babylonian Talmud, which is followed to this day, from the printed codices of canonical law of the Roman Catholic Church. He also transferred the division of biblical texts into chapters and verses customary in Christian editions, distinguished different texts typographically, and designed a fixed double-page layout in which all texts were arranged in a visually meaningful way according to their content. Previously, the design had depended on the oral and manuscript traditions of frequently rival rabbis (→ Rabbinate); with Bomberg's system, the authority of the word was removed from the individual teacher and transferred to the continuous and documentable printed text.

North of the Alps (→ Ashkenaz), the first printed Hebrew texts were produced in → Prague. There, Gerson ben Solomon Kohen founded the printing dynasty of the Gersonides in 1512; in 1527 he published the first Pesah Haggadah (→ Course of the Year) with woodcut images in the style of Hans Holbein and Albrecht Dürer. Most of these were created by the illustrator and itinerant printer Chaim ben David Shachor (16th cent.) and would influence the style of many later Haggadot. Many of Gerson's printed works include flyleaves featuring hands raised in prayer, which became something like his trademark. Unlike printed texts from Venice, the Gersonides exclusively employed

Ashkenazi square type; however, due to a decline in the quality of Prague print products from the 17th century onward, these gradually disappeared.

Other cities that became important locations for Hebrew book → printing, and, consequently, for Hebrew typography, were → Cracow and Constantinople, where Jews opened the first printing press of the Ottoman Empire as early as 1493. Jews were explicitly permitted to produce books in Hebrew types for their own use while they were prohibited from printing in → Arabic letters until 1727.

Beginning in 1630, Amsterdam (→ Esnoga) came to be known as the most significant center of Hebrew book printing. By 1730, more than 1,300 works in Hebrew and → Yiddish had been published here. The Lisbon-born rabbi and scholar Menasseh ben Israel (→ Recife) founded the city's first Hebrew printing shop in 1626, producing books in four additional languages as well in order not to be dependent on just one clientele. In 1651 a church council banned him from printing in Dutch as this was interpreted as an offense to pious Christians. In order to delimit his output from Bomberg's typographical style, ben Israel designed his own Hebrew type; in addition, his books included numerous illustrations and were much sought after by the public [3. 92].

The non-Jewish punchcutter Christoffel van Dijck designed a typeface of high quality, mainly influenced by Sephardi square types, which was used by the printing dynasties Athias (from 1654 onward) and Proops (from 1708 onward). For a long time, these *otiyot Amsterdam* (Amsterdam types) set the standard in Hebrew typography, superseding the Ashkenazi square types. Frequently, items printed in Germany, Poland, Bohemia, and Moravia were given the quality mark *be-otiyot Amsterdam* (in Amsterdam types), often with the name Amsterdam printed in large letters and the actual place of production in small ones.

A lively trade in matrices, woodcuts, and decorative material, offered at fairs in cities such as Frankfurt am Main, was an additional source of income for Amsterdam printers. In 1785 Joseph Proops sold his stock of letters to Joseph Kurzböck in → Vienna, who had taken over his father Gregor's university printing press and now began publishing books in Hebrew as well. The production of Hebrew books in Vienna promised a lucrative market as the → Edict of Toleration issued by Emperor Joseph II in 1782 banned the import of Hebrew books produced abroad and prohibited Jews in the Habsburg Empire from producing any kind of printed papers. Further printers followed Kurzböck's example, among them Joseph Hraschanzky, who did not buy used Hebrew letters but had his manufactured specially by the renowned type founder and copper engraver Johann Ernst Mannsfeld. Many Jewish printing houses in Amsterdam, Fürth, Sulzbach, and Eastern Europe suffered losses in revenue as a result of the import ban. At the same time, larger numbers of matrices from all over Europe came to Vienna, where they were reworked and offered to clients; in this way the city's printing houses were able to produce high-quality items in a wide variety of styles and type sizes.

Kurzböck sent two of his journeymen to the Orientalische Akademie (Oriental Academy) of Vienna University with the specific task of acquiring a sufficient level of knowledge of Hebrew. After Kurzböck's death, one of them, Anton Schmid, bought the type collection and founded his own printing house, which became well-known in its own right. All these printing houses managed by non-Jews in Vienna and in Brno worked closely with Jewish typesetters and proofreaders. However, they were in direct competition with one another, so that they pointed out the quality of their own lettering as an advertisement or accused their competitors of using inferior typefaces.

Over the course of the 19th century, → Leipzig – a city of fairs as well as a center of book printing, book trading, and publishing businesses – also established itself as a production center of Hebrew texts on a large scale. In 1908 the Leipzig type foundry introduced an entirely novel typeface, the → Frank Rühl font, which met with widespread approval due to its typographical design. To this day, it is one of the most frequently used typefaces.

3. Zionism, tradition, and modern style

The renaissance of → Hebrew and its new encoding at the hands of Zionism (→ Basel) also changed the demands made on Hebrew typography. In discussions about possible reforms, there were demands for emancipation from previous typefaces, and historicizing references were rejected. The classical square style of the letters was now even seen as an obstacle to the flow of the script [6. 12f., 25f.].

In view of the limited stock of typefaces available, members of the → Bezalel School of Arts and Crafts founded in Jerusalem in 1906 devoted themselves to typography from an early date. Young Zionist artists, such as Ze'ev Raban (Wolf Rawicki), Avraham bar Adon, and Shmuel Ben David (Samuel Davidov), designed typefaces that were still oriented toward traditional type faces, but they were unable to take hold. Franzisca Baruch, who had studied at the Staatliche Unterrichtsanstalt des Kunstgewerbemuseums (State Academy of the Museum of Decorative Arts) in Berlin in the 1920s and emigrated to Palestine in 1933, first designed the Stam font for the Berlin type foundry H. Berthold AG on the basis of the typefaces used in the Pesaḥ Haggadah by Gershom ben Solomon Kohen. Together with the publisher Salman Schocken (→ Schocken Bücherei), she created another font style based on one of Bomberg's types for a volume of short stories by the writer Samuel

Agnon (→ Shira). While it was not used at the time, it was developed further after she emigrated, becoming the proprietary typeface of the daily paper → Ha'aretz.

For a long time, the close link between the established type styles and religious tradition constituted an obstacle in the development of modern Hebrew typography. Jewish graphic designers and typographers who had studied at progressive academies of arts and crafts, such as the Bauhaus in Dessau or the Moscow Art Academy VKhUTEMAS (*Vysshie khudozhestvenno-tekhnicheskie masterskie*) provided an impetus to create and distinguish modern Hebrew scripts and typefaces. The → art nouveau aesthetic of many printed items, which was felt to be outdated, was abandoned. The Zionists' enthusiasm for all things oriental (→ Orient), which had often been reflected in the typefaces, likewise found an end when violent unrest between Jews and Arabs broke out at the end of the 1920s.

In Mandatory Palestine, Hebrew advertising typography played a key role in the renewal of Hebrew typefaces. As many notices and official publications were bilingual, the Hebrew letters used were often based on the then popular Futura types designed by Paul Renner that was frequently used in English publications, or on the Gill Sans font created by Eric Gill. In 1929 the graphic designer Jan Le Witt from Poland developed these into the geometric Chaim type, which was entirely free of curves and is still used for headings of newspaper articles. The Aharoni font created by the typographer Tuvia Aharoni, who had immigrated to Palestine from Poland in 1932, contributed another radically ahistorical approach. Due to their elegance and readability, these letters are regarded as a successful instance of a transformation from modern Latin to Hebrew type [5. 73].

After the foundation of the State of Israel, young graphic designers set themselves the task of creating modern typefaces. New styles came on the market and were soon integrated into production. In the early 1960s, Eliyahu Koren (Eliyahu Korngold) introduced the Koren Bible Type, a modern typeface based on Hebrew manuscripts and early printed types. Due to its precision and good readability, it became the standard type in Bible printing. Together with Rudolf Koch, Henri Friedländer began as early as the 1930s to work on a modern Hebrew typeface. At that time, he was a typesetter with Teubner in Leipzig, with Wirth in Dresden, and with the in-house printers at the Klingspor type foundry. The typeface was published as Hadassah in 1958, a modern as well as distinguished typeface popular to this day. Later, Friedländer also developed Shalom, Aviv, and Hadar as typewriter fonts. The Bezalel graduate Zvi Narkiss designed the family of Narkiss types in the 1950s, which were adopted by Microsoft for its Hebrew word processing programs in the 1990s. The new Hebrew typefaces were designed to express a clear break with the traditions of → exile; the designers sought to convey the delimitation and particularity of the nation-state while at the same time looking to the aesthetics of modernism and its universalist principles.

Bibliography

[1] R. Frank, Über hebräische Typen und Schriftarten, Berlin 1926. [2] L. Fuks/R. G. Fuks-Mansfeld, Hebrew Typography in the Northern Netherlands, 1585–1815. Historical Evaluation and Descriptive Bibliography, vol. 1, Leiden 1984. [3] C. Harris, The Way Jews Lived. Five Hundred Years of Printed Words and Images, Jefferson (NC) 2009. [4] P. Messner, Tel Aviv und die Revolution des hebräischen Schriftbilds, in: PaRDeS 15 (2009), 22–38. [5] P. Messner, Von der Form der Sprache. Hebräische Renaissance und typografischer Diskurs in Deutschland zur Zeit der Weimarer Republik, in: K. Bürger et al. (eds.), Soncino – Gesellschaft der Freunde des jüdischen Buches. Ein Beitrag zur Kulturgeschichte, Berlin et al. 2014, 41–74. [6] H. Schonfield, The New Hebrew Typography, London 1932. [7] M. Steinschneider/D. Cassel, Jüdische Typographie und jüdischer Buchhandel, Jerusalem 1938. [8] I. J. Tamari, Die Erforschung eines typographischen Ausdruckssystems, in: H. Klocke/I. J. Tamari (eds.), Hebräische Typographie im deutschsprachigen Raum, Gummersbach 2001, 17–26. [9] I. J. Tamari, Das Volk der Bücher. Eine Bücherreise durch sechs Jahrhunderte jüdischen Lebens, Munich 2012.

ITTAI J. TAMARI, MUNICH

U

Übervolk

The idea of the Jewish people as "Übervolk" (Aḥad Ha-Am) derives from a direct transfer of Nietzsche's term "Übermensch" to the Jewish situation. It emerged from a debate between Micha Josef Berdyczewski and Aḥad Ha-Am in the 1890s about Nietzsche and Judaism and can be seen as the linchpin of Jewish Nietzscheanism, which formed a central element of the anti-bourgeois rebellion against Jewish tradition between 1890 and 1933. Jewish Nietzscheans, from Georg Brandes and Georg Simmel to Martin Buber and Oscar Levy, played a major role in spreading Nietzschean thought throughout Europe.

1. Nietzsche and the Jews
2. Jewish Nietzscheanism
3. Übermensch and Übervolk

1. Nietzsche and the Jews

Friedrich Nietzsche (1844–1900), the son of a protestant pastor and a radical atheist, is perhaps the most significant case of a non-Jew who through Jewish interpretations was gradually adopted into the canon of Jewish intellectual history. The fact that he later became an important reference for the National Socialists and that both Mussolini and Hitler viewed themselves as Nietzscheans, is no contradiction. The many voices of the reception are not just a consequence of misunderstandings by the interpreters but are intrinsic to Nietzsche's own "nomad thought" (Gilles Deleuze), which does not align itself with any particular political ideology. His project of a "transvaluation of values," [8g. 52] which aimed at the renewal of a culture mired in torpidity and decadence, could be claimed by the most diverse and antagonistic ideologies and movements.

Contrary to the National Socialist appropriation (Alfred Baeumler, *Nietzsche der Philosoph und Politiker*, 1931), Nietzsche had no part in the antisemitic discourse of his time. In a letter to his sister he called himself an "incorrigible European and anti-antisemite" [9. 178] and understood antisemitism as the doctrine of the "underprivileged" [8f. 460]. In *Morgenröte* (1881; "Daybreak," 1982) he predicted that the European Jews would be "called the inventors and signposts of the nations of Europe" and produce "great men and great works" [8a. 206]. They were desperate to give up their nomadic life; European nations should "go out to meet it: for which it would perhaps be a good idea to eject the anti-Semitic ranters from the country" [8b. 183].

At the same time Nietzsche saw the ancient Jews as the originators of "the slave revolt in morality" [8c. 34] – a people under political oppression whose "priests" used religion to effect a "denaturalizing of natural values" in the sense of a "falsification" of and alienation from the traditional system of morality [8d. 146–150] in order to avenge the powerlessness of the Jews vis-à-vis their oppressors. Paradoxically it is precisely this criticism of the post-biblical, rabbinical, "priestly" Judaism which the Jewish Nietzscheans accepted quite freely [20. 79], while his idea of modern Judaism as a positive counter-concept to the Christian culture of his day was cited more often with apologetic intentions.

The Jewish reception however was not limited to Nietzsche's statements about Jews; much more relevant was the suggestive power of his project to replace the ossified European culture with a new and vibrant one. This new culture, through a circular historical process, was to remain continually in a mode of renewal and rebirth – the "eternal return" is a central motif of the later Nietzsche – and not one that would cause it to stagnate and ultimately to disintegrate. This ambition defines his early attempt to contrast the Dionysian with the Apollonian (*Die Geburt der Tragödie*, 1872; "The Birth of Tragedy," 1909), as much as his struggle against the predominance of history and the emphasis on the antagonism between writing and living (*Vom Nutzen und Nachteil der Historie für das Leben*, 1874; "On the Use and Disadvantages of History for Life," 1983); his spectacular pronouncement that God was dead (*Die fröhliche Wissenschaft*, 1882; "The Joyful Wisdom," 1910, retranslated as "The Gay Science," 2006), and *Also sprach Zarathustra* (1883–1885; "Thus Spoke Zarathustra," 1909), which was intended as a parody of biblical prophecy and established the new, secular religion (→ Secularization) of the Übermensch. Facing the Übermensch was the figure of the "Ultimate Man," the metaphorical embodiment of the most contemptible man – an asymetrical pair of opposites which in the process of reception could be filled with any type of content [8e. 45].

In *Also sprach Zarathustra* we also find the motif of the old and new tablets, of tremendous significance for the Jewish reception of Nietzsche, as it takes up the Jewish origin story while documenting Nietzsche's determination to put a new narrative in its place: "Here I sit and wait, old shattered law-tables around me and also new, half-written law-tables" [8e. 214]. The motif refers to a situation in which the tradition has been upset but new values have not yet taken its place. The old values and distinctions live on even though they have lost their foundation and legitimacy with the death of God. The cry, "O my brothers, shatter, shatter the old law-tables!" [8e. 219] became the guiding principle of the Jewish Nietzscheans at the turn of the 20th century.

2. Jewish Nietzscheanism

The Jewish Nietzsche reception of the early 20th century is not only defined by the fact that Jews were *also* readers of Nietzsche but by the peculiar alliance of Nietzscheanism and Judaism, together with the various branches of Zionism (→ Old New Land; → Basel). The "transvaluation of all values" [8g. 57] offered a program to those who neither found their home in the Jewish tradition nor wished to commit themselves to the future expectations of socialism.

The term Nietzscheanism was coined during Nietzsche's lifetime by Ola Hansson, who in 1889 used it to characterize the Danish-Jewish philosopher Georg Brandes (1842–1927) [20. 17]. Nietzsche's fame in Europe began to spread rapidly with Brandes (*Friedrich Nietzsche: En Afhandling om aristokratisk Radikalisme*, 1889; "An Essay on the Aristocratic Radicalism of Friedrich Nietzsche," 1914). As a result, Nietzsche was given epithets such as "proclaimer," "apostle," and "savior"; for example in the first publication by the subsequent head of the Bavarian government Kurt Eisner (→ Bavarian Council Republic), *Friedrich Nietzsche und die Apostel der Zukunft* (1892), which argued that one had to renounce the "false god" Nietzsche to opt for socialism. Another detractor was Max Nordau (→ Muscular Judaism), who attacked Nietzsche in the second part of his work *Entartung* (1893; "Degeneration," 1895). Such polemical outbursts however were by this stage directed against the hosts of imitators who viewed Nietzsche as their new God.

The idea of a specifically Jewish Nietzscheanism was first formulated in Aḥad Ha-Am's (→ Cultural Zionism) essay *Li-she'elot ha-yom* (On the Questions of the Day), which appeared in the journal *Ha-Shiloaḥ* in 1898 and in → German in → *Ost und West* under the title *Nietzscheanismus und Judentum* (1902). The key → Hebrew phrase was *nitsheanizm Yehudi*. Jewish Nietzscheans were largely indifferent to the concepts of the eternal return and the "will to power." They were attracted first and foremost by Nietzsche's critical stance on ascetic ideals, his statements condemning the denial of sensuality and of life, and by ideas promising a liberation from the yoke of tradition.

For Western European Jews Nietzsche became an invaluable resource for surmounting the disintegrating project of → assimilation. His pathos of affirmation became the blueprint for the campaign to "say yes" to Judaism (Chaim Müntz; *Wir Juden*, 1907). Nietzsche offered a way to escape Jewish self-hatred, a prospect of freedom from tradition, and from the sense of guilt over this break. Robert Weltsch (→ Jüdische Rundschau) as late as 1933 and in the face of the National Socialist assumption of power still called on Jews to "say yes to your Jewishness" [14. 79]. Theodor Lessing's diagnosis of Jewish → "self-hatred" was as firmly stated in Nietzschean categories as his recommended antidote, Zionism: "Do not cheat your destiny but love it" [6. 33].

Theodor Herzl (→ Old New Land) found little to admire in Nietzsche but shared with him a major assumption about politics. About a conversation with the founder of the Magyar Általános Munkáspárt (General Workers Party of Hungary), Leo Frankel (→ Budapest), he wrote: "I explained to him why I am against the democracies. 'So you are a disciple of Nietzsche?' he said. 'Not at all. Nietzsche is a madman. But one can

only govern aristocratically'" [5. 191]. Chaim Weizmann (→ Chemistry), in contrast, was full of admiration in 1902, when he wrote an enthusiastic letter to his fiancée, with a gift of Nietzsche's writings [15. 103].

A crucial voice leading Zionists to embrace Nietzsche was Martin Buber (→ Dialogue), who conceived of his Jewish → Renaissance as a "redemption" [19. 16] from the spirit of Nietzsche's *Geburt der Tragödie*. As a 17-year old, Buber had translated Nietzsche's *Zarathustra* into → Polish and a few years later had composed a solemn tribute to the recently deceased Nietzsche, which concluded with the words: "When he left us, life had become greater and more worth living" ("Ein Wort über Nietzsche und die Lebenswerte," 1900) [19. 158, n. 160]. Buber based his *Erlebnismystik* (mysticism of experience) on the idea of the eternal return, while he opposed any "*Übermensch* fantasies" [19. 147, n. 2]. Like Micha Josef Berdyczewski (→ Anthology), he too found the Nietzschean spirit of rebellion in the tales of → Hasidism.

Gershom Scholem (→ Kabbalah) noted about *Zarathustra* in 1914: "Yet *Zarathustra* is in fact a new Bible [...]. To write something like it is my ideal. That's it! But who can write a *Zarathustra* of [...] a modern Jew (in the deep sense of the word)?" [13. 36]. In 1915 he read the text again and discovered in it "a holy book" [13. 86]. Later he claimed to despise Nietzsche and that he had never been influenced by him [20. 90–105]. Franz Rosenzweig (→ [The] Star of Redemption) would only recognize Nietzsche as a new type of philosopher, who had forged a union of "man and thinker." His actual doctrine was of no interest to him: "What he philosophized has by now become almost a matter of indifference. Dionysiac and Superman, Blond Beast and Eternal Return – where are they now? But none of those who now feel the urge to philosophize can any longer bypass the man himself" [12. 9].

This however did not yet provide a decisive argument against stronger affinities in content between Nietzsche and Judaism. Isaac Heinemann (→ Classical Studies) in 1925 made an attempt to extract the notion of an Übermensch from Jewish sources, which he was adamant should be kept separate from Nietzsche's "Gewaltmoral" (morality of violence). In Philo (→ Alexandria), Judah ha-Levi (→ Kuzari), and Maimonides (→ Guide for the Perplexed) he located the idea of a small circle of greater human beings whose philosophical insight was superior but who remained bound to others by their solidarity [3. 17]. This "Nietzscheanization of Judaism" [15. 99] reached its apex in Heinrich Berl's essay *Nietzsche und das Judentum* (1932), which styled Nietzsche into a prophet of the Jewish spirit.

The epitome of a Jewish Nietzschean, and a life-long proponent, was Oscar Levy (1867–1921), a physician and essayist of German-Jewish origin, who from 1909 onward published the first complete edition of Nietzsche in English. With the onset of the First World War, at a time when Nietzsche was widely seen as the stooge of German militarism, it earned him the harsh condemnation of his critics, while London bookshops advertised his edition with the slogan "read the devil to fight him the better" [7. 42]. Levy's idea of Judaism, heavily influenced by Nietzsche's aristocratic affectations, was ambivalent. On the one hand he argued that only an individual could be chosen and not, as the Jewish tradition holds, an entire people [20. 195]. On the other hand he claimed the National Socialist ideology of the Germans as the chosen people demonstrated that Hitlerism was a Jewish heresy rooted in the Old Testament [7. 28]. In Nietzsche's works, he wrote from his French → exile in 1937, there were views expressed for which he would now "find himself in a concentration camp or in the misery of emigration" [7. 76].

To counteract the National Socialist monopolization of Nietzsche that his sister Elisabeth Förster-Nietzsche had orchestrated with her husband, the antisemite Bernhard Förster, Leopold Schwarzschild published the journal *Das Neue Tage-Buch* from his exile in Paris; joining him in this mission were the Acéphale group around Georges Bataille ("Elisabeth Judas-Foerster," 1937). Others, however, did view Nietzsche as an intellectual precursor of National Socialism. Karl Zickendraht (*Sieben Thesen wider den Nietzsche-Geist*, 1945) described him unceremoniously as a war criminal. The period after the Second World War saw an arduous process of re-appropriation taking place in Germany that was often accompanied by attempts to situate Nietzsche in a context with Karl Marx (→ Jewish Question) and Sigmund Freud (→ Psychoanalysis). The French Nietzsche reception (Paul Ricœur, Gilles Deleuze, Michel Foucault) began to make significant contributions from 1961. The Jewish reclamation of Nietzsche was profoundly shaped by Walter Kaufmann's *Nietzsche: Philosopher, Psychologist, Antichrist* (1950).

3. Übermensch and Übervolk

At the turn of the 20th century Nietzsche was one of the most influential thinkers for the Jews of Eastern Europe [20. 35–52]. While some Hebrew writers (→ Hebrew; → Literature) such as Berdyczewski, Josef Chaim Brenner (1881–1921), and David Frishman (1859–1922) read Nietzsche's works in the original German, others first came into contact with his ideas through the Russian translations of the books about Nietzsche by Georg Brandes and Georg Simmel (→ Type) [20. 37]. Either way, key terms such as Übermensch, "transvaluation of all values," or the "death of God" quickly found their way into the Hebrew language.

The most powerful manifestation of Nietzsche's reclaimed status came in the figure of the New Hebrew who was no longer defined by his connection with the Jewish tradition but exclusively by a specific contemporary way of life (→ Nimrod). As early as 1894 the religious scholar David Neumark (1866–1924) described the "New Hebrew" in the Nietzschean spirit and coined the translation *adam elyon* for Übermensch. Even the type of the New Hebrew propagated in "practical" Zionism, who distinguishes himself by physical strength and a healthy robustness, exhibits traits of the Übermensch; through the absence of aristocratic ideals and his faith in progress, however, he is concurrently diametrically opposed to it.

The poems of Sha'ul Tchernichovsky (1875–1943; → Poetry) from the turn of the 20th century clearly show the influence of Nietzsche. In *Le-nokhaḥ pesel Apolo* ("Before the Statue of Apollo," 1923), which ends with a bow "to life, to strength, to beauty," he emphasizes the vitality of Greek culture. The god's embodiment combines traces of Nietzsche's Apollo with those of his counterpart Dionysus into a beautiful God who is drunk on life, in contrast to the God of the Jewish tradition. Zalman Shneour's (1886–1959) poem *Luḥot gnuzim* (1948; Hidden tablets) emphasizes the conflict of the ancient Hebrews with their priests and prophets [20. 38, 55f.].

Also sprach Zarathustra also had a considerable impact on the style and symbolism of modern → Hebrew. David Frishman's Hebrew translation of *Zarathustra* (publ. 1909–1911) was composed in the biblical style, which illustrated the extent to which the figure of Zarathustra was already seen as a Jewish prophet. Frishman's own stories emphasize the conflict between the → law and the expression of individuality and took the side of the outcast and marginalized individual.

The central event in the reception history of Nietzsche in Hebrew publications was the debate between Berdyczewski and Aḥad Ha-Am in the 1890s. Berdyczewski, who had published a collection of essays under the title *Shinui arakhim* (Transvaluation of Values), was a quintessential Nietzschean and regarded Nietzsche as his "rabbi." In the essay *Stira u-vinyan* ("Wrecking and Building," 1959) he describes how the Jewish people had come close to being eradicated by → assimilation and were now faced with a stark choice: either to "be the last Jews or the first Hebrews" [4. 293]. Faced with this alternative, he favored individuality over the impositions of the collective, physical strength over the intellectual values of Jewish ethics, spontaneity over the yoke of the Law and the Scriptures, and the need to absorb European ideas over the rigidity of the Jewish canon.

Berdyczewski and Aḥad Ha-Am agreed in their endeavor to "restore the Jewish People on thoroughly secular foundations," as Berdyczewski explained in 1905 [2. 283]. He lamented that Jews are "always leering at" the cultures of other people because we don't have a secular culture of our own. And this division within ourselves and the longing to reach beyond ourselves will still exist in our own country unless and until the spiritual core of the Jewish people is completely changed and a transvaluation of all values has taken place; we must envisage the creation of a secular culture for ourselves, a sovereign authority to govern our lives, as religious Judaism once did" (cited in [20. 23]). Moreover, Berdyczewski shared Aḥad Ha-Am's perspective regarding a revitalization of the Jewish people, which could only take place on a cultural understanding. Both therefore viewed Judaism in European categories; to them it was one culture among many and, more importantly, not a primarily religious community, that is, not one defined by the Revelation on Mount Sinai. However, while Aḥad Ha-Am saw the religious genesis narrative as integral to the body of traditions underlying the new Jewish culture, Berdyczewski demanded a radical break not only with the religious tradition but with all elements of the Jewish genesis narrative – to him the epitome of false values. In this, too, he followed Nietzsche, who had described the Revelation on Mount Sinai as a "falsification" that the Jewish priests of the postexilic period (→ Exile) used to secure their power [8d. 148f.].

Berdyczewski concluded that "nothing new can be begun, no total transvaluation and no revolution in the life of a people can be instigated without prior interrogation of and reckoning with the past. The fundamental error of Zionism was that it hoped to combine its thoroughly *new* drive with the *established* one" [2. 283]. The transvaluation of all values was to effect a revolution which would place Jews above Judaism and the living person above the legacy of his ancestors. "We must cease to be tablets on which books are transcribed and thoughts handed down to us – always handed down." A fundamental revision of the conditions for the existence of the Jewish people was to revitalize their souls: "Transvaluation is like a flowing spring. It revives whatever is in us, in the secret places of the soul. Our powers are filled with a new, life-giving content. Such a choice promises us a noble future; the alternative is to remain a straying people following its erring shepherds. A great responsibility rests upon us, for everything lies in our hands! We are the last Jews – or we are the first of a new nation" [4. 295].

Aḥad Ha-Am initially criticized the Jewish Nietzscheans for importing the idea of a Jewish transvaluation of all values virtually unchanged from European culture, instead of carefully transferring it into Jewish literature. It was impossible, he argued, for European content to take on a Jewish form simply by having it "read from right to left." [1. vol. 1, 40]. In his essays "Eitzah Tovah" (Good Advice) and "The Transvaluation of Values" he developed his own hermeneutics for such a transfer. It was his contention that Nietzsche contained ideas of a universal character as well as "merely German or aristocratic ones"; the task was to "free the human element from its subordination to the German form, and subordinate it instead to our own form. Thus we shall have the necessary assimilation, and we shall be importing into our literature ideas which are *new, but not foreign*" [1a. 224]. Nietzsche's veneration of physical strength and of "'the fair beast' (*die blonde Bestie*)" meant that when he confronted the Jews, it was "no longer the philosopher as such who speaks; it is the man of Aryan race" [1a. 225]. While at the same time directing his attack against Berdyczewski's poor knowledge of the tradition, Aḥad Ha-Am pointed out that "there is no necessity now for the creation of a Jewish Nietzscheism of this kind, because it has existed for centuries" [1a. 226]. He was referring to the Just One, the → tsaddik described in the moral literature, in the → Talmud, and in the → Midrashim. This figure was to him the concrete Jewish incarnation of the "Übermensch."

Aḥad Ha-Am, who adopted many ideas and concepts from his Nietzschean opponents, nevertheless made them uniquely his own by referencing their roots in the Jewish tradition. The fusion of Übermensch and tsaddik allowed him to stress the ethical values of solidarity and community which he claimed Nietzsche and the Nietzscheans had overlooked in borrowing from the tradition. A Nietzschean Jewish Übermensch thus led him to the Jewish people as the "Übervolk," whose moral force had prepared the ground for the emergence of the Übermensch: "If we agree, then, that the Super*man* is the goal of all things, we must needs agree also that an essential condition of the attainment of this goal is the Super*nation*: that is to say, there must be a single nation better adapted than other nations, by virtue of its inherent characteristics, to moral development, and ordering its whole life in accordance with a moral law which stands higher than the common type. This nation will then serve as the soil essentially and supremely fitted to produce the fairest of all fruits – the Superman" [1a. 228].

The Übermensch ideology thus became the perfect vehicle for reintroducing the faded idea of the Chosen People. The construct of the Jews as "Übervolk" gave to the curio of intellectual history that is Jewish Nietzscheanism a clearly defined function within modern post-traditional Jewish thought, which could be said to have discovered itself via the detour of Nietzsche. The idea of Jewish chosenness had become increasingly awkward to assimilated Jews of the 19th century, as it seemed to postulate a Jewish exceptionalism that would only undermine the growing confessionalization of Judaism as well as the equality of assimilated Jews. "[T]hey have tried to adapt Judaism to modern requirements by inventing the famous theory of 'the mission of Israel among the nations.' Thus they reconcile the idea of the national election with that of human equality, by making the one a means to the other" [1a. 230]. This universalist reinterpretation of the doctrine of the Chosen People, however, had the disadvantage that it could no longer grasp the deeper layer of the antisemitic prejudice that drew its strength from the old, Christian-influenced hatred of Jews. Against this backdrop Aḥad Ha-Am, who had given a sharp-eyed account of antisemitism in connection with the → Dreyfus Affair (Avdut be-tokh ḥerut, 1891; "Slavery in Freedom," 1898), chose to approach the traditional meaning of the dogma from an entirely modern perspective. He would allow the moral superiority implied in the chosenness to exist only as an inner feeling as long as the vision of → cultural Zionism remained unfulfilled.

By 1910 both Aḥad Ha-Am and Berdyczewski had lost the central position they once occupied in the Hebrew literary discourse. Aḥad Ha-Am was working in London for the Wissotsky Tea Company; Berdyczewski had withdrawn to Germany and was publishing → anthologies of Jewish tales which still preserved faint traces of the Nietzschean spirit. In subsequent collections of his earlier works he often deleted all references to Nietzsche [15. 111]. The debate was carried on by their disciples, albeit with different priorities; for instance in the stories of Josef Chaim Brenner characters often discuss Nietzschean ideas. Many Jewish interpreters developed their own intellectual conceptions through Nietzsche, but after a Nietzschean phase most of them left this influence behind. The translations by Israel Eldad, which appeared in Israel in the 1960s and 1970s, gave rise to a new phase in the Hebrew reception of Nietzsche. Eldad had in the 1940s been a member of the underground organization *Lehi* and first developed an interest primarily in the German philosopher's political outlook before gradually discovering Nietzsche's positive image of Judaism.

Bibliography

Sources

[1] Achad Ha'am, Am Scheidewege. Gesammelte Aufsätze, vol. 2, Berlin 1924. [1a] Ahad Ha'am, Selected Essays, trans. by L. Simon, New York 1912. [2] M. Berdyczewski, Zur Klärung, in: Die Stimme der Wahrheit. Jahrbuch für wissenschaftlichen Zionismus, ed. by L. Schön, Würzburg 1905, 279–287. [3] I. Heinemann, Der Begriff des Übermenschen in der jüdischen Religions-Philosophie, in: Der Morgen 1 (1925), 3–17. [4] A. Hertzberg (ed.), The Zionist Idea. A Historical Analysis and Reader, New York/Philadelphia 1960. [5] T. Herzl, The Complete Diaries of Theodor Herzl, vol. 1, ed. by R. Patai, trans. by H. Zohn, New York/London 1960. [6] T. Lessing, Jewish Self-Hate (1930), trans. by P. C. Appelbaum, New York 2021. [7] O. Levy, Die Exkommunizierung Adolf Hitlers. "Ein offener Brief (1938)," Berlin 2012. [8] F. Nietzsche, Sämtliche Werke. Kritische Studienausgabe in 15 Bänden, ed. by G. Colli/M. Montinari, Munich

1999. [8a] F. Nietzsche, Daybreak, trans. by R. J. Hollingdale, Cambridge 1982. [8b] F. Nietzsche, Beyond Good and Evil, trans. by R. J. Hollingdale, London 2003. [8c] F. Nietzsche, On the Genealogy of Morals, trans. by R. J. Hollingdale, W. Kaufmann, New York 1989. [8d] F. Nietzsche, Twilight of the Idols and The Anti-Christ, trans. by R. J. Hollingdale, London 2003. [8e] F. Nietzsche, Thus Spoke Zarathustra, trans. by R. J. Hollingdale, London 1969. [8f] F. Nietzsche, The Will to Power, trans. by W. Kaufmann and R. J. Hollingdale, New York 1967. [8g] F. W. Nietzsche, The Antichrist, trans. by H. L. Mencken, New York 1931. [9] F. Nietzsche, Selected Letters, ed. by O. Levy, trans. by A. M. Ludovici, New York 1921. [10] M. Nordau, Degeneration (1892–1893), trans. anon. from the second edition of the German Work (1895), Lincoln (NE) 1993. [11] M. Rabinoviz, Ha-yahadut we-"ha-adam ha-elyon" [Judaism and the "Übermensch"], in: Ha-Shiloaḥ 9 (1902) 4, 376–382. [12] F. Rosenzweig, The Star of Redemption, trans. by W. Hallo, New York 1970. [13] G. Scholem, Lamentations of Youth: The Diaries of Gershom Scholem, 1913–1919, ed. and trans. by A. D. Skinner, Cambridge (MA) 2007. [14] R. Weltsch (ed.), Ja-Sagen zum Judentum. Eine Aufsatzreihe der "Jüdischen Rundschau" zur Lage der deutschen Juden, Berlin 1933.

Secondary literature

[15] S.E. Aschheim, The Nietzsche Legacy in Germany: 1890–1990, Berkeley 1994. [16] A.J. Band, The Ahad Ha-Am and Berdyczewski Polarity, in: J. Kornberg (ed.), At the Crossroads. Essays on Ahad Ha-Am, New York 1983, 49–59. [17] J. Golomb (ed.), Nietzsche and Jewish Culture, New York 1997. [18] J. Golomb, Nietzsche and Zion, Ithaca 2004. [19] P. Mendes-Flohr, From Mysticism to Dialogue: Martin Buber's Transformation of German Social Thought, Detroit 1989. [20] W. Stegmaier/D. Krochmalnik (eds.), Jüdischer Nietzscheanismus, Berlin/New York 1997.

PHILIPP VON WUSSOW,
FRANKFURT AM MAIN

Ultra-Orthodoxy

Ultra-Orthodoxy is a broad religious-cultural current within Orthodox Judaism that emerged during the 19th century in reaction to the Reform movements throughout Western Europe. While neo-Orthodoxy kept itself open to various acculturation tendencies, traditional Orthodox Jews defended their strict religious practice first in Hungary and later across Eastern Europe as well. Initially espousing an anti-Zionist stance, the ultra-Orthodox movement diversified in the interwar period to form several distinct groups which today span the political spectrum from anti-Zionist to Zionist-nationalist orientations.

1. Emergence
2. Hungarian Orthodoxy
3. Ultra-Orthodoxy in the 20th century

1. Emergence

Under the influence of the Jewish Enlightenment (→ Haskalah) and the debate surrounding legal equality, Jews, since the early 19th century, had focused their efforts on acculturation to Christian middle-class society first in Germany and later in other regions of Western Europe. The initiatives of the → Reform movement, for instance, concerned the → liturgy; the first Reformed service in the → German language was celebrated in Hamburg in 1818 (→ Hamburg Temple Dispute). Following → emancipation, both traditional and Reform-oriented Jews belonged to unified congregations, now subject to public law.

From the middle of the 19th century onward, increasing disputes over the appropriate measure of acculturation and the powers of the congregations put an end to the initial cooperation. Traditionally-minded rabbis and members of the community established their own independent congregations. The Israelitische

Religionsgemeinschaft in Frankfurt am Main (→ Neo-Orthodoxy) was the first such congregation in 1850. It was led from 1851 onward by Rabbi Samson Raphael Hirsch. Under his dictum *torah im derekh erets* (Torah with the way of the land), Hirsch held that, in addition to their traditional studies (→ *talmud torah*), male members of the congregation should also attend school to receive a general education and participate in vocational training. Those in favor of Hirsch's philosophy originally referred to themselves as "law abiding" or "Torah abiding"; Hirsch, for his part, first used the term "Orthodox" in 1885 to denote traditional religious practice and as a distinction from the followers of Conservative Judaism (→ Breslau). The Prussian "Austrittsgesetz" of 1876 (secessionist law) permitting Jews to change their congregation without losing their religious affiliation did not lead all orthodox Jews to establish their own independent communities; many remained in the unified congregations (*Einheitsgemeinde*; → Orthodoxy).

Both the Orthodox in the unified congregations and the members of the separatist congregations were more willing to compromise than many Torah-abiding Jews in Eastern Europe, where strict observance of the → Halakhah remained normative. Rabbis in the East opposed the Jewish reformers from the start, but they also mistrusted the liberal tendencies among the Orthodox in the German and Western European unified congregations. To them, such a degree of acculturation was only acceptable as an emergency measure, a Halakhic commandment "to avert a looming threat" (*hora'at sha'ah*; "in the hour of need"), not as a lasting innovation. The chief rabbi of Pressburg (today Bratislava) and influential Halakhic scholar Moses Sofer (also called Ḥatam Sofer, 1762–1839) rose to prominence by fiercely opposing the work of the reformers, whom he characterized as "misguided," or even as "renegades." Sofer felt compelled to counterbalance the trend by creating a stern

variant of traditional Judaism. It prescribed, for instance, the exclusive recognition of the – Orthodox – rabbi as the sole religious authority and the *Shulḥan Arukh* (Set Table; → Halakhah) as the reference on religious law, which demanded the strict and absolute obedience to the religious laws and rejection of the prevailing positive-historical studies (→ Wissenschaft des Judentums). Many of his rigid → responsa, however, initially remained theoretical in nature, since their practical application collided with the laws of the state.

Moses Sofer and his disciples directed their polemic not only at the reformers but also at Moses Mendelssohn (→ Bi'ur), the pioneer of an early, cautiously moderate Orthodox position, and against → neo-Orthodox leaders such as Samson Raphael Hirsch and Esriel Hildesheimer, rabbi of the influential Berlin secession congregation of Adass Jisroel. Sofer even viewed their attempts to reconcile ultra-Orthodox Judaism with the modern way of life as the most dangerous proposition because he feared that small concessions would ultimately lead to apostasy. Consequently, Sofer rejected German-language → sermons and generally endorsed the use of → Yiddish in everyday life.

Moses Sofer can be seen as the spiritual founder of ultra-Orthodoxy, even if the term itself was not in use during Sofer's time. In apodictic fashion, Sofer used the Halakhic argument from the Mishnah (→ Talmud), *ḥadash asur min ha-Torah* (innovation is forbidden by the Torah; Orla 3,6) against any ritual and Halakhic innovation; with reference to the Reform movement it became the watchword of Eastern European Orthodoxy. It also reflects the dialectic of preservation and change; its adherents saw themselves merely as the faithful followers of a religion they had inherited, unchanged, from their fathers and forefathers. In actuality even the traditional Orthodox rabbis had introduced considerable changes to the traditions (→ Minhag) and religious practice. For the now ultra-Orthodox faction, the deliberate demarcation from liberal Jewish life was reinforced primarily through ever-more restrictive religious laws. In this respect they have been described as a fundamentalist movement [4].

2. Hungarian Orthodoxy

As the most distinguished leader throughout the eastern regions of the Habsburg Empire, Moses Sofer had chosen the city of Pressburg (today Bratislava, in what later became the Hungarian part of the Empire) for a new yeshivah in 1803 – at a time when the centers of the Enlightenment were progressively shifting eastward. Recognized by the Habsburg authorities, the Pressburg yeshivah became one of the most influential Talmud academies in Europe and a bastion of anti-Modernism. Unlike the students at Russian yeshivot, the Talmud students in Pressburg were exempt from serving in the → military. The traditional seminary instruction did not comprise a general education. The students came from different European countries to which the graduates returned; some also went on to hold office in German breakaway congregations. The Pressburg yeshivah was closed down in 1938 after it had trained many hundreds of scholars and rabbis.

However, the early success of the Pressburg yeshivah did not make up for the fact that by the beginning of the 1860s, if not earlier, the Hungarian traditional Orthodox Jews had become a minority within the increasingly acculturating Jewish community. This development was aided significantly by the introduction of compulsory school attendance in 1849 and, from 1860, by the state propaganda push for Magyarization (→ Hungarian). Most Hungarian Jews working as merchants or in the liberal professions tended to lean toward the moderate and liberal → Neolog school; many German-speaking middle-class Jews from Budapest looked to → neo-Orthodoxy for guidance.

The → Austro-Hungarian Compromise of 1867, which saw Hungarian Jews achieve far-reaching equality before the law, accelerated their acculturation. The → Hungarian National Israelite Congress, held in Pest (1868–1869), finally sealed the fate of the unified Jewish Orthodox communities in Hungary.

In light of this development, Sofer's successors began in the 1860s to view themselves as the defenders of the Hungarian traditional Orthodox against moderate or acculturated forms of Judaism, and they upheld a rigid interpretation of Talmudic law. It formed the basis for their particular brand of Halakhic decision-making, which was rejected by the representatives of other Orthodox denominations for being authoritarian and, ultimately, non-traditional. The ultra-Orthodox thus ignored the exegetic discourses so typical of the Talmud, where contradictory positions are a matter of debate and can sometimes remain undecided. Another innovation by ultra-Orthodox rabbis was the use of non-Halakhic textual sources to justify their decisions. In contravention of traditional practice they drew on quotations thought to be appropriate from Aggadic narrative passages of the → Talmud, the → Midrashim, or the *Zohar* (→ Mysticism). A characteristic of the Hungarian ultra-Orthodoxy was its reinterpretation of Jewish tradition for the purpose of creating a new ultra-Orthodox worldview [7. 26].

Between 1864 and 1872, the Hungarian Orthodox groups publicly debated matters of theological and institutional concern, but several of their confrontations also touched on issues of religious practice, such as the concept of the Messiah, the creation of a neo-Orthodox rabbinical seminary, and sermons held in German. Traditional Orthodox rabbis tended in some points to side with the conservative or Neolog party rather than their natural allies in the neo-Orthodox camp, who were in fact their fiercest rivals. In Michalovce (today located in Slovakia) at the end of 1865, the dispute over German-language → sermons precipitated a momentous rabbinical decision (*psak din*). Among other things, it prohibited moving the *bimah* (podium for Torah reading) from the center of the → synagogue, inadequate dividers (→ *mehitsah*) between men and women, synagogal marriages, and generally any deviation from the traditional service; synagogues permitting such practices were deemed a "house of heresy" [7. 40].

Knowing full well that precisely those changes had just been introduced for neo-Orthodox services in Pressburg, this decision of the rabbis became a type of manifesto for ultra-Orthodox Judaism. Its most ardent advocates were the rabbis Hillel Lichtenstein, Chaim Sofer, and especially Lichtenstein's son-in-law Akiva Yosef Schlesinger. The latter had spent part of his studies at the Pressburg yeshivah and since 1863 wrote several treatises in which he sought to familiarize a broader public with the views of Moses Sofer. Of these, his best known work was *Lev ha-Ivri* (Heart of the Hebrew, 2 vols., 1864–1868), which comprised a commentary on Moses Sofer's testament and on the Michalovce decision and spread rapidly as far as Eastern Europe. Schlesinger emphasized the importance of external, "national" characteristics as the visible expression of the complete "Hebrew," specifically the name (*shem*), language (*lashon*), and dress (*malbush*), which he combined in the Hebrew acronym *shalem* (complete, whole).

Even though Schlesinger harshly criticized the neo-Orthodox for "submitting" to the Hungarian nationalist policy of Magyarization, in making his own demands he was himself not averse to including nationalist, albeit Jewish-nationalist, undertones. In 1863 he had suggested founding an ultra-Orthodox "Alliance of the Hebrews." This alliance was to lend spiritual support to the faithful in Western European cities who faced the "pollution" of the modern age,

as well as material support to enable them to settle in Eastern Europe and lead a law-abiding life. Initially publishing in → Hebrew and in Judeo-German (with Hebrew script), Schlesinger began to write in → Yiddish at the end of the 1860s in an effort to engage the Jewish population of Eastern Europe. Because he saw the ultra-Orthodox community as a minority "persecuted" by the Jewish majority [1. vol. 1, fol. 109a], Schlesinger argued that, for their own protection, ultra-Orthodox Jews should separate themselves entirely from their non-ultra-Orthodox coreligionists.

In 1870 Schlesinger left Hungary for Jerusalem. Continuing in the spirit of his previous work, he founded a school and named it *Kol Nehi mi-Tsiyon* (Wailing Voice of → Zion) in 1872 with the express aim of combating the secular schools of the → Alliance israélite universelle and especially those of the neo-Orthodoxy. Schlesinger's own curriculum attracted many ultra-Orthodox students from Hungary and Eastern European countries. Inspired by Zvi Hirsch Kalischer's → messianism, Schlesinger moreover addressed himself to facilitating the "return" of ultra-Orthodox Jews to Erets Israel. It was the goal of his 1873-founded, nationalistic *Hevrah Mahzire Atarah le-Yoshnah, im Kolel ha-Ivrim* (Society for the Restoration of the Ancient Glory, or Community of the Hebrews) to create a national commonwealth which, with its own flag, army, and elected assembly of representatives, would guarantee the preservation of "traditional" Jewish culture. Schlesinger formulated the idea of a Jewish State in Palestine – albeit under Ottoman suzerainty – in a letter to Moses Montefiore (→ Board of Deputies) in 1874, but his reputation was irreparably damaged when, in 1875, he called for the removal of the medieval Halakhic prohibition on polygyny (→ Marriage). In the following years, Schlesinger focused instead on raising funds to support Jewish agricultural settlements in Palestine (→ Halukkah).

In Hungary, however, the majority of Orthodox Jews could never fully align themselves with the maximum demands of the ultra-Orthodox. The religious schism between neo-Orthodoxy and ultra-Orthodoxy initially benefitted the traditional Orthodox camp, which represented the Orthodox majority in subsequent decades and in 1867 went on to establish the first pan-Orthodox society *Shomre ha-Dat* (Guardians of the Faith). Ultra-Orthodox voices in their turn derided them as *shomde ha-dat* (Destroyers of the Faith) [7. 45].

Enlightenment (→ Maskilim) and acculturation little affected the authority of ultra-Orthodox rabbis in Eastern Europe. With power structures remaining essentially intact, influence and standing of the rabbis even increased among their followers. A number of them came to be known for espousing a virtually militant stance against any expression of liberal tendencies and the Zionist movement. Some, including the Mitnagged (→ Vilna) Ḥayim Ozer Grodzenski from Kaunas (Kovno), went so far as to discourage any inclination to settle in countries where Jewish observance was presumably lax. The United States fell into this category for being a *treife medine* (non-kosher land), as well as Palestine. The leaders of the Hungarian and Romanian Hasidim, the Munkács Rebbe Chaim El'azar Shapira (Elazar Spira) and the Satmar Rebbe Joel Moshe Teitelbaum, shared the conviction that for Jews any "pilgrimage to the [Temple] Wall" was forbidden because it constituted a transgression against historical events the shaping of which was the privilege of God alone.

3. Ultra-Orthodoxy in the 20th century

Under the influence of new movements, the → renaissance of Jewish secular culture or political ideologies such as Zionism (→ Basel) and socialism (→ Bund), around the turn of the 20th century, more and more Jews abandoned their traditional way of life. In view of these developments, the different Orthodox and ultra-Orthodox communities increasingly tended to cooperate, even if the split between the followers of → Hasidism and their non-Hasidic Orthodox opponents (Hebr. *mitnaggdim*) remained unchanged. One result of such a cooperation was the educational network → Bais Ya'akov, established in Warsaw in 1917, which provided opportunities for Hasidic as well as non-Hasidic Orthodox girls. Bais Ya'akov was also under the patronage of *Agudat Yisra'el* (Association of Israel, in short: *Agudah*), a transnational, pan-Orthodox community of interest, founded in Katowice in 1912, which became the most important Orthodox institution of the 20th century. Initially, however, it did not meet with a positive response from the ultra-Orthodox camp, since the latter believed it detected an overabundance of overly intense religious-Zionist leanings in the ranks of the *Agudah*.

In the 1920s and 1930s the Soviet regime closed down Orthodox educational and religious institutions; moreover, legal restrictions made the observance of the → Shabbat, Jewish holidays (→ Course of the Year), and dietary laws (→ *kashrut*) difficult. It caused some Hasidic rebbes, among them Joseph Isaac Schneerson and many of his followers, as well as Joel Moshe Teitelbaum (→ Kasztner Affair), to flee the Soviet Union.

The majority of ultra-Orthodox Jews fell victim to the National Socialist extermination (→ Auschwitz) of Jews (→ Holocaust). After the war, the Eastern and Central European states and Soviet allies offered no perspective for the survivors. Many settled in the United States, where they established new congregations. While the moderate (neo-)Orthodox Jews who had arrived in the country before the Second World War had become strongly assimilated, ultra-Orthodox Jews sought to maintain their segregation from American society and insisted on their traditional way of life. Not least because of their demographic growth, ultra-Orthodox Jews today constitute the largest group within North-American Jewish → Orthodoxy.

The anti-Zionist ultra-Orthodox felt threatened by the growing influence of the Orthodox Zionist wing, which had in 1902 produced the Mizraḥi organization (acronym of *MerkaZ RuHanI*; religious center). It began operating in Palestine in 1918 and motivated ultra-Orthodoxy and *Agudah* to forge a closer relationship after the First World War and especially from the 1930s onward. Despite its explicit anti-Zionism, the Palestine-based *Agudah* became a member of the national organs of Jewish Palestine. As such, it received a share of the immigration certificates and support for ultra-Orthodox schools.

Since the beginning of the 1920s the ultra-Orthodox in Palestine had been organized as *edah ḥaredit* ("Congregation of God-Fearers," i.e. the Charedi Council of Jerusalem) and strictly kept their distance from the *Agudah*. At the same time, ultra-Orthodox representatives were politically active in the mandate (→ Balfour Declaration): they opposed the creation of secular Jewish institutions and of the chief rabbinate, which in its early phase assumed a moderate pro-Zionist stance. A large part of the ultra-Orthodox infrastructure moreover emerged during the mandate. The seeds were sown with the founding of Lithuanian yeshivot in Jerusalem, Hebron, and Bnei Brak. Yosef Kahaneman and El'azar Menachem Schach (Elazar Menachem Man Shach), leaders of the *Ponevezh Yeshivah* in Bnei Brak, went on to head the ultra-Orthodox movement.

In reaction, Amram Blau and others founded the extreme anti-Zionist ultra-Orthodox group *Neturei Karta* (Guardians of the City), but they were unable to stop the rapprochement between Israeli ultra-Orthodoxy and the State in the 1950s and

1960s. At the other end of the ultra-Orthodox spectrum, members of *Po'ale Agudat Yisra'el* (Agudat Israel Workers, i.e. ultra-Orthodox Workers' Party, originally formed in interwar Poland) established Zionist socialist kibbutzim and moshavim; some becoming the first port of call for *Agudah* members who left Germany in the 1930s to settle in mandate Palestine.

On the eve of the foundation of the State of Israel, *Agudah* and associated groups cooperated with the majority Zionists. The *Agudah* member Yitzhak Meir Levin signed the Declaration of Independence and, in 1948, became Minster of Welfare in the first Israeli government

The question of military service was time and again a source of conflict. Prime Minister David Ben-Gurion (→ Raison d'État) had agreed in 1948 that for an initial period ultra-Orthodox women and yeshivah students would not be compelled to serve. His reasoning was that since ultra-Orthodox Jews had been diminished to a small minority in Israel and around the world, their exemption from military service would have very little impact. This led the ultra-Orthodox community to conclude that they had been granted a general exemption, and they felt vindicated by the fact that, since the 1950s, studying at a yeshivah or a *kolel* was considered an equivalent substitution for young men and for married persons, respectively. In the 1960s and 1970s the leaders of Shas, a party representing the ultra-Orthodox faction among the Oriental → Mizraḥim, were recruited from among the graduates of the ultra-Orthodox yeshivot.

Demographic growth and the full use of their political influence meant that ultra-Orthodox political parties were, with minor interruptions, coalition partners in every Israeli government; often their participation ensured the formation of a viable majority. Today only a small minority still see in such "political maneuvers" a violation of ultra-Orthodox values and continue to boycott elections.

Despite their considerable religious and social heterogeneity, in Israel today all ultra-Orthodox and Hasidic denominations (→ Hasidism) are numbered among in the "ultra-Orthodox congregation." Most of them, however, acknowledge Akiva Yosef Schlesinger as their common spiritual precursor or founder. Their respective group identities find expression in their external appearance and in their traditions, which are derived from their respective countries of origin in Eastern Europe (Russia, Lithuania, Poland, Galicia, Hungary) or in the Islamic world. They differ in their degree of separation from secular society. The Satmar Hasidim and the members of *Neturei Karta* are at the most radically anti-modernist and anti-Zionist end of the spectrum, while those in the Israeli settlers' movement are keen to blend Zionism, or Messianic nationalism, with ultra-Orthodox beliefs.

Both in the United States and in Israel the ultra-Orthodox community is experiencing strong demographic growth, with a statistical five-and-a-half to seven children (in Israel) per family (→ Demography). Especially in Israel, where many ultra-Orthodox men dedicate themselves primarily to the pursuit of religious studies (*talmud torah*) even after marriage, a large number live in poverty. Females, as service providers or educators, contribute significantly, if not exclusively, to the family income. Ultra-Orthodox communities have set up additional support networks to provide economic assistance to their members and to fund their educational institutions. A movement advocating the return (Hebr. → *teshuvah*) to tradition has inspired tens of thousands of secular Jews in Israel and the Diaspora to join the ultra-Orthodox community since the 1980s. While ultra-Orthodox Jews reject the modern global culture, they nevertheless avail themselves freely of modern technologies, means of transport, and new media to coordinate their efforts on a global scale.

Bibliography

Sources
1] A. J. Schlesinger, Lev ha-Ivri [Heart of the Hebrew], 2 vols., Ungvár/Lemberg 1864/1868.

Secondary literature
[2] M. Breuer, Modernity within Tradition. The Social History of Orthodox Jewry in Imperial Germany, trans. by E. Petuchowski, New York 1992.   [3] M. Friedman, ha-Ḥevrah ha-ḥaredit: mekorot, megamot ye-tahalikhim [The Haredi Ultra-Orthodox Society: Sources, Trends and Processes], Jerusalem 1991.   [4] S. C. Heilman/ M. Friedman, The Case of Haredim, in: M.E. Marty/R.S. Appleby (eds.), Fundamentalism Observed, vol. 1, Chicago 1991, 197–264.   [5] J. Katz, A House Divided. Orthodoxy and Schism in Nineteenth Century Central European Jewry, Waltham 1998.   [6] M. K. Silber, The Historical Experience of German Jewry and its Impact on the Haskalah and Reform in Hungary, in: J. Katz (ed.), Toward Modernity. The European Model, New Brunswick 1987, 107–159.   [7] M. K. Silber, The Emergence of Ultra-Orthodoxy. The Invention of a Tradition, in: J. Wertheimer (ed.), The Use of Tradition, Jewish Continuity in the Modern Era, New York 1993, 23–82.

YAAKOV ARIEL, CHAPEL HILL, NC

Undzere Kinder

Title of a Yiddish feature film produced in Poland in 1948. The leading parts were played by Shimen Dzigan (1905–1980) and Yisroel Shumacher (1908–1961), a comic duo exceedingly popular among Polish Jews during the interwar years. *Undzere Kinder* (It Will Never Happen Again; lit. "Our Children") describes two entertainers who returned to Poland from the Soviet Union and their encounter with survivor children in a Jewish children's home on the outskirts of → Łódź. While the comics originally intended to visit the home in order to entertain the children and gather new material for sketches, they are stunned when they learn how the children survived the → Holocaust. In 1950, Dzigan and Shumacher emigrated to Israel, where they continued their successful careers. However, they never revisited the Holocaust as an event again in their performances.

1. Dzigan and Shumacher
2. *Undzere Kinder*
3. Legacy

1. Dzigan and Shumacher

Dzigan and Shumacher were famous in Poland during the interwar years, all over the Yiddish-speaking world, and later in the State of Israel. They both came from → Łódź, a city known for its earthy Jewish → humor as expressed in the lively and descriptive Yiddish dialect spoken by its inhabitants. From the late 1920s onward, the two entertainers, who had met in Moyshe Broderzon's Ararat Theatre, performed as a duo in cabarets, initially in Łódź, then in Warsaw, where they founded their own cabaret in the Nowości Theatre in 1935. They also appeared in several Yiddish films of the late 1930s, among them the successful melodrama *Al khet* (1936), the comedy *Freylekhe kabtsonim* (Jolly Paupers, 1937), and the film version of Jakob Gordin's (→ Sibirya) drama *On a heym* (Without a home, 1939). As these productions usually also made their way to American audiences, Dzigan and Shumacher were soon known to a greater Yiddish-speaking public beyond Poland.

Incisive wit, biting satire, and mockery – *khoyzik* (Yidd.; derision), a legacy of the Galician → Haskalah – became their trademark. It was not, however, the followers of → Hasidism, but the descendants of the → maskilim, the Polish Jews striving for assimilation, who were the favorite object of their mockery. In addition, their sketches, which were typically inspired by newspaper articles, also took aim at Polish (and German) antisemites and officials. One routine was about a hunting accident in which Hermann Göring was mistaken for a wild boar; while the piece "*Der letster yid in Poyln*" ("The Last Jew in Poland") depicted a Jew showered with attention by Polish citizens when they realize that the exodus set in motion earlier entailed the loss of Jewish culture in Poland [11. 145f.].

On stage, the two comedians assumed the parts of two characters who became their trademark. Dzigan, usually wrapped in a black caftan, played a hyperactive and outraged simple Jew, whose torrent of words recalled Groucho Marx (→ Marx Brothers), while the bespectacled Shumacher remained phlegmatic and reserved, countering Dzigan's outbursts with Yiddish sayings and gestures. Some of their pieces were based on their own material, while

Shimen Dzigan (l., 1905–1980) and Yisroel Shumacher (1908–1961)

they adapted classics like Sholem Aleichem (→ Tevye) and others. Moreover, Yiddish authors of their generation, among them Itzik Manger (→ Shtern oyfn dakh), Moyshe Broderzon (→ Yung-yidish), and Moyshe Nudelman, wrote sketches for them.

When the German army invaded Poland in 1939, Dzigan and Shumacher escaped to Soviet-occupied Białystok, where they rebuilt their cabaret, and toured Soviet cities, where they played to packed Jewish audiences hankering after a word of Yiddish. When they attempted to leave the Soviet Union with the Polish forces under Władysław Anders in 1942, they were arrested and imprisoned for four years, first in an Uzbek prison and later in a Kazakh labor camp. There, too, they performed for their guards as well as for Jews from the surrounding area. Further proof of their continuing importance is that the documents of Jewish life collected by Emanuel Ringelblum and his comrades-in-arms in the Warsaw underground archive → *Oyneg Shabbes* included texts of their sketches from the interwar years.

Released in 1946, Dzigan and Shumacher returned to Warsaw the following year. On their numerous tours around Poland, they performed before Jewish audiences hoping to be cheered up by the humor of the two comics.

2. *Undzere Kinder*

Around this time, Shaul Goskind (1907–2003), the energetic founder of the Jewish film cooperative *Kinor*, approached Dzigan and Shumacher to sign them onto a production in which they would star. Goskind's director Natan Gross (1919–2005), who had survived the war hiding in Poland, opposed a classic comedy in the style of the 1930s so shortly after the → Holocaust. It was his idea to feature surviving children as the focus of the film. While the comics famous from before the war played the starring roles, the children cast were real survivors from Jewish institutions in postwar Łódź, among them the Helenówek children's home, which was also used as the set for the film. Although → Yiddish was the language of the film, hardly any of the children were able to speak it. They learned their lines with the aid of transliterations from → Polish.

The plot of the 68-minute black-and-white film starts with Dzigan and Shumacher performing a sketch about life in the ghetto on stage in front of an audience of Holocaust survivors. In one episode of the routine, they beg for food and are surprised to receive a challah, the traditional plaited yeast bread for → Shabbat dinner. While the piece amuses the adult audience members, a boy attending the show together with a group of surviving children from a local home reacts by whistling. The attempts of the other children to calm their companion result in an even greater disruption. Admonished by the matron of the children's home to apologize, the children go on stage after the end of the performance. When the comics ask the children why they did not like the show, the boy who whistled to express his displeasure says "because that's not how it was." Asked if they knew how it really was, two girls spontaneously perform how they were begging for a slice of bread in the ghetto. Moved, Dzigan and Shumacher accept the matron's invitation to visit the children in the home.

In the home, the visitors perform a sketch based on a humorous story by Sholem Aleichem about the imaginary → shtetl Kasrilevke burning down because the Jewish inhabitants are unable to put out the fire. The children laugh and applaud. Afterwards the comics ask the children if one of them has seen a real fire before, and the response is overwhelming. After some children have described the fires set by the Germans in the → Warsaw ghetto, Dzigan and Shumacher suggest a competition for the most enthralling description of the war years. At this point the matron abruptly ends the discussion: "Now children," she says, "don't think about anything and go to bed." However, instead of going to sleep, the children talk far into the night.

When Dzigan and Shumacher pass the children's dormitory on the way to their own room, they witness three children acting out how they survived in front of the others. Breathlessly, the two follow the account of a girl who was saved when a truck full of children from the ghetto stopped for repairs in a Polish village and an SS officer sneeringly offered to sell the girl to the inhabitants. After a Polish farmer spontaneously buys her, the girl sees the truck continue its journey without her – to certain death for the other children, as Dzigan and Shumacher know. The comics are devastated by what they learn listening to the conversations. "This is not a children's home," a distraught Dzigan exclaims, "it is a house of nightmares!" The film ends with the two awakening after a restless night to the sounds of children playing. Looking out of the window into the courtyard, they see the children re-enacting the performance of the previous day. Unlike the shtetl Jews caricatured by Dzigan and Shumacher, however, they succeed in putting out the fire.

The film alludes to the fact that there were few children among Jewish Holocaust survivors. Around 28,000, most of them orphans, had survived, statistically speaking about three percent of all Polish-Jewish children [1. 15]. As a consequence, Jewish institutions in Poland were particularly interested in taking in surviving children, especially those saved by Christians, and guiding them back into the Jewish community. As the Israeli historian Shimon Redlich (b. 1935) – himself a surviving child in the cast of *Undzere Kinder* – wrote, children "were considered to

be walking miracles. They were everybody's children" [9. 152]. This is why the film's voiceover begins with the words: "*Undzere kinder, undzere kinder, vifil inhalt ligt ot in di tsvey poshete verter!*" ("Our children, our children, how much meaning lies in these two simple words!")

In its efforts to establish an image of the surviving Jewish child that would serve as an inspiration, *Undzere Kinder* was not produced to convey a realistic image of the surviving children. Both the dormitory scene and that of the children sharing their stories of survival with each other when they were among themselves and not encouraged by adults were unlikely to have occurred in reality. A year after the children were liberated, the social worker Maria Hochberg-Mariańska (1913–1996), who cared for surviving children, wrote: "In the end, they did not want to talk about the suffering they had experienced; they kept it to themselves" [5]. Indeed, the author Henryk Grynberg (b. 1936), who was housed in the Helenówek children's home and also appeared in *Undzere Kinder*, described the flashback scenes in the film during which the children tell each other stories from their nightmarish past as fiction. "And neither in school nor in the orphanage did we talk about our worst experiences. If we ever mentioned events from the Holocaust, it would be optimistic anecdotes about fooling the persecutors, winning food, cheating one's way out of trouble" [8. 328].

The film was apparently screened only once privately in front of a selected audience in Poland. By the time it was finished in 1949, the communist regime there had begun an extensive campaign against Jewish institutions. An independent film about the Holocaust created by Jews and conveying a decidedly positive image of Jews was not particularly welcomed politically. The film was smuggled out of Poland and shown in 1951 in → New York and → Tel Aviv. After-wards it was believed to have been lost until a version was found in Paris in 1979 and another one was discovered a few years later in Israel. These made it possible to restore the film.

3. Legacy

In 1950 Dzigan and Shumacher emigrated from Poland to Israel, where they encoun-tered public opposition to → Yiddish as the language of the Jews of the Diaspora. Yiddish-speaking Israelis, however, many of them survivors, welcomed the duo enthu-siastically. After performances all over the world and the construction of their own the-atre in → Buenos Aires in 1951/1952, Dzigan and Shumacher finally established a cabaret in → Tel Aviv in 1958.

In Israel the motifs of their jokes and skits shifted from Polish politicians and gener-als to Israeli officials; rather than the chal-lenges and pitfalls of assimilation, they now focused on the immigration experience. Dzigan and Shumacher presented the char-acters of comic heroes who came up with cunning plans in order to outwit Israel's notorious bureaucracy. In 1960 they parted ways. Shumacher died shortly afterwards, while Dzigan pursued a successful solo career until his death on stage in 1980.

Dzigan's autobiography *Der koyekh fun yidishn humor* (The power of Yiddish humor), published in 1974, does not refer to *Undzere Kinder*. Maybe Dzigan did not see the sense in writing about a long-lost film that had been forgotten soon after it was made. After they left Poland, Dzigan and Shumacher took great care to avoid referring to the → Holocaust in their sketches. Audi-ences all over the world who have seen the film *Undzere Kinder* since its rediscovery, including in Poland, have been profoundly moved. The film is a testament to Dzigan and Shumacher's comic dexterity, demon-strated especially in their presentation of Sholem Aleichem's Kasrilevke motif; but, above all, it bears witness to the lifeworld of Jewish children after the Holocaust.

Bibliography

[1] N. Bogner, At the Mercy of Strangers. The Res-cue of Jewish Children with Assumed Identities in Poland, Jerusalem 2009. [2] J. M. Efron, From Łódź to Tel Aviv. The Political Satire of Shimen Dzigan and Yisroel Shumacher, in: The Jewish Quarterly Review 102 (2012) 1, 50–79. [3] G. N. Finder, Überlebende Kinder im kollektiven Gedächtnis der polnischen Jüdinnen und Juden nach dem Holocaust. Das Beispiel "Undzere Kinder," in: C. Bruns et al. (eds.), "Welchen der Steine du hebst." Filmische Erinnerung an den Holocaust, Berlin 2012, 47–64. [4] N. Gross, Toldot ha-kolnoa ha-yehudi be-Polin 1910–1950 [The Jewish Film in Poland: 1910–1950], Jerusalem 1990. [5] N. Grüss/M. Hochberg-Mariańska (eds.), Dzieci oskarżają [The Children Accuse], Kraków et al. 1947. [6] I. Konigsberg, "Our Children" and the Limits of Cinema. Early Jewish Responses to the Holocaust, in: Film Quarterly 52 (1998) 1, 7–19. [7] L. L. Langer, "Undzere Kinder." A Yiddish Film from Poland, in: L. L. Langer, Preempting the Holocaust, New Haven/London 1998, 157–165. [8] J. B. Michlic, Bearing Witness. Henryk Grynberg's Path from Child Survivor to Artist. An Interview with Hen-ryk Grynberg, in: Polin. Studies in Polish Jewry 20 (2008), 324–335. [9] S. Redlich, Together and Apart in Brzezany. Poles, Jews, and Ukrain-ians, 1919–1945, Bloomington 2002. [10] S. Redlich, Life in Transit. Jews in Postwar Lodz, 1945–1950, Boston 2010. [11] R. Wisse, No Joke. Making Jewish Humor, Princeton 2013.

GABRIEL N. FINDER, CHARLOTTESVILLE

Universities

In most European countries, Jews were accepted in universities in the early mod-ern period. Although many academically trained Jewish doctors already practiced from the 16th to the 18th centuries (→ Medicine), but entry into other academic careers (→ Professions) was not open to Jews until the 19th century. In any case, the success of Jewish academics turned out to be ambivalent, since it was soon used as a justification for restrictions on their opportunities for study and careers. At the same time, the encounter with the secular → sciences also had a reactive effect on Jewish society as well: it placed the study of their own religion and culture on a new methodological and institutional foundation.

1. Historical survey
2. Jewish students
2.1 The German states
2.2 The Russian Empire
2.3 Great Britain and the United States
3. Co-opting and restricting Jewish academics
4. The founding of Jewish institutions of higher learning

1. Historical survey

The European institution of the university, shaped by Antiquity, Christianity, and the *lingua franca* of Latin, developed out of the medieval personal relationships between teachers and students (*universitas magistrorum et scholarium*). They enjoyed autonomy, first through papal and later through imperial privileges. Entry into a university was fundamentally denied to Jews and other *infideles* ("infidels") in the Middle Ages. However, since baptism was taken so much for granted that it was not stipulated in university statutes [15. 230], Jewish students were repeatedly able to attach themselves to a teacher, especially in southern France and in Italy, where no formal enrollment was required. The dominance of the subjects of medicine and law, and the less clerical character of the universities there as compared to German areas, likely went hand in

hand with greater openness toward Jewish students.

In the early modern period, it was the University of Padua, which, after the Reformation developed into the academic center for non-Catholics, that had the highest number of Jewish students. As was usual in medieval universities, they too were assigned to the *natio* of their respective places of origin. The city remained the center of academic training for Jewish physicians until the 18th century; more than 250 graduated here, including many from the German territories and Poland-Lithuania [11. 420, 422]. In the process, they always came into contact with Christian students, and these contacts were often maintained after their course of studies.

Although the Council of Basel forbade the granting of academic degrees to Jews in 1434, since, in addition to the authorization to teach, the jurisdiction of students was also associated with it, increasing numbers of Jews graduated in philosophy and medicine. The philosopher Elia Delmedigo (1458–1497) even obtained permission from the authorities to teach at Padua, Florence, Venice, and Perugia. To be sure, Jewish students were discriminated against by high tuition fees; nevertheless, as academic citizens (*cives academici*) they were at the same time dispensed from the obligation to wear distinctive clothing (→ Dress Regulations). Since as early as the mid-17th century, primarily Sephardic, but then, around 1700, Ashkenazi Jews as well, studied at the Dutch universities in Franeker, Harderwijk, Utrecht, and Leiden, which took over from Padua the title of center of Jewish medicine.

From the early modern period, the universities developed into territorial institutions. They increasingly lost their autonomy and became subject to state regulations (although this was not the case for British universities until the late 19th century). In the Russian Empire, universities were set up from the outset as state institutions. In

UNIVERSITIES

the age of national states and nationalism, universities were also "nationalized": on the one hand, this trend originated with the State, for instance in the wake of the Russification of Warsaw and Dorpat (today Tartu/Estonia), and on the other from national movements, which were able to impose the language of the majority or dominant population on previously supranational institutions, as in the Polonization of Cracow and → Lemberg or the division of the University of → Prague into a German-speaking and a Czech-speaking institution.

In the wake of increasing acculturation, but also as a result of the → Haskalah with its striving for the reform of Jewish education and and access to secular knowledge, the attraction of universities to Jews was strengthened. Especially in the German states and the Russian Empire, the privileges acquired by university graduates and the high social prestige that accompanied them intensified the Jews' striving for a university education (→ Bildung) in the 19th century. At the same time, education developed, even more than trade, into the area in which Jews and non-Jews most often came into contact.

2. Jewish students

2.1 *The German states*
Jews were first enrolled in a German university in Frankfurt an der Oder in 1678, in the person of the later physicians Tobias Hakohen (→ Ma'aseh Toviyah) and Gabriel ben Moses. Jews in the German states were granted access to secondary schools and universities from the end of the 18th century. Some universities, especially more recent ones, made enrollment easier by waiving the customary oath; in Göttingen it was replaced by a non-confessional invocation of God; in Erlangen and Heidelberg by a special Jewish oath formula (→ Oath More Judaico). Catholic universities were the last to grant access to Jews: here, they followed the lead of the Habsburg institutions, which did not abolish entrance restrictions for non-Catholics until the → Edicts of Toleration issued by Joseph II.

As registered students, Jews enjoyed the same rights as Christians. They were subject to university jurisdiction, and were exempt from the usual protection money. In the early modern period, Jewish printers (→ Printing) and readers alsomade use of this by enrolling too. Privileged compared to their correligionists as students, some of them even lived permanently in cities in which it was actually forbidden for Jews to settle, as for instance in Utrecht and Freiburg im Breisgau. Nevertheless, many universities maintained their high fees for Jews, as did Königsberg for enrollment, and Erlangen for graduation.

With increasing acculturation, the numbers of Jewish students increased sharply. In 1886/1887, almost 10% of students at Prussian universities were Jews and 25 years later still almost 6%. The proportion of Jewish women among female students was 11% in Prussia in 1911/1912, and even almost 18% in Bavaria [4. 321, 14]; [3. 113].

Jews belonged to student organizations in much lower numbers than Christians. Yet regionally organized corps had long accepted Jews, while the attitude of the fraternities, which emerged later and were more strongly politically oriented, varied. Members of Jewish fraternities included Heinrich Heine (→ Entreebillet), Johann Jacoby, Berthold Auerbach, and Theodor Herzl (→ Old New Land). In the late 19th century, more and more corps and fraternities refused membership to Jews in the context of growing antisemitism and after the model of the associations of German students (Kyffhäuser-Verband 1882). Jewish students reacted to this exclusion by founding their own → student corporations of both German-Jewish and Jewish Nationalist orientations: they aimed at self-affirmation as Jews, by means of conviviality and cultural activities.

Under Nazi rule, a *numerus clausus* was introduced for "non-Aryans" in 1933, and, from April 1938, a "proof of Aryanness" was demanded for enrollment. Jews were denied the doctorate in 1937, and after the → November Pogrom they were forbidden to study in general. Even before this, many were stripped of their doctoral degree for "unworthiness," which, for its part, could be justified by the revocation of → citizenship. From 1943, forced expatriation was accompanied by "Depromotion" (revocation of the doctorate).

2.2 *The Russian Empire*

In the Russian Empire, home of the largest Jewry of Europe (→ Pale of Settlement) after the divisions of Poland and until the → February Revolution of 1917 a feudal system that stipulated the legal inequality of peasants, the universities had basically been open to Jews since 1804. The Jewish Statute of 1804, by which the authorities aimed at closing "the big gap" between Jews "and their fellow citizens" through cultural assimilation, explicitly guaranteed access to higher educational institutions (cited in [9. 150]). Even the Jewish Statute of 1835, which declared Jews to be "aliens," and hence second-class subjects, confirmed the right to attend state educational institutions up to and including university. However, few took advantage of this at first: at the beginning of the 19th centuryprimarily at the German-speaking University of Dorpat, and then from the 1840s, also at other universities of the Czarist Empire.

Since the Great Reforms under Alexander II (r. 1855–1881) the number of Jewish students rose rapidly. In 1886, they represented approximately 15% of the student body [1. 16]. Jews gained important privileges with a university degree, such as the right to live outside the Pale (1861), as well as a reduction of military service (→ Military). The Jews were largely integrated within the multinational student body of the Czarist Empire,

as well as in their relief funds and regional associations and found support precisely as victims of discrimination. Nevertheless, in the early 20th century, surveys of the Jewish student body of several universities point to dissatisfaction with personal relations.

Since 1864, Russian universities set quotas on the admission of Poles; from 1882, some universities extended the quotas to Jews as well. In 1887, the Ministry of Popular Enlightenment also introduced a *numerus clausus*: in the universities of the Pale of Settlement, in which Jews represented approximately 40% of the urban population, only 10% of newly admitted students could be Jews. In other areas, their proportion was limited to 5%, and to 3% in Moscow and St. Petersburg. The quotas, temporarily increased again between 1901 and 1903, remained in effect until 1917, but were not consistently implemented everywhere.

In subsequent times, many Russian Jews decided to study in Central and Western Europe, especially in Switzerland, the German Reich, and France. After an initially generous admissions policy, the universities of these nations tried to limit the influx by means of higher requirements for previous education (Germany, France), raising tuition fees (Switzerland), and, finally, a maximum number for Russian subjects (Bavaria 1911/1912, Prussia 1913).

In the interwar period, the setting of quotas for Jewish students in the Czarist Empire was taken up in other East European nations. A → *numerus clausus* was introduced specifically for Jews in Hungary after the First World War, while a similar limitation was informally practiced in Poland and Romania.

2.3 *Great Britain and the United States*

Until well into the 19th century, most English universities excluded non-Anglicans – and hence Jews – from attending institutions of higher learning. It was the Universities Tests Act of 1871, which abolished the

UNIVERSITIES

ubligation to comply with the Thirty-Nine Articles of Religion of the Anglican Church and compulsory attendance at mass, that first enabled enrollment and the achievement of academic degrees regardless of religious confession. Previously, this had only been possible at the University of London, founded in 1836 and supported by Jewish financiers.

To be sure, Jews, who did not demand the abolition of religious exclusivity in England until rather late, were also able to study in Oxford and Cambridge after the reforms of higher education in the 1850s. However, this did not yet mean unimpeded access, since the various colleges themselves made decisions on admissions, and did not guarantee any unlimited rights to graduate. Until the First World War, there were never more than 25 to 30 Jews studying at both elite universities, where they represented less than 1% of the students. The first graduation of a Jew at an Anglican institution of higher learning took place at Trinity College, Dublin in 1836. In Edinburgh, Scotland, the physician Joseph Hart Myers (1758–1823) had already successfully completed his studies in 1779.

In the United States, Jews did not seek out a university education in fairly large numbers until the late 19th century. At the elite private schools of the East Coast, quotas for Jewish students coexisted with the new, but also restrictive principle of regional balance, and of selective admission, directed toward individuals. Catholics also encountered discrimination, while African Americans were to the greatest extent denied access. At first, Jews were only very rarely accepted into American student associations, which, like their German counterparts, were conceived as lifelong associations; in the 1880s, they began to be excluded in principle, which led to the formation of a parallel system of Jewish student associations.

3. Co-opting and restricting Jewish academics

Already in the early modern period, converts (→ Conversion), and, quite seldom, Jews as well, acted as teachers of → Hebrew at various German and English universities. As late as the 19th century, the statutory Christian nature of institutions of higher learning was used to justify the exclusion of Jewish teachers. In the wake of the → Prussian Emancipation Edict, Prussia granted access to academic teaching positions in 1812 but withdrew it again in 1822. The re-authorization of 1847 was initially valid only for → mathematics, the natural sciences, geography, and linguistics. Until the abolition of this restriction a year later, most of the presumed 18 Jewish private lecturers at German universities were therefore in territories that had belonged to the Confederation of the Rhine or the Kingdom of Westphalia during the Napoleonic expansion and were influenced by French legislation. Full legal equality was not achieved until 1869/1871, when access to all government offices was opened.

In 1910, the proportion of Jews among teachers at institutions of higher learning stood at 8%, thus corresponding to their proportion in the student body. When one differentiates by status groups, as well as inclusion of university professors who had converted to Christianity and had achieved their positions only on that condition, the pressure to be baptized becomes clear. Thus, in 1909/1910, 2.5% of full professors in Prussia were Jews, but 6% were converts; among the 292 associate professors, Jews were represented at a rate of 10%, but converts at 6.5% and of the 675 senior lectures, 14.5% were Jews, but only 9% had converted to Christianity. Jews were also stucturally disadvantaged since around 1870, when they obtained genuine access to professorships; many chairs had just been newly filled, so that no changes took place for decades. In addition, in medicine, a field in which Jews represented a greater share of those who had obtained teaching qualifications than in any other faculty, proportions shifted to the detriment of non-full professors. Finally, because of their exclusion from student associations, Jews also lacked the connections that were important for appointments. Here, the fact that in Prussia, where most of the Jewish senior lecturers worked, neither the ministry nor the universities pursued a clear policy of official discrimination or consistent equality, made the careers of Jews more strongly dependent on chance. Even so, when it came to justifying the "incompetence" of candidates, their Jewishness seems to have served not as a *prima ratio*, but only as an *ultima ratio* [8. 468].

Largely excluded from senior professorships, Jews were by and large barred from decisions on the system of instruction and the institutions of university life. The fact that their scholarly potential was readily exploited, in contrast, is attested by their free access to the habilitation and taking over leadership functions in extra-university research institutes (→ Chemistry).

The pressure in Germany to be baptized corresponded, in Russia, to an actual obligation to undergo baptism. To be sure, lecturers of Jewish descent who had converted to Russian Orthodoxy or to Lutheranism taught at all Russian universities, but no obstacles seemed to impede their university careers. Nevertheless, Jews were still exceptions in the teaching faculty, even among lecturers. In accordance with a regulation enacted in 1866, and which remained in effect until 1917, they were not generally excluded from teaching, but were nonetheless not to be accepted into the faculties of law, history, or political science since these were considered to be based on the truths of the Christian religion.

In England, the philosopher Samuel Alexander (1859–1938) was the first Jew to be admitted as a fellow to a college of a traditional university in 1882. In the following year, the mathematician James Joseph Sylvester (1814–1897) become the first Jew to receive a professorship at Oxford, after he had already worked as a professor from 1837 to 1841 at University College in London, and later at American universities, without any university degree.

Corresponding to the transmission of Christian values and norms in American colleges and universities, potential instructors were subject to informal or explicit religious tests. As a consequence, career possibilities for Jews did not open up there until the late 19th century, when professional competence moved into the foreground.

4. The founding of Jewish institutions of higher learning

To circumvent external limitations and prevent the menace of alienation from Judaism, Jews developed plans for the founding of their own institutions of higher learning. In the 15th century, despite royal authorization in 1466, a university in Sicily, which belonged to the Crown of Aragon, could not be brought to fruition. Instead of the Collegium in Ferrara, planned by the Mantuan rabbi and scholar David Provençal (Provenzali) and his son Abraham ben David in 1564, in which both secular and Jewish subjects were to be taught, only a yeshivah (→ Talmud Torah) came into being.

Not until the 19th century were academic rabbinical seminaries created, first, on the initiative of the Habsburg government, the → Collegio Rabbinico in Padua in 1829, which had the rank of a university. In Germany, it was followed in 1854 by the Jewish Theological Seminary in → Breslau, by the → Hochschule für die Wissenschaft des

Judentums in 1872, and, in 1873 by the ortho-dox → rabbinical seminary in Berlin, after efforts to create a Jewish theological faculty at a German university, or at least a profes-sorship, had failed. The rabbinic seminaries followed the model of German universities in their entrance prerequisites and cur-ricular organization and cooperated with them. Most of the students attended their respective local universities in parallel and received their doctorates from them.

Similar establishments emerged in other nations, such as the → Hebrew Union Col-lege and the Jewish Theological Seminary in the United States. The orthodox rabbini-cal seminary in New York, which at first was more of a yeshivah, developed by 1945 into Yeshiva University through the annexation of secular studies; there the → Halakhah is followed, but it is also open to non-Jews.

In 1908, the "Higher Courses for Oriental Studies" opened in St. Petersburg, which, however, in accordance with their self-con-ception and their Hebrew name, taught the → Wissenschaft des Judentums. Only some of their students attended the university at the same time.

Especially in the 20th century, Jewish → patrons took part in the establishment of new, transconfessional universities, as for instance in the case of the universities in Frankfurt am Main (1914), Hamburg (1919), and → Brandeis University (1948). They pro-vided Jewish scholars with substantially better opportunities for a career in higher education. The → Hebrew University in Jeru-salem adopted elements from various types of universities. At the same time, its founda-tion as the national Jewish university fol-lowed the reasoning of the development of universities in the Age of Nationalism.

Bibliography

Sources
[1] Statistisches Archiv, in: Zeitschrift für Demo-graphie und Statistik der Juden 1 (1905) 8, 15f.

[2] N. Hammerstein, Antisemitismus und deutsche Universitäten 1871–1933, Frankfurt am Main/New York 1995. [3] H. Häntzschel, Frauen jüdischer Herkunft an bayerischen Uni-versitäten. Zum Zusammenhang von Religion, Geschlecht und 'Rasse', in: H. Häntzschel/H. Bußmann (eds.), Bedrohlich gescheit. Ein Jah-rhundert Frauen und Wissenschaft in Bayern, Munich 1997, 105–136. [4] C. Huerkamp, Jüdische Akademikerinnen in Deutschland 1900–1938, in: Geschichte und Gesellschaft 19 (1993), 311–331. [5] A. E. Ivanov, Yevrejskoe studenchestvo v Rossijskoj imperii nachala XX veka. Kakim ono bylo. Opyt sotsiokul'turnogo portretirovaniya [The Jewish Student Body in the Russian Empire at the Beginning of the 20th Century. How it was. An attempt at a Socio-Cul-tural Portrait], Moscow 2007. [6] T. Maurer, Diskriminierte Bürger und emanzipierte "Fremd-stämmige." Juden an deutschen und russischen Universitäten, Graz 2013. [7] D. A. Oren, Join-ing the Club. A History of Jews and Yale, New Haven ²2001. [8] A. Pawliczek, Akademischer Alltag zwischen Ausgrenzung und Erfolg. Jüdis-che Dozenten an der Berliner Universität 1871–1933, Stuttgart 2011. [9] M. Rest, Die russische Judengesetzgebung von der ersten polnischen Teilung bis zum "Polozenie dlja evreev" (1804), Wiesbaden 1975. [10] M. Richarz, Der Eintritt der Juden in die akademischen Berufe. Jüdis-che Studenten und Akademiker in Deutschland 1678–1848, Tübingen 1974. [11] D. B. Ruder-man, The Impact of Science on Jewish Culture and Society in Venice (With Special Reference to Graduates of Padua's Medical School), in: G. Cozzi (ed.), Gli Ebrei e Venezia secoli XIV–XVIII, Milan 1987, 417–448. [12] D. B. Ruder-man, Jewish Thought and Scientific Discovery in Early Modern Europe, New Haven/London 1995. [13] M. Rürup, Ehrensache. Jüdische Studentenverbindungen an deutschen Univer-sitäten 1886–1937, Göttingen 2008. [14] M. R. Sanua, Going Greek. Jewish College Fraterni-ties in the United States, 1895–1945, Detroit 2003. [15] R. C. Schwinges, Zugang für alle? Jüdische Studenten und die mittelalterliche Uni-versität, in: M. Konradt/R. C. Schwinges, Juden

in ihrer Umwelt. Akkulturation des Judentums in Antike und Mittelalter, Basel 2009, 229–253.

TRUDE MAURER, REGENSBURG/GÖTTINGEN

Utopia

Originally a Greek term (*ou-tópos*, no-place) and the title of the 1516 novel by Sir Thomas More, utopia denotes an imaginary ideal political community. In Marxist tradition, the term had negative connotations for a long time, being associated with unrealistic and naïve ideas. The philosopher Ernst Bloch (1885–1977) took up a prominent counter-position, championing in his work, above all in the book *Geist der Utopie* (1918; "The Spirit of Utopia," 2000), an emphatic concept of utopia that incorporated elements of Christian and Jewish messianism.

1. Ernst Bloch
2. An epistemology of the future
3. Utopia as the "not yet"
4. The theory of non-contemporaneity

1. Ernst Bloch

Ernst Simon Bloch was born in 1885 into an assimilated Jewish family in the industrial town of Ludwigshafen. His parents Markus (later Max) Bloch and Barbara (Berta, née Feitel) had both grown up in village communities in the Palatinate and Rhenish Hesse. After their marriage in 1883, they moved to Ludwigshafen, where Markus Bloch worked as a railway employee. Although he grew up in a traditional Jewish environment and was a member of the Jewish community in Ludwigshafen, Ernst Bloch received a secular education.

After attending elementary school, Bloch discovered that he was interested in → philosophy during his education at the humanist secondary school. He also became fascinated by the world of fantasy and fairy tales; later these features would be common in his works. At the age of 17 and 18, the young Bloch wrote letters to the historian of philosophy Wilhelm Windelband (→ Neo-Kantianism), who advised him to write a dissertation, and to the founder of empiriocriticism Ernst Mach (→ Vienna Circle), whose works on the concept of matter provided extraordinary inspiration for him. Bloch's parents, especially his father, whom he later described as authoritarian [9. 20], showed little empathy with their son's interests.

In 1905 Bloch began studying philosophy and German philology in Munich. His teacher Theodor Lipps was one of the most influential university professors of his time. Attracted to Sigmund Freud's → psychoanalysis, Lipps focused on the cognitive dimension of emotions and feelings, initially in their relationship to art and aesthetics. Some of his students, Bloch among them, felt Lipps's psychologism to be insufficient and oriented themselves towards Edmund Husserl's → phenomenology. It was this interest that ultimately led Bloch to Würzburg to the psychologist of thought Oswald Külpe, who awarded him his PhD in the sixth term. In July 1908 Bloch moved to Berlin in order to study under Georg Simmel (→ Type).

Repelled by the "Prussianism" of the capital and attracted by the Alpine landscape, Bloch moved to Garmisch-Partenkirchen in 1911, where he composed the first drafts of *Der Geist der Utopie*. On a visit to → Budapest, Bloch made the acquaintance of Georg Lukács (→ Class Consciousness), who introduced him to Max Weber (→ Pariah People) in Heidelberg. Bloch left a lasting impression. "'Just now a new Jewish philosopher came to see us,' Max Weber recalled, 'a youth with a formidable head of black hair swept up from his forehead and equally formidable self-confidence. He clearly believed himself the precursor of a new Messiah and wished to be recognized as such'" (cited in [9. 49]). At the same time, Bloch met his first

Ernst Bloch (1885–1977)

wife Else von Stritzky, whom he married in 1913. They lived in Garmisch, Munich, and Heidelberg in turn. In 1917 Bloch moved to Switzerland, where he lived until 1919, eking out a living by writing journalistic pieces for the *Freie Zeitung*, which also published texts by Hugo Ball, among others.

In their writings, Simmel, Lukács, and Weber had focused on the crises of the modern age in different ways. Ernst Bloch developed his own strategy for overcoming the crisis and for reviving the utopian impulse to create a just and humane society – an impulse he had recognized to be fundamental. During the years 1918 to 1920, he developed his original variant of Marxism, for which he eclectically drew on Kant, Fichte, Schelling, and Hegel, as well as Marx (→ Jewish Question) and Engels, and even texts from religion and → mysticism. By the end of this development period, he had completed the book *Thomas Müntzer als Theologe der Revolution* (1921) and the new version of *Geist der Utopie* (1923), which he had revised in accordance with Marxism. Literature, art, and folk stories always provided him with material as attested by Bloch's many references to, among others, Karl May and his adventure fiction set mainly in the American Wild West. Together with Bloch's constant interest in showing utopian potential in the present, these varied sources in all their breadth and depth found their way into Bloch's three-volume magnum opus *Das Prinzip Hoffnung* ("The Principle of Hope," 1995), which he wrote between 1938 and 1948 in exile in the United States.

Bloch was acquainted with the most famous left-wing intellectuals of the Weimar Republic, among them Bertolt Brecht, Kurt Weill (→ Misuk), Alfred Döblin (→ Alexanderplatz), Walter Benjamin (→ Angelus Novus), and Theodor W. Adorno (→ Dialectic of Enlightenment). Together with Döblin and Brecht as well as Johannes R. Becher, Max Brod, Robert Musil, Erwin Piscator (→ Piscator Stage), Ernst Toller (→ Bavarian Council Republic) and others, he founded the left-wing Gruppe 1925. While traveling in 1927, Bloch met → Łódź-born Karola Piotrkowska, a member of an upper-middle-class Polish Jewish family, who became his third wife; this marriage lasted until his death. Else von Stritzky had died in 1921, and Bloch's second marriage to the painter Linda Oppenheimer had ended in divorce in 1928. In the 1930s he was part of the Expressionism debate conducted, above all, on the theories of Georg Lukács (→ Weltende); he also composed his study of fascism *Erbschaft dieser Zeit* (1935; "Heritage of Our Times," 1991). While he never joined the Communist Party, he expressed agreement with the Stalinist purges, the Moscow trials, and later supported the Soviet Union as well as the GDR.

He returned from the United States when the University of Leipzig offered him the professorship for philosophy in 1948, becoming the official philosopher of the newly founded East German state, as it were. After Khrushchev's secret speech on the crimes of Stalin in 1956 and the popular uprising in Hungary the same year, he found himself increasingly at odds with the ruling Marxist ideology; in the end, he was prohibited from teaching and publishing his writings. After a lecture in West Germany in 1962, he did not return to the GDR, instead accepting a professorship in Tübingen. In his last two books, *Das Materialismusproblem, seine Geschichte und Substanz* (1972) and *Experimentum Mundi. Frage, Kategorie des Herausbringens, Praxis* (1975), he returned to the subjects of his early works. Until his death at the age of 92 in 1977, Bloch remained in Tübingen.

2. An epistemology of the future

While Bloch had been an avowed atheist since his youth, he still retained a profound appreciation of the religious imagination. In his doctoral dissertation *Kritische Erörterungen über Rickert und das Problem der modernen Erkenntnistheorie*, published in 1909, he pointed to biblical eschatology as an anticipation of an epistemology of the future. This work, which preceded his orientation towards Marxism, already contained the seeds of his subsequently formulated utopian perspective. The dissertation is a critical appreciation of Heinrich Rickert's (→ Neo-Kantianism) endeavor to liberate historical studies from the grasp of positivism, with Bloch regarding the latter as the "new religion" of the middle class (Bürgertum) and the primary cause of the cultural malaise of his generation. Rickert, he held, had failed in the task he set himself as he limited historiography to the ideographic description of individual historical events, identifying what had happened in history as what was necessary [1. 64].

The 24-year-old Bloch countered that empirical reality also included negative elements, for instance, an "event that did not come to pass although it would have been expected in accordance with the universal course of human experiences" [1. 64]. Recognizing and negating these events would then open a view to an alternative reality

beyond strict causality. The means of this sort of view of history, Bloch argued, could be discerned in individual psychology, which Rickert had rejected as being irrational and irrelevant for the understanding of the "objective" structure of history. Bloch initially spoke of a *Glücksdifferenz* (difference in happiness), a sensation sporadically appearing in history indicating that "the present state" did not provide "absolute satisfaction." One could then contrast the "historical rightness of life" by countering it with a "utopian demand" [1. 74].

In Bloch's view, arbitrary individual acts of will correlated with the *Glücksdifferenz* – acts that could be coincidental or even irrational in that they stubbornly disregarded historical reality. According to Bloch, the "ought" at which these actions aim can neither be discovered in the real development of history nor as a regulative idea a priori, as the Marburg School of Neo-Kantianism, led by Hermann Cohen (→ Concept of God), advocated. Rather, that ought must be sought in a "mystery that is still uncalled and unnamed" [1. 88]. The future, he held, possessed an appeal all its own, which distinguished it radically from the past and the present. However, as reason and history were not able in and of themselves to show the way to this future in which humanity would leave the state of constant suffering behind, philosophy faced the urgent question of whether there was an epistemological faculty that could serve to achieve this knowledge. Once philosophy discovered this faculty, humanity's cultural activity might acquire "apocalyptic power," and utopia might come within reach [1. 82].

3. Utopia as the "not yet"

The task Bloch had already formulated in his doctoral dissertation – of achieving an epistemology of the future – formed the constant subject of Bloch's life's work and culminated in his intensive investigation of the concept of utopia. This investigation is expressed in *Geist der Utopie* ("The Spirit of Utopia," 2000) and the three-volume study *Das Prinzip Hoffnung* ("The Principle of Hope," 1995). *Geist der Utopie* was written in the time of the First World War; Bloch completed the original version in 1918. "There has never been a more dismal military objective than Imperial Germany's [...]. The War ended, the Revolution began, and along with the Revolution, doors opened. But of course, they soon shut" [2. 1]. *Das Prinzip Hoffnung*, in turn, was composed during the Second World War, which Bloch observed from his American exile. Both works are characterized by a singular combination of virtually Expressionist presentation, Marxist rhetoric, and elements of Christian as well as Jewish eschatology. In 1963 Bloch wrote about *Geist der Utopie* that it was "an attempted initial major work, expressive, Baroque, devout, with a central subject matter." He had intended it as a "*Sturm and Drang* book entrenched and carried out by night"; indeed, he regarded it as nothing less than a "revolutionary gnosis" [2. 279].

In Bloch's eyes, utopia was not a construct projected onto the future. While the literal meaning of the term suggests a "non-place," he regarded utopia as being present in the Now. As a painful perception of something missing, just as hunger points to a lack of food, it corresponded to what Hegel called "unhappy consciousness" [5. 126]. Thus, utopia was both a phenomenological and a political category. There are both subjective and objective reasons for dissatisfaction with one's own present, so this emotion carries the seed of a utopian corrective within itself.

This premise led Bloch to turn to the historical images and ideas of the utopian future as found in the (theist as well as heathen) religious imagination – namely, in fairy tales, myths and legends, songs, and

the "realm of fancy" in all its manifestations. While Sigmund Freud investigated the nightmares of humanity, Bloch focused on the daydreams in which he saw an expression of the longing for an alternative, perfected reality. The perceived shortcoming of the lived moment – the "not here" – assumed the form of the "not yet" in these daydreams. "Above all in days of expectancy," Bloch stated in the second version of *Geist der Utopie*, "when the imminent itself intrudes into the Now [...], above all within artistic labor itself, is that imposing boundary with *the not-yet-conscious* clearly overstepped" [2. 192].

In his investigations into the utopian imagination, Bloch repeatedly circled around the peculiarly human capacity of comprehending the "absolute" future. He called this capacity "hope" – it was based, he said, in the existence of humanity, and, indeed, of the world itself. The original foundation of reality that preceded the distinction between matter and spirit, object and subject, was moved by a cosmic impulse or "hunger" constantly seeking satisfaction and propelling the world with undiminished momentum. This insatiable impulse, according to Bloch, was the ontological cause of the two realms – the material one and the spiritual one. In the latter the impulse manifested itself as the principle of hope constantly urging its fulfillment in the absolute future. Following this path of investigating the ontological dynamic of hope, Bloch gradually adopted Hegelian dialectics and Marxism as coherent historical strategies for the concrete realization of hope, and of the realm of humans. "It is a question of learning hope [...]. The work of this emotion requires people who throw themselves actively into what is becoming, to which they themselves belong" [3. 3].

Apart from the introduction headed "Objective," it is not until the last chapter that Bloch employed Marxist rhetoric in

Geist der Utopie. It was, however, Bloch's intention to accompany the "cold stream in Marxism" [3. 205] with a purpose of humanity that would put into relief its corporeal, cultural, moral, and fantastic side: "Man does not live by bread alone" [2. 243]. This allowed him to link Marxist concepts with theological thought figures (→ Messianism). Metaphorically, Bloch spoke of a "Church, [...] oriented toward the new content of revelation," by means of which the community could transcend the "society that merely disburdens and a communistically restructured social economy" [2. 246]. With reference to Ba'al Shem Tov's Hasidic tales (→ Hasidism), which had come to enjoy new popularity thanks to Martin Buber (→ Dialogue) shortly before, Bloch wrote, "It is as the Baal Schem says: the Messiah can only come when all the guests have sat down at the table; [...] – in the philadelphian Kingdom the organization of the earth finds its ultimately coordinative metaphysics" [2. 246].

4. The theory of non-contemporaneity

The realization of the utopian future requires a political strategy that joins the analysis of the concrete material conditions of the present – class composition and exploitation patterns – with a keen eye for the utopian fantasy of the masses (→ Crowds). The historical moment is frequently nourished, according to Bloch, by past experiences of humiliation and unfulfilled hopes. Although very vague, they are still present and retain a material and potentially also a spiritual force. A confrontation between past and present political systems and their respective utopian impulses, Bloch held, hones one's awareness of the "non-contemporaneous contradiction" [4. 113] of capitalism. Already in his dissertation on Rickert, Bloch had perceived a "strong non-contemporaneity"

[1. 71] in the course of historical events. The challenge was consequently "to release those elements even of the non-contemporaneous contradiction which are capable of aversion and transformation, namely those hostile to capitalism, homeless in it, and to remount them for functioning in a different connection" [4. 113].

The German Left of the Weimar years lacked the insight that the masses could not be mobilized in their entirety by taking only their material circumstances taken into consideration. Bloch lamented that the Nazis, in contrast, had understood the inexhaustible power inherent in the deeply rooted, "non-contemporaneous" utopian images in the heads of the masses. The Left dismissed the fascist Right's propensity for imagery all too easily as being atavistic and irrational. "It is not the 'theory' of the National Socialists," Bloch said, "but rather their energy which is serious, the fanatical-religious strain which does not merely stem from despair and stupidity." If the Marxists had "dialectically transformed" this energy and not merely "abstractly cordoned [it] off," the world would have been spared the horror of the "Third Reich" [4. 60].

Bibliography

Sources

[1] E. Bloch, Kritische Erörterungen über Heinrich Rickert und das Problem der Erkenntnistheorie [1909], in: E. Bloch, Tendenz – Latenz – Utopie, Frankfurt am Main 1978, 55–107. [2] E. Bloch, The Spirit of Utopia, trans. by A. A. Nassar, Stanford 2000. [3] E. Bloch, The Principle of Hope, trans. by N. Plaice, S. Plaice, P. Knight, Cambridge Massachusetts 1995. [4] E. Bloch, Heritage of Our Times, trans. by N. Plaice, S. Plaice, Breinigsville Pennsylvania 2009. [5] G. W. F. Hegel, Phenomenology of Spirit, trans. by A. V. Miller, Delhi 1998.

Secondary literature
[6] I. A. Boldyrev, Ernst Bloch and His Contemporaries. Locating Utopian Messianism, London 2014. [7] J. O. Daniel/T. Moylan (ed.), Not Yet. Reconsidering Ernst Bloch, London 1997. [8] D. Horster, Ernst Bloch. Eine Einführung, Wiesbaden 2005. [9] A. Münster, Ernst Bloch. Eine politische Biographie, Berlin/Vienna 2004. [10] S. Unseld (ed.), Ernst Bloch zu ehren. Beiträge zu seinem Werk, Frankfurt am Main 1965. [11] W. Voßkamp (ed.), Utopieforschung. Interdisziplinäre Studien zur neuzeitlichen Utopie, vol. 3, Frankfurt am Main 1985.

PAUL MENDES-FLOHR, CHICAGO/JERUSALEM

V

Vaudeville

Eclectic genre of entertainment theatre that provided the most popular form of entertainment in North America from the 1880s to the emergence of talking films and radio in the 1920s. Its heyday coincided with a mass influx of immigrants into the United States, among them four million Jews from Eastern Europe. Initially the preserve of long-established Americans of Anglo-Saxon extraction, vaudeville increasingly attracted Jewish performers, song writers, music publishers, and theatre managers. A Jewish audience in the process of integrating into the American mainstream was able to identify with the issue of acculturation and the development of national affiliation they brought to the stage.

1. The voice of the city
2. From the stage Jew to the Jewish stage
3. Jewish vaudeville

1. The voice of the city

In the second half of the 19th century, vaudeville spread mainly in the cities in North America, above all in → New York. The etymology of the word "vaudeville" is not absolutely certain. It is frequently traced back to the French phrase "voix de ville," voice of the city, or to the drinking songs of the *Compagnons gallois*, a French literary and musical society flourishing in the 15th century in the Vire valley in Normandy, which were called "vaudevire." Taken together, both explanations indicate the character of vaudeville

as entertainment theatre that at the same time radiated European finesse and thus met two different expectations of the audiences, most of whose members came from the working classes.

Vaudeville has its roots in older forms of entertainment such as minstrel and burlesque performances or the variety stages of the 19th century. While in America these genres were at first dominated by white Anglo-Saxon Protestant men, after the → American Civil War (1861–1865) other population groups, women, and even children, made their way onto the stage and into the audiences. Vaudeville offered a mix of different numbers such as short sketches, songs, dances, acrobatic interludes, or jokes. Around 1900 the first films were shown, which soon became an integral part of the shows. Performances were characterized by lively interaction between the performers and the audiences. However, vaudeville distanced itself from the vulgarity of its predecessors, tailored to all-male audiences, presenting instead refinement and elegance that also appealed to women. The enterprising New York theatre manager Tony Pastor was the first to advertise vaudeville as edifying entertainment suitable for the whole family.

While vaudeville was aimed at a new type of the serious theatregoer, it struggled to find the boundary between frivolous and respectable. City audiences liked the fast, pounding tempo, the witty songs, the opulent costumes, and the magnificent shows, but they also accepted the clichéd caricatures, dialect jokes, and ethnic descriptions typical of the hierarchies of the time based as they were on racist ideologies. At the same time, vaudeville was egalitarian and democratic; its stage was open to almost anyone with performing skills. In a non-stop show made up of numbers repeated from mid-morning to late evening, acrobats took turns with jugglers, bicycle artists, minstrels, and dialect comedians, with the showmen rather than the virtuosos being more popular with the audiences. The unrestricted access allowed even outsiders who possessed neither financial means nor advantageous descent, social status, or → education to earn a decent income.

Each entertainer addressed cultural differences by parodying ethnic markers of the origins of others. African-Americans as well as Irish, Italian, Jewish, or Chinese immigrants played and competed with each other. The Irish comic Julian Rose delivered "Hebrew monologues," his fellow-countrymen Edward Harrigan and Tony Hart sang new "Hebrew songs" [3. 19]. Jews in turn played Irishmen – and all of them performed in → blackface, made up as African-Americans. The two Jewish comics Joe Weber and Lew Fields began their career as the "colored pair," then became the "Irish pair," and almost overnight the "Double Dutch" duo of Mike and Meyer. In their "Dutch Act" ("Dutch" being a malapropism of "deutsch," German), a slapstick, knockabout number, they played on ethnic characteristics by juggling German-accented English intended to evoke → Yiddish: "Say, vot is dis going to be, a vedding or ein funeral?" [3. 20]. The Jewish singer Nora Bayes, who appeared as one of the Ziegfeld Girls performing sentimental ballads, sang with a strong Irish accent "How Can They Tell that Oi'm Irish?" sprinkled with Jewish names ("How Do You Know Oi'm not Levi or Cohen?"), performed a number in the guise of a Chinese woman, and then a black "mammy," finally belting out George M. Cohan's anthem *Over There* (written expressly for her) dressed up as Uncle Sam, dancing the cakewalk and waving a flag.

2. From the stage Jew to the Jewish stage

The standard character of the stage Jew in vaudeville was the *sheeny* (pej.: Itzig), a figure of fun symbolizing the pariah marginalized as the result of his inability to assimilate. The caricature fitted perfectly with the image current in late 19th-century America, depicting Jewish immigrants from Europe as helpless, vulgar, and scruffy intruders. In contrast, there was the figure of the "beautiful Jewess," the *belle juive* (→ Deborah) made popular by performers such as Sarah Bernhardt, Adah Isaacs Menken (→ America), and Ida Rubinstein, who appeared as an exotic oriental or *femme fatale*, alluring and dangerous in equal measure.

Both characters dominated the depiction of Jewish figures in 19th century American theatre. Male Jews were mainly based on stage conventions of Shakespeare's → Shylock, who was usually shown with anti-Jewish clichés such as a hooked nose, a long, pointed beard, peculiar physique and gait as well as aggressive behavior and speech. Female stage parts often used the image of Shylock's daughter Jessica as seen on the 19th-century stage, with plays highlighting her → conversion, her love life, or her taming.

This "theatre of appearances" (Tadeusz Kantor) was adapted by Jewish vaudeville artists who softened it at the same time. Frank Bush, a Jew of German descent, popularized comic Jewish stage characters from the 1870s onward, wearing a black bowler hat, a crumpled suit rather too large for him, a tousled beard, and curly wig. His characters "Luvinsky the old clothes man" and "Abraham Mendel Cohn the pawnbroker" spoke → English interspersed with → Yiddish, their forced grin and shambling gait referring back to earlier performance conventions. His "Pesock the pawnbroker," however, was a serious figure claiming respectability. Bush's bespectacled, good-hearted "Levy Solomon Moses the door-to-door salesman" finally marked the move away from the Jewish characters previously brought to the stage by non-Jews. Following in Bush's footsteps, the comic duo Weber and Fields wore exaggerated costumes and juggled dialects, but avoided explicitly Jewish references. They played characters such as the clownish "Dutch" immigrants in ill-fitting check suits and lederhosen, thinking up absurd plans of how to make it big in America.

Later Jewish performers increasingly gave dignity to the part of the male Jew, avoiding the strong emphasis on physical stereotypes. Important vaudeville artists such as Barney Bernard, David Warfield, or the brothers Ben and Julian Welch accentuated the positive characteristics of their Jewish stage characters by bestowing them with even more heart and respectability. In the 1920s, the positive representation of Jewish characters became established on all theatre stages, contributing to the transformation of the way in which Shylock was portrayed, the character whose stage genealogy had been the starting point of antisemitizing performances in American theatre. Warfield's Shylock was noble, even majestic. For male Jewish vaudeville artists, playing Shylock became the starting point of a serious stage career, at the same time signaling the transformation and indeed disappearance of the negatively-depicted stage Jew.

Unlike their male colleagues, female Jewish vaudeville performers avoided grotesque appearances, preferring to present ethnic ambiguity attired in glamorous opulence. Good-looking young women avoided → blackface, finding other forms of masquerading which included not only ethnic productions but also performances wearing men's clothes. These strategies appealed to Victorian culture with its fascination with secrecy and confession and corresponded to the desire for extravagance and a certain escapism during the time before the First World War.

The most famous comediennes such as Anna Held, Stella Mayhew, Eva Tanguay, Nora Bayes, Sophie Tucker (→ Humor), and Fannie Brice had Florenz Ziegfeld manage them. Ziegfeld, a theatre manager of Jewish descent who had been born in Germany, was also the producer of the *Ziegfeld Follies*, a musical revue inspired by vaudeville that ran on Broadway every year from 1907 to 1931. His show empire was based on a combination of opulence and extravagance that he sold as tasteful elegance. He groomed dancers from burlesque theatres to become glamorous showgirls, acquiring the title "The Great Glorifier of the American Girl." The strategies he employed of concealing on the one hand and revealing on the other, turned America's first female sex symbols and fashion stars into sensations. The cult of celebrity nurtured by them and the reports of their European chic, their jewelry, astronomical salaries, affairs, and global travel fascinated the female readership of *Vanity Fair*, *Theatre Magazine*, and *Vogue*.

→ Tin Pan Alley provided vaudeville with witty novelty songs or the so-called coon songs parodying African-American slaves accompanied by the fashionable cakewalk – the social dance of the slaves – a nod to the old-established minstrel shows, adorned with the more angular notes of → jazz. The ambiguity of slavery and freedom, Jewishness and "blackness" was sophisticated, hinted at alluringly, and zealously denied. The idiom of Tin Pan Alley simultaneously expressed nostalgia and future-oriented patriotism. Ragtime, combining the sighs of Jewish melodies in minor keys and bold syncopation, pointed to the harsh past in the Old World, while at the same time harboring the promise of a better future in the New World.

3. Jewish vaudeville

As a result of the evolution of Yiddish theatre on → Second Avenue around 1900, decreasing audience numbers, and the spread of low-cost entertainment, from 1901 onward Yiddish vaudeville stages emerged on New York's Lower East Side, the part of Manhattan in which the majority of the population were Jews. Public meeting halls that could be rented for a variety of occasions and where simple food and drink were sold became the first vaudeville theatres which combined a bar and entertainment for indigent workers and barely educated people.

Important artists from the Yiddish theatres of the Lower East Side were already involved in the foundation of the first Yiddish vaudevilles. For instance, Boris Thomashefsky, the manager of the Yiddish National Theatre, founded the People's Music Hall together with the actor Jacob P. Adler and the actor–manager Joseph Edelstein. Thomashefsky produced Yiddish-language adaptations of classic works for vaudeville, thereby introducing a new era. Among these were his *Der yeshivah bokher* (The yeshivah student), based on Shakespeare's *Hamlet*, or his parodies of fashionable melodrama such as *Uncle Thomashefsky's Cabin* (1906), a pastiche of Harriet Beecher Stowe's novel *Uncle Tom's Cabin* (1852). Plays like these evoked patriotic sentiments on two levels. They acknowledged the difficulties of immigrants assimilating in the New World (→ Assimilation), and at the same time affirmed their nostalgia for their countries of origin and their faith in their own traditions.

The entertainer Sophie Tucker called vaudeville one large family whose inspiration came from one and the same source of experiencing prejudice, persecution, and immigration [3. 15]. New York-born Fanny Brice invented a → *shtetl* character, and in her famous rendition of Irving Berlin's (→ White Christmas) *Sadie Salome Go Home* repeatedly sprinkled the exclamation "Oy!," which became her trademark. The daughter of Hungarian Jewish immigrants, she did not speak → Yiddish, but the Yiddish accent assured her of the audience's favor. The *mame-loshn* (mother tongue) gave them a sanctuary that enabled them to overcome the trials of migration, poverty, and the struggle to survive in a foreign land (→ Yiddishland). Similar to Tony Pastor, managers such as Julius Prince, Morris Heine, and Abraham Tantzman also marketed Jewish vaudeville as a kind of respectable variety show for Jewish families.

By 1906, Jewish vaudeville was considered an essential attraction on the Lower East Side and had become a lucrative business. At the same time, immigration brought increasing numbers of Jewish artists from Eastern Europe to → America. Yiddish actors had responded to this development in 1899 by founding the Hebrew Actors Union. This union implemented regulations excluding new arrivals from positions in Yiddish theatres. However, these regulations did not apply to vaudeville theatres, and numerous talented artists began their careers here, for instance Molly Picon (→ Second Avenue), who performed on Yiddish vaudeville stages until the 1930s before becoming successful in film (*Yidl mitn Fidl*, 1936; *Mamele*, 1938) and on → Broadway.

In Yiddish vaudeville, too, film screenings were incorporated into the program early on. From 1907 onward, the first Yiddish Nickelodeons were established on the Lower East Side – movie theatres that competed with the vaudevilles as places of light entertainment. Film screenings became central components of vaudeville – just as elements of vaudeville made their way into the Nickelodeons. Changes in recreational behavior, the rise of → cinema, as well as the increasing numbers of Jews moving away from the Lower East Side encouraged the rapid Americanization of the immigrants and ushered in the end of Yiddish vaudeville in the 1930s. From then on it would exist only in the summer months as entertainment in the holiday villages of the Catskill Mountains in New York state (→ Borscht Belt).

Bibliography

[1] M. Alison Kibler, Rank Ladies. Gender and Cultural Hierarchy in American Vaudeville, Chapel Hill 1999. [2] J. Berkowitz/B. Henry (eds.), Inventing the Modern Yiddish Stage. Essays in Drama, Performance, and Show Business, Detroit 2012. [3] P. Brown Lavitt, Vaudeville, in: P. Buhle (ed.), Jews and American Popular Culture, Vol. 2: Music, Theater, Popular Art, and Literature, Westport et al. 2007, 15–35. [4] F. Cullen (ed.), Vaudeville, Old and New. An Encyclopedia of Variety Performers in America, 2 vols., New York 2006. [5] A. L. Erdman, Blue Vaudeville. Sex, Morals and the Mass Marketing of Amusement, 1895–1915, Jefferson/London 2004. [6] H. Erdman, Staging the Jew. The Performance of an American Ethnicity, 1860–1920, New Brunswick et al. 1997. [7] L. A. Erenberg, Steppin' Out. New York Nightlife and the Transformation of American Culture, 1890–1930, Westport 1981. [8] A. Fields, Sophie Tucker. First Lady of Show Business, Jefferson 2003. [9] S. A. Glenn, "Give an Imitation of Me." Vaudeville Mimics and the Play of the Self, in: American Quarterly 50 (1998) 1, 47–76. [10] L. Harrison-Kahan, The White Negress. Literature, Minstrelsy, and the Black-Jewish Imaginary, New Brunswick et al. 2011. [11] J. Melnick, A Right to Sing the Blues. African Americans, Jews, and American Popular Song, Cambridge (MA)/London 1999. [12] L. Mizejewski, Ziegfeld Girl. Image and Icon in Culture and Cinema, Durham 1999. [13] K. Peiss, Cheap Amusements. Working Women and Leisure in Turn-of-the-Century New York, Philadelphia 1986. [14] R. W. Snyder, The Voice of the City. Vaudeville and Popular Culture in New York, Chicago 1989. [15] J. Thissen, Liquor und Leisure. The Business of Yiddish Vaudeville, in: J. Berkowitz/B. Henry (eds.), Inventing the Modern Yiddish Stage. Essays

in Drama, Performance, and Show Business, Detroit 2012, 184–201.

PAMELA BROWN LAVITT, SEATTLE

Venice

Spiritual and cultural center of Italian Jewry in the early modern period with European-wide influence. The city of lagoons, scene of the notional coinage "ghetto" in the early 16th century as the designation for a closed Jewish residential quarter, had, in the world of the premodern Italian states, the role of a model for the way secular authorities dealt with Jews in an urban context.

1. History of the settlement and spread
2. Cultural and intellectual life

1. History of the settlement and spread

The presence of Jews in Venice is attested since the early 14th century. Except for a settlement → privilege granted for ten years in 1387, until the end of the 15th century individual Jewish money lenders (→ Money Lending), physicians (→ Medicine), merchants, and scholars, but also pilgrims on their way to and from the Holy Land were tolerated as temporary residents in the city. When, in 1509, the League of Cambrai declared war on Venice with the goal of recapturing Venetian mainland holdings in northern Italy, many Jewish money lenders who had settled on the mainland fled from the advancing troops to the city of lagoons. The Venetian government had a strong economic interest in the Jews, who, as a lucrative source for taxes and as lenders, promised to mitigate the laguna city's strained financial situation. Within the population and the church, however, their influx inspired anti-Jewish resentments (→ Anti-Judaism). In 1516, the government therefore granted them the right to settle in an isolated area of the island, situated on the periphery of the city, known as Ghetto Nuovo (New Ghetto).

The term "ghetto," derived from the Italian verb "gettare" ("to pour," here in the sense of the casting of copper), referred to the circumstance that until 1434, the residential district assigned to the Jews had been used for the disposal of waste products from the copper foundry. It was located in an immediately adjacent quarter, the Ghetto Vecchio (Old Ghetto), linked by a wooden bridge over a small canal. The Ghetto Nuovo, established in 1516, was inhabited by members of the Nazione Tedesca (→ Ashkenazim), composed of German and Italian Jews (→ Ashkenaz), to whom the Senate granted the right to practice money lending and pawnbroking, as well as trading in used goods (→ Shmattes). Owing to housing shortages, in 1541 the authorities assigned a second residential area in the Ghetto Vecchio to immigrants of Sephardic origin (→ Sepharad) from the Ottoman Empire, who joined the Nazione Levantina (→ Sepharadim). An additional expansion of the residential area, requested by the Jews of Venice, took place in 1633 with the establishment of the Ghetto Nuovissimo for well-to-do merchants from Spain and Portugal, primarily the descendants of New Christians (→ Conversos), who constituted themselves as the Nazione Ponentina (derived from the Italian noun "ponente," for "West"). They were usually active in overseas trade, and were therefore particularly important economically for Venice. In 1589, the government granted them the right to return to Judaism.

All three districts were joined to one another by footbridges, and with the new function assigned to them, underwent structural alterations, especially in the form of the construction of gates and walls, the costs of which, including pay for the Christian gatekeepers posted at night, were imposed upon the Jews. Added to this was a series of other discriminatory regulations, such as high tax contributions, the regular purchase of an extension of the residence permit, the prohibition of specific careers, or nocturnal curfews. During the day, however, the Jews were able to move freely in the city and pursue their business as money lenders, merchants, or craftsmen (→ Crafts); nevertheless, they were obliged to wear yellow or red head coverings (→ Dress Regulations).

In subsequent times, the term "ghetto," as a designation for a residential district spatially separated from the Christian population, to which Jews were forcibly relegated, spread throughout the entire Italian peninsula. Until 1600, there were ghettos in the Papal States (Rome, Ancona 1555), the Republic of Venice, and the Grand Duchy of Tuscany (Florence, Siena 1571). Only in → Livorno and Pisa did the Medici dispense with the establishment of a ghetto. There were many other new foundations in north and central Italy in the 17th century, for instance in → Mantua 1612, Modena 1638, Genova 1660, Reggio Emilia 1669, Conigliano 1675, Torino 1679, and → Trieste 1696, as well as in the cities of the Duchies of Ferrara and Urbino, which were annexed to the Papal States in 1598 and 1631, after the House of Este died out (Ferrara 1627, Urbino and Senigallia 1633, Lugo 1639). Many of the quarters established in larger and smaller cities were arranged as if in a closed rectangle around an inner courtyard, with an underpass as the entrance. The location of the ghettos in the urban area varied widely: often, it was in the outskirts of the city (Venice, Lugo), other times in the city center (Florence, Siena, Mantua, Verona). In addition, the founding of ghettos was not always accompanied by resettlement, as places were chosen in which Jews had traditionally long resided. The process of ghettoization concluded in the realm of the Dukes of Savoy, where, in 1724, Victor Amadeus II ordered the establishment of separate residential areas (as in Acqui, Alessandria, Chieri, Fossano, and Vercelli).

2. Cultural and intellectual life

By conservative estimates, the number of Venetian Jews in the late 16th and 17th centuries stood between 2,000 and 3,000 persons, hence 1 to 2.5% of the entire urban population [3. 22]. The three "Nazioni," named after their respective ethnic origin, did not form a community in the proper sense of the term, but a corporation ("università"). They differed clearly from one another with regard to their legal status, economic activity, and financial situation, which formed the background for many internal conflicts. Increasing administrative requirements, and the need to defend common interests against the outside world finally necessitated the establishment of superordinated institutions. In addition to the plenary assembly ("congregatione grande"), the key executive organs included the lesser council ("congregatione piccola"), the tax committee ("tansadori"), and the banking committee ("i venti" – the Twenty). A preserved minute book provides a glimpse of the complicated, sometimes strained interplay among the three groups for political influence and economic room for maneuver. This evidence shows that German and Italian Jews (→ Ashkenazim) lost their political dominance to the → Sephardim in the first third of the 17th century [7. 13–15].

Since the three nations continued to cultivate their languages (→ Yiddish; → Ladino), traditions of dress and cuisine (→ Dress Regulations; → Kashrut), and religious rites and customs (→ Minhag), and since each maintained their own → synagogues and other community facilities as well as institutes of teaching and study, a pluralistic Jewish life developed within a restricted space. It was visibly reflected in the architectural structure and design language of the eight synagogues, the oldest of which, the Scuola Grande Tedesca (1528/1529), as well as the Scuola Ponentina or Spagnola, erected in the late 16th century, and the Scuola Levantina,

are to be emphasized as particularly important from an artistic perspective.

Among the personages working in Venice was Leone Modena (1571–1648). Born in the Ghetto Vecchio, Modena, already considered exceptionally gifted in the early years of his life, enjoyed a comprehensive education from private tutors, including instruction in music and singing. In 1593, Modena became the rabbi at the Synagogue of the Nazione Tedesca. Endowed with great oratorical talent, he developed an active preaching activity that was appreciated in Christian circles as well. This brought him fame but no financial security. Contributing to this was his obsessive passion for gambling, strongly condemned by Jewish law (→ Halakhah), and only permitted at Hanukkah, Purim, and certain other holidays (→ Course of the Year), about which he provided frank information in his account of his life entitled *Ḥaye Yehudah* (Life of Yehuda), one of the first Jewish autobiographies. Constantly in need of extra income, Modena pursued many intermittent activities (→ Professions), the number of which he himself estimated at 26, including prayer leader, translator, scribe, bookseller, merchant, matchmaker (→ Marriage), and director of a singing academy ("Maestro di Capella"). Nevertheless, Modena left behind an extensive, multifaceted œuvre, which included many works on the secular branches of knowledge. His best-known work was the *Historia de Riti Hebraici* (History of Jewish Rituals). Written in Italian at the instigation of the English ambassador Henry Wotton, the work was translated into several European languages after its first printing in Paris (1637) and Venice (1638). Modena was also an attentive observer of the intellectual and religious currents among his coreligionists. In his work entitled *Ari Nohem* (Roaring Lion, completed in 1639) he carried out a critical confrontation with the Kabbalah (→ Mysticism), which had undergone an enormous surge in popularity in northern Italy and other countries beginning in the early 17th century. In this book, which did not appear in a complete printed version until 1840 in → Leipzig under the editorship of Julius Fürst (→ [Der] Orient), he castigated the Kabbalists' appropriation of the philosopher Moses Maimonides (→ Guide for the Perplexed), the practice of sorcery and magical acts, the belief in the transmigration of souls, as well as the cult of personality carried on around Isaac Luria (→ Safed) and Moses Cordovero.

Simone Luzzatto (1580–1663) may be named as another representative of Venetian rabbis who were characterized not only by comprehensive secular culture (→ Bildung), but also by a wealth of Jewish knowledge. In what was probably his best-known work, *Discorso circa il stato de gl'Hebrei et in particolar dimoranti nell'inclita Città di Venetia* (Discourse on the Status of the Jews, and Especially Those who Live in the Excellent City of Venice), which appeared in Italian in 1638, Luzzato set forth political reflections on the situation of the Jews in the → Diaspora and formulated suggestions for their improvement. In his work, dedicated to the Venetian government and written in the chronological context of an imminent expulsion, Luzzato pleaded for considering the Jews as an integral component of the Republic of St. Mark. Through their trading and their role as importers who paid customs dues on foreign goods, Jews would provide an important contribution to raising the state finances, and since these were of benefit to all, to social well-being. Luzzato thus formulated thoughts and arguments that paved the way for the debates over the future and opportunities of the Jewish community in the Diaspora, and were taken up by Menasseh ben Israel and John Toland, among others, in the discussion over accepting Jews back into England (→ Jew Bill) [10. 203–210].

The works written by scholars and rabbis such as Luzzatto and Modena spread quickly in both Jewish and non-Jewish learned circles. The reason for this was that Venice was a location of → printing and the book trade (→ Pakn treger) of European status, which represented an important industry in the ghetto. Of the approximately 4,000 → Hebrew books printed in Europe down to 1650, almost one third (about 1,300) were printed in Venice; of these, prayer books accounted for around 290 titles, Talmudic-Rabbinical (→ Talmud) writings, including → responsa and → sermon literature, for 460, Bibles (→ Tanakh) and biblical → commentaries 246, Hebrew grammars 47, works for moral and ethical edification 46 (Musar), philosophical works for 37, Kabbalistic works for 35, and, finally, historiographical presentations (→ Historiography) for ten titles [3. 172]. Also contributing to Venice's role as a religious, spiritual, and intellectual center of early modern Judaism was the large number of eminent doctors (→ Medicine) who stayed in the city, either temporarily or for longer periods. The background for this was the nearby University at Padua, where since the early 16th century Jews were admitted to study and obtain doctoral degrees at the famous Faculty of Medicine.

With the devastating plague of 1630/1631, in which Venice lost one third of its inhabitants and which also claimed many victims in the ghetto, the "università" had already passed its prime. In the wake of the decline of the political power and economic force of Venice, which sank to the status of a port for domestic Italian trade in the course of the 17th century, Jewish merchants suffered considerable losses from the elimination of trade routes and partners. Declining income, combined with rising demands by the Senate for taxes and contributions, brought about a clear deterioration of the financial situation and led to tendencies toward impoverishment in the ghetto. This development entailed further emigrations, so that by the time of Napoleon's invasion in 1797, celebrated in the Ghetto by the raising of a tree of freedom, the number of Jews had shrunk to about 1,600. Napoleon's entry was accompanied by the demolition of the ghetto gates and the broad attainment of → emancipation. After the formation of the Kingdom of Italy in 1861 in the process of national unification (→ Risorgimento), Europe's last early modern Jewish ghetto was dissolved with the end of the Papal States in Rome in 1870.

Bibliography

[1] F. Backhaus et al. (eds.), Frühneuzeitliche Ghettos in Europa im Vergleich, Berlin 2012. [2] R. Bonfil, Jewish Life in Renaissance Italy, Berkeley/Los Angeles 1994. [3] R. C. Davis/B. C. I. Ravid (eds.), The Jews of Early Modern Venice, Baltimore 2001. [4] J. Deventer, Zwischen Ausweisung, Repression und Duldung. Die Judenpolitik der "Reformpäpste" im Kirchenstaat (ca. 1550–1650), in: Aschkenas 14 (2004) 2, 365–385. [5] Y. Dweck, The Scandal of Kabbalah. Leon Modena, Jewish Mysticism, Early Modern Venice, Princeton/Oxford 2011. [6] J. Heyde, The "Ghetto" as a Spatial and Historical Construction. Discourses of Emancipation in France, Germany, and Poland, in: Simon Dubnow Institute Yearbook 4 (2005), 431–443. [7] D. J. Malkiel, A Separate Republic. The Mechanics and Dynamics of Venetian Jewish Self-Government, 1607–1624, Jerusalem 1991. [8] B. C. I. Ravid, Studies on the Jews of Venice, 1382–1797, Aldershot 2003. [9] D. B. Ruderman et al. (eds.), Essential Papers on Jewish Culture in Renaissance and Baroque Italy, New York/London 1992. [10] G. Veltri, Die Stadt, die Regierung und der Rabbi. Venedig im jüdischen Denken zwischen Renaissance und Aufklärung, in: Z. Andronikashvili/S. Weigel (eds.), Grundordnungen. Geographie, Religion und Gesetz, Berlin 2013, 193–212. [11] M. J. Wenninger, Grenzen in der Stadt? Zu Lage und Abgrenzung mittelalterlicher deutscher Judenviertel, in: Aschkenas 14 (2004) 1, 9–29.

JÖRG DEVENTER, LEIPZIG

Verein für Cultur und Wissenschaft der Juden

The Verein für Cultur und Wissenschaft der Juden (Society for the Culture and Science of the Jews), founded in Berlin in 1819 and active until 1824, served a new generation of Jewish scholars and intellectuals as an academic and social forum and is regarded as the first institution of the → Wissenschaft des Judentums. Its members were among the first Jewish students at Berlin University and were influenced substantially by the → Haskalah, classical studies, and German idealism. In view of the emancipation debates and the discussions on the "civic improvement" (→ Improvement) of the Jews, the Verein's objective was to spread science and education among the Jews and, systematically, to apprehend the universal relevance of Jewish history and culture, and at the same time to counteract ignorance and prejudice against Judaism among the non-Jewish population.

1. Origin and objectives
2. Activities and actors
3. Reception and significance

1. Origin and objectives

The foundation of the Culturverein was a direct response to the → Hep-Hep riots in the summer and autumn of 1819, which were pogrom-like attacks directed against the emancipation of the Jews. Isaak Levin Auerbach, Eduard Gans, Joseph Hillmar, Isaak Markus Jost (→ Historiography), Joel Abraham List, and Leopold Zunz had already met with other Jewish students and guest auditors at Berlin University in 1816 and 1817 in an informally organized reading circle, the Wissenschaftszirkel (Science circle). On November 7, 1819, they founded a society significantly first named the Verein zur Verbesserung des Zustandes der Juden im Deutschen Bundesstaate (Society for the Improvement of the Jewish Condition in the German Federation), which had its roots essentially in the premises of the contemporary philological and philosophical debates. In 1822, Heinrich Heine (→ Entreebillet) – at the time a student at Berlin University – joined the (by then renamed) society.

The majority of the Verein's founders were influenced by the ideas of the → Haskalah and the European → Enlightenment and were inspired by the promise of → emancipation. All the same, they found themselves confronted with everyday exclusion, finding an overall negative image of Jews and Judaism even with their academic teachers. The members of the Verein endeavored to counteract this and at the same time to encourage the inner renewal of Judaism. They were critical of the traditional authorities and the constraints of "Rabbinism." They met the challenges of internal and external emancipation by means of → science and education (→ Bildung), trusting in the power of reason. They sought a deeper understanding of the singularity of Judaism beyond its exclusive interpretation as a religion, specifically also discussing contemporary ideas and concepts such as *Nation* (nation) and *Kultur* (culture), *Volksgeist* (national character) and *Wesen* (essence).

Despite the restrictive German association law (*Vereinsrecht*), which ruled out any political activity, the Verein came into being during a golden age of German societies. Some members feared governmental restrictions and sought official permission. As a result of the necessary drafting of statutes and the establishment of formal association structures, conflicts between the members arose, which, among other things, led to the withdrawal of Hillmar, Jost, and later List as well. The disagreements developed around the program and objectives of the Verein, individual society activities as well as concrete responsibilities, especially

regarding the planned journal, but also the name of the society. It was not until July 1821 that the members agreed on the final name Verein für Cultur und Wissenschaft der Juden, immediately causing confusion among the Prussian authorities who misunderstood *Cultur* as *Cultus* (faith, worship). Considering the academic tendency of the Verein's objectives, official permission was ultimately not required; however, the application for official recognition as a legal entity was rejected [10. 5].

In the course of the debates regarding the Verein's objectives, its scholarly tendency became increasingly important. Even before its foundation, Zunz had begun in his 1818 paper *Etwas über die rabbinische Literatur* to apply the perspectives and methods of → classical studies to Judaism, devising a wide-ranging program of study of Jewish → history, culture, and → literature. Zunz's vision found a continuation and systematic formulation in the Culturverein. Immanuel Wohlwill's (originally Immanuel Wolf) treatise "Ueber den Begriff einer Wissenschaft des Judenthums" ("On the Concept of a Science of Judaism," 1957) published in the Verein's own journal *Zeitschrift für die Wissenschaft des Judentums* in 1822, immediately made this evident. Influenced by Hegelian philosophy, Wohlwill described Judaism as the bearer and preserver of a "divine idea," the "idea of unlimited unity in the all," vouched for in biblical monotheism [3. 194f.]. Judaism, he said, carried this idea into the world and also preserved it. Based on this premise, Wohlwill developed a program for the systematic study of Judaism, divided into its "historical and literary documentation" and the "statistical study of Judaism," the latter building on the former [3. 202]. The methodological foundation was provided by historical criticism and therewith philology. It laid the foundations of the → Wissenschaft des Judentums that would concentrate essentially on three fields of study over the following decades – history, literature, and → philosophy including Jewish theology.

2. Activities and actors

The Verein's activities reflect the cooperation between education and scholarship, and simultaneously document the Verein's everyday work, frequently riven with conflicts. The members provisionally agreed an immediate program to serve the society's objectives and lay the foundations for its long-term activities. It comprised a teaching institute, a journal, a research institute, and an archive for correspondence which had the task of collecting material with a view to the further development of the Verein [9. 64]. In addition there were plans for a scientific → library and a women's association. As to its activities, the Culturverein did not differ essentially from comparable scholarly and education associations of the time which were voluntaristic societies seeking moral improvement through education and civic sociability.

The protracted drafting of the statutes and program delayed the start of the Verein's practical work, carried out in particular through the activities of the Wissenschaftliche Institut, the teaching institute, and the journal. The most productive phase was between March 1821 and April 1823, accompanied by a focus on scholarly work. The latter was also due to the understanding that all practical educational work must be based in scholarly methodology. At the same time the political climate and the restrictive association law had the effect that a stronger political tendency of the Verein's work was not possible.

The Wissenschaftliche Institut consisted of regular meetings of Verein members, who took turns giving lectures on various subjects and putting them up for discussion. Many of these lectures were later published in the *Zeitschrift für die Wissenschaft*

des Judentums (1822/1823), led by Zunz as the managing editor. Only after an official notification from the Verein to the government authorities could the journal be submitted to the censorship authority, which then demanded a separate notice that the journal primarily addressed a Jewish readership, with the aim of preventing "Christians taking the side of Jews and Judaism" [9. 77]. Nonetheless, the journal was also sent to Christian readers, meeting the Verein's implicit aspiration of reaching out to the educated public and consequently everyone dedicated to the scholarly investigation of Judaism.

While not all the articles of the journal corresponded to contemporary scholarly standards, it did gather a series of remarkable contributions, among them Wohlwill's deliberations on the concept of an academic discipline of Judaism as well as Zunz's exposition on a future → statistics of Judaism or his study on the medieval Halakhic authority Rashi (→ Worms). It was here above all that the consistent historization of Judaism and its sources was demonstrated, which characterized the Wissenschaft des Judentums and had its origins in the Culturverein.

The teaching institute of the Culturverein which opened in November 1921 accompanied the scientific program. It was addressed primarily to young Jews from Eastern Europe who were preparing for university studies. The subjects taught included German, Latin, geometry, arithmetic, Greek, → Hebrew, French, history, geography, and declamation. The question of religious instruction was a controversial one. Some Verein members like Gans rejected it out of principle, while others such as Zunz believed that this responsibility could be covered more effectively within the family or elsewhere [2. 16–19]. Formally, the Verein's members were obliged to teach three lessons a week, but only a few actually complied with this requirement. Even among the few pupils who could be enrolled, most did not meet the requirements either. The financial situation also remained precarious. Zunz's suggestion of uniting the teaching institute with the Jewish → Freischule, which found itself in financial difficulties as well, found no interest. In May 1823, lessons were concluded after the last pupils had been suspended; the suggestion of restarting teaching in October 1823 was rejected by the members. The journal was discontinued after three issues.

While the Culturverein united some of the most important protagonists of German-speaking Jewry – in addition to those named above, David Friedländer (→ Oriental Printing Press), Eduard Kley (→ German), Gotthold Salomon, and as adjunct members Joseph Perl (→ Megalle Temirin), Samuel Meyer Ehrenberg, and Lazarus Bendavid (→ Self-hatred) – in the end there was a lack of active members and also of the necessary financial resources. The 1821 establishment of the Specialverein in Hamburg as a branch changed nothing. Two thirds of the Hamburg members had ties to religious → reform and were committed to the Tempelverein (→ Hamburg Temple Dispute). Also in Berlin some members were active in similar circles, such as the Beersche Temple. Even more numerous were pedagogues and headmasters. Around a quarter of the members worked in this sector, most of them during their membership. In addition from 1840 onward, Zunz was director of the Jewish teachers' seminary in Berlin founded by him and Rabbi Meyer Landsberg. Between 1819 and 1824, 81 persons are documented as having been regular or adjunct members at least temporarily; only a minority among them, however, took regular part in the society's activities [9. 174–189].

3. Reception and significance

The fact that it was never formally dissolved is characteristic of the history of the Verein; rather, it stopped existing in 1824 when its relevant activities came to an end. Although the Culturverein did not enjoy great success, it exerted a lasting influence on its members and contemporaries, above all in the context of the idea of the → Wissenschaft des Judentums that first emerged here. With a view to the reasons why the Verein failed, some twenty years after his activity in the society, Heinrich Heine wrote in his commemoration of the Orientalist Ludwig Marcus that it was ultimately founded on a "soaringly great but unfeasible idea" [1a. 33]; [1. 267], referring to the circumstance that the project of a small, educated elite with an interest in scholarship was ultimately ahead of its time. In some ways, the Verein also failed due to everyday life, occasional harsh personal disagreements between individual members, and thus ultimately the inability to unite the different perspectives on Judaism and its role in a fundamentally changing time into a coherent vision.

Irrespective of its failure, the Verein is historically significant if only because of the foundation of the Wissenschaft des Judentums, as repeatedly emphasized over the course of the 19th century. Thus the Verein and the *Zeitschrift für die Wissenschaft des Judentums* it published were an important reference point for following generations. This was also due to the prominent significance accorded to Leonard Zunz as the founding father of the Wissenschaft des Judentums.

Bibliography

Sources

[1] H. Heine, Ludwig Marcus, in: H. Heine, Historisch-kritische Gesamtausgabe der Werke, ed. by M. Windfuhr, Vol. 14/1: Lutezia, Hamburg 1990, 265–272. [1a] R. Schlesier, Homeric Laughter by the Rivers of Babylon. Heinrich Heine and Karl Marx, in: The Jewish Reception of Heinrich Heine, ed. M. H. Gelber, Tübingen 1992, 21–44. [2] S. Ucko, Geistesgeschichtliche Grundlagen der Wissenschaft des Judentums,

in: Zeitschrift für die Geschichte der Juden in Deutschland 1 (1935), 1–34. [3] I. Wolf, On the Concept of a Science of Judaism (1822), in: Year Book - Leo Baeck Institute, 2(1), 1957, 194–204.

Secondary literature

[4] O. Bertrams, Der Verein für Cultur und Wissenschaft der Juden (1819–1824). Zur ersten Konzeption einer "Wissenschaft des Judentums" und ihrer Bedeutung für die Neubestimmung jüdischer Identität im Kontext autoemanzipatorischer Apologetik, in: M. Konkel et al. (eds.), Die Konstruktion des Jüdischen in Vergangenheit und Gegenwart, Paderborn 2003, 29–47. [5] M. Graetz, Renaissance des Judentums im 19. Jahrhundert: "Der Verein für Cultur und Wissenschaft der Juden" 1819 bis 1824, in: M. Averbuch (ed.), Bild und Selbstbild der Juden Berlins zwischen Aufklärung und Romantik, Berlin 1992, 211–227. [6] A. Greenbaum, The "Verein für Cultur und Wissenschaft der Juden" in Jewish Historiography. An Analysis and Some Observations, in: M. Fishbane/P. Flohr (eds.), Texts and Responses. Studies Presented to Nahum N. Glatzer on the Occasion of his Seventieth Birthday, Leiden 1975, 173–185. [7] R. Livneh-Freudenthal, Kultur als Weltanschauung. Der Kulturbegriff der Begründer der "Wissenschaft des Judentums," in: B. Greiner/C. Schmidt (eds.), Arche Noah. Die Idee der "Kultur" im deutsch-jüdischen Diskurs, Freiburg im Breisgau 2002, 59–84. [8] E. Lutz, Der "Verein für Cultur und Wissenschaft der Juden" und sein Mitglied H. Heine, Stuttgart 1997. [9] H. G. Reissner, Eduard Gans. Ein Leben im Vormärz, Tübingen 1965. [10] I. Schorsch, Breakthrough into the Past. The Verein für Cultur und Wissenschaft der Juden, in: Leo Baeck Institute Year Book 33 (1988), 3–28.

KERSTIN VON DER KRONE,
BERLIN/BRAUNSCHWEIG

[Der] verwaltete Mensch

Title of a 1974 study by H. G. Adler (1910–1988) in which he investigated the deportation of the Jews under National Socialist rule and formulated a theory of the administration in modern nation states. Himself a survivor of the Shoah, Adler drew on his personal experiences by acting simultaneously as witness, scholar, and author. His work revolves around the question of the relationship between the academic research into the Shoah and its literary presentation.

1. Introduction
2. H. G. Adler
3. Administration and extermination
4. Poetry and memory

1. Introduction

At the center of Adler's work is the persecution and murder of European Jews. He decided early on to report on his experiences: "When it came to the deportations, I told myself: I won't survive this. But if I do survive, I want to represent it, and in two different ways: I want to explore it in a scholarly manner and so separate it from myself completely, and I want to portray it in a literary manner" [cited in 3a. 25]. Over the following forty years, this project found expression in the two parts of his œuvre, a literary one and a sociological-historical one.

In literature and research, Adler focused on the phenomenon of the administration which he analyzed in *Der verwaltete Mensch* (1974), especially with reference to the question of the possible "proximity [...] of murder and administration" [2. 867]. These deliberations as well as his theory of mechanical materialism he had already developed in his 1955 study *Theresienstadt 1941–1945* were the building blocks of a comprehensive theory of modernity in which the → Shoah appears as the most extreme consequence of inhumane developments in contemporary societies.

Adler's poetic works repeatedly took up the linguistic aspect of persecution. On the one hand he described, similar to Victor Klemperer's (→ LTI) analyses, how a certain utilization of language dehumanizes fellow human beings, turning them into objects; on the other he explored – in his poetry and lyrical prose in particular – the possibilities of a poetical language suited to humans. In contrast to the usual practice in postwar literature, Adler already addressed the topic of the universe of concentration and extermination camps (→ Bearing Witness) in the 1940s and 1950s. Consequently his work is among the earliest and most comprehensive accounts of the Shoah in German; its reception, however, did not begin until comparatively late.

H. G. Adler (1910–1988)

2. H. G. Adler

Adler was born in → Prague in 1910 into an assimilated German-speaking Jewish family. He grew up without significant religious ties. Because of his mother's ill health, he spent a long time in educational institutions outside Prague from the age of ten onward, for example from 1921 to 1923 in the strictly managed boarding school of the Freemasons' Institute in Dresden. As Adler emphasized in 1950, these were "notwithstanding Auschwitz – the two most horrific years" of his life (cited in [12. 366]). Back in Prague he attended the Gymnasium, but left at his own request in 1927 in order to acquire the Matura (secondary school exit exam) by self-instruction.

During these years he joined the Prague Neupfadfinder, a movement within the German Scouts who embraced a life in tune with nature. Between 1928 and 1935, he also attended the debating circle around the Czech poet Emanuel Lešehrad and the photographer František Drtikol. Here Adler developed a temporary enthusiasm for Buddhist, Christian, and Hindu mysticism. From 1930 to 1935, he studied musicology, literature and art history, philosophy, and psychology at the German University of Prague. From 1935 to 1938, he worked at the Prague Volksbildungshaus Urania, where his close friendship with Elias Canetti (→ Crowds) began in 1937. Adler already wished to become a writer at this time, composing his first literary texts and presenting them at public readings.

After the German occupation of Prague in March 1939, Adler's long-prepared plan to emigrate failed. In 1941 he was called up to → forced labor in railway construction. In the same year he married the Jewish physician Gertrud Klepetar (1905–1944). Both of them were deported to → Theresienstadt in February 1942 [3. 41]. Together they were transported to → Auschwitz, where Adler's wife and her mother were suffocated in the gas chambers immediately after their arrival in October 1944. Adler's parents had already been murdered in 1942; he lost 18 members of his family in the Shoah. At the end of October 1944, he was first taken to Niederorschel, and later in February 1945 to Langenstein-Zwieberge (both subdivisions of → Buchenwald), where American troops liberated the completely enfeebled prisoner. After the liberation, Adler consistently abbreviated his given names – Hans Günther – because he could not bear having the same name as the National Socialist head of the Zentralstelle für jüdische Auswanderung (Central Office for Jewish Emigration) in Prague, Hans Günther, who had organized the deportation of the Jews of Bohemia and Moravia.

In June 1945 he returned to Prague, where neither his family nor the majority of his friends were still alive. Because he was a member of the German-speaking population, his Czechoslovak citizenship was revoked. Adler worked as a teacher and tutor in Štiřín in one of Přemyzl Pitter's homes for Jewish and German war orphans and as a research assistant in the Jewish → Museum in Prague. The National Socialists had collected stolen cultural artifacts from Jewish homes and communities in warehouses intended for the planned Jüdische Zentralmuseum (Central Jewish Museum) of the SS. Adler helped with the inventory of items in order to restore them – in part to the Jewish Museum.

In 1947 Adler succeeded in emigrating to Great Britain, where he lived as a writer and private scholar from then on. The majority of his literary and scholarly works were composed here. Even before settling in → London, he married the artist Bettina Gross (1913–1993) who had emigrated in 1938, a friend from his youth in Prague and with whom he had exchanged letters since October 1945. Their correspondence is a moving contemporary historical source. Adler now had close contact to his childhood friend Franz Baermann Steiner and to Elias and Veza Canetti. After Steiner's death in 1952, Adler published his works. He also belonged to a circle of Jewish poets dedicated to the

synthesis of traditional and modernist as well as German and English poetry. Besides Steiner, other members were Hans Werner Cohn, Georg Rapp, Hans Eichner, and Erich Fried, as well as, for a short time, Tuvia Rübner [11]. Adler died in London at the age of 78.

In an "Obituary in My Lifetime" (1970) Adler wrote about himself in the third person, that he had been granted "to understand his existence as a witness, and to bear witness to this existence as he experienced and observed it, as he endeavored in many attempts [...] to depict it academically and artistically" [4. 11]. This also explains his political engagement: membership in the International Auschwitz Committee, his lectures and his informative contributions to broadcasting in the early Federal Republic of Germany, and his support for several legal actions against National Socialists, among them the → Eichmann trial in Jerusalem and the → Frankfurt Auschwitz trial.

3. Administration and extermination

Adler began his work of bearing witness in Theresienstadt, systematically collecting documents of life in the camp. They provided the foundation for his study *Theresienstadt 1941–1945* which he completed in London in the → Wiener Library. In this study he undertook the first comprehensive depiction of a National Socialist camp, under three aspects. First, he sketched the camp's background and history. Second, in a sociological section, he addressed the organization of individual departments of the camp, including the controversial Jewish self-administration (→ Judenrat). Third, under the title "The psychological face of the coerced community," he investigated the effects everyday camp life had on the personality, the character, the ethos, and the social contacts of those interned.

As in all his scholarly works, Adler relies on source material he presents in detail and analyzes critically. Part of this is always the assessment of language. To this end he analyzes the regularity and systematic character of life in the camp, but always with recourse to concrete phenomena and individual experiences.

In addition, Adler positions the Theresienstadt phenomenon within his theory of "mechanical materialism." According to him, wherever humans are perceived as a → crowd, as is increasingly the case in the modern era, they are denied their organic vitality and thus their individuality – they are experienced as a "mechanical quantity." This mechanization of organic life, according to Adler, is combined with the administration, and in National Socialism became murderous by means of transforming people into numbers and life into a mere thing: "Instead of serving to create order in life, administration imperiously becomes an end in itself [...] Once overmechanization is taken seriously [...] National Socialist treatment of human beings is only a small step away." This found expression in state slavery and the "complete extermination of all Jews" [1. 562, 680].

Like all those living in the modern age, however, the Jews also had a part in "the psychology of a humanity contaminated by mechanical materialism." Their → assimilation, in particular, accelerated the "decay of values" analyzed by Hermann Broch (1886–1951) [1. 569, 564]. In the coerced conditions of the camps they, too, were entangled in guilt. Adler demonstrates this by reference to the three chairmen of the council of elders in Theresienstadt – Jakob Edelstein (1903–1944), Paul Eppstein (1902–1944), and Benjamin Murmelstein (1905–1989) – accusing in particular the latter two to have taken harsher action against the prisoners than demanded by the SS. There were objections against these evaluations after the first edition of the book, which Adler discusses in the foreword to the second edition, but does not retract the substance of his accusations

[1. XIII–XXII]. Berthold Simonsohn, for instance, objected that Eppstein harbored the hope that the deportees in Theresienstadt might be saved in due course; his behavior had been due to the coerced situation [9. 24]. Adler replied that Eppstein acted beyond the enforced limits, especially because he allowed leeway for corruption. Adler cited the case of Vladimír Weiss, who in 1943 had sent a memorandum concerning corruption to Eppstein and had, as a result, been sent on a transport to Auschwitz by the latter. Adler concluded: "This was not an instance in which Eppstein succumbed to tragic circumstances; these were actions that he deliberated over and undertook out of his own free will" [1. XIX].

Looking back upon the camp, Adler indicates hypothetically and in a generalizing manner how a spiritual renewal of Judaism under the banner of faith could look – and that it could have started in Theresienstadt, although conditions there were the most difficult imaginable. The persecutions suffered could have led to a human catharsis, whereby mechanical materialism would have been countered with a "Jewish organism" that should not, however, be understood as exclusive but rather, in accordance with the revelations of Judaism, "strives to achieve concrete salvation for all of humanity, together and indivisible" [1. 577]. Passages of this kind testify to Adler's universalist humanism with a Jewish foundation.

The study of Theresienstadt was mainly favorably received by contemporaries and regarded as a seminal work: to begin with by Leo Baeck (→ Leo Baeck Institute), who had himself been a prisoner in Theresienstadt and wrote a supporting foreword, and later by Hermann Broch and Hannah Arendt (→ Judgement). The study won Adler the reputation of being an expert in the historiography of the camps. To this day, *Theresienstadt 1941–1945* and the collection of documents *Die verheimlichte Wahrheit* published in 1958 with the support of the Conference on

Jewish Material Claims Against Germany (→ Claims Conference) hold a firmly established position in the historiography of the Theresienstadt ghetto.

After the investigation of a concrete camp, Adler moved on to *Der verwaltete Mensch*, a description and analysis of the deportations that took place in similar fashion all over Europe. Once again he integrated the view on individual victims, but it is "the persecutor's point of view" that is at the core of this study [2. XXIII]. A considerable portion is dedicated to the disenfranchisement of the victims as well as the confiscation and exploitation of their possessions. In case studies, Adler reconstructed individual experiences of deportation as well as investigating specific places of deportation (→ Auschwitz, Lublin, → Riga, and → Theresienstadt).

The study achieves philosophical and socio-critical depth in its final part which was intended "to contribute to a new theory of administration." To this end, Adler first demonstrated the productive sides of the administration. In principle, it facilitates coexistence. It is necessary and desirable in that it regulates and documents the interchanges constantly taking place within every society. The concept of administration is distinguished from those of governance, the executive, bureaucracy, and the state, above all with reference to their respective relationship with power. Administration is regulated, limited power, "power that does not rule and govern, but is entirely controlled and governed" [2. 955, 957].

The situation was different under National Socialism. Here, the administration played an essential role in the planning and implementation of the Shoah. Adler wished to understand "how a hierarchically controlled official operation" could remove humans "from the network of society and send them where [...] the business of killing took over." To this end he uncovered those points at which the administration had been historically led astray and become harmful. Based on his theory of mechanical materialism, Adler wrote that only things but never humans may be managed: "The slave, in modern terms the prisoner in the concentration camp, becomes a 'thing'; and besides the slaves, – and within clearly definable boundaries – a legally condemned human for the duration of his imprisonment [...]. Under no circumstances may the free human become a thing, not even someone who is a minor, disenfranchised, or physically or mentally ill." A second point Adler makes states that administration may not be permitted to exercise power and must therefore be separated from the government theoretically as well as politically and practically: "If power rules where only administration has to function, then the administration is being abused" [2. 868, 976, 977].

Within National Socialism, administration as government practice, had the most harmful consequences. Adler demonstrated in particular how the deportation of the Jews was achieved using the administration. It was the fusion of leadership and administration, Adler said, that led to the latter becoming "the silent but true master in the state [...]. For the people, the result of an overbearing administration is the managed man even in a 'normal' state; in a totalitarian state [...], the totally managed man, and not infrequently [...] the man managed to death." Adler was especially analyzing the role played by the police who were able to exercise protective custody and later deportation as an administrative act. His conclusion was: "A human imprisoned by the Gestapo and in a concentration camp is the perfectly managed human. The logical conclusion of imprisonment is the physical destruction of the managed human," if his life appears useless to the administrators [2. 986, 1034].

4. Poetry and memory

Adler's literary work comprises mainly poetry and prose. His most important works, written in the 1940s and 1950s, could be published only much later, an indication of the sentiment among the general public in the Federal Republic of Germany, where a literary approach to the → Shoah was confronted with little interest and even a tendency to cover up past events for a long time. His poetic works include poems he composed in the camps and later edited and arranged into cycles, such as "Theresienstädter Bilderbogen 1942." Another part of his works reflects Adler's subsequent investigation of the Shoah. Three of his great postwar novels have been published: *Eine Reise* (1962; "The Journey," 2008), *Panorama* (1968; "Panorama," 2010), and *Die unsichtbare Wand* (1989; "The Wall," 2014). *Die Ansiedlung* (written 1949) remains unpublished. In these works of art in their own right, connections with the academic works are clearly visible, for instance in the consideration of language.

In *Eine Reise*, Adler focuses on the euphemistic words used for the deportations, without explicitly naming National Socialism. The tone of the work follows the perspectives of the deported and the administration officials, alternating between despair and sarcasm. Adler provides a platform for suffering, but also for those aspects described as demonic, namely that inside a camp, nothing was like the reality one had known. The novel *Die unsichtbare Wand* puts the topic of memory at the center: Adler creates debates about looted art and → restitution, at the same time describing in detail the psychological symptoms of the survivors long before psychology defined the phenomenon of traumatization. He also deliberates on the murder of his first wife in Auschwitz and the difficulties of beginning his new private life, trying on the one hand to be faithful to the memory of the woman he lost and achieving a life-affirming frame of mind in his new marriage on the other. In his last monograph *Vorschule für eine Experimentaltheologie*, a theoretical draft, he also provided a theological foundation for this affirmation of life.

In *Panorama*, Adler spans a historical period from the beginning of the 20th century to the time of the Second World War. His own experiences of persecution find their way into two of the chapters. He describes the → forced labor building railways that he experienced in the labor camp Sázava/Velká Losenice in 1941 on the one hand, and the murderous conditions in a camp similar to Langenstein-Zwieberge, where he was interned during the last two months before the liberation on the other. The novel, which looks back not least onto the Bohemian world that perished in the Shoah as well, shows him as a late successor of the → Prague circle around Franz Kafka, Max Brod, and Felix Weltsch (→ Kunstwart Debate), whose legacy he embodied and helped to preserve [6].

Bibliography

Sources

[1] H. G. Adler, Theresienstadt, 1941–1945. The Face of a Coerced Community, trans. by B. Cooper, New York 2017.   [2] H. G. Adler, Der verwaltete Mensch. Studien zur Deportation der Juden aus Deutschland, Tübingen 1974.   [3] H. G. Adler, Es gäbe viel Merkwürdiges zu berichten. Interview mit Hans Christoph Knebusch, in: J. Adler (ed.), H. G. Adler. Der Wahrheit verpflichtet, Gerlingen 1998, 32–55.   [3a] J. Adler, "The World of My Father's Memory Writing: The Gesamtkunstwerk of H. G. Adler," in H. G. Adler: Life, Literature, Legacy, ed. by J. Creet, S. R. Horowitz and A. Bojadjija-Dan. 2016, 23–46.   [4] H. G. Adler, Nachruf bei Lebzeiten, in: J. Adler (ed.), H. G. Adler. Der Wahrheit verpflichtet, Gerlingen 1998, 7–16.   [5] H. G. Adler, Andere Wege. Gesammelte Gedichte, ed. by K. Kohl/F. Hocheneder in coop. with J. Adler,

Klagenfurt/Vienna 2010. [6] H.G. Adler, Literární tvorba pražské školy = Die Dichtung der Prager Schule, Brno 2003. [7] H.G. Adler, Nach der Befreiung. Ausgewählte Essays zur Geschichte und Soziologie, ed. by P. Filkins in coop. with J. Adler, Konstanz 2013. [8] H.G. Adler, Orthodoxie des Herzens. Ausgewählte Essays zu Literatur, Judentum und Politik, ed. by P. Filkins in coop. with J. Adler, Konstanz 2014. [9] B. Simonsohn, Sein Andenken wird weiterleben, in: Jüdische Sozialarbeit 4 (1959) 3/4, 23–26.

Secondary literature
[10] H.L. Arnold (ed.), H.G. Adler, Munich 2004. [11] M. Atze, "... alten Vorsatz ausgeführt und eine Gruppe jüngerer deutscher Dichter gesammelt" (Erich Fried), in: M. Atze (ed.), "Ortlose Botschaft." Der Freundeskreis H.G. Adler, Elias Canetti und Franz Baermann Steiner im englischen Exil, Marbach 1998, 87–98. [12] F. Hocheneder, H.G. Adler (1910–1988). Privatgelehrter und freier Schriftsteller, Vienna et al. 2009. [13] F. Krämer, Die Poetik des Gedenkens. Zu den autobiographischen Romanen H.G. Adlers, Würzburg 2012.

SVEN KRAMER, LÜNEBURG

Vichy

After the defeat of France in the summer of 1940, the small French town of Vichy was, until August 1944, the seat of government of the État Français, which collaborated with Nazi Germany. "Vichy" became a synonym for the authoritarian regime established there, whose representatives, above all Marshal Henri Philippe Pétain and Pierre Laval, leader of the government, called for the project of an anti-republican "révolution nationale," which united within itself right-wing conservative, militant Catholic, and antisemitic traditions. In its territory, the Vichy regime successively abrogated the basic civil rights of French Jews, interned all foreign Jews, and supported Nazi Germany in the implementation of the "Final Solution" in France. This was the culmination of an antisemitism that had become more virulent in the immediate pre-war years, and a policy which, paradoxically, had focused obsessively on the preservation of national sovereignty.

1. The end of the Third Republic
2. Vichy against "anti-France"
3. Les années noires
4. After 1945

1. The end of the Third Republic

In view of the German "Western campaign," which was surprisingly successful, and the fall of Paris, Marshal Philippe Pétain, who was by then 84 years old, requested a cessation of hostilities from Germany. On June 22, France signed a ceasefire in Compiègne that amounted to a capitulation. As a result, three-fifths of France – the North and the entire Atlantic coast – came under German military administration; Alsace-Lorraine was in effect annexed. The unoccupied zones remained French.

The government established itself in the central French health resort of Vichy and maintained a kind of independence in the so-called Free Zone in the South of the country. On July 10, the deputies of the National Assembly, convened at Vichy, put an end to the French Republic by transferring unlimited governmental power to Marshal Philippe Pétain by a vote of 569 to 80; this step spelled the end of the separation of power and amounted to a self-disempowerment of Parliament.

From here, Pétain pushed through the transformation into an authoritarian *État français*; the republican triad "liberté, égalité, fraternité" was replaced by "travail, famille, patrie," the "ordre nouveau" ("New Order"). From now on, Marshal Pétain, as head of state and of the government, exercised a power, understood as charismatic, over a national community seen as homogeneous and organic. France's conservative right greeted this "révolution nationale" as "salutary," since only by its means was the "necessary renewal" and "purification" of political community made possible [13. 40]. In the process, the collaboration undertaken with Nazi Germany was not unwillingly accepted, but also carried out by the French government with the intention of ensuring for itself a place in the "New Europe" under the aegis of Germany. The Vichy regime was recognized diplomatically by more than thirty states, including the United States, the Soviet Union, and the Vatican.

The Vichy regime made use of the events of the summer of 1940 to demolish the institutions of the Third Republic. In its view, parliamentary democracy of a traditional type, and above all its Jewish representatives, bore the blame for France's defeat. Such leading politicians as Léon Blum, the socialist and former Premier of the → Popular Front government, and the conservative deputy Georges Mandel were arrested. The charges brought against them included both sabotage of the war efforts and warmongering [10. 75].

Thus, in the summer of 1940, the Third Republic ended the way it had begun, seventy years previously: as the result of a military catastrophe. Since its proclamation after the lost Battle of Sedan in the Franco-German War of 1870–1871, the Third Republic had repeatedly been the target of attacks from anti-parliamentarian, royalist, and militant Catholic movements. In this context, its antagonists believed they could identify primarily Jews as a group that had conspired against the "ancien régime" and were therefore to blame for the historical decline of throne and altar. Politically, the antagonists of the Third Republic organized themselves into associations such as the Ligue de la patrie française, Ligue antisémitique de France, or the Ligue des patriotes,

all of which had emerged in the aftermath of the economic and social crises of the 1880s or after the → Dreyfus affair. The latter had created a lasting split in the French political environment between pro-republican Dreyfusite and an anti-Dreyfus camps hostile to both Jews and democracy.

It was particularly the Action française, founded in 1898, that conveyed the aspirations of the anti-Dreyfusards into the Vichy regime. Its spokesman, the author Charles Maurras, coined the term "nationalisme intégral" in 1900, which – in contrast to the universal, integrative notion of the proponents of the Republic – sought to bring about the unity of the nation in an anti-pluralistic way and with ethnically homogenizing intent. For Maurras, Freemasons, foreigners, communists, and cosmopolitans were "métèques" (from the Greek *métoikos*, an unwelcome alien without civic rights), and embodied "anti-France"; in his extremist thought, all these groups somehow appeared as Jewish, which solidified into a gigantic conspiracy of Jews against France [12. 64].

Action française and other extreme right-wing mass movements such as the Croix de feux or the fascist Parti social français, which emerged from it in 1936, were expressions of the political instability of the Third Republic. After the economic crisis which began in 1931, this instability became more dramatic and brought with it increasing social and political polarization. In this process, antisemitism crystallized above all as the primary ideological feature that united all anti-parliamentary groups. As a result of the takeover of government affairs by the Popular Front, the accession to office of the Jewish premier Léon Blum in 1936, as well as the increasing number of Jewish refugees from Germany, antisemitic tendencies were considerably radicalized.

Prominent politicians and intellectuals who rose to become officials of the Vichy regime after 1940 had already adopted stances directed against the Third Republic in the 1930s, which included the removal of Jews from public life and the deprivation of French → citizenship. Their spokesmen included the deputy Xavier Vallat, as well as the Paris city councilor Louis Darquier (better known by the noble title "de Pellepoix," which he himself added), the publisher of the antisemitic weekly *La France enchaînée* (1936–1939), and founder of the Rassemblement antijuif de France (Anti-Jewish association of France). In the Vichy regime, Vallat was appointed as head of the "Commissariat général aux questions juives" (Commissariat-General for Jewish Affairs) in 1941, while Darquier de Pellepoix succeeded him in this position in 1942. Correspondingly, opponents of the Republic welcomed the Vichy regime; Maurras himself called Marshal Pétain's regime a "divine surprise" (cited in [5. 140f.]).

2. Vichy against "anti-France"

German rule served the politicians of the Vichy regime as a convenient justification for immediately implementing their anti-republican, xenophobic, and antisemitic views. In this process, they also had recourse to measures that had already been prepared in the 1930s, and had to some extent already been decided upon. Thus, in his term of office from 1935 to 1936, Prime Minister Pierre Laval had introduced steps to establish an apparatus of repression, free of juridical safeguards, to retreat from France's tradition as a land of asylum. Thanks to almost unrestricted powers, which the National Assembly granted him in 1935, Laval was able to govern by decree. As early as August of the same year, he enacted a decree that allowed prefects to arrest enemy aliens in the case of war. Any regulations favorable to victims of political and racist persecution, like the approximately 25,000 refugees from Germany, were not envisaged. The decree was an expression of a mistrust

that was widespread among politically right-leaning Frenchmen with regard to those specific groups of persons who, as *boches*, left-wingers or Jews, were already suspicious to them in many respects. During his term of office (1938–March 1940), Prime Minister Édouard Daladier succeeded in intensifying this legislation concerning foreigners, so that the Camp de Rieucros, the first internment camp on French territory, came into existence as early as January 1939 [4. 21f.].

Vichy's first measures were thus directed against communists, foreigners, refugees from the Spanish Civil War, and Freemasons, but especially against the Jews. Most of estimated 330,000 Jews living in France in June 1940 originated from Eastern Europe or had fled from the German sphere of influence after 1933. Only about 90,000 had already held French → citizenship for several generations; 70,000 had first obtained it in the 1920s and 1930s, while 120,000 were refugees who had sought refuge in France before the war broke out. Added to these were several tens of thousands of Jews who had fled from the Netherlands, Luxembourg, and Belgium with the outbreak of hostilities [10. 1f.].

On July 17, 1940, it was decided that only persons who could prove they had a French father could find employment in the public sector; on August 16 and September 10, 1940, these provisions were extended to the medical and legal professions. In addition, the Commission de révision des naturalisations, appointed on July 22, 1940, was to scrutinize all naturalizations since 1927 and formulate corresponding legal recommendations. The *Loi Marchandeau* of April 21, 1939, which penalized antisemitic reporting, was immediately revoked.

On October 3, 1940, Minister of Justice Raphaël Alibert (1887–1963) issued the first *Statut des juifs* (Law on the status of Jews, known as *Loi Alibert*). According to it, every person was to be considered a Jew who belonged to the Jewish confession or had belonged to it or descended from more than two grandparents "of the Jewish race" ("race Juive"; → Race). In the case of persons with a Jewish spouse, two Jewish grandparents were sufficient to declare them to be Jews. Successively, they were excluded from all public offices, the media, and the corps of officers and NCOs (→ Military). A quota system applied to freelancers, which made an exception for veterans, those who had been awarded the Ordre National de la Légion d'honneur (National Order of the Legion of Honour), or persons who had rendered extraordinary services to the French State in the fields of → literature, → science, or the → arts [7. 159f.].

The Vichy legislation was more radical than the anti-Jewish regulations which the Germans had issued for the occupied zone in September 1940. Thus, the French version was based on a "Jewish race" whereas the occupying force used the formulation "Jewish religion." This was intended to include persons of Jewish origin whose ancestors not longer considered themselves as belonging to the Jewish religious community. The Vichy laws were in effect for all of France, while the German regulations only applied in the occupied zone, so that a twofold antisemitic legislation resulted from this combination: one for the occupied zone alone, and the other that was in force in both areas. The rivalries which arose between Germans and French with regard to the anti-Jewish legislation intensified the effects of these measures.

For their part, the German occupiers had enacted many antisemitic regulations on September 27, 1940; they introduced a registration of persons, as well as identification by documents and ration cards that included the word "Jew" and demanded an externally visible identification of all businesses and enterprises that were under Jewish ownership.

The *Statut des juifs* forbade Jews who had fled to the territory of Vichy to return to occupied France. This applied to immigrant Jews as well as to Jews with French citizenship and relegated them to an interior status. Unlike the → Nuremberg laws, Vichy did not declare a prohibition of mixed → marriage.

One day after the first *Statut des juifs*, a second law was enacted in the form of the *Loi sur les ressortissants étrangers de race juive* (Law regarding Foreign Nationals of the Jewish Race), which enabled the prefects to place foreign Jews in internment camps without giving reasons; at the same time, it allowed French police in the occupied zone to carry out arrests ordered by Germans. In October 1940, the Décret Crémieux (→ Crémieux Decree) of 1870 was also revoked which meant that 33,000 Jews in Algeria lost their French citizenship. An additional regulation instructed Jews to register their businesses before October 31, 1940, and to visibly identify them.

Both laws were rigorously applied and subsequently tightened by additional regulations. Thus, from December 1940, nearly 3,000 Jewish employees were dismissed from the civil service; a grand total of 18 persons were exempted. In addition, 40,000 foreign Jews were interned in camps or placed under house arrest. On May 14 and August 20, 1941, alone the French police arrested about 8,000 Jews in the occupied zone and displaced them to Pithiviers, Beaune-La-Rolande or → Drancy, relying on lists that were based on a Judenkartei (register for Jews) compiled by the prefectures in accordance with a German ordinance of September 27, 1940. Except for Royallieu in Compiègne, each of these camps was under French administration.

All of these laws and measures went back to the initiative of the authorities at Vichy; their implementation was immediate and rigorous. They were an expression of an indigenous French antisemitism as well. Not until the beginning of sabotage activity against the German occupiers by the → Résistance in the summer of 1941 can the beginnings of increased influence by the

Germans on French agents be observed. In this process, the actions of French authorities were often guided by the intention to preserve state sovereignty, at least domestically; for this reason, they made themselves actively available to the German occupiers for the implementation of their Jewish policies.

Only two months after the publication of the first *Statut des juifs*, the French administration announced the successful completion of their "purifications." In 1941, 36,000 foreigners were held in the internment camps of the Vichy territory, 13,000 of whom were Jews [7. 31, 80]. With respect to the German occupiers, in contrast, Vichy resisted accepting more Jews for example on the occasion of the deportation of 6,500 Jews from the Gau Baden and the Gau Saarpfalz to the French internment camp of Gurs, known as the Wagner-Bürckel-Aktion; yet such French protests fell on deaf ears among the German authorities.

In a second phase, Vichy intensified the institutionalization of its antisemitic policies. For this purpose, in March 1941, after discussions with the German ambassador in Paris Otto Abetz (1903–1958), the Commissariat général aux questions juives (Commissariat-General for Jewish Affairs) was founded, which served as an liaison between Vichy and the occupying power; Xavier Vallat was named as its director.

As his first measure, Vallat sharpened the policies against foreign and stateless Jews and ordered an increasing number of raids. It was on his initiative that the second *Statut des juifs* of June 2, 1941 (known as the *loi Vallat*) was passed. Henceforth, children born from relations between Jews and non-Jews, whether within or outside wedlock, were also considered to be Jews if they had been raised in the Jewish faith. The list of professions which Jews were no longer allowed to practice was expanded to financial services providers, architects, dentists, and actors: a → *numerus clausus* of three percent was

supposed to restrict Jewish access to → universities. In addition, Jews in the non-occupied zone had to register from now on as well. This meant an expansion of the ordinances passed by the German authorities in the occupied zone on September 27, 1940, to the Jewish population throughout France.

As a militant Catholic nationalist, Vallat felt that his duty was to Pétain alone and sought to emphasize French sovereignty through autonomous action. Thus, he conceived of a genuinely French expropriation policy in order to hinder the occupying power's access to Jewish assets and to achieve complete French control over them. On July 22, 1941, a special law was passed in this regard, the *Loi relative aux entreprises, biens et valeurs appartenant aux juifs* (Law on Jewish-owned businesses, property and assets). On the pretext of eliminating any Jewish influence on the national economy, the French initiated their own process of Aryanization, and temporary administrators were now also installed in all Jewish enterprises within the unoccupied zone, as had been current in occupied France since a German ordinance of October 18, 1940. They had the right to administer, liquidate, or dispose of Jewish property to interested non-Jewish parties; since the beneficiary was Vichy, these measures amounted to expropriation in favor of the State.

In addition, all Jewish organizations, with the exception of the Consistoire central israélite (→ Israelite Central Consistory), were forcibly united by law in November 1941 into the Union générale des israélites de France in both the occupied and the unoccupied zone. They were made subject to the Commissariat général; their headquarters were in Paris and Marseille.

3. Les années noires

Beginning in the spring of 1942, German authorities exerted increasing influence both on the composition of the government in Vichy and on its anti-Jewish policies. With his ulitimately anti-German concerns for independence, Vallat fell out of favor in early 1942 with Theodor Dannecker (1913–1945), head of the Judenreferat of the SD (secret service), and with Abetz. Vallat was replaced by Louis Darquier de Pellepoix in May. Laval, who had been acting Prime Minister since July 1940 and Pétain's designated successor, was stripped of his position by the Marshal in December 1940 because of his demands for even closer collaboration with Germany and placed under arrest; following the intervention of the German authorities, he returned to the government as Prime Minister in April 1942, and henceforth drove Pétain into the background.

Symptomatic of Laval's pro-German stance was his radio address on June 22, 1942, in which he expressed his hopes for a quick German victory. As the new Prime Minister, he was simultaneously Minister of the Interior, Foreign Minister, and Minister of Information, all in one. Laval strove intensely for an agreement with Germany so as to ensure a place for France in the "New Europe."

The German occupying power, in cooperation with the French police, had begun the internment of foreign Jews in occupied France in 1941. 3,600 Polish Jews were arrested in May 1941 and moved to the camps of Pithiviers and Beaune-La-Rolande in the Département of Loiret, south of Paris; following raids in Paris, an additional group of over 4,000 mainly foreign Jews were sent to the concentration and transit camp of → Drancy. After a series of attacks by the → Résistance, the German military commander Otto von Stülpnagel (1878–1948) ordered the execution of 100 hostages: 95 persons were shot, including 51 Jews. A compulsory payment of one billion francs was imposed upon the Jewish community in Paris. Subsequently, the Germans murdered over 1,000 persons in the context of retaliatory measures, most of whom were Jews [10. 209f.].

In March 1942, a group of 565 stateless persons from the concentration camp of Drancy (nominally under French control until July 1943), together with 547 Jews from Royallieu-Compiègne, the second largest internment camp in occupied France, were deported to → Auschwitz.

In view of the annihilation of the entire Jewish population of Europe, which had now been set in motion, such numbers were no longer enough for the Nazi regime. On June 11, 1942, Adolf Eichmann therefore summoned Dannecker, together with the *Judenreferenten* for Belgium and the Netherlands, to a meeting in Berlin, where it was agreed to deport 100,000 Jews from both zones of France to Auschwitz [10. 254]. On June 30, 1942, Eichmann himself travelled to Paris to gain a firsthand impression of the situation, whereupon he demanded the deportation of all Jews from France.

At first, the German commanders in Paris were content with the roundup of the foreign Jews and postponed the deportation of the French Jews to a later date. Meanwhile, the Vichy regime continued to pursue its strategy of collaboration and autonomy, and thus permanently avoided the compulsory marking of Jews with a yellow "Jewish star," which the German occupying power had ordered in early June 1942, to be extended to the "free zone."

The Vichy regime was committed to excluding French Jews from the deportations; at the same time, it sought to rid itself of interned foreign Jews in the unoccupied zone. It was especially the young and ambitious Prefect of the Marne, René Bousquet (1909–1993), General Secretary of the Vichy Police since early May 1942, who endeavored to achieve the independence of a French police united under his command. In the infrastructure of the French police, the German authorities saw an important independent body for relieving them in the implementation of persecution of the Jews better. In the infrastructure of the French police, the German authorities saw an important, independent authority who could relieve them in carrying out the persecution of the Jews. This was decided on July 2, 1942, in the course of negotiations between German and French police commanders. Bousquet renewed the proposal made in mid-June to deliver 10,000 foreign Jews from the unoccupied zone to the Germans and declared his agreement that the French police would take part in the detention of 20,000 Jews in the occupied zone. Soon afterwards, the French police, together with the SS, had already carried out the mass raid of July 16–17, which went down in history as the "Rafle du Vel' d'Hiv'." Over 13,000 mainly stateless Jews, now including women and children as well, were driven into the Parisian Vélodrome d'Hiver, whence they were deported, first to French camps and finally to Auschwitz.

It had not been planned to include children in the first deportation trains. On July 6, 1942, Laval suggested, on the occasion of the evacuation of Jewish families from the unoccupied zone, to deport children under sixteen years of age as well, adding that the fate of the children who remained behind in the Free Zone did not interest him. On the contrary: "Not one of them must remain in France," as he declared on September 9 1942 [10. 256]. At the same time, Vichy's antisemitic propaganda became radicalized; twice weekly, on the initiative of Darquier de Pellepoix, its radio stations broadcast contributions on the subjects of racial hygiene and the biology of race, in order to support the inferiorization of Jews.

The deportation of the Jews from the provinces of the occupied zone had the highest priority in the German plans for the summer of 1942; next on the agenda came the area of Greater Paris and finally the unoccupied zone. The Vichy Regime complied with these plans by making available information on the Jews in northern France. In the case of attempts to escape to the unoccupied zone, more than 800 persons were apprehended by the police and immediately deported to Drancy [10. 272].

At the same time, Vichy sought to rid itself of all foreign Jews: consequently, on August 4, 1942, Laval instructed the prefects to transfer to the occupied zone "Russian refugees and Israelites from Germany, Austria, Czechoslovakia, Poland, Estonia, Lithuania, Latvia, Danzig, the Saar-Palatinate, and the Soviet Union having entered France after January 1, 1936." In August and September 1942 alone, this affected 10,614 Jews, which meant that even the target of 10,000 negotiated with the Germans in June was surpassed [10. 275f.].

In November 1942, German and Italian troops occupied the previously unoccupied southern zone of France: the immediate occasion was the Allied landing in French North Africa. Nevertheless, the government in Vichy remained in office until August 1944. Until early 1944, its police forces also continued to carry out individual and mass arrests throughout France. In the process, they were supported by militants from collaborationist groups and the paramilitary Milice française, an auxiliary police force subordinate to the French police that had been created by Marshal Pétain in early 1943 to fight the Résistance and soon afterwards collaborated closely with the Germans as well.

The increasing Fascistization of the regime was manifested on December 30 1943, in the naming of its leader, Joseph Darnand (1897–1945), who was also a Sturmbannführer (major) in the Waffen-SS, as secrétaire général au Maintien de l'ordre (General Secretary for the Maintenance of Order) and hence as commander of the French police forces, as well as the extreme right-wing journalist Philippe Henriot (1889–1944) as Secretary of State for Information and Propaganda. Despite their continuing disempowerment, neither Pétain nor Laval had deviated from the political course they had embarked upon, including the observance and sharpening of antisemitic ordinances and laws. In December 1942, Laval enacted a decree that obliged Jews to have their identity cards and ration cards marked with "Jew," in order to identify them more easily in raids, and hence be able to make arrests with less difficulty.

At the beginning of 1943, Vichy politicians and officials took the initiative to deprive Jews of their French → citizenship, in order to comply with German demands. Here, the date of naturalization on which the measure was based was controversial. Darquier de Pellepoix represented the most radical position in the process, demanding the review of all naturalizations since 1870, but he then put forth a draft law intended to cancel naturalizations since 1927. Laval rejected the draft, since it also affected spouses and children who had been French since birth. Bousquet suggested January 1, 1932, as the date of reference, which the Germans did not accept since only 20,000 Jews would have been affected by it. A reference date of August 10, 1927, was agreed upon, which enlarged the group of persons concerned to 50,000. Laval signed it on June 20, 1943, but withdrew his signature since this compromise would also have affected women whose ancestors were French citizens. For that reason, a revised version of Bousquet's suggestion then came into effect [7. 302f.].

As late as May 1944, the Minister of the Interior decided to create another Judenkartei, in order to better control the remaining Jews. In February 1944, Darquier de Pellepoix himself was replaced as head of the Commissariat général aux questions juives by Charles du Paty de Clam, son of the prosecutor of Alfred Dreyfus (→ Dreyfus Affair) Armand du Paty de Clam.

The liberation of French territory began with the Allied landing in Normandy in June 1944. The last inmates left the Drancy camp on August 20, 1944, and on August 26, General de Gaulle held his triumphal parade along the Champs Elysées. In September 1944, a provisional republican government assumed office in a henceforth liberated France. With the German retreat from France in August 1944, the members of the Vichy government had transferred their headquarters to Sigmaringen Castle in Württemberg, where it continued to exist as a puppet regime until the German surrender.

In total, over 76,000 Jews were deported from France to Poland in the "années noires" from 1940 to 1944; only 2,600 survived the extermination camps. In addition, over 3,000 died in the French internment camps alone, as well as more than 1,000 additional victims as hostages or resistance fighters. Two thirds of the victims were foreign Jews; however, among the one third who had French citizenship, two thirds had been naturalized prior to 1940 or came from immigrant families [12. 93f.].

Vichy primarily sacrificed foreign Jews without protecting French Jews; the anti-Jewish laws passed on their own initiative had worsened the situation of all Jews in France. At most, it could be said that the Vichy authorities somewhat slowed down the occupiers' access to Jews of "old French ancestry" by influencing the decision-making processes themselves.

4. After 1945

After the war, the Vichy authorities, above all Laval, sought to justify themselves with the argument that the life of French Jews had been preserved by handing over foreign Jews to the Germans. While Laval was held to account and sentenced to death in 1945, the participation and collaboration of many other actors remained unpunished. Vallat was sentenced to ten years imprisonment in 1947 but was freed two years later; Darquier de Pellepoix had decamped to Spain in 1944 and was sentenced to death in absentia in 1947. Maurras, who was among the "spin doctors" of Vichy, still exclaimed, on the occasion of his sentencing to life in prison in 1945: "[This is] the revenge of Dreyfus!" [15. 56].

The novel *Treblinka: La révolte d'un camp d'extermination* ("Treblinka," 1967) by Jean-François Steiner (b. 1938), published in France in 1966, shattered the French post-war narrative and contributed to a reconsideration of collaboration under the Vichy regime (→ Treblinka). However, not until end of the 1970s did the Vichy regime, its collaboration with Nazi Germany, and the participation of the French in the "Final Solution" become the subject of public debates in France; until then national reconciliation had priority. Even afterwards, the nation struggled for many years with the reappraisal of the "années noires." As late as the 1980s, the dominant thesis was that of a German diktat of Jewish legislation, as well as collaboration in the case of internment and deportation. Political responsibility for the crimes of the French State was first assumed by President Jacques Chirac on July 16, 1995, in a speech in which he mentioned France's complicity in the persecution of the Jews.

Bibliography

[1] J.-P. Azéma/F. Bédarida (eds.), La France des années noires, 2 vols., Paris 1993. [2] P. Birnbaum, Affaire Dreyfus. Culture catholique et antisémitisme, in: M. Winock (ed.), Histoire de l'extrême droite en France, Paris 1993, 83–124. [3] M. Curtis, Verdict on Vichy. Power and Prejudice in the Vichy France Regime, New York 2002. [4] C. Eggers, Unerwünschte Ausländer. Juden aus Deutschland und Mitteleuropa in französischen Internierungslagern 1940–1942, Berlin 2002. [5] J. Jackson, France. The Dark Years, 1940–1944, New York 2001. [6] M. Marrus/ R. Paxton, Vichy France and the Jews, New York 1983. [7] M. Mayer, Staaten als Täter. Ministerialbürokratie und "Judenpolitik" in NS-Deutschland und Vichy-Frankreich, Munich 2010. [8] R. Paxton, Vichy France. Old Guard and New Order, New York 2001. [9] R. Poznanski, Être juif en France pendant la Seconde

Guerre mondiale, Paris 1994. [10] R. Poznanski, Jews in France during World War Two, trans. by N. Bracher, Hanover 2001. [11] H. Rousso, The Vichy Syndrome. History and Memory in France since 1944, Cambridge (MA) 1991. [12] H. Rousso, Le régime de Vichy, Paris 2007. [13] R. Schnur, Vive la République oder Vive la France. Zur Krise der Demokratie in Frankreich 1939/1940, Berlin 1982. [14] W. Seibel, Macht und Moral. Die "Endlösung der Judenfrage" 1940–1944, Constance 2010. [15] J. G. Shields, The Extreme Right in France. From Pétain to Le Pen, New York 2007.

RENÉE POZNANSKI, BEER SHEVA

Vienna

In the late 19th and early 20th centuries, the capital of the Habsburg monarchy and, after 1918, of the Republic of Austria, was home to the largest German-speaking Jewish community in Central Europe. Vienna was a focal point of Jewish integration into modern European culture and society, characterized unmistakably by regional and local particularities. Jews made an immense contribution to the cultural achievements in Vienna at the turn of the 20th century; at the same time the city was one of the centers of political antisemitism. Due to their specific position, the Jews of Vienna felt especially obliged to anticipate and formulate answers for the modern age.

1. Until the mid-19th century
2. Immigration and integration
3. Professions and education
4. Jews in turn-of-the-century Vienna
5. Antisemitic and socialist Vienna
6. "Vienna around 1900"

1. Until the mid-19th century

The earliest evidence of Jewish life in Vienna dates from the late 12th century. Around

1203 two → synagogues already existed in the city; by the mid-13th century, the community had grown to become the largest of German-speaking Jewry, numbering nearly 1,000 members. However, unlike in other Jewish centers of Central Europe during the Middle Ages and the early modern era such as Prague, the Jews in Vienna were not continuously present as a visible community in the city. In 1421 in the course of the Hussite Wars, confiscations, forced conversions, and expulsions of the Jews were set in motion under Duke Albrecht V. They were alleged to have supported the Hussites and of host desecration, accusations that were also used to justify the execution of numerous Jews. Subsequently a small and, at times, only secretly practicing community survived in Vienna until the middle of the 17th century.

Influenced by the archbishop Leopold Karl von Kollonitsch, the Habsburg Emperor Leopold I expelled all Jews from the city once more in 1670, and had the Great Synagogue reconsecrated as a Catholic church. Due to military and financial necessity, however, soon after 1670 the Habsburg monarchs invited Jewish financiers like Samuel Oppenheimer back to Vienna as → court Jews. During the 18th century they were influential among the upper bourgeoisie and at the imperial court. In addition several important persons who had converted to Catholicism were living in the city, among them Joseph von Sonnenfels, a prominent adviser to Maria Theresa as well as her son Joseph II and a great advocate of the → Enlightenment in Austria, or the Wetzlar von Plankenstern family who were among Mozart's most important benefactors. In general, Jews were only permitted to settle in Vienna after paying a high annual tolerance tax. As a consequence the Jewish community consisted of no more than around 500 persons by the middle of the century. Even so, "tolerated persons" such as Fanny von Arnstein (→ Salon) acquired a considerable reputation in cultural and social life. Besides

the tolerated persons, most of whom had come from Germany, from the 18th century onward there was also a small Sephardic (→ Sephardim) community in Vienna which was under the diplomatic protection of the Ottoman Empire.

The reform legislation passed by Joseph II (→ Edicts of Toleration) in 1781 marked the first step to abolishing some restrictions. Over the following years, a Hebrew press was established, publishing several central works of the → Haskalah, among them → *Bikkure ha-Ittim* (The first fruits) and Peter Beer's *Imre shefer* (Words of beauty). By the beginning of the 19th century, the growing community of tolerated Jews had become influential in Austria's economic affairs, above all the → Rothschild dynasty and their partners. Evidence that the climate in Vienna was improving for Jews was provided not least by the construction of the city's first modern synagogue in 1826; there are indications that many more Jews lived and traded in Vienna in the 1840s than the officially tolerated 179 families. Many Vienna Jews were active in journalism and literature, for instance Moritz Saphir, or graduated from universities, such as the later activists of the 1848 revolution Joseph Goldmark, Hermann Jellinek, and Adolf Fischhof. It was not until 1848 that the Jews of Vienna were permitted to unite as a religious community. The 1849 constitution enacted the following year gave Jews and Christians equal rights; however, it was repealed two years later. Full → emancipation came with the Basic Law after the → Austro-Hungarian Compromise of 1867, which allowed the Jews unhindered exercise of religion and free movement within the realm. The Jewish community of Vienna grew considerably during the second half of the 19th century.

2. Immigration and integration

According to the census of 1857, of the 476,220 inhabitants of Vienna, 6,217 or 1.3%

were Jews in that year. By 1890 their percentage of the population, numbering 827,567 citizens, had grown tenfold; there were a total of 99,441 Jews living in Vienna. The city went through years of rapid growth, and of its over two million inhabitants in 1910, approximately 175,000 were Jews (8.6% of the entire population). During the 1920s the number of Jewish inhabitants was highest as a result of the waves of refugees caused by the First World War. In 1923, just over 200,000 Jews were living in Vienna (10.5% of the population). Ten years later, most of the refugees had left the city once more. The number of Jewish inhabitants fell to 176,000 of 1.9 million (9.3%) in 1934, and to about 170,000 in March 1938 [11. 34]; [12. 154].

The influx into Vienna from the second half of the 19th century onward was fed by many regions of the realm. Around 20% of the Jewish inhabitants of the city before 1914 came from the Lands of the Bohemian Crown (especially Moravia); at first, a quarter was of Hungarian origin, by 1910 they made up 15%. The proportion of Galician-born Jews in Vienna increased to 23% by 1910, growing noticeably once more due to the waves of refugees during the war, but gradually sank during the 1920s. The percentage of Jews born beyond the borders of the empire always remained in single digits; this contradicts the account of the great influx of Russian Jews after the → pogroms of the 1880s, which was supposed to have caused the rise of antisemitism [11. 28]; [13. 36].

Vienna was a hub of a variety of Jewish cultures and traditions. Marriage registers document a high number of marriages between the various groups of Viennese Jews. The diversity of their origin was accompanied by a range of differing approaches to integration. Jews from the West of the realm tended to acculturate fully, even converting to Christianity, while Jews from Galicia (→ Cracow) and northern Hungary in particular cultivated a more separate Jewish culture.

The confluence of different Jewish traditions found its most visible expression in the mid-19th century in the form of the "Vienna rite," a compromise between Orthodox Judaism (→ Orthodoxy) and → Reform Judaism that achieved some degree of fame. Families of German origin, like that of the philosopher Ludwig Wittgenstein (→ Critique of Language) led an overall assimilated life next to Orthodox followers of → Hasidism from Galicia who had close ties with their culture of origin.

Nevertheless, many Galician Jews came to Vienna precisely in order to escape the backwardness of the Jewish communities of their homeland. Many regarded the city as a place where they would find a way into the modern world. This also partially explains the comparatively high numbers of conversions among Viennese Jews. In 1914, around 20,000 converted Jews were living in the city [11. 32].

Presumably the conversion rate was driven even higher because marriage between partners of different religions were forbidden under civil law in Austria; either one of the partners had to convert or the couple had to jointly declare themselves as "konfessionslos" (not affiliated with any denomination). → Conversion and *de facto* mixed marriages were found especially among the economic, social, and cultural elites of the Jews of Vienna. In the community as a whole, the prevailing tendency was to combine a secular lifestyle (→ Secularization) with a loose connection to religious institutions. These "two-day" Jews did not share the formal tenets or practices of the Jewish faith but officially remained Jewish; among them were Sigmund Freud (→ Psychoanalysis), Arthur Schnitzler, and Otto Bauer (→ Question of Nationalities).

The geographical and cultural spectrum was, to some degree, also reflected in the geographical distribution of the Jews in the city. They lived mainly in three districts. In the city center (1st district), where, increasingly, the Vienna elite lived, there were roughly 11,000 Jews in 1910, amounting to 20% of the district's inhabitants. Jewish families who were part of the establishment, most of whom were Viennese-born, lived along the Ringstraße and in the financial district. There were 21,600 Jews living in the Alsergrund (9th district) near the city center, the university, the general hospital, and the Palace of Justice, also amounting to 20% of the inhabitants of the districts. This was where Sigmund Freud lived as well as members of the liberal professions and academics. The more traditionalist Jews, primarily from Galicia, lived in Leopoldstadt (2nd district), colloquially called "Mazzesinsel" (matzo island). In 1910 Leopoldstadt was home to 56,800 Jews, the largest Jewish population of any district in Vienna and around a third of the total Jewish population of the city. Even so, numerous Jews living in the 2nd district did not have Galician origins, were wealthier and less Orthodox. The "Jewishness" of the district was a matter of atmosphere rather than of absolute figures, as no more than a third of the inhabitants of Leopoldstadt were Jewish. As in other districts, Jewish residents were disproportionately represented in some streets, but there was no Jewish majority population in any of the districts of Vienna [11. 29–33].

3. Professions and education

Within the Habsburg elite of financiers and industrialists, Viennese Jewish bankers such as the → Rothschilds played a leading role in the economy of the Dual Monarchy. Families of Jewish industrialists such as the Mautner-Markhofs or the Gutmanns as well as the department store owners Gerngross and Herzmansky ensured a high economic reputation for the Jews. However, the number of poor Jews in Vienna was considerably higher [1]. According to an estimate [13. 79] two thirds of the Jewish population

were affected by poverty in that they could not afford to pay the Jewish community tax. Besides these there was a broad Jewish middle class of members of the liberal → professions, salaried employees, and businessmen.

The Jews of Vienna were strongly represented in the financial sector and in trade. In 1910 just under a third of independent businessmen in the → trade and transport sectors (→ Transportation) were Jews. According to the census of that year, 76% of Catholics working in the industry and trade and transport sectors were wage-earners, 14% were self-employed, and only 9% were salaried (white-collar) employees. Among the Jews in these sectors, on the other hand, only 31% were wage-earners, while 36% were self-employed and 33% salaried employees [11. 36]. Compared to the other inhabitants of the city, the majority of whom were working-class, the Jews of Vienna displayed a noticeably middle-class profile (→ Middle Class).

The most noticeable difference between Jews and most of the other inhabitants of Vienna was the former's enthusiasm for education (→ Bildung). In the 1880s, a full third of all students at Vienna University were Jewish; in 1890 nearly half (48%) of all medical students were of Jewish origin. In subsequent years the numbers gradually decreased: in 1904, just under a quarter of all students were Jewish, nevertheless ten years later still numbered 41% of the medical students. During this period, a quarter of the students in the law faculty were Jewish. Before 1914, around 16% of the students of the philosophical faculty were of Jewish origin, in 1926 they amounted to over a third [4. 34].

The number of Viennese Jews at secondary schools (Gymnasium) was also remarkably high. From the 1880s until 1914, more than 30% of the pupils at Vienna's boys' secondary schools were Jews: three times the Jewish proportion of the population as a whole. Jews were nearly five times as likely to send their offspring to secondary schools than non-Jews and three times as likely to send them to the Realschule. While more than half of all Jewish schoolboys aged 13 and 14 in 1910 attended a secondary school of some sort, only 14% of non-Jewish boys did [4. 52]. Secondary education for girls shows even greater disparity: in 1910 nearly half (45%) of all girls in secondary educational facilities came from Jewish families [13. 121]. The Jewish pupils mainly came from the Viennese liberal middle class, who were most closely connected to the modern economy. According to estimates, of the pupils from middle-class families in the years from 1870 to 1910, 65% were Jews (71% from 1900 to 1910) [4. 53].

4. Jews in turn-of-the-century Vienna

In Karl Popper's words (→ Open Society), turn-of-the-century Vienna was the result of a collision between the cultural values Jews had brought to Vienna and the clearly different cultural values of non-Jewish Vienna with its Habsburg and Catholic Counter-Reformationist traditions. The modernizing tendencies within the Jewish communities, which often dated back to before their arrival in Vienna, gained dynamism in the capital of the Habsburg Empire.

The first mass migration of Jews to Vienna in the 1860s had been concomitant with the liberalization of the monarchy. From the 1870s onward, political liberalism had been pushed into a defensive position, its influence waning at the imperial court in the 1880s until it lost its preeminent position in Vienna to the Christian Social Party. German liberal Vienna had to give way to a noticeably more reactionary variant that had never really disappeared: the Vienna that was the imperial protector of the Roman Catholic Church and ally of the landed nobility whose palaces dominated the inner city. In spite of the reform endeavors

by the Habsburg rulers Maria Theresa and Joseph II at the end of the 18th century, the Baroque culture of this Habsburg "Trinity" had remained a predominant element of life in Vienna. This was the Vienna that had become famous for universal hedonism and a lack of intellectuality.

The embrace of enjoyment, entertainment, beauty, and serenity, which preferred appearance over substance, imbued traditional Viennese culture with its own attraction in many ways. However, it went against Jewish cultural values, even regarded them antagonistically, for instance in its prohibition of searching for truth beyond appearances, and its censorship of all critique of the authorities. Jewish critics regarded the political success of antisemitism in 1895 as a return of this traditional Baroque culture. Turn-of-the-century Vienna emerged if nothing else as a Jewish answer to "Baroque" Vienna.

It was less the traditional wine taverns and more the coffee houses, which were considered modern, that became the secular meeting places for the Jews of Vienna. To be sure, the Viennese coffee houses could look back over a long tradition, but that Jews frequented the relatively mundane coffee house with the aim of engaging in commercial as well as literary or cultural exchanges (→ Chess) led to it being perceived as a "Jewish" domain. The tradition of the comic theatre (→ Jargon Theatre), too, combined with musical numbers, had been popular in Vienna before the 1860s when the → operetta first arrived from Paris. Due to the considerable contribution Jews made to popularizing the operetta from the days of Jacques Offenbach (→ Offenbachiaden) on, it, too, was regarded as a mainly Jewish *metier* in Vienna in the 1900s.

The Jewish business elite endeavored to gain access to Viennese high society by adopting traditions of social life and sponsorship of the arts already existing among the nobility. While aristocratic salons in

Vienna were a great social attraction, they had hardly had any intellectual significance until Jewish *salonnières* such as Fanny von Arnstein established the tradition of the intellectual literary → salons, continued by women like Josephine von Wertheimstein, Bertha von Zuckerkandl, and Eugenie Schwarzwald. Sponsorship of music and the visual arts had become established among the nobility during "Baroque" Vienna in particular. Jewish → patrons of the arts – the first of whom was Karl Abraham Wetzlar von Plankenstern – also followed this tradition. More than their non-Jewish counterparts, however, they sponsored modern artists and musicians, in some cases with the aim of encouraging progressive, emancipatory values. The numerous Jewish patrons of Secession artists hoped that art would bring them a future in which they would find their place as *doyens* of taste. As a result the → art nouveau of the Vienna Secession was given the epithet "le goût juif" ("Jewish taste") not because of its artists but because of its patrons and supporters.

The Jewish contribution to the cultural and intellectual life of Vienna was concentrated on certain areas. There were hardly any Jews among the most famous visual artists and architects in turn-of-the-century Vienna, but many among their sponsors. This may have been linked to their cultural inclinations and traditions based on religion, which in turn explained their strong presence in the field of music (→ Cantor). Gustav Mahler (→ Resurrection) and Arnold Schönberg (→ Twelve-Tone Music) were most certainly among the greatest composers in Vienna at the time and joined by several operetta composers such as Emmerich Kálmán.

In the world of academia, qualified Jewish researchers often found themselves excluded from prestigious positions or professorships, despite formal legal equality. Even so, the informal restrictions could not prevent a strong presence of Jews in research and teaching. In 1910 a fifth of the teaching staff of the philosophical faculty, over a third of the physics faculty, and half of the chemistry faculty were of Jewish origin [4. 36]. Where informal discrimination did prevent a career in academia, Jewish scholars often moved to other fields of academic research.

There was ongoing resistance to Jews being appointed to respected positions in government authorities, bureaucracy, and the administration, too. This may have contributed to the comparatively high percentage of Jews in the liberal professions of law and medicine as well as journalism. The majority of the liberal press in Vienna was staffed with Jews. Around 1900 more than half the editorial staff of the *Neue Freie Presse*, the city's most respected newspaper, was Jewish, as was its publisher and editor-in-chief Moriz Benedikt (1849–1920). The literary → feuilleton, which was also becoming established as an institution of the Viennese journalistic landscape at the same time, was

Arthur Schnitzler (1862–1931)

shaped to a significant degree by Jewish writers. This prompted the author and critic Alfred Polgar (1873–1955) to call it a synthesis of Viennese lifestyle and Jewish intellect [2. 36].

Jewish writers played a very important role in modern literature in Vienna around 1900. Among them were Arthur Schnitzler, Stefan Zweig (→ [The] Royal Game), Jakob Wassermann, Hermann Broch, Elias Canetti (→ Crowds), Richard Beer-Hofmann, Felix Salten, Friedrich Torberg, Franz Werfel (→ Musa Dagh), and also – contrary to his self-understanding as the grandson of a Catholicism convert – Hugo von Hofmannsthal, and the self-proclaimed antidote to all of them: Karl Kraus (→ [Die] Fackel). The orientation of influential non-Jewish writers tended to be more conservative, less "avant-garde," and less modern. They frequently pursued a (German) nationalist agenda or stressed their own down-to-earth nature. Robert Musil's fame in contemporary perception, for instance, was based on him being a great *modern* Viennese writer who was not Jewish.

Jewish authors of political literature also tended to lean towards the more modern and progressive end of the political-cultural spectrum. While most non-Jewish political authors were more likely to side with the conservative or nationalist right, Jews became the most important intellectual leaders of the socialist and liberal-progressive left. Josef Popper-Lynkeus (1838–1921) inspired a type of social liberalism, and the Austro-Marxist thinkers Otto Bauer (1881–1938) and Max Adler (1873–1937) urged a more individualist and pluralist form of Marxist socialism. In the field of philosophy, the non-Jewish Ernst Mach (1838–1916) developed influential theories; most of those who, inspired by him, founded the → Vienna Circle of logical positivism were, in turn, of Jewish origin, such as Otto Neurath, Philipp Frank, Hans Hahn, and Friedrich Waismann. In the fields of psychology

and psychiatry, Jews were similarly numerous. Several methodological approaches were developed nearly exclusively by Jews, with Sigmund Freud's → psychoanalysis being the most famous. His pupils, in turn, founded their own schools, such as Alfred Adler's individual psychology.

5. Antisemitic and socialist Vienna

In 1933, Hans Tietze wrote: "Without Jews, Vienna would not be what it is, just as without Vienna, Jews would lose the brightest aspect of their existence during recent centuries [15. 282f.]. A decade later, Viennese Jewry had been practically extinguished through expulsion and genocide. While the Austrian capital had once justly been regarded as the symbol of the successful integration of Jews into modern European society and culture, now Vienna embodied the failure of assimilation.

In the Habsburg monarchy, there had long been hostility to Jews based mainly on Christian doctrine (→ Anti-Judaism). While enlightened theories, modern economic and social forms, and the success of political liberalism had led to full legal equality in 1867, as early as the mid-1870s, types of cultural and later also racial antisemitism began to spread, especially among German nationalists and Viennese university students. A virulent economic and social antisemitism, also in the lower middle class, increasingly assumed a political character. Georg von Schönerer, who rose to become the leading German nationalist in Austria in the 1880s, incorporated radical antisemitism into the party platform of his Alldeutsche Bewegung (Pan-German Movement; renamed Alldeutsche Vereinigung [Pan-German Federation] in 1896).

Schönerer and German nationalism were more successful in the provinces than in Vienna. In the 1890s, however, Karl Lueger succeeded in uniting a broad antiliberal alliance under the banner of antisemitism, uniting German nationalists and social-conservative Catholics to form the Christian Social Party. In the 1895 communal elections in Vienna, the Christian Social Party achieved the majority in the city council for the first time. Lueger himself held the position of mayor of Vienna from 1897 until his death in 1910. He had succeeded in establishing a political hegemony that anchored political antisemitism in Vienna as well as the central Austrian hereditary lands. Among those who greedily absorbed the propaganda of the German nationalist press in Vienna was the young Adolf Hitler.

Subsequently Jewish integration fell into a profound crisis. One of the cultural and political reactions was the growing popularity of Theodor Herzl's (→ Old New Land) political Zionism. In the case of Austria, this was more strongly motivated by the Vienna crisis than by the → Dreyfus Affair. The Viennese rabbi Joseph S. Bloch (1850–1923) instead endeavored to reformulate Austrian self-understanding along the lines of an ethno-pluralism that comprised all the ethnic groups and nationalities of the realm. Otto Bauer indicated a similar direction; however, as a socialist, his formulation of the (→ Question of Nationalities) denied the status of nationality to the extraterritorial "religious" minority of the Jews.

Before 1914 many Viennese Jews continued to support (Austrian) German liberalism as the best chance for progress. Especially in the three districts with a high Jewish proportion of the population, the 1st, 2nd, and 9th districts, liberal progressive candidates continued to be successful in elections. At the same time there was already a certain readiness to vote socialist against "class interests," not least because socialism promised to protect the equality of all humans regardless of → "race," nationality, and religion. When urban election politics resumed after the end of the First World War, Jews together with the majority of the considerable Viennese working-class population voted in great numbers for socialist candidates.

Under the Social Democratic Workers' Party (SDAP; Sozialdemokratische Arbeiterpartei) government, Vienna developed into a bastion of socialist economic and social policy after 1919. While the attitude of "Red Vienna" to the Jewish population and its religion was not particularly positive, the city returned to a climate of relative progressiveness and integration. Simultaneously, Jewish national consciousness noticeably increased during the interwar years; explicitly Jewish cultural and sporting associations such as S.C. → Hakoah Vienna (founded 1909) flourished, and Zionism gained in popularity. Nevertheless, a considerable percentage of Viennese Jews continued their support of social democracy and remained integrated in social life.

The problem for Austrian Jews consisted in the fact that the impact of Viennese socialism was hardly felt beyond the city boundaries. After 1920, anti-socialist, conservative, and antisemitic forces held the majority of seats in the Austrian National Council. Influenced by the development in Germany, they carried out a coup in 1933, which ultimately resulted in the Austrofascist Federal State in 1934. Besides the antisemitic, albeit comparatively mild, discrimination that set in now, the threat of National Socialism from beyond the country's borders became more apparent. The Austrian "Anschluss" (annexation) in March 1938 was supported actively or passively by a considerable portion of the non-Jewish population. A particularly shocking experience for Viennese Jews was the enthusiasm which an overwhelming number of citizens showed for the mass persecution of the Jews that was now developing. Indeed, Austrian National Socialists were pioneers of the "Aryanization" of Jewish possessions, of plundering Jews, deporting them, and of murdering them in the extermination camps. Of the approximately 170,000 Jews living in Vienna in 1938, around 130,000 fled the city. Many of them would later find themselves under National Socialist rule once again. Nearly 65,000 Viennese Jews were murdered during the → Holocaust [6].

6. "Vienna around 1900"

The greater part of Viennese Jews were able to escape. In the United States, in Great Britain, and other parts of the British Empire, a considerable number of them succeeded in developing their talents and knowledge in → science, art, and entertainment.

In many instances the image of "Vienna around 1900" originated with Jews who had emigrated from Vienna and Central Europe in the 1930s. As a multi-lingual and multi-national empire, the Habsburg monarchy had been virtually predestined to be a laboratory of diversity and pluralism, but also of the "destruction of the world." Independent of Jewish culture, the convergence of the (German-Protestant liberal) culture of the word and the (Habsburg-Catholic Baroque) culture of the image developed a considerable dynamic in itself. However, Jewish experiences and reactions contributed decisively to the relevance of the modern Vienna of the turn of the century. Due to their special position, the Jews of Vienna became aware sooner than others of the reverse, the dark side of the modern age, of the unstable nature of language and belonging, of the deceptiveness of "truths" maintained by science, scholarship, and social conventions, and especially of the perverse logic of nationalism and "scientific" racism. This meant that they, in particular, felt the need to anticipate and formulate answers for the modern age.

The Jewish contribution to turn-of-the-century Vienna centered on two trends. The first one, which became known as "critical modernism," emphasized the ethical responsibility incumbent on an artist or thinker to seek the truth behind the phenomena, the conventions, and the false totality of nationalism and ideology. It demanded the recognition of the boundaries of what modern humanity was able to achieve. Authors like Karl Kraus, Arthur Schnitzler, Sigmund Freud, Karl Popper, and Ludwig Wittgenstein, each in his own way, shared this insight. The second trend was more constructive in its character. It was aimed at discovering and recognizing differences in the development of culture, thought, and society, in order to integrate different groups and cultures and enable collective action as well as mutual understanding. The emphatically pluralistic character of turn-of-the-century Vienna could be observed in the literary culture of the coffee house, in the exuberant, anti-conventional character of the Viennese operetta, and in Mahler's "eclectic" polyphony. Both trends were personified jointly by, for instance, Otto Neurath, who ultimately returned to the fundamental ideas of the encyclopedists who regarded the diverse yet unified languages of science and scholarship as the path to universal understanding (not only among scientists and scholars). Despite great differences, Neurath's pragmatic approach to truth was rather close to Popper's idea of the → open society, particularly in the context of the closed, totalitarian ideologies of the time.

The modern culture of Vienna around 1900 fitted easily into the broad tide of modern culture that spread all over the English-speaking world during the second half of the 20th century. The Viennese culture of the turn of the century which the migrants brought with them – individualism, logical empiricism, "critical modernism," and (liberal) pluralism, the culture of Popper's open society – encountered attitudes in the West that welcomed this affirmation. While Vienna, after 1945, was no longer able to reconnect with its former cultural and intellectual status, the "Vienna around 1900," which had been profoundly shaped by Viennese Jewry, became a symbol of global modern culture.

Bibliography

Sources

[1] A. Jellinek, Der jüdische Stamm. Mittheilungen aus einer ethnographischen Studie, VI [Part], in: Die Neuzeit, 13. Dezember 1861, 179–181. [2] A. Polgar, Sperrsitz, ed. by U. Weinzierl, Vienna 1980. [3] F. Schiller, The Collected Works of Friedrich Schiller, Dinslaken 2015.

Secondary literature

[4] S. Beller, Vienna and the Jews, 1867–1938. A Cultural History, Cambridge 1989. [5] S. Beller (ed.), Rethinking Vienna 1900, Oxford/New York 2001. [6] G. Botz, The Jews of Vienna from the Anschluss to the Holocaust, in: I. Oxaal et al. (eds.), Jews, Antisemitism and Culture in Vienna, London 1987, 185–204. [7] J. Fraenkel (ed.), The Jews of Austria. Essays on Their Life, History and Destruction, London 1967. [8] K. Hödl, Als Bettler in die Leopoldstadt. Galizische Juden auf dem Weg nach Wien, Vienna 1994. [9] A. Lichtblau (ed.), Als hätten wir dazu gehört. Österreichisch-jüdische Lebensgeschichten aus der Habsburgermonarchie, Vienna 1999. [10] C. Magris, Lontano da dove. Joseph Roth e la trad. ebraico-orientale, Torino 1971. [11] I. Oxaal, The Jews of Young Hitler's Vienna. Historical and Sociological Aspects, in: I. Oxaal et al. (eds.), Jews, Antisemitism and Culture in Vienna, London 1987, 11–38. [12] B. F. Pauley, Political Antisemitism in Interwar Vienna, in: I. Oxaal et al. (eds.), Jews, Antisemitism and Culture in Vienna, London 1987, 152–173. [13] M. L. Rozenblit, The Jews of Vienna 1867–1914, Assimilation and Identity, Albany 1983. [14] C. Schorske, Fin-de-siècle Vienna. Politics and Culture, New York/London 1980. [15] H. Tietze, Die Juden Wiens, Vienna/Leipzig 1933.

STEVEN BELLER, WASHINGTON D.C.

Vienna Circle

Name of a discussion circle of approximately 20 members around the philosopher Moritz Schlick (1882–1936) promoting the scientification of traditional philosophy in the context of the → Theory of Relativity, quantum physics, symbolic logic, and language analysis. While the role of clarifying the meaning of statements was assigned to philosophy, its claim to a leading position in the concert of the sciences was challenged within the framework of an encyclopedia of unified science. Many members of the group were of Jewish origin, a fact that soon led external observers to the derogatory connection between the logical-empirical method and Judaism.

1. Introduction
2. Vienna Circle, Judaism, emigration
3. Antisemitism at the University of Vienna

1. Introduction

The core of the Vienna Circle (Wiener Kreis), which met regularly at the Mathematical Institute at Boltzmanngasse 5, consisted of men and women from the fields of → philosophy, the natural sciences, → mathematics, and logic, as well as the social sciences, endeavoring to redefine the philosophical trends of rationalism and empiricism with the aim of joining them together as "logical empiricism." In the wider circle, numerous guests from Austria and abroad – among them for instance Ludwig Wittgenstein (→ Critique of Language) and Karl Popper (→ Open Society) – gave lectures contributing to the discussions. The name of this modernist trend originated with the 1929 manifesto *Wissenschaftliche Weltauffassung: Der Wiener Kreis* ("The Scientific Conception of the World. The Vienna Circle," 1973).

In the same year, the Verein Ernst Mach was founded under the chairmanship of Moritz Schlick, which contributed to the popularization of the ideas of anti-metaphysical scientific philosophy and unified science at many events in the context of Viennese popular education until its forced dissolution in February 1934.

From 1935 onward, the Vienna Circle organized six international congresses for the unification of science in Paris, Copenhagen, Cambridge, Harvard, and Chicago. Members of the group edited the journal *Erkenntnis* (Rudolf Carnap, Hans Reichenbach) and the book series *Schriften zur wissenschaftlichen Weltauffassung* (1928–1937; Moritz Schlick and Philipp Frank) and *Einheitswissenschaft* (1933–1939; Otto Neurath). These endeavors culminated in the project, pursued above all by Carnap, Neurath, and Charles W. Morris from 1938 onward, of the *International Encyclopedia of Unified Science*; however, as a result of the Second World War, only 19 of 260 planned monographs were ever published, leaving the project unfinished.

Because of its contentual program, the political and ideological attitude as well as the largely Jewish origin of its members and followers, the movement of logical empiricism faced much hostility in → Vienna, → Prague, Berlin, and → Warsaw, while achieving strong internationalization and broad recognition in Western and Northern Europe and, above all, in the Anglo-American language area. Without this dramatic prehistory, present-day analytical philosophy and philosophy of science are hardly comprehensible.

2. Vienna Circle, Judaism, emigration

The majority of the Jewish members of the Vienna Circle came from assimilated families and felt committed to universalism and cosmopolitanism. Politically and ideologically located between socialism and liberalism, they represented a typical phenomenon of Vienna Modernism, as the philosopher of science Gustav Bergmann judged: "Seen in this way, the important scientific movements, which until now had their common center of radiation in Vienna – psychoanalysis, the philosophy of the Vienna Circle and Kelsen's legal and political philosophy – really belonged together and they determined the specific intellectual atmosphere of the Austria that vanished, just as did, in the artistic sphere, the authors Broch, Canetti and Musil" (Letter to Otto Neurath, 1938) [1. 199]. The range of political self-understanding extended from the left wing aligned with the workers' movement (Carnap, Frank, Neurath, Hans Hahn, Edgar Zilsel) to the conservative-liberal wing (Schlick, Friedrich Waismann, Felix Kaufmann). This was one of the reasons for the negative imputation that the logic-empiristic → theories originated in a "Jewish circle."

Moritz Schlick attracted pupils most of whom had been born during the first decade of the 20th century, whose interests were interdisciplinary and who would develop considerable influence at their subsequent places of activity, often founding schools of their own. There were several women among them as well (Else Frenkel-Brunswik, Rose Rand, Marie Reidemeister, Hilde Spiel, Olga Taussky-Todd et al.), atypical among the younger generation in contemporary philosophy. Most of those who had ties to the Vienna Circle had to emigrate because of their Jewish origin and/or political convictions, unless they had come to Vienna to study and research from another – usually European – country.

In this generation, Josef Schächter (1901–1995) was an exception. He was born in Kudrynce in Galicia and moved to Vienna after the First World War, where he studied to be a rabbi until 1926. He worked as a Talmud teacher at the Hebräische Pädagogium and at the Bibel Rambam Institut in

Vienna, simultaneously studying philosophy, geography, ethnology, and history from 1925 onward. He attended lectures by Moritz Schlick and Rudolf Carnap among others, and was invited by Schlick to join the meetings of the Vienna Circle while still a student. In 1931 Schächter finished his doctoral dissertation on the subject of Nicolai Hartmann's epistemology. Four years later he published his linguistic-philosophical book *Prolegomena zu einer kritischen Grammatik* (as vol. 10 of the *Schriften zur wissenschaftlichen Weltauffassung*; Karl Popper's *Logik der Forschung* had also appeared in the series in 1934) closely following Schlick and Wittgenstein. From 1936 onward, Schächter occasionally taught philosophical courses as a substitute for Friedrich Waismann.

Schächter emigrated to Palestine in 1938, working as a teacher in middle schools and as a school inspector in → Tel Aviv and Haifa until 1952, and from 1953 onward as a lecturer at the teacher training college in Haifa, finishing his professional career as a high-ranking civil servant in the Israeli education system. He also published on the subjects of classical Judaism as well as language, meaning, and faith. He was a member of the Hebrew Writers Association, of the Israeli PEN Club, and was awarded the Ruppin Prize of the city of Haifa. In the spirit of his teacher and mentor Schlick, Josef Schächter focused on the connections between → philosophy, → science, and religion, which he regarded as the expression of a specifically Jewish consciousness [2].

Regardless of the Jewish self-understanding of those linked by the Vienna Circle, their fate was predetermined by the growing antisemitism (→ Conspiracy) and by Austrofacism and National Socialism coming to power: After the "Anschluss" (annexation) of Austria in March 1938 at the latest, all the Jewish members in Vienna – as well as followers in Berlin and Prague – were dismissed from their positions and forced to emigrate. As early as 1931 Schlick's favorite

student Herbert Feigl had moved to the United States on his teacher's advice, where he founded the Minnesota Center for Philosophy of Science in 1953.

Between 1933/1934 and the beginning of the Second World War, 13 of the 20 members of the inner Circle left their home cities of Vienna, Prague, and Berlin. Victor Kraft was able to survive in inner emigration in Vienna. The mathematicians Hans Hahn and Theodore Radaković had already died before the "Anschluss." Many intellectuals and scientists who had been on the periphery of the circle also shared the fate of having to leave Vienna no later than 1938, as becomes clear from the biographies of Egon Brunswik, Josef Frank (→ Vienna Werkbund Estate), or Hans Kelsen (→ Pure Theory of Law).

In spite of Victor Kraft's brief academic career, none of the members of the former Vienna Circle were invited to return after 1945. Instead, a continuity of elites (from the "corporate statism" via National Socialism) dominated philosophy in Vienna for a long time, supported by the conservative restoration of the "long 1950s" and a continuing antisemitism. This, in addition to the purely quantitative survey, illustrates the enormous intellectual loss at the beginning of the Second Republic.

3. Antisemitism at the University of Vienna

A most dramatic case occurred when Moritz Schlick was murdered in the main building of the University of Vienna by one of his students for personal, philosophical, and ideological reasons on June 22, 1936. The right-wing press applauded the act, while the university board remained silent. Antisemitism was widespread at the university since the 19th century, and it had become a powerful apparatus of discrimination during the interwar years [4]; [8]. The public reactions to and comments on the murder trial in 1937 illustrate the racist culture war of the time and at the same time the phenomenon of antisemitism that finds expression as a cultural code even in the absence of Jews [6]. Schlick, himself, after all, not a Jew, was considered Jewish solely because of his followers and his "radically destructive philosophy" – as a newspaper article published pseudonymously after the crime described it (cited in [7. 602]). The effect of this act of violence is reflected in the shocked reactions of young Jewish intellectuals such as Hilde Spiel or Jean Améry (→ Breendonk), who emigrated to England and Belgium, respectively, in the same year [5. 289].

As the chairman of the Vereinigung sozialistischer Hochschullehrer (Association of Socialist University Teachers) and member of Vienna's municipal education authority, the mathematician Hans Hahn (1879–1934) fought in the institutions as well as in the press against the intensifying nationalist climate. He championed the equality of all students and teachers, turning against the university authorities which tolerated the violent actions of the Deutsche Studenschaft (German Student Union). As early as 1922, together with a number of colleagues he protested to the rector of the university against the discrimination of Jewish and socialist students and professors. Rightwing groups met this unfaltering attitude with defamation campaigns. Thus in 1924, for instance, the antisemitic *Deutschösterreichische Tageszeitung* published a list of 200 Jewish university teachers, which included not only Hans Hahn but also Felix Kaufmann.

Hahn demanded unrestricted freedom of study and teaching, free public education and – as a reaction to the tendentious personnel politics against a number of Social Democratic university lecturers – a habilitation process that only took scholarly competence into account. However, his endeavors remained unsuccessful, also in the context

of the Verein für Sozialistische Hochschulpolitik (Federation for Socialist Policies in Higher Learning) founded in 1925. This became clear for instance in 1927, when the criticism voiced by Hahn and other professors against antisemitic violence committed by the Deutsche Studentenschaft was denigrated as "agitation of Judeo-Marxist professors" (cited in [7. 291]). Two years later, pamphlets circulated among the students once again, which warned against attending lectures by Karl Bühler, Hans Kelsen, Julius Tandler, and Sigmund Freud (→ Psychoanalysis). Hans Hahn's chair remained vacant after his death in 1934, and a request to appoint a new professor in 1937 was denied.

In this climate, Vienna Circle member Edgar Zilsel's (1891–1944) attempt at qualifying as a professor failed in 1923/1924 as well. In his studies on the concept of genius he had focused on latent antisemitism. As a consequence, Zilsel worked full-time in popular education in Vienna until 1934, then as a teacher at middle schools, before emigrating with his family to the United States, where he committed suicide in 1944.

The philosopher of science Victor Kraft (1880–1975) was twice left empty-handed in appointment procedures against other applicants favorably inclined toward National Socialism. In 1937 Schlick's chair was abolished; Alois Dempf, a champion of the Austria ideology with the task of establishing a philosophy of a Christian worldview, became his successor. Karl Menger and the influential logician Kurt Gödel were not able to achieve tenured professorships for → mathematics in Vienna. Despite Schlick's support, Menger failed in his 1936 attempt to be appointed as successor to Wilhelm Wirtinger's chair and left Austria for the United States as a consequence. The professorship went to the National Socialist Karl Mayrhofer who – after a brief absence for denazification – was permitted to continue his academic work in the Second

Republic. Menger's fate was symptomatic of the entirety of Viennese mathematics, which was destroyed at the latest with the National Socialists coming to power in 1938.

Schlick's murder in 1936 spelled the *de facto* end of the by then world-famous Vienna Circle in Austria, although a smaller group of pupils continued to meet until 1938 under the auspices of Waismann, Schächter, and Zilsel, before National Socialism drew a final, violent line under this modernist movement. The consequences of the dissolution and expulsion of logic-empiristic academic culture were felt for a long time in the Second Republic – and in postwar Europe. It was not until much later that the remigration of the ideas of those protagonists of the Vienna Circle who had found sanctuary in the English-speaking world would lead to a new reception of their ideas in German-speaking scholarship.

Bibliography

Sources

[1] G. Bergmann, Memories of the Vienna Circle. Letter to Otto Neurath (1938), in: F. Stadler (ed.), Scientific Philosophy. Origins and Development (Vienna Circle Institute Yearbook, vol. 1), Dordrecht 1993, 193–208.

Secondary literature

[2] J. S. Diamond, Yosef Schächter. An Approach to "Jewish Consciousness," in: The Reconstructionist 30 (1964), 17–24. [3] C. Limbeck-Lilienau/F. Stadler (eds.), The Vienna Circle. Texts and Pictures at an Exhibition, Hamburg 2018. [4] O. Rathkolb (ed.), Der lange Schatten des Antisemitismus. Kritische Auseinandersetzungen mit der Geschichte der Universität Wien im 19. und 20. Jahrhundert, Göttingen 2013. [5] K. Sigmund, Sie nannten sich Der Wiener Kreis. Exaktes Denken am Rand des Untergangs, Wiesbaden 2015. [6] L. Silverman, Becoming Austrians. Jews and Culture between the World Wars, Oxford 2012. [7] F. Stadler,

The Vienna Circle: Studies in the Origins, Development, and Influence of Logical Empiricism, Cham (CH) 2015. [8] K. Taschwer, Hochburg des Antisemitismus. Der Niedergang der Universität Wien im 20. Jahrhundert, Vienna 2015.

FRIEDRICH STADLER, VIENNA

Vienna Werkbund Estate

Model housing estate of modern single-family homes built in the Lainz quarter of Vienna in 1932. At the initiative of the Austrian Werkbund, 33 architects, many of whom were of Jewish origin, designed a total of seventy town house units and detached single-family houses. As an expression of undogmatic modernism and the striving for a liberal and humanistic society, both the buildings and the layout of the estate represented the endeavor to accommodate new individual housing and lifestyle requirements.

1. History and characteristics
2. Jewish architects
3. After 1934

1. History and characteristics

The Vienna Werkbund Estate was the culmination of a number of Werkbund exhibitions held in various European cities from the late 1920s onwards. The starting point was the exhibition "Die Wohnung" (The Dwelling) opened in Stuttgart in 1927 at which the controversial design of the Weißenhofsiedlung was presented. In 1928, the Czechoslovakian Werkbund's "Nový dům" (The New House) estate followed in Brno. When the Silesian branch of the Deutsche Werkbund presented the estate "Wohnung und Werkraum" (Dwelling and Workspace) to the public, the Österreichische Werkbund (ÖWB) decided to invite their German counterpart to the conference in → Vienna the following year and to construct an estate there for the occasion.

The 1930 Werkbund conference was accompanied by a large-scale exhibition in the grounds of the Österreichisches Museum für Kunst und Industrie, where the architects Ernst Lichtblau, Karl Hofmann, Felix Augenfeld, Josef Frank, Walter Sobotka, and Oskar Strnad, among others, presented temporary buildings and facilities. The Vienna Werkbund Estate was part of the original exhibition design but could be realized only in 1932 due to economic and bureaucratic obstacles. The basis of the designs was to present spatial and typological plans for a modern middle-class living culture in tune with nature. Optimum living quality was to be achieved in limited space, with particular consideration given to the needs of the individual.

In this way, the Werkbund reacted on the one hand – with some delay – to the housing situation in Vienna, that was extremely tense due to the mass influx after the First World War, and on the other hand to the town planning concepts of so-called "Red Vienna," in the context of which the social-democrat dominated Vienna city council had implemented a number of representative community construction projects for the working classes, such as Karl-Marx-Hof (1927–1930), from 1918 onward. Members of the Werkbund rejected these large-scale projects as too opulent and dysfunctional. Instead, the core cultural living space of humans should be a place where recreation, contemplation, and the hope of a life fit for human beings could be realized. As a consequence, the Werkbund and the Estate refused to conform to any stylistic or formal diktat contrary to free association and functionality.

At the invitation of the vice president of the Werkbund Josef Frank, who oversaw the Werkbund Estate project, a number of architects presented their own constructions in the Estate, some of them for the first time. Gerrit Rietveld came from the Netherlands, Hugo Häring from Germany, André Lurçat and Gabriel Guévrékian – an architect of Armenian origin who had studied in Vienna – from France. The United States were represented by two emigrated Jews from Vienna, Arthur Gruenberger, who had emigrated to → Hollywood in 1923 and worked primarily as a set designer, and Richard Neutra. The originally Austrian Karl Augustinus Bieber and Margarete Schütte-Lihotzky, who were by then working in Eindhoven and Moscow, respectively, also emphasized the internationality of the architects involved.

Frank's housing and road layout, which followed Camillo Sitte's principles and was not unlike that of the Weißenhofsiedlung, envisaged non-axial, curving paths, small square-like areas with open spaces of varying size, as well as varied vistas. The architects mainly designed townhouses comprising between two and four units. Technical experiments of the kind carried out in Stuttgart were explicitly not the purpose of the cooperatively funded Estate. Most houses followed Frank's principle of providing the greatest possible spaciousness over a small area. The smallest and most affordable ones were the two townhouse units by Walter Loos with thirty square meters (approximately 323 sq. ft.) floor space on the first and second floors. Ernst Plischke worked in accordance with Adolf Loos's floor plan, incorporating staggered floor levels in order to better utilize space; Heinrich Kulka, who designed two semi-detached houses for Adolf Loos's firm, designed a living space over two floors with a workspace in the loft. Lurçat's houses followed the French concepts of external stair towers influenced by Le Corbusier, while Richard Neutra's and Hugo Häring's designs laid all rooms out on the first floor, as did Anton Brenner, in two L-shaped atrium houses.

In keeping with Frank's adherence to Sitte's concept, the Estate was intended to

Advertisement poster for the Vienna Werkbund Estate (1932)

convey the impression of being a naturally evolved town rather than a planned settlement. The direct connection between the houses and the garden, adopted from English country house design, was aimed at the houses fitting into their surroundings in a harmonic fashion. Frank commissioned well-known horticultural firms to create the gardens and green spaces, for instance the Staudengärtnerei Windmühlhöhe owned by Hanny Strauß and the privately run horticultural school Hortensium led by Grete Salzer, a graduate of the Höhere Gartenbauschule für Frauen (higher horticultural school for women) founded by the Jewish feminist Yella Hertzka in 1912. The concept of a modern living garden space embraced by both followed principles such as open-air living, abolishing symmetrical axes and representative ornamentation, and integrating areas for growing fruit and vegetables and for exercise and relaxation.

In the public perception, the Estate, which was visited by around 100,000 interested parties in 1932 alone, was often referred to as a "garden city." From the very beginning, the initiators endeavored to engage laypersons in conversation, for instance through a radio talk hosted by the journalist Max Eisler and Oskar Strnad called "Was gefällt Ihnen an der Werkbundsiedlung nicht?" (What don't you like about the Werkbund Estate?). The main criticism voiced here was the limited space in the houses. In the Monday paper *Der Morgen*, which discussed reservations concerning the Werkbund Estate a number of times, the critic Paul A. Rares mocked the project as a "Zwergsiedlung" ("dwarf settlement"; *Der Morgen*, July 11, 1932).

2. Jewish architects

A not inconsiderable number of the architects of the Werkbund Estate and members of the Vienna Werkbund came from Jewish families. Many of them understood → architecture not only as the prospect of

a secure existence but also as the opportunity to express progressive and liberal ideas through architectural form.

Josef Frank provides an exemplary reflection of this understanding. Born in 1885 in Baden near Vienna as the son of a merchant from the Hungarian part of the monarchy, Frank studied architecture under Carl König at the Vienna University of Technology. König's understanding of the classical tradition lastingly informed Frank's artistic development, inspiring him throughout his life in his designs for furniture and buildings. Furthermore it found expression in Frank's emphasis on the individual and the social dimension of his design concepts, deliberations which always gave precedence to the individual over abstract norms and formalizations of aesthetic theories. In this way, Frank explicitly turned his back on New Objectivity and constructivism as embraced by the Deutsche Werkbund and parts of the Bauhaus movement (→ Tel Aviv). Frank accused them of overlooking human needs in favor of doctrinal notions of efficiency and rationality. "Modern German architecture may be objective, practical, correct in principle, and sometimes even appealing," he wrote in 1930, "but it remains lifeless" (cited in [2a. 134]; [10. 653]).

At the Vienna University of Technology, Frank found like-minded companions in Oskar Strnad and Oskar Wlach, with whom he realized several buildings before the First World War. Frank showed a particular interest in the issue of workers' housing. In his polemic and rather famous essay "Der Volkswohnungspalast. Eine Rede, anläßlich der Grundsteinlegung, die nicht gehalten wurde" (1926; "The People's Apartment Palace. A Speech to Mark the Groundbreaking That Was Not Delivered," 2012), he used the example of the garden city of Jedlesee (1926–1932) to criticize the endeavors of the city of Vienna to remedy the housing shortage by constructing monumental communal structures:

And now the palace! We think of the giant stone cubes in Florence, half ceremonial hall, half fortress, in which the lord of the house could gather his followers during times of unrest; we think of Vienna's princely palaces, which have today been transformed into whole ministries, with loads of civil servants; however, it must be repeatedly stressed here that these buildings uncompromisingly document the honest ethos of the feudal era, and, in this sense, are still exemplary works of a total culture for us. But its time has passed [...]. [2. 255–259]

The Werkbund Estate, a considerable portion of which was designed by Frank, also saw itself as a counter-design to the endeavor, misguided in his view, of planning workers' dwellings along the lines of the magnificent and opulent housing units of the middle class.

There was a further dimension to the conflict over the "people's apartment palace" that encouraged Jewish architects in their inclination towards modern approaches. The masterclass at the Vienna Academy of Arts taught by Otto Wagner, a close friend of the severely antisemitic former mayor Karl Lueger, was considered to be overall antisemitic and was consequently avoided by Jewish students. The alternative was to study at the Vienna Technical University whose head, König, was of Jewish origin himself. While many of Wagner's students found work as architects in "Red Vienna," later frequently cooperating with the Nazis, König's approach of a sober, late historicist neo-Baroque resulted in the emergence of a separate Vienna School. Its founders Oskar Strnad, Josef Frank, and Oskar Wlach were soon surrounded by a circle of like-minded architects who, like themselves, came from a liberal Jewish middle-class background. Adolf Loos's mainly Jewish students and employees constituted a significant part of the Wiener Moderne too, which found

its most eloquent champions in the Jewish journalists Max Eisler, Else Hofmann, and Max Ermers (Maximilan Rosenthal).

Besides open hostility, Jewish architects also faced more subtle discrimination, for instance when applying for public positions. Thus, despite his achievements as an art historian and architecture critic, Eisler was denied the chance of a tenured professorship at the University of Vienna, as the faculty did not wish him "to take root" [6. 75]. Some sought to evade the discrimination by leaving the Jewish community and converting to Catholicism or Protestantism (→ Conversion), for instance Ernst Lichtblau and Richard Bauer, the architectural director of the Gemeinnützige Siedlungs- und Bauaktiengesellschaft (GESIBA). Occasionally, as in the cases of Hans (Samuel) Schlesinger or Ernst Korner (Kohn), people changed their first or last names (→ Naming) in such a way that they no longer indicated their denominational background.

3. After 1934

The crisis of the First Republic, characterized by troubles similar to civil war and growing antisemitism and culminating in the February Uprising in 1934, did not spare the Österreichische Werkbund. As early as mid-1933, Hermann Neubacher, the general director of the GESIBA responsible for the execution of the Estate, resigned from his post as president due to the alleged "Semitization" of the Werkbund. Neubacher, a National Socialist and mayor of Vienna for two years after the "Anschluss" (annexation), represented the wing of the Werkbund that pursued a stronger orientation towards supporting national construction traditions. In late 1933, the representatives of this trend retired, founding the Neuer Werkbund Österreichs in February 1934. The statutes of 1912 were adopted, adding a sentence which declared the encouragement of home-grown culture to be their objective.

Politically, the Neuer Werkbund was based in the corporate state of Austria; this did not, however, rule out the inclusion of Jews and Social Democrats. One of the co-founders of the Neuer Werkbund was the bank director Sigmund Rosenbaum, father of the architect Fritz Rosenbaum. Hanny Strauß also contributed to exhibitions by the Neuer Werkbund. At the → world's fairs in Brussels in 1935 and Paris in 1937, the Österreichischen Werkbund and the Neuer Werkbund were represented together. A reunification, however, did not take place. A few Jewish architects had no problems integrating into the corporate state, some, for instance, took part in the competition for the labor monument that was to replace the Monument of the Republic on Ringstraße that had been dismantled the previous year. Some were exposed as Social Democrats and consequently in danger, such as Josef Frank, who already emigrated to Stockholm with his Swedish wife Anna Regina (née Sebenius) at the end of 1933. Other Social Democrats such as Josef Berger or Helene Roth, the first female engineer and architect in Austria, but also Zionists like Loos's student Paul Engelmann moved to Palestine after the February Uprising of 1934.

After 1938, all Werkbund branches were dissolved. Hugo Gorge, Oskar Strnad, and Max Eisler had died before then. Around half of the architects who had contributed to the Werkbund Estate emigrated, most of them to America, England, and Palestine. Others committed suicide, such as Loos's student Otto Breuer, who had also studied at the Bauhaus, or were murdered in concentration camps, like Breuer's wife Grete Neuwalder-Breuer, who had come from Berlin and studied under Strnad. Arthur Gruenberger's partner in his Vienna firm, Loos's student Erich Ziffer, was deported to → Treblinka.

Paradoxically, as mayor of Vienna the former Werkbund president Neubacher saved the Werkbundsiedlung from being dismantled or altered under the Nazis; among other things he had the houses repainted in a uniform light color. Towards the end of the war, six houses were razed to their foundations by aerial bombs. In 1953/1954, the modular home model estate Veitingergasse, designed by the architects Roland Rainer and Carl Auböck, was constructed with American support, deliberately immediately next to the Werkbundsiedlung.

When architects such as Friedrich Achleitner, Friedrich Kurrent, Johannes Spalt, and Hermann Czech rediscovered the exiled Wiener Moderne, a new and increased appreciation of the Werkbundsiedlung began in the 1980s. In honor of Josef Frank's centenary in 1985, a small exhibition about the construction of the Estate was shown in the context of its restoration. After suffering from structural damage and a long stagnation period, renewed, gradual, and exhaustive restoration was begun in 2012.

Bibliography

Sources

[1] J. Frank (ed.), Die internationale Werkbundsiedlung Wien 1932, Vienna 1932.   [2] J. Frank, The People's Apartment Palace. A Speech to Mark the Groundbreaking That Was Not Delivered, in: J. Frank, Writings, Vol. 1: Published Writings from 1910 to 1930, ed. by T. Bojankin et al., Vienna 2012, 255–267.   [2a] J. Frank, Architecture as Symbol. Elements of the German New Building, in: J. Frank, Writings, Vol. 2: Published Writings from 1931 to 1965, ed. by T. Bojankin et al., Vienna 2012, 134.

Secondary literature

[3] W. Dreibholz, Die internationale Werkbund-Siedlung Wien 1932, unpublished dissertation, Graz 1977.   [4] A. Gmeiner/G. Pirhofer, Der österreichische Werkbund, Vienna/Salzburg 1985.   [5] A. Krischanitz/O. Kapfinger, Die Wiener Werkbundsiedlung, Düsseldorf 1989.   [6] I. Meder, Lebens- und Arbeitsbedingungen jüdis-

cher Architekten in Österreich, in: A. Senarclens de Grancy/H. Zettelbauer (eds.), Architektur. Vergessen. Jüdische Architekten in Graz, Vienna et al. 2011, 69–75. [7] I. Meder, Offene Welten. Die Wiener Schule im Einfamilienhausbau 1910–1938, unpublished dissertation, Stuttgart 2004. [8] I. Meder (ed.), Josef Frank 1885–1967. Eine Moderne der Unordnung, Salzburg et al. 2008. [9] A. Nierhaus/E.-M. Orosz (eds.), Werkbundsiedlung Wien 1932. Ein Manifest des Neuen Wohnens, Vienna 2012 [exhibition catalogue]. [10] W. Posch, Josef Frank, in: F. Stadler (ed.), Vertriebene Vernunft. Emigration und Exil österreichischer Wissenschaft, 1930–1940, Münster 2004, 645–658. [11] M. Welzig, Josef Frank (1885–1967). Das architektonische Werk, Vienna/Cologne 1998.

IRIS MEDER, VIENNA

Vilna

In the second half of the 18th century, the Jewish community in Vilna (today Vilnius) prospered thanks to political stability and demographic growth, becoming a renowned center of Jewish scholarship. A significant part in this process was played by the eminent rabbinical scholar Elijah ben Solomon (1720–1797), known as the "Gaon [head, leader] of Vilna" and most prominent opponent of Hasidism. Elijah's intensive dedication to the Talmud set an example for the yeshivot newly established in Lithuania in the early 19th century, thanks to which religious studies were open to the broad majority of Jewish men for the first time.

1.	The Jewish community of Vilna
1.1	History
1.2.	Community administration
1.3	The Jerusalem of Lithuania
2.	Elijah ben Solomon
2.1	Biography
2.2	Writings and other activity
2.3	The fight against Hasidism
3.	Influence

1. The Jewish community of Vilna

1.1 *History*

In Vilna (Pol. Wilno; Lit. Vilnius), capital of the Grand Duchy of Lithuania since 1323, a Jewish community is documented from the end of the 15th century onward. Its members had come to Vilna from German-speaking regions, settling as merchants, traders, and craftsmen. The Christian guilds perceived them as competition and agitated with Grand Duke Sigismund II to revoke the Jews' right to settle in 1527, although there is evidence of individual Jews remaining in the city which developed into a cultural and economic center of the Polish–Lithuanian Commonwealth. In 1633, King Władisław IV Vasa (1595–1648), who had been elected King of Poland the previous year – the Grand Duchy of Lithuania and the Kingdom of Poland were joined in a real union since 1569 –, permitted Jews to settle in a district of the city delimited by three streets, to erect a → synagogue from stone, and to engage in mercantile as well as artisan activity (→ Crafts). The rapid growth of the Jewish community – in 1645 around 3,000 of the 15,000 inhabitants of Vilnius were Jews – led to anti-Jewish reactions and violent attacks from the Christian population [5. 3–17]. In 1655, the city was laid waste in the course of the Russo–Polish War (1654–1667); many Jews as well as Christians had previously fled the city. After the Polish reconquest in 1661, Jews settled in Vilna once again. In order to support the development of the community, King Jan II Kazimierz Vasa permitted the Jews to settle outside the district previously allocated to them. By the end of the 17th century, the community had once again grown to the size it was before the war [5. 25f., 30–33, 36–40].

During the Great Northern War, the city came under Swedish occupation (1702–1707). The economic consequences of this war were disastrous for Lithuania and would be felt until well into the 18th century. In 1738, King Augustus III granted the Jews of Vilna a far-reaching trade privilege, which met with opposition from non-Jewish merchants. While expulsion could be prevented, the Jewish community had to accept a limitation of its residential district. In addition, several fires destroyed parts of the city around the middle of the 18th century. Some citizens accused the Jews of having started these and used the accusation as a justification for anti-Jewish violence. From the late 1750s onward, aggressive Catholic proselytization started, directed in particular at Jewish women. Conversions to Catholicism did indeed increase significantly during the 1760s. Relief for the Jewish community of Vilna arrived in 1783 when the settlement and professional restrictions were abolished (→ Professions). The Jews in Vilna were from this point forward able to live and flourish in freedom [5. 49, 54–56, 60f., 79].

Under these favorable conditions, the Jewish community grew significantly until it made up nearly half the population of the city. Its economic relevance as well as political influence were similarly considerable. This may have been the reason why the enlightened Catholic Ignacy Massalski, appointed bishop in 1762, put an end to his predecessor's conversion activity. Massalski was in friendly contact with the Vilna chief rabbi Samuel ben Avigdor and was generally well-disposed towards the Jews – an attitude in keeping with Vilna's reputation as a tolerant city. In the context of the First Partition in 1772, the territorially diminished Commonwealth increased its reform endeavors. Thus, the Commission for National Education (Komisja Edukacji Narodowej) was established in 1773, assuming the supervision of universities as well as the over 1,500 educational institutions of the recently disbanded Jesuit order. New, enlightened curricula were devised for all schools and new schoolbooks in the Polish language were commissioned; from 1781 onward, younger lay teachers began to replace the remaining Jesuit teachers.

Soon afterwards, the Jewish education system was fundamentally transformed too. Traditionally, Jewish primary schools (→ Ḥeder) and higher education institutions were part of the respective Jewish community and financially supported by it. Rabbinical study houses in particular were open to a small group of select pupils only (→ Talmud Torah). Around the turn of the 19th century, private yeshivot were established in Vilna as well as in other parts of Eastern Europe, which allowed every male adolescent or adult to devote himself to study. This universal availability of religious study was linked to a decline in the authority wielded by the traditional community leaders.

1.2. *Community administration*

The *va'ad medinat Lita* (Lithuanian Council) founded in 1623 represented the Jews with the Lithuanian authorities and managed the internal affairs of the Jewish community (→ Autonomy). To begin with the *va'ad* recognized three large communities: Brisk (Yidd. for Brest-Litovsk), Grodno, and Pinsk; these represented the smaller communities in their respective regions. The Jewish community of Vilna was granted equal status in the *va'ad* only in 1687, with Sluzk following in 1691. Over the course of the years, the

Vilna community achieved the leading position it would retain until the *va'ad* was dissolved in 1764 [5. 20, 36, 70f.].

The internal administration of the Vilna Jewish community was led by the → *kahal* (Hebr.; community representation). Its members were elected annually; among their duties was intercession (→ Shtadlanut) with the government and local authorities as well as representing the community in the *va'ad*. In addition, it had to oversee the internal community administration, which included levying taxes as well as – in cooperation with the rabbinical court (→ *bet din*) and the chief rabbi – ensuring the → Halakhah was observed.

1.3 The Jerusalem of Lithuania

In the 18th century, the size and comparative wealth of the Jewish community of Vilna attracted scholars from Lithuania and other parts of Eastern Europe. It was above all the reputation of Elijah ben Solomon as the greatest scholar of his time which spread through all of Europe in the first decades of the 19th century and illuminated the community with the splendor of his scholarship. The reputation of Vilna among the Jews is reflected in its byname of *Yerushalayim de-Lita*, "the Jerusalem of Lithuania" [5. 73–78]. This phrase was introduced by → maskilim, followers of the secular-oriented Enlightenment, only in the last third of the 19th century, with the intention of presenting themselves as the heirs of traditional Lithuanian scholarship. The scholar and Lumière Samuel Joseph Fuenn (Finn; 1818–1890) had published his history of the Vilna Jewish community under the title *Kirya Ne'emana* (Faithful city) in 1860. In addition to the title (Isa 1:21, 26), Fuenn used several biblical paraphrases of Jerusalem in his praise of the city. If the phrase "the Jerusalem of Lithuania" had existed at the time, Benjamin Harshav argued, Fuenn would certainly have known it and used it in his book. It is most probable, however, that this honorific

was introduced with reference to Fuenn's successful work (it was reprinted in 1900 and 1915 with additions by M. Strashun and H. N. M. Steinschneider) and used above all in secular circles [6. XXXI].

In the 20th century, Jewish historians introduced the phrase to a wider public: years before Israel Klausner made it famous in his studies, David Livni (Weissbord) published his two-volume history under this title in Tel Aviv in 1930. With reference to the by then popular phrase and to the comparative wealth of cultural life in the Vilna ghetto under the Nazis, the inhabitants of the ghetto called the city "the Jerusalem among ghettos" (cited in [7. 102, 398]). The ghetto itself was established in September 1941. After around 40,000 Jewish inhabitants of Vilna had been murdered during the second half of 1941, around 20,000 were still living in the ghetto from December of that year onward. In September 1943, the ghetto was dissolved by the Nazis and its last inhabitants deported.

2. Elijah ben Solomon

2.1 Biography

Due to Elijah's own reticence when it came to autobiographical information, and the hagiographical exaltation with which he was presented by his followers, there is only little reliable information about his life. He was born on the first day of Pesaḥ (April 23) 1720 either in Selets (today Sialiec, Belarus), his mother's home town, or in Vilna, where he lived with his parents from early childhood. His well-to-do family, which included several respected Vilna scholars of the 17th century, was highly regarded in the city. He was considered a child prodigy and apparently never attended ḥeder or Talmud school. He only had a few select teachers during his childhood and only few fellow students later on. Even so, he was said to have memorized the entire → Talmud as well as the Kabbalistic *Zohar* (→ Mysticism) by the age of ten, and, entirely self-taught, mastered "external" subjects such as logic, arithmetic, music, and astronomy. In 1737, he spent some months studying in Kėdainiai (Kiedan), where he married Hannah in 1738. They remained married until her death in 1782, and she bore him at least eight children. After her death he remarried.

After the marriage with Hannah, Elijah at first continued his studies in Kėdainiai and then in various places in Eastern Europe, among them Königsberg (today Kaliningrad) and possibly also in Berlin. In 1748, he settled in Vilna for good. Thanks to a family allowance and support from the *kahal*, he was financially independent and at first dedicated himself exclusively to his studies. He appears to have cultivated the image of a reclusive, ascetic Kabbalist. His wealth allowed him not only to feed his family but also to open a study house in 1758, situated directly next to the synagogue which had been rebuilt as a magnificent edifice that year. This documents the great esteem in which Elijah was held by the Jewish community even then [10. 21]. It was not until a few years later that Elijah himself began to teach in the study house. In the following years, his students included his sons as well as more distant male relatives and especially gifted young scholars from Vilna and its surroundings, including some who had already earned a high reputation. His subsequently most famous and influential student was Chaim ben Isaac of Volozhin (1749–1821), who opened a yeshivah in Volozhin in Lithuania in 1802 with a curriculum that would have a significant influence on the → Litvaks' (Yidd.; Lithuanian) yeshivot.

One episode in Elijah's life that remains obscure is his reputed attempt to visit the Holy Land. It is not clear when he set off and which route he took [9. 263–306]. In any case, Elijah returned to Vilna without having set foot in Erets Israel and never explained what made him change his mind.

Elijah ben Solomon (1720–1797), the Vilna Gaon

Elijah held no official position in the Jewish community of Vilna. Due to decades of internal controversy concerning the Vilna chief rabbi Solomon ben Avigdor, and in particular after he had lost his office for good in 1782 and no successor was appointed, the *kahal* asked Elijah more and more frequently to intervene in internal community matters as an advisor and mediator. Elijah's spiritual authority was recognized, and many of his Halakhic rulings accepted by the community. His reputation as a prominent scholar had grown too. While he had previously been referred to with the rabbinical title *he-ḥasid* (the pious one), in the late 1750s this was joined by the traditional high honorific "gaon" (from Hebr. *ga'on* for leader, majesty) or "Gaon of Vilna," which soon became established.

Elijah's involvement in the community also held risks. At the end of 1787, the wealthy Abba ben Wolf, a man of some influence in the community whose son had converted to Christianity of his own free will, asked Elijah for help. Elijah, the *kahal*, and Abba together had the son abducted from a monastery and taken to a place outside Vilna. In the course of the subsequent official investigation, Elijah and Abba were initially put into prison for a month; the trial in the autumn of 1789 resulted in three months imprisonment for both of them. It is not clear whether these events were the reason why he spent some time with his son in Sereje (today Seirijai) in Lithuania afterwards.

Elijah spent the last years of his life in Vilna. He died in October 1797 and was buried in a cemetery near the city. After the Second World War, his grave was moved at the orders of the Soviet city administration and is now in the Jewish cemetery in Šaltoniškių in Lithuania. After Elijah's death, his study house passed into the possession of the Vilna Jewish community who established the *Kloyz he-Ḥasid* (Yidd./Hebr.; study house of the pious) there, which continued to exist until 1940.

2.2 *Writings and other activity*

Elijah left an impressively comprehensive literary heritage; tradition attributes seventy (→ Number) books to him [10. 1]. It is true that he composed commentaries on works of nearly all genres of traditional Jewish literature. Their outstanding significance consists in his novel and independent way of thinking and commenting; in addition they reflect an extraordinarily comprehensive and in-depth knowledge of the sources. There is hardly any text of the rabbinic or Kabbalistic canon to which he did not refer in some part of his extensive output. Astonishingly, Elijah does not quote rabbinical texts of the 18th century, possibly in order to conceal every kind of influence and present himself as an independent thinker. All the same, his writings reflect his close links with scholars such as the Kabbalist Moshe Ḥayyim Luzzatto (1707–1746) and the Lumière Raphael Levi from Hannover (1685–1779), who were, in turn, influenced by Leibniz's idealism. Elijah followed the latter

in his understanding of God as a principle of mathematical motion on which nature was based (→ Mathematics) [10. 10]. In none of his writings did he refer explicitly to the ideas of the → Enlightenment (→ Haskalah) or any of its representatives; his famous contemporary Moses Mendelssohn (1729–1786; → Bi'ur) was not mentioned either. While Elijah may not have rejected the Haskalah in general, he probably felt only little interest in it. The followers of the Enlightenment shared Elijah's interest in the sciences; however, his interest was instrumental in that he regarded them merely as a means to more in-depth understanding of the Torah. Thus, in 1778 he received the maskil Baruch Schick of Shklov, who had used his time in Berlin to make the acquaintance of Lumières such as Naphtali Herz Wessely (→ Divre Shalom ve-Emet), and encouraged Schick's Hebrew → translation of Euclid's works.

Elijah commented a large number of works of classical rabbinic literature, among them the Babylonian and Palestinian → Talmuds, the Tosefta, and a multitude of → Midrashim but also of Kabbalistic literature, such as *Sifra di-Tsni'uta* (Book of Concealment) and *Sefer Yetsirah* (Book of Formation) as well as the *Zohar* (→ Mysticism). His great affinity with the Kabbalah was demonstrated not only in his commentaries on Kabbalistic texts but also in his belief that insight gained as a result of intellectual endeavor was the highest expression of divine revelation [3. 3]. He also composed texts on → Hebrew grammar, astronomy, trigonometry, and the geography of the Holy Land. He wrote his manuscripts in a narrow hand that was difficult to decipher. His typical style used sparse, economical language without digressions.

While Elijah preferred a logical approach and rational deductions, his hermeneutic practice was manifold. His method was to examine through comparison several sources he assumed to be "old." In order to understand rabbinic and Kabbalistic works, he liberally emended transmitted versions that appeared to him to be false and in his commentaries ignored the classic interpretations of medieval exegetes (→ Commentary) or the Kabbalist Isaac Luria (→ Mysticism). Moreover, he had no qualms challenging the Halakhic rulings of traditional decisors; for his commentary on the Halakhic compendium of laws, the *Shulḥan Arukh* (1570, Set Table; → Halakhah), he verified the written source of every single rule of religious law.

Although familiar with various philosophical classics, Elijah considered them to be worthless for the understanding of the Torah [3. 22]. He did, however, set great store by the study of Jewish → ethics (Hebr. *musar*). He exhorted his pupils to lead an ethical life and to study the classic moralist works. His attitude had a significant influence on the work of the founder of the ethical → Musar movement Israel Salanter [3. 342].

Elijah did not have any of his works published, which his contemporaries interpreted as his unwillingness to waste time. After his death, his sons inherited a giant legacy of manuscripts. All his manuscripts were published only years, in some cases many decades, after he had written them, many by his sons Abraham (1765–1808) and Yehudah Leib (1764–1816). Some of Elijah's pupils had previously transcribed his lessons and now published these separately entitled *Ma'ase Rav* (Narrative from the master) as well as interspersed in their own works.

2.3 The fight against Hasidism

The center of popular-mystical → Hasidism had shifted from Podolia to Volhynia after the death of the founder of the Hasidic movement Ba'al Shem Tov (ca. 1700–1760). In this period of universal religious awakening, it increasingly gained followers in Belarus and Lithuania too. The Hasidim attributed much greater importance to divine immanence, to prayer as the immediate communication of the individual with God, to ecstasy, and jolly sociability than to the → Halakhah, to traditional study (→ Talmud Torah), and the ascetic aspects of Judaism. The ideas and practices of the Hasidim, who submitted to the leadership and personal charisma of their rebbes, were in conflict with the authority of the traditional community leadership. Consequently, to begin with, rabbis and community lay elders found themselves particularly challenged by the Hasidim.

Elijah's strict rejection of the Hasidim was predominantly based on theology and a reaction to the existence of two heterodox Jewish movements, namely the Messianic crypto-Sabbatianism (→ Smyrna) and the antinomian → Frankism founded in emulation of the former. In 1771, the first Hasidic *minyan* had been established in Vilna and could at first meet unchallenged – led by, among others, the community preacher Chaim ben Solomon. In the same year, however, the Hasidic interpretation of a passage from the Kabbalistic *Zohar* (→ Mysticism) was submitted to Elijah, who regarded it as heretical – presumably the first time he publicly spoke out against the Hasidim. For further clarification, the *kahal* had the members of the *minyan* search for Hasidic texts and collect witness statements. The search brought to light "nefarious acts," among them heterodox customs such as amending prayer texts, praying ecstatically, inserting non-Hebrew (i.e. Yiddish) words into prayers, standing on one's head while praying, abolishing *talmud torah*, disrespecting scholars, and unbridled debauchery. As a consequence, the Vilna *kahal* and the rabbinical court (→ *bet din*) closed the *minyan* and expelled the preacher from the community by means of a → ban. When in the following year the Shklov community representatives informed Elijah of an incident during which a Hasidic preacher in Shklov had denigrated Elijah in 1770, the latter felt compelled to act and in the same year signed a ban against the Hasidim. In addition, letters signed by Elijah, the chief rabbi, and the *kahal* were sent to all larger communities in Lithuania, to Shklov and Minsk in Belarus, and to → Brody in Galicia in order to have the ban implemented there too. Apart from the positive reception of the letter by the *kahal* in Brody, it is not known how the other communities reacted to the letters, but the ban against the Hasidim appears to have been effective in Lithuania and Belarus at least in the short term.

The head of the Belarusian Hasidim, Menaḥem Mendel of Vitebsk (1730–1788), who regarded Lithuania as an important region for the dissemination of the Hasidic movement, presumably travelled to Vilna in the 1770s. He intended to convince the Gaon personally that the ideas and practices of the Hasidim had no foundation at all in heresy. However, Elijah refused to receive him. In the following years, there were repeated reports of violent attacks on Hasidim and their opponents (Hebr. *mitnaggdim*) as well as of their respective texts being burnt; apparently there were even death threats against persons on both sides (including Elijah).

The argument appeared to have been defused when Menaḥem Mendel of Vitebsk decided in 1777 to leave Minsk and establish a Hasidic community in the Holy Land. However, the first Hasidic text appeared in print in 1780, *Toldot Yaʿakov Yosef* (Life story of Jacob Joseph), in which Jacob Joseph of Polonne not only described Hasidic ideas and practices but also attacked the traditional religious leadership. On the basis of this proof of Hasidic heresy, the Vilna *kahal* issued a much more stringent ban against the Hasidim in 1781, this one, too, signed by Elijah. Unlike in 1772, all Hasidim of Vilna were now ordered to leave the city; Jews were also forbidden to let apartments to them in the suburbs of Vilna. Simultaneously, the most important communities in Lithuania were once again asked to repel and persecute the Hasidim in the same way.

Two messengers were sent out bearing a letter from the *kahal* and signed by Elijah to ensure that all communities in Lithuania were able to pronounce a corresponding ban. This decision was in fact taken during a meeting of the *vaʿad* in Selva (Zel'va, Grodno district). The decision led to much disquiet among the Hasidim, with many renouncing the Hasidic movement – which was in any case rather small in Lithuania. Some leaders of Hasidic communities left Lithuania for Volhynia [5. 85].

However, this, too, was merely a partial victory. Shne'ur Zalman of Liadi, the head of the Hasidim in Belarus, was only the first of those who tried to discredit Elijah's authority, comparing him to the Talmudic rabbi Eliʿezer, who had been banished because he would not submit to the majority opinion. Soon after a further ban, Hasidim began to spread rumors that Elijah regretted this verdict and now regarded Hasidic ideas favorably; another rumor had him beg forgiveness for the ban and simultaneously for acceptance among the Hasidim. From 1784 onward, Elijah composed several letters in which he called these rumors completely unfounded. In response to the unstoppable rumors, but probably also the constantly increasing interest in the Hasidic movement in Lithuania in the 1790s, he composed another letter in 1796, once again sharply condemning the Hasidim. He asked his pupil Saʿadya ben Nathan to travel with the letter through Europe, making its contents public everywhere.

Elijah's death in 1797 and the decision of the Russian government that Hasidim, too, had the right to establish their own *minyanim*, put an end to the Mitnaggdim's organized fight against the Hasidim. In fact, the latter's attractiveness for a broad majority of religious Jews in Eastern Europe could hardly be stopped: at the core of the Hasidic message was the submission (*dveykus*) to God, which could be achieved above all through prayer and for which the intellectually challenging study of the holy scriptures was no longer required. The popular-mystical practices held a great attraction for young men, who left the traditional study institutions in droves [3. 153f.].

3. Influence

From the mid-18th century onward, Elijah's reputation had spread beyond the Lithuanian borders, at least among scholars. However, he became known to a wider public only during the first decades of the 19th century, mainly as the result of the gradual posthumous publication of his writings, until he was the most famous and influential Jewish scholar in all of Eastern Europe. A considerable part in establishing his aura was due to the hagiographical works of his closest pupils and followers who positively idolized him.

Elijah's focus on rabbinic literature and the Kabbalah played a significant part in the early modern normative legal codices (→ Halakhah) and the community → rabbinate adhering by them losing their singular authority. From the beginning of the 19th century onward, Elijah's independent investigation of the most important Halakhic codex, the *Shulḥan Arukh*, encouraged students and scholars in Eastern Europe to dispense with studying these normative texts and instead turn to the Talmud, which encouraged individual decisions. To begin with, this practice was implemented by Elijah's pupils at the Volozhin yeshivah (→ Musar) and later in many privately-run yeshivot in Lithuania. Unlike the traditional institutions run by the communities, which admitted only a small elite to study, these were open to all Jewish men. Opening up scholarship was due not least to Elijah's modernizing influence; classifying him, as has frequently been done, as a "traditionalist" does not do justice to his contribution [10. 11].

With Elijah's death, the Mitnaggdim lost the most respected and influential personality in their fight against Hasidism. Nevertheless, some of Elijah's pupils endeavored to carry on his legacy. Recognized as Elijah's successor even during the latter's lifetime, Ḥayyim ben Isaac (1749–1821) employed a different approach. Rather than relying on the ban, he offered reformed Talmud studies at the yeshivah he had founded in Volozhin (today Valozhyn in Belarus), endeavoring to connect Jewish men to non-Hasidic, Orthodox Judaism. His concept was successful; in fact, yeshivot in Lithuania experienced a great boost during the 19th century, accompanied by methodological and subject-oriented innovations the Musar movement incorporated into the traditional curriculum. While Hasidism did take permanent roots in Lithuania after Elijah's death, the country remained a stronghold of the Mitnaggdim [12]. The Litvaks' traditional scholarship, informed as it was by the spirit of rationalism, even became a cornerstone of Jewish → Orthodoxy. While Hasidism grew into a broader Jewish trend in the decades after the Second World War with followers all over the globe, the yeshivah's (→ Talmud Torah) victory over the Hasidic courts – even within Hasidic communities – indicates Elijah's continuing influence.

Bibliography

Sources
[1] S.J. Fuenn, Kiryah Ne'emanah. Korot Adat Yisra'el be-Ir Vilna [Faithful City. Sources on the Jewish Community in Vilna], Vilna 1860.

Secondary literature
[2] I. Etkes, Rabbi Israel Salanter and the Mussar Movement. Seeking the Torah of Truth, Philadelphia 1993. [3] I. Etkes, The Gaon of Vilna. The Man and his Image, Berkeley 2000. [4] I. Klausner, Vilna, in: Encyclopaedia Judaica, Vol. 16, Jerusalem 1971, 138–147. [5] I. Klausner, Vilnah,

Yerushalayim de-Lita. Dorot rishonim 1495–1881 [Vilna, the Jerusalem of Lithuania. The Early Generations], Tel Aviv 1988. [6] H. Kruk, The Last Days of the Jerusalem of Lithuania. Chronicles from the Vilna Ghetto and the Camps, 1939–1944, ed. by B. Harshav, New Haven/London 2002. [7] A. Lipphardt, Vilne. Die Juden aus Vilnius nach dem Holocaust. Eine transnationale Beziehungsgeschichte, Paderborn et al. 2010. [8] D. Livni (Weissbord), Yerushalayim de-Lita [The Jerusalem of Lithuania], 2 vols., Tel Aviv 1930. [9] A. Morgenstern, Mysticism and Messianism. From Luzzatto to the Vilna Gaon, Jerusalem 1999. [10] E. Stern, The Genius. Elijah of Vilna and the Making of Modern Judaism, New Haven 2013. [11] M. Wilensky, Hasidic and Mitnaggdic Polemics in the Jewish Communities of Eastern Europe. The Hostile Phase, in: B. K. Kiraly (ed.), Tolerance and Movements of Religious Dissent in Eastern Europe, New York 1975, 89–113. [12] M. Zalkin, Mekomot she-lo mats'ah adayin ha-ḥasidut ken la-klal? Ben ḥasidim le-mitnagdim be-lita ba-meah ha-19 [Places Where Hasidism Did Not Settle Down Yet? Between Hasidim and Mitnagdim in Lithuania in the 19th Century], in: I. Etkes/D. Assaf (eds.), Be-ma'gele ḥasidim. Kovets meḥkarim le-zikhro shel professor Mordekhai Vilenski [Within Hasidic Circles. Studies in Hasidism in Memory of Professor Mordecai Wilensky], Jerusalem 1999, 21–50.

BEN-TSIYON KLIBANSKY, TEL AVIV

Vilna Troupe

Yiddish theatre company performing between 1916 and 1935 mainly in Poland as well as touring Europe. Its aim was to develop Yiddish theatre art not only for a broader audience but also for more discriminating viewers. Productions were dominated by Jewish topics and a modernist aesthetic. Its tours as well as those of its eponymous spin-offs contributed to the change in perception of Yiddish theatre: while the focus was on artistic quality in Eastern Europe, in Western Europe the troupe was also seen as the expression of authentic Jewish culture.

At the beginning of the First World War, the Russian authorities implemented repressive measures against the Jewish population of → Vilna. When German troops occupied the city in the autumn of 1915, they were welcomed by the Jews who hoped that the occupiers would end the anti-Jewish policy of the Czarist Empire. The German military at first endeavored to counteract the remaining Russian influence. They prohibited teaching the Russian language in schools and closed Russian cultural institutions, encouraging instead the establishment of non-Russian cultural associations, trade unions, associations, libraries, and theatre companies. In the course of these measures, the actor Aleksander Azro (Asro, originally Orliuk) and the painter Leib Kadison were granted permission to found a Yiddish theatre. They benefited from the fact that the German authorities regarded → Yiddish as a politically neutral language compared to → Russian and its speakers as potential allies [6].

The original name of the theatre troupe founded by Kadison and Azro was *Fareyn fun Yidishe Dramatishe Artistn in Vilne* (FADA; Union of Yiddish Dramatic Artists in Vilna). The ensemble consisted mainly of amateurs some of whom had been active in Yiddish theatre clubs. The majority among them had little or no stage experience. Only those actors who had previously worked at Russian theatres brought a certain degree of practical experience to the troupe. Some members of the ensemble were educated workers in sympathy with the *Algemeyner Yidisher Arbeter-bund* (General Jewish Labor Bund; → *Bund*).

Shortly after the foundation, Mordechai Mazo joined FADA, becoming its manager and impresario. Mazo and his actors delimited themselves from the predominant

Yiddish theatre that was primarily dedicated to light entertainment (→ Pomul Verde). In contrast, FADA aimed at theatre productions that could compare to those of prominent European stages. As a result, the troupe first endeavored to broaden the members' literary knowledge. Based on the practice of the Moscow Art Theatre, they introduced intensive rehearsals and committed to ensemble-style performances with the actors exchanging parts as a matter of course.

The first production FADA staged in February 1916 was *Der landsman* (The compatriot) by Sholem Asch (→ Motke), a play about Jewish immigrants in America, in which adherence to the Jewish culture of the Old World triumphs over Americanization [6. 253]. People from all walks of life made up the audience of the premiere: Jewish workers, tradesmen, and intellectuals as well as Russian-speaking inhabitants of Vilna and German soldiers. Due to the presence of the German occupying forces, the performance was mentioned in the German press.

In May 1917, FADA went on tour through regions of Lithuania and Belarus, which were under the control of the German military administration of "Ober Ost." Performances here were also reviewed in the German press. Reviews were written by German-Jewish intellectuals such as Hermann Struck, Sammy Gronemann (→ Tohuwabohu), Herbert Eulenberger, and Arnold Zweig, who were deployed to the Eastern front as soldiers and had supported FADA since it was founded. They were part of a generation of young German Jews who looked critically at the → assimilation embraced by their parents' generation. Thanks to their encounters with Jews from Eastern Europe during the First World War, they had gained a positive image of these → "Ostjuden" with which they countered their individualized existence as acculturated Jews.

In the summer of 1917, the ensemble had its first performance in Warsaw. Jewish writers, journalists, and activists attended the premiere in order to see *Der dorfs-yung* (The village boy) by Leon Kobrin. The press

Members of the Vilna Troupe around 1919, among them David Hermann (standing, 1st left), Sonia Alomis (seated, 1st left), and Leib Kadison (seated, 1st right)

now referred to the ensemble succinctly as the "Vilna Troupe" (Yidd. *Vilner Trupe*). The reviewers delightedly reported on the artistic and literary Jewish theatre as, after all, its existence was proof that Jewish culture did not consist merely of folkloristic entertainment but could be regarded as a veritable national culture.

The productions of the ensemble's first years were characterized by scenic Naturalism and educational tendencies, inspired by the stage aesthetic of the Moscow Art Theatre (→ Habima) led by Konstantin Stanislavsky. Performances pursued a realistic approach, representing locations and environments with as much faithful detail as possible. The company endeavored to shape the artistic tastes of the Jewish audiences, which is why adaptations of literary pieces were often introduced by members of the ensemble. When selecting plays, the Vilna Troupe primarily looked to more sophisticated Yiddish → literature written by, among others, Leon Kobrin, Sholem Asch, Sholem Aleichem (Shalom Yakov Rabinovitch; → Luftmenschen; → Tevye), and Jacob Gordin (→ Sibirya). It also staged works featuring Jewish subjects that had been translated from European languages, such as by Theodor Herzl (→ Old New Land).

In 1918, two of the founding members, Sonia Alomis (Lubotski) and Aleksander Azro, left the troupe. Azro subsequently directed several groups named "Vilna Troupe," performing in Germany, the Netherlands, Great Britain, the United States, Canada, Belgium, and elsewhere. In the following years, several subgroups split from the ensemble, with former actors founding their own "Vilna Troupes." Thanks to the numerous tours of the original troupe and its spin-offs, the phenomenon of the Vilna Troupe spread in Europe, North and South America, Australia, and South Africa over the following decades.

The troupe achieved its greatest success with An-Ski's *Der dibek: Tsvishn tsvey veltn* ("Between Two Worlds," or → "The Dybbuk," composed 1914–1916), premiered in Warsaw under the direction of David Herman in 1920. By 1935, almost 200,000 spectators had seen the production. With *The Dybbuk*, the Vilna Troupe also changed its aesthetic. It abandoned Stanislavsky's naturalism, turning instead to Meyerhold's grotesque anti-realism, creating a stage aesthetic that displayed affinity with the neo-Romanticism predominant in Poland. Herman conjured up a mysterious universe on stage, with constant changes between realistic and symbolic scenes as visual implementation of the plot of the play "between two worlds."

In 1922, the troupe was the first Jewish art theatre to travel to Galicia. As in all its performances in Eastern Europe, it was able here to also reach acculturated as well as traditional Jewish audiences. This was also true of the guest performance in Vienna in 1923, although the fascination for the acculturated audiences here was rather fed by exoticism and nostalgia. Similar to the performances by a derivative group of the Vilna Troupe in Berlin in 1921/1922, they were perceived in Vienna, too, as an expression of the authentic Jewish lifestyle.

Between 1924 and 1927, the Vilna Troupe toured Romania, where it was able to win local sponsorship and great popularity among the non-Jewish population as well, in spite of the economic crisis and growing antisemitism (→ Iaşi). During this time the ensemble affirmed its surrealist style, for instance with the stylized production of Osip Dymov's *Der zinger fun zayn troyer* (1925; The singer of his sorrow). In 1927, several actors broke away from the troupe to emigrate to the United States. Some members rallied round Mazo in Lviv (→ Lemberg), signing new actors, among them graduates of Michał Weichert's *Yidishe dramatishe shul* (Yiddish acting school) in Warsaw.

The productions of the late 1920s focused primarily on Jewish life in Eastern Europe. The adaptation of Sholem Asch's *Kiddush ha-shem* (Sanctification of the name of the Lord) first performed in 1928, for instance, told the story of a Jewish community during the → Cossack persecutions. It glorified the → martyrs who met their ends at that time as national and universal heroes in the face of anti-Jewish threats. The 1930 production of *A mayse mit Hershele Ostropolyer* (A story about Hershele Ostropolyer) by Moshe Lifshitz played on Hasidic legends about → tsaddikim and the → Ba'ale Shem (→ Hasidism).

During the 1930s, the Vilna Troupe endeavored to establish itself as a social and political theatre, especially in Poland. The impulse was given by Jakub Rotbaum joining the troupe in 1929. Rotbaum had studied theatre direction in Moscow with Stanislavsky, Meyerhold, Alexander Tairov, and Solomon Mikhoels (→ GosET; → King Lear) and soon rose to becoming artistic director of the Vilna Troupe. Under his direction it moved on from focusing on only Jewish subjects, expanding its repertoire with plays with which Rotbaum had become familiar in Moscow and translated into → Yiddish. In 1930, he staged *Shvartse geto* (Black ghetto), an adaptation of Eugene O'Neill's *All God's Chillun Got Wings*. This was followed in 1933 by the premiere of the activist play *Shray, Khine* (Scream, China!) by the Soviet author Sergei Tretyakov, which was a great success with the audience. When audience numbers began to dwindle beginning in 1935 due to economic crises and growing antisemitism, the Vilna Troupe ceased its activities.

Bibliography

[1] Art. "Vilner Trupe," in: Z. Zylbercweig [Zilbertsvayg], Leksikon fun yidishn teater [Encyclopedia of Yiddish Theatre], vol. 1, New York 1931, 704–718.   [2] L. Kadison/J. Buloff, On Stage, Off Stage. Memories of a Lifetime in the Yiddish Theatre, Cambridge (MA) 1992.   [3] Z. Reyzen, Der yudisher [!] teater in Vilne [Yiddish Theatre in Vilna], in: T. Shabad (ed.), Vilner zamlbukh [Vilna Anthology], vol. 2, Vilna 1918, 165–174.   [4] N. Wejnig, Piętnaście lat "Trupy Wileńskiej," in: Miesięcznik Żydowski 4 (1930–1931), 359–364.   [5] A. Azro, Der onheyb [The Beginning], in: I. Manger et al. (eds.), Yidisher teater in Eyrope tsvishn beyde velt-milkhomes. Poyln [Yiddish Theatre in Europe during the Interbellum. Poland], New York 1968, 23–34.   [6] D. Caplan, "Reinkultur" in Yiddish. World War I, German-Jewish Encounters, and the Founding of the Vilna Troupe, in: Aschkenas 24 (2014) 2, 243–259.   [7] Y. Vayslits, Der gang in der velt [Direction in the World], in: I. Manger et al. (eds.), Yidisher teater in Eyrope tsvishn beyde velt-milkhomes. Poyln [Yiddish Theatre in Europe during the Interbellum. Poland], New York 1968, 35–49.   [8] S. Zer-Zion, The Dybbuk Reconsidered. The Emergence of a Modern Jewish Symbol between East and West, in: Leipziger Beiträge zur jüdischen Geschichte und Kultur 3 (2005), 175–197.

MIROSŁAWA M. BUŁAT, CRACOW

Vitebsk

Situated on the periphery of the Russian Empire, the Belarusian city of Vitebsk (Viciebsk) became a metropolis of the arts between 1917 and 1922, attracting leading artists of the Russian Soviet avant-garde. At the heart of the "Vitebsk Renaissance" (*vitebskij renesans*) was the artist Marc Chagall (1887–1985), who had been born here. In 1919, while he participated in the socialist utopia of reshaping the world, he founded an art school in the city. In Chagall's texts and images, Vitebsk occupied a central position as a mythicized memory topos and as a signifier of Jewish belonging.

1. Jewish Vitebsk
2. Marc Chagall
3. Vitebsk in Chagall's œuvre

1. Jewish Vitebsk

The first mention of Jews residing in Vitebsk dates back to the 16th century. In 1627 they were granted permission to build a → synagogue; they were allowed to engage in commercial activity from 1634 onward. In the Council of Four Lands (→ Autonomy) of the Polish–Lithuanian Commonwealth, Vitebsk was part of the *va'ad medinat Lita* (council of the land of Lithuania). As a result of the First Partition of Poland in 1772 the city fell to the Russian Empire. Through the activities of the rabbis Shneur Zalman of Liady and Menachem Mendel of Vitebsk, the city and its surroundings became a center of the emerging → Hasidism movement. When the → Maskilim were expelled from Moscow and began to settle in Vitebsk, the ideas of the → Haskalah also began to influence Jewish life in the city from the second half of the 19th century onward. Around this time the city's rapid economic growth began with industrialization, shipping on the Daugava, and the connection to the railway network.

By 1900 the number of Jews in Vitebsk had risen to over 34,000, representing more than half of the population; in 1915, over 43,000 Jews lived in the city, which equaled around 40% of the inhabitants. They made significant contributions to the economic and cultural flourishing of Vitebsk [6. 25f., 44]. A broad range of Jewish musical associations, theatres, and societies emerged; at the center, between 1918 and 1920, was the I. L. Peretz society named for the author Isaak Leib Peretz (→ Bontshe). Headed by the painter and graphic artist Solomon Iudovin (1892–1954), it was dedicated to facilitating Jewish and, above all, Yiddish culture. Iudovin, who like Chagall or the Yiddishist Khayim Zhitlovski (→ Language Conference) had grown up in Vitebsk, regarded → art entirely in the spirit of his uncle S. An-Ski (→ Dybbuk). With his exertions on behalf of popular culture and → folklore, he became a major protagonist of the Jewish → Renaissance in Eastern Europe.

Between the → February Revolution of 1917 and the foundation of the Soviet Union in 1922, Vitebsk developed into a center of the Russian Soviet avant-garde in spite of civil war and famine. Marc Chagall and the People's Art College (*Narodnoe khudozhestvennoe uchilishche*) he founded in January 1919, an institution open to all nationalities and all art forms, played an essential part in the "Vitebsk Renaissance." Unlike Iudovin, Chagall was not concerned with the reconstruction of folk art in order to strengthen a Jewish national culture, but rather with its aesthetic transformation in the context of an international avant-garde. Under Chagall's leadership, Vitebsk became the center of the artistic elite in the young Soviet state.

The flourishing of art in Vitebsk was, however, short-lived. As early as 1924, the People's Art College was forced to Sovietize. At the same time the Jewish section of the Communist Party (*Yevsektsiya*; → Birobidzhan) largely suppressed religious life in the city. In the atheistic atmosphere of the Stalin era, only nine of the once fifty synagogues of Vitebsk survived until 1936; the Lubavitch Chabad movement continued its activity underground. In the autumn of 1941, the city fell under German occupation, which entirely obliterated the Jews. It was not until after the fall of the Soviet Union that a modest Jewish life began to emerge in the city once more.

2. Marc Chagall

Born Movsha Shagalov (Yidd. Moyshe Shagal) as the son of a herring-seller and a shopkeeper in 1887 in Vitebsk, Marc Chagall grew up in a traditional Jewish milieu of

Marc Chagall (1887–1985)

Eastern Europe. Its popular, folklorist, and humorous reality (→ Humor; → Jokes) had a lasting influence on his understanding of aesthetics.

In 1906/1907 Chagall studied at the School of Drawing and Painting (*Shkola risovaniya i zhivopisi*) in Vitebsk. The first Jewish art school in the Czarist Empire, it had been founded by Yehudah Pen in 1898 and continued to exist until the foundation of the People's Art School (1919). Pen later introduced Russian-Jewish avant-garde artists, many of whom would find international fame – including Chagall, Ossip Zadkine (→ École de Paris), and El Lissitzky (→ Wolkenbügel) – to the fundamental techniques of drawing and painting. His symbolically exaggerated realism, expressed mainly in portraits and genre paintings, provided important inspiration for their own work.

Chagall's decision to become a *khudozhnik* (Russ.; artist) [3. 119] was equivalent to a twofold rite of passage. On the one hand he ignored the traditional → aniconism, on the other, the decision is exemplary of the attraction Russian modernism exerted on young Jewish intellectuals in Vitebsk. Chagall's future wife Bella Rosenfeld (1895–1944) was full of enthusiasm for Russian culture, too, while her father remained a practicing Hasid who regarded any interest in a secular way of life with suspicion. However, it was precisely the break with tradition that characterized the East European Jewish revivalist movement, encouraged by the activity of the → *Bund* – which already had 400 members in Vitebsk in 1898, one year after its foundation – and by the 1905 revolution [11. 10].

From 1910 onward, Chagall lived and worked in Paris, experiencing a "revolution of the eye," as he called it, in the direct encounter with Western European avant-garde art (→ École de Paris). During a trip to Vitebsk in 1914, he was overtaken by the outbreak of the First World War, which, for the time being, prevented his return to Paris. He documented the onset of the war in civilian life of the garrison city in oppressively erratic sparse black-and-white drawings. Besides these miniatures of mobilization and mourning, he also created the portraits *The Jew in Black-and-White*, *The Jew in Green*, *The Jew in Red*, and *The Jew in Bright Red* in 1914/1915. In these archetypical figures, Chagall symbolized the recurring fate of the Jews to be obliged to carry their pack and, as the → Yiddish authors Sholem Y. Abramovitsh (Mendele Moykher-Sforim; → Fishke) and Sholem Aleichem (→ Tevye) as well as popular songs (→ Folk Music) repeatedly invoked, the "goles tsu shlepn," that is, to bear the burden of → exile.

Caught up in the euphoria of the revolutions of 1917, which for the first time granted the Russian Jews full legal equality (→ February Revolution), Chagall saw → art, which he believed to be universal, as offering the opportunity of a humanist all-encompassing union of humanity beyond race or nation. As an active supporter of the October Revolution, he was appointed People's Commissar for Fine Arts for the Vitebsk governorate in

1918. By means of the People's Art School he founded, Chagall hoped to transform everyone into artists and new beings and to unite the different styles under one roof. Artists of the most varied aesthetic inclinations followed his call to cooperation, among them the symbolist painter Mstislav Dobuzhinsky, Cubo-futurists like Vera Yermolayeva or Ivan Puni, Yehudah Pen as the representative of academic realism, as well as such prominent personalities as El Lissitzky and Kazimir Malevich. Lesser known artists like David Yakerson and his wife Elena Kabishcher-Yakerson also came to Vitebsk. Even though Chagall was determined not to pursue a specifically Jewish program, the high proportion of Jewish students and teachers at the Art School was noticeable.

Malevich brought Suprematism with him when he came to Vitebsk in 1919. Together with Chagall's famous images of green cows and flying horses, its geometric forms, called "Suprematist confetti" by contemporaries [4. 345f.], adorned the city that had been transformed into a kind of revolutionary stage. However, the impression of a pleasant cooperation was misleading. By the time the Suprematist artists' group *UNOVIS* (acronym of *Utverditeli novogo iskusstva*; Champions of the New Art) was founded in February 1920, Malevich had eclipsed Chagall, not least because the latter was overwhelmed with administrative tasks. Malevich's abstract visualization of the absolute and the concept of salvation associated with Suprematism appeared to exert a greater fascination on the many secularized Jewish artists who were still familiar with religious traditions. Chagall's art students all moved to Malevich, believing their (art) utopias to be expressed more clearly in the radical reduction of his visual language than in Chagall's representations which, while also abstract, always contained a dreamy quality. Chagall responded with paintings that contained self-portraits. In his *Cubist Landscape* (ca. 1918), he immortalized himself under a green umbrella on the way to the People's Art School. Subject and figurative representation – which Malevich had banned from painting – remained subtly present in Chagall's art.

In June 1920 Chagall left Vitebsk, as the socialist co-opting of the art school proved to be incompatible with his idea of "art for everyone." He taught war orphans in Moscow for a time, and created stage sets for the → GosET (*Gosudarstvennyj yevrejskij teatr*) theatre led by Alexandr Granovskii. Artistically isolated and confronted with the growing Sovietization of culture, Chagall left Russia for good in the summer of 1922. After a short stay in Berlin, he settled in Paris in 1923, where he continued to make a name for himself. Thanks to the assistance of Varian Fry and his friend the author Joseph Opatoshu, he and his family were able to emigrate to the United States in 1941.

After his return to France in 1947, where he made his home in the southern artists' village Saint-Paul-de-Vence as well as in Paris, Chagall's career as an internationally recognized artist reached its peak. Until his death in 1985, he created an extensive œuvre on several continents. Among his most famous works are the interior design of the synagogue at the → Hadassah University Hospital in Jerusalem, of major churches in Metz, Zurich, and Mainz, the opera in Paris as well as the United Nations building in New York. Besides illustrations of the Bible and texts by La Fontaine, Gogol, and many other Yiddish and French authors, his main focus continued to be on painting and graphic art. He also created Gobelins (tapestries), mosaics, ceramics, sculptures, murals, and stage sets. The colorful stained-glass windows of the last years of his life were often expressions of Jewish-Christian dialogue. Like the Musée national du message biblique Marc-Chagall, opened in Nice in 1973, they reveal Chagall's deep religious and cultural influence the Hebrew Bible had exerted on him.

3. Vitebsk in Chagall's œuvre

There is hardly any other (Eastern European) Jewish artist in whose work artistic originality, aesthetics, and place of origin were fused so tightly together as in Chagall's. His pictures and writings capture the *genius loci* of Vitebsk and, beyond that, reveal a second face of the city, nourished by Chagall's own private mythology. Be it the coachman (→ Balegule), the *shoḥet* (→ Sheḥitah), or the fiddler, be it → birth, → marriage, or funeral (→ Death), be it → synagogue, *sukkah* (Sukkot), or a wooden house typical of the region – the everyday world of Vitebsk with its strongly Hasidic character frequently provided the motifs for his paintings. Especially the impressions of his childhood and adolescence, which were often characterized by humor, furnished a reservoir brimming with Jewish motifs and scenes. The real Vitebsk and Chagall's fictionalizations in word or visual art fused into a unified whole that abolished the boundaries between art and life.

Conversely, during his Paris years from 1910 to 1914, Chagall reinvented himself as the cultural other in recourse to his Eastern European Jewish background – which was seen as exotic from a Western point of view. In order to do so, however, he used the aesthetic tools of the European avant-garde, above all Orphism, Fauvism, and → Cubism. His *Self-Portrait with Seven Fingers* (1913/1914), for instance, shows the artist in a fashionable, eccentric pose in front of his easel. Behind him to the left, the Eiffel Tower represents the Paris of his reality, while the Orthodox church with its green dome to his right stands for the imagined and inspiring Vitebsk. The Russian provincial city becomes a signifier of the French art metropolis: "Paris, you are my second Vitebsk," as Chagall put it later in *Ma Vie* (1957; "My Life," 1960) [2. 116]. From a Jewish perspective, however, the traditional hierarchies remained in place: Vitebsk functioned for his entire life as the terrestrial "second Jerusalem" that entered into a dialogue with the heavenly Jerusalem (→ Zion) in later years.

When creating Jewish figures and characters, Chagall knew how to combine earthly and celestial, ostensible material poverty and sublime spiritual riches. Thus his painting *Over Vitebsk* (ca. 1914; see image vol. 5, 388) shows a snow-covered street and church in the city, with a Jew wearing a peaked cap and carrying a cane and a pack floating in the air above it. This was Chagall's visual translation of the Yiddish phrase *iber di hayzer geyn* (walking over the houses), meaning "to beg." His visualization, offering a wealth of interpretations, of the Jewish → "Luftmenschen" with the dominating attitude toward life of flying and hovering in the air, provides the subject matter for many more paintings in which the laws of space and time are suspended, such as *Over the Town* (1914–1918), *Anywhere out of the World* (1915), and *The Walk* (1917/1918). Chagall's perception of Vitebsk and its aesthetic transformation obey above all the principles of alogic, recalling the city's Hasidic living environment.

Chagall's intensive involvement in Jewish cultural life in Moscow at the beginning of the 1920s also drew significantly on the Eastern European-Yiddish → folklore and popular art with which he was familiar from Vitebsk and its surroundings. In the Russian capital, the international avant-gardist from the Jewish provinces became an avant-gardist Jew. He met representatives of the Kiev *Kultur-Lige* such as Yekhezkl Dobrushin and illustrated Dovid Hofshteyn's cycle of poems *Troyer* (Mourning) on the 1919 pogroms in Ukraine (→ Schwarzbard Trial). In his interior design for the Moscow Yiddish State Theatre, he continued the work he had done as a set designer for the Vitebsk Theatre of Revolutionary Satire (*Teresvat*).

After emigrating, Chagall depicted the real Vitebsk, now supplemented by manifold symbolizations from a distance. Besides his wife, the former center of his life became his second muse and a fixed topos in his memorial art. Chagall imagined and mythicized the city in oil and engravings, in poems and in his autobiography which he wrote in → Yiddish, → Russian, and later in French. Despite his multiple cultural and linguistic affiliations, for this purpose he preferred Yiddish as his *mame-loshn* (mother tongue). Thus in 1938 he composed a poem to Vitebsk *Di shtot di vayte* (The spacious town or The town so distant): "Within me rings / the town so distant, / The cloisters white, / the synagogues. The door / is open. The sky blooms. / Life flies ever onward" [1]. Jewish and Christian ideas, but above all verbal and visual art, were closely linked in his creation and recreation of Vitebsk.

During the Second World War, the city became for Chagall a symbol for the extermination of the Jews (*The Falling Angel*, 1923–1947; *War*, 1964–1966). Like Bella's death in the same year, the destruction of Vitebsk during its recapture by the → Red Army in June 1944 was a tragedy for him. In the gouache *The Crucified* and the dedication *Tsu mayn shtot Vitebsk* (To my city Vitebsk, both 1944), Chagall composed his farewell to his former homeland. He derived the imagery of the Second World War directly from the iconography of anti-Jewish → pogroms developed by realists like Maurycy Minkowski and Samuel Hirszenberg (→ Bezalel) before the First World War, before Issachar Ber Ryback took it to extremes in his primitivist images after the horror of having been a witness (→ Bearing Witness). Chagall painted burning houses and synagogues, Jews with their *torbe* (pack), and mothers fleeing with their children. Because of their color schemes and motifs, these comparatively conventional representations of war and annihilation not infrequently harbor an eschatological dimension influenced by the crucifixion of Christ – with Vitebsk, Chagall's archetype of Jewish life, as an integral component. The

image, which he had acquired of Vitebsk during the First World War, dominated other established motifs of the → Shoah.

Chagall never saw Vitebsk again. Persona non grata in the Soviet Union for decades, he declined to visit the rebuilt city on a journey in 1973 – for fear of not recognizing it. After the fall of the Iron Curtain, the Marc Chagall Art Center (*Art-Tsentr Marka Shagala*) was founded in Vitebsk in 1992, where some of his graphic works as well as contemporary art are displayed. On the occasion of the artist's 110th birthday in 1997, the Marc Chagall Museum (*Dom-muzej Marka Shagala*) opened in the house in which the artist had spent his childhood.

Bibliography

Sources

[1] M. Chagall, Di shtot di vayte [The Town so Distant], in: Di goldene keyt [The Golden Chain] 60 (1967), 92f.   [2] M. Chagall, My Life, Scranton, PA 1960.   [3] M. Chagall, My Own World, in: B. Harshav, Marc Chagall and His Times. A Documentary Narrative, Stanford 2004, 85–166.   [4] S. Ejzenshtejn, Vitebsk 1920 goda [Vitebsk in 1920], in: I. A. Vakar/T. N. Mikhienko (eds.), Malevich o sebe. Sovremenniki o Maleviche [Malevich on Himself. Contemporaries on Malevich], Vol. 2, Moscow 2004, 345f.

Secondary literature

[5] I. Dukhan, El Lissitzky and the Search for New Jewish Art (Vitebsk – Moscow – Berlin), in: J. Malinowski (ed.), Jewish Artists and Central-Eastern Europe, Warsaw 2010, 291–298.   [6] B. Harshav, Marc Chagall and His Times. A Documentary Narrative, Stanford 2004.   [7] H. Kazovskij, Masterpieces of Jewish Art. Artists from Vitebsk, Moscow 1992 [Russ./Eng.].   [8] S. Koller, Marc Chagall. Grenzgänge zwischen Literatur und Malerei, Cologne et al. 2012.   [9] A. S. Shatskich, "Blagosloven bud', moj Vitebsk." Ierusalim kak proobraz shagalovskogo goroda ["Blessed are You, My Vitebsk." Jerusalem as Prototype of the City in Chagall's Work], in:

M. B. Mejlakh/D. V. Sarab'yanov, Poeziya i zhi-
vopis'. Sbornik trudov pamyati N. I. Khardzhieva
[Poetry and Art. Anthology in Memory of N. I.
Khardzhiev], Moscow 2000, 260–268.   [10] A. S.
Shatskich, Vitebsk. Zhizn' iskusstva 1917–1922
[Vitebsk. Life of the Art 1917–1922], Moscow
2001.   [11] A. Zel'tser, Yevrei sovetskoj provincii.
Vitebsk i mestechki 1917–1941 [Jews of the Soviet
Province. Vitebsk and the Surrounding Shtetls
1917–1941], Moscow 2006.

SABINE KOLLER, REGENSBURG

Völkerpsychologie

A term contained in the title of the *Zeitschrift für Völkerpsychologie und Sprachwissenschaft*, founded in 1860 by Moritz
Lazarus (1824–1903) and Chajim Heymann
Steinthal (1823–1899), and a key concept in
a comprehensive sociopsychological scientific ideal, which sought to investigate the
cultural imprint of the individual through
language and society. Their approach was
focused on a theory of modernity and is not
to be confused with the dichotomous char-
acterology of peoples and nations that was
dealt with under the same term in the early
20th century.

1. A forgotten journal
2. Moritz Lazarus and Heymann Steinthal
3. Inside and outside at the same time: towards
    universal linguistics
4. Contrasting connections

1. A forgotten journal

The *Zeitschrift für Völkerpsychologie und
Sprachwissenschaft* was published beginning in 1860, for a period of thirty years, in
a total of twenty issues. With this journal,
its founders Lazarus and Steinthal created
an intellectual forum in which they brought
their insightful questions and psychological
interests into a universal historical context.

Contrary to what seems implied by the
term in the title, both scholars were not
concerned with typological or antagonistic differences between peoples or states,
although they were interested in sociological and cultural differences between collective milieus and experience.

From the viewpoint of the history of
ideas, their basic assumptions followed
the linguistic studies of Johann Gottfried
Herder (→ Orient), Wilhelm von Humboldt,
and the developmental psychologist Johann
Friedrich Herbart, and were based on the
idea of "multiplicity," which they transferred
to the overarching theme of the sociopsychological relations between collectivity
and the individual. Lazarus's ideal in political science was the universal-historical and
legal equality of all human beings. He also
defended this in debates on → emancipation, and in his struggle against antisemitism (→ Conspiracy; → Berlin Debate on
Antisemitism). While a student in a gymnasium, in 1845 he wrote to his cousin that
when studying the past it always seemed to
him, "as if the overall spirit of all mankind
were a single spirit" [13. vol. 1, 7]. Steinthal
was close to this optimism, but at the same
time was also committed to protecting difference and → alterity. Both understood
their journal as the ideal forum in which this
constitutive, irresolvable tension between
the two basic values of modernity could be
resolved.

The numerous studies by the two founders published in the journal provide a precise impression of the basic concepts of
Völkerpsychologie. Lazarus wrote "Über
den Ursprung der Sitten" (1860), "Über das
Verhältnis des Einzelnen zur Gesamtheit"
(1862), the studies "Verdichtung des Denkens in der Geschichte" (1862) and "Über
die Ideen in der Geschichte" (1865). No less
eloquent are the titles of Steinthal's essays.
In the first issue, he came to the fore with
"Assimilation und Attraktion, psycholo-
gisch betrachtet" (1860), while in the second

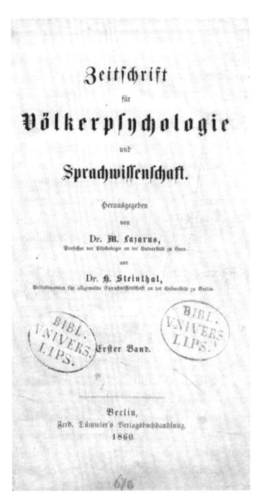

Titel page of the Zeitschrift für Völkerpsychologie und Sprachwissenschaft *(1860), edited by Moritz Lazarus and Chajim Heymann Steinthal*

volume he introduced the terms "fusion," "interconnection," and "apperception" which are typical of early Völkerpsychologie. The editors also gave fundamental expression to the approach and program of their journal; for instance, right from the opening volume, with their text "Einleitende Gedanken über Völkerpsychologie und Sprachwissenschaft" (1860), and soon afterward, with "Einige synthetische Gedanken zur Völkerpsychologie" (1865). At the center of their Völkerpsychologie was the individual appropriation of the "objective spirit" of the given material and ideal culture.

The textual corpus, many thousand pages long, that emerged under the title "Völkerpsychologie" is a unique document of scholarly → enlightenment. According to Heymann Steinthal, following the model of the French *Journal des débats*, there was to be room in the journal for "all that is human" [13. vol.. 2/2, 383]. Both subjects and authorship were, accordingly, highly diverse. Thus, Adolf Bastian, the ethnologist and founding director of the Königliche Museum für Völkerkunde (Royal Museum for Ethnology) in Berlin, set forth his theory of "Völkergedanken" or "elementary ideas" ("Zur vergleichenden Psychologie," 1868), which emphasized the unity of the human mind across all temporal and geographical borders. The epistemologist Wilhelm Windelband ("Die Erkenntnislehre unter dem völkerpsychologischen Gesichtspunkte," 1875) and the philosopher Wilhelm Dilthey ("Über die Einbildungskraft der Dichter," 1878) also published in it, along with contributions by Lazarus's student, the neo-Kantian Hermann Cohen (→ Concept of God), the Islamologist Ignaz Goldziher (→ Muslim Studies), and works by Georg Simmel (→ Sociology; → Type). The editors solicited articles on the history of religion, → ethics, logic, empiricism, and the philosophy of history, and commisioned works on → sermons and homiletics, as well as on notions of fate in various parts of the world and epochs. Following Herder, they were interested in folk songs, but also in ancient rituals and, generally, in questions of cult and all forms of folk beliefs and superstitions. In the journal, they devoted just as much attention to the idea of → science as to the history of individual sciences and disciplines, such as → chemistry or physics. They were particularly interested in the meaning of feeling, emotion, and intuition; psychology, therefore, featured most prominently. There were also essays on aesthetic → phenomenology and the cultural significance of beauty and ugliness, comedy and fear. Every kind of human objectivation, whether books or social studies, works of → art or proverbs,

→ architecture or → music, aroused the editors' interest. Thus, the contents of the journal broadened to the borders of the known, investigated geography and ethnography, and traditional travelogues of festivals, dances, costumes, ceremonies, and masks, on measures and → numbers, the → calendar, and time reckoning of other peoples could also be read here.

However, the journal was not destined for lasting fame. The Leipzig-based physician, philosopher, and psychologist Wilhelm Wundt (1832–1920), for instance, registered the "most serious hesitations" with regard to the wide-ranging approach [17. 43], but adopted the title term "Völkerpsychologie" for his own four-volume magnum opus. In 1891, Lazarus and Steinthal ended their activity as editors and handed over the journal to their successors, who renamed the periodical *Zeitschrift des Vereins für Volkskunde*. Only a few years later, its founders' cultural model, social doctrine, and image of humankind had become outmoded. In 1916, the historian Georg von Below (1858–1927) remarked that when reading Lazarus and Steinthal, one "could not help but smile" [1. 432]. And even Martin Buber (→ Dialogue), who had attended Wundt's lectures on Völkerpsychologie in the winter semester of 1897/1898, retrospectively called Lazarus merely "a clever and amiable popular philosopher" [2. 146].

2. Moritz Lazarus and Heymann Steinthal

The works of Lazarus and Steinthal on Völkerpsychologie were based not only on scholarship but also on the German-Jewish constellation in the age of → emancipation [18. XLVI]. Studies have often and rightly interpreted Lazarus-Steinthalian Völkerpsychologie as a striking example of the influence of the lebenswelt (world of lived experience) on the formation of theories and as the academicization of a Jewish experience [23]; [22. 86]; [24. 4]; [19].

Heymann Steinthal was born in 1823 to a family of merchants in Gröbzig, near Dessau (Anhalt); Lazarus a year later as the son of a merchant and Talmud teacher in Filehne, a small village in the province of → Poznań. In reminiscences of their childhood, both told of how their intellectual development was marked by the lebenswelt of their native villages, characterized by a mixture of religions and plurality of languages. Steinthal remembered his experiences in the Jewish elementary school in Dessau and pointed to the eminent importance of the languages which he had to master as a young boy in order to open up intermediate spaces of affiliation for himself. He spoke of often switching between languages in his everyday life at school, on the street, and at home, where – according to his environment and situation – he had to speak either the local dialect, → Yiddish, moderate Yiddish, or → German; he also learned → Hebrew [15. 290] in class. Lazarus called the difference and coexistence of the three religious communities in Filehne (Catholics, Protestants, and Jews) "the deepest root of Völkerpsychologie" [8. 32]. As he later recalled, the key moment of his childhood was his entry into the linguistic and intellectual traditions of his homeland. Soon after they were granted legal equality, the Jews had "attained the henceforth inseparable unity of the national soul of the German people with unprecedented energy" and had become "receptive of, and at home in, German arts and sciences" [6. 21f.]. In the gymnasium, Lazarus came to know the works of Herbart, which strongly influenced his thought. In the early 1850s, he worked on a treatise on Spinoza (→ Tractatus Theologico-Politicus); Steinthal, too, called called himself a "Spinozist" [13. vol. 2/2, 408f.]. Both, however, reserved their greatest veneration for the works of Humboldt, on whom Steinthal, for instance, worked throughout his life, for instance in *Die Sprachwissenschaft Wilhelm von Humboldts und die*

Hegel'sche Philosophie (1848), *Die Classifika-tion der Sprachen* (1850), and *Die sprachphi-losophischen Werke Wilhelm von Humboldts* (1884).

Whereas Steinthal was a scholar who shied away from publicity, Lazarus considered himself to be a representative of the rights and demands of assimilated, acculturated German Jewry. In the early 1880s he spoke out prominently against Treitschke in the → Berlin debate on antisemitism. Although Steinthal also suffered from neglect in the university environment and from the antisemitic hostilities of his time, his ambitions remained of the academic variety, and he saw himself as a "historian of our science" [13. vol. 2/2, 405]. Both thinkers considered letters to be the most important medium of reflection; they felt their correspondence between each other and with third parties as their "true vital element" [13. vol. 1, 304]. Their substantive connection was reinforced by family ties: in 1863, Steinthal married Lazarus's sister Jeanette (1840–1925).

In addition to considerations of assimilation and independence, language and thought, religion and modernity, it was a reflection on the diasporic *conditio* of Judaism and on antisemitism (→ Conspiracy) that gave 19th century Völkerpsychologie its intellectual form. Lazarus, for instance, experienced the specificity of the Jewish lebenswelt as a prism that enabled particularly colorful observations. In his lecture "Was heißt und zu welchem Ende studiert man jüdische Geschichte und Litteratur" (1900) he made use of this metaphor from optical physics to explain the relevance of Völkerpsychologie studies for Jewish history and culture: "Because of its interweaving with very different cultures, the refraction of Judaism is much more variegated than that of the Jewish religion. Here there are many interesting tasks of the Völkerpsychologie, which the Jewish lineage, more than any other lineage of the human race,

provokes" [7. 20]. Steinthal also saw knowledge of Völkerpsychologie outlined in the example of the Jews and summarized the collective history of the Jews in the image of the *Bildungsroman* (coming-of-age-novel): "The Jews are truly God's chosen people, for where has a people been educated as they have! First a willfully disobedient child, who neither understands nor obeys (the Age of the Prophets), then a ignorant boy, who prides himself on that which he has learned (Purim); then a hot-blooded but still uneducated youth (Age of the Maccabees and the Romans), finally, in the Middle Ages, it becomes a man of pervasive hardness and softness; studies and experience produce a character and a soul" [13. vol. 1, 306].

Between cultural "intensification" and "alignment" to the language and culture of Germany, and the "apperception" (perception, but also a conscious assumption of the unknown) of the new period, both scholars repeatedly felt a crisis in Judaism. "Now, I am often overcome by fear (or rather, others frighten me)," Steinthal wrote to Lazarus, "that there is no more strength left in the Jews, no living Jewish general spirit" [3. vol. 1, 330]. In 1890, he observed, with regard to the "Jewish question" that was being widely discussed: "The Jew cannot be a noncommissioned officer, says the major: well then, no. He cannot be a full professor, says Treitschke; well then, no. What can he be? Well, no one can prevent him from being a competent man. Thus, let him strive to become one. [...] Whatever nation I belong to, that is completely my business" [13. vol. 2/1, 303f.]. For the generation of the children of Steinthal and Lazarus, this conviction, expressed entirely in the awareness of the 19th century, no longer held true. Whereas the fathers died a natural death, respected and advanced in age, at the end of a still-peaceful Saeculum in March 1899 and 1903, the daughter Irene Steinthal, born in 1873, was murdered at → Auschwitz in 1943, at the age of 70.

3. Inside and outside at the same time: towards universal linguistics

The true point of convergence of all themes dealt within the journal was language, which, for Lazarus and Steinthal, was not one object among others, but rather the medium of knowledge itself. It forms the individual from within, molds the individual's thinking and ethical standards, and, as a social bond, ensures the mutual connection of human beings. On the occasion of a possible lengthy stay in China, Steinthal wrote in this sense: "Moreover, I also believe that I shall, so to speak, be able to to get a better look inside the heads of the Chinese when I am among them; that, by means of innocuous questions, I can bring forth from them what they think when they speak, what they feel in the the process; what categorical movement takes place in them" [13. vol. 1, 286]. Language could be used to investigate diachronic-historical questions as well as to make synchronic comparisons between groups and types. In addition, language was also the model for the fundamental historicization that was also advocated by Lazarus as the co-founder of the → Wissenschaft des Judentums. Steinthal once got to the heart of the matter when he wrote: "For me, religion is just as subject to a historical process of becoming as is language, morality, science, and art" [13. vol. 2/2, 302]. Mankind, including Lazarus, is a "historical being," and no word nor idea is spoken or thought that is not "dependent on historical conditions that are infinitely varied in their derivation" [10. 109]. All of the key concepts of early Völkerpsychologie – circulation, diversity, spirit, intensification, interweaving, knowledge, and apperception – become historically visible and recognizable in and through language. The theorem of the "intensification of thought in history" enabled scholars to grasp history, things, and everyday phenomena of all kinds as "products" of the spirit, or objectivations of a linguistic genius (the weekly market as much as a constitution or → literature).

One finds in the journal not only works on lexis and phonetics, on grammar and morphology, but also on usage and the meaning of the subjunctive, as well as on the origin, use, and acquisition of meaning of metaphors. Above all, however, the subject was hermeneutics, semantics and pragmatics, and the difference between everyday, group, and technical language, vernacular and dialect: that is, everything that is today summed up under sociolinguistics. Language also included communication and body language, a semiotics of human expression such as facial expression, gestures, and blushing. More than anything else, however, it was the philosophy of language that interested both editors. Following Humboldt, Steinthal simply called the connection between language and → philosophy "philosophical linguistics," which he considered the "most noble matter" of all [13. vol. 2/2. 405]. Furthermore, by means of language, it was possible to formulate the degree of belonging, that had unlimited validity for the Jewish minority without forcing them to renounce themselves. Lazarus wrote the oft-quoted sentence: "The German language is our mother tongue, the German nation is our fatherland as we speak and think in German, as our soul is filled and formed by German poetry and science: thus, we work with spirit and heart, as much as our strength allows, on German works: the greatness, loftiness, and power of the German nation is the yearning of our minds" [5. 19f.]. As early as the beginning of the 20th century, this emphatic invocation of → German had lost much of its power of persuasion (→ Critique of Language).

To be sure, Lazarus and Steinthal themselves chose an idealistic language for their undertaking, but they were not enthusiasts. In his famous interjection "Was heißt national?" (1880) Lazarus interpreted antisemitism as the expression of a mental denial of reality on the part of its spokesmen, castigated the "entire theory of race and blood" as "the outflow of the gross materialism of the outlook on the world and life" [9. 24, 32] and had written: "There is no nationality whatsoever that is pure and unmixed in its origins." Unlike the ethnography of the early 20th century, Lazarus did not consider the "people" as an ontological or natural entity, but as the spiritual result of a lasting, dynamic process: "The spirit of a people creates the conception, and hence also the reality, of a people" [9. 24].

4. Contrasting connections

In the early 20th century, Ferdinand Tönnies still included Völkerpsychologie in the history of sociology [16], as a matter of course. Soon, however, the history of science and the history of ideas split into two divergent lines: one continued the work of Lazarus and Steinthal, often rather implicitly; while the other, abandoning the sociological and language theoretical path, developed a "characterological" approach and was soon assigned to ethnography, ethnology, and → anthropology.

The substrate of Lazarus's and Steinthal's ideas did not live on in the form of the term that they had made known, but was scattered in quite different fields of knowledge, often outside of Germany and not infrequently with a completely different terminology. Early Völkerpsychologie exhibits echoes of the writings on cultural psychology by Sigmund Freud (→ Psychoanalysis) and the theme of the dissertation by Erich Fromm, written under the direction of Alfred Weber, *Das jüdische Gesetz. Zur Soziologie des Diaspora-Judentums* (1922); it inspired language theoretical, philosophical, and sociopsychological figures of thought by Ernst Cassirer (→ Philosophy of Culture), Hermann Cohen (→ Concept of God), and Norbert Elias (→ Civilizing Process), and it paved the way for essential aspects of the structuralism of Ferdinand de Saussure and Maurice Halbwachs's theory of memory.

In → sociology, Völkerpsychologie was continued in France primarily by Émile Durkheim, and in Germany, mainly by Georg Simmel (→ Type). The former replaced the guiding concept with social psychology, thereby offering a more adequate one that has remained current until today. The latter formulated his sociological thesis of the "hybridization of social circles" in literal connection with Lazarus and declared his indebtedness to his teacher in personal correspondence, but did not make the importance Lazarus had for his thought as evident in his published works [25].

The "characterological" line of reception developed in an opposite direction. It took over the term for its ethnographic perspective on human culture but filled it with different contents. Especially around the time of the First World War, there was a wide range of ideological literature that understood Völkerpsychologie as a collective *Wesensschau* (intuition of essences and essential structures) and antagonistic *Volkscharakterologie* (national psychology), as in the two-volume work entitled *Die Amerikaner. Eine Studie der Völkerpsychologie* (1913) by Maurice A. Law, Werner Sombart's war pamphlet *Händler und Helden* (1915; "Traders and Heroes," 2021), or Ernst Troeltsch's (→ Secularization) *Das Wesen der Deutschen* (1915). The aforementioned Wilhelm Wundt was midway between both conceptions. He was still a cultural and linguistic psychologist and researcher of morals and customs, but in 1920, in keeping with the *zeitgeist*, he contrasted the Western European "utilitarian morality" and the German "morality of conscience." The academic supporters of the Nazi regime in particular – such as Hans F. K. Günther, Max Hildebert Boehm (→ European Congress of Nationalities), Egon von Eickstedt, or Friedrich Keiter – understood Völkerpsychologie as the determination of collective entities, whose history of origin and differentiation were to be researched. Thus, they actuated the physiognomy of peoples and "ethnopolitics," whether through cultural-historical reversions to early and primeval eras, or in the style of natural sciences, in which the notions of heredity and → "race" had been dominant since the 1930s and 1940s. The long-lived German line of tradition, which, under the heading "Völkerpsychologie," subsumed and rationalized all that which allegedly separated human groups from one another in a categorial-natural way, extends down to the most recent present.

Exceptions in the reception history of Völkerpsychologie include *Die Psychologie des jüdischen Geistes. Zur Völker- und Kulturpsychologie* (1913) by the Zionist Samuel Max Melamed and *Die Seelen der Völker. Ihre Eigenarten und Bedeutung im Leben der Völker* (1920) by the Russian-Jewish sociologist Elias Hurwicz. Melamed wrote his pamphlet explicitly against Houston Stewart Chamberlain's *Die Grundlagen des 19. Jahrhunderts* (1899; "The Foundations of the 19th Century," 1912) and Werner Sombart's *Die Juden und das Wirtschaftsleben* (1911; "The Jews and Modern Capitalism," 1913). However, he also sought to defend his interest in "differences in the dispositions of consciousness" [14. V] against the "antisemitic fables about ritual murders [...] in the jargon of national economics" [14. IX]. Hurwicz, who came from Kiev to Berlin in 1905, where he obtained his doctorate in law, wrote against the prejudice of his time and especially against the identification of Judaism with Bolshevism. Thus, he polemicized against Oswald Spengler and his work, which, he claimed, was "full of the most bizarre conceptual shifts" [3. 59]. Hurwicz also sharply rejected the Sombart's book on economics, describing its kind of → statistics as "a numerical creature" and "phantom" and as a procedure that was only ostensibly exact and must "be considered a failure" [4. 126]. During his time in Berlin

in the 1920s, Hurwicz also translated works by Simon Dubnow into German, and published his autobiography *Mein Leben* in 1937 (→ Weltgeschichte).

Overall, however, his book *Die Seelen der Völker* was no mere journalistic protest, but a wide-ranging, learned treatise, which explicitly followed Lazarus and Steinthal. Like them, he understood Völkerpsychologie as "the psychic differences between peoples" not without their plurality and universality. Like his role models, he accepted differences and sought to historically justify them. Ultimately, he admitted that there was something hidden in the psyche of a people "that could not be completely analyzed into individual elements, nor could it be deduced from them," and that researchers must recognize this [4. 86]. According to Hurwicz, this type of Völkerpsychologie was "in the tradition of classical German philosophy" and was "the opposite of chauvinism." The only law of nature that Elias Hurwicz accepted was that of "differentiation." Therefore, the author provided his text with a plea for "psychological tolerance" and advocated "the coexistence of different collective-psychological units" [4. 155]. It is significant that he concluded with Goethe (→ Elective Affinities) "who coined the phrase that the whole truth is not given to an individual people, but to the whole of mankind" [4. 154].

Bibliography

Sources

[1] G. v. Below, Untitled [Literary Report], in: Vierteljahrsschrift für Sozial- und Wirtschaftsgeschichte 13 (1916), 430–437. [2] M. Buber, The Martin Buber Reader. Essential Writings, ed. by A. D. Biemann, New York 2002. [3] E. Hurwicz, Völkerpsychologie, in: Der Jude 5 (1920) 1, 57–59. [4] E. Hurwicz, Die Seelen der Völker. Ihre Eigenarten und Bedeutung im Völkerleben. Ideen zu einer Völkerpsychologie, Gotha 1920. [5] M. Lazarus, Unser Standpunkt. Zwei

Reden, Berlin 1881. [6] M. Lazarus, An die deutschen Juden, Berlin 1887. [7] M. Lazarus, Was heisst und zu welchem Ende studirt man jüdische Geschichte und Litteratur? Ein Vortrag, Leipzig 1900. [8] M. Lazarus, Aus meiner Jugend. Autobiographie, Frankfurt am Main 1913. [9] M. Lazarus, Was heißt national? Ein Vortrag, Berlin 1925. [10] M. Lazarus, Grundzüge der Völkerpsychologie und Kulturwissenschaft, ed. by K. C. Köhnke, Hamburg 2003. [11] M. Lazarus, Ueber das Verhältniß des Einzelnen zur Gesammtheit, in: M. Lazarus, Grundzüge der Völkerpsychologie und Kulturwissenschaft, ed. by K. C. Köhnke, Hamburg 2003, 39–129. [12] M. Lazarus, Verdichtung des Denkens in der Geschichte, in: M. Lazarus, Grundzüge der Völkerpsychologie und Kulturwissenschaft, ed. by K. C. Köhnke, Hamburg 2003, 27–38. [13] M. Lazarus/H. Steinthal, Die Begründer der Völkerpsychologie in ihren Briefen, ed. by I. Belke, 2 vols., Tübingen 1971/83. [14] S. M. Melamed, Die Psychologie des jüdischen Geistes. Zur Völker- und Kulturpsychologie, Berlin 1913. [15] H. Steinthal, Über Juden und Judentum, ed. by G. Karpeles, Berlin ³1925. [16] F. Tönnies, Die Entwicklung der Soziologie in Deutschland im 19. Jahrhundert, in: Entwicklung der deutschen Volkswirtschaftslehre im 19. Jahrhundert. Gustav Schmoller zur siebzigsten Wiederkehr seines Geburtstages dargebracht in Verehrung von A. P. Altmann (et al.), Leipzig 1908, 1–42. [17] W. Wundt, Völkerpsychologie. Ein Reader, ed. by C. Schneider, Göttingen 2008.

Secondary literature

[18] I. Belke, Einleitung, in: M. Lazarus/H. Steinthal, Die Begründer der Völkerpsychologie in ihren Briefen, vol. 1, Tübingen 1971, XIII–CXLII. [19] M. Berek, Neglected German-Jewish Visions for a Pluralistic Society. Moritz Lazarus, in: Leo Baeck Institute Year Book 60 (2015), 1–15. [20] E. Beuchelt, Ideengeschichte der Völkerpsychologie, Meisenheim 1974. [21] G. v. Graevenitz, Verdichtung. Das Kulturmodell der "Zeitschrift für Völkerpsychol-

ogie und Sprachwissenschaft," in: Kea 12 (1999), 19–57. [22] U. Jensen, Gebildete Doppelgänger. Bürgerliche Juden und Protestanten im 19. Jahrhundert, Göttingen 2005. [23] I. Kalmar, The "Völkerpsychologie" of Lazarus and Steinthal and the Modern Concept of Culture, in: Journal of the History of Ideas 48 (1987), 671–690. [24] E. Klautke, The Mind of the Nation. Völkerpsychologie in Germany, 1851–1955, New York/Oxford 2013. [25] K. C. Köhnke, Der junge Simmel – in Theoriebeziehungen und sozialen Bewegungen, Frankfurt am Main 1996. [26] H. Wiedebach/A. Winkelmann, Chajim H. Steinthal. Sprachwissenschaftler und Philosoph im 19. Jahrhundert / Chajim H. Steinthal. Linguist and Philosopher in the 19th Century, Leiden et al. 2002.

Nicolas Berg, Leipzig

Voskhod

Title of a Jewish monthly journal in → Russian founded by Adolf Landau, which was published in St. Petersburg from 1881 to 1906, that reported on Jewish history and literature as well as contemporary developments of Judaism in the Diaspora. The moderately nationalist *Voskhod* (Sunrise) saw itself as a bridge between Russian and Jewish culture. It repeatedly came into conflict with Russian censorship, not least because of the reports on → pogroms and anti-Jewish regulations (→ May Laws).

1. Publication history
2. Editors and contributors
3. Topics
4. Russian censorship

1. Publication history

In October 1880 the publisher Adolf Landau (1842–1902) was granted permission to transform the annual series *Yevrejskaya biblioteka* (Jewish library), which he had been editing since 1871, into a Russian language monthly. From early 1881 onward, the journal appeared under the title *Voskhod* subtitled *Zhurnal uchyono-literaturnyj i politicheskij* (Journal for science, literature, and politics), in St. Petersburg. In view of the → pogroms that followed the assassination of Czar Alexander II, in June 1881 Landau applied for permission to publish a weekly supplement that appeared under the title *Nedel'naya khronika Voskhoda* (Weekly chronicle of *Voskhod*) the following year, focusing more strongly on current political developments. In addition to the short-lived magazines → *Rassvet* (Dawn, 1879–1883) and *Russkij yevrej* (The Russian Jew, 1879–1884), *Voskhod* became the most significant and, in fact between 1885 and 1889, the only Jewish periodical in → Russian, exerting considerable influence on the acculturated Russian-Jewish elite.

A semi-annual subscription to the voluminous *Voskhod* was priced at six rubles, a yearly subscription at ten rubles. Sales figures rose from 2,300 issues in 1882 to over 3,900 in 1893; by 1895 almost 4,400 subscribers received the journal, most of whom were living in Kiev, Kherson, and St. Petersburg [5. 14]. It thus reached the majority of the Russian educated elite and the → maskilim.

Due to illness, Landau was unable to be present for long periods of time, and in the mid-1890s, the physician Samuel Grusenberg took over the editorship. In 1899 Landau sold the journal to the lawyer and journalist Maximilian G. Syrkin, who acted as its editor from then on. From the eleventh issue of that year, the increasingly literary-scholarly monthly was published under the title *Knizhki Voskhoda* (Books of the *Voskhod*) but retained its previous subtitle. The title *Voskhod* was transferred to the journal's supplement which appeared as a weekly publication until 1906 and even twice weekly between 1899 and 1902.

2. Editors and contributors

Born in 1842 in Rossieny (Kovno Governorate, today Raseinai in Lithuania), Landau graduated from the rabbinical seminary in → Vilna in 1862, where he wrote his first contributions on Jewish topics for Russian-language journals such as → *Rassvet* and *Sion* (Zion). Subsequently he studied law in St. Petersburg. From 1871 onward, Landau edited the series *Yevrejskaya biblioteka* containing historical and literary papers written by members of the → Haskalah; in 1873 he founded his own publishing house. With regard to content, Landau championed the → emancipation of Russian Jews, supporting their being granted equal status in the state while retaining their Jewish religion and tradition [2. XLVIf.]. He acknowledged contemporary societal developments while likewise defending the Jewish people's ethical principles and spiritual heritage. He rejected the emigration to Palestine promoted by associations (→ Aliyah; → Hoveve Tsiyon) as well as the idea of *Palestinofil'stvo* (Palestinophilia) embraced by the publishers of *Rassvet*.

In the 1890s *Voskhod*'s thematic focus was increasingly influenced by a younger generation of Russian Jewish intellectuals, among them the lawyers and politicians Leon Bramson (→ ORT) and Maksim Vinaver (→ Duma), the physician Julius Davidovich Brutzkus, and the historians Alexander Isayevich Braudo, Solomon Posener, and Shaul Ginsburg. In addition, the historian Simon Dubnow (→ Riga; → Weltgeschichte), the Orientalist Avraam Garkavi (Abraham Harkavy), the lawyers Mikhail G. Morgulis and Mikhail Kulisher, and the author Rashel Khin also wrote for the journal. Over time, Leib Yaffe, Hayim Nahman Bialik (→ El hatsippor; → Kishinev; → Lamentation), Saul Tchernikhovsky (→ Poetry; → Sonnet), and Semyon Yushkevich became regular authors as well.

3. Topics

The contributions in *Voskhod*, as well as its supplement, advocated the civil and political equality of the Russian Jews, and, to this end, supported initiatives for the dissemination of the → Haskalah and universal education (→ Bildung) and for the transformation of employment structures (→ Professions). *Voskhod* itself was divided in two sections: one containing scholarly essays, research reports, → novels, and → poetry; the other containing reviews, compilations of → Yiddish, → Hebrew, and → Russian recent publications, reports from correspondents from various countries, and discussions on the political situation of the Jews. Subjects ranged from → Bible translations and biographical studies on famous Jews to detailed analyses of the living conditions in the → Pale of Settlement and of anti-Jewish ordinances (→ May Laws). Several articles criticized the negative image of Jews in Russian society but also polemicized against Zionism (→ Basel) and emigration to Palestine (→ Aliyah). Nevertheless, articles on the subject of emigration were also included in *Voskhod*.

Under Syrkin as its new editor and as a weekly journal beginning in 1899, *Voskhod* introduced new sections for reviews, accounts of Jewish community life, and → folklore, as well as of Russian laws applying to Jews. In addition a press review focused on developments in the global Jewish → Diaspora. Permanent foreign correspondents for the journal were, among others, Simon Rapoport from → London, Isaac Max Rubinow from → New York, and Menashe Meyerovitch (Meerovitch) from Palestine.

In view of discrimination and anti-Jewish violence, the new editorial team regarded Zionism more positively overall but still did not see emigration to Palestine as the solution of the "Jewish question."

A growing number of articles in *Voskhod* promoted emigration to America. Aḥad Ha-Am (→ Cultural Zionism; → Odessa), Israel Zangwill (→ Melting Pot), and Arthur Ruppin (→ Brit Shalom; → Palestine Office; → Statistics) engaged in heated debates on issues of Jewish national life in the journal. The conflict between Diaspora nationalists and Zionists led to a parting of the ways in 1904; Ginsburg, Brutzkus, and Miron Davidovich Ryvkin, who favored Zionism, left the editorial board. From then on, the management of the journal was in the hands of the champions of greater assimilation; led by the future chairman of the → Jewish Society for History and Ethnography (*Yevrejskoe istoriko-etnograficheskoe obshchestvo*) Maksim Vinaver, they maintained close ties with liberal Russian circles [6. 174].

One of the core topics from the 1890s onward was the education of the younger generation of Jews, who were encouraged to develop close ties to both the Russian state and the Jewish community. The journal championed a contemporary style of Jewish community life with a public presence, striving for general recognition within Russian society through its religious practice as well as its social and charitable commitments [7. 69].

The literary focus of *Voskhod* was on Russian translations of Hebrew and Yiddish works, making it the medium of the mainly still young representatives of Russian Jewish → literature. Nearly all works of Russian Jewish prose and poetry of this period, from Lev Levanda (→ Rassvet) to Vladimir Ze'ev Jabotinsky (→ Altalena), from Yushkevich to Ryvkin, appeared in *Voskhod*. The journal was also open to non-Jewish writers and published contributions by, among others, the critic Vladimir Stasov, the historian Sergei Alexandrovich Bershadsky, and the philosopher Vladimir Solovyov.

During the pogroms of 1881/1882, which dimmed the hopes for an improvement to the situation of the Russian Jews, *Voskhod* supported the Jews of Russia. The journal reported the events, called for the creation of a Jewish self-defense organization, and denounced the authorities as well as those who appeared to look down on their suffering fellow-believers, particularly Western European Jews. *Voskhod* also reported on the expulsion of the Jews from Moscow in 1891, on the → Kishinev pogrom in 1903, and on the wave of pogroms after the defeat in the Russo–Japanese War.

4. Russian censorship

Initially Landau was permitted to print *Voskhod* and *Nedel'naya khronika Voskhoda* without prior inspection by the → censorship authority. Soon, however, disagreements arose with the censors, as the weekly publication in particular repeatedly reported on campaigns directed against anti-Jewish prejudice and laws and criticized the actions of public authorities. Although Landau endeavored to avoid printing overtly critical texts, the Ministry of the Interior issued official warnings against *Voskhod* in 1884 and 1885 [4. 411–414]. After a further warning in 1891, publication was suspended for six months. Once the journal was resumed, the censors monitored the galley proofs, ensuring, above all, that nothing was written about pogroms, anti-Jewish laws, or the Christian religion [8. 97–114].

After the change of editorship, the censorship measures were sharpened once again from 1899 onward. With the founding of the Zionist rival publication *Budushchnost'* (The future, 1899–1904) by Grusenberg, *Voskhod* felt compelled to become more polemical. In November 1901 the censorship authority once again issued a warning. When, in reaction to renewed pogroms, some articles were published in 1903/1904 which accused the authorities of bearing a share of the

responsibility, several issues were confiscated and another six-month publication ban was imposed on the weekly *Voskhod*. Once it reappeared, the journal was subject to pre-censorship and remained subject to official pressure because of continued reports of violence against Jews, such as an article about the Białystok pogroms by S. An-Ski (→ Dybbuk; → Jewish Society for History and Ethnography) [8. 115–125].

The publication of the monthly *Knizhki Voskhoda* stopped in March 1906; the last issue of the weekly *Voskhod* appeared in June of that year. Numerous new Russian-Jewish journals attempted to fill the resulting vacuum, among them the weekly journal *Novyj Voskhod* (New Voskhod), which appeared between 1910 and 1915 and on which some former *Voskhod* editors collaborated.

Bibliography

Sources
[1] Iz pisem A. E. Landau. Materialy dlya istorii "Voskhoda" (1884–1896) [Material from the Letters of A. E. Landau on the History of "Voskhod" (1884–1896)], in: Yevrejskaya starina [Jewish Antiquities] 9 (1916), 102–117. [2] G. Landau, Pamyati A. Landau [In Memory of A. Landau], in: Yevrejskaya biblioteka [Jewish Library] 10 (1902), XVII–LXVI.

Secondary literature
[3] M. Beizer, The Jews of St. Petersburg. Excursions through a Noble Past, Philadelphia/ New York 1989. [4] D. A. Elyashevich, Pravitel'stvennaya politika i yevrejskaya pechat' v Rossii. 1797–1917 [Government Politics and the Jewish Press in Russia, 1797–1917], St. Petersburg/Jerusalem 1999. [5] V. Kelner, Zhurnal "Voskhod" i ego izdatel'-redaktor A. E. Landau [The Magazine "Voskhod" and its Editor A. E. Landau], in: A. R. Rumyantsev (ed.), "Voskhod" – "Knizhki Voskhoda." Rospis' soderzhaniya 1881– 1906 ["Voskhod" – "Knizhki Voskhoda." Table

of Contents 1881–1906], St. Petersburg 2001, 7–43. [6] S. Markish, Voskhod. Glavnyj zhurnal russkogo yevrejstva [Voskhod. The Main Journal of Russian Jewry], in: Cahiers du monde russe et soviétique 28 (1987), 173–182. [7] Y. Slutsky, Ha-itonut ha-yehudit-rusit ba-me'a ha-esrim, 1900–1918 [The Jewish-Russian Newspaper Industry of the 20th Century, 1900–1918], Tel Aviv 1978. [8] A. Strakhova, The Image of America on the Pages of the Russian-Jewish Journal Voskhod (1881–1906), unpublished thesis, Budapest 2013. [9] B. Valdman, Russko-yevrejskaya zhurnalistika (1860–1914). Literatura i literaturnaya kritika [Russian-Jewish Journalism (1860–1914). Literature and Literary Criticism], Riga 2008.

EKATERINA NORKINA, ST. PETERSBURG

W

Wadi Salib

Wadi Salib (Arab.; Valley of the Cross) is originally a poor Muslim neighborhood in the Israeli port of Haifa. Over the course of the 1948 war, the Arab inhabitants either left the district or were expelled from it; afterwards it became home to Jews who had immigrated from North Africa and developed into a focus of social tensions, which came to a head in the summer of 1959 in a series of violent protests. These events raised awareness in Israeli public and political sphere of the socially disadvantaged → Mizraḥim for the first time. Projects to improve the living situation and integrate the recent North African immigrants, however, ignored their cultural characteristics and traditions, consequently revealing the shortcomings of the ethos of modernization embraced by the Ashkenazi political establishment. "Wadi Salib" became a symbol of the internal Jewish intra-ethnic tensions in Israel.

1. The events of 1959
2. Background
3. Afterwards

1. The events of 1959

In the early hours of July 9, 1959, a violent incident occurred in the Haifa neighborhood inhabited mainly by Moroccan Jewish immigrants: a police patrol shot at the drunkenly rampaging David Alkarif, seriously injuring him. This disproportionate violence against an unarmed man led to spontaneous protests by the residents.

During the same night, police were attacked with rocks and a police vehicle destroyed. After the situation temporarily calmed down, more violence erupted the following day. This time, the demonstrators' fury was also directed against the building of the all-powerful labor union Histadrut (→ Davar) and the club of the ruling workers' party Mapai. There was also damage to shops and cafés in the Hadar HaCarmel district located above Wadi Salib, a quarter inhabited by middle-class → Ashkenazim. In the course of the violence, dozens of civilians and police officers were injured; several people were arrested [4. 129].

While the Israeli media did not report on the incidents, news of the events rapidly spread throughout the country, leading to protests and unrest in several cities such as Acre and Tel Hanan. There were demonstrations in some towns including Be'er Sheva and Migdal HaEmek. A demonstration of solidarity planned for July 23 in the Musrara district of Jerusalem was forbidden by the police. On July 24, there were demonstrations against an event organized by Mapai with a view to the elections for the Fourth Knesset due the following November.

On July 31, a Mapai election rally in Haifa once again coincided with violent clashes. Together with the police, members of workers' brigades took action against demonstrators from Wadi Salib. The sixty demonstrators arrested included David Ben-Haroush, born in Casablanca in 1924 and raised there, who was the leader of the Union of North African Immigrants (*Likud Yots'e Tsfon Afrika*) founded only months previously. Further leading activists of the organization were also arrested, namely Ḥaim Mamman, Naftali Sabag, and Yosef Shem-Tov. The Union of North African Immigrants had originally been founded as an apolitical self-help organization but quickly found itself becoming politicized. During the Wadi Salib riots, it called for demonstrations and for the closure of businesses, denouncing the social situation of the → Mizraḥim in the country. Awaiting trial in prison, Ben-Haroush tried to have himself elected to the Knesset but just missed the electoral threshold. In spite of attempts by the Israeli media to present David Ben-Haroush's activities as criminal and not politically motivated, he became a figurehead for the Jews of Moroccan origin.

On July 18, 1959, the government appointed a public commission to investigate the events in Wadi Salib, the findings being published in a report on August 17, 1959. It concluded that the protests had originally been of a spontaneous nature but had subsequently been incited by the Union of North African Immigrants.

2. Background

Wadi Salib had developed in the second half of the 19th century in the vicinity of the port of Haifa. In the 1880s, wealthy Arabs began to build their homes here. After Haifa was linked with the Hijaz Railway (1905) and a railway line to Egypt had been constructed (1918), a railway station and engine repair workshops were built in the immediate vicinity of Wadi Salib, whereupon numerous Arab railway workers settled in the district. In the 1920s and 1930s, the population of Wadi Salib and Haifa in general experienced rapid growth. Its transformation into a British naval base and further large-scale projects such as the construction of an oil refinery and oil transport terminals drew thousands of Arab migrant workers to Haifa. In 1918, the city had had a mere 18,000

Protest in Wadi Salib, 1959

inhabitants, but thanks to its economic attractiveness as well as Jewish immigration from Europe, the population had grown to over 100,000 by 1939. In early 1948, an equal number of Jews and Arabs were living in the city [6. 303].

According to the United Nations Partition Plan of November 29, 1947 (→ Exodus), Haifa was to be part of the Jewish state territory; as a consequence, the Arab population began to leave the city. After the British began to withdraw troops from April 20, 1948 onward, violent clashes between Arab and Jewish armed groups erupted, culminating in a mass flight on April 22, 1948, during which around 15,000 Arab inhabitants left the city. Many of them attempted to reach Nazareth, Jenin, or Nablus via the overland route; others tried to reach Acre or the Lebanese coast by boat. By July 1948, only around 3,500 Arabs were left in Haifa.

At first the abandoned Arab homes were used as housing for Jews from Haifa whose apartments had been damaged in the course of the hostilities. In addition, about 24,000 recent Jewish immigrants settled in Haifa in the months between May 1948 and March 1949 alone, many of them, too, in houses that had been in Arab ownership [6. 304]. There were various reasons for this: there was not enough residential space to accommodate the 687,000 Jews, 331,000 of these from Muslim countries, who had arrived in the country in the course of the mass → Aliyah between 1948 and 1951 [3. 281]. Moreover, the abandoned Arab homes were in the immediate vicinity of the Jewish urban center of Haifa, and new immigrants were deliberately housed there. An additional intention was to prevent the return of the Arabs who had fled.

These measures were given statutory support by emergency regulations enabling the confiscation of real estate for military purposes and so-called security reasons; later they would be used to legalize the acquisition of private property. The Absentees'

Property Law of March 1950 defined absentees as those persons who had been on enemy territory or outside of the mandated territory between December 29, 1947, and September 1, 1948. Their real estate would henceforth be administered by a trustee and transferred to a development agency or to the Jewish National Fund. In Wadi Salib, 394 buildings with 1,754 apartments – the majority of houses in the district – fell to the development agency.

Town planning considerations of early May 1948, which had still assumed the legal return of the Arabs who had previously fled, were now invalid. The original intention had been for Wadi Salib to remain a residential district for Muslim Arabs, while neighboring Wadi Nisnas had been allocated to Christian Arabs. Even so, in the months after the foundation of the State, numerous Jewish immigrants from Europe and North Africa moved to Wadi Salib. Unlike most other places where Arabs had previously lived, it retained its → Arabic name rather than using a Hebraized version (→ Hebrew).

At the beginning of the 1950s, the demographic in Wadi Salib changed once more, when European → Holocaust survivors gradually succeeded in improving their social status and moved to more favorably situated districts. They were at first replaced by destitute Jewish immigrants from Romania and subsequently by increasing numbers of Jews from Morocco (→ Marrakesh; → Tangier). The latter had not been settled in the area by the authorities but moved to Wadi Salib of their own accord. Originally, the plan had been for them, like many other immigrants, to move to newly founded development towns and agricultural settlements on the periphery in accordance with a settlement concept decided by the public planning authority based on an initiative by the architect and town planner Arieh Sharon (1900–1984), who had studied at the Bauhaus in Dessau. The objective of the concept was to take pressure off the conurbations on the coast and to demographically strengthen the peripheral regions of Israel.

This project failed for two reasons. On the one hand, many were put off from settling near the Israeli borders by the tense security situation. On the other hand, the majority of the immigrated North African Jews had been part of the urban population in their countries of origin (→ Mellah). They were not accustomed to life and work in agricultural settlements. Many of them left the places assigned to them and found new homes in the houses left by Arabs in the urban centers – among them Wadi Salib, where around 15,000 inhabitants of nearly exclusively Mizrahi origin lived in confined spaces and exceedingly precarious social conditions in 1959 [1. 63].

The North African immigrants' refusal to work in the agricultural sector strengthened the prejudice against them among the Ashkenazi elite (→ Ashkenazim). In addition, they were inclined to give precedence to immigrants from the states of the then European Eastern Bloc, for fear that these might stop Jews emigrating to Israel at any moment.

At a meeting of the Jewish Agency in March 1952, selective immigration discriminating against → Mizrahim was considered; the latter regarded this as an affront. Many of them had relatives in their countries of origin who were waiting for the requisite emigration documents. In any case, they saw the reason for their marginalization in the Ashkenazi elites' dismissive attitude towards them. Immediately after the foundation of the State, Mizrahim had already drawn attention to their situation through protests, for instance in April 1949 in → Tel Aviv and in May 1956 in the development town of Kiryat Shmona, where an angry mob set fire to the local Mapai offices. The protests that erupted in Wadi Salib soon afterwards brought the ethno-social inequality in Israel to public notice.

3. Afterwards

In its report, the commission of public enquiry convened to investigate the events in Wadi Salib stated a remarkable socio-economic discrepancy in Haifa that was reflected topographically as well as ethnographically. While the lower situated Wadi Salib had the worst results regarding employment figures, living conditions, and level of education (→ Bildung), the financially better-off inhabitants lived in the districts situated higher on the hillside. Although the North African origin of the majority of the socially disadvantaged population groups was noted, members of the commission did not regard the ethno-social inequality as a result of discrimination. The sociologist Shmuel N. Eisenstadt (1923–2010; → Sociology), who led the commission, interpreted the protests as the result of universally existing difficulties in the integration of immigrants from less developed societies, which could be changed only by means of modernizing their lifeworld. Correspondingly, the commission recommended that the living conditions in Wadi Salib should be improved, especially for families with many children who had to live in run-down accommodation in a district without suitable infrastructure. Convinced that social differences could be remedied by means of town planning, the commission recommended unanimously that Wadi Salib be cleared and the inhabitants be provided with state-funded accommodation.

The recommendations of the inquiry commission were quickly implemented, and from 1961 onward, a "public-communal society for restructuring the poor districts of Haifa" ensured that the population of Wadi Salib was housed in a number of publicly-funded residential estates in the city. However, the project could only be partially enacted. Many residents refused to leave their old homes, and as there was no legal basis for forced evacuation, they could not be forced to move elsewhere. In fact, the majority of the inhabitants of Wadi Salib had no interest in accommodation in the publicly funded estates. This was due to some extent to their preference for urban homes but above all to the fact that the resettlement would have entailed the kind of long-term financial commitment incompatible with their insecure labor situation. Those who did accept the offer were greatly disappointed. The apartments did not meet the requirements of their new inhabitants. They were too small for large families, and the surrounding area was not designed to be child-friendly. The religious requirements of the new inhabitants had not been taken into consideration either. The residents were far away not only from their → synagogues but also from the city center and from their sources of income. Above all, however, modern town planning ignored the communal living traditions the immigrants had brought with them from the → mellah of Morocco (→ Marrakesh), a way of life they had preserved in the formerly Arab district of Wadi Salib despite great poverty.

While one of the aims of evacuating the population of Wadi Salib had been to dilute the specifically Moroccan-Jewish affiliation, the opposite was achieved. The nickname "evacuees" would stay with them, hampering the integration process. It was also not possible to renovate the evacuated district and make it fit in with the urban landscape of Haifa. This failure appears rather like a repetition in that a similar plan had already been launched by a so-called Haifa Commission in 1937 under the mandate administration. According to the recommendations of the Peel Comission regarding the partition of Palestine, Haifa was not intended to be part of the future Jewish state. The Haifa Commission planned to move the Arab population of Wadi Salib to an agricultural

area east of the city and to have the evacuated area transformed into a "modern city" by Jewish investors. The mandate administration did not appear interested in this project. During the 1950s, such plans could not be realized because of the disorderly immigration of destitute Jewish immigrants, and in the 1960s the project foundered due to bureaucratic obstacles in state and communal authorities. While political discourse and sociological curiosity focus on the inhabitants of Wadi Salib as objects of research and the status of the district as a symbol of the struggle of → Mizraḥim against Ashkenazi domination (→ Ashkenazim) in Israel grows, it still bears its Arabic name. Consisting of crumbling Arab structures, the district will continue to preserve the memory of its original inhabitants and thus of its Arab past.

Bibliography

[1] S. Chetrit, Intra-Jewish Conflict in Israel. White Jews, Black Jews, London 2010.   [2] B. Morris, The Birth of the Palestinian Refugee Problem Revisited, Cambridge 2004.   [3] S. Smooha, Israel. Pluralism and Conflict, Berkeley 1978.   [4] E. Sprinzak, Brother against Brother. Violence and Extremism in Israeli Politics from Altalena to the Rabin Assassination, New York 1999.   [5] Y. Tzur, The Brief Career of Prosper Cohen. A Sectorial Analysis of the North African Jewish Leadership in the Early Years of Israeli Statehood, in: P. Medding (ed.), Sephardic Jewry and Mizrahi Jews, New York 2007, 66–99.   [6] Y. Weiss, Conflicting Memories, Unrestituted. Wadi Salib as an Israeli Political Metaphor, in: D. Diner/ G. Wunberg (eds.), Restitution and Memory. Material Restoration in Europe, New York 2007, 301–319.   [7] Y. Weiss, A Confiscated Memory. Wadi Salib and Haifa's Lost Heritage, New York 2011.

YFAAT WEISS, JERUSALEM

Warburg Library

Private research institution in Hamburg, Germany, that emerged from the art historian Aby Warburg's (1866–1929) scholarly library and was funded by the Warburg family, who were involved in banking business in Germany and the United States. The Kulturwissenschaftliche Bibliothek Warburg (K.B.W.) had been established with a view to Warburg's research interest – art history with a stronger focus on cultural studies and the → iconology devised by him. In Warburg's library and archive (now in London) there are many indications that one of Warburg's reasons for establishing the institution was to work against the antisemitism of his time by means of cultural politics.

Ever since his 1892 dissertation on Botticelli's *Venus* and *Primavera*, Aby Warburg's research had focused on issues at the center of art historiography of the time – the Italian Renaissance. These were his starting point to opening additional and methodologically new perspectives, which included questions of cultural exchange, the interaction of words and images, the interpretation of the contents of images, and the role classical tradition played for European culture. Before Warburg permanently settled in Hamburg in 1902, he had lived and researched in Florence from 1897. During a journey to the United States in 1895 and 1896, he spent some time visiting the American southwest, meeting the Puebloans and the Hopi, studying their cultic practices and artistic production. This considerable broadening of the range of art history to include the disciplines of religious history, ethnology, and historical and other cultural sciences soon persuaded Warburg, who had almost infinite means to procure books at his disposal, to establish a unique scholarly library.

Even before the First World War it became clear to Warburg that the intended function

The Reading Room of the Kulturwissenschaftliche Bibliothek Warburg in Hamburg, photo of 1926

of the library as a research tool required it be institutionalized. He began to employ assistants and from 1911 onward included the Vienna art historian Fritz Saxl in his plans.

The First World War and Warburg's subsequent mental illness postponed the process to transform the library into an institution. Warburg himself spent time in a number of psychiatric hospitals between 1918 and 1924, among them the Sanatorium Bellevue in Kreuzlingen. Together with the literary scholar Gertrud Bing and with the support of the family, in particular Max M. Warburg, the head of the Hamburg Bank, in 1921 Fritz Saxl undertook the reorganization and gradual opening of the library, which was still in Warburg's private house, to the scholarly community in Hamburg and beyond. In 1924, it comprised 28,000 volumes. Warburg had a separate building erected for the continually expanding library in Heilwigstraße 116, next to the house in which he lived. When it opened to the public in 1926, the K.B.W. was physically visible as an institution as well. The four-story new build had been designed in accordance with Warburg's conception of the classification of knowledge.

The K.B.W.'s declared aim was to research the *nachleben* of classical Antiquity in Europe. Warburg called this task "the problem that commands us" and believed it could be solved by means of a comprehensively informed → iconology in the strict sense. The library reflected this new disposition of knowledge by arranging its holdings in an original and novel way. The great fields of "word," "image," "orientation," and "action" or "dromenon," as the field of history was called, shelved books and separate essays together in a system thought through to the smallest detail, for library users regularly to come across sources they had not actively sought but which gave new impulses to their research. Warburg called this "the law of the good neighbor." Another characteristic of the library was the tension between "Detailforschung" (research focusing on details)

and the great questions on which defining concepts such as "orientation" are based, a tension that also characterizes Warburg's own comparatively slim œuvre.

A considerable part of the success of the K.B.W. in the 1920s was due to the work of Saxl and Bing; they continued to run the library after Warburg's death in 1929. Together with the Warburg family, they also ensured that the collection of books, photographs, and diapositives could be brought to safety in London on two freighters in 1933. This undertaking succeeded thanks to an "Ausleihe" (loan) requested initially for three years from political bodies in Hamburg. In London, donations and the support of influential people meant that the greater part of the library could be resettled; acquiring legal status in 1944 as the Warburg Institute, a foundation of the Warburg family, affiliated to the University of London. In the 1950s, it found its long-term home in a new building on Woburn Square.

During the Weimar Republic, the K.B.W. was part of an intellectual new beginning based on private initiatives trying to react to urgent issues of the postwar years. Among these was the Institut für Auswärtige Politik (Institute for Foreign Policy) in Hamburg, founded in 1923 and co-funded by private parties (especially Max M. Warburg), which was headed by the expert on international law and political scientist Albrecht Mendelssohn-Bartholdy, and the Institut für Sozialforschung (→ Institute for Social Research) in Frankfurt am Main, inaugurated the same year. All those involved in the K.B.W. project worked on increasing the public visibility of the young institution and its perception in a variety of disciplines. The K.B.W. was the venue for the Fourth German Oriental Studies Conference in late September 1926. From 1922/1923 until 1932, the lecture series hosted every winter were published by Saxl under the title *Vorträge der Bibliothek Warburg*; a series of *Studien der Bibliothek Warburg* by authors such as Ernst Cassirer, Erwin

Panofsky, Percy Ernst Schramm, Wilhelm Gundel, Hans Liebeschütz, and Wolfgang Stechow totaled 24 volumes over the same period. Other events with public visibility were exhibitions on subjects researched in the K.B.W., for instance on the part played by astrology in the history of astronomy or on Ovid's *Metamorphoses* as a source of the transmission of ancient topics, which were organized with great enthusiasm. There were regular guided tours of the library for visitors and scholars from out of town. In addition Warburg and Saxl offered seminars at the university's art history department. Plans for the library's own journal were only realized in London in 1937, when the first *Journal of the Warburg Institute* appeared.

Warburg's political beliefs and their connection with his scholarly interests and activities did not receive much attention for decades, not least because he never publicly commented on them. The fact that the K.B.W. had many Jewish employees and that the circle of those interested and involved in it included numerous scholars of Jewish origin was a barely covered subject until the 1990s when the art history department at Hamburg University began to study the exile of German art history and the diary of the K.B.W. was completely edited. Above all, documents in Warburg's archive, which is kept at the Warburg Institute in London, but also his correspondence show that the aims he pursued with his studies and his institute included not only the publicly proclaimed research objectives but also socio-political ones. Thus, there are many references to Warburg – who had dissociated himself from Jewish religious practice early on – being sensitive to all expressions of antisemitism in the German Empire and of documenting them throughout his life. Among the aspects of history of religion, history of ideology, history, and art history, his library contains frequently unexpected material on → anti-Judaism and antisemitism (→ Conspiracy), on the accusation of ritual murder (→ Blood Libel) as well as other elements of enduring anti-Jewish attitudes.

Warburg and many scholars and researchers in the circle of the Warburg Library could hope that their Jewish background would be irrelevant in a modern constitutional state. The achievement of cultural studies was intended to be a contribution to this enlightened and secularized political, scholarly, and scientific culture of the German Empire and the Weimar Republic. By studying atavistic aspects of European culture, such as the belief in astrology, but also the exchange processes at the basis of all cultures, which Warburg emphasized in the context of the threats he clearly perceived in nationalism and racism, he hoped to halt the threat he recognized antisemitism to be. On the occasion of a positive review of the K.B.W.'s publications in the conservative *Süddeutsche Monatshefte*, Warburg wrote a letter to his brothers Max and Fritz characterizing the work of the K.B.W. as a part of the struggle for recognition of the German Jewry. He was confident that his productive and innovative contribution to scholarship in Germany would endure as such.

Bibliography

[1] M. Diers (ed.), Porträt aus Büchern. Bibliothek Warburg & Warburg Institute, Hamburg – 1933 – London, Hamburg 1993 [catalogue]. [2] K. Michels, Die Kulturwissenschaftliche Bibliothek Warburg, in: R. Faber/C. Holste (eds.), Kreise, Gruppen, Bünde. Zur Soziologie moderner Intellektuellenassoziation, Würzburg 2000, 225–238. [3] F. Saxl, A Memoir on the History of the Library, in: E. H. Gombrich, Aby Warburg. An Intellectual Biography, London 1970. [4] C. Schoell-Glass, Aby Warburg and Anti-Semitism: Political Perspectives on Images and Culture, trans. by S. P. Willcocks, Detroit 2008. [5] T. v. Stockhausen, Die Kulturwissenschaftliche Bibliothek Warburg. Architektur, Einrichtung und Organisation, Hamburg 1992. [6] A. Warburg, Tagebuch der Kulturwissenschaftlichen Biblio-

thek Warburg, ed. K. Michels/C. Schoell-Glass, Berlin 2001.

Charlotte Schoell-Glass, Hamburg

Warsaw

Before the Second World War, Warsaw was home to a socio-culturally, denominationally, and politically exceedingly varied Jewish community that was at the same time the largest in Europe. Immediately after the surrender of Poland, the persecution of the Warsaw Jews at the hands of the German occupiers began. In November 1940, the latter closed off several streets in the city center to form the ghetto in which at times up to half a million people were forced to live. Ghetto life was characterized by forced labor, extreme malnutrition, epidemics, smuggling, corruption, the constant threat of persecution, and death. The inhabitants sought to counter this by establishing a well-organized social and cultural life supported by numerous self-help organizations. When mass deportations began in the summer of 1942, Jewish underground fighters prepared for military resistance, culminating in the unparalleled uprising against the German occupants in the spring of 1943.

1. Jewish Warsaw before 1939
2. German occupation
3. The ghetto
3.1 Establishment and administration
3.2 Everyday life
4. Deportations and resistance
5. The Uprising

1. Jewish Warsaw before 1939

Around 370,000 Jews were living in Warsaw in 1938, constituting just under 30% of the total population of the city [2. 15]. They were the largest Jewish community in Europe, and the second largest in the world after → New York. → Polish- and → Yiddish-speaking Jews, followers and opponents of → Hasidism, → Litvaks, an acculturated Jewish → middle class, and also one of the largest concentrations of poor Jews in Europe all came together here.

Warsaw was the religious (→ Tłomackie Synagogue) as well as the economic (→ Nalewki Street) center of Polish Jewry; at the same time, it was the home of numerous charitable organizations and various political trends among Polish Jews. The largest number of Yiddish newspapers in Europe were published here, but also numerous Polish-Jewish ones, such as → *Haynt* (Today), *Der Moment* (The moment), *Dos yudishe togblat* (The Jewish daily paper), *Nasz Przegląd* (Our review), and *Opinia* (Opinion). Jewish representatives in the → Sejm as well as on Warsaw city council – there were twenty Jewish city councilors on this body in 1938 – fought against the rising antisemitism, especially after the death of the state founder Jósef Piłsudski in 1935; however, they had barely any political influence.

2. German occupation

In the course of their invasion of Poland, German troops besieged and shelled Warsaw at the end of September 1939; as members of the Polish armed forces, Jewish soldiers played a part in the defense of the city. On October 4, 1939, the Polish mayor Stefan Bronisław Starzyński appointed the engineer, politician, and Jewish community councilor Adam Czerniaków head of the Jewish community council, replacing Maurycy Mayzel who had fled. While Czerniaków was a practicing Jew, he spoke hardly any → Yiddish and was felt to be distanced and unapproachable by the less affluent majority of Jews in Warsaw.

Shortly after the surrender of Warsaw on September 28, 1939, the occupying forces' persecution of the city's Jews, at that time still around 360,000, began [2. 48]. They were pressed into → forced labor, many of their homes were confiscated, bank accounts were blocked, and companies dispossessed. They were forbidden to travel on long-distance trains and forced to wear a white armband with a blue → Star of David. In October 1939, civilian German authorities took over the administration of Warsaw, which was from then on part of the district of the same name in the newly created General Governorate. Many Warsaw Jews who had fled to the eastern parts of the country, among them a considerable number of members of the political elite, found themselves under Soviet occupation as a result of the invasion of the → Red Army starting in mid-September.

3. The ghetto

3.1 *Establishment and administration*

As early as November 1939, the SS endeavored to contain the Jews in a ghetto; however, the army administration suspended this decree. At the beginning of 1940, the German administration declared an area in the center of Warsaw to be a restricted infected area and ordered walls to be built. This was followed on October 12 by the announcement that a ghetto would be established. 113,000 non-Jewish Poles had to vacate their homes in the area affected, which then took in a further 138,000 Jews [2. 76]. From November 16, 1949, the ghetto was blocked off. Around 380,000 people, around 30% of the population of the city of Warsaw, now crowded into the area, which at first covered 340 hectares – around three percent of the total area of the city. In March 1941, the number of Jews living in the ghetto reached its highest number of 460,000. From among them, the competing German civilian administration and the SS recruited forced laborers for the German war economy sites in the city [3. 63].

As early as October 4, 1939, Czerniaków was ordered by the Gestapo to establish a → Judenrat (Jewish council) with 24 members as the administrative organ of the Warsaw Jews [8]. Among the members of the body were Joseph Jaszuński, director of the Polish → ORT, and the entrepreneur Abraham Gepner. The Judenrat faced titanic challenges from the very first: on the one hand, it had to obey the German instructions on order and hygiene and provide Jewish forced laborers; in addition it was responsible for the police, medical services, and the postal service after the establishment of the ghetto. On the other hand, it faced the necessity of organizing provisions and shelter for the inhabitants of the ghetto. The financial basis was dependent on indirect taxes such as duties on food coupons, burial and hospital fees, and electricity and gas bills. These exacerbated the social inequality in the ghetto as they hit poor Jews hardest, sparing Jews who had become wealthy through speculations and smuggling. The Judenrat grew to include 25 departments with over 6,000 employees [2. 166–190]; [3. 77–94].

One object of particular loathing among the ghetto population was the Jewish Police Service founded in November 1940 independent of the Judenrat. Directly responsible to the Polish police, it was headed by the police major and Catholic convert (→ Conversion) Józef Andrzej Szeryński. Up to 2,000 persons, mainly university-educated middle-class Jews with little affinity for Jewish culture, served in the ghetto police without pay. They soon became notorious because of corruption and arbitrary arrests. In the summer of 1942, the Police Service took an active part in the deportations of Warsaw Jews to → Treblinka [2. 190–216]; [3. 86–90]. In addition, there was a network of spies and collaborators in the ghetto collecting information for different institutions, among them the Gestapo-funded authority to combat usury and speculation known as "Thirteen" (Pol. Trzynastka; Yidd. *Das Draitzental*) after its headquarters at 13 Leszno Street. Led by Abraham Ganzwajch, it competed with the Judenrat and the Jewish police.

3.2 Everyday life

Living conditions in the ghetto proved to be catastrophic for most of the Jews living there. On average, seven persons shared a room, there was a shortage of heating fuel, and the lack of hygiene resulted in typhus epidemics. While Germans and Poles were officially entitled to 2,613 and 699 calories per day respectively, just 184 were allocated to the Jews, which was not enough to survive on [3. 66]. The mortality was particularly high among Jews from the environs of Warsaw who had been relocated by force, of whom there were around 130,000 in April 1941.

The deep social differences were clearly visible in the ghetto. While a small elite lived comparatively well despite the circumstances and around 200,000 Jews were able to get along by selling personal belongings or through work – 70,000 in July 1942 –, the rest faced death from starvation [3. 77]. Desperate children begged for food by the doors of smart restaurants; beggars, the dying, and the dead were part of the streetscape. In May 1942, a kilo of white bread cost 20 złoty, two or three times the daily income of a forced laborer in one of the German factories [2. 434]. In 1941 alone, over 41,000 people died in the ghetto; by the time the mass deportations started in July of the following year, their number had risen to 80,000.

The fact that around 80% of the ghetto inhabitants had survived until then was due to a multifarious underground economy and the efforts of the numerous Jewish self-help organizations as well as the Judenrat. The foundation was a system of smuggling financed in part by the sale of Jewish possessions but also through businesses located in the ghetto exporting goods. In his diary, Czerniaków noted that the ghetto obtained foodstuffs worth 1.8 million złoty legally each month, but 70 to 80 million złoty illegally [2. 457f.].

An important self-help organization that was firmly independent from the Judenrat was the *Yidishe Sotsyale Aleynhilf* (Jewish Social Self-Help; *Aleynhilf* for short), which received support from the American → Joint Distribution Committee until the United States entered the war at the end of 1941. It organized soup kitchens, contact points for newly arrived Jews, as well as facilities for children and adolescents. Among the organizations active under the aegis of the *Aleynhilf* in the ghetto were the Żydowskie Towarzystwo Opieki Społecznej (ŻTOS; Jewish Association for Public Welfare) and the Centralne Towarzystwo Opieki nad Sierotami (CENTOS; Central Office for the Care of Orphans), which worked with the Judenrat and the Jewish Police Service to help street children and ran children's homes as well as daycare centers [6. 100f.]. After receiving permission from the German administration in September 1941, 19 primary schools were established, many of them supported by political parties; however, only a small number of the children in the ghetto were able to attend theses schools.

The organizational foundation of the work done by *Aleynhilf* was provided by the house committees. Their number increased to 1,600 by January 1942 [7. 65]. The committees held regular meetings of the occupants of the house, organized charitable events, and founded children's day care centers. However, their work was also affected by the increasing lack of resources and by blackmail at the hands of the Jewish as well as the Polish police, who were known to react to the refusal of protection money by threatening the dreaded "párowka," the disinfection of an entire house originally introduced from fear of typhus. While the inhabitants had to go to bathhouses in such cases, where they had to strip and remain for up to 24 hours, their belongings would be ransacked and destroyed.

Many writers, intellectuals, and members of social associations of the prewar years found employment with *Aleynhilf*. The management included representatives of the Joint Distribution Committee as well as leading figures from the political parties active in the underground. An active underground press, including publications in → Hebrew, Yiddish, and Polish published by the → *Bund*, the Communists, the Zionist workers, the Revisionists, and youth groups like *Hashomer Hatzair* (The young guardian) and *Dror* (Freedom), supported the organization's work. *Aleynhilf* also encouraged the use of → Yiddish, supporting the *Yidishe Kultur Organizatsiye* (IKOR; Yiddish cultural organization) as well as the underground archive → *Oyneg Shabbes* established by Emanuel Ringelblum. *Aleynhilf* regarded itself as the true representation of Warsaw Jews; its members accused the Judenrat of corruption and unjust social and tax policies, but they were themselves accused of favoritism too. Dwindling resources and pressure from the Germans finally forced *Aleynhilf* to become more dependent on the Judenrat in 1942.

Despite the most adverse circumstances, a rich cultural life developed in the ghetto. Well-known actors and singers appeared in theatres such as the Eldorado, Nowy Azazel, Na Pięterku, and the Nowy Teatr Kameralny. A symphony orchestra directed by Adam Furmánski and Marian Neuteich gave numerous concerts; people thronged to the recitals of the talented young singer Marysia Ajsenstadt, and several cafés staged sophisticated → cabaret. Café Sztuka achieved particular popularity as the venue for performances by the pianist Władysław Szpilman and the poet Władysław Szlengel, who was known for his satirical texts about ghetto life. The practice of religion decreased in the ghetto overall. The department for religious matters of the Judenrat headed by Alexander Soscha Friedman tried to counteract this, and religious studies were continued in

secret; famous Hasidic rabbis (→ Hasidism) such as Kalonymus Kalman Shapira were active as preachers.

4. Deportations and resistance

The mass deportations of the Warsaw Jews to → Treblinka began on July 22, 1942; at this point, the SS took over the majority of the administration of the ghetto. Czerniaków, who had previously been given the assurance that the ghetto was safe, now received instructions that 6,000 Jews had to be sent to so-called labor service to the East every day. Employees of the Judenrat were exempt, as were those of the Jewish Police and forced laborers in German factories. When Czerniaków heard that children were also to be deported, he committed suicide on July 23. The representatives of political parties and youth groups were divided as to whether resistance was called for under the circumstances or not, as allegedly only a limited number of unemployed ghetto inhabitants were being deported. The exemptions announced by the Germans gave some Jews a deceptive feeling of security, while others spent their last remaining money to find employment in a German factory.

During the deportations, at first the Jewish police and, over time, increasingly German units and their helpers rounded up Jews on the so-called "Umschlagplatz" (transfer site), a siding on the corner of Dzika and Stawki Streets. After an announcement of July 29 which promised volunteers for the deportations three kilograms of bread and one kilogram of margarine, thousands of ghetto inhabitants reported there. By the end of August, it had become known that the Jews were taken to Treblinka extermination camp [3. 221–223]. The first phase of deportations reached its peak between September 5 and 12. The 120,000 Jews remaining in the ghetto had to assemble for selection; 30,000 were given work cards while the others – unless they went underground or worked for the ghetto administration – were deported. Between July 22 and September 21, 1942, around 265,000 Warsaw Jews arrived in Treblinka in this way as well as 11,000 in labor camps; around 10,000 were murdered in Warsaw. Around 8,000 had gone underground outside the ghetto. Legally remaining in the ghetto were 35,000, together with 20,000 others who lived there without food vouchers and work cards [1. 914].

The ghetto decreased in size after the deportations of the summer of 1942, several unconnected enclaves remaining, which contained the German businesses of W. C. Többens, Schultz & Co. GmbH, Bernhard Hallmann & Co., and others, as well as the living quarters for the Jewish forced laborers. Every day, Jews found on the streets during working hours were shot, with other terror measures instituted as well. The survivors searched the apartments of those who had been deported for goods they could offer in Poland in exchange for food. Facing death, some of the remaining ghetto inhabitants sought refuge in alcohol and promiscuity, while others were tortured by the question of why they had allowed the deportation of their relations and friends without resistance.

As early as July 28, 1942, the three Zionist youth organizations *Hashomer Hatzair*, *Dror*, and *Akiba*, had founded the Żydowska Organizacja Bojowa (ŻOB; Jewish Fighting Organization). The group intended to fight not only in Warsaw but also to bring the resistance to other ghettos. On August 20, the ŻOB injured the leader of the Jewish Police Service Józef Szeryński. As representatives of the → Polish Home Army insisted on linking the negotiations on supplying weapons to the ŻOB to the establishment of a coordination post to which all Jewish parties belonged, the Żydowski Komitet Narodowy (ŻKN; Jewish National Committee) and the Żydowski Komitet Koordynacyjny (ŻKK; Jewish Coordination Committee) were founded, the latter being joined by

the → *Bund*. The Revisionists could not be persuaded to join the ŻOB; instead, they founded the Żydowski Związek Wojskowy (ŻZW; Jewish Military Association), a separate militant organization. Mordechai Anielewicz, a member of *Hashomer Hatzair*, was appointed commander of the ŻOB. The militant organization liquidated several Jewish collaborators, among them the director of the economic department of the Judenrat Izrael First, Szeryński's successor as the head of the Jewish police Jakob Lejkin in 1942 and, in the following year, Alfred Nossig (→ Statistics), who wrote reports for the Germans. Its authority in the ghetto increased steadily.

In January 1943, Himmler ordered the transfer of machinery and workers from the Warsaw ghetto to the SS labor camp in Trawniki near Lublin. When SS units invaded the ghetto on January 18, 1943, intending to deport around 8,000 Jews without work papers, Jewish militants resisted in a few locations. For instance, Anielewicz, together with a small group of fighters, joined a line of Jews headed for deportation on their way to the transfer site, from which they opened fire on the German guards. Some fighters of the *Dror* attacked the SS too. Entirely surprised by the Jewish resistance, the SS left the ghetto temporarily after deporting about 6,500 Jews. The January battles marked a psychological turning point for the terrorized and traumatized Jews: they believed that with their fight they had prevented the liquidation of the ghetto (at this time not yet planned by the Germans) for the time being. News of the Soviet victory at → Stalingrad and the allied advance in North Africa (→ El-Alamein) also fed their hopes of survival.

Unlike the ghettos in → Vilna and Białystok, the majority of the Jews remaining in Warsaw supported the fighters, built shelters and connecting passages between cellars, and started stockpiling provisions. A campaign by German industrial firms calling on their workers to volunteer for deportation to the Lublin labor camps with allegedly good conditions, which did not meet with much success, was countered by a poster campaign by the ŻOB and the ŻZW.

The resistance of the ŻOB was also recognized by the Polish Home Army, who sent fifty pistols, explosives, and instructions for the manufacture of grenades to the ghetto. Negotiations over further arms deliveries suffered a setback with the arrest of Arie (born Izrael Chaim) Wilner, the ŻOB member who was the main contact person with the Polish side. In the end, the ŻOB and ŻZW bought their arms on the black market, having extorted the money from wealthy Jews.

5. The Uprising

On the eve of the Warsaw ghetto uprising, the ŻOB had 500 fighters ready, armed mainly with handguns, grenades, and Molotov cocktails. They were organized in line, per their political party and youth group affiliations, into 22 task forces. The Żydowski Związek Wojskowy (ŻZW), led by Leon Rodal and Paweł Frenkiel, numbered around 250 fighters who were overall better armed. In accordance with previous agreements, the ŻZW held the sections facing Muranów Square. The ŻOB divided the remaining ghetto area into three sectors. The central ghetto was under the command of Izrael Kanał, the area containing the German firms W. C. Többens and Schultz & Co GmbH under Eliezer Geller's, and the region around the brush factory on Świętojerska Street under Marek Edelman's. The ŻOB assumed that its fighters would die in the confrontation; there was no plan for retreat.

On April 19, 1943, the day before Pesaḥ (→ Course of the Year), SS and police units invaded the ghetto in order to complete the evacuation. ŻOB and ŻZW fighters kept them under heavy fire as well as grenades and Molotov cocktails. The ŻZW raised a flag showing the → Star of David and a Polish flag over their positions on Muranów Square. A majority of the Jewish population retreated

into bunkers. Once again, the organized Jewish defense found the SS unprepared. After the commanding SS and police chief Ferdinand von Sammern-Frankenegg had been relieved, SS Brigadeführer Jürgen Stroop took over in order to quash the uprising. To begin with, he ordered to have the factories evacuated, but only 6,000 Jewish workers could be deported in this way. On April 23, Stroop changed his tactic, having the ghetto burned down systematically. This forced the Jewish fighters in houses and bunkers, if they did not perish from the heat and the smoke, to retreat or surrender. Subsequently, the remaining resistance fighters began to attack German units at night. On May 8, SS units discovered Anielewicz' ŻOB headquarters in 18 Miła Street. After the call to surrender, over a hundred Jewish fighters died, most of them by suicide. With the help of the contact man Simcha Rotem, at least a few dozen ŻOB fighters were able to flee the ghetto through the sewer system. All ŻZW leaders lost their lives.

On May 16, 1943, Stroop had the famous → Tłomackie Synagogue blown up and declared the operation at an end. In his final report he noted that there was no longer a Jewish residential district in Warsaw. Of the around 40,000 Jews at the beginning of the uprising, 10,000 met their end in the ghetto; 30,000 were deported to Treblinka, Majdanek, Trawniki, and Poniatowa. Most of the Jews in the three last-named camps were killed on November 3 and 4, 1943, during the so-called "Aktion Erntefest" ("Operation Harvest Festival"). According to Stroop's report, the German dead numbered 16, the injured, 85 [3. 393].

After the destruction, a few hundred Jews continued to live in the ruins of the ghetto; around 20,000 were hiding underground in other city districts. Although many of them received aid through the Polish-Jewish refugee aid organization Rada Pomocy Żydom (Council to Aid Jews), active under the code name Żegota, most of them did not survive the end of the war because of denunciation as well as traps set by the German security apparatus. In addition, many lost their lives during the Polish uprising in 1944, in which ŻOB fighters took part as well.

After the end of the war, the Warsaw ghetto uprising became the most important symbol of Jewish resistance during the → Holocaust. Shortly after the liberation, many autobiographical and literary works began to focus on the subject, among them *Getto walczy* ("The Ghetto Fights," 1946) published by the former commander of the ŻOB Marek Edelman in 1945, or John Richard Hersey's 1950 novel *The Wall*. Aleksander Ford's *Ulica Graniczna* ("Border Street") of 1948 is among the first films to focus on the Warsaw ghetto.

Bibliography

[1] H. Dreifuss Ben Sasson, Art. "Warsaw Ghetto," in: G. Miron/S. Shulhani (eds.), The Yad Vashem Encyclopedia of the Ghettos during the Holocaust, Jerusalem 2009, 897–921. [2] B. Engelking/J. Leociak, The Warsaw Ghetto. A Guide to the Perished City, New Haven/London 2009. [3] Y. Gutman, The Jews of Warsaw 1939–1943. Ghetto, Underground, Revolt, trans. by I. Friedman, Bloomington 1983. [4] C. A. Kaplan, Scroll of Agony. The Warsaw Diary of Chaim Kaplan, ed. by A. I. Katsh, Bloomington/Indianapolis 1999. [5] S. D. Kassow, Who Will Write Our History? Rediscovering a Hidden Archive from the Warsaw Ghetto, New York 2009. [6] M. Roth/A. Löw, Das Warschauer Getto. Alltag und Widerstand im Angesicht der Vernichtung, Munich 2013. [7] R. Sakowska, Komitety domowe w getcie warszawskim [House Committees in the Ghetto of Warsaw], in: Biuletyn Żydowskiego Instytutu Historycznego [Bulletin of the Jewish Historical Institute] 61 (1967), 59–86. [8] I. Trunk, Judenrat. The Jewish Councils in Eastern Europe under Nazi Occupation, New York/London 1972. [9] Y. Zuckerman/B. Harshav, A Surplus of Memory.

Chronicle of the Warsaw Ghetto Uprising, Berkeley 1993.

SAMUEL D. KASSOW, HARTFORD

Watchmaker

Especially in Switzerland, the production and sale of watches developed into characteristic professions of Jews. Since the mid-19th century, Jewish traders, craftsmen, and manufacturers established themselves there. When, in the 1870s, with the advent of inexpensive watches from the United States, the skilled manual production of Switzerland proved to be outdated, it was easier for the Jews, as immigrants, as opposed to the long-established, tradition-oriented dynasties of craftsmen, to take up modern manufacturing methods. The tradition of Jewish watch producers lost its former importance with the emergence of quartz watches in the second half of the 20th century at the latest.

1. Beginnings and establishment
2. Crises and successes
3. From 1914 to 1945
4. The postwar period

1. Beginnings and establishment

The production of clocks by Jews is already attested in 13th century Spain. During the reign of King Alfonso X, the scholar and engineer Samuel Ha-Levi Abulafia prepared a water clock and translated instructions for the use of candle clocks from → Arabic. In 1359, the scholar Isaac Nafūsī, who lived in Mallorca, was invited to Barcelona by King Pedro IV of Aragón, in order to manufacture clocks and instruments for observing the celestial bodies. The fact that Jews were active as clockmakers from an early date can be traced back to the need to determine → time more precisely for reasons of → liturgy and worship. In the modern period, Jews found their way to careers as clockmakers primarily by way of traditional → craft activities and as retailers and jewelers (→ Peddlers). The important influence that Jews exerted on the Swiss clock industry, however, was a consequence of Jewish labor immigration to Switzerland, and to that extent was a specifically modern development.

In Switzerland, Jewish watchmakers were present primarily in the Neuchâtel and Bernese Jura, as well as in the cities of Biel (Bienne) and → Geneva, close to the French border. The presence of Jews in the watch city of La Chaux-de-Fonds in the Canton of Neuchâtel can be presumed as early as the 1780s: these were merchants from Alsace (→ Metz), who, despite the ban on residence, continued to live in that place in small numbers. Beginning in the 1830s, increasing numbers of Jews arrived in individual Swiss towns as merchants of livestock, drapery, and watches [3]. The first significant upswing in watch manufacturing took place in the Jura Arc, concomitantly with the settlement of Alsatian Jews. Subsequently, immigrant Jews began to trade in watches and their parts and went on from there into producing them themselves.

In the early 19th century, watchmakers in small towns such as La Chaux-de-Fonds or Biel took advantage of the strict guild laws in Geneva, until that time the center of Swiss watchmaking, which permitted only adult male citizens to practice the career of watchmaking. In order to reduce production costs, orders for the fabrication of small parts were placed with the surrounding rural population. Harsh, cold winters and infertile lands forced the peasants to find additional sources of income. Under these conditions, the division of labor in individual production stages known as *établissage* emerged, which became characteristic of Swiss watch manufacturing. A learned watchmaker, often a merchant known as the *établisseur*,

ordered individual parts from independent workers and made tools and often the raw material available to them as well. The watches were then assembled in his workshop by him or under his supervision.

One of the first Jewish trading houses for watches (*comptoir d'horlogerie*) was founded in 1850 by the brothers Marc Marx and Emmanuel Didisheim in Saint-Imier, canton of Bern. The brothers also owned a workshop and were considered as promotors and developers of watch manufacturing. They therefore belonged to the new generation of watch traders, who were active in the production of watches. To that extent, they differed in respect of their economic function as well from the Jewish retail merchants already based there, who, as intermediaries between countryside and town, supplied the watch centers with everyday objects and materials for watch production, and at the same time sold their watches to middlemen or end-users outside the Jura. In contrast, the owner of a *comptoir* produced, developed, and presented his own range of products as the proprietor.

2. Crises and successes

In 1872 Switzerland exported 18.3 million francs worth of watches and watchparts to the United States, but only four years later the export value amounted to a mere 4.8 million francs [4. 159]. In the early 1870s, American watch companies had begun automated mass production. At the latest, the presentation of a fully automatic screw machine by the Waltham Watch Company at the 1876 Centennial International Exhibition (→ World's Fair) in Philadelphia showed that the Americans could not only produce larger quantities at lower prices per item, but they were also able to manufacture watches of high technical quality that were extremely precise. In Switzerland, family businesses that had been active in watchmaking for many generations held fast to the skilled manual modes of production that had previously been the basis of their success. Not only *établisseurs*, but also highly trained workers initially balked at modernization. The idealized image of the independent watchmaker working in his workshop and the belief in the superiority of craftsmanship over mass production of watches were the reasons for a crisis in sales that lasted for years.

The 1880s saw the beginnings of a slow but then all the more durable process of modernization. Especially Jewish manufacturers who had first entered into the local economy beginning in the mid-19th century, and therefore, unlike the Christian watchmaking elites, were less attached to traditional modes of production, transferred modern modes of production into Switzerland. From 1880 to 1914, eight of the 17 businesses with more than 20 hired workers in the canton of Neuchâtel belonged to Jewish proprietors. In 1922, there were ten watch factories in the region with more than 50 employees each; only two of them were not in the possession of Jewish families [4. 195, 203]. Among the successful Jewish enterprises were names such as Ebel SA, Paul Ditisheim SA, and Tavannes Watch Co. SA, which co-founded the myth of Swiss watches.

One of the first modern factories in the region was founded in 1892 by the brothers Léopold, Achilles, and Isidore Ditesheim, who merged their separate enterprises into L. A. & I. Ditesheim, Fabricants. The family had first settled in La Chaux-de-Fonds in 1876. By 1897, the company had more than 80 employees and was well-known for its broad program of pocket watches. At around the same time, it began to develop the first wristwatches, which necessitated even more intricate mechanisms. In the wake of the resulting growth, one of the first large industrial buildings arose in La Chaux-de-Fonds in 1905, for what were now more than 150 employees. In the same year, the

Headquarters of the Swiss Watch Company Movado in La Chaux-de-Fonds (photo montage, 1948)

Ditesheim brothers gave their company the name Movado: the term, which came from the world language → Esperanto, means "constantly in motion," and was programmatic for the company's approach.

Smaller firms with fewer than 20 employers, to which Jewish business likewise particularly tended to belong, also profited at the turn of the century from the boom driven by technical innovation. Thus, of the 180 mid-sized family businesses existing in La Chaux-de-Fonds in 1887, about 10% were in the hands of Jewish families. Until 1912, the Jewish proportion rose to 30%. From 1880 to 1914, over 40% of the Jews in La Chaux-de-Fonds were employed in the production of watches; added to these were somewhat more than 20% who took care of world-wide sales as watch dealers. Almost half of Jews employed in the watch industry worked as specialized craftsmen [4. 198–199]. Companies based on family alliances continued to operate for generations. At the municipal vocational school in La Chaux-de-Fonds, trainees could learn specialized crafts, such as those of engraver, gilder, and casings maker, or else they trained to qualify as watchmakers, capable of producing all components of a clock, down to the end product.

Economic success attracted more Jewish immigrants. Whereas 541 Jews lived in La Chaux-de-Fonds in 1880, 20 years later the number had risen to 900. The Jewish share in the population was especially high in the upper middle-class and prestigious neighborhoods of the town. Four out of five Jewish households had domestic service staffs. The new synagogue in the grandiose Byzantine-Romanesque style, consecrated in downtown La Chaux-de-Fonds in 1896, also testified to the social rise of the Jewish population. In 1914, there were ten Jews among the 50 most wealthy inhabitants of La Chaux-de-Fonds; a proportion that far surpassed the Jewish share of the population, which was about three percent [4. 194–198].

3. From 1914 to 1945

During the First World War, watchmakers in the Jura Arc initially experienced a rapid upswing. The plants designed for the production of precision mechanics primarily manufactured armaments, especially precision detonators for artillery shells, which were delivered to the states of the Entente. After the end of the war, armaments orders largely stopped. Because of the socially and economically difficult postwar situation, watches hardly were sold in Germany and the lands of the former Danube Monarchy or in Soviet Russia. Added to this were protectionist limitations on the market in other states, such as Spain. In the 1920s and 1930s, the businesses reorganized themselves in the form of comprehensive cartel, which was supported by industry, bankers, federal authorities, and social groups. On the basis of price fixing, controls on exports, and a corporatist balance between the interests of manufacturers and workers, the Swiss watch industry recovered, while maintaining its structure of products, based on smaller and middle-sized businesses.

In 1930 federal statistics recorded 104 Jews among a total of 3,950 persons self-employed in the watch industry, 2.6% of Jewish manufacturers and watch sellers, which corresponded to five times their share in the population (0.5%) [6. 177–179]. At the beginning of the Second World War, out of 51 delegates in the Chambre Suisse de l'Horlogerie (Swiss Chamber of Watchmaking), the main association of watch manufacturers, seven were Jews; the twenty-man Central Committee and the Financial Commission included three Jewish entrepreneurs [8. 342].

From the end of the 1930s, Jewish manufacturers of pocket watches and jewelry watches in Switzerland had to struggle with the fact that trade licenses were denied to their representatives in Germany, Italy, and Spain. The Swiss government accepted this anti-Jewish discrimination without protest. When, in the course of 1941, the "Aryanization" of the property of foreign Jews began in France, this once again raised the question of diplomatic protection for Swiss citizens. In this regard, an intervention in favor of the rights of Swiss Jews abroad was presented by the social democrat Ernest-Paul Graber, who lived in La Chaux-de-Fonds. The state government replied to his question in the Nationalrat (National Council) that Swiss Jews abroad were subject to legal conditions in the respective countries, thereby confirming *de facto* the antisemitic measures in the areas occupied by Germany as *ordre public* (→ Helvetic).

With the fall of France in 1940, Switzerland came under considerable pressure from Nazi Germany. Except for a small gap in the southwest, which bordered on → Vichy France, the nation was surrounded by Axis powers. In addition to the immediate military threat, the alpine state's dependency on supplies and technology was therefore intensified. The interest of the "Third Reich," in turn, focused on Swiss high-tech products, pharmaceuticals, and electricity, as well as the unimpeded use of transalpine transportation routes. Switzerland organized a war economy, which, despite maintaining the principle of neutrality, primarily took into account an understanding with Germany. In 1940, Switzerland committed itself to Germany not to sell any war material to the Allies. Nevertheless, entrepreneurial leeway remained, which continued to allow deliveries to Germany's enemies. In June 1941, in response to German pressure, the Bundesrat (Federal Assembly) prohibited exports of goods by normal postal transport, which spelled an end to the usual practice of breaking the German blockade by transport of smallparcels. This also affected watchmakers, who had previously sold watch jewels, important for the war effort, and other precision and small mechanical components to the Allies in this way.

Jewish watch manufacturers adapted to the specifications of the Swiss wartime economy, and, at the same time, sought in a semi-legal way to support Germany's wartime opponents, as for instance in the case of the Tavannes Watch Co. SA, which, nevertheless, by way of the private equity firm Tavaro SA, became one of the main suppliers of the timing devices to the German military beginning in 1940. In October 1940, the two Jewish industrialists Isaac and Maurice Schwob had withdrawn *pro forma* from the Board of Directors. In a report by the German foreign intelligence, however, the firm was still considered Jewish and hostile to Germany and was suspected of illegally exporting war materials to the Allies.

Theodor Schwob, corporate director of Tavannes Machines SA, a spinoff from the Tavannes watch factory that had been independent since 1937, reacted by a tactical strategy to the German interest in one of the firm's products that was particularly valuable for arms production. Tavannes Machines SA produced the precision milling machine Gyromatic – a machine tool that enabled rapid processing of watch casings, but also of gun barrels, detonators, projectiles, or bombshells in large quantities. Beginning in 1942, the Wehrmacht tried to order large quantities of the Gyromatic, but the company's directors stalled, so that the goods were only delivered with an obvious delay.

4. The postwar period

After the war, the success story of Jewish watch manufacturers from Switzerland initially continued. International attention was ensured by the Museum Watch by American designer Nathan George Horwitt. Radically simplified in its design and inspired by the Bauhaus style (→ Architecture), it was distributed from 1948 by the Movado company, and accepted into the collection of the Museum of Modern Art in New York in 1960. The Schweizer Bahnhofsuhr (Swiss railway clock), designed in 1944 by Hans Hilfiker and later produced and sold as a wristwatch by the Mondaine Group of the Jewish entrepreneur Erwin Bernheim, founded in Neuchâtel in 1951, also attracted worldwide attention. Finally, watches of the Swatch brand also testify to the achievements of Jewish watchmakers. The mass production of these watches, commercially successful since the 1980s because of their colorful design, relies, among other factors, on the automatization methods of the Polish watchmaker and Auschwitz survivor Léon Reich, who had settled in the region around Biel in the 1950s.

However, the tradition of Jewish family businesses broke off in the second half of the 20th century. This process was accelerated by the replacement of mechanical watches by the electronic quartz watch and the emerging trend toward digital displays beginning in the 1970s. In the wake of this development, many medium-sized watch producers from Switzerland fell behind compared to vendors from Japan and had to liquidate their firms. Previously renowned names of Jewish watch companies such as Movado and Ebel partly survived as brands and labels of globally active capital holding companies.

Bibliography

[1] A. Brunschwig, Heimat Biel. Geschichte der Juden in einer Schweizer Stadt vom Spätmittelalter bis 1945, Zurich 2011. [2] P.-Y. Donzé, History of the Swiss Watch Industry. From Jacques David to Nicolas Hayek, trans. by P.-Y. Donzé/R. Watkins, Bern 2015. [3] M. Fallet-Scheurer, Geschichte der Uhrmacherkunst in Basel 1370–1874. Ein Beitrag zur Entwicklungsgeschichte der Uhrmacherkunst im allgemeinen, sowie zur Wirtschafts- und Kulturgeschichte Basels, Bern 1917. [4] S. Mahrer, Handwerk der Moderne. Jüdische Uhrmacher und Uhrenunternehmer im Neuenburger Jura 1800–1914, Cologne et al. 2012. [5] M. Perrenoud, Problèmes d'intégration et de naturalisation des Juifs dans le canton de Neuchâtel, in: P. Centlivres (ed.), Devenir Suisse. Adhésion et diversité culturelle des étrangers en Suisse, Geneva 1990, 63–94. [6] J. Picard, Die Schweiz und die Juden 1933–1945. Schweizerischer Antisemitismus, jüdische Abwehr und internationale Migrations- und Flüchtlingspolitik, Zurich 1994. [7] J. Picard, Swiss Made oder Jüdische Uhrenfabrikanten im Räderwerk von Politik und technischem Fortschritt, in: M. Bosch (ed.), Alemannisches Judentum. Spuren einer verlorenen Kultur, Eggingen 2001, 150–161. [8] J. Picard, Gebrochene Zeit. Jüdische Paare im Exil, Zurich 2009. [9] Independent Commission of Experts – Second World War (eds.), Switzerland, National Socialism, and the Second World War. Final Report, Zurich 2002.

STEFANIE MAHRER, JERUSALEM
AND JACQUES PICARD, BASEL

Weintraubs Syncopators

Popular → jazz band that came to fame in the Weimar Republic thanks to its wide-ranging repertoire. Seven band members, six of whom were of Jewish origin, emigrated from Germany in 1933. A long tour of Europe, Russia, and the Far East brought them to Australia in 1937. In spite of opposition from the Australian musicians' union, the band was a great success there. Australia's entering into the war put an end to the ensemble's career as they were identified with the enemy due to their country of origin.

In 1924 Berlin, Stefan Weintraub (1897–1981) founded the "Tanzkapelle Stefan Weintraub" together with Horst Graff (1905–1994). It was made up of music-loving amateurs who constantly changed during the first years until a permanent ensemble had come together. At first, the dance band played only at dances and private parties. By 1927, the "Weintraubs Syncopators," as they called themselves by then, had acquired a reputation as the best jazz band in Berlin [1. 1]. Their cooperation with Friedrich Hollaender (1896–1976), a leading composer and cabaret performer of the Berlin → cabaret scene, contributed to their fame. Hollaender signed the band in the spring of 1927 for his cabaret revue *Was sie wollen*, directed by Max Reinhardt (→ [The] Great World Theatre) at the Komödie am Kurfürstendamm. In February 1928 they made their first recording with Hollaender on piano [1. 11]. Hollaender's work as a film composer also provided the group with access to talking films, which increasingly competed with stage entertainment from the late 1920s onward. The group's involvement in the film industry contributed to its international presence and also to the development of its own style. The musicians shared numerous characteristics – such as their great stylistic range and their clownery – with Hollaender, who was famous for being a supremely gifted impersonator and a master of witty wordplay.

In Berlin the ensemble moved between smaller cabarets and larger variety stages. It performed together with the cabaret performer and musician Rudolf Nelson and with the cabaret artist Trude Hesterberg in the Deutsches Künstlertheater, as well as playing in Max Reinhardt's second cabaret Schall und Rauch and in Hollaender's revues. It accompanied Josephine Baker during her performances in Berlin and played a part in Erik Charell's large-scale stage shows in his Varietétheater Wintergarten. When on tour, the group played in theatres, hotels, cafés, and in → department store restaurants. The musicians appeared in several films, including as the stage band in Josef von Sternberg's classic *Der blaue Engel* with Marlene Dietrich. They also had their own stage show in the Berlin cabaret Kabarett der Komiker.

At the heart of their performances was a three- to five-minute instrumental or vocal act. As this format was equally suited to the variety theatre, cabaret revue, film, records

(corresponding to the duration of a 78-rpm disc), or dance, the Weintraubs could move seamlessly between the different media and genres. Their range included a 30-minute stage show (comedy, burlesque, music), a two-hour evening concert (a symphony of hot rhythms), "Whispering Swing" (music for dancing), a teatime concert (entertainment program), as well as radio broadcasts [2. 11].

Their performances stood in the tradition of variety and → vaudeville shows. They favored short, innovative pieces that relied on visual comic effects, coupled with extreme musical precision and great flexibility in the choice of instruments as well as musical genres. This was precisely what was expected of jazz musicians: excellent entertainment, wit, and the humorous twists that characterized the so-called "nut jazz" (jazz parody). It seems that the Weintraubs excessively paraded this element. One of the musicians was so exasperated by the Weintraubs' continual gimmicks that he left the group after only a few months [3. 15].

The Weintraubs gave every audience the imitation it expected of them. With their sketches and parodies, they fit into the cabaret scene of the Weimar Republic. By employing bowed stringed instruments, they simultaneously connected with older styles of coffee house and salon dance music. Their repertoire covered a wide range from American swing and "gypsy" melodies to Viennese waltzes and Cossack songs, with each genre potentially being both the subject and the medium of parody.

In late March 1933, after Goebbels's announcement of anti-Jewish measures in the film industry, the Universum Film AG (UFA; → Cinema) canceled its contract with the group. The Weintraubs, who were guest performers in Prague at the time, initially extended their tour to include Switzerland and the Netherlands, where they decided not to return to Germany. The four-year tour that followed took the group across all of Europe, twice to Russia, and finally via Japan to Australia. Besides Stefan Weintraub and Horst Graff, the band now consisted of the musicians Kurt Kaiser (Sydney John Kay), Cyril Schulvater, Leo Weiss (Leo White), Emanuel Frischer (Mannie Fisher), and Freddie Gordon Wise (an American and the only non-Jewish band member); they were accompanied by Fritz Goldner as stage director and Heinz Baruch (Henry Barger) as tour manager.

"The Weintraubs," as the band called itself in Australia, were signed by the cinema managers Snider & Dean in Sydney for sixteen weeks in 1937. According to the licensing regulations negotiated between the Australian musicians' union and the government in 1929, employers of foreign musicians were obliged to ensure that these musicians left the country after their contracts ran out. A polio epidemic led to the closure of public cinemas and to the premature end of their contract, so the band went on tour to New Zealand in 1938, re-entering Australia in May 1938. Wise left the band and returned to Europe. In spite of ongoing and vehement opposition from the musicians' union, the band succeeded in securing employment with Prince's, a prominent restaurant and night club in Sydney in December 1938, consolidating its reputation as one of the best small bands of Australia. In addition, the band appeared on the radio numerous times and was hired to accompany dance events. The band members' flexibility and virtuosity, their skill on a considerable number of instruments, their well-coordinated ensemble play, and their idiosyncratic mix of music and comedy meant that they became a something of an attraction in the local music scene.

As a member of the British Commonwealth, Australia declared war on Germany in September 1939. Because of their German origin, the Weintraubs were identified with the wartime enemy in Australia. In addition, there were concerns in Australia about "fake refugees" who might engage in subversive behavior, as well as anti-German resentments dating back to the time of the First World War. In this climate of extreme tension in Australia, a British businessman living in Sydney accused the Weintraubs of having spied for the German government during their tour in Russia in 1936. The accusations were inconsistent and the informer was not considered reliable, but the smears had grave consequences.

In 1940 Weintraub, Graff, and Kaiser were arrested during a country-wide crackdown aimed at German citizens. The other band members were not bothered. While Weiss and Frischer as well as his brother Adolf (Ady [Eddie] Normand), who had joined the band after playing with a different jazz band in Germany, had all been born in Berlin, they were of Polish descent on both their father's and mother's side; Schulvater was the son of a German father and an English mother and had been born in South Africa. Kaiser's parents were German, but he could point out that his father had been born in Peru and was soon released. Graff and Weintraub, however, were of undoubtedly German origin and were detained in the Tatura internment camp in the state of Victoria. While they both appealed and were discharged in September 1941, the musicians' union made sure that the two founders of the band had no opportunity to perform again and had to abandon their musical profession.

Weiss and the two Frischer brothers founded a new ensemble together with three other Australian musicians, playing at Prince's as the "Polish Sextette." Between 1946 and 1951, Weiss also led his own band at Prince's. In 1948 they recorded a series of songs with well-known Australian singers; the music magazine *Tempo* crowned them the best night club band of Australia. Kaiser successfully sued the musicians' union for refusing to accept him as a member. He founded the Mercury Theatre in Sydney, where he worked with a number of celebrated Australian actors and writers. He composed several film scores for the Australian Commonwealth Film Unit as well as for private producers. He left Australia in 1955 to continue his career in London. Schulvater had already been replaced in the Weintraub ensemble by Adolf Frischer in 1938; after 1946 he was a member of the Sydney Symphony Orchestra and acquired a reputation as an outstanding cello teacher.

Bibliography

[1] H. J. P. Bergmeier, The Weintraub Story. Incorporated the Ady Rosner Story, Menden 1982. [2] K. Dreyfus, Silences and Secrets. The Australian Experience of the Weintraubs Syncopators, Clayton 2013. [3] M. H. Kater, Different Drummers. Jazz in the Culture of Nazi Germany, Oxford 2003.

KAY DREYFUS, MELBOURNE

Weißensee

Inaugurated in 1880 and in use to the present day, the Jewish cemetery in the Berlin district of Weißensee is one of the largest in Europe, numbering 115,000 graves. Its layout, graves, and monuments reflect the changeable history of the Jewish inhabitants of Berlin as well as their self-understanding oscillating between tradition and modernism since the days of the German Empire. Immigration of Jews from Eastern Europe above all, but also the persecution during the National Socialist years, lastingly influenced the cemetery's sepulchral culture. After 1945, the site also became a place of collective remembrance.

1.   Initial phase and layout
2.   Sepulchral culture
2.1   The site and its special characteristics
2.2   Graves and gravestones
3.   "Monument to cultural history"

1. Initial phase and layout

Due to the rapid increase in the number of Jewish inhabitants in Berlin, it became clear from the mid-19th century onward that the second cemetery of the modern Jewish community, inaugurated on Schönhauser Allee in 1827, would soon be fully occupied. In order to establish a new cemetery, the community acquired an area of over 40 hectares in the, at the time, independent village of Weißensee northeast of Berlin.

In the spring of 1878, the Jewish community announced a competition to the members of the Association of Architects in Berlin for the area purchased to include a cemetery complete with a mortuary, a celebration hall, an office building, porter's quarters, and a sturdy boundary wall. It was not intended to be a place of rest for the dead only but also a place for reflection and public representation that would be in line with the contemporary trend in cemetery art "in landscaped style as far as possible" (cited in [2.171]). After several revisions, the design of the architect and later Stadtbaurat (director of urban development) in Leipzig Hugo Licht (1841–1923) was selected. It envisioned the cemetery as a renaissance garden with a strictly geometrical network of paths separating it into individual sectors. Major paths were projected as tree-lined avenues, crossroads presented as decorative squares, and the buildings faced with yellow brick were built in the style of the early Italian Renaissance. Unlike the original design, which was criticized as not being sufficiently solemn, this one added an octagonal tambour to the dome of the mourning hall, raising it to a more representative height. A water tower and a toilet wing were added to the site. The total cost of establishing the cemetery amounted to 230,000 marks.

On September 9, 1880, the community solemnly inaugurated the site; the first burial took place two weeks later. In view of the fact that the burials had moved a long way into the area, an additional mourning hall, a waiting room, and a flower room were built in the rear part of the cemetery between 1910 and 1912; in 1912 a further entrance with a porter's lodge and visitors' toilets opened on present-day Indira-Gandhi-Straße.

Also in Weißensee, but separate and some distance from the cemetery of the Jewish community, the neo-Orthodox "Austrittsgemeinde" Adass Jisroel (→ Neo-Orthodoxy) established their own burial place. The first burial in this area, which covered around two hectares and had been purchased in 1873, took place in February 1880. Grave design was dominated by simple forms; there were no representative family graves at all. Besides prominent rabbis of Adass Jisroel such as Esriel Hildesheimer (1820–1899; → Rabbinical Seminary), this was also the final resting place of the strongman Zishe Breitbart (1893–1925; → Samson).

2. Sepulchral culture

2.1 *The site and its special characteristics*
The extensive burial and cemetery regulations of the Jewish community of Berlin, published in 1909, show clearly the compromises between the self-understanding of the rising Jewish → middle class (Bürgertum) and the traditional Jewish laws (→ Halakhah) and customs (→ Minhag) [4. 33–37].

As had been the custom in many Jewish cemeteries from ancient times, the community reserved individual burial sites in each of the seven sectors for specific groups of people. As had been done in the two older

cemeteries on Große Hamburger Straße and Schönhauser Allee, a row of honor for rabbis and famous people was located in the first and later also in the sixth sector; this is where the philosopher Hermann Cohen (1842–1918; → Concept of God), the composer Louis Lewandowski (1821–1894; → Organ), the founder of → Völkerpsychologie Heymann Steinthal (1823–1899; → Critique of Language), the writer Mikhah Yosef Berdyczewski (Micha Josef Bin Gorion, 1865–1921; → Anthology), and the painter Lesser Ury (1861–1931), among others, were laid to rest.

Married couples could reserve graves on designated lots, while lots with graves arranged in rows were mainly reserved for unmarried, young, and poorer Berlin Jews. Prestigious family tombs were erected along the boundary walls as well as the main paths and squares and from the 1890s onward also on side paths due to increased demand. It was permitted to build vaults, but the coffins had to be placed on unmade ground and be covered completely in soil in order to meet the requirements of religious law. Children were buried in separate sections, while stillborn and miscarried infants were buried in unmarked graves in a separate field along one of the boundary walls.

Following a decision by the community council, a field of honor for fallen Jewish soldiers of the First World War was established in 1915. The final layout of the terraced grounds was implemented following a design by the Imperial and Community Architect in Chief Alexander Beer (1873–1944). The graves for over 370 of the around 3,500 fallen Jewish soldiers from Berlin are marked by uniformly designed simple gravestones. The inside of the wall enclosing this site is also decorated with uniform memorials, while prestigious tombs with Jewish symbolic decoration were integrated along the outside. The ashlar memorial stone in the form of a biblical horned altar,

Jewish cemetery Berlin-Weißensee, memorial to the wine merchant and restaurateur Berthold Kempinski (1843–1910)

decorated with the sleeping lion of Judah and the words "Mächtig wie der Tod ist die Liebe" ("For love is fierce as death"; Song 8:6), completed the presentation of the site. The memorial was donated by the → Reichsbund jüdischer Frontsoldaten and is the most important memorial for fallen soldiers in the First World War in Berlin, simultaneously symbolizing the patriotic self-understanding of the Berlin Jews that had been challenged, above all by antisemites, even during the war (→ Judenzählung).

In 1914 and 1917, the community established the first two of a total of four urn burial fields in a prominent position near the New Mourning Hall. While cremation was contrary to the Jewish understanding of → death as well as the religious rules and had thus been the subject of a controversial discussion since the 19th century, it was practiced in Weißensee in isolated cases as early as 1883. The cemetery regulations officially permitted urn burials as long as the rules of *toharah* (Hebr.; cleansing), the ritual washing of the body, had been observed before cremation. Before the urn burial fields were established, the ashes were buried in coffins.

In order to do justice to the requirements of the particularly strictly religious Jews in the community, most of whom had immigrated from Galicia, a so-called "Sonderfeld" was established where urns could not be buried. While burials of non-Jewish wives next to their Jewish husbands had been permitted since 1909 due to an increase in interconfessional → marriages, this was also forbidden on the Sonderfeld. The increasing influence of Orthodox community members (→ Orthodoxy) and their endeavors to delimit themselves from the widespread trend to → assimilation is also illustrated in the grave positions. While men and women were buried in the same rows in the 1920s, by the 1930s they were buried in separate rows in accordance with the separation of the sexes (→ Meḥitsah) common in → synagogues. The graves of rabbis and scholars at the beginnings of the rows formed their own row of honor along the path. While the cemetery as a whole does not arrange the gravestones uniformly in accordance with Jewish tradition, all those on the Sonderfeld are oriented southeasterly towards Jerusalem (→ Zion), the place of the anticipated resurrection at the end of time.

2.2 Graves and gravestones

There were detailed cemetery regulations on the acquisition, design, maintenance, and safeguarding of gravesites, which were marked with a headstone in accordance with tradition. During the first decade after the inauguration of the cemetery, the gravestones of those buried there, the majority of whom came from Berlin and its environs, were mostly tapering stelae with pyramidal tops or flat slabs from Silesian marble or Saxon sandstone. Family tombs often based their design on façade architecture with classicist motifs; they were less often designed as mausoleums and always remained open to the outside either by means of stained glass in the roof, or column placement – one of the special characteristics of Jewish sepulchral culture. The family tomb that the newspaper publisher Rudolf Mosse (1843–1920; → Advertising Agency) had designed by the architect Gustav Ebe (1834–1916) for his family is a typical example of this. The structure, consisting of red granite and Carrara marble, is built like the vestibule of a Doric ancestral temple.

Free-standing stones had to be placed at the head of the grave and state the German name of the person buried on the side facing the grave. During the first years, around half the headstones still bore → Hebrew inscriptions; however, by the end of the 1880s, these constituted 20% at most and by 1914 had fallen to 5% [7. 35]. This marked the peak of a development that had begun to spread out of Berlin around 1800, in which → German inscriptions increasingly replaced traditional Hebrew ones. Only the headstones on the grave lots of immigrant Jews from Eastern Europe nearly all bore long Hebrew inscriptions on the front, while the back of the stone often merely stated the name in German letters.

While symbols not conforming with Jewish traditions, figural decorations, and three-dimensional images were officially forbidden by the cemetery regulations of 1909, this rule was not always observed in practice, or compromises were found. Urns, for instance, were not permitted as memorial but as decoration. The practice of adding photographs of the deceased to the tombs, which emerged primarily as a result of the influence of less strictly traditionalist immigrants from Eastern Europe, was permitted as long as the images were concealed by a metal cover. Floral tributes, which became established in Jewish cemeteries in Germany in the 19th century, were also permitted in Weißensee. The cemetery management established a dedicated greenhouse on the site for this reason in 1887; a larger complex of greenhouses, cold frames, and open-air spaces was added in 1906. In the summer months, large potted plants decorated many graves as well as the entire cemetery.

From the last decade of the 19th century onward, tomb design began to favor not only massive stone constructions but increasingly also metal latticework with floral decoration, sometimes colored, as for instance in the family tomb of the Lewinsohn and Netter families. They were a peculiar characteristic of the Weißensee cemetery; the choice of material reflected not only the industrialization but also the prosperity of the Jewish → middle class. At the beginning of the 20th century → Art Nouveau, later also Art Deco, Bauhaus, and New Objectivity (→ Architecture) took the place of the traditional headstone styles. However, until the First World War the most frequently used form of gravestone, which greatly influenced the overall impression of the cemetery, was still the stele, now more frequently also made from darker hard stone. The traditional tablets were increasingly replaced with slanted headstones; the height of individual standing headstones was limited to around chest-high.

As the variety of forms grew, criticism was also expressed. The Regierungsbaumeister and architect at the → Technion in Haifa Alexander Baerwald (1877–1930) lamented the decline in sepulchral culture giving Weißensee as an example, with its "ill thought-out" geometric layout, but above all "misguided taste and unculture" and "architectural stylistic blunders" in grave lots and headstone forms together with the flowers planted throughout the cemetery preventing a monumental overall impression [1].

From the 1920s onward, simple stones with rough surfaces on three sides and polished only on the front were increasingly used; they usually bore only a German inscription. They were joined by low rectangular slabs and headstone markers. Artificial stone increasingly replaced the materials previously used. In the 1930s the influence of immigrant Galician, Polish, and Baltic Jews resulted in a return to older gravestone traditions. The number of classic stelae increased, and besides German inscriptions there were also those combining German and Hebrew.

Numerous architects and sculptors, Jewish as well as non-Jewish, designed memorials for the Weißensee cemetery, among them Alexander Beer, Hans Dammann (1867–1942), Gustav Eberlein (1847–1926), Benno Elkan (1877–1960), Louis Fränkel (1863–1922), Paul Levy (1876–1943), or Alfred Messel (1853–1909). The ties between Berlin Jews and the international avant-garde also left their imprint. The future head of the Dessau Bauhaus, the architect Ludwig Mies van der Rohe (1886–1969), for instance, designed the family tomb for Laura Perls in the form of a simple shell limestone ashlar set on a wider pedestal – his first work consistently implementing the stylistic elements of early Modernism. The founder of

Bauhaus Walter Gropius (1883–1969; → Copper House) designed the family tomb of the merchant Albert Mendel (1866–1922). The monument for Hugo Elkeles (1896–1937), exemplary of the combination of Hebrew and German calligraphy that became increasingly rare in the 20th century, was designed by the architect Erich Mendelsohn (1887–1953; → Einstein Tower).

Social differences between Berlin Jews were demonstrated by the sepulchral culture as well. Thus for the poorer deceased, the Jewish community set merely simple uniform headstones, small cuboids originally made from sandstone and after 1912 serially produced from concrete, frequently featuring only the burial number. In the years before the First World War, this type accounted for around 35% of all headstones. From 1921 onward, and in particular as a result of the Great Depression, their number rose until it reached over 40%, making it the most widely used type of headstone of all [7. 53].

3. "Monument to cultural history"

During the period of National Socialism, the cemetery was a place of sanctuary to the ostracized Berlin Jews during the day. In the greenhouse section, young Jews prepared for their emigration to Palestine (→ Aliyah). The year 1943 saw the highest number of annual burials, 3,226, due not least to numerous murders, violent deaths, and suicides. Containers with the ashes of Jews who had lost their lives in → Auschwitz, → Buchenwald, Dachau, Mauthausen, → Ravensbrück, and Sachsenhausen had to be bought back by the relatives before they could be buried in Weißensee, usually in unmarked plots. At the same time, due to its size and complex layout the cemetery provided a refuge for individual Jews in hiding. During the Second World War, over 500 of the originally 608 decorative railings as well as the metal fences of many plots were removed and melted down. Bombs and grenades damaged almost 4,000 graves; large parts of the New Mourning Hall and the cemetery nursery were destroyed.

The Shoah put an abrupt end to the German-Jewish sepulchral culture, which had grown since the → Enlightenment and reflected the permanently fruitful exchange between Jewish tradition intent on conservation and commemorating the dead on the one hand and the social as well as artistic influences of Modernism on the other. Private and personal commemoration was increasingly replaced by collective remembrance in Weißensee. Memorial stones recall, among others, the six million victims of the Shoah, the Jewish communist Herbert Baum (1912–1942) who was moved to the cemetery in 1949, as well as around 90 Torah scrolls buried here, which were hidden in the New Mourning Hall when it was destroyed by bombs. Many reserved burial places in grave plots and family tombs remain unclaimed. Other headstones bear posthumous memorial inscriptions for deported and murdered family members. In addition, the Jewish community ensured that further special fields were established for non-Jews to be buried who had remained faithful to their Jewish partners during the time of persecution. While the Jewish community of West Berlin buried its dead in the Weißensee cemetery during the first years after the war, once the cemetery in Charlottenburg had been inaugurated in 1955, the administration fell to the East German Jewish community alone.

In 1977, the East Berlin municipal authorities recognized the cemetery, which was still in use, as a "Denkmal der Kulturgeschichte." From then on, they supported the small Jewish community by defraying the labor costs of the cemetery maintenance to which the city's department for public gardens and parks contributed as well. The community also received support by increasing the number of volunteer gardening hours. On the occasion of the cemetery's centenary in 1980, the destroyed New Mourning Hall was removed and the site redesigned into a low, plant-covered hill against which older headstones from the closed cemetery in Köpenick were rested from 1986 onward. The "field of honor" for the fallen of the First World War was restored too. The partially collapsed wall bordering Indira-Gandhi-Straße was replaced in 1983/1984 with a wall constructed out of porphyry red prefabricated concrete sections featuring a → menorah and decorative wrought iron railings designed by the architect Gerd Pieper.

At the beginning of the 1980s, however, the Berlin authorities revived their plans for building a connecting road across the site, which had been considered even before the cemetery had been established. As a consequence, the Jewish community had undertaken in 1915 not to occupy the area designated for this project; in 1921 the Berlin municipal authorities had been entered as the owner in the register of real estate. After global protests, the plans were abandoned and the unused land re-allocated to the Jewish community for use in perpetuity. The care and maintenance of the Weißensee cemetery is among the duties of the trust Stiftung Neue Synagoge Berlin – Centrum Judaicum founded in 1988.

After 1990, the Jewish community of Berlin grew as the result of the immigration of Jews from the former Commonwealth of Independent States (CIS) states. By 2015, they constituted around two thirds of the more than 10,000 community members. Their graves and headstones in the plot previously reserved for the construction of the thoroughfare reflect this development in their style and inscriptions. It remains to be seen, however, whether an independent German Jewish sepulchral culture will develop once again in the future.

Bibliography

Sources

[1] A. Baerwald, Der Friedhof in Weißensee, in: Allgemeine Zeitung des Judentums, 12. July 1912, 333f.

Secondary literature

[2] M. Brocke et al., Stein und Name. Die jüdischen Friedhöfe in Ostdeutschland (Neue Bundesländer/DDR und Berlin), Berlin 1994. [3] A. Etzold et al., Jüdische Friedhöfe in Berlin, Berlin ²1988. [4] A. Etzold, Ein Berliner Kulturdenkmal von Weltgeltung. Der jüdische Friedhof Berlin-Weissensee, Teetz/Berlin 2006. [5] W. Gottschalk, Die Friedhöfe der jüdischen Gemeinde zu Berlin, Berlin 1992. [6] A. Nachama/H. Simon (eds.), Jüdische Grabstätten und Friedhöfe in Berlin. Eine Dokumentation, Berlin 1992. [7] Technical University Berlin/Berlin Monument Authority (eds.), 115.628 Berliners: The Weissensee Jewish Cemetery. A Documentation of the Comprehensive Survey of the Burial Sites, Berlin 2013.

NATHANJA HÜTTENMEISTER, ESSEN

Weizmann Institute

The Weizmann Institute in Rehovot is considered the leading research center of Israel. Founded as Daniel Sieff Research Institute in 1934 at the initiative of the chemist, leading Zionist, and future president of the State of Israel Chaim Weizmann (1874–1952), it is engaged in fundamental research on numerous fields of science. Weizmann thus realized his ideas of a Zionism based on a combination of practical groundwork with research and technical progress. Furthermore, he wanted to offer a new place of work to Jewish scientists persecuted in Europe and to encourage them to immigrate to Palestine.

1. Weizmann's initiatives
2. Before and after the foundation of the State of Israel
3. New fields of research and cooperation

1. Weizmann's initiatives

Founding an internationally leading scientific institution in Jerusalem had been Weizmann's vision even at a young age. Together with the philosopher of religion Martin Buber (→ Dialogue) and the publicist Berthold Feiwel, he had championed the establishment of such an institution as early as 1902 in the publication *Eine jüdische Hochschule*.

Born in Motal near Pinsk in Belarus, Weizmann had studied → chemistry in Darmstadt, Berlin, and Fribourg from 1892 onward. After his first position as an assistant lecturer at the University of Geneva in 1901, he moved to Manchester in 1904 where he was employed in the department of organic chemistry. Now based in England, Weizmann consolidated his position within the Zionist movement. It was primarily thanks to his successful research into the production of acetone, which soon aroused the interest of the British military and led to his appointment as director of the Admiralty laboratories in London, that he acquired the connections with British government circles which ultimately made the → Balfour Declaration possible.

In his function as the chairman of the Zionist Commission for Palestine, Weizmann set out on an exploratory journey to the Near East even before the end of the First World War. In July 1918, he attended the ceremony of laying of the foundation stone for the → Hebrew University in Jerusalem. After it was officially opened in 1925, disagreements arose between Judah Magnes (1877–1948), first chancellor of the university until 1935, and Weizmann, who objected to Magnes's curriculum on the grounds that it placed too much emphasis on Jewish Studies and the humanities while neglecting the – in his view – much more relevant sciences. Although a microbiology as well as a chemistry department were part of the Hebrew University from the very beginning, Weizmann repeatedly deplored the inadequate equipment of the laboratories [3. 206f.]. In addition, Magnes insisted on the university being independent of the Zionist movement, while Weizmann, president of the World Zionist Organization from 1921 to 1931 and again from 1935 to 1946, aimed for the exact opposite, regarding the Hebrew University as an integral part of the Zionist project.

In the early 1930s, Weizmann decided to establish a new institute to be led by himself and with an exclusively scientific orientation. His project became possible thanks to the Sieff family from Manchester who had been his close friends since 1913. The wealthy businessman Israel Sieff (1889–1972) was a member of the Manchester School of Zionism, a section of the Zionist movement with reservations concerning socialist tendencies, and editor of the journal *Palestine*.

With a donation of £2,500, the Sieff family provided a major portion of the institute's first annual budget of £4,770 [1. 36, 440]. It was named the Daniel Sieff Research Institute in memory of the Sieffs' son who had died in 1933. The location Weizmann chose was Rehovot where an agricultural research station had been established by the Jewish Agency in 1921 and which became integrated into the new institution.

2. Before and after the foundation of the State of Israel

In his speech on the occasion of the opening ceremony in April 1934, which was attended by, among others, the British High Commissioner for Palestine Sir Arthur Grenfell

Wauchope, Weizmann emphasized that the institute's main objective was to improve the agricultural performance in Palestine [1. 42f.]. His models were the great European research institutions, above all the Kaiser Wilhelm Institutes, which he had previously visited a number of times. "I was comparing in my mind those mighty institutions which served the agriculture of Germany with our little Agricultural Experiment Station at Rehovoth, and hoping that the new Institute which I contemplated might help to fill some of the gaps in our reconstruction" [2. 435]. The staff originally consisted of eleven members; its research focus was on organic chemistry and biochemistry.

By founding the institute, Weizmann began competing with the → Hebrew University for scientists and funds, which he endeavored to raise in the United States and Great Britain. He simultaneously worked on the administrative board of the Hebrew University between 1925 and May 1948, when he became the first president of the State of Israel, and was the chairman of the British Friends of the Hebrew University society which, founded in 1926, also endeavored to secure international donations. Hoping to defuse the resulting conflict of interest, Weizmann appointed the American journalist Meyer Weisgal as his personal representative responsible for this issue. In 1949, Weizmann appointed him administrative head of the research institution; from 1966 to 1969 he was the president and until his death in 1977 chancellor of the Weizmann Institute.

One of Weizmann's objectives for the institute was to bring Jewish scientists who were persecuted in Germany and expelled from their → universities to Palestine: "In the context of my work in Palestine, my main concern – indeed, my only interest – was focused on the Jewish German scientists," he noted in his memoirs [2. 431]. In the first year alone, seven researchers from Germany were employed at the institute [1. 52]. Weizmann also hoped to be able to persuade well-known scientists such as the physicists Albert Einstein (→ Theory of Relativity), Georg Placzek, and James Franck, or the mathematician Hermann Weyl whose wife Helene was Jewish [2. 438]. However, they preferred the established institutions in the United States, Great Britain, or Switzerland, or they did not want to leave their homes, such as the Nobel laureate for chemistry Richard Willstätter. He travelled to Rehovot on the occasion of the inauguration ceremony but returned to Germany afterward. Weizmann was able to engage Fritz Haber, another Nobel laureate for chemistry and contributor to the development of nitrogen fertilizer as well as German poison gas weapons during the First World War, as scientific director, but Haber died unexpectedly in January 1934 in Basel.

He was replaced by Ernst David Bergmann who declined a tailor-made position in Oxford in 1933, emigrating to Palestine instead together with his wife Ottilie Blum-Bergmann and his brother Felix, all of them chemists. In their work, they focused on the conversion of the waste products of the distillation of aromatic hydrocarbons or dyes out of oil. On the basis of their research, new ways of producing synthetic rubber, among other things, were discovered.

Among the first scientists working in Rehovot were also the biochemist and Sorbonne graduate Leon Haskelberg who succeeded in producing an artificial fiber similar to nylon out of castor oil, the microbiologist Esther Hellinger from London who studied the fermentation of dry whey, as well as Yehuda Hirshberg who held a Ph.D. from Brussels and was an expert in physical chemistry engaged in fundamental research on the field of photochromism, as well as being the first president of the Israel Chemical Society from 1948 to 1955. Other early staff members such as Frieda Goldschmidt

and Chaim Weizmann's sister Anna Weizmann had studied chemistry in Berlin and Zurich. Their research was directly linked to the groundwork in Palestine, aimed especially at improving agricultural yield as well as substituting rare or valuable raw materials.

When the war broke out, a department of pharmaceutical development was established, specializing in medicines previously manufactured in Germany that now needed to be substituted. The institute also began producing the anti-malaria drug Atabrine as well as the barbiturate Evipan. However, this was not enough for Weizmann [6. 214]. He was already planning for the postwar years, hoping that by expanding the institute he would be able to encourage further Jewish scientists to move to Palestine from abroad.

During the Second World War, Ernst David Bergmann left Palestine in order to work on Allied armament projects; he returned to Rehovot in 1946. Thanks to the experience acquired abroad as well as his close contact with David Ben-Gurion, he was appointed head of the research department of the Israel Defense Forces in 1948. In 1952, he received a call to the Hebrew University and founded the Israel Atomic Energy Commission in the same year.

Weizmann's 70th birthday in 1944 provided an occasion to expand the institute into a multidisciplinary institution. The funds raised to this end made it possible to lay the foundation stone for a new building complex in June 1946. As suggested by Weisgal, this was called the Weizmann Institute [6. 214] and housed departments for physical chemistry, physics, and mathematics. In 1949, both parts of the institute were joined under Weizmann's name with the agreement of the Sieff family. Weizmann himself continued to hold the position of president of the institute until his death in 1952; until 1966 his successor was the politician and diplomat Abba Eban.

3. New fields of research and cooperation

Immediately after the first computer was introduced in the United States in 1946, the new technology became a matter of interest in Rehovot too. Together with the game theorist Aviezri Fraenkel born in Munich in 1929, the mathematician Leib Pekeris, who had studied at the Massachusetts Institute of Technology (MIT), developed the WEIZAC (Weizmann Automatic Calculator) by 1954, one of the world's first large-scale computers. In 1949, the Weizmann Institute employed almost 1,000 staff and was home to nine scientific departments with a total of sixty laboratories [4. 706].

One of the most prominent researchers of the Weizmann Institute was Ephraim Katzir, born in Kiev in 1916. A former pupil of Chaim Weizmann's brother Moshe Weizmann, who had taught organic chemistry at the → Hebrew University in the 1920s, he was the founder and head of the biophysics department with research focus on proteins and synthetic polypeptides. From 1966 to 1968, Katzir headed the research department of the Israel Defense Forces; between 1973 and 1978 he was the fourth person to hold the office of president of the State of Israel.

An expert in physical chemistry, Israel Dostrovsky, born in Odessa in 1918, whose father Arieh was one of the founders of the medical faculty at the Hebrew University, headed the isotopes research department in Rehovot for 17 years. In 1949, Dostrovsky founded the first commercial enterprise on the campus, producing and distributing water enriched with heavy oxygen isotopes for medical diagnostics. From 1965 to 1971, Dostrovsky was the director general of the Israel Atomic Energy Commission. As the president of the Weizmann Institute during the 1970s, he provided the impulse for increasing the focus on researching renewable sources of energy, ultimately leading to the establishment of the WIS Center for Energy Research, which he headed from 1980 to 1990.

In 1958, the Feinberg Graduate School opened as part of the institute for students of natural and computer sciences and medicine to acquire a Master of Science or Ph.D. degree. To provide an interface with the industry sector, the Yeda Research and Development Company was founded in 1959, marketing patents and research results.

The start of German-Israeli science cooperation was marked in 1959 by the visit in Rehovot of a delegation of the Max-Planck-Gesellschaft led by its president Otto Hahn. The connection had been established by Weizmann's former assistant Josef Cohn, who had previously approached Konrad Adenauer with a letter of recommendation from the Chancellor's friend Dannie N. Heinemann, a Jewish industrial entrepreneur and patron of the Weizmann Institute. Cohn hoped to be able to include the Federal Republic in the circle of sponsors of the Institute. The Max-Planck-Gesellschaft was considered as a possible cooperation partner; Wolfgang Gentner, the head of the Max Planck Institute for Nuclear Physics made the proposal to commission research from the Weizmann Institute with the aim of providing it with additional funding from a German source [5. 153]. In this way, exchanges between scientists of both states predated the beginning of diplomatic relations between Germany and Israel (1965). On the occasion of his meeting with David Ben-Gurion in New York in 1960, the chancellor also promised one million Deutsche Marks in funds for three years as well as the means for establishing a new department of molecular biology; in recognition, Adenauer was awarded honorary membership of the Weizmann Institute during his visit in Rehovot in 1966.

Bibliography

Sources

[1] B. Litvinoff (ed.), The Letters and Papers of Chaim Weizmann (Series B: Papers), Vol. 2: December 1931–April 1952, Jerusalem 1984.
[2] C. Weizmann, Trial and Error. The Autobiography of Chaim Weizmann, London 1949.

Secondary literature

[3] D. Kotzin, Judah L. Magnes. An American Jewish Nonconformist, New York 2010. [4] S. Nery, Weizmann Institute of Science, in: C. Summerfield/M. Devine (eds.), International Dictionary of University Histories, New York 1998, 705–707. [5] D. Nickel, Wolfgang Gentner und die Begründung der deutsch-israelischen Wissenschaftsbeziehungen, in: D. Hoffmann/U. Schmidt-Rohr (eds.), Wolfgang Gentner, Festschrift zum 100. Geburtstag, Berlin 2006, 147–170. [6] M. Weisgal, ... So Far. An Autobiography, New York 1971.

RALF BALKE, BERLIN

Weltbühne

In the Weimar Republic, the weekly *Die Weltbühne* represented a key forum for independent journalistic and political debates. Over time, the paper - initially founded in 1905 as the theatre journal *Die Schaubühne* – made a turn toward politics and contemporary criticism. The *Weltbühne* was deeply influenced by its founders Siegfried Jacobsohn (1881–1926) and Kurt Tucholsky (1890–1935), who with it created a melting pot for left-wing intellectuals of primarily Jewish origin, who thereby found a political and spiritual home that was denied to them elsewhere. Prohibited in 1933, the journal radiated as a lost place of longing until well into the second half of the 20th century.

1. Profile of a magazine
2. Siegfried Jacobsohn and Kurt Tucholsky
3. Legacy and posterity

1. Profile of a magazine

On September 7, 1905, an edition of the weekly *Die Schaubühne* appeared for the first time. From the outset, it was entirely the product of the theatre critic Siegfried Jacobsohn, who – as he later did *Die Weltbühne* as well – called it his "rag," and – because of its brick-red cover – his "coagulated lifeblood" [16. 165]. Jacobsohn, who came from a family of Jewish merchants, placed the theatre, the object of all his passion, at the focal point of the first eight volumes. Thus, as *Die Schaubühne* was dominated by cultural and aesthetic questions during its first decade, it aimed at a small, cultured audience. However, it was not an apolitical paper. As he emphasized as early as 1905 in his introduction to the first issue, Jacobsohn showed himself to be convinced that the "spirit of a people and of a specific time is expressed more vividly in drama than in the remaining literature" and therefore "the current of new intellectual values springs from the theatre" [2. vol. 1/1, 1].

The entry of Kurt Tucholsky, who had also grown up in a Jewish family, into the circle of collaborators in 1913, brought about a push toward politicization, which was indicated not only by the orientation of its content, but also by the modified subtitle of the weekly. According to it, the magazine saw itself from now on as responsible not only for the "overall interests of the theatre" but "for politics, art and economics." The First World War intensified this change of course, which Jacobsohn promoted deliberately and aggressively, and whose orientation tended toward the political and the social. Thus, this was the time not only of the omnipresent debate over the world war, but also of two series of articles on the immigration of Orthodox Jews from Eastern Europe, who increasingly left their mark on the street scene of the Berlin → Scheunenviertel. Jacobsohn understood these articles as a necessary labor of enlightenment, in order to brighten the image of the → Ostjuden, which was gloomy even in left-wing political circles, and to combat antisemitic tendencies and prejudices, whatever their origin or mode of expression.

Meanwhile, from 1914 to 1918, the magazine, which, from April 4, 1918, appeared under the new main title *Die Weltbühne*, had to exercise restraint in view of censorship and the threat of a ban. A considerable backlog of criticism thereby had to accumulate, which during the postwar years made *Die Weltbühne* undertake a "good clearing out" [1. vol. 26/2, 378] in Germany, as Tucholsky recalled on September 9, 1930, on the occasion of the magazine's 25th anniversary.

After the adoption of the Weimar Constitution, *Die Weltbühne* had initially welcomed the new republic. To be sure, some of the authors harbored, as before, sympathy for the Spartacus League of Rosa Luxemburg and Karl Liebknecht or the → Bavarian Council Republic; in contrast, Jacobsohn rejected them as uncivilized and violent [8. 74]. Nevertheless, he imposed editorial guidelines according to which the change of system from the autocratic Empire to the new democratic order was not enough. With the 1920 Kapp putsch in Berlin, the editors saw a confirmation of their thesis of the perseverance of the powerful remains of the old order in the military, the judiciary, and administration. As a direct reaction to the attempted overthrow, Tucholsky demanded the immediate dismissal of all "conservative Prussian officers" from the Reichswehr, and the transformation of the army into a "reliable people's militia," as well as the rigorous

education of the populace with regard to the past and present crimes of the Nationalists [1. vol. 18/2, 25].

That, with this last demand, Tucholsky had also partially outlined the journalistic claim of *Die Weltbühne* became clear in the following years and especially in 1925. By means of a series of articles, initially published anonymously by Carl Mertens, a former member of the Free Corps, the magazine initiated a public debate of the activities of right-wing secret organizations, above all the Black Reichswehr. This group had originated from units of the Free Corps in the early 1920s out of fear of an expected Polish attack, but under Major Bruno Buchrucker had increasingly resorted to the preparation of a putsch. Mertens's report in *Die Weltbühne* now revealed that the Küstrin putsch attempted on October 1, 1923, was not to be blamed on ultra-left forces, as was represented in the press, but on conservative units. At the same time, Mertens pointed to the assassination attempts committed by the Black Reichswehr and its affiliated organizations against presumed traitors in their own ranks, critics, and political opponents. Inspired by *Die Weltbühne*'s reporting, the Prussian State Parliament, under the auspices of the Social Democrats, set up a Committee of Inquiry, which led to the conviction of some of the suspects [8. 119f.].

Although the magazine, with a circulation of almost 15,000 copies [3. 18], was not a popular publication even in the Weimar Republic, it nevertheless achieved the status of one of the key intellectual media of the time. The renown of *Die Weltbühne*, the influence of whose thematic focus extended to the daily and regional press, was especially furthered by the fame of its authors, who included some of the leading writers, journalists, and critics whom the first three decades of the 20th century had produced. In addition to texts by political editorialists such as Kurt Hiller (1885–1972) or Heinrich Ströbel (1869–1944), works appeared by such authors as Julius Bab (1880–1955), Alfred Döblin (→ Alexanderplatz), Leo Lania (→ Piscator Stage), Else Lasker-Schüler (→ [Das] Hebräerland), Lion Feuchtwanger (→ Jud Süß), Walter Mehring (→ Cabaret), Erich Mühsam (→ Bavarian Council Republic), Alfred Polgar (→ Vienna), Ernst Toller (→ Bavarian Council Republic), and Arnold Zweig (→ Ostjuden). For many of the authors, who were often Jewish, *Die Weltbühne* became the spiritual home that was denied to them in public institutions. This did not change even with Jacobsohn's death, as early as it was surprising, following an epileptic attack in 1926. Of necessity, Kurt Tucholsky succeeded him as the magazine's editor but derived little pleasure from his editorial activity. As a result, Carl von Ossietzky (1889–1938) took over the leadership few months later "with the collaboration of Kurt Tucholsky" as was announced on the cover beginning in October 1927.

As much as the journalistic wrath of *Die Weltbühne* was directed against rightwing, restorative, and reactionary forces, or objected to the persistent subservient mentality among the population, it also struck at defenders of gradual change and of majoritarian Social Democracy. The sometimes violent polemics against politicians such as Friedrich Ebert, who was reproached with "betrayal of the working classes" [1. vol. 21/2, 893] and was attacked as "petty bourgeois" [1. vol. 22/1, 54], turned after the election of Paul von Hindenburg as President of the Reich in 1925 into a fundamental critique of the party and majoritarian democracy of Weimar. Until the dawn of the period of Presidential Cabinets, beginning in 1930, however, the hope of being able to preserve the existing democracy did not completely disappear from *Die Weltbühne*; only after that time did *Die Weltbühne* increasingly endorse the creation of a new political order, which it combined with increased

calls for a merger between Social Democrats and Communists.

Even prior to the transfer of power to Hitler, the magazine found itself the target of repression by the state, not least in the famous *Weltbühne* trial for alleged treason. The occasion was Walter Kreiser's 1929 article "Windiges aus der deutschen Luftfahrt," in which the author had reported on secret attempts by the Luftwaffe to arm itself in contravention to the Treatise of Versailles. The trial ended with Ossietzky's sentencing to one and a half years in jail, of which, however, he only had to serve six months, because of the Christmas amnesty of 1932. At the same time, the magazine argued vehemently for pacifism, against the growing antisemitism, and raised awareness about the challenges of the "social question" and capitalism's vulnerability to crises, as had become apparent after "Black Friday" in 1929. As had already happened in previous years, but now increasingly so, one could hear disparaging remarks about the "Jew's paper" in radical right-wing circles. However, the editorial board did not allow itself to be intimidated. Until its definitive prohibition shortly after the Reichstag fire in February 1933, it raised its "warning voices," ready to assume the "reputation of eternal rumblers." In a manner as defiant as it was pugnacious, one could read at the end of the last issue, delivered on March 7: "[T]he work continues because the spirit prevails after all" [1. vol. 29, 376].

Shortly thereafter, the magazine had to cease publication: many authors were soon doubly stigmatized by the National Socialists as "Jews" and "left wing intellectuals." Arrests, abuse, and murders ensued unless they succeeded in fleeing into exile. The best known of them, Carl von Ossietzky, detained and abused in various concentration camps from 1933 to 1936, died in May 1938 from the effects of a lung disease which he acquired in captivity.

2. Siegfried Jacobsohn and Kurt Tucholsky

Jacobsohn, born in Berlin in 1881, came from a Jewish merchant family that accorded little importance to religious upbringing and defined itself primarily as German. The mere choice of the name "Siegfried" for their eldest son reflected a corresponding desire for acculturation on the part of the parents.

From an early age, Jacobsohn was fascinated by the world of the Berlin theatre. Between 1901 and 1904, he rose, without any secondary school or university graduation, to the position of one of the leading stage critics and theatre reporters for the Berlin daily, *Welt am Montag*. However, a damper was placed on his promising career when, in late 1904, he was accused of plagiarism in the influential *Berliner Tageblatt*. Faced by continually intensifying debate over his work, sometimes tinged by antisemitism, Jacobsohn found himself obliged to withdraw from the Berlin daily press. After a few months abroad, Jacobsohn returned to Berlin in June 1905, and founded his own theatre journal under the title *Die Schaubühne*.

However unambiguous the → theatre criticism in the magazine sometimes turned out to be, it avoided all obstinate dogmatism. Nevertheless, a clear tendency could be identified: it was directed against Naturalism, did not hesitate to criticize Expressionism, and instead favored a renaissance of the classical idealist theatre. For many years, the editor of *Die Schaubühne*, who in 1910 had devoted an entire monograph to Max Reinhardt, considered the latter – to whose Jewish background, in accordance with Jacobsohn's own self-understanding, he paid no attention – as an exemplary representative of German culture. Reinhardt's stagings in the German theatre were long the subject of lavish praise until Jacobsohn turned away from the mass spectacle of the "Reinhardt circus" [1. vol. 16/1, 563] and his → [The] Great World Theatre.

In his 1928 study *Juden auf der deutschen Bühne*, Arnold Zweig, who wrote for *Die Schaubühne* beginning in 1914, interpreted Jacobsohn's path toward theatre criticism as a consequence of a general Jewish experience "at a time when all political activity was closed to the young, middle-class Jew." For this reason, Jacobsohn's "creative instinct" soon reached the point "where group passions can be spiritually expressed, where love and hate, the radical Yes and the radical No could be used educationally, propulsively: in theatre criticism, in a theatre journal." Jacobsohn can be considered a representative of German-Jewish awareness defined by → Bildung, language, culture – in this case, especially the theatre – which sought a common and, as it were, integrative denominator in the tradition of an enlightened → middle class (Bürgertum) and liberal Humanism. Not until – especially with the founding of the Weimar Republic and the consolidation of a left-wing, urban-oriented liberalism – "the times deepened, revealed, relaxed," did an open interest in politics become possible, and "the theatrical aspect lost importance in his paper, but not in his life" [7. 7f.]. A year after Jacobsohn's death on December 3, 1926, an admiring Tucholsky called him the "most ideal German editor our generation has seen" [1. vol. 23/2, 811].

Tucholsky, born in Berlin in 1890, came from upper middle-class families on both his father's and his mother's side, but did not have a faith-based upbringing. He left the Jewish community in July 1914, and four years later, without giving his reasons, had himself baptized as a Protestant. He always emphasized that he was a secular man, and that he attributed no particular importance to religious influences – especially Judaism – as far as his person was concerned.

Tucholsky began to write his first journalistic works in his school days, but his breakthrough as an author occurred in 1912, with the publication of his short story *Rheinsberg*. In January 1913, he published his first work in Jacobsohn's *Schaubühne*. After completing his studies with a law degree at the University of Jena, he found himself forced to interrupt his journalistic career when called up for military service. Although Tucholsky, who rose to become one of the best known pacifist journalists after the First World War, worked for many journals – thus, for instance, he edited the satirical journal *Ulk* from 1918 to 1920 – his name remained closely associated with *Die Weltbühne*. In all, he wrote 1,629 contributions for *Schaubühne* and *Weltbühne*, and their variety of form extended from political prose and court reporting, through → feuilletons, to satires and lampoons. With his notorious polemics, he distributed "on the little typewriter, knife thrusts, sabre strokes, punches," as Erich Kästner recalled in the first edition of the East Berlin *Weltbühne* of June 4, 1946.

Tucholsky's critique, formulated during the Weimar period, was directed against the "accidental republic" [1. vol. 18/2, 25–30]: the former USPD member (1920–1922) was at odds with the parties and politicians of the Republic, because, in his view, they perpetuated the Empire in veiled form in all too many areas. This, and what he regularly complained of as the lack of a decent mindset in the country, and instead the presence of an often nationalistic one, also found expression in the book of collages he created together with John Heartfield: *Deutschland, Deutschland über alles* (1929).

He increasingly avoided Berlin. In 1924, he went to Paris as a correspondent for *Die Weltbühne* and the *Vossische Zeitung*, while in 1930 he moved to Sweden, to which he dedicated his last, literarily sensitive 1931 book *Schloss Gripsholm*. It verified once again how little Tucholsky, as powerful in his language as he was witty, could be reduced to the political literati. After the transfer of power to Hitler, his books fell victim to book burning, and he himself was expatriated from Germany. After two failed marriages and other unhappy relations, he died in his Swedish exile in 1935, alone and plagued by depression, from an overdose of pills: presumably a suicide.

Shortly before his death, he had written a letter of farewell to Arnold Zweig, the interpretation of which is still controversial today; it has repeatedly been interpreted as a harsh reckoning with Judaism and a testimony to Jewish → self-hatred. Apart from the virulence of the attacks, however, the letter was in line with the polemics against Jewish acculturation which Tucholsky and Jacobsohn formulated still during the time of *Die Weltbühne*. The attacks by both editors had basically been directed against the drive to assimilation, which went as far as servility, of many Jews and their organizations, namely the → Reichsbund jüdischer Frontsoldaten (Reich Federation of Jewish Front-Line Soldiers), the Verband nationaldeutscher Juden (Association of German National Jews), and the → Centralverein deutscher Staatsbürger jüdischen Glaubens

Kurt Tucholsky (1890–1935)

(Central Association of German Citizens of Jewish Faith). Against the background of the ruthless antisemitism and the extermination policies of Nazism, in 1966 Gershom Scholem (→ Kabbalah) called Tucholsky one of "the most talented and nasty Jewish antisemites [who] achieved at a high level what the antisemites themselves could not" [12. 17]. In fact, Tucholsky had formulated in drastic terms reproaches against a ghettoization of the Jews, for which they only had themselves to blame, and, like the left-wing intellectuals, had attributed to them partial responsibility for the fall of the Weimar Republic. The author's isolation in exile and the psychological damage he had sustained, as had already been Zweig's interpretation, must have contributed to his harsh, exaggerated polemics.

3. Legacy and posterity

Prior to the prohibition of the Weimar journal, a parallel edition appeared, beginning in the autumn of 1932, in the form of the *Wiener Weltbühne*, under the direction of William Siegmund Schlamm (1904–1978). After the brief interlude in Vienna, he moved the paper, now entitled *Neue Weltbühne*, to Prague in the spring of 1933. There, led by Hermann Budzislawski (1901–1978) from 1934 onward, it was continued, with its editorial headquarters now in Paris, until it was prohibited once again in 1939. After the end of the Second World War, *Die Weltbühne* was re-founded in East Berlin in 1946. From then on, the East German *Weltbühne* was published with a high circulation, under the control of the SED (Socialist Unity Party), and presented itself as largely conformist and adhering to the party line.

There was no direct successor in the old Federal Republic. Nevertheless, in 1978–1979, the former *Weltbühne* author Axel Eggebrecht (1899–1991) organized a complete reprint of the Weimar editions, published by Athenäum Verlag. This major undertaking enjoyed some public resonance and promoted a debate over what responsibility the left-wing intellectuals represented by *Die Weltbühne* circle had in the maintenance or decline of the first German democracy. The answers turned out to be widely divergent, not least because of varying normative criteria: what some praised as radically democratic and conducive to the Republic, others condemned as hostile to the state and the Republic.

Only a small number of regular contributors to *Die Weltbühne* continued to work as journalists after 1945. These included independent-minded contrarians such as Kurt Hiller and William Schlamm, who had turned toward conservativism during his exile in America. However, for him, as for all those who still understood themselves as old-fashioned, non-conformists, disruptive outsiders, and incorruptible social critics, *Die Weltbühne* remained a political place of longing.

Bibliography

Sources

[1] Die Weltbühne, 1918–1933, complete reprint, 16 vols., Königstein 1978. [2] Die Schaubühne, 1905–1918, complete reprint, 14 vols., Königstein 1979. [3] F. Greis/S. Oswalt (ed.), Aus Teutschland Deutschland machen. Ein politisches Lesebuch zur "Weltbühne," Berlin 2008. [4] S. Jacobsohn, Briefe an Kurt Tucholsky 1915–1926. "Der beste Brotherr dem schlechtesten Mitarbeiter," ed. by R. v. Soldenhoff, Reinbek 1997. [5] S. Jacobsohn, Gesammelte Schriften 1900–1926, ed. by G. Nickel/A. Weigel, 5 vols., Göttingen 2005. [6] K. Tucholsky, Gesamtausgabe. Texte und Briefe, ed. by A. Bonitz et al., 22 vols., Reinbek 1996–2011. [7] A. Zweig, Juden auf der deutschen Bühne, Berlin 1928.

Secondary literature

[8] I. Deak, Weimar Germany's Left-Wing Intellectuals. A Political History of the Weltbühne and Its Circle, Berkeley 1968. [9] A. Enseling, Die Weltbühne. Organ der Intellektuellen Linken, Münster 1962. [10] A. Gallus, Heimat "Weltbühne." Eine Intellektuellengeschichte im 20. Jahrhundert, Göttingen 2012. [11] W. B. van der Grijn Santen, Die Weltbühne und das Judentum. Eine Studie über das Verhältnis der Wochenschrift "Die Weltbühne" zum Judentum hauptsächlich die Jahre 1918–1926 betreffend, Würzburg 1994. [12] M. Hepp (ed.), Kurt Tucholsky und das Judentum, Oldenburg 1996. [13] R. Hosfeld, Tucholsky. Ein deutsches Leben, Munich 2012. [14] U. Madrasch-Groschopp, Die Weltbühne. Porträt einer Zeitschrift, Berlin 1983. [15] G. Nickel, Die Schaubühne – Die Weltbühne. Siegfried Jacobsohns Wochenschrift und ihr ästhetisches Programm, Opladen 1996. [16] S. Oswalt, Siegfried Jacobsohn. Ein Leben für die Weltbühne, Gerlingen 2000.

ALEXANDER GALLUS, CHEMNITZ

Weltende

The Jewish poet Jakob van Hoddis's (1887–1942) poem *Weltende* ("End of the World," 1994) is considered the original text of literary Expressionism. First published in 1911, it was perceived as the prototype of a new poetry and in 1919 introduced the definitive → anthology of Expressionist → poetry *Menschheitsdämmerung* ("Dawn of Humanity," 1994). Numerous Jewish poets contributed to this work, edited by Kurt Pinthus (1886–1975), in particular as well as to literary Expressionism in general. In their works they combined traces of Jewish tradition with sharp-witted observations of the individual in the modern age, Jewish historical thought with anti-bourgeois criticism, and messianic hope with the power of poetry.

1. Marginal status and anti-bourgeois rebellion
2. Jakob van Hoddis
3. Simultaneity and the perception of history
4. Messianism in literature
5. A female Jewish poet in the modern age
6. Debating Messianism

1. Marginal status and anti-bourgeois rebellion

Of the 23 authors Pinthus included in the volume *Menschheitsdämmerung*, ten were of Jewish origin. Overall, nearly half of all the authors and artists considered Expressionist came from Jewish families [9. 136]. This disproportionately high contribution of Jews to a dominant epochal style was often attributed to the marginal status of Jewish intellectuals, which went hand-in-hand with Expressionist authors' anti-bourgeois rebellious attitude. In this context, one of their most important representatives, Alfred Wolfenstein (1883–1945), pointed to the "comparability of the Jewish and the poet's fate" [8. 12].

Concrete traces of Jewish tradition can certainly be found in these authors' texts. This is true also of the probably best-known text of Expressionist → poetry, Jakob van Hoddis's poem *Weltende*, which attracted the attention of his contemporaries and met with enthusiastic approval when it was first published in 1911. Pinthus placed it at the head of his collection of texts intended to represent a synthesis of the times [6. 61]. Even in those days the poem, according to the Expressionist poet Johannes R. Becher (1891–1958), was felt to be the "slogan" of the movement that "was to initiate an immense renaissance of humanity" (cited in [4. 408]). This canonization of the text was primarily due to the universal spirit of optimism of the young generation before the First World War. The contemporary reader is unable to discern neither an apocalyptic end of the world nor a messianic new beginning in the poem. Rather, it primarily expresses anti-bourgeois rebellion, as made clear in its very first verse: "The hat flies off the bourgeois' pointy head" [4. 15]. The following verses listing unconnected misadventures are above all the expression of a meaningless social event. In them the contingency characteristic of the modern age is made evident through the unconnected coexistence of small and large catastrophes of everyday life. The "flood tide" on the coast, the storm, railway accidents, a head cold – the asyndetic sequence of such events, as can be read in the Berlin daily papers of the time, bestows on the poem written in early 1910 its grotesque character [4. 248f.]. Van Hoddis himself intended, as Becher recalled, to capture "a new world-feeling [...], the sense of the simultaneity of events." He had already detected this world-feeling in Homer's epic analogies (cited in [4. 409f.]). In the bourgeois world of the early 20th century and its catastrophes, the poet utilizes this stylistic device in order to give expression to the absurdity of the world around him.

2. Jakob van Hoddis

Jakob van Hoddis, who had formed his pen name from the anagram of his civic name Hans Davidsohn, adding the name of the biblical patriarch Jacob as his first name, was born in Berlin in 1887 as the son of the physician Hermann Davidsohn, who came from a poor background. The tension between the sickly father who considered himself an atheist and the highly educated mother Doris (neé Kempner), who came from a family of Jewish landowners and had – as she wrote in an autobiographical account – "grown up in a traditionally Jewish home" (cited in [4. 286]) influenced the eldest of five siblings from his earliest childhood. At the humanities-oriented Gymnasium, he became acquainted with the world

of the ancient Greeks. In a later letter, he confessed: "At that time I loved only Homer" [4. 239].

From 1908 onward, Van Hoddis studied classical philology in Jena and Berlin, among other locations. In Berlin he joined the Neuer Club founded by Kurt Hiller (1885–1972), where, during its poetry evenings entitled "Neopathetisches Cabaret," he began to read his new poems beginning in 1910. In 1912 the first signs of a mental disorder began to manifest themselves. Van Hoddis travelled to Munich and Paris, from where he wrote letters acknowledging his conversion to Catholicism. He now believed, he said, in "the holiness of the sacraments." At the same time, however he maintained: "I still believe in the Jewish people" [4. 234]. On his mother's initiative, he was admitted into a psychiatric institution for the first time in 1912, from which he fled after a brief stay. He did not settle during the years 1913 and 1914, living in Berlin, Paris, and Munich alternately, frequently presenting new works in the Neuer Club and during authors' evenings of the Expressionist journal *Die Aktion*, in which the last poem he published, *Indianisch Lied*, appeared in 1914. In the autumn of the same year, his mother arranged for him to be taken in by the family of a teacher in Thuringia; from this point forward, his family and other people around him treated him as mentally ill. In 1918, 16 of his poems previously published in *Die Aktion* were collected under the title *Weltende* in the Expressionist series "Der rote Hahn."

His sister Marie, who had studied in Tübingen, ensured that he was housed with an innkeeper there beginning in 1922. The sick man, considered harmless, spent his days going for walks, drawing, and what he called "Spitzenmathematik" (elite mathematics). After a quarrel he was first admitted to the psychiatric university hospital in Tübingen in 1927 and later to an institution for "Nerven- und Gemütskranke" (nervous and emotional disorders) in Göppingen. His mother, who had in the meantime become a confirmed Zionist, visited him one last time in August 1933, before emigrating to Palestine (→ Aliyah). In September of that year, he was moved to the Israelitische Kuranstalt (Jewish sanatorium) in Sayn near Koblenz. He was deported from there in 1942 and murdered in one of the National Socialist extermination camps, Chełmno, Belzec, or → Sobibór [10. 162].

3. Simultaneity and the perception of history

The fixation with Greek Antiquity from his secondary school days appears to have distorted van Hoddis's view of the cultural foundations of his own origins. Ultimately the category of "simultaneity" determined by Becher, and in which van Hoddis himself discerned the novel aspect of his poems, has its origins in the Jewish understanding of → history. The moment in which past and present coincide, and in which consequently the "simultaneity" of all historical moments is present, proves to be the opposite of the occidental concept of history, secularized from Christianity. This concept, understood as a continuum, moves in a linear way towards an aim that can only be reached in the infinite. The messianic force of history, however, is concentrated within the "moment," as conceived by Jewish mystical tradition. Martin Buber (1878–1965; → Dialogue), who was in contact with the generation of young Expressionists – he read excerpts from his translation of Zhuangzi in the "Neopathetisches Cabaret" during the same evening as some of Jakob van Hoddis's poems were recited [4. 331] – invoked the "irrupting force of simultaneity" in the spirit of Judaism, but with Expressionist pathos, in a text written in 1914 and entitled *Der Augenblick*. In the mystical moment "where times unite" he felt the "tolling bell of 'All Time'," which bids him "do the the work of the morrow" [1. 94–96].

What this passage describes from the the tradition of Judaism as an experience of fulfilled time and is elaborated in its ethical consistency also appears in a modified form in the poem *Weltende*. Here, however, in accordance with the Greek world, "simultaneity" becomes the bad time, during which the meaninglessness of all history is revealed. In this blurred trace of original tradition not even perceived by the author himself, the cultural endangerment of all → assimilation becomes apparent.

4. Messianism in literature

By including poems by Walter Hasenclever (1890–1940) and Alfred Wolfenstein under the heading "Liebe den Menschen" ("Love to Human Beings") in his → anthology, Pinthus had selected works for his anthology which expressed the messianic hopes of Jewish tradition poetically much more directly than others (→ Messianism). Wolfenstein, for instance, initially focused in his great poem *Die Friedensstadt* ("The City of Peace") on the motif of the doomed city, which was central to Expressionist → poetry, and expressed above all by Georg Heym (1887–1912) in his poems from the volume *Umbra Vitae*. However, in the last four-lined rhymed stanzas, as in Heym's work, he addresses the city itself as a place of peace where a new humanity achieves perfection. The light metaphors of the last line – "Loved and loving, enlighten and enkindle us!" – emphasizes the mystical character of this vision [6. 331.]. Similar ideas are expressed by Hasenclever, whose poem *Du Geist, der mich verließ* ("You Spirit Who Abandoned Me") ends with the verse: "I am promise! I am eternally here!" [6. 352]. The numerous poems by Franz Werfel (1890–1945; → Musa Dagh), which Pinthus also included in this category all end with an optimistic Utopian prospect.

Even contemporary observers noticed that Wolfenstein's work alluded to "some passages from the Jewish prophets" [7]. In his → essay *Jüdisches Wesen und neue Dichtung*, first published in Buber's journal *Der Jude*, and then in an extended version as a separate booklet in 1922, he himself pointed to the kinship between the → literature of the new generation and the Jewish world-feeling that fluctuated "between messianic melancholy and ultimate optimism" [8. 48]. Poetry was to shape the ideal community; only then would it achieve its objective of generating a new humanity and a new world: "In poetry God wanders as in a human paradise" [8. 46]. This utopian exuberance is due to the universal sense of departure and new beginning that was widespread among Jewish intellectuals and writers as a consequence of Buber's → cultural Zionism. Buber himself formulated this new understanding of the "messianic" most precisely in his correspondence of 1917: It was, he said, "the belief in the fulfilment at the end of days, which eschews the ephemeral, but yet may, and must, work through the ephemeral" [2. 120].

Numerous texts by authors such as Albert Ehrenstein (1886–1950), Paul Adler (1878–1946), Alfred Lichtenstein (1889–1914), and Salomo Friedlaender (1871–1946), who wrote under the pseudonym Mynona, convey messianic visions in a disrespectful and provocative combination of the irreconcilable. At the same time they exhibit a tendency to include bizarre and contradictory passages, to use puns and grammatically incorrect syntax, mixing babblings and colloquialisms with mystically inspired allusions to the power of the poetic word to transform reality.

5. A female Jewish poet in the modern age

By referring directly to Jewish tradition in her verses, Else Lasker-Schüler (1869–1945; → [Das] Hebräerland) stands out from the other Expressionist poets. Besides many love poems, Pinthus included three poems from her volume *Hebräische Balladen*: *Mein Volk*, *An Gott*, and *Abraham und Isaak* in *Menschheitsdämmerung* ("My People," "And Seek God," and "Abraham and Isaac") [293, 306, 224]. Particularly *Mein Volk*, a poem she had already published in 1905 in the volume of poems *Der Siebente Tag* but now programmatically placed at the beginning of her 1913 collection of poems [5. vol. 1.1, 157], reflects the precarious relationship between the emancipated Jewish woman and her origin. In the first verse as well as at the end of the poem, she describes her people as a "rock," simultaneously applying a negative perspective by adding the adjective "decaying" and then "bones." As a citizen of the modern age and as a poet she is lonely – "And murmur deep withing / Seaward, distant, and alone / Over the wailingstones." However, the screams of her people "to the East" evoke a "echo" within her [5a. 177].

These images express the situation of the Jewish woman isolated within acculturation, who is reminded of a shared fate by the Ostjuden seemingly persisting in their traditional way of life. The first three verses of the second stanza should be understood in their ambivalence: "I have flowed so far away / From the must, the ferment / Of my blood." [5a. 177]. The current of life and poetry of the lyrical I rises among the Jewish people, with the metaphor of the blood, which frequently occurs in the Zionist context and in Buber's works in particular, in order to emphasize the close ties to this people. The blood, however, is "mostvergoren" ("fermented"), indicating on the one hand that it has spoiled, but on the other highlighting fermentation as the process that turns "must" into wine. This positive connotation is emphasized by Lasker-Schüler in 1920 having changed "vergoren" ("fermented [and spoiled]") to "gegoren" ("fermented [and turning to wine]") [5. vol. 1.2, 136f.].

Thus the process of the "Gärung" ("fermentation") of the Jewish people in the East as well as the West emerges as the true origin of her poetry, a cause for despair and hope at the same time.

The short poem, which reflects the situation of the female Jewish poet in the modern age like no other, also contains an implicit reference to the German cultural tradition of which Lasker-Schüler knew herself to be a part as well. With its basic motif of the river flowing to the sea as an image of the life and work of the poet, as well as with individual motifs, it refers in the form of a text contrafact and refutation to one of the canonic texts of the German educational tradition (→ Bildung), Johann Wolfgang Goethe's (→ Elective Affinities) "Sturm und Drang" hymn, *Mahomets Gesang* [3. 22–26]. The poetess, however, does not appear as the brook dancing "with youthful energy" or as the magnificently resplendent great river in the plain which carries its "brothers" with it to the sea. On the contrary, she appears as entirely self-focused, uttering lonely lamentations and, reduced to a small rivulet, "trickling faraway" to the sea. In Lasker-Schüler's poem, the "marble cliff" from which the "rock spring" in Goethe's hymn "rejoices up to the heavens," becomes "rocks of lamentation," recalling the Western Wall in Jerusalem, at which the Jews weep for their diasporic fate.

The modernity of Lasker-Schüler's poetry is demonstrated most impressively in her use of the Jewish tradition of biblical texts. In *Hebräische Balladen*, she transforms it into the medium of anti-bourgeois rebellion and the pronouncement of her own values inspired by her life as a bohemienne and avant-garde poet. In these poems she rejects the Enlightenment ideal of a universal brotherhood of man in favor of a messianic hope of salvation through a poetry sustained by religious and erotic intensity. Thus in the poem *Abraham und Isaak* ("Abraham and Isaak," 2002), first published in *Hebräische Balladen* in 1913, and placed by Pinthus in *Menschheitsdämmerung* together with her poems *An Gott* and *Zebaoth* ("To God" and "Sabaoth") [5. vol. 1.1, 157f.]; [6. 223], she presents the biblical story of the patriarch in a new light. The desert nomad Abraham builds "a city out of leaves and sod" [5a. 181]. If the "leaves" alludes to a leaf or sheet on which something could be written, the biblical figure of the patriarch would have been modelled on the character of the "great prophet St. Peter Hille." Peter Hille (1854–1904) was a nomadizing bohemian and anarchist writer who introduced Lasker-Schüler to the Berlin literary scene. In 1906, two years after his death, she wrote *Das Peter Hille-Buch* about him; furthermore, *Abraham und Isaak* is dedicated to Hille "in reverence." The close connection with the sea, too, from whose "crest" Abraham, as the fourth stanza tells, "broke" "shells" and "sponge" to decorate his altar, indicates Hille, to whom Lasker-Schüler referred as "Petrus-Poseidon" in the *Peter Hille-Buch* [5. vol. 3.1, 3.2]. Isaac, however, who appears as the innocent victim of God's arbitrariness and Abraham's obedience, is portrayed as a child "playing sacrifice" and tormenting the sacrificial beasts, the "rams," while God in his kindness, propitiated by the work of art that is Abraham's altar, shows the latter his love. In this way Lasker-Schüler transfers the canonical biblical text into a statement on the power of poetry. It generates reconciliation and improvement in society, abolishing the archaic human sacrifice, and thus achieves what according to the Hebrew Bible (→ Tanakh) only the power of God can do. Her poetry here, as well as in many others of the *Hebräische Balladen* with biblical motifs as their subject, is commentative writing reiterating the original written tradition of diasporic Judaism, in which a canonical text, the Torah, is interpreted by means of a commentary oriented towards one's own experience [11. 9–14].

6. Debating Messianism

In the context of German-speaking → cultural Zionism, an intensification of theoretical discussions on messianism may be observed toward the end of the First World War, concurrent with later Expressionism. It was triggered by, from a German perspective, the deteriorating war situation and the renewed hope of settling in Palestine fed by the → Balfour Declaration of 1917. Karl Wolfskehl (1869–1948), a poet close to Stefan George (→ George Circle), expressed the universal excitement that had taken hold of Jewish intellectuals at the time with literal Expressionist pathos in a letter to Buber: "I am no Zionist [...] but my blood cries out and rebels these days, for now the great crisis of mankind has also stepped under our star and shield, and it sways in the new night." [2. 226]. Buber himself, whose writings from this period – such as the book *Ereignisse und Begegnungen* (1917) – were also based in the general mood of the time sustained by apocalypticism and optimism for the future, made several remarks on the messianic question in his correspondence during the latter months of the year. Thus in 1917 he wrote to "Landgerichtsrat S.": "The world is unredeemed-don't you feel that, as I do, in every drop of blood? Don't you feel as I do that the messianic cannot be something that has happened [...] but only something toward which we gaze when we look into infinity" [2. 223]. A few days later he remarked to the Prague philosopher Hugo Bergmann (1883–1975; → Brit Shalom; → Prague): "In the redeeming function, the redeeming act of the messianic human being, the absolute future is being prepared in the present, in every present" [2. 224]. Buber's father Carl, an emancipated land owner and industrialist, commented on the sense of messianic anticipation expressed in these sentences in his response to his son who had sent him his autobiography *Mein Weg zum Chassidismus* at the end of 1917:

"You are virtually announcing yourself as the Messiah. That cannot possibly stand" [2. 226].

However, the messianic dimension in the work of Jewish Expressionists retains a universalist dimension by maintaining the hope for a renewal of all humanity. In addition, its rebellious character, which sometimes goes against good taste, indicates the anarchistic, revolutionary, and apocalyptic potential it carried from Jewish messianism to one of the most impressive forms of expression found in the literature and art of the modern age in the German-speaking world.

Bibliography

Sources

[1] M. Buber, Ereignisse und Begegnungen, Leipzig 1917.   [2] N. N. Glatzer/P. Mendes-Flohr (eds.), The Letters of Martin Buber. A Life of Dialogue, trans. by R. and C. Winston et al., New York 1991.   [3] J. W. Goethe, The Collected Works, Vol. 1: Selected Poems, ed. by C. Middleton, trans. by M. Hamburger et al., Princeton 1994.   [4] J. van Hoddis, Dichtungen und Briefe, ed. by R. Nörtemann, Zurich 1987.   [5] E. Lasker-Schüler, Werke und Briefe. Kritische Ausgabe, ed. by N. Oellers et al., 11 vols, Frankfurt am Main 1996–2010.   [5a] E. Lasker-Schüler, Selected Poems, trans. by A. Durchslag-Litt and J. Litman-Litman-Demeestère, Los Angeles/ Copenhagen 2002, 177, 181.   [6] K. Pinthus (ed.), Menschheitsdämmerung: Dawn of Humanity. A Document of Expressionism with Biographies and Bibliographies, trans. by J. M. Ratych et al., Columbia 1994.   [7] E. Weiß, Über Alfred Wolfenstein, in: Feuer. Monatsschrift für Kunst und künstlerische Kultur 2 (1920) 2/3, 136.   [8] A. Wolfenstein, Jüdisches Wesen und neue Dichtung, Berlin 1922.

Secondary literature

[9] H. O. Horch, Expressionismus und Judentum. Zu einer Debatte in Martin Bubers Zeitschrift "Der Jude," in: T. Anz/M. Stark (eds.), Die Modernität des Expressionismus, Stuttgart/Weimar

1994, 120–141. [10] H. Hornbogen, Jakob van Hoddis. Die Odyssee eines Verschollenen, Munich 2001. [11] B. Witte, Jüdische Tradition und literarische Moderne. Heine, Buber, Kafka, Benjamin, Munich 2007.

VIVIAN LISKA, ANTWERPEN
AND BERND WITTE, DÜSSELDORF

Weltgeschichte

Weltgeschichte des jüdischen Volkes is the title of the Russian-Jewish historian Simon Dubnow's (1860–1941) ten-volume magnum opus, published between 1925 and 1929. First published in German, the *Weltgeschichte* is regarded as the historiographical foundation of a "sociological" → historiography of the Jews, focusing on their lebenswelten (worlds of lived experience) and institutions primarily from a Russian-imperial and Jewish diasporic perspective. The work of the autodidactic historian and popular political educator Dubnow allows insights into the complex transformation of a history of the people of Israel, *am Yisra'el*, permeated by liturgy and following mainly biblical narrative patterns into the secular historiography of a global Jewish people living in the Diaspora but nevertheless regarding themselves as a national entity. A historian on the threshold between tradition and modernity, Dubnow proved to be a mediator between ancient and modern Judaism, as well as between the cyclical and the linear concept of profane time.

1. Terminology
2. Simon Dubnow
3. Theory of history
4. Politics of history
5. Tradition and modernity

1. Terminology

Entitled *Weltgeschichte des jüdischen Volkes* (World history of the Jewish people) in the German edition, the Hebrew title of Dubnow's great work of history is *Divre yeme am olam* – Chronicle of the eternal people. Both were shaped by different traditions of interpreting time and the world. In addition, they indicate the influence of different people to whom Dubnow was close.

After moving to Berlin in 1922, Dubnow dedicated himself to the publication of his magnum opus, which was originally to be titled "Allgemeine Geschichte der Juden" (Universal history of the Jews). Influenced by the Russian-Jewish philosopher David Koigen (→ Ethos), who had chosen exile in Berlin in 1921, one year before Dubnow, he changed the title of the work to *Weltgeschichte des jüdischen Volkes* in 1924 [3. vol. 3, 93f.]. Koigen had completed his dissertation on the history and philosophy of the Young Hegelians in 1900 and had also written on, among others, Bruno Bauer, Ludwig Feuerbach, Moses Hess (→ Geldwesen), and Karl Marx (→ Jewish Question). The professor of philosophy, who had emigrated from Soviet Russia, edited the journal *Ethos* from 1925 onward, which focused on issues of the cultural self-definition of man, the so-called theory of the cultural act [17]. In the context of Hegel's philosophy of history, which, though secular, was at the same time imbued with Christian thought, the concept of *Weltgeschichte* is accompanied by an eschatological echo. Friedrich Schiller, for instance, wrote in his poem *Resignation* (1786): "The world's history / Is the world's judgment doom" [9. 205]. Dubnow used a similar phrase, which would appear in the introduction to the Russian edition of his *Weltgeschichte*. In one passage, he declared historical judgment to be subject to ethical criteria, which represent a "court of history" [3. vol. 3, 93].

In September 1924, the first volume of Dubnow's work was published in a Russian edition under the title *Vsemirnaya istoriya yevrejskogo naroda* (World history of the Jewish people), translated from German by the Russian-Jewish publishing house

Gescher, based in Berlin. However, due to inflation and the Great Depression, they were unable to continue publishing the Russian version [14. 492f.]; the entire work was thus first published in German by the publishing house → Jüdischer Verlag in Berlin.

In 1929, the first Hebrew edition of Dubnow's *Weltgeschichte* was published by Dvir publishing house. The tradition behind the Hebrew title is different from those of the German and Russian editions. *Divre yeme am olam* sounds decidedly biblical. The world *olam*, in fact, has a secular and a sacred meaning, denoting both "world" as well as "eternity." *Am olam* is linked to the idea of Israel as God's eternal people – eternal in time and ubiquitous in space. The first part of the title, *divre yeme*, too, is of biblical origin. Its literal meaning is "things of the days," with the "days" referring to narrated history as a sacred chronicle. This sacrally charged, liturgical-sounding title probably goes back to Ḥayim Naḥman Bialik (→ El ha-tsippor), who was the head of the Dvir publishing house and in charge of the publication of the Hebrew translation of the *Weltgeschichte*. Bialik would have found it unbearable if the work did not have a profound Hebrew title that derived from biblical tradition. As early as 1913, he had insisted in his essay *Ha-sefer ha-ivri* (1951; The Hebrew Book), published in the journal *Ha-Shiloaḥ* (The Messenger), that Jewish authenticity could only be expressed in → Hebrew. In 1924 Bialik criticized the → Wissenschaft des Judentums for abandoning Hebrew – the one and only language that guaranteed the "spiritually intimate contact with the living tradition." Using biblical vocabulary, he campaigned against the "mortal sin" of displacing Hebrew, which he said was the "true oral teaching" [1. 567, 569].

Dubnow, who wrote most of his works in → Russian, was rather agnostic on the language question. Besides Russian, Hebrew, and → Yiddish, he also accepted other languages due to the dispersal of the Jews [20].

The philosophical and religious connotations of the titles of his *Weltgeschichte* indicate the conception of his → historiography, which oscillates between sacral Jewish and secular, universal semantics, images, metaphors, and narrative forms.

2. Simon Dubnow

Simon Dubnow was born in 1860 in the Belorussian → shtetl of Mstislavl, at that time part of the → Pale of Settlement. He was murdered by the Nazis and their henchmen in → Riga in 1941. His lifetime encompasses the decisive period in the history of the Russian-Jewish experience in the modern era. His early life was shaped by the Great Reforms initiated by Czar Alexander II in the wake of the Crimean War (1853–1856), along with the historically pivotal abolition of serfdom in 1861. The assassination of the Czar in 1881 led to a wave of anti-Jewish → pogroms and to the 1882 → May Laws directed against the Jews, along with the quota on admissions to institutions of higher education (→ Universities). In 1891 the Jews living in Moscow were expelled from the city. The Duma granted by the Czar in 1905 gave rise to great hopes of a constitutional regime in Russia. The achievements of the February Revolution of 1917, above all, the decree of universal equality, which included the Jews, corresponded to Dubnow's ideas, which leaned toward the Constitutional Democrats (Cadets) and were liberal in the Western sense. However, he could not agree with the politics of the Bolsheviks from the October Revolution onward (→ Red Cavalry). In 1922, the year in which the Soviet Union was founded, Dubnow left the "red autocracy"; coming from Petrograd, he settled in Berlin [7. vol. 10. 531]. After the transfer of power to Hitler, he left the city in August 1933 for Riga, Latvia.

The fundamental upheavals in Russian history provide the outlines of Dubnow's education and development, as well as the political and intellectual conditions that shaped how his works came into being. Hopes for individual → emancipation, blocked by the prevailing circumstances in Russia, turned into frustration about unfulfilled civic longings. In diasporic conditions, this disappointment converted to a nationally preformed Jewish longing for collective selfhood. Dubnow's own experience and education may be understood as exemplary of the collective biography of a generation of intellectual Jews in the Russian Empire who suffered under the authoritarian restrictions on individual emancipation, unfurling a collective future horizon in response. Dubnow's historiographical work presents an ideologically processed reflex of this constellation. The historian's enlightening memoirs from the 1930s provide clear information about this in a teleological retrospective [3].

Dubnow's impetus for individual emancipation in his education under the shadow of Alexander II's Great Reforms emerges in his early schooling. After his traditional education in the ḥeder (→ Talmud Torah), the young Dubnow requested that his parents – his father worked in the timber trade and was consequently rarely present as an authority figure – send him after his → bar mitzvah to a public crown school, which was an educational institution for young Jews that aimed at acculturation to the Russian language. Dubnow's traditionalist parents and grandfather Benzion agreed only on the condition that he continue to attend the Talmud lessons his grandfather taught in the yeshivah of the local → synagogue. As an adolescent, Dubnow immersed himself in literature and poetry that was informed by the Jewish Enlightenment (→ Haskalah). Above all, he read the works of Abraham Mapu (→ Ahavat Tsiyon), Micah Joseph Lebensohn, and Moses Leib Lilienblum. In the autumn of 1874, the public crown schools were closed, and Dubnow had to continue his education at a Russian community

school. From 1876 to 1877, he attended the district school in Mstislavl.

In the following three years Dubnow tried in vain to be accepted at a secondary school. During this time, he set himself an enormous amount of reading. Full of optimism for progress, he saw himself as a positivist like many other Jews of his generation. He was greatly influenced by the works of the Russian Nikolay Chernyshevski, the Briton Henry Thomas Buckle and his *History of Civilization in England*, as well as the ideas of John Stuart Mill and Herbert Spencer. He felt a particular connection with the writings of August Comte. Utilitarianism and the doctrine of freedom made a lasting impression on him. For example, he described Mill's work as "the gospel of individualism" [3. vol. 1, 142]. Influenced by the philosopher of religion Vladimir Solovyov, Dubnow later moved away from Positivism. However, his early adolescent reading led him to renounce religion as an expression of atavism and superstition.

Failing the entrance exams for secondary schools, Dubnow was not qualified to study at a university. As a consequence, he was unable to achieve the status as a member of the intelligentsia, and, thus, was not legally permitted to live outside of the Pale of Settlement. From 1880 onward, he lived illegally in St. Petersburg with forged documents, working as an author for Russian-Jewish publications, primarily the periodical → *Voskhod* (Sunrise). The insult he felt from these circumstances seems to have hurt him even more deeply than the pogroms that began in 1881, which spread terror among the Jews of the Russian Empire. In any case, Dubnow left no trace of any appropriate contemporary reaction to these drastic events.

In St. Petersburg, Dubnow published articles in newspapers and journals advocating the individual integration of Jews in the Czarist Empire, combining this with domands for modernization and making them productive. Accordingly, he was highly critical of Leon Pinsker's 1883 text → *Auto-Emancipation* with its national Jewish leanings [3. vol. 1, 188]. After that, Aron Ginzburg's circle commissioned him in 1884 to conduct an anonymous survey of the legal situation of the Jews in Russia with the aim of influencing the High Commission for the Revision of the Current Laws Concerning the Jews in the Empire that Czar Alexander III had convened [3. vol. 1, 195–197]; [14. 117f.].

Only later, when he was regarded as a great historian of the history of the Jews, did he classify the pogroms of the first half of the 1880s as a fundamental historical caesura and turning point that broke with Jewish expectations of emancipation in Russia. He put the following words in the mouth of the protagonist of his 1916 *Geschichte eines jüdischen Soldaten*, a character constructed in the mold of collective history: "I was born in 1881. Later I grasped the symbolic import of this fateful date in my life: it was, after all, the very year in which the time of pogroms began – and various kinds of pogroms have accompanied me from the cradle to the grave" [8. 44f.].

Dubnow's shift from the project of individual emancipation and toward regarding Jews as a collective occurred during the second half of the 1880s. It is connected not least to a personal crisis that coincided with him getting married in 1884 and returning to his home town Mstislavl. Until then, Dubnow had seen himself as *aḥer* (other) in the sense of Jewish Epicureanism (→ Epikoros), basing his views on the Tannaite Elisha ben Abuja and the deist Baruch Spinoza (→ Tractatus Theologico-Politicus). In this way, he embodied an apostatizing affiliation with paradoxical participation in the Jewish collective that would later be called the → non-Jewish Jew.

3. Theory of history

Dubnow rationalized his renewed closeness to the Jews as a collective in terms of a historical-theoretical purpose by drafting a dialectical constellation of Jewish historical development, analogous to his own transformations. He called this an "evolutionary triad" [3. vol. 3. 183–187]. He expanded this methodology in his *Pis'ma o starom i novom yevrejstve* (1907; "Nationalism and History. Essays on Old and New Judaism," 1958), which constitutes a reflexive foundation of his historiography. He counters traditional Judaism – the "thesis" – with the modern concept of a secular self-understanding aimed at the emancipated individual – the "anti-thesis." The two mutually exclusive approaches are ultimately abrogated in the "synthesis"; this offers Jews a new kind of belonging with a secular as well as a national Jewish self-understanding. The bearer of this self-understanding is the Jewish people. Being the most historical of all historical peoples, the Jews move through space and time with religion as a mere vessel of their continued existence. As a nation of the spirit rather than of rootedness in the ground, the centers of the Jewish people move in chronological sequence to Babylonia, → Sepharad, and → Ashkenaz.

Dubnow considered America a potential future center. He was not convinced by Zionism (→ Basel). To him, Palestine presented no alternative, certainly not as a future home for the masses of destitute Jews from Eastern Europe. At best, he could imagine a spiritual center becoming established there, approaching the thoughts of the Cultural Zionist Aḥad Ha-Am (→ Cultural Zionism). Dubnow's political activities were informed by the imperial and multinational composition of the Russian Empire; here, individual liberty was supposed to be combined with collective, national self-organization. His biographical experience affirmed this, and his understanding of history contributed the necessary theoretical tools.

Dubnow pursued the direction of Jewish nationalization (Russ. *natsionalizatsiya*) whose intellectual home was → Odessa. In 1890, he moved there with his family from Mstislavl after endeavoring in vain to obtain a residence permit for St. Petersburg. In Odessa he soon became part of an illustrious debating circle consisting of literary figures and writers of a Jewish-nationalist bent. Besides Mendele Moykher-Sforim (→ Fishke) and Ḥayim Naḥman Bialik (→ El ha-tsippor), he also met Aḥad Ha-Am, to whom Dubnow dedicated his only book in → Hebrew, the two-volume *Toldot ha-ḥasidut* (1930/1932; History of Hasidism), written in Berlin in the early 1930s.

In Odessa Dubnow also embarked on translating the *Volkstümliche Geschichte der Juden* by Heinrich Graetz, who died in 1891 (→ Historiography), into Russian. While he was at first impressed by the historiographical achievements of the German-Jewish historian, who had been trained in the tradition of the → Wissenschaft des Judentums, he later distanced himself from Graetz's approach to intellectual history, developing his own, distinct, "sociological conception" of Jewish history [7. vol. 1, XVII]. Part of this undertaking was his appeal *Naḥpesah ve-naḥkorah* ("Let Us Seek and Investigate," 2008), published in Russian in 1891 and in Hebrew the following year, in which he called upon the Jewish public to search for and collect the "hidden treasures" of history [4. 363]. Treasures of history referred primarily to pinkasim in which traces of the religious, institutional, and social life of the Jews might be discovered. Dubnow regarded the pinkas as the foremost source of Jewish historiography. Rather than focusing on the intellectual, spiritual, and liturgical literatures, as Graetz had done, he directed his research interest at the community records of the → kahal, the administration of the autonomous community. For Dubnow, the pinkas became the reservoir of information on the material Jewish lebenswelt.

In Dubnow's "sociological" historiography, the *kahal* thus played a central role. As the fundamental institution of the traditional, premodern autonomy of Jewish communities, it became the abstract, non-telluric, diasporic surrogate of the statehood that the Jews as an "intellectual-historical nation" lacked [6. 40].

4. Politics of history

Dubnow's 1907 *Pis'ma o starom i novom yevrejstve* originated in a series of publications in the monthly journal → *Voskhod*, which he had begun in 1897 – the iconic year of modern Jewish history when the First Zionist Congress convened in → Basel and the *Algemeyner Yidisher Arbeter-bund* (General Jewish Labor → *Bund*) was founded in Vilna. In his fundamental deliberations on historiography, he drew conclusions from the preceding decades. Accordingly, his historiographical work went hand in hand with political activity, whereby political and historical-philosophical interventions frequently intermingled.

Dubnow had first come in contact with members of the *Bund* after moving to Vilna in 1903. Once he returned to St. Petersburg in 1906, he took part in establishing the → Jewish Society for History and Ethnography (*Yevrejskoe istoriko-etnograficheskoe obshchestvo*), edited the journal *Yevrejskaya starina* (Jewish antiquities) from 1909 to 1918, and briefly taught at a private institute for Jewish studies sponsored by Aron Ginzburg, where the classes were entitled "Courses in Oriental Studies" [14. 335–338]. In 1906 he also took part in establishing the increasingly Yiddishist Jewish autonomist and constitutional *Folkspartey*, which, however, met with little success. In 1925 he supported the founding of → YIVO and became a member of its honorary board of trustees, together with, among others, Albert Einstein (→ Theory of Relativity).

In politics, Dubnow was always a liberal. His attitude to Marxism was reserved. He also kept his distance from the *Bund*, although he agreed with the principle of *doikayt* it propagated, engaging in political activity in the here and now, as well as with its stance on issues of national-cultural autonomy. His daughter Sophia's marriage to *Bund* politician Henryk Erlich certainly ensured he would be close enough to the *Bund* to be knowledgeable about it.

During the interwar years, Dubnow championed the 1919 minority treaties (→ Minority Rights). However, these were not identical with his concept of the *kahal*, which he transferred onto contemporary political conditions. In Dubnow's view, the *kahal* ought to be granted the authority to legislate. As in his construction of history, this modern *kahal* seemed to him the guarantor of the autonomous national existence of the Jewish communities in Eastern Europe. Yet, it could correspond to the *kahal* of premodern times in name only. After all, premodern Jewish autonomy had been part of a vertically structured corporate order that had already begun to disintegrate during the period of late absolutism. The horizontal order of the polity significant for the modern era, however, rested on the premise of the civic equality of all individuals – a type of society in which corporate residues no longer had any place. If Dubnow's *kahal* hoped to find a place in the new world of nation-states, it would have to adapt to horizontally-oriented integration. If it was possible at all, this transformation could be realized only within the framework of the minority protection treaties imposed from the outside onto the newly established nation-states of Eastern Central Europe. In the crisis-ridden 1930s, however, these arrangements were already crumbling. The end of the multinational empires seemed to have precipitated the historical end of the corporate residues surviving within them.

5. Tradition and modernity

Dubnow was a historian of the transition between tradition and a Jewish modern age that he helped to shape. The movement of transforming from one lebenswelt and cultural age into the other runs through his person as well as his works. He used images and metaphors scattered throughout his work with biographical as well as historiographical intentions, constructing an affirmation of the modernity he represented – for instance, when he compared himself to his grandfather Benzion, a severe opponent (*mitnagged*) of → Hasidism in the mold of the Gaon of → Vilna, to contrast the traditional with his "new" wisdom. Dubnow held that the "wisdom of the Talmud and rabbinic texts" that his grandfather personified is transmitted orally, whereas he, the grandson Dubnow, produces "the new wisdom of the century," imparting it to a numerous and highly dispersed audience thanks to the "printing press" (→ Printing) [3. vol. 1, 207]. By juxtaposing oral and written transmission as well as the different possibilities inherent in them, including the material ones, Dubnow here symbolizes the change that had occurred, linking it to his own person, as well.

His differentiation between sacred and profane texts also seems to be material and secularistic, although he considered only the latter to be relevant for historiography. Accordingly, he employed religious symbolism in his appeal *Naḥpesa ve-naḥkorah* when he contrasted the scripture considered sacred (→ Tanakh), which was written with a goose quill, to the → pinkasim "incised ... with iron stylus and lead" (Job 19:24). These he exalted to be the primary original source for modern Jewish historiography [5. 226].

In his historical works, Dubnow frequently relied on traditional, biblical, and Talmudic semantics in order to describe modern or historical phenomena. In *Naḥpesa ve-naḥkorah*, he wrestled with the appropriate collective designation for the Jews. He employed the traditional terms *Yisra'el saba* (Grandfather Israel, Bereshit Rabba 68:11), *am Yisra'el* (People of Israel), *bet Yisra'el* (House of Israel), and *bne Yisra'el* (Children of Israel); there are also biblical terms like *Yisra'el* (Israel) and *Yehudim* (Jews) [5]. In order to affirm the semantic alignment with the modern age, Dubnow invoked Ernest Renan's concept of nation, yet omitting its core (*le plébiscite de tous les jours*), that established the political will of the nation. Indeed, the political formula of the "daily plebiscite" based in the concept of the territorial state cannot properly be applied to the Jews as a "spiritual nation."

In spite of his avowed secularism, Dubnow could not evade the ulterior validity of the biblical narrative, certainly not its cyclical narrative form [12. 153–159]. An example is his 1939 article, with the haunting title *Vos darf men ton in Homens tsaytn?* (What should we do in Haman's times?), published in the Yiddish journal *Oyfn sheydveg* (At the crossroads), which briefly appeared in Paris. Dubnow uses Haman, the iconic negative character in the Book of Esther, to personify the catastrophes threatening the Jews. Haman, who represents → anti-Judaism in a way similar to the biblical collective figure of Amalek, historically appears in varied forms [13]. The happy ending of the story of Esther, in which God does not appear explicitly at all, can hardly be transferred to the tribulations befalling the Jews elsewhere. Nevertheless, in the form in which Dubnow makes use of it, it possesses a kind of explanatory mode also with regard to the historical catastrophes he names in the article – be they the persecutions as a result of the Crusades and the plague, the expulsion from Spain (→ Sepharad), the Khmelnytsky persecutions in the Polish–Lithuanian Commonwealth (→ Cossack Persecutions), the Russian → pogroms beginning in the late 19th century, or the pogroms in Ukraine in 1919 (→ Schwarzbard Trial), which he lists using the dates of both the common and Jewish eras. This mode appears, albeit less explicitly, throughout the narrative of Dubnow's work. In the article published in *Oyfn sheydveg* on the eve of the war – that is, the most terrible catastrophe ever to befall the Jews – Dubnow professes his enduring trust in Western democracies, expecting that they would oppose Hitler as the new incarnation of Haman. To the disappointment of his students as well as the editors of the journal whose view of history was by now deeply pessimistic, Dubnow continued to the very last to embody a profound faith in democracy and liberalism shaped by the 19th-century concept of linear progress. In Dubnow, two worlds and the linguistic cultures connected with them diverge – on the one hand, the religiously-based language of catastrophism, employing an essentially historiosophical rhetoric, and, on the other, an unyieldingly dominating faith in the promises of the → Enlightenment. Both moments are equally reflected in Dubnow's works and impact.

Bibliography

Sources

[1] C. N. Bialik, Jüdische Wissenschaft in fremder Sprache. Ein Brief an die Herausgeber des "D'wir," in: Der Jude 8 (1924) 10, 566–574. [2] C. N. Bialik, The Hebrew Book. An Essay, trans. by M. Halkin, Jerusalem 1952. [3] S. Dubnow, Buch des Lebens. Erinnerungen und Gedanken. Materialien zur Geschichte meiner Zeit, 3 vols., ed. by V. Dohrn, Göttingen 2004/05. [4] S. Dubnow, Let Us Seek and Investigate [1892], in: Simon Dubnow Institute Yearbook 7 (2008), 353–382. [5] S. Dubnow, Naḥpesah ve-naḥkorah [Let Us Seek and Investigate], in: Ha-Pardes. Osef sifruti [The Garden. Literary Collection] 1

(1892), 221–242. [6] S. Dubnow, Die Grundlagen des Nationaljudentums, Berlin 1905. [7] S. Dubnow, Weltgeschichte des jüdischen Volkes. Von seinen Uranfängen bis zur Gegenwart, 10 vols., Berlin 1925–29. [8] S. Dubnow, Geschichte eines jüdischen Soldaten. Bekenntnis eines von vielen, ed. by V. Bischitzky/S. Schreiner, Göttingen/Bristol (CT) 2012. [9] F. Schiller, The Poems and Ballads of Schiller, trans. by E. B. Lytton, Edinburgh 1844.

Secondary literature

[10] D. Diner, Ambiguous Semantics. Reflections on Jewish Political Concepts, in: Jewish Quarterly Review 98 (2008), 89–102. [11] A. Greenbaum et al. (eds.), Writer and Warrior. Simon Dubnov. Historian and Public Figure, Jerusalem 2010 [partially in Hebrew]. [12] A. Hilbrenner, Diaspora-Nationalismus. Zur Geschichtskonstruktion Simon Dubnows, Göttingen 2007. [13] J. Karlip, In the Days of Haman. Simon Dubnow and His Disciples at the Eve of WW II, in: Simon Dubnow Institute Yearbook 4 (2005), 531–564. [14] V. E. Kelner, Simon Dubnow. Eine Biografie, Göttingen/Oakville 2010. [15] D. Miron, Simon Dubnow as a Literary Historian, in: Simon Dubnow Institute Yearbook 10 (2011), 433–445. [16] R. M. Seltzer, Simon Dubnow's "New Judaism." Diaspora, Nationalism and the World History of the Jews, Leiden et al. 2014. [17] M. Urban, Religion of Reason Revised. David Koigen on the Jewish Ethos, in: Journal of Jewish Thought and Philosophy 16 (2008), 59–89. [18] J. Veidlinger, Simon Dubnow Rexontextualized. The Sociological Conception of Jewish History and the Russian Intellectual Legacy, in: Simon Dubnow Institute Yearbook 3 (2004), 411–427. [19] D. H. Weinberg, Between Tradition and Modernity. Haim Zhitlowski, Simon Dubnow, Ahad Ha-Am, and the Shaping of Modern Jewish Identity, New York 1996. [20] S. Werses, Zwischen Wilna und Jerusalem. Simon Dubnow und die jüdische Sprachenfrage, in: Jahrbuch des Simon-Dubnow-Instituts 11 (2012), 413–439.

DAN DINER, JERUSALEM/LEIPZIG

West Side Story

West Side Story is considered the pinnacle of the American musical and characterized the new dynamic in the cultural life of → America that began in the 1960s. The play, set to music by Leonard Bernstein (1918–1990), about the conflict between Puerto Ricans and Anglo-Americans in → New York, embodies the composer's ideological and artistic values, which resulted from his double affiliation, both American and Jewish. With his socially-committed liberalism, his plea for ethnic and religious tolerance and his striving for a new American → music based on the nation's ethnic variety, Bernstein was exemplary of the second generation of Jewish immigrants to America.

1. East Side Story
2. Leonard Bernstein
3. "A new way of living"
4. The double man

1. East Side Story

West Side Story was a joint effort by the American-Jewish creative artists Leonard Bernstein, Stephen Sondheim (1930–2021), Jerome Robbins (1918–1998), and Arthur Laurents (1917–2011). All four were united by a critical liberal perspective on society and culture, which stemmed from their Jewish experience, especially after the Holocaust.

The idea for *West Side Story* goes back to Robbins, the choreographer. In 1949, he suggested to Bernstein to bring to the stage a version of Shakespeare's *Romeo and Juliet*, adapted to modern American conditions. "East Side Story," as the play was entitled, was to deal with the clashes between a Jewish and an Irish-Catholic gang in the slums of → New York's Lower East Side (→ Kosher Nostra) on the occasion of the celebrations of Pesaḥ and Easter (→ Course of the Year) [3. 20–25]. Robbins tried to win over the composer Bernstein and the playwright Laurents to his project, but the three could not initially come to an agreement. He therefore abandoned his idea at first, especially since the conflict between Jews and Catholics in New York had lost some of its topicality.

Robbins re-initiated discussion of the project in 1955. A breakthrough finally occurred on the occasion of a chance meeting between Bernstein and Laurents in Los Angeles, when a headline in the *Los Angeles Times* on the gang violence raging in the city between Mexican immigrants and Anglo-Americans caught his eye. Both of them immediately saw parallels between the West and the East Coast, and drafted a new concept: they transferred the story line to New York's West Side – the slums of the East Side had been demolished in the meantime – and picked up on the smoldering ethnic conflict there between Puerto Ricans and Anglo-Americans. Bernstein was thoroughly electrified by the idea of taking up Latin-American rhythms, which were very popular at the time in American popular culture [4. 249f.]. Stephen Sondheim, as lyricist for *West Side Story*, as the play was now to be called, completed the team. Instead of the relations between Jews and non-Jews, the musical now had as its theme the tensions between Anglo-Saxons and Latinos. However, the central idea, as Bernstein noted right at the top of the first page of his copy of *Romeo and Juliet*, of being "'an out and out plea for racial tolerance'" (cited in [3. 127]), was preserved.

2. Leonard Bernstein

Leonard Bernstein was born in 1918 in Lawrence (Massachusetts), as the child of Ukrainian-Jewish immigrants. His father Samuel Joseph Bernstein, son of a rabbi influenced by → Hasidism, worked successfully in Boston as a businessman in the field of hairdressing and cosmetic articles.

Leonard Bernstein (1918–1990)

Leonard grew up in the suburbs of Boston, and attended the city's most prestigious school, the Boston Latin School. Not until relatively late, at the age of ten, did he find his way to → music. He studied piano, and developed near-virtuoso abilities on that instrument. In 1935, he began to study music at Harvard University and gave his first public concert in 1937. In addition, he distinguished himself as director of the musical productions of the Harvard Dramatic Club. Through his friendship with the composer Aaron Copland, he gained access to the American musical avant-garde.

With the goal of pursuing a career as a conductor, Bernstein enrolled in the renowned Curtis Institute of Music in Philadelphia. His career as a conductor received a decisive boost from his meeting with Serge Koussevitzky, music director of the Boston Symphony Orchestra, who in 1940 accepted Bernstein into his conductors' class in the summer camp of the prestigious Tanglewood Music Center for rehearsals, concerts, and training. In 1943, Artur Rodziński, music director of the New York Philharmonic Orchestra, engaged the young musician as his assistant and auxiliary conductor. When, in November 1943, Bernstein stood in for Bruno Walter, who had fallen ill, and conducted a concert broadcast nationwide by radio, he became famous overnight. Bernstein also distinguished himself early on as a composer. His first symphony *Jeremiah*, his ballet *Fancy Free*, and his first musical *On the Town* had their debut in 1944. In 1945, the now celebrated star conductor took over the position of music director of the New York City Symphony Orchestra.

In the McCarthy era (→ Rosenberg Trial), the politically liberal Bernstein was suspected of communist activities, but avoided more serious trouble. In 1951, he took over the leadership of the conductors' class at the Berkshire Music Center in Tanglewood, as well as a teaching position at → Brandeis University. In addition, he wrote many other compositions, covering a broad spectrum of genres and styles, including his second symphony *The Age of Anxiety* (1949), his first opera *Trouble in Tahiti* (1951), the popular musical *Wonderful Town* (1953), the musical score for Elia Kazan's dramatic film *On the Waterfront* (1954), the *Serenade* for solo violin, string orchestra, harp and percussion, with the violinist Isaac Stern in the debut performance (1954), and the comic operetta *Candide* (1956). The musical *West Side Story* (1957) developed into a brilliant success.

In January 1958, Bernstein took over the position of music director of the New York Philharmonic Orchestra; this was the first time a musician born and trained in the United States held that leading position. During his twelve years of activity with the Orchestra, Bernstein distinguished himself by, among other thing, his interpretations of the works of Gustav Mahler (→ Resurrection), through which he made an essential contribution to the late recognition of the composer. In addition to his activity as a conductor, he wrote other important compositions, such as his Symphony No. 3 *Kaddish* (Hebr.; Prayer for the Dead 1963; → Kaddish), dedicated to the assassinated John F. Kennedy, the choral work *Chichester Psalms*, which included texts from the Hebrew Psalms (1965), the musical theatre piece *Mass* (1971), commissioned by Jacqueline Kennedy, the ballet *Dybbuk* (1974; → Dybbuk), the musical *1600 Pennsylvania Avenue* (1976), and his second opera *A Quiet Place* (1983).

In addition to his regular appearances with the New York Philharmonic Orchestra, Bernstein gave many concerts as a guest conductor with other great orchestras in America and Europe. The fact that for Christmas 1989, on the occasion of the fall of the Berlin Wall, he performed Beethoven's Ninth Symphony with an international orchestra in the former East Berlin *Schauspielhaus*, where he replaced the word "Joy" in Schiller's Ode with the word "Freedom," can be considered both a political and a cultural highlight of his career [4. 508f.]. With Bernstein's death in 1990 in New York, the city lost one of its greatest sons.

3. "A new way of living"

West Side Story was entirely in the tradition of the Broadway musical, and can in many respects be considered representative of Bernstein's work. Similar to the Viennese → operetta, the strong presence of Jews on → Broadway favored the entry of liberal, pluralistic, and antiracist values into the American entertainment industry. Examples of this are musicals such as *Finian's Rainbow* by Yip Harburg, Burton Lane, and Fred Saidy (1947), or, more strongly, *Show Boat, South Pacific*, and *The King and I*, whose libretti, written by Oscar Hammerstein II, explicitly emphasized the need for understanding among ethnic groups and denounced racism.

In Bernstein's words, *West Side Story* is "'a tragic musical comedy'" (cited in [4. 275]), yet conveys an essentially positive message. It finds expression in the ballet number "Somewhere," the utopian vision of a peaceful, harmonious future, "a new way of living [...] a way of forgiving" [2. 201], which became famous beyond the musical: on the night after the murder of Martin Luther King Jr. on April 4, 1968, the African-American group The Supremes sang the song on the Ed Sullivan Show [3. 105]. In addition, many liberals and progressives turned to "Somewhere" as a means of political mobilization. The song expressed Bernstein's optimistic outlook on life, typical of the second generation of Jewish immigrants to America.

The young Bernstein saw himself as a committed member of the American musical avant-garde, as is attested by his friendships with the composers Copland, Marc Blitzstein, and many others. In his first years as a conductor, and later in the New York Philharmonic Orchestra, he set great store by including works by American avantgarde composers in the program. The newly acquired venue of the New York Philharmonic Orchestra, in the modernistic Lincoln Center for the Performing Arts, Bernstein's expressive athletic style as a conductor, and his resolve to build a bridge between the "high culture" of Carnegie Hall and the popular culture of → Broadway, symbolically stood for the dynamic new age, which he welcomed. He went to concerts by Jimi Hendrix, attended the rock opera *Tommy* by The Who, and included electric guitars, bass guitars, and keyboards in the orchestral instrumentation of *Mass*, which was first performed in 1971 for the opening of the John F. Kennedy Center for the Performing Arts in Washington.

Bernstein advocated stronger support for public music education, for which he viewed radio and television as the appropriate media. Through his concert series *Young People's Concerts* (1958–1972), broadcast on CBS, and his dynamic appearances on the TV series *Omnibus*, he made his own contributions to this agenda. He became involved with the musical summer camp in Tanglewood, where he taught and gave concerts for fifty years, but also felt a duty to promote classical music in America.

Bernstein described his political orientation as socialist, but anti-communist; he later understood himself as a liberal [5. 42]; [4. 506]. He advocated liberal and progressive goals with great enthusiasm; his opposition to the atomic bomb (→ Manhattan Project) and the Vietnam War were particularly important to him. His pacifism and convinced internationalism partly explain the great popularity he enjoyed in his numerous tours in the Soviet Union, Japan, or South America. Bernstein's left-wing political optimism explains his pro-Zionist attitude – at a time when Israel symbolized the chance for a socialist future and a new society, or, better yet, "a new way of living."

Bernstein dedicated himself to the intra-American project of cultural and ethnic synthesis. He graduated from Harvard in 1939 with a work on *The Absorption of Race Elements into American Music*, in which he wrote, with reference to → jazz, that "'Negro music has finally shown itself to be the really universal basis of American composition'" (cited in [5. 37]). He regarded American culture from an inclusive perspective, and used jazz elements, for instance, both in his popular music and in his more classical compositions. As a result, the connection between jazz and Latin American music was natural in *West Side Story*. Bernstein was also committed to the integration of African Americans and women into the world of classical → music. His nature was best expressed in the statement he made in 1985, that "the Will to Love guides my living from day to day, always has" [4. 479].

However, Bernstein's life also testifies to the fact that the 1960s did not fulfill their political and social potential. In 1969, Bernstein, who in 1947 had spoken out strongly in favor of musical training for African-American children, and whose *On the Town* was famous because its casting came from both sides of the "color-line," received a summons to a hearing before the New York Commission on → Human Rights: after a job advertisement, two Black musicians had sued the New York Philharmonic Orchestra, which consisted exclusively of white members, for racial discrimination. Despite his pioneering efforts for the recognition of the foundational influence of the music and culture of minorities on American music, for which *West Side Story* stands as an example, he found himself subjected to academic reproaches for lack of authenticity and disparagement of Puerto Rican society and culture.

In 1970, Bernstein's wife Felicia (born Cohn Montealegre), who was involved in the → civil rights movement, opened the couple's home for a solidarity event for the African-American party of the Black Panthers to collect money for the legal costs of many of their wrongfully arrested members. However, because of the Black Panther Party's anti-Zionism, the result was extremely bad publicity among many New York Jews. Tom Wolfe's commentary *Radical Chic* – a term describing that mixture of glamor and social behavior which the journalist encountered at the Bernsteins' event – caused additional damage to Bernstein's reputation [5. 54–57]; [4. 396–397, 491].

In early 1989, Bernstein's political optimism with regard to developments in Israel suffered another let-down: during an event at the Holocaust memorial → Yad Vashem, he was dismayed by the speech of Prime Minister Yitzḥak Shamir, which was filled with ardent nationalism. He confided his impressions to a friend: "'They are burning books again [...] What has happened to my Israel? For the first time I feel old'" [4. 562].

4. The double man

From an early date, Bernstein was among the admirers of the music of Gustav Mahler (→ Resurrection). His tireless advocacy for Mahler's creation, attested, for instance, by the Mahler Festival organized at the New York Philharmonic in 1960, or his choice of the Adagietto from Mahler's Fifth Symphony as accompanying music for Robert F. Kennedy's funeral in 1968, were of the greatest importance for the composer's reception into the pantheon of classical music [5. 173–191]. Bernstein sometimes saw himself as the medium for Mahler's spirit when he conducted the latter's music. He empathized with the composer, identifying with what he called Mahler's "double man": "'It's like being two different men locked up in the same body; one man is a conductor and the other a composer, and they're both one fellow called Mahler (or Bernstein). It's like being a double man'" (cited in [5. 175]).

This deep insight perhaps held true even more for Bernstein than for Mahler. Throughout his entire career, Bernstein oscillated between the agitated, glamorous existence of a maestro and the rather stationary, isolated life that composing art music demanded. This was combined with his careers as a Broadway composer, television moderator, and, in general, as a celebrity. To be sure, he was able to combine all this, but his many-sided, exuberant talent not infrequently brought problems along with it. Bernstein proved to be a "double man" in other areas of his life as well. His bisexuality caused many complications, especially in his relations with his wife Felicia. As a composer, he alternated between a conventional tone and new avant-garde tendencies such as atonality, seriality, or experimental forms. At the beginning of his career, he cultivated a strong commitment to the American avant-garde, yet in his own compositions, and in the choices of the pieces he conducted, he became more conservative as he grew older. He found himself torn between his existence as an outstanding New York personality and a member of America's social and cultural elite, on the one hand, and, on the other, his partly socialistic, partly liberally-motivated support for many radical, left-wing projects. Even if the nickname Tom Wolfe attached to him connoted an unjustified reproach of hypocrisy, Bernstein was in fact "radical chic."

Another parallel to Mahler's "double man" is represented by Bernstein's attitude toward his → Diaspora Judaism, which he affirmed much more self-consciously than did Mahler. On the one hand a proud, even idealistic American, on the other hand he made no effort to conceal his Jewishness. His initial fame in 1943 had little to do with his Jewish origins but applied to the brilliant conductor born in the United States. Through his tours overseas, he brought America's cultural and political values to the world. At the same time, he travelled to → Tel Aviv in 1947, one year before the founding of the State of Israel, to conduct the → Palestine Symphony Orchestra or, as he called it, "the Jewish orchestra" [4. 163]. During the Arab-Israeli War of 1948, he gave a concert with the orchestra for Israeli troops at Beer Sheva, in which he appeared as pianist and conductor. The position of permanent Director of the Israel Philharmonic Orchestra, as the Palestine Orchestra was called after the foundation of the state, was offered to him many times. The enthusiastic Zionist certainly considered accepting, but repeatedly declined. After the Six Day War, Bernstein gave three special concerts in July 1967 in Jerusalem on Mount Scopus (→ Hebrew University), on the occasion of the administrative unification of the city, previously divided between Jordan and Israel, but now placed under Jewish authority; he included movements from Mahler's "Resurrection Symphony" on the program. He was deeply moved to stand before the Wailing Wall for the first time. He considered Israel his second home [4. 185, 365f.].

A dualism was also reflected in Bernstein's compositions. In his younger years, he was driven by the desire to develop an authentic "American" compositional style on the basis of "Black" → jazz. He devoted most of his career to the attempt to make a name for himself in this new world of American art music. He harbored the particular ambition of composing a great American opera, in which serious music would be paired with easy comprehensibility [4. 171] – a goal which he pursued from 1948 until the premiere of *A Quiet Place* in 1983. In the process, Bernstein deliberately integrated various different musical traditions into his American works, including jazz, Latin-American rhythms, and many obviously Jewish elements and themes. *Jeremiah, Kaddish, Jubilee Games, Chichester Psalms, Dybbuk*, and even *Mass* are all strongly influenced by Bernstein's Jewish background, and often contained texts in → Hebrew or → Aramaic. *Arias and Barcarolles*, moreover, includes a song in → Yiddish. Jewish music is also discernible in *West Side Story*: the series of three notes with which the prologue to the musical begins, and which is taken up again in songs like "Cool" and "Maria" as inversion and reflection, corresponds precisely to the traditional shofar blast *teki'ah gedolah*, blown on the eve of Rosh ha-Shanah and Yom Kippur (→ Course of the Year) [4. 274]; [3. 84]. Shortly before his death, he was still thinking about an opera on the → Holocaust, which was to be called *Babel* [4. 502]. Bernstein's work can be considered the most important corpus of specifically Jewish works created by a Jewish composer in the field of classical music [4. 487].

Through the inclusive character of his world view and the innovative accomplishments of his career, Bernstein also helped this "Jewish" music find its place in the mainstream music of the 20th century [4. 487]. Just as the musical *West Side Story* drew its forward-looking vigor from the mixtures of the most varied musical traditions [5. 75], so the potentialities that Bernstein's contribution to modern music and culture developed sprang precisely from the affirmation of his "doubleness," rather than the attempt to flee from it.

Bibliography

Sources
[1] L. Bernstein, The Joy of Music, Pompton Plains (NJ) 2004. [2] A. Laurents et al., Romeo and Juliet. West Side Story, New York 1965.

Secondary literature
[3] M. Berson, Something's Coming, Something Good. West Side Story and the American Imagination, Milwaukee 2011. [4] H. Burton, Leonard Bernstein, London 1994. [5] B. Haws/B. Bernstein, Leonard Bernstein. American Original. How a Modern Renaissance Man Transformed Music and the World during the New York Philharmonic Years, 1943–1976, New York 2008. [6] J. B. Jones, Our Musicals, Ourselves. A Social History of the American Musical Theatre, Lebanon 2003.

STEVEN BELLER, WASHINGTON D.C.

Westerbork

Village in the northeastern region of the Netherlands, approximately 30 kilometers from the German border. In 1939, on the orders of the Dutch authorities, a camp was established there to house Jewish refugees from Germany. During the German occupation from 1940 to 1945, Westerbork served as a transit camp from which more than 100,000 Jews were deported to German extermination camps in Poland and Germany. As such,

Westerbork has become a symbol of the → Holocaust in the Netherlands.

1. Installation of the camp
2. The Netherlands under German occupation
3. Westerbork Transit Camp
4. Westerbork after 1945

1. Installation of the camp

As a result of the transfer of power to Adolf Hitler and the ensuing persecutions, the first Jewish refugees from Germany began arriving in the Netherlands in the spring of 1933. The Dutch government was not prepared to provide food and shelter for the refugees. To address the situation, the Comite voor Bijzondere Joodsche Belangen (CBJB; Committee for Jewish Special Interests) and the Comité voor Joodse Vluchtelingen (CJV; Committee for Jewish Refugees) were initiated in March 1933 by David Cohen, professor of ancient history at the Municipal University of Amsterdam and member of the permanent committee of the Ashkenazi community in the Netherlands. Cohen himself assumed the presidency of the CJV and asked his friend Abraham Asscher, a prominent businessman and chair of the Nederlands-Israëlitisch Kerkgenootschap (Organization of Jewish Communities in the Netherlands), to head the CBJB.

Between 1933 and 1939, the Netherlands saw 33,000 Jewish refugees arriving from Germany, nearly one third of whom came from Eastern Europe and some were stateless, but 13,000 found a way to leave the country before the outbreak of the war [10. 32].

When the number of refugees rose rapidly after the → November pogrom of 1938 and thousands fled across the border from Germany, the Dutch government faced the problem of having to provide accommodation and, in February 1939, decided to establish a Central Refugee Camp for Jews. Since there were no plans to integrate those Jews coming from Germany into Dutch society, the camp was supposed to be remote. In July 1939 the order came that the camp be built on land belonging to the municipality of Westerbork, near the village of Hooghalen in the province of Drenthe. The CBJB was to bear the costs of more than one million guilders. On October 9, 1939, the first 22 refugees from Germany reached the barren heaths of Westerbork, where they were housed in small wooden huts. The refugees themselves managed the camp's internal affairs in cooperation with the committee. Administrative oversight lay with the Dutch Ministry of the Interior, whose administrative officer, D. A. Syswerda, was responsible for the camp.

At the time of the German invasion of the Netherlands, on May 10, 1940, about 750 refugees were staying in Westerbork; from then on they sat there definitively trapped. The responsibility for the camp was transferred to the Dutch Ministry of Justice in July 1940. Command of the camp was assigned to Jacques Schol, a Dutch army captain in the reserves, who organized the internal administration of the camp by "Dienstzweige" (service branches), each headed by a "Dienstleiter" (service head). The services leaders reported to the German Jew Kurt Schlesinger, whom Schol appointed as chief administrator in February 1942 better: In February 1942, he appointed the German Jew Kurt Schlesinger as the head of the "Dienstleiter." Schlesinger and his wife Thea Francis Klein had arrived at the camp in February 1940. Like the other "Dienstleiter" Erich Zielke, Fritz Spanier, Heinz Todtmann, and Arthur Pisk, who had come to the camp as German refugees, Schlesinger remained in this position until the end of the German occupation. Schol set up a Jewish "Ordnungsdienst" (OD; security service), which functioned as a police force in the camp. While the German occupiers initially exerted little influence on the running of the Westerbork Central Refugee Camp, they intensified the measures against the entire Jewish community in the Netherlands.

2. The Netherlands under German occupation

Whereas Belgium and the occupied part of France came under German military administration in the aftermath of the "Western Campaign," Hitler decided to swiftly appoint a civilian administration for the occupied Netherlands. By the end of May 1940, after the royal family and the Dutch cabinet had gone into exile in London, the "Reichskommissariat für die besetzten niederländischen Gebiete" (Reich Commissariat for the Occupied Dutch Territories) was established. Filling the position of Reichskommissar (Reich Commissioner) was the Austrian National Socialist Arthur Seyß-Inquart, who in the days before the "Anschluss" (annexation) of Austria in March 1938 had briefly held office as Chancellor of Austria.

The new regime gradually tightened the measures against the approximately 140,000 Jews living in the Netherlands. Beginning on July 15, 1940 Jews were no longer allowed to work as wardens in the civilian air-raid protection service; on July 31 a prohibition against ritual slaughter (→ Kashrut; → Sheḥitah) was issued. In the autumn of 1940, the Reichskommissariat gave the order that all persons active in the Dutch civil service had to present a declaration of their ancestry; subsequently, by the end of November all public institutions were forced to dismiss their Jewish employees. The criteria determining who was a Jew and therefore subject to removal had been decreed in October, with the purpose of registering Dutch Jews. Facing the threat of punishment and the high probability of being caught by the Germans anyway, nearly all the country's Jews complied with this regulation [10. 58, 64–65].

At the end of 1940 the *Weerafdeling* (military division) of the Nationaal Socialistische

Beweging in Nederland (NSB; National Socialist Movement in the Netherlands) mounted a parallel campaign of harassment against the Jewish population. In February 1941 this led to violent clashes in the Jewish working-class neighborhood of Amsterdam. Aided by non-Jewish residents and workers' organizations, Jews were able to counter provocations in cafés and dance halls, for instance when a direct confrontation erupted with the German Ordnungspolizei (Order Police) on February 19. The occupiers resorted to retaliatory measures and, on February 22 and 23, 1941, in a massive raid on the Jewish quarter, arrested more than 400 young Jewish men who were abused, publicly humiliated, and finally deported to Mauthausen by way of → Buchenwald; only two of them survived [3. 187f.].

This first anti-Jewish raid caused protests to flare up, and a general strike was organized in Amsterdam and surrounding cities by the Dutch Communist Party. The strike lasted from February 25 to 26, 1941, before it was brutally put down by the German police and SS units.

Between March and October 1941, the Reichskommissariat issued a total of eleven decrees to engineer the so-called "Aryanization" of the economy, enabling the authorities either to transfer Jewish businesses into German trusteeship or to liquidate them entirely. The decree "on the handling of Jewish assets and property" of August 8, 1941, used the name of a bank established in Amsterdam before the occupation and now under German control, Lippmann, Rosenthal & Co., to set up a fake bank that would dispose of the confiscated Jewish property. All Jewish private individuals had to sign their assets over to this bank, which operated under the guise of a regular financial institution rather than the instrument of extortion that it was. The Jewish property seized by the Germans in the Netherlands had an estimated value of 700 to 900 million guilders, making this operation even more profitable than the looting campaigns in Belgium and France [5. 221–224, 411].

On November 7, 1941, a prohibition came into effect that ended freedom of movement for Dutch Jews unless they obtained a permit to travel or to change their address. Issuing the permits fell to the *Joodsche Raad* (Jewish Council; → Judenrat), which had been created during the Amsterdam Riots of February 1941. Led by Abraham Asscher and David Cohen, this body was to handle the affairs of the Jewish community but had no say in religious matters.

Beginning in December 1941 the German regime began to intensify the geographic concentration: non-Dutch Jews were interned at the Westerbork Camp and male Dutch Jews transferred to labor camps in the north and east of the country; Jews residing in various towns and villages were ordered to relocate to those districts of Amsterdam in which 60% of the Jewish population of the Netherlands were already located [11. 111–114, 216–220]. The introduction of mandatory identification by the wearing of the yellow star at the end of April 1942 finally revealed to the entire Dutch population the extent to which the situation had been allowed to progress.

The population reacted differently to the persecution of the Jews. Both Protestant and Catholic churches offered active resistance. Students at the University of Leiden and of the Technical University of Delft went on strike in November 1940 to protest the dismissal of Jewish faculty members. During the riots in February 1941 various groups as well as individuals stood by the Jews of Amsterdam or helped them evade impending capture by the Germans. In contrast, Dutch authorities were cooperating; registration offices and, crucially, regular police had a major role in executing the German measures. Especially top-level ministerial aides, the so-called secretaries-general, obeyed the German orders after the Dutch High Court recognized the dismissal of Jewish civil servants as lawful.

3. Westerbork Transit Camp

The orders issued by Hermann Göring ordering Reinhard Heydrich to begin preparations for the deportation of the Jews from the German-controlled territories in Europe had reached the Reichskommissariat of the Netherlands by the middle of August 1941. To ensure a smooth implementation of the plans, the existing facility at Westerbork was designated a transit camp, and an additional 24 large barracks were built using confiscated Jewish funds. On July 1, 1942, the "Befehlshaber der Sicherheitspolizei und des SD" (Chief of the Security Police and the Security Service) in the Netherlands, Wilhelm Harster, transferred it to the German authorities. At this point the camp housed some 1,500 Jews. Henceforth a domain of the SS, it became a "transit camp under police jurisdiction." The site, approximately 25 hectares in size, was secured with barbed wire and fortified with seven watchtowers. Dutch military police (*Marechaussee*) and the Jewish Ordnungsdienst were responsible for maintaining order within the camp.

Initially, SS Obersturmführer Erich Deppner was put in charge of the camp. On July 15, 1942, he had command of the first deportation of Jews bound for the → Auschwitz-Birkenau extermination camp from the nearby train station at Hooghalen, approximately 5 km from the camp; Westerbork proper was connected to the rail network in early November [10. 93]. After two months, Deppner was relieved by Josef Hugo Dischner as camp commander. Dischner was drunk most of the time and displayed extreme brutality towards the inmates. Chaos erupted when almost 12,000 Dutch Jews were transferred from labor camps to Westerbork in October 1942. Dischner was able to restore order only through violence [9. 731–734].

Dischner was replaced that same month by SS Obersturmführer Albert Konrad Gemmeker, who commanded the camp until the end of the occupation. Gemmeker played the part of the "decent German" treating the detainees correctly and letting the German-Jewish personnel manage the camp's internal affairs. Thus, inmates were allowed to keep their papers and continued to wear their own clothes. The camp-attached farming operation supplied meat, potatoes, and vegetables for the central kitchen. There was also a post office, which permitted camp dwellers to correspond with relatives and to receive food parcels, as well as a hospital with, in the meantime, 1,725 beds. Living conditions, however, were extremely poor. Only a small number of privileged prisoners could share private screened-off spaces in wooden barracks, or, as "Dienstleiter" had small wooden huts at their disposal [1. 589].

Except on Sundays, camp inmates had to work in industrial shops, in the agricultural operation that was part of the Westerbork complex, or on neighboring farms. Prior to the onset of deportations in the summer of 1942, temporary exemptions could be granted to individual Jews if they had been baptized (→ Conversion), were married to a non-Jewish spouse, were considered indispensable for daily camp life, worked in war-relevant industries, or had been placed on one of the lists of names to be spared by the *Joodse Raad* in Amsterdam [10. 95–96].

Keen to avoid tensions in the camp wherever possible, Gemmeker encouraged inmates to take up a variety of activities. Religious services were celebrated for Jews as well as Christians of Jewish ancestry, the "Camp Westerbork Theatre Group," which counted among its members artists such as Willy Rosen, Max Ehrlich, and Erich Ziegler, Camilla Spira, Esther Philipse, Otto Aurich, and Liesl Frank, had the backing of the camp authorities to organize evenings of entertainment featuring a → cabaret and musical performances, an orchestra, and a ballet.

Additionally, there were athletic competitions in football, track and field sports, and boxing.

The calm management of Westerbork followed a clear strategy: the hope of a time after (Westerbork) was to be maintained in order to ensure the smooth implementation of the deportations. Everything about the camp was designed to make the Jews believe they would be brought to labor camps in Eastern Europe. Short messages from relatives who had arrived at Auschwitz appeared to confirm this. While the *Joodse Raad* soon realized that the letters and postcards had to have been written by third parties and that none had been sent by old people, children, or women with children, they did not communicate this suspicion to the detainees in the camp [10. 112]. Serious doubts about the official version of events began to spread among inmates, especially when trainloads of the elderly and the sick, as well as children, left the camp. Rumors of a terrible fate awaiting the deportees resulted in desperate attempts to escape deportation. Only 210 of those attempting to flee succeeded [9. 740].

Date, destination, and size of the transports were determined by Department IV B4 of the Reichssicherheitshauptamt (RSHA; Reich Security Main Office) under Adolf Eichmann (→ Eichmann Trial) in Berlin and conveyed to Gemmeker, who largely left it to the Jewish camp organization and its "Ersten Dienstleiter" Kurt Schlesinger, to draw up the deportation lists. Schlesinger, who also kept the general register, was therefore the most influential prisoner at Westerbork. So as not to cause alarm, the decision about each deportation materialized only hours before the planned departure; the final deportation lists were hastily compiled and delivered to the barracks chiefs. Members of the "Ordunungsdienst," under the command of Arthur Pisk, and the so-called "flying brigade" led the named individuals, with their belongings, to the freight train which awaited them alongside the camp's main thoroughfare, also known as the "Boulevard des Misères." Within the camp, because official positions had been given to the first inmates, a quasi-aristocracy composed predominantly of German Jews was formed. The great majority of "Transportfreie" (inmates scheduled for deportation), primarily Dutch Jews, thoroughly despised the "Altekampinsassen" (long-term camp inmates).

From the first deportations in July 1942 to the last one in September 1944, a total of 65 trains left Westerbork destined for → Auschwitz with 58,549 Jews, of whom only 854 survived; 19 trains with 34,313 Jews went to → Sobibór, all but 18 of whom perished. Nine further trains went to → Theresienstadt (4,894 deportees, an estimated 1,980 survivors), seven to Bergen-Belsen (3,751 deportees, about 2,050 survivors) [8]. The camp's population reached its greatest size in early October 1942, after Jewish men from Dutch labor camps were rounded up and brought to Westerbork with their families. That same month also saw the number of people deported within one month rise to almost 12,000, the highest rate recorded for the entire time of the occupation.

Among the 1,019 deportees who were on the last transport to Auschwitz on September 3, 1944, were Anne Frank (→ Diary) and her family, as well as the van Pels family with whom they had shared their Amsterdam hiding place, and Fritz Pfeffer. All but Anne's father Otto were murdered in German concentration camps. The last train left Westerbork on September 13, 1944, bound for Bergen-Belsen. Overall, more than 100,000 persons were deported in 93 trains from Camp Westerbork, including 245 Sinti and Roma. Fewer than 5,000 survived the ordeal. When the camp was liberated by Canadian troops on April 12, 1945, there were 876 prisoners left.

4. Westerbork after 1945

In the post-war period, the compound was used first for internment of members of the Nationaal-Socialistische Beweging in Nederland (NSB); later as a military camp and reception center for repatriates from the Dutch East Indies. Between 1951 and 1971 it housed former servicemen of the Koninklijk Nederlands Indisch Leger (KNIL; Royal Netherlands East Indies Army) and their families from the Southern Moluccan Islands, who were being resettled in the Netherlands. With the departure of the last occupants, the time had come for the camp to be liquidated. Only the former house of the German camp commander has been preserved.

In 1970 Queen Juliana of the Netherlands dedicated the Westerbork National Memorial, designed by the former inmate Ralph Prins. For a long time, the monument, the only reminder of the acts committed on the site, remained where the train line ended that ran between Hooghalen and the camp from 1942 to 1945. Public access to the area had been restricted due to the construction of the Westerbork Synthesis Radio Telescopes in 1969. In 1978 a small collective led by the legal scholar Manja Pach, the daughter of a Jew who fled Germany in the 1930s and camp survivor, set up a working group to explore the site and its surroundings from a historical perspective. In 1981 the working group became the Stichting Voormalig Kamp Westerbork (Former Camp Westerbork Foundation); the Lower House of the Dutch Parliament passed a resolution according to which the Permanent Exhibition in the Dutch Pavilion of the State Museum Auschwitz-Birkenau (Państwowe Muzeum Oświęcim-Brzezinka) should also be shown in the Netherlands.

In 1983, on the 38th anniversary of its liberation, Queen Beatrix inaugurated the Camp Westerbork Memorial Center near Hooghalen. In the following years, the outline of the camp area was made more recognizable and the entire area rededicated as a monument in 1992. A refurbished and further expanded memorial center opened in 1999.

Bibliography

Sources

[1] E. Hillesum, Etty. The Letters and Diaries of Etty Hillesum 1941–1943. Complete and Unabridged, trans. by A. J. Pomerans, ed. by K. A. D. Smelik, Ottawa/Grand Rapids 2002. [2] P. Mechanicus, Im Depot. Tagebuch aus Westerbork, Berlin 1993. [3] B. A. Sijes, De Februari-staking, 25–26 Februari 1941, The Hague 1954. [4] H. Verdoner-Sluizer, Signs of Life. The Letters of Hilde Verdoner-Sluizer from Westerbork Nazi Transit Camp, 1942–1944, ed. by Y. Verdoner/F. Verdoner Kan, Washington D.C. 1990.

Secondary literature

[5] G. Aalders, Geraubt! Die Enteignung jüdischen Besitzes im Zweiten Weltkrieg, Cologne 2000. [6] J. Boas, Boulevard des Misères. The Story of Transit Camp Westerbork, Hamden 1985. [7] A. Hájková, Das Polizeiliche Durchgangslager Westerbork, in: W. Benz/B. Distel (eds.), Terror im Westen. Nationalsozialistische Lager in den Niederlanden, Belgien und Luxemburg, 1940–1945, Berlin 2004, 217–248. [8] G. Hirschfeld, Niederlande, in: W. Benz (ed.), Dimension des Völkermords. Die Zahl der jüdischen Opfer des Nationalsozialismus, Munich 1991, 137–165. [9] L. de Jong, Het Koninkrijk der Nederlanden in de Tweede Wereldoorlog, Vol. 8.2: Gevangenen en gedeporteerden, The Hague 1979. [10] B. Moore, Victims and Survivors. The Nazi Persecution of the Jews in the Netherlands 1940–1945, London 1997. [11] J. Presser, Ashes in the Wind. The Destruction of Dutch Jewry, London 2010.

PIM GRIFFIOEN, AMSTERDAM

Westminster

Westminster, as the seat of the Parliament of the United Kingdom, provided the setting for a debate that began in 1828 and continued for three decades regarding the question whether Jews could hold a seat in the House of Commons. In 1858 Lionel Rothschild became the first Jewish Member of the House of Commons. It would, however, be misleading to characterize the surrounding controversies as a struggle for the → emancipation of the Jews. Since their resettlement in the 17th century, the legal status of Jews born in England had been equal to that of Christians not affiliated with the Anglican Church. The course of Jewish legal equality in Great Britain, and the significance of the legislation inspired by this process, differ fundamentally from the developments in most other European states.

1. Before the "emancipation" debate
2. Admission to Parliament
3. The English model of emancipation

1. Before the "emancipation" debate

After the expulsions of 1290, Jews had been allowed to return and settle in England since the latter half of the 17th century. Unlike their counterparts elsewhere in Europe, Oliver Cromwell and the monarchs of the House of Stuart who followed him did not spell out the conditions of their readmission. The state did not impose any restrictions, general or specific, on Jews regarding their right to own property, take up certain professions, practice their religion, or interact socially with their Christian neighbors. By the same token, there was no official recognition of Jewish communal institutions that would have been able to discipline their members or whose task would have been to collect taxes. The legal status of English Jews was from the beginning more individual

than collective, their communal organization voluntary rather than prescribed.

In the Georgian era (1714–1830), English-born Jews enjoyed the same rights as Christians, with few exceptions. They paid the same taxes and levies and were subject to the same civil and criminal laws as all others; they were free to choose their place of residence and trade in goods of all types. Legal restraints existed for Jews because, as non-Christians, they were unable to swear oaths of loyalty to the ruling monarchs which included the formula "upon the true faith of a Christian" or similar expressions (→ Oath More Judaico). Such oaths had been introduced in the 17th century to mark those Catholics who sympathized with the contenders of the House of Stuarts for the throne.

Therewith it had the effect of barring Jews from public office, including local administrations, the House of Commons, the Inns of Court, and colleges of the ancient universities of Oxford and Cambridge. → Universities required matriculating students to respect the Thirty-Nine Articles of the Church of England. For the vast majority of English and foreign-born Jews in England, however, the exclusion by obligatory oaths was irrelevant because their inferior social status or lack of acculturation meant they did not strive for public office or elevated occupations. The only significant constraint experienced by individual Jews unable to swear the obligatory oath was to be denied the liberties of a *freeman* and, thus, the right to operate a retail trade in the City of London, the historic center of trade and finance. An alternative solution was for the retailer to work from a purported wholesale warehouse within the City or set up shop at the entrances of the district. The City itself limited the number of Jewish commodity brokers at the Royal Exchange to twelve; again, this affected only the wealthiest members of the community.

Often erroneously described as a bill addressing naturalization in general, the → Jew Bill of 1753 did in fact deal exclusively with overseas merchants who were not born in England and were seeking British citizenship. Their main concern was to avoid the trade tariffs imposed on foreigners; here, too, the majority of English Jews remained unaffected.

Full emancipation for English Jews was not accomplished by means of major legislative efforts and only rarely through an Act of Parliament. In 1830 Jews won the right to become "Freemen of the City of London" because the Common Council of the City allowed them to take an oath that made no reference to the Christian religion. Two years later Jews were admitted to the bar after the Honourable Society of Lincoln's Inn exempted the jurist Francis Henry Goldsmid from the obligation to swear a Christian oath. In 1835 Parliament enabled the financier David Salomons, who had been newly elected Sheriff of the City of London, to assume the office without reciting the Christian form of oath. That same year, Parliament also removed the compulsory Oath of Abjuration at the ballot box; this gave the vote to all Jews eligible under the general rules of the property-based franchise. In some constituencies Jews were already able to vote. The Jewish Municipal Relief Act, passed by Parliament in 1845, allowed Jews to assume public office without taking a Christian oath. Here, too, legislation followed what was the practice, at least outside London. Jews had previously been elected to public office in Southampton (1838), Birmingham (1839), and Portsmouth (1841). The Religious Opinions Relief Act of 1846 conferred the same legal protection on Jewish schools and welfare organizations that it gave to Nonconformist institutions. It also established the entitlement of Jews to own land, once more codifying what had been a fact in reality. The right to take academic degrees and be admitted as Fellows at the historic universities was conferred on Jews within the framework of a wider legal reform of the universities in 1854, 1856, and 1871. Such changes in the legal status of Jews were seldom surrounded by controversy.

2. Admission to Parliament

By contrast, the three-decades long campaign for Jews to be admitted to the House of Commons met with resistance both from within Parliament and from without. This happened primarily because the campaign was part of a larger struggle for political reforms in the Victorian era. In this connection, it was a matter of eliminating blatant manifestations of electoral corruption, of limiting the hegemony of the Church of England, the privilege of the aristocracy, and that of the landed gentry, as well as strengthening the urban, largely Nonconformist middle class.

The first attempt to admit Jews to Parliament came after the successful abolition of the Test and Corporation Acts by the reformers in 1828/1829 and the passage of Catholic Emancipation Act. This legislation allowed Nonconformists and Catholics to assume public office both on the local and on the national level.

The first bill for the emancipation of the Jews reached Parliament in 1830 but was defeated on its second reading in the House of Commons. A new attempt was made one year after the passage of the Reform Act in 1833. The reformed House of Commons passed the law, the conservative House of Lords, however, rejected it. The pattern thus established was repeated in 1834, 1836, 1841, 1848, 1851, 1853, 1856, and 1857: Members of the House of Commons passed regulations to abolish restrictions still in force against Jews, only to be overruled by the House of Lords on every occasion.

Four groups with four sets of motives offered their backing for the full legal → emancipation of the Jews: Whigs, who were ideologically committed to religious freedom and civil rights; progressive Tories who had broken with their party; evangelical Tories who, by means of total integration, hoped to convince Jews to embrace → conversion, and radicals and Nonconformists who were against the influence of the Church of England. The most important opponents of Jewish emancipation were High Churchmen from the ranks of the Tories as well as ultra-conservative evangelicals. They rejected Jewish ambitions for religious reasons, railed against the emancipation of Catholics and Nonconformists, and were angered by the growing amount of exertion of influence of the state in the affairs of the Church. For these reasons, they blocked, for decades, any legislation that would have enabled Jews to enter Parliament.

The banker and stockbroker David Salomons played a significant role in the eventual admission of Jews to Parliament. Having been appointed Sheriff of the City of London, he became the first Jewish Lord Mayor of the City in 1855. As the Liberal Party candidate, Salomons campaigned for election in the constituencies of New Shoreham in 1837 and in Maidstone in 1841, but he lost both elections. In 1847 he stood again, this time in Greenwich. For the Liberal Party there were four more Jewish candidates, Lionel → Rothschild in the City of London, his brother Mayer Rothschild in Hythe, Isaac Lyon Goldsmid in Beverley, and his son Francis Henry, the first Jewish barrister, in Great Yarmouth. Of these five candidates, Lionel Rothschild alone won the election, but it took four more election victories before he was allowed to take his seat in Parliament in 1858. In the meantime, the more combative Salomons had won Greenwich at a by-election in 1851, made his way into the House of Commons, taken the Oath of Abjuration (without the Christian references), given a speech, and proceeded to vote with other Members of Parliament before being forcibly removed from the House.

Rothschild's and Salomons's election victories now shifted the debate to a practical matter: how could Parliament reject members who had been legally elected by British voters to represent them? The question was intensified in that Parliament itself endorsed the admission of the newly-elected members. In 1858 the Conservative leadership wearily relented since they realized that their intransigence was harming the party and agreed to a compromise: each chamber would devise its own form of oath. Rothschild entered the House of Commons; by 1860 four of the five Jewish candidates of 1847 had taken their seats there.

In view of the support shown by Liberal politicians for Jewish emancipation, it comes as no surprise that of the Jews elected to Parliament before the First World War the majority were Liberals. Most Jewish Members of Parliament in these decades came from the families of financiers who had grown wealthy, or they were successful solicitors. The first Jewish Member of Parliament for the Conservatives, in 1874, was Saul Isaac, the owner of a coal mine in Nottinghamshire. When William Ewart Gladstone, who served multiple times as Prime Minister, and the Liberal Party became increasingly unsympathetic to Jewish concerns – especially during the Bulgarian Uprising of 1876 – the number of Jewish Conservative Members of Parliament rose in the 1880s. The leading figure to emerge from the Conservative Party, and its eventual Prime Minister (1868, 1874–1880), was Benjamin Disraeli (→ Tancred), who had been christened at the age of twelve and remained a member of the Anglican Church.

The majority of English Jews in the middle of the Victorian period were not, themselves, enthusiastic supporters of the campaign for emancipation – largely because they had little to gain from the removal of the few remaining legal restraints. Whether or not a Rothschild was admitted to Parliament seems not to have concerned them in any meaningful way. Even members of the Jewish elite themselves were lukewarm about emancipation, if not outright opposed to it. As a wealthy religious traditionalist, Moses Montefiore (→ Board of Deputies) disapproved of Jewish participation in public life because he feared it would weaken Jewish religiosity. Consequently, Montefiore refused to support the campaign and to mobilize the Board of Deputies of British Jews, where his was the dominant voice, on the issue. Chief Rabbi Solomon Hirschell and his successor Nathan Adler shared this outlook.

The campaign for Jewish emancipation was not so much a broad-based communal effort as an elite project undertaken by a circle of ambitious men in the City of London with close contacts to influential politicians. Only after Rothschild's fourth election victory in 1857 did the demand for Jews to be admitted to Parliament find more widespread approval among the Jewish population of London, which was the largest in the country. In the significantly smaller provincial communities, where Jews of lesser rank took an active part in the local administration, the interest in total emancipation was more strongly developed.

3. The English model of emancipation

The history of the emancipation of the British Jews differs markedly from the pattern followed in other European states, where the granting of legal equality had either explicitly or implicitly set conditions. In return for equal rights Jews were expected to transform and make themselves "less Jewish" by forswearing their tribal social consciousness, their distinctive ritual practices, and their "typical" → professions. Indeed, German opponents of Jewish equality had claimed since the Romantic period that equality could never lead to complete → assimilation, which to them was the measure of all things.

In Britain, by contrast, those who favored → emancipation already viewed Jews as loyal citizens who were contributing to the good of the nation. Whether Jews prayed for their messianic return to Zion, whether they married among themselves or Christian partners, and whether they earned their living by trade or in the financial sector was of little interest to them. To be sure, Conservatives, who opposed the admission of Jews to Parliament, emphasized their "otherness," but Jewish efforts for acculturation and integration were irrelevant to them; solely baptism was of importance. What disqualified Jews from playing a part in the legislative processes of the nation was their religion. In British politics, the emancipation debate focused less on Jewish social and economic habits than on the status of the established church *vis-à-vis* that of other confessions.

Of course English Jews felt compelled to conform with English norms and customs. The pressure to assimilate was however largely of a social and cultural, rather than a political, nature. Because the legal position of Jews in Britain was not officially regulated by the state or in any agreements, their religious structure also developed differently than in the German states, for instance. Since the call was not usually raised in England to take away their "national" character, there was also little reason to press for a → reform of Judaism. Prior to the arrival of Jewish refugees from National Socialist Germany in the 1930s, Reform Judaism barely had a presence in Britain. Nearly all congregations up to that point observed the traditional synagogal → liturgy and viewed their own self-understanding accordingly.

Bibliography

[1] G. Alderman, The Jewish Community in British Politics, Oxford 1983. [2] T. M. Endelman, The Jews of Britain, 1656–2000, Berkeley 2002. [3] I. Finestein, Anglo-Jewish Opinion during the Struggle for Jewish Emancipation,

in: Transactions of the Jewish Historical Society of England 20 (1964), 113–143. [4] I. Finestein, Jewish Emancipationists in Victorian England. Self-Imposed Limits to Assimilation, in: J. Frankel/S. J. Zipperstein (eds.), Assimilation and Community in Nineteenth-Century Europe, Cambridge 1992, 38–56. [5] A. Gilam, The Emancipation of the Jews in England, 1830–1860, London 1982. [6] H. S. Q. Henriques, The Jews and the English Law, London 1908. [7] M. C. N. Salbstein, The Emancipation of the Jews in Britain. The Question of the Admission of the Jews to Parliament, 1828–1860, London 1982.

TODD M. ENDELMAN, ANN ARBOR

White Christmas

Title of a song by Irving Berlin (1888–1989) also at the center of a musical film (1942), a film musical (1954), and a stage play (2004). As a naturalized US citizen, Berlin expressed the assimilation experiences of Jewish immigrants in *White Christmas* by drawing on established tropes of the American popular song and imbuing them with new attributes. The song stands out from among American songs not only because of its extraordinary popularity, its media presence, and its unprecedented commercial success. It also contributed to upholding America's morale during the Second World War and to the secularization of American Christmas traditions in the postwar years.

1. *White Christmas*
2. Irving Berlin and his song
3. Jewish migration experiences
4. Resonance in America

1. *White Christmas*

White Christmas was first broadcast nationwide on Christmas Day 1941 in the US radio show *The Kraft Music Hall*. The song, which invokes the dream of a white Christmas in longing words, was sung by Bing Crosby, whose voice remains closely linked to *White Christmas* to this day. In the following year, the song was heard again in the musical film *Holiday Inn* starring Bing Crosby and Fred Astaire; *White Christmas* is the emotional and musical center of a total of twelve vocal numbers composed by Irving Berlin on the subject of the most important American holidays. The reviews after the premiere in August 1942 were lukewarm. Shortly before the film came out, Crosby recorded an album featuring singles of *White Christmas* and five other vocal numbers from *Holiday Inn*. After a slow start, *White Christmas* became the bestselling song nationwide by October 1942. In the radio show *Your Hit Parade*, it stayed at number one for ten weeks from Christmas 1942 onwards.

In 1945, the US forces' great interest in the song led to its being included in the V-Disc (Victory Disc) program initiated by the government, which distributed records among US soldiers stationed abroad. Because of the great demand for Crosby's original recording, Decca pressed five million copies until 1947 by which time the master disc was worn out. The record company then gathered all the musicians who had been involved in the original version and produced a new recording that only differed from the old one in few details. Until the reissue of the original recording in 1998, the 1947 one was regarded as *the* classic Bing Crosby version.

Until the beginning of the 1960s, *White Christmas* stormed the charts every year in December (with the exception of 1953), spending 86 weeks in the charts altogether, with 38 weeks at number one. When the Academy of Motion Picture Arts and Sciences nominated *Holiday Inn* for three awards in March 1943, the song won the award for best original song. *White Christmas* also achieved commercial superlatives: 125 million copies of the sheet music for the song were sold, and at 100 million copies, the version sung by Bing Crosby in 1942 is considered the bestselling single of all time. In addition, versions in languages such as Hungarian, Japanese, Swahili, and → Yiddish were recorded.

The career of *White Christmas* continued beyond the charts. In 1954, Paramount Pictures (→ Hollywood) produced the film musical *White Christmas* starring Bing Crosby and including other musical numbers by Irving Berlin besides the title song. The plot recalls *Holiday Inn* but is tinged with post-war nostalgia. *White Christmas* became the highest-grossing US film of the year. A stage adaptation of the film version, entitled *Irving Berlin's White Christmas. The Musical*, enriched with further Berlin classics besides the songs from the film, premiered in San Francisco in 2004. After stage productions in the United States, Canada, and Great Britain, it finally ran on → Broadway for nearly two months in both the 2008/2009 and 2009/2010 seasons.

2. Irving Berlin and his song

The son of a → cantor, Irving Berlin was born in 1888 in Mogilyov in Russia (today Mahilyow, Belarus). In 1892, the family fled from the → pogroms in the Russian Empire to the United States, settling in → New York. After his father's early death, Berlin left the family home at age 13 years, taking various low-paying jobs as a vaudeville singer and waiter among others. He taught himself to play the piano by focusing on the black keys and playing nearly always in F sharp major. In 1907, the first song with lyrics written by him was published; in 1911 he composed *Alexander's Ragtime Band* which became his first enduring success. Over the course of the following 40 years, he composed innumerable songs, wrote the scores for successful musical comedies on → Broadway and songs for several → Hollywood film musicals. When → rock 'n'

Irving Berlin (1888–1989)

roll began to supersede earlier forms of popular music in the 1950s, Berlin concluded his composing career and lived on the high revenues from his royalties until his death in New York in 1989.

As a child, Berlin had been fascinated by the Christmas traditions of his Irish neighbors on New York's Lower East Side. As early as 1910, he wrote about the Christian holiday in his lyrics to the song *Christmas-Time Seems Years and Years Away* (music by Ted Snyder). On Christmas Eve 1916, his *Santa Claus. A Syncopated Christmas Song* appeared in a New York newspaper. Berlin had his three daughters from his second marriage to Ellin Mackay, who was of Irish descent, raised in the Catholic faith. Extensive Christmas ceremonies were part of the family tradition. After their only son died as an infant on December 25, 1928, the holiday became overshadowed for Berlin and his wife. According to the recollections of their eldest daughter Mary Ellin Barrett, her parents visited the child's grave every year on Christmas Eve. In 1937, Berlin was unable for the first time to celebrate Christmas in New York, as he was working on a film score for RKO studios in Hollywood.

In 1939, Berlin sketched two musical revues (which were never performed), heading the finale of both *White Christmas*. One of the revues presented holidays with musical and comedic scenes to characterize each one in satirical exaggeration. It is possible that Berlin had this idea in mind when in January 1940 he first formulated the lyrics in a version that opened in sharp contrast with the one used today, rather in the style of an urban joke: "The sun is shining, / the grass is green, / The orange and palm trees sway. / There's never been such a day / in Beverly Hills, L.A. / But it's December the twenty-fourth, / And I am longing to be up north." [3. 351]. The visualization of the warm Californian winter indicates Christmas 1937, which Berlin spent in Los Angeles. It turns the introduction into an ironic prelude to the longing for snow expressed in the chorus. The opening verse has hardly ever been sung to this day; most recordings as well as the classic films and sound recordings begin with the chorus.

3. Jewish migration experiences

At first glance, there is no connection between *White Christmas* and the experiences of Jewish migration, as there are no Jewish references in the text at all. However, this very absence may be interpreted as a sign of → assimilation: as an outsider's adaptation to the norms of middle-class society of which he would like to be a part. The song also characterizes the transformation of American song styles typical of the Jewish songwriters of → Tin Pan Alley during the first half of the 20th century. Most noticeable is the re-imagining of the familiar trope of nostalgic longing for a lost home that ran through the popular American songs of the 19th and early 20th centuries. In the character of the former slave transferred to the

North and longing for his home on the plantations of the South, → blackface minstrelsy had added masquerade to this nostalgia – the subject of, for instance, Stephen Foster's song *Old Folks at Home* (1951). Berlin's verse quoted above sets the scene in California's warm climate, where the first-person singer longs for a snowy landscape.

Jewish references may also be found in the music of *White Christmas*. Many of Berlin's early songs are ethnic novelty pieces (→ Jazz) – humorous songs about ethnic minorities in US society, especially immigrants of Irish, German, Italian, and Jewish origin. While these songs went out of fashion after the First World War, certain traits of the Jewish novelty songs persisted in the songs Berlin and other songwriters from Tin Pan Alley wrote after 1920, although these were ethnically neutral. The most important "Jewish" characteristic is the use of minor keys, standing out against the major keys customary in popular songs. The fact that minor chords in the ethnic novelty song were commonly understood as a Jewish characteristic may be due to their closeness to several traditional synagogue melodies (→ Cantor; → Organ).

In the 1920s, changes between major and minor keys signaled "Jewish melancholy" to many music critics, and probably to a wider audience as well. Even so, major-minor changes had evolved into an omnipresent stylistic device in American popular song. There are two places in *White Christmas* where we find a brief shift from major to minor: firstly at "children listen" ("I'm dreaming of a white Christmas / [...] Where the treetops glisten / And children listen / To hear sleigh bells in the snow"), and then on the word "bright" ("I'm dreaming of a white Christmas / With ev'ry Christmas card I write / May your days be merry and bright / And may all your Christmases be white") [3. 351]. By having a passing cloud of minor chords darken the seemingly sunniest part of the song, Berlin creates emotionally complex music at the very point where the lyrics are in danger of sliding into greeting card banality. Characteristically, it is the melancholy undertone – a resonance of migrant nostalgia, even while seeking assimilation – that gives the song its brilliance, making it appear as an expression of Jewish affiliation while allowing it to influence the American national consciousness of the mid-20th century.

4. Resonance in America

The fact that *White Christmas* was first broadcast publicly during the same month in which the United States entered the Second World War had considerable influence on the song's reception and its position in US history and culture. Its melancholy longing for an apparently lost holiday tradition – the first-person singer does not experience the desired Christmas but only dreams of it – touched a nerve with the nation. For many soldiers, 1942 was the first time they spent Christmas far from home. The song addressed their feelings of homesickness and longing that would intensify during the course of the war. For members of the US forces, especially those stationed in the Pacific, the longing for snow expressed in the song was a part of the annual Christmas celebrations. In the decades after the war, this melancholy longing was joined by the nostalgia of the war years, glorified as a time of great social solidarity in films such as *White Christmas* of 1954.

White Christmas moreover contributed to the secularization of American Christmas traditions accelerated by the war. Among the results of the propagandistic emphasis on the Jewish-Christian ecumene during the war years was that Hanukkah (→ Course of the Year) achieved its present-day status as a kind of Jewish Christmas and that the mass media increasingly presented Christmas as a secular event. *White Christmas* stood out from a series of popular songs with holiday subjects created in the 1940s and 1950s that

influence American Christmas music to this day. The majority of songs such as *I'll Be Home for Christmas* (1943), *Have Yourself a Merry Little Christmas* (1943), *Let It Snow! Let It Snow! Let It Snow!* (1945), *Rudolph the Red-Nosed Reindeer* (1949), *Frosty the Snowman* (1950) and *It's Beginning to Look a Lot Like Christmas* (1951) originated with Jewish songwriters, and all of them are part of the aesthetic initiated by *White Christmas*.

White Christmas is thus emblematic of the Jewish immigrants of the first and second generation who became active in the arts sector in America and shaped American national consciousness by introducing their experiences of migration into American mainstream culture. The influence Jewish entertainers had on the mainstream's self-perception is hinted at in Irving Berlin's song *Let Me Sing and I'm Happy* of 1928: "What care I who makes the laws of a nation: / [...] As long as I can sing its popular songs" [3. 261]. Through their endeavor to adapt to the social norms of the American middle class, Jewish immigrants also contributed to a redefinition of these norms. This social transformation is the basis of Berlin's response to a journalist's question how he as a Jew was able to compose *White Christmas*: "I wrote it as an American" [5. 69].

Bibliography

[1] M. E. Barrett, Irving Berlin. A Daughter's Memoir, New York 2009.   [2] J. Gottlieb, Funny, It Doesn't Sound Jewish. How Yiddish Songs and Synagogue Melodies Influenced Tin Pan Alley, Broadway, and Hollywood, Albany 2004.   [3] R. Kimball/L. Emmet (eds.), The Complete Lyrics of Irving Berlin, New York 2005.   [4] J. Magee, Irving Berlin's "Blue Skies." Ethnic Affiliations and Musical Transformations, in: The Musical Quarterly 84 (2000), 537–580.   [5] J. Rosen, White Christmas. The Story of an American Song, New York 2002.

LARRY HAMBERLIN, MIDDLEBURY

Wiener Library

The Wiener Library is the oldest archival and library collection for the documentation of the National Socialist persecution of Jews. Its concept was a continuation of the "Büro Wilhelmstraße," set up in Berlin in 1929. It was established by Alfred Wiener in Amsterdam in 1934 as the Jewish Central Information Office and transferred to London in 1939. In its new home, the collection named after him served as a significant source of information for the British Government during the Second World War. Over the following decades, it developed into an important center for contemporary historical and Holocaust research.

1. Berlin
2. Alfred Wiener
3. Amsterdam
4. London
5. Since the 1960s

1. Berlin

The origins of the Wiener Library are closely linked to the → Central-Verein deutscher Staatsbürger jüdischen Glaubens (CV). In view of the growing National Socialist agitation, which specifically targeted Jewish → department stores and the Jewish vice president of the Berlin police Bernhard Weiß at the end of the 1920s, the Central-Verein felt compelled to establish an office for counterpropaganda. The remit of the institution, which started its activity in 1929, was to inform the republican parties about the Nazis' machinations by means of collecting relevant publications and undertaking additional research. In order to protect the office from attacks by the radical right, it operated mostly in secrecy.

In the CV, the initiative had been started by its in-house lawyer Alfred Wiener and the lawyer Hans Reichmann. There was no formal link with the CV, not least in order to prevent the impression that this was a Jewish institution. Because of the location of the office premises in Wilhelmstraße in Berlin – near the foreign office – it was often referred to as "Büro Wilhelmstraße." The former police officer and politician of the Deutsche Demokratische Partei (German Democratic Party) Max Brunzlow was invited to act as its titular head. The work of the offices was coordinated by the journalist and archivist Walter Gyssling, a member of the republican defensive alliance Reichsbanner Schwarz-Rot-Gold, which also undertook the distribution of the posters, leaflets, and flyers the office produced by the millions, for instance on the occasion of the federal election in 1930. In addition, the office published the information brochure *Anti-Nazi* under the imprint "Deutscher Volksgemeinschaftsdienst." The leaflet provided details of the NSDAP's party manifesto, information on leading National Socialists' activity in parliament, and on crimes committed by them. Its format and content were based on the looseleaf edition *Anti-Anti: Blätter zur Abwehr. Tatsachen zur Judenfrage* published by the CV and updated several times.

From 1929 onward, the archive collated approximately 200,000 pieces of information from newspapers and documented appearances by National Socialists, until the office in Wilhelmstraße was closed due to security concerns. In February 1933, it was hurriedly transferred to Munich, where the documents were either deliberately destroyed in order to prevent them falling into the Nazis' hands [5. 225], or they were lost during the war.

2. Alfred Wiener

While Alfred Wiener was only loosely connected with the work of the "Büro Wilhelmstraße"; this was the conceptual origin of the research institution that would later be named for him. Born in Potsdam in 1885, Wiener studied history and Oriental languages at the → Hochschule für die Wissenschaft des Judentums and at the University of Berlin. In 1931, he wrote his PhD thesis in Heidelberg on Arabic literature. He had previously spent two years in the Middle East, which resulted in him holding decidedly anti-Zionist opinions. This corresponded to his work in the → Hilfsverein der deutschen Juden, where he worked as chairman Paul Nathan's private secretary from 1911 to 1914. The philanthropic commitment of the Hilfsverein, which established a number of schools and higher education establishments in Palestine (→ Language Conflict; → Technion), confirmed Wiener in his assimilatory and anti-Zionist attitude. He also gained early experiences in the fight against antisemitism (→ Conspiracy), for instance when Nathan spoke out firmly against the → blood libel lies in the Beilis affair of 1911 to 1913, a peak of antisemitic agitation in Russia. During the First World War, he fought as a soldier in the Middle East and in France.

After the end of the war, Wiener dedicated himself to fighting the increasing right-wing extremism in Germany. In 1919, he published the pamphlet *Vor Pogromen? Tatsachen für Nachdenkliche* ("Prelude to Pogroms? Facts for the Thoughtful," 2021) and joined the CV, becoming its in-house lawyer and vice chairman in 1923. In these positions, and as the editor of the *C.V.-Zeitung*, and also in speeches given in public and in political and industrial circles, he warned of the National Socialist menace.

After the publication of Hitler's *Mein Kampf* (1925), this commitment acquired priority for Wiener. In the "Büro Wilhelmstraße," among the initiators of which he had been, Gyssling and his colleagues acted in a manner even more aggressive than Wiener's own approach. After the transfer of power to Hitler in January 1933, Wiener suffered a nervous breakdown; a few months later he fled to Amsterdam with his wife Margarethe and their children.

Alfred Wiener in his London office (1952)

3. Amsterdam

In Amsterdam, it was once more Wiener's concern to provide documentary evidence to shed light on the Nazis' persecution of Jews. To this end, he collaborated with the professor of ancient history at the University of Amsterdam David Cohen, who provided organizational support for Jews fleeing from Germany. In October 1933, Cohen took part in a conference in London organized by the Joint Foreign Committee (→ Conjoint Foreign Committee) of the → Board of Deputies of British Jews and the → Anglo-Jewish Association, which adopted a resolution demanding the establishment of a central office for the collection and distribution of information on the Nazi regime. At first, Wiener stored the material in a hotel room and then in Jan-van-Eyckstraat in the south of Amsterdam, where he lived with his family in an apartment under the office premises. The Jewish Central Information Office (JCIO) was officially founded and established as a legal entity in February 1934.

The JCIO collected all relevant material about the Nazi regime, such as daily papers including regional and local ones, trade and professional journals, books, leaflets, photographs (→ Photography), and personal records. Wiener himself travelled extensively, introducing Jewish organizations to the work of the JCIO and organizing financial resources. A first journal, *Die jüdische Informationszentrale*, provided insights into National Socialist rule; the multitude of published accounts included titles such as *Six Years of Hitler* (1939) or *Briefe aus Shanghai* (1939).

Between 1933 and 1935, one of the topics to which the JCIO was particularly committed was the Bern trial of the distributors of an edition of the notorious antisemitic libelous text → *Protocols of the Elders of Zion*. Wiener supported the Schweizerischer Israelitischer Gemeindebund (Swiss Federation of Jewish Communities) and the Israelitische Kultusgemeinde Bern (Jewish Community Bern) in their legal action against the Bund Nationalsozialistischer Eidgenossen (Association of Swiss National Socialists); the material he provided contributed to exposing the forgery. Subsequently, the JCIO dedicated itself to the affair surrounding the assassination of the leader of the Swiss National Socialists Wilhelm Gustloff in February 1936. The murder committed by the Jewish student David Frankfurter served as a pretext for the National Socialists to exacerbate the persecution of the Jews; however, because of the propaganda effect of the Olympic Games in Berlin (→ Sport), no immediate retaliatory action was taken. In the context of the international debate surrounding the murder, the JCIO published the *Dokumentensammlung über die Entrechtung, Ächtung und Vernichtung der Juden in Deutschland* (1936) as well as a further volume with photographic material. After the so-called *Kristallnacht*, the → November pogrom of 1938, the JCIO collated approximately 350 eyewitness accounts from all over Germany and Austria (an edited version was published in 2008 [1]). Wiener opened his archive to the journalist Konrad Heiden, whose report *The New Inquisition* informed the English-speaking public of the extent of the pogroms. The publication of a Dutch version was stopped by order of the Dutch prime minister Hendrikus Colijn.

In view of the imminent war, Wiener had the collection transferred to London in the summer of 1939. It comprised 8,000 books, numerous journals, a photographic collection, and an outstanding collection of cuttings from journals arranged according to subject. A total of 17 persons had worked for the JCIO. An Amsterdam office was maintained until shortly after the German invasion in May 1940. Wiener's deputy Kurt Arthur Zielenziger and the accountant Bernhard Krieg were later arrested and deported to Bergen-Belsen concentration camp, where Zielenziger was murdered in 1944; Krieg died after his return to Amsterdam in 1945 as a consequence of his imprisonment. Wiener's wife and their daughters Ruth Hannah and Eva Elise were trapped in Amsterdam and also deported to Bergen-Belsen; all three were freed as part of an exchange of prisoners in January 1945.

4. London

In London, the collections of the JCIO were housed in a building on Manchester Square. During the entire war, the documents initially known as "Dr. Wiener's Library" served the British government as its most comprehensive source of background material about Nazi Germany. Numerous Jewish organizations all over the world subscribed to the office's publications.

Alfred Wiener spent part of the war in the United States to establish networks through which the library would regularly receive books and other materials from Germany and the occupied regions. During the war, the JCIO regularly published the journal *The*

Nazis at War. The additional journal *Jewish News*, published from January 1942 onward, appears to have been Wiener's response to the fact that the British authorities accorded comparatively inferior relevance to the fate of the European Jews in the course of their fight against Nazi Germany. Shortly after the Wannsee Conference, for instance, *Jewish News* printed a report by the Jewish Telegraphic Agency that already pointed to the high mortality in the camp near Oświęcim (→ Auschwitz) (Jewish News, No. 2, January 29, 1942).

Immediately after the end of the war, the JCIO published six accounts of Holocaust survivors entitled *Jewish Survivor Reports: Documents of Nazi Guilt.* In 1946, now officially called the Wiener Library, the institution collated important materials for the prosecutors at the → Nuremberg trials; in return, the library was given a series of case records connected with the murder of the Jews. The first issue of the *Wiener Library Bulletin* was published in November 1946, gaining fundamental relevance for the investigation of the Nazi era and the → Holocaust and appearing until the 1980s. Further publications ranged from short reports such as *Germany's New Nazis* and *Jewish Population in the US Zone of Occupation of Germany* to voluminous works, among them the bibliography *European War Crimes Trials* (1951) edited by Inge S. Neumann and Lionel Edmond Kochan's study *Pogrom. 10 November 1938* (1957).

In 1950, Wiener began negotiations with the → Hebrew University in Jerusalem regarding the library's move to Israel. Talks continued over five years and were unsuccessful. To Wiener, the intention of the → Yad Vashem Holocaust Remembrance Center of removing individual pieces from the collection for its own purposes was not acceptable. This would have dissolved their context. As a consequence, the library and archive remained in London, their future uncertain. A significant project in the second half of

the 1950s, led by Eva Gabriele Reichmann, the academic director of the library, was the organization of an extensive collection of eyewitness accounts of the murder of the Jews.

5. Since the 1960s

Alfred Wiener died in 1964. One year later, he was succeeded by Walter Laqueur, under whose chairmanship the library reached its peak as an outstanding research center. Laqueur expanded the → library's remit to include contemporary research and, together with George L. Mosse, started *The Journal of Contemporary History*, which appears to this day.

In the 1970s, the institution struggled due to financial difficulties. In 1980, a considerable portion of the collection was handed over to Tel Aviv University, where it is available to researchers under the name Wiener Library for the Study of the Nazi Era and the Holocaust. Thanks to subsidies from Germany and the United States, a large part of the documents were able to be copied onto microfilm before the transfer. The smaller institution in London still had to fight for survival in the 1980s but succeeded in establishing a new solid foundation for its work and the quality of the collection.

The Wiener Library now serves as Great Britain's library and archive of the → Holocaust; since 2012 it has housed the digital copy of the archive of the International Tracing Service (ITS) owned by the British government. Moreover, it is an internationally renowned education and commemoration institution. The collection comprises approximately 70,000 volumes, 300 journals, 20,000 photographs, and 2,000 collections of documents.

Bibliography

[1] B. Barkow et al. (eds.), Novemberpogrom 1938. Die Augenzeugenberichte der Wiener

Library, London, Frankfurt am Main 2008. [2] B. Barkow, Alfred Wiener and the Making of the Holocaust Library, London 1997. [3] W. Laqueur, Dr. Wiener's Library 1933–1960, in: 50 Years of the Wiener Library [Special Issue of the Wiener Library Bulletin], London 1983, 3–9. [4] A. Paucker, Der jüdische Abwehrkampf gegen Antisemitismus und Nationalsozialismus in den letzten Jahren der Weimarer Republik, Hamburg ²1969. [5] A. Paucker, Das Berliner liberale jüdische Bürgertum im "Centralverein deutscher Staatsbürger jüdischen Glaubens," in: R. Rürup (ed.), Jüdische Geschichte in Berlin. Essays und Studien, Berlin 1995, 215–228. [6] E. Reichmann, Alfred Wiener. The German Jew, in: 50 Years of the Wiener Library [Special Issue of the Wiener Library Bulletin], London 1983, 10–13. [7] H. Reichmann, Der drohende Sturm. Episoden aus dem Kampf der deutschen Juden gegen die nationalsozialistische Gefahr 1929 bis 1933, in: H. Tramer (ed.), In zwei Welten. Siegfried Moses zum fünfundsiebzigsten Geburtstag, Tel Aviv 1962, 556–577.

Ben Barkow, London

Wirklichkeit der Hebräer

Title of the philosopher of religion Oskar Goldberg's (1885–1953) 1925 programmatic major work, which combines ancient concepts of Hebrew tradition with the idea of a radical new beginning influenced by Expressionism. Goldberg's historical thinking contradicted that of → Orthodox as well as liberal Judaism (→ Reform). He was convinced that by harking back to the pre-rabbinic era, it could be possible to end the present catastrophic → history and bring about the beginning of a new era in which miracles would be part of reality. During the first decades of the 20th century, Goldberg was a well-known personality in the cultural and intellectual circles in Berlin, especially as a result of the activities of his pupil Erich

Unger (1887–1950), who led the Philosophische Gruppe Berlin.

1. Introduction
2. Oskar Goldberg and *Die Wirklichkeit der Hebräer*
3. Erich Unger and the "Philosophische Gruppe"
4. Reception and impact

1. Introduction

In Berlin in 1908 some students led by the author Kurt Hiller resigned from the Freie Wissenschaftliche Vereinigung, the first student association (→ Student Corporations) explicitly against antisemitism that had been founded in 1881. The establishment of the Neuer Club in the following year marked the birth of literary Expressionism (→ Weltende). The German-Jewish physician and philosopher of religion Oskar Goldberg and the philosopher Erich Unger – who was also born into a Jewish family – were directly involved in these activities and the influence exerted by the Neuer Club. Unger was one of the founding members of the club, while Goldberg was its last chairman before its dissolution in 1914.

Born in Berlin in 1885, Goldberg received a traditional upbringing from his grandfather after his father's early death. He learned → Hebrew and → Aramaic, observed the → mitsvot, and at the same time followed the latest developments in → literature, biology, → mathematics, and → anthropology. At the Gymnasium, Goldberg joined a group of students interested in literature that also included the poet Jakob van Hoddis and there became acquainted with Erich Unger. He first graduated from the → rabbinical seminary before attending lectures in medicine, Oriental studies, and → Völkerpsychologie. Goldberg and Unger were both active in artistic circles of the city and took an active part in debates on philosophy and → art, but also mathematics. Goldberg's theories had been debated by small groups in Berlin since 1903. His fiercest opponent Gershom Scholem (→ Kabbalah) later wrote: "In the circles of the modern and hypermodern writers and artists of the coffee houses or clubs in Berlin's west, where the Expressionist movement was born, he was, quite simply, *the* Jew" [11. 182].

Goldberg had gained this reputation primarily through lectures on *Die Wirklichkeit der Hebräer*. At the last public event of the Neuer Club in 1914, Unger gave the unpreserved lecture *Zur Frage der Prüfbarkeit der Metaphysik*, discussing Goldberg's fundamental idea; Unger's masterpiece *Politik und Metaphysik* (1921) also contains clear traces of Goldberg's thought. Unger attracted the interest of Walter Benjamin (→ Angelus Novus), who quoted him in his essay *Zur Kritik der Gewalt* (1921; "Critique of Violence," 1978); they first met in Switzerland during the First World War. As a result of Scholem's dislike of Unger's mentor Oskar Goldberg, however, the relationship remained tense. In the 1930s, Unger began to distance himself from Goldberg when the latter began to transfer his theories of the singularity of the Hebrew people to other "mythenfähige" (lit. capable of bearing myths) peoples. In Thomas Mann's novel *Doktor Faustus* (1947), Goldberg became the model for the figure of Chaim Breisacher, who volubly rejects culture altogether.

2. Oskar Goldberg and *Die Wirklichkeit der Hebräer*

The premise for all of Goldberg's deliberations was the divine origin of the Torah. In 1908 he published a brochure on *Die fünf Bücher Mosis ein Zahlengebäude* in which the Torah is presented as a comprehensively devised numerical construction (→ Number) that could not have been imagined by any human but still accessible with the aid of scientific methods. This theory led

to a public debate with Josef Wohlgemuth and Abraham Berliner, both of whom were active at the → Rabbinical Seminary of Berlin. While Berliner regarded Goldberg's demonstrating numerical connections in the Torah as dangerously playing with the Holy of Holies, Wohlgemuth pointed to the tradition of viewing the Pentateuch as the unfurled name of God and consequently its numerical value. Goldberg's second fundamental conviction was that the events described in the Torah were by no means to be understood metaphorically but did, in fact, reflect reality. What today is regarded as a "miracle," had been, at that time, actual history and direct contact with God possible. The physical and metaphysical worlds were not yet completely separate; metaphysics was not yet purely spiritual and descriptive but real and active. While the gods of other peoples had a limited sphere of influence and limited biological possibilities, the God of the Hebrews was a force that "generated biology." This "biological universalism of Hebrew metaphysics" [4. 140] would have to be re-established. Here, a positively Fichtean radicality of thought is combined with the latest ideas of the vitalists but also the cultural pessimists.

While *Die Wirklichkeit der Hebräer* – only the introductory chapter of the second part survives – had been completed before the First World War, it was not published until 1925 and, in its more demonstrative than argumentative style, was perceived as a work of the 1920s when modern progressive thinking found itself in crisis. While the subtitle of *Die Wirklichkeit der Hebräer* presents itself as *Einleitung in das System des Pentateuch*, it is in fact a new conception of world history, rich in quotations. Since God could not enter into his → creation directly – here, Goldberg hinted at his view of the Kabbalah (→ Mysticism) – many peoples with their own (national) deities evolved on earth. If God, as the "principle that generates biology," the "origin of all laws of life" [4. 6], intended to perpetuate his power on earth, he had to do this in the uninhabited desert and choose a people who would have to abandon their tribal god and instead recognize him as God. These were the desert people of the Hebrews, exhorted by God to follow his laws and enable God's presence on earth in their manifestation as the quasi-metaphysical Israelites: "As opposed to the 'historically' established people of the Hebrews, the people of Israel is a *teleological* creation that consists in the fact that a break with the center of *origin* took place, followed by gravitation towards the center of *destination*, the chosen God, is to occur" [4. 88f.].

Only in this way was it thinkable to Goldberg that something new could enter → history. He described the beginning of the history of humanity as polytheistic; only once the unlimited presence of the one (creator) God had been achieved would "history" end. Only then would it be possible to overcome the natural biological cycles, ultimately even the cycle of life and death. According to Goldberg, the creator God was "the *enemy* of death, whom YHWH [the creator God] annihilates in the eschatological era" [4. 67]. Until that time, however, God, together with the people of Israel, would have to wage a veritable war against the tribal gods of other people: "The Pentateuch is, thus, the 'Sefer milkhamot YHWH', *the book of YHWH's wars*" [4. 36].

However, Goldberg held that the Chosen People had failed and thus brought about the post-metaphysical, non-metaphysical, technical age. In this context the term "metaphysics" denotes something not inferable from the existing physis, but rather referring to a reality of a different kind, namely the reality of YHWH on earth. As a result of turning its back on metaphysics, the world found itself in a process of "fixation" ever more strongly at the mercy of mechanical laws of nature, until it finally reached the state that we now know and during which

any kind of miracle and intermittent presence of God are impossible. If it was actually possible during the mythical period to transform a staff into a serpent, today we are able to interpret it only as a "legend." The objective Goldberg pursued with his book was nothing less than to initiate a repeat of the founding act of the people of Israel – if the Jews proved incapable of achieving this, then with another people capable of metaphysics. Consequently "in finite reality, the breakthrough of a new law of life" would have to take place [4. 274]. Only the "principle that generates biology" could produce a truly "new organism" in an "act of (orderly, creative) *organizing explosion*" [4. 285].

Goldberg literally took the Torah seriously, but in a way that differed markedly from other interpretations, including orthodox ones. He rejected all moral interpretation; in his view, the commandments and laws (→ Ceremonial Law) were really technical instructions with the objective of allowing a real encounter with God. His dissertation *Die anomalen biologischen Vorgänge bei orientalischen Sekten* (1915), which has not survived, as well as Erich Unger's dissertation *Das psychophysiologische Problem und sein Arbeitsgebiet. Eine methodologische Einleitung* (1922) were dedicated to this task. The fundamental idea was that particular figures such as fakirs, shamans, and other miracle workers, but also priests were able to use their spiritual powers to control involuntary bodily functions and thus could overcome biological cycles. If humans with such "supernatural" abilities could be collected into one people – in accordance with the divine instruction: "but you shall be to Me a kingdom of priests and a holy nation" (Exod 19:6) – and to deploy these powers as a "transcendentally political force," a new beginning of history would be possible. The rejection of morality and technology, the uncompromising break with continuities that appeared to have no alternative, the suddenness of discontinuity, combined with the possibility of a radical new beginning: For these reasons, Goldberg's introduction to the Pentateuch may also be interpreted as the hidden manifesto of the cultural-revolutionary, experimental Expressionism.

In 1932, Goldberg moved to San Remo for health reasons, where he met Walter Benjamin (→ Angelus Novus) among others. In 1939 he had to leave Italy as a result of the race laws introduced the previous year; with the help of Marcel Mauss and Lucien Lévy-Bruhl, he was able to flee to France. Only a few months after his arrival, Goldberg was interned (→ Drancy). In 1941 he managed to emigrate to the United States via Marseille; on the first ship organized by the Emergency Rescue Committee (→ Lisbon), André Breton and Victor Serge crossed the ocean along with Goldberg. In addition, in 1941, he endeavored to secure a grant for his work on the second part of *Die Wirklichkeit der Hebräer*. Thomas Mann supported him with a recommendation to the Guggenheim Memorial Foundation. Mann had read Goldberg as early as 1927, when he began work on his Jacob novels, and borrowed some of his individual formulations [7]. Goldberg also wrote for the exile journal *Maß und Wert*, which was edited by Mann and Konrad Falke (originally Karl Frey) from 1937 onward. In his diary, however, Mann had explicitly criticized him some years previously from a humanist and universalist perspective. Later Mann, who had intensively studied *Die Wirklichkeit der Hebräer* [6. 269–274], wrote that he had always felt it was the work of a "typical Jewish fascist" [2a. xxxiv].

Mann had probably arrived at this verdict on the basis of Goldberg's second book *Maimonides. Kritik der jüdischen Glaubenslehre* (1935). On the occasion of the 800th anniversary of Maimonides's birth (→ Guide for the Perplexed), Goldberg spoke in his book of the profound crisis brought about by Maimonides's connection of Jewish and Greek thought. Not only did he claim that Judaism owed "its lack of originality, its dependency,

its powerlessness, and the barricading of its future" [3. 159] to Maimonides, but at a time when the persecution of Jews in Germany could not be ignored anymore, he also wrote: "Their deletion from the 'book of history' is imminent. [...] It must be said to the Jews in no uncertain terms: The Torah is not dependent on you. [...] Either the Jews do their duty, or they will be eliminated. There is no third option" [3. 217].

With that Goldberg drew the political conclusions of the philosophy of *Die Wirklichkeit der Hebräer*, according to which God did not inevitably have to choose the Jews as a people capable of metaphysics. Surely also under the impression of the victory of National Socialism, Goldberg relativized the significance of the founding of the Jewish people (rather than descent, as in the case of other people), considering a transfer of the capability for metaphysics onto other peoples to be possible. This transformation did not remain uncontested. His friend Erich Unger increasingly distanced himself from Goldberg's "people's metaphysics." When Goldberg published an essay from the context of the Maimonides book in → *Aufbau*, there was criticism as well, and the article, which was to have been published in several parts, was not continued.

Goldberg increasingly found himself isolated in exile. In 1949 he returned to Europe on behalf of the International Society of Naturopathic Physicians of America in order to strengthen ties with the World Health Organization; however, he was increasingly suffering from a heart condition. He died in Nice in 1952 and was buried in the Jewish cemetery in Monaco; after thirty years, his grave was levelled.

3. Erich Unger and the "Philosophische Gruppe"

Erich Unger, who wrote an introduction to *Die Wirklichkeit der Hebräer* immediately after its publication [15], transferred

Goldberg's exegetic ideas into a philosophical → theory. For him, the superiority of the intellect over nature was the definitive precondition to implement the "idea of a catastrophe-free order" and achieve the "conception of world justice" [16. 70]. "The path to a new mythical era leads through Socrates, philosophy, and the discoveries of reason" [5. 285].

Unger was an active member of literary Expressionism – and esteemed as such by Kurt Hiller – until 1925 when he turned his back on Expressionism in his book *Gegen die Dichtung* in which he repeatedly referred to Goldberg. The background to this change lays in the recourse to a Jewish tradition according to which God had created several other worlds before creating this one, but destroyed them because of their shortcomings, and that consequently the same fate might threaten our world [9. 32, 35]. Poetry, Unger was convinced, was uniquely suited to conceal this possibility; the "miraculous nature" of poetry was a "compensatory act" that distracted from the task in hand [14. 8]. In *Wirklichkeit, Mythos, Erkenntnis* (1930), Unger first critically dealt with the mythography of Oswald Spengler, Ernst Cassirer (→ Philosophy of Culture), Émile Durkheim (→ Sociology), and Lévy-Bruhl, before returning to the topic of poetry and philosophy.

The book's ultimate objective was to prove the necessity and potential of a more comprehensive consciousness. To Unger, the highest aim of knowledge was "*to produce reality* – 'enabling experience' not merely in the *thinking* but in the *literal* sense, in the real sense" [16. 199]. This is Goldberg's "metaphysical action" and "experimental religion" translated into philosophical terms. In Unger's eyes, the human, being the "center of the world" was also the "end point of creation" [16. 266]. As the epitome of all life force, he was the interface of all elements of reality and, as a result, responsible for this world. He had to live up to this responsibility by experimentally producing the New, which would no longer be affected by catastrophes.

Unger had already published a smaller text in similar terms in 1921, *Politik und Metaphysik*, whose basic premise was that only the combination of politics and metaphysics could provide the foundation for a "catastrophe-free human order" [17. 3]. In spite of his strained relationship with Unger, Walter Benjamin was deeply fascinated by the text, quoting it in central passages of his essay *Zur Kritik der Gewalt* (1921).

Around 1925, a lecture and discussion circle grew up under Unger's leadership, named Philosophische Gruppe Berlin. The discussion group, which met nearly every week, was advertised in public and occasionally reviewed in the press. The writer H. G. Adler described it as the "center of Berlin's cultural life" [1. 68]. The participants, lecturers, or discussants panel came from various fields of German intellectual life: for instance the writer Alfred Döblin (→ Alexanderplatz), the Marxist theorist Karl Korsch, the physicist Hans Reichenbach, the historian Arthur Rosenberg, the political jurist Carl Schmitt, the philosopher Günther Anders (→ Hiroshima), and the dramatist Bertolt Brecht (→ Misuk). Topics ranged from Marxism (→ Class Consciousness), → sociology, and theory of science to art theory, → mathematics, and the works of contemporary intellectuals such as Cassirer, Husserl (→ Phenomenology), and Heidegger (→ Davos Disputation). In 1937, Unger emigrated to England via Prague. He lived in Oxford in straitened circumstances, where he continued to publish essays and books until his death in 1950.

4. Reception and impact

A differentiated and appropriate reception of Goldberg and Unger was carried out best by H. G. Adler. Walter Benjamin was interested only in a part of Unger's deliberations, and Scholem, if anything, considered Goldberg an opponent to be fought [18]. In 1928 he commented on *Die Wirklichkeit der Hebräer*, attesting to the book's "confusion of true insights with undisguised madness into a 'system'" [10. 235], without, however, having studied the book in any depth and attacked Goldberg personally. Despite of his severe rejection of Goldberg, he wrote an article about him for the *Encyclopaedia Judaica* (→ Encyclopedias).

Even though in 1937/1938 Goldberg contributed to the humanistic and anti-fascist journal *Maß und Wert* edited by Thomas Mann and Konrad Falke, Mann satirized him as Dr. Chaim Breisacher in *Doktor Faustus* (1947). There he is described as a "polyhistor, who knew how to talk about anything and everything, concerned with the philosophy of culture whose views were anti-cultural, insofar as he pretended to see in the whole history of culture nothing but a process of decline. The most contemptuous word on his lips was the word 'progress'; he had an annihilating way of pronouncing it" [8. 279]. While until 1942 Mann's relationship with Goldberg had been characterized by cautious interest and a certain fascination, he ultimately rejected Goldberg's convictions for moral and ethical reasons.

Karl Wolfskehl (→ George Circle) was profoundly impressed by Goldberg, despite the considerable distance between them – Goldberg's factual, dry style was anathema to him. All the same, he clearly expressed Goldberg's strict separation between the historical Jews and the metaphysical people of the Hebrews in a letter to Margarete Susman (→ Hiob): "And of the actuality of the Jews, this immense find and finder knows nothing but everything about that of the Hebrews." Even so, he did see signs of the "true reality of life of the Jews in which everything is preserved and nothing is lost of the Hebrew essence, and everything becomes a symbol" [21. 349] in Goldberg's work. Susman herself recognized Goldberg as an important voice

of the interwar years. Just as Heidegger had an idea of the "twilight of Christianity," Goldberg had found "a powerful revelation of the being of God in the revelation of the Pentateuch at a time of decline in Judaism" [12. 333]. Franz Rosenzweig (→ [The] Star of Redemption), too, was impressed by Oskar Goldberg's reasoning, which influenced the Bible translation he carried out together with Martin Buber (→ Dialogue) [20. 221].

In 1938 Goldberg travelled from Italy to Zurich, where he met the rabbi of the Israelitische Cultusgemeinde Zwi Taubes and also became acquainted with his son Jacob Taubes, who, influenced by Goldberg's writings, wrote his first article on the Kabbalah (→ Mysticism) in 1942. In 1954 he brought Goldberg to wider public notice in *From Cult to Culture* [13]. When the writer H. G. Adler, who would later become known for his book on → Theresienstadt, spent time in Berlin in the early 1930s, he came into contact with the Philosophische Gruppe Berlin and met Unger. His theoretical magnum opus, *Vorschule für eine Experimentaltheologie* (1987), which was decades in the making, is hardly comprehensible without knowledge of Unger's and Goldberg's books [19].

Bibliography

[1] H. G. Adler, Erinnerungen an den Philosophen Erich Unger, in: E. Unger, Politik und Metaphysik, ed. by M. Voigts, Würzburg 1989, 65–69. [2] H. Bürgin, Die Briefe Thomas Manns. Regesten und Register, vol. 3, Frankfurt am Main 1982. [2a] B. Rosenstock, Transfinite Life. Oskar Goldberg and the Vitalist Imagination, Bloomington 2017. [3] O. Goldberg, Maimonides, Kritik der jüdischen Glaubenslehre, Vienna 1935. [4] O. Goldberg, Die Wirklichkeit der Hebräer. Einleitung in das System des Pentateuch, vol. 1, ed. by M. Voigts, Wiesbaden 2005. [5] O. Goldberg, Zahlengebäude, Ontologie, Maimonides und Aufsätze 1933 bis 1947, ed. by M. Voigts, Würzburg 2013. [6] C. Hülshörster, Thomas Mann und Oskar Goldbergs

"Wirklichkeit der Hebräer," Frankfurt am Main 1999. [7] H. Lehnert, Thomas Manns Vorstudien zur Josephstetralogie, in: Jahrbuch der deutschen Schillergesellschaft 7 (1963), 458–520. [8] T. Mann, Doctor Faustus. The Life of the German Composer Adrian Leverkühn as told by a Friend, trans. by H. T. Lowe-Porter, New York 1948. [9] G. Scholem, Major Trends in Jewish Mysticism, New York 1995. [10] G. Scholem, Briefe, Vol. 1: 1914–1947, ed. by I. Shedletzky, Munich 1994. [11] G. Scholem, Von Berlin nach Jerusalem. Jugenderinnerungen. Erweiterte Neuausgabe, Frankfurt am Main 1994. [12] M. Susman, Leben, in: M. Susman, Vom Geheimnis der Freiheit, ed. by M. Schlösser, Darmstadt 1965, 330–335. [13] J. Taubes, From Cult to Culture, in: M. Voigts (ed.), Jacob Taubes und Oskar Goldberg. Aufsätze, Briefe, Dokumente, Würzburg 2011, 73–84. [14] E. Unger, Gegen die Dichtung. Eine Begründung des Konstruktionsprinzips in der Erkenntnis, Leipzig 1925. [15] E. Unger, Das Problem der mythischen Realität. Eine Einleitung in die Goldbergsche Schrift "Die Wirklichkeit der Hebräer," Berlin 1926. [16] E. Unger, Wirklichkeit Mythos Erkenntnis, Berlin/Munich 1930. [17] E. Unger, Politik und Metaphysik, ed. by M. Voigts, Würzburg 1989. [18] M. Voigts, Eine nicht ausgetragene Kontroverse. Die Beziehung Gershom Scholems zu Oskar Goldberg und Erich Unger, in: Aschkenas 25 (2015) 2, 313–364. [19] M. Voigts, H. G. Adler und Erich Unger. Versuch eines Zuganges zur "Vorschule für eine Experimentaltheologie," in: brücken. Germanistisches Jahrbuch Tschechien – Slowakei N.F. 19 (2011), 253–271. [20] M. Voigts, Oskar Goldberg. Der mythische Experimentalwissenschaftler. Ein verdrängtes Kapitel jüdischer Geschichte, Berlin 1992. [21] K. Wolfskehl, Briefe an Margarete Susman, in: M. Schlösser (ed.), Auf gespaltenem Pfad. Für Margarete Susman zum 90. Geburtstag, Darmstadt 1964, 340–355.

MANFRED VOIGTS, POTSDAM

Wissenschaft des Judentums

From its beginnings in Berlin during the first third of the 19th century to its forced end during the period of National Socialism, the Wissenschaft des Judentums (science or study of Judaism) produced a multitude of eminent scholars in the German language area as well as scholarly works on the fields of Jewish history, literature, and philosophy. In their predominantly historical, philological, and literature-based interpretations of Jewish tradition, its representatives – who adhered to a variety of religious-cultural self-understandings – drew on contemporary European academic cultures. They contributed to the reinterpretation of Jewish history and tradition, insisted politically on the completion of the emancipation of the European Jews, and intellectually defended the right of Judaism to exist in the modern era. While it faced much criticism around the turn of the 20th century because of its apologetic nature, the Wissenschaft des Judentums continued to challenge German academic culture and its Protestant background. All its endeavours to become institutionalized at universities failed; however, with its Jewish educational institutions, scholarly networks, and publication venues, the discipline provided a significant impetus for the emergence of modern Jewish scholarship and exerted a lasting influence on the cultural life of Jews in many regions of Europe as well as in North America and Palestine.

1. 19th century
1.1 Beginnings
1.2 Conflicting understandings of science and scholarship
1.3 Transnational networks
2. The struggle for recognition as an academic discipline
3. Defensive activities and the critical debate with Protestantism
4. Between reorientation and destruction
5. After the Shoah

1. 19th century

1.1 *Beginnings*

The Wissenschaft des Judentums – the term was probably coined by Eduard Gans (1797–1839) – is considered the precursor of the modern discipline of Jewish (or Judaic) Studies. Despite close connections with traditional Jewish scholarship, it owed its existence, above all, to internal Jewish modernization processes concomitant with the → Haskalah and the intense encounter with German Idealism and Romanticism, which revolutionized Jewish historical awareness. Oftentimes under the influence and in confrontation with the ideas of Immanuel Kant (→ Enlightenment), Jewish intellectuals such as Lazarus Bendavid, Salomon Maimon (→ Lebensgeschichte) and Saul Ascher (→ [Die] Germanomanie) emphasized the compatibility of the Jewish religion with enlightened ethical rationalism and consqeuntly with modern European culture.

The concept of the history of ideas, which had been influenced by Romanticism – that is, the idea of the development of the the history of ideas, which had been influenced by Romanticism determined forms – opened up the possibility of historically legitimizing the existence of Judaism in the period of enlightened rationalism. Understanding the history of peoples and religions as a part and historical expression of the divine history of revelation (→ History) made it possible to emphasize the creative part Jews had played in the history of mankind. This also proved to be necessary because in the debates on → improvement and → emancipation, non-Jewish politicians, theologians, historians, and philosophers regarded Judaism as religiously, historically, and morally obsolete and therefore repeatedly challenged the equality of Jews.

The emergence of the Wissenschaft des Judentums can thus best be understood as the reaction of young Jewish scholars who, on the one hand, had hoped for obtaining civic equality in the beginning of the period of restoration after 1815, but on the other hand, were confronted once again with manifestations of → anti-Judaism (→ Hep-Hep Riots), as well as with the continuing expectation even among the liberal sections of non-Jewish society that the abolition of discriminatory regulations for Jews was tied to an extensive abandonment of Judaism (→ Assimilation). In its orientation towards the contemporary understanding of science and scholarship, it likewise marked the progressive acculturation of a new Jewish educated elite. It was from this circle that the → Verein für Cultur und Wissenschaft der Juden (Society for Jewish Culture and Science) was founded in the autumn of 1819 in Berlin, on whose behalf the historian Leopold Zunz edited the *Zeitschrift für die Wissenschaft des Judentums* in 1822/1823. Although it existed for only a short time because its efforts to promote the cultural integration of the Jews and the Jewish religion by means of universal science lacked social acceptance, the Verein left as its legacy the concept of a scholarly discipline that would shape Jewish intellectual and cultural history for more than a century. This concept spread first in the German regions but soon also in other European states as well as North America.

In the 19th century, Moritz Steinschneider (→ Bibliography), Abraham Geiger (→ Quran), and above all Zunz were among the most prominent exponents of the Wissenschaft des Judentums. In his programmatic text of 1818, *Etwas über die rabbinische Litteratur*, Zunz laid out guidelines by calling on Jews to research Jewish literature and tradition using the methods of classical philology and → historiography. In doing so, he argued, they would have to entirely disregard "whether its entire content should or can also be the norm for our own judgment" [14. 5]. Only by means of critical, methodologically contemporary Jewish scholarship could the Jews participate in German culture on equal terms and overcome the prejudices that still existed against them. At the same time, Zunz also linked his universal academic ideal with the reformist intention of separating the lasting aspects of Jewish history from all that was transitory and human. In this way, a contemporary Jewish self-understanding liberated from the burden of rabbinic tradition could be established. Consequently, the radical innovation of the Wissenschaft des Judentums consisted in the fact that, in its confrontation with contemporary universal and cultural history, it developed a scholarly ethos based on the ideal of a systematic-secular and historical-relativizing approach to the Jewish past. This meant firmly renouncing the traditional forms of Jewish erudition since the new scholarly approach also aimed to critically and impartially address historical sources. As Zunz stated in his 1845 text *Die jüdische Literatur*, it had "to emancipate itself first of all from theologians and rise to historical understanding" [13. 57].

Immanuel Wolf, who later changed his name to Wohlwill and was also a member of the Verein für Cultur und Wissenschaft der Juden, expanded this postulate in his foundational article in the society's journal in 1822, *Ueber den Begriff einer Wissenschaft des Judenthums*, by demanding a critical reduction of the "ceremonial practice that had become mechanical and thoughtless through a thousand-year-old habit," that is, a

return to the true core of Judaism. Wohlwill intended to replace the existing theological approach with a historical presentation of Jewish religion, culture, → literature, and societal existence. He hoped that he could in this way counter Christian scholars who studied Judaism "always only for the sake of a historical understanding of Christian theology" or cast it "in a hateful light" [12. 16]. The philological, historical, and philosophical penetration of Jewish tradition on the basis of rational science, which alone was "raised above the partisanship, passions, and prejudices of the lower life," promised to promote the Jews' integration into the free humanist culture of Europe because "if there is ever a bond that encircles the whole human race, it is the bond of science, the bond of pure reasonableness, the bond of truth" [12. 23f.].

From the very beginning, the Wissenschaft des Judentums unavoidably fulfilled an emancipatory-apologetic function, which persisted into the 20th century due to the continued existence of distorted images of Jews and Judaism. The bible scholar Max Wiener emphasized in 1933 that the field's main function was to "dig up the treasures of the Jewish past and cleanse them of their rust in order to raise the steeply dropped esteem of one's tribe in the eyes of non-Jews and to fill one's community with self-respect and confidence" [11. 16]. Accordingly, the representatives of the Wissenschaft des Judentums fought against traditional negative value judgments of Jews, instead emphasizing the cultural and ethical significance of their religion in order to demand its equality in society. Furthermore, they endeavored to counteract the alienation from Jewish tradition that was widespread especially among young Jews, while at the same time critically dealing with tradition themselves. On the one hand, the scientific-critical investigation of Jewish history served to limit the authority of rabbinic tradition and to counteract the impression that one's own religion exhausts itself in normative "Rabbinism." On the other hand, it revealed the potential for renewal inherent in Jewish history, which in their eyes was a means of returning to the central religious ideas and the heroic historical figures, in order to counter the danger of the Jewish society dissolving itself.

1.2 Conflicting understandings of science and scholarship

From the beginning, different Jewish understandings of science and scholarship came into contact in the Wissenschaft des Judentums: Zunz's and Steinschneider's secular philological-historical approach differed from the concept of Jewish theology as a science of faith that Abraham Geiger and Zacharias Frankel had championed. Furthermore, conflicts arose when determining the relationship between scholarship and Judaism, namely, the question of whether research into Jewish tradition should be oriented towards the requirements of the Jewish people and the strengthening of the Jewish religion, or whether it should aim at being integrated into academic study while largely ignoring specifically Jewish interests [21]. Steinschneider, in his works on Jewish cultural history and his bibliographical studies, and Zunz, in his monumental trilogy on synagogue poetry (*Synagogale Poesie des Mittelalters*, 1855; *Der Ritus des synagogalen Gottesdienstes*, 1859; *Literaturgeschichte der synagogalen Poesie*, 1865), in which he endeavored to document the continuity of the Jewish people's creative religious and poetical spirit in the post-biblical period, chose a more secular approach based on literary history. The emergence of conflicting religious trends within German Judaism around the middle of the 19th century, however, laid the foundations for divergent theological concepts of science and scholarship.

As for the → Reform movement, it was Abraham Geiger, above all, who laid the theoretical foundations of a Jewish-liberal scholarship and a Jewish theology based on academic standards. He called for the consistent application of philological and historiographical methods to all aspects of Jewish tradition and history, including the rabbinic texts and the Hebrew Bible (→ Tanakh). With this historicization of the normative tradition of religious law, he associated the hope for a purification of Judaism that would restore its essence by means of recourse to its biblical origins and at the same time historically legitimize its reform. Geiger's approach rested on a dynamic concept of revelation and tradition developing constantly and vividly in the different periods of Jewish history, which meant that a contemporary redefinition of Jewish self-understanding would not have to constitute a break with tradition. He found the necessary foundation for this in → prophecy, with its universal religion and ethics, which constituted the true content of Pharisaic and rabbinic teachings. The Halakhic tradition, however, which had been necessary as a protective cover in the past, would have to be shed in order to unfurl the true essence of Judaism as a universal prophetic religion for humanity. His ethnicizing interpretation of the choosing of Israel and traditional → Messianism culminated in the view that the Jews, as the "people of the revelation," had always been predestined to preserve pure monotheism in dispersal (→ Diaspora) and to prepare for the unity of faith of all humans. With this model of thought, the Jewish religion's claim to legitimacy and the right to continue to exist equally alongside Christianity could also be justified. With groundbreaking studies such as *Was hat Mohammed aus dem Judenthume aufgenommen* (1833; "Judaism and Islam: A Prize Essay," 1898), *Urschrift und Uebersetzungen der Bibel in ihrer Abhängigkeit von der innern Entwickelung des Judenthums* (1857; The Original Text and the Translations of the Bible: Their Dependence on the Inner Development of Judaism), and the three-volume *Das Judenthum und seine*

Leopold Zunz (1794–1886)

Geschichte (1865/1871; "Judaism and its History," 1985), Geiger also created the framework for the Wissenschaft des Judentums to participate with confidence in the contemporary study of Islam and Christianity.

Unlike Geiger, Zacharias Frankel advocated anchoring contemporary → reforms in revealed Jewish tradition. He endeavored to establish a synthesis between a firm belief in the Torah as the positive foundation of the Jewish religion and modern scientific and historic thought. The concept of positive-historical Judaism that he coined rested on the idea of a positive law established by the Torah and its historical effect; this law embodied the Jewish spirit and was not to be dissolved in favor of the zeitgeist. In order to regain the vitality of religious tradition and thus counteract the growing indifference in Jewish communities, the Wissenschaft des Judentums would have to take the written Torah as the revealed and inviolable foundation of faith and life and as the basis for applying "the principles of general science to the study of the doctrine of God and other Jewish religious sources" and develop "Jewish knowledge into Jewish science." Frankel also hoped to resolve the seemingly irreconcilable contradiction and to show "how true science can very well be combined with genuine piety and pure religious sentiment to form a harmonious whole" (cited in [1. 32]). In his work *Darke ha-Mishnah* (1859; The Ways the Mishnah), in which he turned to the history of the → Halakhah and interpreted rabbinic tradition as being shaped in part by human influences, he removed the Torah entirely from the realm of critical study. This was characteristic of his understanding of the Wissenschaft des Judentums as a historical science of faith that also relied on contemporary scholarly methods. He was instrumental in shaping the conservative scholarly tradition of the Jewish Theological Seminary in → Breslau, which was influential in large parts of Europe and also in North America.

The attitude of Jewish → Orthodoxy in Germany toward the Wissenschaft des Judentums was "partially in unison with it, partially parallel to it, but also fundamentally opposed to it" [16. 175]. Samson Raphael Hirsch, the founder of → neo-Orthodoxy, rejected the idea of historical development of the liberal and reform-oriented Wissenschaft des Judentums as being a transgression against the principle of the Torah as revelation. He regarded the concept as merely the "fine dust wafting from the sarcophagi of moldering corpses over the arid steppes of the present day." [7. 45]. Instead, he conceived of scholarship as "true" research into the Jewish tradition based on the theonomous exegesis of the transmitted texts and oriented towards the way people structure their lives. Esriel Hildesheimer, the founder of the Berlin → Rabbinical Seminary, who contributed significantly to the conception of a dialectic relation between tradition and change, faithful adherence to tradition, and scholarly methodology, occupied a less apodictic position. While his approach ruled out in principle any challenge to the divine authority of the normative sources, he did allow the development of serious Orthodox research in the areas of biblical exegesis, Talmudic studies, and Oriental studies, as long as historical criticism followed the framework laid out by the revealed specifications of the written and oral Torah. This approach was represented by respected scholars such as Abraham Berliner, Jacob Barth, and David Zvi Hoffmann.

At the end of the 19th and beginning of the 20th centuries, representatives of the Zionist movement (→ Basel) subjected the Wissenschaft des Judentums to criticism that was devastating in parts. As early as 1862, Moses Hess (→ Geldwesen) had rejected Abraham Geiger's universalist interpretation of the Jewish people's messianic mission as a dangerous surrendering of the national element of the historical Jewish religion, which would only lead to a rationalistic variant of Christianity. Later Zionist attacks were directed against the philological-historical and theological trends within the Wissenschaft des Judentums. Intellectuals such as Ozjasz (Joshua) Thon or Aḥad Ha-Am (→ Cultural Zionism) unanimously accused Steinschneider and Zunz of making a museum of Judaism as a long-dead and buried phenomenon forgotten in the present. They regarded Geiger and Frankel as proclaiming uncreative, imitative apologetics. The alternative they had in mind was a "jüdische Wissenschaft" ("Jewish science and scholarship") – as Martin Buber (→ Dialogue) called it [2] – which would take into account → sociology, ethnology (→ Anthropology), cultural history, economics, → medicine, and psychology. Moreover, it would conduct research on the contemporary life of the Jewish people as well. Their objective was to provide the foundation for the development of a Jewish national consciousness by making use of the philological-historical disciplines. Last but not least, Zionist intellectuals from Eastern Europe, such as Ḥayim Naḥman Bialik (→ El ha-tsippor), insisted on → Hebrew as the language of scholarship, pointing to Samuel David

Luzzatto (→ Collegio Rabbinico), Nachman Krochmal (→ Guide for the Perplexed of Our Time), and Solomon Judah Rapoport as pioneers. They accused the Western-influenced Wissenschaft des Judentums of betraying Jewish culture.

1.3 Transnational networks

Despite the dominant position of → German language and culture, the Wissenschaft des Judentums grew into a transnational phenomenon during the 19th century. Networks of scholars emerged who had acquired their education not only in German seminaries – above all, the conservative Jewish Theological Seminary of Breslau, as well as the → Hochschule für die Wissenschaft des Judentums and the → Rabbinical Seminary of Orthodox Judaism in Berlin – but also in Padua, → Budapest, and → Vienna. In many cases, they maintained close intellectual exchanges across religious divides by means of letters and publications in numerous journals, including, most prominently, the *Monatsschrift für Geschichte und Wissenschaft des Judentums* (1851–1939). This transnational Jewish *res publica literaria* extended from the German language area to France, England, the Netherlands, Eastern and Southeastern Europe – in particular, Hungary – and also Scandinavia.

After the First World War, in particular, the Wissenschaft des Judentums also extended its influence to Palestine, where its representatives played a part in founding the → Hebrew University. From the middle of the 19th century onward, cultural transfers also prompted the foundation of new centers of Jewish scholarship in the United States. Due to the immigration (→ Ellis Island) of German rabbis and scholars, as well as translations of German-Jewish publications, the close connection between the Wissenschaft des Judentums, the German language, and European scholarly traditions came to characterize the religious profile of the American reform movement. It was not until the turn of the 20th century that

American-Jewish culture and scholarship became more independent, which manifested itself in the founding of numerous scientific institutions, such as the → American Jewish Historical Society (1892), the Jewish Theological Seminary in New York (1903), and the Dropsie College for Hebrew and Cognate Learning founded in 1907 in Philadelphia. The publication of the New York *Jewish Encyclopedia* (1901–1906; → Encyclopedias), was characteristic of the field's ongoing ties with German scholarship, but it also emphasized the increasing independence of the American Wissenschaft des Judentums.

2. The struggle for recognition as an academic discipline

The aspirations of the Wissenschaft des Judentums to see the field established as a discipline at German → universities went largely unfulfilled in the 19th and early 20th centuries. Geiger and Zunz had already endeavored to overcome the correlation between Jews' being refused social equality and the disparagement of Jewish research by demanding that a Jewish theological department be established, or at least that their discipline be represented by a full professorship. According to Zunz, the "equality of Jews in customs and life [needs to] arise from the equality of the Wissenschaft des Judenthums" [13. 59]. In 1848 he applied to the Prussian Ministry of Religious and Educational Affairs to establish a chair for the study of Jewish history and literature in the Department of Philosophy of the University of Berlin. The rejection of his application reflected the predominant attitude in education policy that any hint of public recognition of the equality of the Jewish religion, including its institutions and any encouragement of Jewish cultural consciousness, was to be avoided.

Until well into the 20th century, renowned representatives of the field repeatedly demanded that the Wissenschaft des Judentums finally be given a home in the *universitas litterarum* because of its high scholarly standards and also to ensure the objective and fair appreciation of Jewish tradition. "The ghetto of Judaism will not fall completely until the ghetto of its scholarly discipline falls," the Bible scholar Benno Jacob stated in 1907. He added that Jewish research would only flourish "when, instead of vegetating in corners, it is placed in the midst of the infinitely rich scholarly life and work of the nation and of humankind" [8. 16]. On the occasion of the centenary of the → Prussian Emancipation Edict of 1812, Hermann Cohen (→ Concept of God) called on the Prussian state to ensure "that the Wissenschaft des Judentums be represented at the universities by those who profess our faith and are academically independent" [3. 227]. Nevertheless, the question of whether only Jewish scholars – being representatives of the living Jewish faith – would hold the anticipated chair remained controversial: Sigmund Maybaum, for instance, who taught at the Hochschule für die Wissenschaft des Judentums in Berlin, feared that instituting a denominational chair could compromise the main argument in the Jewish struggle for academic equality, namely, that university appointments must be independent of the appointee's faith. Consequently, he regarded the Wissenschaft des Judentums not as a "Jewish academic discipline" but rather as a discipline dependent on secular research that could of course be practiced by non-Jews as well [9. 643]. The majority of non-Jewish scholars, however, were more supportive of establishing Judaic Studies as an area of research dominated by Christian scholars that could, for example, be located within the discipline of Protestant theology. Jewish researchers would only be able to work as research assistants. Accordingly, philosophical and theological faculties merely established lectureships for rabbinic literature.

During the First World War, certain initiatives in education policy that went along with the increased public presence of the Wissenschaft des Judentums since the beginning of the 20th century raised new hopes. The liberal theologian Martin Rade supported the establishment of a Jewish theological department at the newly founded university in Frankfurt am Main. However, by the end of the Weimar Republic, only a few lectureships or honorary professorships had been established. In contrast, in England, Solomon Schechter (→ Conservative Judaism) was granted a professorship for Hebrew at University College London as early as 1899; in the United States, Harry Austryn Wolfson was appointed to the Nathan Littauer Chair of Hebrew Literature and Philosophy at Harvard University in 1925, and Salo W. Baron (→ Jewish Social Studies) to the Nathan Miller Chair for Jewish History at Columbia University in New York in 1930.

3. Defensive activity and the critical debate with Protestantism

At the turn of the century, the growing antisemitic movement (→ Conspiracy) and the increasingly anti-liberal political climate in the Wilhelmine Empire prompted the Wissenschaft des Judentums to become more actively involved than before in supporting German Jews in asserting themselves religiously, culturally, and politically. Within the scope of the defensive activities of the → Central-Verein deutscher Staatsbürger jüdischen Glaubens (Central Association of German Citizens of Jewish Faith) and the Verband der deutschen Juden (Association of German Jews), especially young rabbis and scholars, who found themselves increasingly marginalized at the universities, fought against prejudices that some of the academic elites harbored (→ Berlin Debate on Antisemitism). Racially (→ Race) motivated attacks against the → Talmud, the continued denouncement of the religious and cultural values of the Hebrew Bible, distorted ideas of the Jewish image of God in the wake of archaeological finds in the → Orient (→ Babel and Bible), as well as a multitude of anti-Jewish historical constructions forced them to place their scholarly expertise – in publications, lectures, or in legal proceedings against antisemites – at the service of apologetics.

Above all, the liberal and positive-historical representatives of the Wissenschaft des Judentums determinedly resisted the cultural hegemony of liberal Protestantism (→ Protestantization), endeavoring to immunize the Jews against the internalization of Christian stereotypes. The dispute with cultural Protestants over their constructions of biblical and post-biblical Jewish history became particularly intense as the political implications of these constructions were reflected in heated debates on the "essence of Judaism" (→ Debate on Essence) in the early 20th century. Leading Jewish scholars like Leo Baeck (→ Leo Baeck Institute), Ismar Elbogen, Josef Eschelbacher, Julius Guttmann (→ Philosophy of Religion), Moritz Güdemann, Benno Jacob, Felix Perles, or Martin Schreiner aggressively insisted that their Protestant colleagues take Jewish scholarship into account and give appropriate appreciation to the Jewish sources, notably rabbinic literature, within the history of religion. They challenged not only Protestant theology in its very own domain – the exegesis of the New Testament, the interpretation of the figure of Jesus, and the presentation of contemporary New Testament history – but also historical-critical Bible studies (→ Biblical Criticism), a discipline particularly susceptible to anti-Jewish interpretations. If the contributions made by the Wissenschaft des Judentums were only hesitantly – or even as an impertinence – acknowledged in the debates on religious history, they did reflect, above all, the politically volatile conflict on the legitimacy of the continued existence of Judaism in Europe in the modern era. Julius Guttmann, for instance, observed that: "In the name of scholarship, a certain current within modern theology today disputes the right of Judaism to exist; it obscures the teachings of Judaism in order to then trace back all progress in the cultural life of mankind exclusively to Christianity while eliminating Judaism" [6. 62].

The public debates of the early 20th century proved to be fruitful for the Wissenschaft des Judentums. Numerous important studies on early Judaism were conducted, and an independent Jewish branch of Bible studies emerged; moreover, they resulted in groundbreaking theological and philosophical concepts for the presentation of the Jewish heritage in the present. Besides Kaufmann Kohler's (→ Hebrew Union College) *Grundriß einer systematischen Theologie des Judentums auf geschichtlicher Grundlage* (1910; "Jewish Theology: Systematically and Historically Considered," 1918) and Hermann Cohen's *Die Religion der Vernunft aus den Quellen des Judentums* (1918; "Religion of Reason: Out of the Sources of Judaism," 1972), these include most prominently Leo Baeck's apologetic study *Das Wesen des Judentums* (1905; "The Essence of Judaism," 1936). The latter gained influence in the Jewish-Christian debate precisely because it implicitly postulated the superiority of Jewish tradition. Baeck saw the essence of Judaism in the ethical monotheism of the biblical prophets. In contrast to Adolf von Harnack, he did not regard Judaism as a particularly legalistic religion (→ Ceremonial Law) but as a forward-looking prophetic faith in which religion, reason, and humanism were inextricably connected.

4. Between reorientation and destruction

In the years of the Weimar Republic, the German Wissenschaft des Judentums accomplished its most important achievements – especially in the fields of rabbinic literature and Jewish historiography – at independent Jewish institutions,

in particular, the → Akademie für die Wissenschaft des Judentums founded in 1919 in Berlin. However, some programmatic reorientations occurred after the First World War in the context of the Jewish → renaissance, Zionist criticism of the existing understanding of scholarship, as well as Franz Rosenzweig's (→ [The] Star of Redemption; → Freies Jüdisches Lehrhaus) deliberations on educational theory. Ismar Elbogen, for instance, postulated that the discipline should also deal with contemporary Jewish life and – in line with Abraham Geiger's understanding – must at its core be conceived as "Jewish theology" [5. 90].

The transfer of power to Hitler in 1933 destroyed all hopes that the Wissenschaft des Judentums might be recognized as an academic discipline. One after the other, its institutions were closed; the Hochschule für die Wissenschaft des Judentums was the last to shutter in 1942. The representatives of the field who survived the → Shoah contributed to establishing and expanding research institutions for the study of Judaism and the Jews in England, the United States, and Palestine.

Meanwhile, in the National Socialist state, the antisemitic → Judenforschung pursued by non-Jewish historians and theologians emerged. Among its institutions were the Institut zum Studium der Judenfrage (Institute for the Study of the Jewish Question; founded in 1934/1935) in Berlin, the Forschungsabteilung Judenfrage des Reichsinstituts für Geschichte des neuen Deutschland (Research Department on the Jewish Question at the Reich Institute for the History of the New Germany) in Munich (founded in 1936), the Institut zur Erforschung und Beseitigung des jüdischen Einflusses auf das deutsche kirchliche Leben (Institute for the Study and Elimination of Jewish Influence on German Church Life) that was founded in 1939 in Eisenach, and the Institut zur Erforschung der Judenfrage (Institute for the Research on the Jewish

Question) in Frankfurt am Main (founded in 1941).

Elbogen, who had fled from Germany to North America in 1938, outlined the history of the German Wissenschaft des Judentums from its beginnings and its impact in the United States in the *American Jewish Year Book*, the publication of the → American Jewish Committee, in 1944. In his concluding passage, he expressed pride in the achievements of German-Jewish scholarship, mingling it with sadness at the destruction of this tradition and the hope that an independent Wissenschaft des Judentums might come to flourish in America [4. 65].

5. After the Shoah

In 1944, Gershom Scholem (→ Kabbalah), a prominent representative of the Zionist branch of the Wissenschaft des Judentums at the → Hebrew University in Jerusalem, who was at the same time one of its most acute critics, wrote his impassioned fundamental critique of the field *Mitokh hirhurim al ḥokhmat Yisra'el* (From within Reflections on the Wissenschaft des Judentums) that appeared in the literary supplement of the newspaper *Ha'aretz* [26. 427]. He pointed to the contradiction between the claim of the Wissenschaft des Judentums to pure scholarship and the role it played in the struggle for emancipation. The historicization of what he saw as the living Jewish past undertaken by Zunz, Geiger, and Steinschneider appeared to him as a "horrifying burial ceremony" [10. 20]. He also took exception to the apologetic character of the discipline as it led to an idealizing and falsifying interpretation of Jewish tradition along the lines of enlightened rationalism so that it suppressed Jewish → mysticism, which was regarded as outdated. Indeed, in the entire second half of the 19th century, Scholem argued, the Wissenschaft des Judentums had produced "not a single original, living, and non-petrified word about the Jewish

religion" [10. 39]. In this, one can discern Scholem's grief over the failure of Jewish endeavors to integrate in Germany despite all the political considerations and enlightened apologetics.

Overall, the glaringly apologetic traits in the interpretation of Jewish history characterized the situation in which the Wissenschaft des Judentums involuntary found itself – as a marginalized discipline mostly ignored by non-Jews or perceived as a Jewish special interest group. In view of the ongoing antisemitic discrimination, it constantly found itself compelled to justify the special religious and cultural value of the Jewish religion. Nevertheless, its representatives exhibited a high degree of intellectual energy and creativity. With it, they confidently demanded their right to participate in general academic discourse and challenged the intellectual hegemony of the Protestant view of history without subjecting the field to the categories drawn up by non-Jewish constructions of Judaism.

Bibliography

Sources

[1] M. Brann, Geschichte des Jüdisch-Theologischen Seminars (Fraenckel'sche Stiftung) in Breslau. Festschrift zum fünfzigjährigen Jubiläum der Anstalt, Breslau 1904. [2] M. Buber, Jüdische Wissenschaft, in: Die Welt 5 (1901) 41, 1f.; 43, 1f. [3] H. Cohen, Emanzipation. Zur Hundertjahrfeier des Staatsbürgertums der preußischen Juden (11. März 1912), in: Hermann Cohens Jüdische Schriften, introduced by F. Rosenzweig, ed. by B. Strauss, Vol. 2: Zur jüdischen Zeitgeschichte, Berlin 1924, 220–228. [4] I. Elbogen, American Jewish Scholarship. A Survey, in: American Jewish Year Book 45 (1943/44), 47–65. [5] I. Elbogen, Neuorientierung unserer Wissenschaft, in: Monatsschrift für Geschichte und Wissenschaft des Judentums 62 (1918), 81–96. [6] J. Guttmann, Die Idee der Versöhnung im Judentum, in: Allgemeine Zeitung des Judentums 74 (1910) 6, 61–63. [7] S. R. Hirsch,

Collected Writings, Vol. 7: Jewish Education, New York 1997. [8] B. Jacob, Die Wissenschaft des Judentums, ihr Einfluß auf die Emanzipation der Juden. Vortrag gehalten auf der Generalversammlung des Rabbiner-Verbandes in Deutschland, Berlin am 2. Januar 1907, Berlin 1907. [9] S. Maybaum, Die Wissenschaft des Judentums, in: Monatsschrift für Geschichte und Wissenschaft des Judentums 51 (1907), 641–658. [10] G. Scholem, Überlegungen zur Wissenschaft vom Judentum, in: G. Scholem, Judaica 6. Die Wissenschaft des Judentums, Frankfurt am Main 1997, 7–52. [11] M. Wiener, Jüdische Religion im Zeitalter der Emanzipation, Berlin 1933. [12] I. Wolf, Ueber den Begriff einer Wissenschaft des Judenthums, in: Zeitschrift für die Wissenschaft des Judenthums 1 (1823), 1–24. [13] L. Zunz, Die jüdische Literatur, in: L. Zunz, Gesammelte Schriften, vol. 1, Berlin 1875, 41–59. [14] L. Zunz, Etwas über die rabbinische Litteratur, in: L. Zunz, Gesammelte Schriften, vol. 1, Berlin 1875, 1–31.

Secondary literature

[15] M. Brenner/S. Rohrbacher (eds.), Wissenschaft vom Judentum. Annäherungen nach dem Holocaust, Göttingen 2000. [16] M. Breuer, Modernity within Tradition. A Social History of Orthodox Jewry in Imperial Germany, trans. by E. Petuchowski, New York 1992. [17] J. Carlebach (ed.), Wissenschaft des Judentums. Anfänge der Judaistik in Europa, Darmstadt 1992. [18] K. v. d. Krone, Wissenschaft in Öffentlichkeit. Die Wissenschaft des Judentums und ihre Zeitschriften, Berlin/Boston 2012. [19] R. Leicht/G. Freudenthal (eds.), Studies on Steinschneider. Moritz Steinschneider and the Emergence of the Science of Judaism in Nineteenth-Century Germany, Leiden/Boston 2011. [20] M. A. Meyer, Response to Modernity. A History of the Reform Movement in Judaism, Detroit 1995. [21] M. A. Meyer, Two Persistent Tensions within Wissenschaft des Judentums, in: A. Gotzmann/C. Wiese (eds.), Modern Judaism and Historical Consciousness. Identities, Encounters, Perspectives, Leiden 2007, 73–92. [22] N. H. Römer, Jewish Scholarship and Culture in Nineteenth-Century

Germany. Between History and Faith, Madison 2005. [23] I. Schorsch, From Text to Context. The Turn to History in Modern Judaism, Hanover/London 1994. [24] C. Wiese, Wissenschaft des Judentums und protestantische Theologie im wilhelminischen Deutschland. Ein Schrei ins Leere?, Tübingen 1999. [25] C. Wiese et al. (eds.), Jüdische Existenz in der Moderne. Abraham Geiger und die Wissenschaft des Judentums, Berlin/Boston 2013. [26] C. Wiese, Challenging Colonial Discourse, trans. by B. Harshav/C. Wiese, Leiden/Boston 2005.

CHRISTIAN WIESE, FRANKFURT AM MAIN

Wolkenbügel

Title of the draft of a futuristic ensemble of several high-rise buildings for the city of Moscow, devised between 1923 and 1925 in Germany by the Russian-Jewish avant-gardist El Lissitzky (1890–1941). With his vision, which transcended the American skyscraper into the horizontal plane, Lissitzky created one of the most original and significant architectural concepts (→ Architecture) of the 20th century. At the same time the Wolkenbügel (lit. "cloud hanger") is exemplary of the strong orientation of Jewish artists toward the Russian Soviet avant-garde, which was soon again limited by the narrow focus on the specifications of Socialist Realism in the early 1930s.

1. The draft
2. El Lissitzky
3. Jews and the Russian Soviet avant-garde

1. The draft

In 1925, Lissitzky presented his spectacular project of "Wolkenbügel" to the public. He planned to erect a total of eight high-rise buildings in the center of Moscow on central intersections of the Boulevard Ring. Each building would consist of a flat three-story structure fifty meters above the ground, together with three massive pillars of 10 × 6 meters supporting it; the longest side of the three-story platform shaped like a letter "h" lying on its side was to be 180 meters long (see image). The design also provided for one of the three pillars to be extended into a deep basement, linking the building to a planned subway station via a staircase.

From the point of view of urban planning, the deliberate rectilinear structures were intended to provide a contrast with the overall curvilinear impression of Moscow's city center whose streets radiate out from the Kremlin, forming a series of open-work concentric circles together with the ring roads. At the same time each of the eight buildings with their city-gate appearance were laid out in such a way that the projecting side looked towards the Kremlin, as if they were pointing at the city center like a series of arrows.

The interior design of the "Wolkenbügel" accommodated the natural movement patterns of humans, being oriented horizontally rather than vertically. It was intended to offer an alternative to the verticality of the skyscrapers in the American mold shooting up from the ground. While he was working on the idea of the Wolkenbügel, Lissitzky experimented with different proportions and configurations of height and width, since spatial balance, he emphasized, resulted "from the contrast of the vertical and

Der Wolkenbügel, *Sketch by El Lissitzky* (1925)

horizontal dimensions" (cited in [3. 215]). Lissitzky also argued that horizontal buildings allowed more effective ventilation and insulation than vertical constructions. All things considered, he regarded his draft as an exemplary solution when it came to satisfying human needs, as propagated by the Bolsheviks in contrast to the capitalist system of sacrificing humans to profit.

Lissitzky completed the draft in cooperation with the Dutch architect, urban planner, and furniture designer Mart Stam (1899–1986), who sympathized with the New Objectivity. Stam had moved to Berlin in 1922, where he met Lissitzky and collaborated with him on a number of projects. It was Stam who transferred the cantilever principle into handicraft, designing the cantilevered tubular steel chair that would be perfected by Marcel Breuer and was the starting point for a new type of chair design. Lissitzky spoke fluent → German and repeatedly stayed in Germany for long periods, as it was respected by a majority of the Soviet avant-garde as a culturally and technologically advanced country. This explains why the Wolkenbügel project was given a German name that is still commonly used in Russian today, and it also fits that the steel construction for Lissitzky's project was to be manufactured by Krupp.

Lissitzky presented a first public draft of his idea in an article and a concept drawing in the February 1925 edition of the German art journal *Das Kunstblatt*; a year later, an image of the project appeared on the title page of Adolf Behne's inventory of functionalist architecture *Der moderne Zweckbau* (1926). At the same time, Lissitzky created several photomontages for the Moscow architectural journal *ASNOVA* showing a Wolkenbügel by the Nikitskaya Gate in Moscow.

Due to a lack of resources – or initiative – in the young Soviet state, the project was never realized. However, the underlying principles, namely the emphasis on cantilevered horizontal elements resting on vertical supports, served as inspiration for a number of later buildings, among them Frank Lloyd Wright's *Fallingwater* house in Pennsylvania (1935), George Chakhava's administration building for the Ministry of Highway Construction in Tbilisi, Georgia (1975), or Steven Holl's "horizontal skyscraper," the Vanke Center in Shenzhen in China (2006–2009).

2. El Lissitzky

Lazar Markovich Lissitzky was born in 1890 in Pochinok, a → shtetl not far from Smolensk. While he was still a child, his family moved to → Vitebsk (today in Belarus). In his early youth he studied at the local art school; its director Yehuda Pen, Marc Chagall's first teacher, was of great significance as both an artist and teacher for the Jewish renaissance in the visual arts in the late 19th century.

In late Czarist Russia, the enrollment of Jews in Russian academic institutions was restricted by means of admission quotas (→ Numerus Clausus). When Lissitzky was rejected by the St. Petersburg Academy of Arts in 1909, he chose the same route as many young Jews; he went to Germany, where he began to study architecture and engineering at the Technische Hochschule Darmstadt. During the summer months he travelled all over Europe, in particular to France and Italy, and he soon joined a Parisian group of Russian-Jewish artists headed by his childhood friend Ossip Zadkine (→ École de Paris). The First World War forced him to return to Russia without a degree. In Moscow he found employment in Roman Klein's and Boris Welikowski's architecture offices. He also attended classes at the Riga Polytechnic Institute which had been relocated to Moscow for the duration of the war. When he received a degree as an architect in June 1918, the fall of the Czarist regime and the Russian revolutions opened an entirely new era.

Thus Marc Chagall, for instance, was appointed People's Commissar for Art in the Vitebsk Governorate. At Chagall's invitation, Lissitzky returned to Vitebsk in May 1919 in order to teach at the People's Art School; Yehuda Pen and the painter Kazimir Malevich were also invited by Chagall to teach in Vitebsk. Malevich's recently developed Suprematism with its angular geometric shapes and limited color spectrum soon presented a challenge to the figurative style favored by Chagall. While Lissitzky was loyal to Chagall, he soon succumbed to the fascination of Suprematism.

Lissitzky began his career as an illustrator of (children's) books. He became known for his placards for the revolution, among them his most famous propaganda poster "Beat the Whites with the Red Wedge" (1919), on which a red wedge (the Bolsheviks) breaks into a white shape (the counterrevolution). This already hints at Lissitzky's style and symbolic vocabulary which, unlike Malevich's non-objective conception, allowed more concrete forms. In January 1920 Lissitzky and Malevich founded the short-lived Suprematist association *MOLPOSNOVIS* (acronym of *Molodye posledovateli novogo iskusstva*, Young Followers of the New Art) renamed *UNOVIS* (acronym of *Utverditeli novogo iskusstva*, Champions of the New Art) a month later.

The development of Lissitzky's visual language during the two years in which *UNOVIS* existed led to his own version of Suprematism in which he confronted its obsession with flat, two-dimensional geometrical forms with the constructivist interest in three-dimensional spaces. The latter were more conducive to addressing the viewer and including him in the question of how to design a new and more Utopian world. This was precisely what Lissitzky regarded as an artist's main task which he called (in German) "zielbewusstes Schaffen" (i.e. "goal-oriented creation"). He called these pieces *PROUN* (probably an acronym of *Proekt utverzhdeniya novogo*, Design for the Confirmation of the New). The forms of three-dimensionality he used to this end, referencing his training as an architect, were also the foundation for his later theoretical works of architecture such as the Wolkenbügel project.

When the Soviet government assigned him to establish contacts between Russian and German artists, Lissitzky returned to Germany in late 1921. Together with the author Ilya Ehrenburg (→ [The] Thaw) he founded the short-lived journal *Veshch/Gegenstand/Objet* which appeared in → Russian, → German, and French, and championed the idea of an international art movement based on constructivism. In October 1923 Lissitzky contracted severe pneumonia, which was diagnosed a few weeks later as tuberculosis. In February 1924 he was able to be moved to a Swiss sanatorium where he experimented with the visual language of typography and → photography, translated Malevich's essays into German, and refined the Wolkenbügel draft while making a living designing advertisements for the Pelikan company. After his Swiss visa was not renewed, he returned to Moscow, where he worked as a lecturer at the state college of art *Vkhutein* (acronym of *Vysshij khudozhestvenno-tekhnicheskij institut*, Higher Art and Technical Institute) until its closure in 1930.

After further sojourns in Germany and the Netherlands, in 1927 Lissitzky married Sophie Küppers, the widow of the director of the Hanover art gallery Kestnergesellschaft which had been the first to exhibit his work in Germany. He also discovered new fields of activity at this time. In 1928 he was in charge of design for the Soviet pavilion at the International Press Exhibition in Cologne – an art form to which he remained faithful until the end of his life. At the same time he pursued the novel technique of photomontage. In the birth announcement of his son Jen in 1930 he superimposed the image of his child over that of a factory chimney, creating a link between his son's future and that of the Soviet state.

Books and book design, however, continued to hold the greatest attraction for him, because a book, according to Lissitzky "goes to the people, and does not stand like a cathedral in one place waiting for someone to approach [...] the book [is the] monument of the future." (cited in [4. 49]). At the same time, letters and words developed into important elements in Soviet art, especially after 1932 when Stalin banned independent artists' associations and the Soviet state tolerated only Socialist Realism in visual → art, → literature, and → music. It did not permit abstract representation, demanding instead heroic illustrations of the Soviet reconstruction work.

Despite his continuing ill health and the increasingly harsh tone from the regime, Lissitzky continued to work designing books and posters. From the beginning of the 1930s, he was responsible for the design of the internationally circulated large-format illustrated propaganda publication *USSR in Construction* that presented major socialist building projects. One of the last posters, created shortly before his death in December 1941, was intended to mobilize support for the home front in view of the German attack on the Soviet Union. Against the backdrop of a factory work floor the faces of a man and a woman are put into relief, above them a plane and in front of them a tank. It is inscribed: "Give us more tanks!" and below: "Everything for the front! Everything for victory!" While the poster was thus in accordance with the requirements of Stalin's decree of 1932, its emphasis on harsh red as opposed to black and white as well as its dynamic diagonals refer unmistakably to the early Soviet style which Lissitzky had influenced significantly.

3. Jews and the Russian Soviet avant-garde

During his career, Lissitzky also dealt with Jewish subjects. In the abstract sense, his art and his artistic ethos of the "goal-oriented creation" focused on the idea of the artist as a force for change and improvement in the world – an idea known in the rabbinic tradition as → *tikkun olam* (renewal of the world).

Lissitzky's interest in Jewish contexts already found expression during his time as a student. Influenced by the expeditions undertaken a few years before by An-Ski (→ Dybbuk) and the → Jewish Society for History and Ethnography (*Yevrejskoe istoriko-etnograficheskoe obshchestvo*), in 1916 he and his university friend Issachar Ber Ryback traveled to the Jewish communities in the Dnieper region to study, among other things, the details of wooden → synagogues. One of his best-known works is the illustration of the traditional Pesaḥ song (→ Course of the Year) *Ḥad Gadya* (1919; One kid). The last picture shows the hand of God smiting the angel of death who is wearing a recognizable Czarist crown, thus establishing a clear connection between the Israelites' liberation from the Egyptian yoke and the deliverance of the Jews from the Czarist oppression. The motif of the hand of God, which Lissitzky would use repeatedly in the following years, continues a long Jewish tradition devoted to solving the problem of how to show an invisible God acting. There can be no doubt that Lissitzky had come across this kind of visualizing of biblical phrases during his ethnographic journeys immediately before the revolution.

Even during the 1920s, when Lissitzky had already become known as a Soviet avant-garde artist, we find Jewish symbols – as a rule variations of Hebrew letters (→ Alef Bet) – in his *PROUNs* as well as in his book design. Even before this time, the members of *UNOVIS* had begun signing their works with a small black square that also adorned their badges and cufflinks. While this undoubtedly represented an homage to Malevich's iconic painting *The Black Square* (1913/1915), it also recalled the black tefillin that were a part of street scenes in, for instance, Jewish Vitebsk, where adult Jewish men would traditionally place these on their forehead and hands for the morning prayer. The Wolkenbügel project, ultimately, suggests the interpretation – considering Lissitzky's interest in the bird's eye view of the form of a building – that the form of the horizontally designed work- and living spaces of the Wolkenbügel recalled less a lower-case "h" and rather the Hebrew letter *Bet*, the initial consonant of the → Hebrew word *bayit* meaning house. Lissitzky could thus be said to have drawn on elements of Jewish tradition even in this project.

This connection between → art and Jewish heritage was not unusual in the context of the late Czarist Empire and early Soviet Russia in which Lissitzky's œuvre unfolded. In → music, Jewish composers had been inspired by the (non-Jewish) director of the St. Petersburg Conservatory Nikolai Rimsky-Korsakov to found the → Society for Jewish Folk Music in 1908, dedicated to creating a national Jewish style within Russian music. The Jewish Historical-Ethnographic Society, also founded in 1908, had the objective of researching the history of the Jews in the Russian Empire. Jewish visual artists also began in the early 1890s to investigate the Jewish legacy in their chosen field, a search that became interwoven with the artistic avant-garde movements in pre-Revolutionary Russia, which promoted variety, individuality, and revolutionary thought.

In addition to Lissitzky, many Jewish artists of the most disparate styles and religious convictions, viewed the revolution with enthusiasm and hope, from the painter and stage set designer Léon Bakst through Marc Chagall and the impressionist Robert Falk to Issachar Ber Ryback and the painter Ruvim Mazel. They perceived it as a path leading out of centuries of hatred of Jews (→ Anti-Judaism) to a new world of social, political, and economic equality. Carried along by the furor and the spirit of optimism of the year 1917 they reveled in the effects of the new creative freedom, leaving behind eloquent testimony in which this promise was expressed. Stalin's crushing of this enthusiasm affected Jewish and non-Jewish artists in equal measure, leading to exile or prison, even to executions in many cases. The idealized future, the most powerful symbol of which had been Lissitzky's Wolkenbügel, became a dystopian present that would define the Soviet art world until the 1980s.

Bibliography

Sources

[1] S. Lissitzky-Küppers (ed.), El Lissitzky. Life, Letters, Texts, trans. by H. Aldwinckle and M. Whittal, London 1968.

Secondary literature

[2] F. Burgos/G. Garrido, El Lissitzky. Wolkenbügel 1924–1925, Madrid 2004. [3] S. O. Khan-Magomedov, Sto shedevrov sovetskogo arkhitekturnogo avangarda [One Hundred Masterpieces of Soviet Avant-Garde Architecture], Moscow 2005. [4] P. Nisbet, El Lissitzky in the Proun Years. A Study of His Work and Thought, 1919–1927, New Haven 1995. [5] N. Perloff/E. Forgacs, Monuments of the Future. Designs by El Lissitzky, Los Angeles 1998 [exhibition catalogue]. [6] N. Perloff/B. Reed (eds.), Situating El Lissitzky. Vitebsk/Berlin/Moscow, Los Angeles 2003. [7] M. Tupitsyn, El Lissitzky. Beyond the Abstract Cabinet. Photography, Design, Collaboration, New Haven 1999 [exhibition catalogue].

ORI Z. SOLTES, WASHINGTON D.C.

Woman Rabbi

According to traditional Jewish interpretation, the position and function of the rabbi are reserved exclusively for men (→ Rabbinate). In the late 19th century, both in Europe and in North America, voices within Judaism were increasingly demanding the active involvement of women in religious practice. In 1935, after completing her rabbinical studies, Regina Jonas from Berlin became the first woman rabbi, but her ordination was highly controversial even in liberal circles. Jonas was not employed as a community rabbi but took care of religious matters and provided spiritual care in the Jewish community of Berlin, which was threatened with destruction. In the United States, the discussion on the rabbinate, which had also been ongoing since the 19th century, resumed after the Second World War, but it was not until 1972 (in Europe until 1975) that the first woman received rabbinic ordination again.

1. Early debates
2. Regina Jonas
3. Reform Judaism in the United States
4. Reconstructionist and Conservative Judaism
5. Developments in Europe, Israel, and America

1. Early debates

The gender perceptions formulated in the Bible (→ Tanakh) and the → Talmud assigned women an inferior status to men (→ Meḥitsah). Women were thus viewed as physically and mentally inferior, which was seen as a consequence of secondary creation and the specific female physique: girls cannot be circumcised at the foreskin and therefore cannot directly enter into the covenant (*brit*; → Circumcision) with God. On grounds of their gender, they were also deemed unfit for ritual services at the → Temple. This interpretation excluded girls and women from equal participation in worship-related activities as well as from the study of the Talmud and the associated → commentary literature (→ Talmud Torah). Since knowledge of the traditional literature was deemed to be a cornerstone of Halakhic competence and thus rabbinical authority, it was simply natural to deem women unfit for the → rabbinate, which is the reason why there is no explicit prohibition of the ordination (Hebr. *smikhah*) of women in the entire rabbinical literature.

However, as women were responsible for observing the religious commandments in domestic and family life, knowledge of these commandments was greatly valued. Thus, the rabbi's wife was traditionally held in high esteem – not primarily because of her husband's status but due to her own knowledge: in many cases she was the daughter of a rabbi herself and, in this scholarly environment, had been educated by her father (and sometimes her mother) in the Bible and Halakhic laws concerning → marriage and family, about her own body (→ Mikveh) as well as dietary laws (→ Kashrut). As the rabbi's wife she instructed other women in liturgical and domestic and family matters. However, her title *rebbetsin* (Yidd.; "wife of the rabbi") was not connected to an official function.

Since the early 19th century, Judaism in Europe had been undergoing a comprehensive modernization process. A liberal trend (→ Reform) developed in opposition to traditional Judaism and led to changes not only in → liturgy and practical → piety but also – under the influence of the women's rights movement (→ Jüdischer Frauenbund) – gave expression to changed gender relations and new gender roles. Reform-oriented community members opposed the Halakhic-religious discrimination against girls and women and demanded their equality in the → synagogue. In 1817, the first → bat mitzvah celebration for girls took place in a Berlin Reform synagogue. At a number of → rabbinical conferences in cities of the German Confederation, the first of which took place in Wiesbaden in 1837, liberal rabbis, in line with their efforts to modernize Jewish traditions, discussed the status of women according to Jewish law. In 1846, the liberal rabbi David Einhorn (1809–1879) spoke out in favor of religious equality of women and demanded changes in religious law. Reform-oriented rabbis subsequently adapted many Jewish marriage and divorce laws to the respective national laws. Most reform-oriented rabbis ultimately favored little more than a comprehensive religious education for female community members – they did not seriously discuss opening up the rabbinate to include women. On the one hand, they feared renewed hostility on the part of the → Orthodoxy, on the other hand, as men of their time, they remained rooted in the prevailing views about female gender roles.

2. Regina Jonas

Regina Jonas was born in Berlin on August 3, 1902, as the daughter of Orthodox parents. She grew up in poor conditions, initially in Berlin's → Scheunenviertel. Her father Wolf Jonas was a destitute merchant who had immigrated from Pomerania; he died when Regina was twelve years old. Her mother Sara, who came from Bavaria, took care of her daughter and her son Abraham on her own. In 1920, roughly two years after completing girls' school, Regina Jonas attended the Oberlyzeum (girls' secondary school) Berlin-Weißensee from which she graduated in 1923 with Abitur (qualification granted at the end of secondary education). After a further year attending a pedagogics seminar class she finally left school receiving a license to teach in girls' schools ("Lehrbefähigung für Lyzeen").

As a student, together with her mother, Jonas had attended service at the Orthodox synagogue on Rykestraße, in whose open-minded atmosphere the moderate liberal rabbi Max Weyl (1873–1942, died in Theresienstadt) was also permitted to preach. He promoted religious education of girls and allowed bat mitzvah celebrations. Weyl gave Jonas private classes in rabbinical literature which they later continued in the form of weekly studies until 1942. In 1924, Isidor Bleichrode (1867–1954), a conservative rabbi at the Kottbusser Tor Synagoge (today the Fraenkelufer Synagoge) and principal of the Annenstraße religious school,

employed Regina and her brother Abraham as teachers of religion in 1924 on grounds of their teaching qualifications. Besides teaching, which later partly financed her studies, she held lectures which were met with great enthusiasm.

Although Jonas followed an Orthodox lifestyle in terms of religious law, in 1924 she enrolled at the liberal → Hochschule für die Wissenschaft des Judentums (HWJ) – as a woman she would not have been accepted into the Orthodox → rabbinical seminary. The Berlin HWJ had already accepted women as students of religious education for several years. Although Jonas was pursuing rabbinical studies at the same time, apparently few among the students or teaching staff believed that she would actually graduate with the *hatarat hora'ah*, the official rabbinical diploma.

The Talmud professor responsible for the ordination, Eduard Baneth (1855–1930), was nevertheless cautiously open to Jonas's aspiration. He accepted her thesis on a Halakhic topic. In 1930, Jonas presented her 88-page thesis with the title *Kann die Frau das rabbinische Amt bekleiden?*. In her thesis, she described the modern rabbi as a scholar, teacher, preacher, and Jewish role model; a well-educated woman, she argued, could assume all these functions as a "woman rabbi" as well as any man. Moreover, she held that there had been pioneering examples in the past – not only the biblical prophetesses but also women from the Talmud such as Beruriah (2nd century) or the learned daughters of the renowned medieval commentator Rashi (→ Worms), who had worked as teachers and interpreters of Jewish law.

Regina Jonas' argumentative strategy was to answer the question about women's ability to become rabbis themselves using religious law. She referred to the Talmud and standard works of the → Halakhah such as *Arba'ah Turim* (Four Rows), *Mishneh Torah* (Repetition of the Torah) and *Shulḥan Arukh* (Set

Table) as well as to → responsa. She built her reasoning on the premise that women and men had received the Torah with all its laws at Mount Sinai together. As a consequence, women could also assume the religious obligations traditionally expected solely from Jewish men. In places where Jonas was not able to overcome objections regarding specific functions denied to women, for example the prohibition of women acting as witnesses, she argued in rabbinic fashion: in such cases the women rabbis could gather men who were deemed suitable to be witnesses [6. 33]. This Halakhic form of reasoning was later used successfully by the American-conservative advocates for the ordination of women.

Jonas was aware of the contemporary trends in women's struggle for emancipation. She considered women of her time who started professional careers to be role models for women rabbis. However, Jonas believed that they should remain unmarried since married women had to support their husbands and raise their children. Despite her conservative attitude towards family life, she believed that "female qualities such as compassion, tact, spirit of sacrifice" should also benefit the community: "Apart from prejudice and unfamiliarity, almost nothing stands [halakhically] in the way of women becoming rabbis" (cited in [6. 34]).

Eduard Baneth accepted Jonas's Halakhic thesis. However, he died before her oral examination in Jewish law, which was obligatory for future rabbis. Neither his successor, the Talmud lecturer Hanoch Albeck, nor any other HWJ professor was willing to take her examination – either out of conviction or for fear of a scandal. In December 1930, Jonas left the HWJ with the only certificate women could obtain there – a diploma certifying her as an academic teacher of religion.

Nonetheless, she remained committed to becoming a rabbi. She finally gained the support of Rabbi Leo Baeck (1873–1956; → Leo Baeck Institute) who taught → Midrash

and homiletics at the HWJ, where he had already advocated the acceptance of female students. Besides attending lectures and Talmud seminars as an auditor, she took part in his practice seminars in homiletics. She held lectures at the → Jüdischer Frauenbund and taught religion and → Hebrew at Jewish girls' schools, which accepted an increasing number of students as of 1933 because they had been expelled from public schools.

In the summer of 1935, the progressive rabbi Max Dienemann (1875–1939) agreed to take Jonas's oral examination in Jewish law and also to ordain her. On December 26 of that year, she took her oral examination – the topic was the *Shulḥan Arukh* – in the presence of Dienemann alone in his apartment in Offenbach; for it to be an official private ordination, three rabbis would actually have had to be present. The Hebrew rabbinical certificate bore the stamp of Dienemann but not of the German Rabbinical Association (Allgemeiner Rabbiner-Verband), of which he was the director (in 1941 Leo Baeck certified the German translation of the certificate). The liberal press covered the incident, and even though friends, companions, and even some liberal rabbis congratulated the "Fräulein Rabbiner" (Miss Rabbi), the "Frau Rabbiner" (Ms Rabbi), or the "Rabbinerin" (woman Rabbi), Dienemann gave a cautionary warning concerning the use of the title "rabbi." He advised her not to submit any applications connected to the office at the Berlin rabbinate or individual rabbis since the majority opposed her ordination.

It was hardly surprising that her ordination was sharply criticized by the Orthodox side. Joseph Carlebach (1883–1942), Chief Rabbi of the Hochdeutsche Israeliten-Gemeinde in Altona and one of the most respected Orthodox rabbis in Germany, described the incident in a polemic article, albeit without specifically mentioning Regina Jonas's name: "Just a few weeks ago [...] Mr. *Dienemann* from Offenbach [...] granted rabbinical authorization to a woman, and the Berlin community invited her to speak at its synagogue. Thus, a Liberal has done something others deem a *betrayal* and *caricature* of Judaism as well as the introduction of hysteria into the hallowed halls of our temple" [1. 4 (emphasis in the original)]. All the more astonishing was the reaction of an Orthodox rabbi, Felix Singermann from Berlin, who wrote her a letter congratulating the *rabbanit* (Hebr.; "woman rabbi") on the "blessing given to you by the Eternal Father" (cited in [6. 44, 62]).

The rejection from the official liberal side – or at least their reluctance to address this sensitive issue – was so great that no Jewish community in Germany was willing to offer her a position as a rabbi. Paradoxically, however, the collapse of Jewish community life as a consequence of the National Socialist measures opened up ways for her to become active as a teacher and preacher. After the Nuremberg Laws were passed in 1935 (→ Nuremberg) and the exclusion of Jews from public life was intensified, rabbis and religious teachers emigrated, leaving their positions vacant. Besides teaching at the religious school of the Jewish community, Jonas held "lectures" and "speeches" in a Jewish retirement home (she was permitted to "preach" in such an institution only once, in January 1936), at the Women's International Zionist Organization (WIZO), the → Jüdischer Frauenbund, in several Jewish sisters' lodges, and in the wedding hall of the Neue Synagoge on Oranienburger Straße where she also organized "youth celebrations" on the → Shabbat. However, even though her audience was impressed by her humility, deep religiosity, and passionate lecturing style, the synagogue board could not bring themselves to invite her to preach from the pulpit.

Gradually and under pressure from the existing conditions, her position lost its scandalous aspect. In August 1937, the Jewish community employed Jonas "for rabbinical spiritual care in the welfare centers of the community," a position that primarily comprised sickbed visits at hospitals and caring for members of the welfare association for Jewish deaf mutes. According to the employment contract, however, the community board was also allowed to occupy her elsewhere "according to her skills and performance." Indeed, she now held services in retirement homes and hospitals and conducted consecrations and funerals (→ Death).

Jonas asked the → Joint Distribution Committee and the Jüdische Winterhilfe (Jewish Winter Aid) for support for individual community members. In addition, the → Reichsvertretung der deutschen Juden, which had been designated by the National Socialists as the official Jewish representative agency in the German Reich in mid-1939, sent her to provide spiritual care to several social institutions or Jewish communities outside of Berlin whose rabbis had emigrated or were imprisoned.

After the → November Pogrom of 1938, several community members advised Jonas to emigrate. Apparently she was neither willing to stop her spiritual care work nor to leave her mother. Moreover, in the summer of 1939 she had met the Hamburg rabbi Joseph Norden (1870–1943), who was 32 years her senior. They visited each other several times; Norden also invited her to preach in the alternative locality of the Hamburg Temple, which was closed in 1938. Jonas was hesitant to get married because it would have brought her into conflict with her rabbinical work, and Norden could not bring himself to ask her for marriage because he believed himself to be too old for her [6. 67]. In the letters he wrote to Jonas, Norden appealed to her not to despair in the face of the dramatic situation of the Jews in Germany and to remain "an advocate and support for the oppressed" (cited in [6. 71]).

Even though Jonas was also subjected to forced labor as of March 1941, she preached in the remaining synagogues or temporary premises. She held her last "speech" on October 10, 1942. On November 6, 1942, Jonas and her mother were deported to the → Theresienstadt concentration camp, where Joseph Norden had also been brought four months earlier; he died there in February 1943. In Theresienstadt, Jonas also provided rabbinical spiritual care and held lectures and presumably also sermons. On October 12, 1944, Jonas and her mother were deported to → Auschwitz and killed shortly after.

In the newly organized Jewish community of Berlin after the war, nobody remembered Regina Jonas – not even the representatives of liberal Judaism in Germany. When the first woman rabbi in the United States was ordained – thirty years after Regina Jonas –, she was not mentioned either; she had fallen into oblivion. In the early 1990s, the German-American theologian Katharina von Kellenbach found the archived papers of Regina Jonas; her publications (first in 1992) and those of Elisa Klapheck, who is working as a rabbi today and who also edited Jonas's thesis (1999), made her known to a wider public.

3. Reform Judaism in the United States

In the United States, too, a debate about religious equality for women began at the end of the 19th century. In 1890, the Jewish teacher and journalist Ray Frank (1861–1948) attracted nationwide attention when the Jewish community of Spokane (Washington) allowed her to preach. Until her marriage a decade later, Frank worked as a preacher and teacher; in the press she was called the "girl rabbi of the golden West."

It was only after the First World War and as a consequence of the ratification of the 19th amendment to the Constitution of the United States, which granted general voting rights to female Americans and opened up new prospects and better chances to women, that the debate on women rabbis became more concrete. This was triggered by a number of women who actively strove to become ordained. The first of these was Martha Neumark (married name: Montor, 1904–1981) who studied in Cincinnati at the Reform-oriented → Hebrew Union College (HUC). The question of whether or not she was allowed to finish her nine years of study with the rabbinical ordination sparked a heated debate at the HUC and among American rabbis in general, which was covered by the English-speaking Jewish press and reached far beyond the Reform circle.

The opponents of the ordination of women, among them well-known Jewish scholars such as Jacob Lauterbach (1873–1942), who also taught at HUC, mainly put forward Halakhic arguments. These included that the presence of women at the seminary would distract men from serious study and that the husband of a woman rabbi would not be able to provide the same domestic and familial support to his wife that a rabbi received from his wife. Lauterbach also claimed that the ordination of women could have no basis in Jewish tradition and that it was an "absurd and ridiculous" innovation that "hurt the feelings of a large part of the Jewish people" (cited in [8. 64]). As a concession to the equality of women, Lauterbach and other representatives of Reform Judaism merely approved of women pursuing religious studies to work as religious teachers and governesses at religious institutions.

Other Reform-oriented rabbis and scientists, including the father of Martha Neumark, David Neumark (1866–1924), who also taught at HUC, were confirmed supporters of opening up the rabbinate to women. Their arguments were of a primarily historical nature: in the comprehensive body of Jewish law, the ordination of women had not been discussed and as such had never been prohibited. Moreover, the leadership roles of the biblical prophetesses Miriam, Deborah, and Huldah demonstrated the possibility of a women becoming rabbis in modern times. Neumark acknowledged that the ordination of a woman violated Orthodox norms but also stressed that the debate was not about the stipulations of the Orthodoxy but rather about reforms, particularly since the rabbis of the modern Reform movement were primarily preachers and teachers rather than *poskim* of the law like Orthodox rabbis. Ultimately, the administrative board of the HUC decided not to allow women to train for the rabbinate; Martha Neumark finished her studies as the future principal of a Sunday school.

A similar approach was taken at the Jewish Institute of Religion (JIR) in New York, which had been founded by the Reform rabbi and political Zionist activist Stephen S. Wise (→ American Jewish Congress) in 1922. This rabbinical seminary did not limit itself to training Reform rabbis but regarded itself as a decidedly liberal institution. Helen Levinthal (married name: Lyons, 1910–1989), the daughter of a famous conservative rabbi, was admitted for rabbinical studies. However, on the occasion of her graduation in 1939, the JIR management also decided that the time had not yet come for a woman's ordination.

After the Second World War, it seemed at first as if the trend was going back to a conservative position: in 1947, Nettie Stolper's application for rabbinical studies at the JIR was rejected with the notification that women in general were no longer accepted for this course of studies. In 1950, the debate was sparked again when the board of the Beth Israel Temple in Meridian (Mississippi) gave the leadership of the community to Paula Herskovitz Ackerman (1893–1989), the widow of the recently deceased rabbi who was venerated as *rebbetsin*, until a new rabbi had been found. Leading Reform rabbis sharply criticized this move, in particular since Ackerman was not ordained and had

not undergone religious training. However, they did not fundamentally oppose the ordination of women. In the wake of the announcement of the Presbyterian Church to ordain female pastors in the future, the Reform Jewish Central Conference of American Rabbis also endorsed the ordination of women rabbis in the following year. The precondition was that women received rabbinical training. For this reason, a corresponding course of studies was introduced at HUC in 1957 which included enrollment at the neighboring University of Cincinnati.

In 1968, Sally Priesand became the first woman to enroll for rabbinical studies at HUC–JIR (the two institutions had merged in 1950). Priesand, who had been born into a Reform-oriented family in Cleveland in 1946, began her studies at a time when the ordination of women coincided with the second wave of feminism in North America and the increasingly strong → civil rights movement. Her rabbinical studies, which were supported by the president of HUC–JIR, Nelson Glueck (1900–1971), attracted nationwide attention: Priesand was invited to hold lectures in which she made it clear that Judaism needed to adapt to the times as well and that religious equality was the inalienable right of women. In her rabbinical thesis, published in 1975 under the title *Judaism and the New Woman*, Priesand examined the legal status of Jewish women in biblical and rabbinical literature and discussed their situation in the modern State of Israel. These topics remained fundamental for the agenda of the first generation of women in the rabbinate. Priesand was ordained on June 3, 1972, by Glueck's successor Alfred Gottschalk. Shortly afterwards, she assumed a position as an assistant rabbi at the Stephen Wise Free Synagogue in New York; however, it was not until 1981 that she assumed her first position as a rabbi at Monmouth Reform Temple (New Jersey).

4. Reconstructionist and Conservative Judaism

The North American debate on the ordination of women had not been limited to Reform Judaism. In the 1920s, Cyrus Adler (1863–1940; → American Jewish Historical Society), the long-standing president of the conservative Jewish Theological Seminary (JTS) in New York, stated that the rabbinical school of → Conservative Judaism would by no means train women rabbis. In view of the imminent ordination of Sally Priesand, the question became relevant again for the JTS, particularly since leading representatives of Reconstructionism announced that they would soon ordain woman rabbis. The Reconstructionist movement, which had been the left wing of the Conservatives for many decades, had split off in 1968 and founded its own rabbinical seminary, the Reconstructionist Rabbinical College (RRC) in Philadelphia. From the beginning, both men and women were accepted at RRC; in autumn 1969 the college accepted its first female student. On May 19, 1974, Sandy Eisenberg Sasso (b. 1947), who had grown up in a Reform Jewish environment but felt drawn to Reconstructionist ideas, was ordained as a woman rabbi.

In 1972, in view of the imminent ordinations of Sally Priesand and Sandy Sasso, the feminist group *Ezrat Nashim* (the Hebrew term literally means "women's aid" but originally denotes the "Women's Court," the forecourt of the historical → Temple in Jerusalem) was founded in New York. Its members were closely related to Conservative Judaism and included Paula E. Hyman and Martha Ackelsberg, who later became well-known scholars. They criticized what they felt to be an obsolete attitude on the part of the Conservatives, who held on to the status quo. They denounced their segregating doctrine "separate but equal," which assigned women an inferior status in Conservative Judaism, and strongly insisted on full religious equality, including admittance to rabbinical training.

Nationwide, members of JTS and members of Conservative communities debated the arguments for and against the ordination of women for over a decade. In 1977, the JTS appointed a committee to resolve this question. In the following year, eleven of its members decided that there were no Halakhic objections to the ordination of women, while three were convinced that it violated religious law and would destroy Conservative Judaism. Finally, in October 1983, the majority of the JTS faculty senate voted to admit women to the rabbinical school. This decision had been preceded by a discussion similar to the topic of Regina Jonas's thesis, namely whether or not women rabbis could observe Jewish law in the same way men traditionally did. In 1985, Amy Eilberg (b. 1954) became the first woman ordained as a Conservative rabbi.

5. Developments in Europe, Israel, and America

After the Second World War, women in Europe and Israel increasingly strove for the rabbinate. The liberal London Leo Baeck College (LBC), founded in 1956, had accepted female students from the beginning. In 1967, the LBC decided that nothing fundamentally opposed the ordination of women but at the same time emphasized that it could not be held responsible if the women did not find a position as rabbis. In 1975, Jackie Tabick (b. 1948) became the first woman to be ordained there; by the turn of the millennium, her example had been followed by more than two dozen women.

Today there are hundreds of women rabbis; some of them graduated from the LBC, others from rabbinical seminaries in the United States, France, Poland, Germany, Austria, Belgium, Great Britain, the Netherlands, and Belarus. In 1992, Naamah Kelman (b. 1955), a graduate of the Jerusalem rabbinical seminary of the HUC–JIR, became the first woman to be ordained in Israel. Two years later, Margit Oelsner-Baumatz (b. 1938 in Germany) was the first woman to finish her rabbinical studies in Latin America – at the conservative Seminario Rabínico Latinoamericano in → Buenos Aires. In Germany, the Swiss Bea Wyler, born in 1955 and ordained in 1995 at JTS, was appointed in the same year to serve the Jewish community of Braunschweig, and later Delmenhorst. While liberal communities welcomed Wyler's inauguration, Orthodox voices sharply criticized her appointment. The first woman rabbi to be ordained in Germany after Regina Jones was Alina Treiger (b. 1979). In 2010, she was ordained at the Abraham Geiger Kolleg in Potsdam and has served the Jewish community of Oldenburg since 2011.

The debate on the ordination of women had already been concluded in Reform-oriented, Reconstructionist and Conservative Judaism when it began within Jewish → Orthodoxy. One of its first advocates was the North American feminist intellectual Blu Greenberg (b. 1936), who made a name for herself with writings such as *On Women and Judaism. A View from Tradition* (1981) and *Will There Be Women Rabbis?* (in: Judaism, 1984). In 1993, Haviva Ner-David (b. 1969; formerly Haviva Krasner-Davidson), who had grown up in a Modern Orthodox family in New York, applied to the Orthodox rabbinical seminary of → Yeshiva University. Her application was ignored, but the university indicated that the debate had gained momentum among members of the Orthodoxy. However, this discussion was solely led within the "Modern" or "Centrist" Orthodoxy, whose members adhered to Jewish law but largely oriented themselves towards modern life. Conversely, members of → Hasidism and the → Ultra-Orthodoxy for the most part separate themselves from modern social developments. Their traditional gender perceptions categorically exclude the possibility of women rabbis.

However, several representatives of Modern Orthodoxy are creative when it comes to enabling women to fulfil tasks similar to those of a rabbi. For example, women are allowed to perform certain tasks within the community or give advice in cases of doubt regarding religious law. When the Orthodox Rabbi Aryeh Strikovsky ordained Haviva Ner-David as the first Orthodox woman in 2006, he did not award her the title of "rabbi"; she herself does not call herself an Orthodox but rather a post-confessional rabbi. Similarly, the Orthodox Rabbi Avi Weiss initially only gave the newly coined title of *maharat* (acronym for *manhigah hilkhatit ruḥanit toranit* – "female leader of Halakhah, spirituality, and Torah") to Sara Hurwitz (b. 1977), whom he ordained in New York in 2010. Later she was granted the title of *rabba* (woman rabbi), which led to considerable outrage in Orthodox circles. In June 2012, Hurwitz appeared at the celebration on the occasion of the 40th anniversary of the ordination of Sally Priesand in Philadelphia, thereby underlining her claim to be the first woman rabbi of Orthodox Judaism. Still, the ordination of women remains controversial in the Modern Orthodox world; recent announcements by the Orthodox American Rabbinical Assembly prohibit further ordinations of women.

Bibliography

Sources
[1] J. Carlebach, Nachbrocho, Der Israelit, 20. Februar 1936, 1, 3–4.

Secondary literature
[2] K. Goldman, Beyond the Synagogue Gallery. Finding a Place for Women in American Judaism, Cambridge (MA) 2000. [3] S. Greenberg (ed.), The Ordination of Women as Rabbis. Studies and Responsa, New York 1988. [4] K. von

Kellenbach, Fräulein Rabbiner Regina Jonas. Eine religiöse Feministin vor ihrer Zeit, in: Schlangenbrut 38 (1992), 35–39. [5] K. von Kellenbach, Fräulein Rabbiner Regina Jonas (1902–1945). Lehrerin, Seelsorgerin, Predigerin, in: Jahrbuch der Europäischen Gesellschaft für theologische Forschung von Frauen 2 (1994), 97–101. [6] E. Klapheck (ed.), Fräulein Rabbiner Jonas. Kann die Frau das rabbinische Amt bekleiden? Eine Streitschrift von Regina Jonas, Teetz 1999. [7] E. Klapheck, Fräulein Rabbiner Jonas. The Story of the First Woman Rabbi, trans. by T. Axelrod, San Francisco 2004. [8] P. S. Nadell, Women Who Would Be Rabbis. A History of Women's Ordination, 1889–1985, Boston 1998. [9] H. Ner-David, Life on the Fringes. A Feminist Journey toward Traditional Rabbinic Ordination, Needham 2000. [10] S. Priesand, Judaism and the New Woman, New York 1975. [11] S. Rubin Schwartz, The Rabbi's Wife. The Rebbetzin in American Jewish Life, New York 2006. [12] S. Sheridan (ed.), Hear Our Voice. Women in the British Rabbinate, Columbia 1994. [13] B. S. Wenger, The Politics of Women's Ordination. Jewish Law, Institutional Power, and the Debate over Women in the Rabbinate, in: J. Wertheimer (ed.), Tradition Renewed. A History of the Jewish Theological Seminary, Vol. 2, New York 1997, 485–523.

PAMELA S. NADELL, WASHINGTON D.C.

World Jewish Congress

Non-governmental organization founded in 1936 in → Geneva with the mission of promoting the unity of the Jewish people in the Diaspora and defending their rights. While the World Jewish Congress regarded itself as an umbrella organization, it was by no means joined by all existing Jewish organizations. On the international level, the organization championed the preservation of Jewish minority rights, organized initiatives to provide protection from National Socialist persecution, and made a significant contribution to representing Jewish demands after the war. Its early history illustrates the upheavals to which Jewish communities worldwide were exposed during the 1930s and 1940s as well as the limitations to the effectiveness of Jewish international politics without their own state.

1. Foundation
2. Nahum Goldmann
3. Activities until 1939
4. Rescue attempts during the Shoah
5. From minority rights to human rights
6. The path to reparations

1. Foundation

The World Jewish Congress (also Jüdischer Weltkongress, Congrès juif mondial) constituted itself in August 1936 during a five-day conference in Geneva. 280 delegates, mainly of national Jewish-Zionist background, from 32 countries joined together with the aim of creating a world Jewish representative body that would act as the first contact in all international issues concerning the Jewish Diaspora. Besides defending the rights of Jewish minorities, the World Jewish Congress was also committed to guiding migration as well as providing economic aid in Eastern Europe. In view of the increasing harassment of Jews in that region, and especially the threat that was spreading from National Socialist Germany all over Europe, the Congress sought to concentrate the representation of Jewish concerns beyond the organizations and bodies active in the individual countries. It was established in the context of the more extensive international diplomacy of the interwar years; in particular the League of Nations in → Geneva had opened to non-state actors, and the World Jewish Congress was only one among over 450 non-state organizations that maintained a permanent office in Geneva or submitted concerns there.

The delegates of the World Jewish Congress had been elected by national Jewish organizations of their countries of origin. In Geneva, they appointed the elder statesman of American Jews, the US federal judge Julian W. Mack (1866–1943), honorary president; the rabbi and chairman of the → American Jewish Congress Stephen S. Wise (1874–1949) became its president, and the Zionist Nahum Goldmann (1895–1982) chairman of its executive board. The charter stipulated a conference every four years; offices in Geneva, Paris, London, and New York were to coordinate activities between these conventions. The permanent staff of the World Congress included Nathan Feinberg, Paul Guggenheim, and Gerhart M. Riegner (Geneva), Kate Knopfmacher, Israel Jefroykin, and Robert Bollack (Paris), Maurice L. Perlzweig and Alex Eastermann (London). They were advised by Jewish minority politicians from states in Eastern Europe such as Robert Stricker (Austria), Emil Margulies (Czechoslovakia), Jacob Robinson (Lithuania), Yitzhak Grünbaum, Henryk Rosmarin (Poland), and Meir Ebner (Romania).

The convocation of the World Congress was founded on older deliberations, some of them dating back to the time before the First World War. At the beginning of the 20th century, the idea of a world Jewish agency had first been put forward by prominent Jews, among them the Diaspora nationalist Simon Dubnow (1860–1941; → Riga; → Weltgeschichte) and the Zionists Max Nordau (1849–1923; → Muscular Judaism) and Israel Zangwill (1864–1926; → Melting Pot). Immediately after the end of the First World War, the Zionist and prominent representative of the → *Gegenwartsarbeit* ("work for the present") concept Leo Motzkin (1867–1933) embraced the idea and ensured that the proposal to found a world Jewish representative body with voting rights in the meetings of the nascent League of Nations was included temporarily in the demands submitted by the Zionist Organization to the Paris Peace Conference. In the 1920s, Motzkin and the → Comité des délégations juives (the institutional predecessor of the World Congress) headed by him were foremost in advancing plans for a global representative body, for instance during a conference organized together with the American Jewish Congress in August 1927 in Zurich, which had the objective of coordinating Jewish initiatives for the protection of the → minority rights of the Jews in Eastern Europe.

At the beginning of the 1930s, the project regained importance due to the threat posed by National Socialism. Now it was Stephen S. Wise who took the initiative. However, a global representative body was once again met with skepticism by associations such as the → American Jewish Committee, the → Board of Deputies, and the → Alliance israélite universelle, who regarded their activities as primarily part of the politics of their respective home countries. As a consequence, the preparatory committee decided to begin by convening preparatory conferences. The man entrusted with this task was the young Nahum Goldmann, who proceeded to consult with leading Jewish organizations in Europe and the United States to this end. The first conferences took place in Geneva in 1932, 1933, and 1934, before the Congress itself was convened in 1936.

2. Nahum Goldmann

After Motzkin's death in November 1933, Goldmann took over as chair of the Comité des délégations juives and the preparatory committee. The World Congress had become his life's work. In this position, he became one of the most important and best-known Jewish politicians of the 20th century. In his view, a World Jewish Congress was necessary in order to represent Jewish concerns in the Diaspora in cooperation with, as well as independently of, the ideas of establishing a Jewish national home

Nahum Goldmann (1895–1982)

in Palestine. Consequently, his aim was to pursue "Gegenwartsarbeit" within the remit of the World Jewish Congress and political work concerning Palestine under the aegis of the Zionist Organization: "We must do both, and we need two organizations to this end: the Zionist Congress for Palestine and the World Congress for matters concerning the Galuth," Goldmann declared in 1933 during the Second Jewish World Conference [1. 36].

Goldmann was born in 1895 in Vishnevo in Lithuania (today Vishnyeva, Belarus). After his family moved to Frankfurt am Main, he studied history, law, and philosophy in Marburg, Heidelberg, and Berlin. He became known early on as a Zionist speaker and journalist; during the First World War he was employed by the German Foreign Ministry in the "Nachrichtenstelle für den Orient" (Intelligence Bureau for the East), a department disseminating pro-German propaganda in the Middle East. Together with the philosopher Jakob Klatzkin, he worked on the project of a Jewish encyclopedia from 1922 onward, which resulted in the unfinished *Encyclopaedia Judaica* published between 1928 and 1934 (→ Encyclopedias). From the end of the 1920s onward, Goldmann, who belonged to the faction of the radical Zionists, occupied high-ranking positions within the Zionist movement, acting as the head of the Jewish Agency's office in Geneva from 1929 and its representative with the League of Nations from 1935 onward. Between 1956 and 1968, he was president of the World Zionist Organization.

Besides championing a Jewish state, Goldmann was a confirmed defender of Jewish rights in the Diaspora all his life. His activities as the leading figure of the World Jewish Congress especially during negotiations with the Federal Republic of Germany on so-called reparations (→ Luxembourg Agreement; → Claims Conference) in the 1950s would subsequently earn him admiration and the honorific "Statesman without a State."

3. Activities until 1939

From 1933 onward, Nahum Goldmann led the activities of the Comité for the protection of by now primarily German Jews from the NS regime, with a chance of success as limited as those of his predecessor Motzkin. The most important means of Jewish diplomacy of those days was still recourse to the Paris treaties for the protection of minority rights. Aside from their shortcomings, in the case of Germany these only applied to Upper Silesia (→ Bernheim Petition), and Poland, by far the most important of the signatories, went so far as to declare in 1934 its unilateral withdrawal from the obligations of minority protection.

After its foundation in 1936, the World Congress succeeded in individual cases at least to make use of the Geneva system for the protection of Jews until 1939. In addition to the effect of the → Bernheim Petition in Upper Silesia, the Congress was able to achieve some important political successes for the Jews in the Saarland and in Danzig (Gdansk) too, although these proved to be of limited duration. The situation of the Jews in the Saarland took a dramatic turn; in the referendum of January 1935, which was monitored by the League of Nations, their fate was indirectly decided too. The massive influx of Saarland Jews to France was proof of the increasing uncertainty and fear of the expected development of the Saar region returning to German control. Consequently, the World Congress went to considerable lengths to awaken an international interest in the uncertain fate of the Jews of the Saar region, championing their cause in the governmental commission as well as in the Tripartite Commission appointed by the League of Nations. With the support of the Italian member of the commission and after Mussolini personally intervened, Goldmann finally succeeded in reaching a transition arrangement under which the Jews of the Saar region were granted a year during which they could emigrate unchallenged while retaining their property. After the landslide victory of the supporters of the Saar region's returning to German sovereignty and the region's incorporation into the Reich, the → Nuremberg Laws and other anti-Jewish orders and decrees came into force in the Saar region in March 1936.

In order to protect the rights of the Jews in the Free City of Danzig, the Congress worked together with the permanent high commissioner who, as the representative of the League of Nations, monitored compliance with the constitution and mediated between Germans and Poles in case of conflicts. The World Congress' attempts at influencing the British representatives in Geneva in particular led to them using their moderating influence in Danzig in order to gain at the very least a postponement of the introduction of the Nuremberg Laws in the Free City. As in the Saar, the Congress managed to obtained a delay in the implementation of the anti-Jewish measures in Danzig,

with the result that parts of the Jewish population were able to emigrate in somewhat bearable conditions.

Romania was another focus of the activities of the Congress. The country's moving closer to National Socialist Germany during the 1930s increased the danger for its Jewish population. The reactionary Partidul Naţional Creştin (National Christian Party), which was the result of a merger between the Liga Apărării Naţional Creştine (National Christian Defense League) and the Partidul Naţional-Agrar (National Agrarian Party) and stood in close contact to Nazi Germany, were in favor of prohibiting Jews from working in agriculture and of gradually expelling Jews from small businesses and trade (→ Iaşi). As the popularity of the Romanian Garda de Fier (Iron Guard), which favored even more ruthless action against the Jews, grew, the political actors around King Carol II supported tightening anti-Jewish measures. These plans were implemented when an extremely right-wing government headed by Octavian Goga came to power in December 1937. During the brief six weeks it existed, the revision of civil rights was pushed through and almost 200,000 Romanian Jews were robbed of their citizenship. Goga furthermore announced far-reaching economic measures against Jews. Since 1935, the World Congress had denounced several pieces of draft legislation that had the objective of denationalizing all Jewish inhabitants of the regions allotted to Romania after the First World War. World Congress experts drew up statistics refuting the claim that illegal immigration had led to the number of Jewish inhabitants growing considerably since the end of the First World War. In spite of the Goga government resigning, the article decreeing the revision remained in force, with the result that 35% of the Jewish population, especially of Bukovina and Bessarabia, became stateless [7. 204f.].

Ever since its establishment, the Congress represented only one facet of Jewish politics. Older internationally active organizations, which simultaneously emphasized their agendas were oriented towards emancipation as well as integration, such as the Alliance israélite universelle, the → Joint Foreign Committee of British Jews, or the American Jewish Committee, continued to oppose the concept of the Congress. The objective embraced by the World Congress of increased closeness to or affinity with the people and democratization of Jewish activities in the world, was regarded as a challenge to their authority, their oligarchical structures, and their philanthropic approach. At the same time, they feared that the mere existence of a global Jewish representative body might encourage one of the fundamental motifs of antisemitic → conspiracy theories. Thus, the World Congress was not successful in ensuring a united Jewish attitude in the context of the → Evian Conference of 1938, which President Roosevelt had called in order to discuss the increased refugee problem due to the "Anschluss" (annexation) of Austria. No fewer than 21 Jewish organizations brought recommendations to the conference, which essentially passed without a decision being reached.

The → Ha'avarah Agreement negotiated between the Jewish Agency and the German Reichswirtschaftsministerium (Reich Ministry for Economics) in the summer of 1933 forced the World Congress to appraise its position. The agreement eased the emigration process for German Jews, allowing them to transfer a part of their property to the → Yishuv in the form of German goods. Large parts of the Jewish world, especially in centers such as Warsaw, London, Paris, or New York, were boycotting Germany. The World Congress with its Zionist orientation, which supported the boycott of Nazi Germany, was thus placed in an invidious position. In the end it exercised restraint, accepting the decision of the Jewish Agency to commit to the Ha'avarah Agreement.

4. Rescue attempts during the Shoah

The Second World War fundamentally changed the conditions in which the World Jewish Congress could act. Exerting influence by means of the instruments of international law came to a complete halt during the war years. After the French capitulation in June 1940, its headquarters were moved to New York. Largely cut off from the European continent, the Congress now depended increasingly on the political and financial assistance of the American Jewish Congress.

In the context of the task of obtaining and publicizing reliable information on the persecution of European Jews and coordinating aid efforts in the countries occupied by Germany, its international structure remained its major asset. It was able to work from its various offices in Geneva, London, Stockholm, and Istanbul, primarily by arranging aid to be delivered by the Red Cross. Simultaneously, the Congress endeavored to persuade governments to provide immigration visas. These projects, however, had to submit to the schedule set out by the Allies, for whom the unconditional surrender of the Axis powers had absolute priority.

The World Congress played a significant part in spreading the news of the mass murder of European Jews. Gerhart M. Riegner, secretary at the Congress's Geneva office, learned from the immediate circle of German decision-makers that the Nazis planned to deport and murder all Jews under their rule. In August 1942, he conveyed this information in a telegram (known as the → Riegner Telegram) to the president of the World Congress Stephen Wise, who passed it on to the State Department. At first, Wise was informed that the message could not be made public until the American authorities had confirmed it was accurate. On December 18, 1942, twelve Allied governments finally published a declaration condemning the National Socialist extermination of the Jews and announced even more resolute military action against Germany.

During this time, the World Congress initiated relief efforts that essentially depended on the cooperation of the International Red Cross. In 1944, it was possible to send food to the inmates of → Theresienstadt with the aid of the Portuguese Red Cross. Thanks to the concerted efforts of the War Refugee Board and the International Red Cross in the autumn of that year, the representative of the World Congress in Sweden, Hillel Storch, succeeded in sending food parcels via ship and railway to the → Ravensbrück, Sachsenhausen, and Bergen-Belsen concentration camps. Towards the end of the war, when news of renewed massacres and the imminent deportation of the Jews of → Budapest became public (→ Kasztner Affair), these endeavors were intensified once more.

5. From minority rights to human rights

With the establishment of the → Institute of Jewish Affairs in New York in the winter of 1941, the World Jewish Congress concentrated its resources in order to prepare the most important Jewish demands for a postwar order. Seminal studies were composed in connection with the Institute, dealing with the minority protection framework of the interwar years (*Were the Minorities Treaties a Failure?*, 1943; J. Robinson, O. Karbach, M. M. Laserson, N. Robinson, and M. Vishniak), the migration patterns of Jewish refugees (*The Jewish Refugee*, 1944; A. Tartakower and K. R. Grossmann), and the question of compensation for material loss since 1933 (*Indemnifications and Reparations*, 1944; N. Robinson).

Members of the Institute also advised the Commission for the Investigation of War Crimes set up by the Allies in October 1942. The definition of war crimes in the Hague Convention of 1907 did not include crimes committed during peace time or committed by a state against its own citizens. It was

of great importance to the World Congress to extend the applicability to ensure that persecution before the beginning of the Second World War as well as crimes committed against citizens of the Axis powers and stateless persons would be prosecuted. The documentations prepared by the legal experts of the Institute of Jewish Affairs had a direct effect on the prosecution during the → Nuremberg trials before the International Military Tribunal. The first item of the indictment (Participation in a common plan or conspiracy for the accomplishment of a crime against peace, "Organisationsverbrechen"), and the fourth item (Crimes against humanity) allowed the concept of war crimes to be extended chronologically as well as territorially, emphasizing the collective dimension of Nazi crimes with their objective of exterminating the Jewish people [12].

As a result of the almost complete extermination of the Jewish population in Central and Eastern Europe, the principle of specific protection of Jewish minorities lost its importance. In view of the ethnical homogenization by extermination during the war and subsequent expulsions, from 1944 onward the legal experts of the Congress increasingly turned to the concept of a protection focused on the individual on the basis of → human rights, although the principle of minority protection was never entirely abandoned. Jacob Robinson, as well as Paul Guggenheim and Gerhart Riegner, were present from the very beginning of the deliberations of the human rights commission and worked on the formulation of the United Nations Charter of 1945.

In 1947, the World Congress was the first Jewish organization with observer status at the United Nations to take part in, among other things, finalizing the Universal Declaration of Human Rights, future human rights agreements, and the → Genocide Convention drawn up by Raphael Lemkin. As the protection of the individual now appeared to replace the protection of minorities, anchoring the Genocide Convention within the UN system of 1948 possessed at least the potential to provide a counterweight under international law [13. 394].

6. The path to reparations

The fact that the Jews had been collectively persecuted during the Holocaust led to them being recognized as a kind of political corporation. At the War Emergency Conference convened under the aegis of the World Congress in the autumn of 1944 in Atlantic City, the most important Jewish organizations formulated the guidelines of their demands for → restitution and compensation: stolen Jewish property without heirs should be demanded back collectively "in the name of the Jewish people" [6]. In order to deal with the heirless property of organizations that did no longer existed due to the Shoah, the World Congress proposed the establishment of a Jewish Agency for Reconstruction. By creating this Agency, it laid the foundations for establishing international Jewish successor organizations.

The work of the Jewish Restitution Successor Organization was mainly led by the Jewish Agency for Palestine and the → Joint Distribution Committee. Both organizations were given the task of providing means to rehabilitate and resettle Jewish Displaced Persons who had found sanctuary in camps established by the Allies primarily in the US occupied zones in Germany (→ Munich) and Austria as well as Italy.

The mass → exodus of Jews from Poland (→ Kielce) and their arrival in Palestine circumventing the British immigration regulations occurred at the same time. While this was supported by the World Congress, its ideas of Jewish reconstruction diverged from those proposed by the Jewish Agency. According to the latter, all political and financial resources should be directed to Palestine. The World Congress, on the other hand, was of the opinion that suitable means, especially those derived from the restitution of heirless Jewish property, should not only be employed for the Jewish national home in Palestine but should also serve to rebuild Jewish communities in the Diaspora.

In this context, Nahum Goldmann was able to assert the position of the World Congress. Having been co-chair of the Jewish Agency since 1948 and president of the World Congress since Stephen S. Wise's death in 1949, he could bring considerable weight to bear. Goldmann was also convinced of the necessity of direct negotiations with German policy-makers. He succeeded in convincing the Diaspora organizations of this necessity by establishing the Conference on Jewish Material Claims Against Germany (→ Claims Conference).

After the foundation of the State of Israel and the implementation of the Reparations Agreement with Germany (→ Luxembourg Agreement), the World Jewish Congress gradually began to lose its significance during the 1960s, a development symbolized to some extent by the death of its charismatic president in 1982. The organization continued to perform important work defending Jewish rights around the world, for instance in the campaign on behalf of Soviet Jews in the 1980s, in repeated efforts to restore Jewish property primarily in the wake of the 1989 upheavals, and in denouncing and condemning antisemitism.

Bibliography

Sources

[1] Comité exécutif du congrès juif mondial (ed.), Protocole de la IIe conférence juive mondiale, Genève, 5–8 septembre, 1933, Geneva 1933. [2] N. Goldmann, The Autobiography of Nahum Goldmann. Sixty Years of Jewish Life, trans. by H. Sebba, New York 1969. [3] L. Kubowitzki, Unity in Dispersion. A History of the World Jewish Congress, New York 1948. [4] N.

Lerner, The World Jewish Congress and Human Rights, Geneva 1978. [5] G. M. Riegner, Never Despair. Sixty Years in the Service of the Jewish People and the Cause of Human Rights, trans. by W. Sayers, Chicago 2007. [6] World Jewish Congress (ed.), Resolutions. War Emergency Conference of the World Jewish Congress, Atlantic City, New Jersey, November 26–30, 1944, New York 1944.

Secondary literature

[7] D. Afoumado, Le Congrès juif mondial face à l'antisémitisme nazi, 1936–1940, in: Revue d'histoire de la Shoah 179 (2003), 190–207. [8] A. Beker, Diplomacy Without Sovereignty. The World Jewish Congress Rescue Activities, in: I. S. Troen/B. Pinkus (eds.), Organizing Rescue, Jewish National Solidarity in the Modern Period, London 2002, 301–324. [9] R. Cohen, Das Riegner-Telegramm. Text, Kontext und Zwischentext, in: Tel Aviver Jahrbuch für deutsche Geschichte 23 (1994), 301–324. [10] P. Graf, Die Bernheim-Petition 1933. Jüdische Politik in der Zwischenkriegszeit, Göttingen 2008. [11] A. Hertzberg, Nahum Goldmann's Zionist Legacy, Community and the Individual Jew, Philadelphia 1978. [12] M. A. Lewis, The World Jewish Congress and the Insitute of Jewish Affairs at Nuremberg, in: Yad Vashem Studies 36 (2008), 181–210. [13] M. Mazower, The Strange Triumph of Human Rights, 1933–1950, in: The Historical Journal 47 (2004), 379–398. [14] M. N. Penkower, The World Jewish Congress Confronts the International Red Cross During the Holocaust, in: Jewish Social Studies 41 (1979) 3/4, 229–256. [15] J. Picard, Zwischen Minoritätenschutz und Menschenrechten. Paul Guggenheims Rechtsverständnis im Wandel, 1918–1950, in: Jahrbuch des Simon-Dubnow-Instituts 4 (2005), 111–130. [16] Z. Segev, Nahum Goldmann and the First Two Decades of the World Jewish Congress, in: M. A. Raider (ed.), Nahum Goldmann. Statesman Without a State, Albany 2009, 107–124.

EMMANUEL DEONNA, LAUSANNE

World Union for Progressive Judaism

International association founded in London in 1926, dedicated to the global support of → Reform-oriented Jewish communities. In 1928 the World Union for Progressive Judaism (WUPJ) held its first international conference in Berlin; in the 1930s and 1940s it promoted the foundation of exile communities in the Netherlands, Australia, South Africa, and South America. The initiator and head of the organization was the British social worker, female rights activist, and author Lily H. Montagu (1873–1963). Like Montagu, the WUPJ pursued the aim of religious revival as an adequate answer to the social and political challenges of the time. After the Second World War, the focus of its activities first shifted to the United States and from there to Israel from the end of the 1960s onward.

1. Foundation
2. Activities
3. Lily H. Montagu
4. Religious innovation as the answer

1. Foundation

As early as 1914 the board members of the Vereinigung für das religiös-liberale Judentum in Deutschland (Association for Religious-Liberal Judaism in Germany), among them Leo Baeck, expressed their interest in establishing an international organization to promote → Reform Judaism. They submitted the suggestion of establishing representation for the progressive Jews of Germany, England, France, and the United States, to the head of the London Liberal Jewish Synagogue, Rabbi Israel Isidor Mattuck. Due to the First World War, the plan was not pursued at first. It was not until 1925 that Lily H. Montagu revived the idea. At the time she was the managing director of the Jewish Religious Union (JRU) which had existed in London since 1901 and endeavored to modernize the Orthodox rite (→ Orthodoxy). In the services organized by the JRU from 1902 onward, gender-separated seating (→ Mehitsah) was abolished; men were permitted to remove their head coverings (→ Dress Regulations); a mixed choir and musical instruments accompanied the → liturgy, much of which was in English. In 1909 the JRU was officially declared a liberal Jewish organization and renamed Jewish Religious Union for the Advancement of Liberal Judaism.

Inspired by the Jewish Religious Union founded in → Bombay (today Mumbai) in 1925 and supported by Mattuck and Claude G. Montefiore, one of the spiritual pioneers of the British Jewish Reform movement, Montagu submitted an application for the foundation of an international union of Reform Jewish communities to the JRU council. In 1926 Montagu, Montefiore, and Mattuck organized an international conference in London, attended by over a hundred representatives of liberal Jewish communities from Germany, France, Great Britain, Romania, Sweden, Czechoslovakia, the United States, and India [4. 176]. Montagu herself brought resolutions to be voted on, calling for the foundation of a joint union. When they were unanimously accepted, the WUPJ was formally founded. Montagu was appointed honorary managing director, Mattuck elected chairman of the board, and Montefiore president. After his death in 1938, Leo Baeck followed Montefiore in this position. During the Second World War, while Baeck was working in Berlin as head of the Reichsvereinigung der Juden in Deutschland (Reich Association of Jews in Germany) (→ Reichsvertretung der deutschen Juden) and later interned in → Theresienstadt, Lily Montagu took over his duties in the WUPJ.

In 1928 the first regular international conference of the WUPJ met in Berlin. The opening session took place in the Preußisches Herrenhaus, then home to the Preussischer Staatsrat (Prussian State Council). During a joint service in the Temple of the Berlin Reform community attended by the delegates, Lily Montagu was the first Jewish woman in Germany to preach from a pulpit (→ Woman Rabbi).

The Great Depression beginning in 1929 and the transfer of power to Hitler in 1933 severely limited the financial scope of the WUPJ, above all because of declining support from Germany. In its early years, around a quarter of its annual budget consisted of a private donation from Montefiore and half was provided by the Central Conference of American Rabbis (CCAR) and the Union of American Hebrew Congregations [5. 391]. Between 1926 and 1959 the offices of the WUPJ and the JRU (renamed the Union of Liberal and Progressive Synagogues in 1944) were located in Lily Montagu's private residence in London.

2. Activities

One of the WUPJ's main tasks was to investigate the requirements for establishing progressive communities in different countries. If local reformers expressed an interest, the organization sent a representative and assumed the financing of a rabbi during the early stages.

The main reason for the growth of the associations founded under the aegis of the WUPJ during the 1930s and 1940s was the emigration and flight of liberal-minded Jews from National Socialist Germany. Thus in 1931 new Reform communities were founded in Amsterdam and The Hague in the Netherlands with the support of the WUPJ; the Verbond voor Liberal-Religieuze Joden in Nederland (Union for Liberal-Religious Jews in the Netherlands) was established in the same year. The number of members of the Reform communities grew by leaps and bounds as the result of Jews fleeing to the Netherlands from 1933 onward. Because of this development, the fourth conference of the WUPJ took place in Amsterdam in 1937.

The WUPJ found particularly promising conditions for expanding progressive Judaism in parts of the British Empire. In 1928 the organization sent an American Reform rabbi to → Melbourne where, however, his radical departure from religious traditions found little support. When over 7,000 Jewish refugees mainly from Germany, Austria, and Czechoslovakia immigrated to Australia in the mid-1930s, the WUPJ sent Rabbi Herman Max Sanger, who emigrated from Germany to London in 1936, to Australia. On the one hand, Sanger introduced religious innovations, such as abolishing the gender-separated seating order (→ Mehitsah) and introducing the *Union Prayer Book* published by the CCAR, on the basis of which Reform services were celebrated. On the other hand, prayer shawls and head covering remained customary in the Beth Israel Temple in Melbourne, and the community members continued to observe the religious dietary laws (→ *kashrut*). The combination of traditional elements and Reform religious practice found many supporters among the Jewish immigrants. Progressive communities were also founded in Sydney in 1938 and in Perth and Adelaide as well as the New Zealand cities of Auckland and Wellington after the end of the war.

A similar development took place in South Africa. At the request of a provisional committee, the WUPJ sent the young Reform rabbi Moses Cyrus Weiler to → Johannesburg. Many of the approximately 6,000 German-Jewish refugees in South Africa were followers of Reform Judaism. In 1946 the progressive community in Johannesburg alone had 3,000 members, and by 1955 8,000 families – 15% to 20% of the Jews in South Africa – belonged to communities that were members of the South African Union for Progressive Judaism (founded 1931) [5. 341].

Due to the large number of German refugees, in 1934 the WUPJ also established an advisory board for Palestine which, however, confined itself to religious issues. The WUPJ occupied a neutral position toward political Zionism but did provide financial support for three Reform communities founded in the mid-1930s by German refugees in Haifa, Jerusalem, and Tel Aviv. There was no mixed seating in the services celebrated in → German and → Hebrew, and it was not permitted to use either a revised prayer book or musical instruments. Upholding traditional elements of the → liturgy had been the precondition set by the Orthodox → rabbinate in order to grant permission for marriages.

The greatest success of Reform Judaism, brought about by the immigration of 50,000 German Jews, took place in South American countries like Argentina (→ Buenos Aires), Uruguay (→ Montevideo), and Brazil. Under the direct aegis of the WUPJ, the Associação Religiosa Israelita was established in 1942 in Rio de Janeiro. It was led by Rabbi Henrique (Heinrich) Lemles who had been released from the → Buchenwald concentration camp in 1938 thanks to an employment contract negotiated by Lily Montagu and emigrated to Brazil via London with financial support from the → Joint Distribution Committee [5. 343].

3. Lily H. Montagu

Lily H. Montagu was born in 1873 as the sixth child of the wealthy Montagu family in → London. Her mother Ellen Cohen Montagu came from a well-known family of British bankers; her father Samuel Montagu was a → banker himself and a member of Parliament for the Liberal Party. In 1907 he was raised to the peerage as Baron Swaythling, the title having been created specially for him. Both parents set great store by their faith. Convinced that religion determined a large part of her life, Lily Montagu quickly came to the limits of religious education and rites that Orthodox Judaism (→ Orthodoxy) imposed on her sex (→ Marriage; → Mikveh).

Lily H. Montagu (1873–1963)

As a result, Montagu devoted herself to studying the works of Victorian writers. They showed her a way to a universal understanding of religion, which combined divine moral doctrine with inner piety and the devotion to social work. After reading Montefiore's theological works and researching the Reform movements in Germany and the United States (→ Hebrew Union College), she arrived at the conviction that she could be Jewish and religious without being Orthodox.

From the age of 17 onward, Montagu dedicated a great part of her time to social work. Together with her older sister Marian, with whom she had a close and productive relationship all her life, she gave private lessons to girls from working-class families in London's East End. In 1893 they founded the West Central Jewish Girls Club together with their cousin Beatrice Samuel (née Franklin), in order to give disadvantaged girls access to education (→ Bildung), faith, and social bonds. While the majority of the members of the club were at first indifferent to religion, Lily Montagu endeavored to awaken their sense of the spiritual. The services led by Montagu took place in English, with the short → sermons focusing on the prevailing conditions of Jewish working-class girls. In 1895 Montagu wrote a pamphlet entitled *Prayers for Jewish Working Girls*. It was dedicated to the members of the West Central Club and included prayers for a variety of days, times, and life situations. In addition she cooperated with Rabbi Simeon Singer of the Orthodox New West End Synagogue, of which she and her family were members, to organize children's services.

The great success of her services among children and women reinforced Montagu's endeavor for the religious revival of the whole British Jewish community. In 1899 she published an article entitled "The Spiritual Possibilities of Judaism Today" in the *Jewish Quarterly Review* edited by Israel Abrahams and Claude G. Montefiore (→ Jewish Historical Society of England). In it she addressed all practicing Jews, traditional as well as liberal, calling on them to commit to the organized renewal of religious life in Great Britain. Subsequently she wrote letters to relatives, friends, and liberal Jewish intellectuals canvassing for support to establish an association. By 1901 Montagu had assembled a steering committee with whom she convened the JRU [1. 37].

In 1903 Montagu and the members of the JRU decided to decline the offer by the West London Synagogue to use its prayer rooms, as men and women had to sit separately there. She encouraged women to take on public positions in the administrative and religious leadership of communities. Eleven years later Lily Montagu's Saturday afternoon services at the West Central Club had become an institution, providing the basis for a separate section of the JRU, which she chaired. She led prayer services, gave sermons, assisted in marriage and funeral ceremonies, and prepared prose-lytes for → conversion. At the invitation of Israel Mattuck, in 1918 she became the first woman to preach in a British → synagogue. In 1928 the section officially renamed itself the West Central Liberal Jewish Congregation and was granted congregational status. Montagu, who never married, was inducted as lay preacher and continued to hold the position until her death in 1963.

Shortly after her death, the Lily Montagu Centre of Living Judaism was inaugurated in her honor, housing the West Central Liberal Jewish Congregation, the European board of the WUPJ, and the office of the Union of Liberal and Progressive Synagogues.

4. Religious innovation as the answer

Montagu's effort to ensure the full participation of women in community life fit into a series of social initiatives (→ Female Hebrew Benevolent Society; → Hadassah) and endeavors to improve education for women (→ Bais Ya'akov; → Leipzig Women's College), not all of them linked to → Reform Judaism only. Simultaneously her commitment to religious self-fulfillment arose from her belief that women have a particular gift for spiritual inwardness. This view was in line with the confessionalization tendencies of the Reform movement which shared the conviction that the Judaism of the future would have its roots in the personal awareness of the constant moral presence of God, rather than in strict adherence to externally imposed commandments.

In this context, Montagu's work fit in with the agenda of Reform Judaism, which regarded facilitating access to religion as a response to → secularization tendencies and socio-political problems. In his 1928 speech, *Botschaft des liberalen Judentums an die Juden von heute*, given during the first regular WUPJ congress in Berlin, Leo Baeck emphasized that the task of liberal Judaism was not aligning itself with the zeitgeist but in reflecting on the religious core of Judaism. By confronting that which exists with the messianic, Judaism could be successfully led into the future [5. 337].

After the transfer of power to Hitler, the contemplation of religious aspects gained renewed relevance for liberal Judaism in Germany. In view of their increasing social marginalization, congregations and services offered the opportunity to come together and as a place for mental support to many Jews. The → November pogrom sealed the end of liberal Judaism in the home of its spiritual roots and strong institutional foundations.

With the Jewish refugees from the regions under National Socialist dominion, the focus of the WUPJ's activities shifted first to America and later to Israel. After the war, the largest progressive Jewish organizations and institutions were in the United States. Consequently it was the American rabbi Solomon B. Freehof who became the fourth president of the WUPJ in 1959. A year later the administration was relocated to → New York, until the organization, led by the managing director Rabbi Richard G. Hirsch, moved to Jerusalem in 1973. The WUPJ increasingly regarded itself as Zionist and sought stronger links with the State of Israel. Since that time, the development of progressive Judaism in Israel – as represented by the Israel Movement for Progressive Judaism – is among its most important concerns.

Bibliography

Sources

[1] L. Montagu, The Faith of a Jewish Woman, London 1943.   [2] L. Montagu, My Club and I. The Story of the West Central Jewish Club, London 1954.   [3] E. Umansky (ed.), Lily Montagu. Sermons, Addresses, Letters, and Prayers, Lewiston 1985.

Secondary literature

[4] P. Fox, Israel Isidor Mattuck. Architect of Liberal Judaism, London 2014. [5] M. A. Meyer, Response to Modernity. A History of the Reform Movement in Judaism, Detroit 1995. [6] W. G. Plaut, The Growth of Reform Judaism. American and European Sources, New York 1965. [7] E. Umansky, Lily Montagu and the Advancement of Liberal Judaism. From Vision to Vocation, Lewiston/New York 1983.

ELLEN M. UMANSKY, FAIRFIELD

World's Fair

Jews have also taken part in world's fairs in diverse ways since 1876. Jewish contributions to exhibitions in the 19th and early 20th centuries primarily presented Jewish religion and culture as integral components of their respective societies. From the 1930s onward, the presentation of a Jewish homeland in Palestine took center stage; after 1948 this position was taken by the State of Israel. Jewish contributions to world's fairs were always accompanied by discourses on the definition and presentation of aspects of Jewishness.

1. World in miniature
2. Religion and culture
3. Staged statehood
4. A state among states

1. World in miniature

The 1851 London Great Exhibition of the Works of Industry of All Nations is regarded as the first world's fair [4. 201], with more than 17,000 exhibitors from 28 nations presenting their products. The predecessor of these exhibitions of industry and technology were the regional and national trade, country, and industry fairs primarily organized by private institutions promoting the trade and industry sectors. For these the emphasis was on the importance of business locations and regional competition. World's fairs, in contrast, presented themselves – especially during the period of high imperialism – as popular exhibitions with wide-ranging impact, showcasing the achievements of nations that believed themselves to be in a competition for progress, development, sophistication, and modernity.

From the beginning, the organization of the grand fairs was arranged primarily by nation. The pavilion layout, according to which each nation presents itself in its own exhibition structure, has been architecturally established since the Philadelphia Centennial Exposition in 1876. The focus was on presenting technical innovation and industrial products, being considered the expression and driving force of modernization; however, art, oddities, and life-worlds were exhibited as well. Staging the world in miniature, they attracted millions of visitors. Up until the Second World War, more than twenty world's fairs had been arranged; first in European cities, in England and France in particular, and from the 1870s onward in the United States and shortly thereafter in Australia.

2. Religion and culture

The Centennial Exposition in Philadelphia in 1876 was the first occasion on which Jewish exhibitors took part in the presentation of their respective countries. In the contribution of the United States, six statues represented the religious and ethnic population groups of America. The → B'nai B'rith order sponsored a project by the American-Jewish sculptor Moses Jacob Ezekiel. Without mentioning Judaism directly, his marble statue *Religious Liberty* was a reference to religious freedom which, while guaranteed under the American constitution, had to be constantly defended. The formal and visual language of the work in the neoclassical style employed republican symbols such as the Constitution and the 13 stars of the founding states. Furthermore, the emphasis on tolerance and social justice coincided with the ideals of the Jewish → Reform movement, which wished to have Jews understood as one denomination among others [11. 86–88].

The presentation of the French Jew Isaac Strauss's collection of Judaica at the Paris Exposition Universelle (1878) is regarded as the first distinctly Jewish contribution to a world's fair. In one of the most impressive structures of the grand exhibition, the Palais du Trocadéro, around eighty Judaica, predominantly cult and ritual items, were displayed in a secular public setting. The organization of Strauss's first Judaica exhibition was according to the "Jewish system" that to this day determines the layout of many exhibitions and → museums. The display was set up in accordance with criteria of art and craftsmanship such as stylistic idioms, materials used, and manufacturing techniques, presenting the items primarily as works of art, *objets d'art religieux hébraiques* [2]. Consequently it evoked two fundamental questions that have been increasingly discussed from the late 19th century onward. On the one hand, what was to be regarded as Jewish → art, and on the other, what was its place in European art history and how could it be described using existing terminologies [5. 192]. The curators stressed that the specifics of Jewish art and stylistic idioms should be included in the history of European crafts. Other exhibitions with similar objectives followed, such as the 1887 Anglo-Jewish Historical Exhibition in London, a joint project of Jewish antique dealers led by Joseph Jacobs and Lucien Wolf (→ Conjoint Foreign Committee).

These exhibitions also aimed at introducing non-Jewish visitors to Jewish culture. Aligned with the calendar of Jewish holidays (→ Course of the Year), the ritual environments in the synagogue and at home, as well as everyday life informed by the faith, the focus of the first contributions to these exhibitions was Judaism rather than the Jews themselves in their divergent lebenswelten [9. 15].

Until the early 20th century, Christian representations of Jews at world's fairs were dominated by the image of the biblical people and by ideas of the → Orient as an exotic world. At the 1893 World's Columbian Exposition in Chicago, for instance, Jews were presented in the ethnographical section of the exhibition as inhabitants of a Turkish village. During the Louisiana Purchase Exposition in St Louis in 1904, around 500 Jewish extras populated the replica of a Middle Eastern village, re-enacting the life of the inhabitants – Jews and others – of ancient Jerusalem.

Jewish initiators, in contrast, endeavored to convey a modern, universal image of the Jews. Thus the Semitic scholar Cyrus Adler's (→ American Jewish Historical Society) strictly scientific exhibition concepts for international expositions such as the Cincinnati Centennial Exposition of the Ohio Valley Central States (1888), Cotton States and International Exposition in Atlanta (1895), or Tennessee Centennial and International Exposition in Nashville (1897) sought to integrate Judaism and Jewish culture into a broad history of religion and civilization. The presentation of the Jewish religion was arranged from the perspectives of its members as modern monotheism without connection to the Holy Land. Some of the objects exhibited were shown entirely out of context [10. 67].

Besides independent projects, Jews also took part in international world and country exhibitions as representatives of their home countries. Jewish newspapers (→ Press) extensively reported on this, emphasizing the contribution made by Jews to technical and civilizational achievements. Occasionally, separate exhibition catalogues were printed in order to draw the attention of Jewish visitors to the displays of particular interest to them. Thus a catalogue published in → Yiddish to accompany the World's Columbian Exposition of 1893, listed numerous modern products and tools for craftspeople as well as a presentation of the economic situation of Jewish migrants in America.

3. Staged statehood

Until the 1930s, religious history and Jewish culture in the → Diaspora were the subject of Jewish displays at world's fairs. With the exhibition A Century of Progress in 1933/1934 in Chicago, the project of establishing a Jewish homeland in Palestine moved to the foreground. The contributions to this second world's fair, also situated on the shores of Lake Michigan, and the New York Fair in 1939/1940, presented the Jewish settlement in Palestine from biblical tradition to the present. Prior to the New York World's Fair, in particular, controversial discussions erupted among the different American Zionist groups contributing to the exposition on the issue of the content orientation of the presentation [6. 37–40]. The exhibitions also served as international platforms against the growing antisemitism (→ Conspiracy) in Europe, above all the anti-Jewish policies of National Socialist Germany. While the contributions designed, in the main, by American Zionists did not explicitly refer to disenfranchisement and persecution, they campaigned for mass emigration to Palestine among the visitors and for support for the emigration of German Jews. In view of antisemitic sentiments in America, the Jewish contribution to the exposition of 1939/1940 also worked towards the positive perception of American Jews.

The most important Jewish contribution to the 1933 World's Fair in Chicago consisted of a pageant, an American type of theatre for advertisement purposes (→ Misuk), entitled *The Romance of a People*. The play by the American Zionist Meyer Weisgal (1894–1977)

was performed on the Jewish day of the Fair by more than 3,500 actors using the most advanced opera technology. In an effective tableaux before a backdrop of a giant → Star of David, the silhouette of the Temple in → Jerusalem, and an oversized Torah scroll, it showed key events from 4,000 years of Jewish history from the beginnings of the settlement of the Holy Land to the Exodus and the path to the → Diaspora, the latter being presented as a rather negligible intermezzo. The performance ended with images of the modern life of Zionist settlers in Palestine and their achievements as well as the presentation of a new, youthful, and self-confident Jewish attitude towards life [13]. By combining biblical and Zionist presence, the spectacle, which was staged as a kind of worship service, expressed a historically and religiously legitimized Jewish claim to Palestine. At the same time the production evoked a connection between the United States and the Zionist movement founded on their shared fundamental values.

On the occasion of the 1939/1940 World's Fair in New York, a separate Jewish Palestine Pavilion was created under Weisgal's aegis. It presented the idea of a Jewish homeland in Palestine as authentically and realistically as possible while the symbolic and visual language employed left it open to interpretation to ensure that Zionists, non-Zionists, and non-Jewish visitors would find it accessible. It generally refrained from clear political statements [6. 47]. The pavilion designed by the architect Arieh El-Hanani (1898–1985; → Yad Vashem) adopted the international style widely used above all in → Tel Aviv and was a symbolic representation of Jewish settlement in Palestine. Its foundation stone had come from the excavation of an ancient → synagogue in Hanita and symbolized the arc between the historical Israelite and the modern Zionist settlement of Palestine. The exhibition followed the narrative of a backward and undeveloped territory that would develop into a modern, prosperous land thanks to the commitment of the Zionist pioneers (*halutsim*), from which the Arab population would benefit as well.

The mere fact that a stand-alone Jewish Palestine Pavilion was set up endowed it with the same status as the pavilions of other states, although it was not located directly adjacent to them. While the Jewish contribution to the 1933 Chicago World's Fair had conveyed the image of a young, self-confident, and modern Jewish settlement in Palestine with a claim to statehood, the Jewish Palestine Pavilion explicitly anticipated this state [12. 98]. The World's Fair was consequently used as a platform for the discussion and manifestation of Jewish political programs and objectives.

4. A state among states

The Israeli pavilion at the EXPO 58 in Brussels was the first Jewish contribution to a world's fair after the Second World War, the → Holocaust, and the foundation of the State of Israel. For the first time, the new state presented itself among other states. The Israeli contribution honored the efforts and achievements during the establishment of Israel. By emphasizing Jewish life in Palestine from ancient times onward, the Israeli state affirmed its historical claim to the area. Thus the pavilion designed by the Israeli architect Arieh Sharon (1900–1984; → Tel Aviv; → Yad Vashem) intended "to set forth the country and people of Israel in a continuous picture, set in their historic context, with one aspect of our life moving naturally into the next, without an artificial break" [1]. Visitors entered the foyer through a "Garden of Antiquities" with plants from Israel and archeological finds relating to Jewish life in Antiquity (→ Archaeology). Along a narrow "Corridor of Exile," at the end of which a fresco was displayed featuring the fifth verse of Psalm 137: "If I forget you, O Jerusalem" in all the languages spoken by the immigrants, they reached the main exhibition hall. Pride of place was given to the presentation of the successes and challenges of the Jewish community, in industry, agriculture, public healthcare, education, and culture, as well as the revival of → Hebrew.

Israel did not take part in the 1964/1965 New York World's Fair due to financial reasons, but an American-Israel pavilion was set up. A number of different American-Jewish groups and individuals had formed the American-Israel World's Fair Corporation, regarding the New York World's Fair as an opportunity for strengthening the narrative of the historically grown, profound connection between America, Jewry, and Israel [8. 137]. Unlike the world's fairs of 1933, 1939/1940, and 1958, the American-Israel pavilion presented the history of the Jews in the → Diaspora as an important part of the Jewish experience. The numerous facets of present-day Jewish life outside Israel made up a significant part of the display as well, which was welcomed by many American Jews in particular.

The New York World's Fair also saw the Arab–Israeli conflict among the topics being presented for the first time. The Jordanian pavilion was dedicated to the conflict, emphasizing the fight over water resources in the region and drawing the visitors' attention to the situation of the Palestinian refugees. Just as the American Jews regarded themselves as ambassadors of Israel at the Fair, Americans of Arab extraction and Jordanians felt themselves advocates of the Palestinian refugees. The Jordanian contribution led to a heated public debate, not least on issues of the significance of American-Jewish or American-Arab self-understanding.

The → Holocaust was not among the topics presented in Jewish contributions to the expositions either in Brussels or in New York. While the American-Israel pavilion in New York commemorated the 20th anniversary of the deportation of the Frank family by displaying some original pages of Anne Frank's → diary and a Hebrew poem by Rachel Silkina written in the → Warsaw ghetto, nevertheless the main focus was on the design of a positive and optimistic future of Jewish life.

Jewish artists, architects, and developers contributed to the displays of other countries besides Israel after 1945 as well. Thus the Israeli-Canadian architect Moshe Safdie (b. 1938; → Yad Vashem) designed the modular living complex Habitat '67 for the 1967 Montreal World's Fair. The building designed in the brutalist architectural style endeavored to be a response to the population explosion in big cities and the problems of modern urban planning.

Bibliography

Sources

[1] The Israel Pavilion at the Brussels 1958 World Exhibition, in: Journal of the Association of Engineers and Architects in Israel 16 (1958), Heft 12. [2] G. Stenne, Collection de M. Strauss. Description des objets d'art religieux hébraïques, Poissy 1878. [3] M.W. Weisgal, ... so Far. An Autobiography, New York 1971.

Secondary literature

[4] C.A. Breckenridge, The Aesthetics and Politics of Colonial Collecting. India at World Fairs, in: Comparative Studies in Society and History 31 (1989) 2, 195–216. [5] R.I. Cohen, Jewish Icons. Art and Society in Modern Europe, Berkeley 1998. [6] J.L. Gelvin, Zionism and Its Representation of "Jewish Palestine" at the New York World's Fair, 1939–1940, in: The International History Review 22 (2000) 1, 37–64. [7] A. C.T. Geppert, Fleeting Cities. Imperial Expositions in Fin-de-Siècle Europe, Basingstoke 2010. [8] E.A. Katz, It's the Real World after All. The American-Israel Pavilion – Jordan Pavilion Controversy at the New York World's Fair, 1964–1965, in: American Jewish History 91 (2003) 1, 129–155. [9] B. Kirshenblatt-Gimblett, Vom Kultus zur Kultur. Jüdisches auf Weltausstellungen, in: Wiener Jahrbuch für jüdische Geschichte, Kultur und Museumswesen 1 (1994/1995), 11–37. [10] B. Kirshenblatt-Gimblett, Making a Place in the World. Jews and the Holy Land at World's Fairs, in: J. Shandler/B.S. Wenger (eds.), Encounters with the "Holy Land." Place, Past and Future in American Jewish Culture, Philadelphia 1997, 60–82. [11] B. Kirshenblatt-Gimblett, Destination Culture. Tourism, Museums, and Heritage, Berkeley et al. 1998. [12] B. Kirshenblatt-Gimblett, Performing the State. The Jewish Palestine Pavilion at the New York World's Fair, 1939/40, in: B. Kirshenblatt-Gimblet/J. Karp (eds.), The Art of Being Jewish in Modern Times, Philadelphia 2008, 98–115. [13] L. Love, Performing Jewish Nationhood. The Romance of a People at the 1933 Chicago World's Fair, in: The Drama Review 55 (2011) 3, 57–67. [14] M. Wörner, Religionen auf den Weltausstellungen, Hanover 2000.

DOROTHEA WARNECK, HALLE, S.

Worms

The Jewish community of Worms was among the most important centers of medieval Jewish scholarship in the German language area. The most famous scholar to have studied at the yeshivah there for some years was Solomon ben Isaac, called Rashi (1040–1105), whose home was in Troyes in northern France. His Bible and Talmud commentaries are of preeminent significance for the study of Jewish traditional literature to this day; his followers founded an influential school of Talmud scholarship. From the early modern era onward, the Jewish community of Worms began to exaggerate the connection of the scholar's life and work to the city, which is why today Worms is considered to be the most important place of remembrance for Rashi.

1. Rashi's life and work
2. Rashi's significance for medieval Judaism
3. Worms and the ShUM communities
4. Worms as a place of remembrance

1. Rashi's life and work

Solomon ben Isaac, called Rashi after the Hebrew acronym of his name (*Rabbi Shlomo ben Yitshak*), is generally assumed to have been born in 1040 in Troyes in northern France, an important cultural and economic center of the medieval Champagne region in the 11th century. His life, about which little is known, coincided with an era of intensive transformation of educational institutions in northwestern Europe. Rashi grew up in Troyes, where he received a basic religious education. Around twenty years old, he left the place of his birth in order to continue his studies at the most renowned Talmud schools (yeshivot; → Talmud Torah) of → Ashkenaz, in Mainz and Worms.

It is not known how long Rashi studied at the respective yeshivot. He returned to Troyes around 1065/1070 where he – according to the view embraced by earlier research – worked in the family's wine growing or trading business; it is also possible that he practiced a different trade. His main concern, however, was the yeshivah he had founded, which soon acquired an excellent reputation. After the destruction of large parts of the Jewish communities of Mainz and Worms at the hands of crusaders in the spring of 1096, more students arrived at his school, which followed the Rhenish tradition. His daughters Yocheved, Miriam, and Rachel, who seem to have been educated in religious matters too, married among his most well-known students. His sons-in-law Meir ben Samuel, Yehudah ben Nathan, and Eli'ezer ben Shemayah, as well as some of his grandsons, later worked as influential scholars at a number of northern French and German yeshivot.

Rashi probably composed the works that are transmitted from him in Troyes, where he died in 1105. Soon after his death he was already seen as the most famous commentator of the Babylonian → Talmud, which was read more widely in the European → Diaspora only after the turn of the millennium. To aid the exegesis of complex passages, Rashi discussed different readings of the texts, elucidated hermeneutic key terms, paraphrased → Aramaic sections in → Hebrew, and explained the intertextual connections contained in abbreviated formulae and allusions. In this way, he created a text that could be understood by students of the Talmud even without the guidance of a teacher.

Even during his lifetime, Rashi was considered the most important biblical exegete of his era. His → commentaries on the Pentateuch (*Torah*), the books of the Prophets (*Nevi'im*), and Writings (*Ketuvim*; → Tanakh) were dedicated to the understanding of the text. The objective was to mediate between the immediate literal meaning (*sensus litteralis*; Hebr. *pshat*) of a verse and the metaphorical interpretation (Hebr. *drash*) from the rabbinic → midrash that went beyond the former.

Rashi's verse-by-verse interpretations included brief lexicographical, in places philological-linguistic, explanations of individual Hebrew words and often the paraphrase of a midrash that interpreted the verse. Rashi's knowledge of Christian biblical exegesis was also impressive; it is unclear, however, to what extent his interpretations contain anti-Christian polemic [9. 105]. In addition, there are explanatory glosses, among them over 5,000 Old French lexical examples as well as around thirty Yiddish terms, which are regarded as the oldest written evidence of → Yiddish. These vernacular glosses testify to language usage among the Ashkenazi Jews; together with many vivid examples of everyday customs (→ Minhag) and habits, his Hebrew Bible commentary allows us a detailed look at Jewish cultural, economic, and social history in northern France in the early 12th century.

Besides his commentaries, Rashi also composed liturgical poetry (→ Piyyut) and a large number of expert opinions on matters of religious law (→ Responsa). It is thanks to the precise and comprehensible language employed in his commentary works that he and his followers became trailblazers of Ashkenazi culture.

2. Rashi's significance for medieval Judaism

Rashi's legacy was continued by his pupils, among them his sons-in-law and his grandsons Samuel ben Meir (Rashbam; ca. 1085 – ca. 1174) and Jacob ben Meir (Rabbenu Tam; ca. 1100 – ca. 1171). They and their followers and successors dedicated themselves to studying the Talmud and to the practical interpretation of the law. The writings of these so-called Tosafists (Hebr. *ba'ale hatosafot*; "masters of additions/supplements") soon spread; their methodology became the most-widely applied in Ashkenaz during the 12th and 13th centuries.

Rashi's Torah commentary was most influential and an indispensable part of the study of the Bible; more than 200 supracommentaries testify to the intensive scholarly interest in it. This is also reflected in the history of Hebrew printed books (→ Printing). The first Hebrew book to be printed was Rashi's Torah commentary in Reggio di Calabria in 1475. This edition employed a semi-cursive Hebrew type that would also be used for all subsequent editions of Rashi's commentaries and which is now known as Rashi script. The first or second printed version of the Torah, published in Bologna in 1482, included not only the Targum (the Aramaic translation of the Bible; → Bible Translation) but also Rashi's commentary.

Rashi's knowledge and exegetic methods also influenced the exegesis of Christian scholars in the 12th and 13th centuries. As Christian Hebrew studies became established, interest in Rashi grew during the late 15th century and can also be found in the works of Martin Luther.

3. Worms and the ShUM communities

In the 11th century, the (arch-)bishoprics west of the Rhine – Mainz, Speyer, and Worms – experienced significant demographic and economic growth, accompanied by the building of the great cathedrals (Mainz 975; Speyer 1030; Worms 1120/1130). The close commercial relations between these cities also resulted in intensified connections between the Jewish communities.

A few Jews had settled in Mainz, the early center of the Rhine–Main region, beginning in the 10th century. Only a few decades later they founded a Jewish community that would remain the largest and most important one in German-speaking lands until the late 11th century. Teachers at its yeshivah included, from the late 10th century onward, Gershom ben Judah *Me'or ha-Golah* ("Light of the exile"; 960–1028), the most important Halakhic authority in medieval Ashkenaz. His presence attracted many prominent scholars, such as members of the originally Italian Kalonymos family, who excelled in the study of the Talmud.

The Jewish community in Worms was presumably founded during the incumbency of Bishop Burchard (1000–1025). The first certain date is the foundation of a → synagogue, documented by an inscription of 1034, by a wealthy couple. The oldest gravestone on the "Heiliger Sand," most of which has been preserved, dates from the year 1058/1059; the cemetery, which contains around 2,500 preserved gravestones (of which about 1,200 date from before 1700 and around 280 alone from the 13th century) was in uninterrupted use until the 20th century. The Salic King Henry IV (r. 1056–1105) bestowed an extensive → privilege of protection on the Jews of Worms, granting them among other things safe passage throughout the Empire; this became the standard for privileges for Jews in the German language area. The yeshivah of the prospering community in Worms attracted prominent scholars, among them Halakhists (→ Halakhah) such as Judah ben Baruch, a pupil of Gershom ben Judah, and commentators like Rashi's future teachers Yaakov ben Yakar (d. 1064) and Isaac ben Eleazar ha-Levi (d. 1070).

The Jewish community of Speyer was founded later, in 1084, thanks to a privilege granted by Bishop Rüdiger Huzmann. During this time, a network based on economic, religious, and personal kinship exchanges grew up between the Jewish communities of Speyer (Hebr. *Shpira*), Worms (*Warmaiza*), and Mainz (*Magentsa*). The three communities were increasingly perceived as a religious and cultural entity, giving rise to the Hebrew acronym *ShUM* composed of their initials, by which they have been known since the Middle Ages.

The persecutions of Jews in the course of the First Crusade affected Worms and Mainz particularly severely. Several Hebrew chronicles record the bloody events. They entered the liturgical memory culture of the ShUM communities in the form of → lamentations (→ Zakhor). At the beginning of the 12th century, Jewish communities were already being re-established here. The restored significance of the community of Worms is documented by several buildings displaying architectural similarity with the city's cathedral (consecrated 1181), among them a synagogue that would remain essentially unchanged until 1938 (1174/1175), a → mikveh (1185/1186), and the first addition of a women's prayer room to the synagogue (1212/1213; one of the first female prayer leaders, Urania

[Urgia], was buried in 1275 in the cemetery in Worms).

The yeshivot of the ShUM communities once again attracted prominent legal scholars. Their expert rulings (*takkanot kehillot ShUM*) became binding for all Ashkenazi Jews, and therefore as far as Eastern Central Europe, from the beginning of the 13th century onward; some are valid to this day. One of the signatories of the *takkanot*, Eleazar ben Judah of Worms (ca. 1165–1238), was also one of the last followers of the mystic-ascetic movement *Ḥaside Ashkenaz* (The pious of Ashkenaz) and author of the book of ethical and religious law *Sefer ha-Rokeaḥ* (Book of the ointment-maker). He contributed significantly to the reputation of the medieval community of Worms, also documented by one of the most important medieval Jewish liturgical manuscripts, the richly-illustrated *Maḥzor Warmaiza* (Holiday prayer book of Worms, 1272/1273), that was used in divine service in Worms until 1938 (→ Liturgy). A Yiddish rhyme recorded in it is, after the lexical glosses in Rashi's Torah commentary, the earliest dated written document in → Yiddish.

The assured legal status allowed the Jews of Worms favorable conditions for further development. However, the municipal council grew increasingly independent of episcopal dominion, finally becoming the determining authority for the Jewish community; this was noticeable not least in the growing tax burden. In addition, kings and emperors increasingly transferred their legal titles to the city from the mid-14th century onward as it developed into a Reichsstadt (free imperial city), which led to a deterioration in the legal status of the Jewish communities. The persecutions of Jews in the spring of 1349, in which Jews were accused of poisoning wells in connection with the plague, were a particularly deep cesura. The account in the "Memorbuch" of the Jewish community of Worms listed nearly 600 persons killed and murdered [1. 923]. In 1377, the Jewish population of the city did not even number 200 persons [1. 919–927].

While the Jews were expelled from Mainz and Speyer during the 15th century, the free imperial city of Worms resisted the expulsions that began around 1390 and 1430. Even so, the Jews were subject to increasing marginalization, intensive supervision by the municipal council (regulations, visitations, taxation, restrictive settlement laws), and, from the end of the 15th century onward, gradual physical segregation of the Jewish quarter. However, until the 17th century, Worms was home to the second largest Jewish community in Germany after Frankfurt am Main. It was probably this continuity of the "holy community at Worms" which – unlike Rashi's home city of Troyes, where there was no Jewish community between the early 14th and the 19th century – that encouraged the recollection of medieval traditions and legends.

4. Worms as a place of remembrance

Ever since the 1580s, legends have circulated among the Jews of Worms about Rashi's years of study in their community. In the mid-17th century, his sojourn was mentioned in connection with the topography of the Jewish quarter for the first time. In a → minhag book dating from the last third of the 17th century, the Worms synagogue assistant Juspa Shammash testified to the attempts of the Jews of Worms "to claim the famous commentator for themselves" [11. 228] and to imbue the legends with an aura of ancient tradition. This tendency increased during the 18th century, when ever more buildings of the Jewish quarter were associated with Rashi. In 1760, a synagogue annex said to have housed the yeshivah in 1623/1624 and known to this day as "Raschi-Kapelle" (Rashi chapel) was first named as the place where

the scholar taught sitting in the so-called "Raschi-Stuhl" (Rashi chair). It is assumed, however, that the building that preceded the present-day "Raschi-Haus," which was situated to the south of the synagogue and pulled down in 1971, was the building in which Rashi studied and taught.

In the post-Napoleonic era, Jews were at first granted only limited equality (→ Emancipation) in Worms, which was part of the Grand Duchy of Hesse. However, a period of acculturation and economic and social advancement began among the Jews of Worms in 1830/1840, accompanied by strengthened civic and communal self-confidence (→ Middle Class). This also provided a renewed stimulus to the Rashi reception in Worms. As early as 1823, Leopold Zunz (1794–1886; → Classical Studies; → Historiography) demonstrated an interest in Rashi's life and work in his influential article *Salomon ben Isaac, genannt Raschi*, published in the journal of the → Verein für Cultur und Wissenschaft der Juden.

Despite Zunz's critical view of local legends, members of the community in Worms perpetuated the romantic image of Rashi's activities in the city. The first, successful call by the Comité zur Renovierung alter Denkmäler in der israelitischen Gemeinde in 1853 provided that "Rashi's chair and synagogue" were to be restored. The ensemble of buildings in the vicinity of the synagogue with their newly enhanced status as well as the Jewish cemetery with its graves of famous scholars and rabbis from the city became a kind of pilgrimage site, Rashi himself becoming the "figurehead" [9. IX] of the Jewish community of Worms.

Around the middle of the century, the subject of Rashi led to a number of controversies. Based on the sources, the rabbinical scholar Abraham Epstein (1841–1918) from Vienna refuted any link between the medieval commentator and the "Raschi-Kapelle" and the "Raschi-Stuhl," only to be refuted in his turn by Ludwig Lewysohn (1819–1901), the rabbi of Worms from 1851 to 1858. Among his achievements was safeguarding and scientifically cataloguing the gravestones in the Jewish cemetery as well as overseeing the restoration of the "Raschi-Kapelle" in 1854/1855 and the entirely new inscription describing Rashi as "Light of the Diaspora."

On the occasion of the 800th anniversary of Rashi's death, the discussion concerning his sojourn in Worms moved into the focus of public attention once more in 1905, continuing well into the 1920s. The teacher Samson Rothschild (1848–1939) from Worms emphasized in a biographical sketch of 1924 that it was irrelevant in which building the scholar had sat in his student days. What was important was only the documented fact "that Rashi is closely connected to the Jewish community of Worms. Therefore we understand the pride of this community that it has been the guardian of this place for centuries and will probably remain so for ever" [3. 12].

The museum of the Jewish community (→ Museums), first envisaged in 1914, was set up in 1924 in the remodeled "Raschi-Kapelle" and existed until it was destroyed during the → November pogrom in 1938. During the National Socialist years, the reference to the great scholar strengthened the communal recollection, thus in 1934 on the occasion of the 900th anniversary of the founding of the → synagogue or in 1935 at the founding of the Jewish district school.

In 1945, the Jewish community, which had numbered around 1,110 members in 1933, did not exist anymore. The synagogue was rebuilt from 1957 to 1961. The Raschi-Lehrhaus-Verein Worms e.V., founded in 1968, endeavored to establish a center for remembrance and research at the place of Rashi's activity. The year 1982 saw the opening of the "Raschi-Haus," which comprised a Jewish museum and city archive.

Bibliography

Sources

[1] Germania Judaica, Vol. 2.2: Von 1238 bis zur Mitte des 14. Jahrhunderts, ed. by Z. Avineri, Tübingen 1968. [2] B. S. Hamburger/E. Zimmer (eds.), Minhagim de-kehillat kodesh Warmayza le-rabbi Yuzpa Shamash [The Minhagim Book of the Jewish Community in Worms by Rabbi Juzpa Shammash], Jerusalem 1988. [3] S. Rothschild, Raschi (Rabbi Sch'lomo ben Isak) geb. 1040 zu Troyes, gest. 13. Juli 1105 zu Troyes. Ein Lebensbild, Worms 1924. [4] L. Zunz, Salomon ben Isaac, genannt Raschi, in: Zeitschrift für die Wissenschaft des Judenthums 1 (1823), 277–384.

Secondary literature

[5] G. Dahan et al. (eds.), Rashi et la culture juive en France du Nord au moyen âge, Paris/Leuven 1997. [6] K. E. Grözinger (ed.), Jüdische Kultur in den SchUM-Städten. Literatur, Musik, Theater, Wiesbaden 2014. [7] P. Heberer/U. Reuter (eds.), Die SchUM-Gemeinden Speyer – Worms – Mainz. Auf dem Weg zum Welterbe, Regensburg 2013. [8] A. D. Kauders et al., Fünfzig Jahre Wiedereinweihung der Alten Synagoge zu Worms. Erweiterter Nachdruck der Forschungen von 1961 mit Quellen, Worms 2011. [9] D. Krochmalnik et al. (eds.), Raschi und sein Erbe. Internationale Tagung der Hochschule für Jüdische Studien mit der Stadt Worms, Heidelberg 2007. [10] H. Liss, Raschi, in: M. Bauks et al. (eds.), Das Wissenschaftliche Bibellexikon im Internet, Stuttgart 2009 (https://www.bibelwissenschaft.de/stichwort/64590/). [11] L. Raspe, Jüdische Hagiographie im mittelalterlichen Aschkenas, Tübingen 2006. [12] F. Reuter, Warmaisa – das jüdische Worms. Von den Anfängen bis zum jüdischen Museum des Isidor Kiefer (1924), in: G. Bönnen (ed.), Geschichte der Stadt Worms, Stuttgart 2005, 664–690. [13] N. H. Roemer, German City, Jewish Memory. The Story of Worms, Waltham 2010.

Gerold Bönnen, Worms

Y

Yad Vashem

Yad Vashem (Hebr.; "memorial and name"), at the *Har ha-zikaron* (Mount of Remembrance), in western Jerusalem, is the central Israeli institution for the remembrance and study of the Shoah. After there had been early initiatives in the → Yishuv for the creation of such a memorial during the Second World War, it was established in 1953 by an act of the Israeli parliament. The efforts to give a physical form to the institution reflect the fundamental questions of the treatment and the commemoration of the Shoah within Israeli society, especially in its early phase. Today the memorial site is home to the most comprehensive documentary archive in the world about the destruction of the European Jews.

1. Founding and development
2. Remembrance or Research
3. Political positions

1. Founding and development

In the summer of 1942 reports were growing ever more urgent about the mass destruction of the European Jews (→ Riegner Telegram). Already at that time plans were being drawn up in Jewish Palestine to commemorate the catastrophe with a national monument. It was initiated by Mordechai Shenhavi (1900–1983), a leading member of the socialist-Zionist youth organization Hashomer Hatzair, who had emigrated to Palestine in 1919. In September 1942 Shenhavi submitted a suggestion to the Jewish National Fund, where it was received with interest, but the Fund requested that fundamental revisions be made.

Concurrently, ideas were being discussed within the → World Jewish Congress on how to memorialize the destruction, which found influential proponents in Chaim Weizmann (→ Balfour Declaration), Stephen S. Wise (→ American Jewish Congress), and Nahum Goldmann. More suggestions came from members of the → Hebrew University in Jerusalem and from private individuals. Fully cognizant of the momentum, the National Fund placed the memorial project on its own agenda in February 1945. This prompted Shenhavi to revise his concept, and he gave it the title "Yad Vashem Foundation in Memory of the Lost Jewries in Europe"; on May 25, 1945, the daily newspaper → *Davar* presented the project to a wider public. The title chosen by Shenhavi, Yad Vashem, followed a suggestion by Rabbi Moshe Bursztyn, chairman of the department for religious affairs at the National Fund, who quoted a verse from Isaiah 56:5: "I will give them, in My house / And within My walls, / A monument and a name / Better than sons or daughters. / I will give them an everlasting name / Which shall not perish."

In June 1945 Shenhavi's concept won the official approval of the Jewish National Council, the most important Jewish body in the → Yishuv; in August of the same year the Zionist Central Committee (→ Basel) followed suit at its first post-war session in London. From a small office in Jerusalem the institution began its work by establishing a collection of Holocaust documents to which it would continually add more material. In July 1947 the leadership, in cooperation with academics of the Hebrew University, organized the International Conference on Holocaust and Martyrdom in Our Time, the first international symposium of its kind attended by many scholars, historians, and representatives of the → historical commissions and documentation centers in Europe. Even at this early stage it became clear that due to lack of funding the institution would be unable to realize larger projects. Thus in 1947 it had to decline the offer made by Alfred Wiener to relocate his → Wiener Library from London to Israel because the young institution could not afford the cost of transport and the annual fee of £5,000 demanded by Wiener for the use of his holdings.

After the foundation of the State of Israel, the appointment of the historian Ben-Zion Dinur as Minister of Education and Culture in the autumn of 1951 infused the project with new energy. Previously it had secured a permanent location for the archival collection of the Jewish Historical Commission in Munich, which had been brought to Israel shortly after the founding of the state. Dinur, who as a professor at the Hebrew University is counted among the founders of a nationalist orientation in Jewish historiography (→ History; → Historiography), had lent significant support to the memorial project in the second half of the 1940s. At the end of 1951, and in consultation with Shenhavi, he drafted a bill that sought to establish the institution publicly; it was endorsed by the government in the spring of 1953, shortly before the tenth anniversary of the → Warsaw ghetto uprising. Passed by the Knesset in August 1953, the "Martyrs' and Heroes' Commemoration (Yad Vashem) Law" instructed the institution to "initiate and direct memorial projects; to study and

publish all the evidence on the Holocaust and heroism and to teach the Jewish people the lessons to be learned therefrom"(citedin [7. 120f.]). In formal terms Yad Vashem was subsumed under Dinur's Ministry of Education and Culture; Dinur was also put in charge of the governing body (directorate). An advisory board, comprised of delegates from the Jewish National Fund, the Jewish Agency, the Jewish World Congress, and members of the government as well as veterans, partisans, and survivor organizations, mainly performed representative and consulting functions.

The cornerstone of the memorial complex was laid in 1954 at the *Har ha-zikaron* (Mount of Remembrance) in Jerusalem. The first building, which housed the library, the Archive, and administration offices, was completed in 1957. The opening ceremony for the Hall of Remembrance took place in April 1961, followed in May 1962 by the creation of an Avenue of the Righteous Among the Nations in memory of non-Jewish organizations and individuals who had opposed the National Socialist policies to save Jews. The year 1968 saw the first steps taken toward the presentation of the names, vital statistics, and origins of documented victims of the destruction in a specially designed room. Completed in 1973, the Holocaust History Museum was expanded in 1981 to include an art section. With the transfer of the museum to a new construction designed by Moshe Safdie (b. 1938) in 2005, the Hall of Names, today a repository of nearly three million first and family names, was incorporated in the building and forms the end of the exhibition. Other monuments are located on the grounds of the memorial site, including the 1987 memorial to the murdered children, as well as the monumental Valley of the Communities, completed in 1992.

The Archive is now recognized as the foremost repository for documents relating to the Holocaust. It comprises more than 154 million pages of material, including more than 112,000 survivor statements and just under 420,000 photographs. The annual scholarly journal *Yad Vashem Studies on the European Jewish Catastrophe and Resistance* was established in 1957; between 1958 and 1960, moreover, a selection of rescued diaries and memoirs of → Shoah survivors went to print, one of these being the diary (*Pinkas Shavli*) of Eliezer Yerushalmi, secretary of the → Judenrat in the ghetto of Šiauliai (Shavli, Lithuania). The first volume of the *Pinkas HaKehilot* ("Encyclopedia of Jewish Communities") appeared in 1969 and has been joined by many more in subsequent years. Several reference works as well as many individual studies have since followed and continue to be published on the history of the Holocaust, such as the *Encyclopedia of the Holocaust* (1990) or *The Yad Vashem Encyclopedia of the Ghettos during the Holocaust* (2009).

2. Remembrance or Research

The basic idea of Mordechai Shenhavi, presented in 1956 by the architects Aryeh Elhanani and Arieh Sharon, envisaged a two-part memorial site: a Hall of Remembrance was to commemorate the annihilated Jews of Europe; a Hall of Heroism was to memorialize the armed resistance and the Jewish fighters against the Nazis. This duality largely followed the view also prevalent in the Yishuv which distinguished categorically between ghetto fighters and → partisans on one side, and victims who were imagined as having allowed themselves to be led "like sheep to slaughter" on the other. While members of the organizations representing former ghetto fighters and partisans supported Shenlavi's plans, others raised objections to such a strict dichotomy, including the secretary general of the Histadrut, Yosef Sprinzak, or Zerach Warhaftig, member of the Yad Vashem council and a leading

Yad Vashem director Ben-Zion Dinur (third from left) presents Israeli President Yitzhak Ben-Zvi (second from right) with documents from the Oyneg Shabbes Collection (photo from 1956)

voice in the religious Zionist workers' party *Mizrachi*. They were of the opinion that Jewish heroism had taken diverse forms and had not been limited exclusively to armed struggle.

In the final version of the 1953 law, the Israeli legislature defined the terms "heroism" and "struggle" during the Shoah in a wider sense and included all active and passive manifestations of Jewish resistance, as well as the daily struggle for survival in the ghettos and camps. Shenhavi's plan was rejected not least because it provoked an emphatic objection from the → Claims Conference since it bore roughly half the cost of the project and was not willing to provide funds solely for a memorial site. Instead the Claims Conference urged the planners to promote comprehensive research on the history of the Shoah.

Apart from the objections of the Claims Conference, the relationship between remembrance and research led to intense controversies about the focus of the institution. Shenhavi's original draft had assigned lesser importance to the tasks of collecting documents and maintaining an archive in comparison to the memorial complex. Inspired by the work of the first → historical commissions in liberated Europe, especially in Poland, and in the Displaced Persons camps in Germany (→ Munich), Warhaftig had even in the founding phase of the project held the view that rather than commemoration, it was documentation and archival work which had to be the central concern of Yad Vashem.

What had up to this point been a mostly latent conflict broke open in the summer of 1958. A report by the State Comptroller's Office had found evidence of administrative and financial misconduct involving the management of Yad Vashem, whereupon the press publicized the institution's internal divisions. Two opposing factions had indeed materialized: Dinur, agreeing with the Claims Conference, believed that

Yad Vashem should be run primarily as a research institution. He received support from prominent Hebrew University scholars, and in particular from a group aligned with the historians Israel Halperin (→ Autonomy) and Shaul Esh and the historian and literary scholar Joseph Melkman.

As early as 1953, when Dinur gave his speech before the Knesset on the passage of the law, the then director-designate declared that one of the key tasks for Yad Vashem would be to convey the "lessons taught by the Shoah." The most important of these insights was a historical confirmation of Zionism [1. 92–94]. For Dinur, the Shoah had shown that a people living among other nations, without a state of their own, ran the risk of being extinguished. The → Holocaust to him was the culmination of a crisis the beginnings of which had been marked by the → pogroms in Russia and the emerging antisemitism in late 19th-century Germany (→ Berlin Debate on Antisemitism), and at the end of which stood the creation of the State of Israel. In accordance with this view, Dinur devised a historiographical research agenda for Yad Vashem which extended far beyond the time frame of the Second World War, embedding the Shoah within the totality of Jewish history.

The research would, according to Dinur and his circle, be undertaken in close cooperation with the → Hebrew University, but not with former members of the historical commissions, whose approach – consisting of a synthesis of remembered experience and scientific if not academic practice – they rejected. Dinur argued that in order to perform the proposed research, it was necessary not only to be a trained professional but also to be able to differentiate between personal experience and objective science. This rationale served to undermine trust in the aptitude of Holocaust survivors to conduct such research at Yad Vashem. Dinur's group viewed ordinary victims of the Holocaust but also academically trained scholars who had themselves experienced persecution and extermination and had begun to document the Shoah in the historical commissions while the war was still ongoing incapable of maintaining their professional distance. At a meeting of the council, Yosef Weitz, representative of the National Fund, even went so far as to proclaim: "I do not think that survivors can express their opinion about Yad Vashem. It does not seem right to me that sick people are the ones who should be discussing their illness" (cited in [6. 352]).

Dinur's approach met with opposition from a group made up mainly of Holocaust survivors who had come to the project immediately after the founding of Yad Vashem. It comprised the historian Józef Kermisz, the former Director of the → Jewish Historical Institute in Warsaw, Nachman Blumenthal, the author and activist of the underground archive → *Oyneg Shabbes* in the → Warsaw ghetto, Rachel Auerbach, and the historian and essayist Nathan Eck. They had the support of Israeli survivor coalitions such as the Organization for the Disabled Veterans of the War against the Nazis or the Organization of Partisans, Underground Fighters and Ghetto Rebels, who feared that with Dinur in charge of the institution and its directorate, which included only one token survivor of the Holocaust, Mark (Meir) Dvorzhetski, Yad Vashem might be transformed into a purely research institute of the Hebrew University.

The group led by Auerbach, Kermisz, and Blumenthal by no means rejected scholarly method, but they were decidedly more flexible in their interpretation of the strict line drawn by Dinur between individual experience and academic objectivity. As a national institution Yad Vashem, in their opinion, should take up the work that was begun during the war in the ghettos and in the underground and continued by the historical commissions after the end of the war. This required, they argued, a cooperative effort from professional historians who had survived the war and Holocaust survivors without any academic training. To justify their approach, the circle around Auerbach, Kermisz, and Blumenthal cited the unique character of the Shoah which they said differed fundamentally from all previous events in Jewish history, especially since the Holocaust constituted a singular crime. This fact alone was sufficient to warrant the participation of survivor organizations.

As a result of the very public debate taking place in 1958 Dinur, and with him the academic wing, increasingly lost influence. The fourth conference of the World Council of Yad Vashem, the meeting of the council's member organizations, ended in October with a resolution declaring it no longer had confidence in Dinur and his methodology, whereupon Dinur resigned as director in 1959; more adherents of the academic faction followed his example, including Shaul Esh and Joseph Melkman. Succeeding Dinur as director was a leading figure of the → World Jewish Congress, Leon Kubowitzki, who emphasized the memorial aspect of Yad Vashem and pursued the historiographical orientation of the survivor organizations.

3. Political positions

Until well into the 1950s, the public perception of the memorial in Israel was limited. The political leadership preferred not to express any great enthusiasm for the idea of a more comprehensive commemoration of the Shoah, pointing instead to the construction effort that gave birth to the State of Israel and the nation's determination to survive. To be sure, in 1951 the Knesset had dedicated the 27th of Nissan as the Day of Remembrance of the Shoah (since 1953 *Yom ha-Shoah veha-Gevurah*); however, since no further ceremonial procedures were stipulated, the day of mourning had little impact on public life in Israel. Neither Prime Minister David Ben-Gurion (→ Raison d'État) nor a single leading member of the cabinet attended the memorial services organized by Yad Vashem on → Holocaust Remembrance Day in the 1950s.

Ben-Gurion had already voiced his concerns in the development phase of Yad Vashem, about a memorial site for European Jewry in Israel. It was more important, he argued, to associate the memory of the Second World War with the Jewish rebirth in Israel than to erect monuments and museums to commemorate the annihilation. When Shenhavi submitted the proposal in the early 1950s, in a gesture of respectful commemoration, to confer honorary citizenship on all victims of the Shoah, Ben-Gurion was drawn to the idea amid fierce controversies over the → Luxembourg Agreement on German reparations. By commemorating the Jewish victims of the Holocaust, Israel was to assert its legal claim to their heirless property (→ Restitution).

Moreover, it was revealed that the French Centre de documentation juive contemporaine (→ Center of Contemporary Jewish Documentation) under the leadership of Isaac Schneersohn was planning to establish a Shoah memorial in Paris. A bitter Shenhavi wrote to Ben-Gurion at the end of 1952: "Paris will commemorate the victims of the Shoah, and Jerusalem will receive reparations" (cited in [7. 50]). Ben-Gurion could not refute Shenhavi's argument, which was also shared by Dinur, that the creation of a memorial to the Shoah in Paris rather than in Jerusalem undermined the leading role to which Israel was aspiring in the Jewish world. However, he did insist that Yad Vashem be built on a site near the re-named *Har ha-zikaron* and not in the Jezreel Valley as originally proposed by Shenhavi. With the installation of the memorial close to the grave of Theodor Herzl (→ Old New Land) and the military cemetery of honor for Israel's fallen soldiers, a symbolic bond was put in place linking remembrance and renewal.

Even before the watershed of the → Eichmann trial in 1961, the significance of the Shoah in the consciousness of the Israeli public was gradually increasing. Contributing factors were the public campaign mounted by survivor organizations about the character of Yad Vashem, and the growing concerns over what was at the time felt to be the alienation of the youth, born in the country, with respect to Jewish history, Jewish existence in the → Diaspora, and the Shoah.

Bibliography

Sources
[1] B.-Z. Dinur, Zakhor. Words on the Holocaust and Its Implication, Jerusalem 1958 [Hebr.].

Secondary literature
[2] M. Brog, In Blessed Memory of a Dream. Mordechai Shenhavi and Initial Holocaust Commemoration Ideas in Palestine, 1942–1945, in: Yad Vashem Studies 30 (2002), 297–336. [3] B. Cohen, Israeli Holocaust Research. Birth and Evolution, London 2013. [4] E. Don-Yehiya, Memory and Political Culture. Israeli Society and the Holocaust, in: Studies in Contemporary Jewry 9 (1993), 139–162. [5] O. Kenan, Between Memory and History. The Evolution of Israeli Historiography of the Holocaust, 1945–1961, New York 2003. [6] R. Stauber, The Debate over the Mission of Yad Vashem as a Research Institute. The First Years, in: Simon Dubnow Institute Yearbook 11 (2012), 347–366. [7] R. Stauber, The Holocaust in Israeli Public Debate in the 1950s. Ideology and Memory, trans. by E. Yuval, London 2007.

RONI STAUBER, TEL AVIV

Yankele

Yankele is the title of a → Yiddish song published in 1936 by the → Cracow poet and composer Mordechai Gebirtig (1877–1942). In the form of a conventional lullaby, it reflects the situation of Polish Jews in the 1920s and 1930s, between tradition and moving into the modern era, troubled by economic hardship and increasing antisemitism. Gebirtig also wrote songs and poems in the Cracow Ghetto. Among his most frequently performed songs, however, are those which, like *Yankele*, recall Jewish life in Poland before the → Shoah in the style of Yiddish folk songs.

1. A Yiddish folk song
2. Mordechai Gebirtig
3. The interwar years in Cracow
4. German occupation and ghetto
5. Reception

1. A Yiddish folk song

A collection of Gebirtig's poems was published under the title *Mayne lider* (My songs) in Cracow in 1936 to mark his sixtieth birthday. The collection also contained the words and melody of *Yankele*, at first glance a conventional lullaby. In the song, verse by verse a mother dreams of her little boy's promising future until he becomes a Talmudic scholar (→ Talmud), an experienced merchant, and a wise bridegroom. The child, however, cries, wets himself, keeps his mother awake – as all infants do – and is a long way from becoming "*a mentsh.*" After every verse the refrain evokes scenarios of events that represent a successful life in the traditional culture of the Jews of Eastern Europe and are among the firmly established topics of Yiddish folk songs (→ Folk Music): → marriage, business acumen, religious education, and learning, all of them united in the male offspring of the family.

In *Yankele*, these traditional *topoi* do not stay within the folklore stereotype. With their melancholy and at the same time humorous undertone, the verses turn away from the idea according to which aspiring to status and faithfully adhering to tradition are the only guarantees of the continued existence of the Jewish community – all the more so in a time when there were hardly any chances of social advancement for young Jews in Poland and religious tradition was less likely to guarantee support in life. In analogy with these changes, *Yankele* displays an inversion of the traditional lullaby motif. Instead of the mother calming the child and singing it to sleep, the child's crying startles the mother out of her dreams. Her expectations now seem hopelessly nostalgic and unattainable.

2. Mordechai Gebirtig

Gebirtig was born in 1877 into a poor merchant family in → Cracow. He grew up in a traditional Jewish environment with → Yiddish as his everyday spoken language. There is no proof of the widely-held assumption that Gebirtig had to earn a living in a cabinet maker's workshop while still an adolescent. It may be regarded as certain that his interest in writing poetry was awakened by an encounter with the Yiddish author Avrom Reyzen, who also lived in Cracow, during the early years of the 20th century. After the First World War, his songs became increasingly popular thanks to their familiar topics and catchy melodies. They made their way into the repertoires of Yiddish stages in Poland as well as the United States (→ Second Avenue). Until 1940, Gebirtig himself lived with his wife and three daughters in the Jewish Kazimierz quarter of Cracow. After the German occupation, presumably in October 1940, the family was forcibly relocated to the nearby village of Łagiewniki. In April 1942, they were deported to the so-called "jüdischer Wohnbezirk" (Jewish residential district) in the Podgórze district of Cracow, the Cracow Ghetto. Shortly before the transport to the Bełżec extermination camp, Gebirtig was shot on June 4, 1942.

His œuvre of approximately 90 songs written in Cracow-Kazimierz, Łagiewniki, and Podgórze, takes its subject matter from nearly all the facets of the experience of the Polish Jews during the first four decades of

Mordechai Gebirtig (1877–1942)

the 20th century. While he himself did not actively seek fame, his songs spread throughout the Yiddish-speaking world, from Poland to Argentina (→ Buenos Aires). The author/composer often remained unknown; they were sung, and sometimes also published, as anonymous folk songs without a name.

3. The interwar years in Cracow

Gebirtig's biography was marked by the Jewish culture of → Cracow, where a mood of intellectual renewal reigned at the beginning of the 20th century. Besides socialist groups, followers of various Zionist tendencies competed with one another, and there were many Jewish press (→ Haynt), education, and cultural activities. Literature and theatre evenings organized by the Jewish labor movement stimulated Gebirtig's interest in secular Yiddish literature. He joined professional actors as an amateur in the Yiddish theatre troupe *Bildung*. From 1918 onward, he attended a circle of artists and intellectuals who regularly met in the house of Mordechai Erlich, a member of the Cracow → *Bund*, to exchange ideas and discuss political issues. Gebirtig's contribution consisted of new songs focusing on poverty, discrimination, and social inequality. Some of them were published in 1920 in a small volume entitled *Folkstimlekh* (In the folk style). The first time one of Gebirtig's poems was printed was in the organ of the Jewish social democratic party of Galicia *Der sotsial demokrat* (The social democrat) in 1905. It is called *Der general shtrayk* (The general strike) and describes the aspirations and struggles of a socially, economically, and politically oppressed segment of the population.

As the situation of the Jewish population in Poland deteriorated due to the economic crisis and the growing antisemitism during the interwar years, the topics Gebirtig emphasized in his songs shifted as well. Rather than, as before, sketching cheerful as well as melancholy images of everyday life in Kazimierz, which recalled the literary worlds of authors like Sholem Aleichem (→ Tevye), Isaak Leib Peretz (→ Bontshe), and Sholem Asch (→ Motke), he now focused on the great emigration movements and his personal experience as a paramedic during the First World War. His songs addressed topics such as the tragedy of all those Jews who regarded it as their highest achievement of assimilation to fight for their homeland (*Krigsinvalid*; War invalid), the drama of those who could not maintain a livelihood through work because of discrimination (*An arbetlozer*; An unemployed man), or the sometimes appalling conditions of the working environment (*In fabrik*; In the factory). In Gebirtig's songs, the attention focuses on outcasts and the hapless, without passing judgment or becoming sentimental. This is borne out by songs such as *Di gefalene* (The fallen woman) or *Avreml, der marvikher* (Avreml, the pickpocket). They tell the stories of a young prostitute and a small-time crook, whose social decline could have been prevented if they had not spent their childhood and adolescence in conditions of existential hardship.

Whether in the form of a lullaby or the traditional marriage and love song, Gebirtig's texts process the social borderline experiences of Jewish life in early 20th-century Poland. This was the time of new secular folk songs (→ Folk Music), many of them charged with social criticism, not tied to anonymous authorship and the traditional association with particular situations anymore. Gebirtig's texts speak in at least two voices. On the one hand they speak of religious and cultural tradition, while on the other insistently pointing out the dangers to it. The verses of another lullaby, *Kleyner yosem* (Little orphan), refer to a desperate situation. The singer asks the crying child to save its tears for the *tsores* (troubles) awaiting it in later life, recalling the book of Isaiah (38:5): seeing the tears of Hezekiah when he feels death approaching, the prophet promises the King of Judah 15 more years to live. In Gebirtig's song, however, the tears do not express the promise of life but the mother and child wishing for eternal sleep.

Gebirtig's poetry employs formulae and imagery transmitted from one generation to the next; not, however, in order to maintain their actuality but rather in order to determine their validity on the basis of contemporary experiences. Embodying the knowledge of the cultural difference that meant discrimination and was closely tied to social hardship, his texts indicate the threat to Jewish life in Poland even before the antisemitism that had taken root there at the end of the 19th century transformed into the National Socialist politics of extermination (→ Madagascar Plan). While Polish antisemitism was comparatively moderate under Marshal Piłsudski, the mood deteriorated considerably after his death. Under the Rydz-Śmigły regime, antisemitism became official policy. Gebirtig's best-known poetic reaction to this situation is the song → *S'brent* (1938; It is burning), which became the anthem of the Jewish resistance.

4. German occupation and ghetto

The texts composed between 1939 and 1942, most of them surviving without melodies, reflect the violent turning point in the lives of the Cracow Jews. *Erev yom kiper* (The eve of Yom Kippur) written in November 1939, for instance, commemorates the persecutions in Spain at the turn of the 15th century when thousands of Jews were forcibly baptized and could only practice their faith in secret (→ Conversos), contrasting it with the violence the Jews suffered at the time, which had never before been seen on such a scale. *Blayb gezund mir Kroke* (Keep well, Cracow) evokes the centuries-long history of the Jews in Cracow that appears to have come to an abrupt end. *In geto* (In the ghetto), written in May 1942, is an allegory of the biblical exodus, with the wanderings in the desert not leading the downtrodden people into freedom but continuing endlessly through sleepless nights. In the same month, only a few weeks before his death, Gebirtig handed the manuscripts he had written since the beginning of the German occupation to the family of his friend Julius Hoffmann, to whom he had already entrusted collections of songs in the past. Salvaged after the war, the material is now in the Moreshet Archive in Israel and at the → YIVO in New York.

5. Reception

During Gebirtig's lifetime, his songs were popular not only in everyday use. They were sung to accompany tableaux vivants and during recitals, performed on *kleynkunst* (little art) stages in → Warsaw, → Łódź, and → Vilna. They were adopted into the 1923 operetta *Di rumenishe khasene* (The Romanian wedding) by Moshe Shor (libretto) and Peretz Sandler (score), which was exceedingly popular all over the Yiddish-speaking world. In the 1920s the actor Jacob Kalich secured the rights to *Kinderyorn* (Childhood years) and *Hulyet, hulyet kinderlekh* (Play, play, children), two of Gebirtig's best-known songs.

Since the end of the Second World War, Gebirtig's work has been seen as bearing poetical witness to a destroyed world. On the basis of the existing collections and salvaged manuscripts, new editions of *Mayne lider* as well as other anthologies were published in Poland, Israel, and the United States, among others. In 1992, the production *Der trubadur fun Galitsye* (The troubadour of Galicia; directed by Gołda Tencer) at the Ester-Rokhl Kaminska Yiddish State Theatre (→ Kaminski Theatre) was dedicated to the poet. New melodies are being created for poems transmitted without music, and the Gebirtig discography continues to grow.

Bibliography

Sources

[1] M. Gebirtig, Mayne lider [My songs], Cracow 1936. [2] M. Gebirtig, Mayn fayfele. Umbakante lider [My little flute. Unknown songs], Tel Aviv 1997.

Secondary literature

[3] I. Fater, Yidishe muzik in Poyln tsvishn bayde velt-milkhomes [Jewish Music in Poland during the Interbellum], Tel Aviv 1970. [4] N. Gross, Mordechaj Gebirtig. The Folk Song and the Cabaret Song, in: Polin. Studies in Polish Jewry 16 (2003), 107–117. [5] R. Rubin, Voices of a People. The Story of Yiddish Folksong, New York 1973. [6] G. Schneider (ed.), Mordechai Gebirtig. His Poetic and Musical Legacy, Westport 2000.

CHRISTINA PAREIGIS, BERLIN

Yekkes

Yekkes is the name given in Israel to Jews who grew up under the influence of German language and culture and who immigrated to Palestine during the 1930s. The term above all aims at a specific habitus – Yekkes were said to have been shaped to a noticeable degree by middle-class culture and by the "German" formal sense of order, and rather disinclined to learn Hebrew. The initially derogatory as well as ironic connotation of the term gradually acquired a more empathetic aspect as the Yekkes disappeared in the course of demographic development.

1. The term and its connotation
2. Re-evaluation
3. Yekkes and literature

1. The term and its connotation

In the years between the transfer of power to Hitler and the beginning of the Second World War, almost 70,000 German-speaking Jews from Germany, Austria, and Czechoslovakia emigrated into British Mandatory Palestine. They made up a significant portion, even if not the majority, of the more than 200,000 immigrants of the so-called Fifth → Aliyah of the 1930s, which, nevertheless, is often called the "German Aliyah." "Yekkes" became popular as the collective term for the "German" immigrants. The origin of the term, however, is ambiguous. According to one theory it is derived from the "Jacke" (jacket), the characteristic item of clothing worn by → middle-class men – supposedly the wearers did not wish to take off their jackets in Palestine even in great heat and during physical labor. In another interpretation, the word originates from the term "Jeck" which denotes the carnival fool in Cologne. Yet another theory regards the word as an acronym of the Hebrew phrase *yehudi kshe havana* (lit. "slow-witted Jew"), and thus as an allusion to the allegation that among the German-speaking Jews, the will to integrate linguistically and habitually into the → Yishuv was not very developed.

A public controversy around the assessment of the term erupted in 1979 on the occasion of the broadcast of the documentary *Ha-Yekim* (The Yekkes) on Israeli television, which made clear that the issue was not merely one of semantics but also of social self-understanding in Israel. Decades after the foundation of the state, Israeli historiography as well as the public discourse in Israel were dominated and shaped by immigrants from Eastern Europe and by those born (especially at the time of the foundation of the state) in the country, the so-called Sabras (→ Ashkenazim). Among them the view prevailed that Yekkes had moved to Palestine out of necessity rather than conviction. In support of this view, it was argued that at the beginning of the 20th century only a comparatively small fraction of German Jews had joined the Zionist movement (overlooking the temporary prominence of German Jews in the leadership of the organization). As early as 1933, the daily paper → *Davar* (Word), which had close ties to the Labor Party, patronizingly reported about the "Adolfs, Richards, Arthurs, Hermanns, Wilhelms, and Philipps" from Germany, who were aloof from everyone else in Palestine. In 1941 the rightist daily *Ha-Boker* (The Morning) called for the Yekkes, who were alleged to be unwilling to integrate, not to distance themselves from the ordinary people, but rather to share their joys and sorrows. Even before the foundation of the State of Israel, the Yekkes' lack of willingness to learn → Hebrew, the national language, was highly criticized. And the fact that some German Jews had succeeded in bringing part of their assets to Palestine (→ Haʻavarah Agreement) led to the view that all educated, middle-class Yekkes were

Café Mugrabi in Tel Aviv, 1935

wealthy. Characteristics considered to be typically German, such as obsession with order, excessive punctuality, pedantry, and a dogmatism were ascribed to them; their customs such as the almost holy hour of a post-meal nap were seen as peculiar and were mocked.

2. Re-evaluation

In the Israeli perception, "Yekke" was for a long time an ambivalent term, frequently used with contempt. Chief Justice Chaim Cohen, originally from Lübeck and thus a Yekke himself, countered this with his interpretation in 1979, stating that the term was in fact an expression of esteem or a fond form of address. This is the view that has meanwhile prevailed among the Israeli public. Among the factors contributing to this positive (re-)evaluation of the German-speaking immigrants were, not least, post-Zionist historiography and the growing self-confidence of the descendants of the German-speaking immigrants.

A number of studies has meanwhile documented the considerable contribution made by the Yekkes to the organization and development of Israel. Before the wave of immigration that was the result of Nazi rule, German-speaking immigrants founded several communal agricultural settlements (*kibbutzim*), among them Beit Zera; after 1933 also Hazore'a, Ma'ayan Tzvi, and Ramot Hashavim. Yekkes were pioneers in several branches of industry such as groceries (Assis, Strauss), textiles and cosmetics (Ata, Taya), cigarettes (Dubek), and pharmaceuticals (Teva, Zori), and contributed to the development of the hotel and banking sectors. They were furthermore involved in the improvement of medical care and the welfare system and played a significant role in the establishment of public administration and universities. Among the scholars who shaped the → Hebrew University were, among others, the philosopher and librarian

Shmu'el Hugo Bergmann from Prague (→ Brit Shalom), the Berlin-born → Kabbalah researcher Gershom Scholem, and the philosopher and pedagogue Ernst Simon also from Berlin. Pinchas Rosen (originally Felix Rosenblüth, from Berlin as well), held the position of the first Israeli minister of justice, and numerous lawyers and judges originally from Germany shaped the Israeli legal system. The jurist Siegfried Moses (→ Leo Baeck Institute) became the first Comptroller of the State of Israel in 1949. While the Yekkes found it difficult to prove themselves in the political establishment, journalism became one of their domains, for instance for Gershom Schocken, Asriel Carlebach, and Uri Avnery. Their contribution to the arts, in particular classical music, is also remarkable; many members of the → Palestine Orchestra, founded in 1936 and renamed the Israel Philharmonic Orchestra in 1948, came from Germany. The museum sector and the visual arts also included a disproportionately high number of Yekkes. Structures by Erich Mendelsohn (→ Einstein Tower), Leopold Krakauer, Richard Kaufmann, and others molded urban architecture. With a network comprising social and cultural institutions as well as self-help groups set up by the Association of Immigrants from Germany (*Hit'aḥdut Ole Germanyah*, established 1932), the Yekkes sought to support their integration into their new homeland. The first issue of the German-language *Mitteilungsblatt* was published in 1932; nowadays it appears as *MB Yakinton* in both Hebrew and German.

3. Yekkes and literature

Hardly any authors among the Yekkes were creatively involved with Hebrew literature. Two of the leading avant-gardists of Hebrew poetry, Yehuda Amichai and Nathan Zach, originally came from Germany but had already arrived in Palestine during their childhood. Integration attempts by

German-speaking authors such as Else Lasker-Schüler (→ [Das] Hebräerland) and Arnold Zweig, who were barely able to learn Hebrew, were mostly unsuccessful. The greatest difficulty German-speaking authors faced was their linguistic medium, as → German was perceived as the language of the tormentors and murderers. "I feel I am in the wrong place," theembittered Arnold Zweig wrote to Sigmund Freud (→ Psychoanalysis) from Haifa in 1936; soon after the end of the war, he returned to (East) Germany [3. 120]. While works (plays in particular) by Sammy Gronemann (→ Tohuwabohu), Max Brod, or Max Zweig were occasionally translated into Hebrew, the authors, for whom the national language became at best the language of everyday communication but never a literary language, remained overall unknown in the Yishuv and the State of Israel. "You can emigrate from a country, but not from your mother tongue," wrote the author Shalom Ben-Chorin [2. 33]. This sentence reveals the fate of German-speaking writers in Israel, among them Lola Landau, Jenny Aloni, Meir Faerber, and others who wrote virtually into a vacuum. While their hearts beat for the Zionist idea and for Israel, many were denied a way of expressing their thoughts and emotions in a language other than German. The readership of the authors writing in German was and still is much greater in the German-speaking world than in their own country. In Israel, immigrants from Eastern Europe rather than the Yekkes themselves, translated German literature into Hebrew and sometimes published it.

In the meantime, contemporary Hebrew literature has undertaken the task of presenting the success story of immigration into Palestine from different perspectives, of recognizing the myth of the melting pot as such, and of questioning the construct of an unequivocal Israeli affiliation. Representations of Yekkes consequently oscillate between the grotesque, empathy, and romanticization. Reflecting on his own experience, the Nobel laureate in literature, Samuel Joseph Agnon, described the world of the expatriate German-speaking academics in Jerusalem in his novel → *Shira* (1971; Eng. translation 1989). Their chronic alienation from Israeli reality is also reflected in, among others, Aharon Megged's novel *Haynts u-veno veha-ruaḥ ha-ra'ah* (1975, Heinz, his son, and the evil spirit), and in Amos Oz's short story *Ga'agu'im* (1975, Longings).

In literary representations at the hands of Israeli authors, the Yekke appears as the outsider *par excellence*. He is stigmatized by society or becomes estranged from it. As a consequence, the character is provided with recurring stereotypical topoi such as strict discipline and cantankerousness as well as passionate involvement in middle-class culture. Art music is often a metaphor for the Yekkes' situation of uprooted homelessness, for instance in Nathan Shaḥam 1987 novel *Revi'yat Rozendorf* ("The Rosendorf Quartet," 1994). The eponymous string quartet, whose members as well as the narrator are Yekkes, is a kind of microcosm of the immigrant society. The escape into chamber music, the most intimate form of classical music, indicates the refusal to join the collective mood and the failed attempt at mastering the Hebrew language as part of a new, Israeli belonging. Music as the universal language becomes "the home of the homeless." While the contrived Yekke of early Hebrew literature was a tragicomical figure, his characterization in later works is tinged with nostalgia, romanticization, or idealization, as for instance in Judith Katzir's short story *Schlafshtunde* (1990; "Schlaffstunde," 1992), in several works by Yoram Kaniuk, and in Abraham B. Yehoshua's *Molkho* (1987; "Five Seasons," 1989). Yoel Hoffmann's works are unique, with the imaginary Yekke taking shape by means of the way in which the language is employed. His 1988 novella *Ketskhen* ("Katschen & The Book of Joseph," 1998) describes the world of the Yekkes as seen through the eyes of a child learning to understand this world through language. His *Bernhart* (1989, "Bernhard," 1989) however, is the philosophical excursus of a fifty-year-old Yekke in which the private and idiosyncratic language of the eponymous character represents the partially conscious refusal to integrate.

Bibliography

Sources

[1] S. Y. Agnon, Shira, trans. by Z. Shapiro, New York 1989. [2] S. Ben-Chorin, Sprache als Heimat, in: S. Ben-Chorin, Germania Hebraica. Beiträge zum Verhältnis von Deutschen und Juden, Gerlingen 1982, 33–49. [3] E. L. Freud (ed.), The Letters of Sigmund Freud and Arnold Zweig, trans. by E. and W. Robson-Scott, New York 1970. [4] Y. Hoffmann, Bernhard, trans. by A. Treister, New York 1998. [5] Y. Hoffmann, Katschen, in: Katschen & The Book of Joseph, trans. by A. Treister and E. Levenston, New York 1998, 97–161. [6] A. B. Yehoshua, Five Seasons, trans. by H. Halkin, New York et al. 1989. [7] J. Katzir, Schlaffstunde, in: J. Katzir, Closing the Sea, trans. by B. Harshav, New York et al. 1992, 1–30. [8] A. Megged, Haynts u-veno veha-ruah ha-ra'ah [Heinz, His Son, and the Evil Spirit], Tel Aviv 1976. [9] A. Oz, The Hill of Evil Counsel, trans. by N. De Lange, London 1985. [10] N. Shaham, The Rosendorf Quartet, trans. by D. Bilu, New York 1991.

Secondary literature

[11] A. Feinberg, Abbild oder Zerrbild? Die Darstellung der Jeckes in der hebräischen Literatur, in: A. Feinberg (ed.), Moderne hebräische Literatur. Ein Handbuch, Munich 2005, 140–163. [12] Y. Gelber, Moledet hadashah [A New Homeland], Jerusalem 1990. [13] G. Greif et al. (eds.), Die Jeckes. Deutsche Juden aus Israel erzählen, Cologne/Weimar et al. 2000. [14] J. Schlör, Endlich im Gelobten Land? Deutsche Juden unterwegs in eine neue Heimat, Berlin 2003. [15] M. Zimmermann/Y. Hotam (eds.), Ben ha-Moladot: ha-Yekim bi-mehozotehem [Between two

Homelands. The Yekkes in their Districts of Settlement], Jerusalem 2006.

ANAT FEINBERG, HEIDELBERG

Yentl

Title character of Isaac Bashevis Singer's (1902–1991) short story *Yentl der yeshive bokher* published in Yiddish in 1963 and in English ("Yentl the Yeshiva Boy") the year before. It tells the story of a woman disguising herself as a man in order to gain entry to the male world of Torah studies. In his works, Singer, who had grown up in Poland, emigrated to the United States in 1935, and was awarded the Nobel Prize for Literature in 1978, discussed subjects and the crossing of boundaries such as the transition of the traditional Eastern European world into a modern world of licentiousness and indeterminate affiliation. The successful film *Yentl* (1983) with Barbra Streisand playing the title role, was based on the story of Yentl, to this day one of Singer's most controversial and well-known works.

1. Isaac Bashevis Singer
2. *Yentl*

1. Isaac Bashevis Singer

Isaac Bashevis Singer (Pol. Izaak Hersz Zynger) was born in 1902 as the fifth child of a religious family in Leoncin, Poland; two daughters born before him died early. From 1908 onward, the family lived in the Jewish quarter of → Warsaw, where his father Pinchas Menachem Singer had become a rabbi in Krochmalna Street. Singer received a traditional religious education. His childhood was influenced by the tensions between his parent's divergent religious orientations. While his father dedicated himself to → Hasidism and the Kabbalah (→ Mysticism), his mother Batsheva (Basheve) Zylberman had ties to the Mitnaggdim, who followed the Orthodox anti-Hasidic Gaon of → Vilna. At the age of twelve, Singer began to read works of world literature translated into → Yiddish and to distance himself from the previously dominant strict observance of Jewish ritual.

In order to escape the famine in German-occupied Warsaw, Singer's mother fled with her two youngest sons Isaac and Moishe to Biłgoraj near Lublin in 1917, where her brothers were rabbis, as their father had been before them. The traditional world of the Eastern European → shtetl Singer found there made a lasting impression on him that was to influence his future work: "In this world of old Jewishness I found a spiritual treasure trove. I had a chance to see our past as it really was. Time seemed to flow backwards. I lived Jewish history" [1. 290]. It was at this time in Biłgoraj that Singer first encountered Zionist ideas and members of the → Bund, although this had no influence on his later political convictions. With great enthusiasm, he read Yiddish authors such as Sholem Aleichem (→ Tevye), Mendele Moykher-Sforim (Sholem Y. Abramovitsh; → Fishke), Sholem Asch (→ Motke), and Ḥayim Naḥman Bialik (→ El ha-tsippor), discovered the classics of Russian and European literature like Tolstoy, Chekhov, Maupassant, and Strindberg, and was most impressed by Spinoza's work (→ Tractatus Theologico-Politicus).

Singer's considerably older siblings Esther Singer Kreitman (1891–1954) and Israel Joshua Singer (1893–1944), both of whom wrote Yiddish prose, also exerted a significant influence on Singer's further development. While Esther had agreed to an arranged marriage and left the family when Isaac was only ten years old, she struggled against the traditional gender roles and is, at least to a degree, the model for the short story *Yentl*. Isaac's brother Israel urged him to move to Warsaw in 1923, where he himself had recently returned from Kiev. He took

him in and introduced him to the literary life of the city by finding him employment as a proofreader with the journal *Litera-rishe bleter* (Literary pages). Two years later, Singer's first short story *Oyf der elter* (In old age) was published by the journal under the pseudonym Tse. In the same year, he began to write his literary texts under the *nom de plume* Bashevis Singer, or simply Bashevis, a reference to his mother's name but also in order to avoid being confused with his better-known brother Israel.

Over the course of the year 1933, his first Yiddish novel *Der sotn in Gorey* ("Satan in Goray," 1955) was published, which described the situation of the Jews after the → Cossack persecutions and the activities of the false messiah Sabbatai Zevi (→ Smyrna). The book appeared in instalments in the literary journal *Globus* published by Singer and his friend Aaron Zeitlin (Arn Tseytlin, 1898/1899–1973) in Warsaw. Two years later, Singer followed his brother to → New York. His common-law wife Runia Pontsch and their son Israel Zamir, who would later become a journalist in Israel, stayed in Warsaw at first and emigrated to Palestine via Russia in the late 1930s, as Singer did not succeed in bringing them to America. While his father had died in 1929 and Esther had moved to England in the meantime, his mother as well as his younger brother Moishe stayed in Poland. In 1939, they were deported from Stary Dzików by the National Socialists; both died in the course of the winter [6. xxii].

During his first ten years in the United States, Singer did not write works of literature but only → essays, reviews, and op-ed columns, most of which were published in the Yiddish daily paper → Forverts (The Forward) with which his brother had found employment. After marrying Alma Wassermann in 1940, he once again came to prominence as the author of literary publications when his two short stories *Di kleyne shusterlekh* ("The Little Shoemakers," 1957) and *Gimpel tam* ("Gimpel the Fool," 1953; → Schlemiel) appeared in 1945.

While Singer never wrote in → English himself, he learnt the language from the first English translation of his novel *Di fami-lye Moshkat* ("The Family Moskat," 1950), according to his own account. Only when Saul Bellow (→ America) translated *Gimpel tam* in 1953 did the Yiddish author Bashevis become the famous American Jewish author Singer. The publication of the English text in the journal for literature and culture *Parti-san Review* (→ City College; → Commentary) marked Singer's breakthrough as an author. There can be no doubt that it was the English translations of his works that made him world famous. Translations into other languages were nearly always based on these English versions, even if they differed considerably from the Yiddish original.

Singer was well-known for cooperating closely with his translators from 1950 until his death, often reworking and rewriting the → Yiddish stories. He followed a certain pattern: with regard to non-Jewish readers, he deleted Jewish religious terms or ensured they were not recognizable as such; he abridged long, frequently repetitive works that appeared in installments in the Yiddish press; he toned down or removed expressions that might possibly have given offence to non-Jewish readers: vernacular, slightly pejorative denotations such as *shik-ses* or *goyim* became simply "women" and "people." He deleted criticism of tenets of the Christian faith such as the immaculate conception.

When Singer was the first Yiddish author awarded the Nobel Prize in Literature in 1978 for his complete works, his texts had been published for over five decades, and he had undoubtedly become the voice of Yid-dish-speaking and Eastern European Jewry (→ Khurbn; → Yiddishland) in the eyes of the Jewish as well as the non-Jewish world after the → Holocaust. The Nobel Committee awarded him the prize "for his impassioned narrative art which, with roots in a Polish-Jewish cultural tradition, brings universal human conditions to life" [8. 163–165]. Until his death in 1991, Singer composed several hundred short stories and essays, the latter mainly under the names of Yitzhok Var-shavski and D. Segal, and at least ten Yiddish books; innumerable translations of his novels and short stories appeared in English and other languages.

His work is apolitical; he rejected left-wing politics as embraced by most of the Yiddish authors of his time and condemned the idea that → literature could or should be put at the service of social, political, or religious aims, as tendentious. Populated by the demons and characters of the old and new worlds, by traditional and rebellious Jews in prewar Poland and Holocaust survivors in America, his stories explore the possibilities of human agency in a culture whose history repudiated teleological assumptions. While many of his texts discuss promiscuity and transgression, Singer was a moralist who countered evil with good, sin with love, messianic desire with human requirements, and what he saw as modern chaos with Talmudic laws and ethical doctrine. He was not optimistic where the future of Yiddish was concerned, as it had lost its foundation in the traditional world, most of which had been destroyed from the inside by the forces of modernization and, more tragically, from the outside by forces intent on its annihilation.

2. *Yentl*

Yentl is the story of the eponymous young woman who disguises herself as a man and calls herself Anshel in order to study the → Talmud. This change of identity increasingly leads to complications when Yentl/Anshel falls in love with a man (Avigdor) who becomes friends with her but loves the woman (Hadass) whom Yentl/Anshel marries and subsequently leaves. The story exists in three versions: as a short story composed in → Yiddish, as an English → translation, and in the version of the film starring Barbra Streisand. The Yiddish original *Yentl, der yeshive-bokher* was published in 1963. The → English translation, completed, as usual, with Singer's cooperation, had already appeared the previous year. Singer himself adapted the short story for the stage in 1977, and later for the film, but Streisand rejected his script in 1983, replacing it with one more suited to the English-speaking audience in her opinion. The changes made to the text in the translation and the film version are very informative in the context of the respective target groups.

There are several differences between the published English and Yiddish versions, the most obvious of these being the Yiddish masculine pronouns for Anshel being changed into English feminine pronouns throughout. When Anshel, in the forlorn hope of becoming closer to Avigdor, decides to marry Hadass, both texts describe how troubled the character feels, being on the brink of performing an action considered a sin. The Yiddish text describes Anshel's state of mind as follows: "Er hot zikh [...] dermont az Avigdor hot im gerotn er zol vern a khosn mit der Hadassn [...]. S'hot im getriknt der dorsht un er iz yedes mol arop tsum vaser ton a trunk. Der shtern iz im geven heys [...]. In boykh hot im geklemt [...]. Er hot vi geshlosn a bund mit dem yotser-hare [...]" [2. 99]. The corresponding passage in English reads: "Only then did Anshel remember that it was Avigdor who had wanted her to marry Hadass [...]. Every few minutes she got up for a drink of water. Her throat was parched, her forehead burned. Her stomach throbbed. [...] It was as if she had sealed a pact with Satan" [4. 217]. The Yiddish masculine pronouns *er* and *im* (nominative and dative) become *she* and *her* throughout. The English reader is reminded that Yentl's transformation is incomplete, while the Yiddish version has Yentl as the man whose identity she hopes to assume.

Sexuality, too, is described differently in the two versions, with the Yiddish one considerably more drastic. Thus, the English text states that in the wedding night the union was "consummated" for "Anshel had found a way to deflower the bride" [4. 220]. The Yiddish text reads "Anshl hot gehat gefunen a fortl vi azoy ibertsuraysn bay Hadasn di bsulim" [2. 101]. A more precise translation would be: "Anshel had found a way in which to tear Hadass's maidenhead." The mutual attraction between Avigdor and Anshel, the complications arising from Hadass being attracted to a woman merely dressed as a man, and the love Anshel/Yentl feels for Avigdor as well as Hadass are also described more explicitly in the Yiddish version.

In Barbra Streisand's film version, the story underwent yet another noticeable transformation. All references to Yentl possibly being a man have disappeared; despite her clothing, no viewer can have any doubt as to the gender of the character played by Streisand. Instead of a torn hymen or a "consummated" marriage, the film only shows two innocent, tipsy young women, giggling girl friends who spill red wine over a sheet. Anshel does not move to a different town in order to study at a different yeshivah but transforms back into Yentl and sets off for → America, singing "Papa, can you hear me?" suggesting that the old world is being transferred to the new one. The Americanization of the story – like the similarly famous Americanization of Sholem Aleichem's → *Tevye* stories in the musical *Fiddler on the Roof* – claims that in spite of all the changes the move from Eastern Europe to America will entail, tradition will cross the ocean too.

Singer was outraged at the film and wrote an incisive, mocking review, asking: "What would Yentl have done in America? Worked in a sweatshop 12 hours a day [...]? Would she try to marry a salesman in New York, move to the Bronx or to Brooklyn, and rent an apartment with an ice box and a dumbwaiter?" [3]. In his criticism of the film, Singer pointed to the protagonist's desire to study, which she could fulfill rather more successfully in Poland or Lithuania than in the United States.

Singer's urge to question boundaries was born of an Eastern European world in which the distinctions between male and female, Jew and non-Jew, shtetl and city were clearer and more determining than was the case in America. By allowing Yentl to transform into Anshel in the Yiddish version, Singer gave her the power of decision over the path she was going to take and freedom from the affiliation imposed upon her by the outside world. And for Yentl, freedom means freedom within Judaism. Towards the end of the original story, Anshel reveals himself to Avigdor. He undresses in order to prove that he is a woman, but then rejects the expectations tied to the female sex, assuming the male identity once more. Anshel refuses to marry the man she/he loves in order to avoid the problems that would arise from marriage and replace the shared life devoted to studying. Anshel's transformation enables Avigdor and Hadass to get married, and, above all, it gives Yentl the freedom to continue living as Anshel. In characteristic fashion, Singer thus affirmed the character's desire of existing within Jewish tradition as well as his urge to break free from the limitations of the law (→ Halakhah) and customs (→ Minhag) tied to it.

The film, quite differently, showed the audiences of the 1980s a story rather less strikingly characterized by the desire to challenge individual boundaries of affiliation. Allowing Yentl to adopt different affiliations at will appears to have been regarded as too realistic and, consequently, threatening. The shift in American culture from the idea of the → melting pot to ethnic particularism also probably contributed to the film's insisting that affiliations cannot simply be exchanged: women remain women, and Jews remain Jews. Singer did not feel

this kind of desire when he wrote his story of crossing boundaries.

Bibliography

Sources

[1] I. B. Singer, In My Father's Court, New York 1967. [2] Y. Bashevis, Yentl der yeshiva-bokher [Yentl the Yeshiva Boy], in: Goldene keyt 46 (1963), 91–110. [3] I. B. Singer, I. B. Singer Talks to I. B. Singer about the Movie Yentl, in: New York Times, 29 January 1984. [4] I. B. Singer, Yentl the Yeshiva Boy. A Story, in: Commentary 34 (1962) 3, 213–224. [5] I. B. Singer, Jentl, der Talmudstudent, in: I. B. Singer, Jentl. Erzählungen, Munich 2002, 5–60. [6] G. Farrell, Isaac Bashevis Singer. Conversations, Jackson/London 1992.

Secondary literature

[7] H. Denman et al., Isaac Bashevis Singer. His Work and His World, Leiden/Boston 2002. [8] T. Frängsmyr/S. Allén (eds.), Nobel Lectures, Literature 1968–1980, Singapore 1993. [9] J. Hadda, Isaac Bashevis Singer. A Life, New York 1997. [10] D. N. Miller (ed.), Recovering the Canon. Essays on Isaac Bashevis Singer, Leiden/ Boston 1986. [11] A. Norich, Isaac Bashevis Singer in America. The Translation Problem, in: Judaism 44 (1995) 2, 208–218. [12] A. Norich, The Family Singer and the Autobiographical Imagination, in: Prooftexts. A Journal of Jewish Literary History 10 (1990), 91–107. [13] E. Pollett/L. Napolin, Yentl. A Play, New York 1977. [14] S. L. Wolitz (ed.), The Hidden Isaac Bashevis Singer, Austin 2001.

ANITA NORICH, ANN ARBOR

Yeshiva University

Founded in 1945, Yeshiva University is a leading academic institution of higher education for modern Orthodoxy in the United States, based in New York. Under the motto "Torah u-madda" (Torah and secular knowledge), the university, like its predecessor institutions dating back to the 19th century, has promoted a combination of Jewish scholarship and worldly knowledge through its curricula.

Yeshiva University's origins can be traced to two schools founded in New York towards the end of the 19th century. The Etz Chaim Yeshiva on the Lower East Side, founded in 1886, was a primary school aimed at boys from more traditionally-minded immigrant families from Eastern Europe. Modeled on the Eastern European ḥeder schools (→ Talmud Torah), the school provided pupils with an introduction to the basics of Judaism and → Hebrew, as well as → English lessons. The Rabbi Isaac Elchanan Theological Seminary (Yeshivat Rabbeinu Yitzchak Elchanan; RIETS), founded by Lithuanian rabbis in 1897, is regarded as one of the first modern high yeshivot in the United States that supplemented traditional → Talmud studies with rabbi ordination programs. The first graduates were ordained in 1906.

In endeavoring to modernize the curriculum of traditional Jewish educational institutions, both schools targeted Eastern European Jewish immigrants who immigrated via → New York in the hundreds of thousands and settled there from the 1880s onward. Most of these immigrants quickly became more liberal and secular. Some joined socialist or communist parties or trade unions. They found meaning and community in the newly emerging Jewish culture of → America with its more worldly outlook. Within a few decades, → Conservative Judaism had become the preferred trend among the children and grandchildren of Jewish immigrants, as it offered a more traditional alternative to → Reform Judaism. The majority of Eastern European immigrants remained moderately traditionalist and continued to attend → synagogues, particularly on the High Holidays. Very few of them, however, regarded themselves as

→ Orthodox, even though they encountered almost exclusively Jews in their Jewish districts. They worked on → Shabbat, for instance, or kept their shops open. Their foremost desire was to become genuine Americans and give their children a better future in a new homeland.

The founders of Etz Chaim Yeshiva and RIETS, who would later maintain close ties with the moderate Orthodox Union founded in 1898, continued this economic, social, and cultural reorientation. Yet, being traditionally-minded Eastern European immigrants, they distinguished themselves from the previously established educational institutions of the Sephardic Jews and those of German origin. One of these was the → Jewish Theological Seminary of America in New York, founded on the periphery of Conservative Judaism, which had a definitively traditional outlook and expanded its rabbinical training at the beginning of the 20th century. The founders of Etz Chaim Yeshiva and RIETS wished to establish a teaching institution that would more strongly preserve the characteristics of their old Eastern European home on the religious and cultural levels. In the style of German → neo-Orthodoxy, they endeavored to combine rabbinical and general university studies. While their modern outlook caused RIETS and the emerging university to be accused of heresy by members of the → ultra-Orthodox wing, such as Lithuanian Rabbi Elchanan Wassermann, they nevertheless also attracted numerous ultra-Orthodox students.

Etz Chaim Yeshiva and RIETS merged in 1915. Rabbi Bernard Revel from Lithuania was the first president of the new teaching institution until 1940. It was during his tenure that "Torah u-madda" – the combination of the traditional yeshivah education and an officially recognized academic college degree – was established. After the Talmudical Academy, a high school that prepared its students for attending college, was founded in 1916, Yeshiva College opened in 1928 on the new site of RIETS in Washington Heights. It was a college in the tradition of the liberal arts colleges in the United States. Four years later, the first graduates left the college with a bachelor's degree that enabled them to study law or medicine at a university.

Students of RIETS and Yeshiva College were required to study religious texts (*talmud torah*) before noon, while they were taught secular subjects (*madda*) in the afternoons and evenings. Jewish → history was another constant element of the curriculum. Unlike at secular colleges, studies followed the Jewish calendar (→ Course of the Year; → Time) and guaranteed observance of → Shabbat as well as Jewish holidays. In the 1930s, the institution also became a contact point for Jewish refugees from Germany, some of whom found teaching positions there. In 1954, the Stern College for Women (SCW) was founded, where Jewish women with an interest in tradition were able to pursue studies previously restricted to men only.

The → novel *The Chosen* (1967) by Chaim Potok provides insight into the atmosphere at RIETS in the 1940s; the author was ordained as a rabbi there. Among the Jewish students with liberal and socialist views were the historian Arthur A. Goren, who enrolled in the Teachers' Institute affiliated with RIETS in 1919, and the → Reform rabbi Dana E. Kaplan.

RIETS acquired its reputation as a famous center of Talmudic scholarship (→ Talmud) and moderate Jewish Orthodoxy in America under Rabbi Joseph Dov Soloveitchik (→ Halakhic Man), who succeeded his father Moses Soloveitchik as the director of the seminary (with the unofficial title of *rosh yeshivah*) in 1941. Many students expressed their esteem for Soloveitchik, the scion of a well-known Lithuanian rabbinical dynasty who held a Ph.D. in philosophy from Berlin University, by calling him *The Rav* (the rabbi). His works, for instance *The Halakhic Man* (1944), gave expression to the values

and objectives of RIETS and Yeshiva University. Soloveitchik also expected Jews not only to observe the religious commandments out of conviction and be knowledgeable in Jewish scripture but also to be at home in the surrounding culture. He ordained hundreds of Orthodox rabbis who went on to occupy influential positions in the American Jewish community. He and other scholars taught the Talmud also in → Yiddish in the → rabbinical seminary which prompted many students to develop an interest in this language.

In 1944, Rabbi Samuel Belkin, an expert in the → Halakhah and the Hellenistic era, took over the post of president of RIETS and Yeshiva College. Both institutions benefited from the expansion of higher education after the end of the Second World War that the 1944 G. I. Bill had precipitated. They also profited from the universal economic boom, which allowed American Jews to prioritize education (→ Bildung). After Belkin succeeded in having the college classified as a university in 1945, it was able to offer master's degree programs and award doctoral degrees.

By introducing new subjects and study programs in the following years, Yeshiva University acquired an international reputation as an important private research university. Among its most renowned institutes were the Albert Einstein College of Medicine, opened in 1955, and the Benjamin N. Cardozo School of Law, established in 1976, which supported a number of institutions and public information centers. The latter became particularly well-known for its Innocence Project in 1992. This project helps wrongfully convicted persons through their appeal process to combat miscarriages of justice.

In order to gain wider recognition among Jews who did not follow Jewish tradition, as well as among the non-Jewish population, and to present itself as an open research institution in line with the pluralistic civil society, the university named many departments after prominent secular Jews. In addition, Yeshiva College and University awarded honorary doctorates to numerous prominent individuals from the political, cultural, and scientific-academic realms, among them Albert Einstein (1934; → Theory of Relativity), Supreme Court Justice Benjamin N. Cardozo (1935), President Lyndon B. Johnson (1961), and Israeli Prime Minister Golda Meir (1973). The Zionist idea, which spread at the university not least through Soloveitchik's influence, prompted the university to honor important figures from Israeli cultural life as well, among them Samuel Joseph Agnon (1967; → Shira), who adhered to religious tradition. Since the 1960s, in particular, numerous graduates have emigrated to Israel or spent long periods there.

Yeshiva University's further development in the second half of the 20th century was supported primarily by Orthodox businessmen from the well-to-do American middle class, who sponsored numerous programs and projects. While non-Orthodox Jews also supported Jewish higher education establishments, they tended to sponsor secular universities, such as → Brandeis University.

As employment structures grew more academic, the work week was shortened to five days, and America became more suburban (→ Levittown) in the second half of the 20th century, the Jewish life-world there underwent a profound transformation. Whereas American Jews took an increasingly flexible approach to the Halakhah in their everyday lives, the degree of religious observance increased at Yeshiva University beginning in the 1960s. Women, for instance, tended to cover their heads more and more; the women's movement, which was influential in American → Reform Judaism, never took root at the university. In view of the rise of the *ba'al teshuvah* movement (→ Teshuvah), the university introduced a third focus of study in the 1980s: alongside "Torah u-madda," a specific program of study addressed Jews who had grown up in non-Orthodox surroundings and had had a secular education but now wished to return (*teshuvah*; repentance) to Jewish tradition.

With the rise of Jewish Studies at American universities from the 1990s onward, Yeshiva University and other traditional Jewish institutions of higher education gradually became less important. Consequently, Orthodox students no longer necessarily feel compelled to study at Yeshiva University.

Bibliography

[1] J. S. Gurock, The Men and Women of Yeshiva. Higher Education, Orthodoxy, and American Judaism, New York 1988. [2] J. S. Gurock, Orthodox Jews in America, Bloomington 2009. [3] S. C. Heilman/S. M. Cohen, Cosmopolitans and Parochials. Modern Orthodox Jews in America, Chicago 1989.

YAAKOV ARIEL, CHAPEL HILL, NC

Yiddish

Yiddish is the historical vernacular of the Ashkenazi Jews, as well as one of their literary languages. The emergence and development of Yiddish are closely linked to the Jewish religion as well as the culture and history of → Ashkenaz. In the late Middle Ages and the early modern era, the region in which Yiddish was spoken as a minority language expanded from southern Germany across large parts of Europe, and from the late 19th century onward onto other continents too. In some countries, processes of linguistic acculturation and assimilation began at different times, leading to Yiddish being superseded. In the German language area this process took place mainly during the 19th century; in other parts of Europe it did not occur until the 20th century. However, there are individual linguistic enclaves in which Yiddish flourishes in a way that guarantees its continued existence in the 21st century as well.

1. Introduction
2. Diglossia
3. Language history
4. Manuscripts and printed texts
5. Decline in the West and flourishing in the East
6. Expansion in the wake of migration and linguistic acculturation
7. Modern Yiddish culture
8. Between language change and revival

1. Introduction

Yiddish is a West Germanic language that emerged as a result of the intensive contacts between a variety of languages among Ashkenazi Jews, and it has continued to develop to a significant degree under the influence of such linguistic contacts. The main contact languages in the history of Yiddish were → Hebrew and → Aramaic, Middle High German and Early New High German dialects, later New High → German, Old Czech, → Polish, Belarusian, Ukrainian, and → Russian. During the first centuries of Ashkenazi Jewry, Romance languages brought from countries of origin were also important. Nowadays the main influences on Yiddish are Modern Hebrew and → English. The Jewish religion and lessons in the traditional school, the ḥeder (Yidd. *kheyder*; → Talmud Torah), where Hebrew and Aramaic texts were translated word for word, also exerted a decisive influence on the language.

Yiddish has always been written in Hebrew characters. The words of the Hebrew-Aramaic component retain the orthography of these languages in Yiddish too. Elements from other contact languages are represented by Hebrew characters that have been adapted to render vowels and diphthongs via certain letters and letter combinations.

2. Diglossia

The linguistic situation of the Jews in → Ashkenaz was characterized by internal and external multilingualism until they acculturated linguistically to the majority or national languages of their surrounding societies. Languages of their internal multilingualism (internal diglossia) were Hebrew cross reference missing and → Aramaic as well as hybrid forms of these traditional standard languages of Judaism, on the one hand, and Yiddish, on the other. Hebrew and Aramaic were used nearly exclusively in their written forms, especially for religious worship, while Yiddish was the vernacular and oral language used in lessons. In its written form, Yiddish was used in the Middle Ages and the early modern era mainly in → Bible translations, edifying texts, handbooks, correspondence, and popular fiction. Yiddish had a lower status although its function overlapped with that of Hebrew and Aramaic. Yiddish was not a subject taught at school.

The languages of the Jews' external multilingualism (external diglossia) changed over the centuries. Until the modern era, contact with non-Jews took place mainly orally. In premodern Germany, contact languages were Middle High German and later Early New High German dialects. In the countries of Eastern Europe, where Ashkenazi Jews settled from the High Middle Ages onward, the most important new contact languages to exert great influence on the further development of Yiddish were → Polish, Belarusian, and Ukrainian. In the 19th and 20th centuries, → Russian and → German became important contact languages, as well as the languages of the new countries of emigration (such as English and Spanish).

3. Language history

During its formation phase, Yiddish as a language was still clearly characterized by the various High German dialects of its environment. In the course of the migrations of the late Middle Ages, these influences were evened out. The modern system of Yiddish dialects emerged in the early modern era.

The main dialect groups are East and West Yiddish (the latter died out in the 20th century). West Yiddish dialects were mainly spoken in the German language area, whereas East Yiddish ones were primarily spoken in the Polish-Lithuanian Commonwealth, including Belarus and Ukraine. The two dialect groups can be distinguished according to the primary stress vowel, some grammatical constructions, and a series of keywords, for example, West Yiddish *ete* and East Yiddish *tate* (father); West Yiddish *harle* and East Yiddish *zeyde* (grandfather); West Yiddish *tfile* (Hebr. *tefillah*; prayer) and East Yiddish *sider* (Hebr. *siddur*; prayer book).

Yiddish was not perceived as an independent language from the beginning. The earliest documentary evidence of the language used by Ashkenazi Jews, however, shows early stages of present-day Yiddish that allow us to trace the lines of linguistic-historical development to the present. Thus, Yiddish studies use the term "Yiddish" for all early stages of present-day Yiddish without denying its loose links to Middle High German dialects. In the early centuries, the language was also called, among other things, *taytsh* (Deutsch, Germanic language, Yiddish), *leshoneynu* (our language), or *loshn Ashkenaz* (the language of Ashkenaz, Yiddish, German). The name *yidish* (Yiddish, Jewish) spread from the 18th century onward. As late as the 20th century, we also find "Jüdisch-Deutsch" (Jewish German), "Judendeutsch" (Jews' German), and "Jargon" (Yidd. *zhargon*). The differences between East and West Yiddish are occasionally exaggerated for ideological reasons, such as when "Jüdischdeutsch" is used to denote West Yiddish while "Yiddish" indicates East Yiddish. Calling West Yiddish "Jüdischdeutsch" is terminologically confusing because, in the past, this terms was also used to describe High German with some Yiddish elements or a Yiddish accent, or German written in Hebrew letters, for instance, by the Jewish Lumière Isaac Euchel (→ Ha-Me'assef). From the point of view of Yiddish linguistics, it makes sense to subsume both dialect groups under the term "Yiddish."

The division into three linguistic stages made by the philologist Max Weinreich is valid to this day: Old Yiddish (ca. 1250 – ca. 1500), Middle Yiddish (ca. 1500 – ca. 1750) and Modern Yiddish (since ca. 1750). During the Middle Yiddish period, book → printing led to the emergence and spread of a transregional written language influenced by West Yiddish. From 1750 onward, a new transregional literary and printed language emerged on the basis of East Yiddish. This language developed further into Modern Standard Yiddish during the 20th century. West Yiddish disappeared during this time.

4. Manuscripts and printed texts

As all Ashkenazi Jews who had learned the Hebrew alphabet were able to read Yiddish (not necessarily, however, Hebrew and Aramaic), the language was used for practical concerns and for popular fiction. The earliest surviving documented instances of the language date from the 13th century. The oldest manuscript (the "Cambridge Codex," 1382) contains texts of Jewish edifying literature as well as a secular epic, the *Dukus Horant*, which is part of the Middle High German Kudrun cycle. Broader transmission of Yiddish texts began in the 15th century, with book → printing gaining importance from 1534 onward. The oldest printed Yiddish text is part of a Haggadah (→ Course of the Year): *Almekhtiker got* (Almighty God; Prague 1526) is one of the three Yiddish songs traditionally sung at the conclusion of the Seder meal during Pesaḥ. The oldest printed book in Yiddish is the Hebrew-Yiddish Bible dictionary *Mirkeves ha-Mishne* (The second riding carriage; also *Seyfer shel Reb Anshel*, The book of Master Anshel) printed in → Cracow in 1534, which contains a considerable Yiddish section. The earliest places Yiddish books are known to have been printed are Prague, Cracow, Isny, Augsburg, Constance, Ichenhausen, → Venice, Zurich, and Sabbioneta. Towards the end of the 16th century, Yiddish books were also printed in Basel, Mantua, Cremona, Freiburg, and Verona. In the 17th century, Yiddish book printing vanished from Italy, and instead Frankfurt am Main, Lublin, Amsterdam, Dyhernfurth (today Brzeg Dolny), Wilhermsdorf, and Hanau gained importance in this field. The number of places where Yiddish books were printed grew significantly in the 18th century – above all, in Germany – although the majority of the readership lived in Eastern Europe.

Printed Yiddish texts of the early modern era are mainly those related to religious edification and popular fiction. Printing allowed works to be circulated much more widely, some of which had been passed down for generations only in manuscript form. Among these texts were aids to Bible comprehension in the form of translations and epic poetry (→ Bible Translation), tales (for instance, the collection *Mayse-Bukh*, first printed in Basel in 1602), fables (for instance, *Kü-Bukh*, Verona 1595; slightly revised as *Seyfer Mesholim*, Frankfurt am Main 1697), translations of popular Hebrew works – often adapted for a less educated readership – but also of popular reading material from the surrounding Christian society, such as *Till Eulenspiegel* and *Die Schildbürger*. The largest part of Yiddish book production was dedicated to religious customs, such as Yiddish prayers or supplications (→ Tkhines). The most popular work of older literature is → *Tsene-rene*, a homiletic biblical paraphrase by Jacob ben Isaac Ashkenazi of Janów. Until the second half of the 19th century, manuscripts remained important alongside printed books in the circulation of texts; thus, for instance, → *purim-shpiln* – comedies and other stage plays performed on the occasion of Purim – were mainly transmitted in manuscript form, as were the memoirs of the Hamburg female merchant Glikl (Glückel von Hameln; → Zikhroynes).

5. Decline in the West and flourishing in the East

In the 18th century, the linguistic circumstances of the Ashkenazi Jews began to change in Central and Western Europe. In places where a class emerged that sought to assimilate with the European bourgeoisie, the traditional internal diglossia vanished as the Jews began to speak the national languages among themselves too. The linguistic transition from Yiddish to → German and other languages followed a variety of different paths. West Yiddish began to decline in the late 18th century. While the ideas of the → Haskalah were not the cause of the language changes, its followers were determined Jewish champions of replacing Yiddish with the respective official languages.

A new transregional written language based on East Yiddish dialects emerged in the late 18th century. Adherents of new trends of → Hasidism and of the Jewish Enlightenment in Eastern Europe (→ Maskilim) used Yiddish for their (propaganda) objectives – for Hasidism, Yiddish was used, above all, in sermons and narratives, whereas it was used for the Enlightenment in general educational texts and anti-Hasidic satires.

In the course of the 19th century, the readership of modern Yiddish literature increased. Ayzik Meyer Dik became the first professional Yiddish author. Other writers used the first Yiddish journal *Kol-Mevaser* (1862–1872; Voice of the Preacher), originally a supplement of the Hebrew weekly newspaper *Ha-Melits* (The Advocate), as their platform. This was where Isaac Joel

Linetzky's anti-Hasidic serialized novel *Dos poylishe yingl* (1867; The Polish boy) and Shalom Jacob Abramovitch's Yiddish debut novel *Dos kleyne mentshele* (1864; The little man) appeared. He wrote most of his works under the pseudonym of the literary character Mendele Moykher-Sforim (→ Fishke) and is regarded as one of the three classic authors of modern Yiddish literature, together with Sholem Aleichem (Shalom Rabinovitch; → Tevye) and I. L. Peretz (→ Bontshe). Under their influence, many writers turned to the Yiddish language, among them Avrom Reyzen (Abraham Reisen) and Shalom Asch (→ Motke).

6. Expansion in the wake of migration and linguistic acculturation

As a result of extensive emigration in the 19th and early 20th centuries, Yiddish spread beyond Europe too, above all in North America, but also in South America (→ Buenos Aires), South Africa, Australia, and Palestine (later Israel), as well as European countries in which Yiddish was either hardly spoken anymore or not at all. This led to linguistic enclaves, some of which acquired great importance, especially in the United States (→ America). Besides Warsaw and → Vilna, New York was one of the most important Yiddish cultural centers. The Yiddish press (→ Forverts; → Groshnbibliotek; → Haynt), Yiddish theatre (→ Pomul Verde; → Second Avenue), and Yiddish film (→ Yiddishland) flourished in the United States during the interwar years; Yiddish radio programs were also broadcast there.

The late 19th century saw a linguistic shift to the majority languages in Eastern Europe and the new immigration countries. On the other hand, there were also attempts to raise the status of Yiddish. Jewish intellectuals, who regarded Ashkenazi Jewry as a cultural and linguistic community and not primarily as a religious one, demanded a right to the free development of their own culture and mother tongue, and even cultural autonomy for Ashkenazi Jews with Yiddish as the national language. "Yiddishists" wishing to transform Yiddish into the national language of the Jews encountered "Hebraists" who were trying to revive Hebrew, and the two camps usually had no hope of reaching an agreement. In 1905, the *Algemeyne Yidishe Arbeter Bund in Lite, Poyln un Rusland* (General Jewish Labor Bund in Lithuania, Poland, and Russia; → Bund) adopted the demand for national and cultural autonomy including Yiddish as the national language as part of the party's manifesto. Books setting out standards for orthography, grammar, vocabulary, and other linguistic issues were created. The first → Czernowitz Language Conference in 1908 had great symbolic significance. It was held on the initiative of the assimilated lawyer Nathan Birnbaum from Vienna. The invitation was signed by prominent Yiddishists and authors from Europe and America, among them the theorist of socialist Diaspora nationalism Chaim Zhitlowsky.

7. Modern Yiddish culture

The interwar period is considered the heyday of modern Yiddish culture. The protection of minority rights required of the newly founded or extended states of eastern Central Europe after the Paris Peace Conference of 1919/1920 allowed open and legal political activity in Yiddish. Political parties that used the language were the Socialist-Yiddishist Bund, the international movement *Agudat Yisra'el* (Union of Israel; → Bais Ya'akov), which operated with traditional internal diglossia, and the middle-class *Yidishe folkspartey* in Poland, but also the left wing of the Zionist Socialist workers' party *Po'ale Tsiyon*. Modern secular and religious schools were founded in which Yiddish was one of the languages of instruction.

The Yiddish press landscape of the interwar years was colorful and diverse. Writers used established literary forms or turned to avant-garde trends (such as *Khalyastre*, → *Di Yunge*, → *Inzikh*, or → *Yung-yidish*). Private scholars and cultural activists increasingly published research on Jewish history and the Yiddish language in Yiddish. In 1925, the *Yidisher Visnshaftlekher Institut* (→ YIVO) was founded.

Thanks to sheet music and records, songs from Yiddish theatres and cabaret were circulated widely; the Yiddish theatre on New York's → Second Avenue, the "Yiddish Broadway," had international influence. Modern art songs such as *Mayn shtetele Belts* (My little town of Bălți) became commonplace in this time, as did the songs by Mark Warshawsky, the author of *Afn pripetshik* (On the hearth), and Mordechai Gebirtig (→ Yankele), which soon acquired the status of popular songs. New, sophisticated dramas like Jacob Gordin's → *Sibirya* were staged in many places. The production of Yiddish films for an international audience flourished in the United States and in Eastern Europe, for instance, *Onkl Mozes* ("Uncle Moses," United States 1932) on the basis of the novel by Shalom Asch, or *Der dibek* (→ "The Dybbuk," Poland 1937) on the basis of the drama by S. An-Ski (Shloyme Zaynvl Rapoport).

8. Between language change and revival

In Palestine, Yiddish was the most widely spoken Jewish language in the 1920s, but once Hebrew had been chosen as the national language (→ Language Conflict), a rapid language change took place, in spite of a number of waves of immigration (→ Aliyah). At the beginning of the 1920s, the establishment of Yiddish socialist culture in the Soviet style ("national in form and socialist in content") was decreed in the Soviet Union in accordance with the remit of the official minority policy. Literature and language usage were subject to strict regulations (→ GosET). The Soviet leadership founded an autonomous Jewish (Yiddish-speaking) region in → Birobidzhan; however, the endeavors to transform the region on the Chinese border, far away from the traditional Jewish settlement area, into a cultural and social center of Soviet Jewry failed. In the course of the repression under Stalin, Yiddish-speaking schools, theatres, and other institutions all over the Soviet Union were closed; newspapers were also discontinued. From 1948 onward, Yiddish cultural activists were arrested and condemned to death or lengthy imprisonment (→ Cosmopolitans) in secret trials, among them the writers David Bergelson and Itsik Fefer. As a result of the → Shoah, the persecution and extermination of the Jews in Europe, as well as global acculturation, the number of Yiddish speakers had fallen from around twelve million before the Second World War to just a few million in the 1950s. The number and extent of Jewish linguistic enclaves fell concomitantly with the diminishing contacts between traditionalist (especially Hasidic) and secular speakers of Yiddish.

Under the influence of new contact languages, Yiddish continues to develop today. In traditional Orthodox circles, which constitute the majority of Yiddish speakers, there is hardly any language cultivation and no systematic instruction in the mother tongue. Secular and modern Orthodox circles (for instance, in Canada, Mexico, Australia, and the United States) employ the modern standard language. Yiddish writers and poets like Abraham Sutzkever continued to produce works of high quality even after the war, but their number and that of their readership fell steadily. The interest in Yiddish among non-native speakers, however, has increased in recent decades because of a growing interest in Jewish culture in general and, not least, thanks to the Nobel Prize for Literature being awarded to Isaac Bashevis Singer in 1978. Since then, there has been an expansion of academic research of Yiddish and Yiddish → literature.

Bibliography

[1] M. Aptroot/R. Gruschka, Jiddisch. Geschichte und Kultur einer Weltsprache, Munich 2010. [2] J. Baumgarten, Introduction to Old Yiddish Literature, ed. by J. C. Frakes, Oxford 2005. [3] S. A. Birnbaum, Die jiddische Sprache. Ein kurzer Überblick und Texte aus acht Jahrhunderten, Hamburg 1974. [4] S. A. Birnbaum, Yiddish. A Survey and a Grammar, Toronto 1979. [5] G. Estraikh, Soviet Yiddish. Language Planning and Linguistic Development, Oxford 1999. [6] D. E. Fishman, The Rise of Modern Yiddish Culture, Pittsburgh 2005. [7] J. A. Fishman, Yiddish. Turning to Life, Amsterdam 1991. [8] K. Frieden, Classic Yiddish Fiction. Abramovitsh, Sholem Aleichem, and Peretz, Albany 1995. [9] B. Harshav, The Meaning of Yiddish, Berkeley et al. 1990. [10] N. G. Jacobs, Yiddish. A Linguistic Introduction, Cambridge et al. 2005. [11] D. Katz, Zur Dialektologie des Jiddischen, in: W. Besch et al. (eds.), Dialektologie. Ein Handbuch zur deutschen und allgemeinen Dialektforschung, vol. 1, part 2, Berlin 1983, 1018–1041. [12] D. Katz, Words on Fire. The Unfinished Story of Yiddish, New York 2004. [13] S. Liptzin, A History of Yiddish Literature, Middle Village 1972. [14] D. Miron, A Traveler Disguised. The Rise of Modern Yiddish Fiction in the Nineteenth Century, Syracuse 1996. [15] K. B. Moss, Jewish Renaissance in the Russian Revolution, Cambridge (MA)/ London 2009. [16] N. Römer, Tradition und Akkulturation. Zum Sprachwandel der Juden in Deutschland zur Zeit der Haskalah, Münster/New York 1995. [17] D. Shneer, Yiddish and the Creation of Soviet Jewish Culture 1918–1930, Cambridge 2004. [18] B. Trachtenberg, The Revolutionary Roots of Modern Yiddish, 1903–1917, Syracuse 2008. [19] M. Weinreich, History of the Yiddish Language, New Haven 2008. [20] I. Zinberg, A History of Jewish Literature, Vol. 2: The Haskalah Movement in Russia, Cincinnati/New York 1978.

MARION APTROOT, DÜSSELDORF

Yiddishland

The term *Yiddishland* that emerged in Eastern Europe towards the end of the 19th century at first referred to a culturally construed space encompassing all Yiddish-speaking Jews. It defined itself above all through the Yiddish language, which was already declining at this time under the influences of modernization, secularization, and acculturation. *Yiddishland* experienced its heyday on the eve of the Second World War in the press, literature, theatre, and film in Eastern Europe and the United States. In the context of the desire to revive and redefine Yiddish culture that emerged after 1945, it developed into a global memorial space highly detached from → Yiddish as an everyday language.

1. Origins
2. Before the Second World War
3. Postvernacular *Yiddishland*

1. Origins

For the Jews of Eastern Europe, Yiddish continued to be the most important everyday language until the early 20th century in spite of their increasing orientation towards the official languages of their environment. By the eve of the Second World War, its native speakers still numbered ten million.

Represented in → literature and the press, Yiddish as the vernacular language advanced to become the *lingua franca* of the → Diaspora nationalists of Yiddishist orientation. They championed the preservation of the Jewish living environment of Eastern Europe but likewise the establishment of a modern Jewish nation. Unlike the Zionists (→ Basel) who worked towards the foundation of a Jewish state in Palestine, the representatives of Diaspora nationalism did not regard a dedicated territory as a prerequisite for the envisioned national rebirth. On the contrary, they regarded the usually criticized statelessness of the Jews (→ Citizenship) as a basis for the desired integration into the community of sovereign nations with equal rights. While the Zionists hoped that → Hebrew would be reborn as the everyday language, the Diaspora nationalists regarded Yiddish as the medium for expressing and supporting modern Yiddish national culture and the exchange between the Jewish middle and lower classes, especially in Eastern Europe [11. VIII, 21]. As the vernacular, it represented the link between national consciousness, cultural affiliation, and authenticity. After controversial discussions between representatives of Hebraism and Yiddishism, → Yiddish found recognition during the → Czernowitz Language Conference of 1908 not as *the* Jewish national language but as *one* of them. This was probably one reason why the confirmed Yiddishist Chaim Zhitlovsky, one of the initiators of the conference, considered the event a call to cultivate *Yiddishland* in retrospect [9. 81]; [12].

The idea of *Yiddishland* as an imaginary space formed by Yiddish – also called "Jargon" – goes back to the end of the 19th century. In 1888 Isaac Leib Peretz (→ Bontshe) chose the phrase *zhargon fun zhargonenland* (jargon of jargon-land) in a letter to Sholem Aleichem (→ Tevye) [18. 33]. In his 1913 essay *In a yidisher medine* (In a Yiddish/Jewish state), Zhitlovsky described the little Belarussian → shtetl of his childhood, Ushachy, as the model of life with Yiddish at its center:

> I spent my childhood years in a purely Jewish/Yiddish environment [*in a reyn yidisher sviv*]. Had I not known that, in theory, we Jews lived in diaspora, and had I been asked to characterize my life's experiences as they appeared at first glance, I would then have had a right to say that I live in a Jewish/Yiddish country [*a yidish land*]. [...] [We] did not live in exile among the Russians, but perhaps quite the opposite-that

> the Russians with whom we interacted lived in exile among us, in our own Jewish/Yiddish country [*in unzer eygn yidish land*]. (cited in [18. 36])

In order to emphasize the widespread perception of the Jews as a people without a country, Zhitlovsky used the word *yidish* to denote the language as well as the ethnic affiliation; this usage is not possible in → English, → German, or → Hebrew, due to the distinction between "Yiddish" and "Jewish" [18. 37]. He equated *Yiddishland* in a mythical discursive fashion with Eastern Europe. However, the question of where to locate it geographically, or whether it should be imagined beyond territorial boundaries, is the special challenge inherent in this concept.

In the 20th century, *Yiddishland* became conflated in two competing Jewish territorialization projects: Zionists as well as communists called on Eastern European and American Jews to support the "Yiddish land." While the former advertised their endeavors in Palestine in the supplement *Dos Yidishe Land* (The Yiddish/Jewish land) in the Zionist Warsaw daily paper → *Haynt* (Today), the latter sought to recruit participants for the project of a socialist Jewish state in Soviet → Birobidzhan with the slogan *Tsu a yidish land* (To a Yiddish/Jewish land) [18. 37].

2. Before the Second World War

In the 1930s, the Eastern European Jews experienced a process of rapid acculturation that included the gradual adoption of the respective national languages and resulted in the decline of Yiddish. The proportion of Jews in the Soviet Union who indicated that → Yiddish was their mother tongue sank from approximately 70% in 1926 to barely 40% in 1939, not least as a consequence of the intensified Russification policy. In Poland, too, as the process of Polonization (→ Polish) gained momentum, Jews increasingly regarded Yiddish as outdated [11. 83–85]. In the United States, a center of Yiddish culture even after 1900 (→ America), the wish for assimilation and the desire to identify with modern American culture around the middle of the 20th century also precipitated a drop in the use of Yiddish.

Parallel to these developments, the term *Yiddishland* became detached from territorial ideas and increasingly denoted a globally existing Yiddish community. The Warsaw Yiddish cultural activist Yitskhok Grudberg wrote about the decline of Yiddish → Vienna: "The borders of Yiddishland are wide, perhaps wider than those of any other empire in the world" [4]. Even so, the point of reference of this dispersed community remained tied to Eastern Europe. On the occasion of the first international conference of → YIVO in 1935, one speaker described the institute – which was known especially for its Yiddish studies – as the "head office" and → Vilna as the capital of *Yiddishland*. In the Warsaw weekly paper *Literarishe bleter* (Literary pages), Yankev Botoshansky reported enthusiastically that the conference "represented and demonstrated 'Yiddishland,' which appeared, despite all crises and assaults, to be alive" [2]; [18. 40]. The historian Lucy S. Dawidowicz, a research fellow with YIVO, expressed criticism of the Yiddishist version of *Yiddishland*. She accused the institute of "[creating] an illusion [...] that there's a Jewish people which earns its daily bread in Yiddish and takes pleasure in using its own language for matters of mind and spirit. I know that it's only an illusion because the headlines in the daily papers belie it everyday" [3. 100f.].

A mystified, stereotypical image of the Eastern European → shtetl became the embodiment of the imaginary *Yiddishland*. In Jewish literature, the shtetl stood for a world delineated entirely by the presence of Jewishness in everyday life and the → course of the year, as well as by the Yiddish language, in contrast to the actual multilingualism of most Eastern European Jews. In this image, everything non-Jewish appeared irrelevant and foreign [16. 3f., 7].

The most comprehensive and fanciful expression of *Yiddishland* was through poetry, where iconic characters of Yiddish literature or Yiddish writers acted as inhabitants of this space. For example, Mina Bordo-Rivkin's poem "Yidish" describes the imaginary journey of the classic Yiddish writer Sholem Y. Abramovitsh (Mendele Moykher-Sforim; → Fishke) with a horse and cart through *Yiddishland* – an image drawn from his own literary creations [1]. Avrom Reyzen also emphasized the importance of the language as the "portable fatherland" and as constitutive of the idea of *Yiddishland* in a poem: "Peretz, Mendele, all the rest, / They're my home – my Yiddishland" [5. 264]; [18. 40].

As a location defined by language, *Yiddishland* enjoyed its heyday in the years before the Second World War. A significant contributing factor was the institutionalization of Yiddish culture linking Eastern European Jews in their homeland and abroad. This included newspapers and journals, publishing houses, → libraries, theatres, literary and cultural associations, schools, and academies [6. 84]. The main media were the Yiddish newspapers → *Haynt* and *Der moment* in Poland, which, by their own account, reached up to 100,000 readers, as well as → *Forverts* in the United States with up to 250,000 readers. In addition, ambitious projects emerged, such as the weekly journal *Literarishe bleter* (1924–1939), in the style of the Polish *Wiadomości Literackie* (Literary News), published by the *Kultur-Lige* (Culture League; → Czernowitz Language Conference). American Yiddish writers (→ America), such as Joseph Opatoshu and H. Leivick (→ Di Yunge; → Shmattes) also published their works with Yiddish publishing houses in Poland due to the high level of professionalism and low cost. Literary works by authors such as Sholem Y. Abramovitsh and Sholem Aleichem as well as translations into Yiddish encouraged the idea of a *Yiddishland* that existed beyond territory and religion [11. 87]; [14. 83]; [18. 40].

The idea of *Yiddishland* also spread thanks to Yiddish theatre (→ Kaminski Theatre) and Yiddish film. Besides popular cabaret and variety performances (→ Shmontses; → Vaudeville), Yiddish dramas and plays translated into Yiddish were performed (→ Sibirya). The stars of the Yiddish stage in America such as Boris Thomashefsky and Molly Picon (→ Second Avenue) toured Eastern Europe, while Eastern European artists such as the → Vilna troupe or Zygmunt Turkow toured the United States. Polish and American productions of Yiddish films, which reached wide audiences on both sides of the Atlantic in the late 1930s especially, recreated a temporary Yiddish nation-state every time they were shown [15. 5].

Journalism, literature, theatre, and film not only spread the illusion of a *Yiddishland* in the Eastern European mold, inhabited nearly exclusively by Yiddish-speaking Jews and offering an alternative sovereignty, as it were [19]; [10. 10, 14]. In Eastern Europe, in particular, this construct also provided an answer to growing nationalism and anti-semitism (→ Conspiracy), which posed a threat not only to the Yiddish language but also to the physical survival of the Jewish community as a whole [19].

On the eve of the Second World War, Yiddish writers and cultural activists were aware of the increasing decline of their language. In the discussion about the crisis, *Yiddishland* was one of the dominating terms during the First International Yiddish Culture Congress (*Ershter Alveltlekher Yidisher Kultur Kongres*) in Paris in 1937. Opatoshu defined it as a virtual-ideal territory that comprised the living environment of Ashkenazi Jewry (→ Ashkenazim). Zhitlovsky alluded to a metaphor of the British Empire, declaring that the sun never set on *Yiddishland* [8. 26, 30].

3. Postvernacular *Yiddishland*

The accelerated acculturation of the Jews, the abolition of Yiddish cultural institutions in the Soviet Union between 1936 and 1938, and, above all, the extermination of Jewish existence in the region during the → Holocaust destroyed the dream of an all-encompassing *Yiddishland* characterized by the → Yiddish language whose point of reference was Eastern Europe.

However, the concept lived on even after the Second World War, now denoting a memorial landscape. In this function, *Yiddishland* conveyed complex (re)constructions of the vanished Yiddish living environments, while the idea of the old *Yiddishland* was superseded by the construct of the → shtetl [17. 5]; [7]. The decline of Yiddish as the vernacular and means of communication also entailed a changed approach to the language as familiarity with it could no longer be presumed. Thus, in order to revive and represent *Yiddishland*, postvernacular Yiddish culture [18. 48] employed other forms, such as → music, theatre, and dance, that were not dependent on the language. → Klezmer, *yidish-vokhn* (Yiddish weeks), *shmues-krayzn* (debating societies), and even virtual shtetlekh allowed people to share in such an imaginary community. Yiddish itself transformed into a quasilect whose function was no longer everyday communication but the cultural-symbolic creation of a shared experience [13].

The new *Yiddishland* was the basis of Yiddishism without Yiddish: The language was no longer spoken but rather invoked [18. 53]. In this form, *Yiddishland* offered a fiction of Jewish "being among ourselves" to postmodern Jews in Israel and America. American Jewish self-understanding, as well as, above all, the renewed increase in Jewish immigration from Eastern Europe, supported this process. The growing interest in the Holocaust in North America and Europe encouraged performative as well as discursive *Yiddishland* practices, combined with the identification with victims and survivors. Yiddishism without Jews spread increasingly in Central Europe, especially in academic circles. Among → ultra-Orthodox speakers of Yiddish, nostalgically romanticizing ideas of *Yiddishland* as a realm of piety and pristine Judaism is widespread [20. 43–123]. In spite of all lines of continuity, postwar *Yiddishland* is characterized by a profound transformation of Yiddish and its significance for Jewish life beyond geographical, chronological, and cultural affiliations [18. 57f.].

Bibliography

Sources

[1] M. Bordo-Rivkin, Yidish, in: S. Rozhansky (ed.), Antologye. Yidish in lid [Anthology. Yiddish in Poetry], Buenos Aires 1967, 50. [2] Y. Botoshanski, A demonstratsye in der hoyptshtot fun Yidishland [A Demonstration in the Capital of Yiddishland], in: Literarishe bleter, 23. August 1935, 543. [3] L. Davidowicz, From That Place and Time. A Memoir, 1938–1947, New York 1991. [4] Y. Grudberg, An untergeyendike shtot in Yidishland [A Declining City in Yiddishland], in: Literarishe bleter, 7th January 1938, 26. [5] A. Reyzen, Di lider fun Avrom Reyzen [Poetry of Avrom Reyzen], New York 1951. [6] A. A. Roback, Di imperye yidish [The Empire of Yiddish], Mexico 1958. [7] G. Silvain/H. Minczeles, Yiddishland, Corte Madera 1999. [8] Yidisher Kultur Farband (ed.), Ershter alveltlekher yidisher kultur-kongres, Pariz 17–21 Sept. 1937, stenografisher barikht [First World Congress of Yiddish Culture, Paris 17.–21. Sept. 1935, Shorthand Report], Paris/New York 1937. [9] Yidisher Visnshaftlekher Institut (ed.), Di ershte yidishe shprakh-konferents. Barikhtn, dokumentn un opklangen fun der tshernovitser konferents 1908 [The First Conference on the Yiddish Language. Reports, Documents and Aftermath of the Czernowitz Conference 1908], Vilna 1931.

Secondary literature

[10] S. DeKoven Ezrahi, Booking Passage. Exile and Homecoming in the Modern Jewish Imagination, Berkeley/Los Angeles 2000. [11] D. E. Fishman, The Rise of Modern Yiddish Culture, Pittsburgh 2005. [12] J. A. Fishman, Attracting a Following to High-Culture Functions for a Language of Everyday Life. The Role of the Tshernovits Language Conference in the "Rise of Yiddish," in: International Journal of the Sociology of Language 24 (1980), 43–73. [13] L. Glinert, Language as Quasilect. Hebrew in Contemporary Anglo-Jewry, in: L. Glinert (ed.), Hebrew in Ashkenaz. A Language in Exile, Oxford 1973, 249–264. [14] B. Harshav, The Polyphony of Jewish Culture, Stanford 2007. [15] J. Hoberman, Bridge of Light. Yiddish Film between Two Worlds, Philadelphia 2010. [16] D. Miron, The Literary Image of the Shtetl, in: Jewish Social Studies 1 (1995) 3, 1–43. [17] D. Roskies, The Shtetl as Imagined Community, in: G. Estraikh/M. Krutikov (eds.), The Shtetl, Image and Reality. Papers of the Second Mendel Friedman International Conference on Yiddish, Oxford 2000, 4–22. [18] J. Shandler, Adventures in Yiddishland. Postvernacular Language and Culture, Berkeley 2006. [19] M. Silber, Narrowing the Borderland's "Third Space." Yiddish Cinema in Poland in the Late 1930s, in: Simon Dubnow Institute Yearbook 7 (2008), 229–251. [20] T. Soldat-Jaffe, Twenty-First-Century Yiddishism. Language, Identity and the New Jewish Studies, Portland 2012. [21] D. Weinberg, Between Tradition and Modernity. Haim Zhitlowski, Simon Dubnow, Ahad Ha-Am, and the Shaping of Modern Jewish Identity, London/New York 1996.

MARCOS SILBER, HAIFA

Yishuv

Term for the pre-statehood Jewish community in Palestine used since the end of the 19th century. The modern understanding of the Hebrew word *yishuv* differs from its classical meaning in rabbinic literature after acquiring a territorializing semantic component. Linguistically, as a verbal noun, it reflects the polysemy of the verb *yishev* while it also occurs widely as a generic term. In combination with the definite article, *yishuv* became a quasi-proper name, *ha-yishuv*, and a basic concept of the socio-political discourse in Israel.

1. Rabbinic and Medieval Hebrew
2. Modern Hebrew

1. Rabbinic and Medieval Hebrew

The word *yishuv* does not occur as a noun in the Bible. Verbs and other types of words with the triradical Hebrew root *Yud – Shin – Bet* are present in large numbers but are entirely derived from other verb stems than the *pi'el*, which was used for the verb form *yishev* and the later verbal noun *yishuv*. Thus, we find biblical forms of the *pa'al* stem (*yashav*) in the sense of "to sit (down)," "to abide," and "to inhabit," or of the *nif'al* stem translating as "to be inhabited" [6. 271f.]. A verb form in the *pi'el* is attested for only one passage in the Bible (Ezek 25:4, *yishvu* in the 3rd person plural), where it has the meaning of "to set up an encampment" [6. 372].

Rabbinic → Hebrew also employs the verb *yishev* for actions that involve placing an object in the correct location or sequence. Thus, for instance in the → Talmud *Yerushalmi* we read that "the builder who set the keystone is liable" (Shabbat 12,13c), and that a city planner must "set the city in advance" (Bava Batra 2,13b) to ensure the correct distance is kept between houses.

In the Midrash literature the verb *yishev* is used in the same way while its meaning expands into new contexts, including metaphorical applications. In one Midrash we are told that oil "enhances" learning (Lekaḥ Tov, Devarim, 66a), in another to be "deliberate

in judgment and set judgments in order" (Avot de-Rabbi Nathan [Schechter] B, 1).

The verbal noun *yishuv* is first documented in rabbinic sources, where it appears in various substantive clauses. Here the *pi'el* word for the first time draws on the meaning of the *pa'al* stem: in the Talmud, *yishuv olam* (Bavli, Eruvin 86a), or *yishuv ha-olam* (Yerushalmi, Bava Batra 2:13c) means ordering (in the sense of cultivation/settlement) of the world, *yishuv medinah* (Bavli, Avodah Zarah 18b) ordering (in the sense of cultivation/settlement) of an area, and *yishuv erets Yisra'el* (Bavli, Bava Kamma 80b) ordering (in the sense of cultivation/settlement) of the Land of Israel. The Midrash *Aggadah Exodus* similarly expands the biblical explanation for God's decision not to expel the Canaanites and other people in the first year of the Israelite settlement – since the land could otherwise become desolate and the wild animals rampant (Exod 23:29) – by adding that humans cultivate the world (*yishuv ha-olam*; Aggadah Exodus [Buber] 23:27) through controlling the growth of the wild animals. The presence of the non-Israelite tribes is thus regarded as a necessary measure to protect the human environment against wild beasts and to preserve it until the Israelites have grown sufficiently strong in number.

The "setting of the world" is also discussed in the context of the Flood. In one Midrash we read, Noah is said to have seen the world "in its ordinary setting [*be-yishuvo*], in its destruction, and in its ordinary setting [*yishuvo*]. [...] Noah would not die until he saw a bird's nest in its ordinary setting [*be-yishuvah*], until he saw seventy nations ranging from his seed" [15. 65].

Another example of *yishuv ha-olam* being used in this way appears in the Talmud *Yerushalmi*, where it concerns a conflict between two neighbors: the cistern of one was affected by the roots of a tree the other had planted. The rabbinic decision in favor of the owner of the cistern is explained as follows: "The rabbis' reason is, that civilization is based on cisterns." The minority opinion of Rabbi Jose is also included in the passage: "[J]ust as you hold that civilization is based on cisterns, so I am holding that civilization is based on trees" (Bava Batra 2:10). In view of the limits imposed by nature on the late ancient agricultural subsistence economy, *yishuv ha-olam* can also be understood as an ordering principle in the struggle to secure the basic means of survival [7. 600].

Another social dimension of *yishuv* emerges in the debate over the question whether dice players are reliable witnesses. Rav Sheshet argues against it since such persons are "not involved in settling the world" (*be-yishuvo shel ha-olam*; Talmud Bavli, Sanhedrin 24b), that is they are not part of the productive community structure. People who do follow a regular occupation besides such diversions are indeed qualified to act as witness as they are not transgressing against the rules of supporting a family and the economy. Sometimes *yishuv ha-olam* can also be interpreted as obeying the commandment to "be fertile and increase" (Gen 1:28).

A more limited use is attested for the phrase *yishuv medinah* (cultivation of the land). In rabbinic Hebrew *medinah* denotes a particular social space, and this can be an area, a city, or also a rural region. The concept is employed in a Halakhic Midrash on the Book of Exodus discussing paternal obligations. According to the Midrash, these include circumcision, the ritual redemption of the first-born son, Torah study, and marriage. However, "R. Akiva says: He must also teach him how to swim. Rebbi says: Also how to get along with others" (Mekhilta d'Rabbi Yishmael 13:13, Pisḥa 18). In this context, *yishuv medinah* describes the etiquette and rules of conduct at a given location.

The nominal phrase *yishuv erets Yisra'el* not only draws on the social-normative aspects but also indicates the correct conduct in the Land of Israel. This includes the obligation to affix a mezuzah to the door frame: the Talmud suggests that anyone staying at a hostel in the Land of Israel or lives in rented accommodation outside the Land is exempt from this rule for a period of 30 days. However, anyone who rents a house in the Land of Israel must affix the mezuzah immediately, as this is customary "due to the settlement of Eretz Yisrael" (*yishuv de-erets Yisra'el*; Bavli, Menaḥot 44a).

Another example is relevant especially in connection with the modern use of *yishuv erets Yisra'el*. The Babylonian Talmud explains that when buying a house in the Land of Israel the contract itself may be concluded on the → Shabbat, and the Jew has to recite the text of the agreement to the non-Jew. While this practice constituted a minor infraction of a → Halakhic rule, it was nevertheless permissible on account of the general "mitzva of settling Eretz Yisrael" (Bava Kamma 80b). The transfer of a house from a non-Jew to a Jew, thus to the expansion of the Jewish presence in the Land of Israel doubtless seemed desirable because by so doing the religious laws of the land could be followed more consistently. In the Land of Israel, where the commandments of the Torah are practiced most diligently, it also expanded the rule of God. In passages such as this the earliest hints of a religious territorial interpretation of *yishuv* can be detected. It must be borne in mind, however, that territorial claims here refer to the Kingdom of God, not the physical territory of a modern state.

In addition to the verbal noun, the Hebrew language also knows *yishuv* as a generic term and here, too, as in many other such cases, we see a narrowing of the semantic context [5. 146]; *yishuv* underwent this semantic specification in rabbinic Hebrew, where it emerged as a generic term for geographic units characterized by the visibility of well-organized public space: thus, for civilized places. Indeed, in this meaning, *yishuv* is frequently contrasted with *ḥurbah* (ruin), *bar* (open field), *yam* (ocean), and *midbar* (desert, void) – areas where principles of social order and legal standards do not exist. The Mishnah states: "With regard to one who robs another or who borrowed money from him, or one with whom another had deposited an item, if any of these interactions took place in a settled area [*yishuv*], he may not return the item to him in an unsettled area [*midbar*], where it is of little benefit to the owner and he cannot safeguard it. If the loan or deposit was given on the condition that the recipient may go out and return it to the owner in an unsettled area, he may return it to him in an unsettled area" (Bava Kamma 10:6). It is generally assumed that the reason for the suspended obligation to repay a debt is the absence of a legal system in the "wilderness," and especially the danger of the repaid sum being stolen by robbers. Only if the lender already knew that the borrower intended to leave the "settled area," in other words was consciously taking the risk that his repayment could readily be lost, the borrower had to make the repayment anyway.

The next stage in the semantic development of the term can be found in Medieval literature. The *Sefer Ḥasidim* (Book of the Pious; → Ashkenaz) from the 12/13th century recommends that when looking for shelter in a city, a Jew "should look into the Jewish communities of that town" (*be-yishuve ha-arets be-otah ha-ir*; Sefer Ḥasidim, § 1301). The author here, in his use of *yishuv*, is clearly referring to a Jewish community in the general sense. Two semantic shifts enabled this new understanding: First, law and order are applied to an exclusively Jewish context; second, the reference denoting a geographic area is limited to indicate a (smaller) community within a geographic area.

As a generic term for "a small number of people in a location, especially a number of Jews residing in non-Jewish villages," *yishuv* was also included in Eliʿezer Ben-Yehudah's

historical dictionary, the first volume of which appeared in 1910 [2. 2181].

2. Modern Hebrew

The era of modern → Hebrew begins with the Jewish Enlightenment (→ Haskalah) and the preference shown by its protagonists for Hebrew rather than → Yiddish as their written common language. The middle of the 19th century also saw the publication of Hebrew newspapers whose political discourse was conducted in the Hebrew language, the earliest being → *Ha-Maggid* (The Courier; also The Preacher) in 1856.

Sometime between 1860 and 1880, *yishev*, *yishuv*, and *moshavah* came into use as Hebrew translations for "colonize/settle," "colonization/settling" and "colony/settlement." In the process, the expression *yishuv erets Yisraʾel* became polysemic as well; the old meaning of "correct conduct in the Land of Israel" was joined by the new meaning of "colonization of the Land of Israel."

Not only did the verbal noun undergo another semantic shift, the meaning of the generic term *yishuv* changed as well, from a Jewish community within a non-Jewish settlement to a Jewish community in Palestine. While the "semantic trace" (*Bedeutungsstreifen*, Reinhart Koselleck) of the Jewish community remained intact, the geographic context was altered.

When combined with the definite article, *ha-yishuv* ("the Yishuv") turns into a quasi-proper name exclusively for the Jewish community in Palestine. The name continues to be used – for the period preceding the creation of the State of Israel – and is maintained until today in political and academic discourse.

The earliest recorded example of this new semantic charge appears in the work of the pioneer of → cultural Zionism, Aḥad Ha-Am (Asher Ginsberg; 1856–1927); it is highly likely, however, that he already encountered the term on his visits to Palestine in 1891 and

1893. At the time it also became customary to distinguish the "new Yishuv" (*ha-yishuv he-ḥadash*) from the "old Yishuv" (*ha-yishuv ha-yashan*; → Ḥalukkah), in recognition of the widening gap between the secular new immigrants and the existing traditional, religious Jewish communities with a long history of settlement in Palestine, predominantly in Jerusalem but also in Safed, Tiberias, and Hebron.

The semantic shift meant that *ha-yishuv* could no longer denote a particular Jewish community in a given location. To refer to such a community, the adjective "Jewish" had to be added. Thus, for a Jewish community outside of Palestine the term *ha-yishuv ha-yehudi* came to be used. A report in the Hebrew newspaper *Ha-Melits* (The Advocate), published in → Odessa between 1860 and 1904, accordingly surmises that throughout history centers of Jewish life had arisen because the Jewish community (*ha-yishuv ha-yehudi*) had grown in that location (*Ha-Melits*, November 28, 1898).

Even though the quasi-proper name *ha-yishuv* constituted an innovation, rabbinic Hebrew retained a certain semantic continuity in the opposition between *yishuv* and *midbar* (wilderness, unsettled area) or similar concepts indicating the absence of a social order, as did Medieval Hebrew where the semantic trace of a specifically Jewish configuration of order was particularly dominant. As a cultural attribution, *ha-yishuv* thus marked the space outside of a Zionist settlement as wilderness (*midbar*) or void (*shemamah*) [14]. Vaguely *yishuv* refers to a place that is not only settled but also civilized [13].

Unlike *ha-yishuv*, *midbar* refers to an object that appears in the Zionist discourse as "symbolic landscape that was defined as a symbolic void." The desert, therefore, becomes a residual category defined by its difference from the settlement; the expressions *midbar* and *shemanmah*, or combined as *midbar shemamah*, describe "landscapes that appeared as desolate, wild, or occupied by Arabs." The negative connotation of "desert" is present in the "narrative of decline" of Zionist discourse, where the settlement of the Twelve Tribes up to the time of the ancient Jewish Kingdom symbolizes the golden age for the Land of Israel, while the centuries of the → Diaspora represent its decline to a desolate wasteland. Since the late 19th century, that golden age has served as inspiration and motivation for Jewish settlement, with a view to "making the desert bloom" and recreating an "earlier state of national bliss" [13. 203–205].

Thus the political significance of the noun *yishuv* derives from the interaction of semantic continuities and discontinuities in its history of meanings. The old symbolic dichotomy between *yishuv* and *midbar* was filled with new content. A collective sense of being Jewish was preserved in *yishuv*, as was the idea of law and order; now it signified being Jewish in the political entity of Palestine, and a concept of law and order fashioned after the standards of Western civilization, which the Zionist colonization shared with forms of European expansion.

The noun phrase *yishuv erets Yisra'el* was a hybrid form. On the one hand it functioned in the Halakhic literature as a principle recalling the classical usage, much like *yishuv medinah* (the creation or maintenance of law and order in an area) and *yishuv ha-olam* (the creation of law and order in the world). On the other hand, it was a neologism which by applying the European idea of colonization to Palestine came to replace the Halakhic concept of *yeshivat erets Yisra'el* (inhabiting the Land of Israel) as the expression of Jewish longing for Zion in the religious sense.

One of the first to introduce this new meaning was Abraham Isaac Kook (Harayah) who after relocating to Palestine in 1904 emerged as the spiritual leader of religious Zionism (from 1921 to his death in 1935 as the first Ashkenazi Chief Rabbi of British

Mandatory Palestine). Kook called on all Jews in the Diaspora to buy their citrus fruits (Etrog) for Sukkot (→ Course of the Year) from "our brothers, the colonizers of the Holy Land" (*erets ha-kodesh*), and by doing so, to honor the mitzvah of *yishuv erets ha-kodesh* as well as the one regarding citrus fruits [3. 145]. Since the rabbi used the term *meyashvim* (lit. "settlers," "colonizers") – a *pi'el* verb form, like *yishev* – it is clear that even when he speaks of *yishuv erets ha-kodesh* (settlement of the Holy Land), he is already employing the verb *yishev* and the verbal noun *yishuv* in the modern, neologized sense. And because there is no mitzvah in the classical, textual tradition expressed as *yishuv erets ha-kodesh*, it is here a case of a paraphrase of the concept of *yeshivat erets Yisra'el*. From this point onward the pro-Zionist Halakhic discourse no longer distinguished between *yishuv erets Yisra'el* in its classical meaning of maintaining law and order in the public space of the Land of Israel and *yeshivat erets Yisra'el* which originally referred to the act of residing in the Land of Israel. The phrases *yishuv erets Yisra'el* and *yishuv erets ha-kodesh* now carried the modern secular meaning of the colonization of Palestine.

In religious Zionist circles both expressions are today used synonymously. While scholars are still mindful of the distinction, the nationalist-religious discourse takes advantage of the conflation because it allows quotations from the religious canon on the religious meaning of the cultivation of the Land of Israel to be used as evidence for the existence of a mitzvah legitimizing its colonization. This has ramifications in the political sphere, where it serves to legitimize Jewish settlements in the West Bank.

Beyond the narrower context of religious Zionism, the historical change in the meaning of *yishuv* is a striking example of the dialectic inherent in the secularization of the Hebrew language. The formerly secular concept, basically not bound to any specific location, upon its arrival in Palestine becomes charged not only with a territorial-colonial component but also an increasingly sacralized one. It is therefore a testament to the political-theological foundation of Zionist discourse.

Bibliography

Sources
[1] A. Ha'am, Truth from Eretz Israel, trans. by A. Dowty, in: A. Dowty, Much Ado about Little: Ahad Ha'ams Truth from Eretz Israel, Zionism, and the Arabs, in: Israel Studies (2000) 5/2, 160–181. [2] E. Ben-Yehuda, Milon ha-lashon ha-'ivrit ha-yeshanah veha-ḥadashah [A Complete Dictionary of Ancient and Modern Hebrew], vol. 4, repr. Jerusalem 1980. [3] A.Y. Kook, Iggrot Harayah [Letters of Harayah], vol. 1, Jerusalem 1961. [4] J. Wistinetzki/J. Freiman (eds.), Sefer Ḥasidim [Book of the Pious], Frankfurt am Main 1924.

Secondary literature
[5] E. Coffin/S. Bolozky, A Reference Grammar of Modern Hebrew, Cambridge 2005. [6] W. Gesenius, Hebrew and Chaldee Lexicon to the Old Testament Scriptures, trans. by S. Prideaux Tregelles (based on orig. German ed. of 1815), London 1857. [7] M. Jastrow, A Dictionary of the Targumim, the Talmud Babli and Yerushalmi, and the Midrashic Literature, London/New York 1903. [8] U. Ram, Israeli Nationalism. Social Conflicts and the Politics of Knowledge, London 2011. [9] J. Reinharz, Old and New Yishuv. The Jewish Community of Palestine at the Turn of the Twentieth Century, in: Jewish Studies Quarterly 1 (1993), 54–71. [10] E. W. Said, Orientalism, New York 1978. [11] J.I. Weinstein, What Is Yishuv Medina? Lecture at the Third International Conference on Political Hebraism, Princeton 2008. [12] R. Williams, Key Words. A Vocabulary of Culture and Society, London 1976. [13] Y. Zerubavel, Desert and Settlement. Space Metaphors and Symbolic Landscapes in the Yishuv and Early Israeli Culture, in: J. Brauch et al. (eds.), Jewish Topographies.

Visions of Space, Traditions of Place, London 2008, 201–222. |14| Y. Zerubavel, The Conquest of the Desert and the Settlement Ethos, in: A.P. Hare/G. Kressel (eds.), The Desert Experience in Israel. Communities, Arts, Science, and Education in the Negev, Lanham 2008, 33–44. [15] C. Albeck (ed.), Midrash Bereshit Rabbati, Parashat Noah, Jerusalem 1940 [Hebr.].

RON KUZAR, HAIFA

YIVO

The *Yidisher Visnshaftlekher Institut* (YIVO) was founded in Vilna (today Vilnius) in 1925 as an interdisciplinary research institute for the past and present history of the Jews in Eastern Europe. The institute was the result of endeavors to establish → Yiddish as a national cultural language and to preserve the Jewish culture of Eastern Europe. It was committed to Diaspora nationalism and was supported by numerous collectors in Vilnius, whose materials provided the foundation of the institute's archive. After the Soviet occupation of Lithuania, YIVO moved to New York in 1940. In view of the destruction suffered during the Second World War and the → Holocaust, it transformed into a more academic organization, dedicating itself to new topics such as the history of Jewish immigrants in America.

1. Background and foundation
2. Vilna
3. New York

1. Background and foundation

The foundation of YIVO in 1925 was preceded by a fundamental change in the attitude to → Yiddish, which slowly transformed from a despised jargon into a recognized language of science, → literature, and theatre (→ Pomul Verde). During the last quarter of the 19th century, writers such as Sholem Aleichem (→ Tevye), Shalom Jacob Abramovitch (Mendele Moykher-Sforim; → Fishke), and Isaac Leib Peretz (→ Bontshe) had raised Yiddish to the level of a literary language in their works. At the same time, a new Jewish workers' movement emerged (→ *Bund*), which tied its political objectives to the appreciation of Yiddish culture.

From the end of the 19th century onward, political activists, artists, and writers such as Peretz and S. An-Ski (→ Dybbuk) endeavored to establish a secular Yiddish culture, which they regarded as a bridge between Jewish tradition and European liberal humanism. With this objective in mind, they increasingly incorporated the lives of the wider population into their works. Unlike the enlightened → maskilim, who tended to look down on Jewish popular culture, they believed that the everyday lives of the Jewish masses represented a reservoir of national energy that could benefit from the establishment of a Jewish nation. For example, the poet and ethnographer S. An-Ski (→ Jewish Society for History and Ethnography), in particular, called for Yiddish historical documents to be collected, songs and stories to be written down, old gravestones to be discovered, and popular customs (→ Minhag) to be observed (→ Folklore). In 1912 he organized an extensive ethnographical expedition into the → Pale of Settlement. In his opinion, traditional Jewish life was gradually disappearing, so he found it all the more important to preserve records of the past in order to establish the foundations for a future national culture. This collecting process, he felt, was just as significant as its result; the determination to establish an archive seemed as important as the archive itself.

Collecting was also the cornerstone of Simon Dubnow's (→ Weltgeschichte; → Riga) call for the development of a new historical consciousness to replace Jews' dwindling religious ties. In 1892 Dubnow published his → Hebrew article *Naḥpesa ve-naḥkora* (Let us search and investigate), which had been published in → Russian the year before, in which he called on the Jews in Russia and Poland to study their history. Every people must know its own history in order to fight for its rights and acquire self-respect, he argued. In the same spirit, Peretz exhorted the Jews at the beginning of the First World War to write their own history to ensure it would not be written exclusively by their enemies. Lacking a state of their own that would take care of collecting documents and preserving them in archives, the Jews would have to take the initiative themselves, he stated.

While his predecessor Heinrich Graetz had given little space to Eastern Europe in his *Geschichte der Juden*, Dubnow regarded this very region as the most significant center of Jewish life. Unlike Graetz, Dubnow emphasized that the → historiography needed to include the lives of all of the people rather than exclusively studying intellectual and religious developments. While Dubnow was not a declared Yiddishist, his call for a new historiography with a focus on the community accorded a new relevance to Yiddish as the language of the majority of the Jewish population.

During the first → Czernowitz Language Conference in 1908, controversial opinions on the importance of Yiddish emerged. While the radical left and members of the → *Bund* regarded Yiddish as the language of the Jewish people *per se*, moderate Yiddishists like Peretz believed it to be an important, but not the only, form of expression of the Jews. In response to this debate, Shmuel Niger (b. Shmuel Tscharny, also Samuel Charney; 1883–1955), A. Vayter (A. Waiter, b. Ayzik Meyer Devenishski; 1878–1919), and Shmarye Gorelik (1877–1942) founded the journal *Literarishe monatsshriftn* (Literary monthly) in Vilna in the same year; it was committed to independent Yiddish high culture but not subject to any political agenda. In 1913 *Der pinkes* (The notebook) appeared

in Vilna as well – an almanac edited by Niger together with the socialist Zionist Ber Borochov (1881–1917). It contained articles and memoranda on the Yiddish language, literature, and theatre, as well as on Jewish history, such as Borochov's influential essay *Oyfgabn fun der yidisher filologye* (The tasks of Yiddish philology, 1813). Both its subject matter and the use of Yiddish rendered *Der pinkes* an important contribution to the development of Yiddish scholarly terminology and syntax.

Der pinkes heralded the growing interest in Yiddish scholarship among members of the younger generation, many of whom would later become founding members of YIVO, such as Zalmen Reyzen (1884–1941), Max Weinreich (1894–1969), Zelig Kalmanovich (1881–1944), Yudl Mark (1897–1975), and Nochum Shtif (1897–1933). These young scholars had ties to various political groups, but they all supported Diaspora nationalism. In spite of their political commitments, they gave priority to their cultural and scholarly work. With the exception of Reyzen, they lived and met in St. Petersburg during the First World War, discovering their shared interest in the Yiddish language. After the October Revolution (→ Red Cavalry), they settled in various places but stayed in close contact. Mark, born in Palanga in Lithuania, was encouraged by Kalmanovich and Shtif to study Yiddish linguistics. Shtif, who came from Rivne in Ukraine, abandoned his legal studies in order to devote himself zealously to Yiddish scholarship and the foundation of a research institute. Weinreich, who came from Courland, where he had grown up with → German as his mother tongue, joined the *Bund*, although he focused on studying Yiddish culture. After completing a doctorate in linguistics at the University of Marburg, he settled in Vilna, which had become part of Poland in 1922. In 1923 he published his first book *Shtaplen. Fir etyudn tsu der yidisher shprakhvisnshaft un literaturgeshikhte* (Steps. Four studies on Yiddish linguistics and history of literature). Kalmanovich, also from Courland, completed his doctorate in linguistics as St. Petersburg University in 1919. By this time he was already a skillful translator into Yiddish and a prominent authority on matters of Yiddish style. Zalmen Reyzen, the younger brother of the writer Avrom Reyzen, performed pioneering work in the field of Yiddish grammar and published bibliographical reference works on Yiddish → literature. During the First World War, he edited the journal *Letste nayes* (Latest news), which promoted a new Yiddish orthography and modern style.

After the First World War and the conclusion of the treaties on minority rights as part of the peace negotiations (→ Minority Rights), an extensive network of Yiddish schools developed in Poland and the Baltic states. This development led to an ever-increasing demand for trained teachers and suitable textbooks. Moreover, it became ever more urgent for Yiddish to be standardized and for terminologies for teaching the natural sciences, history, and literature to be developed. The creation of Yiddish journals with a focus on education science as well as a teachers' college, and, above all, an academic institute with the authority to set normative standards seemed to be all the more necessary.

In late 1924 Shtif composed a memorandum concerned with the establishment of such an institute, stating that dedicating a center of scholarship to the language spoken by millions of people and enabling the study of Yiddish philology as well as Eastern European Jewish popular culture, history, economics, psychology, and education science was long overdue. In addition, he called for the establishment of a central → library affiliated with the institute, as well as an archive. While Shtif intended for the institution to be located in Berlin or New York, it soon became clear that its headquarters would be in Vilna. The center of Lithuanian Jewish scholarship (→ Litvaks), – the

city was called the "Jerusalem of Lithuania" for this reason – was home to an active Jewish community and a core of scholars and intellectuals such as Weinreich, Reizen, and the physician Zemach Shabad (1864–1935), who was highly respected due to his commitment to serving the community.

In March 1925, Jewish intellectuals discussed Shtif's memorandum and published their *Vilner tezisn vegn a yidishn visnshaftlekhn institut* (Vilna theses on a Yiddish academic institute). They agreed with Shtif's call for the foundation of a research institute but emphasized that it would have to be linked closely to community life. Accordingly, the institute was to support new Yiddish schools in writing appropriate textbooks complete with modern terminologies, educating teachers, and organizing public lectures.

On the basis of the Vilna theses, the organizational framework of YIVO was established in August 1925 in Berlin. The management of the institute was entrusted to the Society of the Friends of YIVO with its headquarters in Vilna. Max Weinreich was the director, supported by Zelig Kalmanovich, who published the institute's journal *YIVO bleter*. As planned by Shtif's memorandum, it consisted of four sections: these were the philological, historical, socioeconomic, later developed into the economic-statistical section, and the pedagogical, later renamed the psychological-pedagogical. The management of the four sections bore witness to the global presence of the Yiddish-speaking community. Weinreich led the philological section; Elias Tcherikower, who lived in Berlin, the historical section; Jakob Lestschinsky – he, too, from Berlin – the economic-statistical; and Leybush Lehrer, who spent part of his time in New York, the psychological-pedagogical section. The New York-based historian Jacob Shatzky headed the American section of YIVO, which provided important funding.

2. Vilna

The scholars of YIVO took care from the very first to delimit themselves from the → Wissenschaft des Judentums, which in their view treated Jewish → history as a closed chapter after Jewish → emancipation and integration into the surrounding societies. YIVO, by contrast, regarded its research activities as a contribution to a living nation. Scholarship, however, was not only supposed to serve the people but also to include them in the scholarly work. Accordingly, YIVO continued the collection activities that had accompanied the establishment and practice of Yiddish scholarship since the 19th century.

In the absence of state funding, YIVO in Vilna was forced to rely on the support of Jews from all over the world and on the dedicated cooperation between scholars and volunteer collectors. The ethos of *zamlen* (Yidd.; "collecting") documents, books, chronicles, idioms, proverbs, photographs, and orally transmitted narratives by enthusiastic volunteer collectors contributed to YIVO's growing archives and → library. In this way, a theatre museum and a newspaper archive were set up as well. Tens of thousands of items made their way to the institute, including recollections of Purim celebrations (→ Course of the Year) in a 19th-century → shtetl, language documents by itinerant actors, and children's rhymes and games. While collectors and financial supporters were found in many regions of Eastern Europe and in Jewish communities of other countries, the overwhelming majority came from Jewish *Lite* (Jewish Lithuania), which comprised northeastern Poland, Lithuania, and Latvia. In spite of the increasing acculturation of a younger generation of Polish Jews to the surrounding culture (→ Polish), the institute succeeded in mobilizing the greatest number of supporters in this area.

In 1928 the institute's management acquired a plot of land to build new institute premises, the foundation stone of which was laid in 1929 during the first international YIVO conference. However, as a result of the global economic crisis, the institute found itself in financial difficulties. Donations

Simon Dubnow (standing, center) at an international YIVO conference, Vilna, 1935

dropped, precipitating drastic cuts in the budget. Even so, it was possible to complete the construction work, and during the second half of the 1930s, the institute's financial situation gradually improved.

Although the new building was spacious and included fireproof storage rooms for the archives, the board of directors realized that additional space would be needed as early as 1937 due to the large amount of material being sent in. In 1934 YIVO established the Zemach Shabad postgraduate program to train the next generation of scholars; this was followed by an introductory program for students who lacked the education for graduate work in 1937. In the late 1930s, YIVO expanded its cooperation with secular Yiddish schools, with the psychological-pedagogical section playing a particularly important part in this.

The second world conference of YIVO in 1935 saw a controversial debate between politically left-leaning supporters and the institute's board of directors. From the perspective of the left, YIVO had become an academic ivory tower whose scientific work ignored the urgent requirements of the Jewish masses and the difficult situation of the Yiddish schools. Weinreich and Kalmanovich defended the institute's policies and warned that politicization would destroy it. In their opinion, YIVO served the people best by adhering to its fundamental academic orientation.

The philological section headed by Weinreich was always the most active branch of YIVO and included a number of subsections, for instance, for terminology and popular culture. Unlike many representatives of the older generation of scholars, Weinreich held an academic degree. He set high standards, and his knowledge ranged from Yiddish linguistics through early modern popular → literature to Freudian → psychoanalysis and social psychology. Influenced by the biographical method of Polish → sociology and time spent at Yale University in 1932/1933, he

initiated an extensive study of youth. Several hundred Jewish adolescents in Poland followed the call to compose autobiographical accounts for this study.

The endeavors of the philological section to establish a modern Yiddish terminology and orthographical standards (→ Czernowitz Language Conference) produced mixed results. It lacked the authority of a state academy, and the Yiddish press ignored the majority of the recommendations. This was due primarily to the mistrust shown to YIVO not only by Zionists challenging its Diaspora nationalism but also by religious groups attacking its secularism. A further controversial subject was the spelling of Hebrew words in → Yiddish; members of the Left and many teachers opposed the YIVO leadership on this. Socialists and communists wanted to follow the example of the Soviet Union, where phonetic transcription was in use. Weinreich and Kalmanovich rejected this suggestion as it might have been seen as politicization, threatening to alienate important groups of supporters from YIVO.

Despite being hampered by Tcherikower's geographical distance, the work of the historical section produced impressive results, especially in the field of the Jewish history of Eastern Europe. Even before the official establishment of YIVO in 1925, young Polish Jewish historians led by Emanuel Ringelblum (→ Oyneg Shabbes) and Raphael Mahler had united to promote historical research in Yiddish. The core of the historical section of YIVO emerged from this group. Besides publishing three large volumes entitled *Historishe shriftn* (1929, 1937, 1939; Historical writings), this section called on Polish Jews in the 1930s to collect Jewish community records (→ Pinkasim), to write the histories of their towns, and to investigate Jewish material culture, including its photographic documentation.

The YIVO historians regarded their field not least as a defensive strategy against the accusation that Jews were aliens without roots in the land in which they had lived for generations. Accordingly, Ringelblum, representing the institute, established links to the *landkentenish* movement, which advocated Jews taking extensive trips through rural Poland in order to gain more in-depth knowledge of their own country. The economic section supported extensive statistical research on the economic challenges confronting Jews all over the world. From 1937 onward, it published the journal *Yidishe ekonomik* (Yiddish economics), overseen by Jakob Lestschinsky (→ Statistics) and Menachem Linder.

By 1938 the institute's financial situation had stabilized, new branches had been founded in → Warsaw and → Łódź, and YIVO had become the leading institute of Yiddish scholarship globally. While the political situation grew increasingly precarious after Germany's annexation of Austria and the Sudeten regions, leading members of the institute such as Weinreich and Kalmanovich declared that dedicated scholarly work was more important to the Jews than ever.

In September 1939, Soviet troops occupied Vilna as part of the Polish regions apportioned to the Soviet Union under the Molotov–Ribbentrop Pact. Instantly Moyshe Lerer, a communist sympathizer, was appointed the new head of the institute. Six weeks later, the city was surrendered to Lithuania, which, in turn, was attacked by the Soviet Union in June 1940. With the establishment of the Lithuanian Socialist Soviet Republic, the institute's independence ended. The new rulers incorporated YIVO into the Lietuvos mokslų akademija (Lithuanian Academy of the Sciences) as the Institute for Jewish Culture. Noah Prilutski (→ Purim-shpil), the former head of the Warsaw branch of YIVO, was appointed professor of Yiddish at Vilnius University and the new head of the institute.

After Vilnius was occupied by National Socialist Germany in June 1941, Johannes Pohl of the Einsatzstab Reichsleiter Rosenberg (ERR) arrived in the city in March 1942 and oversaw the looting of the cultural treasures of Jewish Vilnius. Germans ordered Kalmanovich, Herman Kruk, Uma Olkenitska, and the young poets Abraham Sutzkever (→ Khurbn) and Shmerke Kaczerginski, among others, to work in YIVO's library. They smuggled, in addition to weapons, particularly valuable books and manuscripts into the Jewish ghetto, where they became known as the "Papierbrigade" (paper brigade). In the Warsaw ghetto, the underground archive → *Oyneg Shabbes* organized by Ringelblum continued to collect historical material and engage in scholarship and research even under the most adverse conditions.

After Vilnius came under Soviet occupation once again after the end of the war, Sutzkever and Kaczerginski, who had survived the → Holocaust, endeavored to establish a Jewish → museum in the city. However, they soon had to acknowledge that Jewish culture did not have much of a future in Soviet Lithuania. In various ways, they succeeded in sending numerous items from YIVO's collection to New York.

3. New York

In September 1939, Max Weinreich and his son Uriel were in Copenhagen and decided not to return to Vilnius. In 1940, they arrived in → New York, where the new YIVO head office was established. Lestschinski and Tcherikower, too, settled there. In view of the move from Vilnius, which had an impoverished but culturally dynamic Yiddish-speaking community, to the United States, where Yiddish had no attraction for the younger, Americanized generation, YIVO faced the challenge of having to develop a new concept for its activities.

Even during the Second World War, the institute had begun to dedicate its work to documenting the persecution and murder of the European Jews at the hands of the National Socialists. As early as 1940, it published a report on the → Warsaw Ghetto, and four years later followed this with a leaflet about the ghetto uprising. After the end of the war, YIVO began a new initiative in New York: it sent a call to the Jewish Displaced Persons (→ Munich) to collect testimonies, thus becoming a pioneer of Holocaust research (→ Khurbn). This new focus also found expression in monographs. Weinreich published his study *Hitler's Professors* in 1946. In addition, the institute began to publish important bibliographies on the history of the Holocaust together with → Yad Vashem.

Weinreich also promoted academic research projects in order to enrich American Jews' self-image. The institute published essays on Jewish immigrants, as well as a two-volume history of the Jewish workers' movement in America, and initiated a study of the experiences of Jewish immigrants in the United States (→ Ellis Island). Furthermore, after the end of the war, the institute managed to secure the restitution of a considerable portion of the materials stolen by the ERR in Vilnius from the → Offenbach Archival Depot (→ Restitution). A large part of the archive of the historical section, hidden by Tcherikower in southern France, also found its way to New York.

In view of the murder of millions of Yiddish-speaking persons in Europe, as well as of the meager interest in the language that the second generation of American Jews showed, Weinreich harbored no illusions regarding the future of YIVO in New York. Even so, he was convinced that at some future time, American Jews would develop an interest in their history and the Jewish culture of Eastern Europe. Consequently, YIVO began publishing the English *YIVO Annual* and continued to publish other significant scholarly monographs: Uriel

Weinreich's textbook *College Yiddish* (1940), Nahum Stutchkoff's *Oytser fun der yidisher shprakh* (Thesaurus of the Yiddish language, 1950; → Radio), Jacob Shatzky's three-volume *Geshikhte fun yidn in Varshe* (History of the Jews in Warsaw, 1947–1953), Uriel Weinreich's *Modern English Yiddish/Yiddish English Dictionary* (1966), which appeared a year after his untimely death in 1967, as well as Max Weinreich's standard work *Di geshikhte fun der yidisher shprakh* (1973), published four years after his death in 1969.

In 1955 YIVO changed its English name from Yiddish Scientific Institute to YIVO Institute of Jewish Research and moved into the former Vanderbilt Mansion on Fifth Avenue. In cooperation with Columbia University (and later New York University) it initiated the Uriel Weinreich Program in Yiddish Language, Literature and Culture in 1968 – the first study program of its kind. With interest in Jewish studies increasing at universities in America, Israel, and Europe, the YIVO archive grew in importance for academic research. Important acquisitions such as the archives of the → *Bund*, the Hebrew Immigrant Aid Society, and the → American Jewish Committee expanded the materials available. In the 1980s, YIVO created a sound archive named for Max and Frieda Weinstein as well as a teaching program on Yiddish popular culture. After the collapse of the Soviet Union, it was found that Lithuanian librarians had actually saved much of YIVO's archive and holdings from before the war that had been believed lost. While the Lithuanian government refused to recognize the institute's ownership of these materials, they permitted the holdings to be copied.

By the 1990s, the institute's collections had grown so voluminous that the Vanderbilt Mansion became too small, and in 1999 YIVO moved to the nearby Center for Jewish History. Its extensive collections and library continue to be an important resource for researchers. Through lectures, exhibitions, and publications about the Jewish history of Eastern Europe – such as the two-volume *YIVO Encyclopedia of Jews in Eastern Europe* published in 2008 – YIVO also addresses a wider public.

Bibliography

[1] L. Dawidowicz, From that Place and Time. A Memoir, 1938–1947, New York 1989. [2] S. Dubnow, Let Us Seek and Investigate [1892], in: Simon Dubnow Institute Yearbook 7 (2008), 353–382. [3] B. Kirshenblatt-Gimblett, Coming of Age in the Thirties. Max Weinreich, Edward Sapir, and Jewish Social Science, in: YIVO Annual 23 (1996), 1–103. [4] C. E. Kuznitz, YIVO and the Making of Modern Jewish Culture. Scholarship for the Yiddish Nation, New York 2014. [5] D. Miron, Between Science and Faith. Sixty Years of the YIVO Institute, in: YIVO Annual 19 (1990), 1–15. [6] J. Shandler (ed.), Awakening Lives. Autobiographies of Jewish Youth in Poland before the Holocaust, New Haven 2002.

SAMUEL D. KASSOW, HARTFORD

Yung-yidish

Name of the first → Yiddish avant-garde group of artists in Poland, active in Łódź from 1919 to 1921/1922, and dedicated to the secular renewal of Jewish art. In their artworks and writings, the members of *Yung Yidish* combined elements of Jewish and Christian tradition with artistic Modernism. They exerted a significant influence on so-called Jewish Expressionism and inspired several Jewish and Yiddish avant-garde art circles of the 1920s.

After the end of the First World War, a rich artistic and cultural life developed in the central Polish industrial city of → Łódź, with Jewish artists and writers playing an influential part. In early 1918, the Stowarzyszenie Artystów i Zwolenników Sztuk Pięknych (Society of Artists and Supporters of the Fine Arts) was founded and organized two exhibitions in the same year. The majority of the works presented there came mainly from Jewish artists. Icchok Brauner's (Yitskhok Broyner) art salon on Piotrkowska Street, founded around the beginning of 1915, was influential as well. Brauner, who had studied at the Berlin Hochschule für Bildende Künste, exhibited his own as well as other artists' works. In his private apartment he gathered a circle of young artists and writers.

After the poet Moyshe Broderzon's return from Moscow, several Jewish artists contributing to the exhibitions, along with Brauner's salon, joined together to form the group *Yung Yidish* (Young Yiddish; Pol. Jung Idysz), which began its activities in February 1919. In addition to Broderzon and Brauner, the approximately 20 members of the group included the painter Jankiel Adler, who returned to Łódź in late 1918 from his studies at the Kunstgewerbeschule in Barmen (near Wuppertal, Germany), and the sculptor Marek Szwarc, who had studied at the Paris École des Beaux-Arts until 1914, as well as Ida Brauner, Pola Lindenfeld, Zofia Gutentag, Dina Matus, and Jecheskiel Neuman. Since most members had spent time in other European countries and were consequently familiar with the new trends in literature and the arts, especially German Expressionism and Russian Futurism, *Yung Yidish* soon became the avant-garde of Jewish artists in the Second Republic.

The leading member of the group was Broderzon who had grown up in Łódź, spent the First World War in Moscow, and played an active part in renewing Yiddish culture after the revolutions (→ February Revolution). In 1917 he was among the founders of the *Krayzl fun Yidish Natsyonaler Estetik* (Circle for Jewish-national aesthetics) and the publishing house Shamir, which published his outstanding epic poem *Sikhes khulin* (Idle chatter). This modernist reworking of a 16th-century Yiddish tale, *Mayse Yerushalmi* (Event in Jerusalem), for which the Russian avant-gardist El Lissitzky (→ Wolkenbügel) provided the illustrations and which was presented in the form of an Esther scroll, is considered a masterpiece of Yiddish modernism. In the old story, Broderzon perceived the tension between → mysticism, demonism, and eroticism characteristic of Expressionist art. In the same year he published his children's story *Temerl* (Little Tamar) illustrated by Joseph Chaikov. His volume of poems *Toy* (Dew), in which he experimentally combined the classical Japanese poetry genre *tanka* with motifs from the Song of Solomon, was published in 1918 while he was still in Moscow. In his artistic creations he endeavored to renew Yiddish → literature formally, to employ Jewish tradition creatively, and to brace together modern and traditional art forms.

Other artists of *Yung Yidish* followed his lead. The group contributed to several exhibitions, for instance in Białystok in 1919 and in Łódź in 1921 – there with its own salon of Futurists, Cubists, and Primitivists –, Warsaw and New York. It was also in contact with the Kiev *Kultur-Lige* (Culture league; → Czernowitz Language Conference), which since its founding in 1918 also sought the renewal of Yiddish culture and influenced the activities of *Yung Yidish*.

In addition to exhibitions, the group also made a name for itself journalistically. In 1919, three editions of the literature and the arts journal *Yung Yidish* appeared, printed on gray wrapping paper in the Futurist manner. The editor responsible was Felicja Szydłowska who hosted a literary salon in Łódź. The journal was richly illustrated with graphics and featured programmatic as well as literary texts composed by members of the group and avant-garde artists connected with them. The publication dates of the three issues of *Yung Yidish* coincided provocatively with Jewish holidays.

In 1920 and 1921, the group focused primarily on publishing. *Yung Yidish* published, among other things, six books by Broderzon, among them *Perl oyfn bruk* (Pearls on the cobblestones) in 1920, whose sonnets referred to the poetics of Symbolism. Additionally, two group declarations, likewise presumably from Broderzon, were published in the journal, as well as his poem *Tsu di shtern* (To the stars), a section of which would become the poetic manifesto of the young avant-garde connected to *Yung Yidish*. It describes the younger generation as a "boisterous gang who love to sing," overflowing with creativity, who reject the rigid value system and tradition, instead treading an "unknown path" towards an uncertain future – "in nights of terror: / Per aspera ad astra" (cited in [2. 166]). Members of the group also contributed to the monthly journal *Tel Aviv*. They arranged evening entertainments in the style of → cabaret, which combined music, dance, recitation, and theatre with detailed stage sets. The members of *Yung Yidish* also produced so-called negative linocuts in which the color black dominated, oil paintings with a frequently fiery color scheme and stark contrasts, and batiks. Their artistic creativity was characterized by bold deformation, flowing contours, and simultaneous geometrization of forms, as well as the conveying of mystical themes and visionary moods.

The main objective of *Yung Yidish* was to renew Jewish art in the context of the artistic modern. They sought to establish a modern, secular Jewish culture as the foundation of a future Jewish national style. Striving for universality, the group also drew on the richness of Jewish → folklore and, encouraged by Martin Buber's (→ Dialogue) works, drew inspiration from → Hasidism, whose irrational-mystical relationship with the world harmonized with their Expressionist attitude. They furthermore accepted the Christian tradition that has emerged from Judaism, frequently referring to motifs from medieval Christian mysticism, Gothic art, and the Mannerist El Greco in their works. The members of the group understood the traditions, on which they drew not without ironic detachment, as the entirety of humanity's cultural achievements, as Broderzon emphasized: "And if we are conservative, we respect our leaders and schools – such as the Tanakh, Greek mythology, the Song of Solomon, Lord Byron, Shelley, French authors (Parnassiens) and Young Belgium, Ernst Theodor Amadeus Hoffmann, Edgar Allan Poe, Cyprian Kamil Norwid" [1].

The members of *Yung Yidish* also appreciated African as well as so-called primitive art. In order to express the intrinsic core of phenomena, they broke with Impressionism and Naturalism, distancing themselves from contemporary social and political *topoi* in their search for new formal and aesthetic solutions. If revolutionary motifs do appear, it was mainly in the context of endeavors for the spiritual renewal of humanity and as a precondition of societal change. The chaotic but nevertheless fascinating conditions in the modern industrial city of Łódź which created a feeling of alienation, were reflected in their works in moods such as isolation and pessimism. They did not avoid moral provocation and were attracted by anarchism. The activities of the artists of *Yung Yidish* were a revolt against the predominating → middle-class culture.

From 1921 onward, the group left the Expressionist style behind, turning instead to Realism or Constructivism. In 1921/1922 it gradually dissolved. A considerable number of its members had left Łódź in the meantime. Adler and Szwarc went to Berlin and Paris, while Broderzon increasingly focused on theatre.

Yung Yidish contributed significantly to the emergence of so-called Jewish Expressionism. The art of Adler and Szwarc and Broderzon's writings, which broke with the form and content of traditional Jewish → literature, provided a source of inspiration for the nascent Warsaw Yiddish avantgarde in the early 1920s, which centered around the Expressionist Yiddish writers' groups *Di Khalyastre* (The Gang) and *Ringen* (Rings). The subsequent generation of artists, who were active from the late 1920s into the 1930s, such as the art and literature group *Yung Vilne* (Young Vilna), were not so much indebted to experimentation, subversion, and formal innovation in art, but rather to the social function of their creative endeavors.

Bibliography

Sources

[1] M. Broderzon, Manifesto, in: Yung Yidish 2/3 (1919), 2.

Secondary literature

[2] A. Eidherr, Sonnenuntergang auf eisig-blauen Wegen. Zur Thematisierung von Diaspora und Sprache in der jiddischen Literatur des 20. Jahrhunderts, Göttingen 2012. [3] J. Malinowski, The 'Yung Yiddish' (Young Yiddish) Group and Jewish Modern Art in Poland, 1918–1923, in: Polin 6 (1991), 223–230. [4] J. Malinowski, Painting and Sculpture by Polish Jews in the 19th and 20th Centuries (to 1939), trans. by K. Z. Cieszkowski, Warsaw 2017. [5] G. Rozier, Moyshe Broderzon. Un écrivain yiddish d'avant-garde, Saint-Denis 1999. [6] J. Suchan (ed.), Polak, Żyd, artysta. Tożsamość a awangarda [Pole, Jew, Artist. Identity and Avant-garde], Łódź 2010. [7] Y. Y. Trunk, Poyln. My Life within Jewish Life, trans. by A. Clarke, Toronto 2016.

JOANNA LISEK, WROCŁAW

Z

Zakhor

The divine imperative *zakhor* ("remember") pronounced in the Bible obligates the Israelites to remember dramatic occurrences and events of their history. During Late Antiquity more recent catastrophic events were also put into a causal religious context and, consequently parallelized in the calendar. The strongest manifestation of the biblical exhortation to remember developed in the → liturgy through commemorative prayers and in ritual in celebration and days of remembrance (→ Course of the Year) serving as historical recollection. This schematizing historical theorem of thought remained a defining aspect of Jewish remembrance and was superseded only by modern historiography.

1. Memory in the Bible
2. Rabbinic innovations
3. The Middle Ages and the early modern era
4. Modern forms

1. Memory in the Bible

In his pathbreaking study *Zakhor: Jewish History and Jewish Memory* (1982), Yosef Hayim Yerushalmi demonstrated that during the pre-modern era, Jewish collective memory was determined less by historiography and more by → liturgy and religious ritual. This was due to God's exhortation to the people of Israel, repeatedly documented in the Bible (→ Tanakh), to "remember" certain events. The best-known formula of this is the Hebrew imperative *zakhor* ("remember"), which occurs about forty times in the biblical text. It is used frequently in the context of divine interventions in history, as at the first time it is mentioned (Exod 13:3): "And Moses said to the people, 'Remember this day, on which you went free from Egypt, the house of bondage, how the Lord freed you from it with a mighty hand'."

The significance of the remembrance of this event in particular is based not least on its connection with the divine revelation on Mount Sinai. God reveals himself to the repeatedly doubting ("grumbling"; Exod 15:24–17:2) Israelites with the words: "I the Lord am your God who brought you out of the land of Egypt, the house of bondage"; Exod 20:2). The imperative *zakhor*, however, refers to remembering the divine commandments as well as the covenant between God and Israel. As God entered into the covenant at Mount Sinai "with those who are not with us here this day"(Deut 29:14) and as the event is not repeatable, it must reach future generations through remembrance [11. 9–10]. Nevertheless, the Israelites were obliged to remember only those occurrences in which divine intervention was manifest. Consequently the biblical narrative codified only select memories, with the result that some events were emphasized in collective commemoration while many others are marginalized or forgotten altogether.

The Bible contains numerous instances of the ritual implementation of the imperative *zakhor*, with the narrative of the first fruits (Deut 26:1–11) being paradigmatic.

During their forty years of wandering through the desert, God commands the Israelites to give part of the first harvest after their arrival in the Promised Land to a priest (Deut 26:1f.). As soon as the latter lays the fruits of the field down before the altar, the people must recapitulate their history (Deut 26:5), namely their Aramean origins (Deut 26:5), the time they spent in Egypt and the bondage suffered there (Deut 26:6), their divine rescue (Deut 26:8), and their entry into "a land flowing with milk and honey" (Deut 26:9). This actualization of Jewish history, referred to as *mikra bikkurim* (recitation of the first fruits), is one of the oldest of all; Yerushalmi pointed out that "fundamental biblical conceptions of history were forged, not by historians, but by priests and prophets" [11. 12]. While the celebration of Passover (→ Course of the Year) retains the memory of its origins as a harvest festival, historical remembrance is in the foreground. Thus the individual rules (Exod 13:3–7) are prefaced with the exhortation: "And you shall explain to your child on that day, 'It is because of what the Lord did for me when I went free from Egypt'" (Exod 13:8).

According to the Bible, historical events worthy of commemoration were primarily those which had negative, frequently also catastrophic, impacts on the life of the Jews. The *locus classicus* for such a commemoration is Deuteronomy 25:17–19, in which Israel is exhorted not to forget the deeds of its most terrible enemy, Amalek (→ Edom):

Remember what Amalek did to you on your journey, after you left Egypt – how, undeterred by fear of God, he surprised you on the march, when you were famished and weary, and cut down all the stragglers in your rear. Therefore, when your God the Lord grants you safety from all your enemies around you, in the land that your God the Lord is giving you as a hereditary portion, you shall blot out the memory of Amalek from under heaven. Do not forget!

The commandment to remember was important not least because "ancient Israel knows what God is from what he has done in history. And if that is so, then memory has become crucial to its faith and, ultimately, to its very existence" [11. 9]. The custom of publicly reading the Amalek narrative once a year, on *Shabbat Zakhor*, the → Shabbat before Purim (→ Course of the Year) probably dates from as early as the 2nd century.

Since Ezra's reorganization of the postexilic community at the very latest, further biblical passages were regularly read out in public in addition to the *mikra bikkurim* or the readings on special Shabbatot such as that on *Shabbat Zakhor*. Their respective historical narrative – Nehemiah 8:13–18, for instance, mentions the feast of Sukkot (→ Course of the Year) which, according to Leviticus 23:42f., also commemorates the exodus from Egypt – thus occupied a fixed place in the collective memory. By introducing a fixed one- or three-year reading cycle of the entire Torah, the biblical historical events – underpinned by the annual festivals – acquired a cyclical character, although → time as such was not imagined in cyclical terms [11. 115].

In addition to Torah readings and festivals, the biblical imperative manifested itself in another form of ritual commemoration, namely the observance of days of remembrance. The prophet Ezekiel established the 10th of Tevet as one at divine behest, as this was the day on which King Nebuchadnezzar's siege of Jerusalem had begun (2 Kgs 25:1), ending with the devastation of the city, the deportation of the Jewish upper class, and, finally, the destruction of the → Temple (586 BCE): "In the ninth year [of exile], on the tenth day of the tenth month [Tevet], the word of the LORD came to me: O mortal, record this date, this exact day; for this very day the king of Babylon has laid siege to Jerusalem" (Ezek 24:1f.).

Fasting was central to these remembrance days in addition to ritual lamentations and mourning. With the exception of Yom Kippur (→ Course of the Year) on the 10th of Tishri, fixed days of fasting were introduced only in the postexilic period. During the time of the prophet Zechariah, they were "[t]he fast of the fourth month [Tammuz], the fast of the fifth month [Av], the fast of the seventh month [Tishri], and the fast of the tenth month [Tevet]" (Zech 8:19). The biblical fast day in remembrance of the destruction of the Temple was probably dated to the 10th of Av according to Jeremiah 52:12ff.; in another passage the event is said to have occurred on the 7th of Av (2 Kgs 25:8ff.). The fast day in the month of Tammuz was observed on the 9th of that month in remembrance of the Babylonian conquest of Jerusalem (2 Kgs 25:3f.).

2. Rabbinic innovations

A fundamental reform of remembrance began after the destruction of the Second Temple in 70 CE. Some cultic actions have since been performed symbolically in Jewish households (→ Kashrut; → Mikveh). Other rituals of temple worship were replaced with synagogue prayers. The greater part of the Jewish liturgy for everyday life, Shabbat, and holidays was fixed during the Amoraic period (5th–7th cents.; → Talmud). During this period, remembrance during divine services acquired a new dimension as certain memories were transformed into a liturgical-symbolic re-enactment of a lost glorious past.

The center of liturgical attention was occupied by the loss of the Temple, which was commemorated with the hope of reconstruction and renewal of the political commonwealth. Some of the oldest prayer forms also recalled historical events. The third blessing *Kedushat ha-Yom* (Sanctification of

the Day) of the *Amidah* (Eighteen Benedictions; → Liturgy), which probably dates from the 2nd century, mentions three different (mytho-)historical occurrences, depending on the occasion on which it is recited. On Friday night it recalls the creation of the world, in the morning prayer the gift of the Torah on Mount Sinai, and in the additional prayer (*musaf*) the sacrificial cult in the Temple, praying for its restoration.

Ritual remembrance was also extended during the rabbinic era. The biblical day of remembrance in the month of Av (→ Tishʿah be-Av) was fixed on the ninth day of the month, with this date being set as the anniversary of the destruction of both Temples (Talmud Bavli, Taʾanit 29a). Three further disasters – the divine doom according to which the forebears would not enter into the promised land, the Roman conquest of Betar during the Bar Kokhba rebellion, and the day on which Jerusalem was razed by the Babylonians – were also dated to this day (Mishnah, Taʾanit 4:6). The biblical fast day in Tammuz was moved to the 17th of the month and dedicated to remembering the first breach the Babylonian besiegers cut into the city walls of Jerusalem and which paved the way for the destruction of the Temple (Mishnah, Taʾanit 4:6). At the same time the rabbis set this as the date of Moses smashing the tablets of the law, of the last sacrifice being brought in the Temple, of the Syrian-Greek general Apostomos erecting an idol in the Temple and burning a Torah scroll (ibid.)

The relationship between the respective events consisted less in chronology or historical causality and more in their religious connection. The ancient Jewish scholars interpreted events as the consequences of a grave and continuing sin, namely the adoration of the golden calf. This perception was the foundation for "[the] need for historical symmetry" [11. 41], which ultimately had an effect on dating as well. By means of the chronological parallelization of (mytho-) historical events, the rabbis created a religious calendar intended to make divine providence comprehensible and to imbue → history with meaning.

3. The Middle Ages and the early modern era

The liturgical and ritual commemoration established during Late Antiquity continued into the Middle Ages but underwent a few innovations. The persecutions that broke out in 1096 with the start of the First Crusade, and that were particularly brutal in the Rhineland where they led to entire communities being obliterated (→ Ashkenaz), were experienced as an unprecedented catastrophe. Accounts of women and men killing themselves and their families in order to avoid forced baptism were particularly powerful. In memory of the → martyrs, a special memorial service was introduced, named *Yizkor* (May [God] Remember) or *Hazkarat Neshamot* (Commemoration of the Souls). This service gradually became a fixed part of Ashkenazi holy day liturgy on the three pilgrimage festivals of Passover, Sukkot, and Shavuot (→ Course of the Year) and on Yom Kippur. In remembrance of the victims of the persecutions motivated by anti-Judaism during the 11th to 14th centuries, Jewish poets furthermore composed new lamentation (*kinot*) and penitence (*selihot*) prayers to be recited on different occasions. Among them were *Av ha-Rahamim* (Father of Mercy), calling for divine revenge, and the elegiac *Eleh Ezkerah* (These I Will Remember).

Various memorial prayers were also composed for the martyrs of Blois in northern France where 32 Jews were burnt at the stake on Siwan 20 (May 26), 1171, as the result of the first accusation of ritual murder (→ Blood Libel) on the European continent. The extent of the violence appears to have been the decisive factor in later catastrophic events being aligned to this non-biblical

date. This applied to the → Cossack persecutions, beginning in 1648, which extended over large parts of Poland–Lithuania and during the course of which an estimated 20,000 Jews lost their lives. Shabbatai Hakohen (1621–1662), a well-known Lithuanian rabbi and → Halakhah scholar, placed these events in the context of the religiously motivated medieval persecution by dating their start – not entirely in accordance with the facts – to the 20th of Siwan. In addition he favored giving renewed meaning to the day of remembrance supposedly introduced in memory of the *auto-da-fé* in Blois in the 12th century for the 20th of Siwan. The leading rabbi in Poland, Yom-Tov Lipman Heller (1579–1654), took even more explicit action. At first he rejected the request of some Jewish communities to compose memorial prayers (he later gave in), arguing that the memorial prayers for the martyrs of Blois should continue to be recited on Siwan 20, for "[w]hat has occurred now is similar to the persecutions of old, and all that happened to the forefathers has happened to their descendants. [...] *It is all one*" (cited in [11. 50]). Thus Heller decided that the Blois *selihot* were to be prayed during the High Holidays between Rosh ha-Shanah (→ Course of the Year) and Yom Kippur. In doing so, he placed the murdered Jews within a chronology of persecutions starting in the Middle Ages, that had not been lost from memory thanks to the liturgical memorial practice of the mid-17th century.

The result of Heller's liturgical traditionalism as well as that of many others was that the memorial prayers for the victims of the Cossack persecutions that had been included in the → liturgy of Polish and Lithuanian communities around 1650 were abandoned once again in favor of the recitation of the medieval prayers during the course of the 17th and 18th centuries. The memorial prayer *El Male Rahamim* (God Full of Mercy; mid-17th century) survived in Ashkenazi ritual in only one version from which all details referring to the Cossacks had been expunged; as a prayer for the souls of the dead, it found its place in the liturgy for burials, memorial services, and in the ritual around visiting a grave.

While the historical-liturgical and ritual memory of the Jews focused almost exclusively on catastrophic events and → death from the Middle Ages until the early modern era, a new tradition emerged out of early modern rituals of remembrance. Along the lines of the biblical festival of Purim (→ Course of the Year) which commemorated the rescue of the Babylonian Jews, communities of the Sephardic → Diaspora, and later also in Ashkenaz, endeavored to establish memorial days commemorating the happy ending of a danger to individuals or an entire community. The first of these *Purim Sheni/Katan* (Second/Small Purim) – among them those celebrated by the Jewish communities in Cairo, Crete, and Algiers – emerged around the middle of the 16th century; in recent years, the existence of comparable customs dating from the Middle Ages has been met with considerable doubt [6. 305f.]. An increasing number of such ritual memorial festivals have been documented in Italy from the second half of the 16th century onward, while the first *Purim Sheni* celebrated north of the Alps took place in the first half of the 17th century and commemorated the triumphant return of the Jews to Frankfurt am Main (→ Fettmilch Uprising).

The liturgical and paraliturgical innovations established by individual communities in the Middle Ages and early modern period prove that the Jews of this era no longer regarded their experiences as a fate shared by all. Various communities introduced their own specific days of remembrance. Regionally impactful events such as the expulsion of the Jews from England in 1290, the expulsion from the Iberian Peninsula in

1492/1496, or the persecutions at the hands of the Cossacks from 1648/1649 to 1656 were reflected in prayers, but they did not occupy an important or permanent place in the Ashkenazic or Sephardic liturgy. Medieval and early modern liturgical memory was as locally defined as it was selective.

4. Modern forms

Enlightenment (→ Haskalah), → emancipation, and → secularization were reflected in religious confessionalization, with the emerging trends also seeing a diversification of liturgical remembrance. Thus, the followers of religious → reform in Germany were the first to demand a reassessment of the historical narratives. The prayer book of the Hamburg Reform congregation either removed or emended phrases in the traditional Siddur that referred to the central significance of Erets Israel and the anticipated the re-establishment of the sacrificial cult; some of the events anticipated were shifted to the messianic era or even given a contrary interpretation. Thus the passage referring to Erets Israel "Bring us home in peace" was reworded as "Guide your blessing to us in all the corners of the earth" (cited in [3. 16]). During the 20th century, especially after the foundation of the State of Israel, this universal view was partially revised. Some Reform prayer books now once again include phrases which show Jerusalem and → Zion as a place of hope – albeit a real rather than a sublime one. In addition, some prayers of the weekday and → Shabbat liturgies employ new phrases: Thus in the *Amidah*, the traditional form of the tenth blessing of the gathering of the "exiles" and "outcasts" has been changed to the "dispersed."

Some of the Jewish festivals and memorial days that were observed in private or in the → synagogue in the → Diaspora have assumed a more publicly celebrated form of ritual remembrance since the foundation of the State of Israel. This change is particularly visible in Hanukkah (→ Course of the Year), the only post-biblical festival, during which traditionally the divine intervention resulting in the renewed consecration of the Temple (175 BCE) and the anticipated redemption are commemorated. The public lighting of the Hanukkah candles that has been celebrated for some decades is accompanied by singing the first and fifth verses of *Ma'oz Tsur* (Strong Rock). This song originated during the 13th century in → Ashkenaz in reaction to anti-Jewish persecutions at the hands of Christians. It mentions several terrible events in Jewish history and their respective happy endings – in the case of Hanukkah the defeat in battle against the Seleucids and the subsequent victory of the Maccabees and the reconquest of Jerusalem (163 BCE). Until the 19th century, the song was exclusively sung in Hanukkah celebrations in the home and later in Reform synagogues.

The → Holocaust (→ Auschwitz) as the key experience of the Jews in the 20th century has not been reflected in standard synagogue liturgy to this day. Reasons cited are the continuing impact of the overwhelming event as well as the generally hostile attitude of traditional religious opinion leaders with respect to liturgical innovations. Only in recent years have some synagogues remembered victims of the Holocaust on special occasions, by reciting an altered version of *El Male Raḥamim* (God, Full of Mercy) or other poems suited to the subject.

While no new prayers were introduced into the standard → liturgy in reaction to the annihilation of European Jews, the debate concerning official commemoration of the Holocaust started only a few years after the founding of the State of Israel. The chief rabbinate favored the 10th of Tevet as being an established day of remembrance, while the Israeli Knesset at first supported the 14th of Nisan, the anniversary of the start of the Warsaw ghetto uprising (1943). However, as this is the day before Passover, in 1951 the Israeli parliament finally voted for the 27th of Nisan, agreeing in 1953 on the official name *Yom ha-Sho'ah veha-Gevurah* (Holocaust and Heroism Remembrance Day). The decision in favor of a date close to the anniversary of the Warsaw ghetto uprising also, and above all, underscored the intention especially to remember the Jewish resistance against the National Socialists. → Lamentations in the form of poems and hymns in the tradition of liturgical *kinot* or → Kaddish are sung and recited at official remembrance ceremonies. The 10th of Tevet also became a day of civil ritual remembrance when it was appointed as *Yom ha-Kaddish ha-Klali* (Day of Universal Kaddish), the day of *yor tsayt* (memorial) of the victims of the Holocaust.

Two more days have been dedicated to more recent national history: The 4th of Iyar is *Yom ha-Zikaron le-Ḥalale Ma'arkhot Yisra'el ve-Ḥalale Pe'ulot ha-Evah*, a "Day of Remembrance for the Fallen of Israel's Military Campaigns and for the Fallen by Enemy Actions"; it commemorates the military and civilian victims of war and terror. *Yom ha-Atsma'ut*, the "Day of Independence," is officially celebrated on the following day. Depending on one's point of view, the civilian remembrance days are regarded as a – modified – continuation of tradition or as breaking with tradition. Especially among the → ultra-Orthodox, the foundation of the State is regarded as an improper attempt at expediting the anticipated divine salvation by human means. Many ultra-Orthodox reject the national days of remembrance, and some particularly radical groups observe the Day of Independence as a Day of Mourning. Members of moderate ultra-Orthodox groups, however, describe the founding of the State of Israel as *reshit tsmiḥat ge'ulatenu* (seed of our salvation).

Bibliography

Sources

[1] Siddur Tefilot Yisra'el = The Hirsch Siddur. The Order of Prayers for the Whole Year, Jerusalem/New York 1997. [2] Siddur Sefat Emet = Daily Prayers. With English Instructions by W. Heidenheim, New York 1928.

Secondary literature

[3] A. Brämer, Judentum und religiöse Reform. Der Hamburger Israelitische Tempel 1817–1938, Hamburg 2000. [4] E. Carlebach et al. (eds.), Jewish History and Jewish Memory. Essays in Honor of Yosef Hayim Yerushalmi, Hanover/London 1998. [5] S. L. Einbinder, Beautiful Death. Jewish Poetry and Martyrdom in Medieval France, Princeton 2002. [6] E. Horowitz, Reckless Rites. Purim and the Legacy of Jewish Violence, Princeton 2006. [7] A. Mintz, Ḥurban. Responses to Catastrophe in Hebrew Literature, New York 1984. [8] M. Nulman, The Encyclopedia of Jewish Prayer. Ashkenazic and Sephardic Rites, Northvale/London 1993. [9] J. Petuchowski, Prayerbook Reform in Europe, New York 1968. [10] G. M. Spiegel, Memory and History. Liturgical Time and Historical Time, in: History and Theory 41 (2002) 2, 149–162. [11] Y. H. Yerushalmi, Zakhor. Jewish History and Jewish Memory, New York 1989.

FRAUKE VON ROHDEN, LEIPZIG

Zeitschrift der Deutschen Morgenländischen Gesellschaft

Journal of the Deutsche Morgenländische Gesellschaft (DMG, German Oriental Society) founded in 1847 to serve the academic community of Oriental scholars in Germany. As a former ancillary discipline of theology, Oriental studies was established as an independent discipline during the 19th century (→ Muslim Studies; → Orient). Unlike theology and history, German Oriental studies distanced itself from contemporary politics, in research as well as in its day-to-day dealings, and it confronted Jewish scholars largely without prejudice. Numerous Jewish scholars came to appreciate the DMG and the *Zeitschrift* (ZDMG) as a forum and place to publish their work beyond the organizations and the periodicals of the → Wissenschaft des Judentums.

1. Oriental studies as an academic discipline
2. Oriental studies and Wissenschaft des Judentums
3. Jewish scholars in DMG and ZDMG prior to 1933

1. Oriental studies as an academic discipline

The discipline of Oriental studies is concerned with the languages and cultures of the Orient, from the Mediterranean to the Yellow Sea. Accordingly, the term "Orient," which provides the discipline with its name, is based on a wide spatial understanding of the area it deals with. The travels undertaken by British and French diplomats, missionaries, and archaeologists in the context of the European expansion and the Napoleonic conquests created an enthusiasm for collecting Orientalia and for the study of Oriental languages, but they also inspired a general interest among educated Europeans in all things → Oriental. Formerly an ancillary discipline of theology and its philological branch, Oriental studies in Europe became an independent academic discipline over the course of the 19th century. Up to that time, the subjects relevant for the study of Jewish history and culture, Hebrew studies (→ Hebrew), Biblical studies (→ Biblical Criticism), and the study of the Holy Land had been the traditional interest and occupation of mainly Protestant scholars and pastors.

At the beginning, oriental studies in Germany had little or no institutional underpinning. After a phase of formation and consolidation at the beginning of the 19th century and specialization in the years between 1870 and 1900, it soon grew to be an emerging new discipline of its own [10. 1–52, 157–211]. Until well into the 20th century the → universities of Berlin, Göttingen, Breslau (Wrocław), Vienna, Leipzig, and Halle an der Saale enjoyed a reputation as centers of Oriental studies in German-speaking areas on account of their outstanding scholars in the field.

Even in the last third of the 19th century the theological and Orientalist professorships were closely intertwined. At the University of Göttingen the theologian and Orientalist Johann David Michaelis had made it a condition when he was appointed as a professor (1750) that his chair for Oriental languages and biblical exegesis be attached to the philosophical faculty. This arrangement lasted until 1848, when it was split again to create a new Oriental chair and a separate one primarily for Old Testament studies; the latter remained at first with the philosophical faculty and was eventually attached to the theological faculty in 1914 with the succession of Rudolf Smend the Elder, a pupil of Julius Wellhausen. Because of such interrelations it was not unusual for scholars to begin as theologians only to find themselves turning increasingly or entirely toward Oriental studies later in their career. Theology, meanwhile, reclaimed the subject areas of Oriental studies as its very own "Oriental ancillary disciplines"; thus, for instance, in the literature overview of the Protestant *Theologisches Literaturblatt* the latter are subsumed under the specialist area "Old Testament."

It made the task of announcing the Deutsche Morgenländische Gesellschaft (DMG) at the Eighth Convention of German Philologists and Educators in Darmstadt in 1845, after twelve months of preparations, an even more important one for German Oriental studies [11]. The official launch of the society followed in October of the same year in Leipzig, and it is to this day the most influential association of the discipline in Germany. Among the founding fathers of the DMG were the Leipzig professors Heinrich Leberecht Fleischer and Hermann Brockhaus, as well as their Halle colleagues Emil Rödiger and August Friedrich Pott. Use of the term *Morgenland* rather than *Orient* in the title was a reference to the word choice in Martin Luther's → Bible translation and reveals the close association with theology. As a professional organization the DMG advocated for the academicization of Oriental studies in the German language area, not least through the Society's own academic journal, *Zeitschrift der Deutschen Morgenländischen Gesellschaft* (ZDMG), in publication since 1847.

Oriental studies became a mainly philological discipline that shared the areas of Hebrew studies and Bible studies, as well as the history and culture of the Orient, with Protestant theology but also with the → Wissenschaft des Judentums. In this way, ancient and medieval Judaism found its academic place in Oriental studies, having been largely excluded from the canon of → classical studies and → philosophy [6]. Unlike the Protestant theologians Franz Delitzsch and Hermann Leberecht Strack, whose Lutheran background and salvific as well as missionary predisposition guided their treatment of Oriental subjects, the discipline itself emphasized its clear linguistic approach and pursuit of cultural studies [17]. Especially Delitzsch, who over time intensified his biblical and Hebraic studies, from 1870 sought to instrumentalize Oriental studies for the → mission to the Jews by offering a course of studies designed to achieve this goal. Following the example of the theologian and Orientalist Johann Heinrich Callenberg and his Pietistic Institutum Judaicum et Muhammedicum in Halle, Delitzsch eventually realized his idea in the shape of the Institutum Judaicum, an educational institution for missionaries to the Jews in Leipzig. Further institutes were established in Erlangen, Halle, Berlin, Breslau (Wrocław), and Greifswald. Stracke headed the Institutum Judaicum in Berlin.

Oriental studies, especially the DMG, did not share the tendency toward thematic constriction observed in ancient history and philosophy and the sometimes missionary aims of theologians working in the Oriental field. Moreover, they generally avoided any involvement in current political matters pertaining to the Orient and its cultures; most members of the DMG acted accordingly and made no public statements on such issues. While contemporary travel accounts were certainly accepted as sources of information, religious and political discussions were deemed the domain of other journals and the newspapers.

2. Oriental studies and Wissenschaft des Judentums

More than many other disciplines, Oriental studies facilitated the fruitful exchange between Jewish and non-Jewish scholars. They often maintained a correspondence or even personal contacts, which included mutual visits and cooperation in research projects.

Under the leadership of Heinrich L. Fleischer and Emil Rödiger the DMG pursued an emphatically research-oriented and historical-philological course which did not allow any anti-Jewish or Christian missionary ideology to come up. Fleischer, for instance, judged Jewish and non-Jewish students and scholars by their academic qualifications and achievements. Religious, cultural, political, and national views were as irrelevant to him as was a person's ancestry. While studying in Paris under the Orientalist Antoine Isaac Silvestre de Sacy, Fleischer himself had made the acquaintance of other renowned Jewish scholars such as Salomon Munk (→ Falsafah). Fleischer's lectures at

the University of Leipzig brought Franz Delitzsch and Moritz Steinschneider (→ Bibliography) into contact. Julius Fürst, who worked, gratuitously, as a language teacher in Oriental studies at the University of Leipzig for decades and who edited the journal → Der Orient (1840–1850/1851), was not close to the circle of Christian scholars, but the university lecturers, it can be assumed, maintained collegial relations [16].

In addition to the thematic proximity of Oriental studies and the → Wissenschaft des Judentums, the largely unprejudiced environment especially under Fleischer and Rödiger made Oriental studies more attractive for Jewish scholars. While there were relatively few doctoral candidates in the area of Wissenschaft des Judentums in the Orientalism faculties at Austrian → universities [1], by contrast numerous Jewish Orientalists obtained their doctorate from the University of Halle; among them were Leopold Zunz (1821; → Verein für Cultur und Wissenschaft der Juden), Azriel Hildesheimer (1846; → Rabbinical Seminary), Leiser Lazarus (1848; → Breslau), Marcus Lehmann (1854 → Jud Süß; → Novel), Marcus M. Jastrow (1856; → January Uprising), Michael Friedländer (1860; → Bible Translation), Sigmund Maybaum (1868; → Hochschule für die Wissenschaft des Judentums; → Sermon), and Pinkus Fritz Frankl (1871; → Karaites) [18]. At the Leipzig Faculty of Oriental Studies, Fleischer wrote the first evaluations for the doctoral dissertations of, among others, Moritz Steinschneider (1851), Ignaz Goldziher (1870; → Muslim Studies), and Adolf Neubauer (1887; → Bibliotheca Bodleiana) [14. 234–236]; he was the second assessor, for instance, in the doctoral degree proceedings for Elieser Lipman Silberman (1874; → Ha-Maggid; → Mekitse Nirdamim) and Richard J. H. Gottheil (1886).

The objective attitude of the discipline in general, and of the DMG in particular, also characterized the editorial regulations of the ZDMG, which readily published papers and studies submitted by Jewish scholars. Many Jewish Orientalists worked on the study of the Holy Land, Hebraic studies, the history of Jewish literature, and the → history and culture of ancient and medieval Judaism. Many of them, including Abraham Geiger, Goldziher, Munk, Steinschneider, Josef Horovitz, Felix Ernst Peiser, Gustav Weil, and Eugen Mittwoch turned to Arabic studies and Quran studies and gained a reputation as trailblazers of modern Islamic studies (→ Quran; → Muslim Studies) [2]; [4]; [13].

3. Jewish scholars in DMG and ZDMG prior to 1933

From its first issue in 1847, the *Zeitschrift der Deutschen Morgenländischen Gesellschaft* saw itself as a publishing forum for the DMG and as a medium for documenting the state of research in the Oriental discipline. Under the leadership of Heinrich L. Fleischer, Emil Rödiger, and Ludolf Krehl there was always room for → Hebrew language studies and Jewish subjects from the rabbinic era as well as topics from medieval Jewish → history and philosophy (→ Falsafah). Many Jewish scholars like Geiger, Goldziher, Gottheil, Samuel Kohn (→ Neolog), and Steinschneider were among the ZDMG's authors in the 19th and early 20th centuries.

Under the heading "Report on the affairs of the DM Society" the ZDMG always included a list with the names of individual and institutional members. Individual membership usually ended with the person's death. Already in the first year of DMG's existence, scholars like Steinschneider, Fürst, Adolf Jellinek (→ Israelitische Allianz zu Wien), Michael Sachs (→ Mekitse Nirdamim), and Zunz were listed as members. Over time, they were joined by numerous scholars of the → Wissenschaft des Judentums, among them Goldziher, Jacob Barth (→ Rabbinical Seminary), Zacharias Frankel (→ Breslau; → Conservative Judaism), Kaufmann Kohler

(→ Hebrew Union College), and Leopold Löw (→ Neolog). They were listed along with the founding and honorary members Fleischer, Rödiger, and Brockhaus, as well as with well-known personalities such as Franz Delitzsch, Adalbert Merx, Hermann L. Strack, Paul Georg von Möllendorff, and Ernest Renan (→ Semitic Studies). Institutional members included the Veitel-Heine-Ephraim'sche Lehranstalt in Berlin, the → Bodleian Library in Oxford, and the Berlin → Rabbinical Seminary for Orthodox Judaism. In the 1880s, scholars such as Gottheil, Hartwig Hirschfeld, and David Simonsen became members.

Honorary memberships were also awarded to Jewish scholars. The first was Julius (Jules) Oppert (→ Semitic Studies) in 1895, who had taught philology and archaeology at the Collège de France in Paris since 1869 and was considered an authority in the field of Assyriology. The second Jewish honorary member in 1911 was Goldziher from the University of Budapest. The British Orientalist and Arabist David Samuel Margoliouth, like Goldziher a pioneer of Islamic studies, became the third Jewish scholar to be awarded an honorary membership in 1934.

The DMG published other professional journals in addition to the ZDMG. Among these, since 1857, is the scholarly journal *Abhandlungen für die Kunde des Morgenlandes*. Motivated by the differentiation of Oriental studies, and in conjunction with the Heidelberg Academy of Sciences and the local Portheim-Stiftung für Wissenschaft und Kunst in Heidelberg the *Zeitschrift für Assyriologie und verwandte Gebiete* (1886–1938) was published; and the *Zeitschrift für Indologie und Iranistik* (1922–1936) and the *Zeitschrift für Semitistik und verwandte Gebiete* (1922–1935) were founded.

An equivalent journal in the German-speaking area was the *Österreichische Monatsschrift für den Orient* (1875–1918), published by the Orientalisches Museum in Vienna. It, too, had Jewish scholars submitting contributions but to a much lesser extent than the ZDMG. Founded in 1898 and continuing to this day, the *Orientalische Literaturzeitung* (OLZ), a research and review periodical, complements the ZDLG for the entire field of Oriental studies. Its first editor-in-chief until 1921 was the Jewish Assyrologist Felix Ernst Peiser; Peiser's successor until his own death in 1935 was the Egyptologist Walter Wreszinski, whose family likewise was Jewish.

The DMG and its *Zeitschrift* depict the many facets and the development of the interrelation between Jewish and Oriental studies until the mid-1930s. Until that time, Jewish scholars, DMG members, and the society's organs cooperated on a largely unprejudiced and collegial basis. Fleischer had supported the work of Jacob Levy on his *Neuhebräisches und chaldäisches Wörterbuch über die Talmudim und Midraschim*, which was published in four volumes between 1876 and 1889 by Brockhaus in Leipzig, with comments and emendations. Even Paul de Lagarde, author of the anti-Semitic *Deutsche Schriften* (1878–1881) encouraged Moses Samuel Zuckermandel to produce an edition of the Tosefta, which was printed in Pasewalk in 1880.

Nevertheless, academic disputes and conflicts also characterized the relationship between Oriental studies and the Wissenschaft des Judentums. A particularly fraught area were the topics of Antiquity and Late Antiquity. Thus, in a series of public lectures between 1902 and 1904 the Assyriologist Friedrich Delitzsch triggered the so-called → Babel and Bible dispute. Delitzsch attempted to show that the → Tanakh and Biblical Judaism were based on the religion and the mythology of Mesopotamia, questioning the status of the Hebrew Bible as an original creation. The anti-Jewish rhetoric culminated in his 1914 work, *Die grosse Täuschung. Kritische Betrachtungen zu den alttestamentlichen Berichten über Israels Eindringen in Kanaan, die Gottesoffenharung vom Sinai und die Wirksamkeit der Propheten* (published in 1920/1921). The more polemical his arguments became, the more Delitzsch positioned himself outside the norms of acceptable scholarly endeavor.

The academically-based antisemitism (→ Conspiracy) and racial doctrine (→ Race) of the late 19th and early 20th centuries did not fail to affect the discipline of Oriental studies, which continued to view itself as apolitical. One early example is a controversy that began in the mid-1880s as a scholarly debate between Lagarde and several representatives from the field of Judaic studies, only to broaden into a public polemical debate about academic epistemology and methodology, with the fields of Oriental studies and Protestant theology on one side and Judaic studies on the other [7]; [14. 227–282]; [15]. In the same vein, subsequent to the → Berlin debate on antisemitism of 1879–1881, Lagarde launched personal attacks against Jewish scholars like Zunz, whose competence he questioned on account of their heritage, disparaged their scholarly achievements, and accused them of a lack of methodology. Even though Lagarde was a controversial figure in his field, a distinction was still made by contemporaries between the Orientalist and the political essayist [3. 184]; the Orientalist scholarly community tolerated Lagarde's antisemitism and did not engage in the debates. Yet in the middle of the century August Friedrich Pott rejected the theses of Arthur de Gobineau on the superiority of the Aryan race in his *Essai sur l'inégalité des races humaines* (1853–1855; "An Essay on the Inequality of the Human Races," 1915; → Assimilation) as unfounded [5].

In Oriental studies, too, it was hardly possible for Jewish scholars to pursue a university career if they did not convert (→ Conversion) to Christianity. The Berlin-based Old Testament scholar Franz Ferdinand

Benary converted to Christianity, as did the Russian Orientalist Daniel Abramovich Chwolson in St. Petersburg.

Scholars who declined to convert found themselves having to accept poorly paid lecturer positions, extraordinary professorships, or a comparatively late appointment to a full professorship. Many outstanding Jewish Orientalists such as Geiger (→ Quran) worked as rabbis or, like Abraham (Albert) Harkavy and Adolf Neubauer, as librarians and editors. The situation was truly dramatic for Goldziher, Orientalist and Islamic scholar (→ Muslim Studies) of worldwide renown, who earned a meagre living as secretary for the Jewish community of Budapest. From 1871 Goldziher taught as a private lecturer at the University of Budapest and was not appointed to a full professorship until 1904 [8a]. Peiser only received his full professorship in Königsberg (Kaliningrad) in 1905, after he had already obtained his habilitation under Friedrich Delitzsch in 1890. In France, Orientalists, who mostly came from Eastern and Central Europe, had comparatively better career opportunities. In Jerusalem, Oriental studies was one of the → Hebrew University's three founding faculties.

The Nazi persecution and mass murder of the Jews also had an impact on Oriental studies in Europe [12]. Some Jewish Orientalists escaped by emigration – one of them was Josef Horovitz's pupil Ilse Lichtenstädter, who fled to Great Britain in 1933 to continue her studies at Cambridge and Oxford before emigrating to the United States, where she enjoyed a successful academic career [8].

Bibliography

[1] W. Bihl, Bibliographie der Dissertationen über Judentum und jüdische Persönlichkeiten, die 1872–1962 an österreichischen Hochschulen (Wien, Graz, Innsbruck) approbiert wurden, Vienna 1965. [2] O. Fraisse, Ignác Goldzihers monotheistische Wissenschaft. Zur Historisierung des Islam, Göttingen/Bristol (CT) 2014. [2a] O. Fraisse, From Geiger to Goldziher. Historical Method and its Impact on the Conception of Islam, in: T. Turán/C. Wilke (eds.), Modern Jewish Scholarship in Hungary. The "Science of Judaism" between East and West, Berlin/Boston 2016, 203–222. [3] M. Gierl, Geschichte und Organisation. Institutionalisierung als Kommunikationsprozess am Beispiel der Wissenschaftsakademien um 1900, Göttingen 2004. [4] D. Hartwig et al. (eds.), "Im vollen Licht der Geschichte." Die Wissenschaft des Judentums und die Anfänge der kritischen Koranforschung, Würzburg 2008. [5] S. Heschel, The Aryan Jesus. Christian Theologians and the Bible in Nazi Germany, Princeton 2008. [6] C. Hoffmann, Juden und Judentum im Werk deutscher Althistoriker des 19. und 20. Jahrhunderts, Leiden et al. 1988. [7] E. Hollender, "Verachtung kann Unwissenheit nicht entschuldigen." Die Verteidigung der Wissenschaft des Judentums gegen die Angriffe Paul de Lagarde's 1884–1887, in: Frankfurter Judaistische Beiträge 30 (2003), 169–205. [8] R. Johnston-Bloom, Symbiosis Relocated. The German-Jewish Orientalist Ilse Lichtenstadter in America, in: Leo Baeck Institute Year Book 58 (2013), 95–110. [8a] G. Komoróczy, The Rabbinical Seminary of Budapest and Oriental Studies in Hungary, in: T. Turán/C. Wilke (eds.), Modern Jewish Scholarship in Hungary. The "Science of Judaism" between East and West, Berlin/Boston 2016, 37–54. [9] S. Mangold, Eine "weltbürgerliche Wissenschaft." Die deutsche Orientalistik im 19. Jahrhundert, Stuttgart 2004. [10] S.L. Marchand, German Orientalism in the Age of Empire. Religion, Race, and Scholarship, Washington et al. 2009. [11] H. Preissler, Die Anfänge der Deutschen Morgenländischen Gesellschaft, Göttingen 1995. [12] J. Renger, Altorientalistik und jüdische Gelehrte in Deutschland. Deutsche und österreichische Altorientalisten im Exil, in: W. Barner/C. König (eds.), Jüdische Intellektuelle und die Philologien in Deutschland 1871–1933, Göttingen 2001, 247–261. [13] I. Schorsch, Converging Cognates. The Intersection of Jewish

and Islamic Studies in Nineteenth Century Germany, in: Leo Baeck Institute Year Book 55 (2010), 3–36. [14] M. Thulin, Kaufmanns Nachrichtendienst. Ein jüdisches Gelehrtennetzwerk im 19. Jahrhundert, Göttingen 2012. [15] M. Thulin, Wissenschaft und Vorurteil. Die Kontroverse zwischen David Kaufmann und Paul de Lagarde, in: H.-J. Hahn/O. Kistenmacher (eds.), Beschreibungsversuche der Judenfeindschaft. Zur Geschichte der Antisemitismusforschung vor 1944, Berlin 2014, 121–148. [15a] M. Thulin, Eine Promotionsbehörde für Rabbinatsstudenten? Die Hallenser Orientalistik und ihre jüdischen Studierenden im 19. Jahrhundert, in: R. Randhofer/C. Lange/K. Eberl-Ruf (eds.), Jüdisches Leben in Sachsen-Anhalt. Kultur – Musik – Gelehrsamkeit, Halle, S. 2023, 234–254. [16] K. Vogel, Der Orientalist Julius Fürst (1805–1873). Wissenschaftler, Publizist und engagierter Bürger, in: S. Wendehorst (ed.), Bausteine einer jüdischen Geschichte der Universität Leipzig, Leipzig 2006, 41–60. [17] C. Wiese, Wissenschaft des Judentums und protestantische Theologie im wilhelminischen Deutschland. Ein Schrei ins Leere?, Tübingen 1999. [18] C. Wilke, Rabbinerpromotionen an der Philosophischen Fakultät der Universität Halle-Wittenberg, 1845–1895, in: G. Veltri/C. Wiese (eds.), Jüdische Bildung und Kultur in Sachsen-Anhalt von der Aufklärung bis zum Nationalsozialismus, Berlin 2009, 261–315.

MIRJAM THULIN,
MAINZ/FRANKFURT AM MAIN

Zelig

Comedy film from the year 1983 by Woody Allen who, as in many of his films, was the screenwriter, director, and lead actor at the same time. In classic documentary style, *Zelig* narrates the fictitious life story of the New York Jew Leonard Zelig using archive footage, voice-over commentaries, and interviews. Zelig rose to fame in the 1920s and 1930s thanks to his chameleon-like ability to take on the physical features and personality traits of any male person with whom he comes into contact. The themes of many of Allen's films reflect phenomena attributable to the dilemma of Jewish belonging, such as the pressure to conform and the ability to adapt, alienation, and neurotic anxiety; in *Zelig*, they are caricatured to the extreme.

1. Woody Allen and his films
2. *Zelig*
3. *Shiksa* complex
4. Between scandal and comeback

1. Woody Allen and his films

Born Stewart Allen Königsberg in the Bronx neighborhood of → New York in 1935, Woody Allen grew up in Brooklyn. His working-class parents were second-generation immigrants whose families had come to the United States from the Czarist Russia and the Austro-Hungarian Empire. For their son they chose a religious education. By the age of 15, Allen began to professionalize his → jokes; at 19, he became a writer for the *Ed Sullivan Show* and the *Tonight Show* and was from the mid-1950s part of the legendary group of writers behind Sid Caesar's *Your Show of Shows*, working alongside Neil Simon, Mel Brooks, and Larry Gelbart among others (→ Borscht Belt). On the rise as a successful standup comedian in the 1960s, he wrote the screenplay for his first major film, *What's New Pussycat?*, in 1965 and also had an acting role in it.

Already in his early films, Allen played the → schlemiel figure he had cultivated since his days as a stand-up comedian. Playing the main role in both *Play It Again, Sam* (1972) and *The Front* (1976), Allen transplanted the schlemiel from the world of the → shtetl to New York. A multiple Academy Award-winning effort, *Annie Hall* (1977) was his seventh film as screenwriter, director, and lead actor and sees him move beyond the schlemiel figure and develop his on-screen character in idiosyncratic ways. For the first time there is an explicit link between the image of the neurotic New York Jew – the ironized *Jew Yorker* – and the public persona of Woody Allen. The protagonist Alvy Singer, a successful comedian, begins a relationship with Annie Hall, a non-Jewish woman, and they soon break up. The film's female lead was Diane Keaton (b. 1946), with whom Allen also had a private liaison. From this point on, fictionalized variations of himself formed a trademark element of all the films in which he appeared.

Significant films exemplifying this tendency are *Interiors* (1978), *Manhattan* (1979), and *Stardust Memories* (1980). Stylistically, but thematically as well, Allen drew inspiration at times from European art film directors, especially Ingmar Bergman and Federico Fellini. Combining the depiction of existential anxieties with Jewish → humor, he turned to questions of power and problems of art but also to the subject of love affairs, which frequently examine the protagonist's susceptibility to the attractions of non-Jewish women and his inability to remain in long-term relationships with them. Other recurring themes are the experiences of belonging and being an outsider.

Where Allen's works turn to the relationship between fact and fiction, form and content meet in novel ways. His first mockumentary *Take the Money and Run* (1969) played with the dialectic of reality and illusion, and he returned to this topic in the 1980s. Jewish themes emerge most clearly when Allen portrays the main character, blending his public persona with the image of the neurotic New York Jew.

An homage to Fellini's *8 ½* (1963), the plot of *Stardust Memories* concerns a filmmaker's professional crisis which in turn becomes the material for the film being watched. The fictional film director Sandy Bates must deal with much the same difficulties that Allen faced at the time: comedies such as *Annie Hall* or *Manhattan* were highly successful, but serious dramatic efforts such as *Interiors* did poorly at the box office and met with rejection by the critics. Many characters in *Stardust Memories* are Jewish and were also played by Jewish actors. Because of their sometimes less than sympathetic depiction, Allen was accused of Jewish → self-hatred. His critics however failed to recognize that *Stardust Memories* is a grotesquerie, whose most vicious barbs the author had directed against himself [5. 57].

Allen's play on the cliché of self-hatred underscores the close connection of persona and on-screen alter ego. Thus in *Deconstructing Harry* (1997) the title character, Harry Block, admits that "Hey, I may hate myself, but not because I'm Jewish," which recalls Allen's own much-quoted *bon mot*: "'I have frequently been accused of being a self-hating Jew [...] and while it's true I am Jewish and don't like myself very much, it's not because of my persuasion'" [7. 196]. The ironic inversion of the accusation of self-hatred is reminiscent of Franz Kafka's (→ Prague) famous diary entry: "What have I in common with Jews? I have hardly anything in common with myself and should stand very quietly in a corner, content that I can breathe" [1. 252]. In the absurd-Kafkaesque *Shadows and Fog* (1991), the bookkeeper Kleinman, played by Allen, is paraphrasing this sentence. When he is mocked for not possessing sufficient faith to believe in the existence of God, he replies: "Listen, I can't make the leap of faith necessary to believe in my own existence."

After *Stardust Memories*, Allen spent the 1980s – his most prolific period – playing with the ambivalence of comedy and tragedy. Comedies such as *A Midsummer Night's Sex Comedy* (1982), *The Purple Rose of Cairo* (1985), or *Radio Days* (1987) were followed by dramas including *September* (1987) and *Another Woman* (1988). Especially in *Hannah and her Sisters* (1986) and *Crimes and Misdemeanors* (1989) he pursued the fusion of comedy and tragedy. The perhaps

2. Zelig

With its visual gags and ironic tone, *Zelig* was designed as an absurdist comedy and was received as such. Its documentary-style presentation, nevertheless, reminds the viewer not to disregard the serious undertone. The kinship between Zelig and protagonists from Kafka's works, notably Gregor Samsa in *The Metamorphosis* and Red Peter in *A Report for an Academy*, emphasizes the film's high aspirations.

In fact, there are numerous links between *Zelig* and Kafka's work, some of which have Jewish connotations. As a result of the strange metamorphoses in his behavior and appearance, Zelig is observed like an insect under a microscope. His nickname, "human chameleon," evokes the zoological dimension of Samsa's transformation into a giant beetle. Moreover, the theme alludes to the widely circulating anti-Semitic notion of Jews as vermin [4]. Zelig's adaptation to his environment, which also includes African Americans and Asians, suggests parallels with the ape Red Peter: it becomes a veritable compulsion. While Kafka's animal stories address the dangers of communities and the uncertainty of belonging in the modern age, Zelig's social adaptation is an outgrowth of his own anxiety. Under hypnosis he confesses that his compulsive adaptation has its roots in the search for security and the need to be liked.

In fictitious interviews with real Jewish intellectuals such as Irving Howe (1920–1993), Susan Sontag (1933–2004), and Bruno Bettelheim (1903–1990), who treat Zelig as a historical figure, the film's protagonist appears to epitomize the Jewish experience. Thus, Howe describes Zelig's condition as a reflection of the "Jewish experience in America" which was characterized by the "great urge to push in and to find one's place in society and then to assimilate into the culture." Sontag evokes the → Talmud in her ironic observation that Zelig's shapeshifting multiple bodily manifestations produced an even greater number of interpretations from media experts who in their turn will be complemented *ad infinitum* by contemporary commentators. Bettelheim universalizes the "ultimate conformist," Zelig, into a person whose "feelings were really not all that different from the normal, what one would call the well-adjusted, normal person, only carried to an extreme degree, to an extreme extent."

Zelig's pathological urge to conform and his need to be liked point to the inner conflict Sandy Bates is facing in *Stardust Memories*, of either having to make comedy films that are guaranteed to be successful or risk financial failure with ambitious dramas. The various characters Zelig assumes incorporate elements of Allen's self-reflexive tendency to emulate and parody other works. Beyond referencing his own earlier films, the cinematic play with fiction and reality also borrows from films by others. Thus at times, *Zelig* recalls the pseudo-documentary beginning of Orson Welles's *Citizen Kane* (1941).

The techniques and themes of other directors are primarily a source of inspiration for Allen. His own characters in films from *Annie Hall* to *To Rome with Love* (2012) always presented distinctly drawn variations of his public persona. Zelig appears both as the subject and the object of a series of alter egos whose origins can be traced back to the assimilation debates and their depiction ultimately refers to the question about the place of the individual in modern society.

3. *Shiksa* complex

Apart from the protagonist in *Oedipus Wrecks*, Allen's contribution to the short film anthology *New York Stories* (1989), his alter egos are attracted to White Anglo-Saxon

Protestant women. *Zelig* falls into the same category, but he does deviate from the pattern: on the one hand, the affair with his psychiatrist Dr. Eudora Fletcher, played by Mia Farrow (b. 1945), ends on a clearly optimistic note and, on the other, there is a reversal of his conventional Pygmalionesque evolution for the lead character in which a cultivated Jewish man schools the uneducated, provincial *shiksa* (non-Jewish woman). Now it is Dr. Fletcher who boosts Zelig's self-confidence, enabling him to love her and in return to make him worthy of her love.

The resolution of the "*shiksa* complex" seems to be reinforced through the successful resolution of his conformity complex. However, the latter is not resolved because Zelig recovers a Jewish self-understanding but because that identity is absorbed into mass culture. By the same token, Dr. Fletcher's occupation as a psychiatrists challenges this assumption. The rhetorical device of → psychoanalysis as a "Jewish science" means that Zelig does not need to play Pygmalion to transform the female character from a gentile into a Jewish woman – Dr. Fletcher already is one by virtue of her occupation. Indeed, their shared characteristics are brought to the fore in the therapy sessions when Zelig becomes a "psychiatrist" and Dr. Fletcher deliberately switches their roles to play his "patient" – a groundbreaking therapeutic move that forces Zelig to become what he is in reality – her patient – and brings him closer to recovery.

Allen's films often feature psychotherapists of either gender. Where the plot also involves his alter ego, the therapists reinforce the link between public persona and film characters by means of the Freudian talking cure. Aside from Dr. Fletcher, three of the other therapist figures are female: Harry's ex-wife Joan and her fictitious twin sister Helen in *Deconstructing Harry*, and Phyllis in *To Rome with Love*. While these three women are portrayed as less personable than Dr. Fletcher, they still assume a similar narrative function. Both Joan and Helen are religiously observant Jewish women, the latter, having turned to faith with the birth of her child, is now citing Hebrew blessings during oral sex and has intimate relationships with her patients. Phyllis, the wife of the opera director Jerry, played by Allen, in *To Rome with Love*, is a kind of Dr. Fletcher-Zelig, turned into a pschoanalytical nag. While therapy sessions are often depicted as comedy routines with their own specific Jewish associations, therapy and comedy have rarely been as closely linked to the Jewish dimension of Allen's persona as in the marital exchange of blows between Phyllis and Jerry after one of her pop-psychological humiliations. Jerry: "My brain doesn't fit the usual id-ego-superego model!" Phyllis: "No, you have the only brain with three ids."

4. Between scandal and comeback

Allen continued to pursue the relationship between documentation and fiction and the difference between the real Woody Allen and his "Woody" persona in several films after *Zelig*, above all, in *Husbands and Wives* (1992) and *Deconstructing Harry*. The former is once again constructed as a pseudo-documentary, but with fewer comedy elements than *Zelig*, and it takes place in the present time.

Husbands and Wives was in production around the time news broke of the scandal involving Mia Farrow and Soon-Yi Previn (b. 1970). The film chronicles the separation of a married couple, played by Allen and Farrow, and the affair of the professor, played by Allen, with a non-Jewish student. About the affair Allen stated in an interview: "Everything about it was wrong. That did not deter me. If anything, as usual, there was something interesting." Public attention was directed not only at the striking parallels suggested by Allen's affair with the 19-year-old South Korean Soon-Yi, the adopted daughter from a previous marriage of his long-time partner and lead actress Mia Farrow. Critics also pointed to similar themes in other films, especially the affair between Allen's character and a non-Jewish student in *Manhattan*, and to the Asian-American *Playboy* model China Lee in *What's up, Tiger Lily* (1966), which led them to deduce in Allen a long-time predilection for underage Lolitas and Asian females.

Consequently, numerous critical reports appeared concerning Allen's private life, and audiences shunned his films. Allen sought to polish his damaged reputation by denying the accusations and by insisting on a strict separation between his public and his private person. The strategy did not have the desired effect and was not helped by the fact that Allen continued to play characters in his own films who become romantically entangled with much younger, non-Jewish women, for example in *Mighty Aphrodite* (1995), *Everyone Says I Love You* (1996), and *Deconstructing Harry*. The last-mentioned film however depicts the romantic and creative tendencies of the anti-hero played by Allen in a way that swayed the viewers in his favor, inviting their identification with the character.

In *Deconstructing Harry*, the protagonist Harry Block is introduced as the celebrated writer of suggestive farces who is constantly conflating life and art. His artistic triumphs contrast with his pitiful private life. Much like Allen, Block has several failed marriages under his belt and has lost custody over the son he loves – also an allusion to Allen's private life; the only biological son he probably had is estranged from him. Block also undergoes intensive psychotherapy and is accused of Jewish self-hatred for the allegedly negative depiction of Jews in his work.

Running through *Deconstructing Harry* is a near-confessional tone tinged with self-irony, and we can read it at least in part as Allen's defense in the Farrow-Previn scandal. The film seeks to garner our sympathies for a life that is subordinated to art and perpetually under threat of being consumed by it. While Harry is not absolved of his guilt in the film, by the end of it his psychological life appears intact [12. 20]. *Deconstructing Harry* proved to be Allen's reinstatement as far as the well-disposed critics were concerned whose conclusions now echoed the sentiment expressed by his character's lover in *The Front*: "And I made this kind of mistake before [...] confusing the artist with the man. I just want you to know I still admire the artist."

Soon Allen's popularity was on the rise again with films such as *Match Point* (2005), *Vicky Cristina Barcelona* (2008), *Midnight in Paris* (2011), and *Blue Jasmine* (2013). This comeback was driven by films that are set in Europe – or, as in the case of *Blue Jasmine*, in San Francisco – and do not feature Allen as an actor. With the disappearance of his alter ego and of the New York setting so rich in Jewish associations, Jewish themes necessarily appear to be reduced, or at best to exist only in subliminal form.

Their reduction notwithstanding, Jewish references and autobiographical elements are far from absent. In *Scoop* (2006) Allen, whose childhood fascination for magic tricks led to developing a professional interest in the subject as an adult, plays a Jewish magician who collaborates with a female Jewish journalist on the hunt for a serial killer. In his most recent → Broadway play Allen was finally able to come full circle on the Jewish themes and connections between his public and private personas. The one-act play *Honeymoon Motel* (2011) takes place in New York and satirizes both the Farrow-Previn scandal as well as one of Allen's long-standing personal demons, the Jewish religion. In *Take the Money and Run*, and again in *Annie Hall* and *Zelig*, the characters played by Allen wore → Hasidic dress as a visual gag. In *Honeymoon Motel* one encounters a rabbi making fun of → ultra-Orthodoxy. As always, Allen does not escape unscathed. In the story about an Allen-esque schlemiel who elopes with the bride of his stepson on their wedding night, the self-ironic allusions to the scandal are unmistakable.

Bibliography

Sources

[1] F. Kafka, The Diaries of Franz Kafka: 1910–1923, trans. by J. Kresh, M. Greenberg, H. Arendt, New York 1988 ([1]1948–1949).

Secondary literature

[2] P. J. Bailey, The Reluctant Film Art of Woody Allen, Lexington 2001.   [3] V. Brook/M. Grinberg, Woody on Rye. Jewishness in the Films and Plays of Woody Allen, Lebanon 2013.   [4] I. Bruce, Mysterious Illnesses of Human Commodities in Woody Allen and Franz Kafka. Zelig, in: C. L. P. Silet (ed.), The Films of Woody Allen. Critical Essays, Lanham 2006, 171–197.   [5] D. Desser/L. D. Friedman, American-Jewish Filmmakers. Traditions and Trends, Urbana/Chicago 1993.   [6] I. Deutscher, Der nichtjüdische Jude, Berlin 1988.   [7] L. J. Epstein, The Haunted Smile. The Story of Jewish Comedians in America, New York 2001.   [8] S. Gilman, The Jew's Body, New York/London 1991.   [9] S. B. Girgus, The Films of Woody Allen, Cambridge et al. 2002.   [10] F. Hirsch, Love, Sex, Death, and the Meaning of Life. The Films of Woody Allen, Cambridge (MA) 2001.   [11] M. P. Nichols, Reconstructing Woody. Art, Love, and Life in the Films of Woody Allen, Lanham et al. 1998.   [12] J. Rubin-Dorsky, Woody Allen after the Fall. Literary Gold from Amoral Alchemy, in: Shofar 22 (2003) 1, 5–28.   [13] M. Shechner, Dear Mr. Einstein. Jewish Comedy and the Contradictions of Culture, in: S. B. Cohen (ed.), Jewish Wry. Essays on Jewish Humor, Bloomington 1987, 141–157.   [14] M. Weinreich, Internal Bilingualism in Ashkenaz, in: I. Howe/E. Greenberg (eds.), Voices from the Yiddish. Essays, Memoirs, Diaries, Ann Arbor 1972, 279–288.

VINCENT BROOK, LOS ANGELES

Zeno

The 1923 novel *La coscienza di Zeno* ("Zeno's Conscience," 2001) about the neurotic protagonist Zeno is among the masterpieces of 20th-century European literature. Like his contemporaries Franz Kafka (→ Prague), Marcel Proust (→ Combray), and James Joyce, its author Italo Svevo (1861–1928) became one of the most important representatives of European literary modernism. Svevo's main œuvre comprises the three novels *Una Vita* (1892; "A Life," 1963), *Senilità* (1898; "As a Man Grows Older," 1932), and *La coscienza di Zeno*. Born Aron Hector Schmitz in Trieste, he adopted the pseudonym Italo Svevo (approx.: "the Italian Swabian") from 1892 onward. In his works Habsburg Austrian, Italian, and Jewish affiliations and alienations are superimposed over each other.

1. Italo Svevo: A biography from Trieste
2. *La coscienza di Zeno*
3. Svevo and Judaism

1. Italo Svevo: A biography from Trieste

Aron Hector (Ital. Ettore) Schmitz was born in → Trieste in 1861. His father Franz came from a Jewish-Austrian family, his mother Allegra (née Moravia) from a Jewish-Italian family; both had grown up in modest circumstances. When Ettore was born, however, his father had already achieved considerable wealth as a businessman. From the second half of the 18th century onward, Trieste was the most important seaport of the Habsburg Empire, acting as a banking and insurance hub for all of Central Europe. In the 19th century, Trieste was the fourth most important city of the Dual Monarchy after → Vienna, → Budapest, and → Prague. Svevo's family were members of the Jewish community in Trieste, which formed the largest ethnic-religious minority in the city according to the census of 1900 with 4,939 members (3.23% of the population). While they were only a small group compared to the Jewish proportion of the inhabitants of Vienna (8.6%), they made a considerable contribution to Trieste's intellectual, social, and economic life.

In the Habsburg Empire at the time of the → Austro-Hungarian Compromise, Jews did have access to the state education system (→ Bildung), but Svevo's parents decided in favor of a Jewish orientation for the education of their sons. From the ages of six to 17, Aron Hector and his brothers Adolfo and Elio attended two Jewish private schools in Trieste and a Jewish boarding school in Germany, the Brüsselsche Handels- und Erziehungsinstitut in Segnitz am Main. Since the paternal grandfather came from the Rhineland, it was a matter of concern for the father that his sons master the → German language. The Schmitz family observed Jewish festivals (→ Course of the Year), was active in the community, and maintained business relations and social contacts mainly with other Jews. The businessman Baron Fortunato Vivante (1846–1926), known to be a generous benefactor, one of the most influential members of the community, and director of the Trieste branch of the Vienna Union Bank, was a relative by marriage of the family and would later become Svevo's employer.

From the 1880s onward, Aron Hector Schmitz wrote plays as well as journalistic contributions for a Trieste newspaper. The positive reception of his first novel *Una Vita* (1892), the first publication under his pseudonym Italo Svevo, was too meager to allow him to exist as a writer. After his father's business went bankrupt, he accepted a position with the Union Bank, where he stayed until 1898, although he disliked the work. Two years after his marriage, he was able to move to his father-in-law Gioacchino Veneziani's ship varnish firm Moravia-Veneziani in Trieste. This position was concomitant with

Italo Svevo (orig. Aron Hector Schmitz, 1861–1928)

the affluence of an established merchant, allowing Italo Svevo to travel to France and England, among other places, where the firm had branches.

In 1896, he married his second cousin Livia Veneziani (1874–1957). Livia's parents were of Jewish origin but had converted to Catholicism (→ Conversion), and their daughter had been brought up a strict Catholic in a convent school. In the second half of the 19th century, so-called mixed marriages were common in the Jewish middle class in Vienna and Trieste, marking a considerable step towards → assimilation. The new Habsburg legislation of 1868 permitted marriages between Catholics and Jews in Austria, if one of the partners embraced the faith of the other. One of the complications was the religious education of the children which frequently led to fierce disagreements in families. This also applied to Svevo and Livia. Even after their engagement, they had painful discussions about religion, culminating in both of them renouncing their faiths and declaring themselves unaffiliated with any religion in May 1896. To the devout Catholic Livia, this was an expression of the deep connection she felt to her Jewish fiancé. However, she soon regretted her decision and returned to the Catholic faith in August of the same year. Having witnessed her, albeit short-lived, gesture of renouncing her religion to show her willingness to enter into marriage with a Jew, Svevo converted to Catholicism. He was baptized in August 1897. While Svevo's conversion may have been motivated by personal reasons, it indicates his desire for their differences to disappear and a denial of his Jewish affiliation.

In her memoirs, Livia omitted any reference to her husband's Jewish origin. After Italo Svevo died in 1928 as the result of a car accident near his home city, he was first buried in the Jewish cemetery; however, Livia had his body exhumed and transferred to the Veneziani family vault in the Catholic cemetery of Sant'Anna. Livia also kept silent about her own Jewish background. When the Italian race laws were passed in 1938, she was excluded from the Fascist Party and, together with her daughter Letizia (1897–1993), declared a member of the "Jewish race," so they were forced to flee Trieste.

2. *La coscienza di Zeno*

Svevo can be viewed as a prototypical Trieste author of his day. The city of his birth informs the physical and psychological topography of his characters; it reflects and determines their destinies. The → novel *La coscienza di Zeno* is set in Trieste in the years before the First World War, and follows the protagonist's walks through the streets leading to the Palazzo Tergesteo, home of the stock exchange, offices, and cafés. The success and material wealth of the Trieste middle class are displayed in the opulent furnishings of Zeno's villa and the residence

of the entrepreneur Malfenti into whose family Zeno marries.

At the same time, *La coscienza di Zeno* is probably the first European novel that uses → psychoanalysis as the narrative frame, albeit ironically. The text is laid out as the life story of the first-person narrator Zeno Cosini, written down at the suggestion of his psychoanalyst Dr. S. and published by Dr. S. as revenge after Cosini breaks off the therapy. The ironic narrative frame reflects Italo Svevo's contradictory relationship with psychoanalysis. His knowledge of Sigmund Freud honed his insight into the human psyche, but ultimately he rejected the psychoanalytic model of self-awareness of self as being too limited; in the novel, this corresponds approximately to the relationship between Zeno and his analyst Dr. S.

Unlike Freud or Arthur Schnitzler, for example, who expressed their reflections on Jews and Judaism in their writings, Svevo did not expressly address his relationship to his Jewish affiliation in his literary work. With the exception of his first article, published under the title → "Shylock" in 1880 for the newspaper *L'Indipendente* on the occasion of a performance of Shakespeare's *The Merchant of Venice*, Jewish themes are not explicitly mentioned in his œuvre. In retrospect, there appears to be irony in the first lines of his sympathetic portrait of Shakespeare's protagonist, as he referred critically to Heinrich Heine's (→ Entreebillet) apostasy, which he himself followed some years later. In the preface to his novel *Senilità* (1898), Svevo even withdrew a reference to the protagonist Emilio Brentani's Jewish origin: "I do not know whether I ascribed the protagonist's senility to his race (I realize that I never knew how to express that he was a Jew) or to his milieu" [4]. In his posthumously published reflections on his marriage with Livia Veneziani and her family *Cronaca di famiglia*, the subject of religion is not touched upon. And in *Profilo autobio-grafico*, published during the last year of his life, the author Italo Svevo does not reveal the Jewish origin of the businessman Ettore Schmitz. Here he obviously reconstructs himself, expunging those aspects of his life that did not sit well with his public image at the time of Italian fascism.

Although the protagonist's Jewish affiliation is not discussed in *La coscienza di Zeno*, in terms of literary history he stands in a tradition of Jewish figures. Svevo's protagonist resembles those of Franz Kafka (→ Prague). He tries to adapt to reality but feels weak and tormented. One peculiarity of Zeno's is that his weakness transforms into strength in the end. In *La coscienza di Zeno*, the protagonist's brother-in-law is his antagonist: Guido Speier, a well-to-do and successful businessman, good-looking and charming as well as self-confident, all of which Zeno envies. Zeno, in his own eyes, sees himself as a limping hypochondriac with a bald patch who feels alienated from everyday life. Guido woos and eventually marries the beautiful Ada, the daughter of the entrepreneur Malfenti, whom Zeno adores as well; Zeno marries her lackluster sister Auguste. This might seem a repetition of a common behavioral pattern of many Jewish characters in → literature: the personable blond heathen prospers, while the Jew suffers. However, the insecure Zeno survives, while the self-confident Guido tragicomically loses his life when attempting to fake suicide. Svevo thus undermines the stereotype of the inadequate Jew. Neurotic Zeno triumphs. His marriage is a success, while Guido's fails; Guido's transactions result in significant losses which Zeno is able to recover, gaining the respect of the Malfenti family. His unshakeable optimism and self-deprecating irony turn defeat into victory. Zeno may thus be understood as "the ostensibly self-denigrating Jew who in the stories he tells on himself invariably manages to come out on top" [15. 45].

3. Svevo and Judaism

The question of Jewish affiliation, meanwhile, developed into a leitmotif in Italo Svevo's private correspondence. While the subject is not discussed extensively, symptomatic sentences reveal that it was constantly present. The frequently self-deprecating and joking tone conceals a sense of the heritage he had rejected. Most of his letters are addressed to his wife and report everyday events during his business travels on behalf of his parents-in-law's firm. He often inserts a remark, such as the repeated analogy: "I was as full of remorse as a Jew at his baptism" [2. vol. 1. 243]. Frequently, he speaks dismissively of the religion to which he converted. As a citizen of the monarchy, Italo Svevo was aware of the growing antisemitism (→ Conspiracy), especially in → Vienna where his youngest brother Ottavio lived, but also in other regions of Europe he visited on business.

In Trieste, too, antisemitism increased with the rise of organizations that had close ties to the Christlichsozialen Partei (CS) founded in 1893 by Karl Lueger. The antisemitism of the Austrian CS became public during Lueger's visit in 1898, when anti-Italian demonstrations were accompanied by chants of "death to the Jews." The antisemitic press of Trieste also spread slogans about the alleged Jewish dominance. Svevo's reaction to antisemitism was to remove all traces of his Jewish origin from his published writings and to endeavor to do the same in his official records. In a letter to Livia dated June 7, 1913, he wrote of his intention to have his Hebrew first name (→ Naming) Aron removed from the electoral register [2. vol. 1, 639]. His first experience of discrimination had been at the age of 19, when he had been refused a position because he was Jewish, as his brother Elio recorded in his diary. During his time in the military he was disparaged by an Austrian officer [6. 28]; an anonymous informer exposed him as a Jew and irredentist [9. 42], and the fascist Italian press showered him in antisemitic invective. He was attacked even posthumously in 1939, when fascist hooligans defiled the bronze memorial bust created by Giovanni Mayer in 1931 and placed in the Giardino Pubblico Muzio de Tommasini.

Italo Svevo had not forgotten his Jewish affiliation. References to Judaism in Kafka's work were among the things that attracted him; both œuvres testify to a pronounced awareness of the contradictions of Jewish affiliation, in Kafka's case with roots in → Prague. He had met James Joyce (1882–1941) at the Berlitz School in Trieste in 1905, where Joyce was employed as a language teacher and taught him → English. They discussed Jewish customs (→ Minhag) and rituals. These conversations found their way into Joyce's *Ulysses* (1922) by way of the character of Leopold Bloom, a Jew living in Catholic Dublin. Svevo was also a member of the Jewish circle founded by Umberto Saba (1883–1957) and Giorgio Voghera (1908–1999), who occupied himself intensively with → psychoanalysis and established Freudianism as a part of Trieste cultural life [13. 135–155].

Over the years, the characters in Svevo's earlier → novels have also been studied with particular emphasis on possible Jewish components: their affinities with the character of the → schlemiel; their propensity for neurosis, hypochondria, passivity, clumsiness; their fear of persecution; their inclination to be self-deprecating. The original title of *Una Vita* was *Un inetto*, meaning "A good-for-nothing." The novel narrates the protagonist's failure to integrate into city life. Alfonso Nitti comes to the city from a village in order to work as a bank clerk. He is introduced to the wealthy world of his boss where he meets the elegant and assertive lawyer Macario, for whom he feels admiration. However, introverted and passive, Alfonso is incapable of emulating Macario's aggressive nature and of seizing opportunities for advancement when they are offered.

He renounces the world and commits suicide. A similar pattern underlies *Senilità*. The insurance clerk Emilio Brentani is overshadowed by his friend, the vibrant sculptor Stefano Balli, who is admired by all women including Emilio's sister and lover. At the end of the novel, both women have disappeared, and Emilio, old before his time, retires into the world of his dreams and fantasies.

While *Una Vita* won great acclaim when it appeared, *Senilità* was accorded less attention. Although Svevo continued to write, it was not until 1923 that he published another work, *La coscienza di Zeno*. He was encouraged by Joyce in particular who supported him as an author. Between 1925 and 1928 Svevo achieved international literary recognition. However, after his death in 1928, his fame transformed into posthumous vilification: Fascist literary critics called his reputation the result of a scheming Jewish cabal. From their point of view, a Jewish writer with a German name writing about weak, awkward, introverts had no place in Italian → literature. Only after the end of the Second World War did Italo Svevo find appreciation as a novelist of unassailable standing.

Bibliography

Sources

[1] I. Svevo, Zeno's Conscience, trans. by W. Weaver, New York 2001. [2] I. Svevo, Opera Omnia, ed. by B. Maier, 3 vols., Milan 1966. [3] I. Svevo, Lettere a Svevo. Diario di Elio Schmitz, ed. by B. Maier, Milan 1973. [4] I. Svevo, As a Man Grows Older, trans. by B. De Zoete, San Francisco 2016. [5] I. Svevo, The Uniform Edition of Svevo's Works, 5 vols., London 1962–1969.

Secondary literature

[6] F. Anzellotti, Il segreto di Svevo, Pordenone 1985. [7] F. Anzellotti, La villa di Zeno, Pordenone 1991. [8] T. Catalan, La comunità ebraica di Trieste (1791–1914). Politica, società e cultura, Trieste 2000. [9] S. Crise, Epiphanies e phadographs. Joyce e Trieste, Milan 1994. [10] L. De

Angelis, Qualcosa di più intimo. Aspetti della scrittura ebraica del Novecento italiano. Da Svevo a Bassani, Florence 2006. [11] J. Gatt-Rutter, Italo Svevo. A Double Life, Oxford 1988. [12] E. Ghidetti, Italo Svevo. La coscienza di un borghese triestino, Rome 1980. [13] E. Schächter, Origin and Identity. Essays on Svevo and Trieste, Leeds 2000. [14] G. Stellardi/E. Tandello Cooper (eds.), Italo Svevo and His Legacy for the Third Millennium, 2 vols., Leicester 2014. [15] H.S. Hughes, Prisoners of Hope. The Silver Age of the Italian Jews 1924–1974, Cambridge (MA)/London 1983.

ELIZABETH SCHÄCHTER, CANTERBURY

Židovská Strana

The Židovská strana (Jewish Party) was founded in January 1919 by Czech Zionists. It acted as the political arm of the Národní rada židovská (Jewish National Council) in → Prague, which had been formed in October 1918. The party sought to represent the Jewish population of Czechoslovakia (ČSR) as a national minority. In practice, it functioned primarily as a lobbying organization for Jewish concerns in the politics of the newly-founded state, to which it felt committed. Roughly half of the Jewish electorate in Czechoslovakia voted for the party; the failure to grow its base beyond that figure was in large part due to the diversity of Jewish self-understandings in the east of the country.

It was in 1929, a full decade after its formation, that the Židovská strana first sent delegates to the parliament in Prague. Protected by a political agreement with the Czechoslovak Social Democratic Party, it managed to re-enter the House of Representatives in 1935.

Even prior to its election success the party's extra-parliamentary activism was considerable. The Židovská strana set up offices to provide legal advice in tax-related matters and to help with questions of citizenship, right of residency, social services, and health insurance. Another party initiative, vocational training centers offered instruction in a variety of crafts to prepare young Jews for their eventual emigration to Palestine. In the 1930s the Židovská strana instigated public protests against the persecution of Jews in Nazi Germany (→ Bernheim Petition), it organized support for Jewish immigrants and tried in various ways to alleviate the economic hardship of the most deprived Jews in the east of the country.

The two seats won in the 1929 parliamentary elections were filled by the Prague Zionist and chairman of the party, Ludvík Singer (1876–1931), and Julius Reisz (1880–1976). As early as 1931, Angelo Goldstein (1889–1947) replaced the deceased Singer, and in 1935 he and Ḥayim Kugel (1897–1966) represented the Židovská strana in parliament.

In parliament, the Židovská strana political sphere of activity included fending off antisemitic ideas and to promote legislation on land reform and citizenship. Its deputies intervened on several occasions against anti-Jewish discriminatory measures, such as attempts to neutralize Jewish competition by re-distributing business licenses, or motions to make the Sunday rest a legally binding obligation. Furthermore it campaigned against the introduction of an anti-Jewish → *numerus clausus* at the universities.

The founding of the party is tied to older discussions concerning the protection of Jewish rights in the Habsburg Empire. In the period leading up to the First World War, efforts had already been undertaken to raise the Jewish community to the status of a corporate entity with full public recognition and to give them a voice in parliament on the local, regional, and national level (→ Question of Nationalities). In 1907, the Jewish National Party was established in Cracow; over time it sent several delegates to the Reichsrat (Imperial Council). After the war, these endeavors saw a resurgence of interest, and based on the concept of → *Gegenwartsarbeit* (also: *Landesarbeit*), that is the campaigning for Jewish rights in the Diaspora, as a parallel thread to the involvement with Jewish goals in Palestine, which had been developed around the turn of the century within the Zionist movement, Jewish → National Councils in Eastern Europe called for the recognition of Jews as national minorities with legally enshrined, collective → minority rights, especially in the areas of education and the creation of Jewish parties. In this, the Czech Zionists could expect a sympathetic stance towards the Jewish minority from the founders of the Czechoslovak state (→ Hilsner Affair).

The Židovská strana was to a large extent the initiative of Bohemian and Moravian Jews; the majority of its leadership was recruited from Zionists of those two regions. This constellation reflected the composition of Czechoslovak Jewry, which was comprised of three distinct groups: a Western-acculturated one in Bohemia and Moravia, a traditional, Orthodox-leaning community in Subcarpathian Ruthenia, a territory annexed by Czechoslovakia in 1919, and a mixture of the two in Slovakia.

The self-understanding of the Bohemian and Moravian Jews was similar to that of the secular acculturated Jews of Western and Central Europe. In the 19th century they had given up → Yiddish in favor of → German, and tradition (→ Orthodoxy) in favor of → reform. They lived predominantly in the cities (50% in Prague alone) and worked mostly in the industrial sector, in trade, and in the liberal professions. Paradoxically, this predestined them, rather than the traditional Jews of Slovakia and Subcarpathian Ruthenia, to cultivate a Jewish national identity of the type represented by the Židovská strana. The emergence of the Czech national movement around the middle of the 19th century confronted the Bohemian and Moravian Jews with the question

whether to choose the German or the Czech camp. As they were loyal to the emperor, and their loyalty was traditionally aligned with Vienna rather than Prague, a majority opted to side with German culture; nevertheless there had always been among them fierce proponents of a Czech-Jewish symbiosis (→ Českožidovské listy). The Czech national movement rarely accepted the Bohemian and Moravian Jews as coalition partners because they were perceived as agents of the Germanization effort. The third option gaining in influence prior to the First World War was the Zionist-inspired commitment to an independent Jewish nation (→ Bar Kochba Association).

By 1919 circumstances had changed substantially. As part of the newly independent country of Czechoslovakia, Bohemia and Moravia came to be administered from Prague, not Vienna; German was no longer the language of the authorities. The roughly three million strong, irredentist-leaning German minority, who lived in compact settlement areas along the German border, did not regard the Jews with sympathy. The growing alienation of Germans and German-speaking Jews correlated with the willingness of the government to recognize the Czechoslovak Jews as a national minority. In view of its irredentist neighbors and large minority groups with ties extending to states beyond the Czechoslovak borders, it was in the interest of the government in Prague to keep the country's 350,000 Jewish citizens on its side. Indeed, wide sections of the Czechoslovak Jewish community soon proved to be staunch Czechoslovaks whose loyalty, unlike that of the Germans, Slovaks, and Hungarians, even increased over the years.

This development also found expression in the political program of the Židovská strana, which defined itself as a non-partisan forum for Jewish voters, who firmly declared their loyalty toward the Czechoslovak state. Accordingly, the Židovská strana supported the government in parliament and took an active part in Czechoslovak legislation; they eventually embraced the Czech language in the same spirit. The National Council, and later the Židovská strana, had an organ in the Czech-language weekly journal *Židovské zprávy* (Jewish News), which appeared from 1918 to 1938. By availing themselves of the Czech language, the Židovská strana sought to countermand the widespread image of Jews as the embodiment of Germanness. In the 1930s, responding to the rapid deterioration in German-Czech relations, it was even more anxious to forge closer ties with the Czech nation. The use of German was increasingly viewed as a stigma, and the leaders of the Židovská strana were expected to speak the official language. Both Singer and Goldstein were fluent Czech speakers. However, Emil Margulies (1877–1943) from Leitmeritz (Litoměřice), who succeeded Singer as party chairman in 1931, epitomized a Bohemian Jewry that was steeped in German culture. Margulies did not master the Czech language and for this reason had declined to fill one of the two parliamentary seats the party had won in 1929.

The Židovská strana was able to attract roughly half of the Jewish electorate in Czechoslovakia (98,793 votes in the 1925 parliamentary elections, and 104,556 votes with the Polish-Jewish List in 1929), but its influence particularly in the east of the country remained extremely limited. As late as December 1934 there was no permanent office in Slovakia, and in Subcarpathian Ruthenia it did not even maintain local associations. The nearly complete absence in the region of an urbanized and reform-oriented Jewish middle class, and the stronger sway of the Orthodoxy, which rejected Zionism, left little room for a secular organization such as the Židovská strana. The traditionally-minded camp in Slovakia and in Subcarpathian Ruthenia, led for the most part by powerful rabbis, instead subscribed to a pragmatic policy of patronage: in exchange

for benefits and concessions it supported the ruling parties, above all the Republikánská strana zemědělského a malorolnického lidu (Republican Party of Farmers and Peasants) As demonstrated by the short-lived alliance of Jewish nationalists and the Orthodox community in the 1928 Slovak district elections, efforts to bridge the differences did materialize in the face of the threat posed by the rise of Slovak separatists, whose stance was decidedly antisemitic. In the long run, however, the Czech Zionists were unable to accommodate the peculiarities of the Jews in the east of the country. Especially in the Slovak context, they behaved awkwardly, and their patronizing policies only served to reinforce existing antipathies toward Prague and its hegemonic ambitions.

The Jewish nationalists, moreover, saw themselves competing against influential non-Jewish parties, such as the Československá sociálně demokratická strana dělnická v republice Rakoúské (Czechoslovak Social Democratic Worker's Party), Deutsche sozialdemokratische Arbeiterpartei in der Tschechoslowakischen Republik (German Social Democratic Worker's Party in the Czechoslovak Republic), the Komunistická strana Československa (Communist Party of Czechoslovakia; → Lied der Partei) and the small, liberal Deutsche Demokratische Partei (German Democratic Party). The difficulties were aggravated by conflicts within the Jewish-nationalist camp over the value, if any, of engaging in *Gegenwartsarbeit*. Voting for the party did not necessarily indicate an acceptance of the party's Jewish-nationalist or Zionist program; more often than not it was an expression of the idea that only a supra-regional Jewish organization would be capable of protecting the rights of the Jewish minority.

The "Anschluss" (annexation) of Austria in March 1938 and the partial mobilization of the Czechoslovak army two months later changed the situation dramatically. The Zionist Central Committee declared its support for the defense of the country: "There are nations that cannot separate the ideal of freedom from the oppression of others. The Czechoslovak nation does not oppress anyone. By defending the freedom of Czechoslovakia, we defend our own freedom. This is our policy inasmuch as we engage in politics at all" is stated in a resolution prepared for the Twelfth Congress of Czechoslovak Zionists in March 1938. In May the Židovská strana held its last congress and likewise declared its unequivocal loyalty to Czechoslovakia. In the final days of its existence, the party organized protests against National Socialist-inspired antisemitism in the country and supported Jews in the border regions, as well as Jewish refugees from Germany and Austria. After the Munich Agreement and the resignation of President Edvard Beneš (1884–1948) in September 1938, the party ceased its political activities even though it officially continued to exist until Germany invaded Prague on March 15, 1939.

Bibliography

[1] M. Crhová, Jewish Politics in Central Europe. The Case of the Jewish Party in Interwar Czechoslovakia, in: Jewish Studies at the Central European University 2 (1999/2001), 271–301. [2] F. Friedmann, Strana Židovská, Prague 1931. [3] E. Mendelsohn, The Jews of East Central Europe Between the World Wars, Bloomington 1987. [4] A. M. Rabinowicz, The Jewish Party. A Struggle for National Recognition, Representation and Autonomy, in: The Jews of Czechoslovakia. Historical Studies and Surveys, vol. 2, Philadelphia 1971, 253–346. [5] M. J. Wein, Zionism in Interwar Czechoslovakia. Palestino-Centrism and Landespolitik, in: Judaica Bohemiae 44 (2009), 5–47.

MARIE CRHOVÁ, OLOMOUC

Zikhron Ya'akov

The three-volume Hebrew study *Zikhron Ya'akov* (Memory of Jacob) published between 1924 and 1930 is a polemic-apologetic work on the history of the Jews in the Czarist Empire. Its author, the ultra-Orthodox Ya'akov Lipschitz (1838–1921) from Kaunas, saw it as offering a religious alternative to modern secular → historiography. In this respect, his work is part of the consolidation process experienced by Orthodox Jewry in Eastern Europe.

1. *Zikhron Ya'akov*
2. Orthodox historiography

1. *Zikhron Ya'akov*

In premodern Judaism, → history was considered a pursuit useful at best when studying the → Halakhah, or acceptable during hours of leisure; in principle, it was seen as being of secondary importance. After its emergence in the late 19th century, Orthodox Jewish historiography addressed a broad readership that would later also include women. Its primary forms of publications initially included chronicles of rabbinic dynasties, lexicographies, works on mystics and the leaders of various of Orthodox trends, hagiographies of Hasidic *rebbes* (→ Hasidism) and tsaddikim ("just men"; → Tsaddik), as well as historiographical publications in the narrower sense.

Ya'akov Lipschitz was among the most influential representatives of this trend in the early 20th century. When his work *Zikhron Ya'akov* appeared posthumously in Kaunas between 1924 and 1930 in three volumes (a fourth part reached the United States in manuscript form only), it represented a fundamental innovation compared to contemporary Orthodox works of history. Containing letters, memoirs, published leaflets, and newspaper articles in → Hebrew, → Yiddish, → German, and → Russian, it combined personal recollections and general opinions about history, presenting traditional historical topics familiar from studying the Torah (→ Talmud Torah) together with reflections on the history of the Jews as well as of humanity in general.

Like all Orthodox religious writings, the individual volumes of *Zikhron Ya'akov* featured rabbinical approvals (→ Censorship), including reviews of preceding volumes. However, it lacked a scholarly apparatus as well as precise bibliographical references of the documents and sources used. Although *Zikhron Ya'akov* cannot be regarded as a historical work in the modern sense, the author did view his book as an objective and faithful, Orthodox → historiography of the Russian Jews in the 19th century. What the modern European readership would probably recognize as *Zikhron Ya'akov*'s weak point, Lipschitz believed to be its strength – namely that he, being a witness to and participant in the events described, was all the more trustworthy and credible: "There cannot be the slightest doubt of the truth of events, facts, and actions that one has experienced" [1. XXXVII]. However, "truth," was according to Lipschitz the opposite of what non-observant historians had written in their modern scholarly works of history: "I am not a chronicler, and for over half of my life I had no intention whatsoever of narrating history. This is regrettable indeed [...], for if I had already had this idea in my youth, [...] I would have had a number of remarkable opportunities to gather large amounts of historical information that would have genuinely enriched the history of the recent past" [1. XXXIII].

In the introduction to his book, Lipschitz is modest and does not rate his capabilities as a historian very highly. In fact, however, one gets the impression of an author inspired by the desire to draft a new picture of the recent past of European Jewry, trying at the same time to get the better of modern Jewish historians with their own weapons.

Although *Zikhron Ya'akov* appeared only decades after the events it essentially describes, it has deep roots in the historical experiences of the Jewish communities of Lithuania in the 1860s and 1870s. A little more than half a century after its publication, critical study of the book led to the coining of the phrase "Orthodox historiography" [5]. The term is used in scholarship today for the emergence and development of historiography throughout the Orthodox Jewish spectrum.

Born in 1838, Lipschitz is among the earliest representatives of → ultra-Orthodoxy in Lithuania. He first made a name for himself as the secretary to one of the leading rabbinical authorities in late 19th-century Lithuania, Yitsḥak Elḥanan Spektor. Lipschitz began his writing and political career in the Russian Empire in reaction to the activities of enlightened → maskilim and later Jewish nationalists in Eastern Europe; he was also involved in founding an anti-nationalist association in Kaunas. Between 1881 and 1900 he contributed to the establishment of a secret news network and provided information about anti-Jewish incidents and → pogroms in Czarist Russia also to foreign newspapers.

2. Orthodox historiography

Zikhron Ya'akov was not the first work of history by a Jewish Orthodox author. As early as the middle of the 19th century, numerous texts of local history such as Samuel Joseph Finn's (Fuenn) *Kiryah Ne'emanah* (1860; Faithful city) about → Vilna or Salomon Buber's *Anshe Shem* (1894; People of God) about Lemberg had already been published. In addition, there were similar works by rabbis and scholars in Galicia, Lithuania, Congress Poland, and the Russian → Pale of Settlement. They addressed an Orthodox readership of educated Jews in Eastern Europe who continued to read traditional Jewish literature while also being open to European scholarship (→ Science). Although the Orthodox historical works were usually composed in the context of a counter-movement to the Jewish Enlightenment (→ Haskalah), at the same time, however, they were significantly influenced by modern historical research.

Lipshitz represented a radically anti-modernist trend within the comparatively broad range of Orthodox historiographical writings. The spectrum ranged from German-Jewish scholarship of neo-Orthodox circles (→ Neo-Orthodoxy) – such as Abraham Berliner's (→ Mekitse Nirdamim) *Aus dem Inneren Leben der Deutschen Juden im Mittelalter* (1871) and his three-volume *Geschichte der Juden in Rom* (1893), or Aron Freimann's (→ Bibliography; → Freimann Collection) *Geschichte der israelitischen Gemeinde Ostrowo* (1896) – through modern, national-religious literature such as Ze'ev Yavetz's (Jawitz; 1847–1924) 14-volume *Toldot Yisra'el* (History of Israel) published beginning in 1906, and texts by proponents of the ultra-Orthodoxy, such as Chaim Meir Heilman's *Bet Rabbi* (1902; The rabbi's house) – to Hasidic hagiographies of a semi-legendary character. The authors from all these trends shared the view that historical events were divinely ordained. Their common, but often unacknowledged, objective was to present a "counter-history" to accepted scholarly historiography. Moreover, they were linked by an ideological agenda that was to provide a clearly structured and operable picture of the past to Orthodox Jewry (→ Orthodoxy). According to this, the Orthodox historian's profound faith was more important than his application of scholarly methods.

Orthodox historians worked like classic rabbinical scholars. In their writings they demonstrated their knowledge of the "external" (modern secular) scholarly literature, namely that written by national-Jewish historians. Thus Lipschitz often referred to Yavetz, not without firmly rejecting the enlightened-national part of his works. In addition, the Orthodox authors furnished their historiographies with extensive annotations which often contained particularly apologetic remarks, anachronistic comparisons, and not infrequently also hagiographical legends and eulogies. They based their works to a considerable degree on meta-historical assumptions and were inclined to enumerate and interpret events of the near and distant past in a harmonizing fashion striving for consensus.

Nevertheless, Orthodox Jewish historians adopted stylistic and structural elements of modern scholarly literature to a greater or lesser extent. Lipschitz and others employed some of the methodological tools of modern historical research such as examining sources under philological-critical criteria and using archival documents in support of their theories. Furthermore, many adopted the periodization established in secular historical research, even if some explicitly rejected the associated implications for theological reasons.

In *Zikhron Ya'akov*, for instance, the modern era begins with the emergence of the Haskalah in Russia and the reforms of Czar Alexander II. This periodization contradicts the opinion Lipschitz expressed elsewhere, according to which the history of the Jews progressed separately and independently of the history of other peoples [1. 2f.]. In fact, this contradiction points to the "modern" character of Lipschitz's approach. Accordingly, the modern age, which started out with the → Haskalah in Berlin in the late 18th century, is an entirely new phenomenon in Jewish history. The defense against this menacing innovation became an important topic within Orthodox historiography.

From the beginning, Orthodox historiography had been concerned with the role assigned to history in modern European discourse. The historicism of the Hegelian and Marxist variety – with which more than a few Orthodox Jewish authors were at least indirectly familiar – was interpreted as an outright denial of faith by the ultra-Orthodox historians, as it had exalted the concept of the laws of → history to the level of dogma. It was precisely this acceptance of historical law that undermined the traditional understanding of Jewish history as divine providence. Furthermore, among the mainly traditional Jews in Central and Eastern Europe, those modernizers who strove for the "improvement" of the Jews in accordance with this very theory of the laws of history on the social, economic, and cultural level, were regarded as the greatest threat.

Their fear of the abolition of Jewish communal → autonomy, of → emancipation succeeding, and of the attempts of Eastern European rulers to restructure the role Jews played in the economic life, which found expression in Orthodox historical works, was not least the result of their anti-historicist attitude. This anti-historicism for its part was the result of their controversy with the maskilim at the end of the 18th century. Paradoxically, a long-term corollary was the legitimation and even endorsement of the study of historiographical texts. Under the auspices of Orthodox historiography it achieved the status of "true wisdom."

In the late 19th century, the conflict with the followers of national movements emerging in Eastern Europe shaped Orthodox historiography. Modern German-Jewish historical research, which developed into a school of national history over the hundred years after its establishment, had from its beginnings contained the seeds of national-historical thought – for instance in Isaak Markus Jost's nine-volume *Geschichte der Israeliten* published from 1820 onward. The anti-national discourse that dominated Orthodox writings was not entirely free from the ideas of the opposing side, since a certain affinity between Jewish nationalism and → Orthodoxy – both postulating

the continuity of Jewish existence – led to overlaps in the depiction of Jewish history. Lipschitz, whose Orthodox path had started out with the struggle against the Haskalah in Lithuania in the late 1860s, turned against the modern Jewish national idea following the emergence of the → *Hibbat Tsiyon* ("Love of Zion") movement. In his understanding, as well as that of other Orthodox historians, Jewish nationalism was nothing but a late variant of the Haskalah, especially as it once again offered Jews a view of history that endangered them.

In Palestine, Orthodox historiography's fight against the national idea took a different form in some ways. Among pre-Zionist Jews (→ Yishuv) which had established themselves in Palestine decades before the national settlement project (→ Aliyah), an alternative to the Zionist view of history developed in the second half of the 19th century. Orthodox authors of this school adopted motifs of the modern national narrative, describing the old Yishuv as the fulfillment of national rebirth even before the beginnings of Zionism (→ Basel). Thus for instance, Chaim Hillel Rivlin in *Ḥazon Tsiyon* (1947; Vision of Zion), El'azar Hurwitz in *Mosad ha-yesod* (1958; Establishing the foundation), or Menachem Mendel Kasher in *Ha-tekufah ha-gedolah* (1969; The great era) mentioned a – fictional – Jewish congress said to have convened in Belarusian Shklov 90 years before the first Zionist Congress took place in Basel. They also exaggerated agricultural endeavors unrelated to either the Haskalah or the national movement and reported about Jewish militias which had protected the Jewish quarter in Jerusalem.

The leader of the Hasidic Chabad movement, Joseph Isaac Schneerson (1880–1950) was also among the authors of Orthodox historiography with his *Sefer ha-toldot* (1947; Book of history). Schneerson, who had awarded one of the approbations for *Zikhron Ya'akov* and praised the work because it provided an image of history that strengthened Orthodox Judaism, regarded modern Jewish historical scholarship as a continuation of the propaganda of → maskilim against traditional Jewish society and its values. He interpreted the Bolshevist persecutions he had experienced in the Soviet Union as an extension of the fight between believers and heretics that had begun with the start of the Enlightenment. According to his account, the maskilim, their Zionist successors, and their Jewish socialist companions played a demonic part in this struggle. Schneerson's writings on the history of the Chabad movement are exemplary of Hasidic Orthodox historiography of the interwar years.

Schneerson was familiar with Simon Dubnow's (→ Riga; → Weltgeschichte) *Geschichte des Chassidismus* (1931) and other relevant texts. He cultivated some conventions of historical scholarship and made use of secular historians' research. At the same time he continued the tradition of hagiographic Hasidic texts, but unlike the eulogies of previous Hasidic literature, his writings championed a fighting spirit. He attacked the assumptions of the opposing side, endeavoring to refute their historical construct, mingling time and again well-founded historical facts and archival findings with legends and supernatural phenomena.

After the Shoah and the destruction of the traditional Orthodox centers in Eastern Europe, new ultra-Orthodox communities (→ Ultra-Orthodoxy) emerged in Western Europe, North America, and Israel. The resulting change in language was a major factor contributing to the large number of publications in → English, among them Zalman Posner's translations of Schneerson's writings entitled *The Tzemach Tzedek and the Haskala Movement* (1962). Some modern historians have conceded that the works Orthodox historians transmitted were mostly unknown documents concerning little-known historical events. In that respect,

it is indeed possible to speak of a continuous, if limited, exchange between secular scholars and Orthodox historians.

The restoration of Hasidic courts (→ Hasidism) and centers of traditional Lithuanian erudition led to increased historiographical activity among those branches of the Orthodox movement that sought a dialogue with academic historical scholarship. Ultra-Orthodox journals in → Hebrew and English published articles from a varied spectrum of topics, in which scholarly methods and philological-historical documentation are linked with Orthodox ideas and tenets in the anti-modernist style. The Hasidic historian Abraham Abish Schorr's writings are typical of these. He researches the history of the most influential Hasidic communities in the Russian Empire, the Karliner and Stoliner Hasidim, and publishes his studies in the ultra-Orthodox journal *Bet Aharon ve-Yisra'el* (The house of Aaron and Israel) printed in Jerusalem over the last three decades.

Bibliography

Sources
[1] Y. Lipshitz, Zikhron Ya'akov [Recollection of Jacob], 3 vols., Kaunas 1924–1930.

Secondary literature
[2] D. Assaf, Yesod ha-Ma'ala. A New Chapter in the Historiography of Hasidism in Eretz Israel, in: Cathedra 68 (1993), 57–66 [Hebr.]. [3] D. Assaf, The Regal Way. The Life and Times of Rabbi Israel of Ruzhin, Stanford 2002. [4] I. Bartal, True Knowledge and Wisdom. On Orthodox Historiography, in: Studies in Contemporary Jewry 10 (1994), 178–192. [5] I. Bartal, Zikhron Ya'akov. Orthodox Historiography?, in: Milet 2 (1985), 409–414. [6] I. Bartal, Shim'on ha-Kofer. A Chapter in Orthodox Historiography, in: Studies in Jewish Culture in Honour of Chone Shmeruk, Jerusalem 1993, 243–268 [Hebr.]. [7] K. Caplan, Absolutely Intellectually

Honest. A Case-Study of American Jewish Modern Orthodox Historiography, in: R. Elior/ P. Schäfer (eds.), Creation and Re-Creation in Jewish Thought. Festschrift in Honor of Joseph Dan on the Occasion of his Seventieth Birthday, Tübingen 2005, 339–361. [8] I. Etkes, The Gaon of Vilna. The Man and His Image, Berkeley et al. 2002, 130–147. [9] H. Gertner, Epigonism and the Beginnings of Orthodox Historical Writing in 19th Century Eastern Europe, in: Studia Rosenthaliana 40 (2007/8), 217–229. [10] H. Gertner, Reshitah shel ketivah historit ortodoksit be-mizraḥ Eropah: ha'arakhah meḥudeshet [The Beginning of "Orthodox Historiography" in Eastern Europe. A Reassessment], in: Zion 67 (2002) 3, 293–337. [11] N. Karlinsky, The Dawn of Hasidic-Haredi Historiography, in: Modern Judaism 27 (2007) 1, 20–46. [12] N. Karlinsky, Historyah she-ke-neged. Igrot ha-Ḥasidim me-Erets-Yisra'el: ha-tekst ve-ha-kontekst [Counter History. The Hasidic Epistles from Eretz-Israel, Text and Context], Jerusalem 1998. [13] A. Rapoport-Albert, Hagiography with Footnotes. Edifying Tales and the Writing of History in Hasidism, in: History and Theory 27 (1988), 119–159.

ISRAEL BARTAL, JERUSALEM

Zikhroynes

In her extensive memoirs (Yidd. *zikhroynes*), Glikl bas Leib Pinkerle (Glikl of Hameln, 1645–1724) described her family life with her many children and her successful commercial activity. Written in West Yiddish, the memoirs were first published in 1896; in 1910 the women's rights activist Bertha Pappenheim presented a translation into German. Since then, Glikl bas Leib has been perceived as the model of a strong female personality. Her *Zikhroynes*, which also record important contemporary historical events, are regarded as a remarkable source for everyday history in Ashkenaz during the late 17th and early 18th centuries.

1. Glikl bas Leib Pinkerle
2. The *Zikhroynes*
2.1 Structure, content, and style
2.2 Language, sources, and significance
2.3 Manuscript, printed versions, and translations

1. Glikl bas Leib Pinkerle

Glikl bas (daughter of) Leib Pinkerle, better known as Glückel of Hameln, became famous as the author of the probably most extensive memoir of a Jewish woman in early modern → Ashkenaz. Glikl was born in → Hamburg in 1645 to a wealthy merchant family with familial and economic ties to → court Jews and their environment. At the age of 12, Glikl was betrothed to Ḥayim of Hameln (Goldschmidt-Hameln, ca. 1642–1689) by her parents Leib (Löb) Pinkerle and Bella Nathan Ellrich. When Glikl was 14 years old, they were married, and she moved into his family home in Hameln. After the first year of → marriage, the couple lived with Glikl's parents in Hamburg, where their first daughter was born. Shortly thereafter, the couple moved into their own house. During their thirty years of marriage, Glikl gave birth to 14 children, two of whom died in early childhood.

Throughout these years, Glikl was an active partner in her husband's business, which mainly consisted in selling jewelry and gemstones, and to a lesser extent in money trade and financial transactions. Her advice and opinion were frequently sought, and she not only independently negotiated with agents but also found possible business associates, drafted partnership contracts, and kept the books. At the same time, she was busy with the care and education of her sons and daughters, sought suitable partners for them once they had reached marriageable age, and ensured they had appropriate dowries. She appeared to have been an active and equal partner in all decisions regarding the family and business.

Consequently she reports that her husband, when asked on his deathbed if he had a last piece of advice to give, responded "I don't know what to say. My wife, she knows everything. She should continue just as she was doing before" [3. 200].

After Ḥayim's → death in 1689, when eight of her children were still unmarried and lived at home, Glikl independently managed the family's business in Hamburg (and established a sock factory here as well) and at the trade fairs in → Leipzig and elsewhere. After eleven years of widowhood, during which, according to her own account, she refused many offers of marriage, and after having married off all her children except the youngest daughter, Glikl married the → banker Cerf (Hertz) Levy from → Metz, where she also relocated. The financial situation of her second husband – to whom she had entrusted her entire wealth including her daughter's dowry – continually deteriorated, until he finally went bankrupt. When Cerf Levy died in 1712, Glikl was utterly destitute and consequently forced to spend the last years of her life dependent on her daughter and son-in-law in Metz and share their home – a situation, in fact, she had always feared and strove all her life to prevent.

2. The *Zikhroynes*

2.1 *Structure, content, and style*
Glikl began to write her memoirs in 1691 at the age of 46 and approximately two years after the death of her first husband. This activity was supposed to disperse her melancholy, "since it afforded me some pleasure when the melancholy thoughts were upon me. I passed many sleepless nights" [3. 43]. She also wanted to record the biography of her parents and family for her children and their descendants. The first chapter gives an introduction to her spiritual world, a kind of manifesto of her faith. It contains the convictions, expectations, motivation, and opinions of a God-fearing, pious Jewish woman concerning God and humans, good and evil, sin and punishment, this world and the world to come, parents and children, and other similar topics.

Even though the second chapter begins with her birth, there is hardly any information about her childhood and upbringing except that she was taught in a ḥeder and that her father ensured that all his children, boys and girls, were educated "in higher matters as well as in practical things" [3. 60]. This chapter comprises mainly descriptions of family occurrences, events in the Jewish communities of Hamburg and Altona – at most of which Glikl was not present herself – as well as information about her immediate ancestors. She often refers to the times of two or three generations ago, for instance in the context of the founding, history, and personalities of the Hamburg Jewish community. The subsequent overview of Ḥayim's family, however, is closer to the present: "My dear children, I write this for you in case your dear children or grandchildren come to you one of these days, knowing nothing of their family" [3. 93]. It is not until after her marriage, and especially after the young family's move to their own home, as described at the end of the second chapter, that Glikl appears as a clearly defined personality with individual self-awareness.

In the third chapter, Glikl describes the servants, salesmen, and partners of the family business as well as several events linked to the business. In the third and fourth chapters, she records episodes and events from family and community life. The fifth chapter is devoted to the illness and → death of her husband and the time immediately following it. Subsequently she describes herself working for the benefit of the family and her children's future, as well as further events from her life.

Bertha Pappenheim as Glikl, *Painting by Leopold Pilichowski* (ca. 1925)

Glikl presumably only wrote the last two chapters about the later years of her life after she had been widowed a second time. First she gives an account about the preparations for her second wedding and her move to → Metz, followed by episodes of her life with her second husband, his economic ruin, his death, and events that occurred afterwards. The last chapter ends, for no apparent reason, in 1719, five years before her death, with her description of an extraordinary celestial phenomenon [3. 310], which was probably the great meteorite fireball that was visible in parts of northwest Europe in March of that year.

Beyond being a family chronicle, Glikl's *Zikhroynes* is a source for contemporary events that took place in the Hamburg and Altona Jewish community. Among these are the reactions to the would-be messiah Sabbatai Zevi (→ Smyrna). The author also reports about her new community in Metz, such as the tragedy that occurred in the → synagogue during the Shavu'ot festival (→ Course of the Year) or of a bitter dispute in the local → rabbinate. A considerable number of events described, however, take place in other cities and communities in Germany, such as Berlin, Frankfurt, and Hanover, or abroad, for instance in Amsterdam (→ Esnoga) and Copenhagen. All these were places Glikl visited in order to arrange and celebrate her children's weddings with friends or relatives, to assist her husband in his business, or to transact business herself. Glikl's narrative furthermore includes events in Jewish communities in Poland (→ Vilna and Lissa/Leszno) or Norway; moreover, there are observations on general historical events in Germany and France, predominantly wars.

While Glikl repeatedly explains that it was her state of mind after her husband's death that motivated her to write, she does not place the portrait of a beloved and revered husband at the center, supplementing it with a modest, brief description of herself – as would have been in keeping with the custom of women writing autobiographical texts in the 17th century. In fact, it is she herself and the story of her own life that are at the center of her account.

2.2 Language, sources, and significance

Glikl's book is written in Old West → Yiddish. It contains a remarkably large number of Hebrew elements, as she included numerous quotations from various Hebrew texts. However, she did not possess comprehensive understanding of → Hebrew texts; in order to understand a Hebrew book, she would have needed someone to translate it into Yiddish for her.

Her impressive literary knowledge was due rather to her traditional education and her intensive attention to the oral culture of her immediate surroundings, in which there was no lack of educated men and religious scholars. Above all, it was probably due to her extensive reading of Yiddish works, especially stories from Jewish as well as non-Jewish sources written in, translated into, or adapted for Yiddish. She had also read works of the ancient Yiddish → *musar* literature, which were her source for dozens of stories, legends, parables, and proverbs which she used in her text with the aim of illustrating and clarifying; her worldview, too, was based on this literature.

At the same time her work testifies to her independent thought and imaginativeness as well as her ability to express wise and empathetic thoughts about her life, giving a multifaceted image of herself, her family, and her community. Thus her memoirs are on the one hand the portrait of an entire society. They show the everyday life of Ashkenazi Jews (→ Ashkenazim) and their behaviors and customs (→ Minhag), their family life, the role of women, the upbringing and education of children, economic and religious life, their tenets of faith as well as views, and relationships between Jews and non-Jews. On the other hand, the *Zikhroynes* allow us an insight into the author's personality, her inner life, and her maturing self-awareness. It tells us about her joys and woes, about crises, conflicts, and despair, but also about moments of fulfilment and satisfaction. It reveals Glikl's sense of humor (→ Jokes) and irony and her sheer enjoyment of writing.

Glikl's memoirs are regarded today as an exceptional historical document and one of the most important Ashkenazi texts of early modern Yiddish – and Hebrew – prose until the end of the 18th century. The *Zikhroynes* is a mosaic of different genres, clearly bearing the mark of contemporary Yiddish → literature in all its eclecticism. Besides references to the form and subject matter of *musar* literature, homiletic prose, and popular literature, we also find the heartfelt tone known from Yiddish → *tkhines* (petitionary prayers) and the immediacy of accounts of contemporary events. It does, however, seem that the literature available to Glikl was not the model for her own autobiographical writing. While she explicitly dedicated the book to her children, several phrases indicate that she was also writing with an eye to other readers.

2.3 Manuscript, printed versions, and translations

Glikl's own manuscript of her recollections has not survived. Two copies made by her youngest son Moshe Goldschmidt-Hameln – the only completely extant one does not have a title – were passed down in the family from one generation to the next, and, finally, in the late 19th century to the scholar David Kaufmann (1852–1899; → Mekitse Nirdamim), who published them in 1896 under the title *Die Memoiren der Glückel von Hameln 1645–1719* ("The Memoirs of Glückel of Hameln," 1977). In the meantime, one of the manuscript copies was nearly entirely lost. The four surviving pages are preserved in the Israeli National Library in Jerusalem. The complete copy is held by the University Library in Frankfurt am Main.

That the *Zikhroynes* became more widely known is mainly due to translations. In 1910 Bertha Pappenheim (→ Jüdischer Frauenbund) presented the first translation into → German (which she called "Übertragung," transcription); as Glikl's distant descendant, she meant it to be read by the family. Around 1923/1924 she posed as Glikl for a portrait by the Polish Jewish painter Leopold Pilichowski (1869–1933).

The German translation by Alfred Feilchenfeld (1860–1923) published three years later highlighted biographical and historical events and supplemented these with numerous footnotes providing the translator's extensive commentary, but he left out the author's own reflections and most of the narrative accounts. Feilchenfeld's translation was the basis for Marvin Lowenthal's (1890–1969) abridged English translation of 1932, which was followed by further abridged translations into French (1971), Italian (1984), and → Russian (2001). Translations overall faithful to the Yiddish original are the → English by Beth-Zion Abrahams

(1962), the → Hebrew ones by Alexander Siskind Rabinovitz (1929) and Chava Turniansky (2006), as well as the modern Yiddish one by Joseph Bernfeld (1967), and the Dutch by Mira Rafalowicz (1987).

Glikl's book was enthusiastically received, especially after Feilchenfeld's German translation, and has been used by many scholars as a historical source for studies on a variety of subjects. It is only since the last two decades of the 20th century, not least thanks to the growing scholarly interest in autobiographical texts and the establishment of gender studies, that the work and its author herself became the subject of more intensive academic research.

Bibliography

Sources

[1] Die Memoiren der Glückel von Hameln 1645–1719, ed. by D. Kaufmann, Frankfurt am Main 1896.   [2] The Memoirs of Glückel of Hameln, trans. by M. Lowenthal and R. S. Rosen, New York 1977.   [3] Glikl Memoirs 1691–1719, ed. by C. Turniansky, trans. by S. Friedman, Waltham 2019. [4] Glikl, Zikhroynes [Memories] 1691–1719, ed. and trans. by C. Turniansky, Jerusalem 2006.

Secondary literature

[5] N. Z. Davis, Drei Frauenleben. Glikl, Marie de l'Incarnation, Maria Sybilla Merian, Berlin 1996.   [6] M. Richarz (ed.), Die Hamburger Kauffrau Glikl. Jüdische Existenz in der Frühen Neuzeit, Hamburg 2001.   [7] C. Turniansky, Descriptions of Events in Glikl Hamel's Memoirs, in: Di goldene keyt 134 (1992), 35–40 [Yidd.].   [8] C. Turniansky, To What Literary Genre Does Glikl Hamel's Work Belong?, in: Proceedings of the Eleventh World Congress of Jewish Studies 3 (1994), 283–290 [Yidd.].   [9] C. Turniansky, Die Erzählungen in Glikl Hamelns Werk und ihre Quellen, in: C. E. Müller/A. Schatz (eds.), Der Differenz auf der Spur. Frauen und Gender in Aschkenas, Berlin 2004, 121–148.

CHAVA TURNIANSKY, JERUSALEM

Zion

As the most associative biblical designation for Jerusalem, the name Zion denotes the mythical-historical place of memory as well as the symbolic-concrete objective of political-sacral action aimed at the reestablishment of the Jewish-Israelite polity. Since the beginning of the Diaspora, the memory of Zion has been kept alive in Judaism through liturgical and other rituals of religious observance. With the decline of the Iberian Diaspora, the longing for an active return of the Jews to Zion was virulently revived. In the modern age, the name of Zion forms the ideal bridge between cultural, practical, and political concepts aimed at establishing a modern Jewish commonwealth.

1.   The names of Jerusalem
2.   Ancient traditions
2.1   Biblical
2.2   Post-biblical
3.   Symbol of modern return movements

1.   The names of Jerusalem

Besides professing the oneness of God (Deut 6:4), the commitment to Jerusalem is one of the central concepts of Judaism (see also Ps 137:5). Zion is the most highly emotionally charged name of Jerusalem. In the Hebrew Bible (→ Tanakh), the word "Zion" (Hebr. *Tsiyon*) occurs 153 times, especially in Isaiah (47), Psalms (37), Jeremiah (17), and Lamentations (15). The origin and meaning of this name, which is not documented outside the Bible, are unclear. It apparently referred to a royal as well as cultic site in Jerusalem and is mentioned, above all, in connection with prophecy and Jerusalem – exclusively Yahwist – worship. It is probable that the fortification of Jerusalem was first called Zion (in 2 Sam 5:7 also called City of David); later the name was also applied to the hill adjoining it to the north that was home to the → Temple.

The name Jerusalem, however, is pre-biblically documented and is used more than 600 times in the Bible, 100 times alone in 2 Chronicles and Jeremiah, but in Psalms it is mentioned only 17 times. In the Torah, the holy city is referred to only once (Gen 14:18) in the form "Salem" (Hebr. *Shalem*), a secondary name for Jerusalem. According to Psalms 76:2, this is understood as another name for Zion.

Jerusalem is called "Jebus" (Hebr. *Yevus*; Judg 10:11; 1 Chr 11:4–5) only in connection with the Davidic conquest of the "stronghold of Zion" (1 Chr 11:5; 2 Sam 5:7). The place-name Jebus is found exclusively in the Pentateuch and sources depending on it; it is possible that this is a later word formation derived from the collective term Jebusite referring to a pre-Israelite population in or near Jerusalem. As in several other biblical narratives of the pre-monarchical period, for instance the account of the Anakites (Hebr. *anakim*; "giants"; Deut 2:11 etc.), this also seems to be an Iron Age legend about Bronze Age conditions.

2. Ancient traditions

2.1 *Biblical*

In the biblical text, Zion has two distinguishable meanings, one historical and one religious. On the one hand, *metsudat Tsiyon* (stronghold of Zion) historically refers to the location of the fortress conquered by David and renamed "City of David" by him (2 Sam 5:7). The story of the conquest, however tendentious and late-monarchical it may be, is certainly based on a historical memory. Characteristically there is no reference to Divine Providence in this narrative. David conquers Jebus, a place of political and strategic rather than cultic importance, and establishes his power base there. The stronghold of Zion provides security, and

it is situated in the border region between the southern tribes over which David initially ruled, and the northern homeland of the Israelites.

Har Tsiyon (Mount Zion), on the other hand, is the sacred divine mountain and terrestrial location of YHWH's enthronement (Pss 9:12, 135:21), where his countenance shall be sought. It is the place from which aid and assistance shall come to the "righteous" believers, and at which the rebuke of the peoples will one day begin. However, it was only as a result of the anti-Assyrian centralization measures under Hezekiah in the late 8th century BCE that this Judean royal city of Zion became the true and only dwelling of YHWH; a century later, Hezekiah's successor Josiah reinforced these measures after the downfall of Assyria (2 Kgs 18–20, 22f.). Zion's rise to become the place of the central sanctuary illustrates some of the most important motifs and tendencies in the development of the official religion of the late royal Davidic dynasty, which left not only literary but also archeological traces (→ Archaeology).

In the Deuteronomistic history (Samuel and Kings), Zion denotes the historical, geographical, and sacral objective of the conquest of the Promised Land. The stronghold of Zion thus becomes the central seat of government of the Davidic kingdom and the location of the Temple of Solomon. From a sacral perspective, Mount Zion refers to the dwelling of God and the location of the Jewish-Israelite monarchy under God's protection, whose defense, peril, destruction, and future restoration, constitute a central motif of Jewish prophecy and historiography (→ History).

If we consider all the books of the Bible, Mount Zion is the place of fulfillment of the Sinaitic legislation. Sinai denotes the condition and Zion the completion of the divinely ordained existence in the Promised Land. Accordingly, the Psalms present Zion as the objective of the liturgical ascension of the pilgrims to the "forecourts of the Lord."

In the Jerusalem prophetic texts, Zion furthermore appears as the destination of a global eschatological pilgrimage and as the home of instruction (Isa 2:3; Mic 4:2). This, as well as the Davidic tradition connected with Zion, is also the source of Christian Zion symbolism, condensed in, for example, the chorus "Zion's Daughter" in Georg Friedrich Händel's *Judas Maccabeus*, and is found more recently in the form of Christian Zionism.

As the place (*mishkan*) where God settled, and the destination of the ascending pilgrimage (*aliyah le-regel*; → Aliyah), Zion survives the destruction of the sacral monarchy and its architectural symbols, remaining the central metaphor of religious-messianic as well as secular movements of returning to the land of the fathers. Due to this line of tradition, it was possible for Zion to become the most concise expression of Jewish → Renaissance movements at the end of the 19th century, among which the idea of founding a modern Jewish state in Palestine was at first merely one of several competing variants.

2.2 *Post-biblical*

Rabbinic Judaism of Late Antiquity and its largely normative legal and exegetic practice neutralized the political thrust of those movements that were committed to the restoration of the → Temple and the liberation of the city of Jerusalem. There were, however, also prominent legal scholars among the champions of Jewish irredentism, such as Rabbi Akiva ben Joseph (mid-1st century – 135 CE; → Alef Bet), whose martyrdom is reported in the Babylonian → Talmud (Berakhot 61b) in the context of the Bar Kokhba revolt. Scholars' opinions differ with regard to the causes and the character (religious-apocalyptic, social-revolutionary, political) of the two anti-Roman uprisings. Coins

minted during the time of the second uprising 132–135 CE cast a messianic-irredentist light on this rebellion against the Roman occupation of Judaea. The Temple had been lying in ruins for two generations when Emperor Hadrian's oppressive measures (in particular the prohibition of circumcision) but also his plans to rebuild the city were answered with a well-organized uprising to liberate Jerusalem. Rabbi Akiva and other leaders of the rabbinic movement welcomed Simon Bar Kokhba's uprising; their reasons, however, are not clear.

Presumably in the wake of the measures taken by Caracalla and Antoninus Pius, whose attitude toward the Jews of Palestine was considered to be friendly, a fundamental agreement between Romans and Jews was concluded at the beginning of the 3rd century, which led to the stabilization of the Jewish presence in → Israel. However, the reconstruction of the Temple was not considered until the reign of Emperor Julian (361–363). Meanwhile, the daily prayers prescribed in the collection of religious laws in the Mishnah (→ Talmud) acted as replacement for the Temple sacrifice. Thus, Tannaitic Judaism established a kind of → diaspora religion in its own country. This compromise allowed the Jews to come to terms with foreign rule without breaking faith with the Mosaic law and the religious duties of the "oral teachings" (Talmud). The model for that was the introduction of a legal system under Ezra (→ Exile). There had also been a compromise under Old Persian rule: the reconstruction of Jerusalem as the temple city adhering to the Torah as its legal system was completed without the restoration of the Davidic kingdom.

In later rabbinic texts, Zion denoted the location where the personified "presence of God" (Hebr. → *shekhinah*) dwelt as well as the City of David and the site of David's tomb. Since Late Antiquity, the latter had been venerated in the southwestern part of the city, comparatively close to the former Herod's Palace and the so-called Tower of David. In the Talmud and → Midrash, there are deliberations concerning the limitation of the holiness of God which had at first covered all of Jerusalem, but was finally limited to the sanctuary alone (→ Kadosh). Zion was sometimes linked to the Temple Mount and sometimes to the House of David.

The Jewish practice of praying on the western side of the temple wall, documented only in later centuries, is based on the belief that the *shekhinah* was present on Mount Zion even when all that remained of the destroyed Temple was the back wall of the sanctuary. The messianic time of the Jews gathering and returning to Erets Israel and rebuilding the Temple, namely the end of exile, is also linked in Jewish tradition with the expectation of the resurrection of the dead (*tehiyat ha-metim*). Consequently the Jewish graves on the southern slope of the Mount of Olives are oriented towards the Temple that still awaits reconstruction and the walled-up Golden Gate, which is expected to be opened upon the arrival of the messiah (→ Messianism). Similar eschatological legends are found among Christians and Muslims.

In the rabbinic Aggadah, Zion assumes cosmic dimensions. It is said to contain the foundation stone or hub of the universe (*omphalos mundi*) on which heaven and earth were created or the world was born (Talmud Bavli, Yoma 54b). Earthquakes occur whenever the Almighty gazes upon the ruins of the Temple on Mount Zion while the sanctuaries of other gods flourish. Furthermore, according to narrative traditions, Jeremiah hid the Ark of the Covenant inside Mount Zion. As early as the Babylonian Talmud (Yoma 78a), the tomb of David is located on Mount Zion, presumably referring to the precipice in the southwest of the city which Empress Eudoxia (ca. 400–460) had incorporated into the Byzantine city

of Aelia Capitolina when it was expanded under her leadership.

Arguably the most enduring transfiguration of Zion as the symbol of Jewish longing to return to the Holy Land is found in Yehudah ha-Levi's (ca. 1075–1141; → Kuzari) *Zionides*. In these hymns and poems dating from the golden age of Andalusian Judaism (→ Sepharad), Zion is sentimentally exalted through a multitude of poetic images. Ha-Levi wrote during a time of strong messianic expectations following the First Crusade. In the end, the poet himself set out for the Holy Land, where he would also die. According to Franz Rosenzweig (1886–1929; → Star of Redemption), who translated and annotated the *Zionides*, ha-Levi's most popular poem *Libi ve-mizrah* ("Between East and West," 2000 or "My Heart is in the East") was heralding a turning point in the history of Jewish exile: "All goods of Spain are/ chaff to my eye, but / the dust on which once stood / the tabernacle is gold to my eye!" [2. 234].

In Christianity, Jerusalem is seen rather more ambivalently as the place where the messiah Jesus of Nazareth was crucified, while Zion enjoys great esteem. The primarily eschatological Christian tradition referred to the Zion mentioned in psalms and hymns as God's dwelling on earth, to which the resurrected Christ will return at the end of time to sit in judgment.

In the early Islamic Jerusalem tradition, the Temple Mount is of pivotal significance as the symbolic center of the world. The deserted Temple Mount is believed to have been the destination of the Prophet Muhammad's nocturnal journey mentioned in the Quran (Surah 17; Arab. *al-isrā'*) and the location of his mystical ascent to heaven (*al-miʿrāj*). It was here that the Umayyad caliph ʿAbd al-Malik had the Dome of the Rock (*qubbat al-ṣakhrah*), the first representative sacred building of Islamic architectural history, built at the end of the 7th century as a symbolic reconstruction of the Temple of Solomon. Islamic legends about the significance of Jerusalem were collected in books on the "merits of Jerusalem" (*faḍāʾil al-Quds*) and in the so-called *isrāʾīliyyāt* (Israelite) literature (→ Tafsīr). From the late Middle Ages onward, however, Islamic scholars began to express doubt concerning Jewish and Christian beliefs that the Jewish Temple had once stood here.

3. Symbol of modern return movements

The biblical and post-biblical Zion tradition continued to be significant in modern Judaism. Mount Zion was linked to the recollection of the Davidic monarchy as well as the Temple of Solomon. Zion was the earthly refuge of Jewish religious and national history, symbolizing the hope of return, the gathering of the dispersed, the reconstruction of the Temple, the resumption of the sacrifices, the resurrection of the dead, and the beginning of the messianic era. Zion was thus not merely a place of memory among others such as Abraham's domicile "Mamre," "Rachel's tomb," or "Mount Gerizim," but the place that structures the Jewish experience of space and time. The distance from Zion corresponded to the distance from the divine presence and salvation; the destruction of Zion was tied to the idea of → exile, and the return to Zion with redemption.

On the foundation of this influential religious tradition, Jewish movements emerged in Western as well as Eastern Europe in the 19th century, which reacted to the social, political, and cultural developments of the time. One of the first groups referring to Zion was composed of Jewish students from Kharkov who called themselves *Bilu* after the acronym of the verse Isaiah 2:5 in the Hebrew Bible. In 1882 they published their manifesto, and in the same year contributed to the foundation of the settlement *Rishon le-Tsiyon* (First to Zion). From the 1880s onward, similar associations were founded in Russia and Eastern Europe under the name of → Ḥoveve Tsiyon (Friends of Zion), whose objectives were at first limited to encouraging Jews to settle in Palestine.

The term "Zionism" was coined by Nathan Birnbaum (1864–1937; → Czernowitz Language Conference) in 1885. This neologism was an expression of the conviction that Zion, being Erets → Israel and the land of the fathers, was the only conceivable place where the → "Jewish question" could be resolved in an organic fashion. Zion stood as a synecdoche for the Holy Land and its biblical roots. The deeply symbolic term Zionism spread as a catchphrase that would come to include the *Ḥoveve Tsiyon* movement.

Nowadays, "Zionism" is usually linked to the modern political movement with the objective of establishing a Jewish polity in Palestine as Erets Israel. → Cultural Zionism, emphasizing spiritual and ethical motifs, emerged in response and opposition to political Zionism. Theodor Herzl's design for a Jewish state had not from the very first been informed by "Zion" (→ Old New Land). By adapting this word to name the first "Zionist" congress in 1897 (→ Basel), however, a preliminary decision in favor of Palestine had been taken based on historical, religious, and sentimental motives, in a fashion that Herzl had not intended. His idea of Zionism had originally been "a returning home to Jewish identity before the return to the country of the Jews," as he himself had put it in his speech at the first Zionist congress [1. 93].

Bibliography

Sources

[1] M. J. Reimer, The First Zionist Congress. An Annotated Translation of the Proceedings, Albany 2019.   [2] F. Rosenzweig, Ninety-Two Poems and Hymns of Yehuda Halevi, ed. by R.A. Cohen, Albany 2000.

Secondary literature

[3] Y. Z. Eliav, God's Mountain. The Temple Mount in Time, Place, and Memory, Baltimore 2005. [4] B. Halpern, The Idea of the Jewish State, Cambridge (MA) ²1969. [5] A. Herzberg, The Zionist Idea. A Historical Analysis and Reader, ¹⁶1986. [6] J. D. Levenson, Sinai and Zion. An Entry into the Jewish Bible, San Francisco 1985. [7] L. I. Levine (ed.), Jerusalem. Its Sanctity and Centrality to Judaism, Christianity, and Islam, New York 1999. [8] M. Zank, Jerusalem in Religious Studies. The City and Scripture, in: M. Adelman/M. Fendius Elman (eds.), Jerusalem. Conflict and Cooperation in a Contested City, Syracuse/New York 2014, 114–142.

MICHAEL ZANK, BOSTON

Żydokomuna

Żydokomuna was an antisemitic catchphrase used by right-wing, clerical, and nationalist circles in Polish society, according to which "Jewish communism" was threatening the Polish nation. Spreading after the First World War, the effectiveness of this enemy image increased, above all, in the wake of the Polish–Soviet War and because of the visibility of Jewish members in the Communist Party. The term Żydokomuna implied a Jewish-Soviet conspiracy to subjugate Poland under Soviet rule. The Soviet occupation of the eastern parts of the country in 1939 was used as proof for the alleged treason of the Jews, leading to numerous pogroms after the Red Army withdrew in 1941. The establishment of communist rule after the Second World War was regarded as the realization of a "Judeo-Polania," and to this day, the existence of a Żydokomuna is alleged in order to relativize Polish responsibility for anti-Jewish attitudes and actions before, during, and after the → Holocaust.

1. History of the term
2. Jewish communists and antisemitism (1921–1939)
3. Żydokomuna in the Second World War
4. After 1945

1. History of the term

Antisemitic enemy images accusing Jews of disseminating Socialist ideas have been ubiquitous in Europe from the second half of the 19th century onward. With the establishment of the Soviet regime in Russia and the growth of revolutionary movements at the end of the First World War in Germany (→ Bavarian Council Republic), Hungary (→ Budapest), and Austria, they gained increasing force.

In the territories of the future Second Polish Republic, the conservative authors Zygmunt Krasiński (*Nie-Boska komedia*; "The Un-divine Comedy," 1923) and Julian Ursyn Niemcewicz were the first to express early versions of this collective allegation against the Jews. In the pamphlet *Rok 3333 czyli Sen niesłychany* ("The Year 3333, or An Incredible Dream," 1996) written in 1817 but published only posthumously in 1858, Niemcewicz depicted the Jews as menacing strangers and imagined a Warsaw ruled by them and renamed "Moszkopolis." The pamphlet invoked the danger of a future "Judeo-Polonia" [10. 47f.]. Called *żydokomuna* (Judeo-Communism) or *żydo-bolszewizm* (Judeo-Bolshevism), this myth grew into one of the most widespread and effective anti-Jewish topoi among conservative, right-wing, and nationalist circles in Poland after the First World War. Their press regarded the revolutionary events in Russia and the establishment of Soviet rule as a "Jewish Bolshevist" threat to Poland and other European nations. Even before the outbreak of the Polish-Soviet War (1919–1921), they regarded Bolshevism and the communist movement as the product of Jewish actions.

In the interwar years, members of the military, journalists, and authors disseminated the Żydokomuna myth. The internment of Jewish soldiers in the Polish army in → Jabłonna during the Polish-Soviet War because of alleged collaboration with the approaching → Red Army was used as proof of the Jews being untrustworthy and devious. Catholic publications, too, such as the monthly journal *Przegląd Powszechny* (General Review) or, even more radically, the daily paper *Mały Dziennik* (Little Daily Paper), painted a picture of treacherous Jews, symbolized by the word Żydokomuna. Among the numerous pertinent publications that spread this trend during the interwar years was the text *O Żydach. Wiadomości pożyteczne* (About the Jews. Useful news), in which Stanisław Rybarkiewicz accused the Jews as early as 1920 of having provoked the Russian Revolution and caused the oppression of the Russian people.

2. Jewish communists and antisemitism (1921–1939)

According to estimates, the proportion of Jews among members of the Communist Workers' Party of Poland (Komunistyczna Partia Robotnicza Polski; from 1925 onward, Komunistyczna Partia Polski; KPP) was between 20% and 40% in the 1920s; members of the Belarusian and Ukrainian minorities also exhibit similarly high proportions. The KPP was attractive above all because it stood up against every kind of discrimination, including on the grounds of nationality. Besides members of socialist Jewish groups such as *Po'ale Tsiyon* and *Fareynikte*, radical left splinter groups of the *Algemeyner Yidisher Arbeter-bund* (General Jewish Labor Bund; → *Bund*) led by Pinkus Minc (pseud.: Aleksander Minc) and Abraham Abel Pflug (pseud., among others: Abe Flug) also joined the KPP in the 1920s. Numerous Jews joined the party between 1926 and

1928, but also into the 1930s. In 1935 more than half the leadership cadre of local party organizations were Jews or persons of Jewish origin. In the 1930s, around 10,000 Jews were members of communist organizations. In spite of this high proportion of Jews in the party, Jewish support for communism overall was very small, even at its highest reaching no more than five to seven percent of the Jewish population. The majority of the approximately three million politically heterogeneous Jews in Poland mainly supported Józef Piłsudski's governing Sanacja (healing) group [12. 95–98]; [8. 106]. A considerable number identified with Orthodoxy, Zionist political groups, or the *Bund*.

That the KPP was internationalist and pro-Soviet, a member of the → Komintern, and included Jews in large numbers who were visible within the leadership, reinforced the illusion of the Żydokomuna. That the party and its predecessors had spoken out against a Polish national state, which led to it being banned in 1919, increased the hostility it faced from the right. While the communist movement carried little weight in Poland, clerical and right-wing nationalist circles held onto the belief that although not every communist was a Jew, every Jew, however, was inclined to be a communist [10. 91]. Even in the early days of the Polish Republic, numerous anti-communist publications circulated in which Jews were particularly singled out. In 1934 Józef Mitzenmacher published the anti-communist text *Historja Komunistycznej Partji Polski w świetle faktów i dokumentów* (History of the Communist Party of Poland in Light of Facts and Documents) under the pseudonym Jan Alfred Reguła. In it he condemned Jewish communists as being particularly disloyal, untrustworthy, and uncultured compared to communists of other national and ethnic origins; the cause, he claimed, was their non-national (*beznarodowy*) or inter-national (*międzynaród*) character.

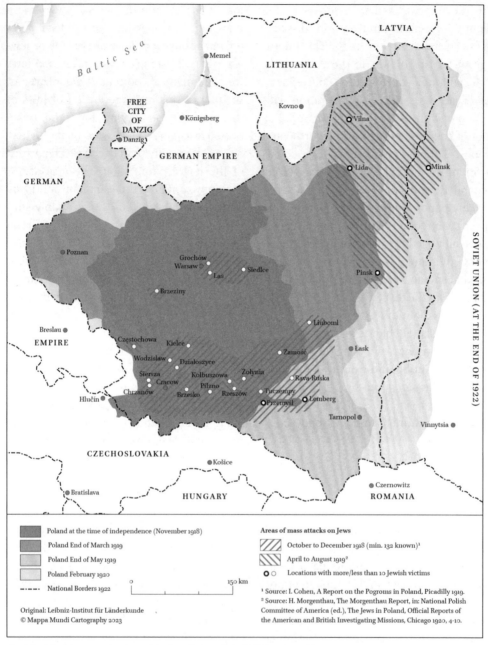

Anti-Jewish violence at the time of the foundation of the Polish state 1918/1919

During the period of deep social and economic tensions from the end of the 1920s onward, this accusation spread further. In 1936, a group of journalists representing 15 right-wing and nationalist publications joined together in the so-called Komitet Prasy Młodych (Youth Press Committee), a collective effort to combat communism and spread Polish nationalism. The movement Narodowa Demokracja (National Democracy) accused the governing Sanacja group of being guided by Jews. To be sure, Jewish politicians, some of whom were members of the → Sejm, protested against the growing number of incidents of antisemitic violence and discrimination beginning in the 1930s (→ Madagascar Plan). However, their influence was limited. By contrast, the belief in

ŻYDOKOMUNA

a "Jewish communism" gained acceptance even in government circles.

3. Żydokomuna in the Second World War

The myth that "Jewish Bolshevism" was responsible for national decline persisted during the Second World War in many countries of Eastern Europe, including Latvia, Lithuania, Romania, Ukraine, and Poland. The occupation between 1939 and 1941 of the eastern areas of the country by the → Red Army seemed to many Polish nationalists to prove the collective responsibility and anti-Polish attitude of the Jews; after all, some – especially younger – Jews had welcomed the invasion in the hope that the restrictions imposed on Jews would now be lifted. Everywhere in the northeastern and southeastern parts of Poland, locally organized → pogroms against Jews broke out, for example in → Jedwabne, Radziłów, or Wąsocz, especially after the hasty retreat of the Red Army as a result of the German attack on the Soviet Union in the summer of 1941.

During the course of the war, the concept of Żydokomuna exerted a considerable influence on the passive attitude of the Poles in the face of the Nazi extermination of Jews. The Polish right, though not inclined to support extermination, regarded help for the Jews as serving the "Soviet enemy." This obsession was expressed with particular virulence in the organs and subsidiary organizations of the National Democrats. In some cases, journals such as *Nurt Młodych* (Youth trend) cited the catchphrase of Żydokomuna to justify the deportation of the → Warsaw Jews as well as the final destruction of the ghetto in April 1943. Just as the Jews were now in the hands of the Germans, the argument ran, the Poles in the eastern region of the country had been in the hands of the Jews during the Soviet occupation. These Jews had allegedly been responsible for the discrimination and internment of Poles as

well as the mass liquidation of Polish officers, police, and intellectuals between September 1939 and the summer of 1941. At the same time intellectuals such as the Catholic historian Feliks Koneczny accused the Jews of having infiltrated National Socialism, which he claimed to be the ultimate product of "Jewish civilization."

The nationalist press escalated the accusation of Żydokomuna by invoking the danger posed by converted (→ Conversion) or "masked" Jews [10. 179–181]. Even in the Armia Krajowa (AK; → Polish Home Army), the attitude towards Jews was ambivalent. While the AK selectively supported the Jewish underground resistance, general anti-Jewish reservations remained.

4. After 1945

In the early postwar period, the most influential underground anti-communist organizations, such as the National Democrats, the far-right Narodowe Siły Zbrojne (National Forces), and, as the successor of the disbanded Home Army, the Wolność i Niepodległość (Movement for Freedom and Independence), regarded the communists and their regime as nothing less than the rule of the "Judeo-Commune." Judeo-Polonia, they claimed, had now become reality. These arguments were used to justify anti-Jewish pogroms in the postwar years (→ Kielce). The fact that some Jews now occupied prominent positions in the leading Polska Zjednoczona Partia Robotnicza (Polish United Workers' Party, PZPR) as well as in the state apparatus was seen as proof of Jewish rule. Among the elected members of the Politburo and Central Committee were Hilary Minc, Jakub Berman, and Roman Zambrowski, who had spent the war years in the Soviet Union. Between 1944 and 1949, Minc acted as Minister of Industry and Trade, and subsequently as deputy prime minister of Poland until his dismissal in the course of de-Stalinization in 1956. As Jews and representatives of the Soviet Union, they were exposed to double hostility.

Parallel with the constant allegation of a Żydokomuna, a reinterpretation of the anti-semitic enemy image was now undertaken by the Communist Party. In the context of anti-Zionist purges in the states within the Soviet sphere of influence (→ Slánský Trial), Jews were alleged to be enemies of the People's Republic of Poland. The campaign reached its peak in 1968 with the closure of Jewish institutions (→ Club Babel). The majority of Jewish party members were expelled from cultural and scientific institutions, among them prominent people like Zambrowski. Jewish party members were accused of having attempted to stop the communist idea from taking roots. This was a reprise of the arguments used by the Polish National Democrats of the interwar period, but this time under communist auspices. The motivations behind it were ethnic in every case.

Even after the revolution of 1989, the slogan of the Żydokomuna was revived. Rightist and nationalist groups used the concept above all in order to justify the history of anti-Jewish violence in eastern Poland in the summer of 1941.

Bibliography

Sources
[1] J. A. Reguła, Historia Komunistycznej Partji Polski w świetle faktów i dokumentów [History of the Communist Party in Poland in the Light of Facts and Documents], Warsaw 1934.

Secondary literature
[2] M. J. Chodakiewicz, Żydzi i Polacy 1918–1955. Współistnienie, Zagłada, Komunizm [Jews and Poles 1918–1955. Coexistence, Extermination, Communism], Cracow 2000.   [3] M. J. Chodakiewicz, After the Holocaust. Polish-Jewish Conflict in the Wake of World War II, New York 2003.   [4] M. J. Chodakiewicz, The Massacre in Jedwabne July 10, 1941. Before, During, and After, Boulder/New York 2005.   [5] J. T. Gross, Fear. Anti-semitism in Poland After Auschwitz; an Essay in Historical Interpretation, New York 2007.   [6] K. Jasiewicz, Pierwsi po diable. Elity sowieckie w okupowanej Polsce 1939–1941 [The First After the Devil. Soviet Elites in Occupied Poland 1939–1941], Warsaw 2002.   [7] K. Jasiewicz, Rzeczywistość sowiecka 1939–1941 w świadectwach polskich Żydów [Soviet Reality 1939–1941 in the Testimonies of Polish Jews], Warsaw 2010.   [8] J. S. Kopstein/J. Wittenberg, Who Voted Communist? Reconsidering the Social Bases of Radicalism in Interwar Poland, in: Slavic Review 62 (2003), 87–109.   [9] J. B. Michlic, The Soviet Occupation of Poland, 1939–1941, and the Stereotype of the Anti-Polish and Pro-Soviet Jew, in: Jewish Social Studies 13 (2007), 135–176.   [10] J. B. Michlic, Poland's Threatening Other. The Image of the Jew from 1880 to the Present, Lincoln/London 2006.   [11] J. B. Michlic, Żydokomuna. Anti-Jewish Images and Political Tropes in Modern Poland, in: Simon Dubnow Institute Yearbook 4 (2005), 303–329.   [12] J. Schatz, The Generation. The Rise and Fall of the Jewish Communists of Poland, Berkeley et al. 1991.   [13] P. Śpiewak, Żydokomuna. Interpretacje historyczne [Żydokomuna. Historical Interpretations], Warsaw 2012.

JOANNA B. MICHLIC,
BRISTOL/WALTHAM, MA